Advances in Intelligent Systems Research 176

Editor-in-Chief

Xun Luo, *Tianjin University of Technology, Tianjin, China*

Series Editors

Akram A. Almohammedi, *South Ural State University, Chelyabinsk, Russia*
Chi-Hua Chen, *Fuzhou University, Fuzhou, China*
Steven Guan, *Xi'an Jiaotong-Liverpool University, Suzhou, China*
Dragan Pamucar, *University of Defence, Belgrade, Serbia*

D1807135

"The proceedings series Advances in Intelligent Systems Research aims to publish proceedings from conferences on all disciplines dealing with and affecting the issue of understanding and reproducing intelligence in artificial systems. The series is also open for publications concerning the application of intelligence in networked or other environments and the extraction of meaningful data from large data sets.

Topics covered by this series:
Artificial intelligence, incl. knowledge representation and logic, Autonomous systems and agents, Machine learning, Neural networks, Evolutionary systems, Robotics, Computer vision and pattern recognition, Fuzzy sets, Semantic web, incl. web services, ontologies and grid computing, Biological systems, Constraint satisfaction, Computational biology, Information sciences, Computational neuroscience"

Ramesh Manza · Bharti Gawali ·
Pravin Yannawar · Filbert Juwono
Editors

Proceedings of the First International Conference on Advances in Computer Vision and Artificial Intelligence Technologies (ACVAIT 2022)

ATLANTIS
PRESS

Editors
Ramesh Manza
Department of Computer Science and IT
Dr. Babasaheb Ambedkar Marathwada
University
Aurangabad, India

Bharti Gawali
Department of Computer Science and IT
Dr. Babasaheb Ambedkar Marathwada
University
Aurangabad, India

Pravin Yannawar
Department of Computer Science and IT
Dr. Babasaheb Ambedkar Marathwada
University
Aurangabad, India

Filbert Juwono
Department of Computer Science
University of Southampton Malaysia
Iskandar Puteri, Malaysia

ISSN 2731-7870   ISSN 1951-6851 (electronic)
Advances in Intelligent Systems Research
ISBN 978-94-6463-195-1   ISBN 978-94-6463-196-8 (eBook)
https://doi.org/10.2991/978-94-6463-196-8

This Atlantis Press imprint is published by the registered company Atlantis Press International B.V., part of Springer Nature
The registered company address is: Van Godewijckstraat 30 3311 GX Dordrecht Netherlands

Preface

The world is marching toward implementation of machine learning algorithms and artificial intelligence for making computing system more responsive and interactive to users. The sensor-based big data analytics is addressing the futuristic needs to mankind. The First International Conference on Advances in Computer Vision and Artificial Intelligence Technologies (ACVAIT 2022) is a biennial conference organized by the Department of Computer Science and Information Technology, Dr. Babasaheb Ambedkar Marathwada University, Aurangabad (MS), India, during August 1–2, 2022. ACVAIT 2022 is dedicated toward advances in the theme areas of *Computer Vision, Image Processing, Pattern Recognition, Artificial Intelligence, Machine Learning, Human Computer Interactions, Biomedical Image Processing, Geospatial Technology, Hyperspectral Image Processing* and allied technologies but not limited to. ACVAIT 2022 invites young and/or advanced researchers contributing in the theme area of the conference and also provides them platform for discussing their scientific contributions/research findings with the domain experts, exchanging ideas with them and fostering closer collaboration between members from the top universities/higher education institutes (HEIs). ACVAIT 2022 invites domain-specific work from research scholars, academician, machine learning and AI scientist and industry experts to contribute their scientific contribution in the following areas but not limited to.

- Shape representation
- Biometrics: face matching, iris recognition, footprint verification and many more.
- Statistical, structural and syntactic pattern recognition
- Brain computer interface and human computer interactions
- Feature extraction and reduction
- Biomedical image processing
- Color and texture analysis
- Speech analysis and understanding
- Image segmentation
- Speaker verification and synthesis
- Image compression, coding and encryption
- Clustering and classification
- Object recognition, scene understanding and video analytics
- Machine learning algorithms
- Image matching (pattern matching)
- Extreme learning machine
- Content-based image retrieval and indexing
- Artificial intelligence trends in deep learning
- Optical character recognition
- Big data

- Image and video forensics
- Information retrieval
- Pattern recognition and machine learning for Internet of Things
- Data mining and data analytics
- Pattern classification through sensors
- Pattern recognition for hyperspectral imaging
- Satellite image processing

There were more than 200 manuscripts in the conference collection developed on conference platform, these manuscripts were blind peer-reviewed, and technical program committee recommended around 30% submission for the conference based in review reports. This selection of the manuscript was based on the criteria of *technical/scientific strength of the work, contribution toward scientific knowledge* and *novelty*. These manuscripts provide detailed discussion on the problem statement pertaining to the thematic area, and the author has justified the work with strong scientific results.

This open access book provides research contributions in the area of Biomedical Image processing, Pattern Recognition, AI and ML, Remote Sensing, GIS and Hyperspectral Image Processing. The manuscripts contributing in Biomedical Image Processing are addressing the research finding including *computer-aided system lung cancer detection, detection of lung cancer nodules from CT images, cantilever-based biosensor for tuberculosis detection, early detection of leukemia using deep hybrid learning techniques, segmentation of pediatric brain tumors using FLSSR, investigation of EEG images for robotic arm, localization of intervertebral disks using deep learning, identification of skin disease using machine learning and early detection of diabetic maculopathy in specific.* Readers may also find good contribution in the potential area of *Pattern Recognition* in general and *printed, handwritten optical character recognition, multilingual optical character recognition, text independent source identification of printed documents, audiovisual speech recognition, handcrafted texture detection, multimodal biometrics, visual cryptography, object detection and classification, gender classification and object identification for block chain application* in general. There are good contributions in the areas of *Remote Sensing, GIS and Hyperspectral Image Processing, the work primarily on extraction and analysis of land elevations and coastal area using spatial data mining, rooftop identification, extraction of road line, road surfaces in complex urban environment based on high-resolution hyperspectral imaging, image segmentation of satellite images, crop prediction, weather analysis and LU/LC analysis.* Moreover, collection also contains couple of manuscripts addressing in the potential areas of text mining and machine learning-related problem statements.

We are sure that this manuscript collection presented in this conference book will be useful to the scientific community working in the potential area of Computer Vision and Artificial Intelligence and also encourage young researchers to undertake challenging problem. We are pleased to provide these selected manuscripts as a part of conference collection on Advances in Computer Vision and Artificial Intelligence Technologies (ACVAIT 2022).

Ramesh Manza
Bharti Gawali
Pravin Yannawar
Filbert Juwono

Organization

Chief Patrons

Pramod Yeole (Vice Chancellor)	Dr. B A M University, Aurangabad, India
M. Ramachandra Gowda (Vice Chancellor)	Rani Channama University, Belagavi, Karnataka, India
Karbhari Kale (Vice Chancellor)	Babasaheb Ambedkar Technological University, Lonare and Savitribai Phule Pune University Pune, India
Uddhav Bhosle (Vice Chancellor)	Swami Ramanand Teerth Marathwada University Nanded, India
Ujwala Chakradeo (Vice Chancellor)	S N D T Woman's University Mumbai, India
Vilas Sapkal (Vice Chancellor)	M G M University, Aurangabad, India
Akshay Shisode	Vivekanand Shikshan Sanstha, Aurangabad, India

Patrons

Shyam Shirsat (Pro-vice Chancellor)	Dr. B A M University, Aurangabad, India
Jayshree Suryawanshi (Registrar)	Dr. B A M University, Aurangabad, India
Kishor Shitole (Chancellors Nominee (Management Council))	Dr. B A M University, Aurangabad, India
Suresh Chandra Mehrotra	Department of Computer Science and IT, Dr. B A M University, Aurangabad, India
Ashish Gadekar (Registrar)	M G M University, Aurangabad, India
Ratnadeep Deshmukh	Department of Computer Science and IT, Dr. B A M University, Aurangabad, India

Honorary General Chair

Sachin Deshmukh	Dr. B A M University, Aurangabad

Conference Chair

Ramesh Manza   Dr. B A M University, Aurangabad

Organizing Secretaries

Bharti Gawali   Dr. B A M University, Aurangabad
Pravin Yannawar   Dr. B A M University, Aurangabad

Finance Chair

Ashok Gaikwad (Director)   I M S I T, Aurangabad

Advisory Committee

Bharti Gawali   Dr. Babasaheb Ambedkar Marathwada
                              University, Aurangabad (MS) India
Ramesh Manza   Dr. Babasaheb Ambedkar Marathwada
                              University, Aurangabad (MS) India
Pravin Yannawar   Dr. Babasaheb Ambedkar Marathwada
                              University, Aurangabad (MS) India
Filbert Juwono   University of Southampton Malaysia, Malaysia
Shivanand Gornale   RCBU, Karnataka, India
Vikas Humbe   SRTMUN, Maharashtra, India
Ganesh Sinha   Myanmar Institute of Information Technology
                              (MIIT) Mandalay
B. Manjula   Kakatiya University, India
Sachin Deshmukh   Dr. B A M University, Aurangabad
Ratnadeep Deshmukh   Dr. B A M University, Aurangabad
Amol Goje   Society for Data Science, Pune
Tuong-Thuy Vu   Curtin University Malaysia
Lenin Gopal   Southampton University Malaysia
Alex Leo   University of Delaware, Delaware, USA
Dragan Cisic   European University Cyprus, Croatia
Sasan Adibi   Deakin University, Australia
Manoj Deore   Amity IIIT, Mumbai, India
P. S. Avadhani   Andhra University, Visakhapatnam, India
P. S. Hiremath   Gulbarga University, Kalburgi, India
S. Murali   MIT Mysore, Mysore, India
Manohar Chaskar   Savitribai Phule Pune University, Pune

Local Organizing Committee

C. Namrata Mahender	Dr. Babasaheb Ambedkar Marathwada University, Aurangabad (MS), India
Sonali Kulkarni	Dr. Babasaheb Ambedkar Marathwada University, Aurangabad (MS), India
Mukta Dhopeshwarkar	Dr. Babasaheb Ambedkar Marathwada University, Aurangabad (MS), India
Seema Kawthekar	Dr. Babasaheb Ambedkar Marathwada University, Aurangabad (MS), India
Sunil Nimbhore	Dr. Babasaheb Ambedkar Marathwada University, Aurangabad (MS), India
Mansi Baheti	Dr. Babasaheb Ambedkar Marathwada University, Aurangabad (MS), India
Dipak Pachpatte	Dr. Babasaheb Ambedkar Marathwada University, Aurangabad (MS), India
Omprakash Jadhav	Dr. Babasaheb Ambedkar Marathwada University, Aurangabad (MS), India
Vijaya Musande	MGM University, India
Prashant Aagnihotri	SRTM University, India
S. P. Shrikhande	SRTM University, India
A. B. Gulwe	SRTM University, India
Mukti Jadhav	Shivaji College of Arts Science and Commerce, Buldhana (MS), India
Parag Bhalchandra	Swami Ramanand Teerth Marathwada University, Nanded, India
Rajiv Mente	Punyashlok Ahilyabai Holkar Solapur University, Solapur, India
Shreeram Raut	Punyashlok Ahilyabai Holkar Solapur University, Solapur, India
Archana Sable	Swami Ramanand Teerth Marathwada University, Nanded, India
Nitin Patil	Savitribai Phule Pune University, Pune, India
Shrikant Mapari	Symbiosis International University, India
Shankar Mali	MIT Pune, India
Gopal Sakarkar	Raisoni College of Engineering, Nagpur, India

Technical Program Committee – International

Abdel-Hameed Badawy	New Mexico State University, USA
Adithya Pediredla	Rice University, Houston, Texas, USA
Ahmed Abdelgawad	Central Michigan University, USA

Aicha Baya Goumeidane   Centre de Recherche en Techno. Industrielles
                               (CRTI), Algeria
Aiman El-Maleh   King Fahd University of Petroleum & Minerals,
                               KSA
Akitoshi Matsuda   Panasonic Communications Corporation Ltd.,
                               Japan
Ala Al-Fuqaha   Western Michigan University, USA
Alba Garcia Seco De Herrera   University of Essex, England
Alex Leo   University of Delaware, Delaware, USA
Alexander Gorban   University of Leicester, UK
Alireza Alaei   Southern Cross University, Australia
Ameni Boumaiza   Qatar Foundation, Qatar
Amjad Gawanmeh   Khalifa University of Science, UAE
Anderson Rocha   University of Campinas, Sao Paulo, Brazil
Anderson Santos   University of Campinas, Brazil
Andres Rosso-Mateus   Universidad Nacional de Colombia, Colombia
B. Uyyanonvara   SIIT, Thammasat University, Thailand
Benoit Naegel   University of Strasbourg, France
Brian Keith   Catholic University of the Nort, Chile
C. Pisarn   Rangsit University, Thailand
Camille Krutz   Institut University de Technologie (IUT de Paris),
                               France
Carsten Maple   University of Bedfordshire, UK.
Chen Chen   The University of Texas at Dallas, USA
Daniel Caballero   University of Extremadura, Badajoz, Spain
Diego Liberati   Polytechnic University of Milan, Milan, Italy
Do Thanh Ha   VNU University of Science, Vietnam
Dragan Cisic   European University Cyprus, Croatia
Ehsan Nedaaee Oskoee   Institute of Advance Studies in Basic Sciences,
                               Zanjan, Iran
Elhadi Shakshuki   Acadia University Wolfville, Canada
El-Sayed El-Alfy   King Fahd University of Petroleum & Minerals,
                               KSA
Eric Llewellyn   University of Wales, Newport, UK
Eugene Borovikov   Intelligent Automation Inc., USA
Evgeny Kostyuchenko   Tomsk State University of Control Systems and
                               Radioelectronics, Tomsk, Russia
Ezendu Ariwa   University of Bedfordshire, UK

Technical Program Committee – National

Abdullah Mohammed Kaleem	Matoshri Pratishthan Group of Institutions School of Engineering, Nanded, India
Abhinav Muley	St. Vincent Pallotti College of Engineering and Technology, Nagpur, India
Ajay Surwade	KBC North Maharashtra University, Jalgaon, India
Ajit Danti	CHRIST (Deemed to be University), Bangalore, India
Ajju Gadicha	P.R. Pote College of Engineering, Amravati, India
Ambika Annavarapu	Kakatiya Institute of Technology and Science, Warangal, India
Amol Goje	Society for Data Science, Pune, India
Anagha Markandey	Abha Gaikwad-Patil College of Engineering, Nagpur, India
Aniket Muley	Swami Ramanand Teerth Marathwada University, Nanded, India
Anita Dixit	Sri Dharmasthala Manjunatheshwara College of Engineering and Technology, Dharwad, India
Anitha H.	Manipal Institute of Technology, Manipal, India
Apurva Desai	Veer Narmad South Gujarat University, Surat, India
Archana Nandibewoor	Sri Dharmasthala Manjunatheshwara College of Engineering and Technology, Dharwad, India
Arjun Mane	Government Institute of Forensic Science, Nagpur, India
Arunkumar K L	Jawaharlal Nehru National College of Engineering, Shimoga, India
Atul Goasi	Saurashtra University, Rajkot, India
Atul Negi	University of Hyderabad, India
B. M. Mehtre	Institute for Development and Research in Banking Technology, Hyderabad, India
Balamurugan Karnan	Vignan's Foundation for Science, Technology & Research, Guntur, India
Bharath Bhushan	Sahyadri College of Engineering and Management, Mangalore, India
Bharathi Pilar	University College Mangalore, Mangalore, India
Bharti Gawali	Dr. Babasaheb Ambedkar Marathwada University, Aurangabad, India
Bhausaheb Pawar	North Maharashtra University, Jalgaon, India
Bindu V. R.	Mahatma Gandhi University, Kerala, India
Chandrani Singh	Sinhgad Institute of Management, Vadgaon, Pune, India

Chaskar Manohar (Dean)	Science and Technology, Savitribai Phule Pune University, Pune, India
C. Namrata Mahender	Dr. Babasaheb Ambedkar Marathwada University, Aurangabad, India
C. P. Sumathi	Shrimathi Devkunvar Nanalal Bhatt Vaishnav College for Women, Chennai, India
Chandrashekhara K. T.	BMS Institute of Technology & Management, Bangalore, India
D. S. Guru	Mysore University, Mysore, India
Daneshwari Mulimani	Karnataka State Women's University, Bijapur, India
Deepak Dhote	Amravati University, Amaravati, India
Dericks Shukla	Indian Institute of Technology, Mandi, India
Dyanand Sawkar	Rani Channamma University, Belagavi Karnataka, India
E Naganathan	Symbiosis Institute of Computer Studies and Research, Pune, India
Ebenezer Jangam	Vignan's Foundation for Science, Technology and Research, Guntur, India
G. P. Hegde	Sri Dharmasthala Manjunatheshwara Institute of Technology, Ujire, India
G. S. Mamatha	Rashtreeya Vidyalaya College of Engineering, Bangalore, India
Ganesh Magar	SNDT University, Mumbai, India
Ganga Holi	Global Academy of Technology, Bengaluru, India
Gireesh Babu	BMS Institute of Technology & Management, Bangalore, India
Gnaneswara Rao Nitta	Vignan's Foundation for Science, Technology & Research, Guntur, India
Gopal Sakarkar	Raisoni College of Engineering, Nagpur, India
H. L. Shashirekha	Mangalore University, Mangalore, India
Haripriya V.	Jain University, Bangalore, India
Joseph Abraham Sundar K.	SASTRA Deemed University, Thanjavur, India
Jude Hemanth	Karunya University, Coimbatore, India
K. K. Chaturvedi	ICAR-Indian Agricultural Statistics Research Institute, New Delhi, India
Kapil Mehrotra	Center for Development of Advanced Computing (CDAC), GIST Group, Pune, India
Karbhari Kale	Babasaheb Ambedkar Technological University, Lonare, India
Kaushik Roy	West Bengal State University, Kolkata, India
Latchoumi Thamarai	Vignan's Foundation for Science, Technology & Research, Guntur, India

M. T. Somashekhar	Bangalore University, Bangalore, India
Mahendra Dhore	Shivaji College, Nagpur, India
Mainak Sen	Techno India University, Kolkata, India
Mallamma V. Reddy	Rani Channamma University, Belagavi, India
Mallikarjun Hangarge	Karnataka Arts, Science and Commerce College, Bidar, India
Mamta Baheti	Hislop College Nagpur, India
Manasi Baheti	Dr. Babasaheb Ambedkar Marathwada University, Aurangabad, India
Manish Joshi	KBC North Maharashtra University, Jalgaon, India
Manisha Saini	G D Goenka University, Gurgaon, India
Manjunath T. N.	Acharya Institute of Technology, Bengaluru, India
Manohar Madgi	K L E Institute of Technology, Hubli, India
Manoj Deore	Amity IIIT, Mumbai, India
Mansi Subhedar	Pillai HOC College of Engineering and Technology, Rasayani, India
Maya Ingle	Devi Ahilya Vishwavidyalaya, Indore, India
Midhula Vijayan	National Institute of Technology, Tiruchirappalli, India
Minakshi Vharkate	MIT Academy of Engineering, Pune, India
Minal Moharir	Rashtreeya Vidyalaya College of Engineering, Bangalore, India
Monali Khachane	Shivaji University, Kolhapur, India
Mukta Dhopeshwarkar	Dr. Babasaheb Ambedkar Marathwada University, Aurangabad, India
Nagaraj Cholli	R.V. College of Engineering, Bengaluru, India
Nagaratna Hegde	Vasavi College of Engg., Hyderabad, India
Nibaran Das	Jadavpur Univ., India
Nitin Patil	Savitribai Phule Pune University, Pune, India
P. S. Avadhani	Andhra University, Visakhapatnam, India
P. S. Hiremath	Gulbarga University, Kalaburgi, India
P. Laxminarayan	Osmania University, Hyderabad, India
Pankaj Agrawal	GH Raisoni Academy of Engineering and Technology (GHRAET), Nagpur, India
Parag Bhalchndra	Swami Ramanand Teerth Marathwada University, Nanded, India
Parag Kaveri	Symbiosis Institute of Computer Studies and Research, Pune, India
Parashuram Bannigidad	Rani Channamma University, Belagavi, India
Parminder Kaur	Jawaharlal Nehru College of Engineering, MGM University, Aurangabad, India

Poornima Patil	Visvesvaraya Technological University, Belgaum, India
Pradeep Bute	RSTM University Nagpur, India
Prajakta Dhamdhere	MIT-ADT University, Pune, India
Prakash Hiremath	KLE Technological University, Hubli, India
Prakash Khanale	DSM College, Parbhani, India
Prakash Unki	BLDEA's Dr. P.G. Halakatti College of Engineering and Technology, Bijapur, India
Praneet Saurabh	Technocrats Institute of Technology, Bhopal, India
Prapti Deshmukh	MGM University, Aurangabad, India
Pratima Manhas	Manav Rachna International University, Faridabad, India
Prema T. Akkasaligar	BLDEA's Dr. P.G. Halakatti College of Engineering and Technology, Bijapur, India
Priyank Saxena	Birla Institute of Technology, Ranchi, India
Pushpa Patil	BLDEA's Dr. P.G. Halakatti College of Engineering and Technology, Bijapur, India
Pushpa S. K.	BMS Institute of Technology & Management, Bangalore, India
Qazi Fasihuddin	Matoshri Pratishthan School of Engineering, Nanded, India
Rajesh Dhumal	Symbiosis University, Pune, India
Rajiv Dharaskar	Indian Institute of Information Technology Kottayam, India
Rajivkumar Mente	Solapur University, Solapur, India
Rajkumar Soundrapandiyan	Vellore Institute of Technology, Vellore, India
Rajkumar Yesuraj	Vignan University, Guntur, India
Rakesh Ramteke	KBC North Maharashtra University, Jalgaon, India
Ramya D.	Sri Krishna College of Engineering and Technology, Coimbatore, India
Rashmi Somshekhar	Karnataka State Women's University, Bijapur, India
Ratnadeep Deshmukh	Dr. Babasaheb Ambedkar Marathwada University, Aurangabad, India
Ratnakar Ghorpade	BRACTs Vishwakarma Institute of Technology, Pune, India
Ravi Hosur	BLDEA's Dr. P.G. Halakatti College of Engineering and Technology, Bijapur, India
Rohini Bhusnurmath	Akkamahadevi Women's University, Vijayapura, India
S. Murali	MIT Mysore, Mysore, India

S. B. Kulkarni	Sri Dharmasthala Manjunatheshwara College of Engineering and Technology, Dharwad, India
Sachin Deshmukh	Dr. Babasaheb Ambedkar Marathwada University Aurangabad, India
Sahana Das	Narula Institute of Technology, Kolkata, India
Sanasam Inunganbi	National Institute of Technology, Manipur, India
Sanjay Jain	Institute of Technology & Management, Gwalior, India
Sarika Sharma	Symbiosis Institute of Computer Studies and Research, Pune, India
Satish Kolhe	KBC North Maharashtra University, Jalgaon, India
Seema Kawthekar	Dr. Babasaheb Ambedkar Marathwada University, Aurangabad, India
Shajee Mohan	Indian Institute of Technology Madras (Chennai), India
Shankru Guggari	BMS Institute of Technology & Management, Bangalore, India
Shanmugapriya Padmanabhan	Saranathan College of Engineering, Tiruchirappalli, India
Shanthi D L	BMS Institute of Technology & Management, Bangalore, India
Sharath Kumar	Mysore University, Mysore, India
Shaveta Thakral	Manav Rachna International University (MRIU), Faridabad, India
Shivananad Gornale	Rani Channamma University, Belagavi, India
Shivani Saluja	GD GOENKA UNIVERSITY, Gurgaon, India
Shridevi Soma	Poojya Doddappa Appa College of Engineering, Gulbarga, India
Siddanagouda Patil	University of Agricultural Sciences, Bangalore, India
Sonali Kulkarni	Dr. Babasaheb Ambedkar Marathwada University, Aurangabad, India
Subhash Kendre	Savitribai Phule Pune University, Pune, India
Suhas Sapate	Shri Guru Gobind Singhji Institute of Engineering and Technology, Nanded, India
Sunanda Biradar	BLDEA's V.P. Dr. P. G. Halakatti College of Engineering and Technology, Vijayapura, India
Suneeta Budihal	B.V. Bhoomaraddi College of Engineering and Technology, Hubli, India
Sunil Muttoo	Delhi University, Delhi, India
Sunil Nimbhore	Dr. Babasaheb Ambedkar Marathwada University, Aurangabad, India

Sureshchandra Mehrotra	Dr. Babasaheb Ambedkar Marathwada University, Aurangabad, India
Tejaswi Potluri	VNR Vignana Jyothi Institute of Engineering and Technology, Hyderabad, India
U. B. Desai	IIIT, Hyderabad, India
Urmila Pol	Shivaji University, Kolhapur, India
Usha B. A.	BMS Institute of Technology & Management, Bangalore, India
Veerappa Pagi	Basaveshwar Engineering College, Bagalkot, India
Vidyagouri Hemadri	SDM College of Engineering and Technology, Dharwad, India
Vijaya Arumugam	Sri Krishna Arts and Science College, Coimbatore, India
Vikas Humbe	Swami Ramanand Teerth Marathwada University, Nanded, India
Vilas Naik	Basaveshwar Engineering College, Bagalkot, India
Vilas Thakare	AMRAVATI University, AMRAVATI, India
Vinay T. R.	Sri Venkateswara College of Engineering, Chennai, India
Virendra Malemath	Gulbarga University, Gulbarga, India
Vishweshwarayya Hallur	Angadi Institute of Technology and Management, Belgaum, India
Y. Jayanta Singh	National Institute of Electronics and Information Technology, NIELIT Guwahati
Yogesh Gajmal	MIT School of Engineering, Ratnagiri, India
Yogish H. K.	SJB Institute of Technology, Bangalore, India
Yannawar Pravin	Dr. Babasaheb Ambedkar Marathwada University, Aurangabad (MS), India

Editors

Ramesh Manza	Dr. Babasaheb Ambedkar Marathwada University, Aurangabad (MS), India
Bharti Gawali	Dr. Babasaheb Ambedkar Marathwada University, Aurangabad (MS), India
Pravin Yannawar	Dr. Babasaheb Ambedkar Marathwada University, Aurangabad (MS), India
Filbert Juwono	University of Southampton Malaysia, Malaysia

Contents

Peer-Review Statements

Ramesh Manza[1]([⊠]), Bharti Gawali[1], Pravin Yannawar[1], and Filbert Juwono[2]

[1] Department of Computer Science and Information Technology, Dr. Babasaheb Ambedkar Marathwada University, Aurangabad, Maharashtra, India
rrmanza.csit@bamu.ac.in
[2] Department of Electrical and Computer Engineering, University of Southampton, Iskandar Puteri, Johor, Malaysia

All of the articles in this proceedings volume have been presented at the First biennial International Conference on Advances in Computer Vision and Artificial Intelligence Technologies (ACVAIT 2022) during 1–2 Aug 2022 in Aurangabad (Maharashtra), India. These articles have been peer reviewed by the members of the Technical Program Committee (TPC) and approved by the Editor-in-Chief, who affirms that this document is a truthful description of the conference's review process.

1 Review Procedure

The reviews were double blind. Each submission was examined by two reviewer(s) independently. The conference collection of were developed using *Easychair* where the authors have made their submissions. The conference chair and has assigned manuscript to the member of technical program committee to review manuscript.

The process adopted by the conference team includes following activities. At the first the submitted manuscript was carefully screened for generic quality, suitableness and plagiarism report of each and every submission was obtained from Turnitin software. The copy of the plagiarism report was made available to authors on to the conference accounts of the author. After the initial screening, they were sent for peer review by matching each paper's topic with the reviewers' expertise, taking into account any competing interests. A paper could only be considered for acceptance if it had received favourable recommendations from the two reviewers. Moreover, the authors are encouraged to revise their manuscript in line with the suggestions/comments of reviewer. All accepted and revised manuscripts are considered for the part of conference collection. The double blinded peer review is adopted therefore initially, the manuscript is allocated to two reviewers, based on the collective decision of reviewer the selection of manuscript was taken as:

Review 1	Review 2	Review 3	Decision
Positive	Positive	-	Positive
Negative	Negative	-	Negative

(continued)

R. Manza—Editor-in-Chief of the [ACVAIT 2022].

© The Author(s) 2023
R. Manza et al. (Eds.): ACVAIT 2022, AISR 176, pp. 1–3, 2023.
https://doi.org/10.2991/978-94-6463-196-8_1

(continued)

Review 1	Review 2	Review 3	Decision
Positive	Negative	Assigned to Review	Positive (1 and 3 are positive)
Positive	Negative	Assign to Review	Negative (1 and 3 are negative)
Negative	Positive	Assigned to Review	Positive (2 and 3 are positive)
Negative	Positive	Assigned to Review	Negative (1 and 3 are Negative)

Positive Score – Manuscript Considered for oral presentation at conference and part of conference collection for proceedings.

Negative Score – Manuscript will not be considered for conference collection for proceedings.

2 Quality Criteria

Reviewers were instructed to assess the quality of submissions solely based on the scientific merit of manuscript along the following dimensions

1. Pertinence of the article's content to the scope and themes of the conference;
2. Clear demonstration of *originality, novelty, relevance* in current time & trend of the research;
3. *Scientific and Technical Strength* of the methods, analyses, and results;
4. Adherence to the ethical standards and codes of conduct relevant to the research field;
5. *Clarity, Cohesion*, and *Accuracy* in presentation of scientific content, use of terms in language and other modes of expression, including figures and tables.

3 Key Metrics

Total submissions	200
Number of articles sent for peer review	190
Number of accepted articles	53
Acceptance rate	27.89%
Number of reviewers	261

Competing Interests. Neither the Editor-in-Chief nor any member of the Scientific Committee declares any competing interest.

An Improved Computer Aided System for Lung Cancer Detection using Image Processing Techniques

Manoj Mhaske[1](✉), Ramesh Manza[1], Pallavi Pradhan[1], and Kavita Khobragade[2]

[1] Department of Computer Science & IT, Dr. Babasaheb Ambedkar Marathwada University,
Aurangabad, Maharashtra, India
mhaskemanoj@gmail.com
[2] Department of Computer Science, Fergusson College, Pune, Maharashtra, India

Abstract. Early detection and prevention is the only way to treat lung cancer to avoid the loss of life. Where Computed Tomography (CT) screening is viewed as perhaps the best technique for discovering the early indications of lung malignant growth. The primary goal of this study is nodule detection and classification of collected CT scans images as benign or malignant. Sometimes some human errors can occur in the checking of a long series of CT slices of a single patient manually. This automated system (CAD-Computer Aided System) can help to radiologist or doctors to know the current stages and condition of the disease to diagnose correctly and quickly on a single click which will useful for radiologists and doctors to avoid the serious disease stage. The key four processes of our proposed system are input CT images, pre-processing, features extraction, and classification. In the proposed approach firstly we read all the CT image database (70 thoracic lung CT scans) having Dicom format then applied some pre-processing techniques of Matlab to enhance the image quality and obtained texture features. Using texture features, we extracted several features. At the end, we classified the dataset as benign or malignant using the K-means clustering method, and we achieved an accuracy of 92.8 percent.

Keywords: ROI · K-means clustering · CAD-computer aided system · Lung · Nodules

1 Introduction

The body text starts with a standard first-level heading like INTRODUCTION or any other heading suitable to the content and context. First level headings are in all caps. Copy the content and replace it for other first-level headings in remaining text. Reference citations should be within square bracket [1]. Headings should always be followed by text. Lung cancer is diagnosed in at least 12 million patients per year. In 2018, cancer will be the primary cause of about 9.6 million deaths. Lung cancer is the second most frequent cause of cancer in comparison to other types of lung cancers. Nearly 1.76 million of the 2.09 million cases of lung cancer reported by the World Health Organization

R. Manza et al. (Eds.): ACVAIT 2022, AISR 176, pp. 4–13, 2023.
https://doi.org/10.2991/978-94-6463-196-8_2

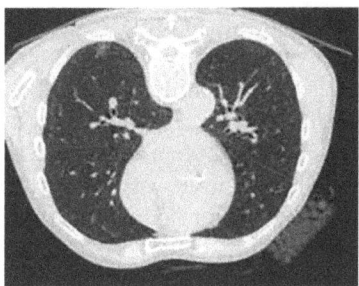

Fig. 1. Lung CT Image

are directly attributable to the disease [1]. The second most common lung disease is persistent malignancy, which affects one in five men and one in nine women. Coughing, coughing up blood, chest pain, weight loss, and shortness of breath are among the most typical lung cancer symptoms [2]. Cancerous cells are eliminated during the production cycle, and red blood cells degrade. Internally, they change the plasma membrane's shape and make-up, which results in a rise in RBCs and a shortening and ultimately rupture of the veins and arteries' walls. Nowadays, CT (computed tomography) is frequently employed in the clinical diagnosis of lung cancer. An unregulated proliferation of lung cells is known as a pulmonary nodule, which appears as a circular formation with a diameter of 3 to 30 mm on lung CT images. The formation of malignant lung tissue comes in two different forms. The first is small cell lung cancer (SCLC), while the second is non-small cell lung cancer (NSCLC).

Lung disease malignancies found around one out of five in men and one out of nine in women and it is the second most regular malignant growth. Malignant and benign are the two structures where tumors comes into. Benign tumors are not dangerous, in this manner they don't develop and spread to the degree of destructive tumors. Benign tumors are normally not perilous or life threatening. The Malignant or cancerous tumors are Harmful tumors, which growth can develop and spread to different parts or regions of the human body. Travelling of the disease cells from the underlying tumor site to different pieces of the body is called as metastasis [3] (Fig. 1).

2   Literature survey

Number of researchers carried out the research on development of lung cancer detection system. In [4], Sayani Nandy and Nikita Pandey put forth a plan for identifying cancer cells in lung CT scan pictures. This research offers a technique for extracting the majority of cancer cells from a CT scan image. In order to identify diseases, Prof. Samir Kumar B. created a system using computer-aided diagnosis (CAD) to extract edges from lung CT scan pictures [5]. Thresholding algorithm [6] offers filtering to notice the sputum cell from the raw image for early detection via Fatm Taher et al. M. Tan et.al [7] proposed CADe (Computer-Aided Detection) system in their work to classify nodules or non-nodules by means of genetic algorithms and Artificial Neural Network; with total of 360 nodules of 3–30 mm in diameter of 134 sufferers enrolled in LIDC society. This CADe system had a sensitivity of 87.5 percent and four FPs (false positives) per scan. In [8], 420 CT scans of 420 individuals were randomly selected from the LIDC database, and the potential malignant nodules were identified by SVM classifier. These scans had 3–30 mm in diameter and 379 possible malignancies. This system achieved a segmentation stage accuracy of 97 percent, a CADe system sensitivity of 94.4 percent with 7.04 FP per scan, and a classification stage sensitivity of 93.9 percent with 7.21 FP each case.

A computerized intelligent method for nodule detection and lung cancer classification in CT images was created by Amjed et al. [9]. They applied morphological image processing methods and geometrical facets in their study. Watershed transform and image mapping were used in [10] by C. Panyindee and W. Chiracharit to identify lung nodules present in PET/CT data. Few studies combined multiple classification techniques with feature extraction from lung CT images using Haralick texture features [10, 11]. For texture quantification, Balaji et al. [11] employed a selective scale-based picture filtration. When classifying the tumors in CT images, Mir Rayat et al. employed a backward search algorithm and the Chi-square distance metric to identify important features [12]. A CAD machine was invented by Tidke et al. for the early detection of lung cancer nodules using chest computer tomography scans. The grey level co-occurrence matrix was used to extract textural components from the lung nodules [13]. With the use of the Sobel component identification methodology, Pandy et al. established a novel method of malignant cell detection from lung CT scan images [14] in those works. Sudha et al. segmented the lung area in their proposed system with use of thresholding and morphological operations [15]. Ada et al. estimated and detected lung cancer survival the usage of neural community classifiers [16]. For the pre-processing of the images, they employed histogram equalization in this. The early stages of the patient's condition are examined using feature extraction techniques and neural network classifiers to determine if it is normal or abnormal. Using a Gabor filter and smart system, Sankar et al. [17] enhanced the structure for lung cancer cell detection. A CAD method was created by Silva et al. [18] to find lung nodules. 33 exams were subjected to the application of SVM as a classification approach. Their suggested strategy has a 95.21 percent accuracy rate.

3 Methodology

The system described here is composed of four fundamental steps. The collection of lung CT scans from the database is the initial phase, which is followed by a quantitative analysis of the images. We used pre-processing methods in Matlab in the second step to improve the quality and clarity of the original lung CT images. These methods included binarizing all CT images, separating the lung parenchyma mask, and binarizing the nodule candidates again.

Finally, we finalized the region of interest to segment the image and obtain the lung nodule candidates. The third step includes feature extraction to produce numerical features. The fourth phase uses K-means clustering to categorize diseases as benign or malignant. Figure 2 shows schematic steps of proposed algorithm of this system.

The database for this study taken from The Cancer Imaging Archive (TCIA), which was sponsored by SPIE, NCI/NIH, University of AAPM, and Chicago. We employed the SPIE-AAPM CT challenge dataset for this study. A total of 70 CT image data from

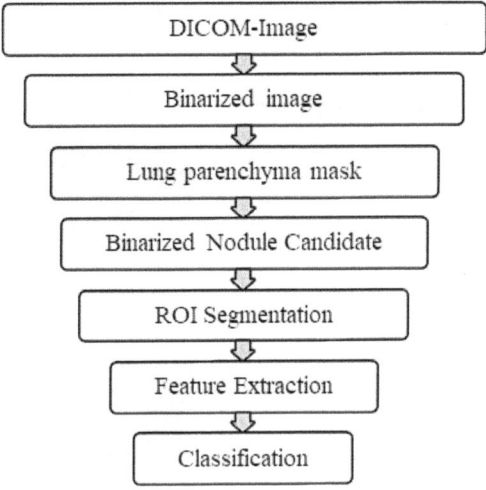

Fig. 2. Flow of Methods

patients are included in the data collection. Out of 70 CT scans of the chest, 10 are used for training and 60 are used for testing [19, 20]. These CT scans include DICOM images with 512×512 pixel size.

4 Result

Based on data from the database for the lung RAD system, the False Positive reduction is initialized as a consequence of the SPIE-AAPM lung CT challenge [19]. We read the original CT pictures using the given lung CT image database, binarized the input images, and then obtained the lung parenchyma mask. Then, lung ROI candidates are obtained by applying the nodule candidate's mask to the initial CT image (shown in Table 1).

This study focuses on the intensity and texture qualities of an image. Mean, variance, and skewness are the intensity feature parameters used in this work, whereas contrast, correlation, energy, and entropy are the texture feature parameters. In addition to these metrics, smoothness and kurtosis properties are also extracted [21, 22]. The segmented lung nodule is used for feature extraction when segmentation is finished. A feature could be a fact that is extracted from image and improves our understanding of it. In this work, the highlights, such as geometric and statistical features based on intensity, are retrieved. Physical dimensions known as shape measurements are used to describe how an object appears. All of these features are produced using the Co-occurrence matrix, which shows when different features occur together [23, 24].

Haralick et al. [25] suggested 14 texture quantities generated from the GLCM matrices for the texture evaluation. These measurements speak to the different dark level types that are connected to images smoothness, consistency, heterogeneity, and distinction. We suggest using ten of the 14 features in total, shown in Table 2, and independent features tests are shown in Table 3.

Table 1. Preprocessing & Image Segmentation

Sr. No.	Image Processing Used	Output Image
1.	Original Lung CT Image	
2.	Binarized Image using Initial Threshold	
3.	Lung Parenchyma Mask	
4.	Lung Nodule Candidates	
5.	Segmented ROIs	

The prosed system uses the K-means clustering method to divide a larger dataset into smaller groups. Unsupervised learning is a method utilized in the K-means algorithm, which is used for classification. It is known as unsupervised categorization since the system automatically categorizes items based on user-defined criteria. We used the K-means clustering technique for image segmentation, followed by morphological filtering for lung nodule detection from lung CT scans [26].

Table 2. Features Extraction

Sr. No.	Type of Feature	Equation
1.	**Contrast:** Measures the local fluctuations in the GLCM, in contrast It determines the difference in intensity between an image element and its neighbour.	$\sum_{i,j} \|i-j\|^2 p(i,j)$
2.	**Correlation:** It calculates the correlation between the joint probabilities of the required image element pair occurrences.	$\sum_{i,j} \frac{(i-\mu_i)(j-\mu_j)p(i,j)}{\sigma_1\sigma_2}$
3.	**Energy:** The GLCM's total square components are provided by energy. Additionally, it is known as homogeneity or the angular moment.	$\sum_{i,j} p(i-j)^2$
4.	**Mean:** For a random variable vector A made up of N scalar observations, it is used to find the average or mean value of the array.	$\sum_{i=0}^{G-1} ip(i)$
5.	**Entropy:** Entropy shows the dissimilarity in the image or ROI. Entropy and energy are inversely related because of this.	$\sum_i p(i)log_2(p(i))$
6.	**Variance:** It gives the variance of the A items along the first array dimension for which the size is not 1.	$\sum_{i=0}^{G-1} (i-\mu)^2 p(i)$
7.	**Smoothness:** Smoothness is a measure of relative smoothness of intensity in a region.	$R = -1\frac{1}{1+\sigma_2}$
8.	**Kurtosis:** Kurtosis measures how prone a distribution is to outliers.	$\sigma^{-4} \sum_{i=0}^{G-1} (i-\mu)^4 p(i) - 3$
9.	**Skewness:** Simply put, skewness is a measurement of how asymmetric the given data is in relation to the sample mean.	$\sigma^{-3} \sum_{i=0}^{G-1} (i-\mu)^3 p(i)$
10.	**IDM:** his is the homogeneity at the local level. It increases when the inverse grey level co-occurrence matrix is large and the local grey level is uniform.	$\sum_{i,j} \frac{1}{1+(i-j)^2} p(i,j)$

The steps below have been used for K-means.

1. Assign the k value to the number of clusters and select the k-cluster centers at random.
2. Determine the cluster's mean or center.
3. Next, determine the separation between each pixel and the center of each cluster.
4. If the cluster is close to the center, move there; otherwise, go on to the next cluster.
5. Re-evaluate the center and continue until it stops moving (Fig. 3 and Table 4).

The trial outcomes and discourse offer the Sensitivity, Specificity, and Accuracy rates attained in the suggested structure after the efficient characterization [27]. The degree of precisely identified negatives is measured by specificity. Sensitivity is often referred to as the true positive rate or the recall rate in various professions. It determines the degree to which real positives are correctly recognized. Accuracy used to represent the ratio of

Table 3. Extracted Sample Features

Feature Extracted	Sample Values				
	Img1	**Img2**	**Img3**	**Img4**	**Img5**
Contrast	0.5042	0.3042	0.3679	0.4883	0.4405
Correlation	0.1032	0.1581	0.1231	0.1329	0.1704
Energy	0.8839	0.8015	0.8318	0.8870	0.8835
Mean	0.0059	0.0041	0.0041	0.0058	0.0063
Entropy	1.8331	2.9567	2.4440	1.3889	1.5578
Variance	0.0081	0.0080	0.0081	0.0081	0.0081
Smoothness	0.9565	0.9385	0.9390	0.9559	0.9589
Kurtosis	47.337	12.393	27.279	47.378	39.148
Skewness	4.4665	1.1712	2.2718	4.3207	3.3964
IDM	6.5730	0.6491	1.4005	3.7505	3.6540

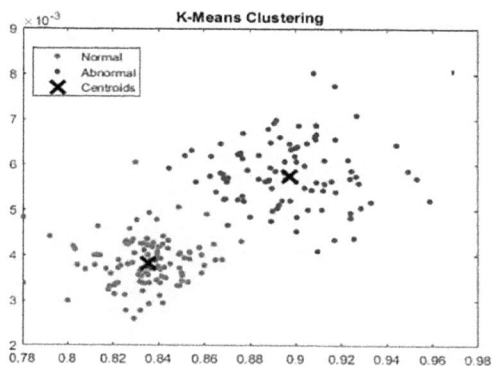

Fig. 3. K-Means Clustering

Table 4. Proposed System Result

True Positive	True Negative	False Positive	False Negative
32	33	3	2

the CT images that are classified correctly. We got overall 92.8% accuracy in proposed system.

5   Conclusion

This suggested CADe framework can speed up the analysis of lung cancerous growth and reduce human error when segmenting and categorizing lung nodules in CT images. This paper's main goal is to categorize the lung CT pictures as normal or abnormal. Radiologists and specialists can avoid the real illness with the help of the proposed technique. For this work, we used the TCIA lung CT scan image database. The texture features are retrieved after pre-purposing. K-means clustering is utilized to classify CT scans as normal or abnormal, and the proposed framework has a great accuracy of 92.8 percent.

Acknowledgments. Thanks to TCIA for providing the lung CT image database and also thanks to Dr. R. R. Manza for supervision and Department of CS & IT Dr. Babasaheb Ambedkar Marathwada University, Aurangabad (MS) India for providing the support.

Authors' Contributions. The main Conceptualization is held by R.M. and M.M., Methodology and framework processed by M.M. and P.P., Database collection, analysis and investigation done by K.K., P.P. and M.M., R.M. did the supervision, Writing-original draft, writing-review and editing is done by M.M.

References

1. Adjei, A. A. (2019). Lung cancer worldwide. Journal of Thoracic Oncology, 14(6), 956.
2. Collins, L. G., Haines, C., Perkel, R., & Enck, R. E. Lung cancer: diagnosis and management. American family physician, 75(1), 56-63, 2007.
3. Elmar Rendon-Gonzalez, Volodymyr Ponomaryov, Automatic Lung Nodule Segmentation and Classification in CT Images Based on SVM, IEEE 978-1-5090-2267, 24 June 2016.
4. Sayani Nandy, Nikita Pandey, A Novel Approach of Cancerous Cells Detection from Lungs CT Scan Images', International Journal of Advanced Research in Computer Science and Software Engineering Volume 2, Issue 8, August 2012.
5. Prof. Samir Kumar Bandyopadhyay, Edge Detection from Ct Images of Lung, International Journal of Engineering Science & Advanced Technology, Volume - 2, Issue - 1, 34 – 37, 2012.
6. FatmTaher, Naoufel Werghi and Hussain Al-Ahmad, Extraction of Sputum Cells using Thresholding Techniques for Lung Cancer Detection, International Conference on Innovations in Information Technology, 2012.
7. M. Tan, R. Deklerck, B. Jansen, M. Bister, J. Cornilis, A novel computer aided lung nodule detection system for CT images, Medical Physics, October 2011, doi: https://doi.org/10.1118/1.3633941 [PubMed Open Access].
8. M. Firmino, G. Angelo, H. Morais, M. R. Dantas and R. Valentim, Computer-aided detection (CADe) and diagnosis (CADx) system for lung cancer with likelihood of malignancy, Journal of Negative Results, 2016.
9. Amjed S. Al-Fehoum, Eslam B. Jaber, Mohammed A. Al-Jarrah, Automated detection of lung cancer using statistical and morphological image processing techniques, Journal of Biomedical Graphics and Computing, 4(2), pp. 33 - 42, 2014.
10. C. Panyindee and W. Chiracharit, Detection of Lung Tumors in Chest PET/CT Images by using Watershed Transform and Image Mapping, The 3rd International Symposium on Biomedical Engineering (ISBME 2008), p. 9–12, 2008.

11. Balaji Ganeshan, Sandra Abaleke, Rupert C.D. Young, Christopher R Chatwin and Kenneth A. Miles, Texture analysis of non-small cell lung cancer on unenhanced computed tomography: initial evidence for a relationship with tumour glucose metabolism and stage, Cancer Imaging, 10(1), pp. 137-143, 2010.
12. Mir Rayat Imtiaz Hossain, Imran Ahmed, Md. Hasanul Kabir, Automatic Lung Cancer Detection using GLCM features, Asian Conference on Computer Vision ACCV14, Singapore, 2014.
13. Ms. Swati P. Tidke, Prof. Vrishali A. Chakkarwar, Classification of Lung Tumor Using SVM, International Journal of Computational Engineering Research (ijceronline.com) Vol. 2 Issue. 5 September 2012.
14. Nikita Pandey, Sayani Nandy, A Novel Approach of Cancerous Cells Detection from Lungs CT scan Images, International Journal of Advanced Research in Computer Science and Software Engineering, Volume 2, Issue 8, August 2012.
15. Sudha. V, Jayashree. P, Lung Nodule Detection in CT Images Using Thresholding and Morphological Operations, International Journal of Emerging Science and Engineering (IJESE) ISSN: 2319–6378, Volume-1, Issue-2, December 2012.
16. Ada, Rajneet Kaur, Early Detection and Prediction of Lung Cancer Survival using Neural Network Classifier, IJAIEM Volume 2, Issue 6, June 2013.
17. K. Sankar, Dr. M. Prabhakaran, An Improved Architecture for Lung Cancer Cell Identification Using Gabor Filter and Intelligence System, International Journal of Engineering and Science (IJES) 2013.
18. Nunes, I. and Da Silva, H.S., Artificial neural networks: a practical course, Springer, 2018.
19. D. Cascio, R. Magro, F. Fauci, M. Iacomi, and G. Raso, Automatic detection of lung nodules in CT datasets based on stable 3D mass-spring models, Comput. Biol. Med., vol. 42, no. 11, pp. 1098–1109, 2012.
20. Public Database Open Access: https://public.cancerimaingachive.net/ncia/searcMain.jsf;jss ionid=128369143ADF4D948378665461898B03, Accessed on 16 Apr 2019.
21. Ciurte and S. Nedevschi, Texture analysis within contrast enhanced abdominal CT images, 2009 IEEE 5th International Conference on Intelligent Computer Communication and Processing, Cluj-Napoca, 2009, pp. 73-78.
22. Manoj M. Mhaske, Ramesh R. Manza and Pallavi K. Pradhan, Detection of Lung Cancer Using SVM with Lung Nodule Segmentation, PENSEE International Journal, ISSN: 0031-4773, VOLUME 51, ISSUE 7 2021.
23. Sawakare, S., & Chaudhari, D., Classification of brain tumor using discrete wavelet transform, principal component analysis and probabilistic neural network, Int J Res Emerg Sci Technol, 1(6), 13-9, 2014.
24. Gonzalez, R. C., Woods, R. E., & Eddins, S. L., Digital image processing using MATLAB, Pearson Education India, 2004.
25. Haralick, R. M., Shanmugam, K., & Dinstein, I. H., Textural features for image classification, IEEE Transactions on systems, man, and cybernetics, (6), 610-621, 1973.
26. Mandwe, A. A., & Anjum, A., Detection of brain tumor using k-means clustering, IJSR, 5(6), 420-423, 2016.
27. MM Mhaske, RR Manza, YM Rajput, Detection of Retinal Images as Normal or Abnormal using Texture Feature Analysis to identify the Diabetic Retinopathy, ISSN No: 2309-4893 International Journal of Advanced Engineering and Global Technology Vol-03, Issue-03, March 2015.

Automated Detection of Tuberculosis Based on Cantilever Biosensor

Bali Thorat[1]([✉]) and Mukti Jadhav[2]

[1] Department of Computer Science, Dr. Babasaheb Ambedkar Marathwada University, Aurangabad, India
balithorat@gmail.com
[2] Department of Computer Science, Shri. Shivaji Science and Arts College, Chikhali, India

Abstract. Mycobacterium Tuberculosis is one of the most hazardous disease. Universally millions of people are suffering from this dangerous disease. Number of detection techniques are available, but due to its complex structure this infectious disease not get diagnose easily and within time. To prevent spreading the bacteria and to stop mortality there is a huge requirement to build an automated and easy technique which can detect tuberculosis at a developing phase. The purpose of the article is to design and simulate the cantilever biosensor for detection of tuberculosis. Micro cantilever biosensor are designed with cylindrical and rectangular shape with silicon substrate. The cantilever surface is coated with antibodies and when patient sample is placed on it, the antigen-antibody gets binds together. When targeted antigen-antibody binds together stress generated and it forms deflection. The displacement achieved by Cylindrical-shape was 2.06×10^6 μm and rectangular-shape was 1.2×10^{26} μm for 100N load force correlates to 28.228×10^{-24} kg weight of antigen. From both the model maximum displacement were recorded and considered the rectangular-shape model as the leading model for tuberculosis detection.

Keywords: Tuberculosis · Cantilever · Biosensor · Simulation · MEMS · Antigen · Antibody

1 Introduction

All around the world Mycobacterium Tuberculosis is one of the hazardous disease [1]. Every year millions of people are suffering from this infectious disease [2, 3]. It comes under the top ten syndromes around the world. Tuberculosis is caused by Mycobacterium Tuberculosis. Tuberculosis classified into Pulmonary Tuberculosis and Extra-Pulmonary Tuberculosis. When Tuberculosis bacteria affect to the lungs organs it is called as Pulmonary Tuberculosis and when it affects to other part of the body rather than lungs it is called as Extra-Pulmonary Tuberculosis [4, 5]. It is also called as airborne disease due to its bacteria get released into the air and people get infection through these bacteria [6]. Tuberculosis is very dangerous disease, if patient not get proper treatment within time, the disease may converted to drug resistant tuberculosis which increases the chance of mortality. For getting proper treatment the disease should get diagnose at an early stage.

R. Manza et al. (Eds.): ACVAIT 2022, AISR 176, pp. 14–22, 2023.
https://doi.org/10.2991/978-94-6463-196-8_3

For this purpose there is a necessity to developed proper diagnosis method, which can diagnose this disease easily and within time. Most of the detection methods have been developed by many researchers. But these methods are insensitive and take lot of time for diagnose the disease. Some methods are laboratory based and some methods are very expensive. Laboratory based methods required proper sample and collection of sample is very tedious job. Laboratory based methods used very heavy and expensive equipment [7, 8]. So researchers are tried to developed biosensor based diagnosed methods. Because various fields used sensor based technologies. In medical field also, to detect various disease biosensors are used. Biosensor sense the biological sensing elements with physicochemical transducer [9]. Work of biosensor is based on antigen-antibodies. Based on the signal transducer the biosensors are categorised as piezo-electric quartz crystal, electrochemical, magneto elastic, breathalyser sensor [10]. Due to its stability and sensitivity biosensor plays a vital role in the medical field. But most of the biosensors are at the developmental stage due to complicated structure of TB bacteria. The objective of the paper is to designed and simulate the Bio-MEMS cantilever sensor for detection of tuberculosis. Cylindrical and Rectangular shapes were used to design Cantilever sensor and analysed the displacement of cantilever for both the shapes and find the best model for quick detection of tuberculosis.

2 Bio-Mems Cantilever Sensor

In the medical field, Micro Electro-Mechanical system plays a vital role to diagnose the molecules. Biosensor consist of a biological diagnose system known as bio-receptor and a transducer. Transducer convert into an electrical signal when bio-receptor and analyte interact with each other. The most common techniques used by transducer are electrical, optical and mechanical detection. The biosensor used bio-receptors which are based on interaction of antigen-antibody.

To diagnose the disease through biosensor antigen-antibodies are required. ESAT-6 and CFP-10 are two main antigens which are used for diagnosis purposed, since these antigens are the sources of tuberculosis. For tuberculosis 6KDa and 11KDa are the molecular weight of ESAT-6 antigen and Anti-ESAT-6 antibodies. The total molecular load is 17KDa, since the value of 1 KDa is near about 1.661×10^{-24} kg, thus considering the value of 1KDa, the total molecular weight of ESAT-6 antigen and Anti-ESAT-6 antibody is 28.228×10^{-24} kg [11]. The surface force range are 10N to 100N for interaction of antigen-antibody whereas the intermolecular force is 10N which generated by single antigen-antibody interaction [12]. Thus the 28.228×10^{-24} kg is the load of 10 antigens. The intermolecular force is estimated by considering the interactions of 10 antigen-antibodies and it applied on the surface of cantilever and demonstrates the value of deformation [13].

A bio-sensing design were produced by cantilever when interaction of biomolecular combined with a micro cantilever platform. The vibrational frequency or variations in cantilever bending can be identify by micro cantilever sensor. The structure of micromechanical and electromechanical sensor associated by micro cantilever sensor [14, 15]. With the collaboration of antigen-antibodies, the stress generated on sensitive aspect of cantilever, which generated displacement on one side of cantilever, as one edge of it is fixed and other edge is free for displacement. The specific antibody is immobilised on the top surface of cantilever, since when sample of patient is drop on it and if sample contain specific elements it binds with antibodies which generated stress on the surface and micro cantilever gets deflected. These defection of cantilever is estimated for 10N to 100N load force and consider the model which generated maximum displacement as a best model for detection of tuberculosis.

3 Experimental Details

The model of micro cantilever biosensor has been made on 3D design where static constraint are applied at one end and hanging free at the other end in COMSOL Multiphysics. The solid mechanics model under structural mechanics the MEMS module were designed. 10N to 100N force were applied to get maximum displacement. The equation for the force in sample is:

$$F_A = {F_{tot}}/{A} \qquad (1)$$

Where, F_A is force per unit area, F_{tot} is total force and A is area of the surface.

The value for Young's modulus $= 170$ Pa and Poisson's ratio $= 0.44$ was deliberated for all the models when load force applied to the sample. Thus when the surface generated stress due to interaction of antigen antibody it forms the deflection [16].

Cylindrical shape and Rectangular shapes of Cantilever has been designed with different dimensions as shown in Table 1 and Table 2 respectively, and the surface of cantilever are made with Silicon material, to analyse the deflection of cantilever by applying same force. To find the maximum displacement, the sensitivity of both the shapes were analysed and the maximum displacement model were consider as a best model for detection of tuberculosis.

Micro cantilever biosensor based on the organisation of Micromechanical and Electromechanical sensor for detection of tuberculosis has been design and simulated in COMSOL Multiphysics. One side of cantilever is used as a static constraint and other side is free for displacement. On the surface of cantilever load force has been applied which is correlates to the weight of ESAT-6 antigen, due to this weight cantilever gets deflects. When the stress generated on the surface of cantilever it produced deflection. Deflection of cantilever is measured using the equation as

$$Deflection = {PL^3}/{3EI} \qquad (2)$$

Where, P is applied load, L is length, E is young's modulus and I is moment of inertia.

Table 1. Dimension of Cylindrical shape geometry

Shape	Dimension	Magnitude
Cylindrical	Radius	1 μm
	Height	1 μm

Table 2. Dimension of Rectangular shape geometry

Shape	Parts	Dimension	Magnitude
Rectangular	Cantilever	Width	5
		Depth	80
		Height	1
	Sample Compartment	Width	20
		Depth	40
		Height	2
	Fixed End	Width	40
		Depth	10
		Height	5

Moment of inertia is measured using the equation as

$$I = BD^2 \big/ 12 \tag{3}$$

Where, B is breadth and D is thickness.

To analyse the deflection cylindrical and rectangular shape with silicon material were design and simulated with load force 10N to 100N. Figure 1 shows cylindrical model with load 10N to 100N. Similarly Fig. 2 shows rectangular model with load 10N to 100N.

4   Result and Discussion

As shown in above Fig. 1 and Fig. 2, due to collaboration of antigen-antibodies stress generated on the surface of cylindrical and rectangular shape of cantilever and it produced displacement for load force of 10N to 100N and these displacement were explored as shown in table 3.

Thus, due to stress displacement generated on the surface of cantilever. The displacement of cylindrical and rectangular shape were analyzed for 10N to 100N as shown in Fig. 3 and Fig. 4.

After analysis it has been observed that, for load force of 100N of both the model it generated highest displacement as compare to lower load. For 100N load of Cylindrical shape produced $2.06 \times 10^6 \mu$m and for same load force rectangular shape produced 1.71×10^{28} μm. After analysing both the models it has been noted that rectangular shape model of cantilever generated highest displacement as 1.71×10^{28} μm for 100N load force. Thus rectangular shape model of cantilever is consider as a best model for tuberculosis detection.

After comparing various biosensors the proposed system that is Micro cantilever biosensor produced an effective result in detection of tuberculosis. As mention in introduction section various biosensors are available for detection. But these biosensors have

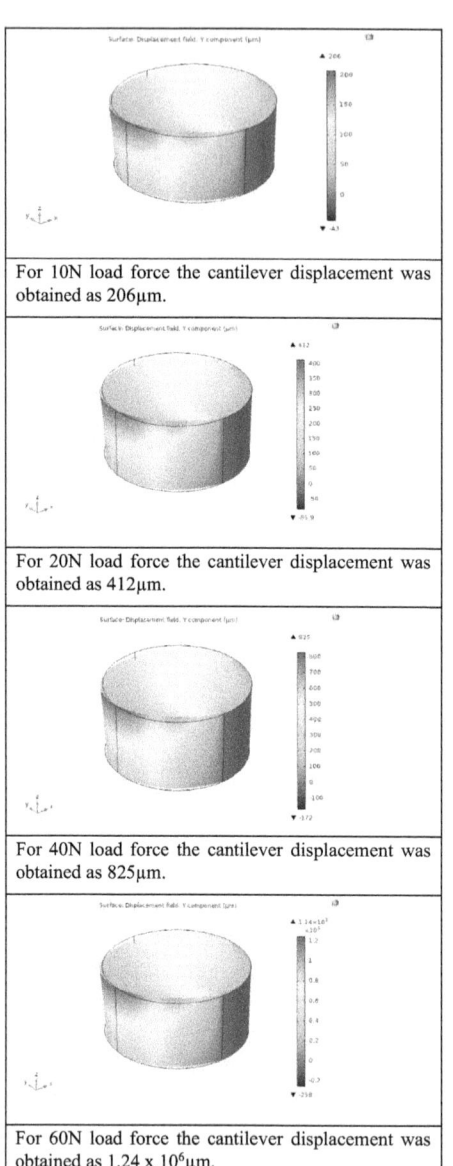

For 10N load force the cantilever displacement was obtained as 206µm.	For 80N load force the cantilever displacement was obtained as 1.65 x 10⁶µm.
For 20N load force the cantilever displacement was obtained as 412µm.	For 100N load force the cantilever displacement was obtained as 2.06 x 10⁶µm.
For 40N load force the cantilever displacement was obtained as 825µm.	
For 60N load force the cantilever displacement was obtained as 1.24 x 10⁶µm.	

Fig. 1. Cylindrical Shape Model with load 10N to 100N.

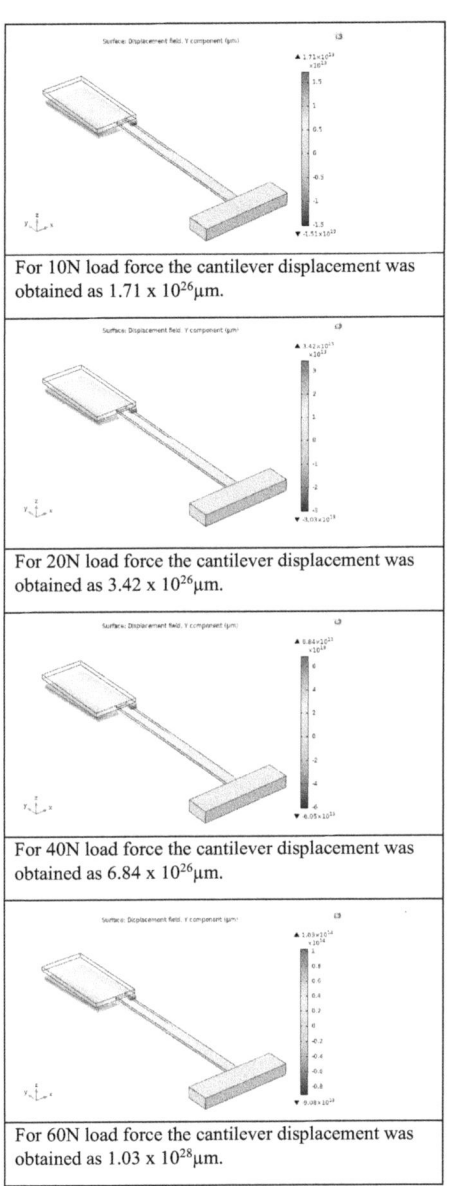

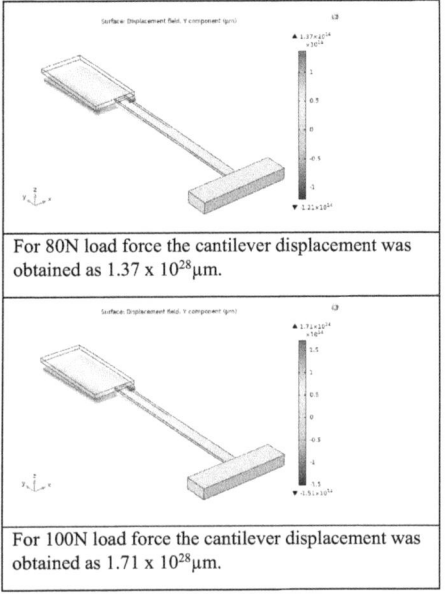

For 10N load force the cantilever displacement was obtained as $1.71 \times 10^{26}\mu m$.

For 80N load force the cantilever displacement was obtained as $1.37 \times 10^{28}\mu m$.

For 20N load force the cantilever displacement was obtained as $3.42 \times 10^{26}\mu m$.

For 100N load force the cantilever displacement was obtained as $1.71 \times 10^{28}\mu m$.

For 40N load force the cantilever displacement was obtained as $6.84 \times 10^{26}\mu m$.

For 60N load force the cantilever displacement was obtained as $1.03 \times 10^{28}\mu m$.

Fig. 2. Rectangular Shape Model with load 10N to 100N.

some limitations such as piezoelectric quartz crystal biosensor is fast, label free but the temperature, density and electrical conductivity of the sample may influence the output. Optical biosensor is rapid sensitive specific but it required complex pre-treatments steps. Electrochemical biosensor is sensitive, label free but low managing ability for complex clinical samples. Most of the biosensors required sample purification and sophisticated

Table 3. Displacement of Cylindrical Model and Rectangular Model

Load	Displacement(μm)	
	Cylindrical Model	Rectangular Model
10	206	1.71×10^{26}
20	412	3.42×10^{26}
40	825	6.84×10^{26}
60	1.24×10^6	1.03×10^{28}
80	1.65×10^6	1.37×10^{28}
100	2.06×10^6	1.71×10^{28}

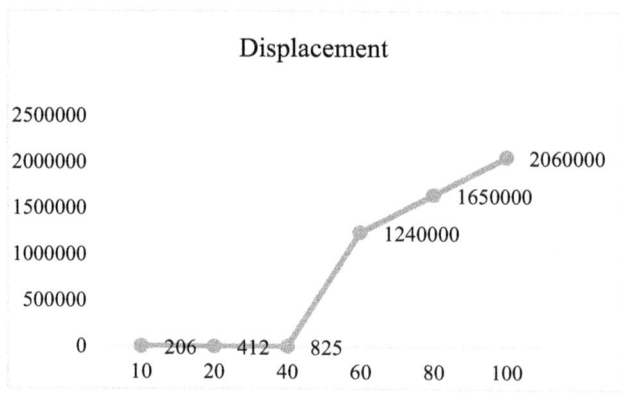

Fig. 3. Displacement of cylindrical shape for 10N to 100N

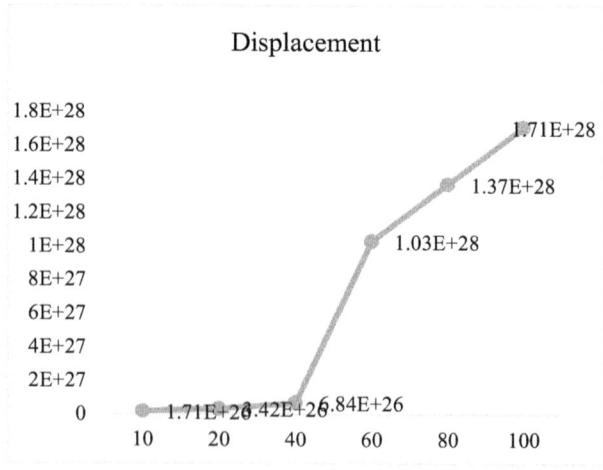

Fig. 4. Displacement of rectangular shape for 10N to 100N

instruments [8]. Whereas our proposed system is a promising tool for directly recognizing bio-molecular collaboration as mention in experiment section.

Conclusion

Mycobacterium tuberculosis is comes under the top ten disease in the world. It is very dangerous disease due to which every year millions of people get infected. Its structure is very complicated, hence tuberculosis bacteria not get diagnose easily. There is a huge need to developed simple detection technique. The purpose of this research is to designed and simulate cantilever biosensor based on MEMS structure. Two models of cylindrical and rectangular shapes cantilever sensor with silicon material were designed and simulated in COMSOL Multiphysics. Various load force were applied to cantilever surface and analysed the displacement for 10N to 100N. From both the models rectangular shape cantilever for 100N load force generates highest displacement as 1.71×10^{28} μm. Therefore, rectangular shape cantilever is consider as a best model for detection of tuberculosis. Since before developing the actual model, simulation helps us to forecast the complete structure and estimate the device performance, which reduced the cost and time.

Acknowledgments. We would like to thank Dr. Babasaheb Ambedkar Marathwada University, Aurangabad (MS) India for providing the publication support.

References

1. Deysel and Martha Susanna Madrey, Structure-function relationships of mycolic acids in tuberculosis, Diss. University of Pretoria (2008).
2. World Health Organization, Global tuberculosis report (2017).
3. Thorat B. A and Jadhav M, "Comparative Study of Global Severity of Tuberculosis" (2018).
4. Fronczek, Christopher F, and Jeong-Yeol Yoon, "Biosensors for monitoring airborne pathogens", Journal of laboratory automation, 390-410, 20.4 (2015).
5. https://ourworldindata.org/hiv-aids#new-infections
6. Radzi, Raja Umi Kalsom Raja Mohd, Wahidah Mansor, and Juliana Johari, "Review of mycobacterium tuberculosis detection", IEEE Control and System Graduate Research Colloquium, IEEE (2011).
7. Hendrick and Nadia Alfitri, "Identifying Tuberculosis through Exhaled Breath by Using Field Programmable Gate Array (FPGA) myRIO", Journal of Automation and Control Engineering Vol. 3, No. 6, December (2015).
8. Srivastava, Saurabh K, Cees JM Van Rijn, and Maarten A Jongsma, Biosensor-based detection of tuberculosis, RSC advances 6.22, 17759-17771 (2016).
9. Thorat Bali, and Mukti Jadhav, "Current Trends In Bio-Sensing Technologies For Tuberculosis Detection", International Conference on Smart Innovations in Design, Environment, Management, Planning and Computing (ICSIDEMPC). IEEE (2020).
10. De Souza and Marcus Vinicius Nora, "Synthesis and biological aspects of mycolic acids: an important target against Mycobacterium tuberculosis", The Scientific World Journal 8, 720-751 (2008).
11. Yashaswini B. M and Dr. Rachana S Akki, "Design of Micro-Cantilever Biosensors for Detection of Latent Tuberculosis", International Research Journal of Engineering and Technology (IRJET) Volume: 07 Issue: 07 | July (2020).

12. Saeed M. A, Khan S. M, Ahmed N, Khan M. U, and Rehman A, "Design and Analysis of Capacitance based Bio-MEMS Cantilever Sensor for Tuberculosis Detection", International Conference on intelligent systems engineering (ICISE), pp. 175-180, IEEE (2016).
13. Monosik Rastislav, Miroslav Stredansky, and Ernest Sturdik, "Biosensors-classification, characterization and new trends", Acta chimica slovaca 5.1, 109-120 (2012).
14. Saranya R, Saranya K, Ceemati D, Chandra Devi K, and Meenakshi Sundaram N, "Design of MEMS-based Microcantilever for Tuberculosis Detection", In Proc COMSOL conference, Bangalore (2013).
15. Murthy K. S. N., Prasad G. R. K. Saikiran N. L. N. V., and Manoj T. V. S., "Design and simulation of MEMS biosensor for the detection of tuberculosis", Indian J Sci Technol 9, 31 (2016).

Diagnosing Microscopic Blood Samples for Early Detection of Leukemia by Deep and Hybrid Learning Techniques

Ebrahim Mohammed Senan[1][(✉)], Mukti E. Jadhav[2], Ramesh R. Manza[1], and Vandana Bagal[3]

[1] Department of Computer Science and Information Technology, Dr. Babasaheb Ambedkar Marathwada University, Aurangabad, India
senan1710@gmail.com
[2] Shri Shivaji Science and Arts College, Chikhli District, Buldana, India
[3] K.K. Wagh Institute of Engineering Education and Research, Nasik, India

Abstract. Blood is an important component of the human, which consists of many important components including White Blood Cells (WBC). Leukaemia is one of the dangerous kinds of cancer that affect the blood and bone marrow, affecting children and adults. Acute lymphoblastic Leukaemia (ALL) is dangerous and deadly type of blood cancer. Hematologists and experts work on diagnosing blood by taking patient samples and analyzing them with a high-quality magnifying lens. However, manual diagnosis is boring, time-consuming, and more prone to errors and differing expert views. Therefore, artificial intelligence techniques solve this problem and support the opinions of highly experienced experts. This research aims to develop diagnostic systems using a Convolutional Neural Network (CNN) and a hybrid CNN and SVM to diagnose the ALL_IDB2 dataset for early diagnosis of Leukaemia. CNN models and a hybrid technique consisting of two blocks were implemented, the first block of CNN models to extract feature and the second block, the SVM algorithm, to classify the feature. All the proposed systems achieved superior results in diagnosing the ALL_IDB2 dataset for early diagnosis of Leukaemia.

Keywords: ALL · Machine learning · CNN · Hybrid method

1 Introduction

Blood is one of the critical components of the human body, and it is the dynamo that moves the human. Blood comprises several elements, namely plasma 55%, RBC 45%, WBC and platelets less than 1% [1]. Plasma transports minerals, hormones, proteins and other nutrients through blood vessels and gets rid of harmful elements in the form of waste products. Blood is produced in the bone marrow, the soft tissue within the bony cavity. When there is overactive or abnormal bone marrow [2], it produces immature cells or multicolored cells. Hematology is diagnosed by extracting WBC information

R. Manza et al. (Eds.): ACVAIT 2022, AISR 176, pp. 23–38, 2023.
https://doi.org/10.2991/978-94-6463-196-8_4

[3]. The diagnosis is made based on increased WBC with immature myeloid or lymphoid cells, low platelets and neutrophils [4]. Therefore, hematologists analyze blood samples under a microscope to diagnose and identify blast cells. Thus, the presence of blast cells in blood smears is one of the most critical symptoms of Leukaemia. There are some types of Leukaemia, the most dangerous of which is ALL. ALL is considered one of the most dangerous and deadly types, prevalent in children and adults. Early diagnosis of Leukaemia and its types is essential for timely treatment. Diagnosis by blood smears and microscopic blood tests is one of the methods that accelerate the detection of Leukaemia without medical risks [5]. There are also many techniques for diagnosing Leukaemia, such as interventional radiology, biopsy, percutaneous aspiration, catheter drainage and other methods that have limitations for the sensitivity of the technique [6]. There are also techniques such as molecular cytogenetics, array-based comparative genetic hybridization (aCGH) and long-distance reverse transcription-polymerase chain reaction (LDI-PCR) that require highly experienced hematologists, time and extensive work to diagnose Leukaemia [7]. There is also a similarity in the characteristics of normal cells and lymphocytes in their early stages, which are challenges for the early diagnosis. Therefore, lymphocytes were categorised into some types: normal, reactive, and atypical. Thus, each type has characteristics that distinguish it from the other type. Since the diagnosis is completed manually, it is a boring and time-consuming method and prone to many errors. Therefore, automated diagnosis using artificial intelligence techniques is essential in the early diagnosis of Leukaemia. Several researchers have proposed automated methods for the early diagnosis of Leukaemia by extracting chromatic, morphological, and texture characteristics from WBC micrographs. Therefore, the diagnosis of microscopic blood sample data set by deep and machine learning techniques will lead to an accurate, reliable and rapid diagnosis of early detection of Leukaemia. CNN models have the ability to solve the deficiencies of manual diagnosis and their excellent ability to differentiate normal and abnormal cells (blast cells). This study focuses on the diagnosis of the ALL_IDB2 dataset; extracting feature and diagnosing them using CNN models, hybrid techniques between CNN models, and machine learning algorithms (SVM).

The significant contributions in this study are as follows:

- Noise and all artifacts were removed using overlapping filters.
- Increasing the dataset images by using the data augmentation method.
- Adjust the parameters of CNN models to extract deep features with accurateness and efficiency.
- Applied a hybrid technique between CNN models and SVM algorithm to obtain superior results for early detection of Leukaemia.

The rest of the article is arranged as follows: Sect. 2 presents a group of related work. Section 3 describes the methods and techniques used to analyze and classify a data set. Section 4 presents the results execution of the systems. Section 5 offers a discussion of the systems. Concludes the work in Sect. 6.

2 Related Work

This section reviews many previous studies related to the diagnosis of microscopic images of microscopic blood samples for the early detection of Leukaemia. CNN and SVM help diagnose microscopic images and identify Leukaemia.

Nizar et al. presented the CNN and machine learning techniques to diagnose the ALL-IDB Image Bank datasets to detect Leukaemia subtypes. The data augmentation method to obtain images was also applied artificially. The CNN got an accuracy of 81.74% [8]. Goutam et al. proposed a model consisting some stages: preprocessing, region of interest, extraction of features, and classification stage for classifying microscopic blood samples. Feature extraction based on Local Directional path (LDP) and feature classification by SVM, which achieved superior results for the classification of microscopic images [9]. Rawat et al. presented a method for diagnosing lymphoid and myeloid cells for the giagnosis of Leukaemia. The system optimizes the images of the AML and ALL datasets and extracts 331 features textures, geometrics, and chromaticities to distinguish between normal and malignant cells. The features were classified by SVM, which achieved good results for classifying the two data sets [10]. Amin et al. discuss an approach to discovering lymphocytic Leukaemia. All dataset images were enhanced, WBC was extracted using k-means, then statistical and geometrical features were extracted from WBC. The features were classified by the SVM algorithm, which got an accuracy of 97% [11]. Zhana et al. proposed two approaches; the first approach is to separate WBCs from the rest of the cells, and the second approach is to extract the most critical geometrical, statistical, and shape features and transform the discrete cosine. The result of systems on the ALL-IDB data set, and it achieved an accuracy of 97.45% [12]. Cecilia et al. presented a new approach to identify WBC from images of the ALL-IDB dataset to diagnose them as normal or leukemic. All images passed through the stages of enhancement, segmentation, WBC recognition and classification; the system achieved an accuracy of 99.7% [13]. Nizar et al. offered a method for diagnosing Leukaemia subtypes using CNN models and machine learning. The data augmentation has been used to augment the images. All models performed well, as the performance of the CNN was more useful than the machine learning algorithms, which reached an accuracy of 88.25 [8]. Aqsa et al. presented a method to detect Leukaemia in its early stages. A color filter was applied to detect white blood cells, and then a wavelet and curvelet descriptor was used to extract structural features. Then feature classification by KNN and SVM algorithms has yielded promising results [14]. Rawat et al. presented a novel method for diagnosing lymphocytes by first isolating white blood cells from other blood cells. The GLCM extracted the texture and shape features algorithm and classified by the SVM classifier. When diagnosing texture features, the system got an accuracy of 86.7%, while the system got an accuracy of 56.1% with shape features [15]. Lakshmi et al. offered a method for early diagnosis of Leukaemia. They applied the K-means clustering to cluster the lesion and isolated it from the rest of the cells. The diagnosis was made using the SVM algorithm, which got an accuracy of 95% [16].

3   Materials and Methods

In this section, the most critical strategies and materials for analyzing and classifying the ALL_IDB2 data set as described in Fig. 1. All images have been enhanced to remove noise and obtain high efficiency in the following stages. After the improvement process, two proposed systems were applied. The first system through two CNN models. The second system is a hybrid between CNN with SVM.

3.1   Description of Two Datasets

All the systems presented were evaluated using the publicly available ALL-IDB dataset using the machine, deep learning, and a fusion them. The publicly available dataset contains images of microscopic blood samples for ALL and normal images. The data set focused on ALL, which were more severe and lethal than other types. Lymphomas were classified and identified for each image by specialized experts. All images were acquired by a Canon PowerShot G5 optical microscope and RGB color at a high-resolution of 1944 x 2592 pixels. This data set consists of ALL_IDB1 and ALL_IDB2; each image contains approximately 39,000 blood cells. This study targets the ALL_IDB2 dataset, which includes 260 images equally divided into 130 images of malignant and 130 normal blood cells [17]. Figure 2.a describes a set of samples for the data set.

3.2   Pre-processing

The data set images were fed before applying the enhancement process; because of the noise and lack of image contrast, the performance of the proposed systems was inaccurate. Thus, all dataset images were enhanced before feeding them into deep learning models [18]. The first step in biomedical image processing is to remove unwanted noise and artifacts. When analyzing blood samples under the microscope, there are light reflections, in addition to liquid samples that are placed with the blood sample, all of which affect the performance of artificial intelligence techniques. Thus, applying filters to enhance the images is required to obtain high performance in the later stages of image processing [19]. In this study, the images were optimized using two filters. First, an

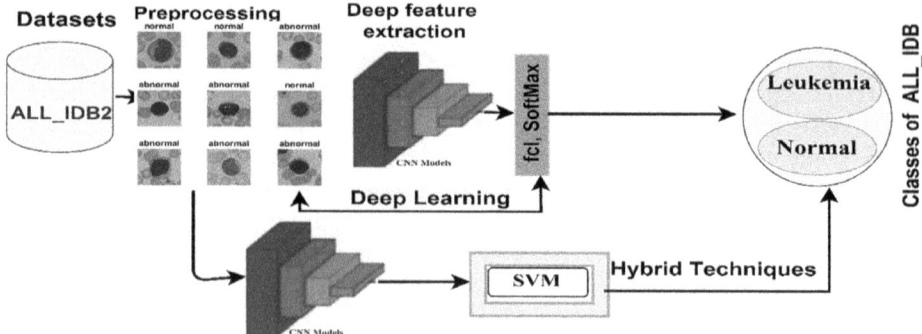

Fig. 1. Methodology for diagnosing the ALL_IDB2 dataset.

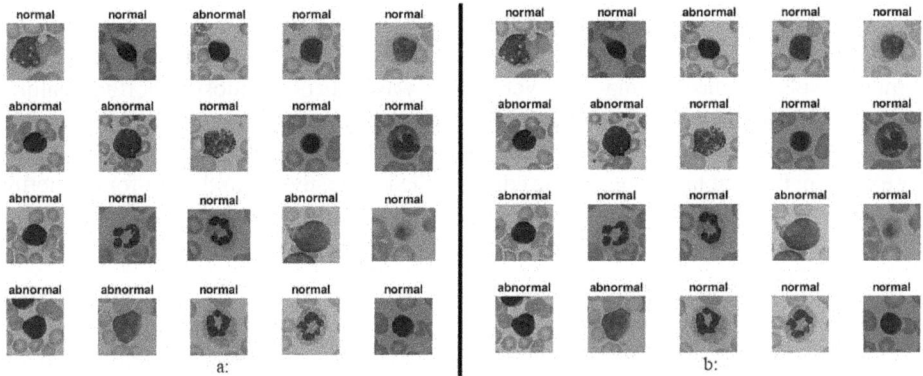

Fig. 2. A set of data set samples before and after enhancement (a) ALL-IDB2 samples and (b) Enhanced ALL-IDB2 dataset images.

average filter is used to improve the contrast of the images. The filter size is set to 7*7 so that the filter replaces each goal pixel by an average of 48 neighbouring pixels, and the process continues for each image pixel. Equation 1 shows how the average filter works [20].

$$z(n) = \frac{1}{N} \sum_{i=0}^{M-1} y(n-1) \tag{1}$$

where $z(n)$ refers to input, $y(n-1)$ refers to earlier input and N is the pixels numbers.

Second, a Laplacian filter was used to detect white blood cells' edges. Equation 2 defines the technique of action of the filter.

$$\nabla^2 f = \frac{\partial^2 f}{\partial^2 x} + \frac{\partial^2 f}{\partial^2 y} \tag{2}$$

differential equation of second order is $\nabla^2 f$ and x, y are the location of the matrix.

Finally, the system produces an improved image using subtracting the images produced by the Laplacian method from the image produced using the average method. Equation 3 describes the final step of producing an enhanced image.

$$EN = z(m) - \nabla^2 f \tag{3}$$

where EN represents the enhanced image

Figure 2.b represents set of images after the enhancement process.

3.3 Convolutional Neural Networks (CNN)

The CNN are called deep learning and have the superior ability to classify, and recognize patterns. CNN work in many fields, such as motion modelling, speech recognition, object segmentation, and biomedical image processing. CNN contain many 2D layers and are suitable for processing and diagnosing 2D images. CNN models differ in the number of layers and the weights of each layer [21]. The work of filters is to convolute around the image to be handle. In each layer, neurons receive associations from the earlier layers and neurons of the same layer. The core of CNN's work is to represent the input images at many levels; To classify images, layers amplify aspects of the most important features and suppress unimportant (irrelevant) differences. Figure 3 shows the architecture for the AlexNet and ResNet-18 [22]. Where layers work on specific processing of images, for example, the first layer detects the edges of the image, the second layer for extracting the geometric features, the third layer extracts the features of texture and shape, and so on. As described in Fig. 3, networks consist of the following most important layers:

- Convolutional Layer: The number of convolutional layers differs from model to another. The name CNN comes from the name of the Convolutional Layer. The convolutional layer is one of the major layers in CNN, and the convolution process is implemented between the filter w (t) and the image to be processed x (t). The mechanism is done as described in Eq. 4. Three critical parameters that define and control the work of convolutional layers are the size of the filter, p-step and zero padding. The larger the size of the filter, will more the filter wrap around the image, while zero-padding keeps the original image size. The p-step operates to specify the number of filter steps on the image [24].

$$s(t) = (x * w)(t) = \int x(a)w(t-a)da \qquad (4)$$

- pooling Layer: This layer reduces the resulting dimensions of the convolutional layer. There are two types of this layer: Max and Average Pooling. Max-Pooling specifies the max pixel from the pixels specified by a filter and represents it in the following stages [25]. Average-Pooling calculates the average weight of the weights set by the filter and represents all values by their average value.
- Fully Connected Layer (FCL): This layer contains millions of interconnected neurons responsible for classifying the input images. It works to convert feature maps from binary representation to mono representation.
- There are also many auxiliary layers, such as the ReLU (Rectified Linear Unit) layer, which comes after the convolutional layers and works to handle positive weights, suppress negative weights, and convert them to zero as explained in the Eq. 5. CNN models produce millions of parameters, which causes overfitting, so the dropout layer solves this problem by setting it to, say, 50%, which means 50% of neurons are passed in each iteration, but one of the disadvantages is that it doubles the training time [26]

$$\text{ReLU(x)} = \begin{cases} x, x \geq 0 \\ 0, x < 0 \end{cases} \qquad (5)$$

- Finally, the Softmax activation layer works to classify each input image into its appropriate class. In this work, the Softmax function will produce two neurons that are either Leukaemia or normal according to the data set classes.

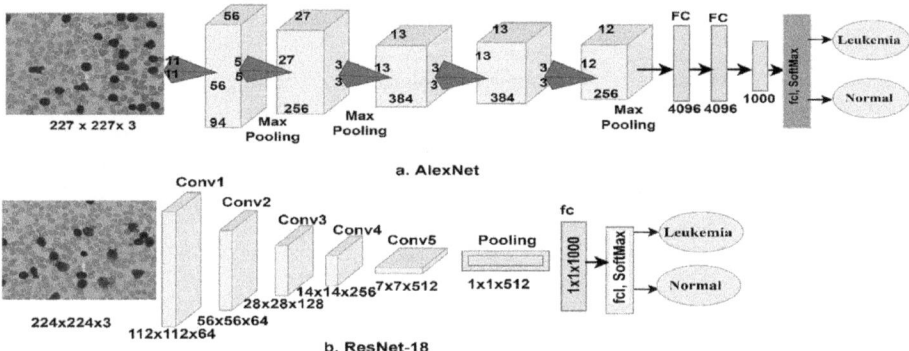

Fig. 3. Structure of a. AlexNet and b. ResNet-18.

3.4 Hybrid of Deep and Machine Learning

This section presents a hybrid method of CNN models and SVM for the diagnosis of Leukaemia. CNN models require high specification computer resource specifications to train the data set, and it takes a long time to train the data set, so these hybrid techniques solve this challenge [26]. The technique removes Fully Connected Layer from the CNN model and replaces them with the SVM algorithm. In this section, the hybrid approach consists of two blocks: the firstly is AlexNet and ResNet-18 models to extract the deep feature [27]. Secondly is the SVM classifier for classifying deep features. Figures 4a and b show the hybrid architecture. The SVM algorithm replaces the fully connected layer of deep learning models.

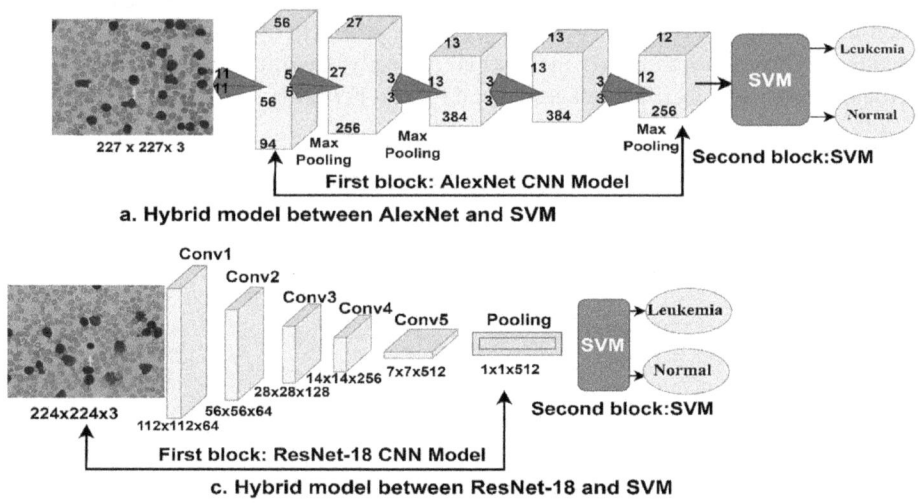

Fig. 4. Hybrid technique a. AlexNet + SVM and b. ResNet-18 + SVM.

Table 1. Splitting the ALL_IDB2 datasets

Phase	training and validation		Testing (20%)
Classes	Training (80%)	validation (20%)	
Leukaemia	83	21	26
Normal	83	21	26

4   Experimental Result

4.1   Splitting Dataset

All proposed systems in this work were evaluated on the ALL_IDB2 dataset that contains 260 images equally divided into two classes, Leukaemia and normal. The data set has been split into 80% for training and validation (80:20, respectively) and 20% for testing. Table 1 describes the splitting of the ALL_IDB2 data set through stages of the training, validation, and testing systems (Leukaemia and normal). The systems were executed on the MATLAB 2018b executable environment and implemented on a computer with Intel ® i5 a 6th generation, GPU of 4 GB, and RAM of 12 GB.

4.2   Evaluation Metrics

In this section, we explain the appropriate statistical measures that evaluate the performance of the networks implemented in this study, whether deep learning models or hybrid method on the ALL_IDB2 dataset for early diagnosis of Leukaemia. Equations 6, 7, 8, 9 and 10 show the most critical measures that evaluate the performance of systems. Each network produced a confusion matrix from which to obtain information for the equations. The confusion matrix includes all correctly classified images named TP and TN and incorrectly classified images named FP and FN [28].

$$Accuracy = \frac{TN + TP}{TN + TP + FN + FP} * 100\% \tag{6}$$

$$Precision = \frac{TP}{TP + FP} * 100\% \tag{7}$$

$$Sensitivity = \frac{TP}{TP + FN} * 100\% \tag{8}$$

$$Specificity = \frac{TN}{TN + FP} * 100\% \tag{9}$$

$$AUC = \frac{TruePositiveRate}{FalsePositiveRate} = \frac{Sensitivity}{Specificity} \tag{10}$$

where:

The true positive (TP) denotes the number of Leukaemia images which correctly classified.

True negative (TN) means the number of normal images which correctly classified.

A false positive (FP) describes the number of normal images incorrectly categorised as Leukaemia.

False negatives (FN) represent the number of Leukaemia images incorrectly categorised as normal.

4.3   CNN Models Results

In this section, the evaluation results of CNN models based on transfer learning are AlexNet and ResNet-18 on the ALL_IDB2 dataset. The dataset contains a small number of images, which affects the accuracy of the diagnosis because CNN models need a large number of images. Thus, a data augmentation technique was used, in which the images artificially increased. There are many operations performed by the image augmentation technique, such as rotation in many angles, shifting, flipping, and other operations [29].

Table 2 describes the tuning of AlexNet and ResNet-18 models. The optimizer "adam" is set for both models and the setting of Max Epochs, Validation Frequency, Mini Batch Size, and Execution Environment.

Table 3 illustrates the results of both AlexNet and ResNet-18, where it is noted that ResNet-18 outperforms the AlexNet model for classifying the ALL_IDB2 dataset. The ResNet-18 model achieved an accuracy of 97.4%, a precision, sensitivity, specificity of 97.5% for all measures, and an AUC of 97.44%. In contrast, the AlexNet model got accuracy, precision, sensitivity, specificity, and AUC with a percentage of 96.2%, 96.5%, 96%, 96%, and 98.82%, respectively.

Figure 5 displays the execution of AlexNet and ResNet-18 for classifying the ALL_IDB2 dataset for diagnosis of Leukaemia.

Figure 6 illustrates the confusion matrix created by the AlexNet and ResNet-18 models for diagnosing ALL_IDB2 dataset for detection of Leukaemia. The confusion matrix includes all rightly classified dataset images represented by the primary diameter called TP and TN and inaccurately classified represented by the secondary diameter FP and FN. Figure 6.a shows the confusion matrix for AlexNet, which reached an overall accuracy of 96.2%, an accuracy of 100% for diagnosing Leukaemia samples,

Table 2. Tuning training options for AlexNet and ResNet-18 models

Options	AlexNet	ResNet-18
training Options	adam	Adam
Mini Batch Size	128	15
Max Epochs	10	4
Initial Learn Rate	0.0001	0.0001
Validation Frequency	50	5
Execution Environment	4 GB GPU	4 GB GPU

Table 3. The results of the CNN models

Measure	AlexNet	ResNet-18
Accuracy %	96.2	97.4
Precision %	96.5	97.5
Sensitivity %	96	97.5
Sepecificy %	96	97.5
AUC %	98.82	97.44

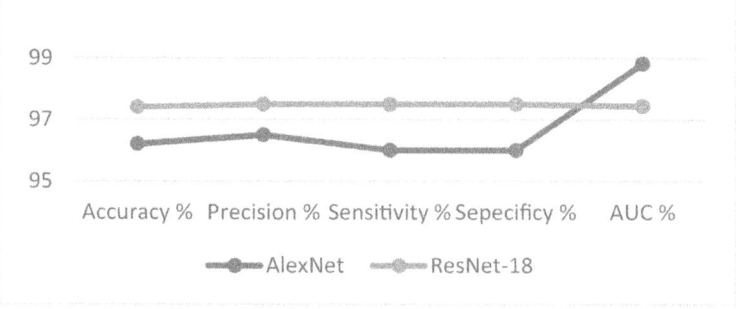

Fig. 5. Display execution of CNN models for classifying the ALL_IDB2 images.

and an accuracy of 92.3% for diagnosing normal images. While Fig. 6.b describes the confusion matrix of ResNet-18, which reached an overall accuracy of 97.4%, an accuracy of 94.9% for diagnosing Leukaemia samples, and an accuracy of 100% for diagnosing normal blood samples.

4.4   Results of the Hybrid CNN with SVM Algorithm

This section reviews the performance results of hybrid technologies between AlexNet and ResNet-18 and SVM machine learning. These techniques worked to overcome the challenges in machine learning models related to their demand for high-performance computer specifications. They are taking a long time to train the data set. This technique consists of CNN for feature map extraction and the SVM for classification. Hybrid techniques have achieved superior results for diagnosing Leukaemia dataset.

Table 4 presents the results of the AlexNet + SVM and ResNet-18 + SVM hybrid technologies. It is noted that these techniques have achieved superior results for the detection of Leukaemia. It is noted that ResNet-18 + SVM has slightly outperformed AlexNet + SVM. The AlexNet + SVM network achieved an accuracy of 98.1% and an equal ratio of accuracy, sensitivity, specificity by 98% for all measures. While ResNet-18 + SVM network achieved an accuracy of 98.7% and an equal percentage of precision, sensitivity, specificity by 98.5% for all measures.

Figure 7 displays hybrid technique performance.

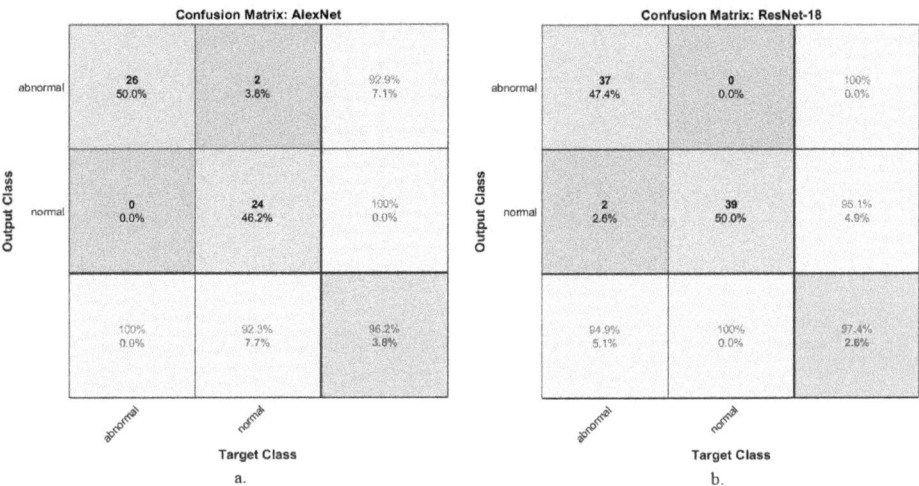

Fig. 6. Confusion matrix for diagnosing ALL_IDB2 data sets (a): AlexNet and (b): ResNet-18

Table 4. The results of the hybrid models on the ALL_IDB2 datasets

Measure	AlexNet + SVM	ResNet-18 + SVM
Accuracy %	98.1	98.7
Precision %	98	98.5
Sensitivity %	98	98.5
Sepecificy %	98	98.5

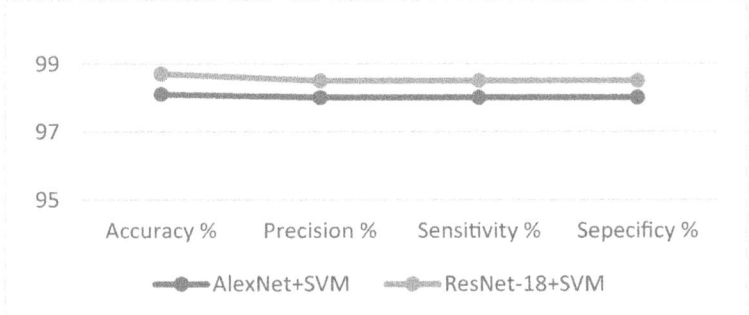

Fig. 7. Displays the performance of the hybrid techniques.

Figure 8a and b describe the confusion matrix produced by AlexNet + SVM and ResNet-18 + SVM hybrid technologies, respectively, to classify the ALL_IDB2 dataset for early diagnosis of Leukaemia. AlexNet + SVM achieved an overall accuracy of

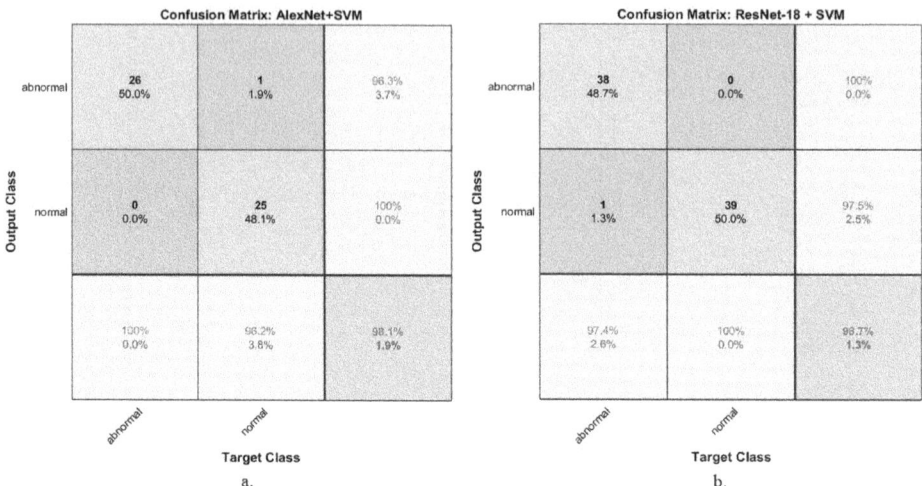

Fig. 8. Confusion matrix for diagnosing ALL_IDB2 data sets (a): AlexNet + SVM and (b): ResNet-18 + SVM

98.1%, an accuracy of 100% for diagnosing Leukaemia, and 96.2% for diagnosing normal blood samples. In contrast, ResNet-18 + SVM reached an overall accuracy of 98.7%, an accuracy of 97.4% for diagnosing Leukaemia, and 100% for diagnosing normal blood samples.

5 Discussion

This section discusses the proposed systems in this paper. Four proposed systems are two CNN models and two-hybrid technologies to classify the ALL_IDB2 dataset for early detection of Leukaemia. All dataset images were subjected to optimization to remove artifacts. A data augmentation method was used to avoid overfitting. The first proposed system is two CNN models based on the transfer learning method, AlexNet and ResNet-18, the two models, have achieved excellent results. AlexNet got an accuracy of 96.2%, while ResNet-18 achieved an accuracy of 97.4%. The second proposed system is two hybrid networks between deep learning and the SVM algorithm. The two networks achieved superior results, with AlexNet + SVM achieving an accuracy of 98.1%, while ResNet-18 + SVM achieved 98.7%.

Table 5 outlines the results of the proposed systems performed on the ALL_IDB2 dataset. First, AlexNet and AlexNet + SVM achieved the best performance and reached 100% accuracy for classifying leukaemia images. Second, for normal class, both ResNet-18 and ResNet-18 + SVM reached 100% accuracy. The table shows that the hybrid systems between CNN and SVM models have better results than CNN models, and this is one of our main contributions in this study.

Figure 9 illustrates the execution of all the proposed systems for classifying each class in the data set.

Table 5. Accuracy of each system in diagnosing each class

Diseases	Deep learning		Hybrid	
	Alex-Net	Res-Net-18	AlexNet + SVM	ResNet-18 + SVM
Leukaemia	100	94.9	100	97.4
Normal	92.3	100	96.2	100

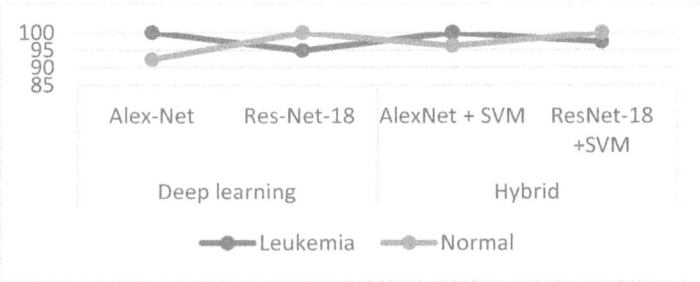

Fig. 9. Display the implementation of the systems for each class in the data set.

6 Conclusion

Artificial intelligence techniques in the medical sector have helped the challenges in manual diagnosis represented by the shortcomings of manual diagnosis, and the taking a long time to track images. Deep and automated learning techniques are considered highly efficient analytical and diagnostic tools. In this study, four different networks were developed between two CNN are AlexNet and ResNet-18, and extracting deep features. Two-hybrid networks between CNN and SVM consist of two blocks, firstly, the CNN model to extract deep features. The secondly deep feature map diagnosis is SVM. All systems have achieved outstanding results, and the superiority of hybrid techniques over CNN models is noted.

Data Availability. In this work, the data were collected from the dataset ALL_IDB2 used to support the results of this work: https://www.kaggle.com/nikhilsharma00/leukemia-dataset.

Conflicts of Interest. No conflict of interest among the authors.

References

1. D. H. Kuan, C. C. Wu, W. Y. Su, and N. T. Huang, A Microfluidic Device for Simultaneous Extraction of Plasma, Red Blood Cells, and On-Chip White Blood Cell Trapping, Scientific Reports 2018 8:1, vol. 8, no. 1, pp. 1–9, Oct. 2018, doi: https://doi.org/10.1038/s41598-018-33738-8.
2. C. L. Sawyers, C. T. Denny, and O. N. Witte, Leukemia and the disruption of normal hematopoiesis, Cell, vol. 64, no. 2, pp. 337–350, Jan. 1991, doi: https://doi.org/10.1016/0092-8674(91)90643-D.

3. S. Agaian, M. Madhukar, and A. T. Chronopoulos, Automated screening system for acute myelogenous leukemia detection in blood microscopic images, IEEE Systems Journal, vol. 8, no. 3, pp. 995–1004, 2014, doi: https://doi.org/10.1109/JSYST.2014.2308452.

4. C. Haworth, A. D. Heppleston, P. H. Morris Jones, R. H. Campbell, D. I. Evans, and M. K. Palmer, Routine bone marrow examination in the management of acute lymphoblastic leukaemia of childhood., Journal of Clinical Pathology, vol. 34, no. 5, pp. 483–485, May 1981, doi: https://doi.org/10.1136/JCP.34.5.483.

5. N. Patel and A. Mishra, Automated Leukaemia Detection Using Microscopic Images, Procedia Computer Science, vol. 58, pp. 635–642, Jan. 2015, doi: https://doi.org/10.1016/J.PROCS.2015.08.082.

6. K. M. Garrett Kevin M., F. A. Hoffer, F. G. Behm, K. W. Gow, M. M. Hudson, and J. T. Sandlund, Interventional radiology techniques for the diagnosis of lymphoma or leukemia, Pediatric Radiology 2002 32:9, vol. 32, no. 9, pp. 653–662, Jul. 2002, doi: https://doi.org/10.1007/S00247-002-0743-2.

7. T. S. K. Wan, Cancer Cytogenetics: Methodology Revisited, Annals of Laboratory Medicine, vol. 34, no. 6, pp. 413–425, Oct. 2014, doi: https://doi.org/10.3343/ALM.2014.34.6.413.

8. N. Ahmed, A. Yigit, Z. Isik, and A. Alpkocak, Identification of Leukemia Subtypes from Microscopic Images Using Convolutional Neural Network, Diagnostics 2019, Vol. 9, Page 104, vol. 9, no. 3, p. 104, Aug. 2019, doi: https://doi.org/10.3390/DIAGNOSTICS9030104.

9. D. Goutam and S. Sailaja, Classification of acute myelogenous leukemia in blood microscopic images using supervised classifier, ICETECH 2015 - 2015 IEEE International Conference on Engineering and Technology, Sep. 2015, doi: https://doi.org/10.1109/ICETECH.2015.7275021.

10. J. Rawat, A. Singh, B. HS, J. Virmani, and J. S. Devgun, Computer assisted classification framework for prediction of acute lymphoblastic and acute myeloblastic leukemia, Biocybernetics and Biomedical Engineering, vol. 37, no. 4, pp. 637–654, Jan. 2017, doi: https://doi.org/10.1016/J.BBE.2017.07.003.

11. M. M. Amin, S. Kermani, A. Talebi, and M. G. Oghli, Recognition of Acute Lymphoblastic Leukemia Cells in Microscopic Images Using K-Means Clustering and Support Vector Machine Classifier, Journal of Medical Signals and Sensors, vol. 5, no. 1, p. 49, Jan. 2015, doi: https://doi.org/10.4103/2228-7477.150428.

12. Z. F. Mohammed and A. A. Abdulla, An efficient CAD system for ALL cell identification from microscopic blood images, Multimedia Tools and Applications 2020 80:4, vol. 80, no. 4, pp. 6355–6368, Oct. 2020, doi: https://doi.org/10.1007/S11042-020-10066-6.

13. C. di Ruberto, A. Loddo, and G. Puglisi, Blob Detection and Deep Learning for Leukemic Blood Image Analysis, Applied Sciences 2020, Vol. 10, Page 1176, vol. 10, no. 3, p. 1176, Feb. 2020, doi: https://doi.org/10.3390/APP10031176.

14. A. Jabeen, S. Jabeen, S. A. Shah, and W. A. Rao, Efficient Features for Effectively Detection of Leukemia Cells, Proceedings - 2020 23rd IEEE International Multi-Topic Conference, INMIC 2020, Nov. 2020, doi: https://doi.org/10.1109/INMIC50486.2020.9318085.

15. J. Rawat, A. Singh, H. S. Bhadauria, and J. Virmani, Computer Aided Diagnostic System for Detection of Leukemia Using Microscopic Images, Procedia Computer Science, vol. 70, pp. 748–756, Jan. 2015, doi: https://doi.org/10.1016/J.PROCS.2015.10.113.

16. V. L. Thanmayi A, S. D. Reddy, and S. Kochuvila, Detection of Leukemia Using K-Means Clustering and Machine Learning, Lecture Notes of the Institute for Computer Sciences, Social-Informatics and Telecommunications Engineering, LNICST, vol. 383, pp. 198–209, Mar. 2021, doi: https://doi.org/10.1007/978-3-030-79276-3_15.

17. R. D. Labati, V. Piuri, and F. Scotti, All-IDB: The acute lymphoblastic leukemia image database for image processing, Proceedings - International Conference on Image Processing, ICIP, pp. 2045–2048, 2011, doi: https://doi.org/10.1109/ICIP.2011.6115881.

18. A. Fink, E. Hung, I. Singh, and Y. Ben-Neriah, Immunity in acute myeloid leukemia: Where the immune response and targeted therapy meet, European Journal of Immunology, vol. 52, no. 1, pp. 34–43, Jan. 2022, doi: https://doi.org/10.1002/EJI.202048945.

19. C. T. Basima and J. R. Panicker, Enhanced leucocyte classification for leukaemia detection, Proceedings - 2016 International Conference on Information Science, ICIS 2016, pp. 65–71, Feb. 2017, doi: https://doi.org/10.1109/INFOSCI.2016.7845302.

20. E. M. Senan and M. E. Jadhav, Techniques for the Detection of Skin Lesions in PH<Superscript>2</Superscript> Dermoscopy Images Using Local Binary Pattern (LBP), Communications in Computer and Information Science, vol. 1381 CCIS, pp. 14–25, Jan. 2020, doi: https://doi.org/10.1007/978-981-16-0493-5_2.

21. Yoshua. Bengio, Learning deep architectures for AI, p. 127, 2009, Accessed: Dec. 15, 2021. [Online]. Available: https://books.google.com/books/about/Learning_Deep_Architectures_for_AI.html?id=cq5ewg7FniMC

22. E. M. Senan, A. Alzahrani, M. Y. Alzahrani, N. Alsharif, and T. H. H. Aldhyani, Automated Diagnosis of Chest X-Ray for Early Detection of COVID-19 Disease, Computational and Mathematical Methods in Medicine, vol. 2021, 2021, doi: https://doi.org/10.1155/2021/6919483.

23. E. M. Senan, F. W. Alsaade, M. I. A. Al-Mashhadani, T. H. H. Aldhyani, and M. H. Al-Adhaileh, Classification of Histopathological Images for Early Detection of Breast Cancer Using Deep Learning, Journal of Applied Science and Engineering, vol. 24, no. 3, pp. 323–329, 2021, doi: https://doi.org/10.6180/JASE.202106_24(3).0007.

24. Deep learning methodology proposal for the classification of erythrocytes and leukocytes, pp. 129–156, Jan. 2021, doi: https://doi.org/10.1016/B978-0-12-822226-3.00006-4.

25. A. Alam and S. Anwar, Detecting Acute Lymphoblastic Leukemia Through Microscopic Blood Images Using CNN, Lecture Notes in Electrical Engineering, vol. 740 LNEE, pp. 207–214, 2021, doi: https://doi.org/10.1007/978-981-33-6393-9_22.

26. M. Ghaderzadeh, F. Asadi, A. Hosseini, D. Bashash, H. Abolghasemi, and A. Roshanpour, Machine Learning in Detection and Classification of Leukemia Using Smear Blood Images: A Systematic Review, Scientific Programming, vol. 2021, 2021, doi: https://doi.org/10.1155/2021/9933481.

27. B. A. Mohammed et al., Multi-Method Analysis of Medical Records and MRI Images for Early Diagnosis of Dementia and Alzheimer’s Disease Based on Deep Learning and Hybrid Methods, Electronics 2021, Vol. 10, Page 2860, vol. 10, no. 22, p. 2860, Nov. 2021, doi: https://doi.org/10.3390/ELECTRONICS10222860.

28. E. M. Senan, I. Abunadi, M. E. Jadhav, and S. M. Fati, Score and Correlation Coefficient-Based Feature Selection for Predicting Heart Failure Diagnosis by Using Machine Learning Algorithms, Computational and Mathematical Methods in Medicine, vol. 2021, pp. 1–16, Dec. 2021, doi: https://doi.org/10.1155/2021/8500314.

29. Z. Liu et al., A survey on applications of deep learning in microscopy image analysis, Computers in Biology and Medicine, vol. 134, p. 104523, Jul. 2021, doi: https://doi.org/10.1016/J.COMPBIOMED.2021.104523.

Lung Cancer Nodules Detection Using Ideal Features Extraction Technique in CT Images

Vikul J. Pawar[✉], P. Premchand, and I. Govardhanrao

Computer Science and Engineering Department, University College of Engineering Osmania University, Hyderabad, India
vikul.pawar@gmail.com

Abstract. In the present time, worldwide the number of patients related to lung cancer disease getting increase exponentially, accordingly the application of Computer Aided Diagnosis (CAD) system building association with medical science to deliver pertinent solution using Image Processing and Machine Learning Techniques. This paper presenting a model for Lung Cancer nodules detection in CT image by employing proposed work in the progressive phases, the first step is image pre-processing which uses standard LIDC-IDRI images as input images, the pre-processing approach employ the denoising technique to remove the speckle noises from images, then by applying adaptive contrast enhancement (CLAhe) technique the quality of input CT image is improved. The second step works on to segment the Region of Interest (ROI) using LevelSet segmentation algorithm, the third step employed the learnable Feature Extraction technique from suspected (ROI) in CT image, the feature to be extracted from CT images are Texture Features such as Grey-Level Co-occurrence Matrix (GLCM), Grey-Level Run-Length Matrix (GLRM), Local Binary Pattern (LBP), Shape-Based Features such as Perimeter, Area, Irregularity Index, Solidity, Equivalent Diameter, Convex Area, and Statistical Features such as Mean, Median, Mode, Entropy, Moment, Skewness, and Kurtosis. The optimized measurable features are offered as input to the Hybrid-Layer Convolutional Neural Network, Hybrid-CNN applied Enhanced Cat-Swarm Optimization algorithm for optimal weight selection. The convolutional neural network trained based on feature values by varying the training percentage of dataset (in the range of 50%, 60%, 70%, 80%, and 90%) and the proposed model attains the elevated accuracy of 92.93%. The performance evaluation metrics are used such as Sensitivity, Specificity, Accuracy and F-Measure to evaluate the robustness of proposed Hybrid-CNN classification model.

Keywords: Lung Cancer Nodules · CT Images · CAD · Pre-processing · Segmentation · Feature Extraction · Classification

1 Introduction

The Lung-cancer disease is becoming prominent source of deaths for human beings in worldwide, research statistics shows that the 2.3 million patients diagnosed with cancer out of which around 1.8 million patents are died due the lung cancer only in the

© The Author(s) 2023
R. Manza et al. (Eds.): ACVAIT 2022, AISR 176, pp. 39–57, 2023.
https://doi.org/10.2991/978-94-6463-196-8_5

year 2020 [1–3]. Detecting Lung-Cancer in early stage of it can raise the prospects of patients to survive up to five years after getting treated, the well-known standard lung cancer diagnosis methods are using X-rays, CT images, Blood sample and Biopsy are used by medical professional. The most impactful scanning method is used in diagnosing the disease is low dose CT scan, the LDCT images are less pertaining to clear the lung nodules in CT images through normal human visual perception and conducting scanning of High Dose CT scan techniques are more hazardous on human body [4, 5], the substantial number of research work is conducted for lung cancer detection in its early stage of it using CAD systems [6]. In such cases computer-based technology is coming with enormous solution, similarly computer assisted diagnosis (CAD) system are becoming more effective for offering the solution to assist the medical system [7, 8]. The CAD system is substitutional system which avoid the situation of indecisiveness in lung cancer disease diagnosis from input CT image of LIDC dataset, consequently the CAD systems assisting medical professionals for precise diagnosis by reducing the erroneous falsification [9–11]. The revolutionary methods of Machine-Learning and Image-Processing techniques maintains detection of nodules and nodules-classification based on their type, shape, dimension, and additional features in CT images [12, 13]. Correspondingly the manual CT scan examination is a time overwhelming and complex task to work on massive amount of dataset for every patient. As the size and structural patterns fluctuates in each slice of CT image becomes difficult for radiologist to categorize the nodules. The basic steps involved in this proposed work for Lung Cancer detection are Image Pre-processing using Adaptive Median Filtering Technique and contrast enhancement using histogram equalization technique, secondly Image Segmentation using improvise LevelSet segmentation method. In segmented ROI possesses the nodules which has certain properties of grey-level intensity, shape, and structure in third stage extracting and optimizing ideal features from CT images, and finally in classification step where the detected nodules are classified whether it is benign or malignant.

2   Related Work

In Ayman E. et al. [14], authors projected model for predicting lung cancer nodules from LIDC-IDRI dataset of CT images, the convolution neural network classification technique is employed for lung cancer nodules detection. The provided input images are converted into stack encoder (SAE) for pro-cessing the input image, then by extracting significant features from input image the proposed model established Convolution Neural Network (CNN) and deep learning neural network classification for detecting the nodules whether it is benign or malignant. The proposed system achieves the accuracy of 84.32%.

B Halalli et al. [15], the authors of paper have stated that computer-aided-diagnosis (CAD) system for detecting cancer in Brest and to assist radiologist by applying artificial intelligence-based algorithm in Image-Processing techniques. The proposed CAD system accomplished the work in several phases such as image-pre-processing, Segmentation-of-images, Extraction-of -Features, classification. This proposed model is more applicable for detecting of accumulation in mammography based on feature extraction, further the accumulated mass is classified whether it in normal or abnormal using classification technique. The present research strengthened the medical image analysis step by developing robust model, the performance evaluation metrics are improving sensitivity rate by reducing the computing cost of the system. The quality of input image is improved using Weiner Filtering and CLAHE histogram equalization technique, then by applying contour-based segmentation method the ROI is segmented. In feature extraction step the measurable features such as Wavelet dB4, GLCM, SFTA features are isolated, those relative features-values offered to classifier (SVM) for classifying the mass type belong cancerous or non-cancerous.

J Wason, et al. [16], this paper comprises of discussion of application of image processing techniques for lung cancer detection using CT images, the use CAD system for lung cancer detection can classify the tumours are belongs to benign or malignant. The steps involved in CAD system are Image pre-processing, Segmentation, Feature Extraction and Classification. Compellingly the authors of this article suggested a path to enrich the superior accuracy by engaging the productive stages of CAD system.

M. Keshani et al. [17], the author has presented feature extraction techniques in CT image, this work has employed the segmentation method known as adaptive fuzzy thresholding to separate the nodules in CT images, then consecutive step acquires hole-free lung-mask by applying widow size 5×5 and 23×23, then in next step to segment large and small size nodules are the masked window is rotated with 45degree by modified dimension of window size 50×50 and 25×25. The fourth step of segmentation allows to apply standard threshold algorithm to separate the region beyond thorax portion of bones province of chest region which are present in inner portion image. Conclusively the established mask returns to the Active-contour model as input. This projected work has successfully extracted the region of interest using adaptive fuzzy thresholding technique with measurable features learning purpose in classification step.

R. Shojaii et al. [18] introduced the segmentation technique to acquires the lung region using watershed segmentation algorithm. The fundamental application of this algorithm is to classify the internal and external boundary of lung region, by marking gradient region of lung image is separated. This work has applied smoothening function using Rolling bar filtering technique, this method has complementary function to filling up the unfilled portion of original boundaries of image.

E. M. van Rikxoort et al. [19], The authors have applied hybrid segmentation model for segmenting lung region, profoundly this method has accomplished in four steps, first step applied the region growing algorithm and morphological methods to automatically segment the lung region. Concurrently, this step found some of the errors in segmentation, but those are promptly removed by tis proposed algorithm. The proposed algorithm is speedy and little intricate to accomplish the task, but the lung region is segmented using multi-atlas technique. Decisively proposed work is evaluated based on error detection method to counteract the error.

J. Lee et al. [20], this work has introduced CAD model which computes the multiple geometric factors to categorize the alleged nodules in CT image based on its structure, elongation, dimension, conjecture, intensity, and some of the more pixel-based features. The further classification step classifies the nodules belongs to benign or malignant. Gurcan et al. [21] the author of this paper has presented the applicability of some of the statistical features to be extracted in 3D object for the purpose of classification nodules using measuring components such as volume, superficial area, grey values, standard-deviation, kurtosis, and skewness of the grey values of each pixel.

3 Methods and materials

The proposed computer assisted diagnosis system for lung cancer nodule detection using ideal feature extraction techniques and Hybrid-CNN classification model is demonstrated in Fig. 1, the intense analysis is conducted to implement the proposed CAD system [22], the methods implicated for accomplishment of proposed work has stated in subsequent phases of it is as follows.

3.1 Dataset

The proposed model uses the LIDC-IDRI dataset in DICOM image format, the size of images is in 512 × 512 pixel, the nodules size is categorized with Nodules ≤ 3 mm, Nodules ≥ 3 mm, Non_Nodules ≥ 3 mm. This dataset comprises of patients having Benign or Non-Malignant cases, Malignant cases, Metastatic Lesion, which are confirmed Malignant cases [23].

3.2 Image Preprocessing

The medical images may consist of different types of noises in it, the adaptive median filtering technique is more pertinent approach to eliminate such type noises from CT images. The proposed work applying the Adaptive Median filtering preserve the useful information in CT image and overcome on the disadvantages of standard Median filtering techniques.

3.2.1 Contrast Limited Adaptive Histogram Equalization (CLAhe)

The histogram equalization technique is employed to improve the contrast of input image, the Contrast-Limited Adaptive Histogram Equalization (CLAhe) is preferably used in this work to enhance the specific region of CT image. The CLAhe method works in several steps, first step is split the image into several similar size of region which should not be overlap, in second step histogram is calculated for each divided region, the third step calculates the Cumulative Distribution (CDF) function in Eq. (1), using Clip-point limit (β), the fourth step performs the Bilinear Interpolation operation to reduce the artificial relics and finally the output image is formed with improved contrast quality.

$$CDF = \sum_{i=0}^{l} f_j(j_i) \tag{1}$$

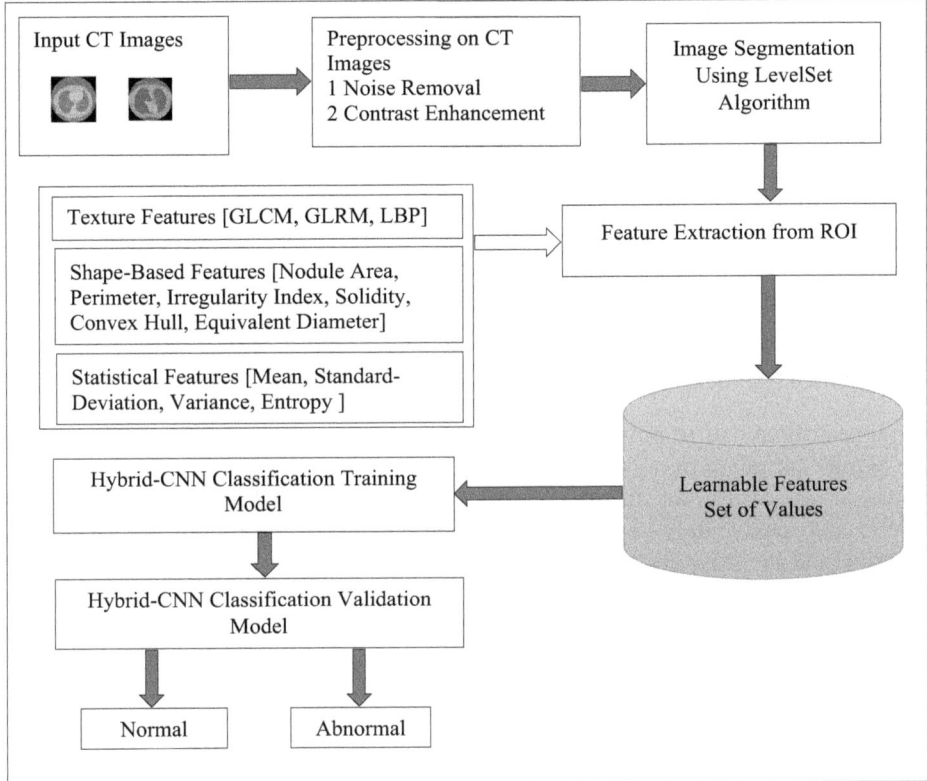

Fig. 1. Block diagram of Computer Assisted Diagnosis System for Lung Cancer Detection Using Hybrid-CNN Classification Model

3.3 Segmentation

The one more valuable step in CAD system is segmentation, which segment the suspicious region from CT image, basically the segmentation is applied on the basis of discontinuity and similarity property type of pattern in any image. The segmentation for discontinuity is applied when there is disordering pixel intensities are reflected, and segmentation for similarity is performed when similar types of pixels patterns are found. The proposed CAD model is applying narrative enhanced LevelSet algorithm for segmentation of region of interest (ROI) in CT images.

The enhanced LevelSet segmentation approach is employed based on the standard Level Set Segmentation method, for separating the exterior region the speed function of standard algorithm is uses moving curve with curving-based velocities. The curve distribution is generated from levelset function, $\phi = (x, y, z) = 0$, initial distribution is set by LevelSet segmentation algorithm is zero. Though, the levelset function, $\phi = (x, y, z)$ is assigned to SDF function, similarly the Signed Distance Function is defined in Eq. (2). For moving curve velocity to develop boundary of exterior region with respect to SDF function the speed function Φ_t is defined in Eq. (3).

$$SDF = (x, y, z) \tag{2}$$

$$\Phi_t = F|\nabla_t| = 0 \tag{3}$$

The LevelSet algorithm is prominently separating the suspicious ROI from CT images by estimating the expectant values of FC-Means and K-means algorithm, the experimental enhancement in proposed work use disaco function isolate the boundary of suspicious ROI.

3.4 Feature Extraction

Major contribution of proposed model is on feature extraction method, feature extraction is a significant phase in nodule detection. The feature extraction endorsed the certain features, those measurable features are used to train the Convolutional Neural Network (CNN), and convincingly based on the parametric feature value nodules are categorized in normal and abnormal class in given input CT image. The preceding step in CAD system extract the suspicious ROI, from the segmented ROI the several features such Texture features, Shape-Based Features, and Statistical Features are estimated the parametric values, these extracted features values are useful for analysis of disease [24, 25].

3.4.1 Texture Features

The texture measures the spatial variation in pixel intensity, the texture features compute the transformation-based model for given object in input image. The texture features compute the Grey-Level Co-occurrence Matrix (GLCM), Grey-Level Run Length Matrix (GLRM), and Local Binary Pattern (LBP) [26] [27].

3.4.1.1 Glcm

The GLCM measures the second order textural features such as Energy, Correlation, Contrast, Homogeneity, and Entropy.

Energy

The energy feature measures the intimacy between the elements which are distributed in spatial pattern of image. The energy feature is measured in Eq. (4).

$$Energy(En) = \sum_{i=1} \sum_{j=1} (px(i,j))^2 \tag{4}$$

Correlation

The correlation measures the probability of pairs of pixels which are connected to each other, this measuring parameter recognizes correlation with neighbouring pixel values, the correlation features estimation equation is defined in Eq. (5).

$$Correlation(Cr) = \sum_{i,j=0}^{G-1} P(i,j)(i - \mu_i)(j - \mu_j)/\sigma_i\sigma_j \tag{5}$$

Contrast
The contrast measures the pixel intensity between neighboring pixels, under contrast estimation equation evaluate the inertia and variance of given input image, the contrast feature values calculation is represented in Eq. (6).

$$Contrast(Co) = \sum_{i,j=0}^{N-1} P(i-j)^2 \tag{6}$$

Homogeneity
The Homogeneity reveals the uniformity in texture of image and organize the local variation in texture of image. The lack of intra-regional variation is observed when the high-level values is indicated by homogeneity in the distribution of texture. The equation for Homogeneity is defined in equation no. (7).

$$Homogeneity(Ho) = \sum_{i,j=0}^{N-1} \frac{P_{ij}}{1+(i-j)^2} \tag{7}$$

Entropy
The entropy measures the uncertainty in pixel distribution in texture of image, entropy calculated the probability of random pixel values at each position of *(i,j)*, entropy calculation shown in Eq. (8).

$$Entropy(En) = -\sum_{i=1} \sum_{j=1} (pl(i,j))log(pl(i,j)) \tag{8}$$

3.4.1.2 GLRM
The Grey-Level Run-Length Matrix (GLRM) feature counts the total number of pixels present with similar intensity values in specific direction [28]. The 2-D matrix of GLRM consist of pixel intensity value i and j, and angle ө indicates the element present in specific direction. The GLRM is extracting and calculating total fourteen features in all (which are known as SRE (Short-Run-Emphasis), LRE(Long-Run-Emphasis), GLN (Gray_level nonuniformity), GLNN, RLN, RLNN, RP(Run Percentage), LGLRE (Low _Gray_Level Run-Emphsis), HGLRE (High_Gray_Level Run-Emphasis), SRLGLE, SRLHGLE, LRLGLE, LRHGLE, and GLV) [29]. The grey-level run length are group of elements of sequential and colinear pixel points having analogous grey level run-length values, the GLRM is calculate the Run-Length (RNL) in Eq. (9).

$$RNL(\theta) = (g(i,j)|\theta), \ 0 \leq i \leq GY_{maxe}, 0 \leq j \leq RNL_{maxe} \tag{9}$$

Here, GY_{maxe} indicates the maximum grey-level values and RNL_{maxe} represents the maximum run-length values.

3.4.1.2 LBP
The LBP feature extraction method calculates the LBP value and validating that the limit of designated value is compared with adjacent pixel and replacing the conclusive binary value. Furthermore, LBP converts the subsequent positive values encode as 1 and negative value is set 0. The binary values are arranged from left in clockwise direction the generated code is accepted as LBP code. The LBP is extracting 100 features.

3.4.2 Shape-Based Features

The Shape-Based features analyzes the attributes at each pixel level, the shape-based features have properties of instinctiveness and optical in nature [30]. This research work is centering to compute the shape-based features such as Nodule Perimeter, Nodule Area, Nodule Irregularity Index, Convex Hull, Solidity, Equivalent Diameter [31].

Nodules Perimeter

The Perimeter is a property is used to calculate the suspicious edges of nodules, if identifies the distance amongst adjacent pixels over the ROI and computing the periphery of nodules shown in Eq. (10), perimeter will return the unknown values when there is incoherence in pixel values [32].

$$Nodule\ Perimeter(PN) = \sum_{i=0}^{L} \sum_{j=0}^{W} p(i,j) \tag{10}$$

Here, L indicates length, W indicates width, and $p(i, j)$ is the pixel values in region.

Nodules Area

The Area of nodules defines the abnormal growth of tissues in CT image, which is calculated using equation no (11), equation evaluates the region in image having binary value as 1.

$$Nodule\ Area(AN) = \sum_{m=0}^{L} \sum_{n=0}^{W} j(m,n) \tag{11}$$

Here, $j(m, n)$ are the pixel values of suspicious region, L indicates length, W indicates width.

Nodule Irregularity Index

The edge of nodule is characterized by computing irregularity index in, the Nodule Irregularity Index is calculated using Eq. (12).

$$Irregularity\ Index(IN) = \frac{4\Pi \times AN}{(PN)^2} \tag{12}$$

Here, AN is Area, and PN is Perimeter of nodule, the nodule identification through Irregularity Index (IN) is evaluating the value of roundedness index $= 1$ only for circle, and for any other shape it should be less than 1. The high probability of object is to be nodule is presumed based on high ranking of circularity of object.

Convex Hull

The convex hull is collection of P points. Which is the tiniest region in convex polygon with the same beginning and end point. The points are collected in counter-clockwise direction around the polygon. Convex area of nodule is ordered the sum of pixel in convex image. The established leaping frame is considered as convex image, and leaping frame is convex hull.

Nodule Solidity

Nodule solidity measure the area wrapped under pixel intensity, though the elements present in nodule regions are highly concentrated in natural surroundings. The nodule solidity is calculated in Eq. (13).

$$Nodule\ Solidity(SN) = \frac{AN}{Convex\ Hull} \tag{13}$$

Here, AN represents the Nodule Area.

Nodule Equivalent Diameter

Equivalent Diameter is typical accumulation method to calculate the diameter of circle having equivalent aggregation of partitioned area, it is calculated using Eq. (14).

$$Nodule\ Solidity(SN) = \frac{AN}{Convex\ Hull} \tag{14}$$

3.4.3 Statistical Features

The statistical features are extracted to evaluate the nodules mathematical parametric value, the statistical property of nodule can be applied for the stage of classification to classify the nodules category. The statistical features calculated through Mean, Standard-Deviation, Variance, Entropy, Moment, Skewness, and Kurtosis. The size of statistical features is 7, which are combinedly applied together as parametric value to the next classification model to classify the nodule [33].

3.5 Classification Using Hybrid-CNN

Convolutional neural-networks are the standard network which applies the mathematical formulation with nonlinear activation functions on the input CT images which are compiled from defined sources, conclusively these neural networks are producing final results as detected nodules are benign or malignant [34, 35]. This research is optimized weight distribution hybrid CNN architecture set with convolutional filters or kernels, the extracted features from input dataset are provided to Hybrid CNN architecture and accomplished feature mapping using transformation function. In fully-connected layer all layers of CNN layer are connected every neuron with all other neuron in impending interlinked layers. The well optimized CNN layers in hybrid layer are in three dimensional, the neurons in CNN are designed in the form of height, width, and depth. In hybrid-CNN layers selects a tiny ROI of image and analyzes the features parametric values of selected portion and subsequently the decision each portion of image will merge together to get the complete result. ReLU layers are used as activation function to stimulates the neuron and Max-pooling layers is applied to optimize the parametric values in hybrid CNN model. Moreover, q^{th} feature mapping is accomplished by the sth layers, the position of feature value (p, r) is defined as F^s_{prq} is exhibited in Eq. (15).

$$F^s_{p,r,q} = W^{s^T}_k J^s_{p,r} + B^s_k \tag{15}$$

where, q^{th} filters value is given in s^{th} layer, W_k is the elective weight in the given equation and B_k is the bias weight. Sequentially, the optimize weight evaluation technique is implemented using Enhanced Cat-Swarm Optimization (ECSO) Algorithm to enhance the accuracy of proposed Hybrid-CNN approach. Crucial layer of CNN model is the Sigmoid layer function, this act as activation function to give conclusive result for detected nodule is normal or abnormal. The sigmoid function is derived in Eq. (16), the sigmoid function is specified as $f(y_k)$.

$$f(y_k) = \frac{1}{1 + e^{y_k}} \tag{16}$$

Training the Hybrid-CNN using ECSO weight optimization model classifies the nodule in conclusive activation known as sigmoid function, it classifies the detected nodule based on the evaluation value 0 and 1. This works has distributed the training percentage of dataset in range of 50, 60, 70, 80, and 90, the subsequent section discusses the performance analysis of proposed work.

4   Result and Discussion

The CT images are most substantial way to diagnose the lungs related diseases, equally in detecting lung nodules LIDC-IDRI dataset images are exclusively used as source of input in CAD computer-based lung cancer diagnosis system. This research work has conducted in distinct stages of it, which are discussed independently in prevalent sections of this research paper, this section is overseeing the performance analysis of proposed work. This work accomplished with minimum software and hardware requirements, Software: Python- Version: 3.7, IDE: pycharm: Version: 2019.2.4, OS-Windows 10. Hardware: Intel Core-i5, RAM-8GB, ROM-More than 100 GB, GPU-Yes,CPU-1.7 Ghz. This research work has used CT images of 793 malignant images and 1323 is benign images. The Fig. 2 shows the transformation of input CT images in (a) and (d), the pre-processed CT images (b), (e) are improved the contrast of images, then by segmenting ROI the measurable features are extracted shown in (c) for benign case and (f) for malignant case. The learnable features are used for training the Hybrid-CNN model with optimizing weight selection method using Enhanced-CSO algorithm, by varying the training percentage with 50, 60, 70, 80, and 90 percentage the experiments is supervised in 50 epochs.

The Hybrid-CNN classification model is trained using ideal features value of Shape-Based Features and Statistical Features, the pattern of extracted feature parameter values are used to analyze the category Benign and Malignant Cases, the benign and malignant cases are discussed in Table 1, the nodules Area and Perimetric values in malignant case are higher as compared to benign cases. The smaller values of irregularity index and nodule Solidity indicates malignant nodules, the diameter of malignant nodules is comparably greater than the benign case. Moreover, Table 2 the statistical parameters such as Mean, Standard Deviation and Entropy are relatively high-ranking values in malignant nodules.

The intent of measuring performance analysis is to investigate the robustness of proposed classification model using ideal feature extraction technique is measured through Accuracy, Specificity, Sensitivity and F-Measure. However, to examine sturdiness of proposed model it is compared with aforementioned standard classification techniques such as DBN [36], SVM [37], and CNN [38]. Table 3, represents the Sensitivity measurement by varying the training percentage of between 50, 60, 70, 80 and 90, the objective of sensitivity is measure the truly classified positive cases amongst all actual positive cases in used dataset. The lower sensitivity ratio for Hybrid-CNN model is 90.37% at 50th training percentage and higher sensitivity ratio is 92.9% at 90th training percentage. Moreover, at 90th training percentage the sensitivity ration for Hybrid-CNN is 4.2% better than CNN, 4.5% is better than SVM and 4.72% higher than DBN.

Input CT Image   Preprocessing on CT Image   Segmented ROI

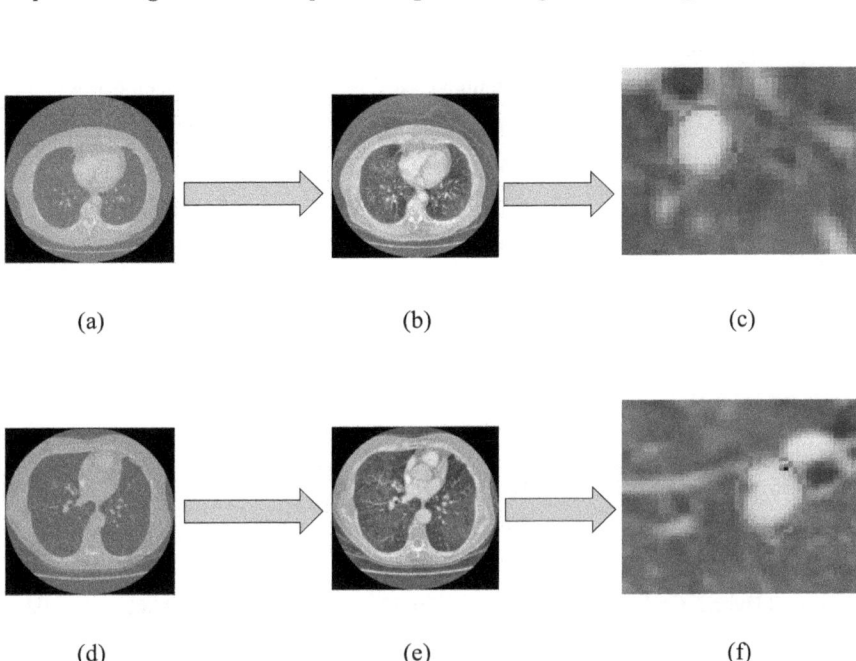

(a)   (b)   (c)

(d)   (e)   (f)

Fig. 2. Feature Extraction: (a) and (d) are the input CT images, (b) and (e) are the pre-processed CT Images, (c) is Feature Extracted in Benign case and (f) Feature Extracted in Malignant case.

Table 1. Shape-based Features Parameter Analysis for categorizing Benign and Malignant Cases

Shape-Based Features		
Shape-Based Parameter	Benign Cases	Malignant Cases
Nodule-Perimeter	56.341	182.362
Nodule-Area	381	699
Nodules-Irregularity index	0.8932	0.2103
Convex Hull	91	689
Nodule-Solidity	0.951	0.556
Nodules-Equivalent Diameter	7.4567	19.9099

The Fig. 3 represents the sensitivity ratio of Hybrid-CNN through graphical analysis in comparison with DBN, SVM and CNN, at distinct training percentage proposed model delivering superior sensitivity ratio which can be clearly visualize in graph.

The Specificity measures the ratio of detecting negative cases or the normal cases amongst all actual normal cases in the given dataset, Table 4 is pertaining the Specificity of Hybrid-CNN model and compared with standard classification model such DBN [36],

Table 2. Statistical Features Parameter Analysis for categorizing Benign and Malignant Cases

Statistical Features		
Statistical Parameter	Benign Cases	Malignant Cases
Mean	0.0218	0.0879
Variance	5.12E + 06	2.19E + 07
Standard deviation	3.06E + 03	5.16E + 03
Entropy	0.0021	0.0039

Table 3. Sensitivity ratio at distinct training percentage

Sensitivity					
Training (%)	50	60	70	80	90
DBN [36]	78.16	78.61	81.77	86.62	88.18
SVM [37]	78.39	79.61	83.53	86.93	88.4
CNN [38]	84.16	87.3	87.31	88.07	88.7
Proposed Hybrid-CNN	90.37	91.13	92.3	92.62	92.9

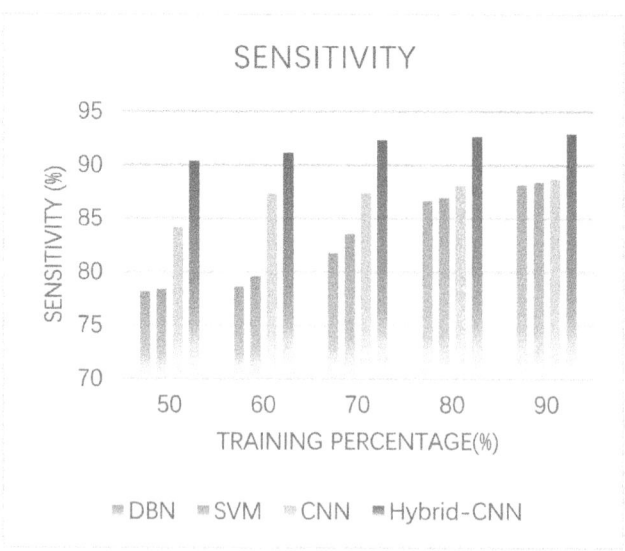

Fig. 3. Sensitivity analysis of Hybrid-CNN in comparison with DBN, SVM and CNN

SVM [37], and CNN [38]. The proposed classification technique is dispensing excellent results for detecting benign cases from all actual benign cases from dataset. The Specificity ratio of Hybrid-CNN attains 10.31%, 10.43%, and 11.18 superior values at 90th training (%) than other customary models such as CNN, SVM, and DBN respectively.

The Fig. 4, explicitly demonstrate the graphical representation of Specificity values for Hybrid-CNN and likening the other conventional classification models such as DBN, SVM, and CNN. The irrefutable analysis reveals the critical study of classification models that exhilarating the companionship within it.

Correspondingly, proposed Hybrid-CNN classification model is highly improved approach, which relatively well distinguishable in comparison with prevalent classification model, the Table 5, includes the results of Accuracy measurement of Hybrid-CNN and contrasted with DBN [36], SVM [37], and CNN [38]. The proposed Hybrid-CNN achieves the 4.4%, 5.02%, 5.05% upper values compare to classical classification model such as CNN, SVM and DBN at 90th percentage.

Table 4. Specificity ratio at distinct training percentage

Specificity					
Training (%)	50	60	70	80	90
DBN [36]	63.47	74.57	83.03	84.62	85.82
SVM [37]	79.76	80.87	84.62	85.64	86.57
CNN [38]	82.77	83.08	85.15	86.28	86.69
Proposed Hybrid-CNN	94.05	95.09	96.13	96.62	97

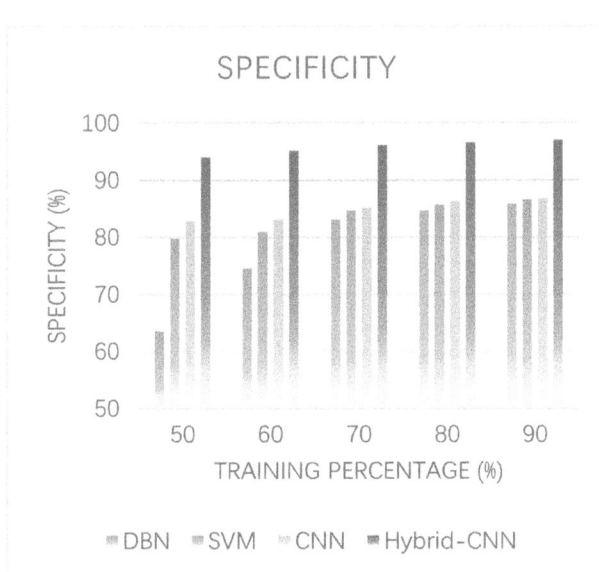

Fig. 4. Specificity analysis of Hybrid-CNN in comparison with DBN, SVM and CNN

Table 5. Accuracy ratio at distinct training percentage

Accuracy					
Training Percentage	50	60	70	80	90
DBN [36]	79.87	79.87	82.42	85.26	87.88
SVM [37]	79.87	79.87	83.43	87.71	87.91
CNN [38]	82.31	85.27	86.79	88.29	88.53
Proposed Hybrid-CNN	90.07	91.08	91.51	92.28	92.93

The influence of vigorous Hybrid-CNN classification model can be evidently validated through the graphical analytical study in Fig. 5, the Accuracy value at all training percentage perceives the improved results, at 90th percentage archiving the best accuracy is 92.93% which exceptionally marginal in comparison with other classification model.

The F-measure calculating the accuracy of classification model based on the Recall and Precision ratio of the classification analysis system, F-measure the single score value for positive nodule prediction amongst all positive cases in dataset. The Table 6 comprises of F-Measure ratio for Hybrid-CNN and differed with DBN [36], SVM [37], and CNN [38] classification model.

The Fig. 6 shows the graphical analysis F-Measure ratio for Hybrid-CNN model and compared with other classification model.

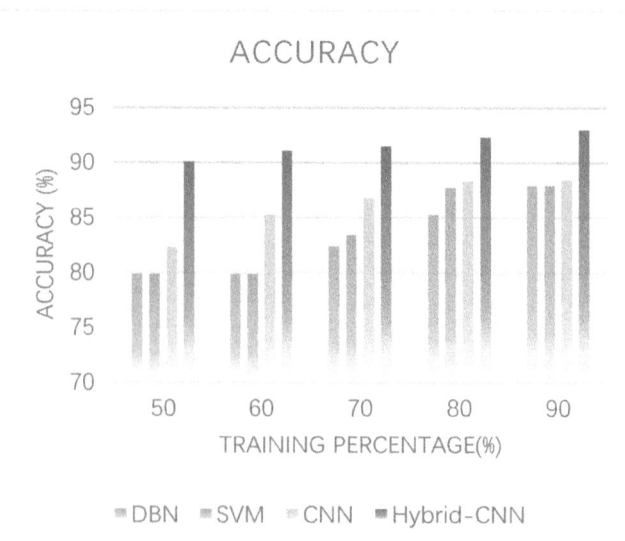

Fig. 5. Accuracy analysis of Hybrid-CNN in comparison with DBN, SVM and CNN

Table 6. F-Measure ratio at distinct training percentage

F-Measure					
Training Percentage	50	60	70	80	90
DBN [36]	84.71	85.92	86.62	86.88	89.67
SVM [37]	84.94	85.94	87.74	87.93	89.71
CNN [38]	88.13	88.15	88.73	89.74	89.84
Proposed Hybrid-CNN	93.76	93.84	93.92	93.94	93.96

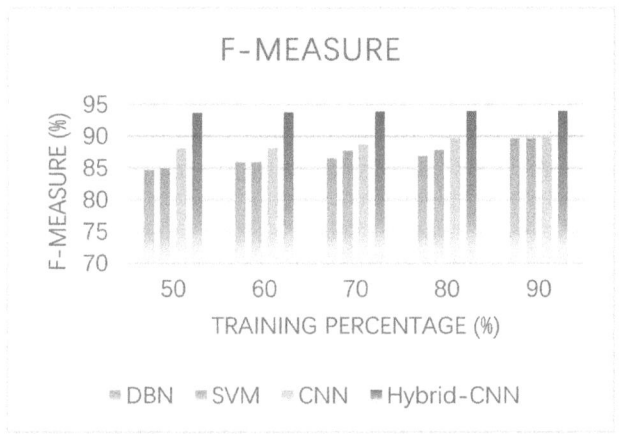

Fig. 6. F-Measure analysis of Hybrid-CNN in comparison with DBN, SVM and CNN

5 Conclusion

This research work has implemented proposed CAD system using Hybrid-CNN architecture for lung cancer detection, the crucial steps involved in proposed models are Preprocessing, Segmentation-(ROI), Extraction of Features, and ending with Classification. Specifically, the first step applies the preprocessing technique using Adaptive-Median Filtering method to eliminate the speckle noises from CT images and applying Contrast-Limited-Adaptive Histogram-Equalization method (CLAhe) to contrast enhancement in input CT image. The enhanced CT images are positively affecting to improve the results of proposed model. Later in the second stage of work is segmenting the Region of Interest (ROI), which is proportionally leaning with suspicious nodules in CT image. The third step of Feature Extraction employs segmented ROI as input to obtain the learnable features-value in ROI, this research model has contributed to extract the Texture Features, Shape-Based Features, and Statistical Features from CT images. The measurable Shape-Based Features are Nodule-Perimeter, Nodule-Area, Nodules-Irregularity index, Convex Hull, Nodule-Solidity, Nodules-Equivalent Diameter, and Statistical Features are Mean, Variance, Standard deviation, and Entropy. The most significant final step is classification using Hybrid-CNN classification model employed

Enhanced CSO algorithm for optimally selecting the weight to improve the performance of proposed system. Analysing critical performance evaluation of proposed model this paper has determined Sensitivity, Specificity, Accuracy and F-Measure ratio. The results proposed model are compared with standard classification model such DBN, SVM and CNN, likewise the Hybrid-CNN model attains the Sensitivity-92.9%, Specificity-97% and Accuracy-92.93% which is remarkably improving the results of proposed model. The crucial F-Measure for evaluating positivity ratio for proposed Hybrid-CNN model is delivering 93.96% ratio. Established performance analytical study exhibits that the proposed model of Lung Cancer detection is a robust model for the diagnosis of disease.

Acknowledgments. The authors would like to thank Head CSE Prof. P. Shyamala, UCE, Osmania University, Hyderabad. And Prof. Suresh Lokhande, Dean BOS in CSE department, UCE Osmania University, Hyderabad, India for their continuous motivation, help and always being there to support for motivation.

Authors' Contributions. The proposed work has major contributions of segmentation of ROI using enhanced Levelset segmentation method, which is consisting of suspicious region in input CT images, secondly is extracting prominent features from region of interest, and thirdly implementing classification Hybrid-CNN model using improved weight optimization algorithm.

References

1. World Health Organization(WHO), Global Health Estimates 2020-Deaths by Cause, Age, Sex, by Country and by Region, 2000–2019. WHO; 2020. Accessed December 11, 2020.
2. Bray F, Laversanne M, Weiderpass E, Soerjomataram,",The ever-increasing importance of cancer as a leading cause of premature death worldwide.", Cancer. In-press in Web of Science.
3. S, Hyuna, Jacques Ferlay, L.Rebecca, Siegel, L Mathieu, I Soerjomataram, Ahmedin DMV, Jemal B Freddie, "Global Cancer Statistics 2020: GLOBOCAN Estimates of Incidence and Mortality Worldwide for 36 Cancers in 185 Countries", A Cancer Journal for Clinician, Pages 209–249, Volume:71, Issue:3, May-June-2021.
4. B. N. Narayanan, R C Hardie, Kebede, T.M, "Performance analysis of a computer-aided detection system for lung nodules in CT at different slice thicknesses." Journal of Medicine-Imaging 2018, 5. 5–10.
5. M. Nishio, M. Nishizawa, O. Sugiyama, R. Kojima , M, Yakami, T. Kuroda,K. Togashi, "Computer-aided diagnosis of lung nodule using gradient tree boosting and Bayesian optimization." PLoS ONE 2018.
6. L. Li,Y Wu, Y Yang, L. Li, and B. Wu. "A New Strategy to Detect Lung Cancer on CT Images" InJune-2018 IEEE 3rd International Conference on Image, Vision and Computing (ICIVC) (pp. 716–722). IEEE.
7. G, Zhang, Z Yang, L Gong, S. Jiang, L. Wang, X, Cao, L. Wei, H. Zhang, Z. Liu, "An Appraisal of Nodule Diagnosis for Lung Cancer in CT Images." Journal of Medicine System 2019, 43-:181.
8. S. A. Regaily, M. A. Salem,M H Aziz Abdel, M. I. Roushdy, "Survey of Computer Aided Detection Systems for Lung Cancer in Computed Tomography," Current-. Medicin Image. Revi.-2018, :14. 3to18.

9. Y. Chunran, W. Yuanvuan, and GX Yi, " .Automatic Detection and Segmentation of Lung Nodule on CT Images," :2018 -11 International-Congress on Imag and Signal Processing.-BioMedical-Engineering and Informaticss (.CISP-BMEI), 1to 6.

10. S.M.B.Netto, A.C Silva, R.ANunes, M. Gattass, "Automatic segmentation of lung nodules with growing neural gas and support vector machine," Computer. Biolo. Medi.: 2012,-42, page-1110–1121.

11. S.L.A. Lee, A.Z Kouzani, E.J Hu, "Automated identification of lung nodules," .In Proceedings-of the 10th Workshop on Multimedia Signal Processing (MMSP), Cairns, Australia, 8,9,10-October 2008; pp:497–502.

12. D. Cascio, R, Magro F, Fauci, M, Iacomi, G. Raso, "Automatic detection of lung nodules in CT datasets based on stable 3D mass–spring models," Compute. Biom. Medic. :2012,-42, pp:1098–1109.

13. S. Akram, M.Y Javed, M. U. Akram, U. Qamar, A. Hassan, "Pulmonary Nodules Detection and Classification Using Hybrid Features from Computerized Tomographic Images," Jou. Of Medic. Imaging Health-Informa. :2016, 6, pp:252–259.

14. Ayman El-Baz, Garth M. Beache, Georgy Gimel'farb, et al. Computer-aided diagnosis systems for lung cancer: challenges and methodologies, International Journal Biomed. Imaging 2013 (2013) 46, https://doi.org/10.1155/2013/942353.

15. Halalli Bhagirathi & Makandar Aziz, "Computer Aided Diagnosis -Medical Image Analysis Techniques", Published on 20December 2017, Intech-Open Book Series, DOI: https://doi.org/10.5772/intechopen.69792.

16. Vasanth Jeyaprakash Wason, Nagarajan Ayyappan, "Image processing techniques for analyzing CT scan images towards the early detection of lung cancer," Bioinformation.:2019; Volume15(Issue-8): pp:-596–599. doi: https://doi.org/10.6026/97320630015596.

17. Keshani M, Azimifar Z, Boostani R, Shakibafar A., "Lung nodule segmentation using active contour modeling" published in 6th Iranian conference on machine vision and image processing, IEEE (2010, October), pp. 1–6.

18. Shojaii R, Alirezaie, P. Babyn "Automatic lung segmentation in CT images using watershed transform" Published in IEEE international conference on image processing-2005, volu. 2, IEEE, September 2005, pp. II:-1270.

19. Van Rikxoort E. M., de Hoop B., Viergever M.A., Prokop M., van Ginneken B. "Automatic lung segmentation from thoracic computed tomography scans using a hybrid approach with error detection", Medicne of Phy, 36(7) (2009), pp. 2934-2947.

20. Lee I J., Gamsu G, Czum J, Wu N., Johnson R., Chakrapani S. "Lung nodule detection on chest CT: evaluation of a computer-aided detection (CAD) system", Korean Jou Radiolog, Volume:6 (Issue-2), 2005 pp. 89–93.

21. N. Metin, Gurcan, B Sahiner, L. Hadjiiski, N. Petrick, C.Heang-Ping, A. Ella, Kazerooni, Philip N. Cascade, "Lung nodule detection on thoracic computed tomography images: Preliminary evaluation of a computer-aided diagnosis system ", Medici. Phy. Volu:29 Issue-11, November 2002.

22. V Pawar, Kailash Kharat, Suraj Pardeshi, Prashant Pathak, "Lung Cancer Detection System Using Image Processing and Machine Learning Techniques" in International Journal of Advanced Trends in Computer Science and Engineering, Scopus Indexed [ISSN 0974–2034] Volume 9, Issue No.4, July – August 2020. Available Online at https://doi.org/10.30534/ijatcse/2020/260942020.

23. A. G.Samuel, G. McLennan, L. Bidaut, M. F. McNitt, C. R. Meyer, A. P. Reeves, B. Zhao, D. R. Aberle, C. L. Henschke, E A Hoffman, "Data From LIDC-IDRI", 2015. Available online: https: //wiki.cancerimagingarchive.net/display/Public/LIDC-IDRI.

24. Priyanka, and Dharmender Kumar, "Feature Extraction and Selection of kidney Ultrasound Images Using GLCM and PCA", Procedi ComputerScience, volu.: 167, 16 April 2020 pp. 1722–1731.

25. K D. Kharat, V J. Pawar, Suraj R. Pardeshi, "Feature Extraction and selection from MRI Images for the brain tumor classification," Presented in IEEE International conference on Communication and Electronics Systems (ICCES) 2016 Coimbatore India.
26. Ojala, T; Pietikainen, M; & Maenpaa, T; "Multiresolution gray-scale and rotation invariant texture classification with local binary patterns" In IEEE Transactions on Pattern Analysis and Machine Intelligence, volume:.24, Issue-no:-7, July 2002, pp. 971–987.
27. Radhakrishnan Manavalan & Kuttiannan Thangavel, "Comparative Analysis of Feature Extraction Methods for the Classification of Prostate Cancer from TRUS Medical Images", IJCSI International Journal of Computer Science Issues, Volume:09, Issue-no.1, Jan-2012.
28. J. K. Kim, M, P. Jeong, S. Koun Song & H P Wook, "Texture Analysis and Artificial Neural Network for Detection of Clustered Microcalcifications on Mammograms," Published in IEEE, 1997;pp.199 – 206,
29. A. J. Masino, A. Kaitlin, Folweiler, "Unsupervised learning with GLRM feature selection reveals novel traumatic brain injury phenotypes", Machine Learning for Health (ML4H) Workshop at Neur IPS-2018.
30. Guo, Z;, Li, Y; Wang, Y; Liu, S; Lei, T; & Fan, Y; "A method of effective text extraction for complex video scene", Math. Problems in Engineering, volume: 2016,Article ID 2187647, 11 pages, 2016.
31. Aarthy, K. P; & Ragupathy, U. S. ; "Detection of lung nodule using multiscale wavelets and support vector machine", International Journal of Soft Computing and Engineering (IJSCE), volume:02, issue-no.03, July 2012.
32. Gozalez R, Woods R. E., "Digital Image Processing Using Matlab," second-edition, Gatesmark, USA, 2002, chat.-12, pp:642–654.
33. https://en.wikipedia.org/wiki/Statistic
34. Wu Jianxin, "Introduction to Convolutional Neural Networks," National Key Lab for Novel Software Technology Nanjing University, China, 01 May 2017.
35. Zeiler, M. D; Fergus, R.; "Visualizing and understanding convolutional networks", in-Proceedings of the European Conference on Computer Vision (ECCV), 2014, pp. 818–833.
36. Shanthi V., Sridevi G., Charanya R. & Josphin, J; "Mary, "Deep Belief Network (DBN) Classi-fication For Lung Cancer Prediction Using KNN Classifier", European Journal of Molecular & Clinical Medicine, ISSN 2515–8260 Volume 07, Issue 09, 2020.
37. Makaju S, Prasad P.W.C., Alsadoon Abeer, Singh A. K., Elchouemi A.,"Lung Cancer Detec-tion using CT Scan Images", sixth International Conference on Smart Computing and Com-munications, ICSCC 2017, 7–8- December-2017, Kurukshetra, India, 1877–0509 © 2018 The Authors. Published by Elsevier B.V.
38. Jin Xin-Yu, Zhang Yu-Chen, Jin Qi-Liang, "Pulmonary nodule detection based on CT images using Convolution neural network," 9th International Symposium on Computational Intelligence and Design 2016, 2473-3547/16 2016, DOI https://doi.org/10.1109/ISCID.201 6.52.

Fuzzy Level Set Search and Rescue Optimization (FLSSR) Based Segmentation of Pediatric Brain Tumor

Rita B. Patil[1]($\boxtimes$), Nirupama Ansingkar[1], Rajmohan Pardeshi[1], and Prapti D. Deshmukh[2]

[1] Department of Computer Science and IT, Dr. Babasaheb Ambedkar, Marathwada University, Aurangabad, Maharashtra, India
rpatil@mgmu.ac.in

[2] Dr. G Y Pathrikar College of CS and IT, Aurangabad, Maharashtra, India

Abstract. Brain tumor disease in children is deadly due to unrecognition at early stage. Hence, a accurate, and less affluent method to detect pediatric brain tumor is necessary. In this paper the theme of model is characterized with stages like Preprocessing and then segmentation of the MRI image by fuzzy level set search and rescue optimization (FLSSR) for an accurate segmentation with high speed and less complexity.

Keywords: CNN · paediatric MRI image · wavelet transform · fuzzy level set · brain tumor

1 Introduction

Brain tumor is a solid tumor which commonly found in pediatric area. The treatment and analysis of brain tumor are based on various factors like age of the patient, position and tumor type. The grade and type of the brain tumor are analyzed with the help of surgical resection method [1, 2]. The surgical resection method provides better analysis and commonly used for various tumor [3]. A pre-reactive analysis make impact on clinical resection and provide adjuvant treatment. A conventional MRI is commonly used for tumor analysis which gives lower accuracy performance [4]. The utilization of MRI increased in the tumor diagnosis field for the previous years, especially in pediatric area. There are various factors like apparatus breakdown and medication feedback causes adversarial events in MRI measurement which act as imaging modality [5]. The tumor occurrence and corresponding risk elements act as important factor for the execution of evidence-based quality development events.

The second cause of pediatric cancer is the pediatric brain tumors which is the leading cause of cancer mortality in children [6, 7]. The major symptom of pediatric brain tumors is occurrence of seizures inside the brain and happens sometime among birth or until they(children) reach the age of 15 [8]. After leukemia, 15% of pediatric cancer is brain cancer. There are four types of brain tumors such as Ependymoma (EP),

R. Manza et al. (Eds.): ACVAIT 2022, AISR 176, pp. 58–68, 2023.
https://doi.org/10.2991/978-94-6463-196-8_6

Medulloblastoma (MB), Pilocytic (PILO) and Diffuse Intrinsic Pontine Glioma (DIPG). Various treatment and prediction approaches are included in these type of tumors [9]. Type of tumor identification is extremely appreciated without the required of surgery. The MRI is most commonly used technique for analysing cancer [10].

Our contributions are given below:

- To identify efficient approaches to handle MRI data for pediatric brain tumor patients.
- To develop the new fuzzy based search and rescue algorithm for an effective segmentation of brain MRI.

2 Related Work

Gayathri et al. [11] suggested a cranial closure assessment on pediatric MRI. During cranial closure imaging technique, CT with 3D reformat applied and used to estimate abnormalities of the brain. The proposed work utilized for calculating the consistency of MRI and CT (Computed Tomography). More than 500 sequential patients are experienced in CT and MRI study. With the help of pediatric neuroradiologist MRI was studied and estimate sagittal, lambdoid sutures and coronal. After the analysis MRI gives better accuracy than CT.

Christine et al. [12] developed a structural brain MRI investigation of pediatric cancer survivors handled with chemotherapy. The cortical thickness, subcortical volumes and morphometry are used as metrics of MRI. The influence of chemotherapy was studied in survivors with non-central nervous structure cancers. Along with functioning memory tasks, evaluations of executive operational behaviour and manual dexterity events are interrelated. The proposed methodology proved that oncology patients show bargain morphometry and cortical thickness which are associated with events of manual dexterity, executive operational behaviour and occupied memory scores.

Michaela et al. [13] developed automated estimation model of imaging biomarker for POPCMS (Post-Operative Cerebellar Mutism Syndrome). The POPCMS occurred within the cerebellum and brain stem. The 2D analysis was limited due to the non-volumetric nature of frequency and leads to complexity in inter-subject and intra-subject analysis. To overcome these issues, computerised image processing and pipeline investigation was introduced. The 4D volumetric MRI database used for offer longitudinal depiction of the brainstem and cerebellum at particular interval points.

Orman et al. [14] proposed progressive method of neuroimaging with MRI and CT. The introduced method discussed about the 17-year patient and he suffered from changes in mental status. During the neuroimaging studies a thrombosed aneurysm was exposed with CT and MRI along with critical left MCA (Middle Cerebral Artery) stroke. Due to the irregularities in SWI(Susceptibility) and DWI (Diffusion Weighted) corresponding with the PWI (Perfusion Weighted Imaging) an ischemic penumbra was recognized.

Ericka et al. [15] discussed the use of brain MRI and spectroscopy for consequence prediction. The proposed method used spectroscopy and brain MRI as forecasters of disability and death. The MRI information was utilized for clinical analysis. The neurological and mortality results were evaluated. The nonparametric tests were employed for the verification of connection between MRI or spectroscopy.

The paediatric brain tumor caused due to the abnormal growth of cells inside the child's brain. Benign and Malignant are the major types of pediatric brain tumors. The chance of recovery and treatment are based on several factors like tumor type, tumor position, tumor spreading nature and child age. Due to the technological development, innovative treatments are established and used at different stages of diagnosis. The pediatric brain tumor treatment is difficult when it compared to adult cases. The cause of tumor is not clear in most children with primary brain tumors. Ependymoma and Medulloblastoma are the major tumor type in pediatric area. The risk of brain tumors increased in some children by family history of genetic syndromes. The supervised learning approaches need labelled information that is costly to accumulate and there is a severe lack of pediatric brain tumor MRI information. Hence, new optimized deep convolutional neural network introduced for the classification of brain images in child's brain.

3   Proposed Methodology

The proposed method undergoes two steps Pre-processing & Segmentation. Initially pediatric MRI data is pre-processed with Extended Adaptive Weiner filter (EAWF) and the tumor portions are segmented using fuzzy search and rescue optimizer. By this concept, we can identify and point out tumor portions. The frame work of proposed methodology is shown in Fig. 1.

3.1   Preprocessing

The initial step followed by our suggested work is pre-processing. Provision of MRI images are given as an input due to its enormous information regarding pediatric MRI data. In a pre-processing stage, the quality of image get enhanced by making it sharper and detach the presence of horrible noise in an image. The superiority of visual appearance and image quality can be recognized by the pre-processing stage. Filtering process will upgrade the oncoming stage such like segmentation. The dominant filter technique i.e. Extended Adaptive Wiener Filter (EAWF) filter to progress the image clarity by eliminating the noises. Visualization of MRI images with good appearance can be maintained by the elimination of unwanted noises. In order to extend the adaptive Wiener Filter, replacement of dispersion index instead of variance has been initiated.

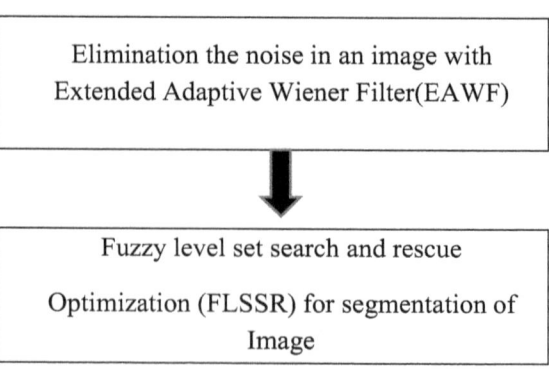

Fig. 1. Frame work of proposed methodology

The use of EAWF filter diminishes any kind of noise recognized in the image along with improving the quality of an image. Let us consider as a pixel location for an input image. In AWF the determination of noise can be done based on mean and noise variance. But the Extended AWF filter utilizes dispersion index to detect the noise from the image. The standard expression of dispersion index can be displayed as:

$$d_i = \frac{\sigma^2}{\mu} \tag{1}$$

If the dispersion index is applied to the AWF filter, the general filter equation get revised like the following:

$$EAW_f\left[X_p(\rho_1, \ \rho_2)\right] = \mu + \frac{d_i - \sigma_n^2}{d_i}\left[X_p(\rho_1, \ \rho_2) - \mu\right] \tag{2}$$

The efficient output after pre-processing can be defined determined through the following formula:

$$EAW_f\left[X_\rho(\rho_1, \ \rho_2)\right] = X_\rho(\rho_1, \ \rho_2) - \mu\left(\frac{\sigma_n^2}{\sigma^2}\left[X_\rho(\rho_1, \ \rho_2) - \mu\right]\right) \tag{3}$$

where designates the mean value and specifies the variance of noise.

The enhanced quality of MRI image can be detected based on Eq. (3). The presence of noise in an MRI image can be tackled by using the suggested EAWF filter. Noise reduction enhance the quality of an image as well as the image appearance is visible and more coherent than the original image. The primary aim of the introduced filter is to remove the speckle noise present in MRI image and it occurs due to the movement of patients and environmental conditions. AWF filter eradicates the speckle noise resourcefully, meanwhile enlightening the image quality.

3.2   Fuzzy Level Set Search and Rescue Optimization (FLSSR) for Segmentation Process:

Segmentation of brain tumor potions can be emphasized by fuzzy level set optimization strategy. Similar to edge parameter representation, fuzzy level set utilizes partial differential equation $f\ (t, \ u, \ v)$ to represent the outlier portions. After tracking the fuzzy level set zero, we obtain an $L\ (t)$ implicit function to validate the outliers in the edges. The implicit function can be expressed as:

$$\begin{cases} \Phi\ (t, u, v) \ < \ 0 & (u, v) \ in \ L\ (t) \\ \Phi\ (t, u, v) \ = \ 0 & (u, v) \ on \ L\ (t) \\ \Phi\ (t, u, v) \ > \ 0 & (u, v) \ to \ L\ (t) \end{cases} \tag{4}$$

Edge indicator function is established based on the regulation of driving force to prevent the optimal solutioin a fuzzy level set method and it is defined as:

$$e = \frac{1}{1 + |\Delta\ (K_\sigma \ * \ I)|^2} \tag{5}$$

I denotes the MRI pediatric image, K_σ indicates smooth gauss kernel and Δ represents the gradient operation of MRI image. The differential partition equation of fuzzy level set method can expressed as:

$$\frac{\partial \phi}{\partial t} = e \ |\Delta\phi| \left[div \left(\frac{\Delta\phi}{|\Delta\phi|} \right) + v \right] \tag{6}$$

$div \left(\frac{\Delta\phi}{|\Delta\phi|} \right)$ denotes the average curvature. Meanwhile, the computational complexity is one of the short coming in an fuzzy level set approach also it extends the two level segmentation problems in to three level segmentation problem. However in order to overcome the complexity issue search and rescue is implemented in fuzzy approach.

The primary aim of this stage is tumor segmentation from MRI images. In accordance with our proposed approach, brain tumor segmentation problem is defined as the position of human which is equivalent to the solution of optimization problem and the importance of clue is termed as best optimal solution. Brain tumor segmentation is emphasized as an optimization problem in SA [16] optimization. The procedure of the suggested approach is processed below:

Clues: The information of clues are gathered by group members during the search operation. The group members with problem dimension is indicated as along with this the dimension matrix is corresponding to. Disseminate of clues indicates the outlier boundary of an MRI image. Initially, the position of founded clues are randomly placed in a clue matrix and it is defined as:

$$CM = \begin{bmatrix} Q \\ P \end{bmatrix} = \begin{bmatrix} Q_{11} & \cdots & Q_{1d} \\ \vdots & \ddots & \vdots \\ Q_{n1} & \cdots & Q_{nd} \\ P_{11} & \cdots & P_{1d} \\ \vdots & \cdots & \vdots \\ P_{n1} & \cdots & P_{nd} \end{bmatrix} \tag{7}$$

Based on the random initialization of clue matrix, generation of new solutions takes place in both social and individual stages. Updation of matrices such as Q, P, CM are evaluated in each search stages. The matrices Q, P denotes the memory and position of humans. Human stages namely, social and individual are preceded as follows:

Social stage: In a social stage, the search direction is procured according to the following equation:

$$SD_j = (Q_j - CM_i) \quad i \neq j \tag{8}$$

Q_j and CM_i symbolize the position of both human and clues also, the search direction of jth human is indicated as SD_j. i represent the random integer number and it lies between the range of 1 and 2. The expression of social stage is defined as:

$$Q_{j,w} = \begin{cases} \left(\begin{array}{l} CM_{i,w} + R_1 \times (Q_{i,w} - CM_{i,w}) \ if \ F(CM_i) > F(Q_j) \\ Q_{i,w} + R_2 \times (Q_{i,w} - CM_{i,w}) \qquad otherwisw \end{array} \right) \\ Q_{i,w} \end{cases}$$

$$if\ R_2 < AB\ or\ w = w_{random}\ w = 1, 2, \ldots d$$
$$otherwise \tag{9}$$

The above equation attains new position in each dimension. For (j^{th}) human and (i^{th}) clue, the new position based on (W^{th}) dimension can be expressed as $Q_{j,w}$ and $CM_{i,w}$. The random numbers R_1 and R_2 lies between the interval of $(-1, 1)$ and $(0, 1)$. The random variable R_1 remains fixed and R_2 get jumbled in all dimensions. The parameter AB ranges between 0 and 1. The values of objective function can be expressed as $F\ (CM_i)$ and $F\ (Q_j)$.

Individual stage: The new position of (j^{th}) human can be obtained by the following equation

$$Q\prime_j = Q_j + R_3 \times (CM_i - CM_n) \qquad j \neq i \neq n \tag{10}$$

The movement along other clues are prevented by the selection of random integers i and j. The random integer R_3 in individual stage ranges between 0 and 1.

Boundary Control: The solutions of individual and social stage are obtained based on the location of solution space. The new position in accordance with (j^{th}) human can be customized by Eq. (11).

$$Q_{j,k\prime} = \begin{cases} \left(Q_{j,k} + Q_k^{max}/2\right) & if\ Q_{j,k\prime} > Q_k^{max} \\ \left(Q_{j,k} + Q_k^{min}/2\right) & if\ Q_{j,k\prime} > Q_k^{min} \end{cases} \Bigg\} \quad W = 1, \ldots .d \tag{11}$$

Q_k^{max} and Q_k^{min} denotes the maximum and minimum threshold values for (W^{th}) dimension.

Information and Position Updation: Based on individual and social stages, searching process done by group members for each iterations. If the position of objective function $Q_{j\prime}\ (F\ (Q_j))$ is greater than $F\ (Q_j)$, the memory matrix P accumulates the previous position Q_j with the aid of Eq. (12).

$$P_m = \begin{cases} Q_j & if\ F(Q\prime_j) > (Q_j) \\ P_m & otherwise \end{cases} \tag{12}$$

$$Q_m = \begin{cases} Q\prime_j & if\ F(Q\prime_j) > (Q_j) \\ Q_j & otherwise \end{cases} \tag{13}$$

Abandoning Clues: In search and rescue optimization, time plays an essential role. The operation searches an enormous space within a short period of time. If the searching process get delayed, the rescue teams will fall in to a critical position. If the search agent is unable to determine new solution under few iterations, then it go towards the current position to new position. Initially, the unsuccessful search agent S is set to zero to determine crucial clues. The fitness function can be evaluated based on following equation:

$$S_j = \begin{cases} S\prime + 1_j & if\ F(Q\prime_j) \\ 0 & otherwise \end{cases} \tag{14}$$

Constraint Managing Mechanism: In this, the penalty function is used to solve the optimization problem. The memory, position and S_j are updated based on the following equations which are as follows:

$$P_m = \begin{cases} Q'_j & \text{if } Q'_j \text{ is better than } Q_j \\ P_m & \text{otherwise} \end{cases} \tag{15}$$

$$Q_j = \begin{cases} Q'_j & \text{if } Q'_j \text{ is better than } Q_j \\ Q_j & \text{otherwise} \end{cases} \tag{16}$$

$$S_j = \begin{cases} 0 & \text{if } Q'_j \text{ is better than } Q_j \\ S'_j + 1 & \text{otherwise} \end{cases} \tag{17}$$

After the updation, Restart mechanism takes place to randomly generate matrices namely human and memory. The fuzzy optimization strategy segment the pediatric MRI brain image for further analysis of an image.

4 Results and Discussions

The proposed pediatric brain tumour classification (PBTC) model is examined with regard of five phases (pre-processing, segmentation) In the pre-processing stage, by the intrusion of EAWF filtering technique the quality of image get enhanced and the horrible nose in image are eradicated. The maintenance of good quality images are done in the first stage. The second stage of proposed model is segmentation. The need of segmentation will provide an accurate classification results and this can be done by FLSSR segmentation technique.

5 Performance Evaluation

Stage 1: Pre-processing
The collected images are corrupted with impulsive noise and the removal of noise is done by stage 1 (pre-processing).To diminish the inadequacies of the image, the stage of pre-processing is essential. The method of pre-processing helps to enhance the visual appearance and quality of an image. The accuracy of an image gets degrade due to the presence of noise. The pre-processing stage helps to rise up the upcoming stages such as segmentation, feature extraction, feature selection and classification. The filtered image is shown in Fig. 2.

Stage 2: Segmentation
For a segmented tumour region, the performance measures of dice similarity coefficient and jaccard coefficients are evaluated. The fuzzy level set optimization approach is intended to segment the tumour region in the collected pediatric MRI image. To balance the computational complexity of the fuzzy level set strategy, the rescue optimization is emphasised to point out the tumour region with high speed and less complexity. Dice and jaccard is termed as a spatial overlapped index and also a reproducibility validation metrics. The metrics of dice and jaccard ranges from 0 to1 and it measures the similarity

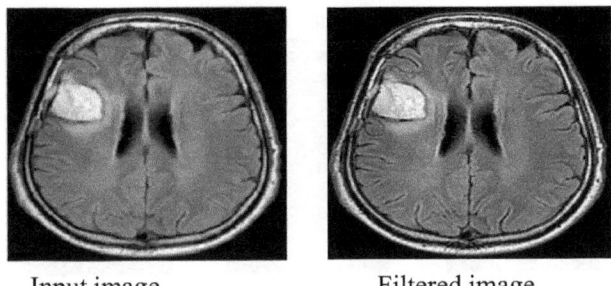

Input image   Filtered image

Fig. 2. Pre-processed image

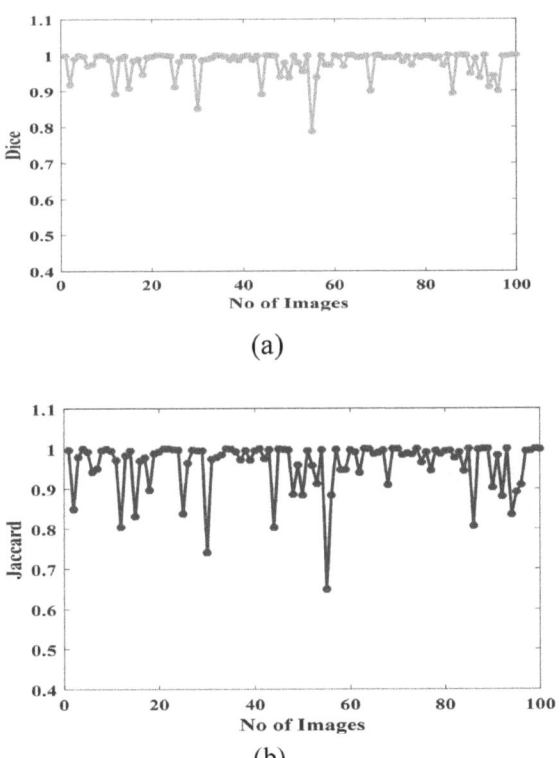

(a)

(b)

Fig. 3. Performance measure of segmentation (3a) Dice similarity coefficient, (3b) Jaccard coefficient

between two images. The range 0 explicate that the no spatial overlap (low) among two images and 1 elucidates high overlap.

$$Dice\,(p, q) \; = \; \frac{2\,|P_1 \cap q_1|}{|p_1 + q_1|} \tag{18}$$

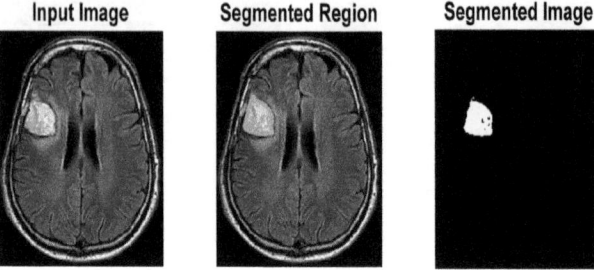

Fig. 4. Segmented image

$$Jaccard\ (p, q)\ =\ \frac{P_1 \cap q_1}{p_1 \cup q_1} \tag{19}$$

The process of segmentation is to partitioning the images in to dissimilar sections. In above equation, ∩ ensembles the logical AND operator. p, q denotes the collected pediatric brain tumour image. Figure 3 illustrates the dice and jaccard similarity coefficient for the proposed segmentation approach under 100 pediatric images. From figure it is observed that it lies between 0.9 to1 and it almost reaches 1. Zero represents imperfect matching and one represents perfect matching. The tumour segmented image is shown in Fig. 4.

6   Conclusion

The major aim of this research is to accomplish an effective child tumour classification system that can be reliable with less computational time and high accuracy. The research is progressed with two stages namely pre-processing, segmentation. The raw input pediatric MRI image is filtered with the assistance of EAWF filtering technique and it upsurge the clarity of an image. After pre-processing, the feature extraction is proceeded for an accurate pediatric tumour segmentation and this can be terminated by FLSSR strategy.

Acknowledgments. I would like to thank Dr. Babasaheb Ambedkar Marathwada University, Aurangabad (MS) India for providing the publication support.

Authors' Contributions.   Rita Patil carried out the experiment and wrote the draft manuscript. Rajmohan Pardeshi and Nirupama Ansingkar edited the draft and verified the results. Prapti Deshmukh mam supervised the project. All authors discussed the results and contributed to the final manuscript.

References

1. AlRayahi, Jehan, Michal Zapotocky, Vijay Ramaswamy, Prasad Hanagandi, Helen Branson, Walid Mubarak, Charles Raybaud, and Suzanne Laughlin. "Pediatric brain tumor genetics: what radiologists need to know." Radiographics 38, no. 7 (2018): 2102-2122.
2. Al-Sharydah, Abdulaziz Mohammad, Hussain Khalid Al-Arfaj, Husam Saleh Al-Muhaish, Sari Saleh Al-Suhaibani, Mohammad Saad Al-Aftan, Dana Khaled Almedallah, Abdulrhman Hamad Al-Abdulwahhab, Abdullah Abdulaziz Al-Hedaithy, and Saeed Ahmad Al-Jubran. "Can apparent diffusion coefficient values help distinguish between different types of pediatric brain tumors?." European journal of radiology open 6 (2019): 49–55.
3. Zarinabad, Niloufar, Martin Wilson, Simrandip K. Gill, Karen A. Manias, Nigel P. Davies, and Andrew C. Peet. "Multiclass imbalance learning: Improving classification of pediatric brain tumors from magnetic resonance spectroscopy." Magnetic resonance in medicine 77, no. 6 (2017): 2114-2124.
4. D'Arco, Felice, Sinead Culleton, Laurens JL De Cocker, Kshitij Mankad, Jorge Davila, and Benita Tamrazi. "Current concepts in radiologic assessment of pediatric brain tumors during treatment, part 1." Pediatric radiology 48, no. 13 (2018): 1833-1843.
5. Remes, Tiina M., Maria H. Suo-Palosaari, Vesa-Pekka Heikkilä, Anna K. Sutela, Päivi KT Koskenkorva, Sanna-Maria Toiviainen-Salo, Liisa Porra et al. "Radiation-induced meningiomas after childhood brain tumor: a magnetic resonance imaging screening study." Journal of adolescent and young adult oncology 8, no. 5 (2019): 593–601.
6. Udaka, Yoko T., and Roger J. Packer. "Pediatric brain tumors." Neurologic clinics 36, no. 3 (2018): 533-556.
7. Lequin, Maarten, and Jeroen Hendrikse. "Advanced MR imaging in pediatric brain tumors, clinical applications." Neuroimaging Clinics 27, no. 1 (2017): 167-190.
8. Wang, Stacie Shiqi, Pratiti Bandopadhayay, and Misty Rayna Jenkins. "Towards immunotherapy for pediatric brain tumors." Trends in immunology 40, no. 8 (2019): 748–761.
9. Vajapeyam, S., D. Brown, P. R. Johnston, K. I. Ricci, M. W. Kieran, H. G. W. Lidov, and T. Y. Poussaint. "Multiparametric analysis of permeability and ADC histogram metrics for classification of pediatric brain tumors by tumor grade." American Journal of Neuroradiology 39, no. 3 (2018): 552-557.
10. Hales, Patrick W., Felice d'Arco, Jessica Cooper, Josef Pfeuffer, Darren Hargrave, Kshitij Mankad, and Chris Clark. "Arterial spin labelling and diffusion-weighted imaging in paediatric brain tumours." NeuroImage: Clinical 22 (2019): 101696.
11. Ladefoged, Claes Nøhr, Lisbeth Marner, Amalie Hindsholm, Ian Law, Liselotte Højgaard, and Flemming Littrup Andersen. "Deep learning based attenuation correction of PET/MRI in pediatric brain tumor patients: Evaluation in a clinical setting." Frontiers in neuroscience 12 (2019): 1005.
12. Ijaz, Heba, Mateusz Koptyra, Krutika S. Gaonkar, Jo Lynne Rokita, Valerie P. Baubet, Lamiya Tauhid, Yankun Zhu et al. "Pediatric High Grade Glioma Resources From the Children's Brain Tumor Tissue Consortium (CBTTC) and Pediatric Brain Tumor Atlas (PBTA)." BioRxiv (2019): 656587.
13. Okada, Keiko, Toshinori Soejima, Hiroaki Sakamoto, Junko Hirato, and Junichi Hara. "Phase II study of reduced-dose craniospinal irradiation and combination chemotherapy for children with newly diagnosed medulloblastoma: A report from the Japanese Pediatric Brain Tumor Consortium." Pediatric Blood & Cancer 67, no. 11 (2020): e28572.
14. Schwake, Michael, Stephanie Schipmann, Michael Müther, Michaela Köchling, Angela Brentrup, and Walter Stummer. "5-ALA fluorescence–guided surgery in pediatric brain tumors—a systematic review." Acta neurochirurgica 161, no. 6 (2019): 1099-1108.
15. Subramanian, Surabhi, and Tahani Ahmad. "Cancer, Childhood Brain Tumors." (2019).

16. Shabani, Amir, Behrouz Asgarian, Miguel Salido, and Saeed Asil Gharebaghi. "Search and rescue optimization algorithm: A new optimization method for solving constrained engineering optimization problems." Expert Systems with Applications 161 (2020): 113698.

Investigating EEG Images of Cognitive Actions for Robotic Arm

Shashibala Tarigopula[1]([✉]), Dipali Chaudhari[2], and Bharti Gawali[2]

[1] MIT College CIDCO, Aurangabad, India
shashibala.rao@gmail.com
[2] Dr. Babasaheb Ambedkar, Marathwada University, Aurangabad, India

Abstract. Brain Computer Interface (BCI) systems works with brain signals. The brain activities are taken into consideration and are used to control external devices These signals are processed to extract features which are then translated to discrete command set to operate some external device like a wheel chair or an application like a speller application, a gaming system etc. In this study an activity of robotic Arm movement (Arm up, Arm down and neutral) is performed. The brain imaging signals are acquired with a low-cost EEG machine as EMOTIV EPOC whereas EEGlab software developed in MATLAB is used for processing the signals. ICA technique is used for pre-processing the acquired data. ICA works on multichannel data and the data used in this study is 14 channels. ICA Algorithm has also helped to find the active components along with the brain area where neural activity was prominently noticed. The study was carried with four participants and a dataset of 1200 events was created and used to obtain the result. During active imagination of the Arm up, Arm down and neutral (the cognitive event i.e. push, pull, and neutral of Emitiv EPOC) movement of the robotic arm the activation was observed in the electrodes F3, F4, FC3, and FC4 placed in the frontal region. Event-related spectral perturbation (ERSP), are noticed in the inter-trial coherence (ITC) which were related to baseline interval. During the imagined movement ERD (Event Related Desynchronization) are observed and ERS (Event Related Synchronization) after the occurrence of imagined movement is noticed in the mentioned electrodes. While performing the study overall 79% accuracy was obtained during arm up, down, and neutral movement. The recognition of pattern on the bases of component map activation is also done to understand the dominant part of the brain while performing a specific movements and it was found that left frontal region is more active during Arm up movement and left & right frontal part is active during an Arm down movement.

Keywords: Brain Computer Interface · Emotiv EPOC · Cognitive events · Event Related Spectral Perturbation · ICA

1 Introduction

Communication takes place when expressions, feelings, thoughts, and intentions are conveyed between people either verbally or non-verbally. Though it is a natural process, it can be proved as a big challenge to people suffering from total paralysis or individuals

© The Author(s) 2023
R. Manza et al. (Eds.): ACVAIT 2022, AISR 176, pp. 69–87, 2023.
https://doi.org/10.2991/978-94-6463-196-8_7

who are suffering from neuromuscular conditions like amyotrophic lateral sclerosis, brain stem stroke, and spinal cord injury. Some of the mentioned diseases are very severe, rendering the individuals motionless thus severely affecting their communication. Thus communication takes place with the help of some assistive devices that rely on nonverbal signals like finger movement and gaze between the signal acquisition and the translation part, with the use of a wireless transmission unit such as Bluetooth and Zigbee modules. By removing wire connections, portability of BCI systems is greatly improved. In recent times more efforts are there for out of lab BCI based research with the help of EEG signals from brain which has provided many applications. This technology converts specific feature of brain activity and transforms into device control actions. The pattern recognition techniques can be applied to the BCI systems for recognition and selection of the correct intentions for BCI control. The developed interface will support individuals with disabilities to become more independent and also enhance their quality of life, and nowadays wireless BCI systems have found a place in entertainment industry also. improving their quality of life, and more recently wireless BCI systems have been applied in entertainments also.

In this study we have attempted to design and develop a robotic arm and interface it with the cognitive state of mind with the help of EEG signals, through Emotiv EPOC. This Emotiv headset is used for cognitive actions of push and pull actions electrical activity which can be captured as EEG signal [2, 3]. The muscle artefacts in EEG signals can be easily decomposed with the help of linear decomposition of EEG signals into source components which is generally used. The aim is to discard the artefact components and focus on neural activity in different components so that the cleaner signals can be reconstructed from the neural components only. To achieve this ICA (Independent Component Analysis) is the most commonly used technique where the blind source separation (BSS) problem is resolved by maximizing the independence of the source components. It is seen that generally, ICA methods yield a useful separation in the maximum number of cases [4, 5]. The pattern recognition technique is also implemented for the classification of the events associated with the movements and identification of the active region of the brain. Along with the active region, dominant part of the brain is also recognised in order to know which part of brain is more dominant and active during performing a respective movement.

2   Literature Review

It is largely acknowledged and widely accepted that volume conduction and reference electrode deteriorate spatial resolution of scalp EEG, other distortions are less widely recognized in the community. As a matter of fact, the time course of brain activities is also largely distorted. For example, spontaneous EEG signals recorded by different electrodes tend to appear more phase-locked than they actually are, inducing artifactually high between site coherence. In what follows, we will show how the timing of averaged event-related potentials (ERPs) is also altered by the same factors. This degraded temporal resolution is seldom acknowledged in the literature, and it is still widely assumed that the timing of scalp potential provides an accurate timing of the underlying sources, since electrical activity propagates instantaneously to the recording electrodes. However, the mixture induced by the spatial smearing also temporally mixes the underlying activities hence making the scalp potential temporal resolution significantly lower than usually assumed. Importantly, we will show that techniques improving the spatial resolution of scalp EEG also secondarily largely improve the temporal one [6].

At present, several types of EEG signals have been classified, such as the sensorimotor rhythm (SMR), slow cortical potential (SCP), event-related potential (ERP), and steady-state visual evoked potential (SSVEP), among others [7].

Since the past few decades work on the functionality of the brain based on the images acquired during capturing the EEG signals have been going on. It is seen that the EEG signal have poor spatial resolution, but an excellent temporal resolution of less than a millisecond. In most of the cases, the process of acquisition of the signals is done using sensors that are non-invasive. The devices used are comparatively easy to use and the entire recording procedure can be done safely.

3 Methodology

Here in our work, we have focused on the use of cognitive actions for capturing the EEG signals using the EEG headset Emotiv EPOC, research edition. The Emotiv EPOC headset is a comparatively simple, portable, cheap, and efficient acquisition device for EEG-based applications. For many EEG based research applications such as Robotic arm control, alphabet recognition using P-300, emotion detection, imagery movements, etc. Emotiv EPOC is used.

The proposed research work is user-dependent, implying that the system will work only for the users who are trained to operate the process and whose databases are already stored. The user can test the system and a comparison between the trained data which is already stored in the databases with the test data is made.

The EEG data were collected using TestBench software of the SDK research kit provided by Emotiv, from the volunteer simultaneously as the events occurred. The created database was further analysed and processed based on the experimental tasks. The pre-processing and analysis of EEG signals was carried out to classify the signals based on the intentions. The active regions of the brain were noted and checked for their relevance based on the functions of the different regions of the brain.

3.1 Participants

The number of participants participating in the proposed study was 4. The selected participants gave their consent to the experimental study. The volunteers were selected from the age group of 22–40 years. Subjects were given a briefing about the proposed study and counseled about the experiments. A log table was maintained for the events, for all the subjects. The training and testing sessions are collected from 4 subjects. Each subject has undergone five training and five testing sessions. In single session 30 events are recorded, thus total of 300 training and testing events are recorded for each subject. A total database of 1200 events is collected.

3.2 Technical Analysis

The EEG file created by using the TestBench tool is saved in the EDF (European Data Format) format. The.edf file can be analyzed in EEGLAB, an analyses GUI developed in MATLAB. BioSig toolbox was used for making our EEG file, saved as.edf compatible with EEGLAB. For processing of biomedical signals like EEG, MEG, EMG, ECG, etc. with SciLab, Matlab, Octave, C/C++, and Python, BioSig is used. More than 30 different data formats are supported by the Signal Viewer.

FIR and IIR filters are the standard pre-processing methods available in EEGLAB. Pre-processing is used for epoch extraction, baseline removal, resampling, and re-referencing for sample analysis. EEGLAB has the strength of strong integration with (ICA). EEGLAB provides ICA algorithm like extended Infomax, JADE, FastICA, and AMICA. We have made use of the default ICA algorithm available in EEGLAB, the extended Infomax. Tools and functions are available for processing and visualization. We can get channel and component data like ERP plotting, time/frequency plots, power spectra, etc.

ICA technique is used to minimize the mutual information among the data projections or maximize their joint entropy. The data projections have minimal temporal overlap. ICA can be viewed as an alternative linear decomposition to principal component analysis (PCA). PCA applied in the temporal domain would specifically make each successive component account for as much as possible of the activity uncorrelated with previously determined components whereas ICA seeks maximally independent sources [8].

In BCI, ICA is a very popular statistical technique that solves the Blind Source Separation (BSS) problem in multiple signal processing applications, like electroencephalographic (EEG) signals for artifact removal procedure. Artifacts like heartbeats, eye blink, muscle activity and noise from a set of signals extracted with some technique like the electroencephalography (EEG), magneto-encephalography(MEG), electrocorticography (ECoG), near infrared spectroscopy (NIRS), functional MRI (fMRI) can be removed with ICA.This method is used to separate a set of linearly mixed multivariate signals and transform it into another set which components are approximately the original signals and independent between them [9].

3.2.1 Independent Component Analysis (ICA)

ICA technique is implemented as follows. Let's assume that there are n linear mixtures of n independent components. Vector x (observed signals) can be written as:

$$x = As \tag{1}$$

where A represents a mixing matrix with the size of, and s is the vector of independent components. The aim of ICA is to find a matrix W (i.e. an inverse of the matrix A) to reverse the mixing effect. Then, after computing the matrix W, one can obtain the independent components by:

$$y = wX \cong s \tag{2}$$

The ICA algorithms generally put some constraints on the mixed signals. First of them is a statistical independence between source signals s; second, a non-Gaussian distribution of the source signals and the third; the equality of the number of source signals and the number of mixture signals. While two first constrains are main assumptions utilized by many algorithms, the third one is introduced only to decrease the algorithm complexity (it causes that the mixing matrix is square). Furthermore, it is assumed that each source signal has the unit variance $E\{si2\} = 1$. To hold this assumption, the matrix of the source signals is whitened before the ICA calculation. One more assumption, introduced only to simplify the algorithm, is that all mixture signals are centered.

ICA does not require any prior information about the source signals. Instead, ICA algorithms utilize the concept of statistical independency of the mixed signals. According to the formal definition, the variables a and b are said to be independent if information about the value a does not give any information about the value b and vice versa. Technically, independence can be defined in terms of the probability density function (pdf):

$$f(x1, x2, \ldots xm) = f1(x1), f2(x2), \ldots fm(xm) \qquad (3)$$

where x1, x2,…xm are random variables.

There are two main approaches to measuring independence: maximization of non-Gaussianity and minimization of mutual information. Most of the existing ICA algorithms are based on one of them.

Different ICA algorithms are used in BCI for artifact removal which generally include: INFOMAX, this algorithm is based on the maximization of entropy and presents a natural gradient form for the independent components computation. FastICA, Hyvärinen's algorithm is often used in 'real time' applications because of the possible parallel implementation. This algorithm converges quickly as it seeks for a component one by one. FastICA uses kurtosis for the independent components estimation. Whitening is usually performed on data before the execution of the algorithm. SOBI, this algorithm relies on second order statistics to explode the time-correlation structure assumption of the signals. It requires computing the following steps: Whitening, Computation of Lagged Correlation Matrices and Joint Diagonalization (JD). JADE (Joint Approximation Diagonalization of Eigenmatrices) JADE, as SOBI does, uses JD and whitening. However, the main difference between both is the set of target matrices on which JD is done [10].

In EEGLAB time analysis or frequency analysis measures like power spectrum, event-related spectral perturbation (ERSP), inter-trial coherence (ITC), and event-related cross-coherence can be done. ERSP visualizes event-related changes in the averaged power spectrum in a broad frequency range relative to a baseline interval whereas ITC measures the amount of event-related phase-locked activity as a function of time and frequency [11].

3.3 Analyzing .edf Files via EEGLAB

Figure 1 demonstrates detailed information of the .edf file selected for analyses in EEGLAB.

The selection of the number of channels and their location has to be mentioned for correct analyses of the components with EEGLAB, as mentioned in Fig. 2. It is based on the location of electrodes of the acquisition device.

```
┌─#1: EDF file ──────────────────────────────┐
│                                            │
│   Filename: none                           │
│   Channels per frame          14           │
│   Frames per epoch            896          │
│   Epochs                      1            │
│   Events                      none         │
│   Sampling rate (Hz)          128          │
│   Epoch start (sec)            0.000       │
│   Epoch end (sec)              6.992       │
│   Reference                   unknown      │
│   Channel locations           No (labels only) │
│   ICA weights                 No           │
│   Dataset size (Mb)            0.1         │
│                                            │
└────────────────────────────────────────────┘
```

Fig. 1. File information after processing by BioSig software

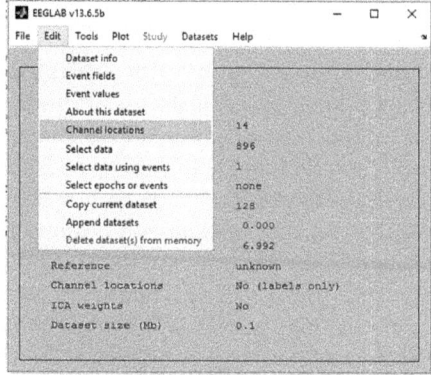

Fig. 2. Information about the channels and their location

After giving the details of the channels, the EEGLAB displays the names of the channels their location and axis details that are shown in Fig. 3. After receiving the channel details, we can execute ICA. The Runica algorithm is selected as it is an extension of the infomax ICA algorithm. Matlab functions allows faster and less memory-intensive computation.

The entire process of executing the ICA technique has been stated in Figs. 3, 4, 5, 6, 7, and 8 stepwise. The particular ICA out of the different techniques has to be selected, in our study as mentioned we have selected "runica". Then the channels out of the available channels for our system for which the component analysis has to be made, have to be selected. The iterations as mentioned in Fig. 6 will be displayed. Then we can view the component maps as stated in Figs. 7 and 8.

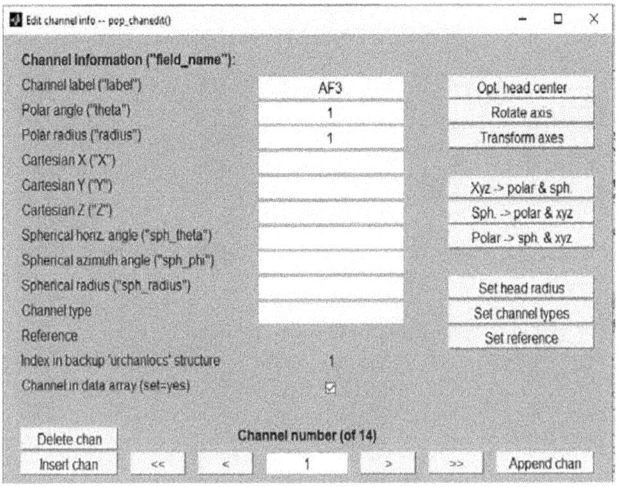

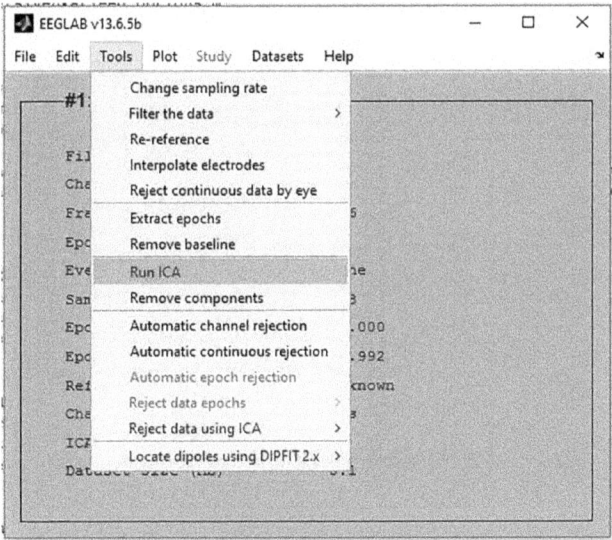

Fig. 3. Channels details

Fig. 4. Execution of ICA through tools

3.4 Robotic Arm Overview

The Technology Uncorked OctaMotion Robotic (TUOM) arm with the degree of freedom as three is considered for this study. The TUOM Robotic Arm DIY Kit was produced from eBay [12]. It contains 84 parts along with Gripper which has the following movements open, close, up, and down movements. Modifications were made in the procured arm, for this experiment. The movements of this arm that are considered are grip open and grip close, up and down movements.

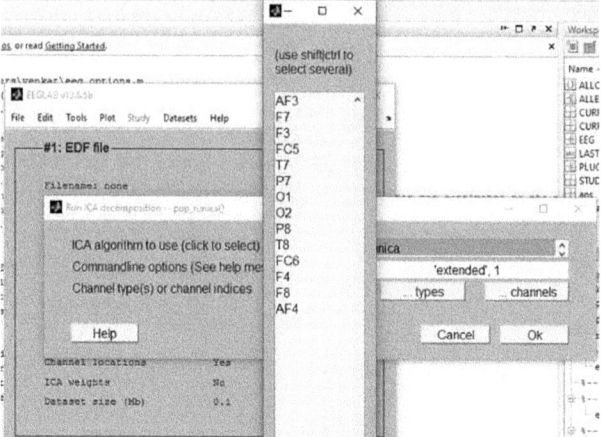

Fig. 5. Select one of the ICA technique

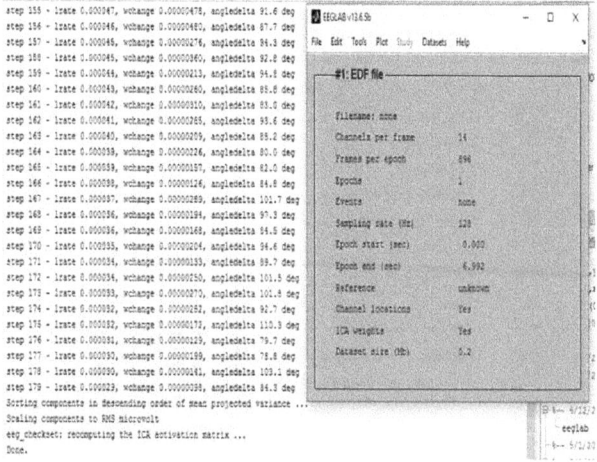

Fig. 6. Iterations observed during ICA

3.5 Active Region Identification

For this study, the region covered by the following electrodes namely F3, F4, FC5, and FC6 is considered. The actual electrodes over the motor cortex are C1, C2, C3, and C4, but these electrodes are not available for Emotiv EPOC, therefore the said electrodes are selected.

As mentioned in Fig. 9, the area of the brain which is involved in motor activity is the frontal lobe, therefore the above-mentioned electrodes are selected. The marked region in Fig. 10 covers these electrodes and the placement location of these electrodes.

The component maps observed during the events of Arm Up, Arm Down, and Neutral of the robotic arm are analyzed. The selected electrode activation has been noted for

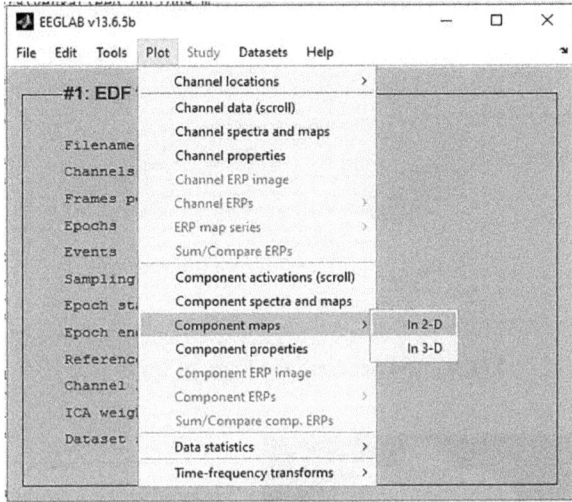

Fig. 7. Component map selection result

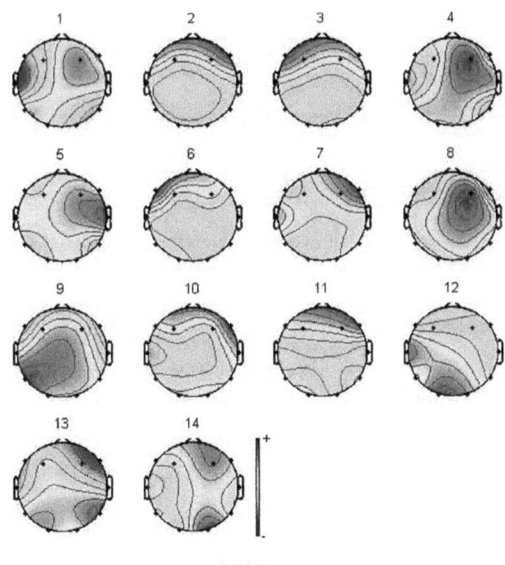

Fig. 8. Component map activation result

different events and a relation between the occurrence of the events and the region of activation is established.

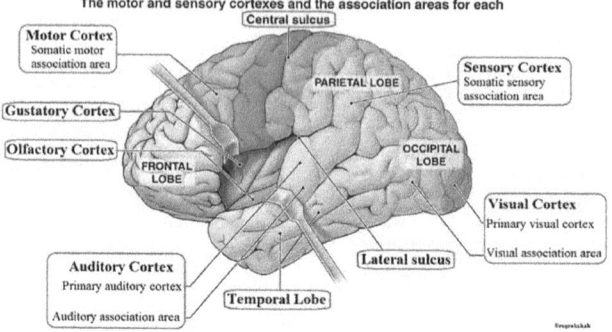

Fig. 9. The Sections and lobes of Brain [13]

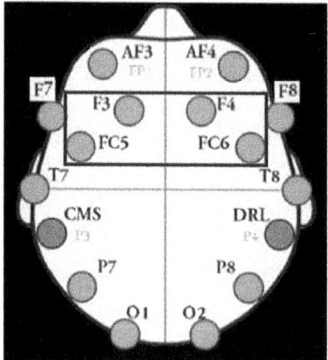

1	AF3
2	F7
3	F3
4	FC5
5	T7
6	P7
7	O1
8	O2
9	P8
10	T8
11	FC6
12	F4
13	F8
14	AF4

Fig. 10. 10–20 system and electrodes of Emotiv EPOC

3.5.1 ARM UP Component Activation

Figure 11 Observations: In Fig. 11 there are four instances of the occurrences of Pull event, of four subjects namely A, B, C, D which results in arm up action in the robotic arm.

11A: Result of Pull event of subject A.
11B: Result of Pull event of subject B.
11C: Result of Pull event of subject C.
11D: Result of Pull event of subject D.

During the occurrence of the pull event of the Cognitive suite, the Arm up action takes place in the proposed robotic arm. Figure 11A, B, C and D display the result of ICA, 2-dimensional components activation. From the figure, it can be observed that the frontal region of the brain is active in most of the components. The 2-dimensional component maps were further classified with reference to the 4 electrodes which were located in the frontal region.

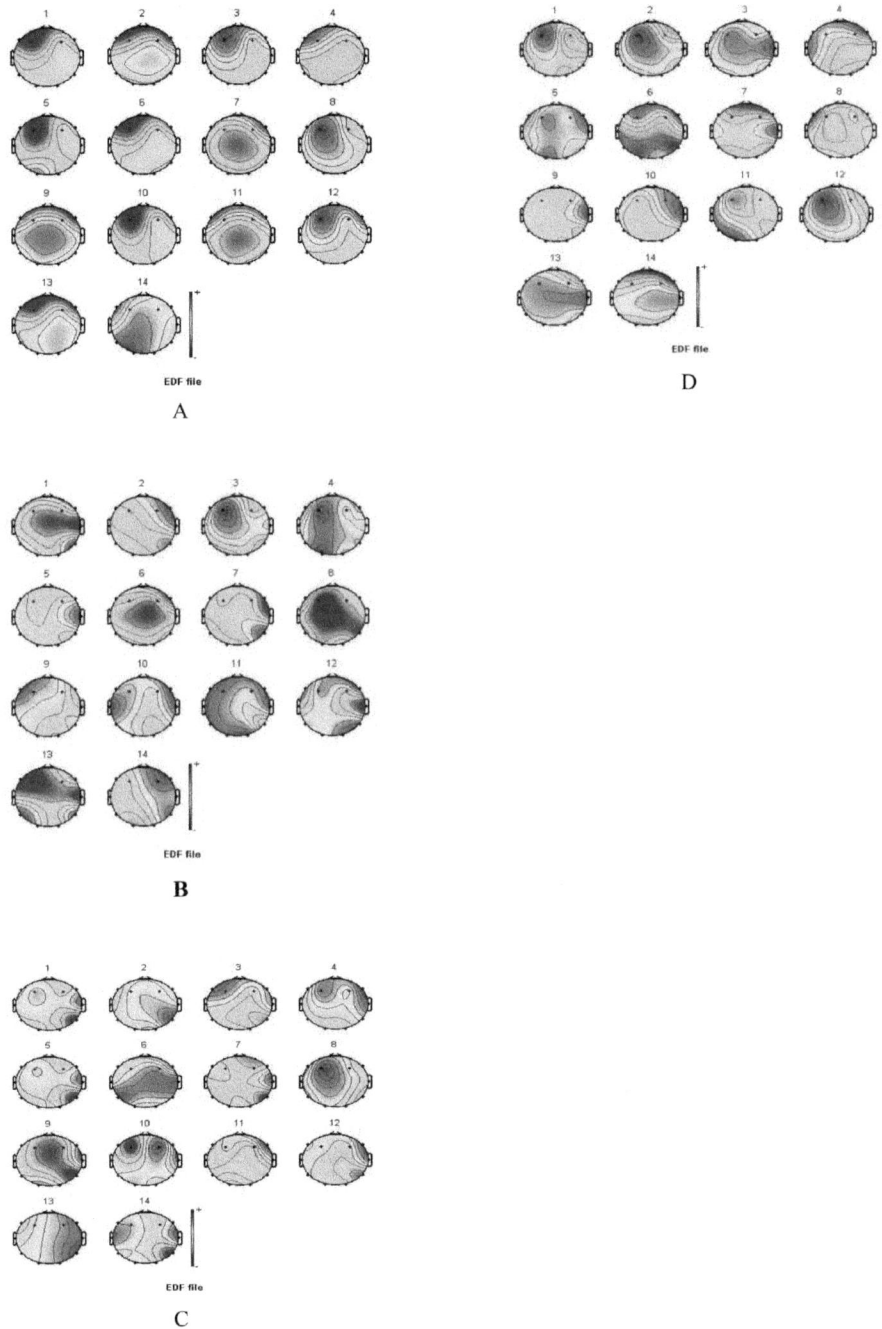

Fig. 11. Component activation during Arm up action

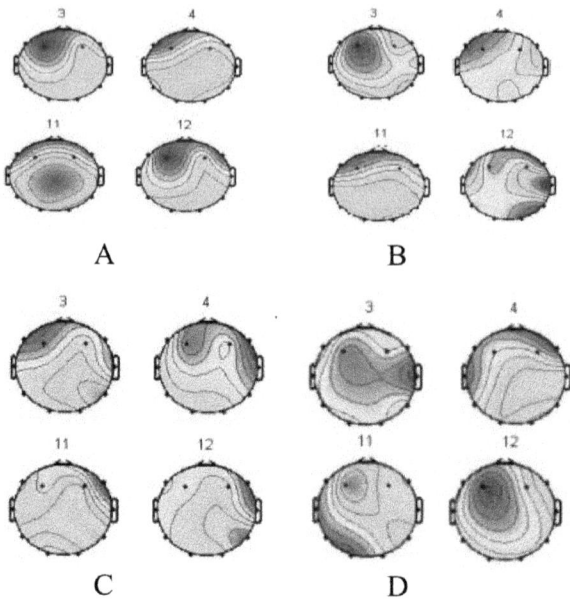

Fig. 12. Frontal region activation during Arm up action

Figure 12 Observations: In Fig. 12 there are four instances of the occurrences of Pull event, of four subjects namely A, B, C, D which results in arm up action in the robotic arm.

12A: Result showing activation in the frontal region of subject A.
12B: Result showing activation in the frontal region of subject B.
12C: Result showing activation in the frontal region of subject C.
12D: Result showing activation in the frontal region of subject D.

From Figs. 12A, B, C, D it can be observed that during imagination of movement that frontal region where the motor cortex is located, becomes active which can be noticed in the results of 2d activation components placed in that region, which we have acquired after running ICA algorithm.

Figure 12 represents the 2D component map that was classified as 4 electrodes located in the frontal region which represents the motor activity while performing the Arm up movement. Form these images it is observed that the red part represents the activity and blue represents no activity. Therefore based on these color patterns it can be observed that more activity is found in the left frontal region.

3.5.2 ARM Down Component Activation

Figure 13 Observations: In Fig. 13 there are four instances of the occurrences of Push event, of four subjects namely A, B, C, D which results in arm down action in the robotic arm.

13A: Result of Push event of subject A.

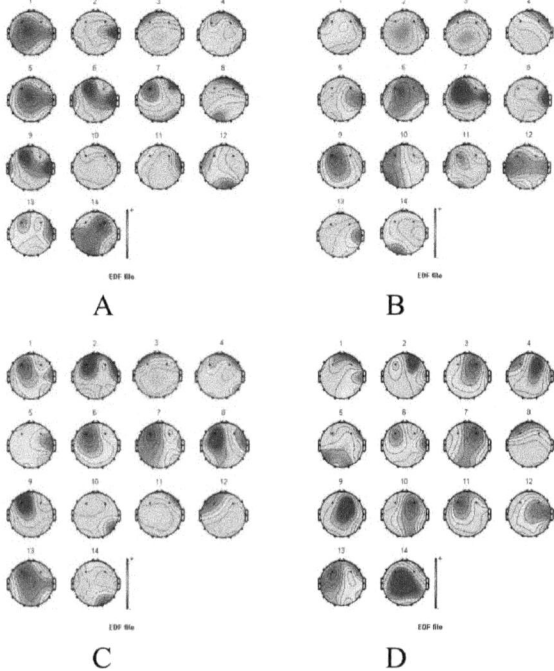

Fig. 13. Component activation during Arm down action

13B: Result of Push event of subject B.
13C: Result of Push event of subject C.
13D: Result of Push event of subject D.

During the occurrence of the push event of the Cognitive suite, the Arm down action takes place in the proposed robotic arm. Figure 13 displays the result of ICA, 2-dimensional components activation. From the figure, it can be observed that the frontal region of the brain is active in most of the components. The 2-dimensional component maps were further classified with reference to the 4 electrodes which were located in the frontal region.

Figure 14 Observations: In Fig. 14 there are four instances of the occurrences of Push event, of four subjects namely A, B, C, D which results in arm down action in the robotic arm.

14A: Result showing activation in the frontal region of subject A.
14B: Result showing activation in the frontal region of subject B.
14C: Result showing activation in the frontal region of subject C.
14D: Result showing activation in the frontal region of subject D.

From Figs. 14A, B, C, D it can be observed that during imagination of movement that frontal region where the motor cortex is located, becomes active which can be noticed in the results of 2-dimensional activation components placed in that region, which we have acquired by implementing ICA algorithm.

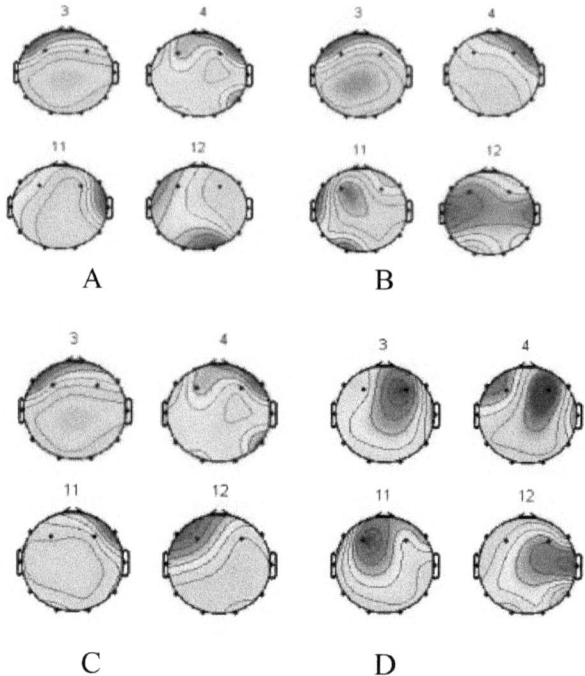

Fig. 14. Frontal region activation during Arm down action

The Fig. 14 it can be observed that while performing the Arm down movement most of the activity is found in the frontal region where both the left and right sides are equally found to be active.

3.5.3 Reduced Frontal Region Activation for Neutral Action

Figure 15 Observations: In Fig. 15 there are four instances of the occurrences of Neutral event, of four subjects namely A, B, C, D which results in no action in the robotic arm.

15A: Result of Neutral event of subject A.
15B: Result of Neutral event of subject B.
15C: Result of Neutral event of subject C.
15D: Result of Neutral event of subject D.

Similarly, during the occurrence of the neutral event of the Cognitive suite, the Arm stops moving and no action takes place in the proposed robotic arm. The Figs. 15A, B, C, and D display the result of ICA 2 dimensional components deactivation as a result of subdued action. From the figures, it can be observed that there is less activity in the frontal region of the brain when the subject is not thinking of any movement as noticed in most of the components. The 2-dimensional component maps were further classified with reference to the 4 electrodes which were located in the frontal region.

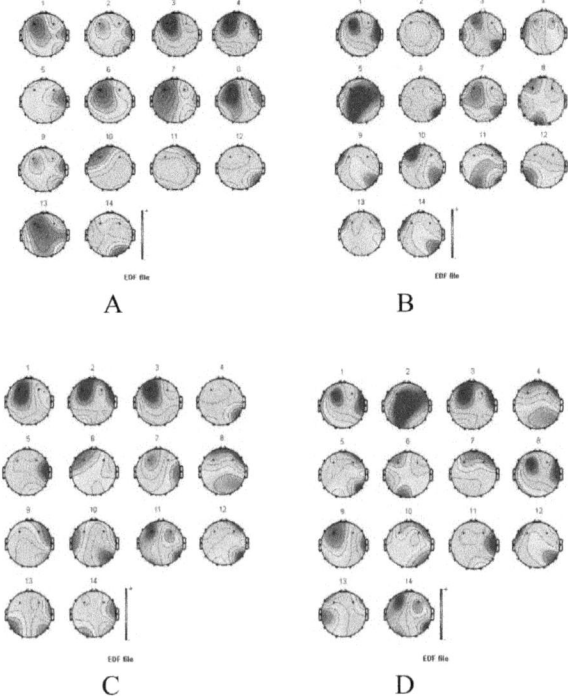

Fig. 15. Component activation during Neutral action

Figure 16 Observations: In Figs. 16 there are four instances of the occurrences of Neutral event, of four subjects namely A, B, C, D which results in no action in the robotic arm.

- 16A: Result showing no significant activation in the frontal region of subject A.
- 16B: Result showing no significant activation in the frontal region of subject B.
- 16C: Result showing no significant activation in the frontal region of subject C.
- 16D: Result showing no significant activation in the frontal region of subject D.

From Figs. 16A, B, C, D it can be observed that when the subject is not involved in the imagination of movement that frontal region where the motor cortex is located, is less active which can be noticed in the results of 2-dimensional activation components placed in that region, which we have acquired by implementing ICA algorithm.

3.6 ERD and ERS for the Components in Frontal Region

As per the literature for the physical movement, ERD and ERS were observed in the electrodes over the motor cortex which is associated with the hand movement. ERD was seen during the actual movement and ERS after the occurrence of movement. ERD were also noticed on the ipsilateral hemisphere. The reason being would have been that during the imagination of the movement of a cube, though there was no physical movement, the natural urge of the movement generated ERD activity, on the contralateral motor cortex,

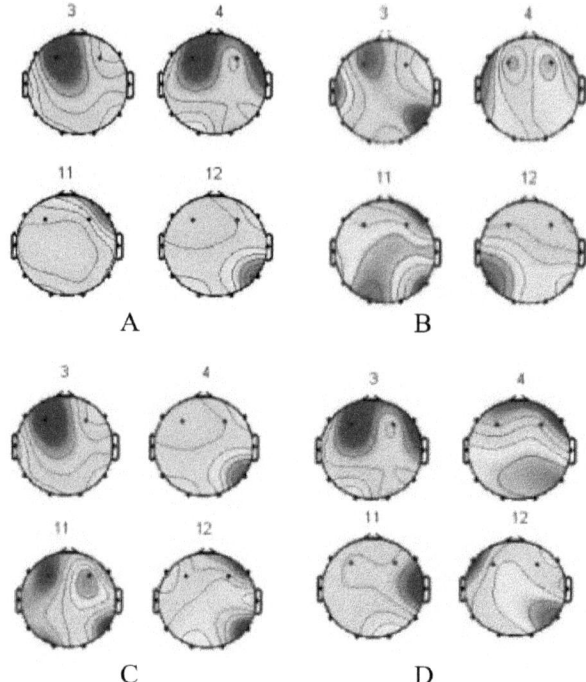

Fig. 16. Reduced Frontal region activation during Neutral action

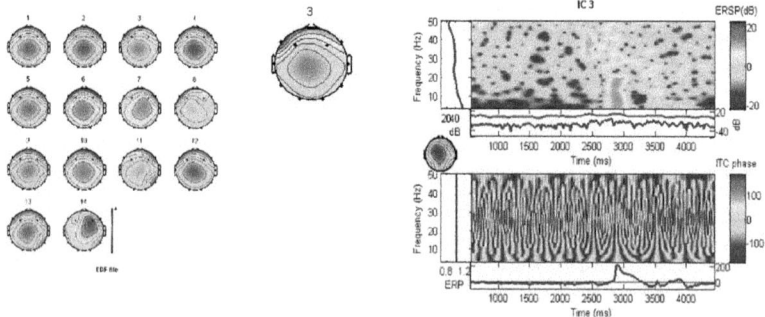

Fig. 17. Activation observed during Arm up event of the robotic arm in electrode F3

which was the ipsilateral side of the moving hand. ERS was prominently noticed after the action had taken place as seen in Figs. 16–18.

As pointed out in Fig. 9, the area or region of the brain that is involved in motor activity is the frontal lobe or frontal region. The activity used in this study is the motor activity/movement for which the frontal lobe is responsible and it is observed that the activation of activity was found in the frontal region.

Figures 16 and 17 show the time-frequency decomposition of the activations of components. Independent components are capable of directly indicating the activity of

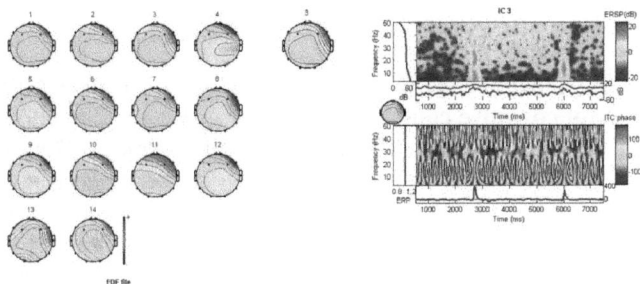

Fig. 18. Activation observed during Arm down event of the robotic arm in the electrode F3

one brain EEG sources. The image represents two images as the ERSP (dB) image and the ITC image. A correlation between the component activity and occurrence of stimulus is also seen. The ERSP (dB) (dB shows the level of waveform in decibels that are relative to digital full scale [14]) image seen in the upper panel represents the phase-lock events [15].

4   Performance evaluation of the Robotic Arm

For doing data analysis the results of all three events were required in the form of TP, FN, TN, and FP as specified in Table 1. The recording of each session five training and five testing is done. The calculations of the parameters important for performance evaluation are sensitivity, specificity, and accuracy as in Table 2.

Table 1. Outcomes Definition

Outcome	Definition
True Positive (TP)	Correct input, Correct Output
False Negative (FN)	Correct input, incorrect Output
True Negative (TN)	Incorrect input, Incorrect Output
False Positive (FP)	Incorrect input, Correct Output

Table 2. Parameter along with the formula

Parameter	Formula
Sensitivity	$\frac{TP}{TP+FN}$
Specificity	$\frac{TN}{TN+FP}$
Accuracy	$\frac{TP+TN}{TP+FN+TN+FP}$

5 Result

In this study, by implementing the ICA technique we were able to classify the region of brain responsible for cognitive control and decision making and pointed out the active region of the brain signals. We were able to get overall accuracy of 76% for Arm Down movement, 76% for Arm Up movement, and 80% for the Neutral movement of the robotic arm during testing sessions. In the same way, overall accuracy obtained during the training session is 76% for Arm Down movement, 77% for Arm Up movement, and 88% for Neutral movement. The overall accuracy rate of this study is 79%.

6 Conclusion

The EMOTIV EPOC provides 3 suites namely Expressive, Affective, and Cognitive. Expressive, reads facial expressions. Affective, reads the user's emotional state. And Cognitive, reads conscious intent for movements. In this study the Cognitive suite and the Expressive suite were considered for controlling the movement of the arm. The Pull, Push, and Neutral events of cognitive and raise eyebrow and clench of expressive events have been taken for experimental work. Looking at the patterns obtained it was found that the left frontal region of the brain is more active while performing arm up movement whereas both the left and right frontal parts of the brain are active during arm down event. The performance evaluation of the proposed robotic arm was done by calculating the sensitivity, specificity, and accuracy values. The analysis was performed with regards to find the activation regions of the brain when the movements were imagined.

References

1. Ujwal Chaudhary et al, "Brain–Computer Interface–Based Communication in the Completely Locked-In State" PLOS Biology l DOI: https://doi.org/10.1371/journal.pbio.1002593 January 31, 2017.
2. Choi B, Jo S (2013) "A Low-Cost EEG System-Based Hybrid Brain-Computer Interface for Humanoid Robot Navigation and Recognition" PLoS ONE 8(9):e74583. doi: https://doi.org/10.1371/journal.pone.0074583.
3. Gerardo Rosas-Cholula et al,"Gyroscope-Driven Mouse Pointer with an EMOTIV ® EEG Headset and Data Analysis Based on Empirical Mode Decomposition", Sensors 2013, 13, 10561-10583; doi: https://doi.org/10.3390/s130810561
4. Laura Frølich, Irene Dowding, "Removal of muscular artifacts in EEG signals: a comparison of linear decomposition methods", Brain Informatics (2018) 5:13–22. https://doi.org/10.1007/s40708-017-0074-6
5. Irene Winkler et al 2014 J. Neural Eng. 11 035013
6. Boris Burle, Laure Spieser, Clemence Roger, Laurence Casini, Thierry, Hasbroucq and Franck Vidal, "Spatial and temporal resolution of EEG: Is it really black and white? A Scalp Current Density view", International Journal of Psychophysiology, doi: https://doi.org/10.1016/j.ijpsycho.2015.05.004 6 May 2015.
7. Alan F. Pérez-Vidal, Carlos D. Garcia-Beltran, Albino Martínez-Sibaja and Rubén Posada-Gómez, "Use of the Stockwell Transform in the Detection of P300 Evoked Potentials with Low-Cost Brain Sensors", Sensors 2018, 18, 1483; doi: https://doi.org/10.3390/s18051483

8. Arnaud Delorme and Scott Makeig, "EEGLAB: an open source toolbox for analysis of single-trial EEGdynamics including independent component analysis", Journal of Neuroscience Methods, Vol. 134, pp. 9–21, doi: https://doi.org/10.1016/j.jneumeth.2003.10.009 16 October 2003.

9. Guillermo SAHONERO-ALVAREZ,Humberto CALDERON, A Comparison of SOBI, FastICA, JADE and Infomax Algorithms, Proceedings of The 8th International Multi-Conference on Complexity, Informatics and Cybernetics (IMCIC 2017)

10. Izabela Rejer, Pawel Górski. Independent Component Analysis for EEG Data Preprocessing - Algorithms Comparison. 12th International Conference on Information Systems and Industrial Management (CISIM), Sep 2013, Krakow, Poland. pp. 108-119, https://doi.org/10.1007/978-3-642-40925-7_11. hal- 01496056

11. Clemens Brunner, Arnaud Delorme and Scott Makeig, "Eeglab – An Open Source Matlab Toolbox for Electrophysiological Research", Biomed Tech 2013; 58 (Suppl. 1) © 2013 by Walter de Gruyter · Berlin · Boston. DOI https://doi.org/10.1515/bmt-2013-4182.

12. http://www.rograkshak.com/BodySystem/Brain.

13. https://www.ebay.com/

14. https://s3.amazonaws.com/izotopedownloads/docs/rx6/07-spectrogram-waveform-display/index.html

15. https://sccn.ucsd.edu/wiki/Chapter_11:_Time/Frequency_decomposition

Localization of Intervertebral Discs Using Deep-Learning and Region Growing Technique

Sujata Satpute[1][✉], Ramesh Manza[1], Ganesh Manza[1], and Anjum Shaikh[2]

[1] Dr. Babasaheb Ambedkar, Marathwada University, Aurangabad, India
`sujatasatpute7058@gmail.com`
[2] Deogiri College, Aurangabad, India

Abstract. Detection and Marking of Intervertebral discs (IVD) of the spinal cord is relevant as it notably enables experts to diagnose spinal cord injury. Many of the experts from medical field do this task manually, therefore there may be risk of wrong labeling of in-vertebral disks and this job is tedious. There are several automated methods are already implemented for CT-SCAN images and MRI images as well. Most of the methods are not freely available and the existing methods fails if the image quality fluctuates. There is another factor that affects the localization go wrong when the algorithms for localization fails to hit discs or it has false positive detection. In this paper we adopted Fully Convolutional Network (FCN), Stacked Hourglass Network with Multi-level Attention Mechanism and region growing technique for vertebral disc localization and segmentation. Deep learning has been used to tackle with false positive detection with the help of pose estimation and semantic segmentation techniques. The accuracy of the results were compared by the ground truth pixel location against predicted pixels location. Spine generic public multi-center dataset was used to evaluate the proposed method.

Keywords: Spinal cord segmentation · IVD localization · Intervertebral Disc · Localization

1 Introduction

The spine is the name given to a bone structure composed of vertebrae that jointly move with each other and extend from the skull to the pelvis. Spine, it starts at the neck and extends to the coccyx. Figure 1 shows structure of spine where it is seen like "S" shaped. It is composed of 33 vertebrae. It is divided into 5 areas: nape (7 vertebrae), back (12 vertebrae), lumbar vertebrae (5 vertebrae), coccyx (sacrum) (5 vertebrae), coccyx (4 vertebrae). The vertebras of the vertebrae join to form the spinal canal. The spinal canal contains the spinal cord. The vertebrae that make up the spine are connected by semi-movable joints. Only the coccyx and coccygeal vertebra have immobile joints between them. The spine protects both the spinal cord and the skeleton from behind. It allows the body to stand upright. It is the cage that protects the lungs through the ribs. It is also a connection point for internal organs. The S-shaped curved structure ensures that the spine is light in jump and balance.

R. Manza et al. (Eds.): ACVAIT 2022, AISR 176, pp. 88–98, 2023.
https://doi.org/10.2991/978-94-6463-196-8_8

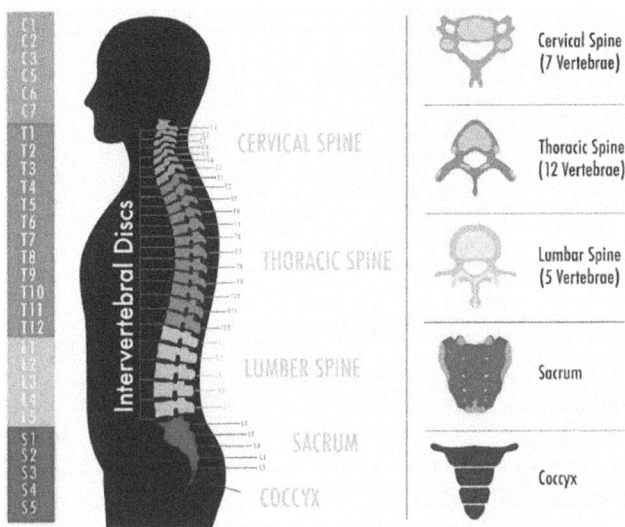

Fig. 1. The Anatomy of the Spine [https://www.motionspineinstitute.com/spine-101/]

Any harm injury to the spinal cord and it's in-vertebral discs lead to major health problems. To diagnose the injury of the spinal cord and in-vertebral discs, images are required. There are two popular methods to acquire images of Intervertebral discs such as Magnetic Resonance Imaging (MRI) and Computerized Tomography (CT). Medical imaging provides images of human spine and its In-vertebral disc to determine the anatomical structure of scoliosis, hernia, disc. It is important for diagnosing diseases such as slippage of disc, disc gaps. Today, the disc in a lumbar MRI image and localization of the vertebrae has been analyzed by radiologists manually. This process takes a long time which may lead to an error. There are several computer aided techniques and tools have been introduced for automatic detection and localization of IVD and Vertebrae. For this reason, many methods have been presented for automatic identification and positioning of the disc. Existing methods are usually based on machine learning. A classifier is used. Recent deep learning methods, men. Most successful in recognizing the structure of the spine. Record the value. In this article, we adopted a fully convolutional network (FCN), Stacked Hourglass Network with a Multi-level Attention Mechanism, and Region Growing techniques for disc localization and segmentation (Fig. 2).

The spine has 23 discs that are situated between the 24 cervical, thoracic, and lumbar vertebrae. Six cervical discs (also known as the cervical spine) are placed in the neck (also known as the cervical spine) between seven cervical vertebrae (C1–C7) just beneath the skull. The lower back (also known as the lumbar spine) has five lumbar discs that are positioned between five lumbar vertebrae.

Each vertebral region performs a specific job in the human body, such as breathing, walking, and protecting the spinal cord. Damage to the in-vertebral disc might result in back discomfort or hypersensitivity in various body areas. The accident or high pressure/tension on the disc usually causes any form of damage to the in-vertebral disc. As a result, diagnosing the in-vertebral disc is critical; assessing the disc form and/or

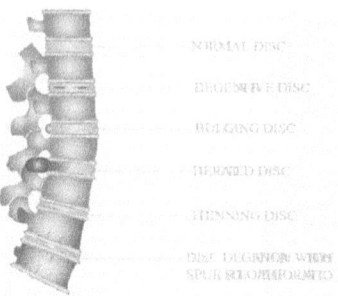

Fig. 2. Damaged IVD

locating the damaged disc may aid in the analysis. The detection of in-vertebral discs is the first step in the diagnosis. Detecting the discs manually is a difficult task. Several strategies have been proposed in existing works to conduct automatic disc recognition and localization mentioned in the Sect. 2.

2   Review of the Literature

Automatic labeling and analysis of the IVD is a critical task. Recently, many methods have been introduced in the field of medical image analysis for Intervertebral disc segmentation and localization [1, 2]. Recent study shows that IVD localization interest have been focused on the deep convolution neural networks (CNNs), and many studies reveals that it outperforming traditional localization techniques. Cohen et. al. [3] proposed 3D Fully Convolutional Network (FCN) to retrieve center coordinates of IVD and segment the disc. In the work proposed in the work proposed by Ji et al. [4] have adopted standard CNN for Intervertebral disc segmentation by using a patch around each pixel. The authors have used 2D patch and impact of vicinity size to evaluate different patch strategies. The authors of [5] adopted deeply supervised multi-scale fully CNN for Intervertebral disk segmentation applied on MR-T2 weighted images. In their work risk of loss of gradients during the training was reduced by use of multi-scale deep supervision in the architecture. In the work proposed by Forsberget. al. [6] clinically annotated spine labels were used for detection and labeling pipelines for cervical and lumbar MR. They have used two distinct pipelines for labeling and detection of vertebrae. And two neural networks (CNNs) were configured for locating lumbar/cervical vertebra. Zhuet. al. [7] introduced a method based on Gabor filter bank for Intervertebral disc localization and segmentation. Alomari et al. [8] employed a two-level probabilistic model for IVD discs localization from MRI images. Michopoulou et al. [9] introduced a semi-automatic method for detection and segmentation of IVDs. In their work they have considered both degenerated and normal lumbar IVDs. Another model based searching method was used to localize entire spine discs by Penget. al. [10]. Castro et al. [11] used active contour model with fuzzy C-means technique to segment the IVDs. Haq et al. [12] used the discrete simplex surface model for segmentation of the IVDs. Anovel anisotropic-oriented flux model employed in the work proposed by Law et. al. [13] to segment the IVDs.

Above mentioned methods needs manual operations or human interaction to refine the results for effective IVDs localization and segmentation. Some studies have proposed early fusion and late fusion techniques of IVD features for Multi-modal segmentation of IVDs [14–20].

3 Proposed Methodology

3.1 Data

We employed MRI spinal cord dataset [3]. The dataset consist of T1w and T2w MRI data from 235 subjects, the dataset includes inconsistent images since, images were captured from 40 different centers. The network was fed an average of each subject's six center slices as input images. For training, testing, and validation, the dataset was divided into three parts: 75%, 10%, and 15%, respectively. Ground truth data was manually formed through *"labelme"* annotation tool [21].

3.2 Pre-processing

The Spinal Cord Toolbox (SCT) v4.0.1 was used to preprocess 3D volumes of the MRI data [22]. The images were re-sampled at 1 mm isotropic resolution and straightened using the spinal cord segmentation method to produce the spinal cord centerline [23]. The image was cropped to 256 * 256 pixels around the spinal region as part of the straightening procedure [24]. To reduce contrast variability in the image, a Contrast Limited Adaptive Histogram Equalization technique was used [25]. We increased the target size to deal with class imbalance by applying a 10-pixel Gaussian kernel to single-pixel labels.

Further we extract the average of 6 sagittal slices (centered in the middle slice) as a data sample for each subject. We normalize each image to be in range [0, 1] to reduce the effect of data variation. In order to prepare the ground truth data for the training process, first, we extract the intervertebral disc position (single pixel) from the ground truth data then we convolve the image with a Gaussian kernel to generate a smooth ground truth with increased target size (radius 10). We repeat this process for each intervertebral disc separately to produce V channel ground truth, where V is the number of intervertebral discs. Since the Spine Generic dataset consists of samples with variable number of intervertebral discs (between 7–11), we extract 11 intervertebral discs for each subject. For any missing inter vertebral disc we consider unknown position and eliminate its effect on the training process by simply filtering out with the visibility flag on the loss function.

The proposed method starts with the pre-processing for the proposed model. The position of the intervertebral discs were extracted using the pose estimation method with attention mechanism of Haourglass model. Figure 3 depicts the proposed method. Steps involved in the methodology are discussed in the subsequent section.

3.3 Proposed Method

The stacked hourglass network [26] learns the object posture using (N-1) intermediate (shown in 3 as intermediate prediction) and one final prediction, as illustrated in Fig. 3. As a result, the multi-level representation is taken into consideration in terms of

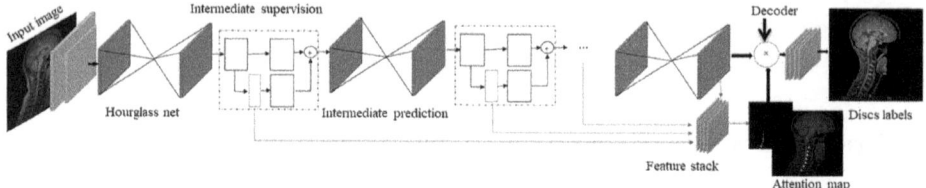

Fig. 3. Proposed stacked hourglass network, An attention mechanism is built into a stacked hourglass network. The model considers the loss function between each hourglass prediction and ground truth mask (intermediate supervision). Further it feds the intermediate representation into an attention layer to produce the attention map (heat map). The attention map guides the decoder layer to focus on the in-vertebral disc.

the N stacked hourglass network. We propose using a multi-level attention technique to enhance the power of representation space. To do this, each hourglass network's intermediate representation (shown in step 2) is concatenated to build a multi-level representation.

This representation can be viewed as a collection of collective knowledge gathered from multiple levels of the network at various scales; consequently, employing this collection of collective knowledge as a supervisory signal to calibrate the final representation can result in a superior representation. We stack all of the intermediate representations to incorporate this supervisor signal. To construct a single channel attention mechanism, this stacked representation is given to the attention block (series of point-wise convolution with sigmoid activation). To re-calibrate the representation space and train the model to pay more attention to the disc position, we multiply this attention channel with the final representation. The attention block fed to region growing technique. Centroid of the block of attention map/ heat map was considered as a seed point for region growing. In the instance of the Region expanding approach, start with a seed pixel and then look at the neighboring pixels. If the neighboring pixels follow the preset rules, that pixel is added to the seed pixel's region, and the procedure continues until no similarity remains. The bottom-up strategy is used in this procedure. The preferred rule might be specified as a threshold in the event of an expanding region. Threshold for region growing is computed using Eq. 1.

$$|Z_{max} - Z_{min}| \leq threshold \tag{1}$$

where, $Z_{max} \rightarrow$ *Maximum pixel intensity value in a region*
And $Z_{min} \rightarrow$ *Minimum pixel intesity value in a region.*

4   Results and Discussion

The Spine Generic Dataset is used to assess the performance of the proposed technique. Each participant has both T1w and T2w contrasts in this sample. Images were taken in 42 various locations across the world. The dataset encompasses a wide range of sample quality, scale, and imaging devices, making it a difficult baseline for intervertebral disc labeling.We use Adam optimization to train the proposed model over 150 epochs with

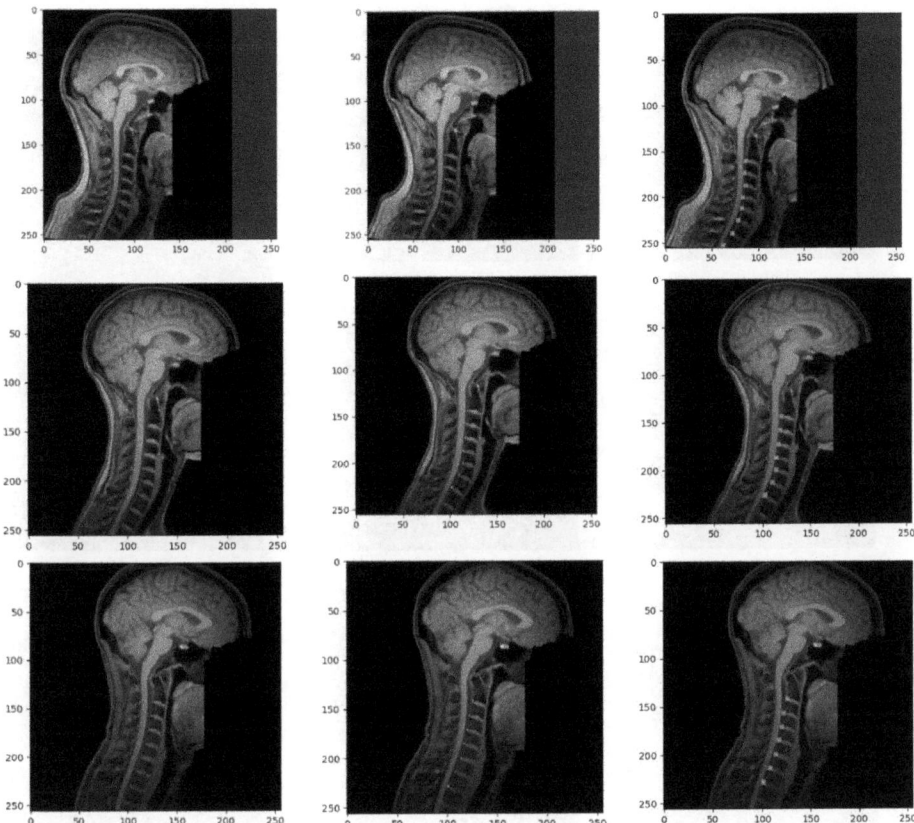

Fig. 4. (**A**) Original image. (**B**) Seed point detected by hourglass network. (**C**) attention map produced by Hourglass Network

a learning rate of 0.00025 and a batch size of 4. In our tests, we found that employing two stacks yielded the greatest results on the validation set. The approach may be easily used via the Spinal Cord Toolbox [22], and the implementation and model training were done in ivadomed [27].

4.1 Evaluation Matrices

Dice Overlap Coefficients
The percentage of successfully segmented voxels is measured using the Dice metric. Dice is calculated using Eq. (1).

$$Dice = \frac{2|A \cap B|}{|A| + |B|} \times 100\% \tag{2}$$

The percentage of successfully segmented voxels is measured using the Dice metric. Where A represents the sets of foreground voxels in the ground-truth data and B

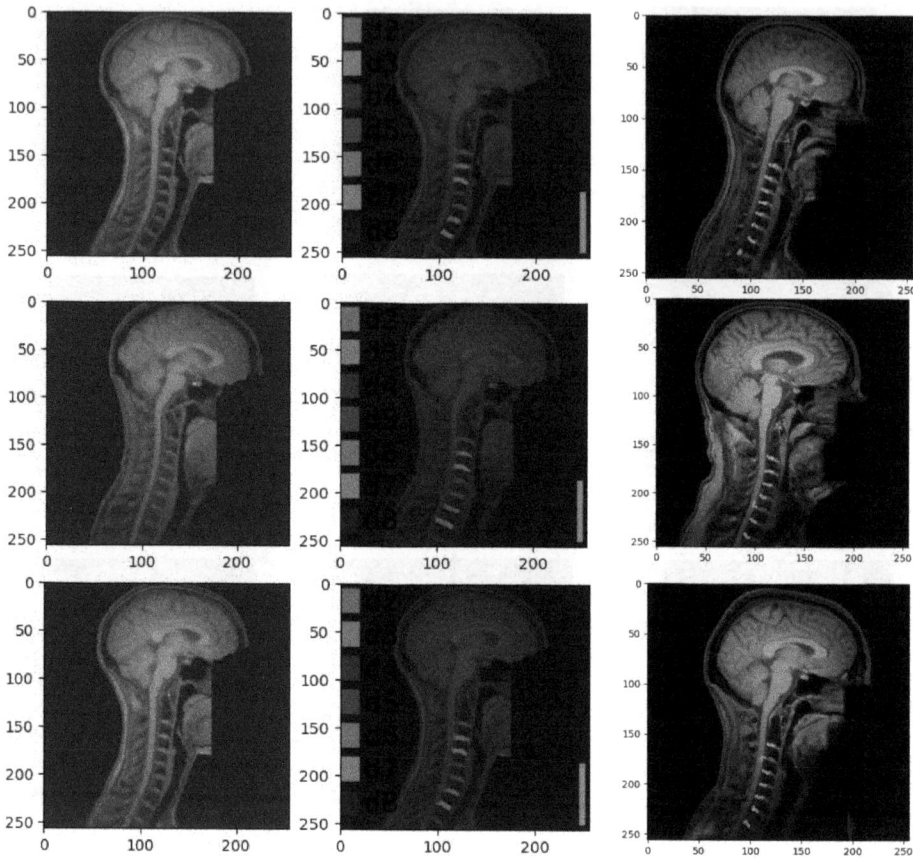

Fig. 5. A) Input images (left), **B)** ground truth image (middle), **C)**output predictions of our proposed method (right)

represents the matching sets of foreground voxels in the segmentation result, Dice is calculated. Better segmentation accuracy is associated with a higher Dice metric. Further, dice value was received by confusion matrix as 1 (correctly identified) and 0 (missed) the target and predicted pixel coordinates. Figure 9(a) and (b) depicts the produced confusion matrix from localization distance technique (Figs. 5, 7 and 8).

4.2   Effect of Hourglass Attention Mechanism

The proposed approach makes use of the attention mechanism to re-calibrate the representation space and focus the model's attention to the target region. We trained the model with and without the attention mechanism to see how it affected the results. The results in Fig. 6 show that the attention mechanism model performance in both T1w and T2w modalities. Figure 4(C) shows a sample attention map on the input images to visualize the influence of the network's attention mechanism.

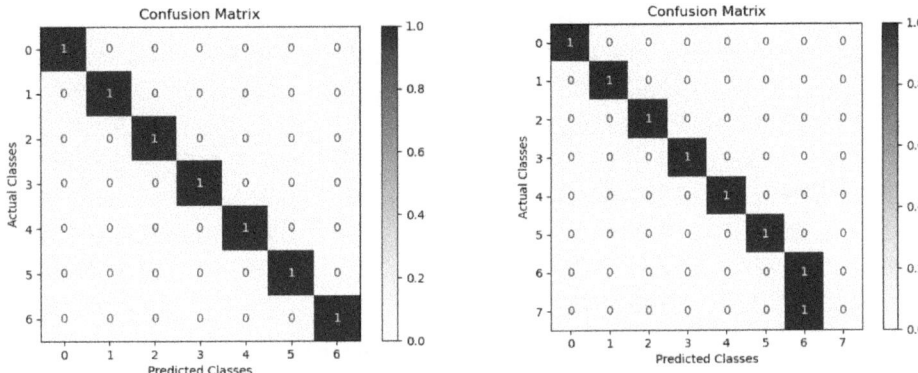

Fig. 6. **(a)** Confusion matrix for testing sample 1, **(b)** Confusion matrix for testing sample 2

	precision	recall	f1-score	support
0	1.00	1.00	1.00	1
1	1.00	1.00	1.00	1
2	1.00	1.00	1.00	1
3	1.00	1.00	1.00	1
4	1.00	1.00	1.00	1
5	1.00	1.00	1.00	1
6	1.00	1.00	1.00	1
accuracy			1.00	7
macro avg	1.00	1.00	1.00	7
weighted avg	1.00	1.00	1.00	7

	precision	recall	f1-score	support
0	1.00	1.00	1.00	1
1	1.00	1.00	1.00	1
2	1.00	1.00	1.00	1
3	1.00	1.00	1.00	1
4	1.00	1.00	1.00	1
5	1.00	1.00	1.00	1
6	0.50	1.00	0.67	1
7	0.00	0.00	0.00	1
accuracy			0.88	8
macro avg	0.81	0.88	0.83	8
weighted avg	0.81	0.88	0.83	8

Fig. 7. **(a)** Precision recall graph for sample 1, **(b)** Precision recall graph for sample 2

	centroid-0	centroid-1	orientation	area	eccentricity	perimeter
0	162.365385	91.403846	1.346391	52	0.937089	33.106602
1	175.761905	91.000000	1.285165	63	0.939756	35.313708
2	189.793651	90.111111	1.278327	63	0.928895	35.520815
3	202.913793	88.344828	1.426224	58	0.956987	33.656854
4	215.712329	87.917808	1.311686	73	0.936319	38.727922
5	229.090909	83.045455	1.087678	44	0.946110	30.349242
6	245.027397	77.315068	0.924879	73	0.930408	37.284271

Fig. 8. Features extracted from sample 1

	centroid-0	centroid-1	orientation	area	eccentricity	perimeter
0	145.968421	124.284211	1.388515	95	0.958702	47.349242
1	160.250000	122.650000	1.479635	80	0.965572	43.242641
2	175.131579	121.092105	1.259736	76	0.953223	40.935029
3	188.400000	120.013333	1.383193	75	0.954316	39.692388
4	202.390244	119.829268	1.286689	82	0.953312	43.142136
5	216.298701	114.883117	1.285865	77	0.897980	38.627417
6	231.367647	107.514706	1.072349	68	0.917693	36.455844
7	245.471429	97.457143	1.048530	70	0.953265	39.420310

Fig. 9. Features extracted from sample 2

5 Conclusion

In this work we fabricated the IVD localization and labeling through region growing and pose estimation technique. The structural information of the IVDs is employed for training and to localize the true location of the discs.

The proposed approach re-calibrates the representation space to focus more on the intervertebral disc area by utilizing the strength of the attention mechanism. To eliminate the FP and FN detection, we presented a skeleton-based post-processing technique.

A new design for recognizing intervertebral discs is presented in this study. The approach improves localization precision while reducing false positives and negatives. Extending the testing of this model to more "real-life" datasets in patients will be a future goal.

References

1. B. Ayed, K. Punitha kumar, G. Garvin, W. Romano, and S. Li, "Graph cuts with invariant object-interaction priors: application to intervertebral disc segmentation," in Biennial International Conference on Information Processing in Medical Imaging. Springer, 2011, pp.221–232.
2. C. Chen, D. Belavy, W. Yu, C. Chu, G. Armbrecht, M. Bansmann,D. Felsenberg, and G. Zheng, "Localization and segmentation of3D intervertebral discs in MR images by data driven estimation," IEEE transactions on medical imaging, vol. 34, no. 8, pp. 1719–1729,2015.
3. J Cohen-Adad. Spinal cord MRI public database (multi-subjects), July 2019.
4. X. Ji, G. Zheng, D. Belavy, and D. Ni, "Automated intervertebral disc segmentation using deep convolutional neural networks, "in International Workshop on Computational Methods and Clinical Applications for Spine Imaging. Springer, 2016, pp. 38–48.
5. G. Zeng and G. Zheng, "DSMS-FCN: A deeply supervised multiscale fully convolutional network for automatic segmentation of intervertebral disc in 3D MR images," in International Workshop and Challenge on Computational Methods and Clinical Applications in Musculoskeletal Imaging. Springer, 2017, pp. 148–159.
6. Forsberg, Daniel, Erik Sjöblom, and Jeffrey L. Sunshine. "Detection and labeling of vertebrae in MR images using deep learning with clinical annotations as training data." Journal of digital imaging 30, no. 4 (2017): 406-412.

7. Zhu, Xinjian, Xuan He, Pin Wang, Qinghua He, DandanGao, Jiwei Cheng, and Baoming Wu. "A method of localization and segmentation of intervertebral discs in spine MRI based on Gabor filter bank." *Biomedical engineering online* 15, no. 1 (2016): 1–15.

8. Alomari RS, Corso JJ, Chaudhary V. Labeling of lumbar discs using both pixel-and object level features with a two level probabilistic model. IEEE Trans Med Imaging. 2011; 30:1–10.

9. Michopoulou SK, Costaridou L, Panagiotopoulos E, Speller R, Panayiotakis G, Todd Pokropek A. Atlas-based segmentation of degenerated lumbar intervertebral discs from MR images of the spine. IEEE Trans Biomed Eng. 2009; 56:2225–31.

10. Peng ZG, Zhong J, Wee W, Lee JH. Automated vertebra detection and segmentation from the whole spine MR images. 2005 27th Annual International Conference of the IEEE Engineering in Medicine and Biology Society. 2005; 2527–2530.

11. Castro-Mateos I, Pozo JM, Lazary A, Frangi AF. 2D segmentation of intervertebral discs and its degree of degeneration from T2-weighted magnetic resonance images. Medical imaging 2014.Comput Aided Diagn. 2014; 9035:17.

12. Haq R, Aras R, Besachio DA, Borgie RC, Audette MA. 3D lumbar spine intervertebral disc segmentation and compression simulation from MRI using shape-aware models.Int J Comput Assist Radiol Surg. 2015; 10:45–54.

13. Law MWK, Tay K, Leung A, Garvin GJ, Li S. Intervertebral disc segmentation in MR images using anisotropic oriented flux. Med Image Anal. 2013; 17:43–61.

14. W. Zhang, R. Li, H. Deng, L. Wang, W. Lin, S. Ji, and D. Shen, "Deep convolutional neural Networks for multi-modality isointense infant brain image segmentation," NeuroImage, vol. 108, pp. 214–224, 2015.

15. P. Moeskops, M. A. Viergever, A. M. Mendrik, L. S. de Vries, M. J. Benders, and I.I˘sgum, "Automatic segmentation of MR brain images with a convolutional neural network," IEEE Transactions on Medical Imaging, vol. 35, no. 5, pp. 1252–1261, 2016.

16. K. Kamnitsas, C. Ledig, V. F. Newcombe, J. P. Simpson, A. D. Kane, D. K. Menon, D. Rueckert, and B. Glocker, "Efficient multi-scale 3D CNN with fully connected CRF for accurate brain lesion segmentation," Medical image analysis, vol. 36, pp. 61–78, 2017.

17. J. Dolz, C. Desrosiers, L. Wang, J. Yuan, D. Shen, and I. Ben Ayed, "Deep CNN ensembles and suggestive annotations for infant brain MRI segmentation," arXiv preprint arXiv:1712. 05319, 2017.

18. S. Valverde, M. Cabezas, E. Roura, S. Gonz´alez-Vill´a, D. Pareto, J. C. Vilanova, L. Rami´o-Torrent´a, ´A. Rovira, A. Oliver, and X. Llad´o, "Improving automated multiple sclerosis lesion segmentation with a cascaded 3D convolutional neural network approach," NeuroImage, vol. 155, pp. 159–168, 2017.

19. N. Srivastava and R. Salakhutdinov, "Multimodal learning with deep boltzmann machines," Journal of Machine Learning Research, vol. 15, pp. 2949–2980, 2014.

20. D. Nie, L. Wang, Y. Gao, and D. Sken, "Fully convolutional networks for multi-modality isointense infant brain image segmentation," in 13th International Symposium on Biomedical Imaging (ISBI), 2016. IEEE, 2016, pp. 1342–1345.

21. LabelMe: a database and web-based tool for image annotation. B. Russell, A. Torralba, K. Murphy, W. T. Freeman. International Journal of Computer Vision, 2007.

22. Benjamin De Leener, Simon L'evy, Sara M Dupont, Vladimir S Fonov, Nikola Stikov, D Louis Collins, Virginie Callot, and Julien Cohen-Adad. SCT: Spinal cord toolbox, an open-source software for processing spinal cord MRI data. Neuroimage, October 2016.

23. Benjamin De Leener, Gabriel Mangeat, Sara Dupont, Allan R Martin, Virginie Callot, Nikola Stikov, Michael G Fehlings, and Julien Cohen-Adad. Topologically preserving straightening of spinal cord MRI, 2017.

24. Charley Gros, Benjamin De Leener, AtefBadji, Josefina Maranzano, Dominique Eden, Sara M Dupont, Jason Talbott, RenZhuoquiong, Yaou Liu, Tobias Granberg, Russell Ouellette,

Yasuhiko Tachibana, Masaaki Hori, Kouhei Kamiya, Lydia Chougar, Leszek Stawiarz, Jan Hillert, Elise Bannier, Anne Kerbrat, Gilles Edan, Pierre Labauge, Virginie Callot, Jean Pelletier, Bertrand Audoin, Henitsoa Rasoanandrianina, Jean-Christophe Brisset, Paola Valsasina, Maria A Rocca, Massimo Filippi, Rohit Bakshi, Shahamat Tauhid, Ferran Prados, Marios Yiannakas, Hugh Kearney, Olga Ciccarelli, Seth Smith, Constantina Andrada Treaba, Caterina Mainero, Jennifer Lefeuvre, Daniel S Reich, Govind Nair, Vincent Auclair, Donald G McLaren, Allan R Martin, Michael G Fehlings, Shahabeddin Vahdat, Ali Khatibi, Julien Doyon, Timothy Shepherd, Erik Charlson, Sridar Narayanan, and Julien Cohen-Adad. Automatic segmentation of the spinal cord and intramedullary multiple sclerosis lesions with convolutional neural networks. Neuroimage, 184:901–915, January 2019.

25. Karel Zuiderveld. Contrast limited adaptive histogram equalization. In Graphics gems IV, pages 474–485. Academic Press Professional, Inc., August 1994.

26. Newell, A., Yang, K., Deng, J.: Stacked hourglass networks for human pose estimation. In: European conference on computer vision. pp. 483–499. Springer (2016)

27. Gros, C., Lemay, A., Vincent, O., Rouhier, L., Bourget, M.H., Bucquet, A., Cohen, J.P., Cohen-Adad, J.: ivadomed: A medical imaging deep learning toolbox. Journal of Open Source Software 6(58), 2868 (2021). https://doi.org/10.21105/joss.02868

Identification of Skin Disease Using Machine Learning

Minakshi M. Sonawane[1(✉)], Ramdas D. Gore[1], Bharti W. Gawali[1],
Ramesh R. Manza[1], and Sudhir N. Mendhekar[2]

[1] Department of Computer Science and IT, Dr. Babasaheb Ambedkar Marathwada University,
Aurangabad, Maharashtra, India
minakshi919@gmail.com
[2] Department of Dermatology, Neurology, and Leprosy, Government Medical College,
Aurangabad, Maharashtra, India

Abstract. Skin diseases are a serious health issue that affects a large number of individuals. In recent years, with the fast advancement of technology and the use of various data mining approaches, dermatological predictive classification has become increasingly predictive and accurate. It is more helpful to dermatologists to identify the disease, As a result, the development of machine learning approaches capable of efficiently the purpose of this study is to make an application of identification of skin disease images by using the machine learning method, Support Vector Machine (SVM), and KNN techniques. Early detection of skin diseases is performed using image processing and machine learning. This study aims to determine the classification of skin diseases in humans. Each skin disease has symptoms. It has five skin diseases, such as acne, psoriasis, wrath, psoriasis, and ulcers. We have collected 314 skin disease images from the government hospital in Aurangabad with the help of a mobile camera and a Sony HD camera. A Gaussian filter is used for image pre-processing. The segmentation method is used for K-Means Clustering and the feature extraction method is used for feature extraction. We have used the haar feature, color feature, FCM, OS-FCM, GLCM, and LBF features for classifications. Based on the result, the SVM is given 92% accuracy for haar feature, FCM, and OS-FCM. And the KNN classifier and K-Means are given 89% and 89% accuracy using a mobile phone camera dataset.

Keywords: Skin Disease · K-Means Clustering · SVM · KNN · Color Feature · Texture feature · Haar Feature

1 Introduction

The skin is the outer layer of the body. It is frequently exposed to the environment, where it may come into touch with dust, microorganisms, and UV radiation. These might be the causes of any disease. Skin-related disorders are made more complicated by genetic instability [1, 2]. The skin is connected to several skin diseases, affecting

R. Manza et al. (Eds.): ACVAIT 2022, AISR 176, pp. 99–113, 2023.
https://doi.org/10.2991/978-94-6463-196-8_9

Skin Structure

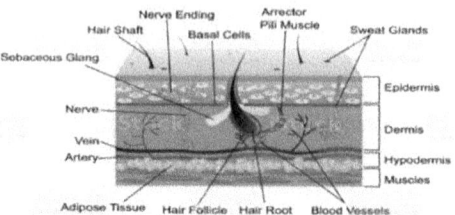

Fig. 1. Anatomy of skin in Human Body.

a person's appearance and capacity to operate. Skin infections are caused by bacteria, fungi, or viruses [3]. As represented in Fig. 1, the human skin has three layers, such as the dermis, epidermis, and hypodermis. The major causes of skin diseases are the most common causes of skin diseases, such as fungal infection, bacteria, allergies, viruses, and other factors. When conditions like infections or chronic diseases are prevalent, the texture or color of the skin generally changes. Skin infections must be identified early to avoid development and spread. It damages the patient both financially and physically [4]. Because of its complexity, dermatology is one of the most difficult fields to diagnose. The widespread use of smartphones in developing countries has opened up new opportunities for low-cost early disease diagnosis. We are obtaining image processing skills for device diagnostics using smartphone and digital camera technologies. We created an application that takes a two-stage approach to solve problems. Machine learning was used in the second step to offer a solution, while image processing was employed in the first stage to detect the issue [5]. The difficulty for the patient to diagnose is that a condition that appears to be a feature of one disease in the early stages may turn out to be a sign of another in later stages. Some disorders need medical attention, yet they all have common flaws. As a result, a dermatologist trained a machine learning model on the assessed properties obtained by a microscope analysis of a skin sample to tackle this challenge.

The key conclusion of this study: The key conclusion of this study: Create a database of images of various skin diseases. ii) A comparison with a mobile phone camera and a digital Sony HD camera.

2 Related Works

Recently, The study of enhanced technological advancement in combination with digital image processing for disease classification. The SVM-based supervised learning system, multi-model, and multilevel technique for analysis were employed by the researchers to identify eczema [6]. Based on the hue of the fingernails, the SVM was used to identify various circulatory infections [7]. Using melisma images as a diagnostic tool, infections were identified [8]. This shows that a method of determining BCC was offered (Basel Cell Carcinoma). The system is capable of accurately recognizing the. Existence of basal-cell carcinoma using adequate thresholding values with a percentage reliability of 91.33 percent in the detection. Three different skin problems keratosis, pyoderma,

Table 1. Different Types of Skin Disease.

Disease Name	Types of Disease	Images	Symptoms
Viral skin Disease	Eczema, Psoriasis, Vitiligo, Hive, Impetigo,	Babies, Plantar warts in adults,	Signs of viralinfection1.cryin, excessive
Fungal Skin disease	Rosacea, lupus, Vitiligo, Melisma	Fungal infection is caused by men and women	Skin changes, red and Possibly
Pigmented skin Disease	Vitiligo, melanocytic, naive (mole), seborrhoea keratosis, skin cancer, melanoma.	There are different categories of pigmented skin benign,	Vitiligo is a condition that causes patches of light skin.

and dermatitis are selected for segmentation using the suggested method, which uses the Sobel operator [9]. Color and texture characteristics and 4,182 color and texture attributes were the two feature sets tested. The average F-measure for the 86 features was 86.67 percent, and for the 4,182 features, it was 84 percent, which was a promising result. As a classification method, the building of an SVM has split the dataset into different classes. Using this method, three groups of skin disease images were categorized skin lesion segmentation, ABCD rules, and GLCM. With the help of KNN, Random Forest, and SVM, the data were categorized. The classifier had a high accuracy of 89.93% when the ABCD Feature Extraction was performed [10]. The literature has made substantial progress in the detection of skin diseases. However, the suggested approach is primarily intended for the identification of a single form of skin disease, making it difficult to apply to the exact identification of many types of skin diseases. We found that even though there is limited research on using one method to describe two or more diseases.

Segmentation, GLCM, color extraction, LBF technique, SVM, KNN, K-Means algorithms, and machine learning-based algorithms to determine whether the skin lesion is useful in the diagnosis of various skin diseases using two different.

Resolutions such as camera photos and Mobile phone images. Diagnosis of skin conditions from a picture is a difficult challenge. There are so many different types of skin disorders, such as acne, psoriasis, eczema, leprosy, wrath, ringworm, and vitiligo. It is presented in Table 1. Challenges: The disease has many skin lesion types. Many diseases may have similar characteristics, which is often confusing for the dermatologist.

3 Method and Techniques

3.1 Input Images

We can take images from the government medical hospital in Aurangabad. We collect photographed patient disease images while dermatologists'. To identify images from the clinical dataset, we have taken five types of skin disease datasets such as acne, psoriasis, eczema, warts, and ulcers (Fig. 2).

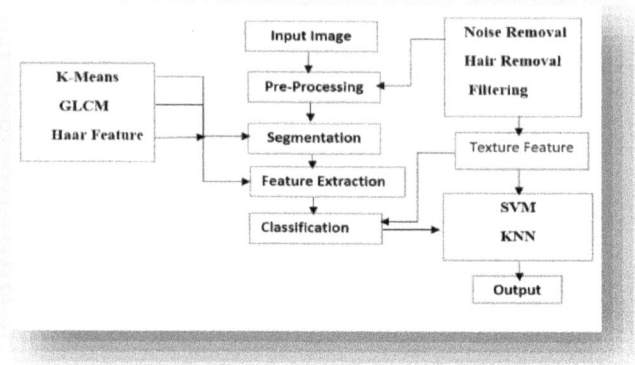

Fig. 2. Block Diagram of Proposed System.

3.2 Image Preprocessing

Improving image quality in the preprocessing step begins with removing unnecessary noise. Hair and bubbles may appear as noise inside the picture photograph. It becomes necessary to filter the picture to remove noise, and some photos contain an undesired feature that is sometimes present in dermoscopic images: hair. Because noise affects categorization accuracy. In this paper, we used filters such as Gaussian filters, adaptive filters, and Median filters for denoising, which include Gaussian noise, salt and paper noise, passion noise, and speckle noise. We go into greater detail about this in previous papers. A Gaussian filter is used to reduce noisy images (Table 2).

The tests were carried out on a variety of standard photographs of various resolutions. Python programming is used to carry out the reproduction. The information is tainted by the harmful impacts of replicated Gaussian, salt and paper noise, speckle noise, and Poisson noise. As the PSNR lowers, the MSE increases, and vice versa. When the peak signal-to-noise ratio increases, the resulting image becomes highly smooth to the eye's perception, and the image returns to its previous state. Images that are highly deformed have a high value.

3.3 Filtering Techniques

To acquire the denoised image and determine the MSE, PSNR, and Entropy values, we applied Gaussian, Median, and Wiener filters to de-noised images on the noisy image.

The MSE, PSNR, and entropy of each examined filter, namely Gaussian, Median, and Weiner filters, are shown in Table 3. Gaussian, speckle, salt, and paper noises were all removed using each filter. On the Gaussian noise, the Gaussian filter performs better than other filters, with 18.67 MSE, 12.81 PSNR, and 5.26 entropy values. On salt and pepper noise, the Wiener filter is given high values, such as 31.56 MSE and 29.10 PSNR.

Table 2. Impact of different Noise types over Image set of Diseases.

Disease Name	MSE	PSNR	Entropy	Noise
Acne	53.67	22.651	7.75	Gaussian Noise
Psoriasis	41.20	38.25	8.26	
Ulcer	31.25	36.58	6.89	
Eczema	51.26	28.96	7.63	
Acne	59.76	20.30	7.05	Salt and Paper Noise
Psoriasis	56.26	51.02	7.49	
Ulcer	32.33	36.92	6.96	
Eczema	49.23	27.70	6.36	
Acne	58.73	27.49	7.43	Poisson Noise
Psoriasis	63.21	59.69	7.52	
Ulcer	36.44	38.24	7.26	
Eczema	33.36	29.63	7.25	
Acne	56.76	20.92	5.48	Speckle Noise
Psoriasis	52.02	49.51	6.89	
Ulcer	32.69	36.41	7.37	
Eczema	33.22	28.63	7.44	

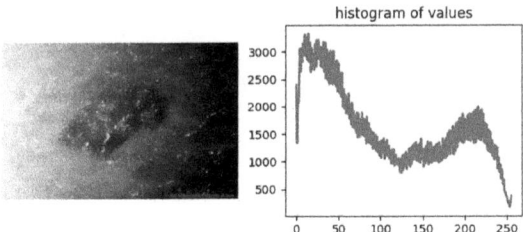

Fig. 3. Detection of Noise using Histogram.

3.4 Gaussian Filter

The image was smoothed and the noise from the artifact was removed using the Gaussian filter, for the influence detected and brought about by an irrelevant backdrop of pictures, a Gaussian filter is required. It is a common method for removing salt and paper noise from photos while preserving edges and being helpful in their creation [11]. A Gaussian filter is a smoothed pixel according to the power-to-power coefficients. The smoothing function can be expressed in an equation.

PSmooth

$$(X, Y) = (C_{NormalA} + C_{NormalB})$$

Table 3. Filter Applied on Noise and Calculated PSNR, MSE, and Entropy values.

Various Filter	MSE	PSNR	Entropy	Name of Noise
Gaussian Filter	18.67	12.81	5.26	Gaussian Noise
	30.81	27.49	5.59	Salt and pepper Noise
	27.84	26.42	6.51	Speckle Noise
Median Filter	20.06	23.64	6.37	Gaussian Noise
	30.32	27.85	6.69	Salt and pepper Noise
	23.98	16.11	7.27	Speckle Noise
Wiener Filter	18.92	15.57	7.44	Gaussian Noise
	31.56	29.10	5.60	Salt and pepper Noise
	18.90	15.58	6.87	Speckle Noise

Table 4. Comparisons of original and filter MSE, PSNR, and Entropy.

Noise	Original MSE	Filter MSE	Original PSNR	Filter PSNR	Original Entropy	Filter Entropy
Gaussian Noise	44.35	23.13	31.61	20.08	6.80	5.07
Salt & Paper Noise	49.40	28.45	33.99	24.53	6.97	5.11
Poisson Noise	47.94	27.44	38.87	25.69	7.63	5.13
Speckle Noise	43.67	26.32	33.76	23.24	7.37	5.51

$$\sum_{in=-2}^{2}\sum_{ik=-2}^{2}\left(C_{i,jA} + C_{ijB}\right)P_{row}(X + i, y + j) \qquad (1)$$

where PSmooth (x, y) and P_row (X + i, y + j) denote the raw pixels, respectively. Represents the approximation Gaussian coefficient(C normal and normal), representing the normalized coefficient. Gaussian noise is found in most skin disease images. We used a Gaussian filter for the removal of the noise and we got better accuracy in MSE and PSNR. Even if the skin disease image displays a better-enhanced image, the PSNR values do not interpret comparable findings, and it is easy to help evaluate them. Table 4 tabulates the average PSNR and MSE values for each tested filter, as well as the computed MSE, PSNR, and entropy. Each filter is applied to remove the Gaussian, salt and pepper, and speckle noises. The Gaussian and Median filters outperform salt and pepper noise when comparing the three filters for speckle noise. Furthermore, the median filter outperforms other filters in terms of PSNR and MSE, but only for salt and pepper noise density levels of less than 30%. Among the others, the Gaussian noise and

Gaussian filter provide great accuracy MSE is given high values in every skin disease, and PSNR is given less than MSE values.

3.5 Image Segmentation

An important component of image recognition is image segmentation. The purpose of picture segmentation is to divide an image into different sections to identify which areas need more attention than the surrounding areas [12]. The K-Means Clustering method is used to segment the skin disease image. Depending on how close the data is to each cluster's centroid, this approach separates the data into different cluster areas. The image segmentation process produces a picture with border detection in the foreground.

The image segmentation with K-Means Clustering results in Fig. 3 is subjected to the post-preprocessing stage. Because these findings are considered less than ideal and could include noise or small things. The method makes use of binary image processing techniques, including the Gaussian filter, noise reduction, border cleaning, the masking process, and cropping images of skin disorders. The post-preprocessing stage is performed on the image segmentation with K-Means Clustering findings in Fig. 4. Since these results are regarded as less than ideal and may contain some noise or small objects. The approach employs binary image processes such as the Gaussian filter, noise reduction, border cleaning, the masking process, and cropping photos of skin conditions.

3.5.1 Contrast

$$A_1 = -\sum_I^{L-1}\sum_I^{L-1}(G(i,j)2.Log(G(i,j)))$$ (2)

whereas G(i,j) is the distribution probability mostly employed in specified in the degree of depth computational mathematical approaches, and I refer to the grey level difference between neighboring pixels. The deeper the groove, the higher the contrast value.

3.5.2 Entropy

$$A_2 = -\sum_I^{L-1}\sum_I^{L-1}(G(i,j).Log(G(i,j)))$$ (3)

where A2 refers to the entropy, which means the quality of information that the image can change with the different textures. The texture of the speck would be sparsely distributed as A2 increased, as shown in Table 4, and vice versa.

The haar features used in Voila and Joneses exhibit a rectangle structure that consists of four subs in a rectangle. Some examples can be seen below. The integral image f is

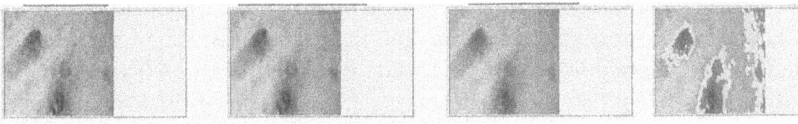

Fig. 4. Image Segmentation Process.

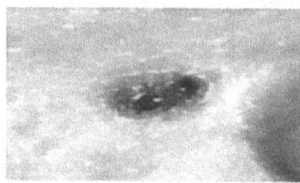 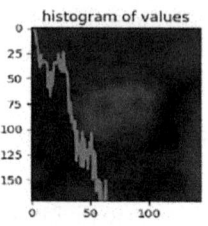

Fig. 5. Haar feature using a histogram.

denoted as Eq. 3 and Fig. 5. The integral F value at position [x, y] is calculated using the sum of the equation of I, which takes into account all pixels inside the rectangular range [0, 0] up to and including [x, y] [17]

$$f(x, y) = \sum\nolimits_{a=0}^{x} \sum\nolimits_{a=0}^{x} I(a, b) \tag{4}$$

The system was trained using 90 photographs from each group to create the training set, and the remaining 10 images from each group were utilized to create the testing set. Using BCC Images, the Haar feature was applied.

We made a conscious effort to display photographs with various dermoscopic image abnormalities when presenting the results. Figure 5 shows a dysplasia nevus with a lesion in the disease region and a boundary indicating the disease region.

3.6 Support Vector Machine (SVM)

The SVM is a machine learning technique that learns by using statistical theory [13]. When compared to other machine learning algorithms in the literature, SVM performs better than others. SVM handles limited quadratic differentiation between two classes, and it can also solve multiclass problems. The SVM method optimizes the distance between data points and hyperplanes. The Support Vector Machine, Fig. 5, is shown below.

Of all the kernels that are accessible, a linear kernel is also among the simplest. Other kernels, such as polynomial kernels, should be used to categorize two classes that share more characteristics to attain more accuracy and precision [14]. The boundary values of the SVM are specified by a gamma kernel [15]. This entails determining the inner products of a fresh input vector (x) with all training data's support vectors [16].The SVM receives all the values that were entered into the database as described as input (Fig. 6).

3.7 K-nearest Neighbor (KNN)

The K-Nearest Neighbor algorithm, which is based on the Supervised Learning technique, is one of the most basic machine learning algorithms. When a new data point is added, the K-NN algorithm classifies it based on how similar the existing data is to it and stores it all. This means that as fresh data is generated, it can be quickly categorized using the K-NN method [17].

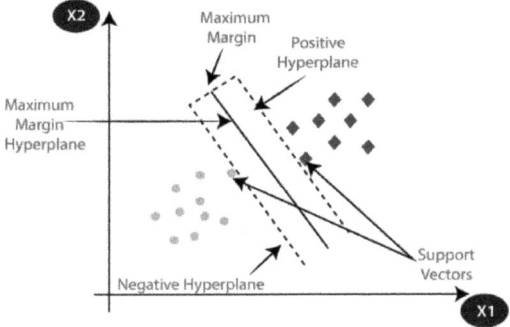

Fig. 6. Support Vector Machine using Linear Regression.

3.8 Feature Extraction

Four groups of human skin illnesses can be distinguished by several distinctive characteristics, including color and texture. For classification, these parameters were used.

3.9 Color Moments

Images of skin conditions can also be categorized according to how each class's colors vary. The color moments are the suggested technique for extracting color features. When describing the color of a picture, color serves as a reliable representation of color characteristics [18]. The color distribution of a picture is thought of as a probability distribution in color moments. Two moments from the color probability distribution of the image, including its mean and standard deviation, will be used in this investigation. The following equation can be used to compute the mean standard deviation.

$$E = \frac{1}{N}\sum\nolimits_{J=1}^{N} P_{ij} \tag{5}$$

$$\partial_1 = \sqrt{(\frac{1}{N}\sum\nolimits_{J=1}^{N}\left(P_{ij} - E_i\right)^2)} \tag{6}$$

In this research [15], the color method that was tested had the best accuracy in recognizing features of skin disease. The color space of YCbCr is a color space component (Y, Cb, and Cr) is a color that is applied in the photography system while Cb and C represent red and blue (Fig. 7).

We have used color feature, SVM, Hopkins, and Elbow techniques for the classification of skin diseases such as Eczema, Acne, Wrath, Psoriasis, and Ulcer. It has given different levels of accuracy in different skin diseases. As shown in Table 6, SVM is given good accuracy in the Acne (94%), wart (83%), eczema (92%), and ulcer (95%) disease, and the color feature is given 100% accuracy in Psoriasis disease. The mobile dataset is given the best accuracy in SVM techniques. Hopkins and elbow techniques give less results for skin disease.

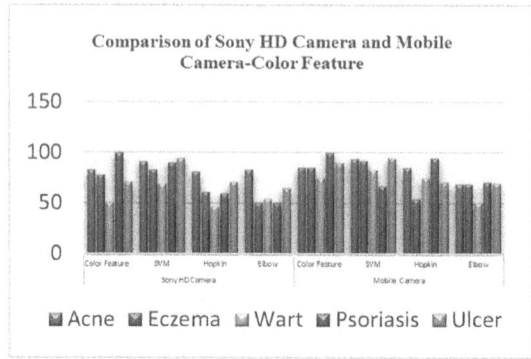

Fig. 7. Comparison of Sony HD Camera and Mobile Camera dataset.

3.10   Texture Feature Extraction

GLCM is an effective tool for analyzing texture features such as entropy and contrast. In this paper, nine different types of disease are chosen as the main research objects, which are acne, psoriasis, leprosy, eczema, wrath, melisma, ringworm, vitiligo, and ulcer, skin cold, respectively, are extracted from photos of a government hospital (Fig. 8).

We have used texture features and techniques for skin diseases such as eczema, acne, wrath, psoriasis, and ulcers. As shown in Table 5, it has given varying degrees of accuracy in various skin diseases. The SVM is given the best accuracy for eczema at 100%, warts at 100%, ulcers at 95%, acne at 93%, and psoriasis at 89% in the mobile dataset.

```
Confusion matrix SVM:
[[ 1  0  0  0  0  0  0  0  0  0  0  0  0  0  0  0  0  0  0  0]
 [ 0  0  0  0  0  0  0  0  0  0  1  0  0  0  0  0  0  0  0  0]
 [ 0  0  6  0  0  0  0  0  0  0  1  0  0  0  0  0  0  0  0  0]
 [ 0  0  0  2  0  0  0  0  0  0  0  0  0  0  0  0  1  0  0  0]
 [ 0  0  0  0  2  0  0  0  0  0  1  0  0  1  0  0  0  0  0  0]
 [ 0  0  0  0  0  2  0  0  0  0  0  0  0  0  0  1  0  0  0  0]
 [ 0  0  0  0  0  0  4  1  0  0  0  0  0  0  0  0  0  1  0  0]
 [ 0  0  0  0  0  0  1  9  0  0  0  0  0  0  0  0  0  0  0  0]
 [ 0  0  0  0  0  0  0  4  1  0  0  0  0  0  0  0  0  0  0  0]
 [ 0  0  1  0  2  0  0  0  1 21  0  0  0  0  0  3  0  0  0  0]
 [ 0  0  0  1  0  0  0  0  0  0  7  0  0  0  0  0  0  0  0  0]
 [ 0  0  0  0  0  0  0  0  0  0  0 12  0  0  0  0  0  0  0  0]
 [ 0  0  0  0  0  0  0  0  0  0  0  0  4  0  0  0  0  1  0  0]
 [ 0  0  0  0  0  0  0  0  0  0  0  0  0  1  0  0  0  0  0  0]
 [ 0  0  0  0  0  0  0  0  0  0  0  0  0  0  3  0  0  0  0  0]
 [ 0  1  0  0  0  0  0  0  0  3  0  0  0  0  0 14  0  0  0  0]
 [ 0  0  0  0  0  0  0  0  0  0  1  0  0  0  0  0  8  0  0  0]
 [ 0  0  0  0  0  1  1  0  0  0  0  0  0  0  0  0  0  3  0  0]
 [ 0  0  0  0  0  0  0  0  0  0  0  0  0  0  0  0  0  0  1]]
```

Fig. 8. Confusion matrix of SVM.

Table 5. Summary of Precision, Recall and F1-score for skin disease classification.

Disease No.	Precision %	Recall %	F1 score%
Acne	1.00	1.00	1.00
Acne Nod	0.67	0.67	0.67
Psoriasis	0.8	0.8	0.8
Eczema	1.00	1.00	1.00
Wrath	0.89	0.89	0.89
Ulcer	0.6	0.6	0.6

4   Performance Measures

For calculating classification performance metrics for skin diseases including accuracy, sensitivity, specificity, positive predictive value, and negative predictive value, confusion matrices are utilized. Information concerning current and anticipated categories can be found in a confusion matrix.

To prevent bias brought on by the uneven distribution of disease, we have additionally computed precision, recall, and F1 scores for each disease.

$$Precision = \frac{TruePositive}{TruePositive + FalsePositive} \tag{7}$$

$$Recall = \frac{TruePositive}{TruePositive - FalsePositive} \tag{8}$$

$$F - measure = 2.\frac{precision.recall}{precision + recall} \tag{9}$$

We have observed the result and we got 1 precision accuracy for Acne and, Eczema disease and less accuracy for Ulcer Ulcers (Fig. 9).

5   Result and Discussion

The classification outcome is significantly influenced by the train-to-test ratio. It has been found that the results get better as the size of the training set rises. According to research on the impact of train/test classification accuracy, an 80/20 train/test ratio produces the best classification outcomes. We found that excessive training might reduce accuracy as well. We not only performed classification but also took a step forward and tried to classify all 314 unique sub-classes as well. We found 100% accuracy for the Color Feature and Haar features in the training data and 99.4 and 97.23% accuracy in the test dataset. We have got less accuracy for texture features in the training and testing datasets, at 86.23 percent and 75%, respectively.

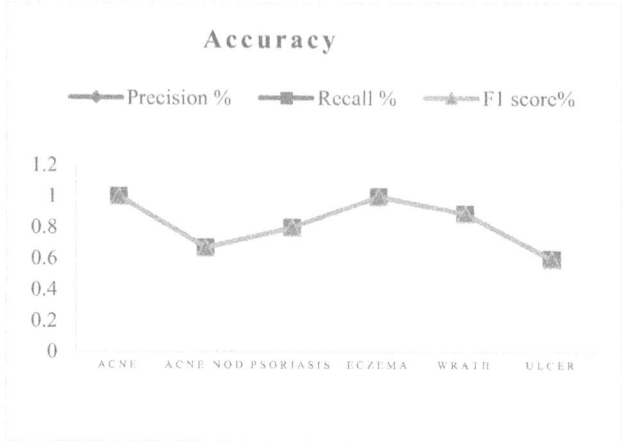

Fig. 9. Performance of classification

The color moment approach was used to extract color features from a variety of color spaces. The color spaces of the picture to be examined are RGB, HSV, and YCbCr. The three-color spaces are tested for correctness.

The RGB, HSV, and YCbCr color feature types exhibit the accuracy gained after the feature extraction experiment using the texture Moments technique in the color space. Color space eliminates the effects of light on the characteristics of skin color, allowing for the extraction of a wealth of feature information. Based on test results, some haar varieties are more accurate than others. The system produces high accuracy when applying multiple skin disease classes with the help of a mobile camera and Sony HD.

Camera resources the results show that the proposed system correctly identified patients' diseases. Acne, eczema, psoriasis, wrath, and ulcerative skin disease are all

Table 6. Feature Type of Skin Disease.

Disease Name	HD Sony Camera				Mobile Phone Camera			
	Texture Feature	SVM	Hopkins	Elbow	Texture Feature	SVM	Hopkins	Elbow
Acne	79	91	82	78	62	93	86	6
Eczema	56	89	67	72	63	100	62	62
Wart	31	85	46	46	25	100	25	75
Psoriasis	50	87	70	40	66	89	88	67
Ulcer	57	90	48	52	76	95	67	76

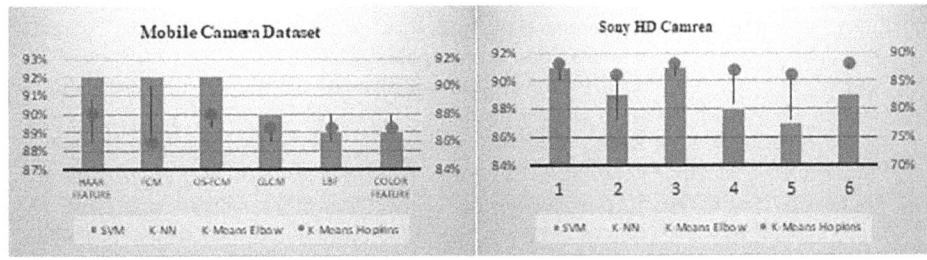

Fig. 10. Classifications Result of Mobile Camera and Sony HD Camera.

correctly identified by the system. We used different types of classifiers like SVM, KNN, and K-Means and used the Haar feature, color feature, FCM, OS-FCM, GLCM, and LBF features for classifications. The classification algorithm was developed to predict the diagnosis system. The Haar feature, FCM, and OS-FCM are given good results in SVM techniques for mobile camera datasets. The GLCM feature is given 90% accuracy in SVM. LBF and color features are given 89% accuracy in the SVM technique. The Sony HD camera dataset performed well in SVM for the Haar color feature, FCM, OS-FCM, GLCM, and LBF features, as shown in Fig. 10. A 92 percent accuracy rating is given to the suggested model. A substance score is also maintained by the SVM classifier.

6   Conclusion

The Research article focused on five skin conditions: eczema, psoriasis, acne, and ulcer. Gaussian noise and Gaussian filter preprocessing techniques are implemented for noise removal and image enhancement. SVM, KNN, and K-Means are used as classification for the features FCM, OS-FCM, GLCM, and LBF features for classification experimental analysis showing that better accuracy is obtained through SVM.

References

1. R. J. Hay, N. E. Johns, H. C. Williams, I. W. Bolliger, R. P. Dellavalle, and D. J. Margolis, "The global burden of Skin disease in 2010: An Analysis of the prevalence and impact of skin conditions", 55 J, Investigative Dermatology, vol. 134, no. 6, PP NO.1527_1534, 2014.
2. Palak Mehta, Bhumika Shah, "Review on Techniques and Steps of Computer Aided Skin Cancer Diagnosis" International Conference on Computational Modeling and Security (CMS2016). https://doi.org/10.1016/j.procs.2016.05.28.
3. Housman TS, Feldman SR, Willi ford PM, Fleischer AB Jr., Goldman ND, et al., " Skin cancer is among the most Costly of all Cancers to treat for the Medicare population", J Am Acad Dermatol 48: pp. 425_429, 2003.
4. Arifin, S., Kibria, G., Firoze, A., Amini, A., & Yan, H. (2012) "Dermatological Disease Diagnosis Using Color-Skin Images." Xian:International Conference on Machine Learning and Cybernetics.

5. Santy, A., & Joseph, R."Segmentation Methods for Computer-Aided Melanoma Detection." Global Conference on Communication Technologies.2015

6. Suganya R., "An Automated Computer-Aided Diagnosis of Skin Lesions Detection and Classification for Dermoscopy Images.2016

7. Kumar, V., Kumar, S., & Saboo, V. (2016) "Dermatological Disease Detection Using Image Processing and Machine Learning." IEEE.

8. Krizhevsky, A., ILYA, S., & Geoffrey, E. (2012) "ImageNet Classification with Deep Convolutional Neural Networks." Advances in Neural Information Processing Systems.

9. Waugh, S.; Purdie, C.; L.B.; Vinnicombe, "magnetic resonance imaging texture analysis classification o primary breast cancer", Eur.Radial, PP No-322–330, 2015.

10. Vamvakas, A,' Tsougo,I,;Arikidis, N.;Kapsalaki,Fezoulidis, "Exploiting morphology and texture 0f 3D tumor models in DTI for differentiating flioblastoma from solitary metastasis, biomed, signal process, control ", PP No-159–173,2018.

11. Deeplearning 0.1 documentation(2018) convolution neural network(leNet).Retrieved sep 16,2017, from http://deeplearning.net/tutorial/lenet.html.

12. Szegedy c, vanhoucke v, loffe s,shlens j, wojna z.rethinking the inception architecture for computer vision.in proceeding of the IEEE conference on computer vision and pattern recognition(pp.2818–2816);2016.

13. M. Srinivas D.Roy and C.K.Mohan, "Discriminative feature extraction from X-ray images using deep convolution neural network ", in proc IEEE International Conference on Acoustic, speech and signal processing,2016,pp-917–921.

14. Sumitra, R.; Sushil,M.Guru, "D.S.Segmentation and Classification of skin lesions for disease Diagnosis", ELSEVIER, Vol-45, PP No-76–85, 2015.

15. Alam, M.; Munia, T.T.K, "Automatic detection and severity measurement o eczema using image Processing", In proceeding of the 2016 38th Annual International Conference of the IEEE Engineering in Medicine and Biology Society (EMBC), Orlando, FLUSA, 16–20;PP NO-1365–1368.

16. Mehdy, M.Ng, P.; Shair,E,;Saleh,N.;Gomes.C., "Artificial Neural in Image Processing for Early Detection of Brest Cancer", Computer and mathematical Methods in Medicine, ArticalID-2610628, PP No-1–6,2017.

17. Harang,B, "Skin Lesion classification with ensembles of deep Convolution Neural Networks", ELSEVIER, Vol-86, PP No-25–32, 2018.

18. Ashu, G.P.H; Anita, J.; P.J, "Identification of Melanoma in Dermoscopy Images Using Image Processing algorithm", International Conference 'on Control, Power, Communication and Computing Technology (ICCPCCT), India, PP No-553–557, 2018.

Apple Classification Based on MRI Images Using VGG16 Convolutional Deep Learning Model

D. Vidya[1]([✉]), Shivanand Rumma[2], and Mallikarjun Hangargi[3]

[1] Department of Computer Science, Govt Women's First Grade College, Kalaburagi, Karnataka, India
vidyasarvottam80@gmail.com
[2] Department of Computer Science, Gulbarga University, Kalaburagi, Karnataka, India
[3] Department of Computer Science, Karnataka Arts, Science, and Commerce College, Bidar, Karnataka, India

Abstract. Apples are considered one of the healthiest fruits worldwide. With the increase in demand for apple, internal quality checking is a most challenging task. In Digital Image Processing different computer vision technologies are used to identify external defects like color, shape, and texture. MRI of apple fruit is the most effective non-destructive and non-invasive method to identify internal defects. In our present study, we have used our own dataset of 196 MRI images of apples. Further, these images are divided into 80:20 for training and testing. These images are classified by using the pre-trained deep learning model VGG16 and with this model, we got 66.21% of validation accuracy and 62.5% of testing accuracy.

Keywords: Apple · VGG16 · Magnetic Resonance Imaging (MRI) · Deep learning

1 Introduction

Apples are the most demanding fruits as health awareness increases around the world. Maintaining the quality parameters in apple is the most challenging task. The external defects like color, size, and texture can be identified using different computer vision technologies [1]. The most challenging task is to detect the internal defect of the apple without harming the fruit. There are different non-destructive technologies are available to detect internal defects in agricultural products like X-ray, sonography, MRI, etc. Whereas Magnetic Resonance Imaging methodology (MRI) is the most accurate and non-invasive and non-destructive technology used to identify internal defects in agricultural products. The analysis of these resulted images and data is carried out manually for a small number of samples. To overcome this issue there are many different robotic methodologies has been applied like Digital image processing for a large number of sample analysis.

In Digital image processing many machines vision-based technologies have been developed to detect defects in agricultural products. Most of the research has been do developed in deep learning technology to identify defects and classify agricultural products most accurately.

Deep learning networking models made drastic growth in digital image processing for classification problems. Mainly Convolutional Neural Networks (CNNs) [2] are broadly used because of their capability to successfully share parameters among different layers inside the deep network model. Various CNN network models have been proposed. Whereas, VGG16 is the simplest network model used for fewer datasets for classification problems.

In our present work, we proposed a VGG16 model for the classification of good and defective apples using MRI images of apples by which we secured 66.2% of validation accuracy and 62.5% of testing accuracy.

2 Literature Survey

Many research has been carried to detect internal defects in agricultural products.

Boan Zion et al., (1995) [3] proposed a technique to identify bruises in apples using the magnetic resonance images (MRI) technique, the author used different sequences of pulse methods to investigate temporal changes in MRI images between bruised & unaffected areas of flesh. They also reported that there is a creased trend between the time contrast of bruised and non-bruised regions in flesh.

Ebrahimnejad Hamed et al. (2018) [4] reviewed the use of magnetic resonance imaging (MRI) in the quality control of food products. The author observed that MRI allows the structure of agricultural products to be imaged non-invasively & non-destructively. This review provides an overview of the most prominent applications of MRI in agriculture. Many advance technologies are available in digital image processing to detect defects in agricultural products. Cheng-Jin Du and Da-Wen Sun (2004) [5] reviewed new advances in digital image processing technology for food product quality evaluation. Anita Raghavendra et, al., (2021) [6] developed a non-destructive technology Near-Infrared spectroscopy (NIR). The author used the wavelength selection method to classify defective and good-quality mango fruits. Mango datasets are collected by using the NIR methodology with a range of wavelength 673 nm–1900 nm. The author used Euclidean distance measure to classify fruits. Different selective technologies are included in the study among which the experiment proved that Fisher criterion-based methods were found to be the good technology for better wavelength selection. With this method, they got 84% of accuracy.

Convolutional Neural Network (CNN) is considered the best network model to use in deep learning methodology to classify images. There are different CNN models used for better classification of images among which VGG models are considered the best models to classify fewer datasets.

Srikanth Tammina [7] developed a VGG16 deep convolutional model for the classification of images of Dogs and Cats. A small set of training samples are used to study the model. With fine-tuned VGG16 CNN model they got a training accuracy of 82% and validation accuracy of 95.40%.

Zabit Hameed et al.,[8] made a study on the classification of non-carcinoma and carcinoma breast cancer histopathology images. The author developed VGG16 and VGG19

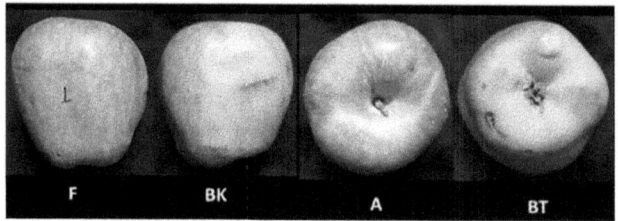

Fig. 1. Apple photography in different directions. (F: Front, BK: Back, A: Arial, BT: Bottom)

deep neural network models. Four trained models are used based on VGG16 and VGG19 pre-trained architectures. Initially, an operation called 5-fold cross-validation is used, namely, fully-trained and fine-tuned VGG16 models. They use an ensemble strategy with an average value of predicted values of probabilities. The author proved that fine-tuned VGG16 and VGG19 ensemble strategies performed good classification. By using VGG16 and VGG19 models, an overall accuracy of 95.29% was obtained.

Edmer Rezende et al.,[9] used the VGG16 deep network model for the classification of thousands of images occurring in malicious software. ImageNet dataset is used for pre-trained VGG16 neural network feature extraction. For experimental purposes, the author used a dataset of 10,136 image samples comprising 20 different families. The author showed that the model can be effectively used to classify malware families got an accuracy of 92.97%.

Shazzadul Islam et al.,[10] used the VGG16 model for feature extraction in Bird species. For experimental purposes collected 1600 images of 27 species of birds from Bangladesh. VGG16 model is used for feature extraction in bird species and then different classifiers like SVM, KNN, and Random Forest algorithms are used to classify bird species.

3   Materials and Methods

3.1 Dataset

21 Apples were collected from the local supermarket. All apples are numerically numbered. Depending on morphological appearance color photographic images are taken from different angles front, back, arial, and bottom (Fig. 1). Then apples were subjected to MR scanning. MR images were obtained using 1.5 T Sieman's Magnetom Spectro MR machine with T2- weighted MR images with a repetition time (TR) of 8980 and Spin echo time of 100.2 with slice diameter of 116.7mm and interslice gap of 8.0mm, which leads to a total of 196 MR images. MRI images were analyzed using RadiAnt DICOM Viewer (64-bit) software. After MR scanning apples were cut into two halves vertically and color photographic images were taken and a manual comparison study was carried out between colored and MRI images (Figs. 2 & 3).

3.2 VGG Model

VGG architecture was proposed by "Simonyan and Zisserman in a Visual Geometry Group of Oxford University" [11]. VGG16 model is having 16 layers containing tuneable

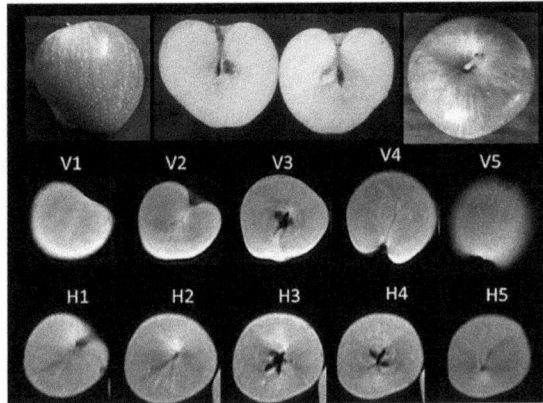

Fig. 2. Photographic images and MR images of good apples

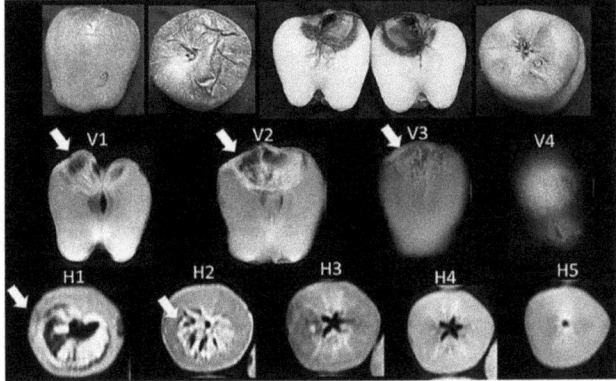

Fig. 3. Photographic images and MR images of defective apples.

parameters. The network model of the VGG16 model is shown in Fig. 4. It contains 13 Convolutional layers used to extract only relevant features from the image. This layer uses a mathematical formula to extract high-level features like color, edges, gradient orientation, etc. Each convolution is followed by one Maxpooling layer used to reduce the dimensionality of the image. The model contains three fully connected layers at the end. The size of the image is fixed to 224 × 224 which passes through the stack of the convolutional layer. Every convolutional filter has a small receptive field 3x3, stride 1. Max pooling layers use 2 × 2 kernels with a stride of 2 followed by the Softmax layer and the output layer (Sixteenth layer) containing 1000 units. The hidden layer in the Convolution layer has Relu as an activation function.

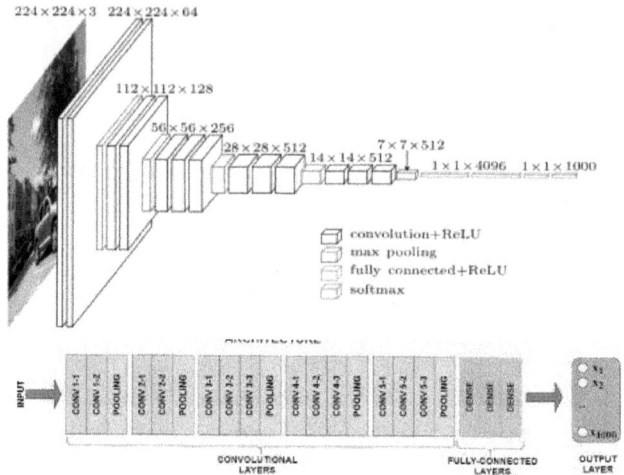

Fig. 4. VGG16 Convolutional network architecture. Source: https://towardsdatascience.com/
step-by-step-vgg16-implementation-in-keras-for-beginners-a833c686ae6c"

4   Results and Discussion

For experimental purposes total of 196 MR images are divided into 80% for training and
20% for testing. VGG16 model was built using the python toolbox in the google colab
platform. The model is tuned with better hyperparameters like the number of epochs,
learning rate, and dropout rate to get better results (Table 1). The model summary is shown
in Fig. 5. The first two input layers contain 2 convolutional layers and 1 Maxpooling
layer followed by the next 3 convolutional layers and 1 Maxpooling layer and so on.
The overall model consists of 13 convolutional layers and 5 Maxpooling layers and 3
activation layers.

Total of 13 Convolutional layer + 3 Activation layer = 16 layers

The resulting history of the model is shown in Fig. 6. After building the model,
Modelcheckpoint methods are called from Keras. The Modelcheckpoint method helps
to monitor the model with specific parameters. In our model validation accuracy is
monitored using the Modelcheck point method and a prediction of apples are made after

Table 1. Hyperparameters for VGG16 model

Hyperparameters	Value
Epochs	72
Batch size	10
Activation function	ReLu
Learning Rate	0.5

building the model (Fig. 7). With this VGG16 deep network, we got 66.2% of validation accuracy and 62.5% of testing accuracy.

```
Layer (type)                    Output Shape              Param #
=================================================================
input_1 (InputLayer)            [(None, 224, 224, 3)]     0

block1_conv1 (Conv2D)           (None, 224, 224, 64)      1792

block1_conv2 (Conv2D)           (None, 224, 224, 64)      36928

block1_pool (MaxPooling2D)      (None, 112, 112, 64)      0

block2_conv1 (Conv2D)           (None, 112, 112, 128)     73856

block2_conv2 (Conv2D)           (None, 112, 112, 128)     147584

block2_pool (MaxPooling2D)      (None, 56, 56, 128)       0

block3_conv1 (Conv2D)           (None, 56, 56, 256)       295168

block3_conv2 (Conv2D)           (None, 56, 56, 256)       590080

block3_conv3 (Conv2D)           (None, 56, 56, 256)       590080

block3_pool (MaxPooling2D)      (None, 28, 28, 256)       0

block4_conv1 (Conv2D)           (None, 28, 28, 512)       1180160

block4_conv2 (Conv2D)           (None, 28, 28, 512)       2359808

block4_conv3 (Conv2D)           (None, 28, 28, 512)       2359808

block4_pool (MaxPooling2D)      (None, 14, 14, 512)       0

block5_conv1 (Conv2D)           (None, 14, 14, 512)       2359808

block5_conv2 (Conv2D)           (None, 14, 14, 512)       2359808

block5_conv3 (Conv2D)           (None, 14, 14, 512)       2359808

block5_pool (MaxPooling2D)      (None, 7, 7, 512)         0

dropout_3 (Dropout)             (None, 7, 7, 512)         0

flatten (Flatten)               (None, 25088)             0

dropout_4 (Dropout)             (None, 25088)             0

dense_2 (Dense)                 (None, 1)                 25089
=================================================================
Total params: 14,739,777
Trainable params: 25,089
Non-trainable params: 14,714,688
```

Fig. 5. Model summary

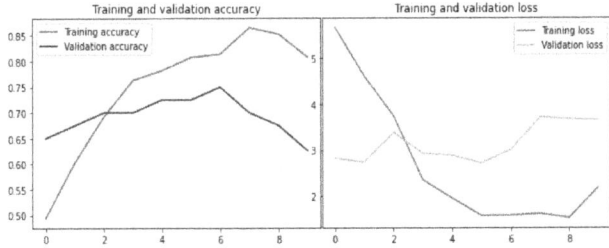

Fig. 6. Model history

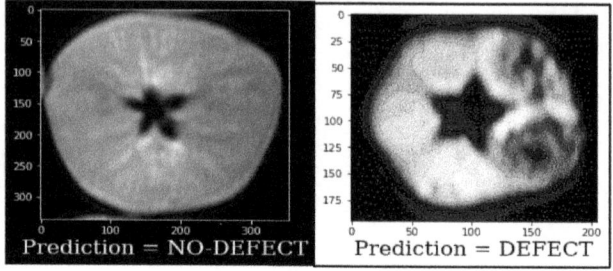

Fig. 7. Model Prediction of apples

5   Conclusion and Future Work

In this study, an experiment was carried out to find the internal defects in apples. A deep learning model VGG16 is used for the classification of defective and good-quality apples. By using the VGG16 network, we achieved 66.2% of validation accuracy and 62.5% of test accuracy. The proposed model is limited to only one fruit and the datasets gathered are fewer. Further, our aim is to improve the number of datasets and use different varieties of fruits and then apply different deep learning algorithms to get more percentage of accuracy.

Acknowledgments. We would like to thank Dr. Kiran Desai, Girish Scanning Center, Kalaburagi, Karnataka, India, for making MRI equipment available for this study.

We also would like to thank Dr. Babasaheb Ambedkar Marathwada University, Aurangabad (MS) India for providing the publication support.

Authors' Contributions.   **Vidya D-** Conceptualization, Methodologies, Software writing, Draft preparation.

Dr. Mallikarjun Hangargi- Supervision, Validation, Draft-review, Editing.

Shivanand Rumma-Supervision.

References

1. Komal Sindhi, Jaymit Pandya, and Sudhir Vegad "Quality evaluation of apple fruit: A Survey" *International Journal of Computer Applications* (0975 – 8887) Volume 136 – No.1, February 2016.
2. Lecun, Y.; Bottou, L.; Bengio, Y.; Haffner, P. Gradient-based learning applied to document recognition. Proc. IEEE 1998, 86, 2278–2324. [CrossRef].
3. Boan Zion, Pictiaw Chen, Michael J, McCarthy, Detection of bruises in magnetic resonance images of apples, *Computers and Electronics in Agriculture* 13 (1995) 289-299.
4. Hamed Ebrahimnejad, Hadi Ebrahimnejad,2 A. Salajegheh,3 and H. Barghi. Use of Magnetic Resonance Imaging in Food Quality Control: A Review. *J Biomed Phys Eng.* 2018 Mar; 8(1): 127–132.

5. Cheng-Jin Du and Da-Wen Sun. Recent developments in the applications of image processing techniques for food quality evaluation. *Trends in Food Science & Technology* 15 (2004) 230–249.
6. Anitha Raghavendra, D.S. Guru, Mahesh K. Rao "Mango internal defect detection based on optimal wavelength selection method using NIR spectroscopy", Artificial Intelligence in Agriculture 5(2021) 43–5.
7. Srikanth Tammina," Transfer learning using VGG-16 with Deep Convolutional Neural Network for Classifying Images", International Journal of Scientific and Research Publications, Volume 9, Issue 10, October 2019 143 ISSN 2250–3153.
8. Zabit Hameed , Sofia Zahia , Begonya Garcia-Zapirain , Jose Javier Aguirre and Ana Maria Vanegas, "Breast Cancer Histopathology Image Classification Using an Ensemble of Deep Learning Models", Sensors 2020, 20, 4373; doi:https://doi.org/10.3390/s20164373
9. Edmar Rezende, Guilherme Ruppert, Tiago Carvalho , Antonio Theophilo , Fabio Ramos and Paulo de Geus, " Malicious Software Classification using VGG16 Deep Neural Network's Bottleneck Features".
10. Shazzadul Islam, Sabit Ibn Ali Khan, Md. Minhazul Abedin, Khan Mohammad Habibullah, Amit Kumar Das, "Bird Species Classification from an Image Using VGG-16 Network", ICCCM 2019, July 27–29, 2019, Bangkok, Thailand © 2019 Association for Computing Machinery. ACM ISBN 978–1–4503–7195–7/19/07
11. K. Simonyan and A. Zisserman, "Very deep convolutional networks for large-scale image recognition,"arXiv preprint arXiv:1409.1556, 2014.

Design a Novel Detection Using KNN Classification Technique for Early Sign of Diabetic Maculopathy

Chetan Pattebahadur[1]([✉]), Ramesh Manza[1], Anupriya Kamble[1], Manoj Mhaske[1], Deepali Lohare[1], and Kavita Khobragade[2]

[1] Department of Computer Science and IT, Dr. Babasaheb Ambedkar Marathwada University, Aurangabad, Maharashtra, India
chetu358@gmail.com
[2] Department of Computer Science, Fergusson College, Pune, Maharashtra, India

Abstract. Scientists call diabetic maculopathy a pathological disorder. It's one of the most serious consequences of diabetes [1]. When diabetic patient having so much sugar level in the body that time its impact on some part of body one part is retina. The retina has macula when near macula having some red dots it's called as microanurysms. Microanurysms is the first sign of diabetic maculopathy it is the initial stage of diabetic maculopathy [2]. In this research paper using image processing technique we can detect the microanurysms and its count using STARE database. For classification used KNN algorithm and got 95.7%good result.

Keywords: Image Processing · Maculopathy · KNN · Microanurysms

1 Introduction

The first ever sign that indicates the development of Diabetic Maculopathy is Microaneurysms. When sugar level increases in the body, the body gives up some signs; one of these sign is the Microaneurysms which signs a red, tiny and circular darkest dot near the Macula of the eye [3]. This red dot with its increase in size may damage the Macula if not detected at an initial stage. So detecting this Micro aneurysm at its initial stage is very important. If at its initial stage Micro aneurysm is not detected then a person has a possibility to lose his or her vision 15 completely as Macula is the central vision of the Retina. That's why diabetic maculopathy detection is very important.

2 Methodology

To detect Maculopathy through the Classification techniques a strong database is required. Collection of this database is not possible at initial stage of research study. If collection of database is considered it may become a different research study as there are many stages in the development of the Macula. So the present study is focused by

R. Manza et al. (Eds.): ACVAIT 2022, AISR 176, pp. 122–129, 2023.
https://doi.org/10.2991/978-94-6463-196-8_11

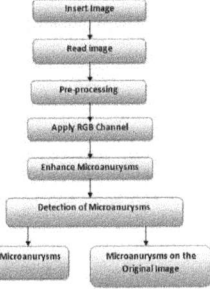

Fig. 1. Flowchart of Detection of Microaneurysms.

getting the Standardized available database. These Standard database that have been considered for the present study are of STARE. STARE is the (STructured Analysis of the Retina) it is the 400 retinal image dataset but for present research study we can use only 100 images [4] (Fig. 1).

2.1 Preprocessing

Images that are present in the Standard Database of STARE are captured through the Fundus Camera. The Images captured through this Fundus Camera always does not give 100% result. So the preprocessing helps to get clear images. With the help of these clear images the detection of the object i.e. the detection of the features is possible. Digital Image Processing helps to detect these features with the Pre-processing technique [5].

2.2 RGB Channel

When the Fundus Camera gives an output Image is captured it consists of 256 colors. These fundus image captured are in pixels. This ranges from 0 to 255. The following is the sample of the retina [6] (Fig. 2).

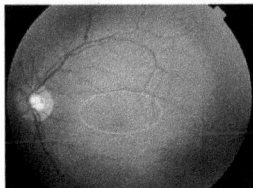

Fig. 2. Microaneurysm on the retina

From these colures only Red, Green and Blue are the three channels which give clarity in the images. The following are the result of the RGB Channel image.

Red Channel
See Fig. 3.

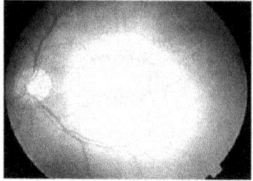

Fig. 3. Red Channel

Green Channel
See Fig. 4.

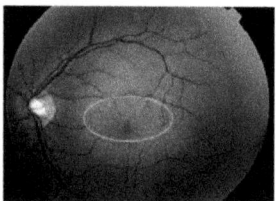

Fig. 4. Green Channel

Blue Channel
See Fig. 5.

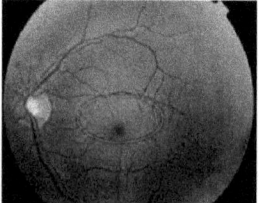

Fig. 5. Blue Channel

2.3 Histogram

Histogram gives the graphical representation of the data points in the data set. For the above three channels the histogram that has been obtained is (Figs. 6, 7, and 8).

With reference to 2.2 and 2.3 above i.e. RGB Channel and Histogram it is very clear that the Red Channel displays only boundary of the Retina while blue channel gives only the noise present in the Retina image but when we take the green channel it perfectly displays whole information that also in detail. So for the further study the Green Channel.

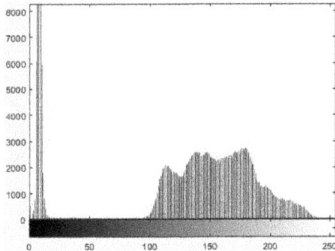

Fig. 6. Histogram of Red channel

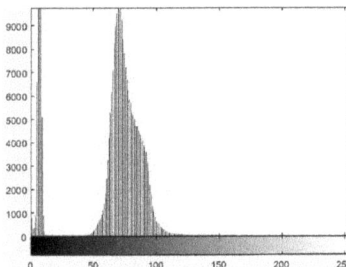

Fig. 7. Histogram of Green channel

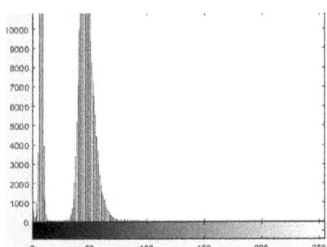

Fig. 8. Histogram of Blue channel

2.4 Enhancement

2.4.1 Intensity Transformation Function

For the enhancement of Microaneurysms, we used the Intensity Transformation Function If the need for an image at a certain period is brighter or darker, it modifies the frequency principles, the frequency metamorphosis purpose, that also improves the contrast with certain values [7]. Pixel pre and post- processing values are denoted as f(x, y) & g(x, y).

$$g(x, y) = T\big[f(x, y)\big] \qquad (1)$$

T converts the pixel value from f (x, y) to Pixel (x, y). The input image is f (x, y) and g (x, y) is the output or processed image [8].

2.4.2 Histogram Equalization

Histogram equalization produces an output image with the same pixel intensity distribution. This means that the histogram of the output image will be compressed and systematically increased [9]. Where ps (s) and pd (d) are image probability density functions. Histogram equalization of an image follows the following equation [9].

$$u = T(s)$$

$$= \int_0^s ps(x)dx \tag{2}$$

The histogram equalization image is acquired by a same transformation function as follows:

$$v = Q(d) = \int_0^d pd(x)dx \tag{3}$$

The values of d for the image is acquired as follows:

$$d = Q^{-1}[u] = Q^{-1}[T(s)] \tag{4}$$

2.4.3 Using Segmentation Detection of Boundaries

The segment label $C(\vec{X}) = K$ for a pixel $(\vec{X})$ is the k which maximizes the ownership of $\vec{F}(\vec{X})$ in the MoG model M. That is,

$$c(\vec{x}) = \arg\max_k \left[\frac{\pi_k g(\vec{F}(\vec{x})|\vec{m}_k, \Sigma_k)}{p(\vec{F}(\vec{x})|M)} \right] \tag{5}$$

2.5 KNN Classification

K-Nearest Neighbor is that the supported Supervised learning technique. This algorithm stores all the available data and classifies a replacement datum supported the similarity. This implies when new data appears then it are often easily classified into a decent suite category by using K-NN algorithm. K-NN algorithms are often used for Regression also as for Classification but mostly it's used for Classification problems. It's a non-parametric algorithm, which suggests it doesn't make any assumptions on underlying data [10].

3   Experiment Result

In this study, we used a publicly available standard database to extract microaneurysms and count them. Depending on the count, after applying the classifier and results, usually determine the Normal and Abnormal grades. If the number of microaneurysms is 0 at this point, this is normal and if this is greater than 1 that time, we said Abnormal.

Extraction of Retinal Microanurysms
See Figs. 9, 10, 11 and Table 1.

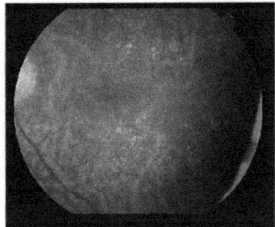

Fig. 9. Original Image

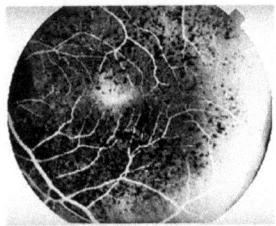

Fig. 10. Pre-processing

Fig. 11. Extraction of Microanurysms.

Classification and Grading

We used KNN classification technique for the classification and Grading, and we got the 95.7 percent accuracy on 100 fundus picture, Fig. 12 shows the classifier Result.

We can see in the figure right-hand side there is the result of the classification is that 95.7%. in the figure left-hand side of the bottom there is two-colour blue and orange, they showing the grading of Microanurysm count. Blue indicates the Abnormal, orange colour indicates the Normal of the maculopathy lesion "Microanurysm" Grading. In that classification, we used five- fold cross-validation.

Table 1. Statistical Count of Microanurysms

Sr.No	Image Name	Microan urysm Count
1	Image	10
2	Image	5
3	Image	1
4	Image	5
5	Image	8
6	Image	0
7	Image	0
8	Image	11
9	Image	9
10	Image	25

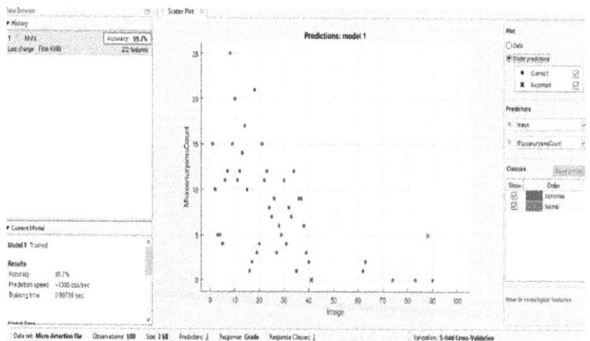

Fig. 12. KNN Classification Technique for Grading of Microanurysms Normal and Abnormal

4   Conclusion

The detection of Microanurysm is extremely crucial in diabetic Maculopathy. Micoa-nurysms are the main indication of maculopathy. Assuming Microanurysm makes close to a macula it tends to be harm a macula and in the event that the macula harmed, the patient can be lost his vision that is the reason identification is vital then the patient will take the treatment on it and the patient will be saved from losing the force of vision. In that exploration work, we utilized the KNN classifier and acquired 95.7% result, on the 100 stare Fundus Image. This current examination is helpful for ophthalmologists.

Acknowledgments. I would like to thank Dr. Babasaheb Ambedkar Marathwada University, Aurangabad (MS) India for providing the publication support.

References

1. Pattebahadur, Chetan & Manza, Ramesh &Kamble, Anupriya. (2019). Design a Novel Detection for Maculopathy Using Weightage KNN Classification. https://doi.org/10.1007/978-981-13-9184-2_32
2. Pattebahadur, Chetan & Manza, Ramesh & Kamble, Anupriya & Verma, Priyanka. (2020). Detection and Counting of Microaneurysm for Early Diagnosis of Maculopathy.
3. Manjiri B Patwari, Ramesh R Manza, Yogesh M Rajput, Manoj Saswade and Neha Deshpande. Article: Detection and Counting the Microaneurysms using Image Processing Techniques. International Journal of Applied Information Systems 6(5):11–17, November 2013
4. Mateen, M.; Malik, T.S.; Hayat, S.; Hameed, M.; Sun, S.; Wen, J. Deep Learning Approach for Automatic Microaneurysms Detection. Sensors 2022, 22, 542. https://doi.org/https://doi.org/10.3390/s22020542
5. Structured Analysis of the Retina. http://cecas.clemson.edu/~ahoover/stare
6. S.muthuselvi, & Prabhu, P.. (2016). DIGITAL IMAGE PROCESSING TECHNIQUES – A SURVEY. 5.
7. CS425 Lab: Intensity Transformations and Spatial Filtering, http://www.cs.uregina.ca/Links/class-info/425/Lab3
8. Kushwaha, Sumit & Rabindra, Kumar &Singh: Study and Analysis of Various Image Enhancement Method using MATLAB, International Journal of Computer Sciences and Engineering (IJCSE). (2015)
9. Rajendra Pal Singh And Manish Dixit: Histogram equalization A strong technique for Image Enhancement. In: International Journal of Signal Processing, Image Processing and Pattern Recognition, pp. 345–352, Vol. 8, No. 8. (2015)
10. Sukanesh, R. & Murugeswari, S.. (2014). Detection of Diabetic Maculopathy Using KNN Algorithm. Applied Mechanics and Materials. 573. 791–796. https://doi.org/10.4028/www.scientific.net/AMM.573.791.

Extraction of Bank Cheque Fields Based on Faster R-CNN

Hakim A. Abdo[1,2], Ahmed Abdu[3], Ramesh Manza[1], and Shobha Bawiskar[4(✉)]

[1] Dr. Babasaheb Ambedkar Marathwada University, Aurangabad, India
[2] Hodeidah University, Al-Hudaydah, Yemen
[3] Northwestern Polytechnical University, Xi'an, China
[4] Government Institute of Forensic Science, Aurangabad, India
`shobha_bawiskar@yahoo.co.in`

Abstract. The cheque field extraction is a critical step in automating bank cheque processing and is the first step in implementing a cheque recognition system. Many approaches for extracting the bank cheques components have been suggested. However, the complexity of the backdrop, the design variety of bank cheques, the variety of font sizes, and different patterns of writing remain a difficulty that necessitates the employment of precise algorithms. In this paper, we present a novel approach to extract the bank cheque components, in presented approach we used an innovative model called Faster R-CNN. This model represents the pinnacle of object recognition since it eliminates the need to manually extract image features and instead segments images to provide candidate region suggestions automatically. The IDRBT Cheque Image Dataset is used to train and test the Faster R-CNN model. The findings demonstrate that the model is capable of properly detecting the bank cheque fields. The extraction of bank cheque fields using Faster R-CNN achieves an accuracy of 97.4%, which outperforms other techniques.

Keywords: cheque fields · Object detection · Faster R-CNN

1 Introduction

A cheque is a document that instructs a bank to transfer a specified amount of money from a person's account to the person named on the cheque. The cheque includes printed identifying information and handwritten information. The printed fields in magnetic ink on the cheques are the number of account and bank code. While, the handwritten fields include the payee, date, courtesy amount (numerical format), the amount to be paid (legal amount), and the signature of the cheque' writer. Extract the bank cheque fields is to locate the bank cheque fields and segmenting this fields by using computer vision technologies.

The extraction of cheque fields is the critical step of automation of cheque processing. Only after completing the extraction step, the process of recognizing the payee, courtesy amount, and signature can be started. Developing an effective cheque fields extraction system, on the other hand, is a challenging undertaking, especially when the cheques

R. Manza et al. (Eds.): ACVAIT 2022, AISR 176, pp. 130–139, 2023.
https://doi.org/10.2991/978-94-6463-196-8_12

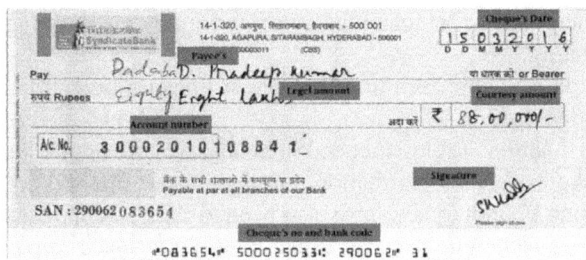

Fig. 1. Fields in a bank Cheque

have intricate and colorful backgrounds. In real applications, bank cheques may contain a variety of colorful backgrounds. In such cases, it is very difficult to find a thresholding method that will produce a satisfactory binarized image. Bank cheques do not conform to a single global standard. Even within the same country, cheques come in a variety of sizes and background colors. Cheques are issued in several sizes, and each bank offers its own collection of background drawings. On an international basis, the cheque fields are not located in the same place on the cheque, and cannot be located in terms of coordinates alone; no special box or icon is provided to help locate the cheque fields. However, a more general method is needed to extract cheque fields or for a system intended to handle international cheques, one that cannot benefit from any particular document structure.

In this paper, we present a novel approach, in this approach we extend the use of deep learning to extract bank cheque content. We use an advanced method called Faster R-CNN. Faster R-CNN is an improved version of R-CNN, which combines region proposals with CNNs. This represents the highest level in the field of object detection by now. The proposed approach is a critical step in automating bank cheque processing, it is an automatic segmentation step of bank cheque regions (Fig. 1).

2 Related Work and Overview

2.1 Related Work

Several methods for extract bank cheque fields are proposed, some of them extract handwritten fields, in [1] proposed a system to detect the handwritten items from bank cheque images; the system adjusted and evaluated for extraction of numeral format amounts in US cheques and Brazilian cheques. This method consists of three stages: arranging data into linked blocks finding possible string candidates and deciding which string best depicts the courtesy amount in [2] Proposed an approach for detecting and recognizing the fields of the signature and amount in the digital format in cheque image, in the proposed approach, the processing is divided into five parts, the courtesy amount and signature are manually selected from a preprocessed cheque image.

In [3] proposed approach for Extraction of Signatures from Cheques image, the sliding window method is used to determine the approximate area in which the signature is located. In this method, a window with adjustable height and width is dragged over the picture one pixel at a time, and the density of pixels within the window is determined.

This density is then used to calculate the entropy, which aids in fitting the box that can segment the signature.

In [4] The proposed approach used the detect lines to the extraction of significant areas from a cheque image..

A collection of heuristic rules encoded in histograms are applied to extract courtesy amount region. Approaches to extraction that make use of linked component analysis and the surrounding bounding box have also been highlighted in research works.[5].

In [6] Proposed technique uses Cartesian coordinate space to partition the cheque picture into interesting areas, at first the converting cheque image into grayscale for the purpose of decrease size, and the vertical and horizontal scanning of grayscale image for locating the AROI, finally, segmentation of the AROI regions.

Some method extract printed fields from cheque image, in [7], the proposed approach utilized cheque template structures to segment the printed items from cheque images. Template structures are determined by extracting the MICR code from the input cheque image. Important fields region is segmented, and the printed data is recognized.

2.2   Faster RCNN

Faster R-CNN [8] is a DCN model, it is using to object detection, this model is an extension of Fast R-CNN [9]. As its name implies, Faster R-CNN outperformed in speed on Fast R-CNN due to RPN.

The Faster RCNN structure consists of ConvNet layers, region proposal generation Network, region of interest pooling [11], and classifier. The structure of Faster R-CNN is shown in Fig. 2.

The Convolutional neural network is used as a feature maps extractor [10], region proposal network aim to generate the region proposal from extracted features map by sharing it with ROI pooling.

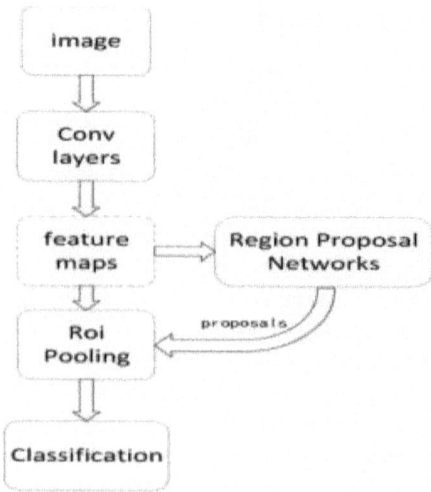

Fig. 2. Structure of Faster R-CNN

3   Methodology

The cheque fields extraction system architecture is described in this part. Figure 3 depicts the structure of cheque fields extraction system, first, the cheque image is fed to backbone convNet to extract the feature map, then the feature map extracted is fed to the PRN network for generates the region proposal, then the Roi Pooling layer uses to extract the proposal feature from feature Maps extracted, finally, the proposal feature is fed to two fully connected layers for predicting the cheque field locations and a class of filed.

3.1   ConvNet Layers

A Convolutional neural network can be used as a feature maps extractor. In the study, we use the VGG16 network as the CNN model for extraction of features map. This serves as a backbone for both the region Proposal network and convNet. The VGG-16 has 13 convolutional layers divided into five network phases by 4 max-pooling layers with relu activation function, which are used to extract various levels and scales of feature maps, we modified it to get the feature map (Feature size: 60, 40, 512) and skip the last 2 fully connected layers.

3.2   Region Proposal Networks

The RPN module [8] is in charge of creating region proposals. It makes use of the idea of attention in neural networks to direct the Fast R-CNN detection module where to seek for items in the image. To generate the region proposals, a 3x3 sliding window from the convNet layer output feature map is passed through the PRN. For each spatial point, the anchor box is sent to the regression and classification layers with varied aspect ratios and varying scales centered, as shown in Fig. 4, let k represent the number of anchors at a location. We estimate three aspect ratios and four scales, yielding k = 12 different anchors at a particular location. The classification layer output is a probability that the anchor box information is object or background, while the regression layer provided anchor boxes offsets.

3.3   Region of Interest Pooling Layer

Region of interest pooling layer purpose is to perform max pooling on inputs of non-uniform sizes to obtain fixed-size feature maps. The proposal suggested by RPN and

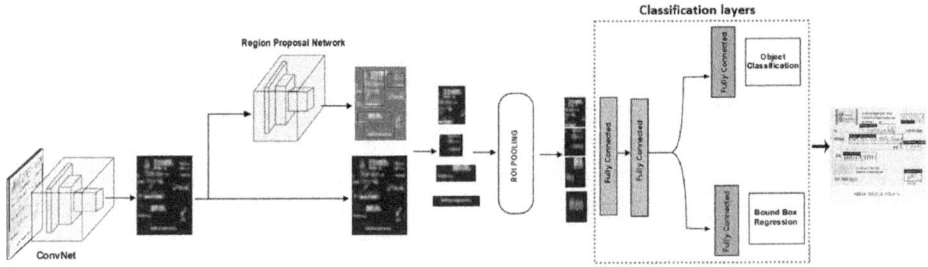

Fig. 3. Cheque fields extraction system architecture

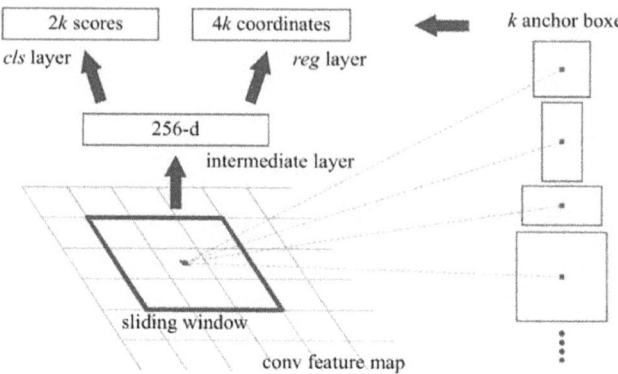

Fig. 4. Region proposal

A fixed-size feature map obtained from backbone convNet are passed to Roi pooling layer, The ROI layer divides the region corresponding to a proposal from the backbone feature map into a specified number of sub-windows, Then, max-pooling is applied to these sub-windows to get a fixed-size output.

3.4 Classification Layers

Classification layers have two fully connected layers, and two parallel sister branches, respectively, for classifying the area proposal and exact bounding box regression. The classification branch is a binary classification layer with a softmax activation function to distinguish respectively between the cheque fields and the background. Once the region proposal is expected to encapsulate cheque fields, the regression branch outputs a tetrad (x,y,w,h), indicating the exact bounding box of cheque fields in the input image based on the region proposal.

4 Experiment and Results

4.1 Dataset

The IDRBT Cheque Image dataset [15] is used in this work. We created an annotation on the dataset to suitable the faster RCNN model, partially presented in Fig. 4, the dataset consists of 112 cheque images collected from Indian banks, the size of original images is 2372×1093, the cheque images written by 9 volunteers in English language, in writing cheques the 14 pens with blue and black ink are used.

To train the Faster R-CNN on IDRBT dataset, we first resized the cheque images into 416×416 for purpose of reducing the model training time, and then we manually annotate them, as the Faster R-CNN demands. To accomplish the annotation task, we use the graphical image annotation application LabelImg designed by [16]. LabelImg is a Python program with a Qt graphical user interface; in LabelImg, the first step is pre-defining the classes of cheque bank fields, and then annotations the image of cheques by drawing a rectangular surrounding the cheque' fields with labeling them as shown in Fig. 4, finally, saving the annotation file as a JSON file.

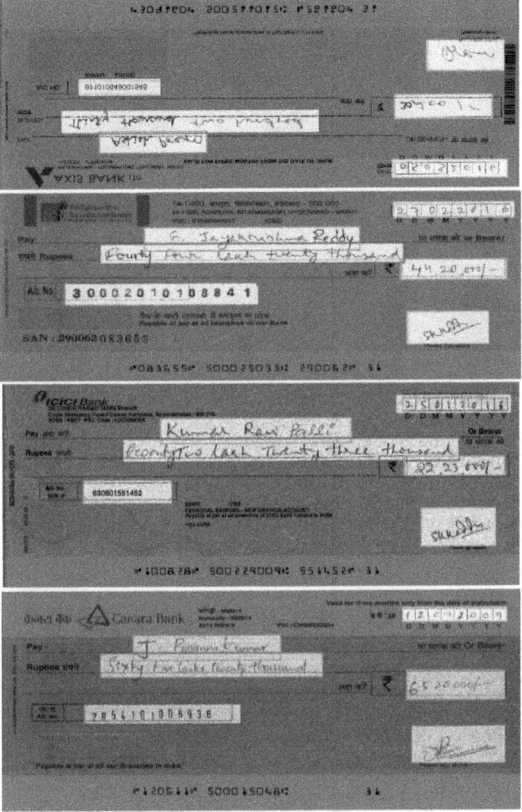

Fig. 5. Samples from modified dataset

4.2 Experiment Results

In this part, the below extraction results have been achieved using Faster R-CNN. Some samples of the model's testing results for extracting bank cheque fields are shown in Fig. 5. It can be observed that the Faster R-CNN is capable of properly detecting the Indian bank cheque fields. Table 1 shows the outcomes of utilizing Faster R-CNN retrained on our dataset, which consists of six classes of cheque fields. The dataset consists of 112 cheque images; 101 images for training and 11 images for testing; all cheques are written in English. The various font sizes and patterns of writing the cheques in the dataset increase the model's ability to extract ROI (fields) from Indian cheques that are written in English. In order to increase the ability of the proposed model to extract the ROI (fields) from Indian cheques that are written in other Indian regional languages, the dataset has to be extended to include various regional languages and retrain the model. The Faster R-CNN model performance is assessed in 2 way: classification precision and bounding box prediction precision, also known as regression accuracy. We can observe that the classification's mean Average Precision (mAP) is reached 97.4 percent. Comparison of different cheque fields extraction methods' Performance is identified in Table 2. As evidenced by the experimental findings, the Faster R-CNN surpasses the other techniques. Figure 6 is shown the outcomes of RPN network loss. The model realizes minimal loss through the training of the model, as can be observed. In the RPN network, the minimal classification and regression losses are 0.0194 and 0.490, respectively (Fig. 7).

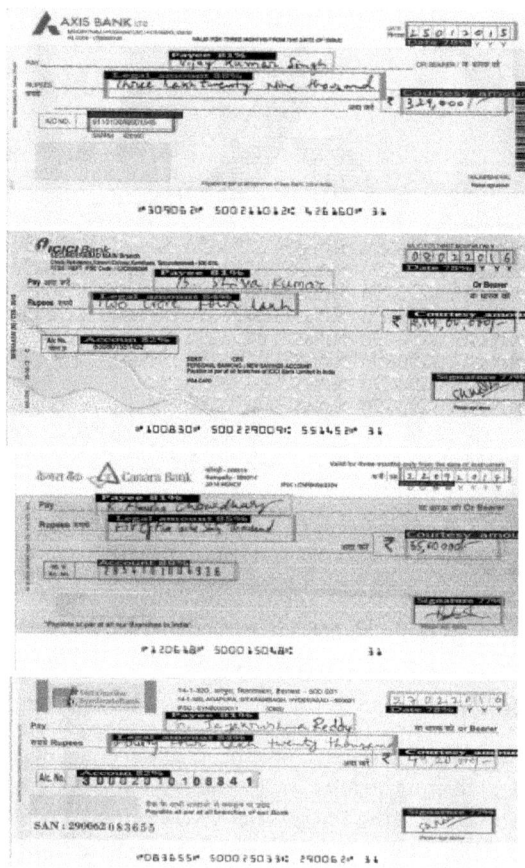

Fig. 6. Samples of cheque fields' extraction result

Table 1. Accuracy rate of classification and regression

Classes	Date	Courtesy amount	Legal amount	Account number	Signature	Time of testing(s)
Classification accuracy	1	0.99	0.91	0.98	0.99	25
Regression accuracy	1	0.99	0.93	.98	0.99	

Table 2. Comparison of different cheque fields extraction approaches' Performance

Cheque field	Method/Accuracy							
	[3]	[12]	[13]	[2]	[14]	[4]	[7]	our
Date	–	Prior knowledge position/NA	–	–	–	based on identification of important lines/NA accuracy	Template Matching method/NA accuracy	Faster R-CNN/97.4%
Courtesy amount	–		ROI based segmentation/95%	Manually selected/NA	recursive thresholding algorithm/90%			
Legal amount	–			–	–			
Payee	–			–	–			
Account No	–	Prior knowledge position/NA	–	–	–			
Signature	Sliding window method /99.26%		ROI based segmentation/91%	Manually selected/NA	–			

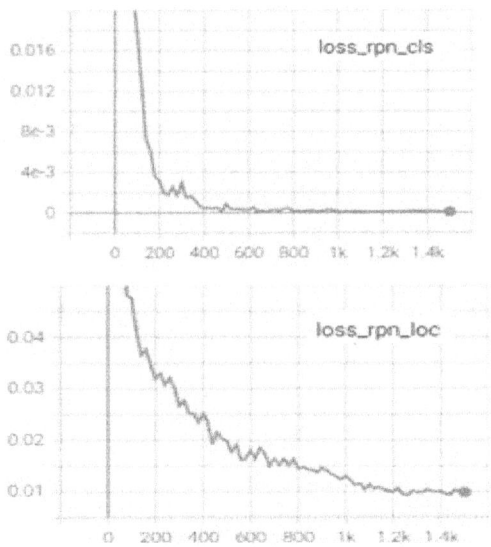

Fig. 7. The RPN network loss outcomes

5 Conclusion

In this work, we used Faster R-CNN to extract bank cheque fields, the Faster R-CNN is a novel object detection method. We modified The IDRBT Cheque Image dataset by creating an annotations to suitable the faster RCNN model. The Faster R-CNN model trained and tested on 112 bank cheque images. The model achieves a mAP value that is 97.4%.The outcomes we got shows that the Faster R-CNN model is capable of properly extracting the bank cheques fields.However, as compared to previous techniques, deep learning improves the effectiveness of the detection method.

References

1. R. Palacios and A. Gupta, "A system for processing handwritten bank checks automatically," *Image Vis. Comput.*, vol. 26, no. 10, pp. 1297–1313, 2008, https://doi.org/10.1016/j.imavis.2006.04.012.
2. M. B. Alam and S. Mia, "Handwritten Courtesy Amount and Signature Recognition on Bank Cheque using Neural Network," vol. 118, no. 5, pp. 21–26, 2015.
3. V. K. Madasu, M. Hafizuddin, M. Yusof, and M. Hanmandlu, "Automatic Extraction of Signatures from Bank Cheques and other Documents," pp. 10–12, 2003.
4. P. Dansena, K. Pramod Kumar, and R. Pal, "Line based extraction of important regions from a cheque image," in *2015 Eighth International Conference on Contemporary Computing (IC3)*, 2015, pp. 183–189, https://doi.org/10.1109/IC3.2015.7346676.
5. L. Chandra, N. Software, T. Limited, S. V. Marg, and Q. I. Area, "Automatic Courtesy Amount Recognition for Indian Banks ' Checks," pp. 6–10, 2008.
6. M. Sankari and M. Benazir, "Verification of Bank Cheque Images using Hamming Measures," no. December, pp. 7–10, 2010.
7. P. M.P, "Automatic Extraction of Attributes from Printed Indian Cheque Images by Template Matching Technique," vol. 5, no. 1, pp. 30–37, 2019.
8. S. Ren, K. He, R. Girshick, and J. Sun, "Faster R-CNN: Towards Real-Time Object Detection with Region Proposal Networks," *IEEE Trans. Pattern Anal. Mach. Intell.*, vol. 39, no. 6, pp. 1137–1149, 2017, https://doi.org/10.1109/TPAMI.2016.2577031.
9. R. Girshick, "Fast R-CNN," *Proc. IEEE Int. Conf. Comput. Vis.*, vol. 2015 Inter, pp. 1440–1448, 2015, https://doi.org/10.1109/ICCV.2015.169.
10. S. Bell, C. L. Zitnick, K. Bala, and R. Girshick, "Inside-Outside Net: Detecting Objects in Context with Skip Pooling and Recurrent Neural Networks," *Proc. IEEE Comput. Soc. Conf. Comput. Vis. Pattern Recognit.*, vol. 2016-Decem, pp. 2874–2883, 2016, https://doi.org/10.1109/CVPR.2016.314.
11. C. Szegedy *et al.*, "Going deeper with convolutions," *Proc. IEEE Comput. Soc. Conf. Comput. Vis. Pattern Recognit.*, vol. 07–12-June, pp. 1–9, 2015, https://doi.org/10.1109/CVPR.2015.7298594.
12. P. Agrawal *et al.*, "Automated bank cheque verification using image processing and deep learning methods," *Multimed. Tools Appl.*, vol. 80, no. 4, pp. 5319–5350, 2021, https://doi.org/10.1007/s11042-020-09818-1.
13. A. K. Talele, "Automatic Extraction of Legal and Courtesy amount , Payee Name and signature in Bank Cheque Processing System," vol. 3, no. 5, pp. 4417–4425, 2011.
14. C. Y. Zhang, Q. Chen, Z. Lou, and J. Y. Yang, "Extraction of courtesy amount item from Chinese check," *2004 8th Int. Conf. Control. Autom. Robot. Vis.*, vol. 1, no. December, pp. 109–114, 2004, https://doi.org/10.1109/icarcv.2004.1468807.
15. Dansena, P., S. Bag, & R. Pal. (2017). Differentiating Pen Inks in Hand-written Bank Cheques Using Multi-Layer Perceptron. *Proc. of 7th International Conference on Pattern recognition and Machine Intelligence, Kolkata, India.*
16. Tzutalin. (2015). labelImg:A graphical image annotation tool. Retrieved from https://github.com/tzutalin/labelImg

Multimodal Deep Learning Based Score Level Fusion Using Face and Fingerprint

Krishna Shinde[1]([✉]) and Charansing Kayte[2]

[1] Department of Computer Science and IT, Dr. B.A.M.U. Aurangabad, Aurangabad, India
shreekriss@gmail.com
[2] Department of Digital and Cyber Forensic, Government Institute of Forensic Science,
Dr. B.A.M.U. Aurangabad, Aurangabad, India

Abstract. In the previous decade, biometrics referred to the automatic recognition of persons based on their physiological or behavioural traits but unimodal biometrics have their limitations. Due to its potential to overcome some of the inherent limitations of single biometric modalities while simultaneously enhancing overall recognition rates, multimodal biometrics has recently gained prominence. In this research, we offer a multimodal biometric person authentication system based on pre-train transfer learning VGG16 with CNN and CNN models, that uses the user's face and fingerprint biometric traits. We have used the own collected samples of same person KVKR face and fingerprint dataset for experimental work. First, we have applied pre-processing data augmentation technique on face and fingerprint data then image enhancement techniques on fingerprint data. In the features extraction, we have extraction the hidden feature of the face and fingerprint images using pre-train VGG16 with CNN and CNN models. The hstack method has been used to combine the features and SoftMax classifier use for features classification. The fusion score is calculated using the fixed-rule-based maximum rule technique, finally we have done comparative analysis of the unimodal and multimodal biometric recognition system.

Keywords: VGG16 · CNN · Deep learning · Score Fusion

1 Introduction

In recent years, biometric-based authentication systems have grown in popularity in several applications that require a reliable verification/identification method. Biometric authentication is a pattern-recognition system that identifies a person using a feature vector obtained from a physiological or behavioural characteristic [1]. The technique is currently used in a variety of high-security identity and individual verification systems. Multimodal biometrics has increased in importance in recent years, due to single modal biometrics' limitation, which includes non-universal, noisy sensor data, substantial intra-user variability and vulnerability to spoofing attacks [2]. The drawbacks of unimodal biometric systems are addressed by multi-modal biometric systems. For example, consider the issue of non-universality: a fraction of users may lack a certain biometrics

© The Author(s) 2023
R. Manza et al. (Eds.): ACVAIT 2022, AISR 176, pp. 140–152, 2023.
https://doi.org/10.2991/978-94-6463-196-8_13

attribute [3]. The multimodal biometric system can be used for combination of multiple modality properties. In the multimodal system sensor-level fusion, feature-level fusion, score-level fusion and decision-level fusion are the four forms of fusion. In a variety of ways, multimodal biometric systems surpass unimodal biometric systems, making them a particularly appealing secure recognition solution [4, 5]. Deep learning is based on an artificial neural network that constructs feature hierarchies using statistical machine learning techniques. There is made up of three layers such as input, hidden layer and output layer and the layers' nodes are all to inter connected. The raw data is transferred to the input layer, where each node stores part of the information they encounter and the information is then passed on to the next layer nodes, which develop abstract knowledge about the data. Deep learning has lately had a significant influence on biometrics systems, generating surprising outcomes. Many of the shortcomings in traditional machine learning methods, particularly in feature extraction procedures, have been solved by deep learning algorithms. Deep neural networks can adapt to changes in biometric images and extract features from raw data [6, 7]. In this article, the Sect. 1 introduced of biometric and multimodal biometric, face and fingerprint recognition. In the next section have related work and existing work of multimodal biometric recognition system. Section 3 about database benchmark, Sect. 4 experimental setup and hyperparameter, Sect. 5 have introduce proposed methodology, features extraction, feature classification and fusion techniques. Section 6 have performance analysis of proposed system, Sect. 7 has result and discussion and last section have conclusion, contribution and acknowledge.

2 Literature Survey

The following Table 1 shows existing work of multimodal biometric system review starting from the author, biometric traits, databases, algorithm, level of fusion, and lastly the recognition result.

Table 1. Literature Survey

Sr. No	Author & year	Biometrics Traits	Database	Techniques	Fusion Level	Result
1	Arun Ross 2003 [8]	Face, Fingerprint, and Hand Geometry	NA	PCA	Score	FAR 0.03%
2	Shi-Jinn Horng 2009 [1]	Face, Fingerprint, and Finger Vein	NIST	SVM	Score	99.8%
3	Mendu. Anusha 2016 [9]	Fingerprint, Face, and Iris	HMM	Doughman's, WLD, and Decision Tree	Features	90.00%

(continued)

Table 1. (*continued*)

Sr. No	Author & year	Biometrics Traits	Database	Techniques	Fusion Level	Result
4	E. Sujatha 2017 [10]	Iris, Palm Print, Face, and Signature	CASIA	DWT	Features	99.90%
5	Supreetha Gowda H D 2018 [7]	Face and Iris	CASIA and ORL	CNN	Feature	99.00%
6	Veeru Talreja 2019 [11]	Face and Iris	NA	CNN	Features	99.00%
7	Nada Alay 2020 [6]	Iris, Face and Finger Vein	SDUMLA -HMT	CNN	Features Score	99.22 100
8	EI Mehdi 2020 [12]	Finger Vein and Face	DB1 and DB2	CNN, RF, SVM	Score	99.98
9	EI Mehdi 2020 [13]	Fingerprint, Finger Vein and Face	SDUMLA -HMT	CNN, SVM, LR, and RF	score	99.49
10	Priti Shende 2020 [14]	Face, Palm Veins, and Fingerprint	Self-Created	CNN and SVM	Features	99.10%
11	Arjun Benagatte 2021 [15]	Fingerprint and Signature	SDUMLA -HMT and MCYT	HOG and CNN	Features	93.33%
12	Mehwish Leghari 2021 [16]	Fingerprint and Online Signature	NA	CNN	Features	99.10%

3   About Database

In this study, we have utilized the KVKR face and fingerprint database for the same person. Under the supervision of Prof. Dr. K. V. Kale, Programme Coordinator, UGC SAP (II) DRS Phase-I, we gathered data in the Multimodal Biometrics Research Laboratory at the Dept. of Computer Science & Information Technology, Dr. B. A. M.U., Aurangabad. Face and fingerprint data were obtained from Research Scholars and PG students aged 21 to 40. The face KVKR database collects 10 various positions of the face such as the frontal face, left 90, left 60, Right 90, Right 60, chin up, Down, small smiling, big smiling, and close eyes, etc. position set and neutral and smiling facial expression. The operation distance 1 m, Resolution of the image is 640*480, the following Fig. 1 show that the sample of face data.

The fingerprint KVKR database collection begins with the left-hand little finger and progresses to the right hand's little finger one by one.

Fig. 1. Face Data sample

Fig. 2. Fingerprint Data Sample

Each dry and natural finger has been gathered and the image resolution is 320 * 480 grayscale images. The sample of fingerprint data is shown in Fig. 2 show that the sample of fingerprint data.

4   Experimental Setup

The proposed method is constructed deep learning with Python 3.6 and other open-source library tools such as Keres, TensorFlow, CUDA and image processing libraries like OpenCV, matplotlib and scikit-learn, among others. The method runs on a laptop window 11 with an Intel Core-i5 CPU, NVidia 2 GB of memory and 8 Gb ram. The training models used Jupyter notebook IDE and the pre-processing was done using spider IDE.

In this study, we have used own collected same person samples of 30 subject KVKR face and fingerprint databases. The features extraction has done using transfer learning pre-train VGG16 with CNN models and CNN model. These extracted features have classified using SoftMax classifier. In the VGG16 model the default input size of the ImageNet wights images is $224 \times 224 \times 3$ but we are allowed to modify this size as per the requirement. Thereby, we are modifying the size as $64 \times 64 \times 3$ as per the experimental requirements. The hyperparameters was kept same for the all-transfer learning as well as CNN based experiments such as Epoch is 8, Batch Size is 64, learning rate is 0.001, Dropout rate is 0.1, activation function ReLU, Optimizer function as Adam, Loss function as categorical cross entropy (as it is multi-class classification) and SoftMax classifier is use as a classifier. The unimodal biometric face and fingerprint-based person identification system, we have used 960 images for training and 240 images for validation (80:20%).

5 Proposed Methodology

In multimodal face and fingerprint score fusion system, we have first applied pre-processing techniques on KVKR dataset, then divided the dataset in to different percentages for models training and used CNN and VGG16 with CNN models for calculating recognition rate. In the multimodal biometric person identification system, first time we have used 960 images for training and 240 images for validation (80:20%), second time used 720 images for training and 480 for validation (60:40%) and last time used 600 images for training and 600 images for validation (50:50%). In Fig. 3 shows general structure of multimodal biometric face and fingerprint fusion system. This system is divided into two phase those are training and testing. In training phase, first load KVKR dataset and resize in to 64 * 64, then used hstack method to combine the resize images features, then to train the networks using the proposed structure. The trained model wights will be stored and use this model wights in to testing phase for test images. In the testing phase, KVKR test dataset image lode and resized into 64 * 64, combine the face and fingerprint images features using hstack technique, then test image using previously stored model wights. Lastly, shown in the screen as the result of person recognition in multimodal biometric system as the person ID belonging to which class and fusion score.

5.1 Pre-processing

In this study, we have used two pre-processing techniques those are data augmentation and image enhancement. The data augmentation technique has used to artificially increase the size of training dataset by making multiple copies of the images. The more data may lead to more proficient deep learning neural network models. The augmentation technique can provide picture variations that help fit models generalize as well as overcome the overfitting problem. This study KVKR face data has applied rotation,

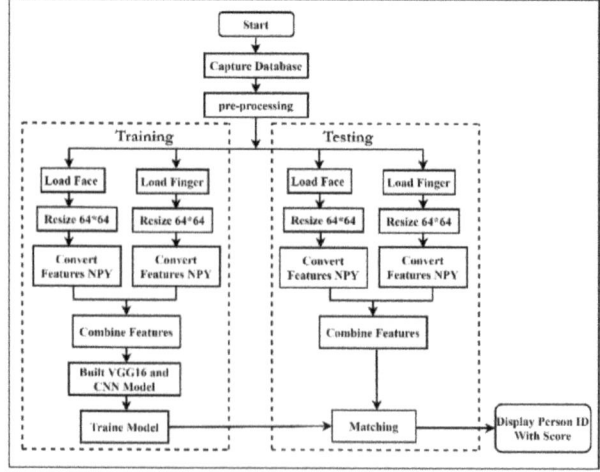

Fig. 3. Proposed Methodology

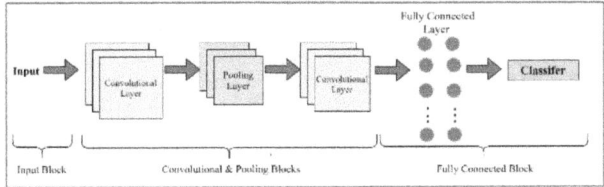

Fig. 4. Convolutional Neural Network Architecture

zoom and horizontal flip operation in the augmentation and KVKR fingerprint data have used cropping and brightness level operation in the augmentation technique. After augmentation the KVKR fingerprint data, we have applied image enhancement technique on KVKR fingerprint database. The image enhancement technique has some ridgelines in fingerprint images flow in various directions by applying Gabor-type filters on these ridgelines no noise between them is introduced and the resultant image is cleaner than the original [19].

5.2 CNN

CNNs are a deep learning approach that consists of numerous layers and is inspired by the biological visual cortex. CNNs are one of the most prevalent forms of neural networks used to detect and classify images and objects. These CNN models are used in a range of applications and domains, but they're especially popular in image and video processing. The building blocks of CNNs are filters and kernels. Using the convolution technique, the Kernels extract the appropriate information from the input. To train and evaluate deep learning CNN models, each input image is passed through a sequence of convolution layers with filters (Kernels), Pooling layers, fully connected layers (FC), and the SoftMax function, which uses probabilistic values to identification an item. These models have used convolutional layers for extracting the image features. Each convolutional contains a set of weighted matrices known as filters or kernels that slide over the input image to identify specific information. Colours and basic patterns are detected by the CNN's initial layers of filters. Then, as they progress through the levels, they begin to see more intricate patterns. Each filter uses a convolution operation to generate a feature map to discover features [17, 20]. In Fig. 4 these three blocks are used to constrict a CNN architecture by varying the size of blocks, addition or removing a block. This model has used three hidden layers and four convolution and max pooling layer.

5.3 VGG16

The VGG models were developed by the Visual Geometry Group at Oxford University. VGG16, one of the most common models, has 16 layers and the ImageNet database was used to train the VGG16 model extensively. This massive database has over 14 million photos divided into 20000 categories Five convolution blocks make up a VGG16 model. The VGG16 model consists of five convolution blocks. Each convolution block has two

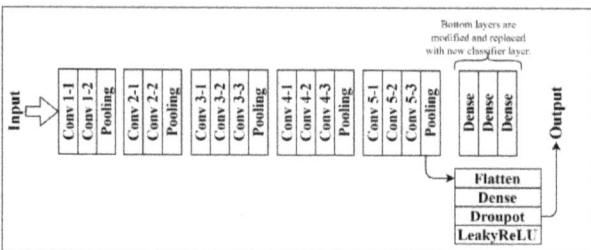

Fig. 5. Modified of VGG16 Model layers using CNN.

convolutional layers (size: 3 × 3) and one max-pooling layer (size: 2 × 2). The prediction and classification tasks are handled by the fully connected (FC) layers [20].

The Fig. 5 shows the architectural block diagram of the convolutional layer's configuration for VGG16 using transfer learning.

The initial layers are frozen layers and we cannot modify them. However, in order to perform transfer learning using this convolution architecture, the bottom layers are modified and replaced with new classifier layer using CNN model. This architecture used eight hidden layer of CNN model.

5.4 Features Classification

SoftMax: Classification of object is very important task normally different literature uses SVM based classifier, which works on the classification score based on hyper plane that separate the data into two categories but, SoftMax classifier predict the class label on the basis of calculated probabilities we used the fully connected layer for final calculation of score, as we calculating probabilities in previous layer and got the value for calculating label. The SoftMax function is the most often utilised activation function at the output layer for multi class classification. When using real values, the SoftMax function calculates the probability distribution and returns a value in the range of 0 to 1, with the total of the probabilities equating 1. The output layer in multiclass issues would have 'n' neurons, where n is the number of classes. Each neuron would provide a probability value for each class, with the predicted class being the neuron with the greatest value.

5.5 Score Level Fusion

In this approach, we have used pre-train transfer learning VGG16 with CNN and CNN model for the fusion of face and fingerprint. In this study, we have calculated similarity score, the fully connected layer is entered into the SoftMax classifier for measuring similar scores, then each subject score is fused using fixed-rule-based maximum rule technique for biometric score fusion. This technique has normalized final score vector and in the output identity of the subject shows who have the largest fusion score. This is a most popular method for fusion, in the maximum rule defined, 'f' is fusion score, 'xm' is the number of modalities used for fusion [17, 18]. This technique has selected the largest value score as fusion score. The following equation shows mathematical description:

$$f = \max(x1, x2, x3 \ldots \ldots x_m) \ldots \ldots \ldots \tag{1}$$

6 Performance Analysis

6.1 Classification and Confusion Matrix

The KVKR face and fingerprint database were used to test the face and fingerprint score fusion multimodal biometric identification system and the results were assessed using several evaluation metrics, including confusion matrix, Precision, Recall, Support, Micro and weighted average, and F1 Score. Precision depicts the model's positive predictive value, whereas recall depicts its sensitivity and true positive rate.

We utilized micro-averages to integrate the findings across the thirty categories to get the overall accuracy and recall. Figure 6 classification report of precision (P) and recall (R) rate of overall classes of VGG16 with CNN data split (80:20%). In the Fig. 7 show that the normalize and without normalize confusion matrix of the face and fingerprint score fusion result of VGG16 with CNN data split (80:20%). The confusion matrix vertical X axis shows that the true labels id of each class and horizontal axis Y show that the predicted labels id of each class.

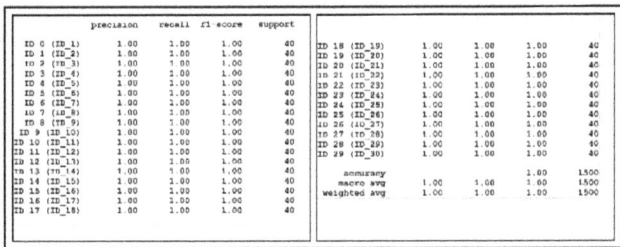

Fig. 6. Face and Fingerprint Classification Matrix of VGG16 with CNN (80:20)

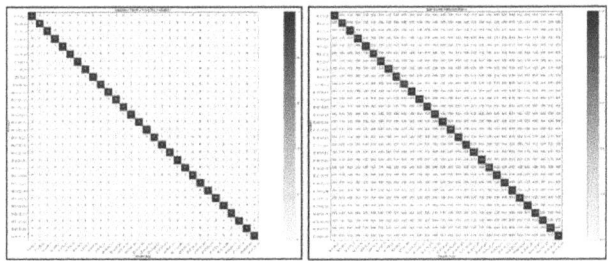

Fig. 7. Confusion Matrix of Face and Fingerprint VGG16 with CNN (80:20)

7 Result and Discussion

Here, the accuracy of the proposed VGG16 with CNN and CNN model. In this study, we have used the KVKR face and fingerprint same person database and calculated unimodal as well as multimodal biometric Accuracy. Figures 8 and 9 shows that the face and fingerprint recognition models accuracy and loss.

Figures 10, 11 and 12 show that the face and fingerprint score fusion model accuracy and loss.

In Table 2 shows, unimodal and multimodal recognition accuracy. In the face recognition we have got 98.86% accuracy and 1.14% equal error rate, fingerprint recognition got 87.08% accuracy and 12.92% equal error rate. In multimodal score fusion first time in VGG16 with CNN got 99.65% accuracy in (80:20) split, second time got 99.30% accuracy (60:40%) split and third time got 99.25% accuracy (50:50%) split. The CNN model using first time got 99.50% accuracy (80:20%) split, second time got 99.10% accuracy (60:40%) split and third time got 98.89% accuracy (50:50%) split.

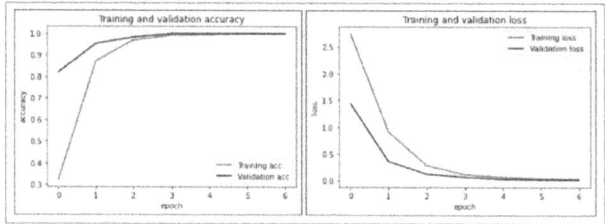

Fig. 8. Face Recognition Model Accuracy and Loss

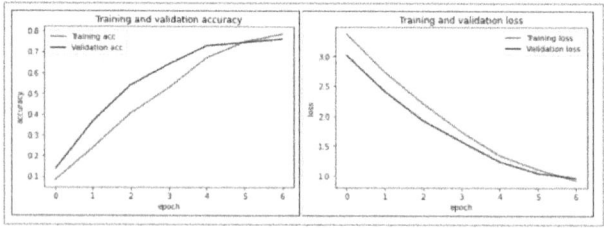

Fig. 9. Fingerprint Recognition Model Accuracy and Loss

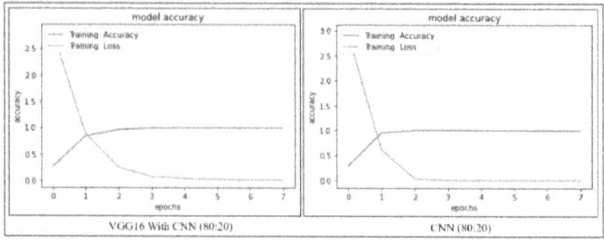

Fig. 10. Face & Fingerprint Fusion (80:20) Accuracy and Loss

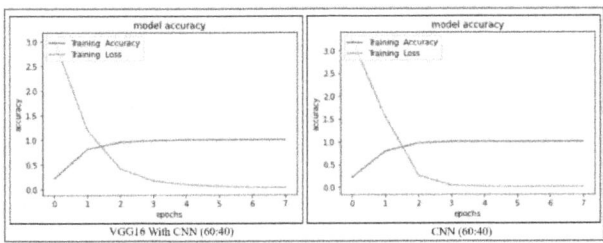

Fig. 11. Face & Fingerprint Fusion (60:40) Accuracy and Loss

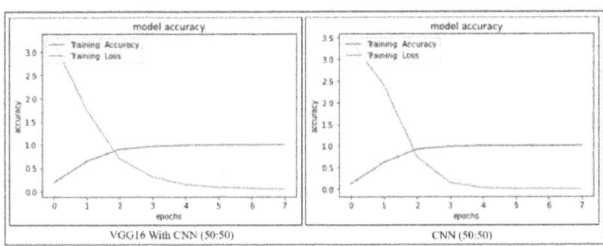

Fig. 12. Face & Fingerprint Fusion (50:50) Accuracy and Loss

In Graph 1 show that the comparative analysis of unimodal and multimodal biometric recognition accuracy. We have got in VGG16 with CNN model split (80:20%) database good recognition accuracy than unimodal biometric.

Table 2. Comparative Analysis of Unimodal and Multimodal Biometric Recognition Accuracy

Data	Techniques/ Algorithm	No. of Subject and data split percentages	EER	Accuracy
KVKR Face	VGG16 and CNN	30 (80:20)	1.14%	98.86%
KVKR Fingerprint	VGG16 and CNN	30 (80:20)	12.92%	87.08%
Face & Finger Score Fusion	VGG16 and CNN	30 (80:20)	**0.35%**	**99.65%**
Face & Finger Score Fusion	CNN	30 (80:20)	0.50%	99.50%
Face & Finger Score Fusion	VGG16 and CNN	30 (60:40)	0.70%	99.30%
Face & Finger Score Fusion	CNN	30 (60:40)	0.90%	99.10%
Face & Finger Score Fusion	VGG16 and CNN	30 (50:50)	0.75%	99.25%
Face & Finger Score Fusion	CNN	30 (50:50)	1.11%	98.89%

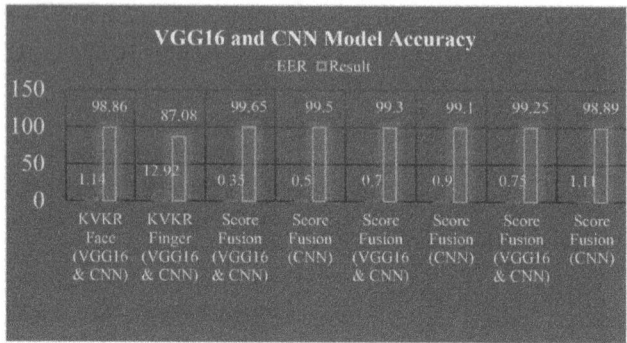

Graph 1. Comparative Analysis of Unimodal and Multimodal Biometric Recognition Accuracy

8   Conclusion

In this paper, we have used a deep learning technique to create a face and fingerprint based unimodal and multimodal person identification system. This work, we have used KVKR face and fingerprint own collected samples of same person database. First, we have applied data augmentation technique on the face and fingerprint database for artificially incurring the size of the database then fingerprint has applied image enhancement for improving ridgelines that run in different directions and the resulting image will be clearer than the original. In this study we have uses 30 subject databases and proposed VGG16 with CNN based face recognition got 98.86% accuracy and fingerprint recognition got 87.08% accuracy. In multimodal biometric person identification system, which uses the user's face and fingerprint using VGG16 with CNN model have got good recognition accuracy in (80:20%) split 99.65%. We have got in multimodal score fusion good recognition accuracy than the unimodal biometric system.

9   Contributions

- Most of the multimodal biometric recognition systems have used traditional methods and very few researchers have attempted the work in deep learning based.
- Our proposed system can be achieved good recognition accuracy in limited as well as larges datasets.
- We have designed a robust multimodal biometric system for person identification using face and fingerprint modality in a deep learning approach.

Acknowledgments. I would like to thank Dr. K.V. Kale for permission for me to collection of databases in the Multimodal Lab. I would acknowledge and thank CSMNRF, Pune for financial support SARTHI an Autonomous Institute Government of Maharashtra. Authors would like to extends thanks to Dr. Babasaheb Ambedkar Marathwada University for the publication support.

References

1. Shi Jinn H., Yuan Chen, Ray-Shine R., Rong-Jian C., Jui-Lin L., and Kevin Octavius S., An Improved Score Level Fusion in Multimodal Biometric Systems, International Conference on Parallel and Distributed Computing, Applications and Technologies, 2009.
2. M. Ahmad, W.L. Woo and S.S. Dlay, Multimodal Biometric Fusion at Feature Level: Face and Palmprint, IEEE, 2010.
3. S. V. and Jules R. Tapamo, Integrating Iris and Signature Traits for Personal Authentication Using User-Specific Weighting, Sensors, 2012.
4. Arun A. Ross, Karthik Nandakumar and Anil K. Jain, Handbook of Multibiometric, springer, 2006.
5. Krishna S. and Sumegh T., Development of Face and Signature Fusion Technology for Biometrics Authentication, International Journal of Emerging Research in Management &Technology, 2017.
6. Nada A. and Heyam H., Deep Learning Approach for Multimodal Biometric Recognition System Based on Fusion of Iris, Face, and Finger Vein Traits, Sensors, 2020.
7. Supreetha G. H D, Mohammad I., and Hemantha Kumar G., Feature level fusion of Face and Iris using Deep Features based on Convolutional Neural Networks, IEEE, 2018.
8. A. Ross and A. K. Jain, Information fusion in biometrics, Pattern Recognition Letters, 2003.
9. M. Anusha and T.V.V. Krishna, Multimodal Biometric System Integrating Fingerprint Face and Iris, International Journal of Innovative Research in Computer and Communication Engineering, Vol. 4, Issue 10, October 2016.
10. E. Sujatha and A. C., Multimodal Biometric Authentication Algorithm Using Iris, Palm Print, Face and Signature with Encoded DWT, Springer, 2017.
11. Veeru T., Sobhan S., Matthew C. Valenti, and Nasser M. Nasrabadi, Learning to Authenticate with Deep Multibiometric Hashing and Neural Network Decoding, arXiv:1902.04149v3 [cs.CV] 7 Mar 2019.
12. El M. Cherrat, Rachid Alaoui, and Hassane Bouzahir, SCORE FUSION OF FINGER VEIN AND FACE FOR HUMAN RECOGNITION BASED ON CONVOLUTIONAL NEURAL NETWORK MODEL, International Journal of Computing, 2020.
13. El M. C., Rachid Alaoui, and Hassane Bouzahir, Convolutional neural networks approach for multimodal biometric identification system using the fusion of fingerprint, finger-vein and face images, Peer J Computer Science, 2020.
14. Priti S. and Yogesh H. D., Convolutional Neural Network Based Multimodal Biometric Human Authentication using Face, Palm Veins and Fingerprint, International Journal of Innovative Technology and Exploring Engineering (IJITEE) Volume-9 Issue-3, January 2020.
15. Arjun B. Channegowda and H N Prakash, Multimodal biometrics of fingerprint and signature recognition using multi-level feature fusion and deep learning techniques, Indonesian Journal of Electrical Engineering and Computer Science Vol. 22, No. 1, pp. 187–195, April 2021
16. Mehwish L., Shahzad Memon, Lachhman Das Dhomeja, Akhtar Hussain Jalbani and Asghar Ali Chandio, Deep Feature Fusion of Fingerprint and Online Signature for Multimodal Biometrics, MDPI, 2021.
17. Nada A. and Heyam H. Al-Baity, A multimodal biometric system for personal verification based on different level fusion of iris and face traits, Biosci. Biotech. Res. Comm. 12(3): 767-778, 2019.
18. Connor S. and Taghi M. Khoshgoftaar, A survey on Image Data Augmentation for Deep Learning, Springer 2019.
19. Muhammad U. Munir and Dr. M. Y. Javed, Fingerprint Matching using Gabor Filters, National Conference on Emerging Technologies, 2004.

20. Karen S. and Andrew Zisserman, VERY DEEP CONVOLUTIONAL NETWORKS FOR LARGE-SCALE IMAGE RECOGNITION, Published as a conference paper at ICLR, 2015.
21. U. Gawande and Yogesh G., Biometric security system: a rigorous review of unimodal and multimodal biometrics techniques, Int. J. Biometrics, Vol. 10, No. 2, 2018.

Enhanced Technique for Exemplar Based Image Inpainting Method

Shivanand Patil[1]([⊠]), V. S. Malemath[1], and Suman Muddapur[2]

[1] KLE Dr. M. S. Sheshgiri College of Engineering and Technology, Belagavi, Karnataka, India
shpatil102@gmail.com
[2] Sangolli Rayanna First Grade Constituent College Belagavi, Belagavi, India

Abstract. Image Inpainting expertise in reconstructing mislaid image parts. It is the technique for filling an unknown area or scratched area of an Image developed on the nearby information present in the image that is not recognizable by ordinary viewer. In proposed method two Inpainting algorithms, the traditional exemplar-based Image Inpainting and structure tensor inpainting technique has been used. The traditional Criminisi's Image Inpainting method is simple and fast but veracity of the image is weakened and the output image results in blurriness's. To resolve this issue structure tensor Inpainting method has been introduced in the proposed method. The structure tensor algorithm gives more accuracy of the image by using Image structure tensor information. The experimental results are obtained by comparing the Criminisi's method and the proposed method by PSNR, SSIM, MSE and SNR. Structure tensor method significantly improves Inpainting quality compared with traditional Criminisi's method.

Keywords: Image Inpainting · Criminisi's algorithm · Structure tensor

1 Introduction

Nowadays, people are much more interested in clicking pictures, images which are stored as memories and lots are the sources of valuable information. With the age, the images, photographs often get damaged. A technique in the Image Processing field which solves this kind of problem known as the Image Inpainting Technique. This technique helps in the reconstruction of the damaged region of images as similar to the original image and used for removing unrequired objects, scratches, superimposed text like dates, subtitles from the image in an undetectable way. The Image Inpainting idea is first proposed by author Criminisi in 2006. Image Inpainting is the algorithm that shows there is no visual discrepancy among the Inpainting and original image and it gives better results. Applications of image inpainting are the recovery of a picture, eliminating an object, compression, restoration, rebuilding the missing places in the photograph, etc. Various categories of image inpainting techniques exist. The primitive method that is Texture synthesis incorporated to consummate the lost portion in the image. This algorithm utilizes similar neighborhoods of damaged pixels imitation and sampling from the nearest region to fill the missing area. Partial Differential Equation (PDE)

© The Author(s) 2023
R. Manza et al. (Eds.): ACVAIT 2022, AISR 176, pp. 153–163, 2023.
https://doi.org/10.2991/978-94-6463-196-8_14

Based Image Inpainting is used to endure geometrical and photometrical informatics seems at the edge of the damaged region. This method gives better results for the small destructive regions and if that region is large then the output results in blurriness. Hybrid Inpainting technique cooperate with two techniques such as texture synthesis and Partial Differential Equation-Based method. Semi-Automatic and Fast Inpainting technique has two steps in the process first is, the user provides mislaid details in the aperture by drawing object edges then texture emulsion is performed. Semiautomatic tactics consume more time from minutes to hours to complete the inpainting of the image. Exemplar based inpainting technique is more efficient for image inpainting than other methods. The algorithm consists of a selection of the unwanted object to be removed and recovering the selected area. It selects the best matching patch in the image apart from the selected area. It consists of steps as figuring the target portion, calculating patch priorities, finding greatest identical patch, and updating in-painted area. When a person takes a snapshot, there might be some unwanted objects in between so to remove such unwanted objects and can fill that area using surrounding patches of the image the software is needed. The proposed method has been used to solve this issue. Where Criminisi's algorithm is improved by adding a structure tensor method. In traditional Criminisi's inpainting method image veracity decreases and the output image results in blurriness's. To resolve this issue structure tensor Inpainting method has been introduced in the proposed algorithm. The structure tensor algorithm gives more accuracy of the image by using Image structure tensor information. Compared to the traditional Criminisi algorithm this proposed improved method gives better results.

2   Literature Review

Criminisi et al. [1] have come up with the Exemplar based image Inpainting method to eliminate huge unrequired portion from the image and to remove small cracks by merging texture synthesis and inpainting technique. The method results in speed efficiency and accuracy of synthesis of texture. Bing Yu and Ding [2] have improved exemplar-based image inpainting algorithms with fastened global optimal search which can effectively maintain the texture and structure characteristics of the lost region. Vidya Krishnamoorthy et al. [3] upgrades the method used for elimination of unrequired portion from the photograph by applying exemplar-based image inpainting techniques and is suitable for images with linear patterns, complete preferred objects. S. Zahra Siadati et al. [4] proposed inpainting algorithm that uses tensor to tackle convoluted structures. This algorithm gives better results in the image accuracy than other methods and information about gradient directions and their coherence. Liu Ying et al. [5] have proposed an improved algorithm that provides a greater advantage in the exactness of figure structure contrast with the Criminisi method. Also, progresses in visual effects. Seema Dixit et al. [6] have proposed an exemplar based image inpainting technique that splits the images and search the region. This proposed clustering method reduces time complications and improves image fidelity. Jayesh Patel [7] have proposed the method where searching pixels procedure reduced to the neighbouring regions rather than exploring the whole image. The user chooses the region to be inpaint and the algorithm automatically starts filling the portion. The process is based on pixel priority. Higher the priority of the pixel region filling is faster. Huaming LIU [12] have proposed a method of screen window propagation for image inpainting. Where the higher layer leads the bottom layer inpainting for various resolution reduction. The priority calculation is upgrade using higher improve results can lead to acquire a superior repair order.

3 Methodology

Implementation of the proposed method shown in following Fig. 1.

3.1 Input Image

Input Image is a photograph, natural image for processing that contain both coloured, black and white images of different sizes. The input image should be in JPG and PNG format. The uploaded image is displayed in the Matlab GUI window to carry out inpainting processes.

3.2 Perform Cropping

The selected image contains unwanted objects or unrequired portions to be eliminated. In Perform Cropping Module, the unwanted region of image is cropped by using "imfreehand" function in MATLAB. It creates mask on selected portion with desired colour.

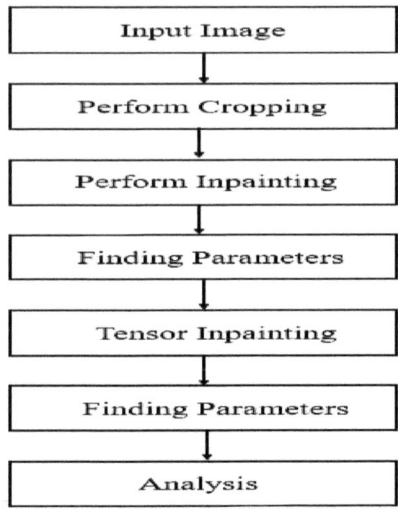

Fig. 1. System Overview

3.3 Perform Inpainting by Criminisi Method

Criminisi's algorithm combines the avails of both texture emulsion and inpainting techniques. The method eliminates unrequired portion from the image by creating a mask known as target region. Pre-setting the priorities for the target part based on image structures and textures. The higher priority pixel is elected as a patch centre with size 9 * 9 for each iteration. The most same patch with the least discrepancies is selected to load the required portion. During this, the patch in the source region content will be imitated into the selected inpainted region. Loading the selected inpainted region by patch degrades the running time (Fig. 2).

The masked object is eliminated by the traditional Exemplar based method. It contains the following steps:

Step1: Computing the Target Region of given Input Image

The user is allowed to select the image to be inpainted. The area that is not required or to be removed is selected and that is made visible by the mask of desired color that is green color (Fig. 3).

Step2: Calculating patch Priorities:

Reconstruction of inpainted portion in the desired image takes place by calculating the pixel priority Pr(p) over damaged region's edge.

The patch priority is obtained by multiplication of confidence term and data term as shown below:

$$Pr(p) = Cr(p) * Dr(p) \qquad (1)$$

where, $Cr(p)$ – confidence term

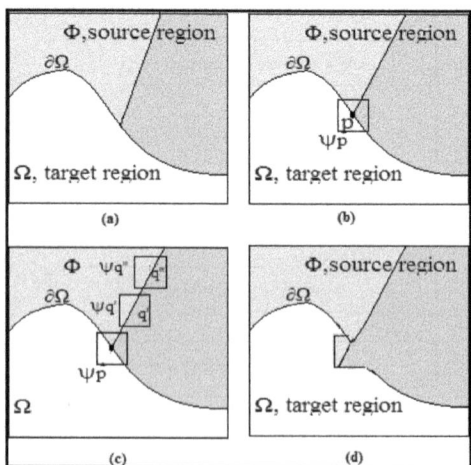

Fig. 2. Patch-based Inpainting, (a) Input Image contains Source region (Φ), Target region (Ω) and the boundary contour ($\partial\Omega$) (b) Patch with highest priority (c) Candidate patches $\Psi q'$ and $\Psi q''$ located approximately either on the same edge or same coloured edge. (d) The patch $\Psi q'$ is the matching patch.

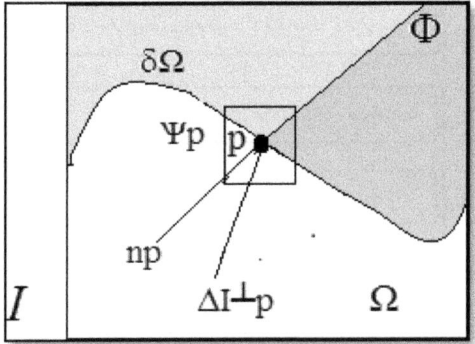

Fig. 3. The image is denoted as I while Φ is the source region, Ω is the target region and $\partial\Omega$ is the borderline between the source and target region. Consider the patch p, normal to the outline of target region is denoted as np and $\Delta I^{\perp}p$ is the gradient at point p.

$Dr(p)$ – data term

$$Cr(p) = \sum q \in \varphi p \cap (1 - \Omega) \frac{c(p)}{\varphi p} \tag{2}$$

where, (p) equals zero for target region and $Cr(p)$ equals one for source region

$$D_r(p) = \frac{\Delta I^{\perp} \cdot n_p}{\propto} \tag{3}$$

where, gradient of pixel is $\Delta I^{\perp}p$ and n p is unit vector perpendicular to the border $\partial\Omega$.

Step3: Finding the greatest identical patch.

The identical priority area in the source region is searched and priority of each pixel is obtained. The pixel having largest priority among they assimilated with the targeted portion over the source area and produced as follows.

$$\varphi_{qr} = arg^{min}_{\varphi p \in \Phi} d(\Psi\mathbf{p}-, \Psi\mathbf{q}) \tag{4}$$

Step4: Updating selected inpainting region.

The obtained best match patch of an image is copied and enhances the target region.

Repetition of all the steps arises till the target part of image is completely processed and produces the inpainting image which is similar to original image.

3.4   Finding Parameters

In this module, the Mean Squared Error (MSE), Signal-to-Noise Ratio (SNR), Peak Signal-to-Noise Ratio (PSNR), and Structural Similarity Index Measure (SSIM) is calculated between original image and inpainted image that is Criminised image (Fig. 4).

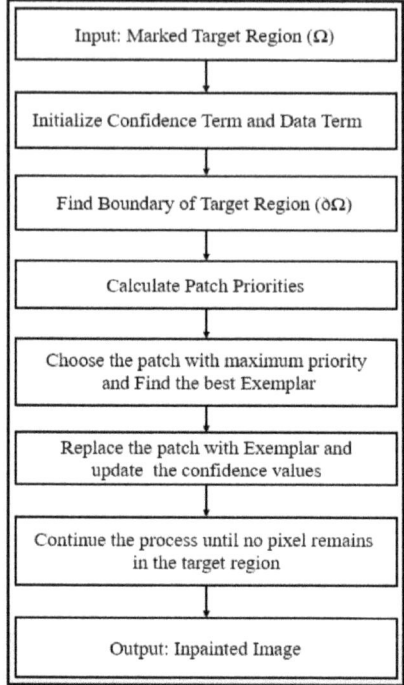

Fig. 4. Flow Chart

3.5 Perform Tensor Inpainting

In this module, same traditional Criminisi algorithm is used with some modification. The product of the confidence and data term in algorithm increases the pixel counts which affects the loading order. If the confidence term is nearly zero for pixel p in the equation of confidence term and data term, the maximum priority will be close to zero. This verdict smaller value of priority. The structure content is added prior to the data term explained by structure tensor algorithm as the data term cannot provide the structure details of an image.

Structure tensor, a second moment-matrix is invented by Forstner and Glush that provides gradients directions and consistency of pixel in the image. The image structure analysis can be obtained by Eigen values. The neighbouring structure content is added to the data term prior the calculation of Patch priorities.

Let I represent the image and the gradient vector is given as follows,

$$\nabla I = \begin{pmatrix} Ix \\ \overline{Iy} \end{pmatrix} \tag{5}$$

The structure tensor is shown as,

$$J\rho = g\rho \otimes Jo \tag{6}$$

where,

$$Jo = \frac{Ix^2 \quad IxIy}{IxIy \quad Iy^2} \tag{7}$$

Gaussian kernel is defined as follow,

$$gp = \frac{1}{2\pi\sigma^2} e^{\frac{x^2+y^2}{2\sigma}} \tag{8}$$

where, Image I contains Ix and Iy as horizontal and vertical vector gradient components of each pixels respectively. The σ represents the breath of the Gaussian kernel and the square of it, $\sigma2$ is the variance and $\otimes$ denotes the convolution operator.

The structure control function is represented as shown,

$$h = (e(1) - e(2))^{\wedge}2 \tag{9}$$

$$F_s(p) = k \cdot h + exp(-h) \tag{10}$$

The patch priorities is shown as,

$$P(p) = C(p)^*(D(p) + F_s(p)) \tag{11}$$

Eigen values of structure tensor provides valuable data for structure analysis. The attributes of tensors are important in the algorithm. Where searching for the matching patch in the image reduces error in matching rate and ensures higher similarity for the target region of the image.

4 Experimental Results

The images that need to be inpainted are selected. The result yields in two output images as Criminisi's method and the proposed method. The evaluation of inpainted images is done by taking MSE, SNR, PSNR and SSIM of both methods. The proposed method compares with to the traditional Criminisi's method as shown in the Fig. 5. The results of proposed approach is tabulated in Table 1. The observation concludes the SSIM values and other calculated values like MSE, SNR; PSNR for proposed approach provides greater results than traditional Criminisi's method. The results are displayed for removing unwanted region in the image with Criminisi's method and proposed method (Tables 2, 3 and Fig. 6).

Table 1. Result images with proposed method and Criminisi's Method

Images	Original Image	Mask	Criminisi's Method	Proposed Method
Image 1				
Image 2				
Image 3				
Image 4				
Image 5				
Image 6				

Table 2. Numerical Analysis of Inpainted Images by Criminisi method

Criminisi's Method	MSE	SNR	PSNR	SSIM
Image 1	497.323	15.6158	21.1644	0.931838
Image 2	209.608	17.4746	24.9167	0.938022
Image 3	43.7815	25.4941	31.7179	0.987476
Image 4	203.134	21.8653	25.053	0.971146
Image 5	293.503	17.4769	23.4547	0.967412
Image 6	253.533	18.4988	24.0905	0.958178

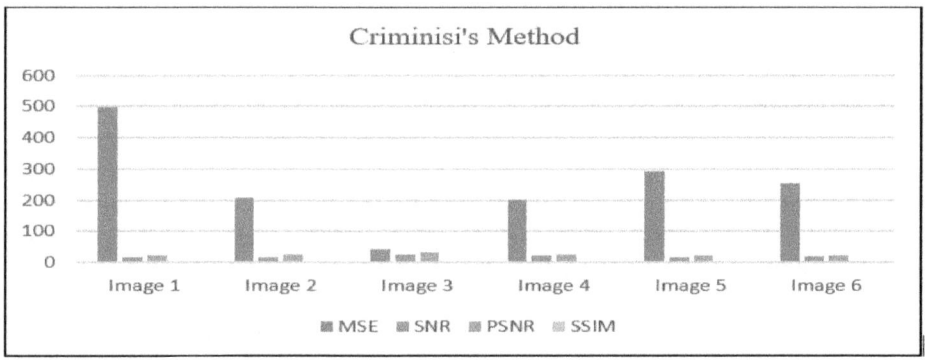

Fig. 5. Graph representation of Numerical analysis by Criminisi Method

Table 3. Numerical Analysis of Inpainted Images by Proposed Method

Proposed Method	MSE	SNR	PSNR	SSIM
Image 1	473.599	15.8281	21.3767	0.940647
Image 2	187.305	17.9631	25.4053	0.938073
Image 3	56.6925	24.3717	30.5955	0.987959
Image 4	140.482	23.4669	26.6546	0.979732
Image 5	326.579	17.0132	22.9909	0.973922
Image 6	190.847	19.7323	25.324	0.964334

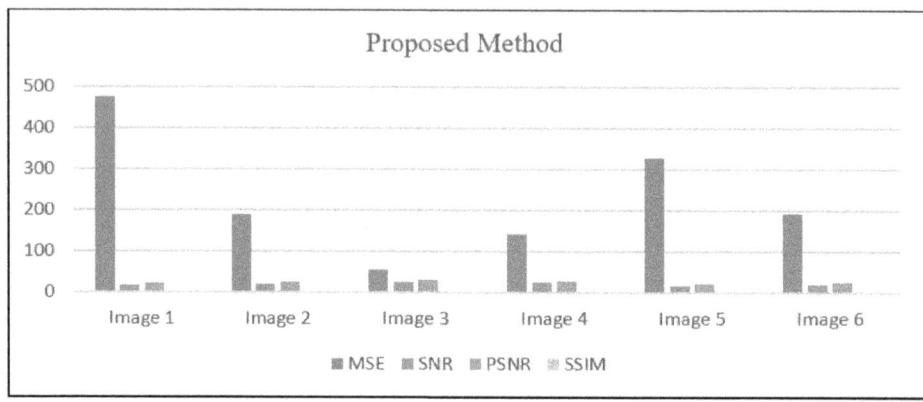

Fig. 6. Numerical Analysis of Inpainted Images by Proposed Method

5   Conclusion

Image Inpainting method perform a measure part in Image Processing. It is a procedure of eliminating unwanted regions or restoring damage area based on surrounding area in the image. The proposed inpainting algorithm provides greater verdicts compared with the traditional Criminisi's method. That is shown by using the Mean Square Error (MSE), Signal-to-Noise Ratio (SNR), Peak Signal-to-Noise Ratio (PSNR), and Structural Similarity Index Measure (SSIM). The future scope for this approach is to reduce the runtime of the algorithm to get more faster results.

References

1. A. Criminisi, Patrick Perez, and Kentaro Toyama, "Region filling and object removal by exemplar-based image inpainting", IEEE, 2004. p 1200-1212 https://doi.org/10.1109/TIP. 2004.83310.
2. Bing Yu, and Youdong Ding, "Exemplar- based Image Inpainting via Fast Global Optimal Searching. "IEEE 2017, DOI: https://doi.org/10.1109/IAEAC.2017.8054110.
3. Vidya Krishnamoorthy, and Senthilkumar Mathi, "An enhanced method for object removal using exemplar-based image inpainting." International Conference on Computer Communication and Informatics (ICCCI), 2017, DOI: https://doi.org/10.1109/ICCCI.2017.811 7690.
4. S. Zahra Siadati, Farzin Yaghmaee, and Peyman Mahdavi, "A new exemplar-based image inpainting algorithm using image structure tensors." Electrical Engineering (ICEE), 24th Iranian Conference on. IEEE, 2016.DOI: https://doi.org/10.1109/IranianCEE.2016.7585666
5. Liu, Ying, et al, "A Novel Exemplar-Based Image Inpainting Algorithm." International Conference on Intelligent Networking and Collaborative Systems." IEEE, 2015, DOI https://doi. org/10.1109/INCoS.2015.15
6. Seema Dixit and Saranjeet Singh, "Exemplar-Based Image Inpainting Technique using Image Partitioning (Search Region Prior) Method." IJSTE-International Journal of Science Technology & Engineering1, 2014.
7. Patel Jayesh, and Tanuja K. Sarode, "Exemplar based image inpainting with reduced search region." International Journal of Computer Applications vol 92 No 12, 2014.

8. Miss S C Bhangale, and Asst Prof PR Thorat, "Image Inpainting Using Modified Exemplar-Based Method." International Research Journal of Engineering and Technology, Vol: 03 Issue: 09,2016.
9. Chhabra, Jaspreet Kaur, and Mr Vijay Birchha, "Detailed survey on exemplar-based image inpainting techniques." International Journal of Computer Science and Information Technologies Vol. 5(5),2014, pp 6350–6354
10. Yu-Ting HE, Xiang-Hong TANG, "Color Image Inpainting by an Improved Criminisi Algorithm." ITM Web of Conferences vol 12 (2017), DOI: https://doi.org/10.1051/itmconf/201 71205023.
11. Hemangini G. Patel, Narendra Limbad, "Object Removal using Image Inpainting" International Journal for Science Research and Development ISSN: 2321–0631. (2015)
12. Huaming Liu, Xuehui Bi, Guanming LU, Weilan Wang, Jingjie Yan, and Zhengyan Zhang, "Screen Window Propagation for Image Inpainting" IEEE Access (2018), DOI: https://doi.org/10.1109/ACCESS.2018.2876161
13. H Chinmayee Rao et al, "Image Inpainting using exemplar-based technique with improvised data term", International Conference on Computational Techniques, Electronics and Mechanical Systems (CTEMS), 2018, DOI: https://doi.org/10.1109/CTEMS.2018.8769238

An Optimal (2, 2) Visual Cryptography Schemes For Information Security

Datta R. Somwanshi[1](✉) and Vikas T. Humbe[2]

[1] Department of Computer Science, College of Computer Science and Information Technology (COCSIT), Latur, Maharashtra, India
somwanshi1234@gmail.com
[2] School of Technology, Swami Ramanand Teerth Marathwada University, Nanded, Latur, Maharashtra, India

Abstract. Visual information security is one of the important security aspects. Secret sharing based schemes of visual cryptography permits secret image encryption and provides a more secure method which allows access to more sensitive visual information. In modern k out of n secret sharing scheme secret image to be encrypted that is partitioned into n different parts or shares. Each part or share is then distributed among the n users are different, and then we can specify at least k out of n shares are needed to get the original secret image. Recently many Secrets Sharing Schemes of visual cryptography have been developed ranging from (2 out of 2 or 2, 2) Visual Cryptography Schemes to Segment based secret sharing schemes of visual cryptography. But most of the schemes are based on processing the binary image as secret, which is not suitable for many applications that are using color information images, and the security of the share is an important issue that is less discussed in previous work. Again there are many problems of secret sharing schemes such as pixel expansions, alignment problems, extensive requirement of the codebook design, flipping issues, distortion problem, and thin line problems are quite unresolved.

In this paper a new secure (2, 2) secret sharing scheme is suggested for securely transmitting the images over the network. The suggested approach can also provide more secured shares and overcome the problems such as pixel expansion, alignment problem, extensive codebook design, flipping Issues, and distortion problem. Finally the result is compared with previously known methods. The Results obtained and the analysis of the suggested method is used to predict the efficiency of the method.

Keywords: (2, 2) Visual Cryptography Scheme · Contrast Optimal Scheme · extensive codebook design · No Pixel Expansion · No flipping Issues

1 Introduction

Visual Cryptography (VC) allows us to encrypt the written material that is in the form of images, printed text, and handwritten notes, etc. in a perfectly secure way and that can be decoded directly by the visual systems of humans [1]. It is one of the most

© The Author(s) 2023
R. Manza et al. (Eds.): ACVAIT 2022, AISR 176, pp. 164–177, 2023.
https://doi.org/10.2991/978-94-6463-196-8_15

powerful cryptography techniques and requires only encryption. Means there is no need for decryption and it does not require huge calculations for the decryption of the text. Because of this, everyone can use the system without acquiring the knowledge about encryption or decryption of cryptography and fail to carry out any computations.

This technique was first introduced by Naor et al. [1], in 1994. In this technique the message or image data to be protected or encrypted is divided into n different parts or shares. Each part or share is distributed among the n different users, and then we can specify at least k out of n shares are stacked together or required to get the original information. The k-1 shares cannot be used to generate the original message. For example, suppose there are six thieves who want to share a bank account, but the problem is they don't trust one another, and they split up the password that is required for transaction from an account and each part of the password is provided to individual thieves. While splitting up the password they implement such a mechanism that at least three or more than that have to come together, they have to provide their part of the password, then it will be combined together and will be provided to the system for performing transactions.

Each Pixel in the original binary image that is to be secured is divided into two or more blocks. There should be the same number of black and white pixel blocks. if any pixel is split up into two shares there will be one black and one white block. Similarly if any pixel is split up into four equal shares then there will be two black blocks and two white blocks [1, 2, 3]. The example Fig. 1 uses pixels that are divided into two parts.

The basic idea of (2, 2) Visual Cryptography is depicted in Fig. 1. The image that is to be secure is split up into 2 equal parts or shares. In each part 2, 4 or 8 sub-pixels blocks which are non-overlapping will be used to represent a single pixel from the original image. All the pixels in the original image are represented in this way and shares will be formed. A user having the single share cannot be able to reconstruct the original secret image. Both two shares are needed to reconstruct the original secret image [1].

For encrypting the pixels of an image, recently many methods have been developed. For one of the methods, every pixel in the image that is to be secured is split up into two pixels in every share. While reading and converting the original image into shares,

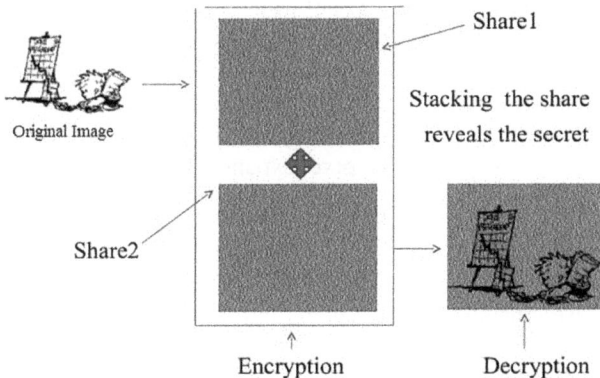

Fig. 1. Basic Idea of Visual Cryptography

Table 1. (2, 2) Secrete Sharing Scheme.

Original Image	Probability	Share1 Sub-Pixel	Share2 Sub-Pixel	Share1 ‖ Share2
☐	0.5	◨	◨	◨
☐	0.5	◧	◧	◧
■	0.5	◨	◧	■
■	0.5	◧	◨	■

if the pixel value encountered is one it means the white pixel then one of the rows from the first two rows displayed in Table 1 is picked up. The probability of this is 0.5 and the 2 pixel blocks mentioned in the third and fourth column of Table 1 are selected and shares are assigned. Similarly, if the pixel value encountered is zero it means the black pixel, then one of the rows from the last two rows displayed in Table 1 is picked up. The probability of this is also 0.5 and the 2 pixel blocks mentioned in the third and fourth column of Table 1 are selected and shares are assigned, in this way shares are formed.

When reconstructing the original image from the two shared images, if the two pixels in two shares images are white, then the reconstructed pixel will white and if the one share image contains black pixels and the other share image contains either black or white then the reconstructed pixel will be black. So, this kind of operation can be achieved using Boolean OR operations. The result of this operation is depicted in the last column of Table 1 when the third and fourth columns are used in the reconstruction process [1].

Problems such as Improper alignment of pixels due to which image may look different, distortions of shares due to which original image may not be reconstructed properly, flipping issues due to which image may not be reconstructed in proper directions. These are some of the issues that may arise while reconstructing the original image from share images, Also for generating the shares there is need of a codebook using which the shares can be created; expansion of the pixels also needs to be taken care of, so that the size of share images will not increase. The Proposed novel (2, 2) methods eliminated all of the problems listed above except little bit pixel expansion.

2 Literature Review

Naor et al. [1] have generalized the scheme into (k, n), in which at least k shares are required from n different shares. In a generalized (k, n) scheme, 'n' shares of the original secret image are created and distributed to all n participants. For the reconstruction of the original image from the share images, at least k shares are necessary, less than k shares cannot be used to reconstruct the original image. This gives flexibility to the user.

if some of the shares are lost, still the secrete image can be formed from share images with only k shares or greater than equal to k and less than equal to n shares.

Ateniese et.al [6] further extended this (k, n) scheme and called it a general access structure. In this type shares generated are bifurcated into subsets of shares and which are called qualified subset and forbidden subset, this is as per the importance given to the subsets of shares. Any k numbers of shares from the subsets of qualified shares can be used to reconstruct the original image, but less than k numbers of shares cannot be used to reconstruct the original image. In case of shares from the forbidden subsets, any k, more than k cannot be used to reconstruct the original image. So the general access structure of visual cryptography can be used to enhance the security of the system. Abhishek p, et al. [7] presented the new scheme called "Recursive threshold Visual Cryptography", The major idea of this type of scheme is, its hides the small secrete information into the shares of the large secrete recursively, it means the secret size doubled at every steps, and therefore it increases the secret information. Every single bit carries n-1/n bits and which is nearer to 100%. Zhi Zhou et al. [4, 5] have profound he new scheme called half-tone visual cryptography, In this scheme every pixel converts into coded form which are simply the array of sub-pixels and called half-tone cell. Using these half-tone cells of suitable size, shares of the image can be more pleasant. Means that there will be good contrast and quality of the image will be maintained and also it improves the security of the shares. Chang-Chou Lin et al. [8] worked on the gray scale image and proposed the scheme for gray level images. In the scheme proposed, a process called dithering technique is used that can be used to transform the gray level image into a binary image and binary image look similar to gray level image. The rest of the method works similar to other methods proposed earlier. In addition to the gray level images the F. Liu et al. [9] introduced the new approach for working on color images which is called color visual cryptography scheme. They proposed the approach of separating the three color channels: red, green and blue and working with each color channel for generating the shares. The approach introduced by them overcomes the pixel expansion problem, but because of the half-toning process the quality of the image gets reduced. To share the two secret information images in two different shares Wu and Chen [10] introduces the new scheme. In this proposed scheme two different binary secrete images are used to hide inside the two different random shares called A, and B. The secrete images are hidden in such a way that, the first secrete image can be reconstructed by superimposing the shares using XOR operation A $\otimes$ B, and the second secret image can be reconstructed by rotating share A anti-clockwise by 90 degree. In addition to this Shyu et al. [11, 12] proposed the scheme for sharing the multiple secret image, through which two or more secret information images can be hidden or secured at the same time in two different shares.

3   Methodology

The proposed research is focused on secure (2, 2) visual cryptography scheme for information security. There are many secrete sharing scheme are designed such as (k, n), Half toning, Multi-resolutions etc. [1, 2]. In k out of n shares scheme, consider the set p from n number of participants, the visual secret image S, that is encrypted or divided in to "n" shadow images, these are called shares or parts where each participant gets a share to be used for getting the original message or visual image. The original message will be visible if only k or more than k is combined or superimposed together. Less than k cannot be used for getting the original message [2].

Consider the message that is to be encoded is composed of a set of white and black pixels and every pixel is processed separately. Each share of the participant is a set of m white and black sub-pixels. The derived image can be assumed as a [n × m] boolean matrix S = [s, i, j].

We can consider that s, i, j = 1 if the jth sub-pixel in the ith share is black and s i, j = 0 if the jth sub-pixel in the ith share is white.

The proposed methodology is as shown in Fig. 3. The information that is to be secure or the image that is to be protected is taken as input. Various applications such as biometric security, online voting system using biometric characteristics, secure banking transaction are the application of visual secret sharing scheme. Pre-processing of input image is performed if there is a need of application. Then next step is to divide the input image into two or more share as per the need of application. Then next step is to divide the input image into two or more share as per the need of application. Each share is then provided to the participants (this can be provided via email or any other application) (Table 2).

Participants will now provide his share whenever needed. Finally shares are combined together and final image is formed. In this proposed study we have used 2, 2 secrete

Table 2. Relative review and study of different scheme of Visual cryptography

Name of Authors	Title of scheme and year of publication	Type of Image	Used techniques
Mahmoud E. Hodeish, Vikas T. Humbe	An Optimized Hal-ftone-Visual Cryptography Scheme Using Error Diffusion-2018 [18]	Binary and Gray Scale Images	Improves and reduces the pixel expansion problems, Eliminate requirement codebook design, They also reduces the random pattern of the share images and Evaluate the performance analysis using different statistical methods

(continued)

Table 2. (*continued*)

Name of Authors	Title of scheme and year of publication	Type of Image	Used techniques
Shivendra Shivani	Verifiable Multi-tone Visual Cryptography- 2017 [17]	Gray Scale and Color Image	For a pixel in share a self-embedding verifiable bit is added for the prevention of cheating and testing the integrity of the pixel. Overcomes the problem of random shares, requirement of codebook.
Mahmoud E. Hodeish, Linas Bukauska, Vikas T. Humbe	An Optimal (k, n) Visual Secret Sharing Scheme for Information Security 2016 [15]	Binary Image	(k, out of n) scheme based on designed codebook, and transport of matrices, n-Vector, and XOR boolean operation are used
Angel Rose, A Sabu, M Thampi	A Secure and Verifiable Scheme for Secret Image Sharing 2015 [14]	Binary Image, gray scale image	Arnold transformation technique Bit-Plane Complexity Steganography, Mean-Square-Error (MSE) and Structural-Similarity-Index value test
Souvik Roy and P. Venkateswaran	"Online Payment System using Steganography and Visual Cryptography" 2014 [13]	Binary Image, gray scale image	text based steganography, and Visual Cryptography
Rajendra A B and Sheshadri H S	"Visual Cryptography in Internet Voting System" 2013 [16]	Gray Level Image	2-out-of-2 Visual Cryptography

sharing scheme and problems such as alignment problem, distortion, thin line problem occurred while combining the share are minimized.

Algorithms for the Proposed Method

1. Read the Input Image as below
2. Calculate the Size of Image
3. Create two empty shares *share1, share2* whose size is equal to the original secrete image and fill with zeros
4. Initialize the two array of 1X2 for creating two shares
   Code1 = [1 0];
   Code2 = [1 0];
5. Check and process the white pixel as below, if pixel value in input image is 1 then get row number and columns numbers where the value is 1
   [x y] = find   (InputImg == 1);
6. Calculate total number of rows where there is 1
   Len = length(x);
7. Iterate through numbers of rows
   For i=1: Len
            a=x (i); b=y (i);
            Call to Share Generation Procedure for getting the pair of pixel if input pixel value is 1as below
            PixelShare=ShareGenration(Code1,Code2);
            share1 ((a), (2*b+1) :(2*b))
   =PixelShare(1,1:2);
            share2 ((a), (2*b+1) :(2*b))
   =PixelShare(2,1:2);
   End
8. Initialize the 2,2 code block for creating two shares
   Code3= [1 0];
   Code4 = [0 1];
9. Check and Process the Black pixel as below, if pixel value in input image is 0 then get row number and columns numbers where the value is 0
   [x y] = find (InputImg == 0);
10. Calculate total number of rows where there is 0 in input image
   Len = length(x);
11. Iterate through numbers of rows
   For i=1: Len
            a=x (i); b=y (i);
            Call to Share Generation Procedure for getting the pair of pixel if input pixel value is 0
            PixelShare=ShareGenration(Code3,Code4);
            share1 ((a), (2*b-1): (2*b))
   =PixelShare(1,1:2);
            share2 ((a), (2*b-1): (2*b))
   =PixelShare(2,1:2);
   End
12. Combine the two Shares as using bitwise OR operator and complement the combined share
    share12=bitor(share1, share2);
    share12 = ~share12;

Share Generation Procedure which is invoked in previous algorithms works as below.

ShareGenration(codea, codeb) Procedure

1. Create two variable from 1x2 array codea as below
   a1 = codea (1);
   a2 = codea (2);
2. Create two variable from 1x2 array codeb as below
   b1 = codeb (1);
   b2 = codeb (2);
3. Assign codea and codeb to array in
   in = [codea
        codeb];
4. Create the out array of size in and fill the zeros
   out = zeros(size(in));
5. Select the random number between 0 and 1 and multiple this with 1.9 to get the floor value either 0 or 1 as below
   RandomNumber = floor(1.9*rand(1));
6. If (RandomNumber == 0)
       out = in;
   elseif (RandomNumber == 1)
           codea(1) = a2;
           codea(2) = a1;
           codeb(1) = b2;
           codeb(2) = b1;
           out = [codea
                  codeb];
   End of IF

7. Finally return the out array as below
   Return out
8. End of Procedure

4 Experimental Result

The result obtained using the above algorithm and procedure is presented as below. Figure 2 shows the input binary sample secrete image, Fig. 3 and Fig. 4 shows the generated share, share 1 and share2, and finally Fig. 5 shows the secrete image after combining the two shares.

5 Discussion and Performance Analysis

5.1 Pixel Expansion

The pixel expansion problem is reduced 100% using the scheme proposed. The size of the secret image and the size of the generated share image, and image after reconstructed using shares is exactly the same size that is represented in Fig. 2, 3, 4 and 5.

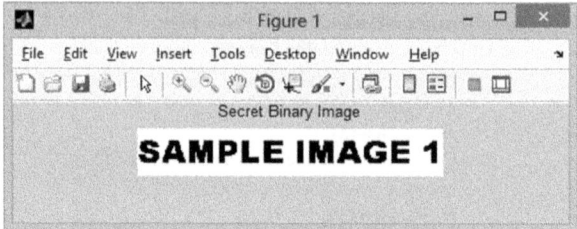

Fig. 2. Input binary sample secrete image

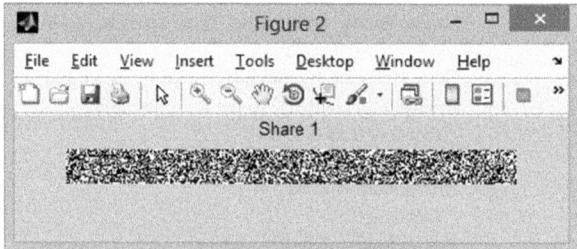

Fig. 3. Generated share, share 1

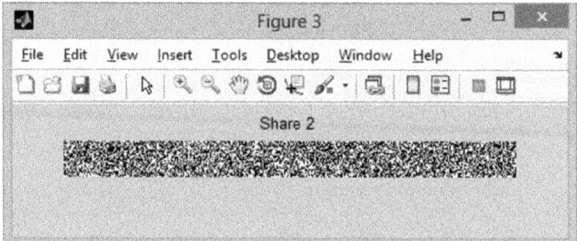

Fig. 4. Generated share, share2

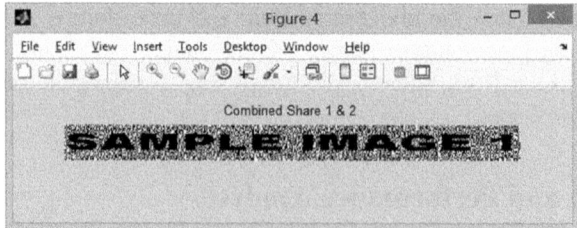

Fig. 5. Secrete image after combing two shares, share1 and share2

5.2 Contrast and Statistical Analysis

The image obtained after reconstruction is without the distortion of pixels, and that is the output displayed in Figs. 1, and Fig. 5. To estimate the quality of a reconstructed secret image and to demonstrate that the reconstructed secret image is of the same quality as of the original secret image, there are a variety of statistical analysis metrics of image restoration as presented below.

5.3 Mean Square Error

The formula to calculate Mean-Square-Error (MSE) [19] mathematically is presented as below.

$$MSE = \frac{1}{M \times N} \sum_{i=1}^{M} \sum_{j=1}^{N} (h_{ij} - h_{ij}')^2 \tag{1}$$

Where h_{ij} and h_{ij}' are the pixel values of original image and reconstructed secrete image, respectively

5.4 Peak-Signal-to-Noise-Ratio

Peak-Signal-to-Noise-Ratio (PSNR) [20] is also a mathematical and or engineering formulation calculated by using MSE and by the help of the Eq. 2 presented below.

$$PSNR = 10 * \log\log \frac{R^2}{MSE} \tag{2}$$

Statistically, when the value of PSNR $= 1$, it indicates that the scheme proposed delivers the extreme visual quality.

5.5 Universal-Index-Quality (UIQ)

Universal-Index-Quality (UIQ) can be calculated with the help of Eq. 3 displayed below[21].

$$UIQ = \frac{4\sigma_{zy}\underline{xy}}{\sigma_x^2 + \sigma_y^2 \left[(\underline{x})^2 + (\underline{y})^2 \right]} \tag{3}$$

Image deformation modeling operation can be performed with UIQ by using the three three parameters listed below.

1. Correlation loss,
2. Luminance distortion, &
3. Contrasts distortion

The range of the UIQ value is between *-1* to *+1*. The positive and a strong Linear-Correlation among the two pictures X and Y exists, if the UIQ values are close to *+1*. The UIQ value is *-1* then it represents there is a negative relationship between the two pictures and at the last the value of UIQ is zero then it represents that there is no any relationship between the two pictures [21].

5.6 Maximum Difference (MD)

This Maximum-Difference (MD) analysis factor is mainly used to determine the error among original secret information images and reconstructed secret information image. This MD factor is straight proportional with the contrast of image given and dynamic range and that can be can be determined using the Eq. 4 as displayed below [22]

$$MD = \max \left| x_{ij} - y_{ij} \right| \tag{4}$$

5.7 Average Difference (AD)

The Average-Difference is used to calculate the differentiation between the two images; that is the original image and image obtained after the reconstruction. The formula to calculate the Average-Difference (AD) of the original secret information image and the image obtained after the reconstruction of the secret image and that is estimated with the Average-Difference metrics as listed below [23].

$$AD = \frac{1}{M \times N} \sum_{i=1}^{M} \sum_{j=1}^{N} (X_{ij} - Y_{ij}) \tag{5}$$

In the above equation, the value of X, and Y are used to presents the secrete image that is in original form and the calculated or the reconstructed secrete image. All those values that are illustrated above are represented in Table 1.

Tables 1 shows the value of MSE, MD and AD are equal and which is zero, The value of PSNR is infinity ∞ and the values of UIQ is 1 presented and persuade that the reconstructed image and the original secret images have been completely extracted without any loss or damage of important and meaningful information of the reconstructed image. Table 3 represented those values.

We compare our method with previously known method the result obtained using different statistical measures are presented in Table 4.

Table 3. Shows the different metrics of statistical analysis metrics Obtained in experiment

Statistical Metrics	Value Obtained in Experiments
MSE	0
PSNR	∞
UIQ	1
MD	0
AD	0

Table 4. Results of comparison between the previously known methods and the proposed method using statistical measures

Scheme	Type of Image	Expansion of Pixel	Super-imposition Method	Aspect Ratio	Quality of Revealed Image
Zhou et al.'s scheme [4]	Binary(m x n)	$p = 4$	OR Operation	Changed	Better quality
Zhongmin Wang et. al.'s [5]	Binary(m x n)	$P = 4$	OR Operation	changed	Lossless
Mahmoud E. Hodeish et. al.'s [15]	Binary Halftone	$P = 2$	XOR Operation	changed	Lossless
Chang-Chou Lin [8]	Grey Level	$P = 4$	OR Operation	changed	Lossy
F. Liu et. al [9]	Color	$P = 4$	OR operation	changed	Lossy
The Proposed Scheme	Binary	$p = 1$	XOR Operation	unchanged	Lossless

6 Conclusion

In this paper a new secure (2, 2) secrete sharing scheme is developed to securely trans-mitting the images over network. The proposed approach provides secured shares and overcome the problems such as pixel expansion, alignment problem, extensive codebook design, flipping Issues, and distortion problem. Shares generated through this system are secure because share are depends on the random value, and while combining the two share problems of share alignment is minimized, also there is no distortion of shares, share size is minimum, and finally flipping issue is minimized. We have compared our results with previously known method, and we found more contrast optimal shares. The proposed method can be further modified for color images, and for creating verifiable shares.

References

1. Moni Naor and Adi Shamir, "Visual Cryptography," Eurocrypt, 1994
2. Jonathan weir and weiQi, Yan "Visual Cryptography and its Application", Ventus Publishing Aps, eBook, pp.1-144, 2012.
3. Ecaterina Moraru (Valica), "Visual Cryptography", Published in: Technology, Art & Photos on Slide share, pp. 1-38, 2008.
4. Zhi Zhou, Gonzalo R. Arce, and Giovanni Di Crescenzo," Halftone Visual Cryptography", IEEE TRANSACTIONS ON IMAGE PROCESSING, VOL. 15, NO. 8, pp. 2241-2453, AUGUST 2006

5. Zhongmin Wang, Student Member, IEEE, Gonzalo R. Arce, Fellow, IEEE, and Giovanni Di Crescenzo, "Halftone Visual Cryptography via Error Diffusion", IEEE TRANSACTIONS ON INFORMATION FORENSICS AND SECURITY, VOL. 4, NO. 3, pp. 383-396, SEPTEMBER 2009

6. G. Ateniese, C. Blundo, A. DeSantis, and D. R. Stinson, "Visual cryptography for general access structures", Proc.ICAL96, Springer, Berlin, 1996, pp. 416-428, 1996

7. Abhishek Parakh and Subhash Kak "A Recursive Threshold Visual Cryptography Scheme", CoRR abs/0902.2487, 2009

8. Chang-Chou Lin, Wen-Hsiang Tsai, "Visual cryptography for graylevel images by dithering techniques", Pattern Recognition Letters, v.24 n.1-3, 2003.

9. F. Liu, C.K. Wu, X.J. Lin, "Colour Visual Cryptography Schemes", IET Information Security, vol. 2,No. 4, pp 151-165, 2009.

10. C.C. Wu, L.H. Chen, "A Study On Visual Cryptography", Master Thesis, Institute of Computer and Information Science, National Chiao Tung University, Taiwan, R.O.C., 1998

11. S. J. Shyu, S. Y. Huanga, Y. K. Lee, R. Z. Wang, and K. Chen, "Sharing multiple secrets in visual cryptography", Pattern Recognition, Vol. 40, Issue 12, p. 3633-3651, 2007

12. Tzung-Her Chen n, Chang-Sian Wu," Efficient multi-secret image sharing based on Boolean operations", Signal Processing Volume 91, Issue 1, pp. 90-97, January 2011.

13. Souvik Roy and P. Venkateswaran," Online Payment System using Steganography and Visual Cryptography", IEEE Students' Conference on Electrical, Electronics and Computer Science, pp. 1-5, 2014.

14. Angel Rose A, Sabu M Thampi," A Secure Verifiable Scheme for Secret Image Sharing 2015", Procedia Computer Science 58, pp.140-150, 2015

15. Mahmoud E. Hodeish, Linas Bukauska, Vikas T. Humbe," An Optimal (k, n)Visual Secret Sharing Scheme for Information Security", Elsevier- Procedia Computer Science 93, pp.760 – 767, 2016.

16. Rajendra A B and Sheshadri H S "Visual Cryptography in Internet Voting System", IEEE, pp. 60-64, 2013.

17. Shivendra Shivani, "VMVC: Verifiable multi-tone visual cryptography", Springer, Multimed Tools Application, https://doi.org/10.1007/s11042-017-4422-6, pp.1-20, January 2017.

18. Mahmoud E. Hodeish and Vikas T. Humbe, "An Optimized Half tone Visual Cryptography Scheme Using Error Diffusion", Springer, Multimed Tools Application pp 1-17, January 2018.

19. Chen, C.Y., Chen, C.H., Chen, C.H., Lin, K.P., 2016. An automatic filtering convergence method for iterative impulse noise filters based on PSNR checking and filtered pixels detection. Expert Syst. Appl. 63, 198–207.

20. Shankar, K., Eswaran, P., February 2017. RGB based multiple share creation in visual cryptography with aid of elliptic curve cryptography. China Commun. 14 (2), 118–130. https://doi.org/10.1109/CC.2017.7868160.

21. Wang, Z., Bovik, A.C., 2002. A universal image quality index, IEEE Signal Process Lett.9 (3), 81–84.

22. Rajkumar, S., Malathi, G., 2016. A comparative analysis on image quality assessment for real time satellite images. Indian J. Sci. Technol. 9, 1–11

23. Ece, C., Mullana, M.M.U., 2011. Image quality assessment techniques in spatial domain, IJCST 2 (3).

A Numeral Script Identification
from a Multi-lingual Printed Document Image

Rajkumar Benne[1]([✉]), Shivanand Gornale[2], and Gayatri Patil[2]

[1] Government Autonomous College, Kalaburagi, India
rgbenne@gmail.com
[2] Rani Channamma University, Belagavi, India

Abstract. India is a multi-lingual multi-script country, where a printed document which contains information in the form of texts, images, etc.; the texts part may have composed with characters and numerals of one or more scripts. So, it is necessary Identify the scripts of numerals/characters from multilingual document before feeding them to their individual script OCR systems. In this paper, the system made an attempt to recognize the script of numerals belongs to Kannada, Devanagari, and English based on structural features like water reservoir, aspect ratio, horizontal and vertical strokes. Initially, Bi-script and tri-script numerals script identification experiments are conducted on a dataset of 2100 numerals string(word), by taking 700 samples for each script and noticed average accuracy for tri-script numerals is 93.62%.

Keywords: Script identification · documents · OCR

1 Introduction

India is Multi-lingual Multi-script country, the Indian printed document which contains information in the form of texts of various scripts and images so we need multilingual OCR system. The problem of developing an OCR system can be simplified by sub-categorizing the problem into script identification fallowed by numeral/character recognition. The characters and numerals recognition is out of the scope this paper. We can understand the recognition process of printed and handwritten numerals and characters is not complete without identifying the script of the numerals or characters, before developing a multi-script OCR.

The various authors have attempted to identify script of the text written in hand-printed or machine-printed at word level/block level/line level for Indian documents with various techniques [2–5, 16]. All these techniques, identifies the scripts of the text words or lines or blocks of text. But no one has reported about script identification of numerals. Meanwhile, many authors have made an attempt to recognize the numerals of single script and multi-script without script identification of numerals. We repeat and highlight some of the works reported for recognition of numerals with different feature sets including template based approaches and they can be seen in [6, 7]. In addition, structural feature based recognition system [8, 9], statistical feature based recognition

R. Manza et al. (Eds.): ACVAIT 2022, AISR 176, pp. 178–186, 2023.
https://doi.org/10.2991/978-94-6463-196-8_16

system [1], and hybrid approach based recognition systems [11, 12] are also seen. The task of numerals recognition without script identification can also be done; this kind of work is reported by Dhandra and U.Pal [9, 13, 14]. But, increase in the number of scripts increases the number of classes. In this case, the search space of recognition system increase and hence time complexity also increases. Therefore, it is not an appropriate way of dealing with multi-script numerals identification. In this direction, only few authors have made an attempt to identify the script of the numerals. For instance, G S Lehal and Nivedan Bhatt [15] presented a bilingual recognition system for handwritten numerals of Devanagari (Hindi) and English scripts and also attempted the problem of identification of numeral's script. They have used a set of global and local features to recognize the script of numerals, which are derived from the right and left projection profiles of the numeral image. The task of Multilingual handwritten numeral recognition using a robust deep network joint with transfer learning is presented by Amirreza Fateh [19] and the proposed system was tested with six different languages. Hangairulappan and others [17] reported work on isolated digits of Handwritten Numeral Recognition System. Shrey Malvi [20] claims the work on Variable Length Digit Recognition system for Gujarati Language. Sk Md Obaidullaha and others [18] reported a system of Numeral Script Identification from Handwritten Document Images only.

1.1 Motivation

All the works available in literature are mainly based on script identification from printed and handwritten documents. Some works are reported on numeral recognition from printed and handwritten documents. Till date very few works has been reported on printed Numeral Script Identification, which inspired us to carry out the present work. It has its applicability in different domain of 'smart computing' like automatic sorting of postal documents based on PIN code script, automatic classification of application forms, examination forms etc. written by native languages based on a numeral string.

2 Proposed Method

In this Section, an integrated approach of script identification of numerals for three scripts is presented. The tri-script numerals recognition problem is the ultimate solution to deal with tri-script documents of India. Such kind of recognition systems are helpful in bank transactions, income tax form processing, postal mail processing and various reservation counters. Recognition of numerals from multilingual document images has two approaches: (1) Recognition of numerals without script identification. (2) Identification of the numeral script is first and followed by the recognition of numerals. In the first approach, recognition of multilingual numerals is carried out by adding number of numeral classes to recognize numerals. In second approach, identification of script followed by recognition of numerals. Here, an attempt is made for script identification of numerals from multi-script document. We have used three scripts for experimentation and identification purpose.

For experimentation purpose, we have created our own printed numerals database. Printed numerals are collected from documents of Kannada, Devanagari, and English scripts of length 10 digits. A dataset of 2100 unconstrained printed numerals of Kannada, Devanagari and English scripts (700 each) are created. The Fig. 1 shows samples of numerals belonging to Kannada, English, and Devanagari scripts.

The India is Multi-lingual Multi-script country, the Indian printed document which contains information in the form of texts and images.

Identification of the script of the numerals consists of the following four stages:

- Acquisition and binarization of document image containing three script numerals.
- Pre-processing and segmentation of numerals from a document using the method proposed by [10].
- Extracted numerals are used for feature extraction.
- Structural features are used to describe each numeral and a single feature vector is formed.
- Using these features, NN classifier is trained. In the same way features are extracted from test numerals and used for identifying the script of the numerals.

The computation of structural feature like aspect ratio, density (fillhole), vertical and horizontal strokes, and water reservoir are discussed in detail.

Water reservoir based principle

If water is poured from one side of a component, the cavity regions of the component where water will be stored are considered as reservoirs. There are four types of water reservoirs, namely Left, Right, Top and Bottom reservoirs. In this chapter, top and bottom water reservoir that are used to identify the script.

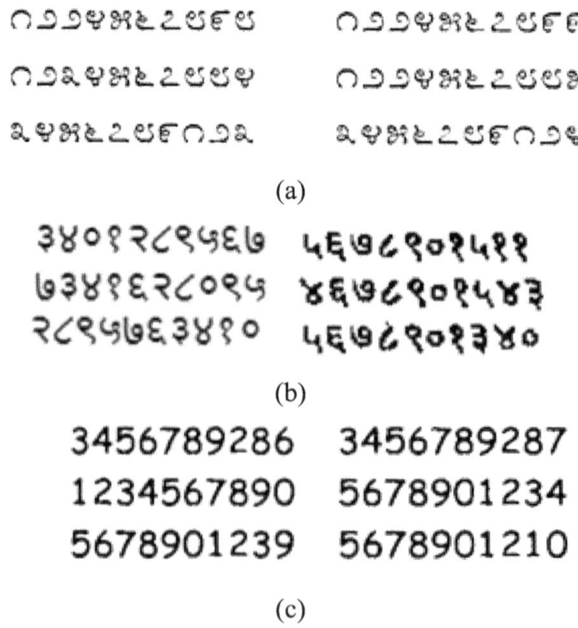

(a)

(b)

3456789286   3456789287
1234567890   5678901234
5678901239   5678901210

(c)

Fig. 1. Sample of numerals: (a) A samples of Kannada numerals. (b) A samples of English numerals. (c) A samples of Devanagari numerals

Top reservoir

The storage region of the water when the water is poured from top of the numeral image. Bottom reservoir: The storage region of the water when water is poured from bottom of the numeral image. Top and bottom reservoir of Kannada, English and Devanagari numerals samples are illustrated in Fig. 2. The observation of the scripts reveals that, the top and bottom reservoirs are present in Kannada script, bottom reservoir is absent in Devanagari script, whereas top and bottom absent in numerals of the English script.

Fill hole density

The looping area of the digits for a numeral is filled with ON pixels, the looping area of the digits varies from script to script. The fill hole density is calculated with respect the image (before fill the hole) and considered as a one of the feature for script identification problem.

Aspect Ratio

Aspect ratio of numeral is calculated by dividing height of the numeral by width of the numeral. The Average aspect ratio is calculated by using the following equation and considered as a one of the feature for script identification problem

Average Aspect Ratio (AVR)

$$(AVR) = \frac{1}{n} \sum\nolimits_{i=1}^{n} \frac{Height(image\ i)}{Width(image\ i)}$$

Directional stroke estimation:

The directional stroke of numeral image computed on vertical and horizontal direction using morphological transformation with line structuring element. Vertical stroke (VS) and horizontal stroke (HS) are extracted from words of numeral image and finally calculate the AVS and AHS features from below equation with respect to total on pixels of image, and considered for script identification problem. The Fig. 3 shows vertical and horizontal strokes obtained from words of numerals of Kannada, Devanagari and English script.

Average Vertical Stoke (AVS)

$$= \frac{1}{n} \sum_{i=1}^{n} \frac{On\ pixel\ from\ VD\ (image\ i)}{On\ pixel\ (image\ i)}$$

Average Horizontal Stoke (AHS)

$$= \frac{1}{n} \sum_{i=1}^{n} \frac{On\ pixel\ from\ HD\ (image\ i)}{On\ pixel\ (image\ i)}$$

Algorithm

The process of identification of script of the numerals is started by extracting a numeral from a document image. On extracted numerals the above proposed features are computed. The computations of features for test and training numerals remain same. The features extracted on trained images inputted to the classifier as a knowledge base. At the end, classifier decides the script of the numerals based on its knowledge base. The complete system of script identification of numerals is briefed out step-wise.

Input: Segmented numeral of three scripts.

Output: Identification of the script of numeral.

Method: Structural feature and Nearest Neighbor classifier.

Step 1. Pre-process the input image [numeral].

Step 2. Fit the minimum rectangle-bounding box to numeral.

Step 3. Extract the Water reservoir based features [Top reservoir and Bottom reservoir] and stored in the library.

Step 4. Calculate Aspect Ratio of numeral and stored in the library

Step 5. Find Fill hole density of numeral and stored in the library

Step 6. Extract the Directional stoke estimation in Vertical direction and Horizontal direction and stored in the library

Step 7. Classify the test image to its appropriate class label using Feature vector stored in the library with NN classifier

Step 8. Stop.

3   Experimental Results

For the purpose of experimentation, 2100 samples of printed numerals of Kannada, Devanagari and English scripts are used. Same data set is used for training and testing purposes, which includes 700-Kannada, 700-English and 700-Devanagari numerals of length ten digits. In the proposed system, simple structural features: Water reservoir, fill hole density, aspect ratio, horizontal and vertical stroke are considered. The classification of numeral's script is carried out with basic Nearest Neighbour (NN) classifier and obtained encouraging results which are shown in the Tables 1, 2 and 3. The result of Kannada-Devanagari script is shown in Table 1, Kannada-English in Table 2, and Devanagari-English in Table 3.

The Tri-script including Kannada-English-Devanagari identification accuracies are presented in Table 4. It can be noticed that, the average bi-script identification accuracies in three cases is high as compared to the results of tri-script identification. It reveals that when combination of more scripts are considered for experimentation, the recognition accuracy falls down. The reason for this is experimentally investigated; it is due to the similarity in shape of the digits of different scripts. For example, the shape of a digit zero of Kannada, Devanagari and English script remains same. Similarly, the shape of a digit four in Kannada resembles to a digit four of Devanagari. These are the reasons for decreased in the script identification accuracies of tri-scripts.

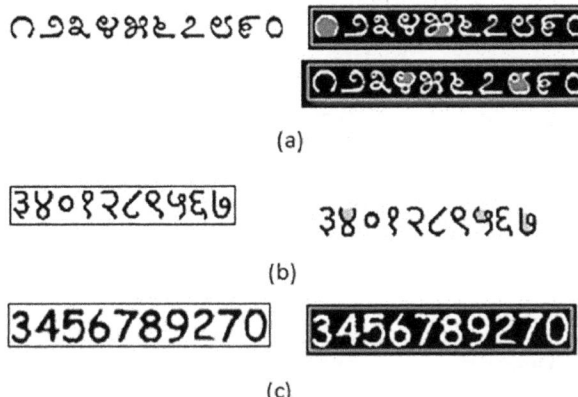

(a)

(b)

(c)

Fig. 2. Water Reservoirs for sample numbers of three different scripts (a) effect of top and bottom Reservoir present in Kannada numeral (b) effect of top and bottom Reservoir present/absent in English numeral (c) effect of top and bottom Reservoir present/absent in Devanagari numeral

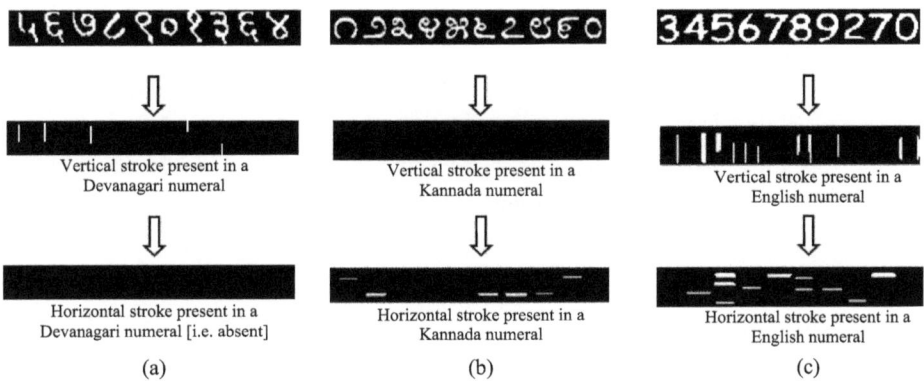

Vertical stroke present in a
Devanagari numeral

Vertical stroke present in a
Kannada numeral

Vertical stroke present in a
English numeral

Horizontal stroke present in a
Devanagari numeral [i.e. absent]

Horizontal stroke present in a
Kannada numeral

Horizontal stroke present in a
English numeral

(a)   (b)   (c)

Fig. 3. Effect of Vertical and horizontal stroke present in a Devanagari(a), Kannada(b) and English(c) Numerals

Table 1. Identification accuracy of Kannada and Devanagari numeral script

Numeral script	Recognition accuracy in %
Kannada	93.14
Devanagari	95.29

Table 2. Identification accuracy of Kannada and English numeral script

Numeral script	Recognition accuracy in %
Kannada	93.14
English	94.14

Table 3. Identification accuracy of English and Devanagari numeral script

Numeral script	Recognition accuracy in %
Devangari	95.43
English	94.29

Table 4. Identification accuracy of Kannada, Devnagari, and English numeral script

Numeral script	Recognition accuracy in %
Kannada	92.58
Devanagari	94.43
English	93.86
Average identification rate	**93.62**

4 Conclusion

This paper summarizes a method of structural features for bi-script and tri-script identification script of numerals. The proposed identification system is to identify the script of the printed numeral belonging to Kannada, Devanagari, and English scripts. The average identification accuracy of the Kannada, Devanagari, and English script is 93.62%. The novelty of the proposed method is that recognition accuracy is high with the simple structural feature and basic nearest neighbour classifier. The work proposed in this paper is an attempt towards recognition of the script of numerals for bilingual/multilingual scripts.

References

1. Ivind Trier, Anil Jain, TorfiinnTaxt, "A feature extraction method for character recognition-A survey ", Pattern Recognition, vol. 29, No 4, pp-641–662.
2. Banashree N.P. and R.Vasanta, "OCR for Script identification of Hindi (Devanagari) Numerals using Feature Sub Selection by Means of End-Point with Neuro-Memetic Model", Proceedings of World Academic of Science, Engineering and Technology (PWASET-July 2007) , ISSN 1307–6884, Volume 22, pp. 78–82, 2007.

3. Banashree N.P. and R.Vasanta, "OCR for Script identification of Hindi (Devanagari) Numerals using Error Diffusion Half toning Algorithm with Neural Classifier", Proceedings of World Academic of Science, Engineering and Technology (PWASET-April 2007), ISSN 1307–6884, Volume 20, pp. 46–50, 2007.

4. R.J.Ramteke, P.D.Borkar, S.C.Mehrotra, "Recognition of Isolated Marathi Handwritten Numerals: An Invariant Moments Approach", Proceedings of the International Conference on Cognition and Recognition, pp.482–489.

5. M.Hanmandlu and O.V. Ramana Murthy, "Fuzzy Model Based Recognition of Handwritten Hindi Numerals", Proceedings of the International Conference on Cognition and Recognition, pp.490–496

6. Anil K.Jain, Douglass Zonker, "Representation and Recognition of handwritten Digits using Deformable Templates", IEEE, Pattern analysis and machine intelligence, vol.19, no-12, 1997.

7. J.D.Tubes, "A Note on Binary Template Matching". Pattern Recognition, 22(4):359-365, 1989.

8. B.V.Dhandra, V.S.Mallimath, Mallikargun Hangargi and Ravindra Hegadi, "Multi-font Numeral recognition without Thinning based on Directional Density of pixels", IEEE International conference on Digital Information Management (ICDIM-2006) Bangalore, India, pp.157–160, Dec-2006.

9. R Sanjeev Kunte and Sudhakar Samuel R.D, "Script Independent Handwritten Numeral recognition". VIE -2006, pp. 94–98, September 2006

10. B.V.Dhandra, and Mallikargun Hangargi, "Morphological Reconstruction for Word Level Script Identification" International Journal of Computer Science and Security, Volume (1) : Issue (1), pp. 41–51

11. Dinesh Acharaya U, N.V.Subba Reddy and Krishnamoorthi, "Multilevel classifier in Recognition of Handwritten Kannada Numerals", PWASET-2008, ISSN-2070–3740, pp.308–313, 2008

12. SubhangiD.C., P.S. Hiremath, "Handwritten English character and Digit Recognition Using Multiclass SVM classifier and Using structural micro features", International Journal of Recent Trends in Engineering. Vol.2, No.2, pp. 193-195, 2009.

13. U.Pal, N.Sharma, F.Kimura, "Handwritten Numeral recognition of six popular Indian scripts" IEEE-explorer, 2008.

14. B.V.Dhandra, R.G.Benne, and Mallikarjun Hangarge, "Kannada, Telugu and Devanagari Handwritten Numeral Recognition with Probabilistic Neural Network: A Script Independent Approach", International Journal of Computer Application, IJCA (0975–8887), Volume 26, No-9, july-2011.

15. G S Lehal and Nivedan Bhatt ,"A Recognition System for Devnagri and English Handwritten Numerals"

16. Mallikarjun Hangarge, Kc Santosh and Rajmohan Arjunsingh Pardeshi, "Directional DCT for Handwritten Script Identification", International Conference on Document Analysis and RecognitionAt: Washington DC, USA, August 2013.

17. Hangairulappan Kathirvalavakumar, M. Karthigai Selvi and R. Palaniappan, "Efficient Handwritten Numeral Recognition System Using Leaders of Separated Digit and RBF Network", Second International Conference MIKE 2014, Cork, Ireland, December 10-12, 2014. Proceedings, pp 135–144.

18. Sk Md Obaidullaha, Chayan Halderb, Nibaran Dasc and Kaushik Roy, "Numeral Script Identification from Handwritten Document Images", Eleventh International Multi-Conference on Information Processing-2015 (IMCIP-2015), Elsevier-Procedia Computer Science 54 (2015) 585 – 594.

19. Amirreza Fateh, Mansoor Fateh, and Vahid Abolghasemi," Multilingual handwritten numeral recognition using a robust deep network joint with transfer learning", Elsevier-Information Sciences, Volume 581, December 2021, Pages 479-494
20. Shrey Malvi, Nirmal Patel and Pratik Prajapati," Variable Length Digit Recognition for Gujarati Language", Easy Chair Preprint no. 7672, March 29, 2022.

A Novel Approach for Object Detection Using Optimized Convolutional Neural Network to Assist Visually Impaired People

Suraj Pardeshi[1(✉)], Nikhil Wagh[1], Kailash Kharat[1], Vikul Pawar[1], and Pravin Yannawar[2]

[1] Department of MCA, Government College of Engineering, Aurangabad, Aurangabad, India
surajrp@geca.ac.in
[2] Department of Computer Science and IT, Dr. Babasaheb Ambedkar Marathwada University, Aurangabad, Aurangabad, India

Abstract. Human race is blessed with the five basic senses such as touch, taste, smell, hearing and the most important of them all 'vision or eyesight'. It is very difficult to survive without any one of them. Unfortunately a mass population across the globe suffers from the ill effects of vision, hampering their daily life. Detecting objects and providing navigational instructions in an indoor environment can considerably improve the day-to-day quality of life of visually impaired people. The motive of this research work is to propose a solution approach for assisting visually impaired population by identifying obstacles in front of them considering indoor environment. This approach focuses on feature extraction and object detection using Convolutional Neural Network (CNN) from a real time video. For this a head mounted image acquisition device may be used to detect the objects from the scene ahead and information of the detected objects is provided to the visually impaired (VI) person through the audio modality. As a first step towards the overall conceptual process, an object detection system is presented in this article, which processes the live video stream captured through the acquisition device. The video is processed frame-by-frame, treating each frame as a separate image and then using the proposed feature extraction and object detection algorithm to identify the objects.

Keywords: Vision · Convolutional Neural Network (CNN) · Visually Impaired (VI) · Feature Extraction · Object Detection · Audio Modality

List of Abbreviations Used

1) Activation Function (AF)
2) Convolutional Neural Network (CNN)
3) Discrete Fourier Transform (DFT)
4) False Discovery Rate (FDR)
5) False Negative Rate (FPR)
6) False Positive Rate (FPR)
7) Gray-Level Co-occurrence Matrix (GLCM)
8) Grey Wolf Optimization (GWO)

© The Author(s) 2023
R. Manza et al. (Eds.): ACVAIT 2022, AISR 176, pp. 187–207, 2023.
https://doi.org/10.2991/978-94-6463-196-8_17

9) High-Level Features (HLFs)
10) Histogram of Oriented Gradients (HOG)
11) Inertial Measurement Unit (IMU)
12) Input Image (I_{input})
13) Interplane Relationships (IPRs)
14) Inverse Discrete Fourier Transform (IDFT)
15) Local Binary Pattern (LBP)
16) Matthews's correlation coefficient (MCC)
17) Mean-Square Error (MSE)
18) Modified Sigmoid Function (MSF)
19) Negative Predictive Value (NPV)
20) Object Detection Model for Visually Impaired (ODMVI)
21) Particle Swarm Optimization (PSO)
22) Peak Signal-to-Noise Ratio (PSNR)
23) Pre-processed Image (I_{prep})
24) Region of Interest (ROI)
25) Scale-Invariant Feature Transform (SIFT)
26) Sea Lion Optimization Algorithm (SLnO)
27) Segmented Image (I_{segm})
28) Speeded-Up Robust Features (SURF)
29) Visually Impaired (VI)
30) Whale Optimization Algorithm (WOA)

1 Introduction

Having a clear vision is a valuable blessing, and it is one of the most important faculties that allow us to gain knowledge from our surroundings. Sadly, vision loss is becoming more and more common. According to the WHO report, there are 314 million people in the world who suffers from visual disabilities. Uncorrected refractive errors or eye conditions are often cited as the main causes of visual impairment. There are 314 million people who are classified as outwardly disabled, 45 million are visually impaired (blind) [1–4]. A maturing population has made visual impairments more prevalent and widespread. As people age, the danger of visual impairments increases, further complicating the challenge of independent mobility. Identifying obstacles without vision is a challenge. The VI person relies on the other senses mostly touch for movements. But in some cases the physical contact between a person and unknown object can be dangerous. A comprehensive framework is needed to help people with visual disabilities presenting with impairments or impedances [5–7]. A simple guide cane is the traditional tool mostly used by VI. The advancements in technology added considerable modifications in the cane such as sensors, vibrating pads etc. The limitation of using cane is distance. Unless the object comes in the perimeter of the cane it is not identified. A computerized system that recognizes objects without touching them and provides auditory feedback to the person giving more accurate understanding of the environment and avoiding threats involved in the overall process is needed [8–12]. Also the need of VI is not only to identify the obstacles but to gain a better understanding of the surroundings. The rapidly increasing research interests in the faculties of computer science such as image processing, machine learning, computer vision and AI is a ray of hope to overcome the problems mentioned so far [13]. Machine vision systems aims to recognize all the objects in an image and collect information about the categories and positions of those objects, so they can understand what the image shows. A number of methods were invented to address these types of situations, mostly based on the principles of computer vision and deep learning. However the overlapping objects and various lighting conditions become another hurdles to overcome [14–16].

2   Related Work

Mehta et al. [17] proposed a cost-effective mobile phone-based device solution which is both cost-effective and noise-resistant. Furthermore, features such as "Local Binary Pattern (LBP), Gabor, and Histogram-based features", among others, can be used to differentiate between different types of obstacles present, such as a chair, vehicle, or human, to improve the efficiency of VI. The optimization algorithms [18–23] are playing a major role in the object detection approach.

Cardillo *et al.* [24] have projected a novel autonomous walking aid for the visually impaired and blind users with the aid of the electromagnetic sensor. The introduction of microwave radar to the conventional white cane aided target identification for the visually impaired while walking. Further, while compared to the state-of-art Electronic Travel Aids, the presented work had consumed fewer dimensions and had better noise tolerance with utmost better performance.

Ye and Qian [25] have implemented a "3-D object recognition method" onto the robotic navigation with the intention of assisting the blind person in indoor structural detection. The researchers have broken a point cloud into a plethora of "planar patches" and extracted the "Interplane Relationships (IPRs)" The authors have specified six "High-Level Features (HLFs)" for each of the patches based on the object's IPRs. Then, using a "Gaussian-mixture-model-based plane classifier", each planar patch belonging to an individual object model was categorized. At last, the classified planes were clustered into model objects using a recursive plane clustering technique. As a consequence, this method was well suited for detecting non-structural structures indoors in a precise way.

Chan *et al.* [26] have developed a new MSF framework on the basis of the "Inertial Measurement Unit (IMU)" for the migration of visually impaired persons within indoor environments. This technique was simpler since it had adopted the Modified Sigmoid Function (MSF) in estimating the blur levels of IMU. Further, the edge detections were made smoother with a moving camera in the MSF topological structure. The authors have evaluated the performance of the MSF framework by means of evaluating the object edges on "video sequences associated with IMU data".

Jindal *et al.* [27] have designed a novel smartphone-based cost-effective system for safe walking along the roads by observing the obstacles along the paths of the visually impaired people in real-time scenarios. The video was captured with the aid of the Monocular vision approach and they have extracted the frames from the video by the meaning of neglecting the blurriness that occurred in the image due to the camera motion. Further, they have extracted the Speeded-Up Robust Features (SURF) after removing the ground plane of the non-ground area. The SURF features matched with the features of the obstacles were segmented with the aid of the active contour model from the non-ground image and these images were referred to as the region of interest (ROI). Moreover, they have verified whether the ROI belongs to an obstacle or not by means of passing the calculated Gray-Level Co-occurrence Matrix (GLCM) features onto the classification model.

Arora *et al.* [28] have developed a new prototype for "real-time multi-object detection" with the aid of the "image segmentation and deep neural network". With the proposed approach, the authors have prompted the blind persons about the entity, its location with reverence to the individual via speech stimulus. Furthermore, the authors have combined the "single-shot multibox detection system" with the "mobileNet architecture" for application construction that's also lightweight, scalable, and has a short response time. As a whole, the proposed approach has performed well in terms of accuracy and latency.

Meshram *et al.* [29] have introduced a new electronic assistive device referred to as the "NavCan" for obstacle-free paths to visually impaired people in both indoor and outdoor settings. The proposed approach provided priority information with no information overloading about the obstacles in the path. In addition, the proposed NavCane approach had also guided the users to recognize the objects in the indoor settings. The NavCane seems to be an effective tool for detecting "snags, ascending and descending flights of stairs, navigating wet floors, and object recognition in both recognized and unknown environments", according to the trial results. Similarly, when compared to a white stick, their evaluation findings show that the NavCane enhances the appearance of a snag-free pathway.

Afif *et al.* [30] have developed a novel indoor object detection system for VI people on the basis of the deep CNN "RetinaNet". The proposed model was significant in localizing as well as categorizing the indoor objects from the collected input image. This approach had gained high detection performances even under most of the challenging conditions like "extreme illumination changes, occlusion, and high inter-class and intra-class variation".

Krishna *et al.* [31] have presented a new "vision system with 3D audio feedback mechanism" to guide the VI people during their navigation. During their movement, the intuitive cognize corresponding to the localization of the object along their path was notified to the blind people via the variation in the intensity of the sounds of earphones. The three main modules of the proposed system were:" depth calculation, object detection, and 3D audio generation. The stereoscopic vision was utilized for discovering the depth map and the localization of doors indoors was detected using CNN. Further, on the basis of the object's location and depth map, the audio vector generates the 3D audio, which guides their locomotion. When tested in a real-life setting, this device proved to be reliable and effective for visually impaired navigation.

3   Architectural Description of the Proposed Object Detection Model for Visually Impaired (ODMVI)

Object Detection Model for Visually Impaired persons aims to provide reliable, fast, and accurate object recognition in real time to assist visually impaired and challenged persons. With this research work, we discuss the black-box functionality of the proposed

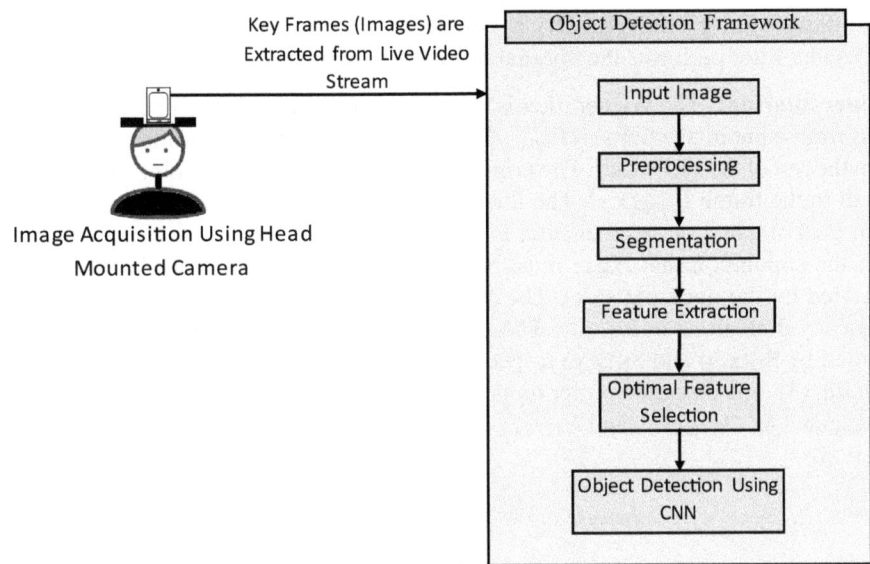

Fig. 1. Architecture of the Proposed Object Detection Model-'ODMVI'

system for handling the complexity of object detection mechanism. The model considers an indoor environment, where objects are stationary.

In the proposed model, a head mounted scene acquisition device captures a stationary indoor scene and provides data (from the scene) to the connected system for the purpose of real-time object detection. We are capturing images from a live video. Checkpoints are added at specific time intervals in the video stream to get the key frames. The key frames are nothing but the two dimensional images that are provided as input to the object detection framework Depending on the specifications of the acquisition device capturing the video, the input image sizes may vary. Hence the images obtained are converted to 255×255 dimensions for uniformity and given to the object detection framework.

The object detection framework processes the input image through five distinct phases: "pre-processing, segmentation, feature extraction, optimal feature selection, and object detection". Figure 1 illustrates the architecture of the proposed object recognition paradigm designed to accommodate the needs of visually impaired individuals.

3.1 Preprocessing

The purpose of image pre-processing is to improve the image data by suppressing unwanted distortions and enhances some important features of the image for further processing. In this research work, wiener filtering is applied to the input image I_{input} for removing unwanted noises. This enhances the quality of the image. The Weiner filter has the highest Peak Signal-to-Noise Ratio (PSNR) (in dB) thus having the lowest

Mean-Square Error (MSE) (in dB), as compared to other compatible ones. Furthermore, the Weiner filter performs the optimal noise smoothing and inverse filtering tradeoffs.

Weiner filtering: The Wiener filter is the most important method for separating blurred areas from input image frames (I_{input}). This distinguishes the interesting points (objects) from the rest of the scene [32]. The original image $orig(x,y)$ and the noisy image $nois(x,y)$ are all in the frame $I_{input}(x,y)$. The image has been degraded according to Eq. (1). The main goal of using the Weiner filter is to get the restored image $r(x,y)$ from $I_{input}(x,y)$, with the stipulation that $r(x,y)$ must be equal to $I_{input}(x,y)$. The pixels' positions are indicated by the notations (x,y). The Weiner filler is mathematically expressed in the frequency domain as in Eq. (2). The power spectra of the $orig(x,y)$ and $nois(x,y)$ are denoted by $S_D(x,y)$ and $S_N(x,y)$ respectively. The solution can be found by lowering K as in Eq. (3). The discrete Fourier transforms (DFTs) of the original image and noise are represented by $O_{DFT}(x,y)$ and $N_{DFT}(x,y)$ respectively. Equation (4) is used to obtain the solution.

$$I_{input}(x, y) = orig(x, y) + nois(x, y) \tag{1}$$

The standard mathematical equation for Weiner filter is denoted by Eq. 2.

$$G(x, y) = \frac{S_D(x, y)}{S_D(x, y) + S_N(x, y)} \tag{2}$$

where: $S_N(x, y)$ is the power spectrum of noise $nois(x, y)$ and $S_D(x, y)$ is the power spectrum of the original image $orig(x, y)$. For simplification we need to take derivative of Eq. (2) reduced to Eq. (3) by computing DFT of original Image $orig(x,y)$ and DFT of noisy image $nois(x,y)$.

$$K = F\left[|ODFT((x, y)) - G((x, y)).NDFT((x, y))|^2\right] \tag{3}$$

$$G(x, y) = \frac{F\left[NDFT((x, y)).ODFT * ((x, y))\right]}{F\left[|NDFT((x, y))|^2\right]} \tag{4}$$

Here, the complex conjugate is denoted by *. In the case of the white noise availability, the numerator gets decreased as per Eq. (5). The denominator reduces as per Eq. (6). The Weiner filter's output is given as in Eqs. (7) and (8), respectively. The inverse transform of DFT is IDFT (Inverse Discrete Fourier Transform). The pre-processed image I_{prep} is subjected to segmentation.

$$F\left[NDFT(x, y).ODFT * (x, y)\right] = \begin{cases} = F\{[ODFT(x, y)] + NDFT(x, y)\} \times ODFT * (x, y) \\ = F[|ODFT(x, y)|^2] \\ = S_D(x, y) \end{cases}$$

$$\tag{5}$$

$$F\left[|ODFT((x, y))|^2\right] = S_D((x, y)) + S_N((x, y)) \tag{6}$$

This helps in increasing the quality of the image, by multiplying input image with Weiner filter as per Eq. (7) and resultant image presented as $Z(x, y)$.

$$Z(x, y) = G(x, y).I_{input}(x, y) \tag{7}$$

Finally, wiener filter need to take Inverse Discrete Fourier Transform (IDFT) as per Eq. (8).

$$z(x, y) = IDFT[Z(x, y)] \tag{8}$$

Subsequently, the resultant image of preprocessing using wiener filtering is to be passed for segmentation.

3.2 Segmentation

The process of segmenting a digital image into several distinct regions comprising each pixel (sets of pixels, also known as superpixels) with identical attributes is known as image segmentation. Objects and boundaries (lines, curves, etc.) in images are usually located using image segmentation. Image segmentation is also the process of assigning a label to each pixel in an image such that pixels with the same label share common values.

The unsupervised K-Means clustering algorithm is used to differentiate the interest region from the context. Based on the K-centroids, it clusters or partitions the given data into K-clusters or segments. It is predominantly used for clustering large sets of images into ROI and Non-ROI regions. The resolution of the image is $I_{prep}(x,y)$, which is clustered into k- the count of clusters. Let $I_{prep}(x,y)$ be the input pixel that is to be clustered and the cluster centre is C_k the steps followed in the k-means algorithm is depicted below:

Step 1: Initialize the cluster centre and the count of clusters k.

Step 2: Compute the Euclidean distance E_{Dist} among every pixel in I_{prep}. In fact, using the relation below, the Euclidean distance between the image's centre and each pixel is computed.

$$E_{Dist} = ||I_{prep}(x, y) - C_K|| \tag{9}$$

Step 3: Depending on the distance E_{Dist}, assign all pixels to the nearest centre.

Step 4: Recalculate the new location of the centre using the relation in Eq. (10), after all, pixels have been allocated.

$$C_k = \frac{1}{k} \sum_{x \in c_k} \sum_{y \in c_k} Iprep(x, y) \tag{10}$$

Step 5: Repeat the procedure before the tolerance or error value is met.

Step 6: Reshape the cluster pixels into the image.

While k-means has the advantage of being simple to be used, it does have some disadvantages. The final clustering results' consistency is determined by the random initial centroid selection. As a result, if the initial centroid is selected at random, the

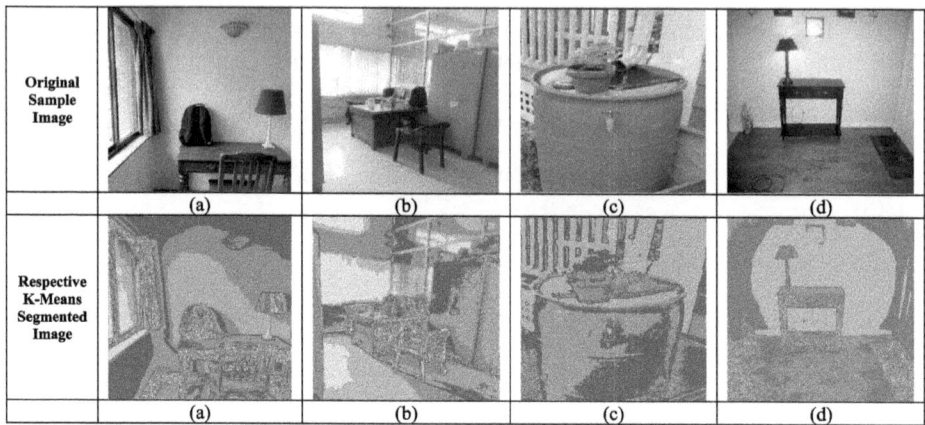

Fig. 2. Sample and Segmented Images

result would be different for different initial centres. Moreover, the K-means algorithm converges at a local minimum and it is highly computationally complex. So, we have introduced a new multi-kernel k-Means algorithm, where we've hybridized both the sigmoid and laplacian kernel. Mathematically, sigmoid and laplacian kernel are shown in Eqs. (11) and Eq. (12), respectively.

$$\text{Sigmoid kernel: } Sk_1(x, y) = \tanh(\beta_0 \langle x, y \rangle + \beta_1) \tag{11}$$

$$\text{Laplacian kernel: } Lk_2(x,y) = \exp\left(-\frac{\|x - y\|}{\sigma}\right) \tag{12}$$

$$Mk(x, y) = \frac{Sk_1 + Lk_2}{3} \tag{13}$$

By combining Eqs. (11) and (12) and by normalizing by Eq. (3) we are obtaining the cluster center using Eq. (13) and the segmented image thus obtained is denoted as I_{segm}, from which the multi-features are extracted.

The sample and segmented images used for evaluation are shown in following Fig. 2.

3.3   Feature Extraction

The segmented image is denoted by I_{segm} from which multiple features (SURF, Scale-Invariant Feature Transform (SIFT), Shape features via Canny edge and gradient features via Histogram of Oriented Gradients (HOG)) are extracted as shown in Fig. 3.

3.3.1   SURF

The SURF feature is extracted from I_{segm}. The SURF method is indeed a stable and accurate technique towards describing as well as contrasting images in a local, similarity invariant manner. The prominent feature of the SURF technique has been its ability

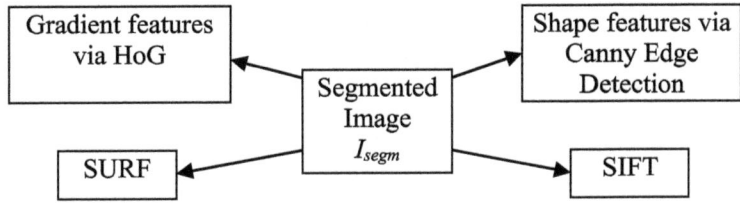

Fig. 3. Multiple Feature Extraction from the Segmented Image

to compute operators quickly using box filters, thereby supporting real-time applications including surveillance and object recognition. The "Feature Description as well as Feature Extraction" are the two major steps in the SURF model [33].

In the feature extraction phase, the "Hessian matrix approximation" has been used for detecting the interest points.

The "SURF descriptor" is generated in two steps: The very first step is to establish a repeatable orientation using data from a circular area surrounding the keypoint. The SURF descriptor is then extracted from a square region aligned to the chosen orientation.

Descriptor Components: (a) The square area creation is the first step, and here the square area is created in the form, which is centered on the keypoint and aligned in the direction of the orientation. (b) The region is then divided into smaller 4 * 4 square-shaped sub-regions on a constant basis. At 5 * 5 regularly spaced sampling points, we compute a few basic features for each sub-region. (c) In the horizontal direction, The Haar wavelet responses referred to as dx, while in the vertical direction it is referred to as dy. In order to enhance the robustness against geometric deformations and localization errors, the responses dx and dy were weighted initially with a Gaussian ($\sigma = 3.3$ s). The extracted SURF feature is denoted as 'f_{SURF}'.

3.3.2 SIFT

The SIFT feature is extracted from I_{segm}. In fact, the SIFT is indeed a simple procedure. The SIFT algorithm consists primarily of four stages:

(a) Selection of a scale-space peak: A possible spot for locating features is selected from the segmented image. The scale shape is defined as per Eq. (14).

$$Q(x, y, \sigma) = Ggaus(x, y, \sigma) * Iseg(x, y) \tag{14}$$

Here, $I_{seg}(x,y)$ is the segmented image with pixels (x,y) and $Ggaus(x, y, \sigma)$ is the Gaussian variable scale.

(b) Keypoint Localization: the feature keypoints from the selected scale-space peak are localized accurately. The keypoints generated in the previous phase result in a large number of keypoints. Some of them seem to be too close to the edge, or there isn't enough contrast. They aren't as useful as features in these scenarios. As a result, we get rid of them. The method is comparable to those used to suppress edge features in the Harris Corner Detector. The extrema location L is given as per Eq. (15).

$$L = \frac{\partial^2 W^{-1}}{\partial d^2} \frac{\partial^2 W}{\partial d} \tag{15}$$

(c) Assigning Orientation to Keypoints: Depending on the scale, a neighborhood is drawn around the keypoint spot, and in this region the gradient magnitude and direction are determined. The result is a 360-degree orientation histogram of 36 bins. Then, the histogram is created. There would be a peak in the histogram at some point. The orientation φ is computed as per Eq. (16).

$$\varphi(x, y) = \tan(O(x, y + 1) - O(x, y - 1)/O(x + 1, y) - O(x - 1, y) \qquad (16)$$

(d) Keypoint descriptor: A high-dimensional vector that describes the keypoints. Each keypoint now has a position, size, and orientation. The next stage is to develop a descriptor for each keypoint's local image area which is strongly distinctive and as invariant as possible to changes in perspective as well as lighting. (e) Keypoint Matching: The closest neighbors of two images' keypoints are identified and paired [34].

The extracted SIFT feature is denoted as 'f_{SIFT}'.

3.3.3 Shape Features via Canny Edge Detection

The shape based features are extracted from I_{segm}. The edge detection phenomena are carried out to estimate the shape of the objects. For this, we've used the canny detection operation. The Canny edge detector is indeed an edge detection operator that recognizes a large variety of edges in images using a multi-stage algorithm. A multi-stage edge detector seems to be the Canny filter [35]. To compute the intensity corresponding to the image gradients, it employs a filter dependent on the derivative of a Gaussian. The Gaussian filter eliminates the influence of image noise. Then, by eliminating "non-maximum pixels" of the gradient magnitude, possible edges are thinned down to "1-pixel curves". Finally, using "hysteresis thresholding" on the gradient magnitude, edge pixels are retained or deleted [36]. The general criteria for edge detection include (a) Edge detection with a low error rate, which ensures that the detection can recognize as much of the image's edges as possible. (b) The operated sensed edge point should be effective in locating the edge's center. (c) Image noise does not produce "false edges". The extracted shape base features via the Canny edge detector are denoted as 'f_{canny}'.

3.3.4 Gradient Features via HoG

In I_{segm}, the HOG (feature descriptor) identifies the homogeneous identical area [37, 38]. The steps followed in HoG feature extraction is depicted below:

(a) Calculate the "histogram of gradient directions or edge orientations" of each pixel in each cell by dividing the pre-processed image into smaller related regions (referred to as cells).
(b) Each cell is discretized into angular bins using gradient orientation.
(c) Each cell's pixel about its angular bin receives a weighted gradient.
(d) Consider a spatial region to be a group of adjacent cells (blocks).
   The block histogram is formed by representing the Normalized type of histograms and is referred to as the descriptor. It is dependent on the classification and normalization of histograms. 'f_{HoG}' represent the extracted HOG characteristics.

4   Optimal Feature Selection

To reduce the computational costs of modeling as well as, in some cases, improve the performance of the model, it is desirable to reduce the number of input variables (features) [39]. All feature subset selection systems use two main components: the search strategy used to choose the subsets of features and the evaluation method employed to measure the quality of those subsets [40–42]. In general, there are four main steps involved in a feature selection procedure. They are (a) generation of the subset; (b) evaluation of the subset; (c) stopping criteria for the procedure; and (d) validation. The step (a) involves selecting subsets based on the approach used for searching. Search direction and research methodology typically determine the approach. Several parameters are taken into consideration in Step (b) such as distance, dependency, consistency, etc. The stopping criteria in step (c) are dependent on other criteria (e.g., less error than required/chosen, complete the search, etc.) In step (d), advanced AI/ML algorithms are used to validate selected attributes. Genetic algorithms (GAs) provide a simple, general, and powerful framework for selecting good subsets of features, leading to improved detection rates.

The overall extracted features are denoted as $F = (f_{SURF}) + (f_{SIFT}) + (f_{canny}) + (f_{HoG})$. The best features '$F*$' can be derived from the overall extracted features 'F'. The extracted best features are $F* = (f_{SURF})* + (f_{SIFT})* + (f_{canny})* + (f_{HoG})*$, and are fed as input to optimized CNN, for training purposes.

5   Object Detection Using CNN

CNN Architecture: Convolutional neural network extracts features from an input image and provides learnable parameters to efficiently do the classification, detection, and many other tasks of an image. The proposed architecture contains five convolutional layers and five pooling layers.

5.1   Convolution Layer

The convolutional layers create a convolution kernel that is convolved with the layer input to produce outputs. The input image is convoluted using filters by using convolution operation. The kernal size is (3,3), specifying the height and width of the 2D convolution window. The convolutional phase will apply the filter on a small array of pixels within the picture. The filter will move along the input image with a shape of 3×3. It means the network will slide these windows across all the input image and compute the convolution. The output matrix is the result of the element-wise operation between the image matrix and the filter. At the end of the convolution operation, the output is subject to an activation function to allow non-linearity. The activation function for our model is the Relu. All the pixel with a negative value will be replaced by zero.

5.2 Pooling Layer

The convolutional layer is followed by pooling layer. The purpose of the pooling is to reduce the dimensionality of the input image. The steps are done to reduce the computational complexity of the operation. By diminishing the dimensionality, the network has lower weights to compute, so it prevents overfitting. In order to down sample images while preserving information, we use pooling layers, we have two types of pooling layers which are max-pooling and average pooling. In our model we are using max-pooling with pool size (2,2). Pool size is nothing but the factor by which to downscale. (2,2) will have the input in both spatial dimensions.

5.3 Fully Connected Layer

Convolution and max pooling is applied to the data set, before sending it to the output layer the model is flattened. Dropout is applied to prevent overfitting of images. The convolutional layers apply different filters on a subregion of the picture. The Relu activation function adds non-linearity, and the pooling layers reduce the dimensionality of the features maps. All these layers extract essential information from the images. At last, the features maps are fed to a primary fully connected layer with a softmax function to make a prediction. We connect all neurons from the previous layer to the next layer. We have used 'softmax' activation function to classify the input image. The overall process is depicted in following Fig. 4.

As discussed in the earlier sections, the extracted $F*$ are given as input to optimized CNN for classifying the objects. Multiple layers of artificial neurons make up convolutional neural networks. Artificial neurons are mathematical functions that measure the weighted number of several inputs and emit an activation value, similar to their biological counterparts. Each neuron's action is determined by its weight. Therefore, we are fine-tuning the weights of CNN to enhance the detection accuracy.

Convolutional kernel defines the entire function map in such a way that r^{th} layer of convolutional layer is mapped with z^{th} feature map as well feature values in the location

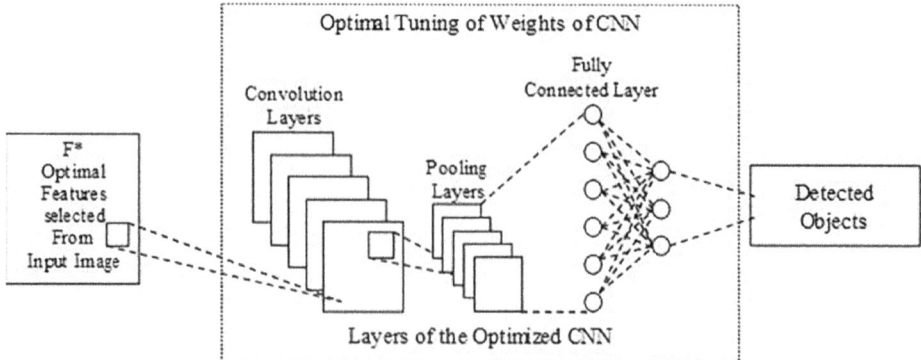

Fig. 4. Schematic Diagram of Optimized CNN for ODMVI

provided to the CNN and being determined by Eq. (17).

$$S^r_{e,x,z} = W^r_z F *^r_{e,x} + B^r_z \tag{17}$$

$$AF^r_{e,x,z} = AF\left(S^r_{e,x,z}\right) \tag{18}$$

$$O^r_{e,x,z} = pool\left(AF^r_{e,x,z}\right), \forall (c, r) \in \Re_{e,x} \tag{19}$$

where W^r_z and B^r_z are the optimum weight vector and bias, which provides the optimal tuning of the weights. Similarly, activation function $AF(\cdot)$ provides prediction of non-linear features of multilayer networks and here it is used to achieve non-linearity and presented in Eq. (18), when processed provides activation value. The Shift variance in the pooling layer is handled by Eq. (19) and it deals with decreasing the resolution of induced feature map by local neighbourhood and presented by $pool$ (). The down sampling operations were also conducted by the pooling layer in CNN with the result collected from the convolutional layers. Additionally, maximum pooling and average pooling were also explored. The higher value was observed in the max-pooling; nevertheless, the average value was observed in the average pooling. Function loss be determined by using CNN as

$$Loss = \frac{1}{Num} \sum_{t=1}^{ms} G\left(\varsigma; V^{(t)}, OUT^{(t)}\right) \tag{20}$$

where, (ς) is the constraints of CNN are associated with required input-output relations and to be operated in limits of $\left\{\left(U^{(t)}, V^{(t)}\right) ; t \in [1, \cdots, IO]\right\}$ and furthermore, output of CNN, t^{th} input data, and the related target values are determined as $OUT^{(t)}$, $U^{(t)}$ and $V^{(t)}$, correspondingly.

The results obtained from the pooling layer are usually given as an entry to the completely fully - connected, and hence the inputs are associated with both layers. The fully connected layer in the work appears at the output of the CNN system. The output layer of CNN is the final layer, and it includes the *softmax* function for performing precise final detection of objects in the images (targets). CNN's loss function (*Loss*) must be minimised in order to get the best result as per Eq. (21).

$$Obj = \min(Loss) \tag{21}$$

In order to have minimization of loss, the efforts were taken for fine-tuning the weight– 'W' of CNN.

6 Dataset

We have used '*ImageNet*' dataset for the simulation of the proposed model [43]. The data in this dataset is available for free to researchers for non-commercial use. ImageNet dataset has 100,000 images across 200 classes. Each class has 500 training images, 50 validation images, and 50 test images provided with the labeling of images. The proposed model is trained and evaluated over ImageNet dataset. 10000 images of over 25 different categories were selected from the dataset for training the model. Initially most commonly used indoor objects were targeted and organized in to respective directories for training. The images were labeled with a string starting with 'n' preceded by a sequence of eight integers e.g. 'n03950228'. Every directory contained 400 different images of a particular object. The images were labeled with the name of directory preceded by underscore and sequence number (e.g. 'n03950228_1, n03950228_2 etc.). The dataset images were separated in to training dataset and testing datasets taking 80%-20% ratio (8000 images for training and 2000 images for testing). After the complete analysis of CNN over the dataset, the model was trained to identify the objects with remarkable accuracy and precision.

7   Results and Discussion

7.1   Simulation Procedure

The proposed model (ODMVI) is evaluated over the existing models like CNN+ PSO (Particle Swarm Optimization), CNN+ WOA (Whale Optimization Algorithm), CNN+GWO (Grey Wolf Optimization) & CNN+SLnO (Sea Lion Optimization Algorithm) in terms of "positive, negative and other measures". This evaluation is carried out by varying the learning percentage from 60 (40% of data was used for training), 70 (30% of data was used for training), and 80 (20% of data was used for training) respectively. The positive measures like "accuracy, specificity, sensitivity, and precision" are ought to be sustained at a higher level, for the most favorable results. The error measures or native measures are False Positive Rate (FPR), False Negative Rate (FNR), and False Discovery Rate (FDR), which need to be as low as possible. The F1-score (harmonic mean of precision and recall), Matthews's correlation coefficient (MCC), and Negative Predictive Value (NPV) are additional value-added indicators that exhibit the supremacy of the proposed work.

7.2   Convergence Analysis

The proposed model should exhibit higher convergence towards the defined objective function in order to better understand its performance. Figure 5 summarizes the results of the convergence analysis of both proposed and existing models for each iteration. Initially, both the proposed and existing models have higher convergence at the lowest iteration count (at 0th iteration). When the number of iterations grows, the cost of the proposed and existing models comes down as they go through more iteration. Comparing the proposed method with the traditional method, the proposed one eventually achieves minimum fitness values. Furthermore, the proposed method achieves fewer fitness values at a maximum of 50 iterations. Thus, the ODMVI model can reduce the CNN loss, representing the superiority of the proposed model in terms of detection accuracy.

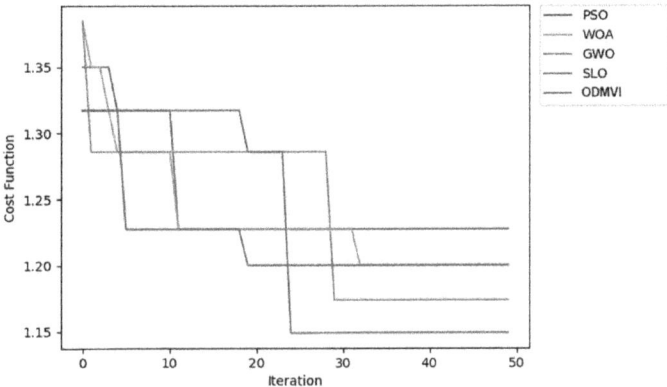

Fig. 5. Convergence Analysis

7.3 Performance Evaluation of ODMVI

The results for accuracy and precision are shown in Table 1, Fig. 6 and Table 2, Fig. 7 respectively as shown below. The obtained results indicate that the ODMVI is very beneficial, since it has indexed the highest percentage for every variation in learning. By focusing on the most important metric, accuracy, the ODMVI shows its superiority. Interestingly, the accuracy of planned work is found higher with any shift in the learning percentage. Additionally, the planned work was at its best even at the highest learning percentage (80 percent).The accuracy of the ODMVI at learning percentage = 80 is 76.78%, which is better than the existing models like CNN +PSO = 65.67%, CNN + WOA = 49%, CNN +GWO = 53.17%, CNN + SLnO = 61.50%.

Moreover, the ODMVI's precision, sensitivity, and specificity increase with an increase in learning percentage. Also the precision outcomes of the model are also exciting. The precision of the ODMVI at learning percentage 80 is 65.67%, which is better than the existing models like CNN+ PSO = 32.33%, CNN +WOA = 0%, CNN+ GWO = 7.33%, CNN+SLnO = 24%. Thus, from the evaluation, it's clear that the proposed work had archived maximal values in terms of positive performance measures, and this is said to be the most favorable outcome.

In addition, the ODMVI has archived the least error measures. The False Discovery Rate - FDR (as shown in Table 3) of the ODMVI is 0.32, which is the least value when compared to traditional works like CNN+ PSO = 0.65, CNN +WOA = 0.99, CNN+GWO = 0.90, CNN +SLnO = 0.74. The False Negative Rate - FNR (as shown

Table 1. Performance Analysis of Proposed and Conventional Work in terms of Accuracy

Learning Rate	CNN +PSO	CNN+WOA	CNN+GWO	CNN+SLnO	**ODMVI**
60	0.698333	0.656667	0.656667	0.601111	0.656667
70	0.573333	0.61963	0.684444	0.61963	0.730741
80	0.656667	0.49	0.531667	0.615	**0.767778**

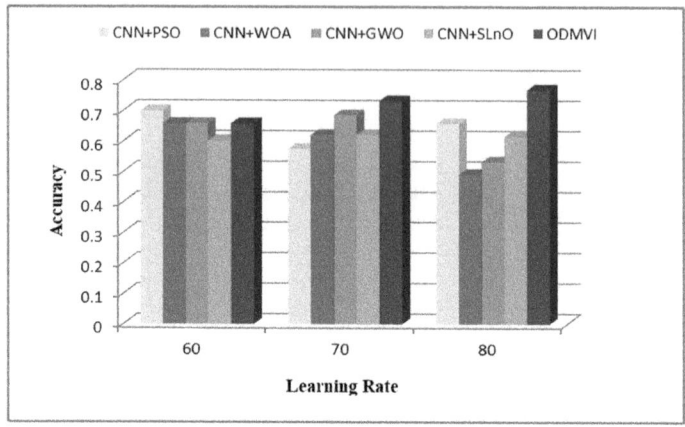

Fig. 6. Performance of Adopted Method Over Extant Models for Accuracy

Table 2. Performance Analysis of Proposed and Conventional Work in terms of Precision

Learning Rate	CNN+PSO	CNN+WOA	CNN +GWO	CNN+SLnO	**ODMVI**
60	0.406667	0.323333	0.323333	0.406667	0.49
70	0.156667	0.434444	0.378889	0.434444	0.601111
80	0.323333	0	0.073333	0.24	**0.656667**

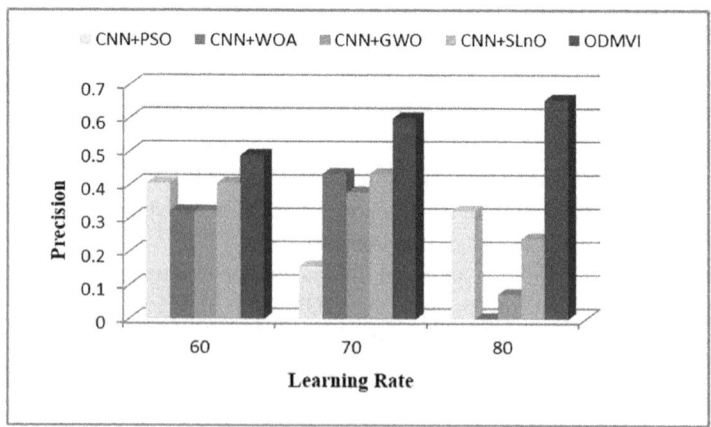

Fig. 7. Performance of Adopted Method Over Extant Models for Precision

in Table 4) of the ODMVI is 0.31 (least value) at 80th learning iteration, which is better than the existing works like CNN+PSO = 0.646, CNN +WOA = 0.98, CNN +GWO = 0.896, CNN +SLnO = 0.73. The False Positive Rate-FPR (as shown in Table 5) of the ODMVI is 0.156 (least value) at 80th learning iteration, which is better than the existing

Table 3. Performance Analysis of Proposed and Conventional Work in terms of FDR

Learning Rate	CNN+PSO	CNN+WOA	CNN+GWO	CNN+SLnO	ODMVI
60	0.573333	0.656667	0.656667	0.573333	0.49
70	0.823333	0.545556	0.601111	0.545556	0.378889
80	0.656667	0.99	0.906667	0.74	**0.323333**

works like CNN+ PSO = 0.212, CNN +WOA = 0.323, CNN + GWO = 0.295, CNN +SLnO = 0.240.

Moreover, F1-score (harmonic mean between precision and recall) = 0.656 (as shown in Table 6), Matthews Correlation Coefficient (MCC) = 0.49 (as shown in Table 7), and Negative Predictive Value (NPV) = 0.823 (as shown in Table 8) are found to be higher with the ODMVI for every variation in the learning percentage. From the overall evaluation, it is clear that the ODMVI had achieved the optimal values; thereby the ODMVI had become much sufficient for detecting the objects.

Table 4. Performance Analysis of Proposed and Conventional Work in terms of FNR

Learning Rate	CNN+PSO	CNN+WOA	CNN +GWO	CNN+SLnO	ODMVI
60	0.563333	0.646667	0.646667	0.563333	0.48
70	0.813333	0.535556	0.591111	0.535556	0.368889
80	0.646667	0.98	0.896667	0.73	**0.313333**

Table 5. Performance Analysis of Proposed and Conventional Work in terms of FPR

Learning Rate	CNN+PSO	CNN+WOA	CNN+GWO	CNN+SLnO	ODMVI
60	0.184444	0.212222	0.212222	0.281667	0.24
70	0.267778	0.267778	0.193704	0.267778	0.184444
80	0.212222	0.323333	0.295556	0.24	0.156667

Table 6. Performance Analysis of Proposed and Conventional Work in terms of F1-Score

Learning Rate	CNN+PSO	CNN+WOA	CNN+GWO	CNN+SLnO	ODMVI
60	0.406667	0.323333	0.323333	0.406667	0.49
70	0.156667	0.434444	0.378889	0.434444	0.601111
80	0.323333	NaN	0.073333	0.24	**0.656667**

Table 7. Performance Analysis of Proposed and Conventional Work in terms of MCC

Learning Rate	CNN+PSO	CNN+WOA	CNN+GWO	CNN+SLnO	**ODMVI**
60	0.212222	0.101111	0.101111	0.115	0.24
70	−0.12111	0.156667	0.175185	0.156667	0.406667
80	0.101111	−0.34333	−0.23222	−0.01	**0.49**

Table 8. Performance Analysis of Proposed and Conventional Work in terms of NPV

Learning Rate	CNN+PSO	CNN+WOA	CNN+GWO	CNN+SLnO	**ODMVI**
0.795556	0.767778	0.767778	0.698333	0.74	0.74
0.712222	0.712222	0.786296	0.712222	0.795556	0.795556
0.767778	0.656667	0.684444	0.74	0.823333	**0.823333**

8   Conclusion and Future Scope

In this proposed model the discussed ODMVI architecture will be working in the background of the final developed system for assisting visually impaired people. The object detection is thus achieved through the major phases comprising pre-processing, segmentation, feature extraction, optimal feature selection and object detection.

The optimal features extracted from the overall features were fed as input to the optimized convolutional network for detecting multiple objects from the image. In order to attain the maximum accuracy and precision in the results, the weights of CNN were optimally tuned. The accuracy (76.78%) and the precision (65.67%) of the proposed ODMVI model at the 80th learning rate was found to be better than the existing models like CNN + PSO, CNN+WOA, CNN +GWO, CNN+SLnO. Thus from the overall performance analysis it can be concluded that the ODMVI had been proven to be more effective for object identification. The proposed work emphasizes object detection in an indoor environment for visually impaired people to assist them to live day-to-day life more easily.

In future the work will be extended by emphasizing on the optimization of time factor of the detection activity and providing the user with notification regarding the detected objects in an audio form. An android application may be developed to capture the video through smartphone and a backend server application may be developed and used to detect real-time objects.

References

1. Seiffert Simões, W. C. S., & de Lucena, V. F. (2016). Indoor Navigation Assistant for Visually Impaired by Pedestrian Dead Reckoning and Position Estimative of Correction for Patterns Recognition. *IFAC-PapersOnLine, 49*(30), 167–170. https://doi.org/10.1016/j.ifacol.2016.11.149

2. Khenkar, S., Alsulaiman, H., Ismail, S., Fairaq, A., Jarraya, S. K., & Ben-Abdallah, H. (2016). ENVISION: Assisted Navigation of Visually Impaired Smartphone Users. *Procedia Computer Science, 100*, 128–135. https://doi.org/10.1016/j.procs.2016.09.132

3. Siddhartha, B., Chavan, A. P., & Uma, B. V. (2018). An Electronic Smart Jacket for the Navigation of Visually Impaired Society. *Materials Today: Proceedings, 5*(4, Part 3), 10665–10669. https://doi.org/10.1016/j.matpr.2017.12.344

4. Connier, J., Zhou, H., Vaulx, C. De, Li, J., Shi, H., Vaslin, P., & Hou, K. M. (2020). Perception Assistance for the Visually Impaired Through Smart Objects: Concept, Implementation, and Experiment Scenario. *IEEE Access, 8*, 46931–46945. https://doi.org/10.1109/ACCESS.2020.2976543

5. Garcia-Macias, J. A., Ramos, A. G., Hasimoto-Beltran, R., & Pomares Hernandez, S. E. (2019). Uasisi: a modular and adaptable wearable system to assist the visually impaired. *Procedia Computer Science, 151*, 425–430. https://doi.org/10.1016/j.procs.2019.04.058

6. Dourado, A. M. B., & Pedrino, E. C. (2020). Multi-objective Cartesian Genetic Programming optimization of morphological filters in navigation systems for Visually Impaired People. *Applied Soft Computing, 89*, 106130. https://doi.org/10.1016/j.asoc.2020.106130

7. Gharani, P., & Karimi, H. (2017). Context-aware obstacle detection for navigation by visually impaired. *Image and Vision Computing, 64*. https://doi.org/10.1016/j.imavis.2017.06.002

8. Zhu, J., Hu, J., Zhang, M., Chen, Y., & Bi, S. (2020). A fog computing model for implementing motion guide to visually impaired. *Simulation Modelling Practice and Theory, 101*, 102015. https://doi.org/10.1016/j.simpat.2019.102015

9. Cordeiro, N., & Pedrino, E. (2019). A new methodology applied to dynamic object detection and tracking systems for visually impaired people. *Computers & Electrical Engineering, 77*, 61–71. https://doi.org/10.1016/j.compeleceng.2019.05.003

10. Chen, X., Xu, J., & Yu, Z. (2019). A 68-mw 2.2 Tops/w Low Bit Width and Multiplierless DCNN Object Detection Processor for Visually Impaired People. *IEEE Transactions on Circuits and Systems for Video Technology, 29*(11), 3444–3453. https://doi.org/10.1109/TCSVT.2018.2883087

11. Cordeiro, N. H., & Pedrino, E. C. (2019). Collision risk prediction for visually impaired people using high level information fusion. *Engineering Applications of Artificial Intelligence, 81*, 180–192. https://doi.org/10.1016/j.engappai.2019.02.016

12. Jimenez, M., Mello, R., Freire, T., & Frizera, A. (2020). Assistive Locomotion Device with Haptic Feedback For Guiding Visually Impaired People. *Medical Engineering & Physics, 80*. https://doi.org/10.1016/j.medengphy.2020.04.002

13. Pardeshi S.R., Pawar V.J., Kharat K.D., Chavan S. (2021) Assistive Technologies for Visually Impaired Persons Using Image Processing Techniques – A Survey. In: Santosh K.C., Gawali B. (eds) Recent Trends in Image Processing and Pattern Recognition. RTIP2R 2020. Communications in Computer and Information Science, vol 1380. Springer, Singapore. https://doi.org/10.1007/978-981-16-0507-9_9.

14. Guimares, C., Henriques, R., & Pereira, C. (2016). Tracking System Proposal of Walking Sticks Aiming the Orientation and Mobility of the Visually Impaired. *IFAC-PapersOnLine, 49*. https://doi.org/10.1016/j.ifacol.2016.11.147

15. Bauer, Z., Dominguez, A., Cruz, E., Gomez-Donoso, F., Orts-Escolano, S., & Cazorla, M. (2020). Enhancing perception for the visually impaired with deep learning techniques and low-cost wearable sensors. *Pattern Recognition Letters, 137*, 27–36. https://doi.org/10.1016/j.patrec.2019.03.008

16. Manjari, K., Verma, M., & Singal, G. (2020). A survey on Assistive Technology for visually impaired. *Internet of Things, 11*, 100188. https://doi.org/10.1016/j.iot.2020.100188

17. Mehta, U., Alim, M., & Kumar, S. (2017). Smart Path Guidance Mobile Aid for Visually Disabled Persons. *Procedia Computer Science, 105*, 52–56. https://doi.org/10.1016/j.procs.2017.01.190

18. Tanweer, M. R., Suresh, S., & Sundararajan, N. (2015). Self regulating particle swarm optimization algorithm. *Information Sciences, 294*, 182–202. https://doi.org/10.1016/j.ins.2014.09.053

19. Rewadkar, D., & Doye, D. (2017). FGWSO-TAR: Fractional glowworm swarm optimization for traffic aware routing in urban VANET. *International Journal of Communication Systems, 31*, e3430. https://doi.org/10.1002/dac.3430

20. Masadeh, R., Mahafzah, B., & Sharieh, A. (2019). Sea Lion Optimization Algorithm. *International Journal of Advanced Computer Science and Applications, 10*, 388–395. https://doi.org/10.14569/IJACSA.2019.0100548

21. Darekar Raviraj Vishwambhar, D. A. P. (2019). Emotion Recognition from Speech Signals Using DCNN with Hybrid GA-GWO Algorithm. *Multimedia Research, 2*(4), 12–22. https://doi.org/10.46253/j.mr.v2i4.a2

22. Sammulal, M. G. & K. M. C. &. (2019). Enhanced Crow Search Optimization Algorithm and Hybrid NN-CNN Classifiers for Classification of Land Cover Images. *Multimedia Research, 2*(3), 12–22. https://doi.org/10.46253/j.mr.v2i3.a2

23. G.Gokulkumari. (2020). Classification of Brain Tumor using Manta Ray Foraging Optimization-based DeepCNN Classifier. *Multimedia Research, 3*, 32–42. https://doi.org/10.46253/j.mr.v3i4.a4

24. Cardillo, E., Di Mattia, V., Manfredi, G., Russo, P., De Leo, A., Caddemi, A., & Cerri, G. (2018). An Electromagnetic Sensor Prototype to Assist Visually Impaired and Blind People in Autonomous Walking. *IEEE Sensors Journal, 18*(6), 2568–2576. https://doi.org/10.1109/JSEN.2018.2795046

25. Ye, C., & Qian, X. (2018). 3-D Object Recognition of a Robotic Navigation Aid for the Visually Impaired. *IEEE Transactions on Neural Systems and Rehabilitation Engineering, 26*(2), 441–450. https://doi.org/10.1109/TNSRE.2017.2748419

26. Chan, K. Y., Engelke, U., & Abhayasinghe, N. (2017). An edge detection framework conjoining with IMU data for assisting indoor navigation of visually impaired persons. *Expert Systems with Applications, 67*, 272–284. https://doi.org/10.1016/j.eswa.2016.09.007

27. Jindal, A., Aggarwal, N., & Gupta, S. (2018). An Obstacle Detection Method for Visually Impaired Persons by Ground Plane Removal Using Speeded-Up Robust Features and Gray Level Co-Occurrence Matrix. *Pattern Recognition and Image Analysis, 28*(2), 288–300. https://doi.org/10.1134/S1054661818020086

28. Arora, A., Grover, A., Chugh, R., & Reka, S. S. (2019). Real Time Multi Object Detection for Blind Using Single Shot Multibox Detector. *Wireless Personal Communications, 107*(1), 651–661. https://doi.org/10.1007/s11277-019-06294-1

29. Meshram, V. V., Patil, K., Meshram, V. A., & Shu, F. C. (2019). An Astute Assistive Device for Mobility and Object Recognition for Visually Impaired People. *IEEE Transactions on Human-Machine Systems, 49*(5), 449–460. https://doi.org/10.1109/THMS.2019.2931745

30. Afif, M., Ayachi, R., Said, Y., Pissaloux, E., & Atri, M. (2020). An Evaluation of RetinaNet on Indoor Object Detection for Blind and Visually Impaired Persons Assistance Navigation. *Neural Processing Letters, 51*(3), 2265–2279. https://doi.org/10.1007/s11063-020-10197-9

31. Aakash Krishna, G. S., Pon, V. N., Rai, S., & Baskar, A. (2020). Vision System with 3D Audio Feedback to assist Navigation for Visually Impaired. *Procedia Computer Science, 167*, 235–243. https://doi.org/10.1016/j.procs.2020.03.216

32. Li, F., Lv, X.-G., & Deng, Z. (2018). Regularized iterative Weiner filter method for blind image deconvolution. *Journal of Computational and Applied Mathematics, 336*, 425–438. https://doi.org/10.1016/j.cam.2017.12.026

33. SURF feature, from : "https://medium.com/data-breach/introduction-to-surf-speeded-up-robust-features-c7396d6e7c4e ", Access Date: 2021–0–17

34. SIFT feature, from :"https://medium.com/data-breach/introduction-to-sift-scale-invariant-feature-transform-65d7f3a72d40", Access Date: 2021–0–17

35. Canny edge detection, from: "https://docs.opencv.org/master/da/d22/tutorial_py_canny. html", Access Date: 2021–0–17

36. Beno, M., R, V., M, S., & Rajakumar, B. (2014). Threshold Prediction for Segmenting Tumour from Brain MRI Scans. *International Journal of Imaging Systems and Technology, 24.* https:// doi.org/10.1002/ima.22087

37. Chandrakala, M., & Durga Devi, P. (2021). Two-stage classifier for face recognition using HOG features. *Materials Today: Proceedings, 47*, 5771–5775. https://doi.org/10.1016/j. matpr.2021.04.114

38. Salve P., Sardesai M., Manza R., Yannawar P. (2016) Identification of the Plants Based on Leaf Shape Descriptors. In: Satapathy S., Raju K., Mandal J., Bhateja V. (eds) Proceedings of the Second International Conference on Computer and Communication Technologies. Advances in Intelligent Systems and Computing, vol 379. Springer, New Delhi. https://doi.org/10.1007/ 978-81-322-2517-1_10.

39. S. Gaikwad, B. Gawali, P. Yannawar and S. Mehrotra, "Feature extraction using fusion MFCC for continuous marathi speech recognition," 2011 Annual IEEE India Conference, 2011, pp. 1-5, doi: https://doi.org/10.1109/INDCON.2011.6139372.

40. K. D. Kharat, V. J. Pawar and S. R. Pardeshi, "Feature extraction and selection from MRI images for the brain tumor classification," *2016 International Conference on Communication and Electronics Systems (ICCES)*, 2016, pp. 1-5, doi: https://doi.org/10.1109/CESYS.2016. 7889969.

41. Pawar, Vikul & Kharat, Kailash & Pardeshi, Suraj. (2019). Enhancement in Brain Tumor Diagnosis Using MRI Image Processing Techniques: Second International Conference, ICAICR 2018, Shimla, India, July 14–15, 2018, Revised Selected Papers, Part I. https://doi.org/10. 1007/978-981-13-3140-4_59.

42. Vivek H. Mahale, Mouad M.H. Ali, Pravin L. Yannawar, Ashok T. Gaikwad, Image Inconsistency Detection Using Local Binary Pattern (LBP), Procedia Computer Science, Volume 115, 2017, Pages 501–508, ISSN 1877-0509, https://doi.org/10.1016/j.procs.2017.09.097. https:// www.sciencedirect.com/science/article/pii/S187705091731921X)

43. Dataset link: https://www.kaggle.com/c/imagenet-object-localization-challenge/data?select= imagenet_object_localization_patched2019.tar.gz

A Machine Learning Based Approach for Image Quality Assessment of Forged Document Images

Gayatri Patil[1,1(✉)], Shivanand S. Gornale[1], and Ashvini Babaleshwar[2]

[1] Department of Computer Science, Rani Channamma University, Belagavi, India
gayatripatil865@gmail.com
[2] Department of Computer Science, Garden City University, Bangalore, India

Abstract. Document Images, such as typed and handwritten documents can be manipulated in various ways using many sophisticated digital technologies and photo editing software's. As a result, one can alter the text in the typed and hand-written documents that leads to degradation of quality of an image. The detection of multiple inherently altering operations in an image is a challenging issue, hence in this work a novel approach is proposed for the ten-class problem in which the alteration of a text can be accomplished through multiple operations, which all create the specific pattern. These operations are analysed with the help of image quality measures and classified using random forests classifier. The proposed app-roach gives a better classification accuracy rate of 94% for forged printed docu-ment images and 98.80% of forged handwritten document images, which is more promising and competitive with state of the art techniques reported in the literature.

Keywords: Document Forgery · Image Quality Measures · Multiple forgery operations · Random Forest tree · Ten Class Classification

1 Introduction

In today's digital environment, the use of printed and handwritten document images in daily human activities is increasing. Manipulation of these document images is also increasing, with many sophisticated digital technologies and photo editing software's being used. As a result, the text in typed and handwritten documents can be changed. In the field of forensic science, altering text document images leads to forging and is considered a crime application [1]. For instance, a property agreement where the contents can be modified to make an illegal trade, or a plane ticket where the date may be changed to gain access to airport terminals by circumventing security. Handwritten documents are also used to produce false suicide letter, answer scripts, and certifications, among other things [2].

In computer vision and image processing, detecting forged videos and images is not a new issue; however, it is not a new problem in research. There are several methods available in literature [3, 4]. However, fraud recognition in document images including printed and handwritten document images is new as compared to video and images. This work receives special attention of the researchers [5]. This is because the document

© The Author(s) 2023
R. Manza et al. (Eds.): ACVAIT 2022, AISR 176, pp. 208–229, 2023.
https://doi.org/10.2991/978-94-6463-196-8_18

images are often used as an authenticated proof evidence for any crime investigation in court rooms. In addition, we the common people believe that the content in newspaper and internet are genuine and authenticated [6]. If the content in these documents is altered, it leads to misinformation and spreading wrong message to society. Therefore, it is necessary to verify authenticity and integrity of the documents automatically without human intervention.

To create forgery or fake documents and tampering original content, usually they use two operations, such as copy-paste and insertion [2]. In case of copy-paste operation they copy from the same document or different document to paste at target words while in case of insertion; people use software tools to edit the words by adding characters at appropriate places. If the document contains forged word with simple operation, there are methods to find solution in the literature [7, 8]. In reality, sometimes document suffers from degradations due to noise, document aging, paper quality, use of ink in case of handwriting etc. When the document contains forged words along with the words affected by the above degradations, the methods do not perform well and fail to detect the forged words [9, 10]. For instance, sample image for printed and handwritten document are shown in Fig. 1 and Fig. 2, where one can see different type of forged words in single document. This challenge remains an open issue for forgery detection.

To address these challenges, we create forged words with multiple operations. For example, for forged word created by copy-paste operation, we add noise to the same word, which is called Copy-Paste + Noise class. In the same way, we create Copy-Paste + Blur, Insertion + Noise, Insertion + Blur, Copy-Paste + Insertion along with copy-paste alone, insertion alone, noise and blur alone. This results in 10 classes of forged typed words and the sample images for each class are shown in Fig. 3 and Fig. 4, respectively for printed and handwriting documents.

2 Related Work

There are several methods for forgery detection in document images. The method can be classified broadly into two categories, namely, the methods which focus on printed document images and the method which focus on handwriting document images. We find hardly the methods focus on both printed and handwriting document images.

Barboza et al. [9] have proposed a color-based model to determine the age of document for forensic purpose based on analyzing the color histograms of sample images. The method works well for the document of age and it is limited to specific applications. However, the color alone is not sufficient to detect forged words in noise Beusekom et al. [11] have presented a tool for detecting forgery based on text-line details Rotation and alignment of text lines can also provide useful hints for discovering altered documents during a questioned text review. Calculating and classifying certain improper alignment and rotations is a time-consuming task. Based on these observations, the authors have presented an automated approach for verification of documents. The features extracted in the method are not robust to the proposed work. Gebhardt et al. [12] have developed a method for comparing the edge roughness of laser-printed and inkjet-printed pages. The work presented here should be interpreted as a foundation for intrinsic document verification in the context of poor resolution scans. The difficult task here is to implement a more robust edge detection to improve the quality of the feature and document

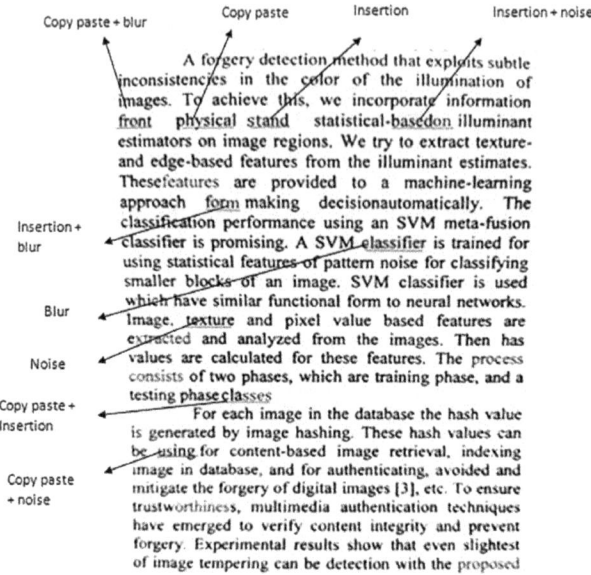

Fig. 1. An example of a forged printed document with ten classes of forgery at word level.

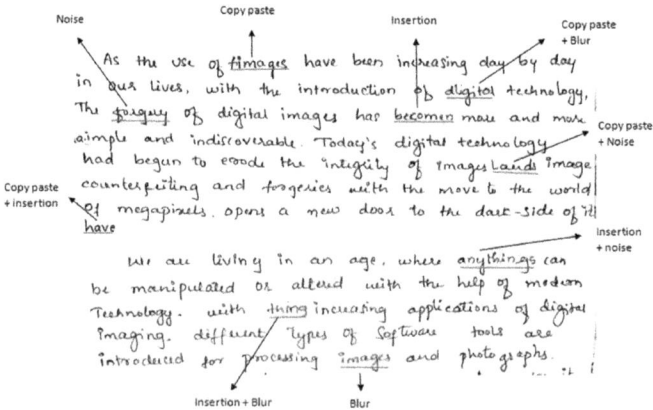

Fig. 2. An example of a forged handwritten document with ten classes of forgery at word level.

processing in order to identify image or italic text, which frequently leads to incorrect source identification. The method may not work for documents with blur and noise. Ryu et al. [13] have presented a method of detecting a forged document created by printers. In this work, seventeen different image quality measures were computed and trained using SVM (Support Vector Machine) classifiers. The method considers the quality measures as features by studying the quality of the images. This is good for the images affected by uniform quality factor else the method may not work well. Sometimes, the document can have different quality at different region in a single image. Chen et al. [14] propose a forensic technique for identifying global blur in entire images using no-reference image

Fig. 3. Example for the forged words of all the 10 classes in order for printed document image shown in Fig. 1.

quality assessment. Using mean subtracted contrast normalized (MSCN) coefficients, the features are extracted and fed into SVM, which can distinguish the altered regions from the original ones and quantify them. Here the tampered images used are well resolution except tempered regions. The method gives false-alarm detection when the entire forged images are of weak resolution. Shang et al. [15] have presented a method of exposing document forgeries using distortion mutation of geometric parameters such as of translation and rotation distortions through image matching for each character. To detect tampered characters with distortion authors have used distortion probability, which is calculated from character distortion parameters. The method is suitable for document examination in both Chinese and English. The drawback of this method is it will work only on printed document which consist of only namely, Chinese and English but the method fails to work on handwritten documents. Cruz et al. [16] Explored classification based forgery detection method, which uses Local Binary Patterns (LBP) for computing discriminant texture features that are common on forged regions and then computed features are fed to Support Vector Machines (SVM) for classification. Author have performed 4 different types of forgery on printed document images namely, Copy-Paste Intra document, Copy-Paste Extra document, Imitation and Region cuts. The method represents much incorrect detection and is not acceptable for real time applications. The

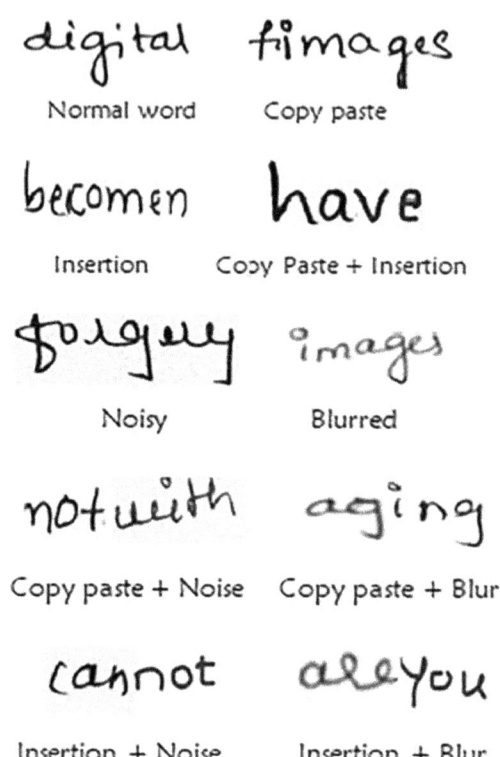

Fig. 4. Example for the forged words of all the 10 classes in order for handwriting document shown in Fig. 2

work is carried out on only printed document images not on handwritten documents. Megahed et al. [17] have proposed a method to detect handwritten forgery in text by detecting different ink using image processing. The features are extracted based on red, green and blue channels. Also computed distance measurements between each pairs of feature vector using Root Mean Square Error. Gorai et al. [18] proposed a method to perform forged handwriting inspection. The three RGB color channels of the handwritten picture were retrieved, as well as the texture features of the grayscale image, and the histogram matching approach was utilized.

It is observed from the preceding work that many researchers have worked for forgery detection in both printed and handwritten document images and raised the following challenges and issues.

- Detecting the altered text in different quality images.
- Handwritten documents written by different ink and pen.
- Document image contains both typed text and handwritten text.
- Document images affected by multiple forgery operations.
- Document images affected by distortion and noise generated by printer overlap.

- Identification altered text in document images rather than printer identification.

Hence to overcome the above challenges and issues the authors have introduced a ten class classification problem in handwritten and printed document images which contains text with variation in different writing styles and affected by multiple forgery operations. The dataset description is explained in detail under Implementation and Results section.

3 Proposed Methodology

The proposed methodology consists of three main steps, pre-processing, Feature Extraction and Classification of computed features as illustrated in the Fig. 5. The distortions in the original images are caused by tampering operations such as insertion, copy paste, copy paste + noise, copy paste + blur, Noise + Insertion, Insertion + Blur, and Insertion + Copypaste on the original images, which all creates complicated patterns. Whereas the Blur and Noise operations are produces the desired patterns on original and forged images using Gaussian distortions. Further, when we perform multiple forgery operations on text, the possibility and degree of image noise multiplies when compared to only one operation on text. Taking these observations into consideration, the traditional features like Image Quality Assessments with the help of a random forest tree classifier has been used to solve the ten-class problem. This is due to the fact that our primary objective is to distinguish between original and forged documents based on specific patterns and distortions created by various forgery operations.

3.1 Pre-processing

For the better understanding of image it is important to pre-process an image which may enhance some important features of an image. In this work preprocessing is carried out by converting color document image into gray scale images and resized to 350X350 for the proper analysis of Documents.

3.2 Feature Extraction

While working on an image it is important to compute the features of an image which is the method of capturing visual content of image for indexing and retrieval. The extraction of features is used to denote a piece of information that is important to solving a computer task related to a certain application. In this work we computed features of pre-processed handwritten and printed document images using MATLAB which results in recognition of accuracy with simple classification modules.

3.2.1 Image Quality Measures

Image Quality Assessment (IQA) is a process of extracting image quality features to determine whether or not an image is genuine. The fake image differs from the real image in numerous ways when a forgery operation is attempted. A number of factors influence image quality. Performance, diversity, and speed are the three characteristics to look at. Predictable quality is defined by varying degrees of sharpness, brightness, covariance,

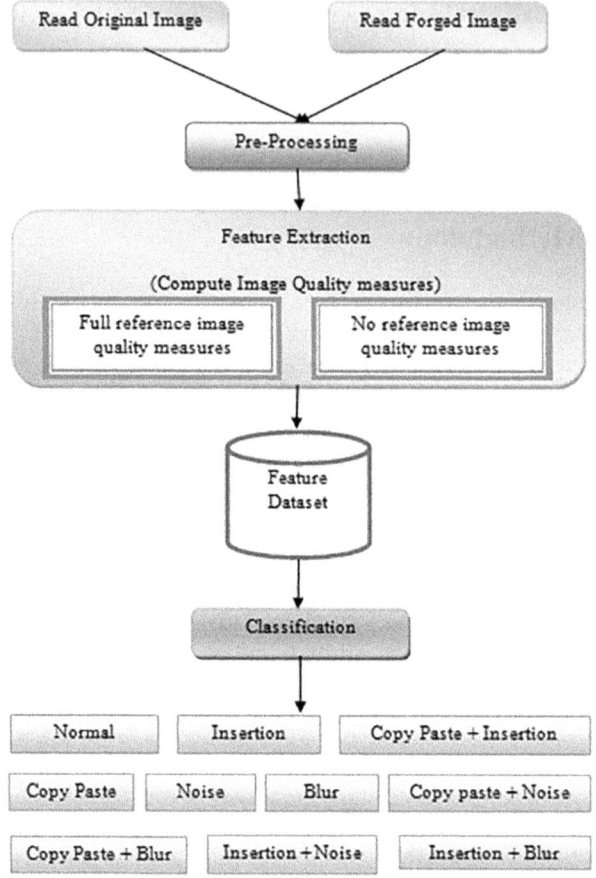

Fig. 5. Block diagram of proposed technique

blur, gradient, distortions, and a strong correlation, and the information generated by both types of images will differ in content. [19].

To assess the quality of distorted images, a variety of methodologies have been developed. Subjective and objective approaches of IQA can be distinguished. Subjective approaches cannot automate the system and are time-consuming and inconvenient because they are depending on human judgment. Evaluation of objective image quality is intended to provide quality measurements that can be used to predict image perception automatically [20]. The objective method is a quantitative strategy in which we utilize the intensity of two images, a reference and distorted type, to create a number that indicates image quality. Based on the availability of a reference image, objective methods are divided into three categories: full-reference, no-reference, and hybrid [21].

3.2.1.1. Full Reference Image Quality Measure
In Full Reference image quality evaluation approaches, the Qualitative aspect of a query image is assessed by contrasting it with a reference image of ideal quality. A number

of Full Reference image quality assessment approaches are available. The most widely used and well-known methods are Peak Signal to Noise Ration and Mean Square error [20]. Some other quality measures are based on 1. Error Sensitivity Measure which includes Pixel Difference Measure, Correlation Based Measure, Edge based Measure, spatial based measures and Gradient Based Measure 2. Structural similarity index and 3. Information Theoretic that includes Visual information fidelity. Following are the full reference image quality measures were computed on forged handwritten and printed document images.

- Mean Squared Error: The mean squared error is measured as the mean of the "errors" squared in original image and reference image as represented in Eq. (1).

$$MSE = \frac{1}{N} \sum_{i=1}^{N} (X_i - Y_i)^2 \tag{1}$$

  Where N is number of samples, X is original image and Y is reference image.
- Root Mean Square Error: The squared root of MSE yields the Root Mean Square Error (RMSE). The root mean square error (RMSE) is a metric that indicates how much a pixel changes as a result of processing, as represented in Eq. (2).

$$RMSE = \sqrt{MSE} \tag{2}$$

- Peak Signal to Noise Ratio (PSNR): Using PSNR, we can calculate the ratio between the greatest possible signal strength and the power of distortion, which has an impact on the quality of its representation [24]. The below Eq. (3) used to calculate the PSNR.

$$PSNR = 10 log_{10} \frac{P^2}{MSE} \tag{3}$$

  Where P is dynamic range of pixel intensity
- Signal to Noise Ratio (SNR): The signal-to-noise ratio is the proportion of desired information (signal power) to undesired information (background noise power). SNR calculates the signal-to-noise ratio (SNR) of a signal X in decibels by dividing its summed squared magnitude by the noise, Y as represented in below Eq. (4).

$$SNR = 10 log_{10} \left(\frac{\sum_{i=1}^{n} X_i^2}{\sum_{j=1}^{n} Y_i^2} \right) \tag{4}$$

- Structural Content (SC): It is calculated as the square of sum of the original and referred image, which is represented in below Eq. (5).

$$SC(X, Y) = \frac{\sum_{i=1}^{N} \sum_{j=1}^{M} (X_i, j)^2}{\sum_{i=1}^{N} \sum_{j=1}^{M} (Y_i, j)^2} \tag{5}$$

- Maximum Difference (MD): The highest value of the absolute difference image is computed i.e. A subtraction is made between the original and the reference image. The below Eq. (6) used to calculate MD

$$MD(X, Y) = max|X_{i,j} - Y_{i,j}| \tag{6}$$

- Average Difference (AD): It is calculated for each pixel in an image to determine the absolute difference average. A subtraction is made between the original and the reference image. The Eq. (7) represents the formulae to calculate AD.

$$AD(X, Y) = \frac{1}{NM} \sum_{i=1} N \sum_{j=1} M (X_{i,j} - Y_{i,j}) \tag{7}$$

- Normalized Absolute Error(NAE): It is calculated by dividing the total of the difference image by the total of the original image as given in below Eq. (8).

$$NAE(X, Y) = \frac{\sum_{i=1} N \sum_{j=1} M |X_{i,j} - Y_{i,j}|}{\sum_{i=1} N \sum_{j=1} M |X_{i,j}|} \tag{8}$$

- Normalized Cross-Correlation (NK): The simplest but most effective similarity measure is normalized cross correlation, which is unaffected by linear brightness and contrast fluctuations which is represented by following Eq. (9).

$$NK(X, Y) = \frac{\sum_{i=1}^{N} \sum_{j=1}^{M} |X_{i,j} \cdot Y_{i,j}|}{\sum_{i=1}^{N} \sum_{j=1}^{M} \lceil X_{i,j} \rceil^2} \tag{9}$$

- Laplacian Mean Squared Error (LMSE): The term Laplacian Mean Square Error refers to the calculation of the normal mean square error. The difference is that the mean square error is determined using the laplacian value of the data rather than the predicted and obtained data [25]. The given Eq. (10) used to calculate LMSE.

$$LMSE(X, Y) = \frac{\sum_{i=1}^{N} \sum_{j=1}^{M} \left(h(X_{ij}) - h(Y_{ij}) \right)}{\sum_{i=1}^{N} \sum_{j=1}^{M} \left(h(X_{ij}) \right)^2} \tag{10}$$

- Total Edge Difference (TED): It's define d as the ratio of the two images' total number of edge differences to the total number of pixels, as given in Eq. (11).

$$TED(X, Y) = \frac{1}{NM} \sum_{i=1} N \sum_{j=1} M |XE_{i,j} - YE_{i,j}| \tag{11}$$

- Total Corner Difference: It is the ratio of the total amount of edge variations between two images to entire pixels in the image, as represented in below Eq. (12).

$$TCD(X, Y) = \frac{|Xtcr - Ytcr|}{max|Xtcr - Ytcr|} \tag{12}$$

- Gradient Magnitude Error: The total number of pixels is used to average the difference between the gradients of the original image, as well as the gradients of the reference image. The following Eq. (13) shows the representation of GME

$$GME(X, Y) = \frac{1}{NM} \sum_{i=1} N \sum_{j=1} M \left(|XG_{i,j}| - |YG_{ij}| \right)^2 \tag{13}$$

- Gradient Phase Error: It is calculated using the overall count of pixels as the mean deviation between the gradient angle of the real image and the gradient angle of the reference image, which is defined in following Eq. (14)

$$GPE(X,Y) = \frac{1}{NM} \sum_{i=1} N \sum_{j=1} M \left| arg\left(XG_{ij}\right) - arg\left(YG_{ij}\right) \right|^2 \qquad (14)$$

- Structural Similarity Index Measure: The notion of image quality assessment based on structural similarity emerged from the idea that the visual system of human is well-adapted for obtaining structural information from the observing field. The most straightforward formulation is the Structural Similarity Index Measure (SSIM), which is broadly used in a variety of relevant implementations. SSIM Means of measuring loss of structure in the image instead of any deviation from the reference. Loss of visual structure as assessed on a local scale using luminance, contrast and structural similarity [26] as represented in Eq. (15), (16) and (17) respectively

$$L(X,Y) = \frac{2\mu_x\mu_y + C1}{\mu_x^2 + \mu_y^2 + C1} \qquad (15)$$

$$C(X,Y) = \frac{2\sigma_x\sigma_y + C2}{\sigma_x^2 + \sigma_y^2 + C2} \qquad (16)$$

$$S(X,Y) = \frac{2\sigma_{xy} + C3}{\sigma_x + \sigma_y + C3} \qquad (17)$$

where $\mu_x\mu_y$ are the mean values of original and reference images, $\sigma_x\sigma_y$ indicates standard deviation of original and reference images, σ_{xy} represents the covariance of original and reference image and C1, C2, C3 are the constants. Depending upon the above three equations the SSIM is represented as in Eq. (18).

$$SSIM(X,Y) = L(X,Y).C(X,Y).S(X,Y) = \frac{\left(2\mu_x\mu_y + C1\right)\left(2\sigma_{xy} + C2\right)}{\left(\mu_x^2 + \mu_y^2 + C1\right)\left(\sigma_x^2 + \sigma_y^2 + C2\right)}$$

$$(18)$$

- Feature based similarity index: Index of Feature Similarity The method compares two images by mapping their features and measuring their similarity.
- Visual Information Fidelity (VIF): Visual images are regarded as natural scenarios based on the VIF model with statistical qualities similar to those of natural scenarios [19]. The Visual Saliency Induced quality measure assumes that image deterioration causes changes in salient regions that are strongly connected to changes in visual quality [27].

3.2.1.2. No Reference Image Quality Measure

This is a method for estimating the quality of a blind image. Without a reference image, the perceived image quality is estimated here [22]. In recent decades, NR-IQA has received a lot of attention. Although NR-IQA algorithms do not have access to a reference image, they can assume things about the distortions inherent in a specific input image [23]. As a result, they can be classified as distortion-specific measures that cope with image quality indexes, traditional-based measures that deal with blind/referenceless image spatial quality evaluator, and Natural image quality evaluator.

Following are the No reference image quality measures were computed on forged handwritten and printed document images.

- Brisque: The Brisque model assesses image quality by employing the locally normalized luminance coefficients that were used to compute image features.
- Natural Image Quality Evaluator: To train the first model, it leverages a priori knowledge extracted from distortion-free images of natural scenes. The Natural Image Quality Evaluator (NIQE) is an absolutely blind quality of the image analyzer that is actually based on the development of a performance aware set of numerical features linked to a multi variate Gaussian natural scene statistical approach.

3.3 Classification

For the experiment, an image dataset of 950 handwritten and forged documents were used, which are classified into ten different classes: Normal, Noise, Blur, Insertion, Copy Paste, CopyPaste + Noise, CopyPaste + Blur, Insertion + Noise, Insertion + Blur and Insertion + Copy Paste. We used the above-mentioned image quality measures as a single feature vector to classify these various forged input images. Various classification techniques such as KNN, Naïve Bayes and Random Forest tree classifiers were used in the experiment. The results of KNN and Naïve Bayes classifiers are insufficient. To improve the accuracy rate we used the Random Forest Classifier and it produced good results.

3.3.1 KNN

One of the least complicated ones is K-Nearest Neighbor. The Machine Learning Algorithm is based on the Supervised Learning procedure, in which the classifier basically obtains the similarity between the test information and the training set [28]. The classification of the class labels depends on calculating the distance between training and testing dataset. KNN classifies the data with Suitable K value thus finds a closest neighbor that provides a class label to un-labeled images [29]. A verity of distance measures was implemented depending on type of problem. City-block distance with K value equals to 3 is considered whose value is empirically fixed. KNN shows the test data M, and then finds the distance D between training sample X and testing pattern N using the following equation.

$$\text{Dcity}(X, Y) = \sum_{j=0}^{n} |X_J - Y_J| \tag{19}$$

3.3.2 Naïve Bayes

Naïve Bayes is a simple probabilistic classifier that predicts on basis of probability of objects which works based on Bayes theorem [30] as given in below equation.

$$P(X|Y) = \frac{P(Y|X)P(X)}{P(Y)} \tag{20}$$

where,

- P (X|Y) is Posterior probability: Provided proof that Y has already occurred, the probability of X occurring.
- P (Y|X) is Likelihood probability: Provided proof that X has already occurred, the probability of Y occurring.
- P (X) is Prior Probability: Probability of X Occurring
- P (Y) is Marginal Probability: Probability of Y Occurring

3.3.3 Random Forest

Random Forest is a well-known and widely used machine learning algorithm. The forest of decision trees is known as Random Forest. This technique can be used for both classification and regression tasks. It is a decision tree ensemble that predicts the outcomes depending on a set of variables as well as rules and aggregates the outcomes of multiple decision trees in order to achieve better performance. The combination of each decision tree's outcomes reduces the total generalization fault and the over fitting issue. [31]. In this experiment random forest tree classifier has achieved better results as compared to other classifiers. The Table 2 provides the detailed analysis and performance test with different number of trees of random forest tree on forged handwritten and printed document images.

The proposed method is represented in form of algorithm as follows.

Algorithm:

Input: Handwritten / Printed Forged Document Image
Output: Classification of handwritten/Printed Forged Document Image.

Step 1: Acquisition of Handwritten/Printed Forged Document Image

Step 2: Pre-Processing i.e. converting into Gray scale and resize the images to 350X350 for further analysis

Step 3: Computation of features using Image Quality Measures I.e. Full Reference and No Reference quality Measures

Step 4: Classification of Obtained Features using KNN, Naïve Bayes and Random Forest classifiers

Step 5: Output of the predicted class.

4   Implementation and Results

The experiment is carried out on own created dataset which consist of 950 Forged documents (500 forged handwritten + 450 forged printed document images) of 10 different classes as discussed Table 1. Full reference and No Reference Image Quality Measures were computed and classified using Classifiers such as Nave Bayes, K-NN and Random Forest. Among these classifiers random forest tree gave good results. Hence the results of random forest tree are predicted.

4.1   Dataset

From the literature review, it has been found that the standard datasets available includes documents with few forgery operations such as noise, blur, copy paste and insertion but they do not contain the handwritten documents with multiple forgery operations. In order to cope up with the problem own dataset has been created with 950 forged document images that includes 500 forged handwritten document images and 450 forged printed document images with 10 different class of different forgery operations like, Copy-Paste, Noise, Blur, Insertion, Copy-Paste + Noise, Copy-Paste + Blur, Insertion + Noise, Insertion + Blur, and Copy-Paste + Insertion and Normal. Each class of forged handwritten document images consist of 50 images and in forged printed document images, each class consist of 45 images. Initially, LaserJet M1136 MFP scanner is used to scan the Handwritten and printed documents were with 200 DPI and then performed 10 different tampering operations on each image.

The description for all the 10 classes is presented in Table 1, where we can see operations are used for creating forged words. When conducting multiple forgery operations on text, one operation uses half portion of the word and another half portion of the word is affected by other forgery operation. If the forged word is created by single operation, the whole word is affected by the operation. It is noted from Fig. 3 and Fig. 4 that it is difficult to notice the difference between original and forged words except blur and noise.

The quantitative classification results of proposed method using fusion of full reference and no reference image quality measures on forged Handwritten and forged printed documents were represented in Table 3 and Table 4 respectively. It is observed from Table 3 and Table 4 that the values present diagonally in table are considered to be correct classification and off diagonal values represents misclassification. Table 5 represents the performance analysis of individual features and fusion of features using KNN, Naïve Bayes and Random Forest tree classifiers on forged handwritten and printed document images. The performance of proposed methodology is evaluated in terms of metrics, such as Precision, F_Score, Recall, and Accuracy as represented in Eq. (21) to Eq. (24) respectively.

$$Precision = \frac{TruePositive}{TruePositive + FalsePositive} \tag{21}$$

$$F_{Score} = \frac{2 * Precision * Recall}{Precision + Recall} \tag{22}$$

Table 1. Ten- Class Classification Problem

Forgery Type	Description
Class 1: Normal Words	Original words without affecting by any forgery operations.
Class 2: Copy- Paste	By using a copy-paste procedure, forged words are formed.
Class 3: Insertion	Words that have been forged as a result of an insertion operation
Class 4: Copy-Paste + Insertion	Both copy-paste and insertion operations result in forged words.
Class 5: Noise	Adding various types of noise to the original images.
Class 6: Blur	Adding blur to the original images.
Class 7: Copy-Paste + Noise	Add different noises to forged words created by a copy-paste operation.
Class 8: Copy-Paste + Blur	Add a different blur to forged words created by a copy-paste operation.
Class 9: Insertion + Noise	Add different noises to the forged words created by the insertion technique.
Class 10: Insertion + Blur	Add a different blur to forged words created by the insertion operation.

Table 2. Performance Analysis Test with Different Number of Trees of Random Forest On Forged Handwritten and Printed Document Images

SL No	Features	Number of Trees	Accuracy (in %)	
			Forged Handwritten Document	**Forged Printed Document**
1	Full Reference + No Reference Image Quality Measures	7	97.05%	92.43%
2		8	97.23%	92.90%
3		9	97.86%	93.03%
4		10	98.00%	93.56%
5		11	98.45%	93.89%
6		**12**	**98.80%**	**94%**

$$Recall = \frac{TruePositive}{TruePositive + FalseNegative} * 100 \qquad (23)$$

$$Accuracy = \frac{TruePositive + TrueNegative}{TruePositive + TrueNegative + FalsePositive + FalseNegative} * 100 \qquad (24)$$

Where the class Abbreviations in Table 3 and Table 4 are: BLUR: Blur, CP + NS: Copy Pate + Noise, INS + NS: Insertion + Noise, NOISE: Noise, CP + BLR: Copy Paste + Blur, NRM: Normal, CP: Copy Paste, CP + INS: Copy Paste + Insertion, INS + BLUR: Insertion + Blur, INS: Insertion.

Where the Abbreviations in Table 5 are: FRIQM: Full Reference Image Quality Measure, NRIQM: No Reference Image Quality Measure.

From the Table 5, it is observed that individual performance of full reference image quality measures on forged handwritten and printed document images using KNN classifier is achieved as 78.2% and 74.7% respectively, using Naïve Bayes achieved as 83.5% and 80.6% respectively and using random forest tree classifier is achieved as 96.8% and 92.2% respectively. For the individual performance of no reference image quality measures on forged handwritten and printed document images using KNN classifier is achieved as 79.2% and 75.3% respectively, using Naïve Bayes achieved as 86.9% and 84.1% respectively and using random forest tree classifier is achieved as 97.4% and 93.11% respectively. The fusion of full reference and no reference image quality measure on forged printed document images and forged handwritten images yields the highest accuracy rate of **94%** and **98.80%** respectively using Random Forest tree classifier whereas, KNN and Naïve Bayes classifiers results in lower accuracy rate as compared to random forest tree classifier. Figure 6 represents the graphical representation of classification performance of individual and fusion of features.

In order to conduct the experiments, MATLAB R2018a image processing tool box was used on a machine equipped with an Intel Core i5-6200U @ 2.40 GHz, 4.00 GB of RAM, and a 64-bit operating system.

Table 3. Confusion Matrix for Fusion of Full Reference and No Reference Image Quality Measures On Forged Handwritten Documents Using Random Forest Tree Classifier.

	BLUR	CP	NRM	CP + BLR	CP + INS	CP + NS	INS + BLR	INS	INS + NS	NOISE
BLUR	50	0	0	0	0	0	0	0	0	0
CP	0	49	1	0	0	0	0	0	0	0
NRM	0	1	49	0	0	0	0	0	1	0
CP + BLR	0	0	0	50	0	1	0	0	1	0
CP + INS	0	0	0	0	50	0	0	0	0	0
CP + NS	0	0	0	0	0	49	0	0	0	0
INS + BLR	0	0	0	0	0	0	50	0	0	0
INS	0	0	0	0	0	0	0	50	0	1
INS + NS	0	0	0	0	0	0	0	0	48	0
NOISE	0	0	0	0	0	0	0	0	0	49

5 Statistical Test of Significance

Statistical test of significance is used to evaluate the experimental findings are statistically significant or no. It's the way of evaluating obtained results to a predictable data assertion. The Chi-Square Test is used to validate the statistical inference in this study at a significance level of 5%.

A chi-square statistic is an assessment that compares a framework to actual observations. The null hypothesis, alternative hypothesis, and degrees of freedom in this test are as follows:

- Null Hypothesis (H_0): There is a strong correlation between the findings of the proposed methodology and the total number of forged document images.
- Alternative Hypothesis (H_1): There is no strong correlation between the findings of the proposed methodology and the total number of forged document images.
- Degree of Freedom (df) = 9, At a 5% significance level, the critical value of x^2 with df = 9 is 16.92. (From the chi-square table).

Table 4. Confusion Matrix for Fusion of Full Reference and No Reference Image Quality Measures On Forged Printed Documents Using Random Forest Tree Classifier

	BLUR	NRM	CP	INS + BLR	CP + BLR	CP + INS	CP + NS	INS	INS + NS	NOISE
BLUR	44	1	0	0	0	0	0	0	0	0
NRM	1	40	0	0	0	0	0	0	0	0
CP	0	0	38	0	0	0	2	0	1	0
INS + BLR	0	1	1	43	2	0	0	0	0	0
CP + BLR	0	0	4	1	43	1	0	1	0	0
CP + INS	0	0	1	0	0	44	0	0	0	0
CP + NS	0	1	1	0	0	0	43	0	0	0
INS	0	0	0	0	0	0	0	39	0	0
INS + NS	0	1	0	0	0	0	0	5	44	0
NOISE	0	1	0	1	0	0	0	0	0	45

Table 5. The Performance Comparison of the Individual Features and Fusion of Features Using KNN, Naïve Bayes and Random Forest Tree Classifier On Forged Printed and Handwritten Document Images (In %)

Feature Set	Classifier	Forged Handwritten Documents				Forged Printed Documents			
		Precision	Recall	F-Score	Accuracy	Precision	Recall	F-Score	Accuracy
FRIQM	KNN	0.7805	0.7621	0.7831	78.2%	0.7463	0.7539	0.7498	74.7%
	Naïve Bayes	0.8301	0.8391	0.8269	83.5%	0.8051	0.8134	0.8083	80.6%
	Random Forest	0.9605	0.9738	0.9692	96.8%	0.9201	0.9386	0.9231	92.2%
NRIQM	KNN	0.7816	0.7864	0.7963	79.2%	0.7502	0.7653	0.7564	75.3%
	Naïve Bayes	0.8521	0.8591	0.8693	86.9%	0.8410	0.8409	0.8406	84.1%
	Random Forest	0.9683	0.9829	0.9761	97.4%	0.9218	0.9435	0.9318	93.11%
FRIQM + NRIQM	KNN	0.7904	0.7896	0.7801	79.8%	0.7621	0.7713	0.7631	76.4%
	Naïve Bayes	0.8742	0.8861	0.8761	87.7%	0.8510	0.8614	0.8493	85.6%
	Random Forest	0.9703	0.9958	0.9834	**98.80%**	0.9400	0.9410	0.9405	**94%**

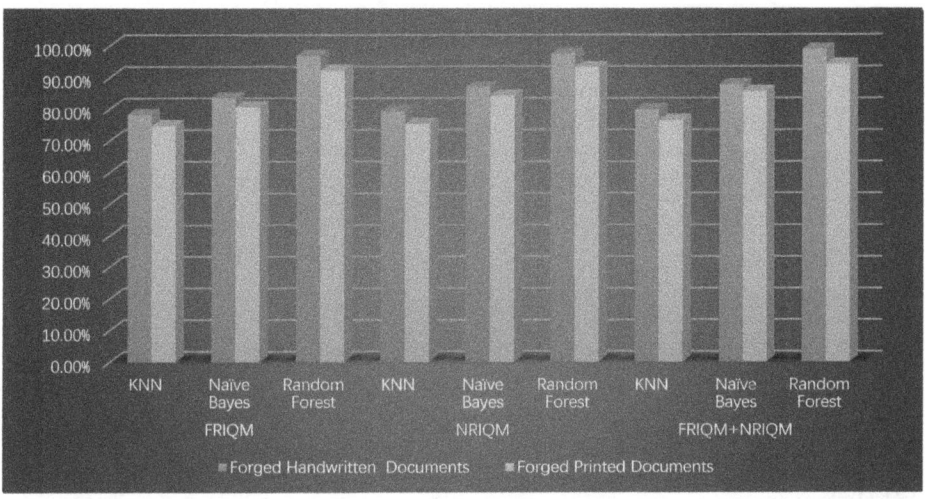

Figure. 6. The graphical representation of classification performance of individual and fusion of features.

If $x^2 < 16.92$, Accept H_0 and Reject H_1, else vice versa.

The Table 6. Represents the performance analysis of Chi-Square examination on total forged document images and proposed algorithm for classification. Eq. (23) defines the computation of Chi-Square Statistics.

$$Chi - Square(x^2) = \sum \frac{(D_o - D_e)^2}{D_e} = 1.392 \qquad (23)$$

The Chi Square statistic's determined value is less than the critical value from the chi square table. As a result, the Null Hypothesis H_0 is acceptable, whereas the alternative hypothesis H_1 is rejected. It illustrates that the proposed approach and the observations provided by the entire quantity of forged document images have a significant association.

Table 6. Performance Analysis of Chi-Square Test On Total Forged Document Images and Proposed Algorithm for Classification.

Forgery Types	Total Forged Images (Handwritten + Printed) Hi	Proposed Method (Handwritten + Printed) Pi	Total (Hi + Pi)	Expected Values (De)	Observed Values (Do)	$x^2 = \sum \frac{(D_o - D_e)^2}{D_e}$
Blur	95	94	189	96	93	0.093
CopyPaste	95	87	182	93	89	0.172
CopyPaste + Insertion	95	94	189	96	93	0.093

(continued)

Table 6. (*continued*)

Forgery Types	Total Forged Images (Handwritten + Printed) Hi	Proposed Method (Handwritten + Printed) Pi	Total (Hi + Pi)	Expected Values (De)	Observed Values (Do)	$x^2 = \sum \frac{(D_o - D_e)^2}{D_e}$
CopyPaste + Blur	95	93	188	96	92	0.167
CopyPaste + Noise	95	92	187	95	92	0.095
Insertion	95	89	184	94	90	0.170
Insertion + Blur	95	93	188	96	92	0.167
Insertion + Noise	95	92	182	93	89	0.172
Noise	95	94	189	96	93	0.094
Normal	95	89	184	94	90	0.170
Total	$\sum Hi = \sum H_i = 950$	$\sum P_i = \sum Pi = 917$	$\sum (H_i + P_i) = 1862$			$x^2 = 1.392$

6 Conclusion

In this paper, we proposed a method for classifying forged handwritten and printed document Images. The proposed method investigates the extraction of image quality measures such as full reference and no reference image quality measures from document images containing words affected by ten different types of forgery operations, including copy paste, Noisy, Blurred, Insertion, copy paste + noise, copy paste + blur, copy paste + insertion, insertion + noise, insertion + blur, and normal. Document images are extremely susceptible to unwanted distortions caused by scanners while scanning documents, as well as distortion caused by forgery operations, which may overlap with distortion in normal images and degrades the image quality. To address these issues, the authors employed techniques that provide an effective method for better understanding and analyzing handwritten and printed document images. Using the Random Forest classifier, the method achieves an accuracy rate of 94% on forged printed document images and 98.80% on forged handwritten document images. In the future, technology for automatic detection of forged words affected by multiple forgery operations in both handwritten and printed document images need to be developed.

Acknowledgement. The authors would like to express their gratitude to all students at Rani Channamma University in Belagavi, Karnataka, India, who willingly shared samples of handwritten and printed documents for this research study.

Authors' Contributions. Gayatri Patil[1]: Conceptualization, Methodology, Software, Field study Shivanand Gornale[2]: Data curation, Writing-Original draft preparation, Software, Validation., Field study Ashivini Babaleshwar[3]: Visualization, Investigation, Writing-Reviewing and Editing.

Compliance With Ethical Standards. • Conflict of Interest: The authors state that they do not have any conflicts of interest.

• Research involving Human and Animal Rights: There are no animal trials by any of the authors in this paper.

• Ethical Standards: All procedures used in research involving human volunteers were compatible with the institution's ethical guidelines.

References

1. S. Sapna, S. Vaibhav , A.K.Gupta "A Review of Trends In Digital Image Processing For Forensic Consideration" International Journal of Software and Hardware Researh in Engineering (IJSHRE), ISSN-2347–4890 Volume 3 Issue 8 August, 2015.
2. S. Kundu, P. Shivakumara, A. Grouver, U. Pal, T. Lu and M. Blumenstein," A New Forged Handwriting Detection Method Based on Fourier Spectral Density and Variation", In Proc. Of Autorité de contrôle prudentiel et de résolution (ACPR)pp 136–150, 2019.
3. L. Su, C. Li, Y. Lai and J. Yang, "A Fast Forgery Detection Algorithm Based on Exponential-Fourier Moments for Video Region Duplication," in IEEE Transactions on Multimedia, vol. 20, no. 4, pp. 825-840, doi: https://doi.org/10.1109/TMM.2017.2760098, April 2018.
4. L. D'Amiano, D. Cozzolino, G. Poggi and L. Verdoliva, "A PatchMatch-Based Dense-Field Algorithm for Video Copy–Move Detection and Localization," in IEEE Transactions on Circuits and Systems for Video Technology, vol. 29, no. 3, pp. 669–682, doi: https://doi.org/10.1109/TCSVT.2018.2804768, March 2019
5. HanyFarid "Image Forgery Detection: A Survey" IEEE Signal Processing Magazine March 2009.
6. B. Sarma, G. Nandi," A Study on Digital Image Forgery Detection", International Journal of Advanced Research in Computer Science and Software Engineering, Volume 4, Issue 11, ISSN: 2277 128X, November 2014
7. Z. Luo, F. Shafait and A. Mian, "Localized forgery detection in hyperspectral document images," 2015 13th International Conference on Document Analysis and Recognition (ICDAR), Tunis, Tunisia, pp. 496–500, doi: https://doi.org/10.1109/ICDAR.2015.7333811, 2015
8. M. J. Khan, A. Yousaf, K. Khurshid, A. Abbas and F. Shafait, "Automated Forgery Detection in Multispectral Document Images Using Fuzzy Clustering," 13th IAPR International Workshop on Document Analysis Systems (DAS), Vienna, Austria, 2018, pp. 393–398, doi: https://doi.org/10.1109/DAS.2018.26, 2018
9. R. d. S. Barboza, R. D. Lins and D. M. d. Jesus, "A Color-Based Model to Determine the Age of Documents for Forensic Purposes," 12th International Conference on Document Analysis and Recognition, Washington, DC, USA, 2013, pp. 1350–1354, doi: https://doi.org/10.1109/ICDAR.2013.273, 2013
10. L. Nandanwar . et al. "A New Method for Detecting Altered Text in Document Image". In: Lu Y., Vincent N., Yuen P.C., Zheng WS., Cheriet F., Suen C.Y. (eds) Pattern Recognition and Artificial Intelligence. ICPRAI 2020. Lecture Notes in Computer Science, vol 12068. Springer, Cham. https://doi.org/10.1007/978-3-030-59830-3_8, 2020

11. Beusekom, Joost & Shafait, Faisal & Breuel, Thomas. "Text-line examination for document forgery detection", International Journal on Document Analysis and Recognition (IJDAR). 16. 189–207. https://doi.org/10.1007/s10032-011-0181-5, 2012

12. J. Gebhardt, M. Goldstein, F. Shafait and A. Dengel, "Document Authentication Using Printing Technique Features and Unsupervised Anomaly Detection," 2013 12th International Conference on Document Analysis and Recognition, Washington, DC, USA, pp. 479–483, doi: https://doi.org/10.1109/ICDAR.2013.102, 2013

13. S. J. Ryu, H. Y. Lee, I, W. Cho, and H. K. Lee," Document Forgery Detection with SVM Classifier and Image Quality Measures",Lecture Notes in Computer Science, Springer-Verlag, PP 486– 495, doi:https://doi.org/10.1007/978-3-540-89796-5_50 ,2008

14. Z. Chen, Y. Zhao and R. Ni, "Forensics of blurred images based on no-reference image quality assessment," 2013 IEEE China Summit and International Conference on Signal and Information Processing, pp. 437–441, doi: https://doi.org/10.1109/ChinaSIP.2013.6625377, 2013.

15. Shang, Shize, Xiangwei Kong, and Xingang You. "Document forgery detection using distortion mutation of geometric parameters in characters." Journal of Electronic Imaging 24.2 : 023008. Doi: https://doi.org/10.1117/1.JEI.24.2.023008,2015

16. F. Cruz, N. Sidère, M. Coustaty, V. P. D'Andecy and J. Ogier, "Local Binary Patterns for Document Forgery Detection," 2017 14th IAPR International Conference on Document Analysis and Recognition (ICDAR), pp. 1223–1228, doi: https://doi.org/10.1109/ICDAR.2017.202, 2017

17. A. Megahed, S. M. Fadl, Q. Han and Q. Li, "Handwriting forgery detection based on ink colour features," 2017 8th IEEE International Conference on Software Engineering and Service Science (ICSESS), pp. 141–144, doi: https://doi.org/10.1109/ICSESS.2017.8342883, 2017.

18. A. Gorai, R. Pal and P. Gupta, "Document fraud detection by ink analysis using texture features and histogram matching," 2016 International Joint Conference on Neural Networks (IJCNN), 2016, pp. 4512-4517, doi: https://doi.org/10.1109/IJCNN.2016.7727790.

19. P. Gupta, N. Gyanchandani, "Image Quality Assessment for Fake Biometric Detection: Application to Iris, Fingerprint and Face Recognition", International Journal of Science and Research (IJSR), Volume 7 Issue 5, May 2017, 2166 – 2169

20. S. Sonawane ,A. M. Deshpande, " Image Quality Assessment Techniques: An Overview", International Journal Of Engineering Research & Technology (IJERT) Volume 03, Issue 04 (April 2014)

21. P. Sejal, S. Shubha, "Survey on Image Quality Assessment Techniques", International Journal of Science and Research (IJSR) , Volume 4 Issue 7, July 2015, 1756 - 1759

22. G. Minakshi , A. Mala , "Image Quality Parameter Detection : A Study," International Journal of Computer Sciences and Engineering, Vol.04, Issue.07, pp.110-116, 2016.

23. Varga, Domonkos.. "No-Reference Image Quality Assessment with Global Statistical Features" Journal of Imaging 7, no. 2: 29. https://doi.org/10.3390/jimaging7020029, 2021.

24. Sara, U. , Akter, M. and Uddin, M. " Image Quality Assessment through FSIM, SSIM, MSE and PSNR—A Comparative Study". Journal of Computer and Communications, 7, 8-18. doi: https://doi.org/10.4236/jcc.2019.73002,2019.

25. Krishnamoorthy, Shivsubramani & Kp, Soman." Implementation and Comparative Study of Image Fusion Algorithms" , International Journal of Computer Applications. 9. https://doi.org/10.5120/1357-1832, 2010.

26. Z. Wang, AC. Bovik, HR Sheikh, EP Simoncelli . "Image quality assessment: from error visibility to structural similarity", IEEE Trans Image Process. 2004 Apr;13(4):600-12. doi: https://doi.org/10.1109/tip.2003.819861. PMID: 15376593, 2004

27. Ding, K., Ma, K., Wang, S., & Simoncelli, E. P. "Comparison of Full-Reference Image Quality Models for Optimization of Image Processing Systems". International journal of

computer vision, 1–24. Advance online publication. https://doi.org/https://doi.org/10.1007/s11263-020-01419-7,2021

28. A. Kesarwani, S. S. Chauhan and A. R. Nair, "Fake News Detection on Social Media using K-Nearest Neighbor Classifier," 2020 International Conference on Advances in Computing and Communication Engineering (ICACCE), Las Vegas, NV, USA, 2020, pp. 1–4, doi: https://doi.org/10.1109/ICACCE49060.2020.9154997.

29. S.Dhivya, B. Sudhakar," Forgery Detection Based on KNN Classifier using SURF Feature Extraction", International Journal of Recent Technology and Engineering (IJRTE) ISSN: 2277–3878, Volume-8 Issue-2, July 2019

30. R. Mallika," Fraud Detection using Supervised Learning Algorithms" International Journal of Advanced Research in Computer and Communication Engineering, (IJARCCE), ISSN (Print) 2319 5940, https://doi.org/10.17148/IJARCCE.2017.6602, Vol. 6, Issue 6, June 2017

31. Yaram, S,"Machine learning algorithms for document clustering and fraud detection", 2016 International Conference on Data Science and Engineering (ICDSE). doi:https://doi.org/10.1109/icdse.2016.7823950, 2016

Comparative Study of Grid-Inverted List Hybrid Indexing Techniques for Moving Objects and Queries

Sulbha Powar[✉] and Ganesh Magar

P. G. Department of Computer Science, SNDT Women's University, Mumbai, India
sulbha_powar@hotmail.com

Abstract. Advancement in GPS technologies and availability of a variety of devices to capture location and other attributes of the objects has led to an enormous development in geo-textual data. Searching through these objects for relevant objects as per the requirement needs efficient indexing technique and searching algorithm. Past queries, Present queries and Future queries are the three types of geo-textual queries. Past queries are responded based on the historical locations of the moving objects stored in the database. Future queries can be answered if the velocity vector of the object is known in advance. But in many real-time applications the position of the objects in future cannot be predicted. In such a scenario capturing movement of the objects and queries in real time and answering queries or updating query answer sets in real time is essential. In this paper three different techniques based on grid index, modified to handle geo-textual queries using hybrid index, YPK-CNN, SEA-CNN and CPM to handle real time queries, are presented. The methods to find kNN based on these three techniques are proposed in this paper and are also compared. Conceptual partitioning along with hybrid index improve the query performance by 30 to 40%.

Keywords: Conceptual Partitioning · Geo-Textual data · Grid Index · Hybrid Index · Inverted List · Moving objects · Nearest Neighbour

1 Introduction

Geo-Textual data is generated abundantly for various objects in our surrounding due to the increase in the wide variety of GPS tracking handheld devices. Each object has location data (spatial) and attribute data (non-spatial) attached to it. Spatial data are 'where things are' data and attribute data are 'what things are'. The movement of these objects can be tracked and can be used to know the current location of the objects. The dynamic objects can be queried and are retrieved based on their location at the query time as well as the query result set can be updated based on the movement of the objects over time period. In case the query point is moving, the result set needs to be updated based on the current location of the query over the time period. This kind of scenario occurs in various applications like emergency management system, traffic management etc.

R. Manza et al. (Eds.): ACVAIT 2022, AISR 176, pp. 230–249, 2023.
https://doi.org/10.2991/978-94-6463-196-8_19

In real-time applications, maintaining location of objects synchronized with time is essential. When the velocity vector of the objects is not known in advance, capturing the current location of the objects and maintaining the results of the queries require efficient indexing techniques and search algorithms. In real time decision support systems, with multiple queries running simultaneously, we need to optimize the query processing time.

2 Related Work

To answer continuous range queries over collections of moving objects, the researchers have used grid index for query indexing and have proved that grid indexing yields better performance than other index structures like R-Trees [1]. A query management technique called MQM (Monitoring Query Management) is used for monitoring real time range-monitoring queries. An object reports its location to the server whenever its movement affects any query results (i.e., crossing any query boundaries) or it moves out of its resident domain [2]. Query Indexing and Velocity constraint indexing are demonstrated for continuous queries on moving objects using R-Tree and safe region, wherein objects report their new locations to the server periodically or when they have moved by a significant distance [3]. MobiEyes answers moving range queries over moving objects using R-Tree with assumption that queries move linearly with fixed velocity and monitors region of moving query [4].

The queries on moving objects can be classified as past (historical), present and future (predicate) queries [5]. The proposed method based on Query Indexing using R-trees answers present queries [3]. YPK-CNN, SEA-CNN and CPM are the solutions given for present queries based on the grid index [6,–8]. When objects' moving pattern of motion is not known in advance, they move in an unrestricted manner. Hence capturing the moved location of the objects and answering the updated query results occurs with some time delay. Techniques are proposed to reduce the time delay in present queries but textual attributes of the objects are not considered [6]–[8]. YPK-CNN re-evaluates an existing kNN query every T time unit and it makes use of its previous result in order to restrict the search space [6]. Shared Execution Algorithm-Continuous Nearest Neighbour Monitoring (SEA-CNN) techniques focuses on monitoring of NN with bookkeeping for answer region [7]. Conceptual Partitioning Monitoring (CPM) techniques does NN-Monitoring with Bookkeeping [8].D-Grid, dual space grid index for moving objects, indexes moving objects using both location and velocity spaces for answering range and kNN queries [9]. In which, authors have proposed D-Grid, an in-memory dual space grid index for moving objects, which indexes moving objects using grid structures in both location and velocity spaces [9].

Scalable INcremental hash-based Algorithm (SINA) implements R-Tree for answering static moving range queries. It uses shared execution and incremental evaluation technique to compute only the updates of the previously reported answers [10]. DISC (aDaptive Indexing on Streams by space-filling Curves) proposes B-tree that uses a space-filling curve to answer static and moving approximate kNN query [11]. Influential Neighbour Sets technique implements R*-tree and VoR-tree to answer moving kNN query by safeguarding objects [12]. In Data Frame Based Spatiotemporal Indexing, spatiotemporal trajectory retrieval algorithm is used to answer moving objects range query [13].

If the trajectories of the moving objects are known in advance, the predictive queries or future queries can be answered at the query processing time. The motion pattern of the objects decides the accuracy of the response to the predictive query. Influential Time Parameterised Indexing, Voronoi cells, updating previously reported answers and approximate nearest neighbour (NN) queries are some techniques used for answering predicate queries. Neighbour Sets are used instead of safe regions to improve performance [10,–12, 14–23]. The time-aware queries considers valid time of the objects and answers Boolean spatial keywords queries [24].

For spatial indexing, most of the techniques use R-tree. But in case of continuously moving objects, the nodes of the R-tree index need to split and merge to maintain the locations of continuously moving objects. This degrades the performance of maintaining R-Tree index structure and answering queries using this index structure. Hence Grid Index is preferred for maintaining locations of moving objects. In this paper the focus is on creating hybrid index structure using grid index and inverted list for spatial and textual components respectively. In case the moving objects movement pattern is not known in advance, the hybrid index helps in answering the geo-textual queries over these objects. The search algorithm based on grid index and inverted list hybrid index, prunes the search space and hence reduces the time delay for answering the nearest neighbours query.

The geo-textual indices combine spatial and text indexing techniques either tightly or loosely [25]. In text-first loose combination, postings in each inverted list is arranged using spatial structure whereas in spatial-first loose combination leaf nodes of spatial index contain inverted files or bitmaps for the textual information of the objects belonging to the region. On the contrary the tight combinations combine both the spatial and text indexes tightly helping to prune search space in an effective manner. R-tree, a grid or a space filling curve are commonly used spatial index structures and inverted files or bitmaps are used commonly for handling text index. In case of tight combinations, one technique integrates a text summary into every node of a spatial index, and another integrates the spatial information into each inverted list [25]. Authors of this paper have implemented a tight combination of hybrid index with text summary into every cell of grid index [5] to handle static and moving objects.

When both objects and queries are static, results do not change over time. When query points and/or objects move the query result changes as some kNN objects go out of scope and new objects come nearer to the query point. Keeping track of data objects moving in and out of the current kNN result set is essential to re-evaluate the queries.

Various hybrid index structures are proposed by researchers and they differ in structures and their effectiveness in answering queries. The indexing structure decides performance of query evaluation depending upon the pruning of the data space. Other factors affecting the query performance include the node splitting technique, search space like Euclidean or road networks. The demand for various kinds of queries like moving queries, approximate query, joint query, predicate query, group query, why not query has grown over the period.

3 Methodology

Geo-textual queries are classified based on the location of data objects with respect to time. If the data objects are queried based on the past locations of the moving objects, are called historical queries and are answered using the past trajectories of the objects. If the trajectories of the moving objects are fully predictable at query processing time, the future queries can be answered to know the position of the objects in future. Present queries are answered in real-time, where the future locations of the objects are not known in advance. Periodically the changes in locations of objects are noted and indexes are updated accordingly. This helps in updating the query results in real-time. In this paper three techniques viz. YPK-CNN, SEA-CNN and CPM, which use grid index for maintaining locations of moving objects, are modified to handle geo-textual queries and are presented [6–8].

Each geo-textual object has a point location defined by latitude and longitude at a particular time stamp and is also described by textual attributes. To answer geo-textual queries, we need to combine textual and spatial structures. While answering the geo-textual queries on moving objects and moving queries following issues need to be addressed with improved execution time.

- the index needs to be updated as the objects move
- affected queries need to be re-evaluated when any objects from its' answer set is moved
- moved query need to be re-evaluated
- queries need to be answered with short execution times for large numbers of moving objects and queries

In every processing cycle, index needs to be updated for all moved objects during the processing cycle, affected queries and moved queries need to be re-evaluated. The technique used for maintenance of result sets needs to optimize the time required for maintaining it.

In case of real-time queries i.e. present queries, the objects' motion patterns and velocity vectors are not known and hence their movements are non-predictable. The query points and data objects being dynamic in nature move frequently and arbitrarily. As the multiple queries are running simultaneously, continuous reporting of its updated results is essential. In this research, the Geo-Textual hybrid indexing techniques are used, with focus on Grid-Inverted List hybrid index, to minimize the index maintenance and query execution time.

Following 3 proposed algorithms are developed, implemented and studied to evaluate their performance against the original techniques:

1. Modified Hybrid Index and modified YPK-CNN search technique – Grid-Inverted List Hybrid Index structure is developed to implement modified YPK-CNN techniques to answer Geo-Textual queries on moving Geo-Textual objects.
2. Modified Hybrid Index and modified SEA-CNN search technique – Grid-Inverted List Hybrid Index structure is developed to implement modified SEA-CNN techniques to answer Geo-Textual queries on moving Geo-Textual objects.

3. Modified Hybrid Index and modified CPM search technique–Grid-Inverted List
   Hybrid Index structure is developed to implement modified CPM techniques to answer
   Geo-Textual queries on moving Geo-Textual objects.

   In this implementation, tight combination is used where text and spatial indexes are
combined tightly. Every cell of the grid-structure has inverted list of all the objects falling
in cells' region.

3.1   Grid-Inverted List Hybrid Index

In grid-based index structure the region of interest is mapped to a 2-dimentional array of
grid (Fig. 1). Each cell of the grid is mapped to some region of space. Let D(t) be a Geo-
Textual data set of objects belonging to the region of interest at time t. Each spatial object
o ∈ D(t) is defined as a pair (o.ρ, o.φ), where o.ρ is a 2-dimensional geographical point
location (longitude, latitude) and o.φ is a text description of the object. The geographical
location of an object o at time t is denoted as o(t).ρ = (o(t).long, o(t).lat). The grid with
cells δ × δ, where δ is the number of cells in each direction, is used to create a Geo-
Textual hybrid index. Each cell of the grid is uniquely identified by c[i, j], where 0 < =
i, j < δ, i denotes the ith cell (column) in horizontal direction and j denotes the jth cell
(row) in vertical direction starting from lower-left corner of the grid. The data objects
are mapped to grid cells by using the Eqs. 1 and 2.

$$i = (o(t).long - minlong) * \delta/maxlong - minlong) \tag{1}$$

$$j = (o(t).lat - minlat) * \delta/maxlat - minlat) \tag{2}$$

In the above formulae, minlong and minlat are the minimum longitude and latitude
respectively of the Region of Interest. Similarly, maxlong and maxlat are the maximum
longitude and latitude respectively of the Region of Interest (Fig. 2).

In each cell c[i, j], an object list is created for all the objects (o(t)) mapped to it and
also an inverted list for all these objects' text description is created and maintained in
this cell as shown in Fig. 3.

Grid-Inverted List hybrid index tightly combines an inverted list to each cell of the
grid index for all objects belonging to the region of interest. Every grid cell maintains
the list of objects mapped to the cell and also the inverted list of textual attributes of the
objects belonging to that cell. Figure 3 illustrates hybrid index structure in which each
grid cell has an object list and inverted list. This tight combination assists in retrieving
objects which fulfil text criteria within the vicinity of the query object by pruning the
search space efficiently as it does not have to check all the objects for responding the
query. Figure 4 demonstrates hybrid index structure for region of interest shown in Fig. 1.

3.2   KNN Query

Let D(t) be a geo-textual data set of objects belonging to region of interest at time t.
Each spatial object $o \in D(t)$ is defined as a pair (o.ρ, o.φ), where o.ρ is a 2-dimensional
geographical point location (latitude and longitude) and o.φ is a text description of the

object [26]. The kNN query $q = (\varphi, \rho, k)$ takes three arguments, where $q.\varphi$ is a set of keywords, $q.\rho$ is a spatial query point, and $q.k$ is the number of objects to retrieve. The result of kNN, q(D(t)), is a set of k objects, each of which covers all the keywords in $q.\varphi$ [26]. Objects are ranked according to their distances to $q.\rho$ at time t. It can be represented mathematically by following relation,

$$\forall o \in q(D(t))((\nexists o\prime \in D(t) \backslash q(D(t)))(dist(o\prime.\rho, q.\rho) \leq dist(o.\rho, q.\rho)) \wedge q.\varphi \subseteq o\prime.\varphi) \quad (3)$$

The performance of creating the Grid-Inverted List Hybrid Index structure for the dataset D(t) and the geo-textual kNN query over this hybrid index structure is studied with three different techniques for index update and search algorithm.

3.3   Hybrid Index Implementation with YPK-CNN Technique

Xiaohui Yu et al. (2005) proposed a method called YPK-CNN for continuous monitoring of kNN queries. In this research work, this technique is modified to handle Geo-Textual queries using Geo-Textual Hybrid Index. In this technique objects are indexed with a grid of cells with size $\delta \times \delta$. Updates are not processed as they arrive and changes are directly applied to the grid. Every kNN query is re-evaluated every T time unit. When a query is evaluated for the first time for its kNN, two step search retrieves the result. In the first step, the cells around the query cell are traversed until k objects are found. In the second step, the search region is set as square with side length 2.d + e, where d is the distance of the farthest object from the query point found in the first step and e is the length of the cell (extent) in the grid index. All the cells intersecting search region are traversed to find the objects satisfying query criteria and the first k objects in the order of the distance from the query point are retrieved as the result.

To re-evaluate the existing query q, YPK-CNN uses its previous result set to restrict the search space. Farthest distance that the current kNN have moved is found and is denoted as d_{max}. The new search region is then the square centred at q with side length $2 \cdot d_{max} + e$. Then all the cells intersecting new search region are traversed to find the objects satisfying query criteria. When query q changes its location, it is evaluated as a new query.

Figure 3 shows the Grid-Inverted list hybrid Index structure implemented for YPK-CNN. As shown in the figure it is a tight implementation of Geo-Textual Hybrid Indexing technique. Every cell has the object list belonging to the cell and Inverted list of keywords of all the objects mapped to the cell. Figure 5 describes the structure of the Query table for YPK-CNN implementation. It maintains the list of all current queries along with the query criteria and current result set.

In case of non-hybrid implementation, all the objects in the search region are evaluated for distance and text criteria separately. This results in false positive hits. In case of hybrid index text criteria of the query is checked with the inverted list of the cell. If any objects are found in the cell satisfying the text criteria, only those objects are checked for the distance from the query point. This pruning in the search space results in reducing the number of actual hits and hence false hits are avoided by using hybrid index structure.

3.4 Hybrid Index Implementation with SEA-CNN Technique

Xiaopeng Xiong et al. (2005) proposed a method called Shared Execution Algorithm – Continuous Nearest Monitoring (SEA-CNN) for continuous monitoring of kNN queries. This technique is modified to handle Geo-Textual queries using Geo-Textual Hybrid Index. In this technique also objects are indexed with a grid of cells with size δ X δ. When a query is evaluated for the first time for its kNN, two step search retrieves the result. In the first step, the cells around the query cell are traversed until k objects are found. In the second step, the search region is set as a circle with diameter $2 \cdot d + e$, where d is the distance of the farthest object from the query point found in the first step and e is the length of the cell (extent) in the grid index. All the cells intersecting search region are traversed to find the objects satisfying query criteria and the first k objects in the order of the distance from the query point are retrieved as the result.

The changes in the kNNs of the existing queries are monitored to re-evaluate the queries, if there are any movements in the search region of the query. The current answer region of the query is set as a circle with q's location as the centre of the circle and with radius as the distance of the current k^{th} NN from the query point. The cells which intersect the answer region of q keep this book keeping information. In the next update cycle, after time T, if any cells intersecting the answer region of the query have been affected due to movements of the objects, this query is re-evaluated by setting the search region based on the following criteria.

1. If some of the current knns of the query move within the answer region or some new objects enter the answer region, the search region of the query is set as the current answer region.
2. If any of the current kNNs move out of the answer region, the radius of the search region is set as the d_{max}, where d_{max} is the distance of the object from the query point, which has moved farthest from the query point.
3. If the query point has moved to a new location q', the centre of the search region is Set as Q', and radius is set as Dist(Q, Q') + k-Dist, where k-dist is the distance of the current k^{th} NN from the query point Q.

All the cells intersecting the updated search region are processed to find the updated kNN set of the query point.

Figure 3 shows the Grid-Inverted list hybrid Index structure implemented for SEA-CNN. As shown in the figure it is a tight implementation of Geo-Textual Hybrid Indexing technique. Every cell has the object list belonging to the cell and Inverted list of keywords of all the objects mapped to the cell. Figure 5 describes the structure of the Query table for SEA-CNN implementation. It maintains the list of all current queries along with the query criteria and current result set. As in the case of YPK-CNN, the hybrid implementation prunes the search space, reducing the number of actual hits and hence false hits are avoided.

3.5 Hybrid Index Implementation with CPM Technique

Mouratidis et al. (2005) proposed a method called conceptual partitioning monitoring (CPM) for continuous monitoring of kNN queries. This technique is modified to handle

Geo-Textual queries using Geo-Textual Hybrid Index. In this technique also, like the previous two techniques, objects are indexed with a grid of cells with size δ X δ. When a query is evaluated for the first time for its kNN, the cells/rectangles around the query cell are added progressively to heap in the ascending order of the distance from the query point. Rectangles from each direction act as boundary boxes. The cells from the heap are removed and checked for the objects satisfying the query criteria till the next cell is at the distance greater than the k-dist, where k-dist is the distance of the kth object in the kNN set. All unexplored regions fall in some rectangle in some direction which is at a distance greater than the k-dist. CPM maintains a query table, wherein for each query it maintains its location coordinates, the k-dist, its current kNN result set, visit list and search heap. CPM is able to monitor the updates to objects and kNN result sets with this book keeping. CPM also maintains an influence list along with an object list in each cell of the grid index. The influence list maintains the list of queries whose influence region contains the cell i.e. the cell is at a distance less than equal to the k-dist of the query.

Figure 6 shows the Grid-Inverted list hybrid Index structure implemented for CPM. As shown in the figure it is a tight implementation of Geo-Textual Hybrid Indexing technique. Every cell has the object list belonging to the cell and Inverted list of keywords of all the objects mapped to the cell. Every grid cell also has the influence list of queries, specifying to which query influence region this cell belongs. It is used for book-keeping. Whenever any object from this cell moves out or any objects enter in the cell, the queries from influence lists are checked if they are affected and are accordingly re-evaluated in each update cycle. Figure 7 describes the structure of the Query table for CPM implementation. It maintains the list of all current queries along with the query criteria, current result set, heap and visit list of each query. Heap and visit list are used while re-evaluating the query and saving the time of creating heap and calculating distance of surrounding cells from the query point. When the query is re-evaluated, cells in the visit list are traversed in the order to find the updated kNN set. If the visit list is exhausted and kNN are not found only then the heap is processed for further search.

As in the case of YPK-CNN and SEA-CNN, the hybrid implementation of Grid Index and Inverted List, helps in pruning the search space, reducing the number of actual hits and hence false hits are avoided. This helps in improving the performance of geo-textual query.

3.6 Differences Between YPK-CNN, SEA-CNN and CPM Techniques

Book keeping is done by the three algorithms to evaluate the kNN query in each update cycle i.e. at every timestamp. Figure 8 shows the difference between the three methods pictorially. As can be seen in the figure, the number of grid cells accessed are varied. YPK-CNN computes the search region bounded by square, around the query point and then accesses the cells intersecting with the search region. SEA-CNN computes the search region bounded by the circle, the query point and then accesses the cells intersecting with the search region. Whereas CPM works with conceptual partitioning and visits the next cell only if required. As can be seen from the figure more number of cells are visited using YPK-CNN technique as compared to SEA-CNN technique and more number of cells are visited in case of SEA-CNN technique as compared to CPM technique. These differences among three methods decide the number of cells visited

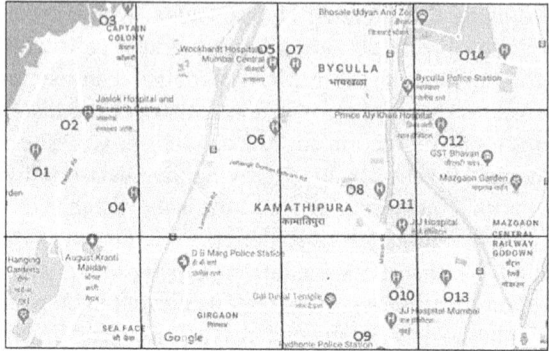

Fig. 1. Region of Interest with Grid

and hence the number of objects evaluated. The hybrid index implementation narrows down the search further by visiting a cell only if it satisfies the query criteria and further objects are evaluated only if they satisfy the query criteria.

In case of modified YPK-CNN and modified SEA-CNN, the speed of the object decides the area of the updated search region, as the farther the object moves, the area of the search region increases. Thus the performance of the modified YPK-CNN and modified SEA-CNN algorithms depends on the speed of the objects whereas the modified CPM is not affected by the speed as it searches for objects only in the influence region of the query.

In case of modified YPK-CNN and the modified SEA-CNN techniques, redundant and more cells are processed as compared to the modified CPM technique which uses conceptual partitioning to restrict the search space. The modified CPM also does the bookkeeping of objects moving inside and outside the influence region in every update cycle. This helps in reducing unnecessary computations. When the query point is moved, the modified YPK-CNN and the modified CPM techniques evaluate the query result like a new query. But SEA-CNN technique uses a formula to find the updated search region to re-evaluate the query. SEA-CNN assumes that the only updates are from incoming objects and/or NNs that move within the distance of kth object from q. It performs redundant computations in several cases.

3.7 Proposed Algorithms

In the beginning, all the objects in the data set are scanned for spatial and non-spatial attributes and the Grid-Inverted List hybrid index is built for the data set. Then all the initial queries are evaluated using the created hybrid index structure. After this periodically, in every update cycle all the movements of the objects and queries are captured and the index is updated with the new locations of the moved objects. Then all the moved queries, new queries and affected queries are evaluated based on the updated index,

Following algorithms are developed for each of the techniques namely, YPK-CNN Hybrid, SEA-CNN Hybrid, CPM Hybrid.

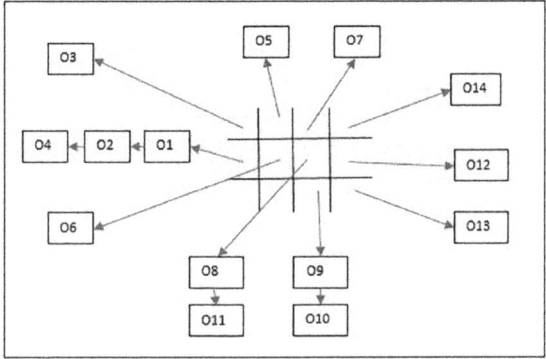

Fig. 2. Grid Index for the region of interest

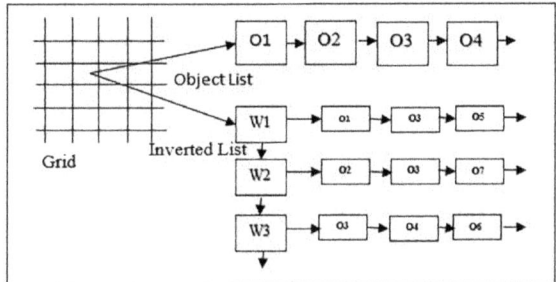

Fig. 3. Grid and Inverted List Hybrid Index

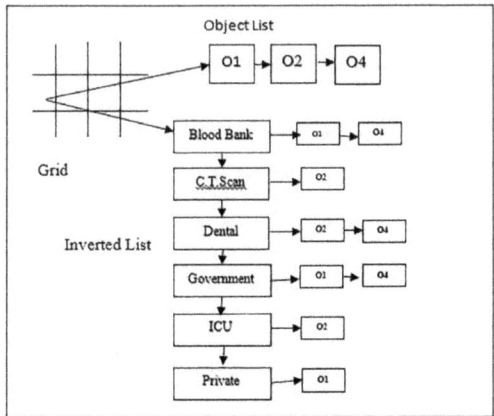

Fig. 4. Grid and inverted Hybrid Index

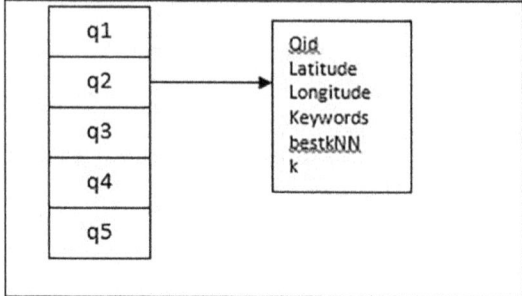

Fig. 5. Query Table structure for YPK-CNN and SEA-CNN techniques

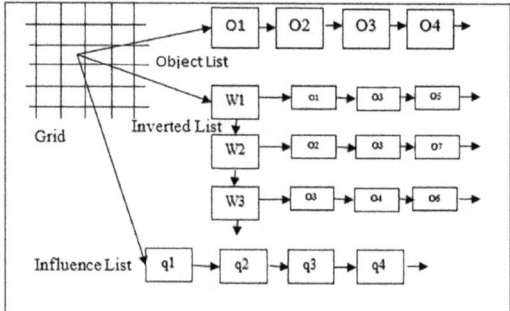

Fig. 6. Grid-Inverted List Hybrid Index Structure for CPM

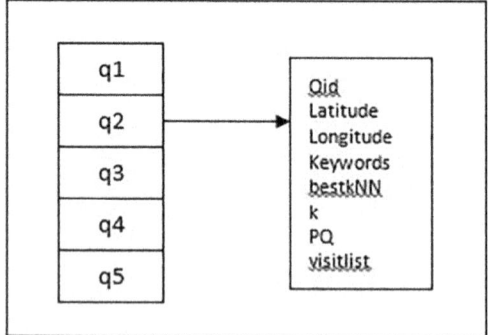

Fig. 7. Structure of Query table for CPM

3.7.1 Hybrid Index Construction Algorithm

This algorithm constructs the hybrid Index for the geo-textual data objects when the grid size m X n and bounding region of interest (spatial coordinates) are provided to the algorithm. It first creates the grid of the provided size and then finds the cell c[i j] for each object in the database using the Eqs. 1 and 2 and then adds this object to the object

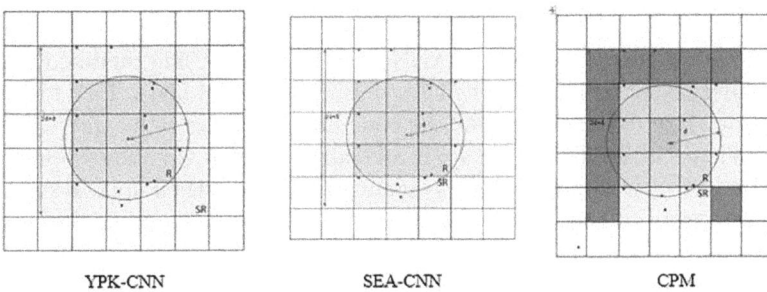

YPK-CNN   SEA-CNN   CPM

Fig. 8. differences between YPK-CNN, SEA-CNN and CPM techniques

list of the corresponding grid cell. Then the inverted list of the cell is updated for the object added to it. This algorithm creates a tight grid-inverted list hybrid index.

3.7.2   Hybrid Index Updation Algorithm

In every update cycle, all the changed locations of the geo-textual objects and queries are captured. If the object is moved in the same cell, the algorithm updates the latitude and longitude of the objects. If the object has moved to a different cell or it is terminated, the algorithm removes the object from the object list of the old cell and also removes its entries from the inverted list of the old cell. If the object has moved to different cell or new object has entered the region of interest, the algorithm finds the new cell c[i j] using the Eqs. 1 and 2 and then adds this object to the object list of the corresponding grid cell and also updates the inverted list of the cell for the object added to it.

3.7.3   KNN Search Algorithms for Modified YPK-CNN

This algorithm evaluates geo-textual kNN query at time t using modified YPK-CNN techniques. It first initializes the kNN set of the query to NULL. Then it finds a query cell using the Eqs. 1 and 2. After initialization, starting with the query cell and its surrounding cells in each direction, it checks for the objects in the cells till k objects are found satisfying query criteria. After the k objects are found, the search region area is initialized as square with side 2 * k-dist + e and query q at the centre. All the cells interesting this search region are then processed to find all the objects satisfying query criteria and the k nearest neighbours of the query point.

3.7.4   KNN Search Algorithm for Modified SEA-CNN

This algorithm evaluates geo-textual kNN query at time t using modified SEA-CNN techniques. It first initializes the kNN set of the query to NULL.Then it finds a query cell using the Eqs. 1 and 2. After initialization, starting with the query cell and its surrounding cells in each direction it checks for the objects till k objects are found satisfying query criteria. Then the search region area is initialized as a circle with diameter 2 * k-dist + e and query point q as the centre. All the cells interesting this search region are then processed to find all the objects satisfying query criteria and the k nearest neighbours of the query point.

3.7.5   KNN Search Algorithm for Modified CPM

This algorithm evaluates geo-textual kNN query at time t using modified CPM techniques. It first calculates the query cell c[i, j] using the Eqs. 1 and 2. First few entries to the heap consist of the query cell and the bounding rectangles to the query cell in each direction. These entries in the heap are in ascending order of key value as the minimum distance between query point and the bounding rectangles. Then in iteration, entries in the heap are removed one by one and are processed till kNN are found or the heap is empty. If the removed entry from the heap is a cell, then its inverted list is checked to see if it has an object satisfying query criteria. If a cell has such objects then these are processed to check if they are kNN of the query, if so kNN and k-dist are updated. Removed entry is added to the visit list of the query and then this query is added to the influence list of the cell. If the removed entry is a rectangle, then each cell of the rectangle is added to the heap and the next level bounding rectangle in the same direction is added to the heap. This algorithm returns the kNN set of the query q as output.

3.7.6   Update Handling Algorithm for Modified YPK-CNN

Update handling of affected queries due to moved geo-textual objects and queries is done in this algorithm using modified YPK-CNN technique. If the query point has moved, it is evaluated as a new query. Otherwise if some kNN objects have moved outside the answer region, new Search Region with formula 2.d + e, is set based on the farthest distance kNNs have travel (d) and grid cell extent e else search region is set as the answer region and the query is re-evaluated.

3.7.7   Update Handling Algorithm for Modified SEA-CNN

If some kNN objects have moved outside the answer region, a new search region with formula 2.d + e, is set based on the farthest moved kNN (d) and grid cell extent e else search region is set as the answer region and the query is re-evaluated. If the query point has moved, a new search region is set based on the movement of the query and farthest moved kNN and query is re-evaluated.

3.7.8   Update Search Algorithm for Modified CPM

This algorithm re-evaluates geo-textual kNN query at time t using modified CPM techniques. It first initializes k-dist to infinity and initializes list kNN to NULL Then for each cell in the visit list of the query, it checks the inverted list to see if any objects exist in the cell satisfying query criteria. If a cell has objects satisfying query criteria, it processes these objects to find kNN. If kNN objects are not found and the visit list is exhausted, then it starts processing the entries in the heap till kNN are found satisfying query criteria.

3.7.9   Update Handling Algorithm for Modified CPM Technique

Update handling of affected queries due to moved geo-textual objects and queries is done in this algorithm using modified CPM technique. First of all, for each moved object, its old cell's and new cell's influence region are checked for affected queries. If the moved object belongs to the kNN of the old cells' influence regions query and it has moved out of the answer region of the query, then out object count of the query is incremented. If this moved object has entered the answer region of the query belonging to the new cell's influence list, then in object count is incremented and object is added to in object list of the query. Once affected queries are marked, for each query from the query table is checked and processed. If the query is moved in the cell itself, search updates the result by processing the visit list. If the query is moved to a different cell its result is evaluated like a new query. If the query is static and sufficient objects are moved inside the answer region of the query, kNN list is updated with existing list and in object list else query is re-evaluated. If the query is static and kNN objects have moved in the answer region itself, the kNN list is updated with the existing list and values are updated.

4   Experimental work

Collecting real-time Geo-Textual data sets is tedious and it usually takes a substantial amount of time and effort. In this research, the python code is written to generate the initial data set and update cycle's data sets by varying parameters and by considering different types of movements of Geo-Textual data. Various data sets are generated using simple random (probability) sampling technique, where every element has an equal chance of getting selected to be the part sample. Various data sets used in experimental evaluation are generated by using 3 different speeds slow, medium and fast for moving objects and moving queries. Algorithms are evaluated by varying parameters like number of objects in a data set (N), number of queries (n), number of nearest neighbours (k), grid cell size (δ), fraction of the objects updates and query updates. Updates to the objects and queries include movements of objects/queries within the region of interest (movement), leaving of objects/queries from the region of interest (terminate) and new objects/queries entering the region of interest (new). Updates are captured and evaluated every update cycle. Each update cycle first captures the updates to location of objects and.

queries. It then updates the index structure for objects updates and then evaluates the affected and updated queries.

Algorithms presented in Sect. 3.7 for proposed solutions of optimization of Geo-Textual queries on Geo-Textual moving queries and objects are implemented in python. These algorithms are analysed using various data sets. Spyder, the Scientific Python

Table 1. Example Data Set

Data set	N	n	k	$\delta \times \delta$	Number of Update cycles	Objects update count	Query update count
7	10000	100	1,2,3,4,5	5 × 5, 10 × 10, 15 × 15, 20 × 20, 25 × 25	3	121, 112, 115	12, 10, 11

Development Environment is used for python code implementation. To visualize the output of Geo-Textual objects, queries and query results, the Jupyter Notebook environment with ArcGIS API is used. In this environment, Geo-Textual experimental data is converted to ESRI shape file and then this shape file is imported as a feature layer on the map for visualization.

For performing experiments various generated data sets are used. One such example is shown in Table 1. Data set 7 consists of 10000 (N) Geo-Textual Objects and 100 (n) queries. This data set is evaluated for 1-NN, 2-NN, 3-NN, 4-NN, and 5-NN with grid sizes [5 X 5], [10 X 10], [15 X 15], [20 X 20], and [25 X 25]. Out of 10000 Geo-Textual objects 121 objects are updated in the first update cycle for their locations, 115 objects moved in the second update cycle and 1441 objects moved in the third update cycle. Out of 100 queries, 12 are moved in the first update cycle, 10 moved in the second update cycle and 11 moved in the third update cycle. In this example the set is processed for 5 kNN values and 5 grid sizes giving rise to 25 combinations.

For each dataset all three techniques namely, modified YPK-CNN hybrid, modified SEA-CNN hybrid and modified CPM hybrid are processed. For each of these techniques, the number of cells visited in the influence region, number of inverted lists accessed, number of cells visited and number of objects processed for kNN computation and re-evaluation of results in each update cycle are measured. On these measured values for each execution, the total CPU performance cost is calculated. The results of the analysis performed are presented in Sect. 5.

5 Results and Discussion

The Geo-Textual hybrid indexing techniques and search algorithm based on these indexing techniques for processing moving objects and queries are implemented and analysed for 3 proposed techniques. Number of Geo-Textual objects, number of Geo-Textual queries, grid size, number of location updates for objects and number of location updates for queries are the parameters evaluated for performance analysis of the algorithms.

Figure 9 shows the actual number of objects evaluated and the number of objects satisfying the query criteria in the search region in case of non-hybrid index. In case of hybrid index, numbers of actual hits are reduced and hence false hits are avoided by using inverted index in hybrid index structure thus pruning the search space.

Varying Grid Size δ. In Fig. 10, the grid size is changed by keeping other parameter values constant. For smaller values of δ, the number of cells in the grid is less, resulting in longer object lists and inverted lists with more number of nodes to be visited. For larger δ, the number of cells in the grid is increased. The time taken to traverse the list is decreased due to the distribution of objects in more number of cells. But when the numbers of cells are increased, there is high overhead due to heap operations. The time of NN computation for a new or a moving query depends strongly on the cell size; a large value for δ incurs high overhead due to heap operations, while a small value implies a high number of objects processed in the influence region.

Varying Value of k. Figure 11 shows the effect of changing the value of k, number of nearest neighbours, on evaluating queries by keeping other parameter values constant.

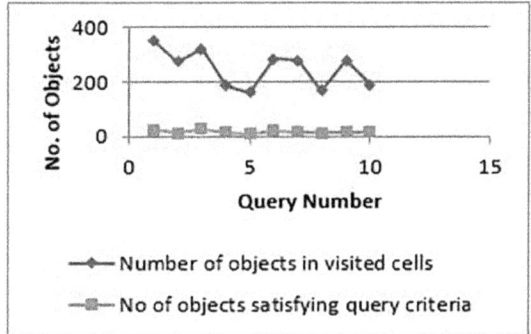

Fig. 9. Number of Objects in visited cells and number of objects satisfying query criteria in Non-Hybrid Index

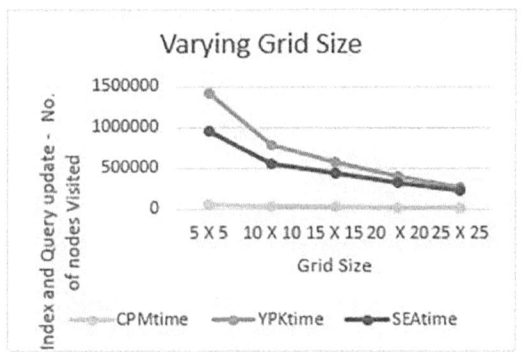

Fig. 10. SEQ Figure * ARABIC Grid Size Vs performance

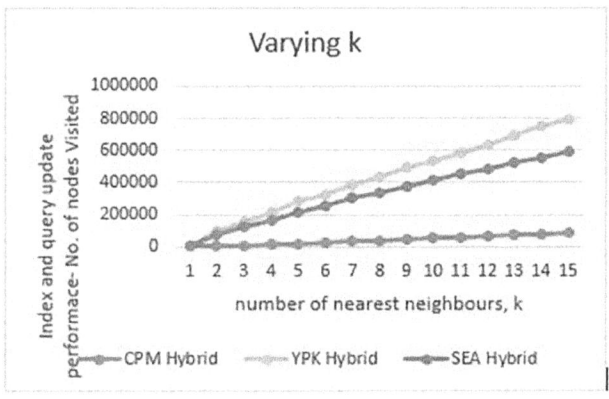

Fig. 11. Number of nearest neighbours (k) vs performance

As the value of k is increased, the time taken to update the result of kNN query is more. To find the k nearest neighbours more cells are visited as the value of k is increased. As the graph illustrates, modified CPM Hybrid Index gives better performance among the 3 algorithms.

Varying N – Index and Query Update. Figure 12 demonstrates index and query update performance dependency on the value of N. The time taken to update indexes and answer queries is directly proportional to the number of objects. Computation cost of the algorithm depends upon N.. Index update time is linear to N and number of updates to objects and increase in object movements does not affect the performance.

Varying n. As shown in Fig. 13, as the number of queries increases, the query result maintenance time is increased. As the number of updates to the query grows, the time required will also be more.

Figure 14 shows example 3NN query with 5 × 5 grid implemented and visualised in Jupyter Notebook.

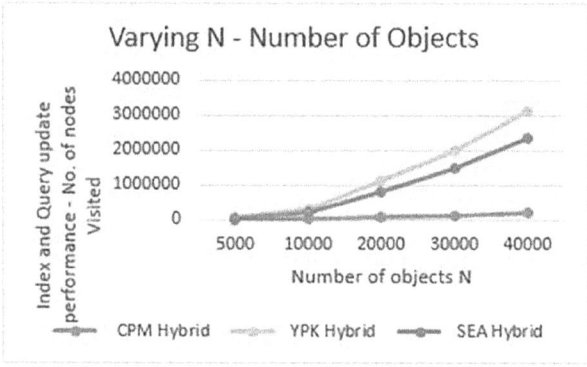

Fig. 12. Number of objects (N) vs Performance

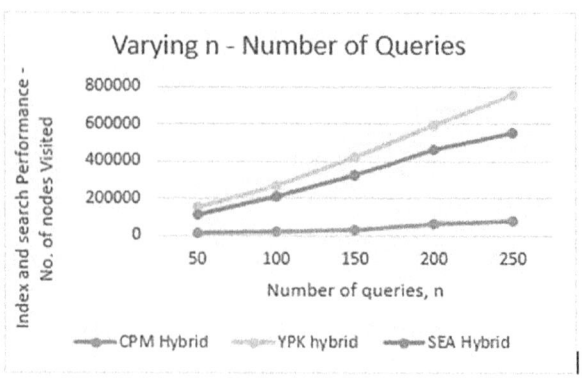

Fig. 13. number of queries (n) vs performance

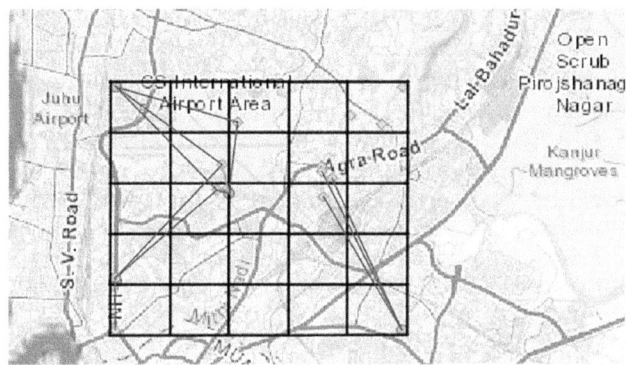

Fig. 14. 3NN query 5 × 5 grid implemented in Jupyter Notebook

6   Conclusion

This paper presents the comparative study of 3 techniques modified to handle geo-textual moving objects with unknown movement patterns using grid-inverted list hybrid index. Uniform grid makes it easy to calculate the cell of a given object with its latitude and longitude in constant time. The Grid index is a space-driven or data-independent method and partitions the data space in a way that reflects the data distribution in a given data set. Hence maintaining grid-index for moving objects can be conveniently by just removing objects from one cell and adding to another. The grid index guarantees that any point query can be answered in, at most, two disk accesses depending on whether the grid file is stored in main memory or disk.

Hybrid indexing having grid and inverted lists tightly combined, the search space narrows down. It reduces the number of false positive hits to database records Conceptual partitioning aids in processing the objects in the vicinity of the query point thereby restricting the search space in kNN processing. NN monitoring using book-keeping information avoids unnecessary processing of objects and further improves the query performance. Hybrid index along with conceptual partitioning improves the query performance by 30 to 40%.

The extensive experiments demonstrate reducing the update and search cost for uniform Grid-Inverted List Hybrid Index. Future work can further improve the cost by implementing the multilevel Grid Index for skewed data. Euclidean space is considered in the search algorithms implemented in this research, extendibility of it needs to be checked for road networks. kNN search query algorithms are implemented in this research, and other types of Geo-Textual queries on hybrid index are in the further research scope. Keyword queries can further be studied for natural language processing (NLP) queries, fuzzy queries and other variations.

Acknowledgments. The author would like to thank Dr. Babasaheb Ambedkar Marathwada University, Aurangabad (MS) India for providing the publication support.

References

1. D. V. Kalashnikov, S. Prabhakar, and S. E. Hambrusch, "Main Memory Evaluation of Monitoring Queries Over Moving Objects," Distributed and Parallel Databases, vol. 15, no. 2, pp. 117–135, Mar. 2004, doi: https://doi.org/10.1023/B:DAPD.0000013068.25976.88.
2. Ying Cai, K. A. Hua, and Guohong Cao, "Processing range-monitoring queries on heterogeneous mobile objects," 2004, pp. 27–38. https://doi.org/10.1109/MDM.2004.1263040.
3. S. Prabhakar, Yuni Xia, D. V. Kalashnikov, W. G. Aref, and S. E. Hambrusch, "Query indexing and velocity constrained indexing: scalable techniques for continuous queries on moving objects," IEEE Transactions on Computers, vol. 51, no. 10, pp. 1124–1140, Oct. 2002, https://doi.org/10.1109/TC.2002.1039840.
4. B. Gedik and L. Liu, "MobiEyes: Distributed Processing of Continuously Moving Queries on Moving Objects in a Mobile System," in Advances in Database Technology - EDBT 2004, vol. 2992, E. Bertino, S. Christodoulakis, D. Plexousakis, V. Christophides, M. Koubarakis, K. Böhm, and E. Ferrari, Eds. Berlin, Heidelberg: Springer Berlin Heidelberg, 2004, pp. 67–87. https://doi.org/10.1007/978-3-540-24741-8_6
5. Sulbha Powar and Dr. Ganesh Magar, "Efficient Geo-Textual Hybrid Indexing Techniques for Moving Objects and Queries," IJRTE, vol. 8, no. 6, pp. 4419–4428, Mar. 2020, doi: https://doi.org/10.35940/ijrte.F9142.038620.
6. Xiaohui Yu, K. Q. Pu, and N. Koudas, "Monitoring k-Nearest Neighbor Queries over Moving Objects," 2005, pp. 631–642. https://doi.org/10.1109/ICDE.2005.92.
7. Xiaopeng Xiong, M. F. Mokbel, and W. G. Aref, "SEA-CNN: Scalable Processing of Continuous K-Nearest Neighbor Queries in Spatio-temporal Databases," 2005, pp. 643–654. https://doi.org/10.1109/ICDE.2005.128.
8. K. Mouratidis, D. Papadias, and M. Hadjieleftheriou, "Conceptual partitioning: an efficient method for continuous nearest neighbor monitoring," 2005, p. 634. https://doi.org/10.1145/1066157.1066230.
9. X. Xu, L. Xiong, and V. Sunderam, "D-Grid: An In-Memory Dual Space Grid Index for Moving Object Databases," in 2016 17th IEEE International Conference on Mobile Data Management (MDM), Porto, Jun. 2016, pp. 252–261. https://doi.org/10.1109/MDM.2016.46.
10. M. F. Mokbel, X. Xiong, and W. G. Aref, "SINA: scalable incremental processing of continuous queries in spatio-temporal databases," 2004, p. 623. https://doi.org/10.1145/1007568.1007638.
11. N. Koudas, T. Labs-Research, B. C. Ooi, K.-L. Tan, and R. Zhang, "Approximate NN Queries on Streams with Guaranteed Error/performance Bounds," p. 12, 2004.
12. C. Li, Y. Gu, J. Qi, G. Yu, R. Zhang, and W. Yi, "Processing moving k NN queries using influential neighbor sets," Proceedings of the VLDB Endowment, vol. 8, no. 2, pp. 113–124, Oct. 2014, doi: https://doi.org/10.14778/2735471.2735473.
13. C. Lv, Y. Xu, J. Song, and P. Lv, "A data frame based spatiotemporal indexing algorithm for moving objects," in 2016 12th World Congress on Intelligent Control and Automation (WCICA), Guilin, China, Jun. 2016, pp. 2592–2597. https://doi.org/10.1109/WCICA.2016.7578643.
14. Simonas ˇSaltenisy Christian S. Jenseny Scott T. Leuteneggerz Mario A. Lopezz, "Indexing the Positions of Continuously Moving Objects." ACM, 2000.
15. R. Benetis, C. S. Jensen, G. Karciauskas, and S. Saltenis, "Nearest neighbor and reverse nearest neighbor queries for moving objects," 2002, pp. 44–53. https://doi.org/10.1109/IDEAS.2002.1029655.
16. C. Shahabi, "Time Parameterized Queries in Spatio Temporal Databases," p. 31.
17. Y. Tao, D. Papadias, and J. Sun, "The TPR*-Tree: An Optimized Spatio-Temporal Access Method for Predictive Queries," p. 12, 2003.

18. K. Raptopoulou, A. N. Papadopoulos, and Y. Manolopoulos, "Fast Nearest-Neighbor Query Processing in Moving-Object Databases," p. 25, 2003.
19. G. S. Iwerks, H. Samet, and K. P. Smith, "Maintenance of K -nn and spatial join queries on continuously moving points," ACM Transactions on Database Systems, vol. 31, no. 2, pp. 485–536, Jun. 2006, doi: https://doi.org/10.1145/1138394.1138396.
20. An Chunming and Li Zongsen, "Studies on kNN query of moving objects for location management in spatial database," Dec. 2013, pp. 2428–2432. https://doi.org/10.1109/MEC.2013.6885443.
21. Y.-K. Huang, Z.-H. He, C. Lee, and W.-H. Kuo, "Continuous Possible K-Nearest Skyline Query in Euclidean Spaces," Dec. 2013, pp. 174–181. https://doi.org/10.1109/ICPADS.2013.35.
22. Y. Park et al., "A New Spatial Index Structure for Efficient Query Processing in Location Based Services," 2010, pp. 434–441. https://doi.org/10.1109/SUTC.2010.64.
23. C. Li, Y. Gu, J. Qi, G. Yu, R. Zhang, and Q. Deng, "INSQ: An influential neighbor set based moving kNN query processing system," May 2016, pp. 1338–1341. https://doi.org/10.1109/ICDE.2016.7498339.
24. G. Chen, J. Zhao, Y. Gao, L. Chen, and R. Chen, "Time-Aware Boolean Spatial Keyword Queries," IEEE Trans. Knowl. Data Eng., vol. 29, no. 11, pp. 2601–2614, Nov. 2017, doi: https://doi.org/10.1109/TKDE.2017.2742956.
25. L. Chen, G. Cong, C. S. Jensen, and D. Wu, "Spatial Keyword Query Processing: An Experimental Evaluation," p. 12, 2013.
26. S. K. Powar and D. G. M. Magar, "Spatial Keyword Query Processing: R*-IF Tree Implementation", Feb 18, pp 65–72, ISSN 2321–3469

Text-Independent Source Identification of Printed Documents using Texture Features and CNN Model

Pushpalata Gonasagi[1]([✉]), Shivanand S. Rumma[1], and Mallikarjun Hangarge[2]

[1] Department of PG Studies and Research in Computer Science, Gulbarga University,
Kalaburagi, Karnataka, India
gonasagi99@gmail.com
[2] Karnatak Arts, Science and Commerce College, Bidar, Karnataka, India

Abstract. Artificial Intelligence (AI) technologies have been used in digital forensic science to resolve disputed documents where one or more human experts would normally be contacted. The purpose of intelligent systems based on printer identification is determined printer created a specific document. Most solutions based on a text-dependent approach may be insufficient in certain scenarios. No study on text-independent based on various word images printed from various laser printer models has been done, as far as the researchers are knowledgeable. As a result, we classify the laser printer models based on the various gray scale word images. 40000-word images of four laser printer models are included in the collection. To classify the different laser printer models, the LBP (Local Binary Pattern) with KNN (K-Nearest Neighbors) and the cubic SVM (Support Vector Machine) classifiers are employed. The deep learning CNN (Convolution Neural Network) model is also used to determine the laser printer models. The experimental results of textural features and the CNN architecture are compared to recent work from a literature survey. We obtained high accuracy from K-NN and cubic SVM classifiers of 97.2% and 97.9%, respectively, and 94.3% accuracy in the CNN model.

Keywords: Printers; Forgery document; LBP · K-NN · SVM · CNN

1 Introduction

We use printed documents for security, instruction, and official work, such as land records, agreements, bills, etc., in our daily lives. The identification of the genuineness of these printed documents is essential. In the present digital era, identifying the authenticity of printed documents is challenging work. Because there is a high possibility of creating fake documents using software, printers, xerox machines etc. The usage of laser printers in day-to-day life is high because of their speed of printing documents, low cost and print quality. However, the use of laser printer devices to create forged documents is also high. Therefore, it is essential to identify the source of documents to authenticate their originality. Each laser printer model has unique printing quality, and this clue is utilized to determine the originality of the documents.

© The Author(s) 2023
R. Manza et al. (Eds.): ACVAIT 2022, AISR 176, pp. 250–261, 2023.
https://doi.org/10.2991/978-94-6463-196-8_20

According to the literature survey, many approaches have been developed using atrifacts. Imperfections in the printing process lead to artefacts in the printed document, which are invisible to the eyes. These artefacts may be observed in the zoomed versions of printed documents. Experts inspected the documents' ink using chemical and physical analysis. The Raman Spectroscopy technique [1] examines the questionable documents in forensic document science. The drawback of this method is that it might be destroyed using chemicals or any physical devices, and it is time-consuming. The code words are embedded in documents for authenticity of documents. These types of methods are known as extrinsic signature methods [2], and there is no need to embed the additional information in the document. But these approaches are expensive and not followed by all industrialists.

Finally, many strategies have evolved to identify the printer devices based on documents. The laser printer models print distinctive noise due to manufacturer imperfection, printing technologies and slight differences in the different printer models. Each printer has unique printing quality. It can be observed at the margin of the characters in printed documents. In text-dependent approaches, various methods for identifying the source printer are used, and these features are used to simulate the printer-specific imperfection [3, 4]. This method is known as the intrinsic signature method or passive method. The intrinsic method exploits that specific signature that can be searched in printed documents using image processing learning techniques [5]. We present the process for identification of printers based on the printed documents at different types of word-level texture descriptors. It is considered a text-independent approach rather than fixing to a specific character or word image.

The remaining part of the paper is as follows. We present related work in Sect. 2. Section 3 describes the proposed technique, pre-processing, and feature extraction. The experimental results are presented in Sect. 4, and the conclusion is seen in Sect. 5.

2   Review of Related Studies

Significant studies have been taken to identify printer models based on documents. A brief literature review is presented below.

Shize et. al. [6] described a method to differentiate the document images produced by laser printers, inkjet printers, and xerox machines. They extracted the features like contour roughness, noise energy and average gradient from the individual letters in the documents. The accuracy is 90% using SVM classifier. Tsai et. al. [7] employed GLCM (Gray-Level Co-occurrence Matrix) and DWT (Discrete Wavelet Transform) to identify the printers based on documents in the Chinese language. They used SVM classifier to classify printer models, and an accuracy 98.64% has achieved. Elkasrawi et. al. [8] used a method to identify printers based on the noise produced by the printer on the documents. They have used statistical features like mean and contour. This system has classified 20 different models of printers and achieved a classification accuracy of 76.75%. Schreyer et. al. [9] detected a method to find the photocopy and described the recognition of printing technique based on machine learning algorithms. They have achieved the target by spatial and frequency domain analysis of the given document. Lambert et al. [10] developed a method to detect counterfeit documents generated using different printers such as laserjet based on the features like text edge roughness, texture, area difference and correlation coefficient. They carried out the classification of the documents using SVM classifier. Mikkilineni et al. [11] used texture features to identify the printer. They examined the font type, size and paper type of document to find the discernment features of documents. The classifier SVM is employed to classify the printers in printing the documents. Wu et. al. [12] described a method to identify intrinsic features of documents for recognizing the printers. Based on the intrinsic properties, they distinguished the documents produced by the type of printer. The geometric distortion and SVM classifier were used for classifying ten printers. Mikkilinen et al. [13] described a method for identifying the printers based on the GLCM texture features. Ten Electro Photographic (EP) printers were used to classify using KNN classifier. Devi et al. [14] proposed an algorithm for distinguished inkjet printers and photocopiers depending on the analysis of the skew and kurtosis of the histogram of text images. They selected five different printers and three different photocopiers to differentiate each other. Tsai et al. [15] presented the technique that analyses the microscopic printed character images for source identification. They have used SVM classifier to classify the printers using different descriptors such as GLCM, DWT, etc. Ferreira et al. [16] developed a method to identify the printers using character images. They have applied raw, median and average filters on character images to obtain features. The CNN is designed to train the data for this problem. They achieved an accuracy of 97.33% for the classification of ten printers. Jain et. al. [17] detected a method for classifying printers by applying geometric distortion techniques at a text-line level. They achieved 98.85% accuracy in classifying the printer models using SVM classifier for pages with different fonts and printers. Joshi et al. [18] proposed a method for document classification based on images of the letter 'e' that uses a single CNN model derived from the combination of letter images and their printer-specific noise residuals. They achieved an accuracy of 90.33% for their created dataset and 98.01% for the available dataset. Bibi et al. [19] presented a printer identification method for printed documents and developed a text-independent method using pre-trained CNN. They achieved 95.52% accuracy on 1200 documents from 20 different printers. Darwish et al. [20] presented a bio-inspired expert system for printer classification that uses the GLCM of the printed Arabic letter 'WOO' and a Niching genetic algorithm. They achieved a 91% accuracy rate.

3   Proposed Method

In recent years, most techniques have relied on a specific letter of document images, which may prove inadequate in real-world scenarios. In this paper, we present the classification of different laser printer models based on the texture analysis of the word of a document. We have segmented various word images from document images to identify the four laser printer models, and it is a text-independent approach. The textural characteristics are derived from the most widely used technique, LBP.

We also used the deep learning CNN model to classify word images from printed documents. Traditional printer recognition systems have depended on handcrafted characteristics and a significant portion of prior knowledge. CNN is the best method for determining printer models based on documents. In this paper, we examined the effect

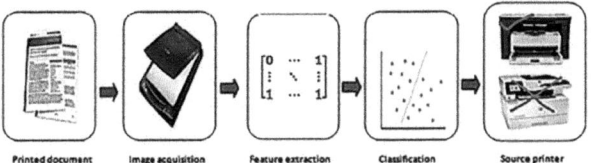

Fig. 1. Overview process of printer identification.

Table 1. Shows the number of word images of four laser printer models

Printer Model	Printed document	Word images	Randomly selected word images
CanoniR2270	100	38690	10000
Canonlbp3108	100	33756	10000
CanoniR7086	100	34540	10000
HPLaserJetM1136	100	30044	10000

of using activation functions ReLU (Rectified Linear Unit) for the inner CNN layer and softmax for the output layer in identifying laser printer models. Figure 1 depicts an overview of the printer identification process.

3.1 Data Collection

The standard dataset is not publicly available to evaluate the proposed method. Hence, we have created a dataset and gathered 100 printed document pages, including research articles. Then, 100 document pages are printed using four different laser printer models: CanoniR2270, CanonLbp3108, CanoniR7086, and HpLaserJetM1136. The word images are segmented from 400 printed document images of laser printer models and generate 137030-word images. To reduce computational complexity and time, we randomly selected 10000 segmented word images from each printer model, and a summary of the dataset is shown in Table 1. Figure 2 shows the samples of four laser printer models. Figure 3 depicts examples of segmented different word images. Figure 3(a) shows a sample of a scanned document image, Fig. 3(b) shows connected bounding box words, and Fig. 3(c) shows an example of segmented word images.

3.2 Pre-processing

The document images are scanned in grayscale and at a resolution of 300 dpi. The printed document image includes images, text, tables, graphs, and equations. The Otsu method [21] converts grayscale document images into binary document images. We used mathematical morphological operations to segment word images from the binary document images. We removed all objects containing fewer than 50 pixels with extraneous pixels along the border from the document images. These pixels have noise such as dots, special symbols, etc. The segmented components are saved as grayscale images to extract the

Fig. 2. Samples of document pages from four laser printers (a) CanoniR2270 (b)Canonlbp3108
(c) CanoniR7086 (d)HPLaserJetM1136

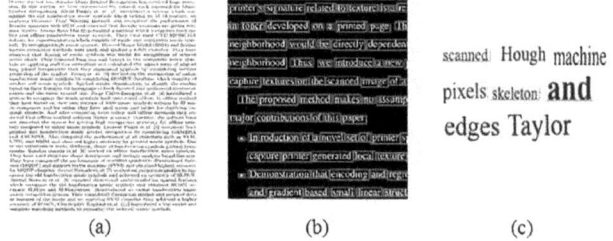

      (a)   (b)   (c)

Fig. 3. (a) Document image (b) Bounding box of connected words (c) segmented word images

discriminated features [22]. These word images represent various scales and directions.
The median filter approach is applied and effectively accomplished by removing the
word images' background noise to improve the dataset's resilience. The word images
are multidirectional, and those have multiple resolutions printed in the documents which
affect the document images' texture.

    This section explains the feature extraction methodology at the word level, using
textural and deep learned methods.

3.3 Feature Extraction

This section explains the feature extraction methodology at the various word level, which
uses the textural and deep learned method.

3.3.1 Textural Level Feature Extraction

Texture-based descriptors produce effective variations for distinguishing between segmented word images printed by different printers. LBP is an efficient technique to capture the texture of the images. LBP is used to recognize blur faces and the age of the persons most efficiently [23] and identify dating of historical documents most efficiently [24]. Hence, we use this to extract word image features from each set of printer's document images separately. LBP descriptor computes a binary code for each pixel in an image by thresholding circularly symmetric to a neighbouring pixel with the central pixel value. It occurs the different binary patterns by creating the histogram. The Eq. (1) of the LBP is given below.

$$LBP_{(P,R)}(Xc) = \sum_{p=0}^{p-1} f(Xp - Xc).2^p \tag{1}$$

where

$$f(y) = \begin{cases} 1, y \geq 0 \\ 0, y < 0 \end{cases}$$

Xc indicates the centre pixel in the above equation, Xp indicates one of its p neighbours. To obtain the LBP labels, we assigned $P = 8$ neighbours spaced equally on a circle of radius ($R = 1$). Then, labelled binary patterns are used as the texture features. A total of 59 features are generated for a word image, and the resulting features are concatenated to form the final feature vector. Finally, this feature vector is fetched into a K-NN and SVM classifier to classify the source printer.

3.3.2 CNN Level Feature Extraction

The deep learning CNN architecture has been used for this problem, and its CNN architecture is shown in Fig. 4. It is highly effective in complex image classification [25]. The advantage of CNN over machine learning is that it reduces the number of parameters [26, 27]. Artifacts for source printer identification are limited to handcrafted methods. As a result, we analyze the CNN architecture for source printer classification. We identified solutions for detecting the pattern of word images segmented from document images of four laser printer models based on the CNN model. CNN is used on multiple representations of document images at a word level, allowing for better data discrimination. CNN extracts the necessary discriminating features directly from the document images. This CNN model learns the bias of characteristics from a group of training document images. We set the training phase with stochastic gradient descent, with an initial learning rate of 0.0001 and a maximum number of epochs of 20. The model created at the epoch with the lowest validation loss is the best choice for each CNN. The size of different word images is 40x227. The various word images are included in the dataset, as discussed in Sect. 3.1. The ReLU layer accelerates training and achieves rapid convergence in CNN training. A pooling layer is then used to summarize the data by sliding a window across the feature maps and performing a max nonlinear operation on the data. Classifiers are fully connected layers, and it is usually followed by a soft-max layer, which determines the input image class. The Soft-max layer is used to normalize input values, and its

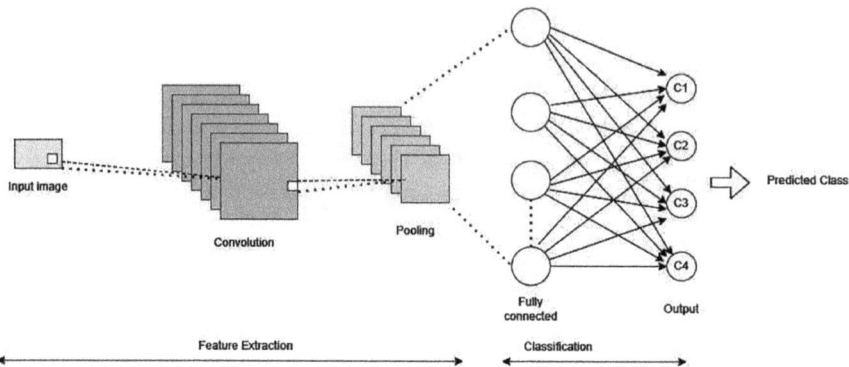

Fig. 4. Basic architecture of CNN model.

output can be interpreted as indicating the probability of a sample belonging to each class.

4   Experimental Results and Discussion

Two sets of experiments are carried out in this section. The experimental setup and results are analyzed in order to evaluate textural and deep learning features. Both experiments are carried out onMatlab software.

4.1   Performance of Textual Features

We used 10-fold cross-validation to classify document images because it is the most accurate and effective validation method and reports the average results of 10 iterations. We considered the randomly segmented various word images from the document images as discussed in Sect. 3.1. Different laser printer models have specific characteristics, and we capture the discriminated 59 features of word images by LBP as mentioned in Sect. 3.3. The features are fed into the K-NN [28] and cubic SVM [29] classifiers for classifying the four laser printer models. The experiment's outcome is measured in terms of overall average accuracy. Table 2 shows four laser printers' classification accuracy. We have attained the average accuracy of words images are 97.2% and 97.9% from classifiers K-NN and cubic SVM, respectively. The confusion matrices are shown in Table 3 and Table 4 for the K-NN and cubic SVM classifiers, respectively.

4.2   Deep Learning CNN Performance Measurement

In a data-driven approach, learn the discriminate features automatically from the readily collected data instead of an enormous training dataset. Extracting the meaningful discriminating data from a set of trained data is also essential for deep learning CNN. The single channel for various word images is used to prepare a CNN model. It works well with small patches of word images. It has been processed by including a Batch Normalization (BN) layer [27] to improve the faster learning of network layer ReLU parameters

Table 2. Classification accuracy of four laser printers using KNN and cubic SVM classifiers

Four Laser Printer models/Classes	KNN-Classifier		Cubic SVM-Classifier	
	Classification rate of words images (%)	Error rate (%)	Classification rate of words images (%)	Error rate (%)
CanoniR2270	95.81	4.19	98.39	1.61
Canonlbp3108	98.49	1.51	98.27	1.73
CanoniR7086	95.12	4.88	96.01	3.99
HplaserJet1136	99.22	0.78	98.73	1.27
Average Accuracy	97.2	2.8	97.9	2.1

and weights because it speeds up the training process. It introduced non-linearity, which improved classification accuracy. When designing the CNN architecture, the combination of BN and ReLU performed admirably in smaller image regions. As examined in Sect. 3.3.2, the CNN model is trained for 20 epochs before selecting the model with the lowest validation loss. The layer has 20 filters with 3X3 dimensions because the CNN's input is single-channel word images. To generate the features maps, a succession of fixed-size filters are applied to the word image. These filters draw attention to patterns useful for image identification, including edges, regular patterns, etc. The classification layer used to classify the CNN characterizes the four-laser printers. We have used 8000-word images for training and 2000-word images for testing to identify the printer models. The evaluation of the deep learning CNN model is estimated by building the CNN architecture. Finally, we achieved 94.3% accuracy in identifying the four laser printer models, promising results. The results are presented as a confusion matrix, as shown in Table 5. The precision, recall, and F1 Score from Eqs. (2), (3), and (4) are also used to evaluate the performance. Precision is measured by how many positives are properly identified out of all positives. The proportion of positive instances that are retrieved is known as recall. The F1 Score is used to calculate the classifier's classification capabilities. It is thought to be a better indicator of the model's performance than the usual accuracy metric.

$$Precision = TruePositive/(TruePositive + FalsePositive) \qquad (2)$$

$$Recall = TruePositive/(FalseNegati + TruePositive \qquad (3)$$

$$F1score = 2 * (Precision * Recall)/(Precision + Recall) \qquad (4)$$

The estimated performance measures of the models are shown in Table 6

4.3 Comparison Analysis

We proposed two experiments in this paper that use handcrafted features and the deep leering CNN model. The developed system is the novel approach for source printer classification for various segmented word images, rather than focusing on a single letter or

Table 3. Confusion matrix using K-NN classifier of four laser printer models

Classes/Printer model	CanoniR2270	CanonLbp3108	CanoniR7086	HpLaserJetM1136
CanoniR2270	**1925**	36	15	24
CanonLbp3108	74	**1853**	24	49
CanoniR7086	66	48	**1660**	226
HpLaserJetM1136	13	5	12	**1970**

Table 4. Confusion matrix using Cubic SVM classifier of four laser printer models

Laser Printers/ Classes	CanoniR2270	Canonlbp3108	CanoniR7086	HplaserJet1136
CanoniR2270	**9839**	51	75	35
Canonlbp3108	17	**9827**	90	66
CanoniR7086	27	105	**9601**	267
HplaserJet1136	6	12	109	**9873**

Table 5. Confusion matrix using CNN model

Classes/printer model	CanoniR2270	Canonlbp3108	CanoniR7086	HplaserJet1136
CanoniR2270	**1955**	13	18	14
Canonlbp3108	74	**1853**	24	49
CanoniR7086	64	48	**1762**	126
HplaserJet1136	13	5	12	**1970**

Table 6. Performance measurement for identifying the four laser printer models using CNN architecture

Precision	Recall	F1 Score	Accuracy
0.9434	0.9440	0.9431	94.3%

word image. As a result, the image quality of laser printer models varies in printed documents. Based on the performance measures such as average precision, average recall, F1 Score, and accuracy obtained. The deep learning CNN model performed well with the train network and achieved a better recognition accuracy rate of 94.3%, lower than the textural approach. The CNN model necessitates massive data and a high computer configuration. Our proposed methodology classified printed documents more accurately and effectively. Table 7 shows the numeric comparative study of our experimental results to the most recent existing methods reported in the literature in [19, 20].

Table 7. Comparison with recent related work

Authors	Techniques	Features	Classifier	Accuracy (%)
Maryam et. al.[19]	Text-independent	Textural features (LBP)	SVM	93.25%
		Deep learning features (Resnet50)	CNN	95.52%
Darwish et. al. [20]	Text-dependent	Textural features (GLCM) and Niching Genetic Algorithm (NGA)	KNN	91%
Proposed Approach	Text-independent	Textural features (LBP)	KNN	**97.2%**
		Textural features (LBP)	Cubic SVM	**97.9%**
		Deep learning features (ReLU CNN)	CNN	**94.3%**

5 Conclusion

The developed textural method LBP and CNN model are the best explorers for determining the source printer. We proved that different printers printed the same document in different ways. This system automatically detects forgery documents based on document images at various word levels. The overall high accuracy classification is 97.9% using the cubic SVM classifier and 97.2% using KNN. We successfully trained the CNN model with a set of parameters to identify the source printer and achieved 94.3%. We plan to improve printer classification accuracy by using a more significant number of printer models and evaluating source mobiles attribution using flatbed and camera-based document images.

References

1. Braz, A., López-López, M., & García-Ruiz, C. (2013). Raman spectroscopy for forensic analysis of inks in questioned documents. *Forensic science international, 232*(1-3), 206-212.
2. Ali, G. N., Mikkilineni, A. K., Allebach, J. P., Delp, E. J., Chiang, P. J., & Chiu, G. T. (2003, January). Intrinsic and extrinsic signatures for information hiding and secure printing with electrophotographic devices. In *NIP & Digital Fabrication Conference* (Vol. 2003, No. 2, pp. 511–515). Society for Imaging Science and Technology.
3. Gebhardt, J., Goldstein, M., Shafait, F., & Dengel, A. (2013, August). Document authentication using printing technique features and unsupervised anomaly detection. In *2013 12th International conference on document analysis and recognition* (pp. 479–483). IEEE.
4. Ferreira, A., Navarro, L. C., Pinheiro, G., dos Santos, J. A., & Rocha, A. (2015). Laser printer attribution: Exploring new features and beyond. *Forensic science international, 247*, 105-125.

5. Khanna, N., Mikkilineni, A. K., Chiu, G. T. C., Allebach, J. P., & Delp, E. J. (2008, August). Survey of scanner and printer forensics at purdue university. In *International Workshop on Computational Forensics* (pp. 22–34). Springer, Berlin, Heidelberg.

6. Shang, S., Memon, N., & Kong, X. (2014). Detecting documents forged by printing and copying. *EURASIP Journal on Advances in Signal Processing, 2014*(1), 1-13.

7. Tsai, M. J., & Liu, J. (2013, May). Digital forensics for printed source identification. In *2013 IEEE International Symposium on Circuits and Systems (ISCAS)* (pp. 2347–2350). IEEE.

8. Elkasrawi, S., &Shafait, F. (2014, April). Printer identification using supervised learning for document forgery detection. In *2014 11th IAPR International Workshop on Document Analysis Systems* (pp. 146–150). IEEE.

9. Schreyer, M., Schulze, C., Stahl, A., &Effelsberg, W. (2009, March). Intelligent Printing Technique Recognition and Photocopy Detection for Forensic Document Examination. In *Informatiktage* (Vol. 8, pp. 39–42).

10. Lampert, C. H., Mei, L., &Breuel, T. M. (2006, November). Printing technique classification for document counterfeit detection. In *2006 International Conference on Computational Intelligence and Security* (Vol. 1, pp. 639–644). IEEE.

11. Mikkilineni, A. K., Arslan, O., Chiang, P. J., Kumontoy, R. M., Allebach, J. P., Chiu, G. T. C., & Delp, E. J. (2005, January). Printer forensics using svm techniques. In *NIP & Digital Fabrication Conference* (Vol. 2005, No. 1, pp. 223–226). Society for Imaging Science and Technology.

12. Wu, Y., Kong, X., & Guo, Y. (2009, November). Printer forensics based on page document's geometric distortion. In *2009 16th IEEE International Conference on Image Processing (ICIP)* (pp. 2909–2912). IEEE.

13. Mikkilineni, A. K., Chiang, P. J., Ali, G. N., Chiu, G. T. C., Allebach, J. P., & Delp, E. J. (2004, January). Printer identification based on texture features. In *NIP & Digital Fabrication Conference* (Vol. 2004, No. 1, pp. 306–311). Society for Imaging Science and Technology.

14. Devi, M. U., Rao, C. R., & Jayaram, M. (2014). Statistical measures for differentiation of photocopy from print technology forensic perspective. *International Journal of Computer Applications, 105*(15).

15. Tsai, M. J., &Yuadi, I. (2016, September). Printed source identification by microscopic images. In *2016 IEEE International Conference on Image Processing (ICIP)* (pp. 3927–3931). IEEE.

16. Ferreira, A., Bondi, L., Baroffio, L., Bestagini, P., Huang, J., Dos Santos, J. A., ... & Rocha, A. (2017). Data-driven feature characterization techniques for laser printer attribution. *IEEE Transactions on Information Forensics and Security, 12*(8), 1860-1873.

17. Jain, H., Joshi, S., Gupta, G., & Khanna, N. (2020). Passive classification of source printer using text-line-level geometric distortion signatures from scanned images of printed documents. Multimedia Tools and Applications, 79(11), 7377-7400 https://doi.org/10.1007/s11 042-019-08508-x

18. Joshi, Sharad, Suraj Saxena, and Nitin Khanna. "Source printer identification from document images acquired using smartphone." arXiv preprint arXiv:2003.12602 (2020).

19. Bibi, Maryam, Anmol Hamid, Momina Moetesum, and Imran Siddiqi. "Document Forgery Detection using Printer Source Identification—A Text-Independent Approach." In 2019 International Conference on Document Analysis and Recognition Workshops (ICDARW), vol. 8, pp. 7–12. IEEE, 2019.

20. Darwish, S. M., & ELgohary, H. M. (2021). Building an expert system for printer forensics: A new printer identification model based on niching genetic algorithm. *Expert Systems, 38*(2), e12624.

21. Otsu, N. (1979). A threshold selection method from gray-level histograms. *IEEE transactions on systems, man, and cybernetics, 9*(1), 62-66.

22. Hangarge, M., Santosh, K.C., Doddamani, S., & Pardeshi, R. (2013). Statistical Texture Features based Handwritten and Printed Text Classification in South Indian Documents. *ArXiv, abs/1303.3087.*

23. Ojala, T., Pietikainen, M., & Maenpaa, T. (2002). Multiresolution gray-scale and rotation invariant texture classification with local binary patterns. *IEEE Transactions on pattern analysis and machine intelligence, 24*(7), 971-987.

24. Gonasagi, P., Rumma, S.S., &Hangarge, M. (2020). Classification of Historical Documents Based on LBP and LPQ Techniques.

25. Krizhevsky, A., Sutskever, I., & Hinton, G. E. (2012). Imagenet classification with deep convolutional neural networks. *Advances in neural information processing systems, 25.*

26. LeCun, Y., Bottou, L., Bengio, Y., & Haffner, P. (1998). Gradient-based learning applied to document recognition. *Proceedings of the IEEE, 86*(11), 2278-2324.

27. Ioffe, S., & Szegedy, C. (2015, June). Batch normalization: Accelerating deep network training by reducing internal covariate shift. In *International conference on machine learning* (pp. 448–456). PMLR.

28. Fix, E., & Hodges, J. L. (1951). *Discriminatory Analysis, Nonparametric Discrimination: Consistency Properties USAF School of Aviation Medicine, Randolph Field* (pp. 1–21). Texas, Tech. Report 4.

29. Cortes, C., &Vapnik, V. (1995). Support-vector networks. Machine learning, 20(3), 273-297

A Vision-Based Sign Language Recognition using Statistical and Spatio-Temporal Features

Prashant Rawat$^{(\boxtimes)}$ and Lalit Kane

School of Computer Science, University of Petroleum and Energy Studies, Dehradun, India
`500065497@stu.upes.ac.in`

Abstract. Those with disabilities should not be characterised primarily by their impairment in modern society; rather, it is the environment that may disable persons with disabilities. As automatic Sign Language Recognition (SLR) develops, digital technology will give more enabling settings. Many existing SLR techniques focus on the classification of static hand gestures, despite the fact that communication is a time activity, as many dynamic gestures demonstrate. As a result, temporal information obtained during the delivery of a gesture is rarely considered in SLR. The studies in this paper look at the challenge of SL gesture identification in terms of how dynamic gestures vary throughout delivery, and the goal of this research is to see how single and mixed characteristics affect a machine learning model's classification abilities. A complex categorization task is presented with 18 frequent movements captured using a Leap Motion Controller sensor. Statistical descriptors and spatio-temporal properties are among the features derived from a 0.6 s time window. Each set's features are compared using ANOVA F-Scores and p-values, then sorted into bins of 10 features each, up to a maximum of 250. The best statistical model chose 240 features and achieved an accuracy of 85.96%, the best spatio-temporal model chose 230 features and achieved an accuracy of 80.98%, and the best mixed-feature model chose 240 features from each set and achieved an accuracy of 86.75%. When all three sets of results are examined, the overall distribution indicates that when inputs are any number of mixed features versus any number of either of the two single sets of features, the minimum outcomes are raised.

Keywords: Sign Language Recognition (SLR) · Spatio-Temporal · Analysis of variance (ANOVA)

1 Introduction

The purpose of applied intelligence for sign language recognition, which is one of the most important subfields of human activity recognition, is to offer systems that can translate sign language to written text by the classification of specific motions that relate to said words and phrases [1]. The capacity to speak is generally taken for granted, and a lack of communication can lead to loneliness and sadness among the deaf community. Computer-mediated communication, or the employment of computational tools to provide a model-in-the-middle strategy for bridging a communicative barrier between

© The Author(s) 2023
R. Manza et al. (Eds.): ACVAIT 2022, AISR 176, pp. 262–277, 2023.
https://doi.org/10.2991/978-94-6463-196-8_21

persons who can and cannot utilise sign language to an effective level, has been proven to minimise isolation. Teenagers frequently experience this when attempting to communicate with their parents and at school, according to the 1992 study, and members of the elderly community who are deaf have also been observed to experience isolation when entering a nursing home designed for hearing residents [4, 25].

More than 1.5 billion people worldwide suffer from hearing loss, according to the World Health Organization. Hearing loss affects 430 million people, which is deemed detrimental in today's culture. It's also worth noting that this is an increasing issue; by 2050, 2.5 billion people are expected to have hearing loss, with 700 million of them regarded to have disabling hearing loss [7]. Given how few educational systems include sign language communication in their curricula, these figures urge for the development of improved ways for sign language communication [6]. This article looks at how different sorts of features can be collected from hand gestures to help with categorization or translating a physical gesture to words on a screen. A system like this would allow those who couldn't communicate using physical gestures to communicate more effectively with those who can. Automatic Sign Language Recognition, unlike voice recognition, which is commercially viable, is still in its infancy, according to a literature assessment [4, 29]. Many issues arise, one of which is the analysis of static gestures using only spatial observations. Studies that go beyond the information provided by sensor APIs tend to produce better results and lower volatility, so this research will look at how other types of characteristics may be utilised to identify hand gestures and how they can be combined to complement one another [29, 20]. Many sign language movements are dynamic and occur at several times, and many studies do not take this into account when analysing hand gesture data. As a result, one of the goals of this research is to see how using spatio-temporal aspects might help with overall classification of dynamic gestures. The following are the work's primary scientific contributions:

- A collection of 18 different gestures was used to extract statistical and spatio-temporal properties.
- The ANOVA F-scores and rankings of the collected gestures, as well as their p-values, were analysed.
- The training and analysis of machine learning models where one or both sets of characteristics have different numbers resulted in a total of 146 models being trained.
- When a mixed set of features is taken into account, hand gesture recognition improves, resulting in an overall mean classification accuracy of 86.75% (240 statistical and 240 spatio-temporal features).

2 Literature Review

The study of how algorithms may be built to automate the translation and interpretation of physical, facial, and hand movements to written text is known as sign language recognition [6]. Automatic voice recognition has improved to the point that it can be commercially viable, while automatic Sign Language Recognition (SLR) is still a newer concept. SLR is yet to be commercially feasible in society, and more effort is needed to develop the technology. The expanding tendency of published papers, which doubled between 2013 and 2017, was observed in Wadhawan and Kumar's 2021 literature analysis on a decade of SLR research [8]. Much of the research has been done on static gestures, which are non-temporal and hence easier to classify than dynamic gestures, which can represent a single word or mood in its entirety. As a result, the studies given in this paper try to identify dynamic features based on statistical and temporal behaviour seen within a time window [17, 23].

RGB cameras [4, 29], depth-sensing cameras [3, 10, 2], smart gloves [15, 17, 19], and biological signal processing of electroencephalography [22] and electromyography [25, 26] have all been considered as options for automatic Sign Language Recognition. The Leap Motion Controller sensor, which is used in this study, is the topic of this literature review. The Leap Motion Controller uses infrared technology and a pair of cameras to determine where the hands are in space [9]. Basic spatial features, as well as the velocity of some points on the hands and arms, can be measured using the sensor's API. The authors proposed utilising KNN and SVM models with a Leap Motion Controller to classify American Sign Language alphabet movements [10]. KNN had a mean accuracy of 72.87% in 4-fold cross validation, but was exceeded by a Radial Basis Function SVM, which had a mean accuracy of 79.83%. To increase categorization capabilities, features were flattened using a sliding window technique. Similarly, the authors offered Bayesian and Deep Learning techniques to jump motion-based Arabic Sign Language identification learned using 5-fold cross validation in [12], with a Naive Bayes classifier scoring about 98% and deep neural networks scoring 99%. The authors of the paper chose half of the functionalities supplied by the Leap Motion API that were most relevant. In addition, feature extraction was used to extract the mean values for the relevant features from each frame. The findings reveal that when such characteristics are created, they improve, implying that further extractions from those provided by the sensor's software produce a set of qualities that are relevant for the task [3]. Long Short-Term Memory models were able to categorise 35 distinct gestures with 89.5% accuracy, leading to 72.3% phrase accuracy in [11], demonstrating the utility of temporal learning in Indian Sign Language recognition. According to the authors of the Indian Sign Language study, three-layer LSTMs were the most likely to extract temporal data for categorization. [13] focused on the categorization of the American Sign Language alphabet using jump motion data after recording 18 different programs, emphasising the efficiency of the Hidden Markov Model for classification, which produced an average accuracy of 86.1%. Similar to the LSTM work, where consecutive (temporal) observations enable greater gesture identification, the model choice is particularly intriguing. Within [15], Geometric Template Matching was proposed as an effective model for the recognition of the American Sign Language alphabet, which achieved around 52.56% accuracy; the authors noted that letters A, B, D, and I were correctly classified by the model, whereas letters P, R, and T were not. The authors in [21] proposed the late fusion of image and leap motion attributes for British and American Sign Language recognition, achieving 94.44% and 82.55% accuracy metrics on the datasets, respectively. Multi-modality is also being considered as a candidate for improving the state-of-the-art in automatic SLR [12]. On the leap motion data alone, the prior study attained 72.73% accuracy, which is the same dataset used in the trials in this article. When combining RGB and Depth data, Zhang et al.'s study [25] revealed that multimodality might dramatically increase sign detection. The study's model was computationally intensive, necessitating the use of two VGG16 convolutional neural networks to handle sensor data. Gao et al. [16] found similar results using a dual-CNN strategy that included picture improvement and pixel mapping. The primary difference between the two research is that Zhang et al. recommended fusing extracted features using a tertiary neural network, whereas Gao et al. fused the predictions of two different models using SoftMax activation vectors as features for a tertiary classifier. [28] advocated using Hidden Markov Models to combine hand gesture and non-manual (facial expressions and non-hand movements) data, resulting in a better outcome when more data was analysed prior to predictions.

With the literature analysis in mind, it appears that feature extraction, temporal event consideration, and multi-modality are three of the most promising possibilities for improving sign language recognition [28]. This is why the distinctions between statistical descriptors and spatio-temporal information as mixed multi-modal inputs to a learning system are the subject of this research [19]. The major study concerns here are how well the two sets of characteristics perform in terms of gesture recognition, and whether blending the traits results in a superior overall result.

3   Proposed Methodology

This section discusses the methods used in this study's experiments. This covers data gathering, feature extraction and analysis, as well as machine learning algorithms for obtaining results before comparing them.

3.1   Data Collection

Data was collected from a prior study [14] that combined hand gesture and image data to classify ASL. Only the data from a Leap Motion sensor is used from this collection. The 18-class problem is demonstrated by the following gestures: Hello/Goodbye, You/Yourself, Me/Myself, Name, Apologies, Good, Bad, Excuse Me, Thanks/Thank you, Airport, Bus, Car, Airplane, Taxi, Restaurant, Drink, and Food. These gestures were chosen because they are useful in communication. The leap motion sensor recorded 3D data for each of the gestures in the form of:

- Arms: Start position of the arm (X, Y, and Z), end position of the arm (X, Y, and Z), 3D angle between the start and end positions of the arm, and velocity of the arm (X, Y, and Z)
- Elbows: Position of the elbow (X, Y, and Z).
- Wrists: Position of the wrist (X, Y, and Z).
- Palms: Pitch, Yaw, Roll, 3D angle of the palm, position of the palm (X, Y, and Z), velocity of the palm (X, Y, and Z), and normal of the palm (X, Y, and Z).
- Fingers: Direction of the finger (X, Y, and Z), position of the finger (X, Y, and Z), and velocity of the finger (X, Y, and Z).

- Finger joints: Start position of the joint (X, Y, and Z), end position of the joint (X, Y, and Z), 3D angle of the joint, direction of the finger (X, Y, and Z), position of the joint (X, Y, and Z), and velocity of the joint (X, Y,and Z).

The following formula is used to calculate 3D angles (θ):

$$\theta = arccos\left(\frac{ab}{|a||b|}\right) \tag{1}$$

where |a| and |b| are:

$$|a| = \sqrt{a_x^2 + a_y^2 + a_z^2} \quad |b| = \sqrt{b_x^2 + b_y^2 + b_z^2} \tag{2}$$

Taking the x, y, and z coordinates of each recorded hand/arm point into consideration, the dataset contains both static (locations in space) and temporal (limited) data (velocity of joints). Further, the dataset does not include motion over short periods of time, which is crucial for grabbing movements [13]. As a result, the purpose of this research is to see how different sorts of features affect categorization abilities.

3.2 Feature Extraction and Learning

The data was collected at a rate of 5Hz, or once every 0.2 s. This study uses time windows of 0.6 (three vectors) for two reasons: (i) shorter time windows cause difficulty with extracting a number of features, and (ii) time windows greater than 3 cause communication to become awkward and slow. This study extracts two types of features: statistical and spatio-temporal. The following statistical features were retrieved from each point:

Histogram: $n = \sum_{i=1}^{k} m_i$, where n is the total number of observations and k is the total number of bins, and m_i depicts the histogram.

Interquartile range: $Q_3 - Q_1$, The first and third quartiles are represented by Q_3 and Q_1, respectively.

$$\text{Mean absolute deviation}: \frac{\sum_{i=1}^{N}|s_i^2 - mean(s)|}{N}$$

Median value: $mean(s)$
Median absolute deviation: $median(|s - median(s)|)$

$$\text{Root mean square}: \sqrt{\frac{1}{N}\sum_{i=1}^{N} s_i^2}$$

Standard deviation: $\sqrt{var}$
Variance: $mean(|s - mean(s)|)^2$
The following spatio-temporal characteristics were retrieved from each point:

$$\text{Area under curve (computed via the trapezoid rule)}: \sum_{i=0}^{N}(t_i - t_{i-1}) \times \frac{s_i + s_i - 1}{2}$$

Autocorrelation: $\sum_{n\in z} s(n)s(n-1)$, where $s(n-1)$ is the complex conjugate of $s(n)$, and l is a lag.

$$\text{Centroid along the time axis :} \quad \frac{\sum_{k}^{N} t_i x s^2}{\sum_{l}^{N} s_i^2}$$

Mean differences: $mean(\Delta s)$
Mean absolute differences: $mean(|\Delta s|)$
Median differences: $median(\Delta s)$
Median absolute differences: $median(|\Delta s|)$

Analysis of variance (ANOVA) testing is performed to rank the attributes retrieved because there are so many and it's unclear which ones are useful [28]. The top 250 features from each set are utilised to build classification datasets, and those with a p-value greater than 0.05 are deleted. The unique set models are created by classifying 10, 20, 30…250 input characteristics (in order of best to worst) for each set. To allow for all features to be present, two approaches are used: first, a total of 250 features are selected by using 10, 10, 30…240 and 240, 230, 220…,10 from each of the sets, and then 10, 20, 30…, 250 from both sets of features. As a result, there are 146 different machine learning models to compare based on the sort of data they use (s). Given the Random Forest of 100 estimators' nature of not overfitting to training data, the classifier chosen for this experiment is a Random Forest of 100 estimators. Future work acknowledges the possibility of studying additional models based on the findings of this study.

Scikit-learn [18] is used for feature selection and model training, whereas the TSFEL package is used for feature extraction. For comparability, all random states are set to 1 in all trials, with random numbers generated by an Intel Core i7-8700K, Python 3.7.9, and scikit-learn 1.0.2.

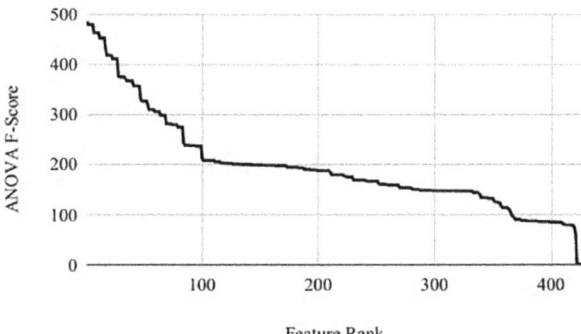

Fig. 1. The number of ANOVA F-Score calculated for hand traits and ordered from highest to lowest.

4   Results and Discussion

The feature analysis and experimental results are given, discussed, and contrasted in this part. This covers raw data preparation, statistical and spatio-temporal feature extraction and analysis, classification of the two sets of features, feature fusion, and an overall comparison and analysis of all outcomes acquired throughout the experiments.

4.1   Raw Data Pre-processing

Because extracting all accessible features from all recorded hand gesture features would result in enormous datasets and resource-intensive experiments, feature selection is done and analysed to offer an initial set of features for statistical and temporal extraction [24].

The F-Scores for each of the features are shown in Fig. 1 by ranking; the first 99 features have comparatively high scores compared to the rest of the data. Several of the features listed lowest near the end of the graph have a clear drop off point, indicating that they are extremely useless for classification when compared to the previous dataset [27]. The p-values for each of these variables are shown in Fig. 2 in the same order as the ANOVA F-Scores; note that the statistically insignificant values correlate with the lowest ANOVA F-Scores. The direction of the left hand on the y-axis ($p = 0.61$), the velocity of the left palm on the y-axis ($p = 0.87$), the direction of the left hand on the z-axis ($p = 0.9$), and finally the velocity of the right palm on the x-axis ($p = 0.98$) were the four features with $p < 0.05$, in order of smallest to largest.

The average ANOVA F-Score for sets of features is shown in Table 1, with the top-ranked features increasing by 50 points as you progress through the groups. When 100 features are analysed, the two first drop-off points have an impact on the value. In all subsequent tests, the top 50 features are used as the feature extraction set; future work suggests that the size of this collection of features be investigated based on the findings of this study.

Table 1. Mean ANOVA F-Scores for the top N-ranked features.

Top N features	Mean ANOVA F-Score
1	485.33
50	407.24
100	342.7
150	297.25
200	262.37
250	239.85
300	256.67
350	231.67
400	361
427(all)	203.8

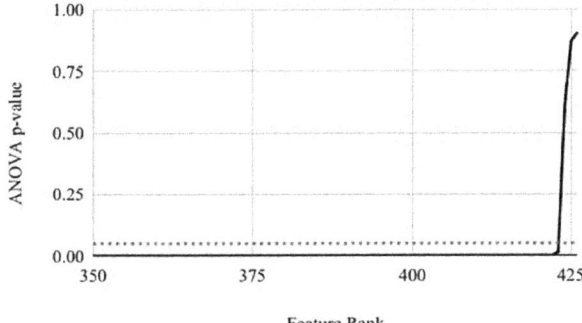

Fig. 2. P-values for hand-drawn features, ordered by ANOVA F-Score ordering, while a significance value of 0.05 is indicated by the dashed line.

Table 2. Classification based on predictions by the most common class compared to a single attribute.

Domain	Attribute	Correct	Accuracy
NA	Most Common Class: "GOOD"	323/3291	9.45%
Statistical	ECDF Percentile 1: Right Hand Pitch	887/3291	26.89%
Spatio-temporal	Absolute Energy: Right Hand Pitch	827/3291	25.1%

4.2   Extraction and Analysis of Statistical and Spatio-Temporal Features

Using feature scoring approaches, features are extracted and analysed in this part. The ANOVA F-scores for each of the retrieved features are shown in Fig. 3 and are arranged by score. The finest 64 statistical features are judged to score higher than all spatio-temporal features, as can be shown. It's also worth noting that there are more statistical features that can be used for categorization than there are useful spatio-temporal features. With $F = 186.54$, four statistical features were ranked first. These were the fourth Empirical Cumulative Distribution of the right index finger's distal end on the z-axis, the fourth ECDF of the right thumb's distal end on the z-axis, the fourth ECDF of the right ring finger on the z-axis, and the fourth ECDF of the right middle finger on the z-axis. The percentile count measurements of these same traits came next. $P < 0.05$ was found in ten statistical features, with the highest being the second histogram of the right hand pitch, which had $p = 0.84$ and $F = 0.66$. The seventh histogram of the right palm's velocity on the z-axis, with $p = 0.0295$ and $F = 1.74$, had the greatest p-value statistical characteristic with p 0.05. Three features were ranked first in terms of spatio-temporal features, with $F = 114.04$. These were the sum of the absolute differences of the right hand pitch, the area under the curve for the right hand pitch, and the zero crossing rate for the right hand's orientation on the x-axis. $p < 0.05$ was found in 137 of the poorest features in this group.

Although many statistical qualities appear to be more beneficial than those that are spatiotemporal, both sets of data include useful features [5]. As a result, classifiers for

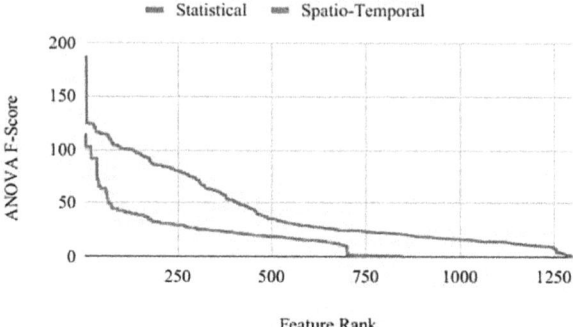

Fig. 3. The retrieved statistical and spatio-temporal features were presented an ANOVA F-Score.

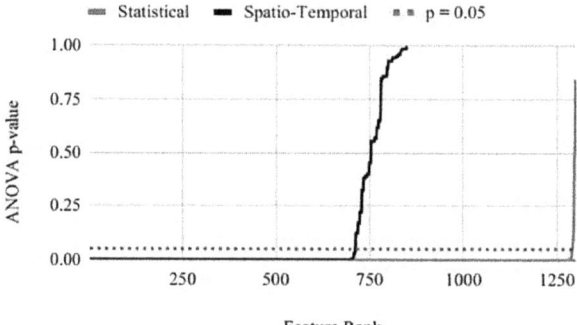

Fig. 4. p-values of ANOVA F-Score for statistical and spatio-temporal features are extracted.

multi-domain classification could benefit from merging the two sets of features. Table 2 compares the lowest mistake rate for a single rule from both sets, as well as classification by the most prevalent class, based on this. The accuracy of classifying based on the most common class is only 9.45 percent, whereas classifying based on a single attribute results in accuracy of 26.89% for the statistical attribute with the lowest error rate and 25.1% for the spatio-temporal attribute with the lowest error rate.

Although there is a difference in ANOVA F-Scores, the single best features from the two datasets have identical classification ability.

4.3 Classification of Statistical Features

When the set of extracted spatio-temporal features is supplied as model training data, this paragraph describes the classification results. Figures 7 and 8 demonstrate the classification metrics when extra spatio-temporal features are included via their ANOVA F-Scores, similar to the results reported in the preceding section. When compared to statistical traits, there is less of an irregular trend. At first, there is a pretty rapid growth in metrics, which then becomes more steady once 80 characteristics have been added. Surprisingly, this was also the amount of characteristics that stabilised the statistical feature set's metrics. While examining spatio-temporal features, the best classifier was

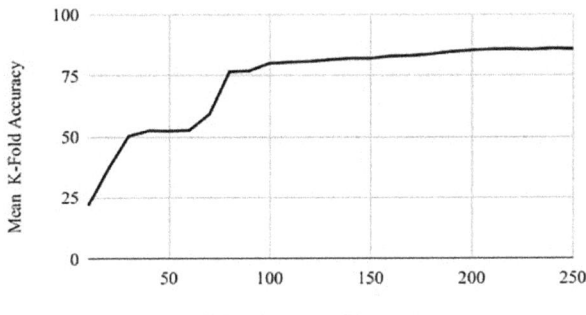

Fig. 5. The mean K-Fold classification accuracy based on the best statistical retrieved features.

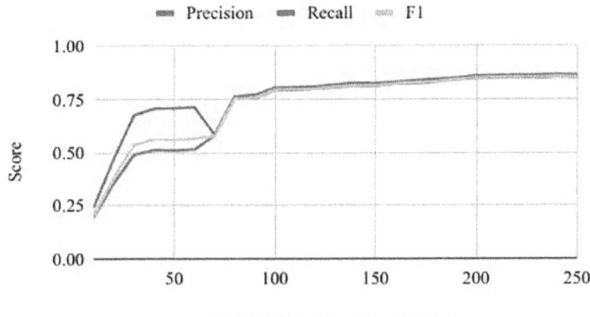

Fig. 6. Mean classification metrics on the best statistical retrieved features.

obtained when inputting 230, with an average accuracy of 80.98%. This model had an F1-Score of 0.805, a precision of 0.814, and a recall of 0.805 Figs. 4, 5 and 6.

4.4 Early Fusion of Statistical and Spatio-Temporal Features

This section explains how to mix both sets of information before creating a prediction based on the input data. Figures 9 and 10 depict a surface relating to the models' accuracy when mixing sets of features. This surface also includes the findings of the single feature set (providing the two relevant edges). The places at which dataset dimensions are equal to or less than 250 are of higher resolution, since there are more combinations examined. When the selected number of features for both sets is equal, the back half of the surface displays the findings. The highest values (darker shades of red) may be found on the front half of the graph, in the direction of equal distribution and more statistical features, as well as for much of the shared feature selection surface.

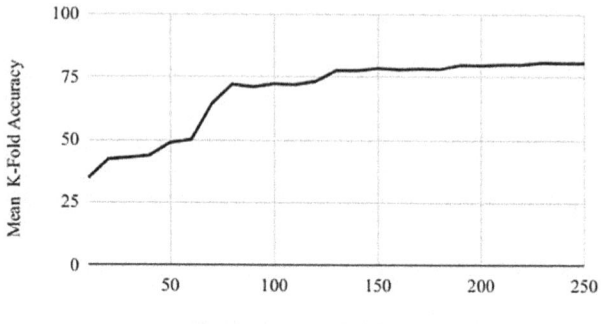

Fig. 7. The mean K-fold classification accuracy for the best spatio-temporal features.

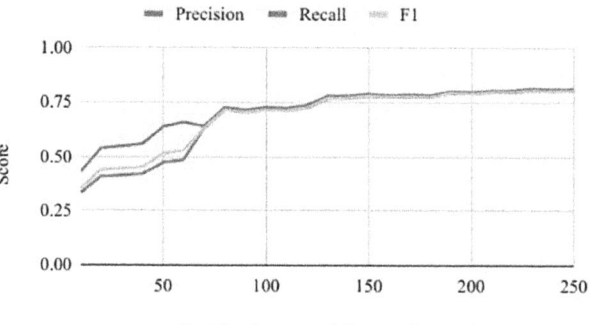

Fig. 8. Mean classification metrics on the best spatio-temporal features.

4.5   Comparison of Results

Table 3 shows the top 10 models from each of the 146 machine learning experiments. By ANOVA F-Score, the best model overall combined the 240 best statistical and 240 best spatiotemporal features. This model had an F1-Score of 0.867 and a mean accuracy of 86.75%, **PRECISION** of 0.876, recall of 0.864, and precision of 0.876. It's worth noting that the 8th best model was the first to achieve a high score by combining information from both domains. This is closely followed by 9th, which considers only 10 spatio-temporal factors in addition to 240 statistical features. Compares the three sets of features in terms of classification accuracy using a scatter and box plot. When characteristics are mixed, a number of outliers appear near the bottom of the plot, but the Q1, median, and Q2 appear to be higher. There were no outliers found towards the top of the findings. Although the statistical features alone outperformed the spatio-temporal set in terms of best results, the worst models for the statistical set outperformed those for the spatio-temporal set; this shows that when features are limited, considering temporal over statistical may lead to better results depending on how many the selection is limited to. The strongest classification models in terms of mean accuracy came from seven different combinations of both statistical and spatio-temporal characteristics (all of which were equal in quantity). Table 4 shows the final best models based on either

Table 3. Ten best models observed from the set of all 146 machine learning experiments (K-Fold standard deviation).

Stat.	Sp.temp.	Acc.	Prec.	Recall	F1
240	240	85.74 (0.9)	0.847 (0.085)	0.852 (0.079)	0.852 (0.066)
230	230	85.65 (0.89)	0.843 (0.087)	0.858 (0.078)	0.853 (0.067)
200	200	85.6 (0.81)	0.849 (0.086)	0.85 (0.082)	0.851 (0.068)
210	210	85.46 (0.84)	0.851 (0.086)	0.853 (0.078)	0.853 (0.067)
190	190	85.32 (0.74)	0.856 (0.094)	0.840 (0.082)	0.858 (0.072)
220	220	85.3 (1)	0.842 (0.093)	0.843 (0.075)	0.856 (0.068)
180	180	85.97 (1.04)	0.858 (0.092)	0.842 (0.085)	0.845 (0.073)
240	0	84.99 (0.51)	0.873 (0.091)	0.847 (0.081)	0.834 (0.069)
240	10	84.92 (0.83)	0.858 (0.098)	0.841 (0.081)	0.862 (0.073)
250	250	84.9 (0.83)	0.852 (0.089)	0.844 (0.078)	0.867 (0.067)

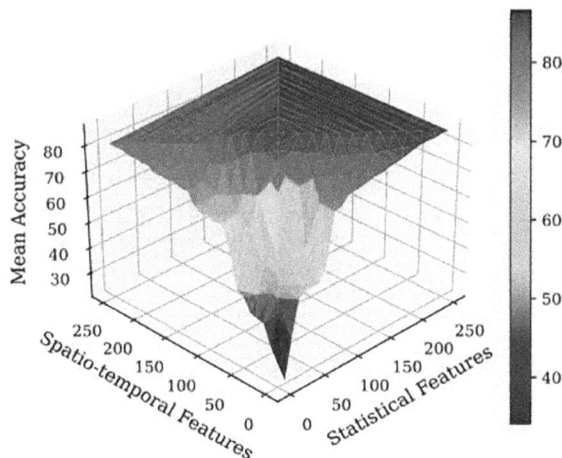

Fig. 9. A 3D depiction of the mean classification accuracy metrics on merging statistical and spatio-temporal features.

both sets of features or just one set of features. Although better metrics are achieved, computational complexity must also be considered; the required number of features can be halved at the cost of 0.79% mean accuracy for a classification capability that is still competitive. Stability is also significantly impacted as can be shown from the standard deviations of the scores when both attribute sets are present.

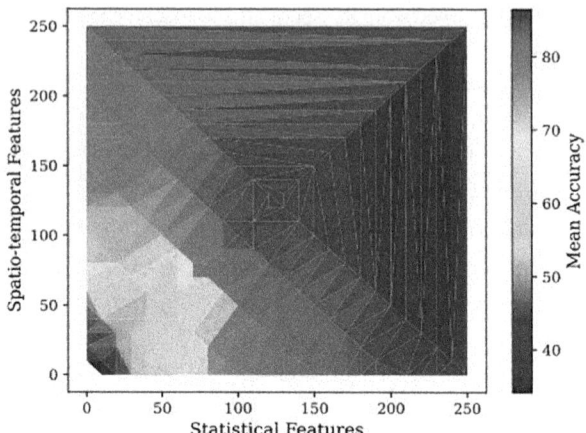

Fig. 10. Heatmap of the mean classification accuracy metrics on merging statistical and spatio-temporal features.

Table 4. Final best models observed when considering either one or both sets of features (K-Fold standard deviation).

Sta.	St. t	Acc.	Pre.	Recall	F1
240	240	83.85 (0.9)	0.862 (0.085)	0.853 (0.079)	0.867 (0.066)
240	0	82.46 (0.51)	0.855 (0.091)	0.848 (0.081)	0.857 (0.069)
0	230	81.68 (0.69)	0.838 (0.101)	0.836 (0.097)	0.805 (0.084)

4.6 Conclusion and Future Work

To conclude, this research investigated how statistical and spatio-temporal feature extraction may be used to classify sign language gestures. In terms of mean classification accuracy, the results showed that combining the two sets and learning through early fusion produced the best models overall. When only single sets of features were evaluated, statistical features improved spatio-temporal classification, however removing statistical features resulted in the global minimum outcome. It was also revealed that the worst models with more than one type of feature as input produced worse outcomes than the worst models with only one type of information as input. When the best 10 out of all 146 trained models were compared by their classification metrics, the top 7 models were all mixtures of mixed features, the eighth best was a model with statistical data exclusively. The ninth and tenth best models, on the other hand, featured a heterogeneous set of learning properties. The findings of this study have enabled much future work, firstly the number of chosen raw features prior to extraction was decided based on an F-score cut-off point, future work could explore this figure to further increase the quality of the extracted features. In terms of feature selection, this study used F-scores for comparability, although alternative techniques of selection might be investigated and compared to the findings. Finally, a random forest model was chosen because of its ability to generalise effectively and not overfit, and additional machine learning approaches could be leveraged and evaluated based on the data revealed by the trained 146 models.

Acknowledgement. This publication is an outcome of the R&D work undertaken project funded by SEED grant UPES/R&D/300320/15 from University of Petroleum and Energy Studies, Bidholi via Premnagar, Dehardun, India.

References

1. Diego G Alonso, Alfredo Teyseyre, Alvaro Soria, 'and Luis Berdun. Hand gesture recognition in real world scenarios using approximate string matching. Multimedia Tools and Applications, 79(29):20773–20794, 2020.
2. Duaa AlQattan and Francisco Sepulveda. Towards sign language recognition using eeg-based motor imagery brain computer interface. In 2017 5th International Winter Conference on Brain- Computer Interface (BCI), pages 5–8. IEEE, 2017.
3. Walaa Aly, Saleh Aly, and Sultan Almotairi. User-independent american sign language alphabet recognition based on depth image and pcanet features. IEEE Access, 7:123138–123150, 2019.
4. Safa Ameur, Anouar Ben Khalifa, and Mohamed Salim Bouhlel. A comprehensive leap motion database for hand gesture recognition. In 2016 7th International Conference on Sciences of Electronics, Technologies of Information and Telecommunications (SETIT), pages 514–519. IEEE, 2016.
5. Mar´ılia Barandas, Duarte Folgado, Let´ıcia Fernandes, Sara Santos, Mariana Abreu, Patr´ıcia Bota, Hui Liu, Tanja Schultz, and Hugo Gamboa. Tsfel: Time series feature extraction library. SoftwareX, 11:100456, 2020.
6. Giuseppe Belgioioso, Angelo Cenedese, Giuseppe Ilario Cirillo, Francesco Fraccaroli, and Gian Antonio Susto. A machine learning based approach for gesture recognition from inertial measurements. In 53rd IEEE Conference on Decision and Control, pages 4899–4904. IEEE, 2014.
7. Umema H Bohari, Ryan Alli, Alejandra Garcia, and Vinayak R Krishnamurthy. Stroke-hover intent recognition for mid-air curve drawing using multi-point skeletal trajectories. Journal of Computing and Information Science in Engineering, 21(1), 2021.
8. Stefania Bracci, Alfonso Caramazza, and Marius V Peelen. View-invariant representation of hand postures in the human lateral occipitotemporal cortex. NeuroImage, 181:446–452, 2018.
9. Zhe Cao, Tomas Simon, Shih-EnWei, and Yaser Sheikh. Realtime multi-person 2d pose estimation using part affinity fields. In Proceedings of the IEEE conference on computer vision and pattern recognition, pages 7291–7299, 2017.
10. Oinam Robita Chanu, Anushree Pillai, Spandan Sinha, and Piyanka Das. Comparative study for vision based and data based hand gesture recognition technique. In 2017 International Conference on Intelligent Communication and Computational Techniques (ICCT), pages 26–31. IEEE, 2017.
11. Weiya Chen, Chenchen Yu, Chenyu Tu, Zehua Lyu, Jing Tang, Shiqi Ou, Yan Fu, and Zhidong Xue. A survey on hand pose estimation with wearable sensors and computer-vision-based methods. Sensors, 20(4):1074, 2020.
12. S´ergio F Chevtchenko, Rafaella F Vale, and Valmir Macario. Multi-objective optimization for hand posture recognition. Expert Systems with Applications, 92:170–181, 2018.

13. Ti Chiang and Chih-Peng Fan. 3d depth information based 2d low-complexity hand posture and gesture recognition design for human computer interactions. In 2018 3rd International Conference on Computer and Communication Systems (ICCCS), pages 233–238. IEEE, 2018.

14. L Minh Dang, Kyungbok Min, Hanxiang Wang, Md Jalil Piran, Cheol Hee Lee, and Hyeon-joon Moon. Sensor-based and vision-based human activity recognition: A comprehensive survey. Pattern Recognition, 108:107561, 2020.

15. Dong-Gyun Hong and Donghwa Lee. Vision-based hand detection in various environments. In RITA 2018, pages 353–360. Springer, 2020.

16. Nada B Ibrahim, Hala H Zayed, and Mazen M Selim. Advances, challenges and opportunities in continuous sign language recognition. Journal of Engineering and Applied Sciences, 15(5):1205– 1227, 2020.

17. Philip Krejov, Andrew Gilbert, and Richard Bowden. Guided optimisation through classification and regression for hand pose estimation. Computer Vision and Image Understanding, 155:124–138, 2017.

18. Rui Li, Zhenyu Liu, and Jianrong Tan. A survey on 3d hand pose estimation: Cameras, methods, and datasets. Pattern Recognition, 93:251–272, 2019.

19. Alexandros Makris, Nikolaos Kyriazis, and Antonis A Argyros. Hierarchical particle filtering for 3d hand tracking. In Proceedings of the IEEE Conference on Computer Vision and Pattern Recognition Workshops, pages 8–17, 2015.

20. Ana I Maqueda, Carlos R del Blanco, Fernando Jaureguizar, and Narciso Garc´ıa. Human–computer interaction based on visual hand-gesture recognition using volumetric spatiograms of local binary patterns. Computer Vision and Image Understanding, 141:126–137, 2015.

21. Anshul Mittal, Pradeep Kumar, Partha Pratim Roy, Raman Balasubramanian, and Bidyut B Chaudhuri. A modified lstm model for continuous sign language recognition using leap motion. IEEE Sensors Journal, 19(16):7056–7063, 2019.

22. Weizhi Nai, Yue Liu, David Rempel, and Yongtian Wang. Fast hand posture classification using depth features extracted from random line segments. Pattern Recognition, 65:1–10, 2017.

23. Maria Parelli, Katerina Papadimitriou, Gerasimos Potamianos, Georgios Pavlakos, and Petros Maragos. Exploiting 3d hand pose estimation in deep learning-based sign language recognition from rgb videos. In European Conference on Computer Vision, pages 249–263. Springer, 2020.

24. Prashant Rawat, Bhupesh Kumar Dewangan, Anurag Jain, and Nitin Arora. Image steganalysis of improvised algorithms based on pixel difference pattern and random embedding.

25. Konstantinos Roditakis, Alexandros Makris, and Antonis A Argyros. Generative 3d hand tracking with spatially constrained pose sampling. In BMVC, volume 1, page 2, 2017.

26. Shahrzad Saremi, Seyedali Mirjalili, and Andrew Lewis. Vision-based hand posture estimation using a new hand model made of simple components. Optik, 167:15–24, 2018.

27. Tsung-Han Tsai, Chih-Chi Huang, and Kung-Long Zhang. Design of hand gesture recognition system for human-computer interaction. Multimedia tools and applications, 79(9):5989–6007, 2020.

28. Aurelijus Vaitkevi˘cius, Mantas Taroza, Tomas Bla˘zauskas, Robertas Dama˘sevi˘cius, Rytis Maskeli¯unas, and Marcin Wo´zniak. Recognition of american sign language gestures in a virtual reality using leap motion. Applied Sciences, 9(3):445, 2019.

29. Ankita Wadhawan and Parteek Kumar. Sign language recognition systems: A decade systematic literature review. Archives of Computational Methods in Engineering, 28(3):785–813, 2021.

Single Image Dehazing Using Haze Veil Analysis and CLAHE

Geeta Babusingh Rajput[✉]

Department of Applied Electronics, Gulbarga University, Kalaburgi, Karnataka, India
rajput.gg@gmail.com

Abstract. Images of the outdoor scene appear hazy due to degradation occurred by atmospheric particles (water droplets, dust, etc.) while capturing the image. Hazing creates lots of problem in the areas of surveillance, tracking and navigation and other applications. Dehazing such images is desired in digital photography and computer vision. Thus, to remove it from an image, single image and multiple images defogging methods have been proposed in the literature. In this paper, we present a single image dehazing approach using haze veil analysis. Contrast limited histogram equalization (CLAHE) technique is used to improve the contrast of the image. The proposed method has been evaluated on different foggy/hazy images. The proposed system yielded better results in terms of preserving the finer details and the color quality of the images.

Keywords: Dehaze · Haze Veil · CLAHE · Contrast Stretching · RGB · YCbCr

1 Introduction

Image processing techniques are widely used to enhance the quality of digital images captured outdoor or indoors. The quality of outdoor images captured is generally degraded due to atmospheric particles scattering the light (bad weather conditions such as fog and dust particles that absorb and scatter light) of the object image in the line of sight. Also, due to defects or movement in capturing device or moving objects, images may get blurred [1, 5]. Further, the images captured in dark or night appear washed out or noisy [2].Images that are foggy or images captured in the haze makes it difficult to identify the objects from those images [3, 4]. Foggy images appear noisy making it difficult in object detection, recognition, and image visualization. Noise-free images are desired in many applications including name plate detection, medical image analysis, surveillance applications and tracking and navigation applications [6]. Image enhancement plays a vital role in improving the quality of images by dehazing or defogging the captured images.

Several single image and multiple images de-hazing techniques have been proposed in the literature [7, 8].A model is proposed in [9] to remove haze from the region of river/sky alike scenes using image negative concept. K-means clustering is used to extract internal and external clues to enhance dark channel values for reconstructing an enhanced

R. Manza et al. (Eds.): ACVAIT 2022, AISR 176, pp. 278–285, 2023.
https://doi.org/10.2991/978-94-6463-196-8_22

image. An algorithm is proposed to preserve the brightness of an image using histogram equalization in [10].

Many of the single dehazing methods use dark channel prior (DCP) approach introduced by He.et. al. [11]. In several cases, DCP approach produces artifacts around regions where the intensity changes abruptly. To eliminate the artifacts He et al. [12] proposed a soft-matting process that suppresses halos and block artifacts. Gibson et al. [13] proposed a DCP method based on the median operator. Zhu et al. [14] introduced linear color attenuation prior, and Ren et al. [15] used a deep multiscale neural network.

This paper presents a single image dehazing method based on haze veil concept introduced by Fan Guo et.al. [16]. The contrast of the de-hazed image is improved using Contrast Limited Adaptive Histogram Equalization (CLAHE) [21] technique. Experimental results demonstrate the effectiveness of the proposed method, and when compared with other methods, the proposed method achieves a higher restoration quality. The paper is organized as follows. In Sect. 2, the methodology is discussed. In Sect. 3, experimental results and analysis are shown. The conclusions are described in Sect. 4.

2   Methodology

The proposed methodology is based on haze veil analysis introduced by Fan Guo et.al. [16]. The method regards haze as a veil layer. Illumination image is generated using retinex algorithm and depth information of the original image is used to remove the veil layer. Lastly, CLAHE technique is applied to the haze removed image to get a clear image. The proposed method is described below.

3   Haze Veil Calculation

Retinex theory deals with compensation for illumination effects in images. Accordingly, the input image, S, can be described as product of reflectance image, R, and illumination image, L, at each point (x,y).

$$S(x, y) = R(x, y) * L(x, y) \qquad (1)$$

where * is the convolution operation. The illumination component can be estimated using smoothening technique. The process involves applying a smoothening function to degraded image to obtain illumination image and is expressed as.

$$L(x, y) = S(x, y) * F(x, y) \qquad (2)$$

$$Where, \ F(x, y) = Ke^{\frac{x^2+y^2}{\sigma^2}}$$

where, K is the normalizing factor and σ is the standard deviation. With w x w window, K is determined so that F(x, y) equals one. L(x,y) is the haze veil assuming the haze is uniform. However, to compensate for color, the uniform haze veil, the degraded image is multiplied by mean of the illumination image to obtain depth-like map as follows

$$L'(x, y) = 255 - S(x, y) * \hat{L}(x, y) \qquad (3)$$

where,

$$\hat{L}(x, y) = \frac{1}{MN} \sum_{x=1}^{M} \sum_{y=1}^{N} L(x, y)$$

And M, N represents number of rows and columns of pixels respectively [18]. For obtaining the final haze veil, $L\prime(x, y)$ is converted from RGB to YCbCr color space and the illumination component from converted space is extracted (Fig. 1(b)). In YCbCr, Y represents luminance component, Cb is difference between blue and luma component and Cr difference between red and luma. Cb and Cr are chromium components. YCbCr component separation of image is given below.

$$Y = 0.299R + 0.587G + 0.114B \tag{4}$$

$$Cb = B - Y \tag{5}$$

$$Cr = R - Y \tag{6}$$

3.1 Computing Reflectance Image

In most Retinex algorithms, the image is converted into logarithmic domain. Accordingly,

$$LogS = logR + log L \tag{7}$$

The reflectance image is then extracted using the expression.

$$R' = exp(logS - Log') \tag{8}$$

Our $R\prime$ represents the haze removed image (Fig. 1(c). Further, image enhancement is carried out as post processing step in order to get clear visual image. For this, we use histogram based technique. Histogram techniques are regarded as simple methods used to enhance the contrast of the image thereby improving the image quality. Many algorithms have been proposed in the literature based on histogram approach [17, 19, 20]. CLAHE an adaptive extension of Histogram Equalization followed by thresholding is a technique which helps in the dynamic preservation of the local contrast features of an image [21, 22, 24]. It operates small regions in the image, called tiles. The contrast enhancement is limited by clipping the histogram through user defined values known as clip limit which describes the amount of noise to be smoothened for contrast enhancement. The technique preserves sharpness details. The method also increases the local contrast pixels. CLAHE has been adopted in our work to enhance the visual quality of the de-hazed image. In RGB color model, CLAHE can be applied on all the three components individually. The result of full-color RGB can be obtained by combining the individual components. In the proposed methodology, CLAHE is applied to reflectance RGB image which yields better haze free image (Fig. 1(d)).

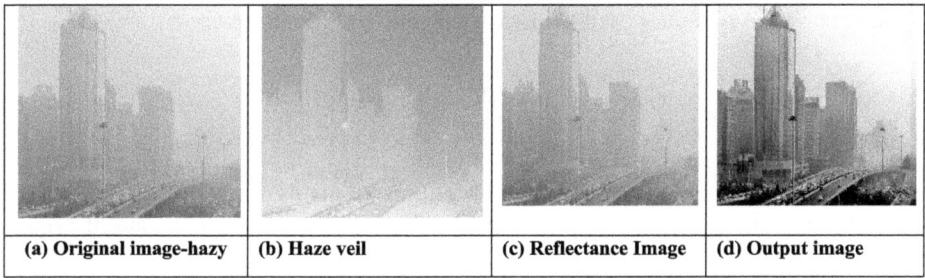

| (a) Original image-hazy | (b) Haze veil | (c) Reflectance Image | (d) Output image |

Fig. 1. Sample image illustrating dehazing process

Fig. 2. Dehazed image samples illustrating dehazing process using proposed method

4 Experimental Results

The proposed methodology yields good results for different hazy images. Sample images are shown in Fig. 2, The resulting images are compared with images obtained by applying different methods presented in the literature. Sample images are shown in Fig. 3.

The results analysis is done in terms of the parameters, PSNR and MSE. "Peak signal-to-noise ratio is the ratio between the maximum possible power of an image and the power of corrupting noise that affects the quality of its representation."

$$PSNR = 10log_{10}(\frac{L-1^2}{MSE})\qquad(9)$$

where, L is the maximum possible intensity levels, and Mean square error (MSE)

$$MSE = \frac{1}{mn} \sum_{i=0}^{m-1} \sum_{j=0}^{n-1} (O(i,j) - I(i,j))^2 \tag{10}$$

where, m, n represents number of rows and columns of pixels respectively. i, j represents index of rows and columns of pixel respectively. O represents matrix data of original image, I represents matrix data of Input image.

The PSNR and MSE values computed for sample images and its comparison with other methods in the literature is given in the Table1.

The proposed methodology is applicable for single image haze removal and the output images provide better result compare to original haze veil analysis [12] and [13]. Here, PSNR values and MSE values show better performance of the proposed method to yield haze free image as an output.

| (a) Original Image | (b) Haze Veil | (c) Fusion based CLAHE | (d) Proposed (modified HazeVeil) |

Fig. 3. Dehazed image samples illustrating dehazing process using different methods

Table. 1. Comparative analysis for proposed method

Method	Image1		Image 2	
	PSNR	MSE	PSNR	MSE
Haze Veil and adaptive contrast strecthing[16]	27.89	100.93	27.76	105.70
Fusion based CLAHE [23]	28.10	98.04	27.66	111.44
Proposed	**28.34**	**95.19**	**27.90**	**105.28**

5 Conclusion

Image Dehazing is one of the challenging issues in digital image processing applications. The paper presents an approach to get dehazed image using haze veil analysis and CLAHE. Here, Haze Veil layer is eliminated from original image and enhanced using CLAHE technique. The results are better than original method because of using CLAHE technique which enhances image adaptively based on clip limit and stops over amplification. The proposed methodology in comparison with existing methods provides better PSNR values, colorfulness and contrast enhancement resulting in better quality dehaze image. The method is applicable for single image and uniformly distributed haze.

References

1. R.Thriveni, "Satellite Image Enhancement Using Discrete Wavelet Transform and Threshold Decomposition Driven Morphological Filter",International Conference on Computer Communication and Informatics (ICCCI -2013), Jan. 04 – 06, 2013, Coimbatore, INDIA,978–1–4673–2907–1/13/$31.00 ©2013 IEEE.
2. Nidhi Gupta, Rajib Kumar Jha, Sraban Kumar Mohanty, "Enhancement of Dark Images using Dynamic Stochastic Resonance in Combined DWT and DCT Domain", 2014.
3. Tripty Singh, "Foggy Image Enhancement and Object Identification by Extended Maxima Algorithm" 2017.
4. JiaSHI,Ke-jianYANG, " An Improved Method of Removing Fog and Haze Effect From Images", 4th International Conference on Machinery, Materials and Information Technology Applications (ICMMITA 2016) Copyright © 2017, the Authors.Published by Atlantis Press..
5. Anusha G K, Rashmi M, Shobha Chandra K, "A Survey on Technique Used for DeblurringLicence Plate of Fast Moving Vehicles Using Sparse Representation", International Journal of Computer Science and Mobile Computing,© 2019, IJCSMC.
6. PadmakantDhage, Prof. M. R. Phegade, Dr. S. K. Shah, "Watershed Segmentation Brain Tumor Detection", International Conference on Pervasive Computing (ICPC), -1–4799–6272–3/15/$31.00(c)2015 IEEE.
7. C. Chengtao, Z. Qiuyu, L. Yanhua, in Control and Decision Conference (CCDC)Qingdao, China, A survey of image dehazing approaches, (2015), pp. 3964–3969;
8. Y. Y. Schechner, S. G. Narasimhan, S. K. Nayar, in IEEE Computer Society Conference on Computer Vision and Pattern Recognition (CVPR), vol. 16, Instant dehazing of images using polarization (Kauai, USA, 2001), p. 325
9. JianZhang,FazhiHe,Yilin Chen, "A new haze removal approach for sky/river alike scenes based on external and internal clues", © Springer Science+Business Media, LLC, part of Springer Nature 2019

10. P. Rajavel, Image Dependent Brightness Preserving Histogram Equalization, IEEE Transactions on Consumer Electronics, Vol. 56, No. 2, May 2010 P. Rajavel, Image Dependent Brightness Preserving Histogram Equalization, IEEE Transactions on Consumer Electronics, Vol. 56, No. 2, May 2010 P. Rajavel, Image Dependent Brightness Preserving Histogram Equalization, IEEE Transactions on Consumer Electronics, Vol. 56, No. 2, May 2010

11. Sungmin Lee, Seokmin Yun, Ju-Hun Nam,Chee Sun Won &Seung-Won Jung, A review on dark channel prior based image dehazing algorithms, EURASIP Journal on Image and Video Processing volume 2016, Article number: 4 (2016).

12. K. He, J. Sun, X. Tang, Single image haze removal using dark channel prior. IEEE Trans. Pattern Anal. Mach. Intell.33(12), 2341–2353 (2010)

13. K. B. Gibson, D. T. Võ, T. Q. Nguyen, An investigation of dehazing effects on image and video coding. IEEE Trans. Image Process.: Publ. IEEE Sig. Process. Soc.21(2), 662–73 (2012).

14. Zhu, J. Mai, L. Shao, A fast single image haze removal algorithm using color attenuation prior. IEEE Trans. Image Process.24(11), 3522–3533 (2015).

15. W. Ren, S. Liu, H. Zhang, J. Pan, X. Cao, M. -H. Yang, in Computer Vision – ECCV 2016: 14th European Conference, Amsterdam, The Netherlands, October 11-14, 2016, Proceedings, Part II, ed. by B. Leibe, J. Matas, N. Sebe, and M. Welling. Single image dehazing via multi-scale convolutional neural networks (SpringerCham, 2016), pp. 154–169https://doi.org/10.1007/978-3-319-46475-6_10

16. Fan Guo, Jin Tang Zi-Xing Cai1, Image Dehazing Based on Haziness Analysis International Journal sof Automation and Computing, 11(1), February 2014, 78-86, https://doi.org/10.1007/s11633-014-0768-7

17. A Review of Histogram Equalization Techniques in Image Enhancement Application, Wan Azani Mustafa, Mohamed Mydin M. Abdul Kader, IOP Conf. Series: Journal of Physics: Conf. Series 1019 (2018) 012026 doi :https://doi.org/10.1088/1742-6596/1019/1/012026

18. W. E. K. Middleton. Vision Through the Atmosphere, Canada: University of Toronto Press, pp. 56–58, 1952.

19. N. S. P. Kong, H. Ibrahim, and S. C. Hoo, "A Literature Review on Histogram Equalization and Its Variations for Digital Image Enhancement," Int. J. Innov. Manag. Technol., vol. 4, no. 4, pp. 386– 389, 2013.

20. S. K. Shome, S. Ram, and K. Vadali, "Enhancement of Diabetic Retinopathy Imagery Using Contrast Limited Adaptive Histogram Equalization," Int. J. Comput. Sci. Inf. Technol., vol. 2, no. 6, pp. 2694–2699, 2011

21. E. D. Pisano, S. Zong, B. M. Hemminger, M. DeLuca, R. E. Johnston, K. Muller, M. P. Braeuning and S. M. Pizer, Contrast Limited Adaptive Histogram Equalization Image Processing to Improve the Detection of Simulated Speculations in Dense Mammograms, Journal of Digital Imaging, vol. 11, pp. 193–200, 1998;

22. Zuiderveld, K., "Contrast Limited Adaptive Histogram Equalization," Chapter VIII.5, Graphics Gems IV, Cambridge, MA, Academic Press, 1994, pp 474–485

23. G. G. Rajput, D. Smruti , "Fusion based single image de-hazing using Laplace Transform and CLAHE", Proceedings of International Conference on Artificial Intelligence and Soft Computing, ICAISC2021

24. E. D. Pisano, S. Zong, B. M. Hemminger, M. DeLuca, R. E. Johnston, K. Muller, M. P. Braeuning and S. M. Pizer, Contrast Limited AdaptiveHistogram Equalization Image Processing to Improve the Detectionof Simulated Spiculations in Dense Mammograms, Journal of Digital Imaging, vol. 11, pp. 193–200,1998.

HiTEK Multilingual Speech Identification Using Combinatorial Model

Naveenkumar T. Rudrappa(✉) and Mallamma V. Reddy

Department of Computer Science, Rani Channamma University, Vidyasangama, Belagavi, India
trnphd2019@gmail.com

Abstract. Speech is a common form of communication as it expresses the feelings, thoughts, and intentions between human beings either verbally or non-verbally. Our research focuses on verbal communication as India is a language diverse country with more than 19500 spoken languages, considered as mother tongue. The diversity in spoken language understanding leads to Speech Processing. Speech retrieval and translation is a subfield of speech processing by which spoken sentences are recorded, stored and retrieved to identify the languages which is a major challenge in natural language processing. This paper presents MFCC-GNN combinatorial model that includes speech segmentation, morphological analyzer and generator, part of speech tagger for language identification. Multilingual speech dictionary is created and consists of 250 spoken sentences for each language. There are ten most spoken languages in India namely Bengali, Gujarati, Hindi, Kannada, Malayalam, Marathi, Odia, Urdu, Tamil and Telugu. This research considers the identification of multilingual speech particularly for Hindi, Telugu, English and Kannada. Once the language being spoken is identified the future scope is the analysis of Morphological structure for each language and then translation. Translation is conversion of the meaning of a source language speech to a target language speech.

Keywords: Phoneme · Phone · Syllable · Speech processing · Articulatory Phonetic

1 Introduction

Human beings express their ideas, feelings and thoughts to one another orally through the movement of speech organ that modifies the voice into an understandable sound. Speech is produced by the muscle coordination of stomach, chest, neck and head. Speech development is a slow and steady process and it improves over years to produce understandable speech. Communication of speech from man-to-man called spoken languages or from man-to-machine called machine readable low level languages. The 8th Schedule [1] of Constitution has declared 22 official languages namely Nepali, Marathi, Manipuri, Malayalam, Konkani, Kashmiri, Kannada, Hindi, Gujarati, Bengali, Assamese, Oriya, Punjabi, Sanskrit, Sindhi, Tamil, Telugu, Urdu, Bodo, Santhali, Maithili and Dogri. As per 2011 Census Ten most Spoken languages in India [2] with the count are as shown in Table 1:

© The Author(s) 2023
R. Manza et al. (Eds.): ACVAIT 2022, AISR 176, pp. 286–303, 2023.
https://doi.org/10.2991/978-94-6463-196-8_23

Table 1. Ten most spoken languages in India as per 2011 Census

Sl. no	Language	No of Speakers in Crores
1	Hindi	52.83
2	Bengali	9.72
3	Marathi	8.3
4	Telugu	8.11
5	Tamil	6.9
6	Gujarati	5.54
7	Urdu	5.07
8	Kannada	4.37
9	Odia	3.75
10	Malayalam	3.48

As per 2021 census [3] English is widely spoken across the globe with a count of 1.35 billion people and the default langugae specified by the world wide web is English. Among the above languages the research focuses on four langugaes namely Hindi, Telugu, English and Kannada referred to as HiTEK languages. When users learn a language some skills are essential for complete communication, they are usually 1. Learn to listen 2. to speak 3. to read 4. to write. These are called the four "Communication Skills" which help to communicate between human beings as shown in Fig. 1:

Fig. 1. Skills of Communication

1.1 Listening: It is the act of hearing a language by human ears. It involves identification of speech sounds (letters, stress, rhythm, pauses), a process of converting it into words, sentences and later human brain converts these into messages that convey the meaning.

1.2 Speaking: It is the delivery of language through the mouth. To speak users create sounds using many parts of human organs including the lungs, vocal tract, vocal chords, tongue, teeth and lips.

1.3 Reading: It is a process that involves motivation, recognition of a word, comprehension and fluency. Readers integrate these processes to make meaning from a printed copy.

1.4 Writing: It is the process of production of symbols, alphabets and punctuations in the brain first and then communicates the same thoughts and ideas onto a printed copy [4].

Linguistics is a systematic analysis of language skills which may be written or spoken. It studies the three viewpoints of a language namely language formation, its meaning and the context in which it is used. Phonetics is a study of acoustic and articulatory properties of speech [5]. Spoken speech are categorized into two sets namely set of vowel and set of consonant. Vowel is a sound formed by pronouncing [6] with an open vocal tract and hence there exists no air pressure at any spot over the glottis. On the other hand consonants are the sounds constructed by restricting the vocal tract that reduces flow of air in and out of the lungs. Place of articulation is the point where the airflow is restricted in the vocal tract. Some of the human speech production terminologies [7] are shown in Table 2.

Human speech processing inculcates Combinatorial Models. This research paper focuses on 1. HMM-GMM, 2.HMM-ANN and 3. HMM-DNN combinatorial model for analysis and experimentation on HiTEK languages for better results.

Table 2. Human speech production terminologies

Sl. no	Terminologies	Explanation
1	Respiration	Breathing is the air pressure inside the lungs that helps in human speech production and to control vocal intensity and loudness.
2	Phonation	It is the determination of how voiced sounds are produced.
3	Articulation	It is the action of producing a speech word clearly.
4	Resonance	Sound produced as it goes through the mouth called oral resonance or nose called nasal resonance.
5	Prosody	It reflects the features of speaker utterance that may be a question or a command or the presence of irony or emphasis, contrast and focus, may reflect elements of language not considered by grammar or vocabulary

2 Literature Review

Cuiling [8] proposed that English Speech Recognition system consists of four steps 1. Voice Acquisition 2. Speech modelling 3. Speech Recognizing 4. Results. English language database utilized was Aurora 2. Hidden Markov model (HMM) was applied for four different noisy environments like subway, babble, Car and Exhibition Hall and utilized Computer Assisted Language Learning (CALL).

Chao [9] proposed English speech recognition by searching the most suitable word sequence depending on a segment of English speech utilizing HMM based Semi-Non Parametric method to enhance performance and accuracy. Word sequences are trained and Probabilistic transition frequency profile matrix and average probabilistic emission matrix calculated. He has elaborated on speech recognition for a cross subject involving, digital signal processing pattern recognition, linguistics, acoustics, information theory and optimization theory. He suggested that signal to noise ratio lies in the range of −5 to 20.

Santosh kumar [10] suggests that speech recognition works for Multlingual environment by combining language specific acoustic models. He has used cross language transfer in addition to cross language adaptation for Monolingual system. Training for English and Tamil languages was carried out separately in bilingual system acoustic models. The combinatorial model used decision tree clustering. Experiments conducted demonstrated that acoustic modelling can be carried out on multiple languages. This reduces computational cost on the search engine because we utilize one acoustic model for multiple languages.

Ling [11] studied and concluded that DNN-HMM is superior than GMM-HMM method. 40 MFCC features were extracted and the tool used was Kaldi toolkit. Signal preprocessing consists of premphasis, subframe windowing and end point detection. In Speech recognition Deep Neural Network is utilized for training the acoustic model. The input to DNN are the acoustic characteristics of current frame for the calculation of each possible HMM state. HMM for Speech Recognition is one way, from left to right, self-ring and can be spanned topologically. HMM works on a composition of multiple phonemes, words and silences. Parameter clustering is carried out using top down method and decision tree. Cool Edit software utilizes a frequency of 16 kHz for sampling using 16 bit encoding.

Trivedi [12] elaborated on the types of Speech, Speech Recognition, S2T conversion, T2S conversion and Speech Translation. Dynamic Time Warping models and HM Models with neural network perform well for classifying of phonemes, recognition of isolated words recognition and adaptation of speaker. Synthesizing of speech performs well for conversion of tokenized words to artificial human speech. Speech production components are phonation, fluency, intonation, pitch variance and respiration. Speech recognition system classification can be performed on the basis of speaker dependency, vocal sound and vocabulary. Commonly used feature extraction methods are Linear Predictive Coding (LPC), Mel- Frequency Cepstrum Coefficients (MFCC) and Dynamic Time Warping. Various pattern classification methods used are template based, Knowledge based, Neural network based and statistical based. The methods utilized Hidden Markov Model and ANN based Cuckoo Search Optimization for S2T conversion. T2S conversion involves processing of text, various speech synthesis techniques namely

Articulatory, Formant and Concatenative. Some of the language translation models are Rule Based, Statistical, Example Based and hybrid machine translation.

Kumar and Aggarwal [13] have proposed Hindi language continuos Automatic Speech Recognition (ASR) system utilizing Recurrent Neural Network (RNN) based Language Modelling (RNN-LM) which uses Maximum Likelihood Linear Regression (MLLR) with Constrained Maximum Likelihood Linear Regression (C-MLLR) by training with Maximum Mutual Information (MMI) and Minimum Phone Error (MPE) methodologies with Two Fifty Six Gaussian Mixture per Hidden Markov Model (HMM) state.

Gopal [14] proposed K-Means clustering algorithm and logistic regression to improve accuracy. Noise reduction was performed using Butterworth low pass filters. Recognition of Hindi Speech utilized Selected Time Delay Neural Network (STDNN) and modeling of acoustics was carried out with i-vector adaptation. Hindi syllables have longer units of acoustics, faster decoding due to reduction in contextual effects and irregularities caused due to phonemes. K-Means clustering is used for segregation of inaudible low quality audio and hence detect human voice and silences.

Jewani [15] talks about speaker dependent and speaker independent models, types of Hindi speech like connected words, isolated words, continuos speech and spontaneous speech and proposes whole word matching and subword matching techniques using Mel-Frequency Cepstrum (MFC) and HMM. MFC and distance minimum algorithm can be combined to improve overall efficiency. Dynamic Time Warping for speech pattern comparison.

Shobha and Anurag [16] have proposed improvement of HMM using hybridization of units like Phones, Syllables which are the acoustic units to improve nasal sounds and Domain Syntactic specific structures that reduce the search space of the recognizer and hence improve performance and are tested for both Speaker Dependent and Speaker Independent Systems.

Sharada and Vijaya [17] have elaborated on Kannada Speech Recognition using tri-state Hidden Markov Model with each state represented by Gaussian Mixture Model. Three approaches for Kannada speech recognition have been identified i.e. Acoustic Phonetics, Pattern Recognition and Artificial Intelligence. They are of the opinion that speech is context dependent and the occurring of a phoneme is dependent on preceding and succeeding phonemes which lead to the development of triphone clustering model. MFCC represents speech parameters better, DTW and HMM are best classifier methods and Viterbi search algorithm is better for pattern matching. Specific language models predict the occurrence of words one after another, which helps to narrow down the search process using Unigram (Normal Search), Bigram (gives statistics of occurrence of words given previous words), Trigram depends on two previous words. Acoustic models represent each distinct sound that make up a word.

Hemakumar and Punitha [18] have elaborated on speech signal segmentation by decomposing a signal into basic phonetic units like phoneme, syllable and subword. Proposed method consists of pre-processing stage, detection of voiced section, feature extraction, model building and testing of an unknown signal.

Prashanth and Ananthakrishna [19] have emphasized on Maximum a Posteriori (MAP) and Gaussian Probability Density Function (GPDF). Baum Welch Forward-Backward algorithm is used for training.

Akhila and Kumarswamy [20] have justified that phoneme level search is effective for searching words/phrases. DBN is used and 16 MFCC features extracted from each speech frame. Conventional acoustic modelling techniques like Multilayer Feed Forward Neural Network (MFFNN) and Support Vector Machines (SVM) utilized. They concluded that performance of any network is affected by the size of phonemes used for training and testing.

Anand and Jangamashetti [21] have focused on speech signal preprocessing to frames and then extracting features using Linear Predictive Coding. MFCC and Euclidean distance is used for isolated word recognition in the first case. MFCC with SVM classifier was used to remove silence in the second case. Gaussian Multivariate Model was utilized in the recognition of an unknown phoneme. Confusion Matrix inferred the performance of classifiers.

Priya and Soumya [22] have used MFCC to extract features and using HMM with triphone acoustic modelling. Baum welch algorithm was utilized for model reestimation to obtain good results in offline recognition mode. They have derived 39 cepstral parameters from speech signal.

Pradeep and Srinivasa [23] have performed a comparative analysis of speech recognition using HMM-GMM, ANN, DNN for various recording modes like reading, lecturing and conversation.

Praveen and Neerudu [24] have recognized Telugu speech speaker independent data using Teager energy operator Delta Spectral Cepstral Coefficients (TDSCC) which is a feature extraction technique and Deep Neural Networks (DNN) feature classification technique. Isolated speech recognition performed using 2 stage Deep Learning Neural Network (2DNN). Stressed speech can be recognized by (TDSCC). Recorded speech consisting of noise is preprocessed using Computation Auditory Scene Analysis (CASA). Artificial Neural Network and Deep Neural Network are used for feature classification.

Jeetendra [25] analyzes speech through signal processing and linguistic processing. Linear Predictive Coding (LPC) and Cepstral Analysis are used for feature extraction of Telugu language and to design speaker independent system. Discrete Fourier Transform (DFT) and Fast Fourier Transform (FFT) is used for calculations. Linguistic processing involves conversion from speech to text or generate speech from text. The basic units involved are allophones string of phonemes and set of string of phonemes called morphophonemes. Morphophonemes are matched with words in the dictionary or various prefixes/suffixes. Wide band spectogram and Narrow band spectrogram are used for the analysis of speech.

Kodali [26] processed continuos speech using open source speech recognition and Kaldi tool kit Static Vector Machine(SVM) and Binary Static Vector Machine(BSVM) were used for Automatic Speech Recognition (ASR) that included Language Models(LM) and Acoustic Model(AM).Training process included Monophone Hidden Markov Model (HMM) for training, aligning training dataset using monophone model and triphone HMM training. Sentimental Analysis was carried out by identifying positive, negative and neutral conversations. Categorized noise into five types namely cough, laugh, noise, breath and background noise. Developed a Multi-Modal that consists of both speech and text.

Sunitha and Kalyani [27] proposed a model that includes five phases namely syllable extraction, building a tri state model for each syllable, a Trie structure through morphological analysis of Telugu language, marking rough boundary of the syllable and syllable recognition. Morphological analysis is carried out by removing prefix, suffix, infix or crucifix from the stem and identification of inflectional and derivational words. Speech segmentation is carried out using linguistic rules. Syllable recognition is carried out using Mahalanobi's distance measure. Trie structure places all words with common prefix under the same path.

Praveen and Ratnadeep [28] focused on continuos speech recognition in two modes namely speaker dependent and speaker independent systems using Melfrequency Cepstral Coefficients (MFCC), Discrete Wavelet Packet Decomposition (DWPD) and Discrete Wavelet Transformation (DWT) for noise removal. Features were classified through Hidden Markov Model (HMM) and Deep Neural Networks (DNN). Word based model was used to recognize continuos data. Vitteri algorithm was used for recognition. Feature classification could be performed through pattern recognition, vector analysis and Artificial Neural Networks.

3 Challenges

Language identification by a human involves listening to spoken speech by another human called as man-man communication, analyze the vocal transcription in the neurons of human brain and then decide the language spoken by the other user. In comparison, language identification by an electronic machine a computer is still more complex as the machine should be trained with different language datasets to identify the spoken speech appropriately. This is performed by given a possible set of languages, their rules and names machine applies classification and comparison techniques so that the exact language is identified by the machine. System accepts input speech and then classifies the language into its predefined class. Hence language identification is a classification problem of data mining. Some of the challenges involved in the identification of spoken speech languages are as shown in Table 3.

Language identification by a machine involves creation of a hybrid HiTEK speech/text dictionary. This involves recording of human spoken sentences in multiple languages by a number of users using a microphone for input and further transforming and storing these recordings in a wave file format in the back end file system. This recorded file should be free from different background noise which poses a major challenge in building a speech dictionary which are detailed as shown in Table 4.

Table 3. Challenges in Speech Identification of HiTEK Languages

Sl. no	Challenges	Explanation
1	Human Speaker Characteristics	Each person has a different set of vocal characteristic features and hence feature extraction for speaker independent speech recognition systems is difficult.
2	Spoken Accent	Each person has a different accent of speaking and hence pattern matching process needs calibration as the process should take into account the non-linear nature of spoken words. Ex: Person A: Hi- 2 s, Person B: Hai- 3 s
3	Linguistic Variation	Each language has a different linguistic pattern and hence difficult to design a generalized model.
4	Sandhi Rules	Different for Hindi, Telugu, Kannada and English has no Sandhi rules but has comparative and superlative degrees for a spoken word.
5	Acoustic characteristics	A thorough knowledge of phonetic units should be known for each language.
6	Syllable Structure	Different and complex for each language.
7	Speech Segmentation	Segments created after segmentation process are of variable size.
8	Noise Removal	Regular Noise: Fan Rotation in the background.
		Irregular Noise: Cough, Laugh, Breath, Wind Speed, and Vehicle Horn.
		An efficient speech recognition system should remove both regular and irregular noise from the recorded speech.
9	Speech Types	1. Isolated Speech: Individual spoken words analyzed, Highest Matching Accuracy.
		2. Connected speech: Combination of two or more isolated words that run with a slight pause. Medium matching accuracy due to the problem of incorrect segmentation at the word boundaries.

(continued)

Table 3. (*continued*)

Sl. no	Challenges	Explanation
		3. Continuos Speech: Human speaks continuously without any gap. Lower matching accuracy due to the problem of incorrect segmentation at the word boundaries as there are no pause and silence between words.
		4. Spontaneous Speech: Human speaks without a written script and hence there are irregular silences, pauses, cough, laugh etc. due to the search of words through intelligence in human brain. Least matching accuracy as the spoken words are unpredictable.
10	Pattern Recognition Techniques	Use indirect methods and hence more time consuming.
11	Data set size	1. Small: Highest Accuracy
		2. Medium: Acceptable Accuracy.
		3. Large: Acceptable accuracy with maximum time for retrieval.

4 Methodology

Multilingual Speech Identification (MLSI) is a process of identifying multiple languages in the pre-recorded speech file. Complexity of MLSI lies in mapping and translation of speech/phone/textual-word with supervised HiTEK dictionary. To improvise matching across various spoken languages it inculcates translation rules for specified languages such as of Hindi [29], Telugu [30], English [31] and Kannada [32].

This research utilizes a combinatorial model consisting of 1. HMM-GMM, 2.HMM-ANN and 3. HMM-DNN for improving speech matching accuracy. The characteristic features of the three models are elaborated as shown.

4.1 Hidden Markov Model- Gaussian Mixture Model

This model is dependent on phoneme recognition while emission distribution is modeled using GMM. Readings are obtained by calculating mean and covariance in Gaussian Mixture. HMM-GMM increases the probability of fetching a sequence of phonemes.

4.2 Hidden Markov Model- Artificial Neural Networks

HM Model is used to obtain the probability of the data under observation for an HMM state that corresponds to a specific sound. ANN training produces posterior probabilities of HM Model state given the speech data.

Table 4. Challenges for building Speech Dictionary

Sl. no	Challenges	Explanation
1	Speech Clarity	Speaking in a way that could be clearly understood by the listeners.
2	Speech Projectivity	Speaking aloud such that every listener can hear the utterance.
3	Speech Enunciation	Clearly pronouncing each syllable with exact emphasis.
4	Speech Pronouncing	Proper word utterance.
5	Expression	Speaking with vocal variation so that listeners are engaged and interested.
6	Speaking Pace	Uttering at a rate that could be clearly heard by the listeners.
7	Filler	Using words that distract listeners. Ex: "Um", "ah" and "you know", "nothing but"
8	Slang	Language understood by a specific group. A listener not part of that group cannot understand the meaning.
9	Buzzword	Frequently used word in a specific context. Ex. "game changer" and "think outside the box" etc.
10	Acronym	Abbreviations used for some phrases CIO: Chief Innovative Officer.
11	Active Listener (Hardware)	Microphone used in recording should be active for the duration till the speaker clicks on stop recording button.
12	Human Speaker Location	Maintaining a correct distance for recording from the microphone.

4.3 Hidden Markov Model- Deep Neural Networks

HM Model is used for phoneme recognition while training of a DNN is carried out in 2 phases as follows:

Phase 1- Unsupervised Pretraining
Phase 2- Supervised fine tuning

MLSI imbibes a Hybrid/HiTEK dictionary consisting of multi lingual Speech/Text. The identification of multilingual speech processing is shown in Fig. 2 and the detailed steps are elaborated below.

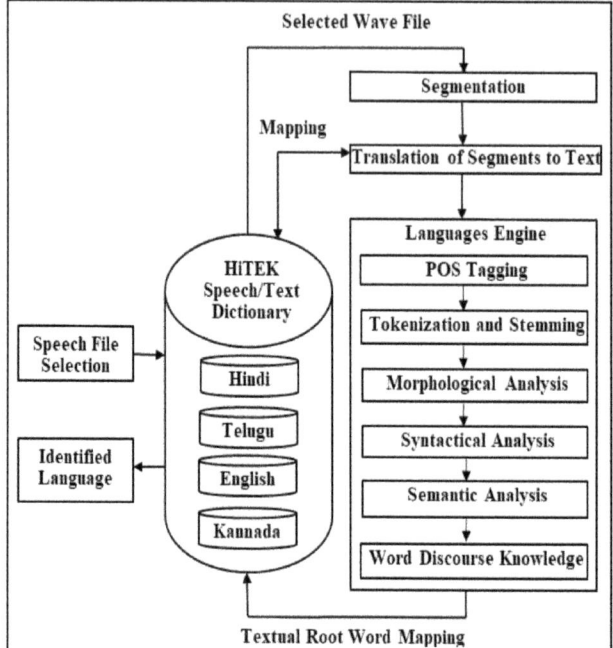

Fig. 2. Block Diagram of Language Identification

Step 1: Speech File Selection Module
The first step is to select a pre-recorded input speech file from Hybrid/HiTEK dictionary. Pronounces out the selected wave file by the activation of speaker and displaying its path.

Step 2: Hybrid/HiTEK dictionary Module
Stores pre-recorded sentences as audio files and textual words.

Step 3: Segmentation Module
This module identifies the boundaries between words, syllables, phones or phonemes in spoken languages to give a proper meaning for a word or a sentence. The challenge during segmentation is to detect boundaries by analyzing the pause between phones which is a minimum one second in our architecture.

Step 4: Translation of Segments to Text Module
The split phones are mapped with the corresponding textual words and if the words are not present in the dictionary transliterated to form the text.

Step 5: Language Engine Module
This is the heart of language identification system and it consists of various steps involved in identifying a language.

4.4 POS Tagging

It is a process of annotating a word to a specific part of speech based on the context, relation with adjacent words within a paragraph, sentence or phrase. Ex In English Vocabulary POS consist of Noun Pronoun, Verb, Adverb, Adjective, Conjunction, Preposition etc.

4.5 Tokenization and Stemming

1. Tokenization is a task of dividing a textual sentence into a predefined set of tokens. It may also break the text on whitespace characters such as a space, tab, or punctuation. Ex: A sentence can be divided into words and a paragraph can be divided into sentences, here words and sentences act as tokens.
2. Stemming is extraction of root word. Ex Making is converted to Make by removing the suffix ing and attaching e as suffix.

4.6 Morphological Analysis

Morphology is the process of formation of words from the smallest primitive chunks by finding a meaningful sub part within the word. These sub-words are called Morphemes as shown in Table 5.

4.7 Syntactical Analysis

Syntactical analysis checks for words, grammar in a sentence and their arrangement among the words by applying grammatical rules. These rules vary from language to language.

4.8 Semantic Analysis

It is an algorithmic activity to understand, merge and analyze the meaning of words, integrate words to form phrases and unite phrases to form a well-structured sentence. This is the most important phase in the full Language Engine as it checks whether the meaning of an input statement is valid in real world as the statement may be syntactically correct but semantically to be validated by the engine as shown in Table 6.

Table 5. Word Conversion to Morpheme

Sl. No	Word	Chunks	Morpheme Count
1	Like	Nil	1
2	Unbreakable	Un + break + able	3

Table 6. Syntactical and Semantical Validity of a Statement

Sl. No	Textual Statement	Syntactical Validity	Semantic Validity in Real World
1	Cat eats Rat	Correct	Valid
2	Rat eats Cat	Correct	Invalid

4.9 Word Discourse Knowledge

The meaning of one sentence depends upon other sentences or may also depend on the immediate succeeding sentence. Ex: She needed it depends on previous discourse context.

Step 6: Textual Root word mapping in HiTEK Speech/Text Dictionary
The obtained root words from the language engine are mapped to an appropriate language dictionary.

Step 7: Identified Language Module
It displays the language of identified sentence if all words are in the same language dictionary or it displays each individual word and its language if the sentence is made up of more than one language.

5 Experimental Setup and Results

Graphical user interface based application is developed with python programming as a front end and file system as back end. The system gives faster results in case of higher hardware system configurations in our case Intel CORE I5 10TH GEN processor and extended RAM Size of twenty Giga Bytes and a file system of One Terra Byte hard disk to store HiTEK pre-recorded Speech/Text dictionary. The expected results are displayed in the last line of each screenshot as shown in Figs. 3, 4, 5 and 6 that indicates the language spoken in a stored wav file which is obtained after pre-training the system using the ISO-639 standard library fused with combinatorial model and stored in a HiTEK Speech/Text dictionary consisting of Hindi, Telugu, English and Kannada languages.

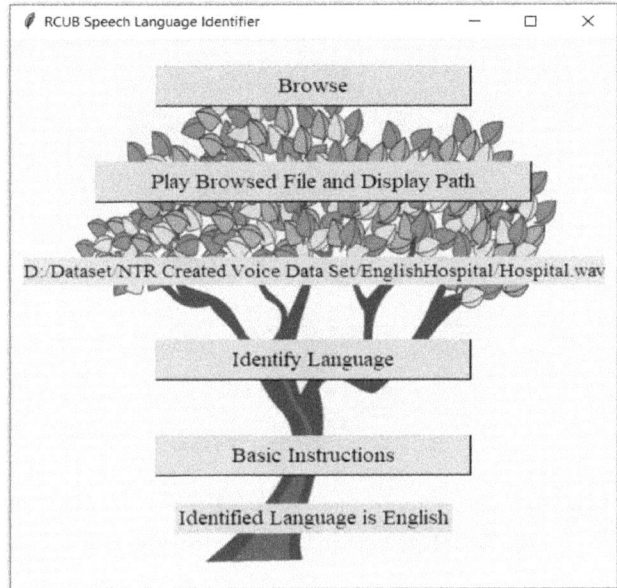

Fig. 3. English Speech Language Identification

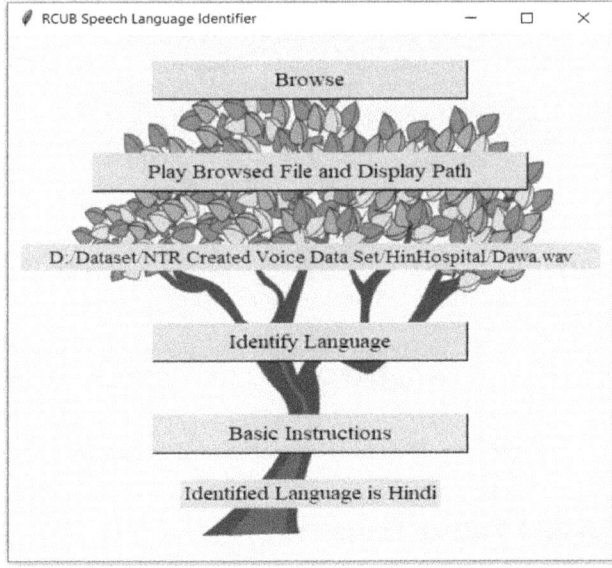

Fig. 4. Hindi Speech Language Identification

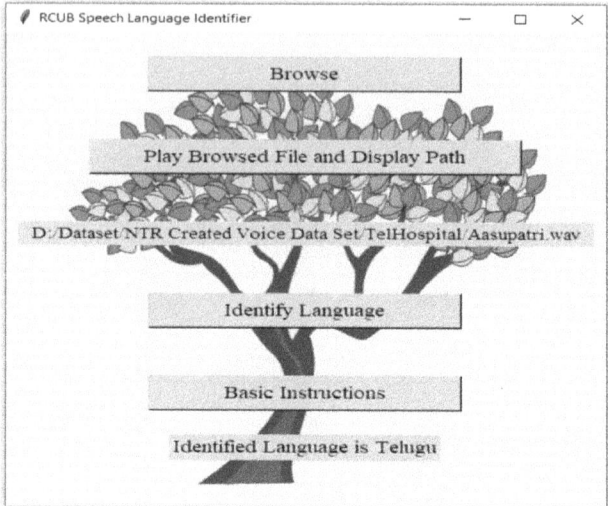

Fig. 5. Telugu Speech Language Identification

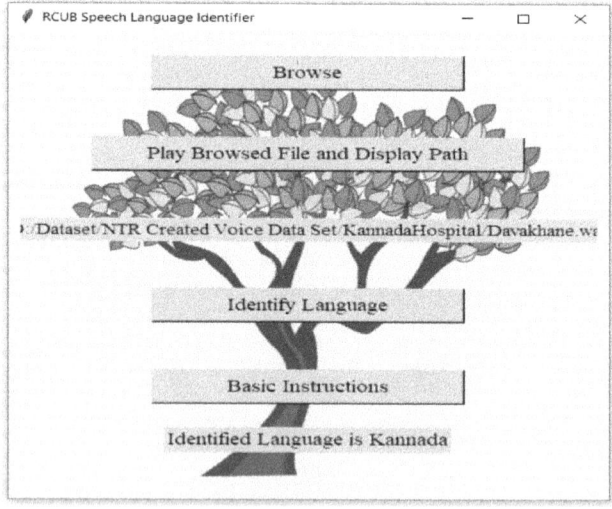

Fig. 6. Kannada Speech Language Identification

6   Conclusion and Future Scope

Variations in speaking accents, speech pronunciation, high dimensional speech feature parameters, computational and evaluation complexity and large speech dataset mandate the need for high end hardware and softwares to train the system to identify the language spoken. This paper focuses on a combinatorial model which is an outcome of combination of HMM-GMM, HNN-ANN and HMM-DNN to convert a speech signal into digital format after extracting various features and then converting to words. We are developing a system that identifies the content of spoken speech and identifies the language of pre-recorded and stored wav file which may be Hindi, Telugu, English or Kannada. Future scope lies in the fact that the system can be used to identify other regional languages of India.

Acknowledgment. Authors thank Rani Channamma University, Belagavi Karnataka for their support to issue a separate lab for Research Scholars. Authors would like to thank NFST wing, Ministry of Tribal Affairs for selecting me as a Research Fellow and providing me the necessary fellowship grant. A special thanks to Dr. Mallamma V. Reddy for her constant support, mentoring and guidance. Special thanks to the entire family of Department of Computer Science, Rani Channamma University, Vidyasangama, Belagavi, Karnataka. I also thank my family members, research scholars and friends for their motivation, moral support and encouragement. Finally the authors would like to thank Dr. Babasaheb Ambedkar Marathwada University, Aurangabad (MS) India for providing the publication support.

References

1. https://indianexpress.com/article/india/more-than-19500-mother-tongues-spoken-in-india-census-5241056/
2. https://www.jagranjosh.com/general-knowledge/most-spoken-languages-in-india-by-number-of-speakers-1541764100-1
3. https://www.statista.com/statistics/266808/the-most-spoken-languages-worldwide/
4. https://www.englishclub.com/learn-english/language-skills.htm
5. Jakobson, Roman, Gunnar Fant, and Morris Halle. "Preliminaries to Speech Analysis: The Distinctive Features and their Correlates", MIT Press. 1976
6. Kingston, John. "The Phonetics-Phonology Interface", in the Cambridge Handbook of Phonology (ed. Paul DeLacy), Cambridge University Press. 2007
7. Neeshali R. Nandarge, Mallamma V. Reddy, Suman Gouda,Gayatri Patil, "Kannada Phonetic Transcription: NLP," Proceedings of 35th IRF International Conference, Bengaluru, India, 2017, pp. 19–21
8. L. Cuiling, "English Speech Recognition Method Based on Hidden Markov Model," 2016 International Conference on Smart Grid and Electrical Automation (ICSGEA), 2016, pp. 94-97, https://doi.org/10.1109/ICSGEA.2016.63.
9. C. Xue, "A Novel English Speech Recognition Approach Based on Hidden Markov Model," 2018 International Conference on Virtual Reality and Intelligent Systems (ICVRIS), 2018, pp. 1-4, https://doi.org/10.1109/ICVRIS.2018.00009.
10. C. S. Kumar and Foo Say Wei, "A bilingual speech recognition system for English and Tamil," Fourth International Conference on Information, Communications and Signal Processing, 2003 and the Fourth Pacific Rim Conference on Multimedia. Proceedings of the 2003 Joint, 2003, pp. 1641–1644 vol.3, https://doi.org/10.1109/ICICS.2003.1292746.
11. Z. Ling, "An Acoustic Model for English Speech Recognition Based on Deep Learning," 2019 11th International Conference on Measuring Technology and Mechatronics Automation (ICMTMA), 2019, pp. 610–614, https://doi.org/10.1109/ICMTMA.2019.00140.
12. A Trivedi, N Pant, P Shah, S Sonik and S Agrawal, "Speech to text and text to speech recognition systems-Areview", IOSR Journal of Computer Engineering, 2018, e-ISSN: 2278–0661,p-ISSN: 2278–8727, Vol. 20, Iss. 2,Ver. I, pp 36–43, www.iosrjournals.org
13. Kumar, A and Aggarwal, "Discriminatively trained continuous Hindi speech recognition using integrated acoustic features and recurrent neural network language modeling". Journal of Intelligent Systems. 2021; Vol: 30(1), pp 165–179, https://doi.org/10.1515/jisys-2018-0417

14. Anuj Gopal, "Automated Recognition of Hindi word Audio clips for Indian children using Clustering-Based Filters and Binary Classsifier", Proceedings of The Fourth International Conference on Natural Language and Speech Processing, Trento, Italy, Publisher Association for Computationl Linguistics 2021,pp 204–208

15. Kajal J , Shreesh Rao, Prashant D, Ronit D and Mrudali B, " Hindi Speech Recognition " International Journal of Advanced Science and Engineering", 2018, Vol 7, Issue No 1, pp-50–55, Available online at www.ijarse.com, ISSN- 2319–8354

16. Bhatt, Shobha & Jain, Anurag & Dev, Amita, "Monophone-based connected word Hindi speech recognition improvement". Journal Sadhana Indian Academy of Sciences (2021) 46: 99, https://doi.org/10.1007/s12046-021-01614-3

17. S. C. Sajjan and Vijaya C, "Continuous Speech Recognition of Kannada language using triphone modeling," 2016 International Conference on Wireless Communications, Signal Processing and Networking (WiSPNET), 2016, pp. 451–455, https://doi.org/10.1109/WiS PNET.2016.7566174.

18. P. Punitha and G. Hemakumar, "Speaker Dependent Continuous Kannada Speech Recognition Using HMM," 2014 International Conference on Intelligent Computing Applications, 2014, pp. 402-405, https://doi.org/10.1109/ICICA.2014.88.

19. P. Kannadaguli and A. Thalengala, "Phoneme modeling for speech recognition in Kannada using Hidden Markov Model," 2015 IEEE International Conference on Signal Processing, Informatics, Communication and Energy Systems (SPICES), 2015, pp.1–5, https://doi.org/10.1109/SPICES.2015.7091382.

20. Akhila K S and R. Kumaraswamy, "Comparative analysis of Kannada phoneme recognition using different classifiers," 2015 International Conference on Trends in Automation, Communications and Computing Technology (I-TACT-15), 2015, pp. 1–6, https://doi.org/10.1109/ITACT.2015.7492683.

21. A. H. Unnibhavi and D. S. Jangamshetti, "LPC based speech recognition for Kannada vowels," 2017 International Conference on Electrical, Electronics, Communication, Computer, and Optimization Techniques (ICEECCOT), 2017, pp. 1–4, https://doi.org/10.1109/ICEECCOT.2017.8284582.

22. K. Jeeva Priya, S. S. Sree, T. Navya and D. Gupta, "Implementation of Phonetic Level Speech Recognition in Kannada Using HTK," 2018 International Conference on Communication and Signal Processing (ICCSP), 2018, pp. 0082–0085, https://doi.org/10.1109/ICCSP.2018.852 4192.

23. R. Pradeep and K. S. Rao, "Deep neural networks for kannada phoneme recognition," 2016 Ninth International Conference on Contemporary Computing (IC3), 2016, pp. 1–6, https://doi.org/10.1109/IC3.2016.7880202.

24. A. P. Kumar, N.U. Maheshwari, Y.Sangeetha and P. Jyothi, " Isolated Telugu Speech Recognition On T-DSCC And DNN Techniques", International Journal of Innovative Technology and Exploring Engineering (IJITEE), 2019, Vol.8, pp. 3419–3422 ISSN:2278–3075, https://doi.org/10.35940/ijitee.K2544.09811119

25. P. Jeethendra, M. Chandrashekar "Linear Predictive Coding and Cepstral Analysis for Telugu Speech Recognition". International Journal of Computer Trends and Technology (IJCTT) V47(1):50–60, May 2017. ISSN:2231–2803. www.ijcttjournal.org. Published by Seventh Sense Research Group.

26. Rohith Gowtham Kodali, 2Durga Prasad Manukonda, 3Rajaraman Sundararajan, Speech and Text Based Analytics in Telugu Language, © 2019 JETIR March 2019, Volume 6, Issue 3 www.jetir.org (ISSN-2349-5162)

27. Dr. K V N Sunitha and N Kalyani. Article: Isolated Word Recognition using Morph Knowledge for Telugu Language. International Journal of Computer Applications 38(12):47–54, February 2012. https://doi.org/10.5120/4765-6940

28. Archek Praveen Kumar, Ratnadeep Roy, Sanyog Rawat and Prathibha Sud-hakaran,"Continuous Telugu Speech Recognition through Combined Feature Extraction by MFCC and DWPD Using HMM based DNN Techniques", International Journal of Pure and Applied Mathematics, Volume 114 No. 11 2017, 187–197 ISSN: 1311–8080 (printed version); ISSN: 1314–3395 (on-line version)
29. https://www.optilingo.com/blog/hindi/everything-about-hindi-language/
30. https://omniglot.com/writing/telugu.htm
31. https://www.englishmirror.com/englishgrammar/vowels-and-consonants.html
32. https://omniglot.com/writing/kannada.htm

Devanagari License Plate Detection, Classification and Recognition

Pankaj Raj Dawadi$^{(\boxtimes)}$, Bal Krishna Bal, and Manish Pokharel

Department of Computer Science and Engineering, Kathmandu University, Dhulikhel, Kavre, Nepal
pdawadi@ku.edu.np

Abstract. This study presents a method for detecting, classifying, and recognizing Devanagari characters based vehicle's License Plate (LP) in Nepalese context. The IWPOD-NET model is used in the detection phase to extract the LP from a vehicle region. After post-processing for contrast adjustment, the extracted LP is fed to a nested classifier for vehicle classification. To reduce the noise around the LP area, several image-processing techniques are used. Finally, the Devanagari LP characters are predicted/recognized using two distinct CNN models. We built a customized LP dataset and character dataset to verify our method. The proposed system has been tested for both stationary and moving vehicles. The robustness of the proposed system is assessed in terms of LP detection, LP classification and character recognition accuracy.

Keywords: License Plate · Devanagari Characters · Convolution Neural Network · IWPOD-NET · nested Random Forest

1 Introduction

The use of vehicles as a mode of road transportation by various stakeholders (government, public, private, etc.) is growing by the day, and the necessity for a robust Automatic License Plate Detection and Recognition (ALPDR) has been a hot topic for each country for some years. The ALPDR includes employing a camera sensor to collect LP from a scene. To get the letter-digit combinations that make up the LP characters, a still image or a frame in which a vehicle is sensed is processed utilizing an image processing pipeline in conjunction with machine learning/deep learning based algorithms whenever necessary. Image acquisition, LP extraction, character segmentation, and character recognition are all steps in a typical ALPDR system [1]. The classification of extracted LP is introduced as an intermediary step before advancing to character segmentation in various ALPDR [2, 3]. The vehicle classification, which is based on an LP's foreground and background (FB) colour combination, confirms the vehicle's ownership by various stakeholders and also aids the researcher/developer in applying a proper image processing pipeline to threshold the LP mask before performing character segmentation. Variance in viewpoint, global and local illumination, occlusion, scaling, and intra-class variation all wreak havoc on the detection, classification, and segmentation phases. The ALPDR process is made

R. Manza et al. (Eds.): ACVAIT 2022, AISR 176, pp. 304–318, 2023.
https://doi.org/10.2991/978-94-6463-196-8_24

more complex by the use of non-standard LPs, such as fluctuating LP size, confusing letter-digit combinations in a specific order to encode a vehicle registration number, writing style, fonts, and the use of different font sizes in several horizontal parts of an LP.

1.1 Devanagari (Nepalese) License Plate

The Nepalese government has classified LPs into seven categories based on vehicle ownership. This is seen in the colour combination of an automobile LP's background and foreground. The vehicles are further sub-classified into groups based on the weight of the load they carry. Also, three types of LP structures are seen; 1-row LP, 2-row LP, and 3-row LP; as vehicle's LP. In DLP, LP characters are read from left to right then from top to bottom in a LP. Figure 1 depicts the sample DLPs used in Nepalese vehicles.

The LP characters arrangement in different LP structures is shown in Table 1. Province is a fixed letter that represents Province (प्रदेश), PN is the 3 digits province identifier, PS is the plate status, L is the three-digits lot number, LD is the load type, and X is one-to four-digits vehicle identity. In 3-row Red (private) LP, the first (top) row has four fixed positional characters.

Province (letter), PN number (a digit), and two digits PS (01 for old registration, 02 and onwards for new registration). The L (3 digits) followed by LD (a letter) are both fixed positional characters in the second (middle) row. Only 1 to 4 digits are used in the final (bottom) row. The first and second rows of the 3-row LP structure contain exactly 4 characters (letter and digits) while the last row contains 1 to 4 numbers. In the case

Tourist   Public   Diplomat

Minister   Private   Government   Public Institution

Fig. 1. DLP characteristics based on ownership, LP structures, fonts, and font size

Table 1. Characters arrangement in DLP

LP Structure	First Row	Second Row	Third Row
3-row	PROVINCE PN PS	L LD	X
2-row	Z LT LD	X	**
	PROVINCE PN PS LT LD	X	
	PROVINCE PN PS	LT LD X	
1-row	Z LT LD X	**	**
	PROVINCE PN PS LT LD X		

**Not Applicable

of zonal format LP for 1-row and 2-row LP structure, Z indicates any fourteen zones (a letter) and LT denotes 1 or 2 digits lot number. Similarly, the province format 2-row LP structure includes either 4 positional characters on the first row and 5 to 8 characters on the second row, or 8 characters on the first row and 1 to 4 digits on the second row. In 2-row LP, the first row of the zonal format comprises 3 to 4 characters, and the second row has 1 to 4 digits as a vehicle identity. The maximum number of characters in a 1-row structure is found to be 12 for both province and zonal format. We should expect a minimum of 4 (zonal format) to a maximum of 12 characters (Province format) in all types of LP structures. In a 2-row (partial) or 3-row LP structure, the last row has just digits, whereas the other rows have both letters and digits in a specific order. For instance, a private truck has an LP with a red background and white foreground characters with load type letter "KA" that indicates a heavy vehicle. A Red LP vehicle with the characters BA (बा) 79 (७९) PA (प) 9544 (९५४४)is a private vehicle with zonal code Bagmati (BA), vehicle's lot no 79, a light vehicle (PA) representing either a motorbike or a scooter, and 9544 as vehicle's identification number. It should be noted that a vehicle that transport heavy load also use a letter "PA" as load type which is specifically seen in a tourist bus. In Nepal, same load type letters may be used to encode intra LP vehicles. For instance, a green BUS and green two-wheelers share same letter "PA" as load type. This ambiguity is also visible in inter LP as a red LP and a green LP share same letter "PA" as load type. The various properties of DLP are tabulated in Table 2.

Both the standardized and non-standardized LP is seen in vehicles. The non-standardized LP uses a variety of fonts to encode vehicle information; the characters may vary in size within the same row, and the space between LP characters varies due to the variety of LPs. Likewise, the space between two characters are not uniform in all kinds of LP. For instance, a minimum distance of 5 to 10mm between two characters within a row and the minimum 5 to 10 mm gap between characters between two successive rows is found to be missing. This lack of uniformity is due to the fact that the LP are written by local painters resulting in non-standard letter distance, font size, fonts, and even with some non-LP characters. Furthermore, we have difficulty recognizing characters due to the use of diverse fonts, as certain characters are too similar even though they belong to different classes. For example, the digits 5, 1, and 9 can be written in a variety of styles. Similarly, the characters (२- ३), (प-०), (बा- ना), (च- ज – अ), and (मे - भे) might look similar and may mislead a character recognizer model.

To address these challenges, we proposed a technique for detecting, classifying, and recognizing Devanagari LP.

The following is a breakdown of the structure of this paper. We take a quick look at some related works in Sect. 2. The proposed ALPR system is described in Sect. 3. The dataset, results, and discussion of the experiments is discussed in Sect. 4. Section 5 wraps up our research work with conclusion.

2   Literature Review

The ALPDR is assumed to be a two-step process in which LP detection and localization is the process of locating a region in an image holding the LP, whereas LP recognition is the process of identifying the text written on it. Both localization and recognition need feature extraction and classification. Automated feature engineering for ALDPR approaches has recently been employed for feature extraction in addition to hand-crafted feature engineering. The hands-on feature engineering approaches use key computer vision algorithms to extract the features specifically. Automated feature engineering, on the other hand, learns features implicitly using machine learning/deep learning approaches.

For automated feature engineering, deep Convolution Neural Networks (CNN) and its derivatives have been widely utilized to detect, segment, and recognize vehicle's LP in recent years. The performance of CNNs in text and optical character recognition has already been demonstrated in [4–6]. One of the deep-learning-based systems for LP recognition is [7, 8] which generate LP region recommendations and perform final selection using a CNN as a binary classifier. Because of the high demand for robustness, some alternative methods use CNN-extracted features rather than hand-crafted features. To increase the character recognition rate, the authors supplement the character dataset with particular hierarchical data augmentation methodologies in [9]. The CNN is similarly trained for the whole character sequence to identify and recognize Malaysian LPs

Table 2. Devanagari LP characteristics

Background (Plate)	Foreground (Characters)	ownership	Load			letters and Digits			
			Type	letters		Zonal Code		Digits	
				English	Devanagari	English	Devanagari	Arabic	Devanagari
Red	White	Private	Heavy	KA		ME	मे	0	०
			Middle	CHA TA	च त	KO	को	1	१
			Light	PA		S	स	2	२
Green	White	Tourist	Heavy	PA		J		3	३
			Middle	YA	य	NA	ना	4	४
			Light	PA		BA	बा	5	५
Yellow	Blue	Public/ National Institution	Heavy	GHA	घ	GA		6	६
			Middle	YNA	ञ	LU	ल़ु	7	७
			Light	MA		DHA	ध़	8	८
Black	White	Public	Heavy	KHA	रव	BHE	भे	9	९
			Middle	JA		RA	रा	**DLP characters used in proposed system	
			Light	THA	थ	KA			
White	Red	Government	Heavy	GA		SE	से		
			Middle	JHA		MA			
Red Blue	White	Minister	Light	BA	व	New Style (3-row LP)			
			Heavy	**					
			Middle	JHA		English	Devanagari		
			Light	**					
Blue	White	Diplomat	Heavy	**		Province	प्रदेश		
			Middle	C D	सी डी				
			Light	**					

[10]. If LP and other general alphanumeric text exist, the algorithms described above will fail to detect them. Furthermore, the program is limited to standard LP due to the fixed-width enclosing box. To detect automobiles and localize LPs, Laroca et al. [11] employed two CNN models. This approach treats the LP as a fixed-length (seven-character) sequence and is only applicable to Brazilian standard LP. For recognition, Zhuang et al. [12] used semantic segmentation and counting refinement. This method works for LP with fixed length characters but not for those with variable lengths. Pant et al. [13] provides a method for detecting an LP in the context of a Nepalese vehicle using various image processing techniques, and the extracted histogram of oriented gradient characteristics (HoG) of DLP character is trained using a Support Vector Machine (SVM). According to the authors, the experiment was conducted on a small number of private LPs with low accuracy. The authors of [14] propose a deep learning method for LP detection and character recognition, but they leave out the full class of DLPs with different FBs, multiple horizontal segments, font, font size, and margin between LP characters. The DLP dataset [15] for private vehicles is also provided by the authors; however it is confined to the Bagmati zone and only for cars and two-wheelers. The approaches presented thus far for foreign LP have only dealt with detection and recognition for standardized designs and sizes. Standard LP is covered to some extent in the literatures that have been reviewed in relation to DLP, but the difficulty of recognizing non-standard LP remains a key gap. As a result, in this study, we propose a method for non-standard LP detection, classification, and recognition that used a variety of plate sizes, foreground and background colours, fonts, styles, and designs. A standard LP and characters dataset is also generated to test the proposed system's robustness.

3   Proposed Method

The details of detection and classification, segmentation and recognition are discussed in the respective sections.

3.1   LP Detection and Classification

The proposed method utilized an Improved Warped License Planar Object Detection Network (IWPOD-NET) [16] which can recognize vehicles in a range of capture scenarios and then rectify them to a fronto-parallel view. The IWPOD-NET is used as a fully convolutional network for recognizing an LP's four corners. The IWPOD-NET approach's network architecture, loss function calculation, vehicle detection, and resizing operation are all used in the proposed LP detection pipeline. Because IWPOD-unwarping NETs provide a nearly frontal image of the LP, it assumes a single FB color and the same size for each LP character, which is not the case with Nepalese LP. Because we expect multiple FB color LP, varying character counts in each segment of detected LP, and dissimilar character height in each segmented row of LP characters, this phase has to be modified. To address these issues, the detected LP is fed into the classification pipeline. To compensate for the low light, an image processing filtering is employed before passing the detected LP to the classification pipeline. The low light compensation process starts with determining whether the image is bright or dim by looking at the expected global average intensity of luminance components in YCbCr colour space and adaptively thresholding the image. The thresholded LP is then sent to the gamma correction filter, which corrects the brightness of the captured LP while leaving the other chrominance components alone. As the gamma value increases, the image transitions from black to white. The resulting image is an RGB colour space image that has been low light corrected. The LP image is resized to 240 pixels by 80 pixels and feed to the classification pipeline.

The initial step in the LP classification process is to determine which category a vehicle belongs to by examining the foreground and background (FB) colour of the LP. To accomplish this, the centre of extracted LP is computed using Eq. (1), where width refers to the width and height refers to the height of the extracted RGB LP. A 120 pixel by 40 pixel LP mask from centre is cropped from the low light compensated image using Eq. (2). The RGB LP mask is transformed into HSV mask. A random forest classifier is used as a FB classifier to determine the ownership of vehicles. The pixel values of hue, saturation, and value components for the cropped HSV image is fed to the random forest classifier. This classifier returns a class based on the hue, saturation, and value components of the LP mask. The returned class value is valid in most of cases except private and government LP. The private and government LPs use the same colour space, with the exception that the colours in the foreground and background are flipped. In such circumstances, another random forest classifier is nested at the end to reduce the ambiguity produced by private-government vehicle uncertainty and to improve vehicle classification results. Four corner patches are extracted as shown in Eq. (3) where TL, TR, BL and BR stands for Top-left patch, top-right patch, bottom-left patch and bottom-right respectively. Each extracted patch is transformed into HSV colour space, and trained with a second random forest classifier. These patches have colour components primarily dominated with the background colour; making it easier to classify the private-government LPs. Figure 2(a) depicts the classification procedure for a vehicle's LP.

$$center_x, center_y = \frac{width}{2}, \frac{height}{2} \qquad (1)$$

$$img = img[centre_y - 20 : centre_y + 20, centre_x - 60 : centre_x + 60] \qquad (2)$$

$$TL = img[0 : 20, 0 : 20], TR = img[0 : 20, 220 : 240],$$

$$BL = img[60 : 80, 0 : 20], BR = img[60 : 80, 220 : 240] \qquad (3)$$

3.2 Character Segmentation and Recognition

Once the vehicles are classified the next task is to clean the noise around LP area and perform character segmentation task. We must apply numerous image processing filters in a sequential order to achieve this. The vehicle classification stage is a critical step for character segmentation since the final binary LP is acquired by applying the appropriate filtering pipeline that threshold the LP according to the class value (categorical) returned by FB classifier. Depending on the LP structure, we must first remove the noise, then segment the LP into a maximum of three vertically discontinuous sections, and finally extract the characters from each row.

The region that is attached to an LP but does not contain LP characters must be removed and the largest contour with LP characters must be acquired. So, the RGB LP is converted to HSV colour space and only the saturation component of the LP is processed. The saturation mask is passed into the Contrast Limited Adaptive Histogram Equalization (CLAHE) [17, 18]. AHE is good for increasing edge definitions and improving local contrast in specific sections of an image however it can enhance noise in more uniform areas. By restricting the amplification, Contrast Limited Adaptive Histogram Equalization (CLAHE), a subset of AHE, prevents this. The coordinates of four points of the thresholded largest contour (top, left, right, and bottom) is logged in this stage and four points perspective projection is applied to generate the actual LP region. The LP is then fed to next image filter which splits the LP structure into a maximum of three vertical segments (3-row LP) based on the numbers of character visible in each row. A Vertical Projection Profile (VPP) test is done in order to check the number of rows for each LP. For instance, the 3-row binarized LP has a valley at starts and later transition to a peak meaning we have encountered the first row LP characters. This process continues for another two rounds meaning the second row and last row LP characters are encountered. The VPP of each column is calculated as a sum along the vertical axis. The plate segmentation pipeline for a 3-row LP structure is shown in Fig. 2(b). The returned class value from nested random forest classifier is critical as the rest of the pipeline rely on FB colour combination of a given LP. We must note that this processing pipeline requires changes in several steps since we have seven types of LP based on vehicle ownership and three types of LP structure. For each vertically segmented binarized LP region the Connected Component Analysis (CCA) [19] is applied which filters out the unwanted blobs before the actual LP characters are segmented. The Connected Components are valid LP characters which must be retained in LP while other connected components must be filtered out. The valid connected component characters satisfy several features such as each candidate LP character must have specific height, breadth, area, aspect ratio and connectivity. At last, each character from vertical rows is segmented using Vertical Projection Profile.

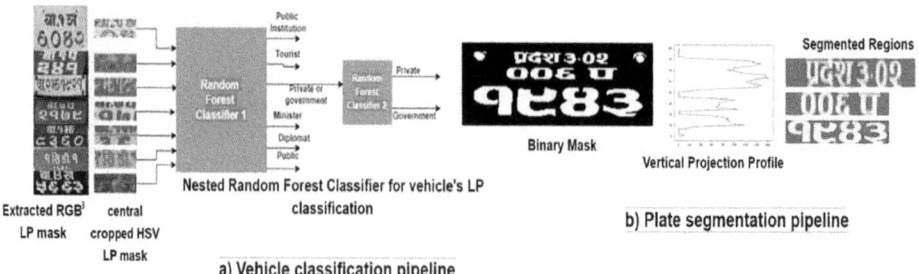

Fig. 2. a) classification pipeline b) vertical segmentation decision

Each segmented character is appended to a single character vector in a conventional character recognition system, which is then fed to a character recognition model for character predictions. We modify this technique by identifying each segmented character as a letter or a digit based on character position in an LP. These characters are then appended to the appropriate character vectors. For instance, the first row in 3-row LP structure has four positional characters where the first character is from the letter class and the remaining three characters are from the digit class. Similarly, the second row is made up of the first three characters from the digit class, followed by a letter from the letter class. In the final row, we expect 1 to 4 digits. Table 1 summarized the positional characteristics of LP. Two character vectors are employed in the proposed system, and all positional characters are merged into their corresponding categories. The Digit Recognizer Model (DRM) is an image container that stores positional digits segmented from each row from various LP structures. Similarly, when the position of the characters cannot be predicted, the letter-digit pair is stored into a Letter and Digit Recognizer (LRDM) model. For instance, because we may encounter zonal or province-based LP, the position of segmented characters in 1-row LP is difficult to predict. LDRM is used in this situation. The processing pipeline for character position decision is shown in Fig. 3.

In proposed ALPDR, each segmented LP character is a 32×32 feature vector that is used for Optical Character Recognition (OCR) and hence sent to the feature extraction subsystem. In the proposed method, the LRDM model has a total of 33 character classes, comprising 10 digits, 12 zonal letters, 10 load letters, and 1 province letter. The DRM model includes a ten-digit class that represents digits ranging from 0 to 9.

The LRDM and DRM are two Convolution Neural Network (CNN) models with identical architecture. The first two layers of LDRM and DRM have 60 filters with kernel size of 3×3. This step extracts the low-level features of LP characters. The 2×2 max-pooling operation down-sample the image input from previous layer. As we move progressively to upper layer of CNN model we capture higher-level image features.

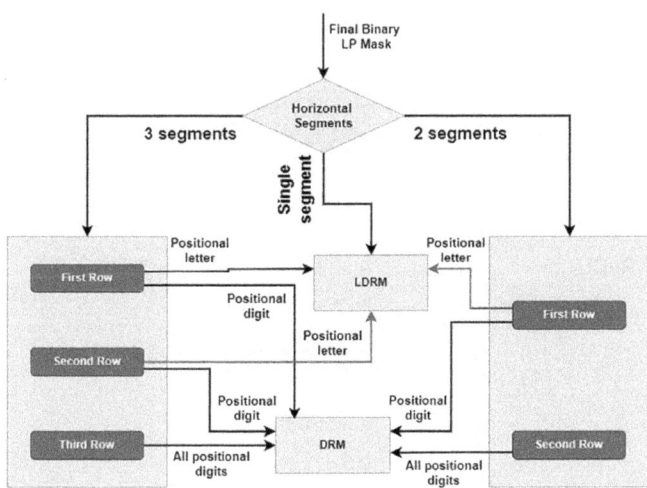

Fig. 3. Positional character decision for different LP structure

The image is further down-sampled in the second max pooling layer. Overfitting during the training is mitigated by introducing a dropout [20] operation once the vector is flattened as one dimensional vector with 480 neurons. A 50% drop-out is applied in the proposed method to prevent the models from overfitting. Later 1×500 one-dimensional feature vector is generated with another 50% drop-out to prevent overfitting. The Softmax activation function is used to predict the LP characters classes. The activation function predicts 33 LDRM classes and 10 DRM classes using the softmax function. Table 3 shows the architecture of proposed LRDM and DRM models.

4 Result and Discussion

4.1 DLP Dataset

The DLP dataset is divided into three parts: 1) the vehicle dataset (VD), 2) the LP dataset (LPD), and 3) the characters dataset (CD). VD, which consists of 3650 vehicles, is used as training data for the LP detection. Cropped LPs segmented during the LP detection, LPD, are used in the classification step for FB training in HSV colour space. The distribution of the VD dataset based on vehicle ownership is shown in Table 4. The VD images were taken in various locations, such as a road, a parking lot, a university, and so on. To avoid the training model from overfitting, the image augmentation technique based on Tensorflow-keras library [21] is used that increase the vehicle counts for vehicles with low vehicle counts. Similarly, the LP and CD dataset are also augmented using the same library to prevent the respective models from overfitting.

The LPs region is detected by IWPOD-NET from vehicles. The extracted LPs are divided into seven classes and then used as LP dataset. The LP dataset is utilized in

Table 3. LDRM and DRM

Layer Type	Parameters
Input	32×32
Convolution + ReLU	28×28, #filters:60, k $= 3 \times 3$
Convolution + ReLU	24×24, #filters:60, k $= 3 \times 3$
Max Pooling	k: 2×2, s: 1
Convolution + ReLU	10×10, #filters:30, k $= 3 \times 3$
Convolution + ReLU	8×8, #filters:30, k $= 3 \times 3$, p:1
Max Pooling	k: 2×2, s: 1
Flattened	#neurons: 480
Dropout	0.5
Dense	# neuron: 500
Dropout	0.5
Fully connected + Softmax	# neuron: 33 (LDRM), #neuron: 10 (DRM)

Table 4. VD for training (without augmentation)

Vehicle Type	Vehicle Ownership	Vehicle Counts
1	Private	1500
2	Tourist	500
3	Public	1000
4	Diplomat	50
5	Government	500
6	Minister	50
7	Public Institutions	50

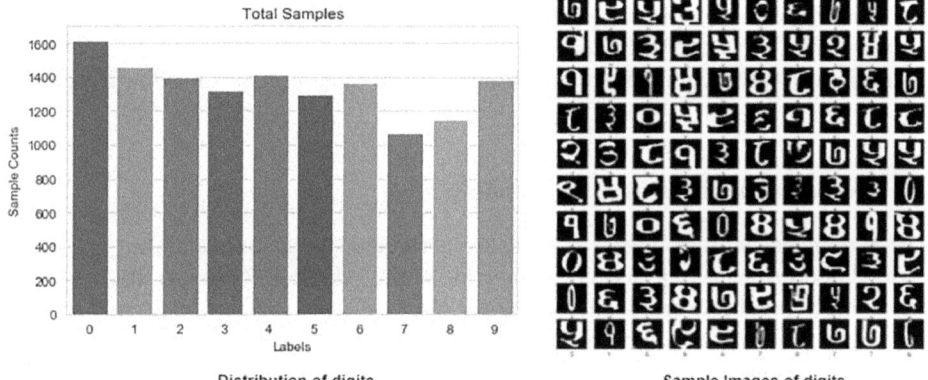

Distribution of digits   Sample Images of digits

Fig. 4. Digit counts along with sample images

training by the nested random forest classifier for LP classification. During the testing, the extracted LP is fed into a nested random forest classifier, with the exception of government and private vehicles, where the first classifier successfully outputs the desired class. The LP is passed into the next classifier to resolve this ambiguity.

The CD dataset contains ten digits and twenty-three letters, which are used to train DRM and LDRM, respectively. These characters are cropped binary images acquired during the character segmentation stage and produced during the segmentation of characters from each rows of a LP. The characters are further classified as a digit or a letter, and each is saved in its own class folder. There are 13489 samples in the DRM model and more than 20000 images in the LDRM model. Each character has been scaled to 32 × 32 sizes. The characters that have low counts are augmented when needed in order to prevent the character recognition model from overfitting. Figure 5 shows the specifics of the number of sample distribution for the digit class. The number of digits with the highest number (0) is around 1600, and the number with the lowest number (7) is around 1100. A random sample of 100 Devanagari digits is also shown in Fig. 4.

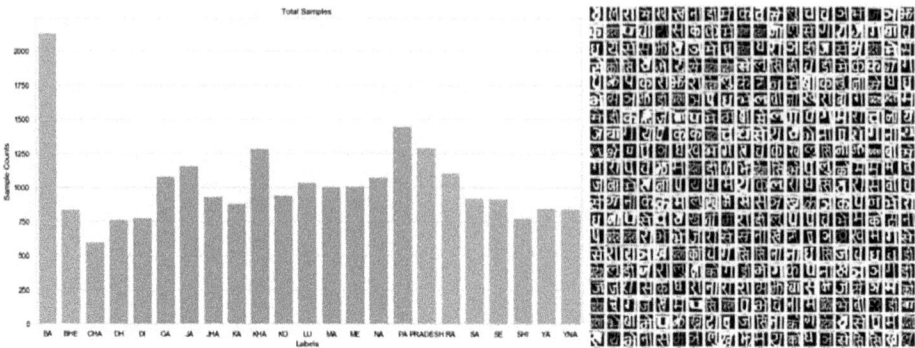

Fig. 5. Letter counts with sample image (digits not included)

The number of samples for each letter class is shown in Fig. 5. The highest number of letters (BA) was over 2200, while the lowest number of characters (SHI, DI) was approximately 800. Figure 5 also illustrates the 200 random letters used in Devanagari LP.

4.2   Detection and Classification Results

The 500 images with vehicle(s) in them are considered for testing, and they are further divided into seven classes based on ownership of the vehicle (FB colour). Because a test image may contain several vehicles, the IWPOD-NET model may detect many LPs in the test image. For each detected LP, the random forest classifier must classify each LP into suitable class.

The detection and classification results are shown in Table 5. The highest detection accuracy is achieved for private vehicles while minister's vehicle has the lowest detection accuracy. Similarly, 217 of the 225 accurately detected Red LPs have the highest FB classification. Overall, 493 LPs out of 537 were classified correctly using the proposed method.

4.3   Character Recognition Results

The character recognition step is performed for the LPs that are correctly classified in their corresponding class. Each LP's characters are split, and the prediction accuracy for each horizontal segment is measured. The character prediction accuracy of the entire (whole) LP is also assessed. For each LP, the entire LP accuracy is determined by correctly predicting the positional letters and digits on each horizontal segment. Table 6 shows the character prediction accuracy for the DLP. In 3-row LP, the availability of both letter and digit in the first and second rows results in lower character prediction accuracy than in the last row. However, in the first and second rows, the character-digit approximation of positional characters reduces prediction confusion, allowing for more accurate digit recognition. The overall LP accuracy for both the 3-row LP and 2-row LP structures is 86.5% and 83.5%, respectively. Because approximating position characters

Table 5. Detection and Classification Accuracy

Vehicle Type	Vehicle Ownership	Vehicle Counts	Ground truth (LP)	Detected LP	LP Detection Accuracy	Correct FB classification	FB Classification accuracy
1	Private	200	230	225	97%	217	96%
2	Tourist	120	130	125	96%	110	88%
3	Public	100	115	109	94%	100	91%
4	Diplomat	20	25	22	88%	20	90%
5	Government	20	22	20	90%	17	85%
6	Minister	20	21	18	85%	15	83%
7	Public Institutions	20	20	18	90%	14	77%
Total		500	563	537	95%	493	91%

Table 6. Character Prediction accuracy

LP Structure	LP Counts	First Row Accuracy	Second Row Accuracy	Third Row Accuracy	whole LP correctly recognized	Whole LP Accuracy
3-row	178	87%	91%	98%	154	86.5%
2-row	200	89%	97.3%	***	167	83.5%
1-row	185	82.7%	***	***	153	82.7%
Classifier	Accuracy					
DRM	97%					
LDRM	84%					

is challenging, and each character is predicted by the LRDM model alone, the 1-row LP structure has the lowest whole LP accuracy with just 82.7%. DRM achieves 97% character prediction accuracy, which is significantly greater than LDRM, due to lower intra-class variation in the digit class.

4.4 Real-Time Implementation Results

In addition, the resilience of proposed method is tested for moving vehicles in a parking lot. A scene in which vehicles are visible in the frame is taken into account. The various LPs from the vehicle with Bagmati zone make up the scene. A total of five videos in which a total of 30 vehicles are present are used to test the system's resiliency. Table 7 shows the results of the real time implementation. A frame with vehicle is captured when a vehicle cross a line. The captured frame is fed to the detection module which detect vehicle first and later a LP region is returned. With four LPs successfully recognized and

Table 7. Accuracy measurement in a dynamic environment

Scene	Vehicles present	Detected LP	Classified LP	Whole LP characters Recognized
1	5	4	4	4
2	8	7	6	5
3	4	3	3	3
4	8	6	4	4
5	5	4	3	3

classified, Scene 1 has the highest detection and classification accuracy whereas Scene 5 exhibits the worst performance.

5   Conclusion

This research presents LP recognition, classification, and character prediction system based on hybrid learning for vehicles with Devanagari LP characters. The IWPOD-NET is utilized as an LP detector and localizer, the nested random forest is used as an LP classifier that used the HSV FB color of an extracted LP region, and the two CNN models are used to predict characters. For LP classification, numerous image processing techniques and machine learning approaches are used. The classified LP is further processed to reduce noise before performing character segmentation. The binary LP is split into the number of rows applying horizontal projection profile. Two CNN models are used to train and predict the positional character: LRDM for letter-digit pairs and DRM for digits only. The Devanagari CD was developed which validate the resilience of the proposed method. In proposed system, total LP detection accuracy was 95%, LP categorization accuracy was 91% for the detected LP, and overall character prediction was over 83% for all LP structures.

In comparison to other DLP investigations [13, 14], this method is more advanced in a number of aspects. To begin, this study looks upon heterogeneous DLP with varying FB colour and plate structure. Second, in order to increase character prediction accuracy the characters dataset support various characters within and between the vehicle ownership classes. This research has included the method to tackle the problem of uncertainty in determining the letter and digit ambiguity and proposed two separate CNN model to improve recognition accuracy. At last, considering the heterogeneous nature of DLP, the overall accuracy in the detection, classification, and character recognition phases is comparably good when compared to available literatures [14] for DLP.

The results of the experiments showed that the proposed strategy could be employed effectively for both static and dynamic situations. This study's findings could be used to recognize an LP in a real-time situation. We intend to deploy this model in the future to detect, classify, and predict all sorts of DLP.

Acknowledgments. This research work is part of the Erasmus+KA107 (https://www.uma.es/icm) mobility program at the University of Malaga in Spain. Professor Enrique Nava Baro provided the research space where the experiments were conducted, which the first author gratefully acknowledges.

Authors' Contributions. This research work's Conceptualization, Methodology, Investigation, Experiment, and Writing were all contributed by Pankaj Raj Dawadi. The final version of the manuscript was approved by all authors after they had reviewed the results.

References

1. S. Du, M. Ibrahim, M. Shehata, and W. Badawy, "Automatic License Plate Recognition (ALPR): A State-of-the-Art Review," *IEEE Trans. Circuits Syst. Video Technol.*, vol. 23, no. 2, pp. 311–325, 2013.
2. B. R. Vasconcellos, M. Rudek, and M. de Souza, "A Machine Learning Method for Vehicle Classification by Inductive Waveform Analysis"," *IFAC-PapersOnLine*, vol. 53, no. 2, pp. 13928–13932, 2020, https://doi.org/10.1016/j.ifacol.2020.12.908.
3. W. Maungmai and C. Nuthong, "Vehicle Classification with Deep Learning," in *2019 IEEE 4th International Conference on Computer and Communication Systems (ICCCS)*, 2019, pp. 294–298, https://doi.org/10.1109/CCOMS.2019.8821689.
4. M. Jaderberg, K. Simonyan, A. Vedaldi, and A. Zisserman, "Reading Text in the Wild with Convolutional Neural Networks," *Int. J. Comput. Vis.*, vol. 116, no. 1, pp. 1–20, Jan. 2016, https://doi.org/10.1007/s11263-015-0823-z.
5. T. Wang, D. J. Wu, A. Coates, and A. Y. Ng, "End-to-end text recognition with convolutional neural networks," in *Proceedings of the 21st International Conference on Pattern Recognition (ICPR2012)*, Nov. 2012, pp. 3304–3308.
6. S. A. Radzi and M. Khalil-Hani, "Character Recognition of License Plate Number Using Convolutional Neural Network," in *Visual Informatics: Sustaining Research and Innovations*, 2011, pp. 45–55.
7. H. Li and C. Shen, "Reading Car License Plates Using Deep Convolutional Neural Networks and LSTMs," *CoRR*, vol. abs/1601.0, 2016, [Online]. Available: http://arxiv.org/abs/1601.05610.
8. Z. Selmi, M. Ben Halima, and A. M. Alimi, "Deep Learning System for Automatic License Plate Detection and Recognition," in *2017 14th IAPR International Conference on Document Analysis and Recognition (ICDAR)*, 2017, vol. 01, pp. 1132–1138, https://doi.org/10.1109/ICDAR.2017.187.
9. Q. Wang, J. Gao, and Y. Yuan, "A Joint Convolutional Neural Networks and Context Transfer for Street Scenes Labeling," *IEEE Trans. Intell. Transp. Syst.*, vol. 19, no. 5, pp. 1457–1470, May 2018, https://doi.org/10.1109/TITS.2017.2726546.
10. T. K. Cheang, Y. S. Chong, and Y. H. Tay, "Segmentation-free Vehicle License Plate Recognition using ConvNet-RNN," *CoRR*, vol. abs/1701.0, 2017, [Online]. Available: http://arxiv.org/abs/1701.06439.
11. R. Laroca *et al.*, "A Robust Real-Time Automatic License Plate Recognition Based on the YOLO Detector," *2018 Int. Jt. Conf. Neural Networks*, pp. 1–10, 2018.
12. J. Zhuang, S. Hou, Z. Wang, and Z. Zha, "Towards Human-Level License Plate Recognition," in *ECCV*, 2018.
13. A. K. Pant, P. K. Gyawali, and S. Acharya, "Automatic Nepali Number Plate Recognition with Support Vector Machines," in *Proceedings of the 9th International Conference on Software, Knowledge, Information Management and Applications (SKIMA)*, 2015, pp. 92–99.

14. P. R. Dawadi, M. Pokharel, and B. K. Bal, "An Approach of Devanagari License Plate Detection and Recognition Using Deep Learning," in *Advances in Computing and Data Sciences*, 2021, pp. 85–96.

15. "Character_dataset." https://www.kaggle.com/pankajdawadi/nepali-lp-dataset (accessed Mar. 18, 2021).

16. S. M. Silva and C. R. Jung, "A Flexible Approach for Automatic License Plate Recognition in Unconstrained Scenarios," *IEEE Trans. Intell. Transp. Syst.*, pp. 1–11, 2021, https://doi.org/10.1109/TITS.2021.3055946.

17. K. Zuiderveld, "Contrast Limited Adaptive Histogram Equalization," in *Graphics Gems IV*, USA: Academic Press Professional, Inc., 1994, pp. 474–485.

18. J. B. Z. S. M. Pizer, E. P. Amburn, J. D. Austin, R. Cromartie, A. Geselowitz, T. Greer, B. ter Haar Romeny, *Adaptive histogram equalization and its variations*, Vol. 39, N. 1987.

19. K. Wu, E. Otoo, and K. Suzuki, "Optimizing two-pass connected-component labeling algorithms," *Pattern Anal. Appl.*, vol. 12, pp. 117–135, 2009, https://doi.org/10.1007/s10044-008-0109-y.

20. G. E. Hinton, N. Srivastava, A. Krizhevsky, I. Sutskever, and R. R. Salakhutdinov, "Improving neural networks by preventing co-adaptation of feature detectors." 2012.

21. "Keras Library." https://www.tensorflow.org/api_docs/python/tf/keras/preprocessing/image/ImageDataGenerator (accessed Mar. 31, 2022).

Pre-trained Convolutional Neural Networks for Gender Classification

Bhuvaneshwari Patil[1,2] and Mallikarjun Hangarge[3(✉)]

[1] Gulbarga University, Kalaburagi, India
[2] Faculty at Presidency University, Bangalore, India
[3] Department of Computer Science, KASC College, Bidar, India
bsp4052001@gmail.com

Abstract. Many researchers have used Convolutional Neural Networks (CNN) models to solve the gender classification problem using pre-trained architectures. In this paper, the author has focused on investigating the success of the custom CNN model with respect to pre-trained deep neural models like VGG16, ResNet152V2, InceptionResNetV2 and EfficientNetV2L with limited data for gender classification.

Keywords: gender classification · keras models · convolution neural network · deep neural network

1 Introduction

Gender classification using facial features has received a lot of attention, but nowadays eye feature-based classification has gained attention among researchers. Feature extraction and classification procedures are crucial for implementing an effective automatic classification system. The traditional machine learning algorithms will give better accuracy, it is necessary to extract accurate features from eye datasets. On the other hand, Deep learning models will automatically extract features from raw data. Deep neural networks can investigate hidden and unpredictable feature sets, which can improve classification performance by exploring hidden and unpredictable feature sets when compared to typical machine learning.

Face traits gathered were from the rich study on human authentication features. In recent years, texture feature extraction (Majumdar & Patil, 2013) from an iris image has gained popularity as a soft biometric trait for determining a person's gender. When combined with related biometric data, the main benefit of employing soft biometrics is that it aids in the faster retrieval of identities by reducing the searching period. Iris data has been utilized productively in a wide range of settings, including airport check-in and refugee control (Bobeldyk & Ross, 2019). It can also be used in cross-spectral matching scenarios (Dantcheva et al., 2016) when comparing RGB and NRI images. By enhancing recognition qualities and accuracy, more semantic information about an unknown situation will be provided, filling the gap between machine and human descriptions of the area.

R. Manza et al. (Eds.): ACVAIT 2022, AISR 176, pp. 319–326, 2023.
https://doi.org/10.2991/978-94-6463-196-8_25

The area of interest has been narrowed to Eye region instead from whole face for Gender classification which reduces the computation complexity and provides the reliable results as the rate of change in eye features is negligible as compared with the changes in facial features. As a result, the dataset and the area of interest have been limited. Keras Applications, deep learning models that come with pre-trained weights and can be used to make predictions, extract features, and fine-tune them. These models can be built according to the required image dataset. Here, we are using VGG16, ResNet152V2, InceptionResNetV2, EfficientNetV2L models for eye images to classify as male and female eyes. The rest of the paper is organized as related work in the field of gender prediction/classification and deep neural network models in Section 2. Section 3 describes the applied methodology and dataset. Section 4 shows results and discussion of results. Finally, completed with conclusion.

2 Related Work

The first publication on gender prediction from geometric and texture aspects of iris pictures was published by Thomas et al. (Thomas et al., 2007). The author considered SVM and NN for classification with an accuracy of 80%. For an improved gender prediction rate, Tapia & Aravena (J. Tapia & Aravena, 2018) presented a modified Lenet-5 CNN model. Four convolution layers and one fully- connected layer with a minimum number of neurons make up the updated network. Bobeldyk and Ross (Bobeldyk & Ross, 2019).

Sreya & Jones (C & Jones B, 2020) investigated the IITD Dataset and employed ANN to recognise iris patterns. The writers went over each phase of the recognition process in great detail. To find the pupil region, the trials were undertaken out on cropped NIR pictures. The accuracy of prediction is said to be dependent on processing, according to the authors.

Singh et al. (Singh et al., 2018) used a variant of an auto-encoder that includes the attribute class label in addition to the reconstruction layer. They used images of NIR Oculars that had been scaled down to 48X64 pixels. For their method, they employed the GFI and ND-Iris-0405 Datasets. The researchers used RDF and NNet classifiers and got an accuracy of 83.17 percent. They claim that The Deep Class-Encoder takes a fifth of the total training time, and that their results exceed Tapia et al.'s (J. E. Tapia et al., 2016).

For an improved gender prediction rate, Tapia & Aravena (J. Tapia & Aravena, 2018) developed a modified Lenet-5 CNN model. Four convolution layers and one fully-connected layer with a small number of neurons make up the redesigned network. To avoid the risk of over-fitting and solve the two-class gender prediction problem, a minimal number of neurons is recommended. The authors used Data Augmentation to boost the size of each eye's Dataset from 1,500 to 9,500 images. The authors find that combining CNN for the right and left eyes results in better prediction than each eye alone.

Deep learning has been used for gender classification from facial images, drawing inspiration from a variety of fields. The study (Janahiraman et al., 2019) develops a dataset consisting of facial photographs of Caucasians and Malaysians, and then applies several Convolutional Neural Networks for gender prediction. Using the VGG-16, ResNet-50, and MobileNet models, it reports accuracy of 88 percent, 85 percent, and 49 percent, respectively. On the Adience dataset (Eidinger et al., 2014), (Akbulut et al., 2017) applied CNN and LRA-ELM methods and achieved 80% and 87.13%, respectively. In the study (Abdalrady et al., 2020), typical CNN models were swapped out for the PCANet model for gender categorization. Furthermore, it is possible to reduce the size of the network architecture in intricate CNN models by employing PCANet.

3 Methodology

Several face datasets have been used for gender classification in the literature, including Adience, FERET (color-feret-database, 2021), Gallagher's dataset (Gallagher et al., 2008), and LFW (Huang et al., 2007). However, they all supply images of the entire face, and segmenting the eyes is an extra task for the researchers. We utilize the dataset labelled "Female and Male" which is referenced in this article since it conducts a comparison analysis between state-of-the-art CNN models simply utilizing eye pictures (eyes-rtte, 2021). The dataset consists of 5202 female and 6323 male eye images.

3.1 Keras Models

The input images are cropped eye portion from UKTFace images and resized to 75 × 75. The model is trained with 8068 images and tested using 3467 images. The dataset consist of 6323 male images and 5202 female images and the parameters used are as listed in Table 1.

The authors of this study want to understand how well different pre-trained deep learning models perform when it comes to gender classification from eye images. Here, we used VGG16, ResNet152V2, InceptionResNetV2, EfficientNetV2L models for this purpose and used dropout layer to protect the network against an overfitting issue. The 'Female and Male' dataset is split in the ratio of 70:30 as training and testing data.

The model's size, accuracy, number of parameters, depth and time inference steps for CPU and GPU as given in Table 2 (Keras applications, 2021). EfficientNetV2L model has a huge number of parameters however the maximum top-1 and top-5 accuracy.

Table 1. Training parameters of CNN models

Parameters	Values
Optimizer	Adam
Loss	Categorical_crossentropy
Shuffle	True
Number of epochs	30
batch_size	32

Table 2. Keras models

Model	Size (MB)	Parameters	Top-1 Accuracy	Top-5 Accuracy	Depth	Time (ms)/inference step (CPU)	Time (ms)/inference step (GPU)
VGG16	528	14,764,866	71.3%	90.1%	16	69.5	4.2
ResNet152V2	232	58,532,354	78.0%	94.2%	307	107.5	6.6
InceptionResNetV2	215	54,413,538	80.3%	95.3%	449	130.2	10.0
EfficientNetV2L	479	117,872,290	85.7%	97.5%	-	-	-

Table 3. Summary of the Custom CNN model

Model: "Sequential"

Layer (type)	Output Shape	Param #
Conv2d_203 (conv2D)	(None, 32, 32, 32)	896
Max_pooling2d_7 (MaxPooling2D)	(None, 16, 16, 32)	0
Conv2d_204 (conv2D)	(None, 16, 16, 16)	9248
Max_pooling2d_8 (MaxPooling2D)	(None, 8, 8, 32)	0
Flatten_4 (Flatten)	(None, 2048)	0
Dense_4 (Dense)	(None, 128)	262272
Dense_5 (Dense)	(None, 1)	129

Total params: 272,545
Trainable params : 272,545
Non-trainable params : 0

3.2 Custom CNN

We have developed a custom CNN to train and test the 'Female and Male' dataset for gender classification. The model is trained using 272,545 parameters as listed in summary Table 3. The model consists of two convolution layers, two maxpooling layers and two dense layers. The modelcheckpoint callback function used to save the weights when there is an improvement during training.

4   Results and Discussion

The authors of this project want to see if they can utilize pre-trained deep networks like VGG16, ResNet152V2, InceptionResNetV2, EfficientNetV2L to classify gender from eye images. In addition, custom CNN model trained with same set of parameters and results are as shown in Figs 1, 2, 3, 4 and 5. The accuracy for these models are tabulated in Table 4.

The Figures 1, 2, 3, 4 and 5 shows that VGG16, ResNet152V2 have similar accuracy for both training and validation data whereas custom CNN has smooth curve for training as compare to validation. It is observed that all the five models, learning rate decreased when the models are trained for more than thirty epochs.

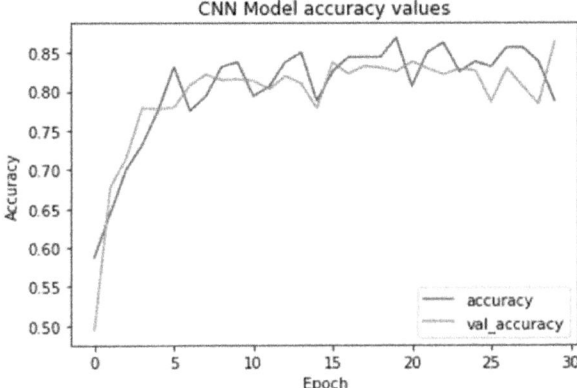

Fig. 1. Accuracy plot for VGG16

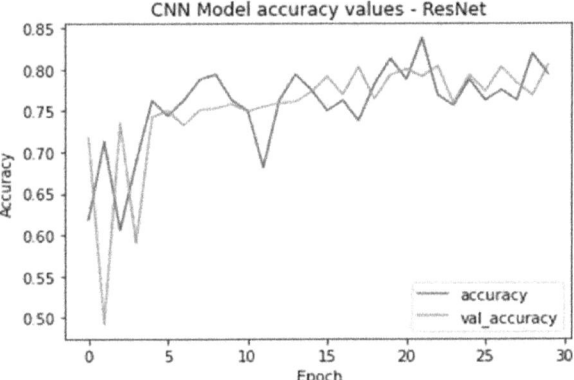

Fig. 2. Accuracy plot for ResNet152V2

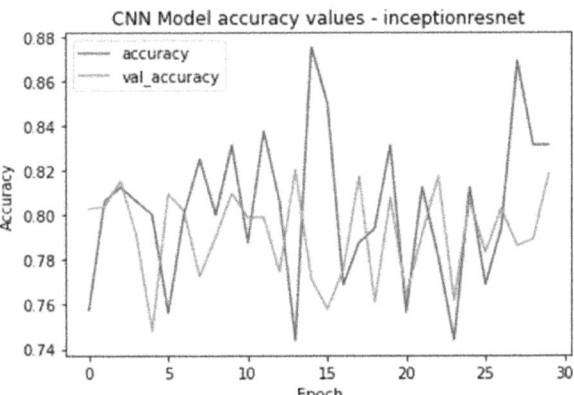

Fig. 3. Accuracy plot for InceptionResnetV2

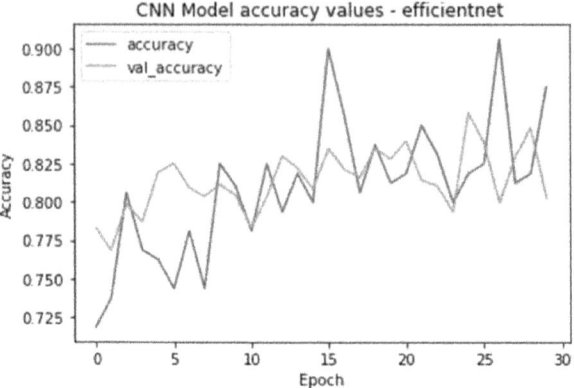

Fig. 4. Accuracy plot for EfficientNetV2L

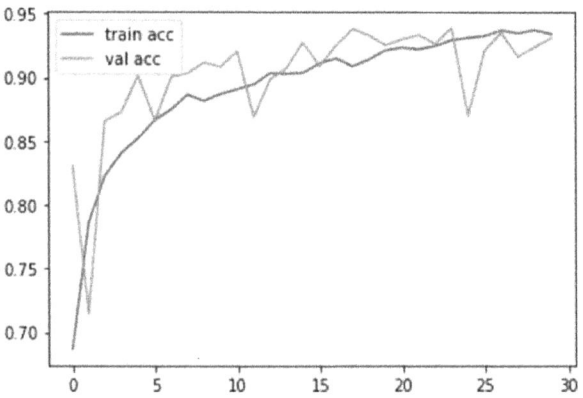

Fig. 5. Accuracy plot for custom CNN

Table 4. Gender Classification results

Model	Trainable parameters	Training duration (h:m:s)	Accuracy (%)
VGG16	50,178	0:37:40.917232	84.05
ResNet152V2	200,706	0:16:34.231426	80.10
InceptionResNetV2	76,802	0:15:50.573017	82.43
EfficientNetV2L	125,442	0:17:19.732781	84.19
Custom CNN	272,545	0:19:43.820124	93.08

5 Conclusion

Based on gender classification from eye images, this study compares the performance of state-of-the- art deep CNN models: VGG16, ResNet152V2, InceptionResNetV2, EfficientNetV2L along with custom CNN model. The "Female and Male" dataset used to train these models. The pre-trained models shows better results for 'imagenet' for thousands of classes and millions of parameters as shown in Table 2. These models can be used to train deep neural network in short period of time with minimum number of parameters as shown in Table 3 by compromising the accuracy. It is also observed that the training time increases with the number of trainable parameters. The pre-trained models are best suited when resources are limited.

References

Majumdar, J., & Patil, B. S. (2013). A comparative analysis of image fusion methods using texture. Lecture Notes in Electrical Engineering, 221 LNEE (VOL. 1), 339–351. https://doi.org/10.1007/978-81-322-0997-3_31

Bobeldyk, D., & Ross, A. (2019). Predicting soft biometric attributes from 30 pixels: A case study in NIR ocular images. Proceedings - 2019 IEEE Winter Conference on Applications of Computer Vision Workshops, WACVW 2019, 116–124. https://doi.org/10.1109/WACVW.2019.00024

C, S. K., & Jones B, R. S. (2020). Gender Prediction from Iris Recognition using Artificial Neural Network (ANN). www.ijert.org

Singh, M., Nagpal, S., Vatsa, M., Singh, R., Noore, A., & Majumdar, A. (2018). Gender and ethnicity classification of Iris images using deep class-encoder. IEEE International Joint Conference on Biometrics, IJCB 2017, 2018-Janua, 666–673. https://doi.org/10.1109/BTAS.2017.8272755

Tapia, J., & Aravena, C. C. (2018). Gender classification from periocular NIR images using fusion of CNNs models. 2018 IEEE 4th International Conference on Identity, Security, and Behavior Analysis, ISBA 2018, 2018-January, 1–6. https://doi.org/10.1109/ISBA.2018.8311465

Thomas, V., Chawla, N. V, Bowyer, K. W., & Flynn, P. J. (2007). Learning to predict gender from iris images.

Dantcheva, A., Elia, P., & Ross, A. (2016). What else does your biometric data reveal? A survey on soft biometrics. IEEE Transactions on Information Forensics and Security, 11(3), 441–467. https://doi.org/10.1109/TIFS.2015.2480381

Abdalrady, N. A., & Aly, S. (2020, February). Fusion of multiple simple convolutional neural networks for gender classification. In 2020 International Conference on Innovative Trends in Communication and Computer Engineering (ITCE), 251-256. IEEE.

Akbulut, Y., Şengür, A., & Ekici, S. (2017, September). Gender recognition from face images with deep learning. In 2017 International artificial intelligence and data processing symposium (IDAP), 1-4. IEEE.

Arora, S., & Bhatia, M. P. S. (2018, July). A robust approach for gender recognition using deep learning. In 2018 9th International Conference on Computing, Communication and Networking Technologies (ICCCNT), 1-6. IEEE.

Eidinger, E., Enbar, R., & Hassner, T. (2014). Age and gender estimation of unfiltered faces. in IEEE Transactions on Information Forensics and Security, 9 (12), 2170-2179, doi: https://doi.org/10.1109/TIFS.2014.2359646.

Eyes-rtte. (23 September 2021). https://www.kaggle.com/pavelbiz/eyes-rtte

Janahiraman, T. V., & Subramaniam, P. (2019, October). Gender Classification Based on Asian Faces using Deep Learning. In 2019 IEEE 9th International Conference on System Engineering and Technology (ICSET) (84-89). IEEE.

Keras applications. (20 October 2021). https://keras.io/api/applications/Color-feret-database. (12 October 2021). https://www.nist.gov/itl/products-and-services/Gallagher, A. C., & Chen, T. (2008, June). Clothing cosegmentation for recognizing people. In 2008 IEEE conference on computer vision and pattern recognition, 1-8. IEEE.

Gallagher, A. C., & Chen, T. (2008, June). Clothing cosegmentation for recognizing people. In 2008 IEEE conference on computer vision and pattern recognition, 1-8. IEEE.

Huang, G. B., Ramesh, M., Berg, T., & Learned-Miller, E. (2007). Labeled faces in the wild: a database for studying face recognition in unconstrained environments. Univ. Massachusetts, Amherst, MA, USA.

AVAO Enabled Deep Learning Based Person Authentication Using Fingerprint

Rasika Deshmukh[1] and Pravin Yannawar[2]([✉])

[1] Department of Computer Science, Fergusson College (Autonomous), Pune, India
[2] Department of Computer Science, Dr. Babasaheb Ambedkar Marathwada University, Aurangabad, India
plyannawar.csit@bamu.ac.in

Abstract. Person authentication based on biometrics has been a major aspect accountable for providing security to cyberspace. The traditional biometric-based systems are based on the usage of single modality, which are potentially devoid of the capability to provide high security. A Deep Maxout Network (DMN) is utilized for performing person authentication on the basis of fingerprint. A novel optimization algorithm, named African vultures-Aquila Optimization (AVAO) algorithm is devised for updating the weights of the DMN. The strategies of the African Vulture Optimization Algorithm (AVOA) are modified according to the expanded exploration capability of the Aquila Optimizer (AO) to develop the proposed AVAO algorithm. The introduced optimization enabled deep learning based person authentication system achieved an accuracy of 0.927, sensitivity of 0.938 and specificity of 0.930,thereby showing superior performance.

Keywords: Person authentication · fingerprint · Deep Maxout Network · AVOA · AO

1 Introduction

Over the last few decades, a digital society has been developed around the globe in which the process of authentication is being made by considering each individual as a distinctive identifier. Authentication can be defined as, "Authentication is the act of confirming the truth of an attribute of a single piece of data claimed true by an entity". Person authentication refers to the procedure of verifying an individual's identity and is highly vital for every individual in this current information world. With the tremendous increase in the number of digital devices, there is a growing concern on the security. Every system or organization requires one type of authentication or other to provide security. The conventional authentication schemes are being replaced rapidly owing to their high vulnerability as these techniques employ PINs, identity cards, passwords, security tokens, etc., which can be easily manipulated, forgotten, copied, stolen or forged. In the past years, there is growing trend in the usage of the biometric-based authentication techniques that use the biometrics or the physical traits of an individual for authentication [1, 2]. Biometrics based approaches can be classified as behavioural as well

R. Manza et al. (Eds.): ACVAIT 2022, AISR 176, pp. 327–346, 2023.
https://doi.org/10.2991/978-94-6463-196-8_26

as physiological, where the behavioral biometrics are based on the unique behaviour of humans, such as signature, keystroke and voice. The physiological biometrics deals with the distinctive physical traits, such as iris, face, or fingerprint. These biometrics are highly unique, unforgettable and non transferable, moreover they are highly difficult to be manipulated, or stolen.

The authentication system which has been hogging the lime light for a long time is those that are based on the hand are highly efficient in recognizing the veins, hand form, hand geometry, palm prints, and fingerprints. These systems are highly successful owing to their robustness, simplicity, acceptance and stability. These systems are being employed by a vast number of government agencies, industries and corporations for providing security, attendance resisters and other purposes [3]. Among the hand based schemes, the fingerprint authentication system is the most extensively utilised system because of its high accuracy and acceptability. Also, the inexpensive and compact nature of the fingerprint scanners has resulted in a tremendous growth in multiple applications [4]. Fingerprint matching is one of the most promising biometric recognition techniques, and it has long been utilised for person authentication [5]. In this paper, fingerprint is pre-processed and then the minutiae are detected from the processed fingerprint. The output obtained is then fed to the DMN, which is tuned by using the proposed AVAO algorithm.

The main contributions of this paper are as follows.

- A **person authentication scheme** is devised for generating the encodings of the fingerprint image.
- A novel **AVAO algorithm** is developed for modifying the weights of the hidden neurons in the DMN. The AVAO algorithm is devised by modifying the AVOA with respect to the AO for enhancing the performance of the classifier.

The rest of the paper is organized in the following structure: Section 2 reviews the literature on the various authentic systems and Sect. 3 elaborates the proposed method along with the AVAO algorithm. Section 4 discusses the experimental outcomes.

2 Motivation

Authentication systems have emerged as a highly critical aspect needed for providing security and privacy to the current digitally interconnected society. Even though there is a growing trend in the usage of biometrics, there exits various attacks that can hamper the security of the system. In this section, the existing techniques of authentication are elaborated with their advantages and their demerits, which formed a major inspiration in the development of an effective authentication technique.

2.1 Literature Review

A large number of researches have been conducted on the development of the authentication schemes using different modalities.

Table 1. Literature Review

Author	Trait	Dataset	Classification Technique	Fusion Level	Average Accuracy
Bouzouina and Hamami, 2017 [6]	Face, Iris	CASIA-IrisV3-Interval iris dataset and ORL face dataset	SVM	Feature level	98.8%
Hezil and Boukrouche, 2017 [7]	Ear, Palmprint	IIT Delhi-2 ear and IIT Delhi palmprint	K-NN, SVM, CRC_RLS.	Feature Level	80.53–100%
Chaudhary and Nath, 2016 [8]	Face, Iris, Fingerprint	CASIA iris dataset, NIST face and fingerprint dataset	SVM	Score Level	99.8%
Veluchamy and Karlmarx, 2017 [9]	Finger knuckle, Finger vein	IIT Delhi finger knuckle dataset and SDUMLAHMT finger vein dataset	SVM	Feature Level	96%
Al-Waisy et al., 2017 [10]	Pair of irises, Face	NIST, CASIA V1.0, MMU1 and SDUMLA-HMT	DBN, CNN	Score/ Rank level	99.91%–100%
Mouad.M.H.Ali et al., [11]	Fingerprint	FVC2000	minutiae matching algorithm	Feature Level	98.55%

3 Introduced Avao Enabled Deep Learning Based Person Authentication Technique

In this paper, fingerprint images are utilized to enhance the efficiency of the authentication system along with providing privacy and security. Figure 1 illustrates the schematic representation of the introduced person.

Authentication technique. Fingerprint authentication module comprises of data acquisition, pre-processing, minutiae detection and person authentication.

These processes are detailed in the following subsections.

3.1 Fingerprint Authentication Module

This section deals with the process of authentication of the fingerprint image. Fingerprint images are most commonly utilized in the process of identification owing to their singularity and invariance. They are extensively utilized as they possess numerous advantages, such as high accuracy, fast and easy operation. In order to make the fingerprint image suitable for authentication, a sequence of operations has to be executed, which are detailed below along with the authentication process.

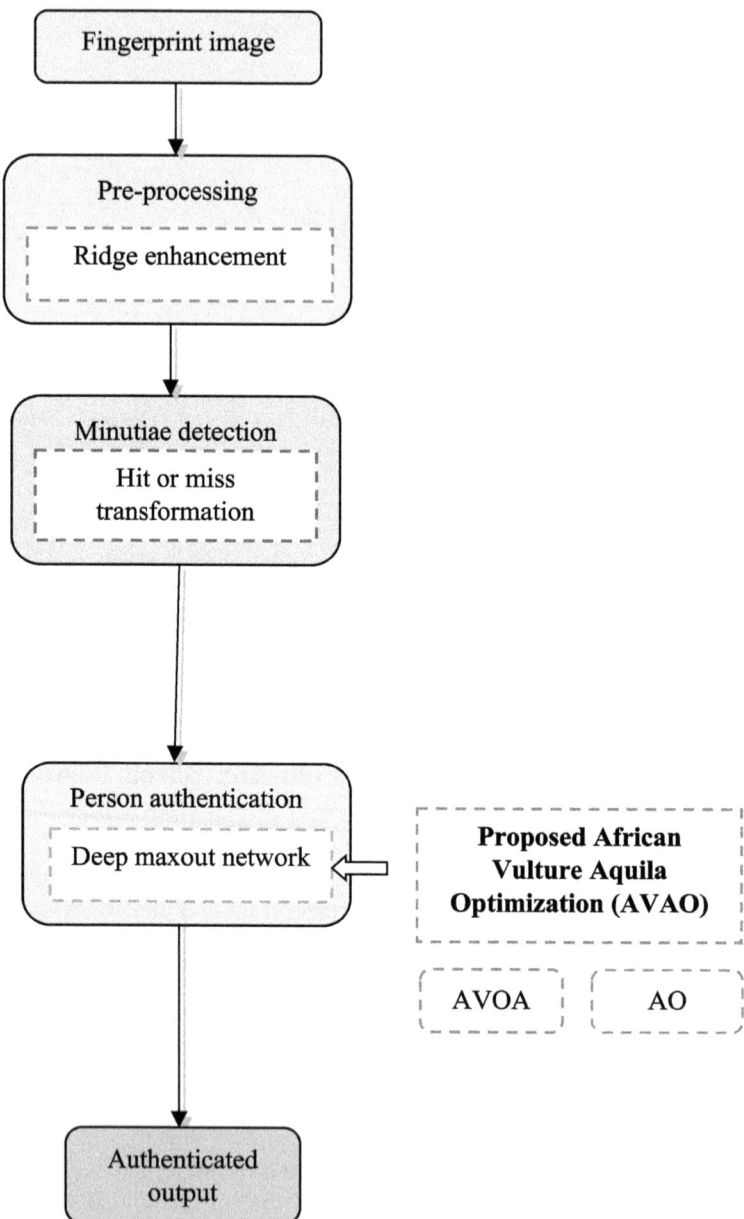

Fig. 1. Schematic representation of the introduced AVAO enabled deep learning based person authentication using fingerprint.

3.1.1 Fingerprint Image Acquisition

Consider a dataset Fp containing n_f fingerprint images and is represented by,

$$Fp = \left\{ fp_1, fp_2, ..., fp_i, ..fp_{n_f} \right\} \tag{1}$$

where, fp_i denotes the ith fingerprint image that will be fed to the preprocessing phase.

3.1.2 Fingerprint Image Pre-processing

The fingerprint image fp_i acquired from the database is subjected to pre-processing. The image acquisition modality has a high impact on the quality of the fingerprint image acquired. If the contrast between the background and the foreground is very poor, it affects the identification process. These noises and artifacts have to be eliminated to enhance the efficiency of identification, which is accomplished by means of pre-processing. Here, a ridge enhancement technique is utilized in pre-processing for obtaining the ridges. Ridge enhancement is highly efficient in smoothing the image without the need of any prior information. A set of processes are used to obtain an enhanced quality image from the poor quality input. The image quality is enhanced by enlarging the objects in the fingerprint image with the help of dilation, where the objects' interior and exterior boundary pixels are added with extra pixels. The ridge enhanced fingerprint image can be obtained by using the following expression.

$$Rid_i = fp_i \oplus l \tag{2}$$

where, l denotes the structuring element. The output obtained Rid_i is fed to the minutiae detection phase.

3.1.3 Minutiae Detection

The ridge enhanced image $Ridge_i$ is forwarded to the minutiae detection phase, where minutia points present in the ridge enhanced images are identified. Minutia refers to the points in the fingerprint, where the ridge lines bifurcate or end. Here, a Gray-scale Hit-Or-Miss Transformation (GHMT) is utilized. The GHMT offers the advantage of utilizing the foreground and the background information to identify the minutia and also it is flexible. GHMT technique is developed by inclusion of gray-scale erosion in the binary HMT technique, so as to make it suitable for gray-scale images. Moreover, template matching concept is utilized to modify the GHMT, whose expression can be represented by,

$$R_i \otimes (l_f, l_b) = \left[\min_{a_1 \in l_f}^2 (R_i + a_1) \right] - \left[\max_{a_2 \in l_b}^2 (R_i - a_2) \right] \tag{3}$$

Here, R_i specifies the gray-scale image, l_f denote the foreground structuring element and l_b is the background in which l_f is present. $\min^2$ and $\max^2$ denote the second minimum as well as the maximum values of the gray-level substitution of binary erosion and dilation operation.

GHMT utilizes sixteen templates, which are oriented and pre-defined for identifying the minutiae. The bifurcations of the ridges in the fingerprint are contained in the templates, which comprises of ridge line that has the background set and the valleys representing the foreground portion. These templates are efficient in detecting the bifurcations alone and do not detect the end point. The end points are identified by considering the inverted images, which is obtained by the following expression,

$$A^{\wedge}(x, y) = Pix_m - A(x, y) \tag{4}$$

Here, Pix_m represents the maximum value of pixel intensity in the original image. The pixel intensity of the original and the inverted images at (x, y) is represented by $A(x, y)$ and $A^{\wedge}(x, y)$.

The minutiae are identified by performing GHMT on both the inverted and the original image using Eq. (3) pixelwise. A total of sixteen filtered outputs are obtained for each of the original as well as the inverted images for each template. This can be expressed by,

$$B^j_{org} = Rid_i \otimes \left(l_f^{\theta_j}, l_b^{\theta_j} \right) \ where \ j \in \{1, 2, ..., 16\} \tag{5}$$

$$B^j_{inv} = Ridinv_i \otimes \left(l_f^{\theta_j}, l_b^{\theta_j} \right) \ where \ j \in \{1, 2, ..., 16\} \tag{6}$$

where, $Ridinv_i$ denotes the inverted ridge enhanced image, B^j_{org} and B^j_{inv} are the outputs obtained from the filtering of the original as well as inverted images and θ^j signifies the orientation of the templates or the structuring elements.

The minutia points are identified by finding the maximum values of the pixel among the outputs obtained from filtering and the pixel value higher than the threshold is selected as the minutiae, which can be represented as,

$$MP = MP \cup \{(x, y)\} \ if \ \max_{1 \leq j \leq 16} \left[B^j_{ori/inv}(x, y) > thresh \right] \tag{7}$$

Here, $B^j_{ori/inv}(x, y)$ gives the pixel intensity at (x, y) of the jth output of the filtered original or inverted image, MP signifies the minutia points and $thresh$ denotes the threshold value. The minutia points MP are subjected to the DMN for person authentication.

3.1.4   Person Authentication with DMN

The DMN [12] is utilized in the process of fingerprint image matching, where the DMN utilizes the minutiae points MP detected in the previous step for performing authentication. This section details the structure of DMN and the introduced AVAO algorithm, which is employed for adjusting the weights of the DMN.

3.1.4.1 DMN

DMN is employed in the authentication process as they produce superior performance in resource constrained environments. A DMN comprises of numerous maxout layers which are connected successively, where the maxout layers contains hidden units which are partitioned into groups, which do not overlap each other. Each layer uses the maxout function to generate hidden activations and the activation functions generated are trainable. The minutia points are fed as the input to the DMN whose activation functions can be given by,

$$c_{s,t}^1 = \max_{t \in [1,h_1]} MP^T k_{...st} + d_{st} \tag{8}$$

$$c_{s,t}^2 = \max_{t \in [1,h_2]} \left(c_{s,t}^1\right)^T k_{...st} + d_{st} \tag{9}$$

$$\vdots$$

$$c_{s,t}^e = \max_{t \in [1,h_e]} \left(c_{s,t}^{e-1}\right)^T k_{...st} + d_{st} \tag{10}$$

$$\vdots$$

$$c_{s,t}^f = \max_{t \in [1,h_f]} \left(c_{s,t}^{f-1}\right)^T k_{...st} + d_{st} \tag{11}$$

$$b_s = \max_{t \in [1,h_f]} c_{s,t}^f \tag{12}$$

where, h_e denotes the number of hidden units in the eth layer, $k_{...st}$ and d_{st} signifies the weight and the bias of the layer. Morover, f represents the total number of layers in DMN and b_s denote the output of the maxout layer. From the above equations, it can be inferred that a max pooling function is applied and hence the maximum value obtained in each layer is fed to the successive ones. The activation used in the DMN has a high potential and can be used in approximating any random continuous activation function. When the number of hidden units is kept greater than 2, the DMN can efficiently approximate non linear functions too. The structure of DMN is depicted using Fig. 2.

3.1.4.2 Proposed AVAO Algorithm for tTaining DMN
A novel AVAO algorithm is introduced in this paper, which is used in the process of updating the weights of the hidden neurons in the DMN. The introduced AVAO algorithm is created by modifying the strategies of the AVOA [13] with respect to the expanded exploration capability of the AO [14]. The AVOA is a population based algorithm which is inspired by the navigation, foraging behaviors and the lifestyle of African vultures. AVOA is implemented in four steps, such as determination of the best vulture, determination of the starvation rate, exploration and exploitation. AVOA aims at finding the best solution and the second best solution to any complex problems. The algorithm has high flexibility and very low computational complexity. Moreover, the algorithm effectively balances variability as well as resonance. The AO algorithm is developed considering the predatory behaviour of Aquila and is implemented in four phases, such as expanded exploration, narrowed exploration, expanded exploitation and narrowed exploitation. The AO algorithm has a fast convergence rate and can effectively tackle

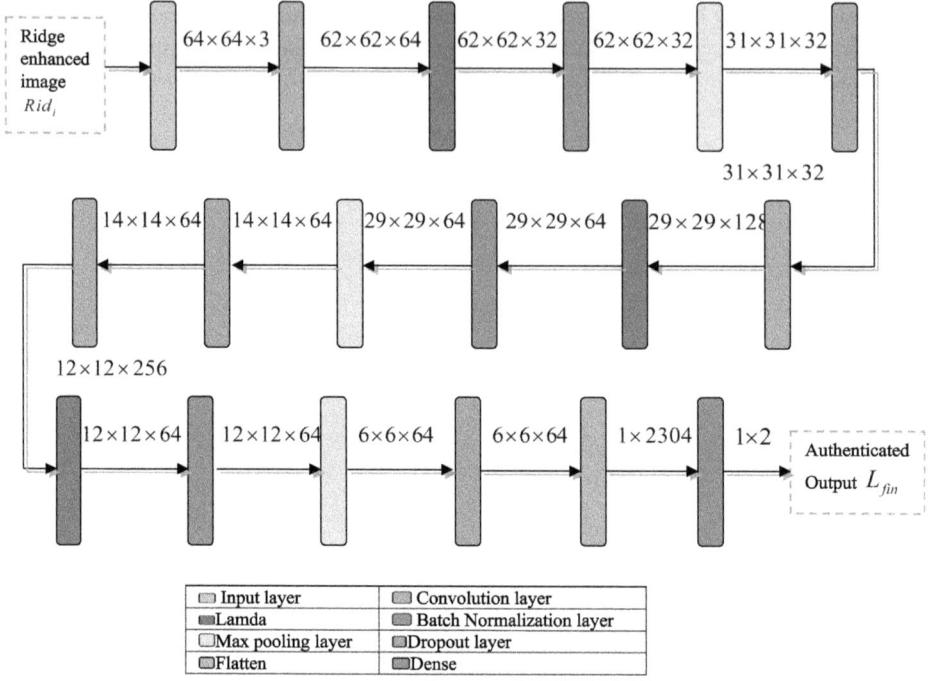

Fig. 2. Structure of DMN

real time applications. The following subsections details the various steps in the proposed AVAO algorithm.

i) *initialization*

Let us assume there are *av* number of vultures. The first step is to initialise the population of vultures in the problem space and can be represented by,

$$V = \{V_1, V_2, ...V_i, ...V_{av}\} \tag{13}$$

where, V_i represents the ith vulture in the population.

ii) *Determine the best vulture*

Once the population is initialised, the best vulture is determined by considering the fitness of all the vultures. The value of fitness is calculated using the following equation.

$$\varepsilon = \frac{1}{n} \sum_{o=1}^{n} [U_o - U_o^*]^2 \tag{14}$$

Here, U_o represents the target output, U_o^* defines the output of the DMN and n designates the overall sample count.

After the fitness is computed, the best vulture of the first group is selected from the group with the best solution and the one with the second best value of fitness is considered the second group's best vulture. The best vultures are determined for every fitness iteration.

$$W(i) = \begin{cases} BestVulture_1, & if \ J_i = K_1 \\ BestVulture_2, & if \ J_i = K_2 \end{cases} \tag{15}$$

Here, K_1 and K_2 are factors that have to be calculated ahead of the search operation and has a value in the range $[0,1]$ and the factors to be computed before the search mechanism with the measures between 0 and 1. The term J_i represents the probability of selecting the best vulture and is calculated using the roulette wheel.

iii) *Determination of starvation rate of vultures*

Vultures normally fly to long distances in search of food when they are full and as a result they have high energy. But in case if they are hungry, they feel shortage of energy of exploring long distances and they become aggressive and seek the food near the powerful vulture. Thus, the rate at which the vulture is starving determines the exploration and exploitation phases and it can be mathematically modelled by using the following equations. The satiated vulture is given by,

$$SR = (2 \times rd_1 + 1) \times w \times \left(1 - \frac{itr_i}{maxitr}\right) + C \tag{16}$$

$$C = D \times \left(Sin^\beta \left(\frac{\pi}{2} \times \frac{itr_i}{maxitr}\right) + Cos\left(\frac{\pi}{2} \times \frac{itr_i}{maxitr}\right) - 1\right) \tag{17}$$

where, *itr* and *maxitr* denote the present iteration count and the overall count of iterations. w, rd_1 and D are arbitrary numbers in the range $[0, 1]$, $[-1, 1]$ and $[-2, 2]$ respectively. Further, β is a parameter, whose value is fixed before the searching process and the probability of exploration enhances with the value of value β. The vultures hunt for food in varied spaces and the algorithm is in exploration phase, if the value of $|SRate| > 1$, otherwise the exploitation phase is encountered.

iv) *Exploration phase*

Vultures have superior eyesight and possess high capability in identifying weak animals, while hunting for food. But, searching food is highly challenging and the vultures have to perform careful scrutiny of their surroundings for a long period over vast distances. Random areas are examined by the usage of two approaches. An arbitrary parameter I_1, which has a value in the range $[0,1]$is utilised to select the approaches. The strategies are selected based on the following equations.

$$R(i + 1) = W(i) - T(i) \times SR \ if \ I_1 \geq rd_I \tag{18}$$

$$R(i + 1) = W(i) - SR + rd_2 \times ((upb - lwb) \times rd_3 + lwb) \ if \ I_1 < rd_I \tag{19}$$

$$T(i) = |Z \times W(i) - R(i)| \tag{20}$$

Here, $R(i + 1)$ denotes the vulture position vector, Z represents the coefficient vector. rd_1, rd_2 and rd_3 are random variable in the range [0, 1]. upb and lwb denote the lower as well as the upper limits of the variable.

Substituting Eq. (20) in Eq. (18),

$$R(i + 1) = W(i) - |Z \times W(i) - R(i)| \times SR \; W(i) > R(i) \tag{21}$$

$$R(i + 1) = W(i) - (Z \times W(i) - R(i)) \times SR \tag{22}$$

$$R(i + 1) = W(i)[1 + Z \times SR] - R(i) \times SR \tag{23}$$

In the AO algorithm, Aquila identifies the position of the prey by exploring by soaring up and then determining the search area. The expanded exploration ability of the Aquila can be given by,

$$H_1(n + 1) = H_{best}(n) \times \left(1 - \frac{n}{N}\right) + (H_r(n) - H_{best}(n) * rnd) \tag{24}$$

$$H_r(n) = \frac{1}{T} \sum_{i=1}^{T} H_i(n) \tag{25}$$

Where,

Assume, $T = 1$.

$$H_1(n + 1) = H_{best}(n) \times \left(1 - \frac{n}{N} - rnd\right) + H(n) \tag{26}$$

$$H_1(n + 1) = R(i + 1). \tag{27}$$

Consider,

$$H(n) = R(i) \tag{28}$$

$$H_{best}(n) = W(i) \tag{29}$$

Substituting Eqs. (27), (28) and (29) in Eq. (26),

$$R(i + 1) = W(i) \times \left(1 - \frac{n}{N} - rnd\right) + R(i) \tag{30}$$

$$R(i) = R(i + 1) - W(i) \times \left(1 - \frac{n}{N} - rnd\right) \tag{31}$$

Substituting Eq. (31) in Eq. (23),

$$R(i + 1) = W(i)[1 + Z \times SR] - R(i + 1) \times SR + W(i) \times \left(1 - \frac{n}{N} - rnd\right) \times SR \tag{32}$$

$$R(i+1) + R(i+1) \times SR = W(i)\left[1 + Z \times SR + \left(1 - \frac{n}{N} - rnd\right) \times SR\right] \quad (33)$$

$$R(i+1)[1+SR] = W(i)\left[1 + \left(Z + \left(1 - \frac{n}{N}\right) - rnd\right) \times SR\right] \quad (34)$$

$$R(i+1) = \frac{W(i)\left[1 + \left(Z + \left(1 - \frac{n}{N}\right) - rnd\right) \times SR\right]}{[1+SR]} \quad (35)$$

Here, N denotes the number of samples.

v) *Exploitation: phase 1*

Exploitation is performed in two phases depending on the value of SR. If the value of $|SR|$ lies between 0.5 and 1, then phase 1 is executed. The first phase comprises of two techniques, such as rotating flight as well as siege-fight. A parameter I_2 is utilised in selecting the strategies, which has to be computed ahead of searching. The parameter is compared to a random variable rd_{I_2} to select the strategies. If $I_2 < rd_{I_2}$, then rotating flight approach is implemented, else siege flight approach is performed.

a) **Contest for food**

The vultures are full and have high energy, if $|SR| \geq 0.5$. When vultures accumulate on a single food source, brutal disputes can occur. The highly powerful vultures wouldn't share the food with the weak vultures, whereas the weak vultures attempt to exhaust the strong vultures by assembling around them and snatching the food leading to conflicts.

$$R(i+1) = P(i) \times (SR + rnd_4) - E(t) \quad (36)$$

$$E(t) = H(i) - W(i) \quad (37)$$

Here, rnd_4 is an arbitrary number in the range $[0, 1]$.

b) **Rotating flight of Vultures**

A rotational flight is made by the vultures for modelling the spiral movement and a spiral motion is formed among the best two vultures and the other vultures and this can be modelled as,

$$P(i+1) = W(i) - (X_1 + X_2) \quad (38)$$

$$X_1 = W(i) \times \left(\frac{rnd_5 \times R(i)}{2\pi}\right) \times \mathrm{Cos}\,(R(i)) \quad (39)$$

$$X_2 = W(i) \times \left(\frac{rnd_6 \times R(i)}{2\pi}\right) \times \mathrm{Sin}\,(R(i)) \quad (40)$$

where, rnd_5 and rnd_6 are arbitrary numbers in the range $[0, 1]$.

vi) *Exploitation: phase 2*

In the second phase, the food source is determined by using the siege and aggressive strife strategy, where, the other vultures aggregate over the food source following the motion of the best vultures. This phase is executed when $|SR| < 0.5$. A parameter I_3 is utilised in selecting the strategies, which has to be computed ahead of searching. The parameter is compared to a random variable rd_{I_3} to select the strategies. If $I_2 < rd_{I_2}$, then the cultures are accumulated over the food source, otherwise aggressive siege-flight strategy is performed.

(i) *Accumulation of vultures over food source*

Here, close examination of the motion of all vultures to the source of food is carried out. When the vultures are hungry, they compete with each other over the food source. This can be represented as,

$$O_1 = BestV_1(i) - \frac{BestV_1(i) \times R(i)}{BestV_1(i) - R(i)^2} \times SR \qquad (41)$$

$$O_2 = BestV_2(i) - \frac{BestV_2(i) \times R(i)}{BestV_2(i) - R(i)^2} \times SR \qquad (42)$$

Here, $BestV_1(i)$ and $BestV_2(i)$ denote the best vultures of the first group and second group. The position of the vulture in the next iteration is given by.

$$R(i+1) = \frac{O_1 + O_2}{2} \qquad (43)$$

(ii) *Aggressive conflicting for food*

The chief vulture becomes famished, when $|SR| < 0.5$, and it becomes too fragile to compete with other vultures, which turn aggressive and move in multiple directions and head to the group head in their search for food. This is modelled as,

$$R(i+1) = W(i) - |E(t)| \times SR \times Levy(E) \qquad (44)$$

Here, $E(t)$ specifies the distance between a vulture and anyone of the best vultures.
Step 8: Termination
    The above steps are kept reiterated till a best solution is achieved. Algorithm 1 depicts the pseudo code of introduced AVAO algorithm.

Pseudo code of devised AVAO algorithm
Initialize the arbitrary population and number of iterations
While **(stopping criteria is not attained)** *do*
Calculate fitness function with Equation (14)
Consider R_{BestV_1} **as the position of first best vulture**
Consider R_{BestV_2} **as the position of second best vulture**
for **(each vulture** $\left(V_i\right)$**)** *do*
Select $W\left(i\right)$ **using Equation (15)**
Update SR **using Equation (16)**
if $\left(\left|SR\right|\geq 1\right)$ then
$if\left(I_1 \geq rd_1\right)$ then
Update the position of vulture using Equation (18)
else
Update the position of vulture using Equation (19)
$if\left(\left|SR\right|<1\right)$ then
$if\left(\left|SR\right|\geq 0.5\right)$ then
$if\left(I_2 \geq rnd_{I_2}\right)$ then
Update the position of vulture using Equation (36)
Else
Update the position of vulture using Equation (38)
Else
$if\left(I_3 \geq rnd_{I_3}\right)$ then
Update the position of vulture using Equation (43)
Else
Renew the location of vulture using Equation (44)
Return P_{BestV_1}
Terminate

The output obtained from the DMN while using the fingerprint image is denoted as L_{fin}.

4   Results and Discussion

The experimental outcomes of the devised AVAO enabled Deep learning based person authentication are elaborated in this section together with the detailed analysis of the devised method.

4.1   Experimental Set up

The innovative AVAO enabled Deep learning approach for the efficient authentication of individual utilising fingerprint is implemented in Python platform on a system with the following specifications: Windows 10 PC, 2GB RAM and Intel i3 core processor.

4.2   Dataset Description

The fingerprint images are collected from the CASIA Fingerprint Image Database Version 5.0 [15]. The database comprises of images acquired from 500 individuals. Eight fingers were considered and a total of 40 images were taken from each individual, thus the database has 20,000 fingerprint images, which are stored as 8-bit gray-level BMP files. These images were taken with the help of URU4000 fingerprint sensors and have a resolution of 328*356.

4.3   Performance Measures

With the usage of the efficiency measures, such as like the accuracy, sensitivity and specificity, the effectiveness of the proposed AVAO enabled Deep learning approach is evaluated. The parameters are detailed in the ensuing subsections.

4.3.1   Accuracy

Accuracy can be defined as the ratio of the modalities successfully classified to the total number of modalities and is represented as,

$$Accuracy = \frac{tp + tn}{tp + tn + fp + fn} \tag{51}$$

where, tp indicate the number of genuine users who are authenticated correctly, tn specifies the number of illegal users classified as such, fp represent the number of non authorized users who are detected as authorized and fn signify the count of authorised users classified as non authentic.

4.3.2   Specificity

Specificity is also known as the True Negative Rate (TNR) and is the ratio of the true negatives to the count of the unauthorized users is expressed as,

$$Specificity = \frac{tn}{tn + fp} \tag{52}$$

4.3.3 Sensitivity

Sensitivity gives the measure of the positiveness of the system and is the ratio of the true positives to the total of the authorized users. It can be found by,

$$Sensitivity = \frac{tp}{tp + fn} \qquad (53)$$

4.4 Experimental Outcomes

In this section, the experimental results of the introduced AVAO enabled deep learning based person authentication method are portrayed. Figure 3 a) depicts the input fingerprint images, 3 b) shows the pre-processed images, Fig. 3c) illustrates the minutiae detection.

The confusion matrix shows the classification of fingerprint dataset. The correctly classified samples percentage is 83.64% and 16.36% samples were misclassified for the population size 5. The performance of the proposed AVAO algorithm using the fingerprint image with different population sizes based on metrics, such as accuracy, specificity and sensitivity and F1-score is discussed in Sect. 4.6 (Fig. 4).

4.5 Comparative Algorithms

The performance of the devised AVAO algorithm in analysed in comparison to the other existing algorithms, such as Sine Cosine Algorithm (SCA) [16] + DMN, Sail Fish Optimization (SFO) [17] + DMN, AO + DMN, AVOA + DMN.

4.6 Algorithmic Analysis

The performance of the proposed AVAO algorithm using the fingerprint image with different population sizes based on metrics, such as accuracy, specificity and sensitivity and F1-score is as follows.

Figure 5 depicts the analysis of the various algorithms using fingerprint images. In Fig. 5 a), the algorithms are evaluate with respect to accuracy for varying population sizes. The existing algorithms, such as SCA + DMN, SFO + DMN, AO + DMN and AVOA + DMN attain an accuracy of 0.887, 0.892, 0.895 and 0.900, while the proposed AVAO + DMN algorithm attained an accuracy of 0.902, with a population size of 5. Thus, an improvement in performance of 1.67%, 1.09%, 0.70% and 0.23% is achieved. Figure 7b) depicts the evaluation while considering specificity. With a population size of 10, the developed AVAO + DMN algorithm calculates specificity of 0.918, but the prevailing SCA + DMN, SFO + DMN, AO + DMN and AVOA + DMN algorithms obtain specificity values at 0.898, 0.900, 0.900 and 0.905. This shows a performance improvement of 2.13%, 1.94%, 1.91% and 1.34% by the proposed algorithm over the existing algorithms. In Fig. 7c), the sensitivity-based analysis of the algorithms is depicted. The values of sensitivity achieved by the existing algorithms, namely SCA + DMN, SFO + DMN, AO + DMN and AVOA + DMN and the proposed AVAO + DMN algorithm is 0.906, 0.908, 0.912, 0.919 and 0.927 respectively for population size = 15. From this it

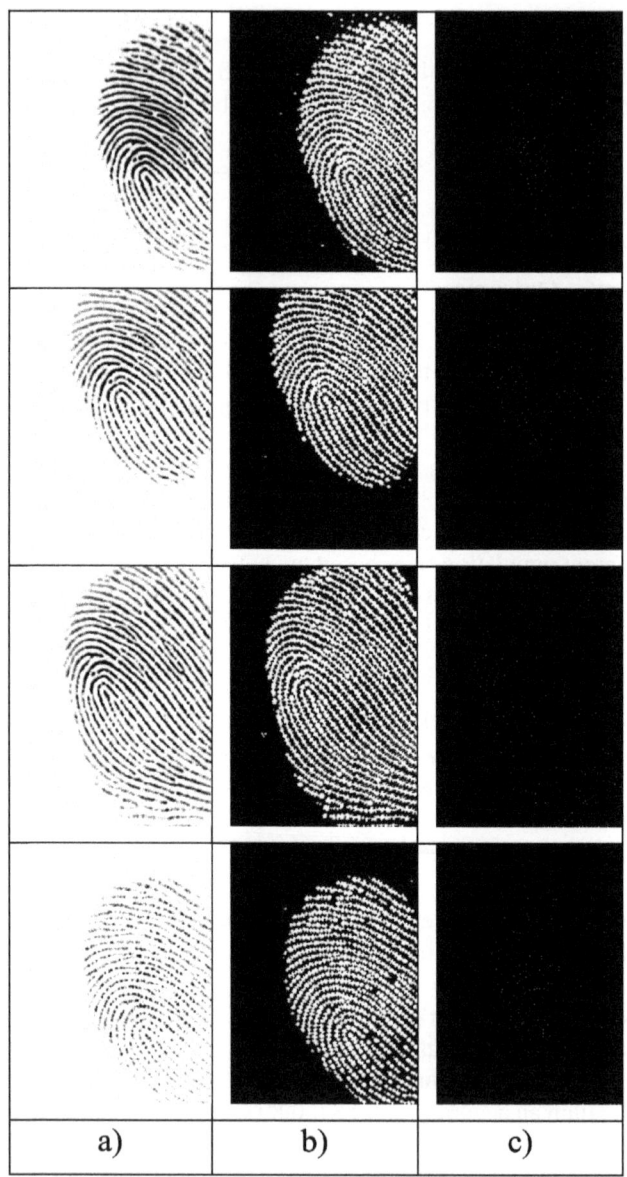

Fig. 3. Experimental results of the introduced AVAO enabled deep learning based person authentication a) input b) pre-processed c) minutiae detected images using fingerprint.

can be inferred that the proposed algorithm produced a higher value of sensitivity than the prevailing methods by 2.22%, 1.95%, 1.52% and 0.83%. Figure 5d) depicts the evaluation while considering F1-score. With a population size of 20, the developed AVAO + DMN algorithm calculates F1-score of 0.912, but the prevailing SCA + DMN, SFO + DMN, AO + DMN and AVOA + DMN algorithms obtain F1-score values at 0.893,

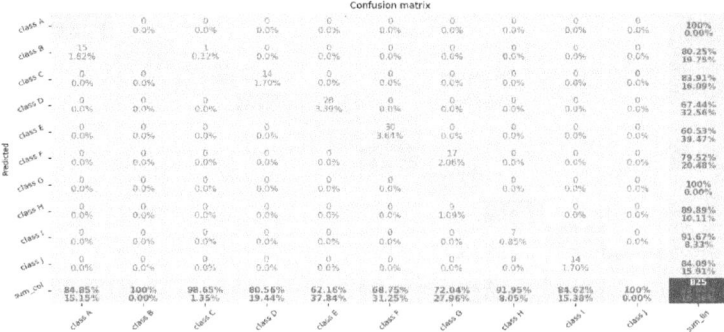

Fig. 4. Confusion Matrix for Fingerprint classification

0.898, 0.904, 0.907 respectively. This shows a performance improvement of 2.12%, 1.6%, 0.8% and 0.5% by the proposed algorithm over the existing algorithms.

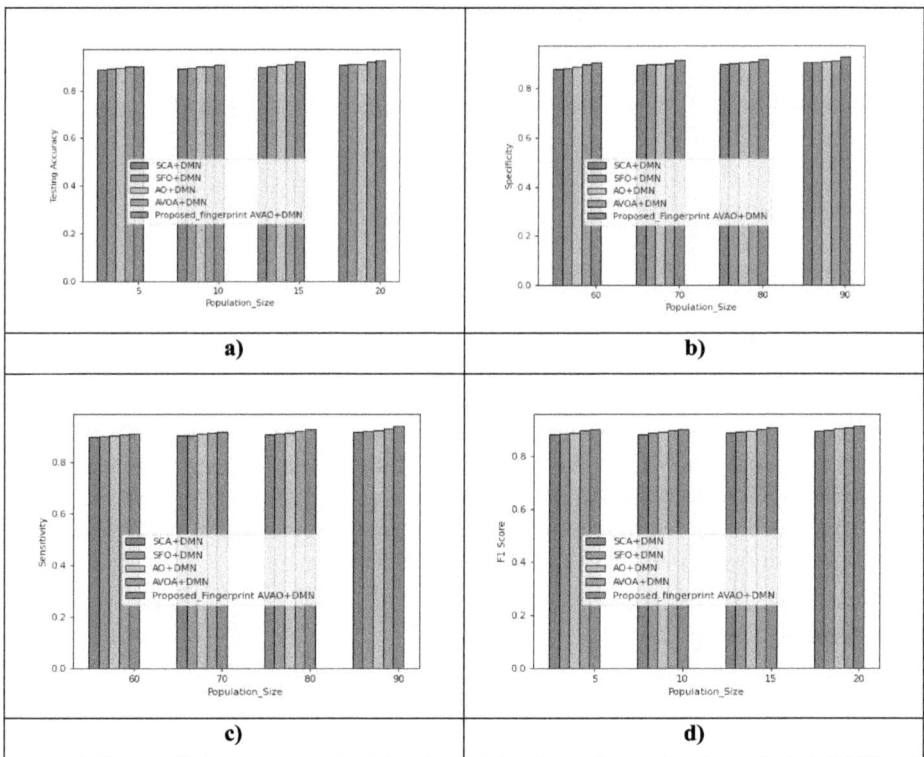

Fig. 5. Algorithmic evaluation using fingerprint image based on a) accuracy b) specificity and c) sensitivity

Table 2. Comparative assessments of the algorithms

Modality	Metrics	SCA + DMN	SFO + DMN	AO + DMN	AVOA + DMN	Proposed AVAO + DMN
Fingerprint image	Accuracy	0.907	0.909	0.910	0.920	0.927
	Specificity	0.906	0.908	0.910	0.915	0.930
	Sensitivity	0.915	0.919	0.921	0.928	0.938
	F1-score	0.836	0.863	0.881	0.890	0.912

4.7 Comparative Discussion

This section deals with the comparison of the developed AVAO optimized person authentication scheme with the prevailing techniques on the basis of various metrics.

Table 1 displays the comparative discussion of the algorithms. The devised AVAO + DMN algorithm is with respect to accuracy, specificity and sensitivity by comparing it with the existing SCA + DMN, SFO + DMN, AO + DMN and AVOA + DMN algorithms. The values of the metrics correspond to the population size of 80 and from the table, the devised AVAO + DMN algorithm is shown to have attained the maximal value of accuracy at 0.927, sensitivity at 0.938, specificity at 0.930 and F1-score at 0.912 (Table 2).

5 Conclusion

In this paper, person authentication scheme is developed by exploiting simplicity of the fingerprint image. A DMN is utilized in authenticating the user based on the fingerprint images using supervised machine learning. The Fingerprint images are pre-processed first, after which the minutia points are identified. Then, person authentication is performed with the DMNs using the detected minutia points and features extracted. A novel AVAO algorithm is devised to generate the optimal weight factor of the DMN, where the AVAO is created by modifying the exploration ability of the African vulture in AVOA in accordance with that of the Aquila in AO. Experimental results show that the devised AVAO optimized deep learning based person authentication achieves a higher accuracy at 0.927, sensitivity at 0.938 and specificity at 0.930.

References

1. Zeynali M, Seyedarabi H., "EEG-based single-channel authentication systems with optimum electrode placement for different mental activities", biomedical journal, vol.42, no.4, pp.261–7, August 2019.
2. Hammad, M., Pławiak, P., Wang, K. and Acharya, U.R., "ResNet-Attention model for human authentication using ECG signals", Expert Systems, vol.38, no.6, pp.12547, 2021.
3. Tarawneh AS, Hassanat AB, Alkafaween EA, Sarayrah B, Mnasri S, Altarawneh GA, Alrashidi M, Alghamdi M, Almuhaimeed A., "DeepKnuckle: Deep Learning for Finger Knuckle Print Recognition", Electronics, vol.11, no.4, pp.513, February 2022.

4. Jomaa RM, Islam MS, Mathkour H, Al-Ahmadi S., "A multilayer system to boost the robustness of fingerprint authentication against presentation attacks by fusion with heart-signal", Journal of King Saud University-Computer and Information Sciences, January 2022.

5. Xuejun Tan∗, Bir Bhanu, "Fingerprint matching by genetic algorithms ", The Journal of The Pattern Recognition Society, Pattern Recognition 39 (2006) 465 – 477.

6. Bouzouina, Y. and Hamami, L.," Multimodal biometric: Iris and face recognition based on feature selection of iris with GA and scores level fusion with SVM", 2nd International Conference on Bio-engineering for Smart Technologies (BioSMART), pp. 1–7,2017

7. Hezil, N. and Boukrouche, A.," Multimodal biometric recognition using human ear and palmprint", IET Biometrics, 6(5), pp. 351–359, 2017

8. Chaudhary, S. ,Nath, R.," A Robust Multimodal Biometric System Integrating Iris , Face and Fingerprint using Multiple SVMs", International Journal of Advanced Research in Computer Science, 7(2), pp. 108–113, 2016

9. Veluchamy, S. , Karlmarx L. R.," System for multimodal biometric recognition based on fi nger knuckle and fi nger vein using feature-level fusion and k-support vector machine classifier", IET Biometrics,6(3), pp. 232–242, 2017

10. Al-Waisy, A. S. et al.," A multimodal biometrie system for personal identification based on deep learning approaches", Seventh International Conference on Emerging Security Technologies (EST). IEEE, pp. 163–168, 2017

11. Ali, Mouad MH, Vivek H. Mahale, Pravin Yannawar, and A. T. Gaikwad. "Fingerprint recognition for person identification and verification based on minutiae matching." In 2016 IEEE 6th international conference on advanced computing (IACC), pp. 332–339. IEEE, 2016.

12. Sun W, Su F, Wang L., "Improving deep neural networks with multi-layer max out networks and a novel initialization method", Neuro computing, vol.278, pp.34-40, February 2018.

13. Abdollahzadeh B, Gharehchopogh FS, Mirjalili S., "African vultures optimization algorithm: A new nature-inspired metaheuristic algorithm for global optimization problems", Computers & Industrial Engineering, vol.158, pp.107408, August 2021.

14. Abualigah L, Yousri D, Abd Elaziz M, Ewees AA, Al-qaness MA, Gandomi AH., "Aquila Optimizer: A novel meta-heuristic optimization Algorithm", Computers & Industrial Engineering, vol.157, pp.107250, July 2021

15. CASIA Fingerprint Image Database available at "https://mla.sdu.edu.cn/info/1006/1195.html"

16. Mirjalili, S., "SCA: a sine cosine algorithm for solving optimization problems," Knowledge-based systems, vol.96, pp.120-133, 2016.

17. Shadravan, S., Naji, H.R. and Bardsiri, V.K., "The Sailfish Optimizer: A novel nature-inspired metaheuristic algorithm for solving constrained engineering optimization problems", Engineering Applications of Artificial Intelligence, vol.80, pp.20-34, 2019.

Tesseract OCR Recognition Based on Arabic Machine-Printed Document

Rakesh Ramteke[✉] and Mohammed Rashed Ali Omar Al Maamari

School of Computational Sciences, Kavayitri Bahinabai Chaudhary North Maharashtra University, Jalgaon, (MS), India
rakeshj.ramteke@gmail.com

Abstract. This paper provides technical aspects and the context of Recognizing and Detecting Arabic characters using Tesseract OCR Engine. OCR engine is freely available and gives a better result and also is supporting many languages such as Arabic etc. The procedure begins by transforming the Arabic documents into machine format (scanning) and then recognizing as well as extracting the text using the PyTesseract library. The OCR is a system that can afford the considerable values of split errors, particularly while working with cursive languages like the Arabic language with repeated overlapping between letters. Moreover, The performance is 99.5 accuracy in OCR-tesseract for converting the Arabic image documents to text editable.

Keywords: PyTesseract · OCR · Arabic · Recognizing · Detecting

1 Introduction

The Arabic language includes 28 letters and it is written differently from other languages such as English, and Hindi these languages can writhe from left to right but the Arabic language is totally different because it's written from right to left. There are many languages that depend on Arabic letters to write those languages such as Jawi, Urdu, and Persian. There are more than 26 nation whose formal language is Arabic and there are more than 280 million people speaks this language this makes the Arabic language so famous and used in the world. Each character has a different written format there are 5 letters from 28 letters written in two formats and the other 23 letters are having four formats(Initial, Middle, Isolate, End) [1]. OCR is a way to recognize the image text that is in a machine document format and transfer it into a machine-readable form to be used for data processing. The OCR system is improved its performance and started to be provided as a software package [2]. Python is the engine that used the PyTesseract library and it is one of the important libraries that are used for Arabic OCR, python is open source and it's easy to implement all the python libraries. Tesseract-OCR Engine is also used to detect the text in images such as line, word and character detection [3]. The optical character recognition to converts the images to the text editable with the.txt extension, then edit.py file is created to be compared between the predicate text and the truth text to check the accuracy of Tesseract OCR for recognizing the characters, that

R. Manza et al. (Eds.): ACVAIT 2022, AISR 176, pp. 347–355, 2023.
https://doi.org/10.2991/978-94-6463-196-8_27

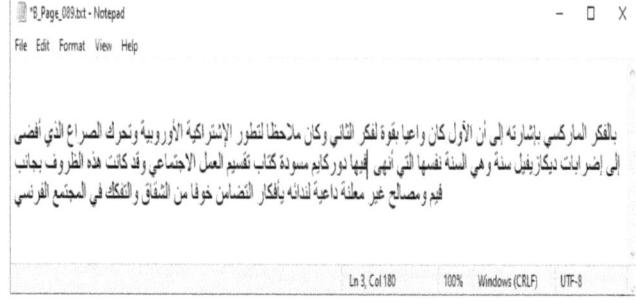

Fig. 1. (Output text)

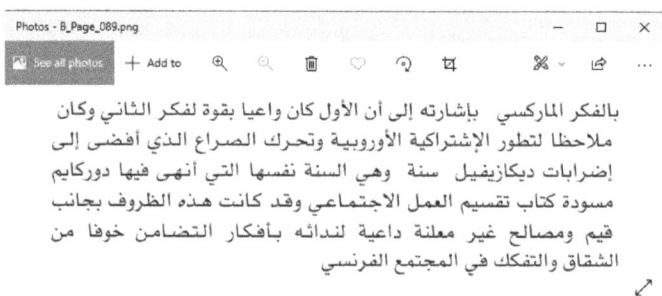

Fig. 2. (Image text)

run the edit.py file by cmd command to check the accuracy and how many characters are recognized wrong and it will account the error of recognizing and issuing the final accuracy the performance of the accuracy is 99.58% accuracy. OCR tesseract is also used in many languages such as English, Hindi, etc., just need to define the language that wants to use it in the OCR engine.

Figures 1 and 2 are the optical character recognition OCR firstly, input the text image that needs to convert to the text editable secondly, make some preprocessing methods as Noise Removal, Skew Correction, Image Resize, Grayscale conversion, Binarization then process it in pytesseract OCR engine to get the accurate text editable output with the .txt extension.

2   Literature Review

This paper, to the best of the authors' knowledge, is the first work in Arabic printed text OCR investigating a novel way to extract word features in the Block-based DCT (BDCT) domain. This is based on using a Discrete one-dimensional Hidden Markov (Bakis) Model (1D-HMM). The results in this area achieved on average 97.65% accuracy [4]. In this paper, the Tesseract engine is analyzed and modified for the recognition of the Urdu language which is a very difficult and cursive writing style of Arabic script. Original Tesseract system has 65.59% and 65.84% accuracies for 14 and 16 font sizes respectively, whereas the modified system, with reduced search space, gives 97.87%

and 97.71% accuracies respectively [5]. In this paper, they had created another OCR approach that depends on HMM for recognition. In their model, a tri-gram model of the character series is implemented. The process achieves a high accuracy rate between 98.9 and 97.71% [6]. In this paper, The system is used on actual printed word images with no overlap between the training and testing datasets. Word advantage vectors are extracted using block-based DCT. A Hidden Markov Models Toolkit (HTK) is used to build the recognizer. Author used Vector Quantization to map every feature vector to the closest symbol in the codebook. The result of the system is various recognition hypotheses (N-best word lattice). The output is hopeful when compared with other published research in this area achieving on average 97.65% accuracy which is significantly higher than previously published results [7]. In this paper, The systems are classified into two groups depending on the operating system MFR and REGIM-LITIS, SP-Curvelet-FR, RDI-CU, GU Font Recognition systems are built under Microsoft Windows environment and MindGarage systems under Linux. They tried to recognize the font size without recognizing the font or the content of the word image. The MindGarage system shows better results with a medium of 99.67% font-size identification rate. The REGIM-LITIS and RDI-CU systems show better results in some tests. The font-size identification rates with the Arabic word images created with bold font, font size 18 are respectively 99.98% and 94.96% with REGIM-LITIS and RDI-CU systems [8]. In this paper, they used rescaling and tesseract OCR to perform accurate Arabic handwritten character recognition. Moreover, used the long short term memory (LSTM) to get better accuracy in Arabic recognition and they got 52% accuracy in Arabic handwritten characters [1]. In this paper, they presented deep learning in OCR techniques to read and recognize text from the tax card image. Moreover, used a convolutional neural network in OCR(Tesseract) model that extracts the features from the tax image card. The score of the CNN-based OCR(Tesseract) model is 80% accuracy [16].

3 Methodology

A. Image preprocessing
The preprocessing step is the second step which is very important in any image detection and recognition system. The objective of this step in handwritten and machine-printed text recognition is to improve and enhance the readability of the text image and remove unnecessary details from it. The preprocessing steps usually include various operations like Image Resize, Grayscale Conversion, Correction Skew, Baseline Detection, and Noise Removal. The system can apply one or more from the preprocessing operations. It can also pass this stage without applying any of the operations if the input data are previously preprocessed [9].

- Grayscale conversion
  The colored image in this step is converted to a grayscale image. So, instead of working with a three-channel image, we can work only with a one-channel image. Color to grayscale conversion algorithm is required to preserve the salient features of the color images, like contrast, brightness and structure of the color images [10].
- Binarization

It is also called thresholding which is the operation of converting a text image into a binary format. Moreover, it is called a black and white image. The values of background pixels are 0 for black and 1 for white, this operation improves processing speed. There are many methods used in image binarization like the fixed threshold method, mean value threshold method and Otsu method [9].

- Image Resize
  The image for the best performance. It is maximum recommended for small images. The scaling property is used to scale the image. It is used to resize. The Tesseract OCR Engine works fully on images with a size of 150, 300 or 600 dpi. The image resize can play well in the image accuracy because the shape of the image helps to recognize the words well [11].
- Noise Removal
  Most of the data acquisition process get affected by noise, so for that most of the data get affected and there is no solution better than process remove noise. There are many ways used to remove image noise and perform smoothing like filtering and morphological operations [9].
- Skew Correction
  Skew correction and text line extraction are the main steps for tesseract OCR applications. For this objective, many access was developed, which conduct the analysis firstly in document images. Text lines in document images are often not aligned with the predictable direction, they are skewed. However, many text lines analysis processes and OCR engines require to skew corrected documents images and credible text line extraction for achieving perfect tesseract OCR performance [12].

B. Image detection and recognition

Image Detection and Recognition is a classic machine learning and Deep learning problem. It is a challenging job to detect an object or to recognize a documents image from a digital image [12]. Tesseract OCR performs in two different steps: recognition and detection. Firstly, we detect rectangular regions in the image potentially containing text. The detect can apply for line detect, word detect and character detect. Secondly, text recognition is performed to extract the text from document images and we can extract and recognize the text in images [12].

C. PyTesseract

OCR_PyTesseract is an optical character recognition engine with open source code, OCR_Tesseract is a more popular and specific OCR library. OCR_Tesseract engine was primarily developed at Hewlett Packard in 1984 to 1994, with many changes made in 1996 to transfer to Windows system. it appeared from nowhere for the 1995 UNLV yearly test of Optical character recognition (OCR) Accuracy, rise brightly with its results, and then vanished back under the gown of secrecy under which it had been developed. It suggested as well as demonstrated that Optical character recognition optical character recognition engines can feature from the use of an adaptive classifier. When the static classifier has to be perfect at generalizing to any form of font, its ability to recognize between various letters or between characters and non-characters is weakened [13]. Tesseract is finding templates in pixels, letters, words and sentences. It uses a two step process that calls adaptive recognition, It requires one data phase for character recognition, then the second phase was to realize any letters, it wasn't covered, by letters that can identify the word or sentence context.

D. Working of Tesseract

pytesseract OCR works in a step by step method, First phase is Adaptive Thresholding which converts the image into binary image form. The next phase is connected component analysis which is used to extract character boundaries. This operation is most useful because it does the OCR of images with text and black background. Tesseract was probable the first, to provide this kind of processing. Then, the outlines are converted into Blobs. Blobs are orderly into text lines, and the lines and regions are analyzed for some fixed area or equal text size. Text is split into words using specific spaces and fuzzy spaces. Recognition of text is started as two-pass. An image with the text is given as input to the Tesseract engine that is a command based tool, Then it is treated by the Tesseract command. Tesseract command takes two cases: The first case is the image file name that contains text and the second case is the output text file in which, the extracted text is stored. The output file extension is given as txt by Tesseract, so it is not required to assign the file extension while assigning the output [14].

Figure 3 is showing the whole work in Arabic Document Recognition and Detection using pytesseract ocr the process is starting to convert the worK as two methods: Detection, Recognition. The detection is starting to use some methods like Thresholding is using to converts the color and grayScale image to binary image simply to black and white form to be easy to use and, and is combined three types of detection in this work like line, word and character will detect all and draw a rectangle for each char in the image. Finally, it recognizes the image text and it will be divided into three: line, word and char for recognition of every char in the image and give accurate output text using pytesseract ocr. Then edit.py file is created to be compared between the predicate text and the truth text to check the accuracy of Tesseract OCR for recognizing the characters

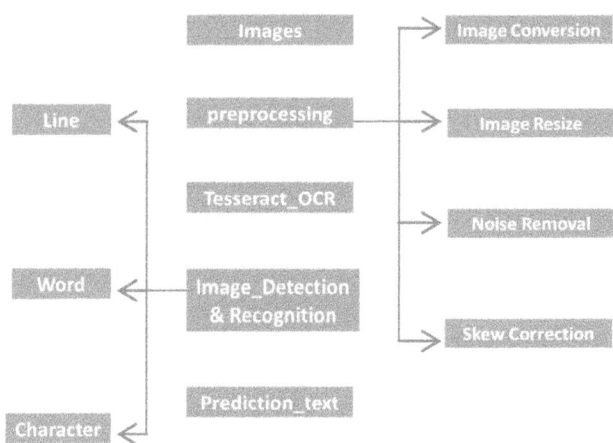

Fig. 3. METHODOLOGY

Table 1. Results And Discussion

No in references	Authors Names	Methodology and Adoptive	Accuracy
4	Krayem, A., Sherkat, N., Evett, L., & Osman, T.	HMM and block-based DCT	97.65%
5	Hussain, S., Niazi, A., Anjum, U., & Irfan, F.	Tesseract engine	97.71%
7	Nashwan, F., Rashwan, M. A., Al-Barhamtoshy, H. M., Abdou, S. M., & Moussa, A. M	Hidden Markov Models (HMM)	97.65%
16	Prawiro, T. G., & Khasanah, A.	Tesseract OCR Based on Long Short Term Memory	52%
17	Uddin, Q.	CNN-based OCR(Tesseract) model	80%
	Proposed method	Preproceesing method,Tesseract engine and cnn model	99.58

then run the edit.py file by cmd command to check the accuracy and how many characters are recognized wrong and it will account the error of recognizing and issuing the final accuracy (Table 1).

4   Results and Discussion

E. Arabic language with pytesseract-OCR

Arabic letter shape is context-sensitive, some Arabic letters have up to four different shapes depending on their relative position in the word, This fact increases the number of classes to be recognized by the OCR Engine. The Arabic language character consists of 28 letters and is written from right to left in cursive. Arabic letters are used to write various languages like Urdu, Persian, and Jawi. Arabic is the official language of more than 26 countries and it is spoken by 280 million people worldwide. Every Arabic letter has two or four shapes depending on its location in the text [1] Arabic writing dots are very important and they are not few as fifteen letters out of twenty-eight have dots above or below them. Arabic writers do not place these dots carefully in their proper place and this leads to much confusion. The Arabic letters are 28 letters that one of the issues is faced in this work and every letter has two or four forms the number f letters with four forms is 22 letters Fig(c), and with two letters are 6 letters Fig(d) (Table 2).

As shown in Table 3 is the letter of ' ب ' is one of the 22 letters with four forms and the letter is written in the start, mid, end and isolated in every form is written differently that making the Arabic OCR is difficult.

As shown in Table 4 is the letter of ' ا ' is one of the 5 letters with two forms and the letter is written in the Initial/isolate same the form and in the mid/end is written same the form.

Table 2. The Arabic letters

No	Characters	Initial	Middle	Isolate	End
1	Alif			ا	ـا
2	Baa	ﺑ	ـبـ	ب	ـب
3	Taa	ﺗ	ـتـ	ت	ـت
4	Thaa	ﺛ	ـثـ	ث	ـث
5	Jiim	ﺟ	ـجـ	ج	ـج
6	Haa	ﺣ	ـحـ	ح	ـح
7	Khaa	ﺧ	ـخـ	خ	ـخ
8	Daal			د	ـد
9	Dhaal			ذ	ـذ
10	Raa			ر	ـر
11	Zaay			ز	ـز
12	Siin	ﺳ	ـسـ	س	ـس
13	Shiin	ﺷ	ـشـ	ش	ـش
14	Saad	ﺻ	ـصـ	ص	ـص
15	Daad	ﺿ	ـضـ	ض	ـض
16	Taa	ﻃ	ـطـ	ط	ـط
17	Zaa	ﻇ	ـظـ	ظ	ـظ
18	Eayn	ﻋ	ـعـ	ع	ـع
19	Ghayn	ﻏ	ـغـ	غ	ـغ
20	Faa	ﻓ	ـفـ	ف	ـف
21	Qaaf	ﻗ	ـقـ	ق	ـق
22	Kaaf	ﻛ	ـكـ	ك	ـك
23	Laam	ﻟ	ـلـ	ل	ـل
24	Miim	ﻣ	ـمـ	م	ـم
25	Nuun	ﻧ	ـنـ	ن	ـن
26	Haa	ﻫ	ـهـ	ه	ـه
27	Waaw			و	ـو
28	Yaa	ﻳ	ـيـ	ي	ـي

Table 3. Letters with four forms

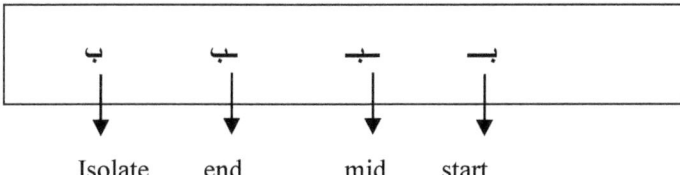

Isolate   end   mid   start

There are three types of the letter with dots in Arabic letters are characters with one dot, two dots, three dots As shown in Table 5.

Table 4. Letters with two forms

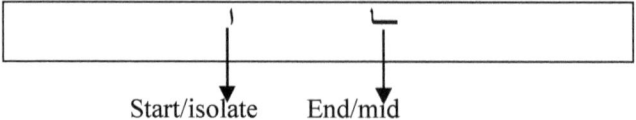

Start/isolate   End/mid

Table 5. Letters with dotst form

Type	Characters
One dot	ن ف غ ظ ض ز ذ خ ج ب
Two dots	ي ق ت
Three dots	ش ث

5 Conclusion

Firstly, Tesseract OCR is used in the Arabic language to convert the document images to the text editable. Secondly, we applied to preprocess techniques to convert the colour image to grayscale colour then image resize or reshape, remove the noises and skew detection. Thirdly, we applied the tesseract OCR to detection the line, word, character from the image and make a rectangle for each line, word and character. Moreover, The performance is a 99.5 accuracy in OCR tesseract for converting the Arabic image documents to text editable.

References

1. Prawiro, T. G., & Khasanah, A. (2020). The Effect of Rescaling on the Performance of Recognition with Arabic Characters Using Tesseract OCR Based on Long Short Term Memory. Journal of Advances in Information Systems and Technology, 2(2), 59-62.
2. Ko, D., Lee, C., Han, D., Ohk, H., Kang, K., & Han, S. (2018). Approach for Machine-Printed Arabic Character Recognition: the-state-of-the-art deep-learning method. Electronic Imaging, 2018(2), 176-1
3. Jayoma, J. M., Moyon, E. S., & Morales, E. M. O. (2020, December). OCR Based Document Archiving and Indexing Using PyTesseract: A Record Management System for DSWD Caraga, Philippines. In 2020 IEEE 12th International Conference on Humanoid, Nanotechnology, Information Technology, Communication and Control, Environment, and Management (HNICEM) (pp. 1–6). IEEE.
4. Krayem, A., Sherkat, N., Evett, L., & Osman, T. (2013, August). Holistic Arabic whole word recognition using HMM and block-based DCT. In 2013 12th International Conference on Document Analysis and Recognition (pp. 1120–1124). IEEE.
5. Hussain, S., Niazi, A., Anjum, U., & Irfan, F. (2014, April). Adapting Tesseract for complex scripts: an example for Urdu Nastalique. In 2014 11th IAPR International Workshop on Document Analysis Systems (pp. 191–195). IEEE.
6. Alkhateeb, F., Doush, I. A., & Albsoul, A. (2017). Arabic optical character recognition software: A review. Pattern Recognition and Image Analysis, 27(4), 763-776.

7. Nashwan, F., Rashwan, M. A., Al-Barhamtoshy, H. M., Abdou, S. M., & Moussa, A. M. (2018). A holistic technique for an Arabic OCR system. Journal of Imaging, 4(1), 6.
8. Slimane, F., Ingold, R., & Hennebert, J. (2017, November). ICDAR2017 Competition on Multi-Font and Multi-Size Digitally Represented Arabic Text. In 2017 14th IAPR International Conference on Document Analysis and Recognition (ICDAR) (Vol. 1, pp. 1466–1472). IEEE.
9. Balaha, H. M., Ali, H. A., & Badawy, M. (2021). Automatic recognition of handwritten Arabic characters: a comprehensive review. Neural Computing and Applications, 33(7), 3011-3034.
10. Güneş, A., Kalkan, H., & Durmuş, E. (2016). Optimizing the color-to-grayscale conversion for image classification. Signal, Image and Video Processing, 10(5), 853-860.
11. Malathi, T., Selvamuthukumaran, D., Chandar, C. D., Niranjan, V., & Swashthika, A. K. (2021, February). An Experimental Performance Analysis on Robotics Process Automation (RPA) With Open Source OCR Engines: Microsoft Ocr And Google Tesseract OCR. In IOP Conference Series: Materials Science and Engineering (Vol. 1059, No. 1, p. 012004). IOP Publishing.
12. Li, W., Breier, M., & Merhof, D. (2015, September). Skew correction and line extraction in binarized printed text images. In 2015 IEEE International Conference on Image Processing (ICIP) (pp. 472–476). IEEE.
13. Chauhan, R., Ghanshala, K. K., & Joshi, R. C. (2018, December). Convolutional neural network (CNN) for image detection and recognition. In 2018 First International Conference on Secure Cyber Computing and Communication (ICSCCC) (pp. 278–282). IEEE.
14. Borisyuk, F., Gordo, A., & Sivakumar, V. (2018, July). Rosetta: Large scale system for text detection and recognition in images. In Proceedings of the 24th ACM SIGKDD International Conference on Knowledge Discovery & Data Mining (pp. 71–79).
15. Smith, R. (2007, September). An overview of the Tesseract OCR engine. In Ninth international conference on document analysis and recognition (ICDAR 2007) (Vol. 2, pp. 629–633). IEEE.
16. Uddin, Q. (2021). Features Extraction of Tax Card by Using OCR Based DeepLearning Techniques (Master's thesis, Itä-Suomen yliopisto).

Design and Generation of Devanagari Script CAPTCHA: Imaginative Technique

Sanjay E. Pate and R. J. Ramteke[✉]

School of Computational Sciences, Kaviyatri Bahinabai Chaudhary North Maharashtra
University, Jalgaon, MS, India
rakeshj.ramteke@gmail.com

Abstract. CAPTCHA (Completely Automated Public Turing Tests to Tell Computers and Humans Apart). Only humans can pass this test, but existing computer systems cannot. It's used in a variety of machine and human identification applications. The most common type of CAPTCHA used on websites is text-based. This protected CAPTCHA script is largely made up of English letters, making it difficult for rural people who only speak their local languages to pass the test. Devanagari characters feature more sophisticated characters than typical English characters and numeral-based CAPTCHAs, considerably increasing the challenge of machine recognition. In India, most government websites present information in the Devanagari language. However, Devanagari CAPTCHAs are not utilized on websites. Therefore, we have designed a new Devanagari script text-based CAPTCHA in this article. There are 33 different varieties of Devanagari CAPTCHA images, of varying lengths (5 to 7), generated using printed and hand-written Devanagari characters and numeral combinations. Using digital image processing techniques, general rules for CAPTCHA generation are utilized to introduce noise to the CAPTCHA image so that it is not recognized or broken. The generation of a single CAPTCHA image requires 1.08 ms and 8 KB of storage. A dataset of 1,10,000 (one million and ten thousand) CAPTCHA images was created, requiring storage of 964 MB.

Keywords: CAPTCHA · Devanagari · BOTs

1 Introduction

Information security is now a key issue around the world. End-users of the Internet improved gradually. General uses of the Internet include searching, e-mail, social networking, e-banking, e-governance, etc.

Internet users have gradually improved. The Internet is generally used for things like searching, email, social networking, e-banking, and e-governance.

Universally, security and authentication are key issues. We are familiar with hackers on the internet who are ready to acquire our valuable information through bots, spammers, and dictionary attacks while operating online accounts, which creates serious issues?

R. Manza et al. (Eds.): ACVAIT 2022, AISR 176, pp. 356–381, 2023.
https://doi.org/10.2991/978-94-6463-196-8_28

Bots and spammers are heavily automated programs that create online accounts without any permission, which unnecessarily increases the damaged space. Resolution is the use of CAPTCHA.

CAPTCHA is a completely automated public Turing test to tell computers and humans apart [21]. Louis Von Ahn et al. proposed CAPTCHA in 2003. CAPTCHA protects websites and online free services (banking, etc.) against bots.

A CAPTCHA is made up of a series of alphabets or numbers that are linked together in a certain order. Random lines, blocks, grids, rotations, and other sorts of noise have been used to distort this image. A human being will have minimal trouble recognizing the set of characters. Computers, on the other hand, should ideally reject this test.

CAPTCHAs are a type of Human Interaction Proof (HIP). This process involves one computer asking a user to complete a test. The CAPTCHA test normally consists of alphabetic characters, numerals, images, or audio. Any user entering a correct response is accepted as a human, and any user who fails to enter the correct response is determined as a robot [21]. If a user fails the test, they will be refused access to the website. English characters and digit-based CAPTCHAs are often used in many applications. In this paper, we have designed a Devanagari CAPTCHA. It's a new Imaginative technique.

The following is how the rest of the paper is organized: The Study of Devanagari Script, a Literature Review on the Different Types of CAPTCHA, a Review of non-English language CAPTCHA research papers, and a review of CAPTCHA generation papers are covered in Sect. 2. Section 3: Devanagari Printed and Handwritten Alphabet and Digit Character Set, Classes of Character Set, Image Processing Techniques Used for Design, CAPTCHA Generation Guidelines, Algorithm for CAPTCHA Generation, and Flow Chart for CAPTCHA Creation are all described in Sect. 3. Section 4 discusses the hardware and software requirements for implementation. Section 5 covers the results and data set, and Sect. 6 closes the paper with a conclusion and future implications.

2 Previous Research Work

2.1 Study of Devanagari Script

The Devanagari script is the foundation of various Indian languages, including Hindi, Sanskrit, Konkani, Marathi, Nepali, Sanskrit, Dogri, Mathili, and Sindhi, among others. Devanagari is a phonetic script that originated from Ancient Brahmi. It links the sounds of alphabets to specific shapes. Except for Urdu, all of these languages are written from left to right. According to data from the year 2022, the Devanagari Hindi script is spoken by over 342 million people worldwide and ranks third among the top 45 languages [20].

Characteristics of the Devanagari Script
There are approximately 11 vowels and 33 consonants in the Devanagari script. The Devanagari script has no upper-or lower-case letters and is written from left to right. A horizontal line connecting the tops of the characters in a word is frequently used to identify it as "Shiro-Rekha". However, not all of the characters are connected in some

way. The difficulty in handwritten recognition is primarily due to the wide range of individual writing styles.

Devanagari CAPTCHA's Importance

The government of India launched the "Digital India" campaign on July 1, 2015, to make government services available to residents electronically, develop digital infrastructure to empower rural areas, notably Indian farmers, and promote digital literacy. The National Agricultural Market (e-Nam) is India's online agricultural commodity trading platform. The Indian government's goal is to build high-speed internet networks in rural areas [13].

The content of most Indian government websites is available in Devanagari script languages such as Hindi, Marathi, Haryanvi, and Gujarathi [11].

However, to protect its contents from being misused by unauthorized computer bots, the user is required to complete a CAPTCHA test. This protected CAPTCHA script is largely made up of English letters, making it difficult for rural people who only speak their local languages to pass the test. As a result, to improve the website's usability and provide easy access to native users, the CAPTCHA test must be designed in their languages, which are based on the Devanagari script [1].

2.2 Types of CAPTCHA

1. Text-based 2. Image-based 3. Audio-based 4. Video-based [11].

1. Text-based CAPTCHA:

It is the most popular type. Background color and distortion and font style are different so that is not recognized by OCR.

Properties of text-based CAPTCHA are a. Font b. Character set c. Distortion d. Tilting e. Waving.

Example: ReCAPTCHA, Gimpy, EZ-Gimpy, Bongo, MSN Captcha, Baffle Text, etc. [11] (Table 1).

2. Image-based CAPTCHA: Require users to identify labeled images or rotated images (Table 2).

3. Audio-based CAPTCHA (Table 3):

4. Video-based CAPTCHA (Table 4):

CAPTCHA methods are divided into two groups:

1. OCR based: The user is shown with a distorted representation of the word and asked to type it in. Words can be recognized and detected by a human user.

Example: Hotmail, Gimpy, Paypal, Persian/Arabic, EZ-Gimpy, Pessimal Print, Scatter type, MSN, Baffle text.

2. Non-OCR based:

i. Visual Non-OCR based: PIX, Single Click Captcha, Collage Captcha, ASIRAA

Table 1. Text-based CAPTCHA

ReCAPTCHA: The reCAPTCHA service asks users to complete on-screen words shown in distorted text pictures and click on "I'm Not a Robot" using the CAPTCHA interface.[11]	
Gimpy: Instead of using automated technologies, Gimpy is founded on the idea that individuals read damaged and corrupted words. It functions by choosing words from a dictionary and showing them to the user in a distorted and corrupted visual form. The user is then prompted to type the words they saw on the screen. works in conjunction with Yahoo.[11]	
EZ-Gimpy: Instead of automated programs that operate by selecting a single word from a dictionary and then making it appear in a corrupted and distorted image format before asking the user to type the term presented in the distorted image format, EZGimpy CAPTCHA bases its operation on the idea that humans can read distorted, textured backgrounds and overwhelmed text.[11]	
Bongo: Bongo is a CAPTCHA designed to address the problem of visual pattern recognition in humans. It displays two separate block series (left and right). The	
user is tasked with identifying the feature that indicates the difference between two blocks. [11]	
MSN -CAPTCHA: Eight (upper case) characters and digits are used. Dark blue makes up the foreground, while grey makes up the background. It i s employed to produce the ripple effect and bend the characters. [11]	
Baffle -Text: At California University in Berkeley, Henry Baird creates the design. It is an altered form of Gimpy. In the Case of Baffle text, alphabets or characters are chosen at ra ndom and combined to create a pronounceable text. After that, the user is prompted to type the right term .[11]	

Table 2. Image-based CAPTCHA

ESP-Pix: created by the reCAPTCHA team and Luis von Ahn. Four warped photos were shown to the user, and they were asked to identify them. [11]	
PIX: It is an application that has a large database of photos that have been indexed and annotated. These photos are photographs of real-life objects (a person, an animal, a flower, etc.) that have been distorted and then introduced to the viewer, followed by a question "What type of images do you have here? or identify which object is included in these images."[11]	
Asirra: It requests that the user clicks on a random image of any chosen random object from the image database.[11]	

Table 3. Audio-based CAPTCHA

Nancy Chan created the first audio-based CAPTCHA as a substitute for text-based CAPTCHAs for those with visual impairments. [11]	

ii. Non-Visual method: Audio-based Captcha.

Advantages and Disadvantages of CAPTCHA Techniques
See Table 5.

2.3 Review of Non-English Language Captcha Research Papers

1. M. Hassan Shirali-Shahreza and Mohammad Shirali-Shahreza proposed a "Multilingual CAPTCHA". The proposed scheme is to recognizer and selects the correct image

Table 4. Video-based CAPTCHA

NuCAPTCHA is a ground-breaking CAPTCHA system that uses video to verify that users are real people and not automated programs.	

Table 5. Merits and Demerits of CAPTCHA techniques

S. No	Type of CAPTCHA	Advantages	Disadvantages
1	Text-based CAPTCHA	1. Implementation is easy. 2. Baffle Text-based CAPTCHA is used to defeat dictionary attacks. 3. Re-CAPTCHA uses new words in the dictionary that cannot be read by OCR.	1. The user has some problem identifying the correct text or characters i. Multiple fonts. ii. Font size. Iii. Blurred Letters iv. Wave Motion [11]. 2. OCR methods can Readily identify it.
2	Images-based CAPTCHA	1. Increases Security than text-based CAPTCHA. 2. An easy system based on clicks, so no need to type. 3. Image recognition pattern is a challenging AI program.	The problem of image identification for those who have low vision or are due to the blurring of images [11].
3	Audio-based CAPTCHA	1. It is used for people that have a visual impairment. 2. Friendly to people.	1. Language support 2. The character that has a similar sound.
4	Video-based CAPTCHA	1. Using OCR (Optical Character Recognition) it cannot crack. 2. Provides greater security.	Because of the big size of the file, users have trouble downloading video and finding the right CAPTCHA
5	Puzzle based CAPTCHA	1. It appears to be enjoyable. 2. It helps monitor the brain of the user.	The job is not simple for users because it takes longer to fix the puzzle-based CAPTCHA.

from among some other images displayed in a grid. Here user interfaces messages "To identify <object name>" are displayed in the user's native language so-called Multilingual. In this method, the user selected his native language than the message shown in the selected language. This strategy can effectively fend off computerized attacks since there are two steps (identification of the object and discovering the object), neither of which can be performed correctly by a bot or spammer. On the other side, as all messages are displayed in their native language, users can operate with this technique readily. This approach was implemented using PHP language. No keyboard is needed. It is like an implicit captcha. This method can also implement on other devices such as mobile phones, PDA (Personal Digital Assistant), and the devices which have touch screens [2].

2. M.Hussn Shirali-Shahreza (2008) proposed "Advanced Nastaliq CAPTCHA". This method uses Arabian, and Persian characters of three to eight characters in length, apply Nastaliq font, and make an image file in PNG format (Portable Network Graphics). No need to add noise or distortion to the image, due to letters being connected, more than half of letters use dots, direction right to left, so OCR programs are unable to recognize the words. Shown image to the user, Compare string, test result pass or fail. Implemented in JAVA programming language [3].

3. Sushma Yalamanchili and Kameswara Rao (August 2011) proposed a "Framework for text-based CAPTCHA using Devanagari script DevaCAPTCHA for Indian languages". It is very easy to operate for Devanagari script users. OCR for Devanagari script is developed but work in progress to recognize distorted or noisy text. Key components used in the proposed framework: Database of Devanagari script text, Query generator (generate random sample), Obfuscator (distorts text and add noise), Interface, Match response. The headline "Shiro-Rekha" unites all the distinct characters of the Devanagari script.

   To obfuscate the image, the obfuscator may remove the headline and add noise using patterns like a mosaic, arcs/jaws, and vertically overlapping over the script.

   The Obfuscator further deceives the system by employing different fonts of different sizes and variable letter spacing.

   Resistant techniques of segmentation will be used in its layout.

   Future research projects will focus on DevaCAPTCHA implementation and involvement in OCR testing initiatives relating to Indian language scripts. Another future research project is to test and recognize Devanagari handwriting [4].

4. S. Ravi Kiran, and Y. Rama Krishna (2012), presented a new approach to protecting users' passwords against spyware attacks in the paper "Combining CAPTCHA and Graphical Passwords for User Authentication". In this paper, the researcher has to only recognize registered CAPTCHA images and graphical passwords to resist spyware attacks. This research is expected to advance the development of graphical passwords from a security standpoint. A Future scope is to increase improve login time and memorability [6].

5. Bilal Khan et al. (2013) presented the paper "Cyber Security Using Arabic CAPTCHA Scheme". The proposed scheme uses Arabic letters and font types to generate an image, a database of selected 2,71,0000 Arabic words, randomly select four to nine characters, create an image of letters in the rectangle with white background and blue foreground color, add light blue color dots and the line also added salt and pepper as a noises make it extremely hard for the OCR to separate noise from the image, display the image to the user for recognition. Uses preprocessing, segmentation, and character recognition techniques. The user has no trouble interacting with the system, and the algorithm is effective. According to the study, a high overall readability rate of the images was determined by a test of 150 people. So this proposed CAPTCHA

scheme can be used in Non-Arabic speaking countries where languages use Arabic scripts such as Urdu, Pashto, Persian, etc. for protecting internet resources [7].

6. Baljit Singh Saini and Anju Bala (May 2013) proposed a "Bot Protection using CAPTCHA: Gurmukhi Script". In this research paper, the proposed scheme is CAPTCHA consists of a sequence of characters in Punjabi font to generate an image. The foreground and background colors are used to distort the image and make the CAPTCHA image attractive by adding noise in the background in the shape of dots. The image is shown to the user. A User enters characters shown with each character there is an appropriate sound attached to it. Surveyed with fifty participants, the average success rate was 75%. This scheme was implemented in C# with the ASP.NET platform. The suggested approach can help secure online resources and is advantageous in countries where Punjabi is spoken. The Future scope is handwritten Punjabi CAPTCHA [8].

7. M.Tariq Bandy, Shafila Afzal Sheikh, Proposed "A model for Indian Regional Multilingual CAPTCHA challenges". In India, there are 22 official languages. Most government websites provide content in the regional language but CAPTCHA is in the English language. The researcher proposed model – i. Get the language ii. Fetch Unicode character set iii. Generate string iv. Add noise (character distortion, cluttering, deformation background, wrapping, dilation, font type, size, color) v. store string vi. Compare – test result pass or fail. Use of handwritten string/words as his future research work [9].

8. Asadullah Kehar, Rafaqat Hussain Arain et al., proposed "Design, and Development of Sindhi Text-Based CAPTCHAs for Regional Websites". In this paper Authors designed a CAPTCHA in Sindhi language, similar to the Arabic language written from right to left, containing 62 characters, Colored ellipses and clutter were inserted. Dots are used in characters so noise is not used. Implemented Sindhi Text CAPTCHA image using C# programming language, Overlapping characters were deliberately used so that CAPTCHA OCR programs could hardly segment the string. Characters string random 3 to 8 characters. Web page created using ASP, and JSP and tested by users [19].

Comparative Analysis of Research Papers on Non-English Language CAPTCHA
See Table 6.

2.4   Review of Captcha Generation Papers

S. A. Alsuhibany and M. T. Parvez, "Secure Arabic Handwritten CAPTCHA Generation Using OCR Operations," [12], In this paper Arabic Handwritten CAPTCHA generated from prewritten Arabic 123,200 part of word (PAW) images extracted from KHATT database. The proposed CAPTCHA generation method takes a PAW image p, a). During the segmentation process, image p is transformed to binary image c b). c is segmented. The centroid of the segmentation spots is used to estimate the baseline of the PAW body, and the segments are then slightly offset from the baseline to distort the segmentation locations. Many Arabic OCR algorithms extract features based on an assessment of the baseline since Arabic words are printed on a baseline. Therefore, if character segments in

Table 6. Comparative Analysis of research papers on non-English language CAPTCHA

SN	Name of Researcher and Year of Publication	Research paper Title	Language	Proposed Method	Distortion/Noise	Implementation/ Security	Success rate
1	M. Hassan Shirali-Shahreza and Mohammad Shirali-Shahreza (2007) [2]	Multilingual CAPTCHA	Multilingual- 7 languages Dutch, French, German, Italian, Portugues and Spanish	The recognizer selects the correct image displayed in a grid. User interfaces messages are displayed in the user's native language		PHP language Resist attacks because recognition is not possible for bots	–
2	M.Hussn Shirali-Shahreza (2008) [3]	Advanced Nastaliq CAPTCHA	Arabian, Persian	String size 3 to 8 characters Uses Nastaliq font, makes an image file in PNG format, User type the word shown in the image, Test result	Colorful background with random lines, Due to letters being connected, more than half of letters use dots, direction right to left, so no need to add noise or distortion to the image.	JAVA language	Most difficult to recognize by OCR
3	Sushma Yalamanchili and Kameswara Rao (August 2011) [4]	Framework for text-based CAPTCHA using Devanagari script DevaCAPTCHA for Indian languages	Devanagari	Devanagari text Database, Random selection of string, Interface, Match response.	Font Variation, Font size, Overlapping character, Shadow Character, background, removal of shirorekha, stretching, and compression of character. Skew	Proposed as a Future work.	Not Implemented
4	S. Ravi Kiran, Y. Rama Krishna (2012) [6]	Combining CAPTCHA and Graphical Passwords for User Authentication	English	Only recognize a pre-registered combination of CAPTCHA and graphical password images	No use	Claim – Resist spyware attack	Not Mentioned

(*continued*)

Table 6. (*continued*)

SN	Name of Researcher and Year of Publication	Research paper Title	Language	Proposed Method	Distortion/Noise	Implementation/ Security	Success rate
5	Bilal Khan et al. (2013) [7]	Cyber Security Using Arabic CAPTCHA Scheme	Arabic 28 Letters	Word written right to left and number left to right, Character is of different size & shape Preprocessing, Segmentation, Character Recognition	Font type, size, vary several characters Background noise arc, lines, dots, clutter. Salt and pepper noise added	Implemented In VB.Net OCR is not developed so secure against brute force attack	Claim – readability rate best. Success rate 99.6%
6	Baljit Singh Saini, Anju Bala (May 2013) [8]	Bot Protection using CAPTCHA: Gurmukhi Script	Punjabi	a string of characters in the Punjabi alphabet that creates a picture. The user is shown the image. A user types the characters that are shown, and each character has a corresponding sound.	By adding noise in the background in the form of dots; foreground and background colors are selected	C# with ASP.NET platform	Success rate 75%.
7	M.Tariq Bandy, Shafila Afzal Sheikh (Dec. 2013) [9]	A model for Indian Regional Multi-lingual CAPTCHA challenges	Multilingual	i. Get the language ii. Fetch Unicode character set iii. Generate string iv. Add noise v. store string vi. Compare – test result pass or fail.	Character Distortion, Cluttering, Deformation background, Wrapping, Dilation, font type, size, color	Proposed Model	–
8	Asadullah Kehar, Rafaqat Hussain Arain et al. (June 2021) [19]	Design and Development of Sindhi Text-Based CAPTCHAs for Regional Websites	Sindhi	52 Sindhi characters, like Arabic, written from right to left,	Colored ellipse and clutter were inserted. Dots are used in characters so noise is not used.	Implemented interface using ASP, JSP, PHP, PYTHON	Usability tested using only Users Interface

a PAW are relocated from their baseline position, the baseline estimation approach will be more difficult. Additionally, characters in a PAW are joined at the baseline to form valleys; if characters are moved (slightly) from their intended positions, the valleys will be distorted. c) all the bounded regions are filled with random colors d) the entire image is distorted with salt and pepper noise e) random rotations are used. f) Broken characters result from some parts (going beyond the upper baseline) being drawn as dotted lines. Broken character pieces in Arabic scripts can be read correctly only in context since they can be mistaken for dots or diacritics. g) Horizontal and vertical displacements of randomly selected characters and polyline approximations.

The accuracy of CAPTCHAs is evaluated for security using a comprehensive word recognition system, with results ranging from 0.00% to 5.49%, which is very less so the researcher claims its secure design. Usability accuracy achieved more than 88%.

Mohinder Kumar1, Manish Kumar Jindal", Benchmarks for Designing a Secure Devanagari CAPTCHA", [18]. In this paper, researchers use www.captcha.com, a famous CAPTCHA designing website is used to design Devanagari CAPTCHA, where just 20 unique designs out of more than 60 available are chosen to design the CAPTCHA. A total of 39 Devanagari letters are used for the design. In each design, 2000 images were generated, and approximately 40,000 images were tested for security (breaking the CAPTCHA).

Steps for breaking the CAPTCHA are: Image converts it into a binary image, for character segmentation pre-processing is used to remove noise. When two or more characters cannot be segmented in the initial stage, post-processing is required. Technical terms included kernel sizes (morphological operations), single, double, and Otsu thresholding values, and vertical projection morphological dilation. All 20 designs have been successfully segmented and de-noised. Segmentation has a high success rate, ranging from 88.14 to 98.06 percent, although it is designed to be easily broken by bots using insecure methods.

Consequently, the researcher creates a set of recommendations for creating a secure text CAPTCHA design: Always Use Background, Similar Pattern Background must be avoided, Larger Character Set, Use of Handwritten Characters, More Use of Similar Characters, Use of Half Characters, Appropriate Use of color, Thickness of Characters, Overlapping, Scaling of Characters, Use of Font, Use of Arcs or Lines, Rotation, Length of CAPTCHA string, Vertical Position of Characters, Use of Noisy Patch [18].

V. K. Yadav, S. Agarwal, J. Uprety, and S. Batham, "SRTS: A Novel Technique to Generate Random Text," [10]. In this paper authors generate CAPTCHA text is completely based on date and time. Here system collects the current date and time, separates each digit, performs the arithmetic operation, and generates code from 62 ASCII values of English alphabets also checks the possibility of repetition of generated text and displays random text. These texts exploit the intelligence of shifting time to construct a unique sequence every time a user sends a request for a new text, making them impenetrable to unsophisticated users and standard code [10].

M. Tang, H. Gao, Y. Zhang, Y. Liu, P. Zhang and P. Wang, "Research on Deep Learning Techniques in Breaking Text-Based Captchas and Designing Image-Based Captcha," [14], In this paper authors, perform analysis of breaking text-based CAPTCHA images of different English, Chinese, Arabic, Roman language top 50 websites using deep learning technique CNN which results from 10% to 90% success rate. Here, authors employing neural style transfer techniques introduced a unique image-based Captcha called SACaptcha. While SACaptcha is based on challenges of semantic information interpretation and pixel-level segmentation, the majority of early image-based CAPTCHA is focused on the problem of image classification. This is a commendable attempt to increase the security of Captchas using deep learning methods [14].

P. Panwar, Monika, P. Kumar, and A. Sharma, "CHGR: Captcha generation using Hand Gesture Recognition," [16]. This research proposes a more efficient methodology for generating CAPTCHAs using hand gesture recognition techniques, as opposed to typical CAPTCHAs. This solution involved displaying a form along with one CAPTCHA image of a hand gesture from the database and a message telling the user to copy the gesture. The user then performed a motion in front of the system's camera, and the model checked to see if it matched the gesture that had been displayed or not. As it is impossible for the robot to learn how to repeat the same move as seen in the image on its own, using this way will undoubtedly ensure the user's identification. These CAPTCHAs can be used in the future by websites to determine if a user is a human being or a robot, requiring less time and effort from humans. The experiments produce findings that are satisfactory for the suggested model. Three steps are involved in pre-processing: 1. Image Conversion 2. Morphological Filtering -dilation and erosion to fetch smooth, closed, and complete contour of gesture. 3. Edge Detection- Canny edge detection algorithm has been used due to the above advantages and it eliminates the risk of multiple responses to one edge. The algorithm first smooth's the image obtained after conversion and morphological filtering to remove any noise if present. The gradient is then calculated by the algorithm to emphasize the areas with spatial derivatives, and by employing this, the maximum pixel values are suppressed. The resultant gradient array was then further decreased via hysteresis to improve accuracy. Hysteresis uses two thresholds to keep track of the pixels that haven't yet been suppressed. The pixel value is set to zero if the magnitude of the pixel is less than the smaller threshold, and to one of the greater thresholds is exceeded. C. Matching: To match the gesture made by the user to the shown as CAPTCHA, pixels were first counted contributing to the edges in the image obtained from the result of canny edge detection. The average number of pixels was then counted for each gesture and this value was further used for matching. Once the pixel count of the input image is obtained, an error has been then calculated for each gesture. We created 100 images using the database of hand gestures from 20 distinct people, each with five different gestures. The model is 80% accurate as a result [16].

Comparative Analysis of CAPTCHA Generation Research Papers
See Table 7.

Table 7. Comparative Analysis of CAPTCHA generation research papers

Sr. No	Researchers' name with Title of paper	Language, Data set	The technique used to survive OCR attacks	Accuracy	Susceptible to attack
1	S. A. Alsuhibany and M. T. Parvez, Secure Arabic Handwritten CAPTCHA Generation Using OCR Operations [12]	Arabic 123,200 part of word (PAW) images extracted from the KHATT database	1. Segmentation, 2. Displacement, 3. Bounded regions filled with random colors, 4. Salt and pepper noise, 5. Random rotations 6. Broken characters	0.00% to 5.49%	Accuracy is a maximum of 5.49%, Means secured from Bots.

(*continued*)

Table 7. (*continued*)

Sr. No	Researchers' name with Title of paper	Language, Data set	The technique used to survive OCR attacks	Accuracy	Susceptible to attack
2	Mohinder Kumar, Manish Kumar Jindal, Benchmarks for Designing a Secure Devanagari CAPTCHA [18]	Devanagari 39 Letters Uses www.captcha. com Website for design CAPTCHA 40,000 images were designed	1. Thresholding 2. Morphological dilation 3. Segmentation Vertical and Horizontal	88.14 to 98.06%	susceptible to break by bots means not secured
3	Virendra Kumar Yadav, Shantanu Agarwal et al., SRTS: A Novel Technique to Generate Random Text [10]	English 62 Letters and Digits Random Generation of Text using server date and time	No image processing technique used	Not Tested	The authors claim it's secure but not verified
4	Pooja Panwar, Monika, Parveen Kumar et al., CHGR: Captcha generation using Hand Gesture Recognition [16]	CAPTCHA image showing some hand gestures from the database, user copies the gesture in front of the camera of the system and then the model has verified whether the gesture made by the user is the same as that shown or not.	1. Image Conversion 2. Morphological Filtering 3. Edge Detection 4. Matching 5. 20 different persons, 6 Gestures of each individual thus making a total of 100 images.	80%	Very Small database used so susceptible for brute force attack

3   Devanagari Captcha Generation Proposed Model

3.1   Character Set

We chose printed Devanagari characters and a handwritten Devanagari character set for our Devanagari CAPTCHA design. Devanagari 53 image processed alphabets
  Each symbol has a size of 65 × 65 pixels (Fig. 1).

Devanagari 53 Handwritten Alphabets
Handwritten 53 Devanagari alphabets: Each symbol has a size of 65 × 65 pixels (Fig. 2).

Rejected Characters from Character Set: 19
We have designed the CAPTCHA in such a way that it does not create any confusion for humans and retains its usability, so rejected 19 alphabets (Fig. 3).

Selected Character Set: Printed PREPROCESSED Characters [34]
See Fig. 4.

Fig. 1. Printed Devanagari Character Set [53]

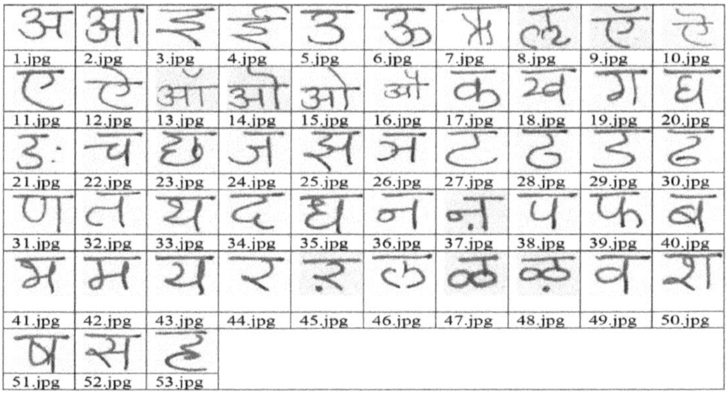

Fig. 2. Handwritten Devanagari Character Set [53]

Handwritten Characters [hc] -34
See Fig. 5.

Devanagari Handwritten 10 Numerals
See Fig. 6.

Devanagari Printed 10 Numerals: PD – 10
See Fig. 7.

Unicodes
See Fig. 8.

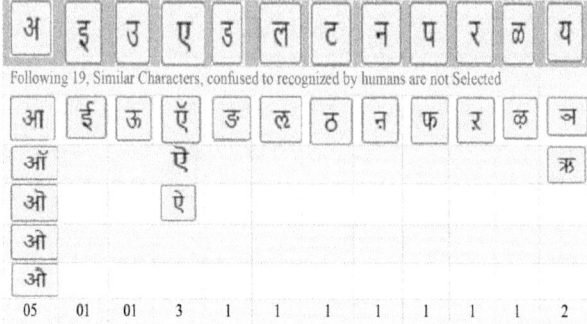

Fig. 3. Rejected Devanagari Characters [19]

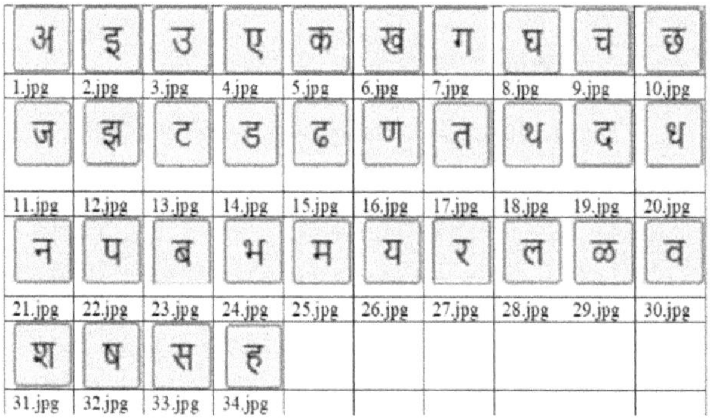

अ	इ	उ	ए	क	ख	ग	घ	च	छ
1.jpg	2.jpg	3.jpg	4.jpg	5.jpg	6.jpg	7.jpg	8.jpg	9.jpg	10.jpg
ज	झ	ट	ड	ढ	ण	त	थ	द	ध
11.jpg	12.jpg	13.jpg	14.jpg	15.jpg	16.jpg	17.jpg	18.jpg	19.jpg	20.jpg
न	प	ब	भ	म	य	र	ल	ळ	व
21.jpg	22.jpg	23.jpg	24.jpg	25.jpg	26.jpg	27.jpg	28.jpg	29.jpg	30.jpg
श	ष	स	ह						
31.jpg	32.jpg	33.jpg	34.jpg						

Fig. 4. Selected Printed Devanagari Characters [34]

अ	इ	उ	ए	क	ख	ग	घ	च	छ
1.jpg	2.jpg	3.jpg	4.jpg	5.jpg	6.jpg	7.jpg	8.jpg	9.jpg	10.jpg
ज	झ	ट	ड	ढ	ण	त	थ	द	ध
11.jpg	12.jpg	13.jpg	14.jpg	15.jpg	16.jpg	17.jpg	18.jpg	19.jpg	20.jpg
न	प	ब	भ	म	य	र	ल	ळ	व
21.jpg	22.jpg	23.jpg	24.jpg	25.jpg	26.jpg	27.jpg	28.jpg	29.jpg	30.jpg
श	ष	स	ह						
31.jpg	32.jpg	33.jpg	34.jpg						

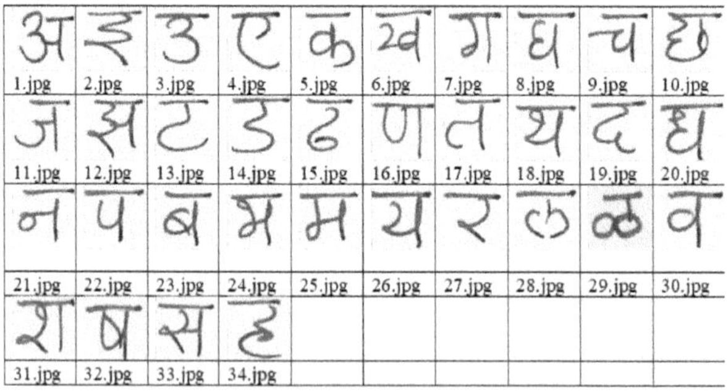

Fig. 5. Selected Handwritten Devanagari Characters [34]

	Printed	Handwritten
Alphabets	34	10
Digits	34	10

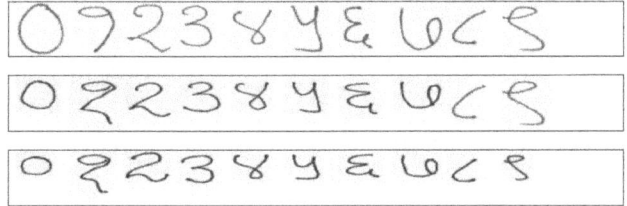

Fig. 6. Three Sets of Handwritten Numerals [10]

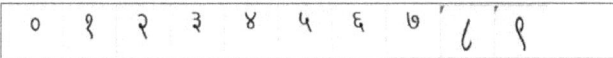

Fig. 7. Set of Printed Numerals [10]

Alphabets Unicodes
["\u0905","\u0907","\u0909","\u090F","\u0915","\u0916","\u0917","\u0918","\u091A","\u091B", "\u091C","\u091D","\u091F","\u0921","\u0922","\u0923","\u0924","\u0925","\u0926","\u0927", "\u0928","\u092A","\u092C","\u092D","\u092E","\u092F","\u0930","\u0932","\u0933","\u0935", "\u0936","\u0937","\u0938","\u0939","\u0966","\u0967","\u0968","\u0969","\u096A","\u096B", "\u096C","\u096D","\u096E","\u096F"]
Digits Unicode
["\u0966","\u0967","\u0968","\u0969","\u096A","\u096B","\u096C","\u096D","\u096E","\u096F"]

Fig. 8. Unicodes of Devanagari Characters and Numerals [34 + 10 = 44]

Table 8. Four Superclasses of charcater set

PA:Printed Alphabet-34	PD: Printed Digit-10
HA: Handwritten Alphabet-34	HD: Handwritten Digit-10

3.2 Classes of Character Set

There are **11** classes of **4** superclasses of the character set (Tables 8 and 9).

3.3 Image Processing Techniques Used

It is a technique for altering images, obtaining enhanced images, or extracting information that can be used later.

The two types of image processing techniques used are analog and digital.

Analog image processing is useful for hard copies like prints and photos.

Computer-based digital image alteration is made possible with the use of digital image processing tools.

Image Acquisition:

Table 9. 11 Classes of charcater set

PA-34	PD-10	PA-34	PD-10
HA-34	HD-10	HA-34	HD-10
PA-34	PD-10	PA-34	PD-10
HA-34	HD-10	HA-34	HD-10
PA-34	PD-10	PA-34	PD-10
HA-34	HD-10	HA-34	HD-10
PA-34	PD-10	PA-34	PD-10
HA-34	HD-10	HA-34	HD-10
PA-34	PD-10	PA-34	PD-10
HA-34	HD-10	HA-34	HD-10
	PA-34	PD-10	
	HA-34	HD-10	

Thirty-Four (34) Devanagari alphabet and Ten (10) digit samples were collected and scanned using a scanner before being converted to a picture format. (.JPG).

In addition, Thirty-Four (34) Devanagari alphabet and Ten (10) digit Devanagari handwritten samples were gathered, digitized, and transformed into image format using a scanner. (.JPG).

Image Pre-processing

I. For printed alphabets following Image preprocessing was performed:

क

i. Each printed alphabet's background was converted using Matlab Program
ii. Each character is enclosed in a square (Image Fusion).

Resizing Image: When an image is resized or distorted from the one-pixel grid to another, it is called image interpolation. When increasing or decreasing the total number of pixels, picture scaling is required.

Using Matlab and Python programs, each printed and handwritten alphabet image is reduced to 65×65 pixels. (1 kb size).

Insert Noise in Image
Noise means, the pixels in the image show different intensity values instead of true pixel values that are obtained from image. []

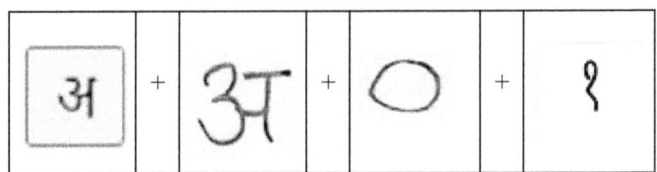

We add noise in CAPTCHA image, because Optical Character Recognition (OCR) recognizer has difficult to break the CAPTCHA image.

$A(x,y) = H(x,y) + B(x,y)$

Where, $A(x,y)$ = function of noisy image, $H(x,y)$ = function of image noise, $B(x,y)$ = function of original image. Following different types of noises are added to the image randomly.

Types of Noise in image:

1. **Gaussian Noise:** Gaussian Noise is a statistical noise having a probability density function equal to a normal distribution, also known as Gaussian Distribution. A random Gaussian function is added to the Image function to generate this noise [22].

$$p_G(z) = \frac{1}{\sigma\sqrt{2\pi}} e^{-\frac{(z-\mu)^2}{2\sigma^2}}$$

2. **Salt and Pepper Noise:** Salt and Pepper noise is added to an image by addition of both random bright (with 255-pixel value) and random dark (with 0-pixel value) all over the image. Because it statistically drops the original data values, this model is also known as data drop noise [22].

3. **Poisson Noise:** The appearance of this noise is seen due to the statistical nature of electromagnetic waves such as x-rays, visible lights, and gamma rays. The x-ray and gamma-ray sources emitted the number of photons per unit of time. In medical x-rays and gamma-ray imaging systems, these rays are injected into a patient's body from the source. The photons in these sources fluctuate at random. The resulting image is spatially and temporally unpredictable. Quantum (photon) noise or shot noise are other names for this type of noise [22].

4. **Speckle Noise:** A fundamental problem in optical and digital holography is the presence of speckle noise in the image reconstruction process. Speckle is a granular noise that occurs naturally in images and diminishes their quality. Speckle noise is produced by multiplying random pixel values with distinct picture pixels [22].

CAPTCHA is noisy image, to break or recognise a CAPTCHA image, noise is removed using a denoising method filter to restore the original image.

3.4   CAPTCHA Generation Guidelines: [17]

1. A Larger Character Set: To construct Devanagari CAPTCHA, we used a printed and handwritten character set. There are 10,34,44,88 symbols in all.
2. Handwritten Characters are used:

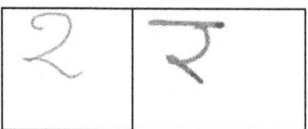

3. CAPTCHA String Length: The length of the CAPTCHA string varies, ranging from 5 to 7. (A random pick is made at runtime.)
4. Characters' Dimensions (Table 10):

5. Font Selection: For the CAPTCHA design, we have only chosen ONE typeface/font. For a single printed character, we get 03 classes of CAPTCHA images.

The number of possibilities of Devanagari CAPTCHA images produced by using more than one typeface/font, increases the complexity of the CAPTCHA image, making it more difficult to read and recognize by OCR.

Table 10. Change Symbol Image Size w.r.t. Captcha string length

CAPTCHA String Size = 5	CAPTCHA String Size = 6	CAPTCHA String Size = 7
54 X 54 Pixel size	45 X 45 Pixel size	39 X 39 Pixel size

6. Scaling: Resizing a digital image is known as image scaling. An image becomes smaller as it is scaled down, and larger when it is scaled up. It employs bicubic and bilinear interpolation. Scale image +5 to +10.

7. Rotation: Bicubic 30° and Bilinear −40° are used.

The effect of scaling and rotation on a Devanagari symbol image in a CAPTCHA drops the accuracy of CAPTCHA image recognition and breaking by OCR.
Use of lines, arcs, polygons, and rectangles:

9. Noisy Patch:
    Noise is typically defined as a random variation in brightness or color information.
    a. Increase and Decrease image contrast
    b. Added randomly any ONE of the noise to CAPTCHA Image: Gaussian, localvar, Salt and Pepper, Poisson, Speckle.

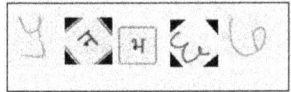

10. The symbol image has a black and white background:

3.5 Algorithm for Captcha Generation

1. PC, HC, PD, HD…..Select any one set from 11 combinations.
2. Set path of character set and CAPTCHA image directories.
3. Set the length of the character set as per the above selection [10 or 34 or 44 or 88]
4. Input required L = number of CAPTCHA images required.
5. Repeat steps 6 to 19, for CI = 1 to L
6. A: = Read square shape box image file (in which CAPTCHA text generated)
7. Randomly select length of CAPTCHA image [5 or 6 or 7] = CL
8. Set folder/directory to store CAPTCHA Image
9. Repeat step 10 to 14, for I = 1 to CL (Length of CAPTCHA is CL = 5 OR 6 OR 7)
10. B: = Read randomly anyone Devanagari character image set.
11. Resize image B
    a. if CL = 5 then 54 × 54
    b. if CL = 6 then 45 × 45
    c. if CL = 7 then 39 × 39
12. Apply any one of the five functions to the above image at random to create noise that OCR Won't recognize.
    a. Rotate image Bicubic 30 degrees.
    b. Rotate image Bilinear −40 degree
    c. Scale image + 5 points
    d. Decrease image Contrast
    e. Increase image Contrast
13. Determine the next image placement in square shape box A.
14. Insert above image B in the A (square shape box) at the calculated location.
15. Resize the image
16. Save the CAPTCHA image, just created in JPG, JPEG, or BMP format.
17. Add any noise to the Image: ["gaussian", "localvar", "poisson", "salt", "pepper", "s&p", "speckle"]
18. Insert line or circle or Polygon or ellipse at specified location in the image.
19. Save a CAPTCHA Image at the specified location.

3.6 Flow Chart

See Fig. 9.

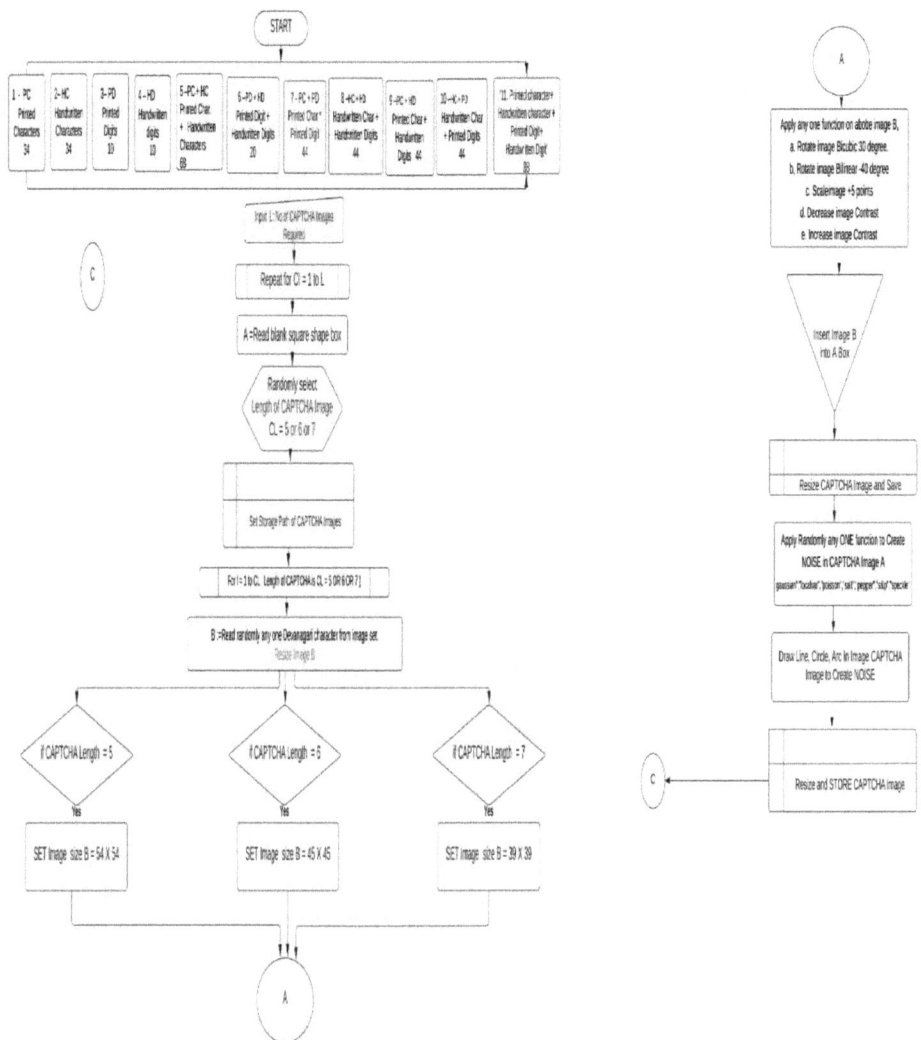

Fig. 9. Flow Chart of Design

4   Implementation

Experimental Environment

This project is implemented in the Jupyter platform in the Windows environment using Python language, with its version 3.0.0 dated 20 Feb 2020.

Computer Hardware requirement: Processor: Intel(R), Core™, i5 or new versions, CPU @ 2.20 GHz,8 GB RAM, 4 GB NVIDIA GEFORCE GTX GPU.

System type: 64-bit Windows operating system.

Software requirement: Python, Tensorflow, Keras.

Table 11. Devanagari Captcha: Generation of Printed and Handwritten Devanagari Characters with Variable Length

Sr. No	Character Set	No. of Char.	CAPTCHA Images Generated of length 5	CAPTCHA Images Generated of length 6	CAPTCHA Images Generated of length 7
1 – PC	Printed Characters	34			
2 – PD	Printed Digits	10			
3 – HC	Handwritten Characters	34			
4 – H D	Handwritten digits	10			
5 – PC + PD	Printed Characters + Printed Digits	34 + 10			
6 PC + HD	Handwritten Characters + Handwritten Digits	34 + 10			
7 – PC + HC	Printed Characters + Handwritten Characters	34 + 34			
8 – PC + H D	Printed Characters + Handwritten Digit	34 + 10			
9 – HC + PD	Handwritten Characters + Printed Digit	34 + 10 = 44			
10 PD + HD	Printed Digit + Handwritten Digits	10 + 10 = 20			
11 PC + HC + HC + HD	Printed Characters + Handwritten Characters + Printed Digit + Handwritten Digits	34 + 34 + 10+ 10 = 88			

Python requires less time to execute the code than Matlab so selected python for implementation.

For implementation used different libraries in Python.

NumPy, Pandas, Scikit-learn (Sklearn), TensorFlow, Keras, OpenCV, PyGame, PyTorch, Tesseract OCR.

OpenCV (Open Source Computer Vision library) technique used Morphing: Merging through a smooth transition different pictures to create a new one.

Used OpenCV functions read, write, display, resize, translate, scale and rotate image.

5 Result: Data Set

A total of 1,10,000 samples of CAPTCHA Images with noise were generated (Table 11).

Devanagari Captcha: Generation of Printed and Handwritten Devanagari Characters with Variable Length: Image Size 250 × 90.

6 Conclusion and Future Work

In this paper, 34 Devanagari Printed, Handwritten characters and 10 digits are used. Image acquisition, Image resize, and Image binarization these basic image processing operations are used. Digital Image processing techniques Bicubic and Bilinear interpolation are used for scaling and rotation. The effect of scaling and rotation on a Devanagari symbol image in a CAPTCHA will drops the accuracy of CAPTCHA image recognition and breaking by OCR.

Various types of noises are added to the image randomly like gaussian, localvar, Poisson, salt, pepper, salt &pepper, speckle. We add above noise in CAPTCHA image, because Optical Character Recognition (OCR) recognizer has difficulties to break the CAPTCHA image.

Standard guidelines for CAPTCHA generations are followed.04 (Four) types of Character Sets are used – Printed Alphabet, Handwritten Alphabet, Printed Digit, and Handwritten Digit. Generated 11 Classes from these 04 combinations. For each class – 03 (THREE) subclasses are created –The string length of the CAPTCHA image considered here is FIVE, SIX, and SEVEN (5, 6, 7). In total there are 11 classes × 3 subclasses = 33 subclasses. So 33 types of images were generated. For each class of selected character set, 10,000 CAPTCHA images were created.

For 11 Classes × 10,000 images = a Data set of 1,10,000 (One Million Ten Thousand) images was created using Python. For a generation of 10,000 CAPTCHA Images 180 seconds are required. So the generation of One (01) CAPTCHA image requires 1.08 milliseconds. Each image is of size 250 × 90 pixels and requires 8 KB storage. Data set of 1,10,000 CAPTCHA images created which requires 964 MB storage. Devanagari CAPTCHA is implemented using Anaconda, Jupiter platform of Python Programming language. This algorithm is helpful to design other languages CAPTCHA. Devanagari CAPTCHA is useful for all Devanagari language users and it is more secure than English CAPTCHA.

The future scope is, Design and develop a framework for recognition or breaking of Devanagari CAPTCHA image and analyze the success rate. Noise in CAPTCHA image is removed using a denoising method filter to restore the original image.

To use more than one typeface/font which increases the complexity of the CAPTCHA image, making it more difficult to read and recognize by OCR, is another future scope.

Design Audio and Video Devanagari CAPTCHA. Also, develop Devanagari CAPTCHA using Alphabets without "ShiroRekha".

References

1. Om V. (2005). Multilingualism for Cultural Diversity and Universal Access in Cyberspace: An Asian Perspective, an Asian Perspective, UNESCO, May 2005
2. Shirali-Shahreza, M.H. &Shirali-Shahreza, M., (2007) "Multilingual CAPTCHA", ICCC 2007 IEEE International Conference on Computational Cybernetics, 19–21 October.
3. M.Hassan Shirali-Shahreza, Mohammad Shirali-Shahreza, "Advanced Nastaliq CAPTCHA", Cybernetic Intelligent Systems 2008, IEEE.
4. Sushma Yalamanchili and Kameswara Rao, "A FRAMEWORK FOR DEVANAGARI SCRIPT- BASED CAPTCHA", Cryptography and Security (cs.CR); Human-Computer Interaction, International Journal of Advanced Information Technology, Vol. 1, No. 4, August, pp. 47–57, 2011.
5. Banday M and Shah N (2011) Challenges of CAPTCHA in the Accessibility of Indian regional websites. Proceedings of the fourth annual ACM Bangalore conference, 1–4.
6. T.S.Ravi Kiran, Y. Rama Krishna, "COMBINING CAPTCHA AND GRAPHICAL PASS-WORDS FOR USER AUTHENTICATION", IJRIM, Volume 2, Issue 4 (April 2012) (ISSN 2231-4334).
7. Bilal Khan, Khaled Alghathbar et al., "Cyber Security using Arabic CAPTCHA Scheme", The International Arab Journal Information Technology, Vol. No.1, January 2013.
8. Baljit Singh Saini, Anju Bala, "Bot Protection using CAPTCHA: Gurmukhi Script", International Journal of Application or Innovation in Engineering & Management (IJAIEM), May 2013, Volume 2, Issue 5. (ISSN 2319-4847)
9. M. Tariq Banday, "A Model for Indian Regional Multi-lingual CAPTCHA Challenges", 9th J&K Science Congress and Regional Science Congress, 1–3 October 2013, University of Kashmir, Srinagar.
10. V. K. Yadav, S. Agarwal, J. Uprety and S. Batham, "SRTS: A Novel Technique to Generate Random Text," 2014 International Conference on Computational Intelligence and Communication Networks, 2014, pp. 268–272, https://doi.org/10.1109/CICN.2014.68.
11. Sanjay E.Pate," A CAPTCHA: A Review ", National Conference on Recent Trends in Computer Science & Applications 2015. Date: 27 & 28 January, 2015. ISBN No. 978-93-84093-76-1(1).
12. S. A. Alsuhibany and M. T. Parvez, "Secure Arabic Handwritten CAPTCHA Generation Using OCR Operations," 2016 15th International Conference on Frontiers in Handwriting Recognition (ICFHR), 2016, pp. 126–131, https://doi.org/10.1109/ICFHR.2016.0035.
13. Seema D. (2017). Digital India Opportunities and Challenges, International Journal of Science & Technology (IJSTM) Special Issue NCIETM – 2017, 6(3): 61–671
14. M. Tang, H. Gao, Y. Zhang, Y. Liu, P. Zhang and P. Wang, "Research on Deep Learning Techniques in Breaking Text-Based Captchas and Designing Image-Based Captcha," in IEEE Transactions on Information Forensics and Security, vol. 13, no. 10, pp. 2522–2537, Oct. 2018, https://doi.org/10.1109/TIFS.2018.2821096.
15. Aldosari M (2018) Innovative multilingual CAPTCHA Based on handwritten characteristics, Intechopen, 72599.
16. P. Panwar, Monika, P. Kumar, and A. Sharma, "CHGR: Captcha generation using Hand Gesture Recognition," 2018 Conference on Information and Communication Technology (CICT), 2018, pp. 1–6, https://doi.org/10.1109/INFOCOMTECH.2018.8722409.
17. Kumar M, Jindal MK and Kumar M (2021a) A systematic survey on CAPTCHA recognition: types, creation and breaking techniques. Archives of Computational Methods in Engineering, Springer, 1–30.
18. Mohinder Kumar1, Manish Kumar Jindal," Benchmarks for Designing a Secure Devanagari CAPTCHA", Published online: 19 January 2021, part of Springer Nature 2021

19. Asadullah Kehar, Rafaqat Hussain Arain et al., Design and Development of Sindhi Text-Based CAPTCHAs for Regional Websites, SJET I P-ISSN: 2616-7069 IE-ISSN: 2617-3115IVol. 4 No. 1 January–June 2021.
20. https://en.wikipedia.org/wiki/List_of_languages_by_total_number_of_speakers, 2022
21. L. Von Ahn, M. Blum, and J. Langford, "Telling humans and computers apart automatically," Communications of the ACM, vol. 47, no. 2, pp. 56–60, 2004
22. Charles Boncelet (2005). "Image Noise Models". in Alan C. Bovik. Handbook of Image and Video Processing.

Color Image Compression Based on Contrast Sensitivity with Quality Factor

A. Christoper Tamilmathi[1][(✉)] and P. L. Chithra[2]

[1] Sri Ramachandra Faculty of Engineering and Technology, Sri Ramachandra Institute of Higher Education and Research (Deemed to Be University), Chennai, Tamil Nadu 600 116, India
actamilmathi@gmail.com
[2] Department of Computer Science, University of Madras, Chennai, Tamil Nadu 600 025, India

Abstract. This paper presents an innovative lossy color image compression based on contrast sensitivity of human visual perception, in which the image contrast sensitivity value (CSV) of each block is determined from Symmetric Gaussian function (SG). Then the outcome of SG is grouped using K-Medoid (KM) cluster to define the adaptive block quantization table (ABQT) for each block in order to provide better quality reconstructed image with good compression ratio (CR). Our experimental result shows that the observed CR is averagely increased by 3 times and visual quality is averagely increased by 9.9% than the existing algorithms namely traditional JPEG and JPEG with contrast sensitivity technique. The tabulated results indicate that proposed methodology out performs very well with the structural content of natural color test images.

Keywords: Adaptive block quantization table · Cluster · Contrast sensitivity · JPEG · Lossy color image compression · Quality factor

1 Introduction

Images make a major portion of modern day digital information processing, storage, and transmission. Compression is essentially required to manage this high data-rate of images without degrading the quality to acceptable level. New compression method based on high degree of correlation between the RGB planes of a color image is reduced by transforming them to O1; O2; O3 planes. Each O plane is then encoded using BTC-PF method proposed [1]. In spatial domain, the JPEG-LS coder in the near-lossless compression mode is modified to make coding errors part of the perceptual redundancy in compressing color images in the RGB space. In the wavelet domain JPEG 2000 coder is refined by minimizing the perceptible distortion involved in the rate control of the compressed image in the YCbCr space stated in [2]. Different formulas were introduced for measuring the contrast sensitivity of an image such as Weber contrast; Michelson contrast and RMS contrast defined [3]. The extended technique of constructing membership functions of fuzzy set proposed in [4]. The color image compression is based on different correlation method in which the existing inter-color correlated is employed to approximate two of the components as a parametric function of the third one, called

R. Manza et al. (Eds.): ACVAIT 2022, AISR 176, pp. 382–399, 2023.
https://doi.org/10.2991/978-94-6463-196-8_29

the base component expressed in [5]. To get the best compression ratio the next step of proposed adaptive scanning providing for each (n, n) DCT block a corresponding (n × n) vector containing the maximum possible run of zeros at its end proposed in [6]. Available statistical quality metrics on compressed data analysis were discussed in [8].

Modified sigmoid function provides better enhancement of low contrast image than the fuzzy ruled based method [11]. JPEG compression algorithm works well when it is combined with K-Means cluster method explained in [12]. Joint Chroma subsampling and distortion-minimization based on Luma modification for RGB color images explained in [13]. The JPEG compression algorithm is improved by modified the luminance quantization table for color images that improved the CR, MSE and PSNR value expressed in [14]. A new lossy compression method PE-VQ is proposed which exploits prediction error and vector quantization concepts. An optimum codebook is generated by using a combination of artificial bee colony and genetic algorithms [15]. Quality of the compressed image using JPEG algorithm mainly depends on the quality factor [16]. In fast and efficient color image enhancement, only V component is stretched under the control of the parameters, namely average intensity value and contrast intensification proposed in [17]. Multiplier less efficient and low complexity 8- point approximate DCT were introduced in which only 17 additions required for both forward and backward transformation discussed in [18]. A new histogram equalization with automated estimate of number of clusters were produced depends on image brightness level displayed in [19] and image contrast enhancement based on intensity expansion-compression. By expanding the intensity, according to the polarity of local edges, an intermediate image of continuous intensity spectrum is obtained in [20].

In this article a novel symmetric Gaussian K-Medoid contrast sensitive (SGKMCS) lossy compression algorithm has been proposed and proved that this method performs well with compression ratio which has been averagely increased by 3 times and visual quality averagely increased by 9.9%. The rest of the paper is organized as follows. Section 2 explains the proposed work. Section 3 discusses the experimental results. Conclusion of the proposed work is given in Sect. 4.

2   Proposed Method

The seed of the proposed compression method is based on the JPEG lossy compression work. The general architecture of the proposed image encoding process is shown in Fig. 1. Since the human eye has different sensitivity to color and brightness, raw RGB image has taken from natural color image data base and it transformed to the YCbCr image [10]. Resultant YCbCr image has been decomposed into luminance and color components.

During the reconstruction process, this decomposition process can be reversible to RGB. Each component of an image is further divided into non-overlapping 8 × 8 image blocks. This compression method has been concentrated on the quantization process, which depends on the contrast value of each block in the component. Implementation of the proposed method has been explained below by the following sections.

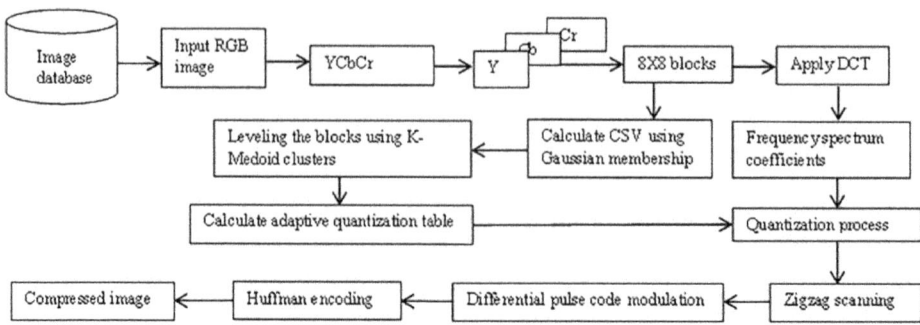

Fig. 1. The general architecture of proposed encoding process.

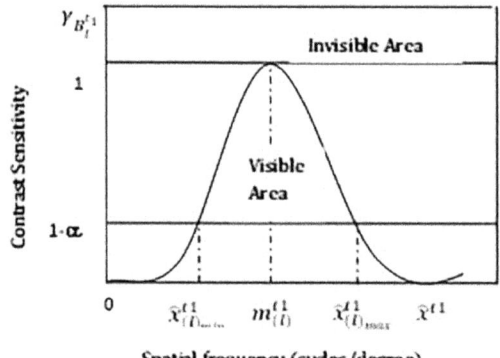

Fig. 2. Contrast Sensitivity function graph.

2.1 Contrast Sensitive Value Identification

Contrast value is the deviated value of brighter part from the darker part of an image [28]. This proposed method describes the new function to determine the contrast sensitive value (CSV) of a block, based on fuzzy activation function. CSV identified by the deviated value which is calculated from the symmetric Gaussian membership function denoted in Eq. (2.3). This method produces bell shaped graph for a block which denotes the contrast sensitivity of each pixel in the corresponding block as shown in Fig. 2. In a graph the contrast sensitivity function has the maximum peak value is 1. Visibility of the human eye perception decreases when increases the contrast sensitivity value from bottom to top with spatial frequency. Inner part of the contrast sensitivity function graph specifies the visibility area and the outer part of the graph as invisibility area. The difference between the visibility appearance and visibility disappearance measured as contrast sensitivity value (deviation). From the contrast sensitivity graph, a CSV value has been calculated using Eq. (2.4). This fuzzy based CS function mainly depends on two parameters, namely spatial frequency value for the corresponding peak contrast sensitive value $\left(m_{(l)}^{t_1}\right)$ and the deviated frequency from the peak value $\left(\sigma_{(l)}^{t_1}\right)$ of each block [4], have been determined by the following Eqs. (2.1) and (2.2).

Spatial frequency of a peak contrast sensitive value $\left(m_{(l)}^{t_1}\right)$ calculated by

$$m_{(l)}^{t_1} = \frac{\left(\hat{x}_{(l)min}^{t_1} + \hat{x}_{(l)min}^{t_1}\right)}{2} \tag{2.1}$$

where $t_1 = 1, 2,..., m_l$ and $l = 1, 2,..., c$. Where m_l is dimensional input vector, l is a band width between $\hat{x}_{(l)min}^{t_1}$ and $\hat{x}_{(l)max}^{t_1}$, $\hat{x}^{t_1}$ is an input vector and c is dimensional output vector. Parameter $\hat{x}_{(l)min}^{t_1}$ referred as a visibility appearance frequency and $\hat{x}_{(l)max}^{t_1}$ referred as a visibility disappearance frequency.

Frequency deviation from $m_{(l)}^{t_1}$ at left side denoted as $\sigma_{L(l)}^{t_1}$ and frequency deviation from $m_{(l)}^{t_1}$ $m_{(l)}^{t_1}$ at right side denoted as $\sigma_{R(l)}^{t_1}$. From these two deviated frequency, $\sigma_{(l)}^{t_1}$ (frequency deviation from this CSV graph) selects the maximum deviated frequency value which has been given in Eq. (2.2).

$$\sigma_{L(l)}^{t_1} = \frac{\left(\hat{x}_{(l)min}^{t_1} + m_{(l)}^{t_1}\right)}{\sqrt{-2\ln(1-\alpha)}}$$

$$\sigma_{R(l)}^{t_1} = \frac{\left(\hat{x}_{(l)max}^{t_1} + m_{(l)}^{t_1}\right)}{\sqrt{-2\ln(1-\alpha)}}$$

where α is a visibility threshold between [0,1]. Using these two equations deviated frequency value has been calculated by the Eq. (2.2).

$$\sigma_{(l)}^{t_1} = \max\left\{\sigma_{L(l)}^{t_1}, \sigma_{R(l)}^{t_1}\right\} \tag{2.2}$$

Contrast sensitivity function $\gamma_{(Bl)}^{t_1}$ of a frequency set $B_{(l)}^{t_1}$ has obtained as follows

$$\gamma_{(Bl)}^{t_1} = exp\left[-\frac{1}{2}\left[\frac{\hat{x}^{t_1} - m_{(l)}^{t_1}}{\sigma_{(l)}^{t_1}}\right]\right] - \infty < \hat{x}^{t_1} < \infty \tag{2.3}$$

After calculating the contrast sensitivity $\gamma_{(Bl)}^{t_1}$ of a block, the contrast sensitivity value has been calculated by using the range of frequency between the lower range(visible part) and the higher range (invisible part) which has been given below in Eq. (2.4).

$$CSV = \max\left\{\gamma_{(Bl)}^{t_1}\right\} - \min\left\{\gamma_{(Bl)}^{t_1}\right\} \tag{2.4}$$

Symmetric Gaussian membership based contrast sensitivity function $\gamma_{(Bl)}^{t_1}$ of the spatial frequency set $B_{(l)}^{t_1} = \left(m_{(l)}^{t_1}, \sigma_{(l)}^{t_1}\right)$ is representing in Fig. 2. CSV calculation explained in Algorithm 2.1.

Algorithm 2.1 CSV calculation

Input: Blocks of a component.

Output: CSV of a component.

1. *for* each block in the component *do*

2.   Calculate central value of the given block using equation (2.1)

3.   Calculate probability density value using equation (2.2)

4.   Draw a bell shaped graph using Symmetric
        -Gaussian member function using equation (2.3).

5.   Find the deviated value from the result of
        -step 4 using equation (2.7)

6.   Deviated value as the contrast sensitivity value

7. *end for*

2.2 CSV Based Block Leveling

CSV based block leveling has done by cluster of blocks using K-Medoid cluster. Procedure of block leveling technique is defined in Algorithm 2.2. This suggested method describes the cluster process which has been uniformly partitioned the whole component blocks into K number of clusters [32]. Blocks have been clustered based on the contrast value of each block and the reference value (number of blocks). Nearest CSV of blocks clustered into the same group. This clustering process continued until the cluster size reached the maximum size mentioned as reference value. During the cluster process, maximum CSV of the previous cluster is considered as the initial minimum CSV (medoid) of the current cluster for finding the minimum distance CSV. Minimum distance blocks identified from Eq. (2.5) and medoid value updated from Eq. (2.6). Level value is assigned to each cluster in the component. A higher level block requires more quantize than the lower level CSV blocks. Level1 is assigned to minimum CSV blocks and level 4 assigned to maximum CSV blocks. Other levels are assigned to the remaining CSV blocks. Block set B expanded as

$$B = B_1^{CSV}, B_2^{CSV}, \cdots, B_N^{CSV}$$

where N = 4096 blocks. K is the number of clusters. Medoids are represented as m1, m2, m3 and m4. Initially the clustering process starts with m1 = 1 and compare the each CSV to determine the minimum distance value. The obtained CSV cluster it into same group. Reference value of each cluster is 1024.

$$Reference\ value\ n\ = N/K = 4096/4 = 1024$$

$$Initially \ m_1 = 1$$

$$K_i = \|B_i^{csv} - m_i\| \leq \|B_i^{CSV} - m_i\| \text{ and } blocks(K_i) < n \tag{2.5}$$

$$j = 1, 2, 3, \cdots, N.i = 1, 2, 3, \cdots, N.$$

$$m_i = maximum \ distance \ CSV(K_{l-1}) \tag{2.6}$$

where N is the total number of blocks in a component, n is the number of blocks in each cluster, K as initialized as four that represents number of clusters in a component.

Algorithm 2.2 Blocks leveling

Input: CSV of a component.

Output: Blocks with leveling value.

    1.   Initialize the K value as 4 Assign first medoid m1=1

    2.   *for* each block in the component *do*

    3.   Determine the minimum distance block by

            -comparing the CSV and check the reference

            -value which is lesser than n using equation (2.5)

    4.   Cluster it as the same and assign the cluster level

    5.   Update the medoid value with maximum CSV

         -    of previous cluster using equation (2.6)

    6.   *end for*

    7.   Assign minimum CSV cluster as the level1.

    8.   Assign maximum CSV cluster as the level4.

    9.   Assign the in-between CSV cluster as the level2 and level3.

2.3   Discrete Cosine Transformation

DCT has been separated the image into spectral sub-bands of differing importance with respect to the image visual quality [6]. This proposed method has transformed every 8×8 block image into high and low level of frequency spectrum to concentrate the compression on the high frequency spectrum [32].

2.4 Adaptive Block Quantization Table

Adaptive block quantization table (ABQT) formation depends on the JPEG standardized quantization table, cluster level and QF value explained in Algorithm 2.3. QF controls the quality of the compressed image with ranging from 1 to 100. Higher cluster level value improved the ABQT value for making better compression on the corresponding blocks. The ABQT calculation given in Eq. (2.8) below

$$q = \begin{cases} \left(\frac{QF}{50}\right) + 1, & \text{if } QF \leq 50 \\ \left(\frac{QF}{50}\right) - 1, & \text{if } QF > 50 \end{cases} \tag{2.7}$$

$$ABQT(i, j) = (QT(i, j) \times q) + \text{cluster level value} \tag{2.8}$$

$QT\ (i, j)$ is the JPEG standard quantization table value [14] for corresponding (i, j) coordinate value of the luminance and chrominance component, q is a quality factor value from Eq. (2.7).

Algorithm 2.3 Adaptive block quantization table calculation

Input: Level value, JPEG quantization table (QT) and QF.

Output: Adaptive block quantization table.

  1. *for* each block in a component *do*

  2.   *if* QF<=50 *then*

  3.   q=(QF/50)+1

  4.   *else*

  5.   q=(QF/100)-1

  6.   *end if*

  7.   ABQT= (QT × q) + cluster level value

  8. *end for*

2.5   Quantization

The Quantization is an essential part in compression algorithm to reduce the number of bits per sample [33]. In this proposed method, quantization process concentrated on contrast sensitive value of each block. ABQT has been created for individual block depends on CSV not like JPEG quantization table which depends on component. This quantization process performed on the DCT spectrum coefficients by ABQT has been given in Eq. (2.9).

$$F(u, v) = round\left(\frac{f(u, v)}{ABQT}\right) \tag{2.9}$$

F(u,v) is an quantized image, $f(u, v)$ is a DCT spectrum coefficient. During the quantization process, the coefficients have been separated into DC and AC coefficients, which have been reordered into 1-D format using a zigzag scanning in order to create long run of zero valued coefficients[29]. All DC coefficients are combined to form a separate bit stream. Encode the difference from the DC component of previous 8 × 8 blocks with the next block, i.e. Differential Pulse Code Modulation (DPCM) [30].

2.6   Huffman Entropy Coding

Huffman coding is popular entropy coding for compressing the data with variable-length codes. This method constructs a set of variable-length code words with the shortest average length and assigns them to the symbols [31]. The symbol with highest probability has assigned the shortest code using symbol table and vice versa. The less sized bit stream has been produced from the Huffman encoding process, which has been considered as the compressed image [32]. Compressed image is the final output of encoding process. The above all explained methods have applied on the proposed SGKMCS compression method is explained in Algorithm 2.4.

Algorithm 2.4 Proposed work

Input: RGB image data base.

Output: Reconstructed RGB image database.

1. Get an input RGB image from the database.

2. Covert the RGB image into YCbCr image format

3. Isolate the individual component Y, Cb and Cr from the YCbCr image format.

4. *for* each Y, Cb and Cr component *do*

5.   Decompose the individual component into

    non- overlapped 8×8 blocks image.

6.   *for* each input 8×8 block image *do*

7.   Call CSV calculation function (Algorithm 2.1)

8.   Call block leveling function (Algorithm 2.2)

9.   Call Adaptive block Quantization

    - table calculation function (Algorithm 2.3)

10. *end for*

11. Transform each input 8 × 8 image block using

    - DCT into frequency spectrum.

12. Quantization process on the frequency

    spectrum using adaptive quantization table

    which is calculated from step 9 using equation (2.9).

13.   Make a single vector values using Zigzag scanning

14. Apply Differential Code Modulation.

15. Produce bit stream using Huffman -Entropy encoding.

16. Calculate CR of an image.

17. Do the inverse process of Encoding.

18. *end for*

19. Reconstruct the YCbCr image.

20. Reconstruct the RGB image.

21. Measure the Quality metrics of all images in the database.

3   Experimental Results

The proposed method has been implemented in Matlab 2017b on 67 input color images which have been taken from the color image database [29] with different QF ranging from 1 to 100. The performance of the proposed work has been compared with the existing color image compression methods, namely JPEG and JPEG with contrast sensitivity function. JPEG compression has been implemented the component based quantization in which the quantization elements are constants. JPEG with contrast sensitivity compression experimented based on the component based quantization in which quantization elements are contrast detection threshold, derived from [10]. Figure 3 shows the 65 input color image database which has 24 bits jpg images with different resolution like 768 × 576, 428 × 569, 300 × 168 and 576 × 768.

In the proposed SGKMCS method, one of the sample RGB input image #13 shown in Fig. 4(a). It has been converted to YCbCr image format, and then converted to an individual isolated Y, Cb and Cr components. Each individual component is further divided into non-overlapping 8 × 8 blocks. Contrast sensitivity function (CSF) applied to every block, the sample output graph shown in Fig. 4(b). From the CS graph the CSV has been calculated. CSV of Y component in image #13 is shown in Fig. 4(c). The blocks are clustered on basis of CSV using K-Mediod Cluster. In this proposed method K represents 4. The whole number of blocks was equally partitioned into 4 clusters in which each cluster has 1024 blocks. The partitioned clusters based on the CSV are shown in 4(d). Parallel work of 8 × 8 block transformed using DCT, as shown in Fig. 4(e).

Adaptive block quantization table generated based on JPEG standard quantization table, block cluster level and QF. Some sample ABQT of proposed SGKMCS method shown below. For example, in an experimental methodology when K = 1, QF = 40 and

Fig. 3. Source RGB image database

first block in Cb component of an image #20 in Fig. 3 obtained the ABQT denoted as
follows.

$$ABQT_{40}^{1}(1) = \begin{bmatrix} 32 & 33 & 44 & 86 & 179 & 179 & 179 & 179 \\ 33 & 39 & 48 & 120 & 179 & 179 & 179 & 179 \\ 44 & 48 & 102 & 120 & 179 & 179 & 179 & 179 \\ 86 & 120 & 179 & 179 & 179 & 179 & 179 & 179 \\ 179 & 179 & 179 & 179 & 179 & 179 & 179 & 179 \\ 179 & 179 & 179 & 179 & 179 & 179 & 179 & 179 \\ 179 & 179 & 179 & 179 & 179 & 179 & 179 & 179 \\ 179 & 179 & 179 & 179 & 179 & 179 & 179 & 179 \end{bmatrix}$$

Quantization process is performed on each block depending on their contrast value
of the transformed image using ABQT. After that zigzag scanning process performed
on the quantized blocks convert the matrices into the vectors for Huffman encoding.
Then the Huffman encoding process encodes the image into stream of bits in the form
of compressed image. Finally compressed image with less size can be transformed from
one place to another through the communication channel. Decompression process is the
inverse process of encoding method.

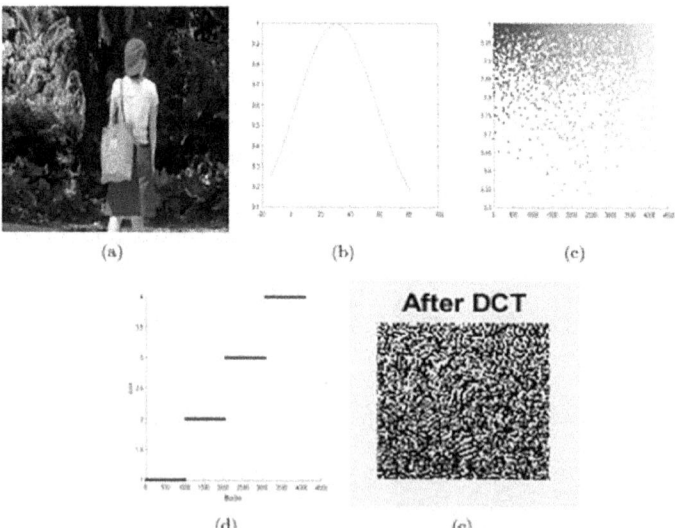

Fig. 4. Process of proposed method on one of the sample of Y component of an image #13 (a)
Original RGB image #13, (b) Sample CSF graph of first block of Y component, (c) CSV of all
blocks in Y component, (d) Block level cluster of Y component and (e) DCT coefficient of image
#13.

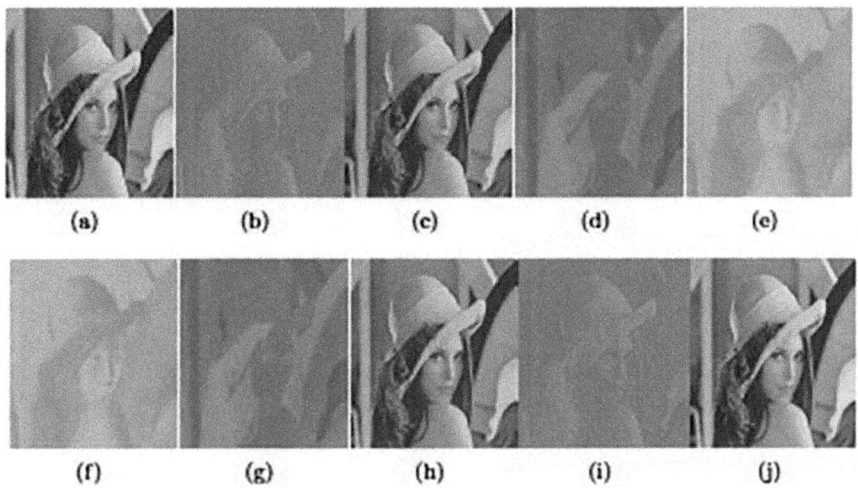

Fig. 5. Output of the proposed method using Lena image (a) Original Lena image (b) YCbCr image (c) Luminance image (d) Cb image (e) Cr image (f) Reconstructed Cr image (g) Reconstructed Cb image (h) Reconstructed Luminance image (i) Reconstructed YCbCr image (j) Reconstructed RGB image.

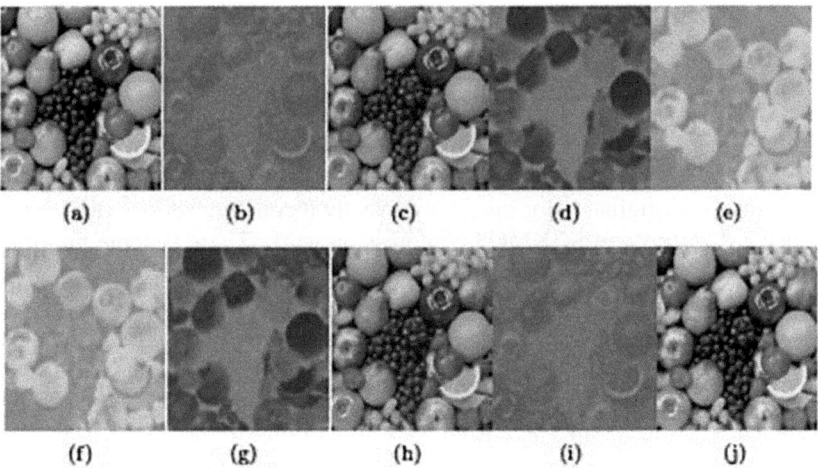

Fig. 6. Output of the proposed method using Fruits image (a) Original Fruits image (b) YCbCr image (c) Luminance image (d) Cb image (e) Cr image (f) Reconstructed Cr image (g) Reconstructed Cb image (h) Reconstructed Luminance image (i) Reconstructed YCbCr image (j) Reconstructed RGB image.

The proposed method has been applied on Lena and Fruits images with 512×512 sizes. Encoding process of Lena and Fruits images shown in Fig. 5(a) to Fig. 5(e) and Fig. 6(a) to Fig. 6(e). Decoding process of Lena and Fruits images shown in Fig. 5(f) to Fig. 5(j) and Fig. 6(f) to Fig. 6(j).

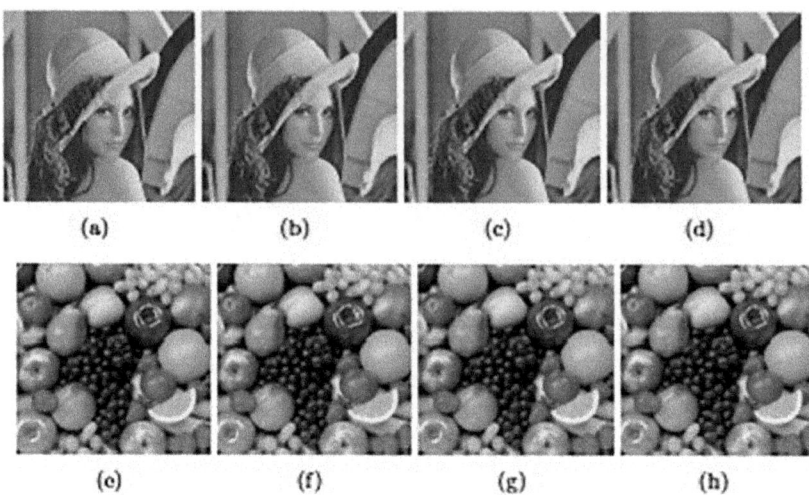

Fig. 7. Comparison of the proposed SGKMCS reconstructed images with the existing methods image (a) Original Lena image, (b) Reconstructed image from JPEG, (c) Reconstructed image from JPEG with contrast sensitivity method (d) Reconstructed image from proposed SGKMCS method (e) Original Fruits image, (f) Reconstructed Fruits image from JPEG (g) Reconstructed image from JPEG with contrast sensitivity method (h) Reconstructed image from proposed SGKMCS method.

Proposed reconstructed Lena and Fruits images have been compared with the existing JPEG and JPEG with contrast sensitive compression methods shown in Fig. 7. We observed that visual quality of proposed reconstructed images as shown in Fig. 7(d) and Fig. 7(h) are more contrast than the other two images. From this figure, this work concluded that the original color image is perfectly reconstructed from the compressed image using the proposed SGKMCS compression work. There is some minimum difference in color information due to the work based on lossy compression method. The performance efficiency of the proposed method compared with the existing methods [10] on the basis of CR and SSIM are tabulated in the Table 1.

Result from the table shows that compression ratio averagely increased by 3 times and visual quality averagely increased by 9.9% than the existing methods JPEG and the JPEG with contrast sensitivity value [10]. According to the Table 1, the proposed work produced better compression ratio and lesser SSIM when QF is 50. Maximum QF (100) has been produced better SSIM of reconstructed image and lesser CR. From the comparison table, this work concludes that the proposed quantization process based on contrast sensitivity value of each block in the component produce better compression ratio than the component based existing method. New SGKMCS compression method applied on all source images in the database with QF is 100 and produced an effective compression ratio that has been displayed using histogram in Fig. 8.

In Fig. 8 image #1(single human image) has the higher CR of chrominance red component than the other images. Image #34(landscape) has the second higher CR of chrominance component value than the remaining 63 images.

Table 1. Performance Comparison of Proposed SGKMCS with Existing PEG and JPEG- CSF

	Parameters	Compression Ratio				SSIM			
		Y-Components	CB Components	CR Components	RGB image	SSIM_Y	SSIM_CB	SSIM_CR	SSIM_RGB
Fruits	JPEG-CSF	15.3723	42.7188	39.696	26.3963	0.9923	09706	09854	0.9861
	JPEG	16.9959	34.611	34.5472	25.7122	0.9717	0.9694	0.9703	0.9422
	SGKMCS (QF=1)	52.4690	68.0457	67.9853	62.9853	0.9864	0.9778	0.9672	0.9623
	SGKMCS (QF=50)	57.7	83.508	81.4305	74.24	0.9679	0.9523	0.9453	0.9412
	SGKMCS (QF=100)	31.7222	45.8771	46.8839	41.4944	0.9993	0.9985	0.9765	0.9753
Lena	JPEG	19.6588	46.2308	41.3889	31.0367	0.9591	0.9464	0.9467	0.9048
	JPEG-CSF	19.7133	58.4927	37.9017	31.8446	0.9889	0.9585	0.9876	0.9507
	SGKMCS (QF=1)	55.7279	88.6366	76.6034	73.6559	0.9768	0.9774	0.9517	0.9500
	SGKMCS (QF=50)	64.9343	119.6279	106.9321	97.1648	0.9563	0.9564	0.9341	0.9312
	SGKMCS (QF=100)	28.6303	59.4415	48.3659	42.1459	0.9989	0.9980	0.9979	0.9954

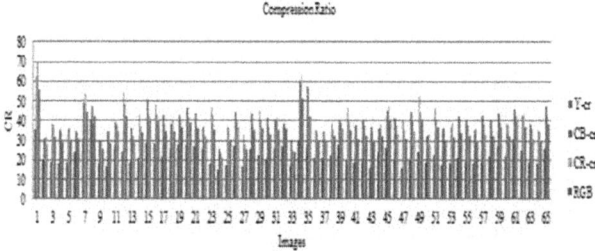

Fig. 8. Compression Ratio of all source images with QF = 100.

These observed results from our experimental method, implied that, this proposed method maximum of images having the higher CR of chrominance red component than the chrominance blue components.

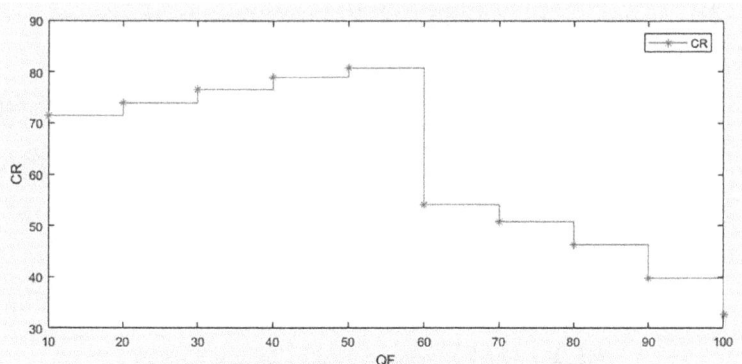

Fig. 9. Stair graph of CR with QF.

The Stair graph in Fig. 9 represents the relationship between CR and QF of the reconstructed image #20. Compression ratio increases as the QF increases from 10 to 50. Once QF reaches 50, CR decreases from the maximum value.

The proposed work has been applied on all the source images with 3 different QF (10, 50 and 100) and calculated the CR which has been plotted in Fig. 10. From this graph, the work concluded that maximum CR has been produced when the QF is 50 and the minimum CR has been generated when the QF is 100. It means that higher QF preserves the quality of the original image.

Figure 11 shows the quality measurement of all test images such as Mean Squared Error (MSE) and Peak Signal Noise Ratio. From that graph, observed that all the test images achieved better PSNR (more than 45 Decibel) value which implies that this proposed work maintains the quality of the original image.

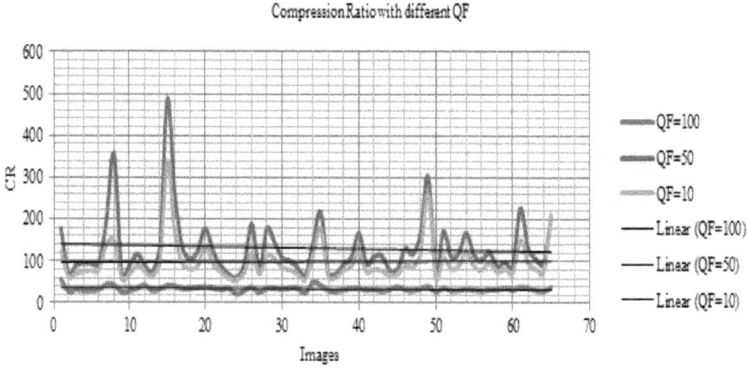

Fig. 10. Compression Ratio (CR) of all test images with three different Quality Factor (QF) values.

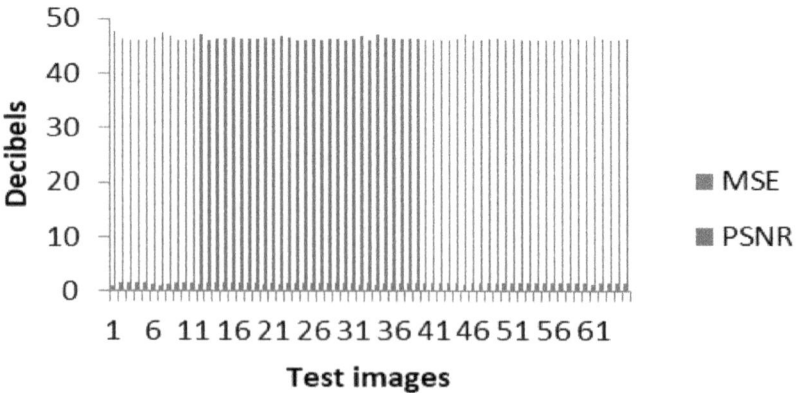

Fig. 11. Quality measurement of all test images.

4 Conclusion

This paper proposed a new methodology SGKMCS lossy compression to improve the compression ratio and visual perception of the decompressed color images. A novel SGKMCS compression algorithm is based on the contrast sensitivity value calculated by symmetric Gaussian member function on a block. ABQT has improved the quantization process than the existing methods namely JPEG and JPEG with contrast sensitivity function. The experimental result shows that proposed work averagely increased the CR by 3 times and SSIM improved by 9.9%. In Future work this method can be extended to 3D Compression with automatic analysis using Artificial Neural Network.

References

1. Bihas C.D., Bhubatosh, C.: Color image construction based on block truncation coding using pattern fitting principle. Journal of the Pattern Recognition Society, 40, 2408–2417, (2007).
2. Chou, C. H., Liu, K.-C.: Color image compression based on the measure of just noticeable color difference. IET image processing, 2 (6), 304–322, (2008). https://doi.org/10.1049/iet-ipr:20080034.
3. Denis, G. P., Peter, B.: Measuring contrast sensitivity. Vision Research, 90, 10 -14, (2014).
4. Dmitri, A. V., Reyhane, T., Aniaksander, D.: Designing Gaussian membership functions for fuzzy classifier generated by heuristic possibility clustering. Journal of information and organizational sciences 37 (2), 127–139, (2013).
5. Evgeny, G, Emilia, L., Moshe, P.: Correlation-based approach to color image compression. Signal processing: Image communication, V. 22, 719–733, (2007). https://doi.org/10.1016/j.image.2007.04.001
6. Fouzi, D., Redha, B, Nabil, B.: Color image compression algorithm based on the DCT transform combined to an adaptive block scanning. International Journal of electronics and communication 65, 16–26, (2011). https://doi.org/10.1016/j.aeue.2010.03.003
7. Haiqiang, W., Ioannis, K., Jiantong, Z., Jeonghoon, P., Shawin, L., Xin, Z., Man-On, P., Xin, J., Ronggang, W., Yun, Z., Jiwu, H., Sam, K., C.-C.Jay, K.: VideoSet: A large-scale compressed video quality dataset based on JND measurement, Journal of visual communication and image representation, 46, 292–302 (2017).
8. Ismail, A., Bulent, S.: Statistical analysis of image quality measures. IEEE, (2015)
9. Joe, Y. L., Lina, J., Sudeng, H., Ioannis, K., Zhi, L., Anne, A., Jay , K. C. -C.: Experimental design and analysis of JND test on coded image/video. Applications of Digital image processing, (2015).
10. Juncai, Y., Guizhong, L.: A novel color image compression algorithm using the human visual contrast sensitivity charecteristics.Photonic sensors, 7(1), 72–81, (2017).
11. Kannan, P, Deepa, S., Ramakrishnan, R.: Contrast enhancement of sports image using two comparative approaches. American Journal of Intelligent Systems, 2(6),141–147, (2012).
12. Karri, T. R., Ramesh, C.: Baseline JPEG compression with K-Means clustering based algorithm. International Journal of computer science and mobile computing, 4 (4), 379–386, (2015).
13. Ku-Liang, C., Tsu-Chun, H., Chi-Chao, H.: Joint chroma subsampling and distortion- minimization based luma modification for RGB color images with application. IEEE transaction on Image processing, 1–3, (2017). PubMed ID: 28650815. https://doi.org/10.1109/TIP.2017.2719945

14. Lamia A., Pranab K. D., Mirza, A.F.M., Rashidul H.,Mohammed G. S. B.,Golam M. D.: An improved JPEG image compression algorithm by modifying luminance quantization table.International Journal of computer science and network security, 17,200–208, (2017).
15. Mohamed, U. A. A., Eswaran, C., Kannan,R.: Lossy image compression based on error and vector quantisation. Eurasip journal on image and video processing, (2017).
16. Rahul, P., Nindhiya, K., Gurjeet, S., Hiteshwari, S.: Image compression and quality factor in case of JPEG image format. International Journal of Advanced Research Computer and communication Engineering, 2(7), 2578–2581, (2013).
17. Raju, G, Madhu, S. N.: A fast and efficient color image enhancement method based on fuzzy-logic and histogram. International Journal of Electronic and communications, 68, 237-243, (2013).
18. Reem, T. H.,Wail, S. E., Hassan, H. R.: Fast approximate DCT with GPU implementation for image compression. Journal of visual Communication and image representation, 357–365, (2016). https://doi.org/10.1016/j.jvcir.2016.07.003
19. Shakeri, M., Dezfoulian, M. H., Khotanlou, H., Barati, A. H., Masoumi, Y.: Image contrast enhancement using fuzzy clustering with adaptive cluster parameter and sub-histogram equalization. Digital signal processing, (2016). https://doi.org/10.1016/j.dsp.2016.10.013
20. Shilong, L., Md, A. R., Ching-Feng, L., Chin, Y. W., Guannan, J., San, C. L., Ngaim-ing, K., Haiyan, S.: Image contrast enhancement based on intensity expansion-compression. Journal of visual communication image representation, 48, 169–181, (2017). https://doi.org/10.1016/j.jvcir.2017.05.011
21. Sreelekha, G., Sathidevi, P. S.: An HVS based adaptive quantization scheme for the compression of color images. Digital signal processing, 20, 1129–1149, (2010). https://doi.org/10.1016/j.dsp.2009.12.003
22. Stefen, W.: Analysis of public image and video databases for quality assessment. IEEE Journal - Signal processing, 6 (6), (2012). https://doi.org/10.1109/JSTSP.2012.2215007
23. Sudeng, H., Haiqiang, W., Jay, K. C.- C.: A GMM-based stair quality model for human perceived JPEG images. IEEE, (2016).
24. Walaa, M. A., Wajeb, G.: Color image compression algorithm based on the DCT blocks. Institution of Engineering and Technology, 52 (20), (2016).
25. Wang, X., Jiang, G. Y., Zhang, J. M., Shao. F., Peng, Z. J., Yu, M.: Visibility threshold of compressed stereoscopic image: effects of asymmetric coding. The Imaging Science Journal. 61 (128), (2013). https://doi.org/10.1179/1743131X11Y.0000000035
26. Yao, J., Liu, G.: An adaptive quantization method of image based on the contrast sensitivity characteristics of human visual system. Journal of Electronics and Information Technology, 38 (5), (2016).
27. http://psy.vanderbilt.edu/courses/hon185/spatialfrequency/spatialfrequency.html   accessed on 10.01.2018.
28. Image samples are taken from https://www.cs.cmu.edu/afs/cs/project/cil/www/V-image.html accessed on 12. 11. 2017.
29. Chithra, PL., Thangavel, P.: A New Efficient Embedded Wavelet Image Codec Based On Multidirectional Traversal Algorithm Based On Multidirectional Traversal. Int. J. Signal and Imaging Systems Engineering, Vol. 5, No. 3, (2012). ISSN online: 1748–0701 ISSN print: 1748–0698
30. Chithra, PL., Christoper Tamilmathi, A.: 3-d wavelet codec (compression/decompression) for 3-d Medical Images. International Journal of Information Technology Convergence and Services (IJITCS),Vol.6, No.1, 45–54, (2016) ISSN 2231–153X: 2231–1939
31. Chithra, PL., Srividhya, K.:A Comparative Study of Wavwlet Coders for Image Compression. Springer International Publishing Switzerland (2013), pp. 260–269

32. PL Chithra, PL., Christoper TamilMathi, A.: Effective lossy and lossless color image compression with multi layer perceptron. International Journal of Engineering and Technology, 7 (2.22) (2018) 9–14, ISSN: 0975–4024.
33. Chithra, PL., Christoper Tamilmathi, A.: Image Preservation using Wavelet Based On Kronecker Mask, Birge-Massart And Parity Strategy International Journal of Innovative Technology and Exploring Engineering (IJITEE) ISSN: 2278–3075, Volume-8 Issue-11, September (2019).

Automatic Classification of Desmids Using Handcrafted Texture Descriptors

Rajmohan Pardeshi[1](✉), Rita B. Patil[1], Nirupama Ansingkar[1], and Prapti Deshmukh[2]

[1] Department of Computer Science and IT, Dr. Babasaheb Ambedkar Marathwada University, Aurangabad, Maharashtra, India
rajmohanji@hotmail.com
[2] Dr. G Y Pathrikar College of CS and IT, Aurangabad, Maharashtra, India

Abstract. Algae plays a vital role in aquatic ecosystem and serves as indicator for various issues related to water quality. In addition to these algae have various application in day to day life such as nutrition, fish feed, agriculture fertilizer, medicine, space research etc. More than 5000 species are discovered by the scientist and still research is going on. Manual classification of microscopic algae is very tedious task as it involves burden of taxonomic investigation whereas machine learning based algorithms play vital role and requires only one-time training. In this paper, we presented a method for automatic classification of desmids using handcrafted descriptors. Our algorithm involves three common steps of Patter Recognition algorithm such as pre-processing, feature computation and classification. We have applied image resize and colour to gray level conversion operation during processing. Histogram of Oriented Gradients, Local Binary Pattern and Local Phase Quantization are used for texture description. Nearest Neighbour Classifier, Linear Discriminant Analysis and Support Vector Machines were tested for classification of desmids. We have achieved encouraging results during our experiments on dataset of five classes of desmids.

Keywords: Unicellular Algae · Computer Vision · Texture Descriptors · Support Vector Machine · Linear Discriminant analysis

1 Introduction

Freshwater wetlands are significant ecosystems, and the benthic, attached microbial communities that live in them, including desmids, are vital habitats that help with primary productivity, nutrient cycling, and substrate stabilisation [1]. Desmids are unicellular biomass algae found in freshwater ecosystem.

As biologists, tiny desmids have piqued their curiosity. It is a complex group of microorganisms found in aquatic environments all over the world. Desmids come in a variety of forms and have applications in a variety of fields. Scientists are attempting to discover how to harness these microscopic creatures for the benefit of humanity's wellbeing, such as an alternative fuel, food, and so on.

Desmids identification has traditionally been performed manually, which is a tough and time-consuming task. And some species' likeness creates human error because they

R. Manza et al. (Eds.): ACVAIT 2022, AISR 176, pp. 400–408, 2023.
https://doi.org/10.2991/978-94-6463-196-8_30

are unable to judge it effectively. On the other hand, computer vision-based systems provide efficient and dependable outcomes, as well as a guarantee of a result. As a result, we proposed an automated technique for classifying desmids from microscopic pictures. In this paper we proposed a system based on popular handcrafted descriptors for classification desmids automatically using computer vision techniques.

2 Literature Review

Classification of microscopic algae is problem of active research since last decade, there few algorithms are presented by researchers based on locally available resources and problems. In [9] presented a method for commonly found algae classification, to do this they applied segmentation using edge detection followed by morphological operations. Various features were computed such Fourier descriptors, Moment invariants, shape features, textures features based on GLCM. SMO classifier was sued for algae classification. Based on contour analysis and scale space features, Imaging cytometry based study was presented in [10], various shape descriptors, texture descriptors and binary shape measures were used with Random Forest Classifier and CNN.

The authors of [11] established a unified paradigm for diatom identification. They also compared their strategy to state-of-the-art descriptors like the Gabor filter and moments, and found that it performed better. On a huge dataset of diatom photos, hand-crafted features are examined [12]. The authors used local binary patterns and log Gabor filters to classify diatoms using several classifiers such as SVM, K-means, Decision trees, Boosting, and Bagging with 10-fold cross validation and reached a result of 98.10 percent. [13] presents convolution neural networks-based deep learning for diatom classification, which demonstrated promising accuracy with a huge dataset of diatoms belonging to 80 categories. Using microscopic algae photos from the Scenedesmus group, [14] authors constructed a system based on statistical features and texture descriptors, achieving a result of 98.63 percent with SVM and 97 percent using artificial neural networks. Authors presented a technique for recognizing and classifying freshwater algae in [15]. To begin, each segmented item is segmented, and binary shape descriptors are extracted from each segmented object. Fourier spectrum descriptors were extracted, and PCA was used to pick features. MLP and ANN were used to classify the data.

Recently authors in [16] evaluated the performance of AlexNet for classification Scenedesmus algae for application to biomonitoring. They have trained the AlexNet on their dataset from scratch with existing weights form ImageNet and achieved the performance with accuracy of 96%.

From the above aforementioned paragraphs, it can be understood that automatic classification algae still have a room for research as studies are carried out based on locally available data and issues. Best of our knowledge this is first study presented for automated desmids classification using image processing machine learning.

3 Proposed Method

A. Pre-processing

In our method we have applied two pre-processing steps, as these steps are important to prepare the image for accurate feature description and most of the times these steps are depends on application. We aimed for desmids classification using texture descriptors and hence we have applied the two operations as pre-processing 1) image resize to size 164 × 164 this is fixed empirically and 2) RGB to gray conversion as gray level conversion allows to reduce the size of memory and texture description become easy with gray values for the feature extraction techniques considered (Fig. 1).

B. Feature Extraction

Local Binary Patterns: Local binary pattern [6] is the texture descriptor which takes a fixed threshold for binary image and gives 8-bit code in terms of binary value; after that, the code is converted into decimal value then this decimal number value of the image is drawn in a histogram and used as features, to make this rotation invariant more compact these descriptor values are classified again into two categories having transition and no transition in binary values and hence we get a total of 59 features which are called as Uniform Local Binary Patterns [5] (Fig. 2).

Histogram of Oriented Gradients: Histogram of Oriented Gradient is well known shape descriptors used for detection human poses [8] based on the principles occurrence of gradient orientation in localized portions of the image. First, the image is divided into small windows are known as cells and these cells are in different sizes in our case we have cell size of 32 × 32 which fixed empirically. And so on it may differ for different applications. Then these cells are connected to form a block from each block values are considered formed a histogram representation (Fig. 3).

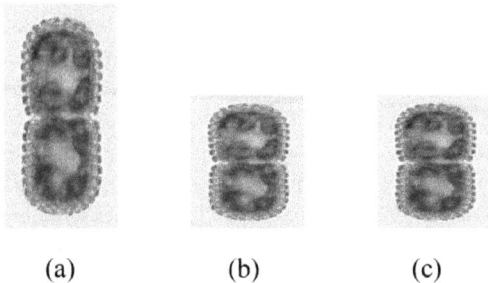

(a)   (b)   (c)

Fig. 1. Original Image of Desmids and Resized and Grayscale Image

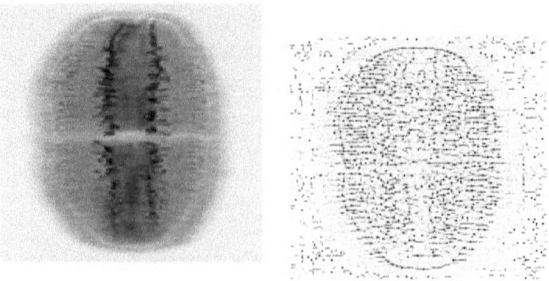

Fig. 2. a) Grayscale Image of Desmid b) LBP Texture Image of Desmid

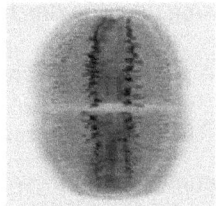 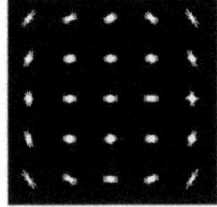

Fig. 3. a) Grayscale Image of Desmid b) HOG Computation

Local Phase Quantization: Local phase quantization [7] is one of the Fourier phase information of blur insensitive property or it is a texture descriptor, which extracts the local information from the images by computing STFT over a rectangular neighbourhood N_x of size M by M. which is nothing but calculating the four frequency coefficients at the four different points on a pixel. And we get four real and four imaginary values in two-bit code and then this two-bit code is converted into 8- bit code. And a histogram of 8-bit code is drawn, pixel position is used as features and here we get 256 features for one image (Fig. 4).

C. Classification

Nearest Neighbour Classifier: The most common and traditional method for classification, the Nearest Neighbour Classifier is utilized. It is a learning algorithm that is supervised in nature. An appropriate distance measure can be used to find the nearest neighbour. We employ Euclidean distance as a distance measure in this study to locate the closest neighbour. If P represents the training data and Q represents the testing sample, then the Euclidean distance between P and Q is:

$$D(P, Q) = \sqrt{\Sigma_{i=1}^{n}(P_i - Q_i)^2} \tag{1}$$

Support Vector Machine: Vapnik [18] developed the SVM classifier. Among the others, SVM is known as the most sophisticated classifier. SVM maps m-dimensional input space X to l-dimensional feature space z. The optimal separating hyper-plane is used to solve the z quadratic programming problem of separating two classes. Kernel strategies can be used to expand the basic SVM [2]. In our experiment, we used SVM with the

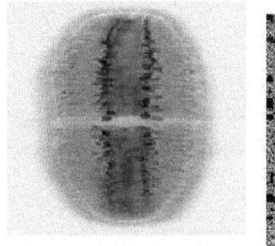 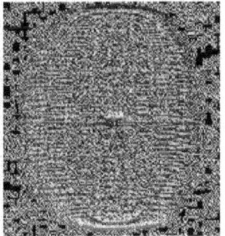

Fig. 4. a) Grayscale Image of Desmid b) LPQ Texture Image of Desmid

RBF kernel function, which gives us the following decision function:

$$D(X) = \sum_{i \in S}^{\infty} \alpha_{iy_i} \exp\left(-\gamma||x_i - x||^2\right) + b \tag{2}$$

In this case, support vectors are centres of RBF, more details are given in [2, 3].

Linear Discriminant Analysis: Linear discriminant analysis is popular classifier due it simplicity, ease of implementation and generalization ability. Higher level of class discrimination is archived in LDA by maximizing the ratio of between class to within class variance [17]. Here we used the LDA to classify the desmids. The classification function for dataset X of desmids and classes C in our case C = 5 given as:

$$g(X) = WTX \tag{3}$$

where W represents the linear projections.
   The between class scatter matrix Sb given as

$$Sb = \sum_{i=1}^{c} n_i(m_i - m)(m_i - m)^T \tag{4}$$

where mi represents the mean of ith class and m is the overall mean.ni are the number of samples in ith class.
   The within class scatter matrix is Sw is given as

$$Sw = \sum_{i=1}^{c} \sum_{x \in X} (X - m_i)(X - m_i)^T. \tag{5}$$

Now, given the Quadratic distance d of g(X) and centers Vi = WT mi compared in LDA space and new sample classified to class label $\omega \in C$, accordingly:

$$\omega = \arg \min_{1 <= i <= c} d(g(X), Vi) \tag{6}$$

D. Dataset and Evaluation Protocol

Dataset: We have used five types of desmids genus with total 88 microscopic images with varied angels, sizes and shapes for automatic classification desmids namely.

1. Closteriaceae (27),
2. Desmidiaceae (23),
3. Gonatozygon (13),
4. Mesotaeniaceae (33),
5. Peniaceae (19)

   This is one of the most versatile data of microscopic image is considered for the experiments and evaluation of our method from [4]. The samples of microscopic images are shown in Fig. 5.

Evaluation Protocol
Most popular method is used for evaluation of proposed approach, named as k- fold

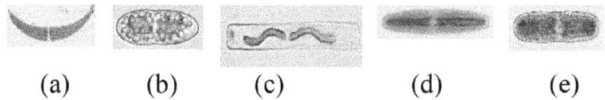

(a)   (b)   (c)   (d)   (e)

Fig. 5. Samples of microscopic images of desmids from our dataset a) Closteriaceae b) Desmidiaceae c) Gonatozygon d) Mesotaeniaceae e) Peniaceae

cross validation. The dataset is randomly partitioned in to k sub folds. Each time one fold is considering for testing and rest for training. Process is repeated until each fold has got opportunity to serve for training and testing. In our experiment we considered k = 10. We have defined accuracy as following:

$$Accuracy = \frac{Correctly\ Classified\ desmids\ in\ class}{Total\ Desmids\ in\ class} \tag{7}$$

4   Results and Discussion

In this work, our aim is to automatic identify the genus of desmids with the hand-crafted descriptors due to their power of texture description. To evaluate our method, we have performed exhaustive experiments with three well known feature extraction methods namely LBP, HOG and LPQ by combining with three popular and efficient classifiers namely NN Classifier, SVM classifier and LDA Classifier. Due to the limited and imbalanced dataset, we have applied the cross validation and error average was computed.

In Table 1 we have details the accuracies given by various classifiers and feature extraction techniques. It can be noted that HoG has given superior performance as compared to LBP and LPQ whereas among the classifiers SVM has given the highest accuracy i.e. 86.1% with HOG, 81.2% with LPQ and 78.3% with LBP. The performance of Nearest Neighbor classifier was also good follwed by SVM with accuracies of 81.7%, 84.3% and 76.1% with LBP, HOG and LPQ respectively. LDA has performed average as compared to NN and SVM and given accuracy of 67.8%, 84.3% and 69.4% respectively with LBP, HOG and LPQ.

For deeper understanding we have also shown the confusion matrix for highest and lowest accuracies obtained during desmids recognition in Figs. 6 and 7 respectively.

Table 1. Desmids Recogntion Accuracy given by Local Binary Patterns

Feature Extraction /Classifier	Nearest Neighbour Classifier	Support Vector Machine	Linear Discriminant Analysis
Local Binary Patterns	81.7%	78.3%	67.8%
Histogram of Oriented Gradients	84.3%	86.1%	84.3%
Local Phase Quantization	76.1%	81.2%	69.4%

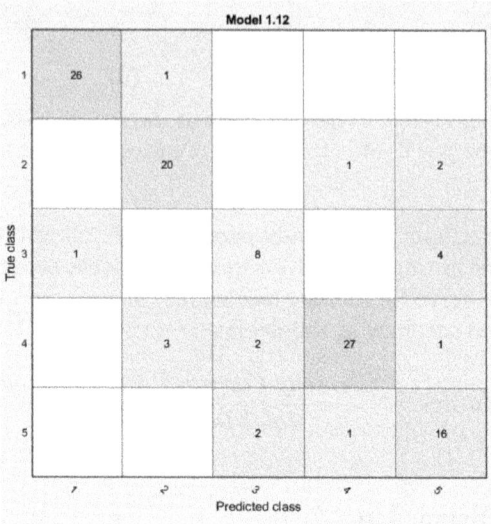

Fig. 6. Confusion Matrix given HOG with SVM for Highest Recognition Accuracy for Desmids

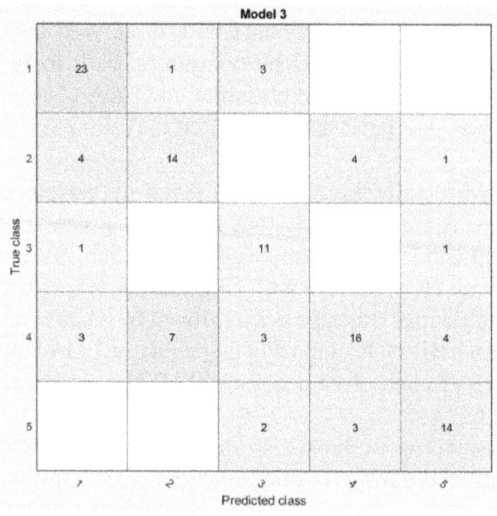

Fig. 7. Confusion Matrix given LBP with LDA for Lowest Recognition Accuracy for Desmids

5 Conclusion

In this paper, we studied the problem of automatic classification of desmids. To solve this problem, we have studies the behavior of three texture descriptors such as Histogram of Oriented Gradients, Local Binary Patterns Local Phase Quantization and with three classifiers namely Nearest Neighbor Classifier, Support Vector Machine and Linear Discrepant Analysis. During our experiments we have observed that Histogram of Oriented gradients and SVM is the best choice for classification of desmids. In future we will extended our work Deep Learning techniques.

Acknowledgments. The Authors thank to Vriendelijke groet, Alfred van Geest from Nederland for providing the Digital Database of desmids used in this experiments and the authors also would like to thank Dr. Babasaheb Ambedkar Marathwada University, Aurangabad (MS) India for providing the publication support.

Authors' Contributions. Rajmohan Pardeshi carried out the experiment and wrote the draft manuscript. Rita Patil and Nirupama Anasingkar edited the draft and verified the results. Prapti Deshmukh Mam supervised the project. All authors discussed the results and contributed to the final manuscript.

References

1. Domozych, D.S., Domozych, C.R. Desmids and Biofilms of Freshwater Wetlands: Development and Microarchitecture. Microb Ecol 55, 81–93 (2008).
2. Shigeo Abe, "Support Vector Machines for Pattern Classification," Springer Verlag,2005.
3. V.N. Vapnik, "The Nature of statistical Learning Theory", Springer 1995.
4. Digital Image Collection of Desmids http://www.digicodes.info/
5. Lahdenoja, Olli, Jonne Poikonen, and Mika Laiho. "Towards understanding the formation of uniform local binary patterns." International Scholarly Research Notices 2013 (2013).
6. Ojala, Timo, Matti Pietikainen, and Topi Maenpaa. "Multiresolution gray-scale and rotation invariant texture classification with local binary patterns." IEEE Transactions on pattern analysis and machine intelligence 24, no. 7 (2002): 971–987.
7. Ojansivu, Ville, and Janne Heikkilä. "Blur insensitive texture classification using local phase quantization." In International conference on image and signal processing, pp. 236–243. Springer, Berlin, Heidelberg, 2008.
8. Dalal, Navneet, and Bill Triggs. "Histograms of oriented gradients for human detection." In 2005 IEEE computer society conference on computer vision and pattern recognition (CVPR'05), vol. 1, pp. 886–893. IEEE, 2005.
9. Promdaen, Sansoen, Pakaket Wattuya, and Nuttha Sanevas. "Automated microalgae image classification." Procedia Computer Science 29 (2014): 1981–1992.
10. Jiuhao Guo, Yaoyao Ma, Joseph H.W. Lee,Real-time automated identification of algal bloom species for fisheries management in subtropical coastal waters, Journal of Hydro-environment Research, Volume 36, 2021, Pages 1–32, ISSN 1570-6443,
11. Colares, Rafael G., Pablo Machado, Matheus de Faria, Am´aliaDetoni, and Virg´ıniaTavano. "Microalgae classification using semi-supervised and active learning based on Gaussian mixture models." Journal of the Brazilian Computer Society19, no. 4 (2013): 411–422.
12. Tan, Ching Soon, Phooi Yee Lau, Siew-Moi Phang, and Tang Jung Low. "A framework for the automatic identification of algae (Neomerisvanbosseae MA Howe): U3 S." In Computer and Information Sciences (ICCOINS), 2014 International Conference on, pp. 1–6. IEEE, 2014.
13. Jalba, Andrei C., Michael HF Wilkinson, Jos BTM Roerdink, Micha M. Bayer, and Stephen Juggins. "Automatic diatom identification using contour analysis by morphological curvature scale spaces." Machine Vision and Applications 16, no. 4 (2005): 217–228.

14. Pedraza, Anibal, Gloria Bueno, Oscar Deniz, Gabriel Crist´obal, Sa´ul Blanco, and Maria Borrego-Ramos. ”Automated Diatom Classification (Part B): A Deep Learning Approach.” Applied Sciences 7, no. 5 (2017): 460.
15. Bueno, Gloria, Oscar Deniz, Anibal Pedraza, Jes´us Ruiz-Santaquiteria, Jes´us Salido, Gabriel Crist´obal, Mar´ıa Borrego-Ramos, and Sa´ul Blanco. ”Automated Diatom Classification (Part A): Handcrafted Feature Approaches.” Applied Sciences7, no. 8 (2017): 753.
16. Pardeshi, Rajmohan, and Prapti D. Deshmukh. "Classification of Microscopic algae: an observational study with AlexNet." In International Conference on Soft Computing and Signal Processing, pp. 309–316. Springer, Singapore, 2019.
17. M. Uray, P. M. Roth and H. Bischof, "Efficient classification for large-scale problems by multiple lda subspaces", Proceedings of International Conference on Computer Vision Theory and Applications, pp. 299–306, 2009.

Recent Advances in Audio-Visual Speech Recognition: Deep Learning Perspective

Diksha R. Pawar[(✉)] and Pravin Yannawar

Department of Computer Science and Information Technology, Dr. Babasaheb Ambedkar Marathwada University, Aurangabad, Maharashtra, India
dikshasalunke97@gmail.com

Abstract. Speech is the powerful engine of communication among human beings and language is meant for communicating with the world. This has motivated new researchers to study automatic speech recognition and expand a computer system so it can integrate and understand human speech. But the problem with speech recognition is the acoustic noisy environment can deeply corrupt audio speech. This polluted audio speech disturbs the whole recognition performance. So, the development of Audio-Visual Speech Recognition (AVSR) aims to solve the issues by utilizing visual pictures that are undisturbed by noise. This review paper's goal is to explain AVSR architectures, which include front-end operations, the utilized audio-visual dataset, and related studies, audio feature extraction, fusion and modeling techniques, and accuracy estimation methods.

Keywords: ASR · audio feature extraction · AVSR · audio-video fusion · HMM · accuracy estimation methods · GNN · etc.

1 Introduction

The computer is now a part of human life and has contributed significantly to creating this world digitally. Language is meant for communicating world. The largest part of human linguistic communication so far occurs as speech. Language is the most popular medium of communication and many languages are used in the world for oral and written communication. Different languages use different approaches to encoding information. Sound signals and visual lip activities are produced by the speaker's vocalization bodies, like the mouth cavity and vocal tract systems. The process of translating a human speech signal into a series of word algorithms for a human-machine interface is known as automatic speech recognition. Since 1920, researchers have been working on how computers can be made to understand the meanings of human language.

Around 1920, the first speech recognition prototype was created using a toy dog that was attached to a magnetic spring. When someone shouted the word Rex, the dog would jump, but it was energy- and frequency-sensitive, operating at around 500 Hz. Speech recognition was categorized in the study [1] as an information extraction method that was developed for the first time at Bell Labs in the 1950s [2]. Noise generally increases the ASR system's primary issue.

© The Author(s) 2023
R. Manza et al. (Eds.): ACVAIT 2022, AISR 176, pp. 409–421, 2023.
https://doi.org/10.2991/978-94-6463-196-8_31

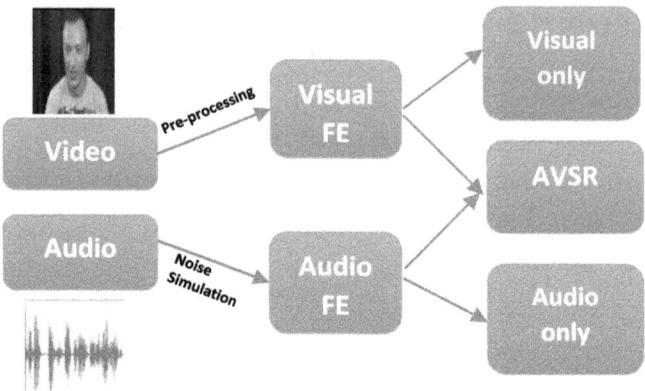

Fig. 1. Block diagram of AVSR

The primary influencing factor in studies of recognition systems is always noise [3]. The ASR, advanced methods take of visual modalities such as a combination of the speaker's lip movements and audio modality, leads to an audio-visual speech recognition (AVSR) system. In order to overcome the limitation of ASR, AVSR uses visual information from the speaker to improve speech recognition when an audio signal is corrupted by noise as shown in the Fig. 1.

To perform speech recognition tasks, and audiovisual speech recognition system (AVSR) integrates auditory and visual data. Lip syncing can be accomplished live on stage, on TV shows, on computer systems, in movies, or through other audio-visual output devices. The term can refer to any of a number of different methods and processes, in the context of live performances and audiovisual recordings. Recent years have seen an increase in the popularity of audio-visual speech recognition, attracting researchers from the fields of pattern recognition, computer vision, and signal and speech processing. However Lip-sync mistake, on the other hand, depends on the ratio timing of audio and visual components throughout production, post-production, distribution, and playback manufacturing as when a challenge or issue arises. Nowadays, Deep learning makes it feasible to convert lip movements into meaningful words. Visual information can improve speech recognition in noisy contexts also. Initially, HMM (Hidden Markov Model) was used by the researcher to represent the movement of the audio and visual patterns for face expression but now DNN (deep neural network), RNN (recurrent neural network), CNN (convolutional neural network), and the newest GAN technology make everything so easy. People were always active on online streaming websites like YouTube after 2015. That had collected hundreds of millions of daily views, Twitch had over 1.5 million broadcasters on it, and YouTube had 2.3 billion subscribers by 2020, so it appeared that the future of video technology was very bright [4].

2 Related Work

The movements of voice and video sequences were represented using simply Hidden Markov Models (HMMs) in a few of the first methods for facial expressions or for movements. Vector quantization was employed by Simons et al. and Cox et al. [5] to obtain a bond description of the audio-visual features that served as the outputs for respective HMM. Even though researchers preferred HMMs as compared to the neural network because they explicitly divide speech down into understandable states. In latest years deep learning has given proper results in neural networks being used in lots of modern approaches. Using the subject-independent method, a deep neural network (DNN) in [6] converts a graphical representation of a pattern into a sequential manner for the lower half of the facial shape.

Using deep neural networks end-to-end approach and other studies were able to solve audio-visual speech recognition "in the wild," [7, 8] which refers to unrestricted open-world speech. Sutskever et al. [9] were the first to use neural networks to solve a sequence-to-sequence challenge. After Bahdanau et al. [10] and Luong et al. [11]. Improvements were brought about with attention mechanisms by newly, Vaswani et al. [12] developed a transformer network and is based on an attention method to identify global connections among outputs and inputs. According to Johnson et al., learning multiple translating techniques raises performance overall, especially for low-resource languages [13]. Recurrent neural networks (RNNs) have relied on deep networks, which were publicized in [14, 15]. These designs produce natural output but are subject-dependent and need reconstruction and retraining procedures to adapt to new faces.

In [16] use convolutional neural networks (CNN) to convert audio data into a 3-dimensional mesh of particular speakers. The CNN approach has comment threads that are in charge of articulating dynamics and mesh point estimation in three dimensions. A CNN based on Mel-frequency Cepstral coefficients (MFCCs) developed by Chung et al. [17] to create subject-independent clips from a simple image and audio signal. This approach includes an L1 loss on the image, which blurs the image and necessitates a de-blurring step too. Along with these, pixel loss discourages deviation from the training clip, which does not encourage the system to create natural emotions and results in essentially static faces with the exception of the lips.

The latest work on GANs in [18] turned machine learning techniques' attention to generative modeling. GANs used adversarial loss that has the ability to produce better images as compared to L1 and L2 losses [19] and straightforward adaptations for audio- visual datasets can be easily modified by swapping out the 2D convolutional networks for 3D convolutional networks. The generator and discriminator networks may represent periodic dependence by using three dimensions convolutional layers however, they require films of a specific length. This drawback is resolved in [20], but constrain be imposed in the latent space to create systematic and proper output. An RNN-based generator with different latent spaces for movement and information was introduced by the MoCoGAN system [21]. At last, Chen et al. in [22] give a Generative adversarial network-based encoder-decoder framework that utilizes CNNs to transform speech signals into frames and frames into spectrograms. In the year 2019- 2020 IIT Hyderabad students created Lip2Wav [60], Wav2Lip [61], LipGAN [62] model using GAN.

3   Data Corpus

Audio-Visual datasets are mostly used in industry such as the Alexa voice service for automatic speech recognition. The voice is routed over a speech-recognition machine for learning lip reading in military services and health care. There are currently many AVSR data corpora available, but some of them have defects in their word analysis, recording quality, illumination, and environmental variations. Although The Tulips1 [23], AVletters [24], M2VTS [25], CUAVE [26], (LUNA-V) [27], TIMIT [28], GRID [29] [30], vVISWa [33, 34], etc. databases are a popular databases used for voice recognition. It permits scientists to use the datasets as a reference, enabling observation and helping judgment of the results of independent tests and AVSR procedures. M2VTS [25] and GRID [29] [30] used MHMM and CHMM classification methods and gives an accuracy result near 97%. The CUAVE [26] speech database w/ith a resolution of 750 × 576 pixels was developed by Patterson et al. in 2002. Tulips1 [23] & AVletters [24] were created in 1995 and 1998 with resolutions of 100 × 75 pixels and 80 × 60 pixels correspondingly. AVletters [24] takes 10 speakers (5 Male, 5 Female) and create A to Z word datasets. Later, the newer speech database Loughborough University Audio-Visual data corpus (LUNA-V) used a geometry approach for lip-syncing audio-visual speech recognition. It has been shown through a Comparing analysis of the LUNA-V [27] and CUAVE [28] datasets that the organized and demonstrated images with high accuracy and significantly advance the task of visual-speech recognition. Vassil Panayoto et al. [31] and Anthony Rousseau et al. [32] provide large open-source speech recognition datasets.

Prashant Borde et.al has created vVISWa [33] data corpus as shown in Fig. 2 and he has explored the role of visual features from the vVISWa data corpus that are generated by Zernike events in combination with MFCC for the recognition of isolated city names [35]. An extensive collection of English, Marathi, and Hindi isolated words are read aloud in this corpus. There were 58 speakers in all that contributed to the corpus, of which 48 were native speakers as shown in Fig. 2(a) and 10 speakers were non-native shown in Fig. 2(b) that is, they are from Iraq and Yemen [33].

4   Visual Front End

Just a while ago, a lot of visual front-end designs have been mentioned in the article [42] such as appearance-based features, geometrical-based features, and a combination of appearance-geometrical-based features [36]. Most of the researchers used appearance-based features, but this feature's imperfection is that it is susceptible to environmental changes like content brightness, shine, and head attitude. However, appearance-based features build a feature vector with reduced dimensionality that contains associated speech information by taking all pixels inside the ROI (region of interest) that are instructive to speech vocalization and linearly transforming their pixel values [37–39].

Geometrical features, such as the size, length, & region of lips movement of the speakers, are used to control audio datasets [40]. More recently, Ibrahim, M. Z et al. [41] show the test-strength of the geometrical and appearance-based aspects using the head posture and brightness increment. The study found that features based on geometry

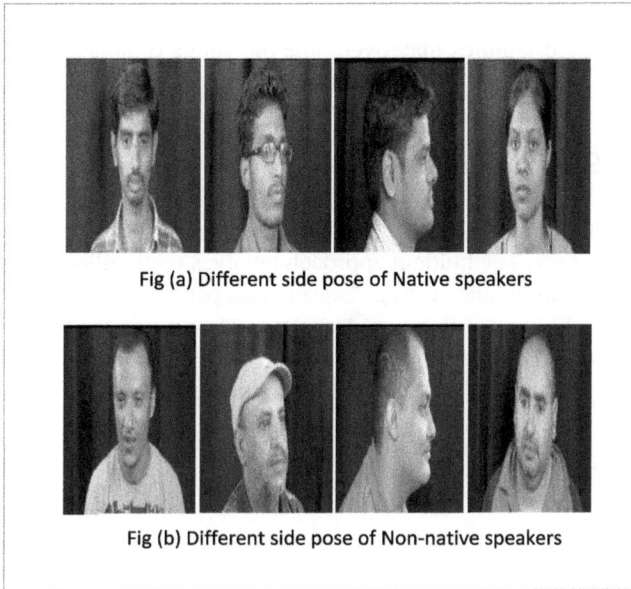

Fig (a) Different side pose of Native speakers

Fig (b) Different side pose of Non-native speakers

Fig. 2. vVISWa data corpus

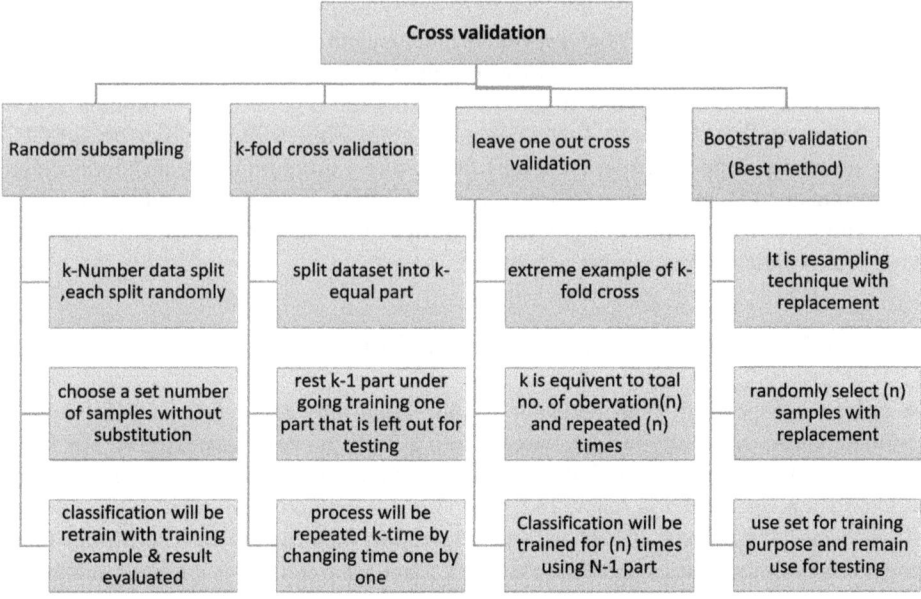

Fig. 3. Types and methods of Cross validation

are more resistant to environmental variations compared with appearance-based features and geometrical-based features may overcome the defect of appearance-based features [41].

5 Accuracy Estimation Methods

The holdout method and the cross-validation are two general methods of evaluating the classifier's accuracy. The holdout approach involves randomly dividing each sample into two training datasets and testing datasets independently. This is a train-and-test experiment, so the holdout estimation may be misleading if the training set samples take corrupted data [42]. By using cross-validation, the holdout method's flaw can be resolved. The description and difference of each method are shown in the Fig. 3

6 Audio Feature Extraction

In the literature review, there are so many features extraction techniques used like linear Predictive Coefficient (LPC) [43], Principal Component Analysis (PCA) [44, 45], Linear Discriminate Analysis (LDA) [46], Independent Component Analysis (ICA) [47] and Mel-Frequency Cepstrum Coefficients (MFCC) [43] [44]. Tripathy.s et al. used linear predictive coding (LPC) and Mel-frequency cepstral coefficient (MFCC) for Hindi speech recognition [48]. In it, datasets were classified into train databases and test databases. Speaker-dependent and speaker- independent systems were each given a portion of the tested data corpus [42]. HMM is demonstrated to perform better than LPC as a classifier for MFCC feature-extraction in the speaker-dependent environment. Therefore, this research work comes to the conclusion that while MFCC outperforms LCP in most situations, it performs worse than LPC feature extraction in speaker-independent environments [42]. In it, datasets were classified into train databases and test databases [48]. The tested data corpus was separated into two different systems: speaker-dependent and speaker-independent systems (Table 1).

7 AVSR Fusion and Modeling Techniques

In order to outperform both audio-only and visual-only recognition, AVSR aims to combine audio-visual modes data stream into a multi-modal classification. For fusion between audio and visual modalities, there are three main approaches: feature fusion, modal fusion, and decision fusion [52, 53]. The best method of integration of audio and video is model fusion, it is higher-level integration than feature fusion. Model fusion integrates both modalities and then classifies them separately. It is a middle integration method that can be demonstrated by multi-stream HMMs that utilize two or more independent streams of audio and visual performance. Decision fusion can't do interaction between two modalities during the classification process, it generally takes place after the spoken utterance is completed, becomes that results come in the delay to generate the classification result and leads to unnatural interaction sessions this is the main drawback of this approach (Table 2).

Table 1. **Some popular methods of feature extraction** [59]

Sr. No	Methods	Property	Procedure for implementation
1.	Linear Discriminate Analysis	Supervised linear map, rapid, Eigen-vector-based nonlinear feature extraction technique	LDA is more effective for classification than PCA [46]
2.	Independent component analysis (ICA)	Iterative non-Gaussian, non-linear feature extraction, linear map	Blind channel separation is employed to separate sources with non-Gaussian distribution [47]
3.	Principal Component Analysis (PCA)	Quick, Eigen-vector based, unsupervised linear map, nonlinear feature extraction technique	Eigenvector base method, or Karhuneu-Loeveare expansion, is a conventional technique that works well with Gaussian data [44, 45].
4.	Mel-frequency cepstral coefficients (MFCC)	By doing Fourier analysis and Spectral analysis, the power spectral is calculated.	Our characteristics are discovered via spectral analysis with a fixed resolution subjective frequency scale [43, 44]
5.	Linear Predictive coefficient	Method for extracting static features with 10 to 16 lower-order coefficients	Lower order feature extraction is done using LPC [43].
6.	Wavelet	Superior to the Fourier transform in time resolution	It improves time resolution at high frequencies compared to Fourier Transform by swapping out its fixed bandwidth for one that is proportional to frequency [49].
7.	Cepstral mean subtraction	Dependable feature extraction	The Mean Statically Parameter is used instead of the MFCC in this case [50].
8.	Integrated phoneme subspace method	PCA + LDA + ICA based on transformation	Greater Accuracy compared to the current approach [51]

Table 2. Different modeling technique

Sr. No	Approaches	Year	Ref. no	Technique
1.	Acoustic-phonetic approach	1996	[18, 22, 23]	Gaussian Mixture Modeling, SVM Classifier Classification, and Problem Phone Recognition
2	Pattern Recognition approach	1993, 1975	[24, 25]	HMM, Pattern training, the Pattern comparison
3	Template-based approach	1979	[26, 27]	Unknown speech is contrasted with a collection of recorded words.
4	Knowledge-based approach	1993	[28, 29]	Vector Quantization(VQ), the lowest distance measure using the VQ codebook
5	Statistical based approach	1998, 2004	[8, 9, 31, 40]	HMM, Statistical learning, learning-VQ, k-mean algorithm
6	Learning-based approach	2006	[14, 16, 18], 0]	Neural network, genetic algorithm, machine learning
7	Artificial Intelligent approach	1987	[26, 41]	Hybrid of acoustic-phonetic & pattern recognition
8	Stochastic Approach	1990	[43]	HMM-based chain model, temporal variability, output distribution, spectral variability

Table 3. Evaluation of Popular Works on the AVSR Speech Corpus

Sr. No.	Ref No.	Year	Dataset	Speakers	Techniques		Task	Accuracy
					Classification	*Feature extraction*		
1.	[25]	2005	M2VTS	25 males, 12 females	MHMM	LDA-PCA	Speaker Recognition	96.57%
2.	[54]	2014	XM2VTS	295 (unknown gender)	MSHMM	MFCC-DCT	Digit Recognition ara>	89%
3.	[55]	2014	CUAVE	19 males, 17 females	HMM	MFCC	Digit Recognition	95%
4.	[28]	2010	VidTIMIT	24 males, 19 females	DCT-MFCC	GMM	Person Recognition	EER = 5.23
5.	[56]	2010	Tulips1	7 males, 5 females	LDB	HMM-SVM	Speech Recognition	EER = 1.74
6.	[29]	2013	GRID	34 (unknown gender)	MFCC	CHMM	Speech Recognition	96.37%
7.	[57]	2014	LUNA-V	9 males, 1 female	HSV	HMM	Digit recognition	92.5% (Visual-only)
8.	[34]	2017	vVISWa	48 speakers native, 10 speaker non-native	K-Means, Random Forest & HMM	MFCC	Speech Recognition	98% (Visual-only)

8 Discussions

In this publication, we see a review of AVSR modeling methods, audio feature extraction, visual front end, and accuracy estimation methods. There are various challenges that are pertinent to the AVSR platforms are training and test datasets. Some typical issues with audio-visual data collection in video. In visual data, the existing spoken database is usually of very poor quality, but now there are high-resolution cameras are used for capturing datasets. Along with that, there are certain difficulties with integrating auditory and visual modalities for speech recognition. Syncing an audio and video and handling asynchrony modality are a big problem in real-world applications and need more work in the future. The research [58] used different validation techniques and conclude that the bootstrap validation method gives the best result compared with other validation methods, and this method is still widely used in real-world applications since it requires less computing work than other techniques like k-fold evaluation and other methods. So we can say, the out-of-sample bootstrap approach is accurate to the others in terms of accuracy and transfer error, but in actual practice, its development is laborious and computerized. In the visual front end section, we can see that researchers used appearance-based features and Geometrical-based features. Appearance-based features are imperfection in that it is sensitive to environmental variation. Compared with appearance-based features and geometrical-based features may overcome the defect of appearance-based features.

9 Conclusion

We conclude from this review paper that the future of video technology is very bright [4]. The AVSR was developed for solving the problem of ASR and the researcher firstly used HMM. After 2006 the learning approach gives the golden changes in AVSR. Recently deep learning has given proper results in neural networks being used in lots of modern approaches. It is just the starting of audio-visual speech recognition and then RNN, CNN-based models are developed by the researcher. This approach uses an L1 loss at the pixel level but the disadvantage of this is creating unnatural expressions and producing output is mostly static faces, with the mouth being the only moving part. Since adversarial loss produces finer, more detailed pictures than L1 and L2 losses, much of the current work on GANs in [18] is related to image generation. There are two networks in it: a generator that creates faces based on speech & a discriminator that determines the produced lip movement and speech are in time or it give proper results with correct syncing. As we discuss in literature review IIT Hyderabad students created Lip2Wav [60], Wav2Lip [61], LipGAN [62] model using GAN. In it, they look at the issue of lip-syncing a random speaking facial video to a specific speech piece and used various type of methods such as in-sync, out-sync and ground truth image. We see different accuracy estimation methods but bootstrap is one of the best methods in cross-validation, it tested each validation technique by looking into bias and variance [42]. According to Table 3 mostly used and accurate methods of classification and feature extraction are HMM and MFCC. Thus, we invite researchers to undertake work on this line for making robust solutions for Lip movement synchronization in a multi-pose AVSR environment.

Acknowledgment. The authors gratefully acknowledge support from the Shree Chhatrapati Shahu Maharaj Research, Training and Human Development Institute (SARTHI), An Autonomous Institute of Govt. of Maharashtra for providing financial assistance for the Major Research Project. This work was supported by Dr. Babasaheb Ambedkar Marathwada University and the vision and intelligence lab. Authors would like to thank Dr. Babasaheb Ambedkar Marathwada University for the publication support.

References

1. Ghadage, Y. H. & Shelke, S. D. Speech to Text Conversion for Multilingual Languages (2016), 236–240.
2. Morgan, N. Deep and wide: Multiple layers in automatic speech recognition. IEEE Trans. Audio, Speech Lang. Process. 20 (2012), 7– 13.
3. Tian, C., Ji, W. & Yuan, Y. Auxiliary Multimodal LSTM for Audiovisual Speech Recognition and Lipreading(2017), 1–9.
4. How many people used YouTube in 2021,backlinko.com/youtube-users.
5. A. D. Simons and S. J. Cox. Generation of mouth shapes for a synthetic talking head. Proceedings of the Institute of Acoustics, Autumn Meeting, 12(January):475482, 1990
6. S. Taylor, T. Kim, Y. Yue, M. Mahler, J. Krahe, A. G. Rodriguez, J. Hodgins, and I. Matthews. A deep learning approach for generalized speech animation. ACM Transactions on Graphics (TOG), 36(93), 2017.
7. Wei Ping, Kainan Peng, Andrew Gibiansky, Sercan O Arik, Ajay Kannan, Sharan Narang, Jonathan Raiman, and John Miller. 2017. Deep voice 3: Scaling text-tospeech with convolutional sequence learning. arXiv preprint arXiv:1710.07654 (2017).
8. Jonathan Shen, Ruoming Pang, Ron J Weiss, Mike Schuster, Navdeep Jaitly, Zongheng Yang, Zhifeng Chen, Yu Zhang, Yuxuan Wang, Rj Skerrv-Ryan, et al. 2018. Natural tts synthesis by conditioning wavenet on mel spectrogram predictions. In 2018 IEEE International Conference on Acoustics, Speech and Signal Processing (ICASSP). IEEE, 4779–4783.
9. Ilya Sutskever, Oriol Vinyals, and Quoc V Le. 2014. Sequence to sequence learning with neural networks. In Advances in neural information processing systems. 3104– 3112
10. Dzmitry Bahdanau, Kyunghyun Cho, and Yoshua Bengio. 2014. Neural machine translation by jointly learning to align and translate. arXiv preprint arXiv:1409.0473 (2014)
11. Minh-Thang Luong, Hieu Pham, and Christopher D Manning. 2015. Effective approaches to attention-based neural machine translation. arXiv preprint arXiv:1508.04025 (2015).
12. Ashish Vaswani, Noam Shazeer, Niki Parmar, Jakob Uszkoreit, Llion Jones, Aidan N Gomez, Łukasz Kaiser, and Illia Polosukhin. 2017. Attention is all you need. In Advances in Neural Information Processing Systems. 5998–6008.
13. Melvin Johnson, Mike Schuster, Quoc V Le, Maxim Krikun, Yonghui Wu, Zhifeng Chen, Nikhil Thorat, Fernanda Viégas, Martin Wattenberg, Greg Corrado, et al. 2017. GoogleâĂŹs multilingual neural machine translation system: Enabling zero-shot translation. Transactions of the Association for Computational Linguistics 5 (2017), 339–351.
14. B. Fan, L. Wang, F. Soong, and L. Xie. Photo-real talking head with deep bidirectional lstm. In IEEE International Conference on Acoustics, Speech and Signal Processing (ICASSP), pages 4884–4888, 2015.
15. S. Suwajanakorn, S. Seitz, and I. Kemelmacher-Shlizerman. Synthesizing Obama: Learning Lip Sync from Audio Output Obama Video. ACM Transactions on Graphics (TOG), 36(95), 2017.

16. T. Karras, T. Aila, S. Laine, A. Herva, and J. Lehtinen. Audio-driven facial animation by joint end-to-end learning of pose and emotion. ACM Transactions on Graphics (TOG), 36(94), 2017.

17. J. S. Chung, A. Jamaludin, and A. Zisserman. You said that? In British Machine Vision Conference (BMVC), pages 1–12, 2017.

18. I. J. Goodfellow, J. Pouget-Abadie, M. Mirza, B. Xu, D. Warde-Farley, S. Ozair, A. Courville, and Y. Bengio. Generative Adversarial Networks. In Advances in neural information processing systems (NIPS), pages 2672–2680, 2014.

19. Y. Li, M. R. Min, D. Shen, D. Carlson, and L. Carin. Video Generation from Text. arXiv preprint arXiv:1710.00421, 2017.

20. M. Saito, E. Matsumoto, and S. Saito. Temporal Generative Adversarial Nets with Singular Value Clipping. In IEEE International Conference on Computer Vision (ICCV), pages 2830–2839, 2017.

21. S. Tulyakov, M. Liu, X. Yang, and J. Kautz. MoCoGAN: Decomposing Motion and Content for Video Generation. arXiv preprint arXiv:1707.04993, 2017.

22. T. Chen and R. R. Rao. Audio-Visual Integration in Multimodal Communication. Proceedings of the IEEE, 86(5):837–852, 1998.

23. Luettin, J., Thacker, N. a. & Beet, S. W. Visual speech recognition using active shape models and hidden Markov models. IEEE Int. Conf. Acoust..Speech, Signal Process. 2 (1996), 817–820.

24. Matthews, I. Features for audio-visual speech recognition. Citeseer (1998).

25. Lucey, S., Chen, T., Sridharan, S. & Chandran, V. Integration strategies for audio-visual speech processing: applied to text-dependent speaker recognition. IEEE Trans. Multimed. 7 (2005), 495–506.

26. Patterson, E. K., Gurbuz, S., Tufekci, Z. & Gowdy, J. N. CUAVE: A new audio-visual database for multimodal human-computer interface research. IEEE Int. Conf. Acoust. Speech, Signal Process.2 (2002), II2017-II-2020

27. M. Z. Ibrahim, "A novel lip geometry approach for audio-visual speech recognition," Loughborough University (2014).

28. Shah, D., Han, K. J. & Narayanan, S. S. Robust Multimodal Person Recognition Using Low-Complexity Audio-Visual Feature Fusion Approaches. Int. J. Semant. Comput. 4 (2010), 155–179.

29. Ahmed Hussen Abdelaziz, Steffen Zeiler, D. K. Twin-HMM-based audio-visual speech enhancement. Digit. Signal Process (2013), 3726– 3730.

30. Receveur, S., Scheler, D. & Fingscheidt, T. A turbo-decoding weighted forward-backward algorithm for multimodal speech recognition (2014), 179–192.

31. Vassil Panayotov, Guoguo Chen, Daniel Povey, and Sanjeev Khudanpur. 2015. Librispeech: an ASR corpus based on public domain audio books. In 2015 IEEE International Conference on Acoustics, Speech and Signal Processing (ICASSP). IEEE, 5206–5210.

32. Anthony Rousseau, Paul Deléglise, and Yannick Esteve. 2012. TED-LIUM: an Automatic Speech Recognition dedicated corpus. In LREC. 125–129.

33. P Borde, R Manza, B Gawali, P Yannawar' vVISWa ' – A Multilingual Multi-Pose Audio Visual Database for Robust Human Computer Interaction.

34. P Borde, P Yannawar. Recognition of Isolated Digit Using Random Forest for Audio Visual Speech Recognition.

35. Borde Prashant, Amarsinh Varpe, Ramesh Manza, and Pravin Yannawar. "Recognition of isolated words using Zernike and MFCC features for audio visual speech recognition." International Journal of Speech Technology (2014): 1-9.

36. Auxiliary Multimodal LSTM for Audio-visual Speech Recognition and Lipreading (2017), 1–9. Tian, C., Ji, W. & Yuan, Y.

37. Galatas, G., Potamianos, G. & Makedon, F. Audio-visual speech recognition incorporating facial depth information captured by the Kinect (2012), 2714–2717.
38. Navarathna, R., Dean, D., Sridharan, S. & Lucey, P. Multiple cameras for audio-visual speech recognition in an automotive environment. Computer Speech and Language 27 (2013), 911–927.
39. Palecek, K. & Chaloupka, J. Audio-visual speech recognition in noisy audio environments. 2013 36th Int. Conf. Telecommun. Signal Process (2013), 484–487.
40. Ibrahim, M. Z. & Mulvaney, D. J. A lip geometry approach for feature fusion-based audio-visual speech recognition. ISCCSP 2014 - 2014 6th Int. Symp. Commun. Control Signal Process. Proc (2014), 644–647
41. Ibrahim, M. Z. & Mulvaney, D. J. Robust geometrical-based lipreading using hidden Markov models. IEEE EuroCon (2013), 2011– 2016.
42. A Review of Audio-Visual Speech Recognition Thum Wei Seong and M. Z. Ibrahim Applied Electronic and Computer Engineering Cluster Faculty of Electrical & Electronic Engineering, University Malaysia Pahang, 26600 Pekan, Pahang, Malaysia (2018).
43. Dave, N. Feature Extraction Methods LPC, PLP and MFCC in Speech Recognition. Int. J. Adv. Res. Eng. Technol. 1 (2013), 1–5.
44. Ittichaichareon, C. Speech recognition using MFCC. Conf. Computer (2012), 135–138.
45. Hongbing Hu, Stephen. A, Z. Dimensionality reduction methods for HMM phonetic recognition (2010), 4854–4857.
46. Mohamed, A. et al. Deep belief networks using discriminative features for phone recognition. Acoust. Speech Signal Process. (ICASSP), IEEE Int. Conf (2011). 5060–5063.
47. Shrawankar, U. & Thakare, V. Feature Extraction for a Speech Recognition System in Noisy Environment: A Study. Comput. Eng. Appl. (ICCEA), Second Int. Conf. 1 (2010), 358–361.
48. Tripathy, S., Baranwal, N. & Nandi, G. C. A MFCC based Hindi speech recognition technique using HTK Toolkit. 2013 IEEE 2nd Int. Conf. Image Inf. Process. IEEE ICIIP (2013), 539–544
49. Feature Detection and Extraction Using Wavelets, Part 1: Feature Detection Video - MATLAB (mathworks.com)2020
50. The effect of reverberation on the performance of cepstral mean subtraction in speaker verification, ScienceDirect Topics(2011)
51. Sannella, M speaker recognition "Project Report" from https:\\cs.pensuu.fi/pages/tkinnu/research/index.html/viewed 23 feb 2010
52. Katsaggelos, A. K., Bahaadini, S. & Molina, R. Audiovisual Fusion: Challenges and New Approaches. Proc. IEEE 103 (2015), 1635–1653.
53. Huang, P. Sen, Zhuang, X. & Hasegawa-Johnson, M. Improving acoustic event detection using generalizable visual features and multi-modality modeling. ICASSP, IEEE Int. Conf. Acoust. Speech Signal Process. – Proc (2011). 349–352.
54. Stewart, D., Seymour, R., Pass, A. & Ming, J. Robust audio-visual speech recognition under noisy audio-video conditions. IEEE Trans. Cybern. 44 (2014), 175–184.
55. Pawar, G. S. Realization of Hidden Markov Model for English Digit Recognition. 98 (2014), 98–101.
56. Kambiz Rahbar. Independent-Speaker Isolated Word Speech Recognition Based on Mean-Shift Framing Using Hybrid HMM/SVM Classifier (2010). 156–161.
57. Ibrahim, Z. A novel lip geometry approach for audio-visual speech recognition (2014).
58. Tantithamthavorn, C., Mcintosh, S., Hassan, A. E. & Matsumoto, K. An Empirical Comparison of Model Validation Techniques for Defect Prediction Models. IEEE Trans. Softw. Eng. 5589 (2016), 1–16
59. Santosh K. Gaikwad, Dr. Bharti Gawali, Dr. Pravin Yannawar, Review of Speech Recognition Technique.(2010)

60. Prajwal K R*, Rudrabha Mukhopadhyay, Learning Individual Speaking Styles for Accurate Lip to Speech Synthesis (CVPR, 2020) arxiv.org/abs/2005.08209.Lip2Wav: https://www.you tube.com/watch?v=HziA
61. [ACM Multimedia, 2020] Wav2Lip: Accurately Lip-syncing Videos In The Wild Wav2Lip:https://youtu.be/0fXaDCZNOJc(2020)
62. Towards Automatic Face-to-Face Translation. Authors: Prajwal K R*, Rudrabha Mukhopad-hyay,LipGAN:https://www.youtube.com/watch?v=aHG6O... (2019)

Deep Learning Based Model for Fire and Gun Detection

Ahmed Abdullah A. Shareef[1]([✉]), Pravin L. Yannawar[1],
Antar Shaddad H. Abdul-Qawy[2], Hashem Al-Nabhi[3], and Ravindra B. Bankar[4]

[1] Vision and Intelligence System Lab, Department of Computer Science and IT, Dr. Babasaheb Ambedkar Marathwada University, Aurangabad, Maharashtra 431004, India
shareef.kin@gmail.com

[2] Department of Mathematics and Computer Science, Faculty of Science, SUMAIT University, Zanzibar, Tanzania

[3] Department of Electronics and Information, Northwestern Polytechnical University, Xi'an, China

[4] Department of Management Science, Dr.Babasaheb Ambedkar, Marathwada University, Aurangabad, Maharashtra 431004, India

Abstract. Real-time object detection is one of the most important applications for surveillance and a prominent computer vision task. This paper proposes a new deep learning-based model for fire, pistol, and gun detection in areas monitored by cameras like home fires, industrial explosions, and wildfires, as they happen frequently and cause adverse effects on the environment. Gun violence and mass shootings are also on the rise in certain parts of the world. Such incidents are time-sensitive and can cause a huge loss to life and property. Hence, the proposed work has built a deep learning model based on the YOLOv5 algorithm that processes a video frame-by-frame to detect such anomalies in real-time and generate an alert for the concerned authorities. Our model has validation with more speed and more accurate manner. The experimental result satisfies the goal of the proposed model and also shows a fast detection rate.

Keywords: deep learning · computer vision · fire detection · pistol detection · gun detection · YOLOv5

1 Introduction

Object detection is a computer vision task that involves predicting the presence of one or more objects, along with their classes and bounding boxes. The object detection has attracted an increased amount of attention in recent years due to its wide range of applications. This mission is subject to extensive investigation both in academic domain and in real-world applications, such as security monitoring, autonomous driving, transportation monitoring, drone scene analysis, and robotic vision [1]. The main purpose of object detection is to indicate, classify and locate the location and type of object in images or videos [2]. There are other purpose of object detection is to detect all states of objects of a known class, such as cars, people, or faces in an image [3]. Fires and guns hit many people and cause damage to their properties in the whole world. Thus,

© The Author(s) 2023
R. Manza et al. (Eds.): ACVAIT 2022, AISR 176, pp. 422–430, 2023.
https://doi.org/10.2991/978-94-6463-196-8_32

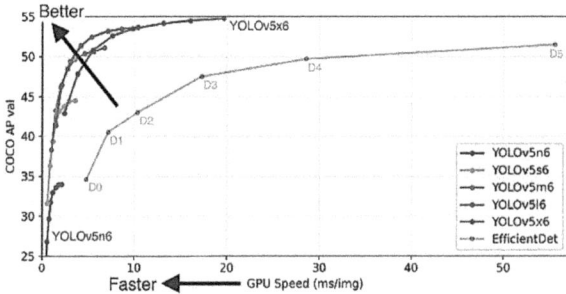

Fig. 1. YOLOv5 (Source [12])

to prevent such loses we need accurate systems to detect the fires and guns early in private and general places. Forest fires are occur always in different countries and cause tremendous damages. Crime rates caused by pistols and guns' fire are increasing as ones of the most common disasters that threaten the world at the present time [5]. The latest statistics reported by the United Nations Office on Drugs and Crime (UNODC) reveal that the number of crimes involving firearms per 100,000 inhabitants is very high in many countries, for example, 21.5 in Mexico, 4.7 in the United States and 1.6 in Belgium [6]. It is very imperative to reduce this type of violence through early detection of guns and pistols' fire.

YOLO "You only look once" is one of the modern and most popular and preferred algorithms for artificial intelligence engineers as object detector that can perform real-time object detection with good accuracy [4]. It has always been the first preference for real-time object detection [7] as one of the finest family of reveal models with start of the art. YOLO algorithm splits images into a grid system. Each cell in the network is responsible for discovering things within itself. The series of YOLO was introduced in May 2016 by Joseph Redmon who released YOLOv1 [8], as one of the biggest advances in real-time object detection. In December 2017 joseph introduced second version which was known as YOLO 9000 [9]. After one year in April 2018 new version called YOLOv3 was released by Joseph and his partner, which was considered as the most popular and stable version [10]. Finally, in April 2020 Alexey Bochkovskiy introduced YOLOv4 [11] with additional amazing features. YOLOv4 outperforms YOLOv3 by a high margin and also has a great deal of average accuracy when compared to the EfficientDet family. After few days on 9 June 2020 Glenn Jocher released YOLOv5. There are a lot of dis-agreements about the choice of the name "YOLOv5" and other things. Glenn introduced a PyTorch-based version of YOLOv5 with exceptional improvements. Hence, he has not released any official paper yet. This version beats all previous versions and comes close to EfficientDet AP with higher FPS as shown in the chart in Fig. 1.

2   Related Work

There are several valuable research articles and project works in Deep learning-based fire and gun detection in images and videos. This section reviews some of the essential articles and research woks on object detection and fire and gun detection.

2.1 Object Detection Methods

The object detection is the process of locating objects in an image or a frame in video sequence [13]. There are many research articles have published recently that explain the accelerated development in object detection field and its approaches. Ross Girshick et al. [14] have proposed method that combines convolutional neural network CNN with regions called R-CNN. This method was good compared with previous methods. Fast Region-Based Convolutional Neural Network, also called Fast R-CNN, has developed by Ross Girshick [15] as a training for object detection, it has written in python and C++. This method mainly fixed the disadvantages of SPPnet and R-CNN. It has more speed and more accuracy than previous methods. Ross Girshicl et al. [16] have proposed a new algorithm that provides a scalable and simple detection. It has been improved in mAp by 30% more than previous algorithms and achieved 53% of mAp. The authors called their algorithm R-CNN. In [17], Jifeng Dai et al. have presented region-based fully convolutional network for accurate and detect objects efficiently. They proposed position sensitive score maps, the achieved competitive results as 83% mAp on the PASCAL VOC datasets. Their method achieved a speed of 170ms per image. In [18], Wei Liu et al. have presented new approach for detecting objects in image using a single deep neural network, their method called SSD. This method work by sorting the output area of bounding boxes into a set of default boxes at different aspect ratios and scales for each feature map location as a simple method compared to others. The SSD results on PASCAL VOC and COCO datasets for 300*300 input images achieved 74.3% mAp. Joseph Redmon et al. [8] have introduced a new unified object detection approach called YOLO (You Only Look Once). YOLO uses a single neural network on the full image to determine classes' probabilities and bounding boxes in a one-time evaluation. This approach is a very fast real-time object detector that can process an image with a rate of 155 frames/second. The authors claimed that YOLO has less probability of predicting false positives on the image background and has shown better detection results than other traditional methods.

2.2 Fire and Gun Detection

Borberto Olmas et al. [5] has presented a system to detect handgun in videos for surveillance and control purpose, the researchers reformulated this detection problem into problem to reduce and resolve false positives by building core training of data set guided by the results of deep convolutional neural networks (CNN). They evaluated the best classification model under two approaches, sliding window approach and area proposal approach. Their results obtained with Faster R-CNN model. Parth Metha et al. [19] have presented a system to detect the fire and gun in public places monitored by cameras. They used yolov3 object detection method that process video frame by frame to detect objects in videos in real-time and generate alarm for the authorized person. The experimental results satisfied the goal of their proposed model with good accuracy, i.e., a loss value of 0.2864 and 85% accuracy. Sanam Narejo et al. [20] have implemented yolove3 based model to detect weapons which trained on their dataset. The training results has confirmed that yolov3 gave results better than yolov2 and traditional CNN. Zhentian Jiao et al. [21] have proposed algorithm to detect forest fire. They have used

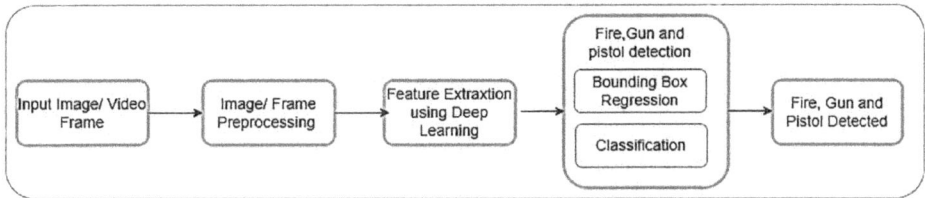

Fig. 2. Fire, gun and pistol detection model

yolov3 and UAV. In their work, CNN has implemented with yolov3 method. The result has given accuracy of 83% and the frame rate of detection was 3.2 fps. Aysegul Yanik et al. [22] have proposed a new machine learning based system to detect forest fire early in low cost and more accurate manner. M.Milagro et al. [23] have presented a system based on faster R-CNN Method. They have compared two approaches as CNN base, a GoogleNet and SqueezeNet architecture. They have achieved results at 85.44% accuracy using squeezeNet and 46.68% using GoogleNet gun and knife respectively. Rana. M. Alaqil et al. [24] have proposed a gun detection system using faster R-CNN model. They have used MobileNet, ResNet, VGG16 and ResNetv2 for feature extraction and compared them with YOLOv2. The results showed that the YOLOv2 is faster than used MobileNet, ResNet, VGG16 and ResNetv2.

3 Methodology

We design a model to detect fire, gun and pistol, based on YOLOv5 object detector. This model works in several stages. It starts by collecting and labelling dataset images for fire, gun and pistol. In this research we used general dataset for fire, gun and pistol, which is available on kaggle [25]. We use YOLOv5 to train our dataset on three classes' fire, gun and pistol. As discussed above. We choose YOLOv5 which is better than previous versions of YOLO. The aim is to train and test dataset to produce new model that can detect fire, gun and pistol in public places such as home fires, industrial explosions and crimes. After model training, our model will be able to detect fire, gun, and pistol by drawing boxes around it and shows the name of object and accuracy of objector. The block diagram of our model for fire, gun and pistol detection is show in Fig. 2. The model starts by receiving image, video or capture live video using dedicated camera. The second step makes reprocessing for input image or frame extracted from video, then do feature extraction from that image depends on deep learning techniques. After detecting the objects which is fire, gun or pistol, the model draws boxes around the detected object. Finally mention the name of the object and the prediction value for the object.

4 Experimental Result

We have trained our model with parameters of YOLOv5 as shown in Table 1.

The training results give very good results compared with previous studies. We have used YOLOv5 which is faster and more accurate than previous family series of YOLO.

Table 1. Model Parameters

Parameters	Description
Image Size	640
Batches	16
Epochs	10
Classes	3

Pistol is represented by label 0, Fire is represented by label 1 and Gun is by label 2. Figure 3(A) presents the training results by showing the number of the class. Figure 3(B) presents the training results by showing the name of class. Figure 3(C) presents the training results by showing both the name of class and the prediction value.

The following charts in Fig. 4 were produced after training YOLOv5 with input size 640x640 on the fire, gun and pistol dataset for 10 epochs.

(A)

Fig. 3. Training results, (A): with the number of the class, (B): with the name of the class, and (C): with the name of class and the prediction value.

(B)

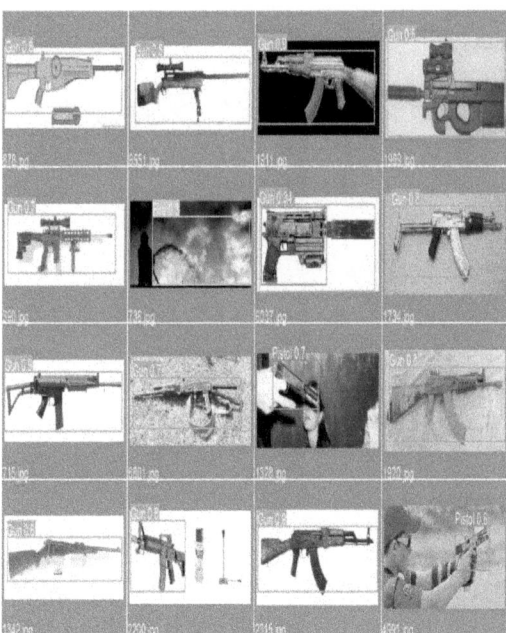

(C)

Fig. 3. (*continued*)

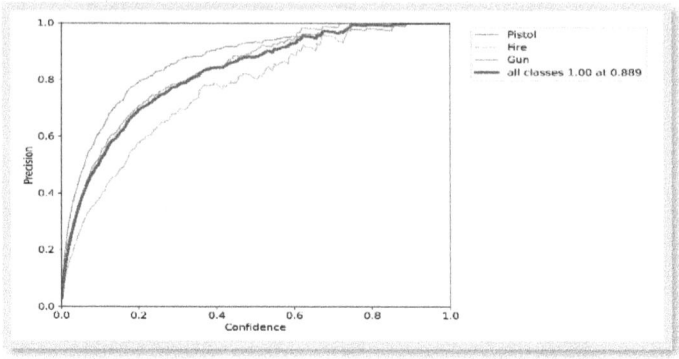

(A) P Curve

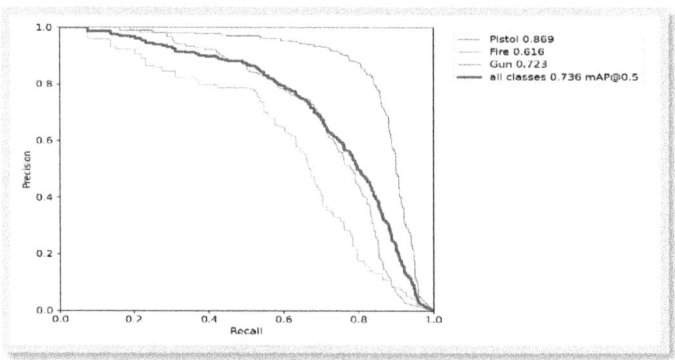

(B) PR Curve

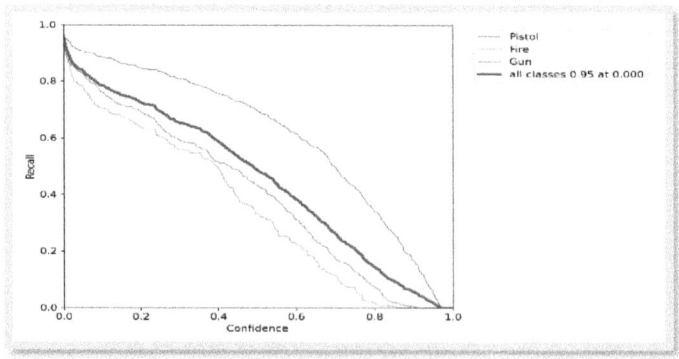

(C) R Curve

Fig. 4. P, PR and R Curves of YOLOv5 trining

The fire, gun and pistols detection results were fairly good even though the model was trained only for a few epochs.

5 Conclusion

In this paper, a YOLO-based model is introduced for detecting fire, pistol, and gun in the real-time. This deep learning-based model is very useful for arears covered by the cameras including industrial areas, forests, homes, etc. to reduces damage, prevent property loses, and save human life. YOLOv5 algorithm has been utilized in this model, where the videos' frames are process and analysed in order to identify one of the three anomalies: fire, gun and pistol. Then, it generates a real-time alert so that preventive actions can be taken by the concerned authorities. The validation results showed the higher accuracy and speed of the provided model compared the existed ones.

References

1. L. Jiao et al., "A survey of deep learning-based object detection," IEEE Access, vol. 7, no. 3, pp. 128837–128868, 2019, doi: https://doi.org/10.1109/ACCESS.2019.2939201.
2. B. Qiang, R. Chen, M. Zhou, Y. Pang, and Y. Zhai, "Convolutional Neural Networks-Based Object Detection Algorithm by Jointing Semantic."
3. Y. Amit and P. Felzenszwalb, "Object Detection."
4. "Yolov5 – Towards Data Science." https://towardsdatascience.com/tagged/yolov5 (accessed Feb. 13, 2022).
5. R. Olmos, S. Tabik, and F. Herrera, "Automatic handgun detection alarm in videos using deep learning," Neurocomputing, vol. 275, pp. 66–72, 2018, doi: https://doi.org/10.1016/j.neucom.2017.05.012.
6. A. Vazsonyi, J. Wittekind, L. Belliston, T. Loh, and Unodc, Global Study on Homicide, vol. 20. 2014.
7. "YOLOv5 is Here!. Elephant Detector Training Using Custom… | by Mihir Rajput | Towards Data Science." https://towardsdatascience.com/yolo-v5-is-here-b668ce2a4908 (accessed Feb. 13, 2022).
8. J. Redmon, S. Divvala, R. Girshick, and A. Farhadi, "You only look once: Unified, real-time object detection," Proc. IEEE Comput. Soc. Conf. Comput. Vis. Pattern Recognit., vol. 2016-Decem, pp. 779–788, 2016, doi: https://doi.org/10.1109/CVPR.2016.91.
9. J. Redmon and A. Farhadi, "YOLO9000: Better, faster, stronger," Proc. - 30th IEEE Conf. Comput. Vis. Pattern Recognition, CVPR 2017, vol. 2017-Janua, pp. 6517–6525, 2017, doi: https://doi.org/10.1109/CVPR.2017.690.
10. J. Redmon and A. Farhadi, "YOLOv3: An incremental improvement," arXiv, 2018.
11. C. Wang and H. M. Liao, "YOLOv4: Optimal Speed and Accuracy of Object Detection."
12. "Ultralytics · GitHub." https://github.com/ultralytics (accessed Feb. 13, 2022).
13. A. A. A. Shareef, P. L. Yannawar, A. S. H. Abdul-Qawy, and Z. A. T. Ahmed, YOLOv4-Based Monitoring Model for COVID-19 Social Distancing Control, vol. 235. Springer Singapore, 2022
14. R. Girshick, "Fast R-CNN," Proc. IEEE Int. Conf. Comput. Vis., vol. 2015 Inter, pp. 1440–1448, 2015, doi: https://doi.org/10.1109/ICCV.2015.169.
15. S. Ren, K. He, R. Girshick, and J. Sun, "Faster R-CNN: Towards Real-Time Object Detection with Region Proposal Networks," IEEE Trans. Pattern Anal. Mach. Intell., vol. 39, no. 6, pp. 1137–1149, 2017, doi: https://doi.org/10.1109/TPAMI.2016.2577031.

16. R. Girshick, J. Donahue, T. Darrell, and J. Malik, "Rich feature hierarchies for accurate object detection and semantic segmentation," Proc. IEEE Comput. Soc. Conf. Comput. Vis. Pattern Recognit., pp. 580–587, 2014, doi: https://doi.org/10.1109/CVPR.2014.81.

17. J. Dai, Y. Li, K. He, and J. Sun, "R-FCN: Object detection via region-based fully convolutional networks," Adv. Neural Inf. Process. Syst., pp. 379–387, 2016.

18. W. Liu et al., "SSD: Single shot multibox detector," Lect. Notes Comput. Sci. (including Subser. Lect. Notes Artif. Intell. Lect. Notes Bioinformatics), vol. 9905 LNCS, pp. 21–37, 2016, doi: https://doi.org/10.1007/978-3-319-46448-0_2.

19. P. Mehta, A. Kumar, and S. Bhattacharjee, "Fire and Gun Violence based Anomaly Detection System Using Deep Neural Networks," Proc. Int. Conf. Electron. Sustain. Commun. Syst. ICESC 2020, no. January, pp. 199–204, 2020, doi: https://doi.org/10.1109/ICESC4 8915.2020.9155625.

20. S. Narejo, B. Pandey, D. Esenarro Vargas, C. Rodriguez, and M. R. Anjum, "Weapon Detection Using YOLO V3 for Smart Surveillance System," Math. Probl. Eng., vol. 2021, 2021, doi: https://doi.org/10.1155/2021/9975700.

21. Z. Jiao et al., "A Deep learning based forest fire detection approach using uav and yolov3," 1st Int. Conf. Ind. Artif. Intell. IAI 2019, pp. 1–5, 2019, doi: https://doi.org/10.1109/ICIAI. 2019.8850815.

22. A. Yanık, M. S. Güzel, M. Yanık, and E. Bostancı, "Machine Learning Based Early Fire Detection System using a Low-Cost Drone," 2021, doi: https://doi.org/10.1201/978100322 1333-1.

23. M. M. Fernandez-Carrobles, O. Deniz, and F. Maroto, "Gun and Knife Detection Based on Faster R-CNN for Video Surveillance," Lect. Notes Comput. Sci. (including Subser. Lect. Notes Artif. Intell. Lect. Notes Bioinformatics), vol. 11868 LNCS, pp. 441–452, 2019, doi: https://doi.org/10.1007/978-3-030-31321-0_38.

24. R. M. Alaqil, J. A. Alsuhaibani, B. A. Alhumaidi, R. A. Alnasser, R. D. Alotaibi, and H. Benhidour, "Automatic Gun Detection from Images Using Faster R-CNN," Proc. - 2020 1st Int. Conf. Smart Syst. Emerg. Technol. SMART-TECH 2020, pp. 149–154, 2020, doi: https:// doi.org/10.1109/SMART-TECH49988.2020.00045.

25. "fire and gun dataset | Kaggle." https://www.kaggle.com/atulyakumar98/fire-and-gun-dataset (accessed Feb. 15, 2022).

Real-Time Detection of Crime and Violence in Video Surveillance using Deep Learning

Ali Mansour Al-Madani[1]([✉]), Vivek Mahale[2], and Ashok T. Gaikwad[2]

[1] Department of Computer Science, Dr. Babasaheb Ambedkar Marathwada University,
Aurangabad, India
ali.m.almadani1992@gmail.com

[2] Institute of Management Studies and Information Technology, Aurangabad, India

Abstract. Since its widespread application, deep learning is a vital part of the machine learning community's toolbox. With so many crimes and wrongdoings going on without adequate oversight in public spaces, various ways have been developed to identify crime and violence in the camera footage. Automated violence detection has become more important in video surveillance research. However, they have several restrictions, and much of the time, it is based on a certain set of circumstances. This research presents a 3D convolutional neural network-based technique for detecting violence in videos. Accuracy is improved by employing machine and deep learning techniques in a suggested manner. Performance evaluations have shown that the suggested technique effectively identifies violence in video clips. ' Experimental data show that the proposed strategy outperforms existing methods for identifying crimes and violence in films. The pre-training models, Inception-V3, InceptionResNetV2, ViolenceNet, and ViolenceNet-OF, were trained on the four datasets. The classification results on the validation data for each model are as follows: ViolenceNet OF 99.40%, InceptionResNetV2 89%, ViolenceNet pseudo 96, and InceptionV3 92%. The DenseNet model was chosen for our application system because it concatenates the feature maps in a simpler method than Inception or InceptionResNet, which are more complicated. It has a more durable design that requires fewer filters and settings to attain high efficiency than other models and achieves the highest accuracy.

Keywords: Crime detection · Violence detection · DenseNet · LSTM · Abnormal detection · Blockchain · InceptionV3 · fight detection

1 Introduction

Even while computer vision has become more interested in identifying human motion in video, identifying criminal behaviour has received far less research attention than other types of human movement. Public and private security can benefit significantly from the capacity to detect criminal activity. There are cameras in almost every public place nowadays, such as schools and jails, hospitals, and retail malls. It's becoming increasingly necessary to have enough staff to monitor these cameras' ever-increasing volume of photos. Usually, this isn't feasible; thus, they lose a lot of their potential.

© The Author(s) 2023
R. Manza et al. (Eds.): ACVAIT 2022, AISR 176, pp. 431–441, 2023.
https://doi.org/10.2991/978-94-6463-196-8_33

Detection of criminal activity is the primary goal of this research. A Spatio-temporal analysis is important to identify criminality and violence in the video because of the abrupt movements associated with strikes and punches. It is possible for violent behaviours to be mistaken for other kinds of actions, leading to false positives. During CPR, for example, quick actions such as punching might be mistaken for punching in a film with minimal motion, leading to a false positive. Detecting these kinds of problems requires a thorough examination of all of the video's temporal context, both before and following the activity.

According to our knowledge, no commercial solution uses artificial intelligence and human operators to identify crimes, despite the fact that substantial research has been done. This is essential from a quality of work standpoint. So that the operators who have to view this sort of film may focus on other productive duties, this method can help alleviate their stress levels. Most importantly, the task cannot be done correctly and effectively because of a basic restriction on the number of movies that can be seen simultaneously and with the required concentration. False positives and false negatives, both of which can lead to the deactivation of a video surveillance system, are the most significant roadblocks to developing a system that can automatically identify violence. A system that has been thoroughly tested across several datasets is thus being considered. There are several sorts of criminal activity, and it is impossible to generalize from a single dataset. Models that have been trained on one dataset may not perform as well when applied to a different dataset. If this is the case, the model cannot be used in production and must be improved.

The following sections depict the flow of this document. Section 2 provides a quick review of the current condition of the problem. Section 3 explains the proposed model's Architecture in great detail. Detailed descriptions of each dataset used to assess the model are provided in Sect. 4. Section 5 includes Training and Validation of the model. Experiment results and discussion are shown in Sect. 6. Finally, in Sect. 7, the most conclusions and probable avenues for future growth are laid bare for the readers.

2   Literature Review

According to this part, an evaluation of the current state of the art in crime and violent action detection using visual characteristics is done. The most generally used references use deep learning techniques, which have consistently produced the best outcomes of any of the other approaches. As a result, there is less control and greater difficulty in creating explainable models utilizing deep learning approaches compared to earlier methods that required manual and typically complex feature extraction.

S. Battiato et al. [1] use a faster version of R-CNN (Region-based Convolutional Neural Network) to identify items within a building in real-time. ImageNet's 12 object classes and Karina dataset were used to assess this study's suggested system's performance. In NvidiaTitanX GPUs, we achieved an average accuracy of 74.33% and a mean detection time of 0.12 s per picture.

L. McClendon et al. [2] The Communities and Crime Dataset were used to develop the linear regression, additive regression, and decision stumbling algorithms utilizing the same limited dataset. The linear regression approach performed the best of the three evaluated algorithms. The study's primary goal is to use machine learning techniques in data mining analysis to forecast violent crime patterns.

A. Chowdhary et al. [3] With feature matching in the videos, this study tries to go beyond simple image-to-image comparisons to locate the query picture in its source image. Recognizing someone or anything is much easier when it comes to this method. It will return just those frames in a given video that meet a specific query characteristic.

S. Chakravarthy et al.; [4] proposed a solution based on neural networks created using the Hybrid Deep Learning (HDL) method. Fragments of video data, such as those showing crowd movement, facial expressions, and object interactions, can be retrieved using this technique. This is done using a Deep Convolutional Neural Network (DCNN) and the HDL method. In conjunction with this feature implementation, a Recurrent Neural Network (RNN) is used to learn object and human recognition. Combining these models and technologies enables an accurate ranking and scoring system for urban crime based on camera footage to be developed. To assess the correctness of the score, the histogram error rate may also be continuously tracked for each instance.

[5] VGGNet19, a pre-trained deep learning model, is used in the proposed system to identify a person aiming a weapon or knife at another person. GoogleNet InceptionV3 was also compared to two other pre-trained models in training. In terms of training precision, the outcomes obtained with VGG19 are superior. For this reason, we decided to use VGG19 with only minor fine-tuning to better detect criminal intent in videos and images than we could with the existing approaches. To construct the bounding box around photos of people, weapons, knives like a knife, guns, and so on, we used the Fast RCNN and RCNN algorithms (also known as Faster RCNN). Object detection and image classification are made easier with the assistance of algorithms.

[6] using SSD and Faster RCNN convolutional neural network algorithms, it implements automatic detection of guns (or weapons). Datasets used in the proposed implementation are split into two types. One dataset contains photographs that have already been labelled, whereas the other contains images that have been labelled manually. When the data is tallied, it turns out that both algorithms produce accurate results. The Faster RCNN has a superior accuracy of 84.6 percent compared to the standard RCNN. For example, SSD has an accuracy of 73.8 percent compared to RCNN, which has a far higher success rate in real-time detection.

[7] The deployed initiative utilizes CCTV video to keep an eye out for any suspicious activity on campus and warns campus security if anything unusual happens. This was accomplished by using CNN to extract characteristics from the frames. Classifying frames as suspicious or regular is done using the LSTM architecture after extraction. For the first 10 epochs of training, the accuracy is 76%. As the number of iterations rises, so does the model's accuracy. For testing, video frames are taken from videos and placed in a single folder. Predicting suspicious or normal behaviour based on our model, the machine classifies the images as either suspicious or normal.

M. K. El den Mohamed et al. [8] Detecting handguns and firearms in video surveillance systems has been made easier with the help of a new method. No intrusive technologies are required for weapon detection in this method. It employs Deep Learning (DL) as part of the classification and detection operations. It employs Deep Learning (DL); using Transfer Learning, the suggested method improves the outcomes that are

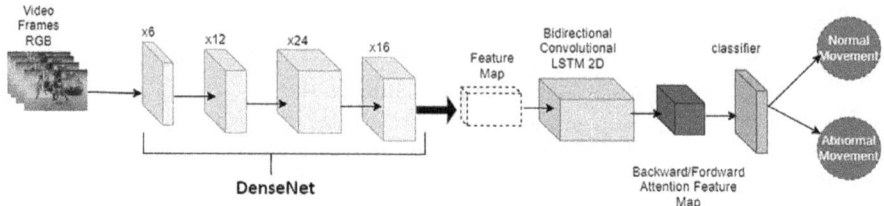

Fig. 1. Model Crime Detection Architecture

generated (TL). Both AlexNet and GoogLeNet are used in this deep learning approach. As demonstrated by experimental data, handguns and weapons may be detected by the same system. Internet Movie Firearms Database (IMFD) was used as a reference point for the tests (IMFDB) (Fig. 1).

P. Sivakumar et al.; [9] Real-Time Crime Detection Technique employing a Deep Learning Algorithm that watches real-time cameras and tells neighbouring cybercrime administrators about the incidence of crime at the current location are suggested. The object detection method utilizes YOLO. In order to compare the proposed YOLO model with the current Fast R-CNN regarding Precision, Recall, and Mean Average Precision, 45 frames per second of real-time processing were used. The suggested work's Mean Average Precision achieved 78.3 percent on the testing set, whereas fast RCNN only achieved 62.4 percent. The proposed work has a final mean average precision of 78.3% in the testing set.

[10] suggested a deep-learning-based real-time violence detector. We present a three-factor (generality, accuracy, and rapid reaction time) CNN-LSTM model that uses spatial feature extraction via CNN and temporal relationship learning via LSTM. The proposed model was 98 percent accurate and ran at a frame rate of 131 frames per second. A comparison of the suggested model's accuracy and speed with earlier studies shows that the proposed model delivers the greatest accuracy and fastest speed in violence detection.

C. S. Sung et al.;[11] suggest constructing an intelligent system for real-time video monitoring without a person's involvement. Once an artificial intelligence server and video surveillance cameras have been constructed, the flaws with the current video surveillance system will be addressed using deep learning technology as part of the data processing model design. In addition, a real-time processing video picture and a notification message will be sent to the web via this design's intelligent surveillance system to promptly and efficiently identify crimes.

3   Model Architecture

Creating a solid video encoding is essential for subsequent classification by utilizing a fully linked network to categorize crime in videos appropriately. To do this, every video is first transformed from RGB into background subtraction. The background subtraction is encoded as a series of feature maps using dense networks [17–19]. Before the attention mechanism is applied spatially and temporally to the video, a multi-head self-attention layer and a bidirectional ConvLSTM layer are applied to these feature maps (forward and backwards pass). Each video's significant spatial and temporal information is extracted using this spatiotemporal encoder's attention algorithm. A four-layer classifier divides the movie into two groups based on the encoded information (normal and abnormal movements).

3.1 DenseNet Convolutional 3D

DenseNet is a 2D convolutional architecture that was created specifically for use with photos [12]. However, it can be extended to handle video. First, the 2D convolutional layers have been replaced with 3D ones, and the 2D reduction layers have been replaced with 3D reduction layers.

For the reduction layers MaxPool2D and AveragePool2D, DenseNet employs (2, 2) as the pool size (7, 7). Maximized Pool3D and Average Pool3D were utilized with a (2, 2, 2)-pool size for the reduction layers (7, 7, 7).

The term "DenseNet" [13] is derived from the dense bricks that form the network's basis. All of a layer's descendants' feature maps are combined in these blocks. To sum it up, we've employed four different-sized dense blocks in our design. This is the succession of layers that make up a dense block: 3-dimensions of batch normalization and convolution -batch normalization-convolution in 3D.

The DenseNet model was chosen from four models, InceptionResNetV2, InceptionV3, and ViolenceNet pseudo-Of, because it concatenates the extracted features more efficiently than models like Inception or InceptionResNet, which are more complicated. It has a more durable design and requires fewer filters and settings to attain high efficiency than other models, unlike others. Compared to previous designs, it has shown superior outcomes when used to handle biomedical pictures. The DenseNet model is more efficient than other models in extracting the features needed to accomplish the detection job in terms of the number of trainable parameters and training and inference times.

3.2 Convolutional LSTM 2d Bidirectional

Bidirectional recurrent cells have two states. The past and the future are the two possible states (forward). Bidirectional recurrent layers are connected to output layers that receive information on both states simultaneously. Bidirectional recurrent layers separate a typical recurrent layer's neurons into two groups, one for positive time and the other for negative time. Having the capacity to go back in time is very helpful when trying to discover crimes and violent acts in the camera footage.

For video and image classification, the bidirectional convolutional LSTM 2D module has been proven to extract Spatio-temporal characteristics. Video gestures may be recognized and classified using long-term Spatio-temporal properties learned from videos. Classification of hyperspectral pictures is accomplished using it; however, spectral characteristics are employed in place of spatial and temporal ones.

One of the most useful features of BiConvLSTM is its ability to concurrently examine time-varying sequences forward and backwards. Layers like BiConvLSTM may look at the video's chronology in both directions. As a result, the video is better understood overall.

3.3 Classification

There are four levels in total in the classifier. There are 1024, 128, 16, and 2 nodes in each layer, arranged in ascending order of a number of nodes. The ReLu activation function is used to activate the layers that aren't visible. An activation function sigmoid is used to classify the input into two classes: Normal Movements and Abnormal Movements. This binary predictor is the last layer's output.

4 Dataset

There were four datasets used in the tests, all of which had been used in previous research on violent action identification. Their usage in comparing methods for identifying aggressive behaviour is widespread. The following are the datasets:

- NHL hockey If you're looking for a selection of games that feature fighting between players, you'll find them here.
- Movies Fights (MFs) A 200-clip compilation of fight and non-fight scenes from action films.
- Violent Flows (VFs): There are a number of videos that feature mob violence. Instead of looking at violence between individuals, this model examines the dynamics between groups of people. It's an intriguing way to see how versatile the model can be.
- A compilation of 1000 violent and 1,000 nonviolent films culled from YouTube, and the violent videos feature numerous genuine street fights in various locales and scenarios. In addition, films of nonviolent human behaviours, such as sports, eating, walking, and so on, are amassed.

They all had the same labels and were split into 80% for training and 20% for testing. Each dataset's details are shown in Table 1. Different weather conditions and indoor and outdoor settings have all been accounted for in these data sets. The Hockey Fights dataset exclusively includes fights that take place in an ice hockey rink. The sequences in the Movies Fights dataset include a mix of indoor and outdoor ones, but none of them is affected by inclement weather. The violence that happens in the open air is what the Violent Flows dataset is focused on. Rain, fog, and even snow may be seen in several of the film's sequences. There are a wide variety of indoor and outdoor settings in the Real-Life Violence Situations dataset, from the street to various sporting event venues, various rooms inside a building, and stages for music shows, among others, and depicts several types of inclement weather, with rain being the most common.

5 Training and Validation of the Model

The weights of all neurons in the model were randomized. In each frame, the pixel values were normalized to be between 0 and 1. All the movies in the dataset had the same number of frames in their input video. This algorithm repeated the previous frame until a satisfactory average was attained [58,59] regardless of whether there were more or fewer frames than average in the input video [58,59]. Using Keras pre-trained models, the frames were scaled to $224 \times 224 \times 3$, the normal size.

Table 1. Dataset Breakdown [14]

Datasets	*Number of videos*	Training	Validation	Frames %
Hockey Fights [14]	1000	**800**	**200**	**50**
Movies Fights [14]	200	**160**	**40**	**50**
"Violent Flows" [15]	246	**196**	**50**	**100**
Real-Life Violence Situations [16]	2000	**1600**	**400**	**100**

Table 2. Results Of The Models

Model Name	*Training Accuracy*	*Validation Accuracy*	Sensitivity	Specificity
InceptionV3	**92%**	**89.23%**	**91%**	**91%**
InceptionResNetV2	**89.12%**	**90.92%**	**91%**	**88%**
ViolenceNet pseudo-Of	**96.23%**	**98.5%**	**98%**	**96%**
ViolenceNet OF	**99.40%**	**100%**	**100%**	**97%**

We settled on a starting learning rate of 14, a batch size of 10 films, and a total of 25 epochs; at 0.1, weight decay was activated. It was also necessary to take advantage of the Adam optimizer's pre-configured settings. A binary cross-entropy loss function and a sigmoid activation function were both selected for use in the classifier's final layer. The training of models has been done using the Python language with deep learning libraries Keras and TensorFlow on a Lenovo laptop named LEGION, which has a GeForce GTX 1650, 4GB GPU.

6 Results and Discussion

By using a robust backbone network in this study, we looked at whether or not the performance might be improved by switching from previous experiments that used optical flow and pseudo-optical flow. It was found that the models with the self-attention module outperformed those without in terms of accuracy and inference time. For those that used only optical flow or pseudo-optical flow input when the attention module was utilized, both accuracy and inference time improved. Convolutional recurrent layer operations required slower to perform on featured maps than on concatenated sequences of attention layers; hence inference time was reduced by the application of attention mechanisms.

It was found that the optical flow input had superior results to the pseudo-optical flow input after the trials were carried out. Table 2 shows the results of a single training and testing iteration for every dataset and type of model input.

Hockey is an extremely fast-paced activity, and our model performed admirably in the HF dataset, where players are constantly moving and occasionally coming into touch with one another. Our model could learn the temporal characteristics of events depending on how energetic they were at the time of their occurrence.

There were differences in the difficulty of generalizing violence in the VF and HF datasets. In the films from the VF dataset, there were instances of violence during large-scale events like marches or concerts. During large-scale events, several acts were taking place at once. Because the vantage points were far away from the action, the images show a large number of individuals in a pixelated form. When seen from a distance, several actions in a single film appear little, making it difficult to tell whether or not a contact motion is aggressive. As a further example, the mass event's setting featured circumstances such as a mob of people grabbing a golf ball (that could seem to be the beginning of a fight). The RLVS dataset also made it impossible to generalize the idea of violence since it is so varied. Because they were not topic-specific, the RLVS scenes

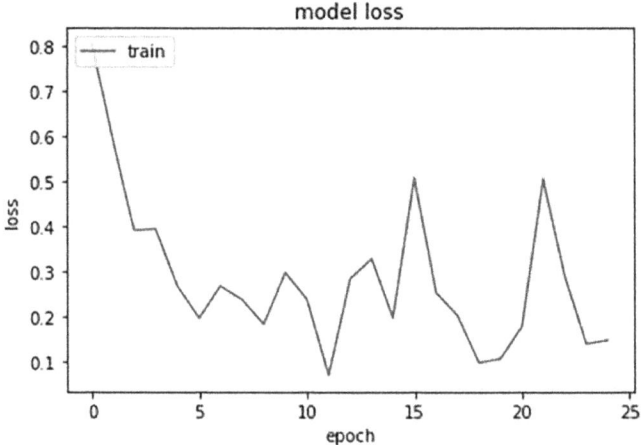

Fig. 2. Training and Validation model loss

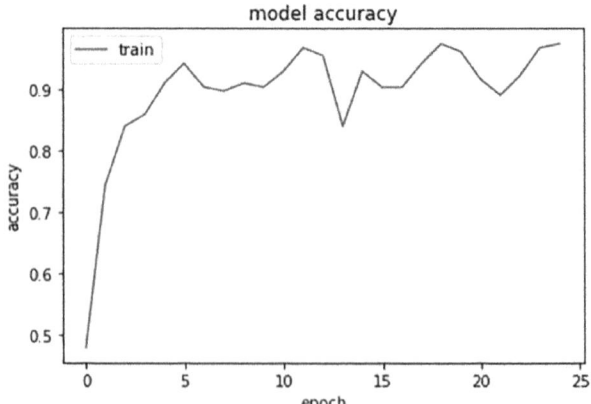

Fig. 3. Training and Validation Accuracy

constituted a unique dataset. The non-violence category showed the most variation in the dataset's heterogeneity, with scenes acting in diverse ways (Figs. 2 and 3).

Violent action detection has benefited more from the model built than from generalizing the idea of violent behaviour. Results from the preceding section show that this is true. It is feasible to increase the generalization of violence in cross-dataset tests if big and diverse cases in a dataset that considers varied settings and circumstances are utilized. The idea of violence cannot be generalized using datasets, For example, whether the input is optical flow or pseudo-optical flow that contains just one context, as in MF and HF.

7   Conclusion and Future Work

Facilities might greatly benefit from this capacity. Using action recognition software, techniques for recognizing individual actors and basic events may now be applied to this more complex scenario. Fight detection on two new datasets is evaluated in this work, including a 1000-video collection of NHL hockey games and a smaller 200-clip collection of action movie sequences. In experiments, researchers have found that the common "bag of words" strategy is 90% accurate in recognizing combat sequences. While accuracy was unaffected by low-level feature descriptors and vocabulary sizes in the hockey dataset, the choice of descriptor was essential for MoSIFT in the second dataset, where it outperformed the top STIP under all circumstances. Because of the encouraging performance of action recognition systems on this difficult job, a commercial and adaptable combat detector appears achievable.

In the future, this research will make use of the decentralised database feature given by blockchain technology [20, 21] to make data available to government for the detection of crime and violence in video surveillance with a high degree of privacy and safety.

Acknowledgments. This research was supported [Dr Babasaheb Ambedkar Marathwada University, Aurangabad (MS) India]. We thank our Teachers from [Faculty of Computer Science and Information Technology] who provided insight and expertise that greatly assisted the research, although they may not agree with all of the interpretations/conclusions of this paper.

The author would like to thank Dr. Babasaheb Ambedkar Marathwada University, Aurangabad (MS) India for providing the publication support.

Authors' Contributions. We have been done Real-time detection of crime and violence in video surveillance using Deep learning. In this research author tested the 200 videos for the experiment based on DNN model. The pre-training models, Inception-V3, InceptionResNetV2, ViolenceNet, and ViolenceNet-OF, trained on the four datasets. The classification results on validation data for each model are as follows: ViolenceNet OF 99.40%, InceptionResNetV2 89%, ViolenceNet pseudo 96.

References

1. S. Battiato, G. Gallo, R. Schettini, and F. Stanco, Eds., Image Analysis and Processing - ICIAP 2017, vol. 10485. Cham: Springer International Publishing, 2017. DOI: https://doi.org/10.1007/978-3-319-68548-9.
2. L. McClendon and N. Meghanathan, "Using Machine Learning Algorithms to Analyze Crime Data," Machine Learning and Applications: An International Journal, vol. 2, no. 1, pp. 1–12, Mar. 2015, DOI: https://doi.org/10.5121/mlaij.2015.2101.
3. A. Chowdhary and B. Rudra, "Video surveillance for the crime detection using features," in Advances in Intelligent Systems and Computing, 2021, vol. 1141, pp. 61–71. DOI: https://doi.org/10.1007/978-981-15-3383-9_6.
4. S. Chackravarthy, S. Schmitt, and L. Yang, "Intelligent crime anomaly detection in smart cities using deep learning," in Proceedings - 4th IEEE International Conference on Collaboration and Internet Computing, CIC 2018, Nov. 2018, pp. 399–404. DOI: https://doi.org/10.1109/CIC.2018.00060.
5. IEEE Circuits and Systems Society. India Chapter and Institute of Electrical and Electronics Engineers, 2018 International Conference on Circuits and Systems in Digital Enterprise Technology (ICCSDET).
6. Institute of Electrical and Electronics Engineers and Hindusthan Institute of Technology, Proceedings of the International Conference on Electronics and Sustainable Communication Systems (ICESC 2020) : 02–04, July 2020.
7. Dayananda Sagar College of Engineering, Institute of Electrical and Electronics Engineers. Bangalore Section, and Institute of Electrical and Electronics Engineers, 2nd International Conference on Innovative Mechanisms for Industry Applications (ICIMIA 2020) : conference proceedings : 5–7 March 2020.
8. M. K. el den Mohamed, A. Taha, and H. H. Zayed, "Automatic gun detection approach for video surveillance," International Journal of Sociotechnology and Knowledge Development, vol. 12, no. 1, pp. 49–66, Jan. 2020, DOI: https://doi.org/10.4018/IJSKD.2020010103.
9. P. Sivakumar, V. Jayabalaguru, R. Ramsugumar, and S. Kalaisriram, "Real-Time Crime Detection Using Deep Learning Algorithm," Jul. 2021. doi: https://doi.org/10.1109/ICSCAN53069.2021.9526393.
10. University of Technology (Iraq). Computer Sciences Department, Institute of Electrical and Electronics Engineers. Iraq Section, and Institute of Electrical and Electronics Engineers, 2019 2nd Scientific Conference of Computer Sciences (SCCS) : University of Technology, Computer Sciences Department, March 27–28, 2019.
11. C. S. Sung and J. Y. Park, "Design of an intelligent video surveillance system for crime prevention: applying deep learning technology," Multimedia Tools and Applications, vol. 80, no. 26–27, pp. 34297–34309, Nov. 2021, DOI: https://doi.org/10.1007/s11042-021-10809-z.
12. G. Huang, Z. Liu, L. van der Maaten, and K. Q. Weinberger, "Densely connected convolutional networks," in Proceedings - 30th IEEE Conference on Computer Vision and Pattern Recognition, CVPR 2017, Nov. 2017, vol. 2017-January, pp. 2261–2269. doi: https://doi.org/10.1109/CVPR.2017.243.
13. F. J. Rendón-Segador, J. A. Álvarez-García, F. Enríquez, and O. Deniz, "ViolenceNet: Dense Multi-Head Self-Attention with Bidirectional Convolutional LSTM for Detecting Violence," Electronics, vol. 10, no. 13, p. 1601, Jul. 2021, doi: https://doi.org/10.3390/electronics10131601.
14. E. B. Nievas, O. Deniz Suarez, G. Bueno García, and R. Sukthankar, "Violence Detection in Video Using Computer Vision Techniques." [Online]. Available: http://visilab.etsii.uclm.es/
15. Y. Itcher, "Real-Time Detection of Violent Crowd Behavior."

16. Jāmi'at 'Ayn Shams. Faculty of Computer and Information Sciences and Institute of Electrical and Electronics Engineers, *ICICIS 2019 : Ninth IEEE International Conference on Intelligent Computing and Information Systems: Cairo, Egypt, December 8–9, 2019.*

17. A. M. Al-madani, A. T. Gaikwad, V. Mahale, Z. A. T. Ahmed and A. A. A. Shareef, "Real-time Driver Drowsiness Detection based on Eye Movement and Yawning using Facial Landmark," 2021 International Conference on Computer Communication and Informatics (ICCCI), 2021, pp. 1-4, doi: https://doi.org/10.1109/ICCCI50826.2021.9457005.

18. M. Tawfik, S. Nimbhore, N. M. Al-Zidi, Z. A. T. Ahmed and A. M. Almadani, "Multi-features Extraction for Automating Covid-19 Detection from Cough Sound using Deep Neural Networks," 2022 4th International Conference on Smart Systems and Inventive Technology (ICSSIT), 2022, pp. 944–950, doi: https://doi.org/10.1109/ICSSIT53264.2022.9716529.

19. Ahmed, Z.A.T., Jadhav, M.E., Al-madani, A.M., Tawfik, M., Alsubari, S.N., Shareef, A.A.A. (2022). Real-Time Detection of Student Engagement: Deep Learning-Based System. In: Khanna, A., Gupta, D., Bhattacharyya, S., Hassanien, A.E., Anand, S., Jaiswal, A. (eds) International Conference on Innovative Computing and Communications. Advances in Intelligent Systems and Computing, vol 1387. Springer, Singapore. https://doi.org/10.1007/978-981-16-2594-7_26.

20. A. M. Al-madani and A. T. Gaikwad, "IoT Data Security Via Blockchain Technology and Service-Centric Networking," 2020 International Conference on Inventive Computation Technologies (ICICT), 2020, pp. 17-21, doi: https://doi.org/10.1109/ICICT48043.2020.9112521.

21. A. M. Al-madani, A. T. Gaikwad, V. Mahale and Z. A. T. Ahmed, "Decentralized E-voting system based on Smart Contract by using Blockchain Technology," 2020 International Conference on Smart Innovations in Design, Environment, Management, Planning and Computing (ICSIDEMPC), 2020, pp. 176–180, doi: https://doi.org/10.1109/ICSIDEMPC49020.2020.9299581.

Adsorption Study of Carbon Monoxide on Modified Metal and Non-metallic Surface Using Density Functional Theory: A Short Review Towards Functional Materials

Amogh A. Sambare[1(✉)], Kunal P. Datta[1], Mahendra D. Shirsat[2], Bharti W. Gawali[1,3], and Ramkisan S. Pawar[4]

[1] Deen Dayal Upadhyay KAUSHAL Kendra, Dr. Babasaheb Ambedkar Marathwada University, Aurangabad, Maharashtra, India
amoghsambare@gmail.com
[2] RUSA Centre for Advance Sensor Technology, Department of Physics, Dr. Babasaheb Ambedkar Marathwada University, Aurangabad, Maharashtra, India
[3] Department of Computer Science and Information Technology, Dr. Babasaheb Ambedkar Marathwada University, Aurangabad, Maharashtra, India
[4] Shreeyash College of Engineering and Technology, Aurangabad, Maharashtra, India

Abstract. Carbon Monoxide is an established pollutant with high indexed hazard potential for human being and environment and its omnipresence in indoor and outdoor air, has garnered specific research interest for real time detection of the same at trace level of existence. Extensive spectrum of research for development of Carbon Monoxide sensors are therefore being carried out and pursuit for efficient and smart materials constitute the core of such research efforts. The most common technique of sensing these gas molecules is to detect them with various adsorption materials, such as metal, semi-conductor metal oxides like MnO_2, MoS_2, and carbon-based materials, among others. Doping transition metal atoms in adsorbent materials has also been shown to be beneficial in the gas adsorption process. In order to have a predictive command over development of smart functional materials for detection of Carbon Monoxide, the Density Function Theory calculation is still a time-tested tool for analyzing the adsorption properties of pollutant molecules on various materials at the microscale levels to comprehend adsorptive reactions, adsorbents reactivity, and structure activity relationships, that can provide theoretical guidance for scientific experiments. This review presents the adsorption models and surface properties of CO gas molecules on metal and nonmetallic surfaces by Density Function Theory calculations in recent years. This review opens up the theoretical background for DFT based molecular adsorption studies and some of the recent reports of research pertinence.

Keywords: DFT · Carbon Monoxide · Functional Materials

R. Manza et al. (Eds.): ACVAIT 2022, AISR 176, pp. 442–458, 2023.
https://doi.org/10.2991/978-94-6463-196-8_34

1 Introduction

Deployment of computational aids for modelling of physical systems dates back to the age of World War II, with is prominent role in Manhattan Project. Through an ever-maturing journey of over seventy years, computational algorithms have succeeded to reach a better apex every other day and have attracted researchers from all strata of science and technology towards applications that encompass initial designing of experiments to complex modelling of subatomic regime. Computational tools have allowed to reveal predictive scenario of hitherto unseen and has allowed to design extremely complicated experiments that could be otherwise costed heavily with definite possible errors. They have allowed to do things, that were otherwise difficult to achieve with direct experiment. As on date, computational tools have emerged as first hand cheaper and faster solution to critical problems, which might have required complex machinery to achieve [1]. Computational tools have not only augmented laboratory experiments as potent precursors but has proved its potency towards in-depth understanding of physical and chemical phenomenon through computer simulation derived from numerical analysis and theoretical considerations to solve problems. The scientific computing approach provides understanding, mainly through the analysis of mathematical models.

Among the different potent areas of application, computational simulations have proved to be an indispensable tool to investigate gas molecule adsorption on the sensing materials at molecular or the atomic level. Density functional theory (DFT), a quantum mechanics-based electronic level computational simulation technique, has garnered tremendous attention among researchers in the domain of chemical sensing. It has notable extent of reliability and broad application arena, which is of great value in material computational simulation [2]. In last ten years, Density Functional Theory have been extensively applied to study of the chemical reaction and interfacial chemical reactions [3, 4]. A large gamut of reports have proved the accuracy of DFT calculations by comparing with experiments [5]. Most of the research papers on gas adsorption by DFT calculations have primarily concentrated on low-index surfaces of pure metals and alloys.

Adsorption study of Carbon Monoxide (CO) on different sensor surfaces is appealing from both scientific and technical interest considering the extreme perilous effect and pervasive presence of CO.

This short review presents recent work carried out for CO gas adsorption and diffusion on metals, metal oxides and non-metallic surfaces by DFT calculations. A brief introduction of the density functional theory followed by review of recent work carried out involving dissociative adsorption of gas molecule, adsorption of atom and diffusion of gas molecule by DFT calculations has been provided. Finally, challenges and opportunities with adsorption and diffusion studies of gas molecule on surface has been given.

2 Density Functional Theory

In 1964, Hohenberg and Kohn studied Thomas-Fermi model for the electronic structure of materials and proposed two fundamental theorems that resulted in Density Functional Theory (DFT) [6]. Experimented through time, DFT has proved itself to be an indispensable tool for theoretical study of solids. Later, Nitya Nanda et.al proposed to derive ground-state energy from Schrodinger equation, which is uniquely determined by the density number of particles [7]. Another theorem is related to condition of constant number of particles, the electron density that minimizes the energy of the overall functional, which is the ground state energy [8]. Thus, by finding charge density wave function in three spatial variables, one can reach to solution of Scrodinger equation. Finally, Scrodinger equation is used to obtain ground-state energy.

Hohenberg-Kohn theorem described energy function as a single electron wave function as -

$$E[\{\psi\}] = E_{known}[\{\psi i\}] + E_{xc}[\{\psi i\}] \tag{1}$$

where,

$$E_{known}[\{\psi i\}] = \frac{h^2}{m} \sum_i \int \psi i^* \nabla^* \psi i d^3 r + \int v(r)n(r)d^3 r + \frac{e^2}{2} \iint \frac{n(r)n(r^*)d^3 rd^3 r^*}{|r - r^*|} + E_{ion} \tag{2}$$

In above formula, the first term represents the electron kinetic energies, second term represents the coulomb interaction between the electrons and the nuclei, while the third term represents coulomb interaction between pair of electrons and last term represents coulomb interaction between pair of nuclei, respectively.

$E_{xc}[\{\psi i\}]$ represents exchange-correlation functional.

In pursuit to correct electron density, Kohn and Sham solved the problem of finding solution to Scrodinger equation wave function [9].

Final form of equation obtained is as follows:

$$\left[-\frac{h^2}{2m} \nabla^2 + v(r) + v_H(r) + v_{xc}(r) \right] \psi i(r) = \epsilon i \psi i(r) \tag{3}$$

Single electron wave function is obtained by solving kohn-sham equation which depends on three spatial variables ψi (r).

The potential term v, v_H, and v_{xc} are present on left side of the kohn sham equation.

The first term v, represents interaction between an electron and all of atomic nuclei.

The Second term v_H represents Hartee potential, and has form

$$v_H(r) = e^2 \int n(r^*) \frac{d^3 r^*}{|r - r^*|} \tag{4}$$

v_H represents Coulomb interaction between pair of electrons.

The third term v_{xc}, represents exchange to the single electron equations.

It is expressed as '' functional derivative'' of exchange correlation energy.

$$v_{xc}(r) = \frac{\delta E_{xc}(r)}{\delta n(r)} \tag{5}$$

An initial charge density, n(r) is applied and solution to Kohn-Sham equation in form of single electron wave function ψi (r).

$n_{ks}(r) = 2 \sum_i \psi i^*(r)\psi i(r)$, single particle wave function is utilized to calculate charge density and calculated charge density nks is compared with initial charge n(r).

If both charge densities are same, it indicates ground state electron density and is used to compute the total energy. If both charge densities are different, then initial electron density is modified in some way [9].

3   Software Packages Based on DFT

Figures and tables should be placed either at the top or bottom of the page and close to the text referring to them if possi In recent years, there have been developments in Computational Technology and improvement of calculation methods. Open- source or Commercial software packages are available that can be used for performing most of the calculations based on DFT. Based upon application, open source software packages such as Quantum Espresso (for investigations with electronic structures, simulation and optimization), ABINIT, SIESTA (Spanish Initiative for Electronic Simulations with Thousands of Atoms), CPMD (Car-Parrinello Molecular Dynamics), MOLPRO and Commercial – Softwares including VASP (Vienna Ab in to Simulation Package), Material Studio (MS), Gaussian, ADF (Amsterdam Density Functional), Crystal or Wien2K are being used by researchers for computation and material simulation [10].

Some software are based on plane waves, whereas, some are based on linear combinations of atomic orbitals. In this paper, we report three programs more frequently used by researchers i.e., VASP, Quantum Espresso, Material Studio, SIESTA. Open source and free software such as Quantum Espresso are used for performing electronic structure calculations and material modelling based on DFT, plane waves (PW)s and pseudopotentials (PPs) [1]. Programming languages such as C++ and Fortran are used in Quantum Espresso. These codes are constructed in such manner that can deal with periodic as well as a periodic boundary conditions. Quantum Espresso can deal with infinite crystal system and treat with efficient convergence of the thermodynamic limit for periodic as well as aperiodic but extended crystal system such as liquids or amorphous materials [11].

As per requirement, open- boundary conditions may be employed by the density-countercharge method. The computations/simulations can be performed using energy for extended/periodic systems or isolated systems, structural optimization of the microscopic (atomic co-ordinates) also macroscopic (unit cell) systems, ground- state condition of magnetic or spin polarized systems, using any arbitrary wavelength second and third derivative of total energy, first principle molecular dynamics study of thermodynamic ensemble, determining transition states and saddle points with help of transition path optimization, calculation of NMR (nuclear magnet resonance) and EPR (electronic paramagnetic resonance) parameters [12].

Material Studio is a commercial software package that offers a platform for computational simulation and modelling. Material Studio helps us in solving important problems in physics, chemistry and material science [13]. CASTEP, $DMOL^3$ modules are used for the first principle quantum mechanics calculations based on DFT. CASTEP is used for solid materials makes full use of the DFT plane-wave prepotentials method and LDA and GGA theoretical methods to explore the exchange correlation energy of electron interaction [13]. Study of band structures, density of states, Mulliken charge distribution, surface chemistry and optical properties (absorption and reflection spectra etc.), study can be performed using CASTEP [13]. Whereas, calculation of surface and solid properties, study of homogenous catalysis, heterogenous catalysis, molecular reaction can be performed using $DMOL^3$. $DMOL^3$ can also be used to predict structures, reaction barriers, reaction energies, thermodynamic properties and vibrational spectra. SIESTA is an open-source software package, which is used for electronic structure calculation

Table 1. Summary of adsorption of CO gas molecules on metal surface

Sr.no	Gas Molecule	Surface	Doped Element on Surface	Exchange-Corelation	Cut-off Energy	K Points	Charge Transfer	Adsorption Energy	Equilibrium Distance between molecule and surface	Computational Package	Site	Method	Ref
1.	CO	Cu		GGA-PW91		8 × 6 × 1		−0.73eV	1.96A	VASP	Cu-C	DFT + U	[17]
2.	CO	Ni		GGA-PBE	500eV	Gamma Points Only		−1.68	4.73	VASP	Ni-C	DFT-PBE + D3	[18]
3.	CO	Au		LSDA			0.25	3.14		Gaussian98	Au-C	DFT	[19]
4.	CO	WO3	----	B3LYP			−0.338	3.264	2.07	Gaussian	W-C	DFT	[25]
5.	CO	ZnO		GGA-PBE	300 eV	1 × 4 × 1		0.89eV	2.089A	CASTEP	Zn-C	DFT	[27]
6.	CO	MOS2		PBE	400	3 × 3 × 1		0.01		VASP	Mo-C	DFT-D2	[26]
7.	CO	Zno (0002)		GGA-PBE	280Ry	4 × 4 × 1	0.23	−0.76	2.108	Quantum Espresso	Zn-C	DFT-D2	[28]
8.	CO	Co3O4		B3LYP			0.757	−3.36	1.93	Gaussian09	Co-C	DFT	[20]
9.	CO	Co3O4	In	B3LYP			0.1	−5.44	1.93	Gaussian09	In-C	DFT	[20]
10.	CO	Co3O4		GGA-PBE	400			−1.94	1.79	VASP	Co-C	DFT	[20]
11.	CO	Pt (211)		GGA-PBE		5 × 3 × 1		−2.41	1.83	Material Studio	Pt-C	DFT	[21]
12.	CO	WO3		GGA-PBE		3 × 3 × 6	0.50	0.35	3.077	DMol3	W-C	DFT	[29]
13.	CO	MgO	Ni	GGA-PBE		Gamma Points	0.557	1.17		DMol3	Ni-C	DFT	[22]

(continued)

Table 1. (*continued*)

Sr.no	Gas Molecule	Surface	Doped Element on Surface	Exchange-Corelation	Cutt-off Energy	K Points	Charge Transfer	Adsorption Energy	Equilibrium Distance between molecule and surface	Computational Package	Site	Method	Ref
14.	CO	MgO	Pd	GGA-PBE		Gamma Points	0.325	1.61		DMol3	Pd-C	DFT	[22]
15.	CO	MgO	Pt	GGA-PBE		Gamma Points	0.217	2.55		DMol3	Pt-C	DFT	[22]
16.	CO	TiO2 (001)		B3LYP		8 × 8 × 8		−9.73 kcal/mol		CRYSTAL06	Ti-C	DFT	[30]
17.	CO	TiO2 (101)		B3LYP		8 × 8 × 8		−6.78 kcal/mol		CRYSTAL06	Ti-C	DFT	[30]
18.	CO	WO3(001)		PW91	400			0.44	2.510	VASP	W-C	DFT	[23]
19.	CO	Alpha-Al2O3		GGA-PBE	400	5 × 5 × 2		0.45	2.26	CASTEP	Al-C	DFT	[24]
20	CO	WO3		B3LYP			0.062	6.256	1.208	Gaussian 09	O-C	DFT	[25]
21	CO	WO3		B3LYP			−−0.302	0.272	2.07	Gaussian 09	W-C	DFT	[25]
22	CO	WO3	MO	B3LYP			−0.338	3.274	3.07	Gaussian 09	Mo-C	DFT	[25]
23	CO	MOS2	Fe	PBE	400	3 × 3 × 1	−0.27	1.60		VASP	Fe-C	DFT-D2	[26]
24	CO	MOS2	Co	PBE	400	3 × 3 × 1	−0.19	1.71		VASP	Co-C	DFT-D2	[26]
25	CO	MOS2	Ni	PBE	400	3 × 3 × 1	−0.16	1.69		VASP	Ni-C	DFT-D2	[26]
26	CO	MOS2	Cu	PBE	400	3 × 3 × 1	−0.02	1.27		VASP	Cu-C	DFT-D2	[26]

(continued)

Table 1. (*continued*)

Sr.no	Gas Molecule	Surface	Doped Element on Surface	Exchange -Corelation	Cutt-off Energy	K Points	Charge Transfer	Adsorption Energy	Equilibrium Distance between molecule and surface	Computational Package	Site	Method	Ref
27	CO	MOS2	Ag	PBE	400	3 × 3 × 1	−0.01	0.79		VASP	Ag-C	DFT-D2	[26]
28	CO	MOS2	Au	PBE	400	3 × 3 × 1	−0.02	1.06		VASP	Au-C	DFT-D2	[26]
29	CO	MOS2	Rh	PBE	400	3 × 3 × 1	−0.16	1.49		VASP	Rh-C	DFT-D2	[26]
30	CO	MOS2	Pd	PBE	400	3 × 3 × 1	−0.06	1.13		VASP	Pd-C	DFT-D2	[26]
31	CO	MOS2	Pt	PBE	400	3 × 3 × 1	−0.08	1.60		VASP	Pt-C	DFT-D2	[26]
32	CO	MOS2	Ir	PBE	400	3 × 3 × 1	−0.16	2.04		VASP	Ir-c	DFT-D2	[26]

and molecular dynamic simulation of molecules, surfaces and solids. SIESTA offers a platform for computational simulation and modelling, based on Density Functional Theory [12]. The basic computation/simulations such as calculation of total energy and local energy, atomic force, stress tensor, electric diploe moment, Mulliken charge distribution, atomic orbital, charge density, energy band and density of states etc. are performed using standard Kohn-Sham method, Local density approximation (LDA) or generalized gradient approximation (GGA) [14]. Two sub-programs of SIESTA code such as FCBUILD and VIBRATOR are used to control phonon frequency of the system. The software programs help us to understand scope of quantum chemistry and enrich the research output based on the density functional theory [12].

In this review, the use of DFT method used to study the adsorption and diffusion behavior of gas molecules on the surface and some examples have been provided (Tables 1 and 2).

4 Adsorption Study of CO Gas Molecules on Metal Surface

Transition metals and precious metals play a significant role in the enhancing catalytic oxidation rate of some gas pollutant molecules such as CO and NOx, and often represents as catalysts with excellent performance [15]. After cleaving the single crystals, the required crystal faces can be obtained, which provides a material basis for the adsorption of the gas molecules. Lattice of the metal is replaced by different forms of crystal planes, which are represented by Miller indices. But on contrary, certain metal oxides may have some properties which are not found in single metal [16]. As a result, study of the adsorption or chemical kinetics mechanism of these pollutants on the surface of pristine metals and their compounds is of great significance for enhancing sensitivity and selectivity of materials for detection of gases. And through last decade, researchers have taken interest in study of the adsorption behaviour of gas molecules on some metal surfaces by DFT theories.

Gajdos et al. studied adsorption properties of CO on transition metal Cu (111) and Cu (001) surfaces by first principle calculations [17]. The structural, vibrational and thermodynamic properties of CO on Cu substrate was analyzed within DFT framework. The conventional DFT method along with DFT + U method result were compared with experiments and underlaying advantages of DFT + U method were discovered. The DFT + U method provided correct prediction of site preference and agreement of adsorption energies with experiments. Amorim et al. carried out atomic level study on Ni nanoclusters and CO molecule to determine how the molecular adsorption of CO affects the energetic, structural and chemical properties of Ni. The results depicted those geometric modifications upon molecular adsorption had significant role in structuring molecular interaction. If adsorbed gas molecules have longer internal bond lengths upon adsorption to Ni nanoclusters, stronger chemical bonding resulted with Ni [18]. X.Wu et al. studied binding of CO molecule with small neutral and charged Au clusters using Density Functional theory [19]. It could be observed that CO binding on small gold clusters could be enhanced or decreased by preparing differently charged gold clusters. Nanostructured Co_3O_4 is one of the prominent functional materials with outstanding properties for gas sensing applications. V. Nagarajan et al. studied CO adsorption on

Table 2. Summary of adsorption of CO gas molecules on non-metallic surface

Sr.no	Gas Molecule	Surface	Doped Element on Surface	Exchange -Corelation	Cutt-off Energy	K Points	Charge Transfer	Adsorption Energy	Equilibrium Distance between molecule and surface	Computational Package	Site	Method	Reference
1.	CO	Graphene	Nitrogen,	Pw-91 GGA				-1.04eV	- 3.39 A	GAUSSIAN 09	N-C	DFT	[31]
2.	CO	Graphene	Boron	Pw-91 GGA				-5.68eV	- 3.28 A	GAUSSIAN 09	B-C	DFT	[31]
3.	CO	Graphene	Fe	GGA-PBE			0.13 eV	1.60 eV		ORCA	Fe-C	DFT	[38]
4.	CO	Graphene	Pt	GGA-Pw91	400eV	5 × 5 × 1		-34.3eV		VASP	Pt-C	DFT	[39]
5.	CO	Graphene	Pt,B							VASP	B-C	DFT	[39]
6.	CO	PentaGraphene	Fe	GGA-PBE		2 × 2 × 1	0.094	0.586	1.939	DMol3	Fe-C	DFT-D2	[32]
7.	CO	Graphene		GGA-PBE + Grimme	300	4 × 4 × 2	0.01	-0.131	4.111	CASTEP	C-C	DFT-D2	[33]
8.	CO	Defective Graphene		GGA-PBE + Grimme	300	4 × 4 × 2	0	-2.046	1.301	CASTEP	C-C	DFT-D2	[33]
9.	CO	Graphene	In	GGA-PBE + Grimme	300	4 × 4 × 2	-0.01	-0.021	3.653	CASTEP	In-C	DFT-D2	[33]
10.	CO	Graphene	Sb	GGA-PBE + Grimme	300	4 × 4 × 2	0.01	-0.002	3.165	CASTEP	Sb-C	DFT-D2	[33]
11.	CO	Graphene		B3LYP/LanL2DZ				-1.28	3.576	Gaussian 03	C-C	DFT	[34]
12.	CO	Graphene	Fe	B3LYP/LanL2DZ				-33.77	1.848	Gaussian 03	Fe-C	DFT	[34]
13.	CO	Graphene	Ru	B3LYP/LanL2DZ				-28.07	2.028	Gaussian 03	Ru-C	DFT	[34]
14.	CO	Graphene	Os	B3LYP/LanL2DZ				-41.62	1.997	Gaussian 03	Os-C	DFT	[34]
15.	CO	Graphene	Co	B3LYP/LanL2DZ				-21.74	1.879	Gaussian 03	Co-C	DFT	[34]
16.	CO	Graphene	Rn	B3LYP/LanL2DZ				-23.35	2.016	Gaussian 03	Rn-C	DFT	[34]
17.	CO	Graphene	Ir	B3LYP/LanL2DZ				-36.30	1.959	Gaussian 03	Ir-C	DFT	[34]

(continued)

Table 2. (*continued*)

Sr.no	Gas Molecule	Surface	Doped Element on Surface	Exchange-Corelation	Cut-off Energy	K Points	Charge Transfer	Adsorption Energy	Equilibrium Distance between molecule and surface	Computational Package	Site	Method	Reference
18.	CO	Graphene	Ni	B3LYP/LanL2DZ				-23.61	1.885	Gaussian 03	Ni-C	DFT	[34]
19.	CO	Graphene	Pd	B3LYP/LanL2DZ				-21.13	2.065	Gaussian 03	Pd-C	DFT	[34]
20.	CO	Graphene	Pt	B3LYP/LanL2DZ				-29.87		Gaussian 03	Pt-C	DFT	[34]
21.	CO	Graphene Pristine		DFTB		$5 \times 5 \times 1$		-4.652	3.467	Quantum Espresso	C-C	DFTB	[35]
22.	CO	Graphene-Stone wall Defective		DFTB		$5 \times 5 \times 1$		-4.661	3.00	Quantum Espresso	C-C	DFTB	[35]
23.	CO	Graphene-Vacancy Defective		DFTB		$5 \times 5 \times 1$		-4.652	1.8	Quantum Espresso	C-C	DFTB	[35]
24.	CO	Graphene		GGA-PBE		$16 \times 16 \times 1$	-0.014	-0.219	3.20	DMol3	C-C	DFT-D	[40]
25.	CO	Graphene	In	GGA-PBE		$16 \times 16 \times 1$	0.033	-0.223	3.118	DMol3	In-C	DFT-D	[40]
26.	CO	Graphene	N	GGA-PBE		$16 \times 16 \times 1$	0.015	-0.152	3.764	DMol3	N-C	DFT-D	[40]
27.	CO	Graphene	Ga	GGA-PBE		$5 \times 5 \times 1$	-0.129	-0.674	2.027	DMol3	Ga-C	DFT-T	[41]
28.	CO	Graphene		GGA-PBE		$5 \times 5 \times 1$	-0.076	-0.210	3.139	DMol3	C-C	DFT	[41]
29.	CO	Graphene		GGA-PBE	400	$4 \times 4 \times 1$	0.015	0.08		VASP	C-C	DFT-D	[36]
30.	CO	Graphene		GGA-PBE	400	$4 \times 4 \times 1$	0.155	1.05		VASP	C-C	DFT-D	[36]
31.	CO	Polymorphins	Mn	B3LYP			1.228	-0.468	1.763	Gaussian09	Mn-C	DFT	[37]
32.	CO	Polymorphins	Co	B3LYP			0.985	-0.334	2.045	Gaussian09	Co-C	DFT	[37]
33.	CO	Polymorphins	Fe	B3LYP			0.000	-1.042	1.743	Gaussian09	Fe-C	DFT	[37]
34.	CO	Polymorphins	Cu	B3LYP			0.593	-0.132	3.050	Gaussian09	Cu-C	DFT	[37]
35.	CO	Polymorphins	Ni	B3LYP			0.000	-0.102	3.225	Gaussian09	Ni-C	DFT	[37]
36.	CO	Polymorphins	Zn	B3LYP			0.000	-0.206	2.656	Gaussian09	Zn-C	DFT	[37]

Co_3O_4 nanostructure with substitution impurity and identified favourable sites for CO adsorption [20]. The adsorption properties of CO on CO_3O_4 nanostructures could be enhanced by incorporation of In atoms [20]. Adsorption energies, structures, and C-O stretching vibrational frequencies are explored by evaluating different probable adsorption sites and comparing them with actual data in a DFT analysis of CO Adsorption on Pt (211) surface by Orita et al. [21]. It could be observed that CO adsorption is preferred on atop site on the step edge of Pt (211) at low temperature [21]. Linghuan Zhao et al. conducted DFT investigation of CO Adsorption on O-terminated and WO-terminated WO_3 surface by Density Functional Theory (DFT) calculations [21]. It was found that O terminated surface had higher sensitivity to CO gas molecule as compared to WO terminated surface [21]. Yang et al. carried out DFT investigation to study interaction of CO gas on transition metal doped MgO nanotube [22]. Addition of transition metal dopant could enhance CO adsorption on MgO nanotube while Pt doping demonstrated significant influence on CO adsorption [22]. Jin et al., conducted systematic DFT investigation of CO molecule on the WO_3(001) surfaces for CO sensing [23]. It had been demonstrated that the top oxygen atom converted CO to CO2 for the ideal WO3(001) surface, resulting in the production of a faulty surface with oxygen vacancy at the surface and a drop in surface resistivity[23]. Rohmann et al. studied the adsorption of CO on α-Al_2O_3(0001) using the DFT-GGA computational method and on α- Al_2O_3 powder experimentally by Infra-red spectroscopy [24]. CO adsorption of α- Al_2O_3 layer results in inward relaxation of Al layers and increase or decrease in adsorption energy is in proportion with structural distortion [24]. V.Nagarajan et al. Performed DFT investigation in order to study structural stability, electronic properties, and adsorption characteristics of CO adsorption on WO_3 surfaces [25]. The structural stability of WO_3 nanostructures was discussed with calculated energy. The electronic properties of WO_3 structures were analyzed in terms of HOMO-LUMO gap, ionization potential and electron affinity. The adsorption characteristics CO on WO_3 were reported in terms of adsorbed energy, average energy gap variation, Mulliken population analysis and density of states spectrum. The authors reported that adsorption characteristics of CO could be enhanced with the substitution of Mo impurity in the WO_3 base material. Fan. et al. reported systematic study of structures and electronic properties of diverse transition metal (TM = Fe, Co, Ni, Cu, Ag, Au, Rh, Pd, Pt and Ir)-embedded monolayer of MoS_2 in the S-vacancy and the adsorption of CO molecules using DFT [26].

5   Adsorption Study of CO Gas Molecules on Non-Metallic surface

In recent years, graphene has garnered specific attention as a prominent sensing material. Lopez et al. conducted a density functional investigation of CO adsorption in B-, N-, and BN-co-doped graphene using a coronene-based model to assess the applicability of these systems as CO-sensors. The results revealed that, while all of the configurations confirmed CO physical adsorption, the relative positions of Nitrogen and Boron gave varied responses to CO adsorption. Since monosubstituted Boron-coronene showed the highest CO adsorption energy, this structure could be potentially a good CO-sensor, as suggested by authors [31]. Arrigada et al. used molecular dynamics to investigate the stability of the FeG-Gas interaction in ambient conditions, as well as the adsorption stability in aerobic conditions. As a reference, the gas adsorption was also studied onto pristine graphene. Through this study, FeG was suggested to enhance the gas adsorption process of toxic gaseous pollutants with negative effects on human health, flora and fauna [31]. Zhang et al. conducted DFT investigation in order to study the adsorption energy, charge transfer, adsorption distance, charge density, density of states (DOS), and partial density of states (PDOS) of CO gas molecules on Fe-doped Pentagraphene. It was found that adsorption of CO gas could be effectively enhanced by the doping of Fe atom in Fe-doped PG substrate. Adsorption energy and charge transfer for CO on the Fe-doped PG was found to be higher than those on the pristine PG, and different adsorption orientations of CO have different adsorption behaviours [32]. Yang et al. studied adsorptions of CO molecules on the pristine, defective, In-doped and Sb-doped graphene through the density functional theory (DFT) calculations [33]. The results demonstrated that the insertion of defects or dopants into graphene has a significant influence on the stable geometries of graphene-based materials. The pure, In-doped, and Sb-doped graphene surfaces had a modest contact with the adsorbed CO. The inclusion of a C flaw into the sensing material might facilitate interaction between the CO molecule and the faulty graphene substantially. The CO favoured to be chemisorbed on the defective graphene with the C atom above the adsorbent surface in the parallel direction, resulting in the defective graphene's sensing performance towards CO, as revealed by the potent crossover of the spikes in the PDOS of the C atom/O atom in CO and the energetic C atom in the defective graphene [33]. Wanno et al. used density functional theory calculations at the B3LYP/LanL2DZ theoretical level to study CO adsorptions on virgin, Fe, Ru, Os, Co, Rh, Ir, Ni, Pd, and Pt doped graphene [34]. This work revealed that the transition metal doped graphene were higher sensitive to CO adsorption than that of pristine graphene. The Os- and Fe-doped graphene displayed the strongest interaction with C and O atoms of CO molecule, respectively [34]. Tit et al. conducted DFT investigation to study adsorption behaviour of CO molecule on Graphene sheet in three forms, namely- (i) pristine graphene, (ii) Stone-Wales defected graphene, and (iii) vacancy-defected graphene. Results showed the occurrence of chemisorption of CO molecules possibly took place on only vacancy-defected graphene, considered to be most active adsorbent one of the highest studied materials. Adsorption of several CO molecules on multiple-vacancy graphene (i.e., which is similar to chemisorption of CO_2 on vG) could be observed was corroborated with rise in total density of states (TDOS) at Fermi level with increase of gas dose. Causing rise of conductance [35]. To investigate the viability of employing Ga-doped graphene for gas sensing, Liang et al. performed DFT calculations on the adsorption of CO gas molecules on pristine graphene and Ga-doped graphene [35]. Because of the poor interaction between graphene electrons and gas molecules, the adsorption of CO gas molecules on pure graphene was weak with little charge transfer. In comparison to virgin graphene, Ga-doped graphene displayed considerably higher affinity for gas molecules. Chemisorption on Ga-doped graphene with relatively high adsorption energies was discovered using the DOS and electron density plots. Adsorption of gas molecules on Ga-doped graphene was discovered to open a significant band gap due to increased electron transport and the creation of strong chemical interactions between the electron cloud and gas molecule orbitals [35]. Ling Ma et al. employed first-principles based on density functional theory (DFT) to investigate sensitivity of pristine graphene (PG) and Pd-doped graphene (Pd-G) toward CO gas molecule [36]. It was found that doping graphene with Pd significantly improved the strength of interaction between adsorbed molecules and the modified substrate. The drastic enhancement in adsorption energy and charge transfer of these systems were expected to induce changes in the electrical conductivity of the Pd-G sheet. The results revealed that the sensitivity of graphene-based chemical gas sensors could be significantly enhanced by introducing the Pd dopants, so Pd-G could be concluded to be more suitable for gas molecules detection compared with PG [36]. Ammar et al. investigated the structural stabilities, electronic and optical properties of TM-doped porphyrin (TM = Mn, Co, Fe, Cu, Ni and Zn) using density functional theory (DFT) method. The binding of the CO gas molecules onto the porphyrin was mainly due to electrostatic and van der Waals interactions and thereby physisorption in nature. The CO adsorption nature on TM-doped substrates was found to be dependent on two factors, - (i) the orientation of CO molecule and (ii) species of the doping. The presence of Mn, Fe, Co, and Zn enhanced the adsorption of CO molecule [37].

6 Conclusion

As evidenced by a slew of major discoveries, first-principles calculations, particularly the DFT approach, have proved tremendously effective for understanding the adsorption process of CO gas molecules on various materials.

The adsorption characteristics of CO gas molecules on the surface of several materials have been discussed in this brief overview.

It has been demonstrated that adsorption energy, change in bond length and molecular configuration before and after adsorption, and adsorption charge transfer can be computationally predicted, and the results can be used for sensor fabrication optimised for selectivity, sensitivity, and response towards CO gas molecules, in particular.

According to the findings described here, CO gas molecules may be adsorbed on metals, metal oxides, graphene, and its derivatives. Metals and Semiconductor Metal Oxides (SMOs) are among those that may achieve excellent adsorption without doping. Furthermore, the adsorption impact of pristine graphene has been shown to be modest, but adsorption performance has been extensively reported to be increased by doping the functional groups or metal atoms in graphene, particularly the transition metal atoms. As a result, it is determined that doping transition metal atoms in these adsorption materials enhances CO gas adsorption.

Furthermore, the DFT, in particular, can provide insight into molecule adsorption parameters such as bond angle, energy band, density of state, and magnetic characteristics, which are not described in this study. Despite the fact that DFT-based calculations have been frequently employed in adsorption in recent years, the following issues require systematic attention:

Metal, Semiconductor Metal Oxides, and graphene have been employed to adsorb CO gas molecules, which have been widely used in experimental research and certain applications in practical engineering. However, the use of doped metals, SMOs, and graphene necessitates a thorough knowledge of adsorption processes.

Although it is generally known that noble metal elements have a very good influence on the adsorption behaviour of CO gas molecules, the overall costs of employing these precious metal materials in the real experiment are very high. As a result, the adsorption behaviour of CO gas molecules on low-cost materials as more attractive adsorbents with trustworthy performance in the development of more cost-effective solutions must be considered.

DFT simulations employ ideal circumstances to simulate molecular behaviour at material surfaces, but real adsorption materials differ from ideal conditions. Furthermore, because the experimental conditions are dynamic and cannot be replicated, the DFT calculation may only reflect an ideal state in some situations. As a result, rigorous optimization is required to get findings that are more compatible with actual tests.

Acknowledgments. The author would like to thank Dr. Babasaheb Ambedkar Marathwada University, Aurangabad (MS) India for providing the publication support.

References

1. C. Cazorla, "The role of density functional theory methods in the prediction of nanostructured gas-adsorbent materials," *Coord. Chem. Rev.*, vol. 300, pp. 142–163, 2015, doi: https://doi.org/10.1016/j.ccr.2015.05.002.

2. H. Over et al., "Atomic-scale structure and catalytic reactivity of the RuO2(110) surface," *Science (80-.).*, vol. 287, no. 5457, pp. 1474–1476, 2000, doi: https://doi.org/10.1126/science.287.5457.1474.

3. A. M. Latyshev, A. V. Bakulin, and S. E. Kulkova, "Adsorption of oxygen on low-index surfaces of Ti3Al alloy," *Phys. Solid State*, vol. 59, no. 9, pp. 1852–1866, 2017, doi: https://doi.org/10.1134/S1063783417090165.

4. V. Nagarajan and R. Chandiramouli, "NiO nanocone as a CO sensor: DFT investigation," *Struct. Chem.*, vol. 25, no. 6, pp. 1765–1771, 2014, doi: https://doi.org/10.1007/s11224-014-0451-1.

5. H. P. Koch, P. Singnurkar, R. Schennach, A. Stroppa, and F. Mittendorfer, "A RAIRS, TPD, and DFT study of carbon monoxide adsorption on stepped Rh(553)," *J. Phys. Chem. C*, vol. 112, no. 3, pp. 806–812, 2008, doi: https://doi.org/10.1021/jp076080b.

6. P. E. Blöchl, "Projector augmented-wave method," *Phys. Rev. B*, vol. 50, no. 24, pp. 17953–17979, 1994, doi: https://doi.org/10.1103/PhysRevB.50.17953.

7. R. Nityananda, ", Vol.136, No.3B, November 1964.," vol. 136, no. 3, pp. 809–811, 2017.

8. P. E. Blöchl, "Generalized separable potentials for electronic-structure calculations," *Phys. Rev. B*, vol. 41, no. 8, pp. 5414–5416, 1990, doi: https://doi.org/10.1103/PhysRevB.41.5414.

9. H. JÓNSSON, G. MILLS, and K. W. JACOBSEN, "Nudged elastic band method for finding minimum energy paths of transitions," pp. 385–404, 1998, doi: https://doi.org/10.1142/9789812839664_0016.

10. Z. Cheng, T. Liu, C. Yang, H. Gan, J. Chen, and F. Zhang, "Ab initio atomic thermodynamics investigation on oxygen defects in the anatase TiO2," *J. Alloys Compd.*, vol. 546, pp. 246–252, 2013, doi: https://doi.org/10.1016/j.jallcom.2012.08.036.

11. P. Giannozzi et al., "QUANTUM ESPRESSO: A modular and open-source software project for quantum simulations of materials," *J. Phys. Condens. Matter*, vol. 21, no. 39, 2009, doi: https://doi.org/10.1088/0953-8984/21/39/395502.

12. E. Artacho et al., "The SIESTA method; Developments and applicability," *J. Phys. Condens. Matter*, vol. 20, no. 6, 2008, doi: https://doi.org/10.1088/0953-8984/20/6/064208.

13. S. J. Clark *et al.*, "First principles methods using CASTEP," *Zeitschrift fur Krist.*, vol. 220, no. 5–6, pp. 567–570, 2005, doi: https://doi.org/10.1524/zkri.220.5.567.65075.

14. B. Delley, "An all-electron numerical method for solving the local density functional for polyatomic molecules," *J. Chem. Phys.*, vol. 92, no. 1, pp. 508–517, 1990, doi: https://doi.org/10.1063/1.458452.

15. J. Ni, M. Quintana, and S. Song, "Adsorption of small gas molecules on transition metal (Fe, Ni and Co, Cu) doped graphene: A systematic DFT study," *Phys. E Low-Dimensional Syst. Nanostructures*, vol. 116, p. 113768, 2020, doi: https://doi.org/10.1016/j.physe.2019.113768.

16. K. Xu, N. Liao, B. Zheng, and H. Zhou, "Adsorption and diffusion behaviors of H2, H2S, NH3, CO and H2O gases molecules on MoO3 monolayer: A DFT study," *Phys. Lett. Sect. A Gen. At. Solid State Phys.*, vol. 384, no. 21, pp. 3–7, 2020, doi: https://doi.org/10.1016/j.physleta.2020.126533.

17. M. Gajdoš and J. Hafner, "CO adsorption on Cu(1 1 1) and Cu(0 0 1) surfaces: Improving site preference in DFT calculations," *Surf. Sci.*, vol. 590, no. 2–3, pp. 117–126, 2005, doi: https://doi.org/10.1016/j.susc.2005.04.047.

18. R. V. de Amorim, K. E. A. Batista, G. R. Nagurniak, R. P. Orenha, R. L. T. Parreira, and M. J. Piotrowski, "CO, NO, and SO adsorption on Ni nanoclusters: A DFT investigation," *Dalt. Trans.*, vol. 49, no. 19, pp. 6407–6417, 2020, doi: https://doi.org/10.1039/d0dt00288g.

19. X. Wu, L. Senapati, S. K. Nayak, A. Selloni, and M. Hajaligol, "A density functional study of carbon monoxide adsorption on small cationic, neutral, and anionic gold clusters," *J. Chem. Phys.*, vol. 117, no. 8, pp. 4010–4015, 2002, doi: https://doi.org/10.1063/1.1483067.

20. V. Nagarajan and R. Chandiramouli, "A DFT study on adsorption behaviour of CO on Co 3 O 4 nanostructures," *Appl. Surf. Sci.*, vol. 385, pp. 113–121, 2016, doi: https://doi.org/10.1016/j.apsusc.2016.05.085.

21. H. Orita and Y. Inada, "DFT investigation of CO adsorption on Pt(211) and Pt(311) surfaces from low to high coverage," *J. Phys. Chem. B*, vol. 109, no. 47, pp. 22469–22475, 2005, doi: https://doi.org/10.1021/jp052583a.

22. M. Yang, Y. Zhang, S. Huang, H. Liu, P. Wang, and H. Tian, "Theoretical investigation of CO adsorption on TM-doped (MgO) 12 (TM = Ni, Pd, Pt) nanotubes," *Appl. Surf. Sci.*, vol. 258, no. 4, pp. 1429–1436, 2011, doi: https://doi.org/10.1016/j.apsusc.2011.09.097.

23. H. Jin, H. Zhou, and Y. Zhang, "Insight into the mechanism of CO oxidation on WO3(001) surfaces for gas sensing: A DFT study," *Sensors (Switzerland)*, vol. 17, no. 8, pp. 1–12, 2017, doi: https://doi.org/10.3390/s17081898.

24. C. Rohmann, J. B. Metson, and H. Idriss, "DFT study of carbon monoxide adsorption on α-Al2O 3(0001)," *Surf. Sci.*, vol. 605, no. 17–18, pp. 1694–1703, 2011, doi: https://doi.org/10.1016/j.susc.2011.05.033.

25. V. Nagarajan and R. Chandiramouli, "DFT investigation on CO sensing characteristics of hexagonal and orthorhombic WO3 nanostructures," *Superlattices Microstruct.*, vol. 78, pp. 22–39, 2015, doi: https://doi.org/10.1016/j.spmi.2014.11.027.

26. Y. Fan, J. Zhang, Y. Qiu, J. Zhu, Y. Zhang, and G. Hu, "A DFT study of transition metal (Fe, Co, Ni, Cu, Ag, Au, Rh, Pd, Pt and Ir)-embedded monolayer MoS2 for gas adsorption," *Comput. Mater. Sci.*, vol. 138, pp. 255–266, 2017, doi: https://doi.org/10.1016/j.commatsci.2017.06.029.

27. O. A. L. Galán and G. Carbajal-Franco, "Energy profiles by DFT methods for CO and NO catalytic adsorption over ZnO surfaces," *Catal. Today*, vol. 360, no. July, pp. 38–45, 2021, doi: https://doi.org/10.1016/j.cattod.2019.08.003.

28. Nugraha *et al.*, "Selectivity of CO and NO adsorption on ZnO (0002) surfaces: A DFT investigation," *Appl. Surf. Sci.*, vol. 410, no. 0002, pp. 373–382, 2017, doi: https://doi.org/10.1016/j.apsusc.2017.03.009.

29. L. Lin *et al.*, "A periodic DFT study on adsorption of small molecules (CH_4, CO, H_2O, H_2S, NH_3) on the WO_3 (001) surface-supported Au," *Commun. Theor. Phys.*, vol. 72, no. 3, 2020, doi: https://doi.org/10.1088/1572-9494/ab690d.

30. R. Wanbayor and V. Ruangpornvisuti, "Adsorption of CO, H_2, N_2O, NH_3 and CH_4 on the anatase TiO_2 (0 0 1) and (1 0 1) surfaces and their competitive adsorption predicted by periodic DFT calculations," *Mater. Chem. Phys.*, vol. 124, no. 1, pp. 720–725, 2010, doi: https://doi.org/10.1016/j.matchemphys.2010.07.043.

31. L. F. Velázquez-López, S. M. Pacheco-Ortin, R. Mejía-Olvera, and E. Agacino-Valdés, "DFT study of CO adsorption on nitrogen/boron doped-graphene for sensor applications," *J. Mol. Model.*, vol. 25, no. 4, 2019, doi: https://doi.org/10.1007/s00894-019-3973-z.

32. C. P. Zhang, B. Li, and Z. G. Shao, "First-principle investigation of CO and CO_2 adsorption on Fe-doped penta-graphene," *Appl. Surf. Sci.*, vol. 469, no. November 2018, pp. 641–646, 2019, doi: https://doi.org/10.1016/j.apsusc.2018.11.072.

33. S. Yang *et al.*, "A DFT study of CO adsorption on the pristine, defective, In-doped and Sb-doped graphene and the effect of applied electric field," *Appl. Surf. Sci.*, vol. 480, no. November 2018, pp. 205–211, 2019, doi: https://doi.org/10.1016/j.apsusc.2019.02.244.

34. B. Wanno and C. Tabtimsai, "A DFT investigation of CO adsorption on VIIIB transition metal-doped graphene sheets," *Superlattices Microstruct.*, vol. 67, pp. 110–117, 2014, doi: https://doi.org/10.1016/j.spmi.2013.12.025.

35. N. Tit, K. Said, N. M. Mahmoud, S. Kouser, and Z. H. Yamani, "Ab-initio investigation of adsorption of CO and CO_2 molecules on graphene: Role of intrinsic defects on gas sensing," *Appl. Surf. Sci.*, vol. 394, pp. 219–230, 2017, doi: https://doi.org/10.1016/j.apsusc.2016.10.052.

36. L. Ma, J. M. Zhang, K. W. Xu, and V. Ji, "A first-principles study on gas sensing properties of graphene and Pd-doped graphene," *Appl. Surf. Sci.*, vol. 343, pp. 121–127, 2015, doi: https://doi.org/10.1016/j.apsusc.2015.03.068.

37. H. Y. Ammar and H. M. Badran, "Effect of CO adsorption on properties of transition metal doped porphyrin: A DFT and TD-DFT study," *Heliyon*, vol. 5, no. 10, p. e02545, 2019, doi: https://doi.org/10.1016/j.heliyon.2019.e02545.

38. D. Cortés-Arriagada, N. Villegas-Escobar, and D. E. Ortega, "Fe-doped graphene nanosheet as an adsorption platform of harmful gas molecules (CO, CO_2, SO_2 and H_2S), and the co-adsorption in O_2 environments," *Appl. Surf. Sci.*, vol. 427, no. 2, pp. 227–236, 2018, doi: https://doi.org/10.1016/j.apsusc.2017.08.216.

39. H. Basharnavaz, A. Habibi-Yangjeh, and S. H. Kamali, "Adsorption performance of SO_2 gases over the transition metal/P–codoped graphitic carbon nitride: A DFT investigation," *Mater. Chem. Phys.*, vol. 243, no. December 2019, p. 122602, 2020, doi: https://doi.org/10.1016/j.matchemphys.2019.122602.

40. X. Sun *et al.*, "Adsorption of gas molecules on graphene-like InN monolayer: A first-principle study," *Appl. Surf. Sci.*, vol. 404, pp. 291–299, 2017, doi: https://doi.org/10.1016/j.apsusc.2017.01.264.

41. X. Y. Liang, N. Ding, S. P. Ng, and C. M. L. Wu, "Adsorption of gas molecules on Ga-doped graphene and effect of applied electric field: A DFT study," *Appl. Surf. Sci.*, vol. 411, pp. 11–17, 2017, doi: https://doi.org/10.1016/j.apsusc.2017.03.178.

A CNN-LSTM Model for Arabic Sign Language Recognition

Basel Dabwan[1](✉) and Mukti Jadhav[2]

[1] Department of Computer Science, Dr. Babasaheb Ambedkar Marathwada University,
Aurangabad, India
baseldbwan@yahoo.com
[2] Shri Shivaji Science and Art College, Chikhali District, Buldhana, India

Abstract. Gesture-based communication is a correspondence of nonverbal sort that involves the utilization of additional body parts. Demeanours of the face alongside Hand, eye, and lip movement is used for passing on data in correspondence with sign language. Individuals with hearing impairment or discourse are significantly dependent on gesture-based communication as a kind of association in their day-to-day existence. Few of the studies dealt with Arabic sign language, so in this work, we developed applied research with its video-based Arabic sign language recognition system that helps deaf and dumb people in the Arabic community. We developed our sign language model by a combination of Long Short Term Memory (LSTM) and Convolutional Neural Networks (CNN), with two distinct neural network architectures. The first architecture is ConvLSTM and the second one LRCN. We used these two algorithms for extracting spatial and temporal features. The first model achieved a training accuracy of 99.66% and validation accuracy of 95%, and the second model achieved 99.5% training accuracy and 93.33% validation accuracy. We tested the performance of these two models in recognition between 28 classes of Arabic sign language.

Keywords: CNN · LSTM · Sign Language · Deep Learning · Machine Learning

1 Introduction

Individual existence without contact is exceptionally difficult to stay. Various conducts are utilized to impart and share their thoughts among sender and recipient. Discourse and sign are the most normal approaches to convey. Contact in the audible method is called discourse and is perceived through hearing. Then again correspondence utilizing body movement parts like hands and expressions of facial is called Gesture. Communication through signing is the language of Gesture that is gotten and perceived via the force of vision. Ordinary individuals have the alternative to utilizing gesture-based communication yet hard-of-hearing individuals utilize communication through signing as the essential language. There are "7099" communicated in dialects on the planet and "142" sign dialects utilized by handicapped individuals [1]. Table 1 show research on different gesture-based communication translation.

Communication via gestures is not a global language. It is unique from one country to another. Signs of the same letter can be performed distinctively in different sign

Table 1. The countries of different sign languages

Sign Language	Country
British Sign Language	United Kingdom (Elliott,2000)
Spanish Sign Language	Spain (. San-Segundo et al., 2008)
American Sign Language	United State of America (Vijayalakshmi and Aarthi, 2016)
Mexican Sign Language	Mexico (Caballero-Morales and Trujillo-Romero, 2012)
Arabic Sign Language	Arab Middle East (Halawani et al., 2013)
Greek Sign Language	Greece (Karpouzis etal., 2007)
Indian Sign Language	India (Vij and Kumar, 2016)

languages. For example letter, 'A' it's present in American sign language with one hand while Hindi sign language used both hands to present the same letter. Gesture-based communication is a significant tool to overcome any barrier between individuals who do not hear and the people who are listening. Gesture-based communication isn't just utilized by hearing the disabled individual, be that as it may, it is additionally utilized by the parent(s) of a hard of hearing youngster, offspring of the hard of hearing individual, instructor of the hard of hearing understudy thus numerous another space of correspondence with hard of hearing [9]. Communication through signing is a cooperative exploration region that incorporates PC vision, normal language handling, design coordinating, and phonetics. Its goal is to foster different logarithms and procedures to recognize the signs and recover the significance. In sign language recognition systems there are two main approaches: (a) sensor-based and (b) image-based. The main benefit of picture-based systems the client doesn't have to wear any devices, but this approach needs many computations in the pre-processing of the images, and also needs some set of constraints such as backdrop color, bright, nearby environment, and skin color [10]. There are many methods and techniques used to detect sign language. Machine learning has been used and it has given good results, such as the Support Vector Machine (SVM) and Key Nearest neighbor (KNN) algorithm, and then the deep learning method, which has very excellent results as it is characterized by many layers for feature extraction. Particularly when the data set size is very large, examples of deep learning algorithms are Convolution Neural Network (CNN), Recurrent Neural Network (RNN), and Long Short Term Memory (LSTM). In this paper, we developed a model by the more powerful algorithms in deep learning to recognize the Arabic Sign Language (ASL). The results will be analyzed in the coming sections. The figure below shows the Arabic Sign Language alphabet.

2   Deep Learning

Lately, essential AI approaches have been for the most part replaced with more significant models that use many layers and pass information in vector design between layers, ceaselessly refining the appraisal until a correct affirmation is cultivated. Such calculations are typically depicted as "deep learning" frameworks or deep neural networks,

Fig. 1. Arabic Sign Language alphabet

furthermore, they work on norms like Machine Learning frameworks portrayed above, even though with undeniably more conspicuous complexity. in light of the development of the organization, two calculations are for the most part used for different endeavors: Convolutional Neural Networks (CNNs) that fuse somewhere at least around one layer of convolutional, and Recurrent Neural Networks (RNNs) that incorporate something one at least like intermittent layer. Contingent upon the number, what's more, sort of layers, these logarithms can show different properties and are generally sensible for different sorts of tasks, while the preparation stage impacts the effectiveness of the calculation The overall standard is that bigger and more explicit datasets consider all the more impressive organization preparing, and thusly, the idea of the preparation set is a huge impact element. Extra tweaking of a model can commonly be cultivated by changing a part of the important hyper-boundaries that describe the training method [11].

2.1 Convolution Neural Network

CNN designs for classification and properties extricated in the CNN models, the main arrangement of layers incorporates low-level features which incorporate a large portion of the fundamental data about edges in the first layers. Also, the second one is more profound than the initial one, etc. A fully connected layer neuron is additional to the convolutional layers to collect the extricated features from the layers of convolutional. Different fully connected layer properties for best discrimination results. After withdrawals, all properties for each picture by CNN profound layers Classification stage is acknowledged with dense/fully connected layers after that activation functions. Finally, in the final phase of the model, the SoftMax function is working to categorize each class. It deals with multiple variety labeling and is a generalization of carrying regression so far because it will be applied to continuous data (rather than a paired category) which may reflect various choice boundaries.

2.2 Long Short Term Memory

Sepp Hochreiter and Juergen Schmidhuber created LSTM in 1997 to address the vanishing gradient issue. LSTM, which was subsequently coordinated and advocated with the commitment of many individuals, is presently generally utilized. LSTM is utilized to keep up with the mistaken esteem from various times and layers in the backdrop. By giving steadier mistake esteem, it permits the learning steps of repetitive organizations to proceed. It does this by opening another channel between causes also impact.

3 Related Work

Few research and studies dealt with the Arabic sign language, we have gathered some studies to show the methods and technology used in this area:

In (Aly et al., 2020) [12] proposed a system to distinguish Arabic gestures using three different architectures for deep learning where the system was trained using an adaptive instantaneous scaling algorithm to classify all gestures. This architecture was created using a mix of a semantic segmentation network, a convolutional SOM, and a two-way deep directional LSTMNetwork network. The hand partitions were done utilizing DeepLab3 +, and as a result of utilizing this approach, the effectiveness was expanded by 70%, and the normal precision was 89.5%.

In (El-Bendary et al., 2011) [13] develop an automated translation model for indications of the manual letter set in the ArSL. The present ArSL Letter sets Interpreter (ArSLAT) structure doesn't base on using visual markings or gloves to achieve the recognition work. As a decision, it oversaw the image of hands that empowered the client to interact with the model characteristically. The present ArSLAT architecture included five fundamental stages; pre-processing, best-frame distinguishing proof, kind identification, properties extraction, and a classification phase. The used extricated properties were the interpretation, transformation invariant, and scale to make the model dynamically adaptable. The proposed ArSLAT model was shown to have the decision to see the Arabic letters generally along with 91.3 percent and 83.7 percent accuracy using MLP classifiers and Minimum Distance Classifier (MDC), autonomously.

In (Omar Al-Jarrah and Alaa Halawani, 2001) [14] built an Alphabet distinguishes system in ArSL. The study was accomplished via teaching the group of ANFIS systems, Each of these ideas was offered for identifying a current sign. In the absence of the need for gloves, the image of the gesture was acquired via a cam connected to the computer. Since pre-processing release from the properties plan is dependent on the calculation of 30 vectors under the gestural foci the region near the helpful gesture segment's edge As a result, the vectors were preserved within the ANFIS framework. To place it in the appropriate category (gesture). The presented model was solid on the changes of the place of the sign, Size, also as a result of the image's orientation. it had been that the extricated properties were positive as translation, invariant movement, and scaling. The results of the simulation showed that their framework with about nine rules for each ANFIS system has had the chance to be recognized Accuracy of 93%.

(Dabwan Basel & Jadhav Mukti, 2021) [15] developed an automated recognition system for Yemeni Alphabets sign language; they used CNN layers to extract the features, A fully connected layer neuron is added to the convolutional layers to gather the extracted properties from the convolutional layers, After extractions, all features for each image by CNN deep layers Classification stage is realized with dense/fully connected layers followed by functions of activation. Lastly, the regression SoftMax function is utilized to category each alphabetical from 32 classes. The system precision achieved 93%.

4   Proposed Model

We used a CNN to obtain spatial properties at a particular time step in the sequence of the input (video) after that used LSTM to discover temporal relationships between frames in our model. Figure 1 shows the proposed model architecture (Fig. 2).

We have taken the Arabic Sign Language (ArSL), and we have used KArSL: Arabic Sign Language Database (Sidig et al., 2021), a dataset which we selected consists of 28 classes of dynamic sign Alphabets. Dataset was performed by three professional signers; the dataset was captured with a state-of-the-art multi-modal Microsoft Kinect V2 device. There are 24 videos (MP4) for each class, As a result, this dataset has a total of 24 × 28 = 672 videos of sign characters with Different variations. The dataset was recorded at 30 frames per second with a resolution of 1920 × 1080 pixels. We did all pre-processing and normalization operations, e.g., resizing the frame to a fixed size (64, 64), reducing the computations, data normalization to rang [0–1] by dividing the values of pixels by 255, also shuffle the dataset and separated it into testing training, training set = 75%, test set = 25%. The two architectures of the model that were utilized for ConvLSTM and LRCN are two algorithms that combine CNN and LSTM, as shown below.

5   ConvLSTM

In this architecture, we have developed the initial approach utilizing ConvLSTM cells in combination, ConvLSTM cell are a type of LSTM network that includes convolutions activities in the neural network. it is an LSTM with convolution implanted in the structure, This makes it appropriate for distinguishing spatial properties of the data while keeping the temporal relationship in mind. Because of this convolution architecture, this approach

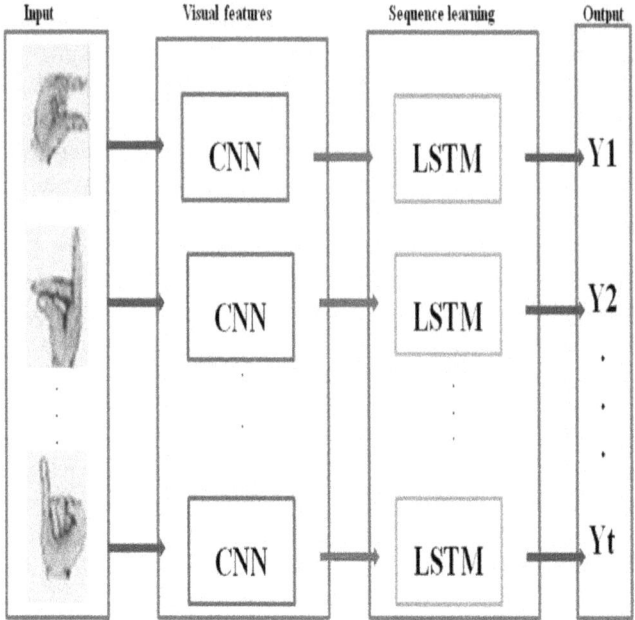

Fig. 2. Model architecture.

is equipped for taking in three-dimensional data (height, width, no of channels) though a basic LSTM just used one-dimensional input subsequently, LSTM is inconsistent for displaying Spatio-transient information all alone.

We developed the model by utilizing ConvLSTM2D Keras, layers with recurrent. The ConvLSTM2D layer additionally takes kernel size and no of filters demand executing the convolutional activities. The result of the layers is flattened in the ending and made it input to the softmax actuation in the Dense layer this gives the probability of each sign category. Also used layers of MaxPooling3D with (2,2) filter size to reduction in feature, decrease the frame's dimensions and avert not important calculations and Dropout layers to avoid the model overfitting. Also to avoid vanishing gradient we used softmax with small batch size for training the model trained with the flowing parameters (x = features_train, y = labels_train, epochs = 20, batch_size = 4,shuffle = True, validation_split = 0.2, callbacks = [early_stopping_callback]). The Fig. 3 shows the ConvLSTM model construct.

5.1   LRCN

In this architecture, we have implemented the LRCN method by joining LSTM and Convolution layers in one model. Another comparable situation methodology utilizes the LSTM model and CNN model trained independently. The CNN model can be utilized to get spatial properties from video frames, and for this reason, it utilized a pre-trained model, that can be fine-tuned for the issue. And the CNN-extracted features can then be used by the LSTM model., to recognize the signing class being acted in the input.

```
Model: "sequential_2"

Layer (type)                    Output Shape              Param #
===============================================================
conv_lst_m2d_8 (ConvLSTM2D)     (None, 20, 62, 62, 4)     1024

max_pooling3d_8 (MaxPooling3    (None, 20, 31, 31, 4)     0

time_distributed_6 (TimeDist    (None, 20, 31, 31, 4)     0

conv_lst_m2d_9 (ConvLSTM2D)     (None, 20, 29, 29, 8)     3488

max_pooling3d_9 (MaxPooling3    (None, 20, 15, 15, 8)     0

time_distributed_7 (TimeDist    (None, 20, 15, 15, 8)     0

conv_lst_m2d_10 (ConvLSTM2D)    (None, 20, 13, 13, 14)    11144

max_pooling3d_10 (MaxPooling    (None, 20, 7, 7, 14)      0

time_distributed_8 (TimeDist    (None, 20, 7, 7, 14)      0

conv_lst_m2d_11 (ConvLSTM2D)    (None, 20, 5, 5, 16)      17344

max_pooling3d_11 (MaxPooling    (None, 20, 3, 3, 16)      0

flatten_2 (Flatten)             (None, 2880)              0

dense_2 (Dense)                 (None, 4)                 11524
===============================================================
Total params: 44,524
Trainable params: 44,524
Non-trainable params: 0

Model Created Successfully!
```

Fig. 3. ConvLSTM model construct

But here, we have implemented another methodology called the Long-term Recurrent Convolutional Network (LRCN), which joins CNN and LSTM layers in one model. The Convolutional layers are utilized for spatial properties extrication from the video frames, then, the extricated spatial properties are directly input to LSTM layer(s) at every time-step for temporal sequence modeling. In This approach the network learns spatiotemporal properties straightforwardly in end-to-end training, resulting in a vigorous model. We were also utilizing the TimeDistributed wrapper layer, which permits applying the same layer to each video frame independently. So it prepares a layer (around which it is wrapped) equipped with taking input of form(no of frames, width, height, no of channels) if originally the layer's input form was (width, height, num_of_channels) which is exceptionally helpful as it permits to include the entire video into the model in a solitary shot. We implemented LRCN approach utilizing Conv2D time-distributed layers which are going to be followed by the MaxPooling2D and layers of Dropout. Flattened the properties extricated from the Conv2D layers using the Flatten layer and input it to an LSTM layer. Then, the softmax activation in the Dense layer will use the result from the LSTM layer to This gives the probability of each sign category. Figure 4 shows the LRCN model construct.

```
Model: "sequential_4"

Layer (type)                    Output Shape                Param #
=================================================================
time_distributed_22 (TimeDis (None, 20, 64, 64, 16)        448
_____
time_distributed_23 (TimeDis (None, 20, 16, 16, 16)        0
_____
time_distributed_24 (TimeDis (None, 20, 16, 16, 16)        0
_____
time_distributed_25 (TimeDis (None, 20, 16, 16, 32)        4640
_____
time_distributed_26 (TimeDis (None, 20, 4, 4, 32)          0
_____
time_distributed_27 (TimeDis (None, 20, 4, 4, 32)          0
_____
time_distributed_28 (TimeDis (None, 20, 4, 4, 64)          18496
_____
time_distributed_29 (TimeDis (None, 20, 2, 2, 64)          0
_____
time_distributed_30 (TimeDis (None, 20, 2, 2, 64)          0
_____
time_distributed_31 (TimeDis (None, 20, 2, 2, 64)          36928
_____
time_distributed_32 (TimeDis (None, 20, 1, 1, 64)          0
_____
time_distributed_33 (TimeDis (None, 20, 64)                0
_____
lstm_1 (LSTM)                   (None, 32)                  12416
_____
dense_4 (Dense)                 (None, 4)                   132
=================================================================
Total params: 73,060
Trainable params: 73,060
Non-trainable params: 0
```

Fig. 4. LRCN model construct

6   Result and evaluation

We used a combination of CNN and LSTM logarithms to implement our models, we used two architectures: ConvLSTM and LRCN to classify the Arabic Sign language (ArSL), the dataset includes 28 classes of alphabetic signs video, 24 videos for each class, with Different variations and dimensions, Total of videos = 672 videos. The dataset was divided into 75% for the training and 25% for the testing, the first model ConvLSTM achieved a training accuracy of 99.66% and validation accuracy of 95%, and the second model LRCN achieved 99.5% training accuracy and 93.33% validation accuracy. Figure 5, 6, 7, and 8 show the accuracy and loss of the two models.

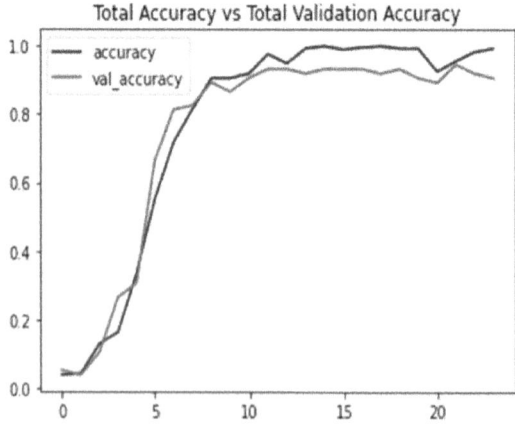

Fig. 5. ConvLSTM model accuracy

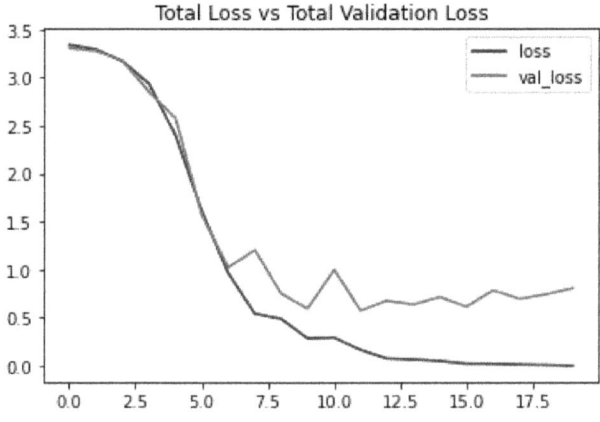

Fig. 6. ConvLSTM model loss

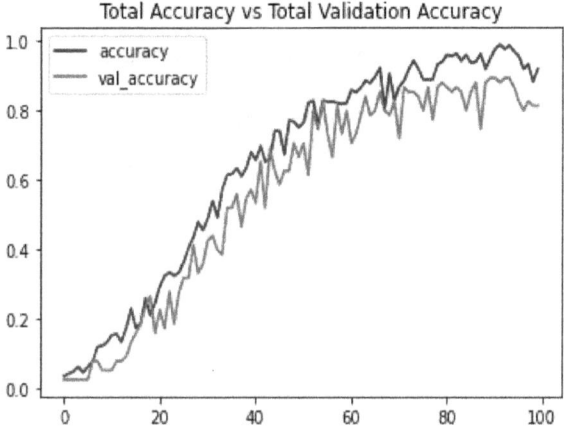

Fig. 7. LRCN model accuracy

In fact, to date, there are no researches that used this architecture to recognize the Arabic sign language, but we will compare it with studies that used the same algorithm in different sign languages, Table 2 displays The Comparing of our models with existing models.

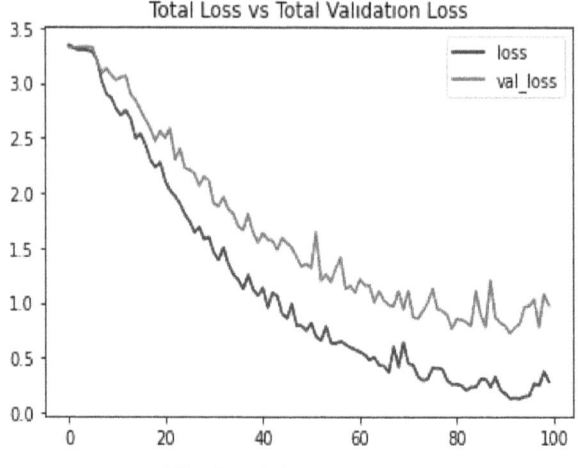

Fig. 8. LRCN model loss

Table 2. Comparing of proposed models with the existing models.

Method	Feature type and Classifier	Accuracy
baseline method (Shipman et al.,2015)	Hand-crafted features + SVM	69.23%
Baseline + RNN (Shipman et al.,2015)	Hand-crafted features + RNN	78.02%
CNN + SVM (Shipman et al.,2017)	2- stream CNN features + SVM	79.15%
CNN + RNN(Borg & Camilleri,2019)	Stream CNN features + RNN	87.67%
Our ConvLSTM model	CNN features + RNN	95%
Our LRCN model	CNN features + RNN	93.33%

7   Conclusion

In this research, the Arabic sign language (ArSL) recognition models were introduced by two architectures of CNN in combination with RNN, the first model is ConvLSTM. A ConvLSTM cell is a variant of an LSTM neural network that includes convolutions activities in the network. it is an LSTM with convolution implanted in the approach, which prepares it to fit for distinguishing spatial properties of the data while keeping into account the temporal relation. Because of this convolution architecture, the ConvLSTM is equipped for interacting in three-dimensional input (height, width, no of channels) though a basic LSTM just interacts in one-dimensional input subsequently LSTM is inconsistent for displaying Spatio-transient information all alone. This model achieved validation accuracy of 95%, and the second model is LRCN, we have implemented the LRCN model by joining Convolution and LSTM layers in one model, The layers of Convolutional are utilized for spatial properties extrication from the video frames, and the extricated spatial properties directly input to LSTM layer(s) at every time-steps for temporal sequence modeling. In This approach the network teaches spatiotemporal properties straightforwardly in end-to-end training, resulting in a vigorous model. We were also utilizing the TimeDistributed wrapper layer, which permits applying the same layer to each video frame independently. So it makes a layer (around which it is wrapped) equipped with taking input of form(no of frames, width, height, no of channels) if originally the layer's input form was (width, height, n of channels) which is exceptionally helpful as it permits to include the entire video into the model in a solitary shot, This model achieved validation accuracy 93.33%. When were compared our architectures with previous research, we found a significant difference in performance. We used CNN algorithm to obtain spatial properties, and we benefited from the RNN algorithm to preserve the frame sequence in the video, and we combined them into one model. The two algorithms also work in the same layer.

References

1. Ehnolgue, 2018,"Sign Language." [Online]. Available:https://www.ethnologue.com/subgro ups/signlanguage. [Accessed: 20- Jun-2018]
2. R. Elliott, J.R. Glauert, J.R. Kennaway, I. Marshall, The development of language processing support for the ViSiCAST project, in: Proceedings of the fourth international ACM conference on Assistive technologies - Assets '00, 2000 , pp. 101–108.
3. R. San-Segundo, et al.,Speech to sign language translation system for Spanish, Speech Commun., vol. 50, no. 11–12, 2008, pp. 1009–1020, 2008.
4. P. Vijayalakshmi, M. Aarthi, Sign language to speech conversion, in: Fifth International Conference on Recent Trends in Information Technology, 2016, pp. 1–6
5. S.O. Caballero-Morales, F. Trujillo-Romero, 3D Modeling of the Mexican Sign Language for a Speech-to-Sign Language System, Comput. y Sist., vol. 17, no. 4, 2012, pp. 593–608.
6. S.M. Halawani, D. Daman, S. Kari, A. R. Ahmad, An Avatar Based Translation System from Arabic Speech to Arabic Sign Language for Deaf People, Int. J. Comput. Sci. Netw. Secur., vol. 13, no. 12, 2013, pp. 43–52.
7. K. Karpouzis, G. Caridakis, S. Fotinea, E. Efthimiou, Educational resources and implementation of a Greek sign language synthesis architecture, Comput. Educ., vol. 49, no. 1, 2007, pp. 54–74,
8. P. Vij, P. Kumar, Mapping Hindi Text To Indian sign language with Extension Using Wordnet, in: Proceedings of the International Conference on Advances in Information Communication Technology & Computing, 2016, pp. 1–5.
9. T. Dasgupta, A. Basu, Prototype machine translation system from text-to-Indian sign language, in the 13th International Conference on Intelligent User Interfaces, no. January, 2008, pp. 313–316.
10. Kausar S, Javed MY, A survey on sign language recognition. In: 2011 frontiers of information technology.,(2011),pp95–98. https://doi.org/10.1109/FIT.2011.25
11. Y. LeCun, Y. Bengio, G. Hinton, Deep learning, Nature, vol. 521, no. 7553, 2015, pp. 436–444, 2015
12. S. Aly, W.A. Aly, DeepArSLR: A novel signer-independent deep learning framework for isolated arabic sign language gestures recognition, vol. 8,2020 pp. 83199–83212.
13. N. El-Bendary, H. Zawbaa, M. Daoud, A. Hassanien, K.. Nakamatsu, ArSLAT: Arabic sign language alphabets translator. Int J Comput Inf Syst Ind Manag Appl 3,2011, pp.498–506.

14. O. Al-Jarrah, A. Halawani, Recognition of gestures in Arabic sign language using neuro-fuzzy systems. Elsevier, Amsterdam, 2001, pp. 117–138
15. B. Dabwan, M. Jadhav, A Deep Learning based Recognition System for Yemeni Sign Language, 2021 International Conference of Modern Trends in Information and Communication Technology Industry (MTICTI),2021, pp.1-5,doi: https://doi.org/10.1109/MTICTI 53925.2021.9664779.
16. A. Sidig, H. Luqman, S Mahmoud, M. Mohandes, KArSL: Arabic Sign Language Database. ACM Trans. Asian Low-Resour. Lang. Inf. Process. 20, 1, Article 14 (2021,pp.19, https://doi.org/10.1145/3423420
17. F. Shipman, R. Gutierrez-Osuna, T. Shipman, C. Monteiro, V. Karappa, Towards a distributed digital library for sign language content, in Proc. .15th ACM/IEEE-CS Joint Conference on Digital Libraries, 2015, JCDL '15, pp. 187–190.
18. F. Shipman, S. Duggina, C. Monteiro, R. GutierrezOsuna, Speed-Accuracy Tradeoffs for Detecting Sign Language Content in Video Sharing Sites, in Proc. ACM SIGACCESS. 2017, ASSETS '17, pp. 185–189, ACM.
19. M. Borg, K. Camilleri, Sign Language Detection "in the Wild" with Recurrent Neural Networks. ICASSP 2019- 2019 IEEE International Conference on Acoustics, Speech and Signal Processing (ICASSP), 1637–1641.

Transfer Learning for Mosquito Classification Using VGG16

Ayesha Anam Siddiqui[✉] and Charansing Kayte

Institute of Forensic Science, Aurangabad, Maharashtra, India
ayeshashaikh74@yahoo.com

Abstract. A challenge in computer vision known mosquito classification hasn't gained much traction. Automatic mosquito species credentials using real-time images is a crucial feature. Mosquitoes are a serious matter of concern since they can spread diseases including dengue fever, zika, and malaria. It's important to control mosquito populations in order to effectively control mosquitoes. The World Health Organization reported that over a million people worldwide experience malaria and dengue fever each year. In this investigation, we analyze a deep learning vgg-16 network architecture for mosquito specifically chosen. On our mosquito dataset, which included six (6) species of mosquito. The pre-trained vgg-16 network architecture with transfer learning technique was studied and proved to identify distinct mosquito species, with an average accuracy rate of 97.1751 percent Loss 0.094359393954277. The results of VGG 16 and CNN are compared. The results show that CNN with multi class classifier is achieving 85.75 percent accuracy and VGG 16 with 97.1751 accuracy. It shows that the VGG 16 model is pretty good in results as compare to CNN.

Keywords: VGG16 · CNN · Mosquito · Transfer Learning · MSCMosquito Species Classification

1 Introduction

Classifying mosquito species is particularly difficult due to the tremendous degree of resemblance in appearance between various species. Because of the visual similarities between distinct species, mosquito categorization presents a wonderful chance to utilize new Deep CNN algorithms. The pre-processing of images uses image processing techniques.

The extraction and classification of visual features has long been an important and essential area of research in the science of computer vision. The Convolutional Neural Network offers a comprehensive learning model. (CNN).[1] (K., 2019).

The classification of mosquitoes is regarded as an area of computer vision that is rarely addressed. The classification of mosquitoes makes use of classifiers and a variety of machine learning techniques. Due to the existing Machine Learning (ML) algorithms' inadequacy to precisely extract the features from the mosquito image, they are still unable to reach optimal performance, making it extremely challenging to increase

© The Author(s) 2023
R. Manza et al. (Eds.): ACVAIT 2022, AISR 176, pp. 471–484, 2023.
https://doi.org/10.2991/978-94-6463-196-8_36

the recognition accuracy of the system. Extraction of features and classifier are the two main processes in the majority of constructed Mosquito classification systems. The difficulty in developing an accurate mosquito classification system is largely due to the longer computing time and distinct feature extraction. Deep learning methods are typically recommended for resolving these issues in a variety of image-based applications since they conduct combined feature extraction and classification tasks. As features are automatically extracted by deep learning algorithms, computation time is decreased and recognition accuracy is increased. The primary innovation of the work is the creation of a new VGG-16 algorithm with transfer learning for mosquito classification using different active layers. Additionally, it creates the Convolutional Neural Network (CNN) for classification of mosquitoes. A fresh classification scheme for mosquitoes was introduced in the proposed work. Three main steps make up the procedure: collecting databases, classifying mosquitoes to identify specific species, and assessing performance. For the first step, we created a dataset of 6 different species of total 5400 mosquito images. Second step, efficient MSC (Mosquito species classification) algorithm is then used to recognize mosquito species. Here, the MSC system is introduced to two distinct deep learning algorithms, CNN and VGG16 with Transfer Learning. Keras and TensorFlow are used to implement this proposed approach. Thirdly, precision, recall, F1-score, accuracy are used to assess how well these two classifiers perform. From results it concludes that proposed algorithm produces higher accuracy results of 97.1751%, whereas the other existing classifiers such as CNN gives the accuracy results of 85.75% values respectively. The project is implemented in Python, along with additional supporting frameworks like Keras and TensorFlow for the analysis of mosquito species image detection and classification.

2 Problem Statement

Mosquitoes are the most common disease vector, accounting for a large number of deaths in both children and adults. Disease affecting about 430,000 people each year, according to a study published in 2015[2].

Scientists have been able to pinpoint where the Zika and West Nile viruses originated because of the clear spread of diseases like dengue and yellow fever. The Zika virus is spread by mosquitoes of the Aedes genus, especially Aedes aegypti and Aedes albopictus. Figuring out whether a mosquito species that transmits disease is present in a particular community seems to be the first step towards an efficient disease prevention plan. Once a carrier mosquito is discovered in the vicinity, it is reasonable to presume that there are others because of how rapidly mosquitoes reproduce.

The mosquitoes *Aedes and Culex* are well-known for the spread of deadly infections that can result in death the worst circumstances.[3] Blood-sucking mosquitoes include the *Aedes, Anopheles, and Culex* species, as shown in a tropical medicine expert.

3 Related Work

- **Mosquito flight Sound (Wingbeat):** Eleftherios Fanioudakis carried out experiment on based on optical recordings of mosquitoes' wingbeat and able to classify classified six species of mosquitoes [33]. D. R. Raman, R. R. Gerhardt constructed a prototype field-deployable acoustic insect flight detector has been constructed [36]

- **Mosquito Image:** Junyoung Park investigated classification of vector mosquitoes of 8 species with Morphological Analysis using deep learning [34] Daniel Motta, Alex A´ lisson Bandeira Santos, studied using CNN-based models with complex architectures, they tried to the automation of the detection and classification of adult mosquitoes [35].

- **Mosquito Genomic Data (DNA barcoding):** Based on information from the ribosomal DNA string's internal transcribed spacer 2 region, an artificial neural network method is proposed for the classification and identification of Anopheles mosquito species by Amit Kumar Banerjee, K.Kiran [31]A study by B T L H van de Vossenberg, A Ibáñez-Justicia shoes, real-time PCR tests for the identification of Ae. Aegypti and Ae. Albopictus are implemented, and two new real-time PCR tests for the identification of Ae. Atropalpus and Ae. j. japonicus are developed.Initial testing revealed that Ae. Aegypti and Ae. Albopictus test elements needed to be optimized [32].

4 Extention to Previous Research and Its Applications

In this paper we selected six species from the three main genera *Anopheles, Aedes, and Culex*. Some mosquito species of these genera are responsible for serious diseases like dengue, zika and malaria and Chikungunya. we study how cnn models can solve the issues associated with mosquito species classification tasks. We want to extend our problem to design automation system to classify and identify the mosquito species. The application will be able predict the mosquito species type. It can further be used in flood areas and in seasonal mosquito borne dieses spread as a prevalent to disease spread by mosquito.

5 Deep Learning

Deep Learning

Deep learning is a feature-based machine learning technology that allows a system to automatically understand the representations required for identification activities using training data [4].

Convolutional Neural Network

In the field of DL, the CNN is the most famous and commonly employed algorithm [5, 6]. The main benefit of CNN compared to its predecessors is that it automatically identifies the relevant features without any human supervision [7]. Numerous industries, including computer vision [8], voice processing [9], face recognition [10], and others have made substantial use of CNNs. Similar to a traditional neural network, CNNs have characteristics with neurons found in human and animal brains. In a cat's brain, the visual cortex is made up of a convoluted series of cells, and the CNN simulates this series [11]. The equal representations, sparse interactions, and parameter sharing of the CNN are its three main advantages. To fully utilize 2D input-data structures, such as image signals, the CNN makes use of shared weights and local connections, in contrast to typical fully connected (FC) networks [12].This technique uses a remarkably minimal number of parameters, which speeds up the network while also making training easier. The visual cortex cells also have this. Notably, rather than detecting the entire image, these cells only detect specific portions of it (i.e., these cells spatially extract the local correlation available in the input, like local filters over the input).[13] (Laith Alzubaidi1, 2021).

Convolutional Neural Network CNN Working

A commonly used type of CNN, which is similar to the multi-layer perceptron (MLP), consists of numerous convolution layers preceding sub-sampling (pooling) layers, while the ending layers are FC layers [13]. The original image can be utilized as input in Convolutional neural networks (CNN) without any image pre-processing. Since it was integrated with deep learning, CNN has showed highest accuracy in large-scale image classification and recognition. [14] Researchers utilize parameters to increase the accuracy of the CNN model structure. The majority of the upgraded models take more time to train and evaluate.[15] (Fig. 1).

There are two main parts to a CNN architecture

- A convolution tool that separates and identifies the distinctive characteristics of an image for investigation using a technique called Feature Extraction.
- A fully connected layer that uses the convolution process output to predict the image's class based on the features extracted in previous steps.

CNN is made up of three types of layers: convolutional layers, pooling layers, and fully-connected (FC) layers. A CNN architecture is formed when these layers are stacked. In addition to these three layers, the dropout layer and the activation function are critical parameters [17] (Gurucharan, 2020).

Transfer Learning

When a model is used as the base for one task but not another, this process is known as "transfer learning." TL is a fantastic technique in which models with identical weights that have been sent on a big amount of data are utilised as a starting point for processing another problem with fewer data and improving the task's predictions. It provides a methodology where a model is first trained on a problem that is similar to the one being solved and then applied to a different task. Even before the emergence of current deep learning, the concept of knowledge sharing amongst machine learning models was well known. [29] (Fig. 2).

VGG16

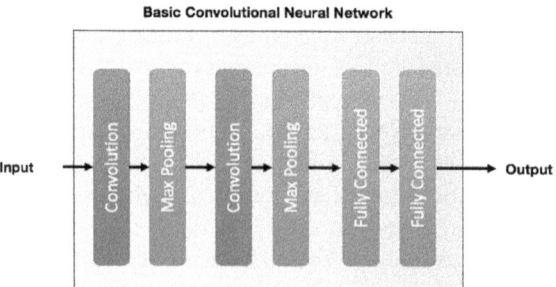

Fig. 1. Convolutional Neural Network CNN architecture [16] (Building a simple CNN, 2022)

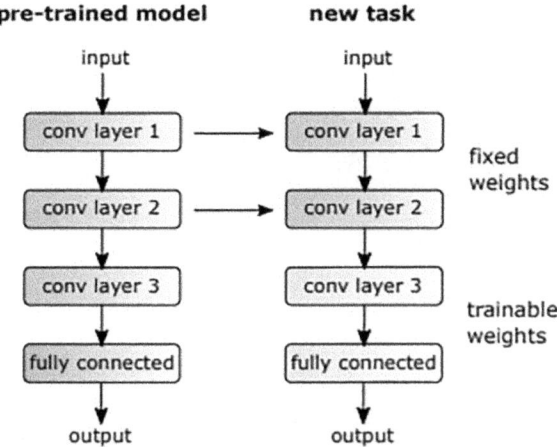

Fig. 2. Schematic View of trasfer learning idea Image source [30]

A ConvNet is a type of artificial neural network that is also known as a convolution neural network. An input layer, an output layer, and various hidden layers comprise a convolution neural network. VGG16 is a CNN (Convolution Neural Network) that is commonly acknowledged as one of the best computer vision models available today.

VGG16 Architecture

The Visual Geometry Group at the University of Oxford and Google DeepMind jointly developed VGGNet, a CNN whose architecture can be thought of as an extended AlexNet and is characterized by 3×3 convolutional kernels and 2×2 pooling layers. To improve feature learning, the network architecture can be further developed by using smaller convolutional layers. VGGNet-16 and VGGNet-19 are the two most popular versions of the VGG Net at the present. [28].

The ImageNet Large Scale Visual Recognition Challenge (ILSVRC) is an annual computer vision competition. Each year, teams compete on two tasks. The first is to detect objects within an image coming from *200* classes, which is called object localization. The second is to classify images, each labeled with one of *1000* categories, which is called image classification. VGG 16 was proposed by Karen Simonyan and Andrew Zisserman of the Visual Geometry Group Lab of Oxford University in 2014 in the paper "VERY DEEP CONVOLUTIONAL NETWORKS FOR LARGE-SCALE IMAGE RECOGNITION". This model won the 1st and 2nd place on the above categories in 2014 ILSVRC challenge (Fig. 3).

The precise structure of the VGG-16 networks shown in Fig. 7 is as follows:

- The first and second convolutional layers are comprised of 64 feature kernel filters and size of the filter is 3×3. As input image (RGB image with depth 3) passed into first and second convolutional layer, dimensions changes to $224 \times 224 \times 64$. Then the resulting output is passed to max pooling layer with a stride of 2.
- The third and fourth convolutional layers are of 124 feature kernel filters and size of filter is 3×3. These two layers are followed by a max pooling layer with stride 2 and the resulting output will be reduced to $56 \times 56 \times 128$.

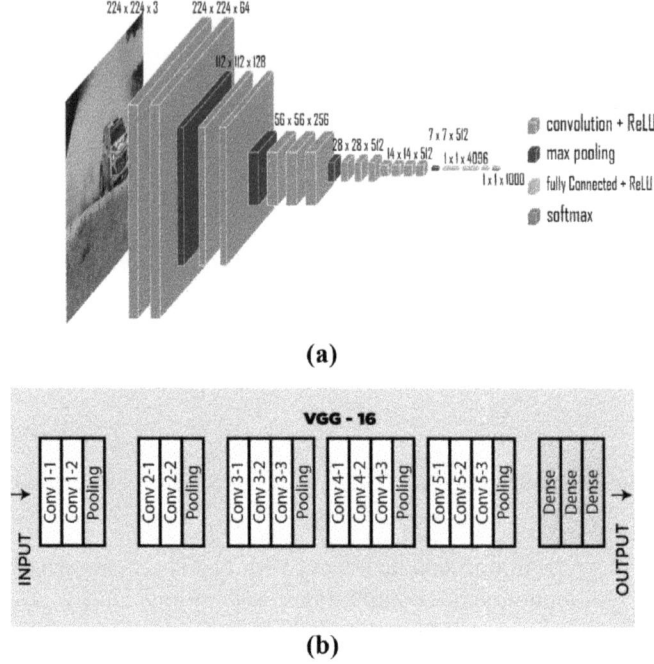

(a)

(b)

Fig. 3. (a) VGG16 architecture (b) VGG16 architecture [18] (pawangfg, 2020)

- The fifth, sixth and seventh layers are convolutional layers with kernel size 3 × 3. All three use 256 feature maps. These layers are followed by a max pooling layer with stride 2.
- Eighth to thirteen are two sets of convolutional layers with kernel size 3 × 3. All these sets of convolutional layers have 512 kernel filters. These layers are followed by max pooling layer with stride of 1.
- Fourteen and fifteen layers are fully connected hidden layers of 4096 units followed by a softmax output layer (Sixteenth layer) of 1000 units. [19] (Tammina, October 2019)

Transfer Learning with VGG-16

Transfer learning is simply a machine learning technique where the knowledge obtained from the previous task can be applied to another related task and at the same time improves the learning operation [27]. The CNN network architecture like ResNet, VGG, AlexNet and so on, are already trained on a huge image dataset of ImageNet comprising more than one million labelled high-resolution images belonging to one thousand (1000) categories. Thus, the knowledge obtained already from a particular task is assigned to learn a new different task. It is especially used where the training data is relatively small. In addition, it shows good performance, especially during classification tasks and the computational complexity is significantly minimized to some extent as the entire operation need not start from the scratch.

6 Proposed System

The mosquito classification system is shown in Fig. 4. The main process is composed of image collection, image pre-processing, feature extraction, train pattern, mosquito species classification (Figs. 5 and 6).

It's important to note that accurate identification of adult mosquito species is essential for identifying disease vectors and designing disease control strategies. [20]. Due to their outstanding capacity to detect patterns from images, CNNs are one of the most prominent deep learning network architectures used in computer vision [21]. New models for the

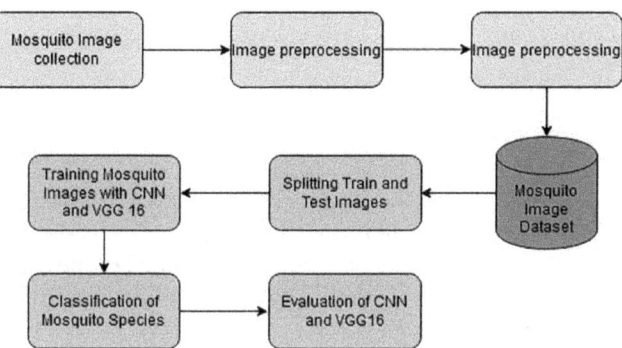

Fig. 4. Overview of Proposed system

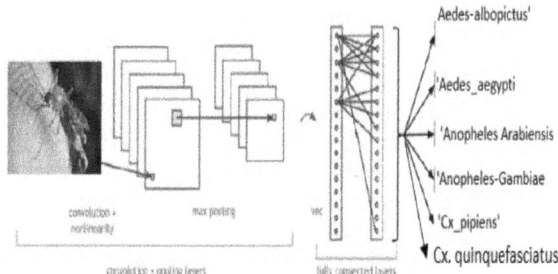

Fig. 5. Mosquito classification system using CNN

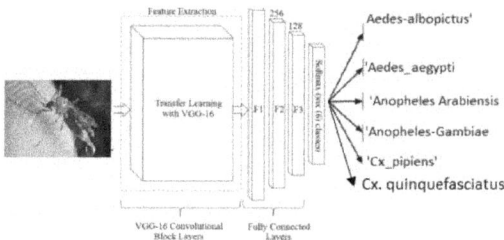

Fig. 6. Mosquito species classification with VGG 16 model

automatic classification of mosquitoes have recently been proposed. The frequency and harmonics of mosquito wingbeats have been used in several studies to classify mosquito species [22]. Techniques based on image feature analysis have also been used as a classification method. In addition, Machine Learning and Deep Learning techniques have been used for mosquito classification [23]. A feature extractor and a classifier that are trained end-to-end can describe the architecture of such networks. Many convolutional and pooling layers make up the feature extractor. Between their inputs and their learnable weights, convolutional layers perform weighted convolutions. As a result, they identify local patterns in the data. Non-trainable pooling layers reduce the dimensionality of their input by mapping a single layer in the input to a single number locally. One or more fully connected layers and a SoftMax function are commonly used to create the classifier [24]. Deep learning methods are essential for the processes underlying general object recognition.[25].

7   Dataset Preparation

Dataset used in this study is created by collecting images from different websites. We use Chrome extension downloads all images for collecting images of different mosquito species. It cannot filter images based on their sizes therefore preprocessing of images is required.

Image Sources

Images were collected from websites/blogs using chrome extension.

Data: Dataset of 5400 images is created. Images of three different genera of mosquito species are collected. Dataset consists of Images of *Aedes, Anopheles* and *Culex*. There are six types of mosquito species included in dataset. The mosquito species images included in dataset are *Aedes-albopictus, Aedes_aegypti, Anopheles Arabiensis, Anopheles-Gambiae and Culex quinquefasciatus and Culex _pippins.*

Pre-processing. Images were converted to uniform format of jpeg. All image size is also changed to uniform size images. Images of each type of mosquito species collected from Google. Then images were rescaled to uniform size. The insect images were rescaled for achieving improved accuracy and eliminate the problems of overtraining. All images are converted into.jpg format.

Data Augmentation for Generating Image Dataset. Image data augmentation techniques such as rotation, flipping, gray scale operators are used to increase the training set for achieving improved accuracy and eliminate the problems of. As shown in Fig. Downloaded image dataset of 6 types of mosquitoes is converted into multiple images by using augmentation by applying different operators. After using augmentation on the training set, datasets contain 5400 augmented mosquito species images. The details are given in supporting information Tables 1.

8   Results and Discussions

Mosquito classification is done with the help of convolution neural network. The dataset of mosquito images were created by downloading images from Google. Then all images were rescaled in uniform size and type. Using augmentation dataset of 5400 images was created. Details of images in dataset are given in Table 1.

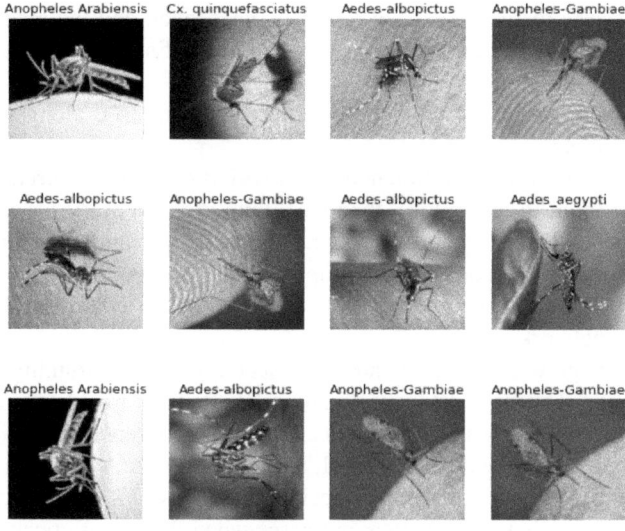

Fig. 7. Images from dataset [26]

Table 1. Types of Mosquito & Sample Count

Mosquito species	Number of mosquitoes
Aedes-albopictus	900
Aedes_aegypti	900
Anopheles Arabiensis	900
Anopheles-Gambiae	900
Culex. Quinquefasciatus	900
Culex_pipiens	900
Total images in dataset	5400

Convolution neural network is applied to dataset and compared the result. Epoch size is 50 for both the CNN and VGG16 module (Fig. 8).

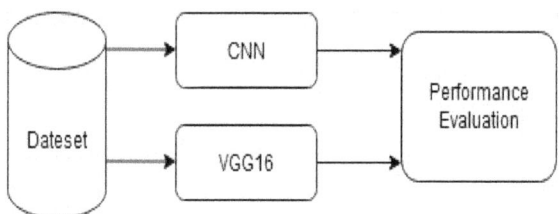

Fig. 8. Performance Evaluation of CNN and VGG 16

The first layer's feature is carried on to the next layer, and the result is sent on to CNN's hidden layers. The process is repeated until the final output in the last layer is obtained.

The screenshot in the fig. Shows the different layers used along with the output shapes and learnable.

The accuracy of this convolution neural network is evaluated by creating predictions and comparing them to test values, then calculating the accuracy based on the mean. The maximum number of epochs considered for experimentation is set to 50, so that the number of iterations required for completing the process increases and the image accuracy improves with each epoch. Table 2 shows the hyper parameter settings used for training the network and.

The input image with the labels are given as a input to the training network in the form of jpg image. The input data which is been labelled as a jpg file and it is been given for the testing purpose. The testing data is taken as the reference and the predicted data is compared to measure the accuracy level.

Figure 9 and 10 shows the plot of accuracy and loss Vs number of epochs. The accuracy plot shows that the accuracy increases when the no. of epochs increases and the maximum accuracy of 85.76% is reached in CNN Model. Similarly, the loss is found to be decreasing from 1.7 to less than 0.2 as number of iterations increases.

The accuracy obtained from this convolution neural network is calculated by making predictions and comparing it with the test values and the accuracy is calculated based on the mean obtained. The maximum epochs considered for experimentation is set to 50 so that the number of iterations taken to execute the process increases and the features was taken more from the signal so that the accuracy of the image gets improved at each epoch. Table 2 shows the hyper parameter settings used for training the network. The accuracy obtained by VGG 16 module is 97.1751 and loss decreased up to 0.094. The results shows that the pre trained model VGG 16 with CNN gives better results than CNN module (Table 3).

Table 2. Parameters and values

Parameter	CNN	VGG16
No of Epoch	50	50
Batch size	100	100
Training sample	4233	4233
Testing sample	1063	1063

Table 3. Accuracy and Loss

Model	Optimizer	Accuracy	Loss	Average time per epoch
CNN	Adam	85.75%	0.280	221s
VGG16	SGD	97.17%	0.094	884s

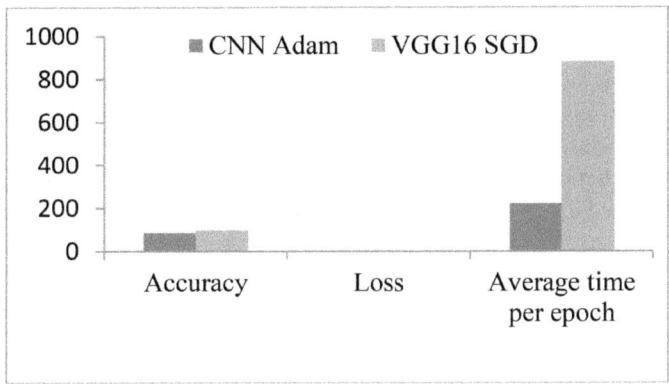

Fig. 9. Graph Accuracy and Loss of CNN

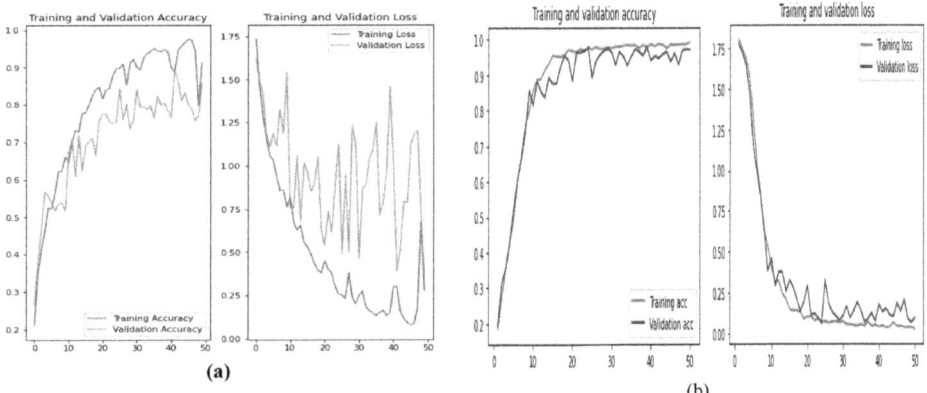

Fig. 10. **(a)** & **(b)** Graph Accuracy and Loss of VGG 16

9 Future Research Directions

Outcome of the study suggest us following suggestions:

I. In this study we used dataset of mosquitoes at resting position. Images are collected from internet.
II. In the next phase we will use the mosquito image captured dataset.
III. Further we want to deploy the mosquito identification system to predict the mosquito species.

10 Conclusion

In this paper, a CNN-based deep learning model is suggested that uses a multi-classifier network to classify six types of mosquito species images. The dataset consists of images of *Aedes-albopictus, Aedes_aegypti, Anopheles Arabiensis, Anopheles-Gambiae and Culex quinquefasciatus and Culex _pippins*. We used Convolution neural network and

VGG16 network to classify the mosquito species images. The confusion matrix is used by the deep learning classifier to classify the number of classes and give the class of the input image to which the class belongs. The human error in data prediction is minimized since the deep learning model does not require any human labeling to extract the features. The results of the classification are compared to those obtained with CNN and VGG 16. The results show that CNN with multi class classifier is achieving 85.75 percent accuracy and VGG 16 with 97.1751 accuracy. It shows that the VGG 16 model is pretty good in results as compare to CNN. In future the research can be incorporating alternative architectures of deep learning models.

References

1. (K., 2019) K., D. J. (2019). Image Classification and Object Detection. *SCIENCE INSIGHTS*, 85–100.
2. (Mosquito-Borne Diseases. , 2014) *Mosquito-Borne Diseases.* . World Health Organization
3. Mosquito-borne diseases information from WHO. [On-line]. Available: http://www.who.int/ neglected_diseases/vector_ecology/mosquito-borne-diseases/en/
4. Andreas Geiger, P. L. (2013). Vision meets robotics *International Journal of Robotics Research (IJRR),*.
5. . Zhou DX. Theory of deep convolutional neural networks: downsampling. Neural Netw. 2020;124:319–27.
6. Jhong SY, Tseng PY, Siriphockpirom N, Hsia CH, Huang MS, Hua KL, Chen YY. An automated biometric identification system using CNN-based palm vein recognition. In: 2020 international
7. Gu J, Wang Z, Kuen J, Ma L, Shahroudy A, Shuai B, Liu T, Wang X, Wang G, Cai J, et al. Recent advances in convolutional neural networks. Pattern Recogn. 2018;77:354–77.
8. Fang W, Love PE, Luo H, Ding L. Computer vision for behaviour-based safety in construction: a review and future directions. Adv Eng Inform. 2020;43:100980.
9. . Palaz D, Magimai-Doss M, Collobert R. End-to-end acoustic modeling using convolutional neural networks for hmm-based automatic speech recognition. Speech Commun. 2019;108:15–32.
10. . Li HC, Deng ZY, Chiang HH. Lightweight and resource-constrained learning network for face recognition with performance optimization. Sensors. 2020;20(21):6114.
11. .Hubel DH, Wiesel TN. Receptive fields, binocular interaction and functional architecture in the cat's visual cortex. J Physiol. 1962;160(1):106
12. . Goodfellow I, Bengio Y, Courville A, Bengio Y. Deep learning, vol. 1. Cambridge: MIT press; 2016.
13. Laith Alzubaidi1, 5. ,.-D.-S. (2021). Review of deep learning: concepts, CNN . *Journal of Big Data*, 8:53
14. Tianming Liang, Xinzheng Xu and Pengcheng Xiao, "A new image classification method based on modified condensed nearest neighbor and convolutional neural networks", Pattern Recognition Letters, vol. 94, July 2017, pp-105-111
15. . X.X. Niu and C.Y. Suen, "A novel hybrid CNN–SVM classifier for recognizing handwritten digits", Pattern Recognition, vol. 45, 2012, pp. 1318-1325.
16. (Building a simple CNN, 2022) *Building a simple CNN.* (2022, Feb 15). Retrieved from oreilly: ttps://www.oreilly.com/library/view/neural-network-projects/9781789138900/ 8e87ad66-6de3-4275-81a4-62b54436bf16.xhtml

17. (Gurucharan, M. (2020, Dec 7). *Basic CNN Architecture: Explaining 5 Layers of Convolutional Neural Network*. Retrieved from upgrad: https://www.upgrad.com/blog/basic-cnn-architecture/

18. (pawangfg, , 2020) pawangfg. (, 2020, Feb 27). *VGG-16 | CNN model*. Retrieved from geeksforgeeks: https://www.geeksforgeeks.org/vgg-16-cnn-model/

19. Tammina, S. (October 2019). Transfer learning using VGG-16 with Deep . *International Journal of Scientific and Research Publications, Volume 9, Issue 10*, , 143-150.

20. Yang HP, Ma C Sen, Wen H, Zhan Q Bin, Wang XL. A tool for developing an automatic insect identification system based on wing outlines. Sci Rep. Nature Publishing Group; 2015; 5: 1–11. https://doi.org/10.1038/srep12786 PMID: 26251292

21. . W. Rawat, Z. Wang, Deep convolutional neural networks for image classification: a comprehensive review, Neural Comput. 29 (2017) 2352–2449

22. Ouyang TH, Yang EC, Jiang JA, Lin T Te. Mosquito vector monitoring system based on optical wingbeat classification. Comput Electron Agric. Elsevier B.V.; 2015; 118: 47–55. https://doi.org/10.1016/j.compag.2015.08.021

23. 20. Schmidhuber J. Deep Learning in neural networks: An overview. Neural Networks. Elsevier Ltd; 2015; 61: 85–117. https://doi.org/10.1016/j.neunet.2014.09.003 PMID: 25462637

24. 18. Loris Nannia , Gianluca Maguoloa* , Fabio Pancinoa, Insect pest image detection and recognition based on bio-inspired methods, *University of Padova, via Gradenigo 6, Padova 35131, Italy*

25. Krizhevsky A, Sutskever I, Hinton GE. ImageNet Classification with Deep Convolutional Neural Networks. Adv Neural Inf Process S

26. Mosquitos and other biting Diptera, *wate sanitation health*. WHO https://www.who.int/water_sanitation_health/resources/vector007to28.pdf

27. R. M. Prakash, N. Thenmoezhi and M. Gayathri. (2019) "Face Recognition with Convolutional Neural Network and Transfer Learning", 2019 International Conference on Smart Systems and Inventive Technology (ICSSIT), Tirunelveli, India, pp. 861–864

28. Simonyan, K.; Zisserman, A. Very deep convolutional networks for large-scale image recognition. arXiv 2014, arXiv:1409.1556

29. Torrey L. and Shavlik J. Transfer learning. Handbook of Research on Machine Learning Applications, 01 2009.

30. Andrzej Brodzicki, Michal Piekarski1,Dariusz Kucharski,Transfer Learning Methods As A New Approach In Computer Vision Tasks With Small Datasets , Foundations Of Computing And Decision Sciences, Vol. 45 (2020) No. 3

31. Amit Kumar Banerjee,K.Kiran, Classification and identification of mosquito species using artificial neural networks,*Computational Biology and Chemistry* Volume 32, Issue 6, December 2008, Pages 442–447

32. B T L H van de Vossenberg [1] , A Ibáñez-Justicia [2] , E Metz-Verschure , E J van Veen [3] Bruil-Dieters [3] , E J Scholte, Real-time PCR Tests in Dutch Exotic Mosquito Surveys; Implementation of Aedes aegypti and Aedes albopictus Identification Tests, and the Development of Tests for the Identification of Aedes atropalpus and Aedes japonicus japonicus (Diptera: Culicidae) , *Oxford University Press on behalf of Entomological Society of America 2015 May;52(3):336–50*

33. Eleftherios Fanioudakis ,Mosquito wingbeat analysis and classification using deep learning

34. Junyoung Park1,3, Dong In Kim,Classifcation and Morphological Analysis of Vector Mosquitoes using Deep Convolutional Neural Networks,*Scientific Reports,*(2020) 10:1012 | https://doi.org/10.1038/s41598-020-57875-1

35. Daniel Motta, Alex A´ lisson Bandeira Santos,Optimization of convolutional neural network hyperparameters for automatic classification of adult mosquitoes,*PLOS ONE* https://doi.org/10.1371/journal.pone.0234959 *July 14, 2020*

36. D. R. Raman, R. R. Gerhardt, J. B. Wilkerson, Detecting Insect Flight Sounds In The Field: Implications For Acoustical Counting Of Mosquitoes, Vol. 50(4): 1481–1485 2007 American Society Of Agricultural And Biological Engineers Issn 0001–2351

An Extraction and Analysis of Land Elevation and Coastal Area using Spatial Data Mining Techniques in DEMs

B. G. Kodge[(⊠)]

School of Science, GITAM Deemed University, Hyderabad, TS, India
kodgebg@gmail.com

ABSTRACT. The earth's land surface is always changing its morphology and characteristics due to its inside and outside movements/activities like earthquakes, volcanic eruptions, tsunamis, cyclones, avalanches, asteroid hits, floods, land sliding, and so on. All these earth's movements/activities are the natural phenomenon and not affected the earth's atmosphere that much which is affecting more than the man made things or global warming. The main causes of increase in the earth's temperature are the industrialization, deforestation, and pollutions which are generating more and more artificial disasters. The melting of land ice such as glaciers and ice sheets are the main reasons of increase in global sea levels and is become a big challenge to the people of cities/villages which are located on the sea coasts. Therefore an attempt is made in this paper to extract and analyse the land elevation data, elevation statistics, number of cities/villages located near the sea coasts in India within a specific distance and elevation classes using spatial data mining techniques in DEMs (Digital Elevation Models). The states wise extracted results of this paper are visualized geographically for better understanding and will be useful to plan, monitor and control the by local administrative of that concern province.

Keywords: Elevation data · Sea coast area/cities/villages · Digital elevation model · Spatial data mining · Geographical Information System

1 Introduction

Earth's landform is changing constantly by the movements of tectonic plates which created the mountains, hills, plateaus, canyons and valleys. The change in earth's surface changing its morphology and characteristics year by year and also affects its atmosphere. The global warming is affecting the land ice and melting the same day by day which is one of the major causes of increase in global sea level.

1.1 Digital Elevation Model

To study and analyze the landform and land elevation of a particular province, we must need to have an elevation/terrain data model with us. Now days there are variety of

© The Author(s) 2023
R. Manza et al. (Eds.): ACVAIT 2022, AISR 176, pp. 485–495, 2023.
https://doi.org/10.2991/978-94-6463-196-8_37

elevation data models are available which are processed by different remote sensing techniques. Digital elevation model is a 3 dimensional metrics (XYZ), in which the X and Y are the spatial coordinates which similarly represents the longitude and latitude of earth surface. The Z coordinate represents the elevation values of that location which is associated with that X and Y spatial coordinates.

Digital elevation model is a 3 dimensional spatial data/image contains three coordinates (*X Y and Z*) which is basically generated from contour lines of terrain data. The terrain elevations data from land surface positions are sampled at specific spaced intervals. The digital elevation models can be represented as a raster image or as a vector data such as TIN (Triangulated Irregular Network). The DEMs can be generated using photogrammetry, IfSAR, LiDAR, land surveying techniques [1, 7].

1.2 Spatial Data Mining

The data mining dealing with traditional data (text and numbers) is different from dealing with spatial data (text, numbers, geometries, images, land coordinates). Working with spatial data mining processes are little bit complicated and than the traditional data mining processes and are need much more knowledge and modelling logics because of their more number of features.

2 Methodology

2.1 Data Source

The primary data of my study area (India) such as DEMs are collected from USGS (United States Geological Survey), vector shape-files are downloaded from ESRI (Environment Space Research Institute, USA), remote sensing images are collected from BHUVAN (Indian Geo-platform of ISRO) and other associated data sets such as India gazette, census, coastal data are collected from Indian official sources.

2.2 Data Processing

The main focus of this study is to process and analyze the spatial data which includes the vector maps (shape-files), terrain data (DEMs), raster maps (satellite images) and some official location based records. All these kinds of data are processed and queried using PostgreSql spatial database using some specific features and associated values. The ImageJ open source software is used to classify, analyze, and plot graphs/maps of 3D DEM data matrices using image processing and mapping toolboxes. The step by step data processing of the analytical study is shown in Fig. 1.

The data acquisition process begins with collecting inputs from different types of associated spatial data sets. The data pre-processing step verifies and validates the geo-reference and projection related data and is done using QGIS 3.22.0. If any associated data is not geo-referenced then it will assigns to the same. The WGS-84 EPSG-4326 geodetic datum/spatial reference system is used in this system. The term WGS stands for 'World Geodetic System' and ESPG stands for 'European Petroleum Survey Group'.

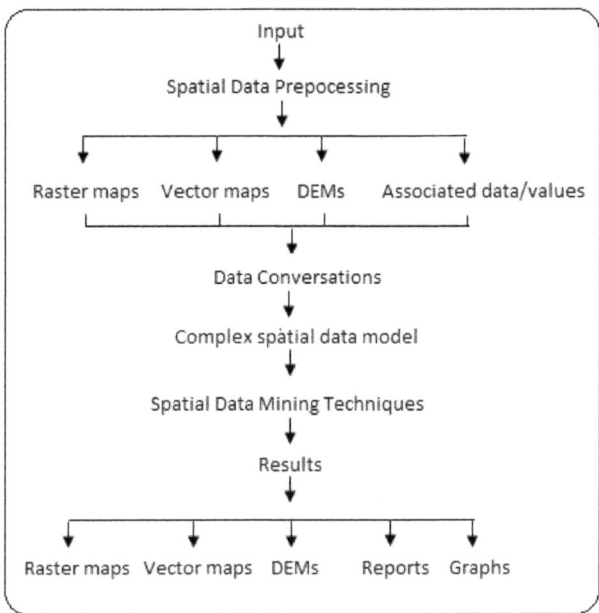

Fig. 1. Methodology used in this analytical study.

Further the system does the required data conversions for compatible spatial computations. Next the validated data will be accessed into a spatial database which is created using PostgreSql. All the associated relations are established between the database fields and spatial data links to form a complex spatial data model. Now we can extract the required information/results by executing queries using spatial data mining techniques [5].

2.3   Spatial Data Mining Techniques

In this study the following spatial data mining techniques are used:

2.3.1   Spatial Classification

This technique assigns an object to a class from a provided set of classes based on the spatial attribute values of this object. The attribute values of the neighboring objects can also be considered in this technique. Using this technique the set of areas and villages are classified differently.

2.3.2   Spatial Clustering

This technique is used to group a set of spatially distributed objects into labeled clusters therefore those spatial objects within a cluster have maximum similarity comparative to others. This technique is applied grouped into 5 classes as shown in the results and discussion section.

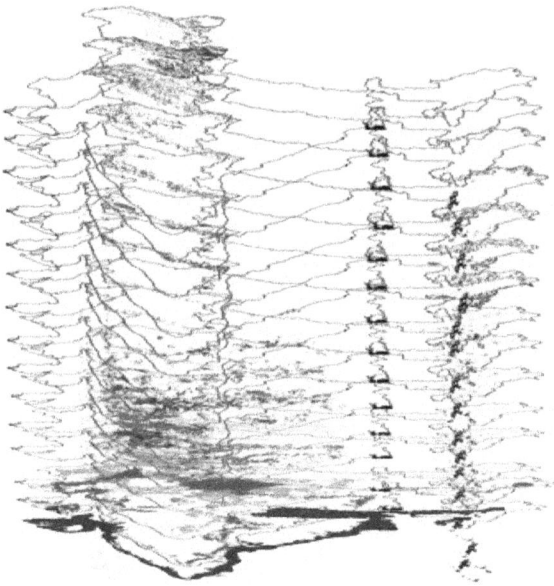

Fig. 2. Elevation sliced map of India.

2.3.3 Spatial Association Rule

Spatial association rule mining is a rule which shows some certain association relationships among a set of spatial and possibly some non spatial attributes/values. A rule must indicate that the model in the rule have relatively frequent occurrences in the spatial database and strong inference of relationships. The spatial attributes are processed which are related to each other like, villages located at specific distances and having the specified elevations [4].

3   Results and Discussion

3.1 Indian Land Elevation

India has a very inconsistent and bumpy land surface elevation. The elevation range begins from 0 i.e. sea level to 8586 m (28169 feet). India's land elevation is to be found increasing in its height as we move from south to north.

The major part of north and north-eastern side consists of highest elevation. The Kangchenjunga is a highest place located at India-Nepal border at 8586 m elevation. The elevation sliced map of India is shown in Fig. 2.

3.2 Elevation Profile

The Fig. 3 showing elevation map (graduated-colored) of India started from the sea level i.e. displayed in blues color and increasing with light-blue, dark-green, light-green, yellow, orange, brown, red, pink, purple to grey as shown in its map legend.

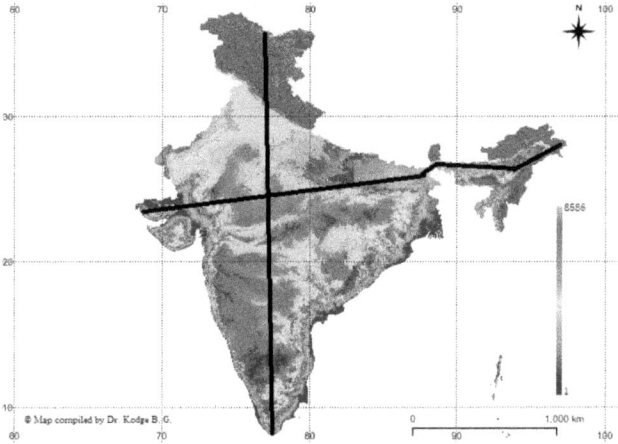

Fig. 3. Elevation map of India

The black lines drawn in Fig. 3 from north side to south (top to bottom) and west side to east (left to right) are used to get the elevation profile of the area. The north to south and west to east line elevation profiles are extracted and shown in Figs. 4(a) and 4(b) respectively.

From Fig. 4(a) and 3(b) it is observed that the India has a very inconsistent and bumpy land surface. The northern and north-eastern part of India is having highest land elevation compared to its other parts. The western and southern part of India is flat in nature and having very small amount of elevated land compared to its north side.

The Fig. 5 showing the slope (in percent) profile of the lines drawn in Fig. 3. Figure 5(a) displaying the slope profile of line north to south, and Fig. 5(b) showing the slope profile of line drawn from west to east.

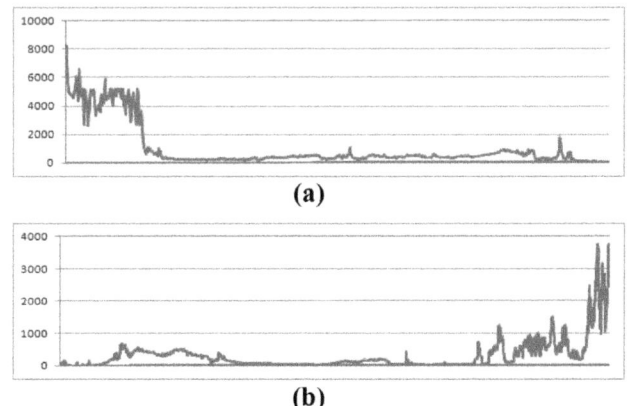

Fig. 4. Elevation profile of India: (a) north to south. (b) west to east.

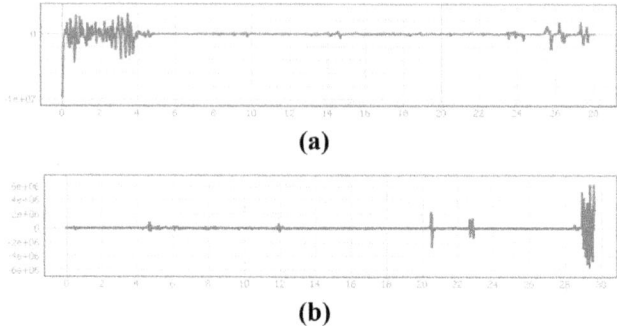

(a)

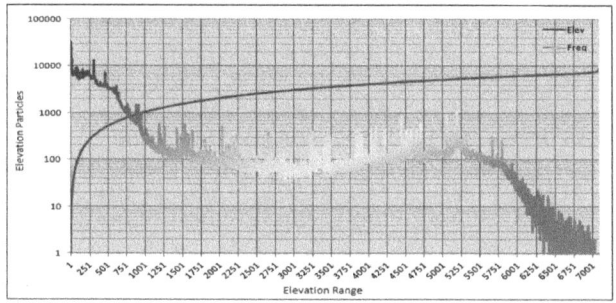

(b)

Fig. 5. Slope profile (a) north to south, (b) west to east.

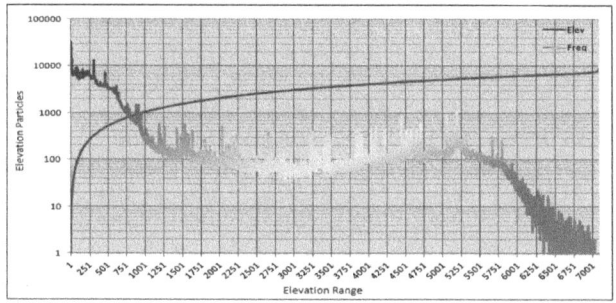

Fig. 6. Frequency of land elevation values with covered area.

3.3 Elevation and Covered Area

According to the Survey of India, India is the seventh largest country having a total area of 32,87,263 square kilometre and has fourth highest mountain in the world i.e. Kangchanjunga located at 8586 m (28,169 feet). The covered area is spreaded with discrete elevation values with different land characteristics.

The Fig. 6 showing the frequency of elevations (graduated) and it's covered area. The elevation range is started from 1 to 8586 m and covered area particles are extracted from a DEM. Majority of the area is in between 500 to 700 m and average elevation is 620 m.

3.4 Coastal Area and Nearby Located Cities/Villages

India contains a vast seacoast line with total length of 7516 km connected to 09 states (Gujarat, Maharashtra, Goa, Karnataka, Kerala, Tamilanadu, Andhra Pradesh, Odisha and West Bengal) and 04 union territories (Dadar & Nagar Haveli and Daman & Diu, Lakshadweep, Pondicherry and Andaman & Nikobar islands).

The coastal area within a specific distance and elevation are classified into 5 classes and are extracted from the spatial database using an association rule and feature extraction techniques. The classes with specific features are defined as follows:

Table 1. Class attributes of extracted coastal area

SN	Class ID	Elevation range (meters)	Color
1	Class_1	0–3.9	Red
2	Class_2	4.0–7.9	Orange
3	Class_3	8.0–11.9	Yellow
4	Class_4	12.0–15.9	Green
5	Class_5	16.0–20.0	Blue

The Fig. 7 showing the extracted coastal area as using specified values as shown in the Table 1. The area of each individual class fall within a specific range of elevation values extracted and their statistical measurements are also calculated. The details of class wise extracted area and their statistical measurements are shown in Table 2.

The extracted values of class wise coastal area such as Total Area Counts, Total Area, Mean, Standard Deviation and Range are shown in Table 2, and the same is displayed in graph as shown in Fig. 8.

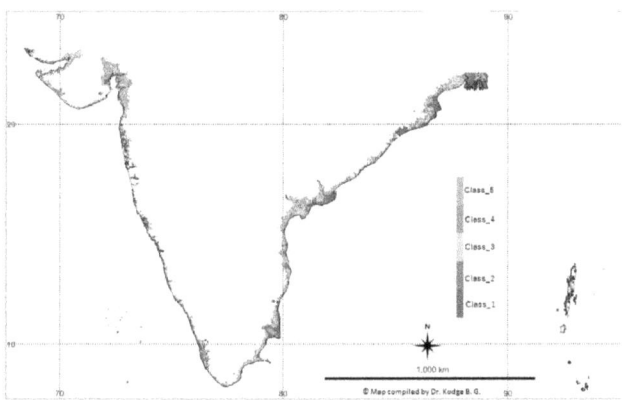

Fig. 7. Specified class wise extracted coastal area.

Table 2. Class wise extracted coastal area and their statistical measurements

	Class_1	Class_2	Class_3	Class_4	Class_5
Area Count	2152	2349	3097	3609	4024
Area	30327	24476	19167	16632	14217
Mean	14.09	10.41	6.18	4.6	3.5
St.Dv.	165	81.18	35.72	30.42	17.6
Range	4219	1843	1070	1308	612

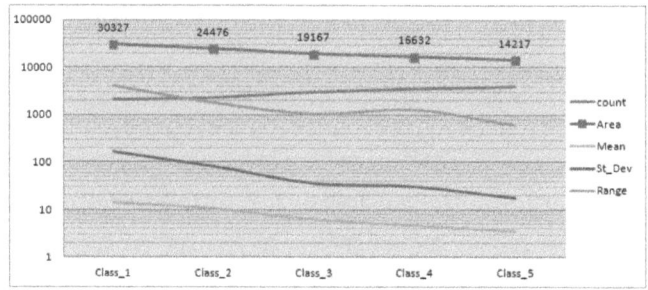

Fig. 8. Class wise extracted area and their statistical measurements.

In Fig. 8, the area of Class_1 (Elevation from 0 to 3.9 m) spread in 30327 square meters which is the highest one and Class_5 has 14217 square meters with lowest area.

From Fig. 9, it is observed that majority of villages are located in nearby coastal areas in India. The villages are shown in red color points are located in just 0 to 3.9 m of elevation. The orange colored points are lies between 4.0 to 7.9 m and yellow points found within 8.0 to 11.9 m. The green colored points are of 12.0 to 15.9 m and blue points are found within the areas of 16.0 to 20.0 m of elevation.

The class wise total number of clustered villages are extracted from the database and shown the following Fig. 10.

From the above Fig. 10, it is found that the major number of villages i.e. 760 belongs to class 'Class_1' which are located very close to the seacoast and are on very short/lowest land elevation. The 'Class_2' villages are 686 in numbers which are lies between the 4.0 to 7.9 m of elevation, and 474 villages belongs to class 'Class_3' are between 8.0 to 11.9 m land elevation. There are 428 villages are found located between the 12.0 to 15.9 m of elevation are of 'Class_4', and 304 number of villages are observed within 16 to 20.0 m of land elevation are of 'Class_5'.

The Fig. 11 showing list of coastal states and union territories on its x-axis denoted as GJ for Gujarat, MH for Maharashtra, GO for Goa, KA for Karnataka, KL for Kerala,

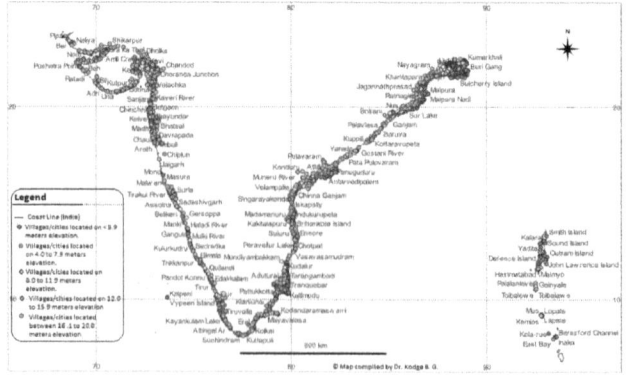

Fig. 9. Class wise extracted cities/villages of specified coastal area.

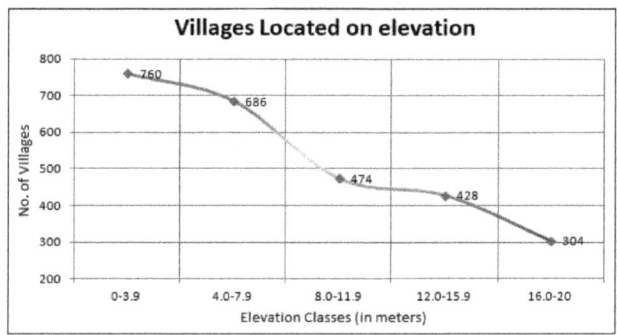

Fig. 10. Class wise extracted number of clustered cities/villages.

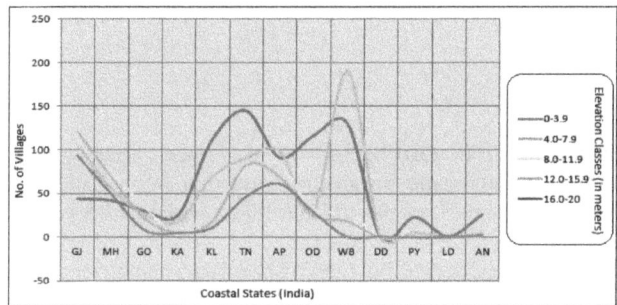

Fig. 11. State wise coastal cities/villages found within their specified classes.

TN for Tamilanadu, AP for Andhra Pradesh, OD for Odisha, WB for West Bengal, DD for Diu Daman, PY for Pondicherry, LD for Lakshadweep and AN for Andaman and Nikobar islands respectively. On y-axis we can see the number of coastal cities/villages associated with their colored graph lines belongs to Class_1 to Class_5. (Refer Table1 for more details).

The values shown in red colored line are belongs to Class_1 and are at high risk or danger zone/locations. These cities/villages are very close to the seacoast and are on very lowest land elevation. If the sea level increases to its 2 to 3 m of more height, then all these 760 villages will be found underwater within the oceans.

According the Fig. 11, the cities/villages of Class_1 in states of Kerala, Tamilanadu, Odisha and West Bengal are more in numbers and are at high risks (Red line). Similarly the orange line (Class_2) is found very high in the state of West Bengal followed by Andhra Pradesh, Tamilanadu and Kerala.

The cities like Mumbai, Thiruvananthapuram, Chennai, Visakhapatnam, Puri, Kolkata are also at high risk. All the shown cities/villages are needs to be move towards a safer location as far as the distance from seacoast and elevation is concern.

4 Conclusion

The proposed study is very important and will be helpful for the planning of location based projects like, formation of new rail lines/routes, installation of wind power terminals, building dams, road networks, coastal area monitoring and other land elevation related movements/activities. The global sea level is increasing day by day due to global warming and the proposed study will help to monitor the extracted coastal areas and their associated cities/villages (Classes 1 to 5) of India.

Acknowledgement. Author is grateful to USGS, ESRI and Bhuvan (ISRO) for providing the required datasets and I am also thankful to providers of open source software such as QGIS, PostGRESQL, ImageJ.

References

1. Ayman Soliman, Ling Han (2019), Effects of vertical accuracy of digital elevation model (DEM) data on automatic lineaments extraction from shaded DEM, Advances in Space Research, Vol. 64, Issue 3, pp-603-622. https://doi.org/https://doi.org/10.1016/j.asr.2019.05.009
2. Christopher J. Moran & Elisabeth N. Bui (2002) Spatial data mining for enhanced soil map modelling, International Journal of Geographical Information Science, 16:6, 533-549, DOI: https://doi.org/10.1080/13658810210138715
3. Dou, Jie and Yunus et.al. (2019), Evaluating GIS-Based Multiple Statistical Models and Data Mining for Earthquake and Rainfall-Induced Landslide Susceptibility Using the LiDAR DEM, Remote Sensing, Vol. 11, No. 6, https://doi.org/10.3390/rs11060638.
4. J Dillipan et al, Spatial Data Mining Techniques, International Journal for Research in Emerging Science and Technology, Vol. 3, Issue 1, 2016.
5. Kodge, B.G. A review on current status of COVID19 cases in Maharashtra state of India using GIS: a case study. Spatial Information Research, 29, 223–229 (2021). https://doi.org/https://doi.org/10.1007/s41324-020-00349-3
6. Lee, Sunmin and Hyun, Yunjung and Lee, Moung-Jin (2019), Groundwater Potential Mapping Using Data Mining Models of Big Data Analysis in Goyang-si, South Korea, Sustainability, Vol. 11, No. 6, https://doi.org/10.3390/su11061678
7. S. M. Gandhi, B. C. Sarkar (2016), Essentials of Mineral Exploration and Evaluation, Elsevier, ISBN: 978–0–12–805329–4, https://doi.org/10.1016/C2015-0-04648-2
8. Shekhar S., Huang Y., Wu W., Lu C.T., Chawla S. (2001) What's Spatial About Spatial Data Mining: Three Case Studies. In: Grossman R.L., Kamath C., Kegelmeyer P., Kumar V., Namburu R.R. (eds) Data Mining for Scientific and Engineering Applications. Massive Computing, vol 2. Springer, Boston, MA. https://doi.org/https://doi.org/10.1007/978-1-4615-1733-7_26.

Extensive Rooftop Expression Identification and Spatial Analysis

Ashok Sangle[1]([⊠]) and Prapti Deshmukh[2]

[1] Department of Computer Science and IT, Dr. Babasaheb Ambedkar, Marathwada University, Aurangabad, India
ashoka4it@gmail.com
[2] Pathrikar College of Computer Science and IT, Aurangabad, India

Abstract. This Research is going to explore innovative ways for Site Evaluation and Potential Assessment to utilize sunlight hitting rooftop extent for green energy potential and agriculture practices. It may intend to green energy, green roofs and water harvesting as per extent area. In this scenario, it is essential to estimate the existing open flat roof surface with full sun on it, hitting light but absolutely no utilization of the surface. The investigation of the urban rooftop extent based on geospatial technology an extensive roof top for solar potential assessment and as to establishing a benchmark for a multifunctional system within one surface area at household level. Those are green energy potential, water harvesting and agriculture practices. A new term Agrivoltaics practice at household level an Agrivoltaics is the process of farming crops under shade of the solar system. In this scenario an Agrivoltaics is an approach for the cultivation of vegetables or portable agriculture system installation at urban rooftop. In this research a major focus on evaluation of site estimation, quantification and potential measure analysis similarly to interpret the role of technology in this scenario. This will be ensure the utilization of existing resources smartly as under stressed resources due to urbanization, population, industrialization and pollution. A specific convinced technology can boost green energy, vegetable food generation, saving water, healthy environment and major effectiveness for the solar energy potential assessment and generation truthfulness can be extended.

Keywords: Geospatial Technology · Spatial Analysis · solar energy · Agrivoltaics · green energy · photovoltaic cell · Rooftop etc.

1 Introduction

Many cities facing the challenges of area so building infrastructure is one over above, its necessity to increase the utilization of available infrastructure smartly so rooftop green (solar) energy as well as farming (Agrivoltaics) is one of the smartest ways of making use of building infrastructure. It does really have such tremendous environmental benefits to the ecosystem at small scale. It's proficient in cities around the world you know it is like a drop in a bucket, but if we gain some momentum we can really create a title shift. A shift like flipping roof gardens to rooftop farming, water harvesting and green energy.

© The Author(s) 2023
R. Manza et al. (Eds.): ACVAIT 2022, AISR 176, pp. 496–510, 2023.
https://doi.org/10.2991/978-94-6463-196-8_38

In case roof gardens, rooftop farming and water harvesting we use existing space as it is but only need a quantification of rooftops. For the green energy case here we need to select right rooftop for placing the solar photovoltaic system.

To select, to quantify the rooftop area of each building and to find out the whole rooftop area of institutional, social and economic infrastructures here Spatial Analysis technique and Geospatial Technology are being used. The estimation of rooftop area is for further analysis and potential assessment and right selection of suitable site also for quick and holistic rooftop potential estimation approaches considered.

The Geospatial technology for handling location based data related to urban resources and site suitability circumstances on various scales will be careful. The claims of Remote Sensing and GIS based approaches in green energy; Agrivoltaics (agro- photovoltaic-A portable farming system) planning and potential measurement analysis is going to be useful. It is being exploring innovative ways to utilize rooftop extent for green energy potential (PV-photovoltaic) system as well as water harvesting and portable agriculture practices too. Primarily it is needed to find out whole area of rooftops which comprises of institutional, social and economic infrastructure of urban. The estimation of rooftop extent in particular sense for potential assessment and planning purposes. A uniqueness of this study is to find and identify a specific building object from other urban infrastructure, counting all buildings as well as findings each building's rooftop area in square meter and then as per area analysing potential assessment of whole. Building resilience at urban level in solar energy and vegetable production is a stuff challenge due to the more investment at a time but beyond in long term sense it is cost effective. Today's changing world, especially growing industrialization and population its again essential to utilize the present space smartly in order to reduce the load on existing resources.

The Potential assessment is specifically essential for planning and installation of green energy, portable agriculture practices as growing vegetables crops in the shadow of solar panel. This can further stimulate food production and effectiveness for water conservation, as a multifunctional system within one surface area at household level is most suitable for sustainable development.

1.1 Survey of Literature

Yosoon Choi, Jangwon Suh and Sung-Min Kim has the paper title "GIS-based solar radiation mapping, site evaluation, and potential assessment: a review" in 2019 were utilized methods for site evaluation i.e. Boolean overlay, Weighted sum, analytic hierarchy process, fuzzy and artificial neural network (ANN), shadow analysis, model validation are used With DEM and DSM dataset [7].

Kakoli Saha was work under the paper title "Smart Solutions" for a Smart City: a GIS Approach" in 2017 A techniques are utilized i.e. Image preprocessing, automated extraction of urban roof area, production of reference map, accuracy assessment of the automated method, estimating potential for smart solutions by use of input data IRS-5 CARTOSAT-1 stereo images of Bhopal, acquiredon 16th Feb 2012 [8].

Rishabh, Harmeet Singh Kathuria utilized multispectral spatial resolution imagery with spatial analysis Techniques solar generation on the rooftop has been calculated in 2016 under the paper title "Application of remote sensing and GIS technique in rooftop mapping and PV module layout design" [9].

Flavio Borfecchia, Emanuela Caiaffa, Maurizio Pollino worked under paper title "Remote sensing and GIS in planning photovoltaic potential of urban areas" used GIS and LiDAR Satellite Data to estimates of PV potential at roofs level in urban areas [10].

Teresa Santos, Nuno Gomes, Miguel Brito Evaluated the roof-top area suitable for installation of solar energy systems in the city of Lisbon, Portugal with paper title "Solar Potential Analysis in Lisbon Using LiDAR Dataset in 2011" [11].

L. Kang,Q. Wang, H. W. Yan has studied under title "Building extraction based on OpenStreetMap tags and very high spatial resolution image in urban area" and compair building extration from OSM and Very high resolution data and they found that the OSM data is rich enough to directly extract almost all the buildings in 2018 [12].

2   Problem Statement

In today's changing world, especially growing industrialization and urban population it is essential to reduce the load on existing resources. Due to the urbanization, pollution, population, existing resources are getting trapped under stress. To overcome this, it is necessary to utilize existing resources smartly. Thousands of open flat roofs surface with full sun spreading light on it, hitting light but absolutely no utilization as example observe in Fig. 1.

The leading problem of the smart city is no healthy surroundings, environment, and other community issues. It's critical because of the emerging certain situations like growing urbanization, its population, industrialization so slow growth of the city etc. It's influences directly on development, so it's necessary to utilize urban rooftop smartly for sustainable development as in view green energy and green rooftop even at household level. See following Fig. 2 is an example it indicating load over resources without development plan and with development as a difference.

So due to this it will limit the return on investment so now here looking forward to an enhanced approach which considers the existing load over resources. To overcome the geospatial technology an enhanced sustainable development approach is to be considered. A precisely measure holistic approach by geospatial based rooftop potential assessment will be suitable for multifunctional system. The multifunctional system

Fig. 1. Indication Building footprints as an open space.

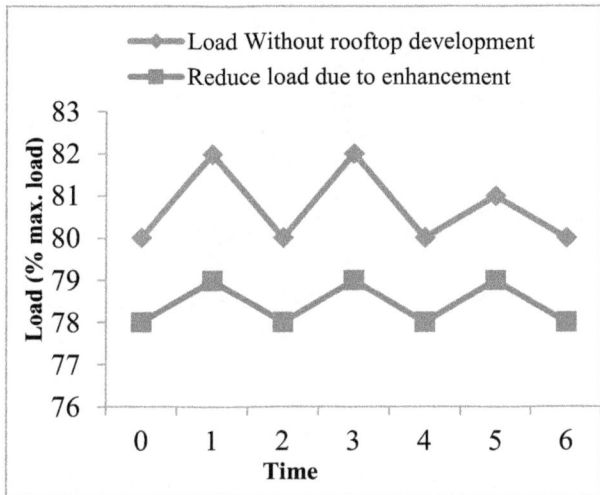

Fig. 2. As an example it indicating load over resources without development and with development as a difference.

means green energy, portable agriculture practices and water conservation within one surface area at household level.

3 Study Area

In this instance initially the study area is considered the urban region of Aurangabad Municipal Corporation. The geographical location of the Aurangabad City situated at latitude 19° 51′ 27.2952"N north and longitude 75° 20′ 36.3228"E East. The Aurangabad city is found at 581mts. From mean sea level. Its area is to be 138.50 Sq. Km. in which for this study the more focus is on the region that starts from divisional sports complex and its surrounding area situated at Gadiya Vihar, Aurangabad, Maharashtra, India, Following Fig. 3 shows study location.

4 Methodology

It's very much essential for selection of the proper procedure for smooth conduction of work. Appropriate evaluation of methodology to apply to frame the research work is most important thing to get targeted accuracy of findings (Fig. 4).

5 Spatial Analysis

5.1 Definition Required Data: Data Finding

To target the required interpretation of theme by applying step by step procedure the data must suitable, content full to extract the appropriate information. There are various types of data available in several scales and resolutions but raw data must compromises the end requirements of the application.

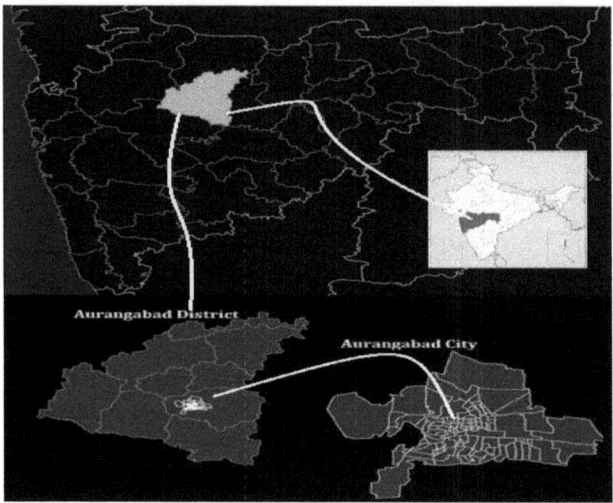

Fig. 3. Indicating Study Location

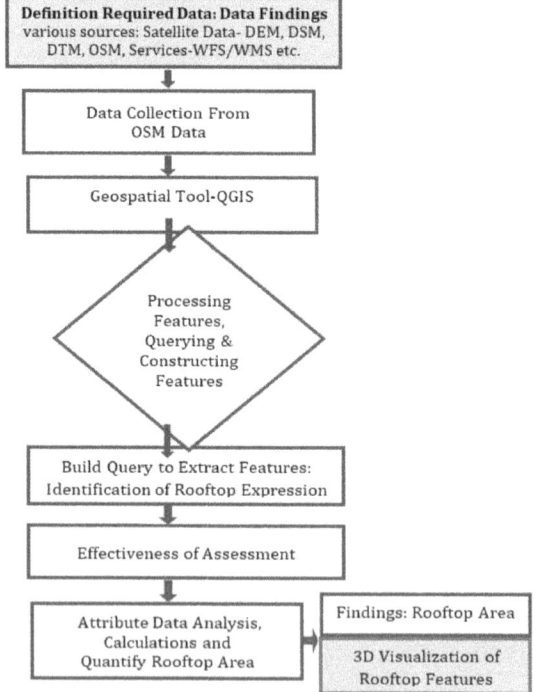

Fig. 4. Indicating the process of Spatial Analysis

There are many sources available from where the researchers can avail the data. The selection of data is totally based on the nature of the application and problem statement.

To fit the purpose here data from various sources is as suitable i.e. Satellite Data- DEM (Digital Elevation Model), DSM (Digital Surface Model), DTM (Digital Terrain Model), OSM (OpenStreetMap). At this stage for this study it is observed that now OSM has bear out the required amount of content so as its packed content it may be helpful for further analysis and interpretations for mining the targeted features.

5.1.1 Description of Data

At the hand a secondary data is available and it is also free at this movement so it has been suitable to utilize. The OSM (OpenStreetMaps) is a systematic updated database by contributors so vector format popular resource is available, again this resource offers Web Feature Service/Web Map Service (WMS) and other web based utility so through which the data is easily accessible in a QGIS environment.

5.2 Data Collection

With the help of GIS environment a as per the extent a required data searching and its collection (observe Table 1) has been completed using the open source tools i.e. QGIS and its plugins see Table 2.

Once the raw data gets selected, it must be packed content for the analysis and interpretations concern. The OSM data is giving an opportunity to utilize it in the GIS environment for further processes, like analysis and quantification of areas.

5.3 Geospatial Tool-QGIS

It's GIS Software to Construct Features. Now a day's lot of software systems offers GIS decision-making capabilities. As a concern, variety of software & hardware tools the important factor is the level of integration of these tools to provide a smoothly operating and fully functional geographic data processing environment.

So on the basis of its processing environment, functionality it's necessary to choose correct tool. As a processing part firstly here need to configure the existing QGIS Version 3.22.8 tool using external plugins. There are three most suitable plugins available for required feature extraction purpose for this study to process the features the required configuration accomplished by QuickMapService, QuickOSM Plugin and Qgis2threejs Plugin. Look in Table 2 it shows its utilization description (Table 3 and 4).

5.4 Build Query to Extract Features: Identification of Rooftop Expression

Think of real world features like streets, roads, Buildings and cities etc. Each feature on OpenStreetMap, is described as one or more geometries with attached attribute data (for example Building the Buildings carries some additional information about what it represents for example its name and its type etc. are its attribute data). In OSM the geometries/ features are described with three different elements i.e. nodes, ways and relations with its associated attribute data (Tags). Nodes are the equivalent to a point, ways are like lines that connect points and relations are collections of points or ways that represent a larger whole. See following Fig. 5. Attributes are described as **tags** that

Table 1. Details of Data used in the study.

Source	Visibility- Geospatial Coverage	Scale	Data Type	Availability	Accessed
OSM Data (OpenStreetMaps)	Public – whole World	Scale-Dependent visibility (Mini 1:500 To Max 1:1000000)	Vector Data	By Web feature Service (WFS) / Web Map Service (WMS)/ In GIS Tool	In QGIS using plugin i.e. QMS
Maxar Preminum Imagery	Public – whole World	Scale-Dependent visibility (50 to 80 cm.)	Raster Data	By Web feature Service (WFS) / Web Map Service (WMS)/ In RapiD Editor	Using RapiD Editor Tool.
Google Satellite	Public – whole World	Scale-Dependent visibility	Raster/Vector Data format	By Web Map Service (WMS) / Web feature Service In GIS Tool	In QGIS

can be part of a node, a way or a relation. These elements carry associated geometry and with its additional information about what it represents to be i.e. in the form **tags**.

5.4.1 Tags

Nodes and ways need to describe the type of feature they actually represent. For this it is possible to attach tags to nodes and ways so due to tag one can understand the type of feature it will be (observe Fig. 5. For example tags like forest, road, hill and Building Auditorium). Tags consist of a key and a value; we usually write down a tag as key = value. An example of a tag is the name tag (more precisely: the tag with the key name), that defines the name of the object. For instance, the way representing the Auditorium building on the above Fig. 5 map has the tag name = Auditorium & building = yes. There are also many tags that do not naturally need a value. Those tags usually take the value yes; for example building = yes means that something is a building which do not have a value or may default value.

Table 2. Details of QGIS Plugins Utilization Description.

QGIS Plugins	Utilization Description
QuickMapService (QMS) Ver.0.19.29	• A QGIS plugin to Insert BaseMap for example from OSM Standard. • OSM- it is open database so to get access it, the supportive services such as WMS – Web Map Service, and WFS – Web Feature Services are helpful so through QMS plugin one can access data using these services. These services are helpful for searching and finding datasets and basemaps. So one can easily insert appropriate BaseMap in QGIS. • Now then you can able to access and find the required extend and its data you are interested in see Fig. 7. • In QGIS As per local zone find out Coordinate reference System (CRS) and Re-Project as per that Local CRS (In this study CRS: EPSG: 4326 - WGS 84 – Geographic, utilized) Projection.
QuickOSM Ver.2.0.1	• QuickOSM plugin allows you to work quickly with OSM data in QGIS due to Overpass API. Overpass API is helpful for execute the query to render required appropriate features. • To write query as per syntax and semantics the Overpass API provides Overpass Query Language. Initially it's a challenging task (due to querying spatial a georeferenced data regarding geometry as being unaware about its attributes i.e. keys and values regarding the dataset) without proper skill set of Overpass Query Language (OQL) but due to QuickOSM plugin a task become handy and easy. • It helps to write some queries for you by providing an interface, key/value of features/preset. (A pair's key/value- it's a Tags means an attributes data of the features means additional information about feature, each feature have at least one tag or more than one tag too). Tag describes the type of feature the concern elements do represent. • With help of interface one can able to select specific required extent boundary of your study area. Likewise one can customize the query and building a query as per end user application, target or geometry the features interested in the extent. • In our case we are interested in the real world geometry i.e. Building object and its rooftop area. So with support of QuickOSM customizing the query and tackle the appropriate feature very quickly due to plugin. • A QuickOSM plugin offers an interface to query interactively on a basemap.

(*continued*)

Table 2. (*continued*)

QGIS Plugins	Utilization Description
Qgis2threejs Plugin Ver. 2.7.1	· This plugin visualizes vector data in 3D on web browsers. · So you can build required 3D objects and generate files for web publishing in simple procedure shown by interface. · In addition, you can save the 3D model in glTF format for 3D printing.

Table 3. As per associated ID a sample attribute table shows each building's footprint roof area in square meter.

ID	Type	Area_Cal (Square Meter)
118729410	building	315
120161637	building	2262
220281897	Hotel Taj Residency	3164
257873002	Garware Company	3029
257879923	Shivchhatrapati College	1680
257960575	Reliance Mall	5686

Table 4. Shows at this stage the extracted total number of buildings and its total area in square meter.

Total No. of Buildings	Area (Square Meter)
1115	328959

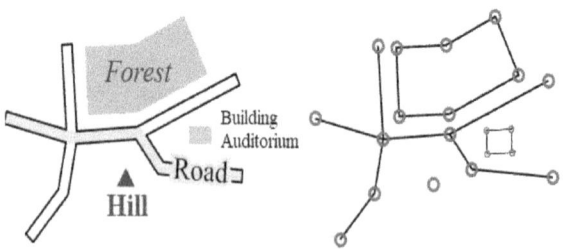

Fig. 5. Representations of real world geometries with its associated additional information in the form **tags** and lastly end up with its node, ways and relations.

5.4.2 Query

Once we know the representation of data with the help of elements and with its tags one can easily query the data. Query can control what information is extracted and output from the OSM database. The QuickOSM allows you to work quickly with OSM data in QGIS and Overpass API can support for this.

A node represents one single point on the map; a node carries its geographical location (latitude and longitude) and a unique identifier number.

A way represents a polyline or (closed) polygon on the map. Ways do not store their own location; instead they carry an ordered list of node identifiers.

When you drill down from relations and ways you always end up with nodes see Fig. 5. Nodes are the most basic element of the data model: a point on the map with some data attached to it as tags (name-value pairs).

In order to extract the geometries here need to build an appropriate queries and with help of nodes, ways and relations (these elements carry associated tags regarding with its geometry) one can able to construct the query to get required features you interested in. The main things are that a query consists of a series of statements which OSM database does have regarding feature elements with tags. Tag describes the type of feature the concern elements do represent. An Overpass Query Language/ Overpass QL (OQL) query is a list of statements that are executed by the API. More complex queries will consist of many more statements of different types. When you use Overpass QL (OQL) you're likely to be querying information based on the location or metadata, rather than their identifiers only. These statements build up sets of results that are then returned to the user.

In this study case we able to get access the OSM data in a GIS format by QGIS as it is possible via the QuickOSM plugin. This plugin support to write some queries by providing preset (geometry features are set in OSM database) and also with key/values see Fig. 6. Through plugin interface then choose required extent and then select features you required to extract like point, lines, Multilinestrings and Multipolygons as per your interest features. Once query get built up then Click on run query option observe Fig. 6. The query starts execution and once finishes it will added new layer to the existing QGIS layers panel, switch to the main QGIS window. You will see a new layer get added to the Layers panel. Now if you aware the canvas will show the extracted geometries feature. Then next step is filter or extract this newly added layer as exactly feature you interested in i.e. the interested feature is Building Rooftop Footprints of the urban buildings. So once get filtered by query the extensive rooftop expression identification gets resolved. In main while a simultaneously attribute data table get generated while processing the query for extraction of features and when query is proper new layer get added with its attribute data. That attribute table resides inside that specific layer property.

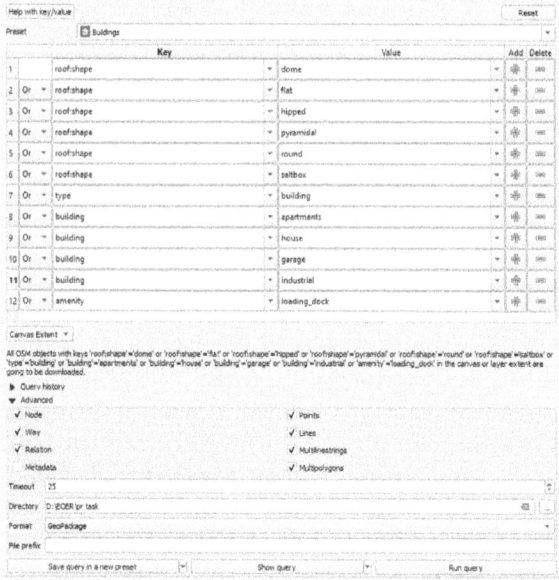

Fig. 6. QuickOsm Plugin Interface to Build Query to Extract Features

5.5 Effectiveness of Assessment

After appropriate features extraction here need to check the effectiveness of the assessment by comparing with the help of google satellite map or with ground truth here checked out and by visual observation it gives the sense of its validness. A valid or invalid meets as per the end users application so the end users purposes get meets then and then it's considered as a valid interpretation.

5.6 Attribute Data Analysis, Calculations and Quantify Rooftop Area

The extracted features/ layer properties displays attribute table option so open it for analysis and examine the attributes data as per associated with features with its locations. Inspect relationships of spatial features in data through overlay and other analytical techniques in order to locate the proper data with its associated features. Observe columns and row data as per specific building rooftop feature for total count and appropriate calculations. Once observed so there no area related information in attribute table. So in order to calculate area of rooftops in attribute table here need to add a new column for area calculation of each building's rooftop as per column of table data as building feature's id for proper quantification of each building rooftop area in square meter. In this way attribute table's data are organized, analyzed and necessary fields are calculated as per the required unit and end target. Finally all buildings are visualized in 3D by use of Qgis2threejs plugin.

5.6.1 Findings: Rooftop Area and 3D Visualization of Rooftop Features

So the final output also expressed and represented in two separate ways. A data analysis phase is originated in attribute tables of the constructed features, the calculated area also expressed with help of graph and another way is with 3D visualization of Buildings (Fig. 8 and 9).

6 Findings and Visualization

Experiment on Input Data to tackle buildings, building footprints and rooftop area.
Attribute Table

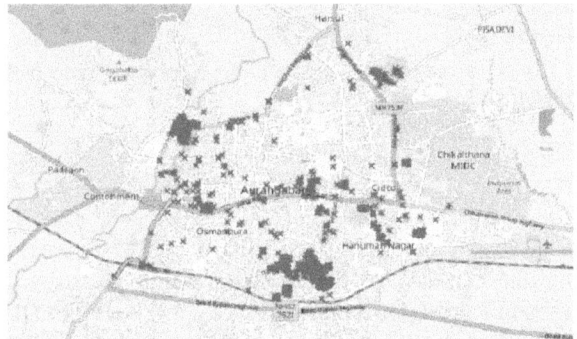

Fig. 7. Study Area shows the physical feature on ground for example settlements, road, buildings etc.

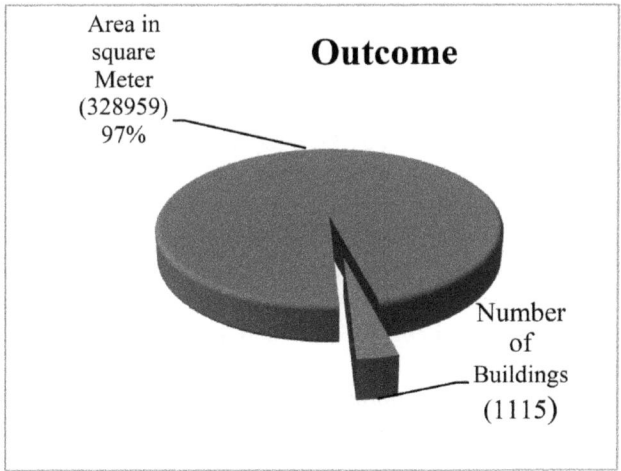

Fig. 8. Graph shows with all together the number of buildings and its collective area in square meter.

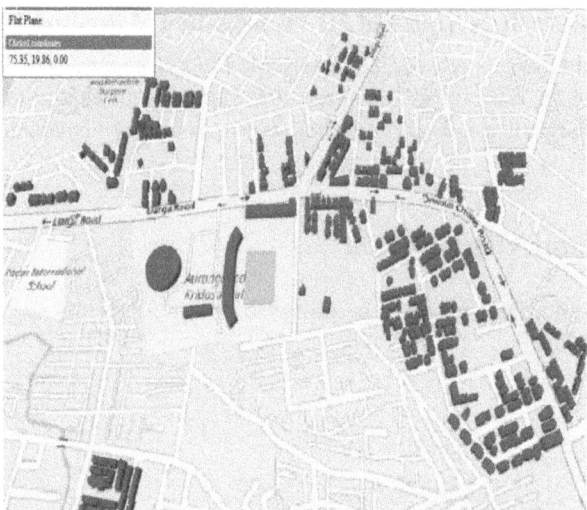

Fig. 9. Shows the Study areas Surrounded Buildings as an Extensive Rooftop Footprint Expression In 3D Form.

7 Conclusion

In this study, we tried to extract building rooftop from OSM here extracted all buildings are almost accurate the accuracy of the extracted buildings is confirmed by comparing the extraction result to google satellite. So here observed that all the OSM's vector data structure is better to describe geological objects rather than raster satellite images. Although the OSM data is constantly under improvement at global scale, the completeness and quality of the data annotations in different regions are different so in our case for this particular region here observed and found total number of buildings are 1115 and its area 328959 Square Meter, but matter of fact that as per theme/region of interest at this stage the quantity concern accuracy is less to retrieve actual number of buildings and its rooftop area as per the urban ROI (Region of Interest). So for more accuracy for this specific location the data is required to be up to date updated with rich contentful. Otherwise, to resolve this type of study here required high resolution data like LiDAR DEM and DSM data then the feature extraction will get resolve with more accurately. Distinctive advantage of this study is that people get aware about OSM for its mapping contribution concern so the benefit is that people get open-source geospatial data easily and updated around us. So geospatial geo-referenced data meets the peoples need for example research, commercial application and daily navigation concern also.

In this scenario it is more suitable for quick and 'holistic' rooftop potential estimation approach. Identifying and finding the area of each building for innovative applications such as solar energy, Agrivoltaics a portable farming and water conservation. Unique benefit of this study to the society/community around us is having opportunity to link urban people in to their solar power energy, food production system and water conservation system.

References

1. George B. Korte and P. E., THE GIS BOOK, Fifth Edition ed., Publisher Onword Press /Thomson Learning, ISBN981–240–228–4, 2001.
2. Ian Heywood, Sarah Cornelius and steve carve, An Introduction to geographical Information System, Third edition ed., Pearson Education India, ISBN 978–81–317–3193–2., 2009.
3. Sujit Choudhury, Deepankar Chakrabarti and Suchand Choudhury, An Introduction To Geographic Information Technology, I. K. International Publishing House pvt. Ltd. ISBN81–88237–66–3, 2010.
4. Abhishek vijayvairgia, Machine Learning with python an approach to applied Machine learning, first edition ed., BPB publications, ISBN978–93–8655–193–1, 2018, 2018.
5. Dr. D. Nagesh Kumar, Remote Sensing - Web course, Department of Civil Engineerin IISc Bangalore, [Online]. Available: http://civil.iisc.ernet.in/~nagesh/rs_gis.htm. [Accessed 16 11 2019.].
6. Smart City Mission Statement and Guidelines, Government of India, Ministry of Urban Development, June 2015.
7. Yosoon Choi,Jangwon Suh and Sung-Min Kim, GIS-Based Solar Radiation Mapping, Site Evaluation, and Potential Assessment: A Review. Applied sciences, 2019.
8. Kakoli Saha, Smart Solutions, for a Smart City: a GIS Approach" ICEGOV '17, March 07–09, 2017, New Delhi, AA, India ACM 978–1–4503–4825- 6/17/03. https://doi.org/10.1145/3047273.3047395.
9. Rishabh, Harmeet Singh Kathuria et.al Application of Remote Sensing and GIS technique in rooftop mapping and PV module layout design International Journal Of Geomatics And Geosciences, ISSN 0976 – 4380Volume 7, No 2, 2016.
10. Flavio Borfecchia, Emanuela Caiaffa, et. Al: Remote Sensing and GIS in planning photovoltaic potential of urban areas. European Journal of Remote Sensing - 2014, 47: 195–216 doi:https://doi.org/10.5721/EuJRS20144713.
11. Teresa Santos, Nuno Gomes et al. :Solar Potential Analysis in Lisbon Using LiDAR Data Lena Halounová, Editor EARSeL, 2011.
12. L. Kang,Q. Wang, H. W. Yan Building extraction based on OpenStreetMap tags and very high spatial resolution image in urban area, The International Archives of the Photogrammetry, Remote Sensing and Spatial Information Sciences, Volume XLII-3, 2018 ISPRS TC III Midterm Symposium Developments, Technologies and Applications in Remote Sensing, 7–10 May, Beijing, China.
13. Kakoli Saha, Smart Solutions" for a Smart City: a GIS Approach, ICEGOV '17, March 07–09, 2017, New Delhi, AA, India ACM 978–1–4503–4825- 6/17/03. https://doi.org/10.1145/3047273.3047395.
14. Kakoli Saha, A Remote Sensing Approach to Smart City Development in India: Case of Bhopal City, Madhya Pradesh, ICEGOV '17 SCII, March 07–09, 2017, New Delhi, AA, India © 2017 ACM. ISBN 978–1–4503–4930- 7/17/03...$15.00 DOI: https://doi.org/10.1145/3055219.3055232.
15. M. Arvind "Green Roofing Technology" published on SlideShare, on August 13, 2015, Retrieved on January 2, 2020. URL-https://www.slideshare.net/alaravanaravind/green-roof-presentation-51577641
16. Nisha, Aneesha, Sahil Kaundal et.al "Roof Garden" published on SlideShare, on Sep.14,2014, Retrieved on January 2, 2020. URL-https://www.slideshare.net/sahilkaundal92/roof-garden-39073651?next_slideshow=1
17. CBC, Andre Mayer "Green roofs and 'agritecture' have potential to transform food supply in cities" CBC News · Posted: Aug 07, 2015, Last Updated: August 11, 2015, Retrieved on January 2, 2020. URL-https://www.cbc.ca/news/technology/green-roofs-and-agritecture-have-potential-to-transform-food-supply-in-cities-1.3179971

18. metsolar "What is agrivoltaics? How can solar energy and agriculture work together?"Published on 2021–05–29, Updated: 2021–09–29, Retrieved on November 12, 2021.URL-https://metsolar.eu/blog/what-is-agrivoltaics-how-can-solar-energy-and-agriculture-work-together/

19. E. Trimaille, "QuickOSM", Docs.3liz.org, 2022. [Online]. Available: https://docs.3liz.org/QuickOSM/. [Accessed: 22- May- 2022].

20. Mapbox, "The OpenStreetMap data model", Labs.mapbox.com, 2022. [Online]. Available: https://labs.mapbox.com/mapping/osm-data-model/. [Accessed: 24- June- 2022].

21. Alga, The Eindhoven University of Technology, "Algorithms, Geometry & Applications", Alga.win.tue.nl, 2022. [Online]. Available: https://alga.win.tue.nl/tutorials/openstreetmap/. [Accessed: 24- June- 2022].

22. L. Dodds, "00 - The Beginning", Osm-queries.ldodds.com, 2022. [Online]. Available: https://osm-queries.ldodds.com/tutorial/00-node-1.osm.html. [Accessed: 24- June- 2022].

23. OpenStreetMap, Wiki contributors, "OpenStreetMap Wiki", Wiki.openstreetmap.org, 2022. [Online]. Available: https://wiki.openstreetmap.org/wiki/Main_Page. [Accessed: 24- June- 2022].

24. NextGIS, "QuickMapServices: easy basemaps in QGIS | NextGIS", NextGIS | Opensource Geospatial Solutions, 2022. [Online]. Available: https://nextgis.com/blog/quickmapservices/. [Accessed: 24- June- 2022].

25. MInh Nguy˜ên, "A turbo introduction to Overpass", Youtube.com, 2022. [Online]. Available: https://www.youtube.com/watch?v=q9QI4AfwHoM. [Accessed: 18- June- 2022].

26. Minoru Akagi, "GitHub - minorua/Qgis2threejs: A QGIS plugin to export 3D maps to Web", GitHub, 2022. [Online]. Available: https://github.com/minorua/Qgis2threejs. [Accessed: 18- June- 2022].

Machine Learning Approach for Road-Line Extraction in Complex Urban Environments from High-Resolution Hyperspectral Image

Amol D. Vibhute[1]([✉]), Karbhari V. Kale[2], Sandeep V. Gaikwad[3], and Arjun V. Mane[4]

[1] Symbiosis Institute of Computer Studies and Research (SICSR), Symbiosis International (Deemed University), Pune 411016, MH, India
amolvibhute2011@gmail.com
[2] Computer Science and IT, Dr. Babasaheb Ambedkar Technological University, Lonere 402103, MH, India
[3] Department of Computer Applications, Charotar University of Science and Technology, Changa 388421, Gujarat, India
[4] Department of Digital and Cyber Forensic, Government Institute of Forensic Science, Nagpur, MH, India

Abstract. Road network extraction and road line extraction from remote sensing images is still challenging task due to the complex structure of urban areas. The spectral response, design, shape, size, shadow, a contrast of roads, and other urban features are similar, which causes inaccurate results. The present paper investigates the asphalt road line extraction from high spatial-spectral resolution hyperspectral imagery. The implemented approach is based on a machine-learning algorithm, i.e., Support Vector Machines (SVM), structural information, and road line filtering. Road and non-road classification have been done using the SVM algorithm, generating a road map. In the second step, mathematical morphology was used to extract the road network with enhanced precision. Unwanted material has been removed using the granulometry approach. Finally, accurate and comprehensive road line extraction has been done by median filtering. The results have shown 85.13% correctness with 79.93% completeness of the implemented methodology. The experimental results are helpful for transportation analysis, traffic management, cartography, urban planning, and its management.

Keywords: Road-line extraction · Machine learning · Hyperspectral image · Mathematical morphology · Support vectors

1 Introduction

Road network extraction using remote sensing is essential in several applications such as transportation analysis, traffic management, urban planning, cartography, and updating the Geographic Information System (GIS), etc. [1–5]. The advancements in remote sensing imagery provide very high spatial and spectral information for road network extraction that can be used to modernize and preserve the GIS in real-time monitoring of

© The Author(s) 2023
R. Manza et al. (Eds.): ACVAIT 2022, AISR 176, pp. 511–520, 2023.
https://doi.org/10.2991/978-94-6463-196-8_39

numerous applications [1, 2]. Several studies have been done on road network extraction, including automatic road detection from remote sensing images. Most of the methods suggested by researchers for road extraction comprise one or more approaches, such as image classification or segmentation, edge detection and preserving, bridging and cleaning broken roads, and matching road templates [1, 3, 5].

Several studies have testified road network extraction using medium or high-resolution remote sensing images following various approaches. For instance, Ünsalan et al. [6] applied probabilistic and graph theoretical methods to detect road networks. They performed experiments on very high-resolution satellite and aerial image sets. The study [1] proposed the framework consisting of three aspects: generation of rod map using pixel-based method, filtering road networks by guided filter and shape feature method, and road center line extraction by merging multiscale Gabor filter and fast parallel thinning method. They used free remote sensing images and restored the discontinued road network. The work reported by [5] focuses on road detection systems using high-resolution IKONOS multispectral images. The performed approach was based on SVM and multiscale structural feature extraction. Das et al. [3] extracted salient features of roads from high-resolution multispectral satellite images using Probabilistic SVM and dominant singular measures. The research carried out by [4] proposed a new method for road network extraction via two remote sensing images using a DenseUNet model using limited parameters. However, the results obtained in their way are difficult to apply to the other issues in road network extraction. On the other hand, Shao et al. [2] have designed the challenging datasets from the GF-2 satellite for road surface and centerline extraction. In addition, multitask convolutional neural network models have been used to extract two tasks simultaneously.

However, road network and road line extraction remain challenging due to several similar urban structures like buildings, trees, vegetation, and the complexity of urban areas. Furthermore, road network extraction and its complete automation are complicated tasks that have not been addressed accurately over a complex and extensive set of remote sensing images. Moreover, the followed methodology varies from acquisition sensor to sensor and geo-location of the area. In this case, the researcher proposes different methods and sets several experimental parameters to obtain accurate results with sufficient accuracy.

The present study aims to implement a machine learning and image processing approach on high-resolution satellite images for asphalt road extraction in complex urban environments. The set objectives are: (1) Pre-processing of hyperspectral image, (2) Classification of road and non-road objects along with road map generation using SVM algorithm, (3) Extraction of road network from a classified image using morphological operations and granulometry approach, (4) Extraction of road line and smoothing of roads, (5) Results evaluation.

The paper is divided into five sections. This section introduces the background of the study, recent advancements, implemented approach, and set objectives. Section 2 briefs the used satellite data. The methodology is provided in Sect. 3, which includes pre-processing, classification, target detection, and extraction. Results and discussions are presented in Sect. 4 with achieved accuracy. Section 5 concludes the study with future scope.

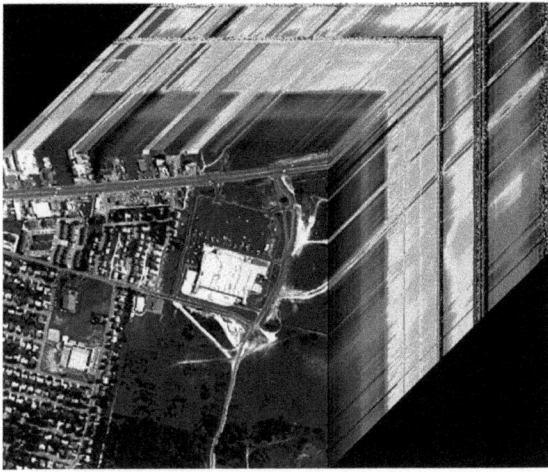

Fig. 1. Urban dataset false-color composite image with bands 47, 26, and 16 for the red, green, and blue wavelength, respectively.

2   Hyperspectral Image Data

In the present study, the hyperspectral digital collection experiment (HYDICE) dataset, Urban of Copperas Cove, Texas [7], has been used to perform the experiments. The HYDICE data consists of complex urban structures, which are used mainly to unmix urban features. There are 307×307 pixels, with a 2×2 m^2 area. This image's 210 spectral wavelength bands range from 400–2500 nm with a high spectral resolution of 10 nm [8]. Figure 1 shows the false composite color of the used image composed of bands 47, 26, and 16 for the red, green, and blue wavelengths.

3   The Methodology

The methodology implemented in the present study is shown in Fig. 2, which includes pre-processing, preparation of primary map using binary SVM classification, road network extraction using morphological operations, road line extraction using median filter, and preparation of the final map.

3.1   Pre-processing

The downloaded raw image has 210 spectral bands with unknown wavelengths and irrelevant values. Thus, firstly we set the wavelengths and FWHM units in nanometres and provided correct wavelength values for each band ranging from 400 nm to 2500 nm. The original HYDICE image has several dense water vapor and severely polluted atmosphere bands. In addition, this image is distorted by heavy Gaussian noise, deadlines, and strips. As a result, the water absorption and polluted atmosphere bands (1–4, 76, 87, 101–111, 136–153, and 198–210) have been eliminated, and the remaining 162 bands were used for further processing [8, 9].

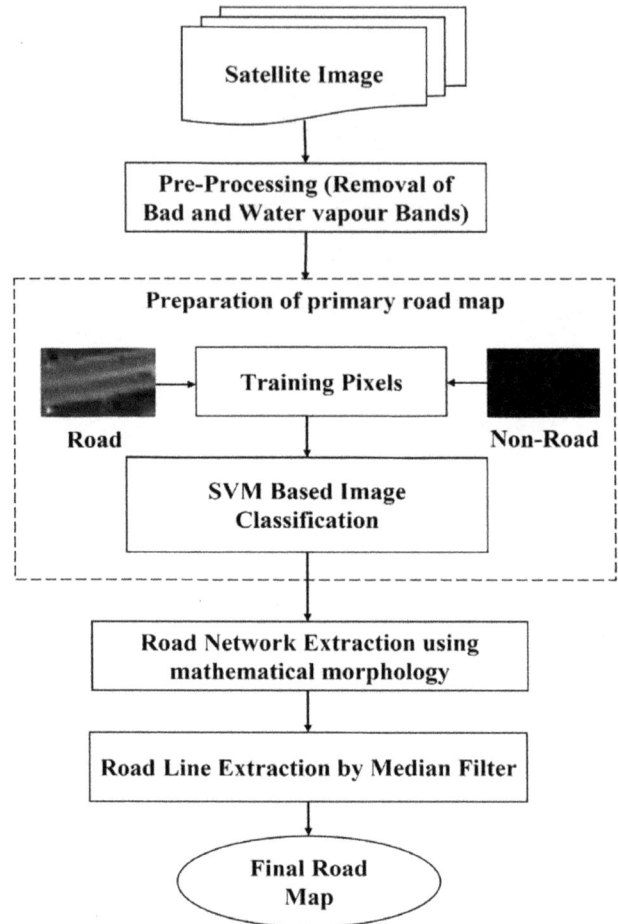

Fig. 2. Workflow of the implemented methodology.

3.2 SVM Based Image Classification

The hyperspectral image has several heterogeneous spectral variations and complex structures like grass, trees, metals, and roofs. These objects generate the asphalt road extraction task more challenging. Consequently, it is essential to identify the road network from high-resolution images using a classification approach. In the present study, we have used a pixel-based machine learning classification approach using SVM. The SVM is a statistical non-parametric method based on a supervised process [10] that requires very few training pixels to produce better accuracy. In addition, SVM works superior in the spectral feature change of the road material and intensity change [11]. The SVM uses the training pixels on the edges of class support vectors. However, the SVM has initially introduced for binary classification. Thus, the binary SVM approach is computed directly for roads and non-roads types in the present study. The SVM method based on Radial Basis Function (RBF) kernel [10, 12] has been used due to its high performance to classify the hyperspectral image into two classes, i.e., road and others using sufficient training pixels with Eq. (1).

$$(x) = \begin{cases} 1 & \text{if } x \text{ is a road class} \\ 0 & \text{otherwise other class} \end{cases} \tag{1}$$

3.3 Road Network Extraction Using Mathematical Morphology

The mathematical morphology of opening and closing operators has been used in this study to extract the existing road network. The road maps (Fig. 3) classified using SVM contain noise and other features due to the spectral similarity of roads and other features such as buildings and asphalt areas. Thus, these similarity issues were resolved using morphological operations [13, 14] to enhance the accuracy of road network extraction. Mathematical morphology filtering is a non-linear method of processing digital images based on shape. Its primary goal is the quantification of geometrical structures. By using the opening operation, no shape noise is created. However, the granulometry approach extracted the shape or size distributions of the image features. Equations (2) and (3) are used to implement the opening and closing operations, respectively.

The opening of set X by structuring element Y, represented by X ∘ Y, is an erosion followed by a dilation given in Eq. 2 [15, 16],

$$X \circ Y = (X \ominus Y) \oplus Y \tag{2}$$

The closing of set X by structuring element Y, represented by X · Y, is a dilation followed by an erosion given in Eq. 3 [15, 16],

$$X \cdot Y = (X \oplus Y) \ominus Y \tag{3}$$

where ⊖ and ⊕ are the erosion and dilation, respectively.

3.4 Road Line Extraction by Median Filter

The extracted road network by morphological operations has several discontinuities due to obstruction affected by trees. Therefore, the median filter has been used to smooth an image while preserving better edge information and removing the outliers without diminishing the sharpness of the view. In addition, it eliminates the speckle noise caused in the previous step [17].

3.5 Performance Evaluation of Methodology

The performance evaluation of implemented methodology has been accessed using three widely accepted metrics such as correctness (A), completeness (B), and quality (C) [1]. Equations (4), (5), and (6) denotes correctness (A), completeness (B), and quality (C) metrics, respectively, and are used to evaluate the methodology.

$$A = \left(\frac{TP}{TP + FP} \right) * 100 \tag{4}$$

$$B = \left(\frac{TP}{TP + FN} \right) * 100 \tag{5}$$

$$C = \left(\frac{TP}{TP + FP + FN} \right) * 100 \tag{6}$$

where TP stands for true positive, FP and FN stand for false positive and negative, respectively.

4   Results and Discussion

The pre-processed hyperspectral image has been used to perform different methodology. The efficiency of the road extraction method has been assessed using ground truth data provided by [8]. It contains an urban hyperspectral image and ground truth of 6 pure classes. The image's 903 and 657 training pixels were used to classify road and other features, respectively. The RBF kernel of the SVM method has been utilized to generate an initial road map. The set parameters of the RBF kernel function were penalty parameters C (100), gamma value (0.1), pyramid level (1), pyramid reclassification threshold (0.90), and classification probability threshold (0.1).

The SVM model has been trained using optimized variables, and the classification map is prepared. The classification map generated by the SVM method is illustrated in Fig. 3, representing classified road networks and non-road classes. The classified road map (Fig. 3) using the SVM method clearly shows other features like roofs and specks of dirt due to their spectral similarities. It is observed from Fig. 3; the map has produced some insignificant outcomes. Furthermore, this road map (Fig. 3) also contains some noises. Thus, the non-road features and shape noises were eliminated using the prior road map's morphological operations and granulometry approach.

Figure 4 shows extracted road network performing morphological operations. It is observed from Fig. 4 that the road network has been successfully extracted, eliminating the noises and spectral similarities. However, Fig. 4 contains building structures along with a road network. The broken road network has been repaired to allocate a precise road network. These discontinued roads have been repaired by median filtering. The 3×3 kernel of median filtering [17] has been used to smooth roads while removing the roadside building structures. The road extracted by median filtering is shown in Fig. 5. It is confirmed by the obtained results (Fig. 5) that the road line has been pulled accurately by the implemented methodology. The extracted road line is evaluated using provided ground truth data. The computed methodologies' performance is evaluated by completeness, correctness, and quality [1] implemented by true positive, false positive, and false negative. The implemented methodology's completeness, correctness, and quality were 79.93, 85.13, and 67.49%, respectively.

The implemented methodology's efficiency is satisfactory compared to recent studies [1, 2].

Fig. 3. Classified image using pixel-based SVM method.

Fig. 4. Image after road network extraction by morphology.

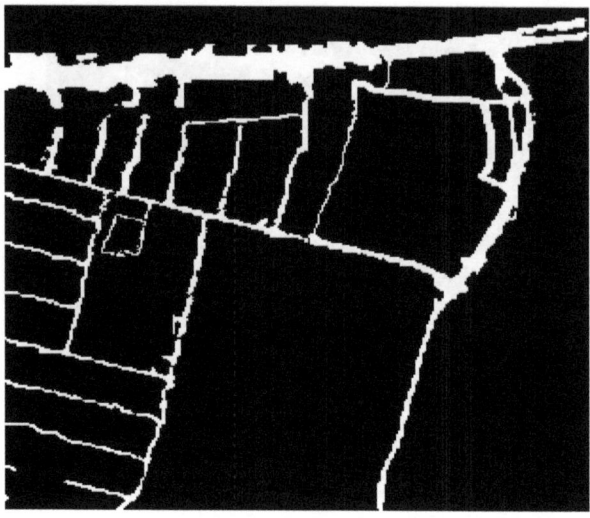

Fig. 5. Image after road line extraction by median filtering.

5 Conclusions

This work uses a composite structure of a machine learning algorithm for pixel-based classification, morphological operations, and median filtering to extract the asphalt road network and road lines from the high-resolution hyperspectral image. This work's novelty consists of using spatial and spectral information for road line extraction using the SVM method and fusion of different information. The experimental results are assessed using three evaluation methods: completeness, correctness, and quality with satisfactory accuracy. The implemented methodology eliminates road line issues like reconstruction of disconnected roads and extraction of the correct and smooth road lines as confirmed by the experimented results. More satellite images will be used in the future, results will be compared with standard literature, and road topology will be analyzed for real-time applications.

Acknowledgments. The authors would like to acknowledge Dr. Le Sun for providing the hyperspectral datasets to carry out this study.

Authors' Contributions.   Amol D. Vibhute: Conceptualization, Data curation, Methodology, Experiments, Writing - original draft, review and editing, **Karbhari V. Kale:** Supervision, Investigation, Technical advice and Scientific validation, **Sandeep V. Gaikwad:** Formal analysis and correction, **Arjun V. Mane:** Formal analysis and correction. All authors read and approved the final manuscript.

References

1. Soni, P. K., Rajpal, N., & Mehta, R. (2021). Road Centerline Extraction from VHR Images Using SVM and Multi-Scale Maximum Response Filter. Journal of the Indian Society of Remote Sensing, 1–14.
2. Shao, Z., Zhou, Z., Huang, X., & Zhang, Y. (2021). Mrenet: Simultaneous extraction of road surface and road centerline in complex urban scenes from very high-resolution images. Remote Sensing, 13(2), 239.
3. Das, S., Mirnalinee, T. T., & Varghese, K. (2011). Use of salient features for the design of a multistage framework to extract roads from high-resolution multispectral satellite images. IEEE transactions on Geoscience and Remote sensing, 49(10), 3906-3931.
4. Xin, J., Zhang, X., Zhang, Z., & Fang, W. (2019). Road extraction of high-resolution remote sensing images derived from DenseUNet. Remote Sensing, 11(21), 2499.
5. Huang, X., & Zhang, L. (2009). Road centreline extraction from high-resolution imagery based on multiscale structural features and support vector machines. International Journal of Remote Sensing, 30(8), 1977-1987.
6. Unsalan, C., & Sirmacek, B. (2012). Road network detection using probabilistic and graph theoretical methods. IEEE Transactions on Geoscience and Remote Sensing, 50(11), 4441-4453.
7. Sun, L., Jeon, B., Zheng, Y., & Wu, Z. (2017). A novel weighted cross total variation method for hyperspectral image mixed denoising. IEEE Access, 5, 27172-27188.
8. http://lesun.weebly.com/hyperspectral-data-set.html, last accessed 2021/06/11.
9. Zhu, F., Wang, Y., Fan, B., Meng, G., & Pan, C. (2014). Effective spectral unmixing via robust representation and learning-based sparsity. arXiv preprint arXiv:1409.0685.
10. Vibhute, A. D., Kale, K. V., Gaikwad, S. V., Dhumal, R. K., Nagne, A. D., Varpe, A. B., Nalawade, D. B., & Mehrotra, S. C. (2020). Classification of complex environments using pixel level fusion of satellite data. Multimedia Tools and Applications, 79, 34737-34769.
11. Shi, W., Miao, Z., & Debayle, J. (2014). An integrated method for urban main-road centerline extraction from optical remotely sensed imagery. IEEE Transactions on Geoscience and Remote Sensing, 52(6), 3359-3372.
12. Vibhute, A. D., Gaikwad, S. V., Dhumal, R. K., Nagne, A. D., Varpe, A. B., Nalawade, D. B., Kale, K. V., & Mehrotra, S. C. (2018, December). Hyperspectral and Multispectral Remote Sensing Data Fusion for Classification of Complex-Mixed Land Features Using SVM. In International Conference on Recent Trends in Image Processing and Pattern Recognition (pp. 345-362). Springer, Singapore.
13. Liu, R., Miao, Q., Huang, B., Song, J., & Debayle, J. (2016). Improved road centerlines extraction in high-resolution remote sensing images using shear transform, directional morphological filtering and enhanced broken lines connection. Journal of Visual Communication and Image Representation, 40, 300-311.
14. Fauvel, M., Benediktsson, J. A., Chanussot, J., & Sveinsson, J. R. (2008). Spectral and spatial classification of hyper-spectral data using SVMs and morphological profiles. IEEE Transactions on Geoscience and Remote Sensing, 46(11), 3804-3814.
15. https://www.cs.auckland.ac.nz/courses/compsci773s1c/lectures/ImageProcessing-html/topic4.htm, last accessed 2021/10/13.
16. https://www.bioss.ac.uk/people/chris/ch5.pdf, last accessed 2021/10/13.
17. https://www.l3harrisgeospatial.com/docs/ConvolutionMorphologyFilters.html, last accessed 2021/07/07.

Analysis of Variable Importance Measurement Techniques for Classification of Road Surfaces

Anupama Jawale[(✉)] and Ganesh Magar

Post Graduate Department of Computer Science, SNDT Women's University, Mumbai 400049,
India
anupama.jawale26@gmail.com

Abstract. The term variable importance refers to the role of an attribute in making accurate predictions. A particular model, when relies majorly on multiple variables, increases variable importance of those variables in positive direction. Variable importance is applied to various classification and regression models using different methods. For example, in regression model, higher value Root Mean Squared Error (RMSE) is the indicator of high importance to that variable, whereas in classification model, higher number of splits associated with a variable determines its importance in the model. In this research study, we have considered a problem of road surface classification depending upon 17 variables associated with vehicle parameters. This is a multiclass classification problem. Different classification and regression models are used, and variable importance of each model is evaluated on the metrics like RMSE, Goodness of fit model. Outcome of this research study shows all models define a common set of 5 to 7 higher importance variable rankings to predict dependant variable.

Keywords: Classification · Decision Trees · Regression · Variable Importance

1 Introduction

Variable importance and its various measures are essential outcome of exploratory data analysis. Variable importance assesses role of a variable in prediction. It helps in improvement of overall performance of predictive model, classification or regression. Variable importance analysis is performed on the dataset. This analysis gives some useful insights about data, for example;

1. To know which variables in the dataset are important for the model – Variables those are not important for model prediction performance can be excluded.
2. For a particular variable, to learn how does it influence model's prediction – Assessing influence of the variable is helpful for examining validity of the model for specific domain
3. To learn if any specific combination of variables or set of observations cause incorrect prediction or is responsible for decrease in accuracy – This may result to generation of new factors or new models.

© The Author(s) 2023
R. Manza et al. (Eds.): ACVAIT 2022, AISR 176, pp. 521–537, 2023.
https://doi.org/10.2991/978-94-6463-196-8_40

4. Comparison of different models based on variable importance – Useful for performance benchmarking of various models

   Methods of variable importance measurement are divided into two groups, viz; model-specific and model-agnostic.

1.1 Model Specific Metrics

1.1.1. Linear Models – Linear models describe y as a continuous variable function of x_i predictor variables. The most common measure for variable importance is t-statistics test. T-statistics is defined as a ratio of the difference of the estimated value of a parameter from its hypothesized value to its standard error. Equation 1 provides formula for computation of t-test.

$$t_{\hat{\beta}} = \frac{\hat{\beta} - \beta_0}{s.e.\left(\hat{\beta}\right)} \tag{1}$$

where $\hat{\beta}$ is estimator for parameter β and s.e. $(\hat{\beta})$ is standanrd error of estimation
   In linear models, absolute value of t-statistics is used for each model parameter.

1.1.2. Random Forests and decision tress - For each tree, prediction accuracy for out of bag data which is left out observation form the bootstrap training set. For regression, Mean Square Error (MSE) is computed on this data for each tree and same is computed by permuting a variable. The difference is normalized with standard error. Equation 2 shows computation of MSE in regression or classification trees

$$\frac{1}{n} \sum_{i=1}^{n} \left(\widehat{Y_i} - Y_i\right)^2 \tag{2}$$

where $\widehat{Y}$ is predicted value, Y is true value label and n is number of observations

1.1.3. Partial Least Squares (PLS) – PLS models use weighted sum of regression coefficients as metric of variable importance. Weights are multipliers used to decrease sum of squares across various PLS variables. To find most important variables can be seen as binary classification problem. According to researcher [1] sensitivity and specificity are considered basic measures of accuracy for a classification task are obtained from confusion matrix.

1.1.4. Recursive Partitioning – Reduction in mean square error is a loss function of recursive partitioning. This function is returns certain value at each partition of tree and then summed up. Along with loss function value, upper competing variables are also added at each split and recorded. Total of these values are used to compute variable importance.

1.1.5. Bagged Trees and Boosted Trees – These models implement same technique as in recursive partitioning method. In bagged trees, total variable importance is computed for all bootstrapped trees, whereas in boosted trees, total variable importance is returned for each boosting iteration.

1.1.6. Multivariate Adaptive Regression Splines (MARS) – MARS models proposed by Friedman, use backward elimination for reduction in cross validation error estimate. This algorithm creates piece wise linear model, sums up GCV error of estimation for each predictor variable. Total loss function given by total reduction of GCV values is used for assignment of variable importance.

1.2 Model – Agnostic Methods

1.2.1. Intuition [2] – The idea behind this method is to calculate change in a models' performance with effect of removal of selected variables. Resampling or permutations are used to remove effect of removal. This is another version of the idea of variable importance measure for random forest [3]. If the important variable is removed, performance of the model will be decreased.

Loss function computation is given by Eq. 3.

$$L^{*j} = L\left(\hat{y}^{*j}, X^{*j}, y\right) \tag{3}$$

Where $\hat{y}^{*j}$ Model Prediction based on X^{*j}, y is the true label value.

In this research study, we have discussed and compared various variable importance measurement methods to generate different metric. Methods understudy are Random-Forest, Partial Least Square, Bagging and Multivariate Adaptive Regression Splines (MARS).

2 Background

The latest study for Variable importance proving it as a useful tool for larger datasets and multi-objective optimization [4], implements differential evolution algorithm on importance ranking basis. Reduction in variable dimensionality has been tried by researchers including various feature selection and feature extraction techniques [5–9]. However, variable importance measurement is the technique that can be applied to dataset before any feature engineering. The advantage is to reduce the pre-processing complexity. As the machine learning accuracy highly dependant upon this stage, for imbalance datasets, accuracy performance becomes a challenging task. Variable importance measurement techniques described in [10], highlights usage of imbalance dataset and shows out performance of proposed method. To achieve high dimensional selection consistency in decision tree algorithm, researchers have presented model selection algorithm named DSTUMP that outperforms in nonlinear additive model settings [10].

There are few research studies carried out on variable importance measurement metrics. Basically model specific variable importance is carried out for various models. A popular model among all is a Random Forest model [11, 12]. The reason behind is only random forests model with conditional inference trees provide unbiased variable importance [13]. In the research study [14], researchers have worked on variable ranking using Mean Decrease in Accuracy (MDA) and Mean Decrease in Gini (MDG) using *random forest*. They have concluded that both the measures are different even if same model is used. They have suggested to use *randomforest* model only once in order to select variable importance based on ranking. Another popular model for classification is Partial Least Square Regression (PLS). To select relevant important predictors, PLS regression coefficients are investigated using Receiver Operating Characteristic (ROC) analysis. The comparison of various variable selection methods for PLS have shown that variable importance methods have outperformed other methods [1].

Variable contribution can be computed at part stages of a model also. For example, research study [15] suggests variable contribution computation at each stage of a multistage process using random forest regression and a new measure of conditional permutation metric. This combination is further used to quantify local contribution of each variable, which is then integrated to calculate global quantification. Even in muti objective optimization problem, variable importance play role in enhancing accuracy of the model [16]. However, it is also observed that if number of ranks in overall observations is small then importance of variable is not predicted accurately. There are many experiments in defining variable importance mechanism. Variable importance are computed on the basis of similarity between margin distributions prior to random permutation and after that [17]. Researchers have noticed more stability in computation of variable importance with this methodology. Based on variable importance calculation, some new feature selection approaches are also presented. Importance combined with prior knowledge parameters to select features, when applied to soft measuring model, these features have shown increase in performance, as stated in [18]. Similarly permutation based framework, a dissimilarities based algorithm is proposed by [10] researchers that computes variable importance using distribution of misclassification errors. In the area of image classification, researchers have proposed method of quantifying of variable importance, employing concept of game theory and metric of Shapely value which is applicable to any type of model [19]. Researchers in research study [14] has presented systematic approach that computes variable importance using optimal number of runs. Shapely method refers to the concept of treating every variable as a player in collaborative game, where the objective of maximum accuracy is followed.

As observed in above theoretical survey, we can conclude that variable importance is not a stable input and is very much model specific. There is a scope of further research in model specific behaviour of variables importance measure. This research study focuses on computation of variable importance for different models like regression trees, random forest, bagged trees and multivariate adaptive regression splines – MARS models on the basis of relative metric of accuracy of these metrics. Next sections describe different algorithmic models and experimental setup of this research study.

3   Methodology

This research study focuses on five different methods of classification/regression and tries to analyse different variable importance ranking for all theses methods. Methods under consideration are explained as below-

i. Recursive partitioning and regression tree model- this model performs successive binary partitions on the basis of various predictor variables. Once the partition is made, prediction on the basis of average of depended variable y in each partition can be made.

This technique is applicable to both classification and regression [20]. For classification, predicted value is based on the formula

$$max(Pr(Y = s|XA_k))$$ (4)

Here, A is a class of road surface conditions (Y = roadSurface), having 3 different values (1 = SmoothCondition, 2 = FullOfHolesCondition, 3 = UnevenCondition)
   Pr is probability value, s is a split or partition of a tree.

ii. Random forest model – The idea behind this model is to grow many classification trees on the basis of probabilistic scheme. Classify the new observation from predictor variable by putting it down each of the tree. The tree votes for that observation thus giving its classification [21].
iii. Bagging – The name bagging stands for bootstrap aggregating. Bagging generated multiple versions of predictors and aggregate them in later phase. These multiple versions are formed by replicating bootstrap of learning sets and using them as new learning sets [22]

   We can formulate bagging as numerical equation, when used for classification. Consider Eq. 5 given below for a predictor $\varphi(x, L)$ predicts the class label j $\epsilon(1, 2, \ldots \ldots .J)$.

$$Q(j|x) = P(\emptyset(x, L) = j)$$ (5)

where P is the probability, $\emptyset$ is the function to predict class label and Q is one of the many replicates of learning set.

iv. Partial Least Squares regression model (PLS) – This model is popular in the situations wherever we have multiple, possibly correlated predictor variables [23]. As shown in the Table 1, we have a dataset of 17 variables, possibly correlated with each other for prediction of road surface condition class. PLS model could be the ideal model to solve this type of problem.
v. Multivariate Adaptive Regression Splines (MARS) model – This approach adopts non linearity of polynomial regression by evaluating cut points that are similar to step functions. Mathematical function of MARS model is shown in below equation

$$\hat{f}(x) = \sum_{i=1}^{k} C_i B_i(x)$$ (6)

   All of the above models have their own set of variable importance ranking. In this research study we have computed variable importance for all the models and compared them. The methodology used in this research study is described in Fig. 1.

i. Data Cleaning and Preparation
   The dataset [24] is collected using various sensors using vehicle running in different road conditions. There are missing values due to hardware failure and/or bad road or other conditions. The very first step includes removal of missing values.

ii. Dataset Exploration

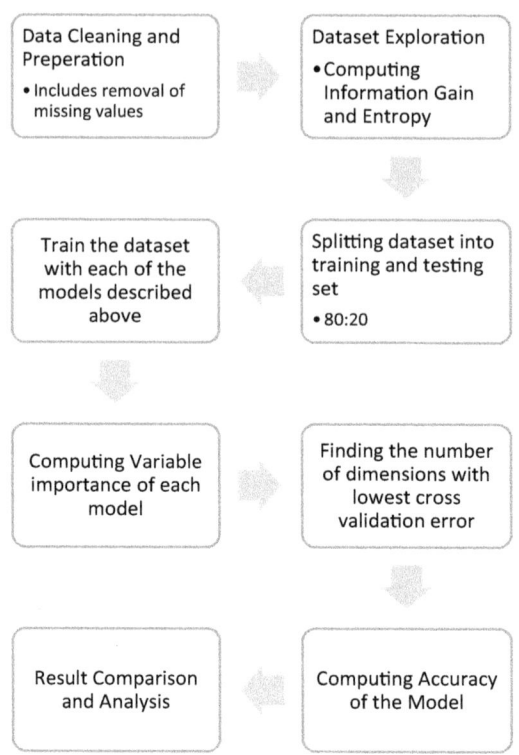

Fig. 1. Flow of Methodology

The dataset used in this research study has dataset with 17 variables. We have computed Entropy and Information gain from the dataset. This step explores intricate nature of dataset. The concept of entropy introduced by Shannon in 1948 is used to quantify the information contained inside the variable. For the datasets used for classification task, entropy is used to determine how balanced the dataset is. In this research study, we have obtained the entropy value 1.547135. The dataset has 3 classes defining road surface condition. Decision Tree algorithms use entropy to calculate information gain at each split to decide variable importance. Table 1 shows information gain for every variable.

iii. Splitting dataset

With 80:20 training – testing proportion, dataset is split for machine learning. Dataset is shuffled to maintain adequate weightage to every class.

iv. Training Dataset with Models

The dataset is trained with five different methods as described earlier in this section.

v. Variable Importance computation

Variable importance calculation for Recursive partitioning is computed using reduction in loss function, like mean squared error. The reduction value is calculated for

Table 1. Information Gain Computation

Variable	Information Gain
IntakeAirTemperature	0.843938644
EngineCoolantTemperature	0.694697585
ManifoldAbsolutePressure	0.369650062
MassAirFlow	0.30801103
VehicleSpeedAverage	0.265671043
EngineRPM	0.194717111
VehicleSpeedInstantaneous	0.165999861
FuelConsumptionAverage	0.149185424
EngineLoad	0.110725003
AltitudeVariation	0.038622989
LongitudinalAcceleration	0.031212503
VehicleSpeedVariation	0.017425414
VerticalAcceleration	0.015265343
VehicleSpeedVariance	0.009659753

each variable and each split and then tabulated to add up. For Random Forest, Gini Importance (mean decrease in impurity) is used to calculate variable importance. Higher value of node probability (calculated as Number of samples to reach that node / Total number of samples) indicates high importance of the feature. In bagged tree models, the variable that appears frequently in splitting function and decrease in squared error is considered for importance. In Partial Least Squares, the variable importance is calculated based on weighted sum of absolute regression coefficients. Weight is computed as reduction of sum of squares across all Partial Least Squares Variables. In MARS models, reduction in generalized cross validation estimate of error is considered to calculate variable importance. The total reduction is used as variable importance.

vi. Finding number of dimensions with lowest cross validation error
Minimum of Root mean squared error of prediction (RMSEP) is used to find out best dimensions. From different estimators, minimum value is taken t consider best predictor variable.

vii. Comparison of Accuracy of various models
Accuracy on test dataset is computed for all models with set of best dimensions

viii. Result Comparison and analysis
Variable Importance obtained from all models understudy are presented in Sect. 5.

Experimental setup and dataset description is covered in the below section.

Table 2. (a): Summary of Dataset

Altitude Variation	Vehicle Speed Instantaneous	Vehicle Speed Average
Min.:-9.900e + 09	Min.:0.000e + 00	Min.:0.000e + 00
1st Qu.:-1.100e + 09	1st Qu.:4.050e + 02	1st Qu.:1.250e + 09
Median:-2.000e + 00	Median:1.890e + 09	Median:2.788e + 09
Mean:-1.405e + 08	Mean:2.617e + 09	Mean:3.452e + 09
3rd Qu.: 6.000e + 08	3rd Qu.:4.140e + 09	3rd Qu.:4.656e + 09
Max.: 9.600e + 09	Max.:9.900e + 09	Max.:9.999e + 09
NA's:63	NA's:9	NA's:415
VehicleSpeedVariance:	**VehicleSpeedVariation**	**LongitudinalAcceleration**
Min.:0.000e + 00	Min.:-9.900e + 09	Min.:-14576
1st Qu.:1.455e + 09	1st Qu.:-9.000e + 08	1st Qu.: 2972
Median:2.510e + 09	Median: 0.000e + 00	Median: 10187
Mean:3.424e + 09	Mean: 3.613e + 07	Mean: 9971
3rd Qu.:5.005e + 09	3rd Qu.: 9.000e + 08	3rd Qu.: 15703
Max.:9.999e + 09	Max.: 9.900e + 09	Max.: 39798
NA's:415	NA's:78	
EngineLoad	**EngineCoolantTemperature**	**ManifoldAbsolutePressure**
Min.:0.000e + 00	Min.: 8.00	Min.: 88.0
1st Qu.:1.098e + 09	1st Qu.:51.00	1st Qu.:103.0
Median:3.412e + 09	Median:79.00	Median:106.0
Mean:4.134e + 09	Mean:65.89	Mean:114.6
3rd Qu.:7.294e + 09	3rd Qu.:79.00	3rd Qu.:124.0
Max.:9.961e + 09	Max.:86.00	Max.:170.0
NA's:5 NA's:5	NA's:5	
EngineRPM	**MassAirFlow**	**IntakeAirTemperature**
Min.: 0	Min.:3.490e + 08	Min.: 7.00
1st Qu.: 1476	1st Qu.:1.699e + 09	1st Qu.:21.00
Median: 7295	Median:2.438e + 09	Median:35.00
Mean: 8392	Mean:2.970e + 09	Mean:32.82
3rd Qu.:14965	3rd Qu.:4.020e + 09	3rd Qu.:41.00
Max.:28025	Max.:9.990e + 09	Max.:65.00
NA's:5	NA's:5	NA's:5
FuelConsumptionAverage	**roadSurface**	**traffic**

(*continued*)

Table 2. (*continued*)

Altitude Variation	Vehicle Speed Instantaneous	Vehicle Speed Average
Min.:1.230e + 06	Min.:1.000	Length:8614
1st Qu.:1.212e + 09	1st Qu.:1.000	Class:character
Median:1.454e + 09	Median:2.000	Mode:character
Mean:2.997e + 09	Mean:1.925	
3rd Qu.:2.035e + 09	3rd Qu.:3.000	
Max.:9.999e + 09	Max.:3.000	
NA's:96		
VerticalAcceleration	**drivingStyle**	
Min.:-27631.0	Length:8614	
1st Qu.: -9796.5	Class:character	
Median: -5357.0	Mode:character	
Mean: -5721.8		
3rd Qu.: -761.2		
Max.: 9999.0		

4 Experimental Setup

In this research study we have taken a dataset of accelerometer sensor from Kaggle [25] for study of safety driving and road condition analysis. There are 17 variables and 8614 objects in the dataset. Table 2 (a) shows summary of the dataset.

We have used VIP package from R Library for variable importance analysis and graphical representation. These computations are model specific. However, all computations can not be compared on the basis of same parameter like accuracy. For example RMSE based importance calculations can not be directly compared with tree models' accuracy score or t-statistics values of linear model [26]. Findings and interpretation of these findings are described in below section.

5 Results and Interpretation

Experimental results for computation of Variable importance are sorted from largest to smallest order and are presented in below Tables. All the models have shown variable sets of important variables, keeping few common. Graphical representation of the same is also shown in Fig. 2.

Fig. 2. (a) – Top 6 feature variables for.Recursive Partitioning and Regression Tree – IntakeAirTemperature, ManifoldAbsolutePressure, EngineCoolantTemperature, VehicleSpeedAverage, EngineRPM, FuelConsumptionAverage

Table 3. (b): Variable importance rankings obtained for different models

a.) Recursive Partitioning and Regression Tree

Variable	Importance value
IntakeAirTemperature	4847.469
ManifoldAbsolutePressure	3293.519
EngineCoolantTemperature	3063.557
VehicleSpeedAverage	1744.039
EngineRPM	1534.012
FuelConsumptionAverage	1012.668
MassAirFlow	537.7126
VehicleSpeedInstantaneous	314.968
VerticalAcceleration	290.1684
AltitudeVariation	102.9991
VehicleSpeedVariance	84.99847
LongitudinalAcceleration	44.21902
VehicleSpeedVariation	0
EngineLoad	0

b) Random Forest Model

Variable	Importance value
FuelConsumptionAverage	47.71845
EngineCoolantTemperature	42.13896
IntakeAirTemperature	38.52865
ManifoldAbsolutePressure	36.4526
VehicleSpeedAverage	35.49989
VehicleSpeedVariance	28.15275
VerticalAcceleration	28.09975
LongitudinalAcceleration	25.96866
VehicleSpeedInstantaneous	24.78347
AltitudeVariation	21.00622
MassAirFlow	19.18455
EngineRPM	17.17326
VehicleSpeedVariation	14.79859
EngineLoad	13.42231

c) Partial Least Square Regression Model

(*continued*)

Table 3. (*continued*)

a.) Recursive Partitioning and Regression Tree

Variable	Importance value
Variable	Importance Value
ManifoldAbsolutePressure	0.0185
EngineCoolantTemperature	0.0133
IntakeAirTemperature	0.00161
EngineRPM	0.00001
LongitudinalAcceleration	0.00001
VerticalAcceleration	0.00001
EngineLoad	0
VehicleSpeedAverage	0
FuelConsumptionAverage	0
AltitudeVariation	0
VehicleSpeedInstantaneous	0
VehicleSpeedVariation	0
MassAirFlow	0
VehicleSpeedVariance	0

d) Bagging Model

Variable	Importance Value
FuelConsumptionAverage	2.361472
IntakeAirTemperature	2.232337
VehicleSpeedAverage	1.571968
ManifoldAbsolutePressure	1.332739
VerticalAcceleration	1.190778
EngineCoolantTemperature	1.178852
MassAirFlow	0.846832
VehicleSpeedVariation	0.534877
VehicleSpeedInstantaneous	0.511967
LongitudinalAcceleration	0.477734
AltitudeVariation	0.3921
EngineRPM	0.391357
VehicleSpeedVariance	0.195058

(*continued*)

Table 3. (*continued*)

a.) Recursive Partitioning and Regression Tree

Variable	Importance value
EngineLoad	0.04444

e) Multivariate Adaptive Regression Splines (MARS) Model

Variable	Importance Value
ManifoldAbsolutePressure	18
EngineCoolantTemperature	18
IntakeAirTemperature	18
FuelConsumptionAverage	16
VehicleSpeedAverage	15
VerticalAcceleration	12
MassAirFlow	7
AltitudeVariation	5
VehicleSpeedInstantaneous	3
VehicleSpeedVariance	0

Table 4. Performance Parameter

	Decision Tree	Random Forest	Partial Least Square Regression	Bagging	Multivariate Adaptive Recursive Spline
Accuracy (All)	93.20%	97.30%	75.80%	22.20%	25.20%
Accuracy (Top 6)	93.83%	98.29%	81.17%	19.28%	24.83%

Fig. 2. (b) – Top 6 feature variables for Random Forest – FuelConsumptionAverage, EngineCoolantTemperature, IntakeAirTemperature, ManifoldAbsolutePressure, VehicleSpeedAverage, VehicleSpeedVariance

Fig. 2. (c) – Top 6 feature variables for Partial Least Square Regression Model – ManifoldAbsolutePressure, EngineCoolantTemperature, IntakeAirTemperature, EngineRPM, LongitudinalAcceleration

Fig. 2. (d) – Top 6 feature variables for Bagging Tree Model – FuelConsumptionAverage, IntakeAirTemperature, VehicleSpeedAverage, ManifoldAbsolutePressure, VerticalAcceleration, EngineCoolantTemperature

Figure 2 (e) – Top 6 feature variables for Multivariate Adaptive Regression Splines (MARS) Model – ManifoldAbsolutePressure, EngineCoolantTemperature, IntakeAirTemperature, FuelConsumptionAverage, VehicleSpeedAverage, VerticalAcceleration.

From Table 1, we can observe there are some variables with low information gain, like EngineLoad, VehicleSpeedVarience etc. We can drop such variables from our machine learning models to save computational resources. Similarly, from Table 2 (b), we can observe that certain variables with very low importance can be omitted from the machine

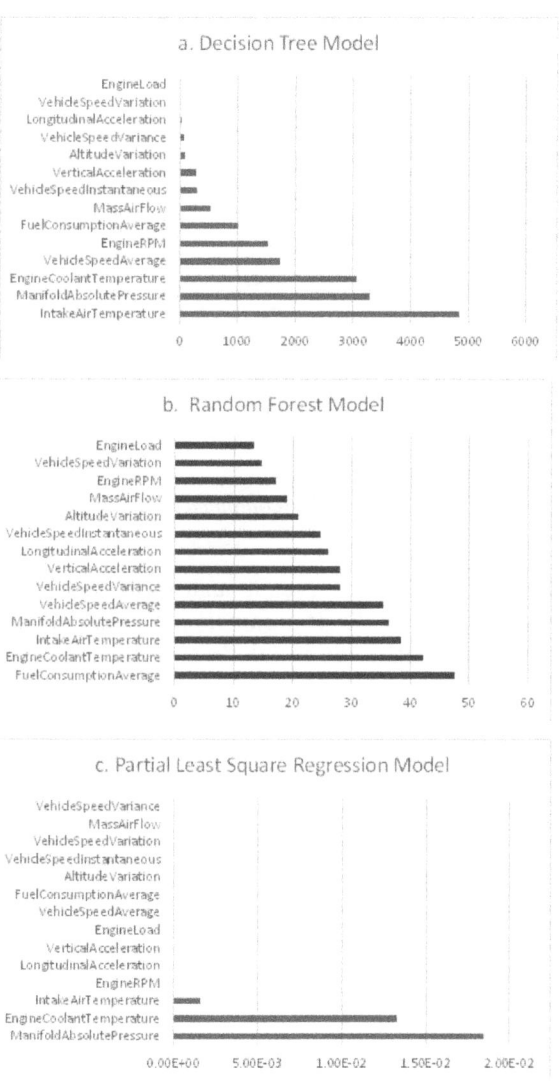

Fig. 2. Variable Importance graphs for different model

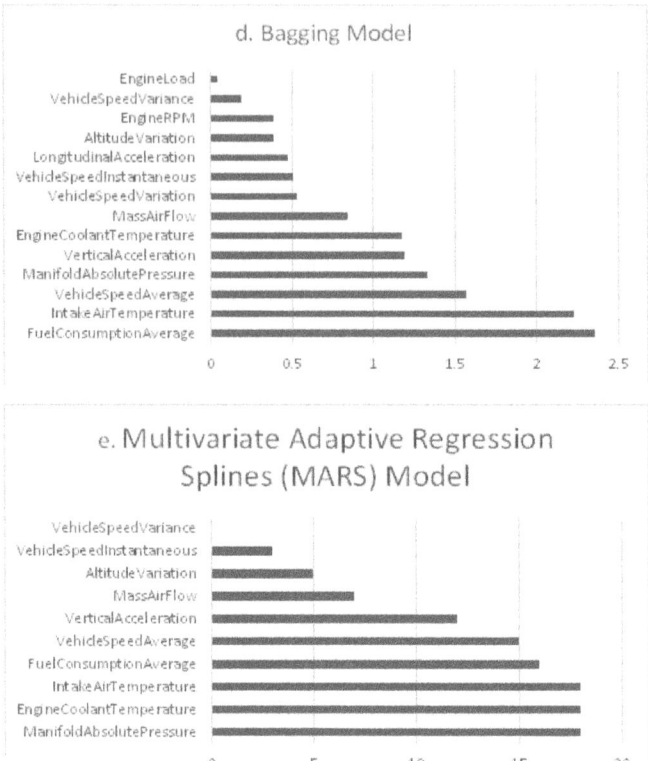

Fig. 2. (*continued*)

learning model. We also observe that, even though variable analysis ranking is model specific, all models have ranked *FuelConsumptionAverage, EngineCoolantTemperature, IntakeAirTemperature, ManifoldAbsolutePressure and VehicleSpeedAverage* as of higher importance. On the basis of these results, we can reform our predictive model formula as Y ~ 6 most important variables, rather than using Y ~ 17 variables. Table 4 shows performance of various models on the basis of above ranked variables.

It is observed that instead of all 17 variables formula in Decision Tree, Random forest, PLS, 6 most important variables formula works better with increased accuracy. However, it is also noticed that the performance of Bagging and Multivariate Adaptive Recursive Spline models are very poor. Bagging has a drawback of sensitivity to variance. A very little addition in number of observations highly impact prediction accuracy. MARS model, when unable to fit the spline function, results in poor accuracy of predictive model.

6   Conclusion

In this research study we have studied a problem of variable importance ranking based on different models. We have studied five different models; decision trees, random forests, PLS, bagging and MARS. Variable importance computation specific to these models can extract a set of 5 to 6 common variables like FuelConsumptionAverage, EngineCoolant-Temperature, IntakeAirTemperature, ManifoldAbsolutePressure and VehicleSpeedAverage and rank them as the highest importance. Accuracy comparison on the basis of these important variables gives us good results for Decision Tree (93.83%), Random Forest (98.29% and PLS models (81.17%) indicates instead of all 17 variables, we can use these ranked variables for computational cost reduction. In future we would like to work on model-independent variable importance ranking methods and quantification of the same.

References

1. G. Palermo, P. Piraino, and H.-D. Zucht, "in selecting variables for each response of a multivariate PLS for omics-type data," Advances and Applications in Bioinformatics and Chemistry, p. 14.
2. A. Fisher, C. Rudin, and F. Dominici, "All Models are Wrong, but Many are Useful: Learning a Variable's Importance by Studying an Entire Class of Prediction Models Simultaneously," p. 81.
3. T. M. Therneau, E. J. Atkinson, and M. Foundation, "An Introduction to Recursive Partitioning Using the RPART Routines," p. 60.
4. S. Liu, Q. Lin, Y. Tian, and K. C. Tan, "A Variable Importance-Based Differential : https://doi.org/10.1109/TCYB.2021.3098186.
5. N. Mlambo, W. K. Cheruiyot, and M. W. Kimwele, "A Survey and Comparative Study of Filter and Wrapper Feature Selection Techniques," p. 11.
6. A. S. Ashour, M. K. A. Nour, K. Polat, Y. Guo, W. Alsaggaf, and A. El-Attar, "A Novel Framework of Two Successive Feature Selection Levels Using Weight-Based Procedure for Voice-Loss Detection in Parkinson's Disease," IEEE Access, vol. 8, pp. 76193–76203, 2020, https://doi.org/10.1109/ACCESS.2020.2989032.
7. J. Cao, G. Lv, C. Chang, and H. Li, "A Feature Selection Based Serial SVM Ensemble Classifier," IEEE Access, p. 1, 2019, https://doi.org/10.1109/ACCESS.2019.2917310.
8. F. Feng, K.-C. Li, J. Shen, Q. Zhou, and X. Yang, "Using Cost-Sensitive Learning and Feature Selection Algorithms to Improve the Performance of Imbalanced Classification," IEEE Access, vol. 8, pp. 69979–69996, 2020, https://doi.org/10.1109/ACCESS.2020.2987364.
9. A. Jawale and G. Magar, "Study of Feature Extraction Techniques for Sensor Data Classification:," International Journal of Information Communication Technologies and Human Development, vol. 13, no. 1, pp. 33–46, 2021, https://doi.org/10.4018/IJICTHD.2021010103.
10. I. Ahrazem Dfuf, J. Forte Perez-Minayo, J. M. Mira Mcwilliams, and C. Gonzalez Fernandez, "Variable Importance Analysis in Imbalanced Datasets: A New Approach," IEEE Access, vol. 8, pp. 127404–127430, 2020. https://doi.org/10.1109/ACCESS.2020.3008416.
11. J. Ehrlinger, "ggRandomForests: Exploring Random Forest Survival," arXiv:1612.08974 [stat], Dec. 2016, Accessed: 21, 2022. [Online]. Available: http://arxiv.org/abs/1612.08974
12. R. Diaz-Uriarte and S. A. de Andres, "Variable selection from random forests: application to gene expression data," arXiv:q-bio/0503025, Jun. 2005, Accessed: 21, 2022. [Online]. Available: http://arxiv.org/abs/q-bio/0503025

13. D. Ollech and K. Webel, "A Random Forest-Based Approach to Identifying the Most Informative Seasonality Tests," SSRN Journal, 2020, https://doi.org/10.2139/ssrn.3721055.

14. A. Behnamian, K. Millard, S. N. Banks, L. White, M. Richardson, and J. Pasher, "A Systematic Approach for Variable Selection With Random Forests: Achieving Stable Variable Importance Values," IEEE Geosci. Remote Sensing Lett., vol. 14, no. 11, pp. 1988–1992, 2017, https://doi.org/10.1109/LGRS.2017.2745049.

15. G. Gazzola et al., "Integrated Variable Importance Assessment in Multi-Stage Processes," IEEE Trans. Semicond. Manufact., vol. 31, no. 3, pp. 343–355, . 2018, https://doi.org/10.1109/TSM.2018.2853586.

16. M. Sagawa et al., "Learning Variable Importance to Guide Recombination on Many-Objective Optimization," in 2017 6th IIAI International Congress on Advanced Applied Informatics (IIAI-AAI), Hamamatsu, 2017, pp. 874–879. https://doi.org/10.1109/IIAI-AAI.2017.158.

17. F. Yang, P. Piao, Y. Lai, and L. Pei, "Margin based permutation variable importance: A stable importance measure for random forest," in 2017 12th International Conference on Intelligent Systems and Knowledge Engineering (ISKE), Nanjing, 2017, pp. 1–8. https://doi.org/10.1109/ISKE.2017.8258842.

18. J. Tang, J. Qiao, and W. Yu, "Selective Ensemble Modeling Approach based on Variable Importance of Projection With its Application 1," in 2018 IEEE International Conference on Information and Automation (ICIA), Wuyishan, China, 2018, pp. 99–104. https://doi.org/10.1109/ICInfA.2018.8812566.

19. S. D. Nandlall and K. Millard, "Quantifying the Relative Importance of Variables and Groups of Variables in Remote Sensing Classifiers Using Shapley Values and Game Theory," IEEE Geosci. Remote Sensing Lett., vol. 17, no. 1, pp. 42–46, 2020, https://doi.org/10.1109/LGRS.2019.2914374.

20. L. Breiman, J. H. Friedman, R. A. Olshen, and C. J. Stone, Classification And Regression Trees, 1st ed. Routledge, 2017. https://doi.org/10.1201/9781315139470.

21. L. Breiman, "Random Forests," Machine Learning, vol. 45, no. 1, pp. 5–32, 2001, https://doi.org/10.1023/A:1010933404324.

22. L. Breiman, "Bagging Predictors," Machine Learning, vol. 24, no. 2, pp. 123–140, 1996, https://doi.org/10.1023/A:1018054314350.

23. B.-H. Mevik and R. Wehrens, "Introduction to the pls Package," p. 24.

24. "Absolutegaming, 'Road_prediction Dataset,' Kaggle, 08-Aug-2021. [Online]. Available: https://www.kaggle.com/code/absolutegaming/road-prediction/data. [Accessed: 02-Jun-2022]." Absolutegaming, "Road_prediction Dataset," Kaggle, 08-Aug-2021. [Online]. Available: https://www.kaggle.com/code/absolutegaming/road-prediction/data. [Accessed: 02-Jun-2022].

25. https://www.kaggle.com/gloseto/traffic-driving-style-road-surface-condition/download.

26. B. Greenwell M. and B. Boehmke C., "Variable Importance Plots—An Introduction to the vip Package," The R Journal, vol. 12, no. 1, p. 343, 2020. https://doi.org/10.32614/RJ-2020-013.

Multifeature Based Satellite Image Segmentation of High Spatial Resolution Remote Sensing Images

Sujata Gaikwad[1](✉) and Vijaya Musande[2]

[1] Department of Computer Science and Engineering, TPCT's COE, Osmanabad, India
sujatagaikwad414@gmail.com
[2] Department of Computer Science and Engineering, JNEC, Aurangabad, India

Abstract. With the continuous development of remote sensing technology, the spatial resolution of the image is getting higher and higher and the characteristic information contained in the image is more abundant. High spatial resolution data provides detailed information about the ground for various applications. Methods of Image segmentation become more and more important in the field of remote sensing image analysis. The structural features and texture information are more obvious. The traditional segmentation method based on a single feature of the image can no longer meet the high requirements. In this work, an efficient algorithm is introduced for evaluating segmentation quality. Multifeature based Satellite image segmentation algorithm is proposed to segment the HSR satellite images into different regions based on the properties of multiple features such as color and texture present in the image. The combination of Multifeature information helps to improve an accuracy of segmentation.

Keywords: High Spatial Resolution · Satellite Image Segmentation · Remote Sensing

1 Introduction

Image Segmentation is very primary and critical task in satellite image processing. Segmentation is a technique of dividing an image into a set of different classes whose characteristics such as intensity, color, texture, etc. are similar. Segmentation is a method that summarizes the pixels based on their similarity in the feature space, but in the image itself (location space). It is a combination of spectrally similar pixels, but at the same time the spatial context is also considered. A segmentation technique thus collects important properties of image understanding, thereby having a great importance for visual interpretation.

High Resolution images have the characteristics of abundant geometric and detail information and have been widely used in many applications. The segmentation of various land cover areas in a satellite image is a complicated task. Generally, this kind of images carry out insignificant illumination feature, and are essential because of various kinds of environmental distributions. Typically, satellite images contain various objects or regions, i.e. vegetation, water bodies, concrete structures, open spaces etc. These areas are not very well differentiated because of the low spatial resolution. Satellite images contain information over a wide range of scales. Therefore, to study satellite images, it is very important to understand how information differentiates over the different scales of imagery. The main goal of the Segmentation consists in the correct mapping of the boundaries of region and the creation of homogeneous segments in order to eliminate the noise. To analyze or classify images, accurate segmentation is usually needed.

Many research scholars have been done a lot of research on the problems of multiple features fusion, multiscale and multitemporal high resolution remote sensing image segmentation.

Image Clustering is done using the segmented regions, instead of the image pixels in "Color image segmentation based on mean shift and normalized cuts" by W. Tao, H. Jin, and Y. Zhang. This work reduces the sensitivity to noise & results in enhanced image segmentation performance. But it is difficult to divide a natural image into important regions to represent different scenes [1].

To perform MultiScale Segmentation for High Resolution Remote Sensing Imagery Based on Statistical Region Merging and Minimum Heterogeneity Rule, the SRMMHR Method was implemented by Haitao et al. There are many other issues that require further investigation, including the improvement of sort function & merge predicate, the study of evaluation index for estimating segmentation results, the determination of parameters for various classes [2].

To perform Per-pixel vs. object-based classification of urban land cover extraction using high spatial resolution imagery, Object –based Methods were implemented by S. Myint et al. In this work, solved the problem of salt and pepper noise [3].

A novel segmentation framework based on bipartite graph partitioning was implemented by Z. Li et al. In this work, author was able to aggregate multi-layer superpixels in a principled & very effective manner but here is scope of future work to the selection of super pixels more systematically & the incorporation of high level cues [4].

A Scale-Synthesis Method was implemented by Lina Yi, Guifeng Zhang, Zhaocong Wu. This method is highly flexible to be adjusted to meet the segmentation requirements of varying image analysis tasks but it is less effective regarding optimal scale selection [5].

For Unsupervised multispectral satellite image segmentation, Region based normalized cut method was implemented by B. Banerjee, S. Varma, and K. M. Buddhiraju. The strategy taken in this method of region based NCuts is usually based on a region adjacency graph, which is actually a single scale graph; therefore the result is heavily dependent on presegmentation process. To make the result more robust, multiple super pixels can be used [6].

Multiscale Object Accuracy Measure and the measure of Bidirectional Consistency Error Method was proposed by Xueliang Zhang et al. in "Toward Evaluating Multiscale Segmentations of High Spatial Resolution Remote Sensing Images". In this work, author presented two discrepancy measures to determine the manner in which geographic objects are delineated by Multiscale segmentation [7].

A conditional random field classification alg. Was proposed by J. Zhao et al. to perform High Resolution Image Classification by integrating spectral spatial location cues by conditional random fields. Here is future scope of presenting more potentially useful details & the use of spatial location cues in other Remote Sensing techniques [8].

Fine Registration Approach was proposed by Youkyung Han, Francesca Bovolo, Lorenzo Bruzzone. The goal of this approach is to estimate& correct the residual local misalignment which affects Multitemporal VHR images after standard registration & improves registration accuracy. But it become less effective when scenes show very tall elements captured with large off nadir angles. Here is scope to design an approach to mitigate the impact of heterogeneous segments& to improve the robustness of the proposed method to use with multi sensor images [9].

To perform Multi-Scale Segmentation of High Resolution Remote Sensing Images by integrating Multiple Features, The Normalized Cuts Method was proposed by Y. Di et al. The method combined with a variety of features for image segmentation but is not yet implemented fully automatic segmentation feature fusion. Future scope is to implement a method to obtain high segmentation accuracy, fast speed of operation & automatic segmentation [10].

Hence the work must be followed by the region based methods. Hence, the study of image segmentation algorithm is gaining more attention under such circumstances.

2   Proposed Technique

This section presents the proposed Multifeature based satellite image segmentation. Multiple features considered in this work are color and texture. The definition of texture is the "spatial repetition of the same pattern in different directions of space ".

2.1   Multifeature Based Satellite Image Segmentation

Image segmentation methods including Multifeature such as color and texture together allow an image to be partitioned while being closer to human perception than those using color or texture separately. In general, the combination& of Multifeature such as color and texture information helps to improve the results of segmentation as compared to using one of the two sources alone.

The Texture superpixels technique improves the superpixels decomposition approach and set locally the spatial regularity of superpixels, in order to automatically adapt to the image content. Finally, we introduce a new pixel to superpixels texture homogeneity in order to measure group pixels in terms of texture. The implementation of the proposed algorithm starts with finding the color difference between the adjacent pixel values (x_a, y_a) and (x_i, y_i) is given by Eq. 2.

$$d_{RGB} = \sqrt{(R_a - R_i)^2 + (G_a - G_i)^2 + (B_a - B_i)^2} \tag{1}$$

The distance between the pixels is given by Eq. 5

$$d_{xy} = \sqrt{(x_a - x_i)^2 + (y_a - y_i)^2} \tag{2}$$

The energy and contrast features are calculated as below:
Energy formula is presented in Eqs. 3, 4 and 5 for the color planes R, G, B respectively.

$$E\frac{R}{n} = \sum_{i,j=0}^{N-1}(R_{ij})^2 \tag{3}$$

$$E\frac{G}{n} = \sum_{i,j=0}^{N-1}(G_{ij})^2 \tag{4}$$

$$E\frac{B}{n} = \sum_{i,j=0}^{N-1}(B_{ij})^2 \tag{5}$$

The combined energy equation is presented in Eq. 6.

$$E_n = E_n^R + E_n^G + E_n^B \tag{6}$$

The contrast for the R, G and B planes is presented in Eqs. 7, 8 and 9.

$$Contrast_R = \sum_{i,j=0}^{N-1}R_{ij}(i-j)^2 \tag{7}$$

$$Contrast_G = \sum_{i,j=0}^{N-1}G_{ij}(i-j)^2 \tag{8}$$

$$Contrast_B = \sum_{i,j=0}^{N-1}B_{ij}(i-j)^2 \tag{9}$$

The combined contrast equation is presented in Eq. 10.

$$contrast = Contrast_R + Contrast_G + Contrast_B \tag{10}$$

The parameter D_s, known as super pixel distance is defined as

$$D_s = d_{RGB} + E_n + Contrast + m/s\, d_{xy} \tag{11}$$

S is the distance between the centres and is given by $\sqrt{\frac{N}{a}}$ the number of image pixels is denoted by N and number of superpixels is denoted by a. 'm' is the parameter influencing the spatial disstance.

2.2 Algorithm

Step 1: Determine the cluster centre C_a, For every pixel in the image that consists of the RGB pixel values and the position in the image.

$$C_a = [R_a, G_a, B_a, x_a, y_a]^T \tag{12}$$

Step 2: Define a neighborhood of size 2S x 2S, for each centre of the cluster.
Step3: Find out the similar pixels in the neighborhood and update the cluster centre until stability is gain by grouping similar pixels in color and texture.
Step 4: Now with all the clusters, create a dataset D.

Step 5: For every unvisited cluster P, if the numbers of pixels in the cluster are less than minimum threshold, then merge the cluster with a neighboring cluster with the closest color and texture matching pair.

Step 6: For each unvisited cluster P, if the numbers of pixels in the cluster are more than minimum threshold, then proceed to the next cluster.

The proposed algorithm is implemented in MATLAB R2018a on real-time Google earth images.

3   Results

3.1   Experimental Analysis on Real-Time High Spatial Resolution Google Earth Satellite Image

The real-time image is collected using Google earth pro software. The resolution of the image is 1920 x 1080. The image is captured from the following coordinates:

19°53′55.65″N, 75°18′52.29″E elev 1906ft eye alt 933ft.

The image is of Dr. BAMU Campus in Aurangabad, India.

The proposed method performs better as compared to the existing techniques. This is proved by the comparison Table 1 provided as.

The proposed technique produced better segmentation result as compared to existing segmentation results. The Segmentation Quality of proposed technique is improved.

Fig. 1. The real-time high spatial resolution google earth input image 1.

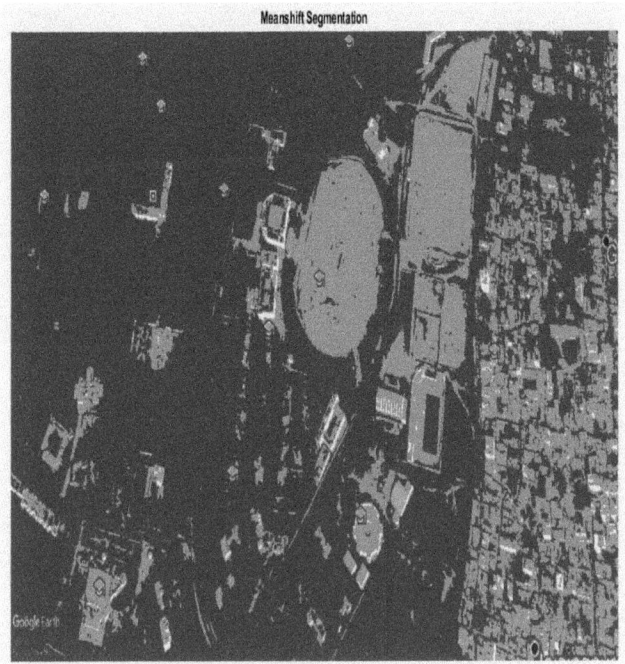

Fig. 2. Mean-Shift segmentation result of input image 1

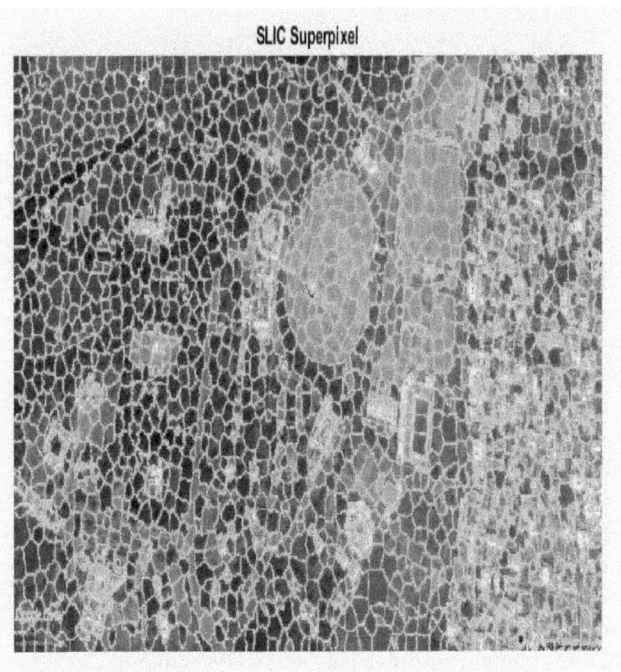

Fig. 3. SLIC-Superpixel segmentation result of input image.

Fig. 4. Multifeature based satellite image segmentation result of input image

Table 1. Comparison Results

Algorithm	Mean Value	Average Deviation from mean value	Entropy	Elapsed time
Mean Shift Segmentation	127.890717	296715.515404	0.288686	470.35
Superpixel Segmentation	112.293302	3223.247003	0.006162	260.172
Proposed Multi feature Based Segmentation Technique (Color and Texture Based)	110.985766	3987.014261	0.002316	1240.073

4 Conclusion

Accurate segmentation of High Spatial Resolution Remote Sensing Imagery identify various patterns, objects, damage assessment due to environmental disasters. This is done by a technique using combination of multifeature information i.e. color and texture. When images are analysed, analysis requires correct segmentation. Color and Texture features information together improves accuracy of segmentation.

References

1. W. Tao, H. Jin and Y. Zhang, Color image segmentation based on mean shift and normalized cuts, IEEE Trans. Syst., Man, Cybern. B, Cybern, 37(5), pp. 1382–1389, 2007.
2. Li Haitao, Gu Haiyan, Han Yanshun, and Yang Jinghui, An efficient MultiScale Segmentation for High Resolution Remote Sensing Imagery Based on Statistical Region Merging and Minimum Heterogeneity Rule, IEEE Journal of Selected Topics in Applied Earth Observations & Remote Sensing, 2(2), 2009.
3. S. Myint, P. Gober, A. Brazel, S. Grossman-Clarke, and Q. Weng, Perpixel vs. object-based classification of urban land cover extraction using high spatial resolution imagery. Remote Sens. Environ., 115 (5), pp.1145–1161, 2011.
4. Z. Li, X. Wu, M., and S.F. Chang, Segmentation using superpixels: A bipartite graph patitioning approach. pp. 789–796, 2012.
5. Yi Lina, Guifeng, Zhang, and Wu. Zhaocong, A Scale-Synthesis Method for High Spatial Resolution Remote Sensing Image Segmentation, IEEE Transactions on Geoscience and Remote Sensing, 50(10), 2012.
6. B. Banerjee, S. Varma, and K.M. Buddhiraju, Unsupervised Multispectral satellite image segmentation combining modified mean-shift and a new minimum spanning tree based clustering technique, IEEE J. Sel. Topics Appl. Earth Observ. Remote Sens., 7(3), pp. 888–894, 2014.
7. G Xueliang Z., X. Pengfeng, F. Xuezhi, Li. Feng, and Ye Nan, Toward Evaluating Multiscale Segmentations of High Spatial Resolution Remote Sensing Images, IEEE Transactions on Geoscience and Remote Sensing, 53(7), 2015.
8. J. Zhao, Y. Zhong, H. Shu, and L. Zhang, High-resolution image classification integrating spectral-spatial-location cues by conditional random fields, IEEE Trans. Image Process., 25(9), pp. 4033-4045, 2016
9. H. Youkyung, B. Francesca, and B. Lorenzo, Segmentation Based Fine Registration of Very High Resolution Multitemporal Images, IEEE Transactions on Geosciences & Remote Sensing, 55 (5), 2017.
10. Y. Di., G. Jiang, L.Yan, H. Liu, and S. Zheng, Multi-Scale Segmentation of High Resolution Remote Sensing Images by integrating Multiple Features., The International Archives of the Photogrammetry, Remote Sensing and spatial information Sciences, XLII-1(W1), 2017.

Deep Learning Based Classification of Microscopic Fungi for Agriculture Application

Mallikarjun Hangarge[✉]

Department of Computer Science, Karnatak Arts, Science and Commerce College, Bidar, Karnataka, India
mhangarge2009@gmail.com

Abstract. Plant diseases are one of the significant reasons that lead to the destruction of crops and plants. These diseases are caused by bacteria, virus, algae, fungi, etc. Among these diseases, fungi causes the major diseases in plants and crops. This article aims to collect the novel dataset of fungi infected leaves of two different fruit plants. To take pictures of the fungus at a microscopic scale, these leaves are carefully grown and examined under a microscope with a 40X objective. By utilizing the machine learning classifiers and deep learning architectures We develop and examine the models on the collected novel dataset. Using 5 fold cross validation experimental results showed the high recognition accuracy of 97.52% for the ResNet-50 model.

Keywords: Fungi · Leaf diseases · Microscopic images · Machine learning · Deep learning · ResNet-50

1 Introduction

Plant diseases are one of the most significant reasons that lead to the destruction of crops and plant. These diseases may be caused by environmental condition, deficiency of nutrient, due to bacteria, virus or fungi. Among the many diseases, fungi cause the major diseases to plants and crops. India being an agriculture country and almost more than half percent of our agriculture provides the majority of the revenue to the inhabitants; it is the need of an hour to identify these diseases at early stage.

The diseases may occur at any part or through the entire crop or plant. Different fungi or bacteria cause different types of the diseases to the plant. Traditional method of identifying these diseases is through knowledge of the domain expert or with the help of farmers. Identifying of these diseases sometimes may lead to the wrong assumption of the diseases and which may lead to usage of wrong fertilizers or chemicals to the plant. The manual method of identifying diseases is tiresome, expensive and time consuming. Hence the need arise to work on automated identification of fungi affected diseases of plants.

Classifying the diseases through visible symptoms of the diseases is done by most of the researchers. Authors in [1–10] have worked on leaf identification of diseases

R. Manza et al. (Eds.): ACVAIT 2022, AISR 176, pp. 546–560, 2023.
https://doi.org/10.2991/978-94-6463-196-8_42

using machine learning (ML) and deep learning (DL) models. [11–15] have worked on feature extraction of the leaf diseases and these features are used to classify the diseases according to the respective categories using machine learning classifiers. The authors in [16] have worked on new method of classifying the leaf diseases by extracting the features from DL model and classifying these images using ML models. This reduces the time complexity of the models.

Microscopic level of fungi classification is done by authors in [17–21]. In such case, the fungi are acquired by tainted food, soil, human body, airborne fungus, etc. Our goal is to recognise fungus at the molecular level by developing a novel fungus dataset of spores and hyphae of fungi. We are the first of our type to focus on plant leaf diseases caused by fungus of fruit plants.

We have considered two fungi infected fruit plants leaves. Anthracanose of mango leaf is caused by fungi Colletotrichum Gloeosporioides (CG) and Leaf spot of Custard apple is caused by fungi Cylindrocladium Colhounii (CC). The dataset consist of 602 images of which are divided into four classes which include spores of Colletotrichum gloeosporioides, hypahe of Colletotrichum gloeosporioides, spores of Cylindrocladium colhounii and hyphae of Cylindrocladium colhounii.

The remainder of the article is divided into two sections: Sect. 2 describes the literature review, preparation of dataset is given in Sect. 3, Sect. 4 gives the overview of dataset, The anticipated technique is described in Sect. 5 utilizing several models and classifiers., experimental results are summed up in Sect. 6, Sect. 7 evaluates the results, Sect. 8 sums up the conclusions and Sect. 9 gives the future scope of our work.

2 Literature Survey

Machine learning techniques are used in a variety of fields, but feature engineering is still the most difficult challenge to solve. With the advent of deep neural networks, promising outcomes for plant pathology are now available without the need for time-consuming feature engineering. Deep neural networks improve visual recognition accuracy considerably. This section describes the many deep learning techniques used by researchers to identify plant diseases. S. Gayathri et al. [22] proposed a CNN based LeNet architecture for leaf diseases classification of Tea leaves, as India is the highest consumer of tea. The dataset of tea leaves consists of three different categories of diseased leaves. And using their proposed approach they got a good result of 90.23%. Maeda-Gutiérrez et al. [23] classified the leaves of tomato plant which is obtained from the Plant village dataset. Their work focused on the fine tuning of the CNN models such as AlexNet, GoogleNet, ResNet 18, Inception V3 and ResNet 50 models. The results from the GoogleNet model obtained are significant with AUC of 99.12%.

Rangarajan et al. [24] studied the Plant village dataset of tomato leaves which has six different class labels. They used the deep learning models of AlexNet and VGG 16 network to train on different hyper parameters. They analyzed the different hyper parameters of the models like weight, bias of learning rate and mini batch size of the models. Mosin Hasan et al. [25] implemented drone based precision farming using CNN to classify the tomato leaves. They used their own dataset and utilized the inception model of Google for training the model. They obtained good accuracy of 99% and the model performed well. Md. Rasel Howl al. [26] studied the guava plant from Bangladesh and created their own dataset of Guava with four different classes. They developed their own customized Deep-CNN. The experimental results show an average accuracy of 98.74% on the test set. R. Sujatha et al. [27] compared the ML and DL models using the leaves of citrus dataset. They used different techniques and analyzed the result on the dataset. The results of trials show that DL models performed well when compared to the ML techniques.

Table 1. Survey of Microscopic Image Identification and Classification

Sl. No.	Name	Utilized database	Utilized technique	Category's	Obtained accuracy
1	Muhammad Waseem Tahir et al, [17]	Private dataset of fungal spores	CNN's unique architectural style	5 different classes of fungi	94.8%
2	Anuruk Prommakhot etal, [18]	Private dataset of fungal spores	CNN's unique architectural style	2 different classes of fungi	98.03%
3	Lin Liu et al, [19]	Private dataset of fungal spores	ANN architecture	One class	Model gives good result
4	Bartosz Zieliński et al, [20]	Digital Images of Fungus Species database	Deep Neural Network (DNN) and Bag of words	10 different classes of fungi	DNN gave good recognition accuracy
5	Robert Kerwin C. Billones et al, [21]	Own aspergillus dataset	Customized CNN architecture	9 different classes of fungi	94.31%

Table 2. Overview of the dataset

Sl. No.	Class labels	Training Images	Testing Images	Total images
1	Spores of Cylindrocladium colhounii (CC)	122	30	152
2	Spores of Colletotrichum gloeosporioides (CG)	180	46	226
3	Hyphae of Cylindrocladium colhounii (CC)	104	26	130
4	Hyphae of Colletotrichum gloeosporioides (CG)	74	20	94
Total Images				**602**

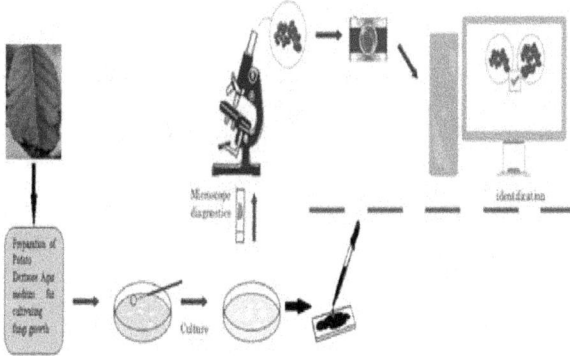

Fig. 1. Flowchart for the proposed method of identifying the spores and hyphae of fungi.

Table 1 summarizes the identification of microscopic images of fungus that are found on human bodies, polluted soil, or food sources. Fungi identification of plant leaf diseases at microscopic level is not addressed.

For the purpose of categorizing the fungus, authors developed a custom designed convolutional neural network. We experiment on transfer learning of DL models such as Alex-Net, SqueezeNet and ResNet50 model. We also evaluate the dataset using the hybrid approach in [16] such as CNN-KNN, CNN-LDA and CNN-SVM. Fivefold cross validation is utilized for all the models to get the optimized results.

3   Preparation of Novel Dataset

In this section, we describe the method utilized to obtain the microscopic images of fungi from plant leaf. The Fig. 1 shows the proposed method for identifying and classifying the spores and hyphae of fungi.

The infected leaf of mango/custard apple is taken and washed thoroughly with distilled water and kept aside. A Potato Dextrose Agar (PDA) medium is prepared and kept in Autoclave for 15min at 121' C. After Autoclave the mixtures is dispensed from the flask of around 10ml- 15ml in Petri dish and incubate the infected leaf in the PDA medium. Allow the fungus on the medium to grow for two days. Using the sterile needle transfer the mycelia mat from the Petri dish to a sterile slide. Observe this slide under 40X objective lens. These are captured using 12Mega pixel camera and this dataset consists of 602 images in total.

4   Overview of Dataset

We have developed a novel fungus database. The database is collected from Dept. of Microbiology, Gulbarga University, Kalaburagi, Karnataka, India. The database is developed from anthracnose disease of mango plant and leaf spot disease of custard apple plant. These are again divided into four different classes, which is on the basis of number of days passed on observation. Fungus spores are observed after 2 days of incubating

Fig. 2. Anthracanose of mango

Fig. 3. Leaf spot of Custard apple

with the infected leaf on the PDA medium. And after 5 days we see the fungal hyphae grown on the medium. This observation is classified into four classes, which are spores of Colletotrichum gloeosporioides, hyphae of Colletotrichum gloeosporioides, spores of Cylindrocladium colhounii and hyphae of Cylindrocladium colhounii. These total counts to 602 images. The novel dataset is not publicly available yet. Below Table 3 shows the summary of the database, Fig. 2 and 3 shows the leaf diseases of mango and custard apple plant caused by fungi. Figure 4, 5, 6 and 7 shows the microscopic images of these four respective classes.

5   Methods/Models Used

Image processing techniques often do not deliver state of the art results in the field of biological sciences like the fungal disease [17]. To detect the microscopic fungi, we employ the Convolution Neural Network (CNN) architecture, which provides the state of the art results. And to establish the novelty and credibility of our novel dataset, we employ different Machine Learning (ML) techniques, Deep Learning (DL) models. The hybrid approach of machine learning and deep learning technique described in [16] is also implemented to evaluate the performance of our novel dataset.

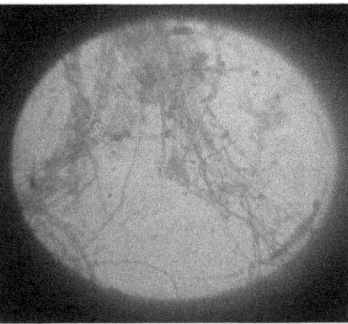

Fig. 4. Hyphae of Cylindrocladium colhounii

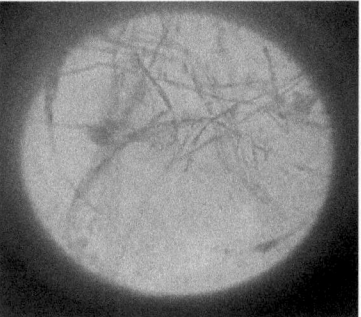

Fig. 5. Hyphae of Colletotrichum gloeosporioides

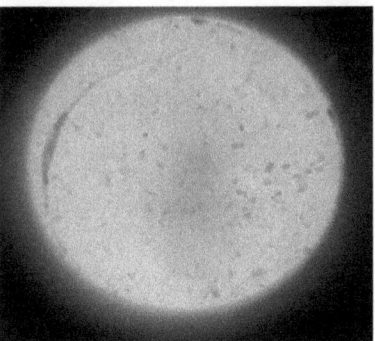

Fig. 6. Spores of Cylindrocladium colhounii

The authors in [17–21] have worked on own customized CNN architectures. We aim to work on transfer learning of Deep learning models such as AlexNet [28], SqueezeNet [29] and ResNet50 [30] model. These models are already trained on thousands of images of different categories. The architectures used are shown in Fig. 8 , 9 and 10 respectively.

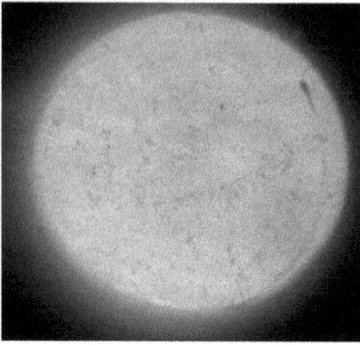

Fig. 7. Spores of Colletotrichum gloeosporioides

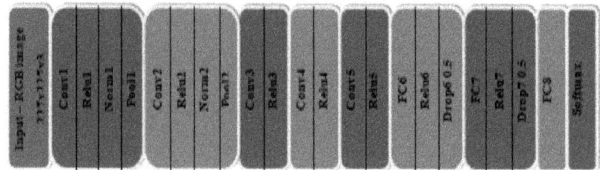

Fig. 8. Overview of AlexNet architectur

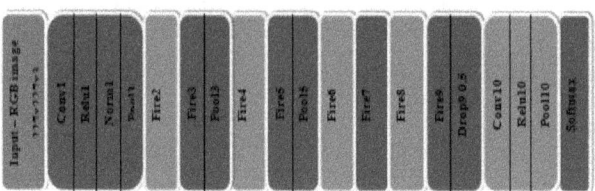

Fig. 9. Overview of SqueezeNet architecture

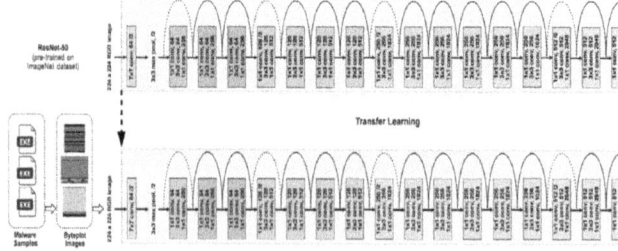

Fig. 10. Overview of ResNet50 architecture. Reprinted from "Malicious software classification using transfer learning of resnet-50 deep neural network" by Rezende, Edmar, Guilherme Ruppert, Tiago Carvalho, Fabio Ramos, and Paulo De Geus, 2017, 16th IEEE International Conference on Machine Learning and Applications (ICMLA).

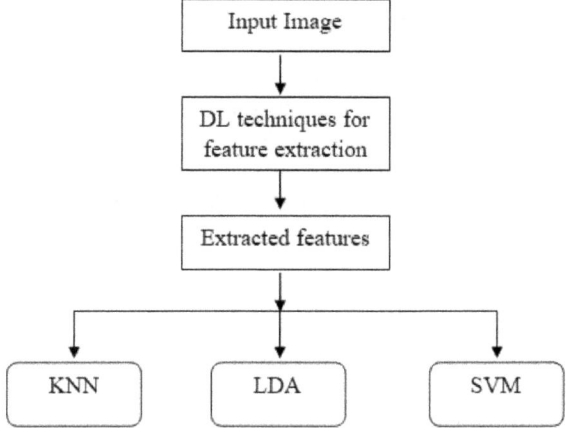

Fig. 11. Hybrid approach using ML and DL technique.

Table 3. Domain Details

Environment	Parameters
OS	Windows 10 Pro
CPU	Intel® Core™ i7–2620 with 2.70GHz
RAM	12GB
Hard Disk	1 TB

In the hybrid approach, the features are collected from Customized CNN architecture which has 5 layers. The collected features are stored and used for classification using machine learning classifiers. We use three machine learning classifiers which are K Nearest Neighbor (KNN), Linear Discriminant Analysis (LDA) and Support Vector Machine (SVM). The below Fig. 11 shows the flow chart for hybrid approach.

The deep learning models are trained on the same execution environment and same hyper-parameters, to compare the models effectively. The Table 3 shows the Domain Details utilized (Table 4).

6   Results of the Experiment

In this part, we assess the hybrid approach's experimental findings and the Deep learning models. For training and testing purpose, the database is divided as 80:20 split. Where 80% of data is given for training and the rest is used for validation purpose. The learning rate of the models is kept at 0.0001. 5 fold cross validation is used to optimize the accuracy and all the models are trained for 25 epochs. Below Table 5, 6, 7, 8 and 9 shows the identification accuracy of class-level recognition for Alex-Net, Squeeze-Net, ResNet50, CNN- KNN, CNN- LDA and CNN- SVM.

Confusion matrix for all the models is given below from Table 10, 11, 12, 13, 14 and 15.

Figure 12 shows the comparative analysis of models.

The derived performance metrics for each model are displayed in Table 16.

From Table 16 it is evident that ResNet50 model gave good recognition accuracy of 97.52% compared to the other models on the collected novel fungus dataset.

Table 4. Identification of categories using Alex-Net

Sl. No.	Species	Accuracy
1	Spore_CG	100%
2	Spore_CC	100%
3	Hyphae_CG	89.5%
4	Hyphae_CC	85.2%

Table 5. Identification of categories using Squeeze-Net

Sl. No.	Species	Accuracy
1	Spore_CG	95.5%
2	Spore_CC	71.4%
3	Hyphae_CG	89.5%
4	Hyphae_CC	90%

Table 6. Identification of categories using ResNet50

Sl. No.	Species	Accuracy
1	Spore_CG	100%
2	Spore_CC	100%
3	Hyphae_CG	94.5%
4	Hyphae_CC	91.2%

Table 7. Identification of categories using CNN- KNN

Sl. No.	Species	Accuracy
1	Spore_CG	82.2%
2	Spore_CC	80%
3	Hyphae_CG	89.5%
4	Hyphae_CC	81.5%

Table 8. Identification of categories using CNN- LDA

Sl. No.	Species	Accuracy
1	Spore_CG	97.8%
2	Spore_CC	93.3%
3	Hyphae_CG	84.2%
4	Hyphae_CC	92.6%

Table 9. Identification of categories using CNN- SVM

Sl. No.	Species	Accuracy
1	Spore_CG	97.8%
2	Spore_CC	93.3%
3	Hyphae_CG	94.7%
4	Hyphae_CC	77.8%

Table 10. Confusion Matrix obtained using AlexNet

	Spore_CG	Spore_CC	Hyphae_CG	Hyphae_CC
Spore_CG	**45**	0	0	0
Spore_CC	0	**30**	0	0
Hyphae_CG	0	1	**17**	1
Hyphae_CC	1	0	3	**23**
Accuracy in %				**95.3%**

Table 11. Confusion Matrix obtained using SqueezeNet

	Spore_CG	Spore_CC	Hyphae_CG	Hyphae_CC
Spore_CG	**64**	2	0	1
Spore_CC	1	**42**	0	1
Hyphae_CG	0	0	**20**	8
Hyphae_CC	2	0	2	**36**
Accuracy in %				**90%**

Table 12. Confusion Matrix obtained using ResNet50

	Spore_CG	Spore_CC	Hyphae_CG	Hyphae_CC
Spore_CG	**64**	0	0	0
Spore_CC	0	**42**	0	0
Hyphae_CG	0	1	**26**	1
Hyphae_CC	0	0	1	**38**
Accuracy in %				**97.5%**

Table 13. Confusion Matrix obtained using CNN- KNN

	Spore_CG	Spore_CC	Hyphae_CG	Hyphae_CC
Spore_CG	**37**	7	1	0
Spore_CC	6	**24**	0	0
Hyphae_CG	1	1	**17**	0
Hyphae_CC	1	0	4	**22**
Accuracy in %				**82.6%**

Table 14. Confusion Matrix obtained using CNN- LDA

	Spore_CG	Spore_CC	Hyphae_CG	Hyphae_CC
Spore_CG	**44**	1	0	0
Spore_CC	2	**28**	0	0
Hyphae_CG	1	1	**16**	1
Hyphae_CC	2	0	0	**25**
Accuracy in %				**93.4%**

Table 15. Confusion Matrix obtained using CNN- SVM

	Spore_CG	Spore_CC	Hyphae_CG	Hyphae_CC
Spore_CG	**44**	0	0	1
Spore_CC	2	**28**	0	0
Hyphae_CG	0	0	**18**	1
Hyphae_CC	1	2	3	**21**
Accuracy in %				**91.7%**

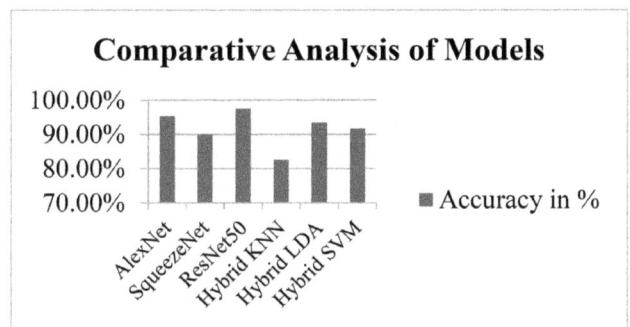

Fig. 12. Comparative Analysis of models

Table 16. Performance metrics utilizing transfer learning: precision, recall, and F1 score.

Using Transfer Learning				
	Precision	**Recall**	**F1score**	**Accuracy**
Alex-Net	0.9366	0.9386	0.9376	95.3%
Squeeze-Net	0.8757	0.8905	0.8832	90%
ResNet50	**0.9634**	**0.9278**	**0.9538**	**97.52%**
Using Feature Extraction				
CNN- KNN	0.8329	0.8362	0.8346	82.6%
CNN- LDA	0.9198	0.9482	0.9338	93.4%
CNN- SVM	0.9091	0.9229	0.9159	91.7%

7 Conclusions

In this study, we created a brand new dataset of fungi. To develop the fungus, we carefully nurture the PDA medium. Under a 40X high power objective lens microscope, the developing fungus are examined. As there is no standard available dataset for fungi which are obtained from leaf, this is one of first of its kind work. We have used different algorithms and techniques to establish the comparison between different ML, DL and the hybrid approach of ML & DL techniques. The novel fungus dataset is evaluated using 5 fold cross validation. According to Table 18's performance metrics, the ResNet50 model did well, with an average classification result of 97.52%.

8   Future Scope

A lot of research on classification of microscopic fungi of plant diseases needs to be done. It includes the microscopic examination of steam, bark, fruit, flower of crops and plants. In this article we have focused only on the leaf part of the plant. Hence, there is a lot of scope to expand and generalize solution for the problem.

Acknowledgement. My sincere gratitude to Vision Group of Science and Technology (VGST), Govt. of Karnataka, India, for funding and supporting the research. I am also thankful to Dr. Dayanand Agsar, Vice-Chancellor, Gulbarga University, Kalaburagi, Karnataka, India, for providing the dataset of microscope images of fungi. The Author would extend sincere thanks to Dr. Babasaheb Ambedkar Marathwada University for publication support.

References

1. Zhang, Shanwen, Wenzhun Huang, and Chuanlei Zhang. "Three-channel convolutional neural networks for vegetable leaf disease recognition." *Cognitive Systems Research* 53 (2019): 31-41.
2. Ferentinos, Konstantinos P. "Deep learning models for plant disease detection and diagnosis." *Computers and Electronics in Agriculture* 145 (2018): 311–318.
3. Karthik, R., M. Hariharan, Sundar Anand, Priyanka Mathikshara, Annie Johnson, and R. Menaka. "Attention embedded residual CNN for disease detection in tomato leaves." *Applied Soft Computing* 86 (2020): 105933.
4. Park, Hyeon, Jee-Sook Eun, and Se-Han Kim. "Image-based disease diagnosing and predicting of the crops through the deep learning mechanism." In *2017 International Conference on Information and Communication Technology Convergence (ICTC)*, pp. 129–131. IEEE, 2017.
5. Sardogan, Melike, Adem Tuncer, and Yunus Ozen. "Plant leaf disease detection and classification based on CNN with LVQ algorithm." In *2018 3rd International Conference on Computer Science and Engineering (UBMK)*, pp. 382–385. IEEE, 2018.
6. Liu, Bin, Zefeng Ding, Liangliang Tian, Dongjian He, Shuqin Li, and Hongyan Wang. "Grape leaf disease identification using improved deep convolutional neural networks." *Frontiers in Plant Science* 11 (2020): 1082.
7. Jiang, Peng, Yuehan Chen, Bin Liu, Dongjian He, and Chunquan Liang. "Real-time detection of apple leaf diseases using deep learning approach based on improved convolutional neural networks." *IEEE Access* 7 (2019): 59069-59080.
8. Sholihati, Rizqi Amaliatus, Indra Adji Sulistijono, Anhar Risnumawan, and Eny Kusumawati. "Potato Leaf Disease Classification Using Deep Learning Approach." In *2020 International Electronics Symposium (IES)*, pp. 392–397. IEEE, 2020.

9. Zhang, Xihai, Yue Qiao, Fanfeng Meng, Chengguo Fan, and Mingming Zhang. "Identification of maize leaf diseases using improved deep convolutional neural networks." *IEEE Access* 6 (2018): 30370-30377.

10. Durmuş, Halil, Ece Olcay Güneş, and Mürvet Kırcı. "Disease detection on the leaves of the tomato plants by using deep learning." In *2017 6th International Conference on Agro-Geoinformatics*, pp. 1–5. IEEE, 2017.

11. Chuanlei, Zhang, Zhang Shanwen, Yang Jucheng, Shi Yancui, and Chen Jia. "Apple leaf disease identification using genetic algorithm and correlation based feature selection method." *International Journal of Agricultural and Biological Engineering* 10, no. 2 (2017): 74–83. 11

12. Sivakamasundari, G., and V. Seenivasagam. "Classification of leaf diseases in apple using support vector machine." *International Journal of Advanced Research in Computer Science* 9, no. 1 (2018).

13. Dubey, Shiv Ram, and Anand Singh Jalal. "Detection and classification of apple fruit diseases using complete local binary patterns." In *2012 Third International Conference on Computer and Communication Technology*, pp. 346–351. IEEE, 2012.

14. Barbedo, J. G. A. "A novel algorithm for semi-automatic segmentation of plant leaf disease symptoms using digital image processing." *Tropical Plant Pathology* 41, no. 4 (2016): 210-224.

15. Islam, Monzurul, Anh Dinh, Khan Wahid, and Pankaj Bhowmik. "Detection of potato diseases using image segmentation and multiclass support vector machine." In *2017 IEEE 30th canadian conference on electrical and computer engineering (CCECE)*, pp. 1–4. IEEE, 2017.

16. Verma, Shradha, Anuradha Chug, and Amit Prakash Singh. "Application of convolutional neural networks for evaluation of disease severity in tomato plant." *Journal of Discrete Mathematical Sciences and Cryptography* 23, no. 1 (2020): 273–282.(fture extrctn)

17. Tahir, Muhammad Waseem, Nayyer Abbas Zaidi, Adeel Akhtar Rao, Roland Blank, Michael J. Vellekoop, and Walter Lang. "A fungus spores dataset and a convolutional neural network based approach for fungus detection." *IEEE transactions on nanobioscience* 17, no. 3 (2018): 281–290.

18. Prommakhot, Anuruk, and Jakkree Srinonchat. "Exploiting Convolutional Neural Network for Automatic Fungus Detection in Microscope Images." In *2020 8th International Electrical Engineering Congress (iEECON)*, pp. 1–4. IEEE, 2020.

19. Liu, Lin, Yang Yuan, Jing Zhang, Haoting Lei, Qiang Wang, Juanxiu Liu, Xiaohui Du, Guangming Ni, and Yong Liu. "Automatic identification of fungi under complex microscopic fecal images." *Journal of biomedical optics* 20, no. 7 (2015): 076004.

20. Zieliński, Bartosz, Agnieszka Sroka-Oleksiak, Dawid Rymarczyk, Adam Piekarczyk, and Monika Brzychczy-Włoch. "Deep learning approach to describe and classify fungi microscopic images." *PloS one* 15, no. 6 (2020): e0234806.

21. Billones, Robert Kerwin C., Edwin J. Calilung, Elmer P. Dadios, and Nelson Santiago. "Aspergillus Species Fungi Identification Using Microscopic Scale Images." In *2020 IEEE 12th International Conference on Humanoid, Nanotechnology, Information Technology, Communication and Control, Environment, and Management (HNICEM)*, pp. 1–5. IEEE, 2020.

22. S. Gayathri, D. C. J. W. Wise, P. B. Shamini and N. Muthukumaran, "Image Analysis and Detection of Tea Leaf Disease using Deep Learning," *2020 International Conference on Electronics and Sustainable Communication Systems (ICESC)*, 2020, pp. 398-403, doi: https://doi.org/10.1109/ICESC48915.2020.9155850.

23. Maeda-Gutiérrez, Valeria, Carlos E. Galvan-Tejada, Laura A. Zanella-Calzada, Jose M. Celaya-Padilla, Jorge I. Galván-Tejada, Hamurabi Gamboa-Rosales, Huizilopoztli Luna-Garcia, Rafael Magallanes-Quintanar, Carlos A. Guerrero Mendez, and Carlos A. Olvera-Olvera. "Comparison of convolutional neural network architectures for classification of tomato plant diseases." *Applied Sciences* 10, no. 4 (2020): 1245.
24. Rangarajan, Aravind Krishnaswamy, Raja Purushothaman, and Aniirudh Ramesh. "Tomato crop disease classification using pre-trained deep learning algorithm." *Procedia computer science* 133 (2018): 1040–1047.
25. Hasan, Mosin, Bhavesh Tanawala, and Krina J. Patel. "Deep learning precision farming: Tomato leaf disease detection by transfer learning." In *Proceedings of 2nd international conference on advanced computing and software engineering (ICACSE)*. 2019.
26. Howlader, Md Rasel, Umme Habiba, Rahat Hossain Faisal, and Md Mostafijur Rahman. "Automatic recognition of guava leaf diseases using deep convolution neural network." In *2019 international conference on electrical, computer and communication engineering (ECCE)*, pp. 1–5. IEEE, 2019.
27. Sujatha, R., Jyotir Moy Chatterjee, N. Z. Jhanjhi, and Sarfraz Nawaz Brohi. "Performance of deep learning vs machine learning in plant leaf disease detection." *Microprocessors and Microsystems* 80 (2021): 103615.
28. Krizhevsky, Alex, Ilya Sutskever, and Geoffrey E. Hinton. "Imagenet classification with deep convolutional neural networks." *Advances in neural information processing systems* 25 (2012): 1097-1105.
29. Iandola, Forrest N., Song Han, Matthew W. Moskewicz, Khalid Ashraf, William J. Dally, and Kurt Keutzer. "SqueezeNet: AlexNet-level accuracy with 50x fewer parameters and< 0.5 MB model size." *arXiv preprint* arXiv:1602.07360 (2016).
30. Rezende, Edmar, Guilherme Ruppert, Tiago Carvalho, Fabio Ramos, and Paulo De Geus. "Malicious software classification using transfer learning of resnet-50 deep neural network." In *2017 16th IEEE International Conference on Machine Learning and Applications (ICMLA)*, pp. 1011–1014. IEEE, 2017.

Crop Prediction Using Machine Learning and Artificial Neural Network

Tanya Saraswat[✉]

Computer Science and Engineering, Amity School of Engineering and Technology, Amity University, Noida, India
saraswat.tanya24@gmail.com

Abstract. *Agriculture Sector* being most vital parts of every Nation. The production of a crop mostly relies on numerous features and result is relied on the end yield and on the selling rate of that crop. In today's world there is a growth of countless technologies which can predict the growth of a crop on a regular basis, what must be added in that type of soil to make it more productive on-the-basis of study of that region. *Crop Prediction* using *Deep Learning* methods is indeed an upcoming challenge in the field of Agriculture.

Deep Learning would increase the efficiency of the workforce, a huge amount of time would be spending in learning analytics, therefore increasing one's concentration leading to predicative analytics also there would be personalized learning, the dependency on others would slowly start to terminate. The main aim of this paper is to focus on crop prediction by using numerous algorithms of machine as well as *deep learning*, and then to draw a comparison on the results and other performance measure of the different algorithms of *Machine Learning* and *Deep Learning*.

Keywords: Agricultural Sector · Crop Prediction · Deep Learning · Machine Learning

1 Introduction

Crop Prediction is a vital part of the Indian economy as nearly all the sectors of the economy are related to the production in the agricultural sector and what sorts of profit happens in the Agricultural Sector. The Crop Prediction mainly hangs upon a few weather situations and circumstances such as:

1. Rainfall Prediction in the near future
2. Temperature variations
   a) Next Heat wave prediction
   b) Next Cold wave prediction

The Crop Prediction is also dependent upon numerous other factors like:

1. Nitrogen Concentration in soil
2. Potassium Dilution in the soil

R. Manza et al. (Eds.): ACVAIT 2022, AISR 176, pp. 561–568, 2023.
https://doi.org/10.2991/978-94-6463-196-8_43

3. Phosphorus present in the soil
4. Ph of the soil

Precise evidence in relation to the historical prediction of the crop is imperative for taking in effective conclusion that are in relation with the hazards that the agriculture sector may face in the near-future and how to pass through those risks and to make the approximate forecasting and prediction of it beforehand to prevent the losses. In the current work, Crop Prediction is being made by using different algorithms of Machine Learning as well as Deep Learning, both of which are an important segment of prediction [1]. In the current work, the predictions have been made on basis of some of the elements which may or may not lead to the increment in the agricultural sector of the economy of India. In India, largely and mainly depends upon the agricultural sector hence forth, there is a huge need for examining the element related to crops which may result to the boon in the primary sector [1].

The key objectives which have been used are divided into five parts, data being pre-processed, data visualization, training and testing of the data, training of the model and then the evaluation of the model with effect of numerous algorithms.

The main objective of the current work is to draw the prediction of the given crops by using random forest, decision tree classifier, Gaussian Naïve Bayes, Gradient Booster, Logistic Regression and Artificial Neural Network to find out which of the models predict the stroke with the highest accuracy. Current work has been divided into following parts, Section 2 tells about the Literature Review, Sect. 3 deals with methodology, which is adopted, Sect. 4 presents the result followed by Sect. 5 which provides the inference of the work presented [15].

2   Literature Review

Crop Prediction deals with several complicated attributes which include the genotype of the crop, environmental changes and conditions, and the interaction of these genomes and ecology. These traits widely describe the properties which are going to be used in this Research Paper [12, 13].

For producing crop on a worldwide scale, crop yield prediction is crucial. In this Research paper, drawing a crucial analysis using the different machine learning algorithms, Ensemble Learning as well as Artificial Neural Network [14].

In this Research Paper, interdependency of the various weather conditions on the Crop is being reviewed and researched upon.

3   Methodology

In the current work, the methodology which is used has been divided into five segments or parts named as, Data being Pre-processed, Data Visualization, Training and testing the data, training of the model and then the evaluation of the model on basis of numerous algorithms [2].

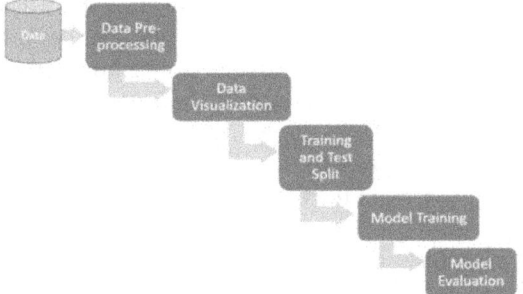

Flow-diagram of Methodological structure used

Details about the dataset used in this work is mentioned below:

a) *Dataset Description* The dataset used in the current work has been taken up from Kaggle. The dataset provides the information which deals with the prediction of the crop.

The dataset consists of seven elements on basis of which the crop prediction is dependent upon, they are: - N (Nitrogen), P (Phosphorus), K (Potassium), Temp (Temperature), Humidity, Ph and Rainfall. The dataset consists of 2200 entities wherein there are 22 crops and seven other elements on which the crop prediction depends upon [3].

There are 100 entries for every type of crop. The size of the Dataset suitable for performing various performance measures such as accuracy and precision, as these performance measures require a dataset with heavy data.

The value count of all the respective crops is shown beneath:

The dataset comprises of these different aspects:

```
blackgram       100
pigeonpeas      100
mango           100
rice            100
chickpea        100
watermelon      100
lentil          100
coconut         100
mothbeans       100
coffee          100
orange          100
muskmelon       100
mungbean        100
pomegranate     100
grapes          100
maize           100
kidneybeans     100
banana          100
cotton          100
apple           100
papaya          100
jute            100
Name: Crop, dtype: int64
```

Fig. 1. Number of Crops in the dataset

Nitrogen: This aspect or property is a numerical attribute, which tells us about how much nitrogen is present in the soil and Nitrogen plays a vital role in the growth and development of the plant as Nitrogen is foremost constituent element which helps in letting the plants generate sugar by the help of sunlight from the presence of water as well as Carbon Dioxide.

Phosphorus: This aspect or property is a numerical attribute, which is used in storing and then transferring of energy in the crops. Henceforth, it is the topmost necessity in crop prediction.

Potassium: This aspect is used to determine the water holding capacity in the plants. The need of phosphorus in plants is to hold-down the water, due to the absorption rate.

Temperature: Temperature is an important aspect which is used to determine at what rate the evaporation will take place. For example, in the daytime when the temperature is more, the evaporation rate is more henceforth, crops whose surface area of leaf is more will need more water as the evaporation rate will be higher, and similarly at nighttime, when the sunsets, the evaporation rate decreases, decreasing the need of water in the soil. It is therefore a key factor in determining the prediction of crop.

Humidity: This is again a numerical aspect which find out the moisture present in the environment, and what is the result of it on the crop.

Ph: The Ph also defines a lot about the crop therefore, it is also an important factor in diffing the type of crop being grown.

Rainfall: Rain consists of many useful nutrients which are beneficial for the crop. It is also observed that the germination process of the crop tends to begin after the monsoon season.

Also, if the rainfall tends to happen for a longer time, then it may result in a havoc for the crops as they can get rot. Farming depends upon the period wherein the rain is occurring. It plays a significant role in deciding as well as predicting the crop.

The amount of rainfall also has a huge positive impact on the rising-up of the water table, as the water table rises, the plants which needs more water, can get water from the soil itself. Rainfall also increases the soils fertility by adding extra nutrients into it, thus enhancing the quality of the soil [4].

b) *Data Preprocessing* Later when the dataset has been collected from several resources, it's a necessity to pre-process the available Dataset after collection. Pre-processing of the available data could be completed at several stages. This starts with the reading and understanding the data which has been gathered.

Next step is the cleaning of the data which is being used in the current work [1, 4]. For example, if the dataset is having a huge amount of NAN values, then those values or the entire column must be dropped down beforehand itself, or it may be filled with the maximum or random values as to get better accuracy [5].

It is foreseen that, a data which consists of larger amount of NAN values, then that doesn't result in higher accuracy as data-cleaning is being performed due to the faults present in the data. If data preprocessing is being performed using python language, then some pre-defined libraries must be imported to the server in order to perform pre-processing [3, 4].

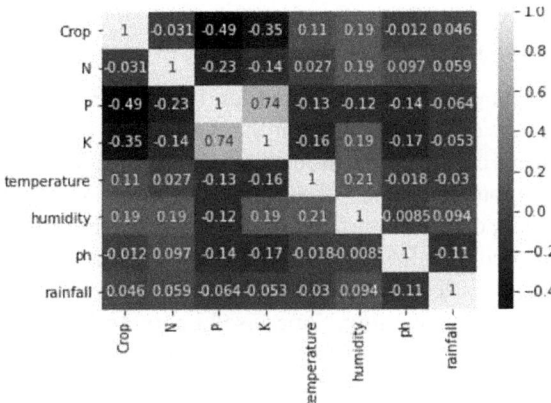

Fig. 2. Heatmap

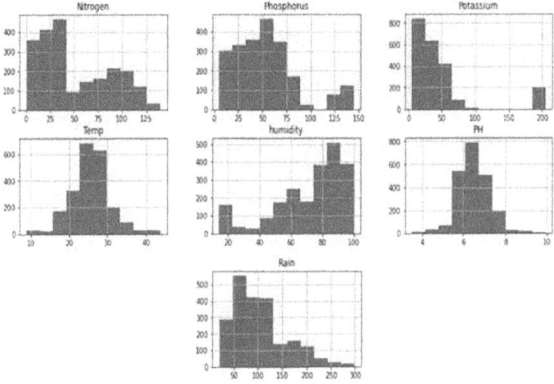

Fig. 3. Histogram of numerical data

c) *Train – Test Split* In this step of the methodology, the data is now categorized into two different segments known as the:
a) Training Data
b) Test Set

Training and test splits main motive is to evaluate and calculate the execution of Machine Learning as well as Deep Learning Algorithms. Training and Test Split technique is beneficial for Regression as well as the Classification problems of Machine Learning.

Technique coming under Supervised Learning [4, 5].

I. Training Set: As the term itself suggest that the training of the entire data is to be done on this particular data.

II. Testing Set: The word is self-explanatory; this work means that the testing is being done on which parameter for providing the forecast or prediction.

The cause behindhand using the train and test split is to accomplish the predictions and forecasting on new data rather than on the data which had by now been used for training purposes. In the current work, the data on which train and split is being performed had been fragmented into proportion of 80:20 which means the training data occupies 80% whereas the testing data occupies 20% [10]. For the fragmentation of the given data, the method that was used was, from 'sklearn.model_selection', the test and train set was imported ant the this was used for training and testing of the dataset 'train_test_split'.

In the subset of Machine learning, Supervised Learning, model training is meant to be feeding the machinery with the different algorithms present along with the training as well as the testing data available so that the targeted value could acquire from it [7].

The main motive of Training of the model is generation of trained model as in to simplify well known to new known to not-known data. The trained-fitted model estimated by the help of these new known data from the beforehand, handheld data as to evaluate the accuracy provided by training of the model.

In the current work, the classifiers used are Random Forest, Decision Tree, Gaussian Naïve Bayes, Gradient Booster, Support Vector Machine, Logistic Regression and Artificial Neural Network (ANN) [6].

4   Results

Machine learning and deep learning are a very useful approach for working with prediction as well as forecasting.

The limitation of these algorithms is that, in dataset the required, data must have enormously a huge number of entries' else, the performance measure will be having lower performance.

In the current work, the methodology adopted is for the prediction of the most appropriate crop with the help of identification of several aspects of element that are essential for the best growth as well as the development of the crop such as the soil containing adequate amount of nutrients or not, also specifications which are related to the atmosphere like, humidity as well as temperature.

This piece of work hereby displays the capability of the algorithms used in the above work for the forecasting as well as the prediction of crops in different sections of India, where in the soil requirement and the atmospheric requirements are fulfilled [11].

5   Conclusion and Future Work

Prediction of crop is a necessity as it is the daily need of everyone. No human being can live a life without being feed on a crop. Also, India's economy is directly indirectly dependent upon Crop thereafter, it is not only a necessity but also the essential requirement of living [8]. In the rising demand of crop prediction, to get precaution and cautious about the near-future risks, the prediction of crop had been done on basis of seven other

Table 1. Comparison B/W Classifiers (Accuracy)

MODELS APPLIED	Accuracy (in %)
Random forest classifier	99.3181818
Decision tree classifier	98.8636364
Gaussian naive bayes	99.5454545
Gradient booster classifier	99.4886364
Support vector machine	96.1363636
Logistic regression	94.5454545
Deep learning ANN	99.3574803

Table 2. Distribution Table verified by different algorithms

Crop Name	N	P	K	Temperature	Humidity	pH	Rainfall
Apple	0-40	120-145	195-205	21.04-24.00	90.03-94.93	5.52-6.50	100.12-124.99
Banana	80-120	70-95	45-55	25.02-29.91	75.04-84.98	5.51-6.50	090.11-119.85
Blackgram	20-60	55-80	15-25	25.10-34.95	60.07-69.97	6.51-7.78	060.42-074.92
Chickpea	20-60	55-80	75-85	17.03-21.00	14.26-19.97	5.99-8.87	065.12-094.79
Coconut	0-40	5-30	25-35	25.01-29.87	90.02-99.99	5.51-6.48	131.10-225.64
Coffee	80-120	15-40	25-35	23.06-27.93	50.05-69.95	6.03-7.50	115.16-199.48
Cotton	100-140	35-60	15-25	22.01-26.00	75.01-84.88	5.81-8.00	060.66-099.94
Grapes	0-40	120-145	195-205	08.83-41.95	80.02-83.99	5.52-6.50	065.02-074.92
Jute	60-100	35-60	35-45	23.10-26.99	70.89-89.90	6.01-7.49	150.24-199.84
Kidneybeans	0-40	55-80	15-25	15.34-24.93	18.10-24.97	5.51-6.00	060.28-149.75
Lentil	0-40	55-80	15-25	18.07-29.95	60.10-69.93	5.92-7.85	035.04-054.94
Maize	60-100	35-60	15-25	18.05-26.55	55.29-74.83	5.52-7.00	060.66-109.76
Mango	0-40	15-40	25-35	27.01-36.00	45.03-54.97	4.51-6.97	089.30-100.82
Mothbeans	0-40	35-60	15-25	24.02-32.00	40.01-64.96	3.51-9.94	030.93-074.45
Mungbean	0-40	35-60	15-25	27.02-29.92	80.04-90.00	6.22-7.20	036.13-059.88
Muskmelon	80-120	5-30	45-55	27.03-29.95	90.02-94.97	6.01-6.79	020.22-029.87
Orange	0-40	5-30	5-15	10.02-34.91	90.01-94.97	6.02-8.00	100.18-119.70
Papaya	31-70	46-70	45-55	23.02-43.68	90.04-94.95	6.51-7.00	040.36-248.86
Pigeonpeas	0-40	55-80	15-25	18.32-36.98	30.41-69.70	4.55-7.45	090.06-198.83
Pomegranate	0-40	5-30	35-45	18.08-24.97	85.13-95.00	5.57-7.20	102.52-112.48
Rice	60-99	35-60	35-45	20.05-26.93	80.13-84.97	5.01-7.87	182.57-298.57
Watermelon	80-120	5-30	45-55	24.05-26.99	80.03-89.99	6.01-6.96	040.13-059.73

parameters. The prediction had been done using seven algorithms. The training and test-ing split data taken for this purpose was in the proportion of 80:20. Highest accuracy was approximately 99.54% which was given by Gaussian Naïve Bayes Algorithm and second highest accuracy was about 99.35% and was given by Artificial Neural Network [9]. Prediction made by these algorithms are particular in every aspect and can be used to perform predictions in-actuality.

References

1. Kaggle.com. 2021. *Crop Prediction Dataset.* [online]

2. Ashwani kumar Kushwaha, Swetabhattachrya "crop yield prediction using agro algorithm in hatoop"
3. Pavan Patil, Virendra Panpatil, Prof. Shrikant Kokate "Crop Prediction System using Machine Learning Algorithms"
4. Girish L, Gangadhar S, Bharath T R, Balaji K S, Abhishek K
5. T "Crop Yield and Rainfall Prediction in Tumakuru District using Machine Learning".
6. Manjula E, Djodiltachoumy S (2017) A model for prediction of crop yield. Int J Comput Intell Inf 6(4)
7. Clarkson, D. T. & Warner, A. (1979). Relationships between root temperature and the transport of ammonium and nitrate ions by Italian and perennial ryegrass (*Lolium multiflorum* and *Lolium perenne*). Plant Physiology 64, 557– 561.
8. Aggarwal Sachin (2001). Application of Neural Network to Forecast Air Quality Index. Thesis submitted in partial fulfillment of requirements for a degree in Bachelor of Technology, April 2001.
9. Everingham, Y. L., R. C. Muchow, R. C. Stone, and D. H. Coomans, 2003. Using southern oscillation index phases to forecast sugarcane yields: a case study for Northeastern Australia. International Journal of Climatology 23(10): 12111218.
10. D.L. Ehret et al, Neural network modeling of greenhouse tomato yield, growth and water use from automated crop monitoring data, 2011.
11. Rice Research and Development Institute (RRDI), *Department of Agriculture-Sri Lanka.Rice Cultivation*, Rice Research and Development Institute (RRDI), Ibbagamuwa, Sri Lanka, 2020.
12. Y. Masutomi, K. Takahashi, H. Harasawa, and Y. Matsuoka, "Impact assessment of climate change on rice production in Asia in comprehensive consideration of process/parameter uncertainty in general circulation models," *Agriculture, Ecosystems & Environment*.
13. S. Khaki and L. Wang, "Crop yield prediction using deep neural networks", *Frontiers in plant science.*
14. T. Senthil Kumar, "Data Mining Based Marketing Decision Support System Using Hybrid Machine Learning.
15. Algorithm", *Journal of Artificial Intelligence*, 2020.
16. V. Pandith, H. Kour, S. Singh, J. Manhas and V. Sharma, "Performance Evaluation of Machine Learning Techniques for Mustard Crop Yield Prediction from Soil Analysis", *Journal of Scientific Research*, 2020.
17. S. D. Kumar, S. Esakkirajan, S. Bama and B. Keerthiveena, "A microcontroller based machine vision approach for tomato grading and sorting using SVM classifier", *Microprocessors and Microsystems*, 2020.

Analysis of Weather Parameters Using Machine Learning

Ramdas D. Gore$^{(\boxtimes)}$ and Bharti W. Gawali

Department of Computer Science and Information Technology, Dr. Babasaheb Ambedkar, Marathwada University, Aurangabad 43104 (MS), India
ramdasgore1888@gmail.com

Abstract. Rainfall forecasts at various time and space scales have been one of the essential ingredients for not only industries, businesses, and politicians but also farmers to minimize losses. For agriculture, forecasts of other atmospheric parameters are also relevant. Atmospheric techniques must be known, measurements improved and ongoing study and improvement to ensure reliable weather predictions. In India, the Ministry of Earth Science (MoES) works to develop forecasting in its separate programs and divisions such as India Meteorological Department (IMD). The efforts have culminated in fairly reliable predictions of rainfall patterns. This research aims to enhance prediction accuracy in different geographical areas ranging from weather subdivisions to agro-climate areas. The machine learning techniques have introduced detailed experimental position forecasts for the Marathwada region of Maharashtra state, India. We have developed prediction model for Marathwada region using machine learning techniques. We have used Autocorrelation and seven machine learning techniques for the prediction of weather model such as Linear, Exponential, Quadratic, Additive seasonality, Additive Seasonality Quadratic Trend, Multiplicative Seasonality, and Multiplicative Seasonality Linear Trend. Linear, Exponential, Quadratic and Additive seasonality are not given good result for weather parameter.

Additive Seasonality Quadratic Trend is best fit model for the highest maximum temperature (1.42), lowest minimum temperature (1.87), wind speed (1.06), relative humidity (5.07), mean station (1.19), and mean sea level pressure (1.43). Multiplicative Seasonality model is the best model for mean minimum temperature (1.12) total rainfall in the month (24.13), heavy rainfall (8.74), and number of rainy days (1.2). Multiplicative Seasonality Linear Trend is given good accuracy for mean maximum temperature (1.2). The linear, exponential, quadratic and additive seasonality are not given good result for weather parameter. Rainfall is not the same every year. Some areas get more rain and some areas get less rain and its effect falls on all Marathwada region. The low rainfall and high temperature in the Marathwada region in most of the year due to this comes under the drought condition. So there is a need to change the crop pattern in this region like temperature tolerant crops.

Keywords: Rainfall · Temperature · Weather · Prediction model · Forecasting Model · Correlation · Autocorrelation · Linear Regression · Data Science · Machine Learning · Marathwada Region

R. Manza et al. (Eds.): ACVAIT 2022, AISR 176, pp. 569–589, 2023.
https://doi.org/10.2991/978-94-6463-196-8_44

1 Introduction

In rapid events, climate research relies entirely on long-run traits. Climate data has risen significantly in the last 30 years due to the rapid expansion of information technology, and the rate of increase will accelerate in the future. [1]. The long-term average of weather patterns, usually assessed over a period of 30–40 years, is referred to as climate. Some commonly measured meteorological variables include temperature, humidity, atmospheric pressure, rainfall, wind, and precipitation. In a broader sense, the climate is the state of the climate system components which includes the Earth's ocean and ice. The climate of a location is influenced by factors such as its latitude, geography, and altitude, as well as adjacent bodies of water and currents. A region's climate is the general state of the present-day climate system at that location [2]. Meteorological parameters such as temperature, humidity, wind speed, and the current climate all influence rainfall. When the temperature is high, rainfall and humidity are both low. Wind speed is high then rainfall is also high and wind speed is low, then average rainfall. Climate parameters (Rainfall, Temperature, Humidity, and Wind) affected living and non-living things. Climate is affected directly or indirectly in various sectors such as Human Health, Agriculture, Forest, Animal, Birds, Business, Environment, Educations, polities, National and International organizations (Private and Government). We have found the number of forecasting techniques in the literature survey. The data science techniques are wildly used for forecasting analysis. The machine learning is the one of the technique in data science [3].

The objective of this research, the machine learning techniques is helped forecasting, it is established prediction models five homogeneous monsoon regions of the district of Marathwada. The analysis's goal is to compare forecasts and assess the model's usefulness. It is possible to compare the findings of both studies to draw acceptable conclusions that show the value and usefulness of models.

1.1 Weather and Atmospheric

The state of the atmosphere is referred to as weather. Most weather occurs in the troposphere or the lowest layer of the atmosphere. Weather is influenced by a variety of elements for example, air temperature, atmospheric pressure, humidity, precipitation, solar radiation, and wind. Each of these factors is monitored in order to assess the quality of local atmospheric conditions and identify common weather patterns [4]. According to recent studies on fluctuations in rainfall over India, the global average yearly rainfall does not follow a clear pattern. Despite the fact that there was no clear pattern in monsoon rainfall in India over time, particularly on a national scale, multiple studies revealed areas with substantial long-term fluctuations in rainfall [5].

1.1.1 Rainfall (in mm)

Rain is an important part of the water cycle since it is responsible for depositing the majority of the world's fresh water. It provides habitat for a variety of habitats as well as water for hydroelectric power facilities and farmland irrigation. In many places of the globe, rainfall or precipitation is the primary supply of water for agricultural production.

Water is required for all crops to grow and provide yields. Rainfall is the most essential source of water for agricultural growth. Rainfall is defined by the amount, intensity, and timing of its occurrence [6].

1.1.2 Temperature (in Degree Celsius)

Temperature, an essential determinant, influences the rate of plant growth. Temperatures predicted by climate change, as well as the potential of more severe temperature occurrences, will have an impact on plant productivity, or agricultural production [7]. The temperature categories are as follows: mean and highest maximum temperature, mean and lowest minimum temperature, and mean and lowest minimum temperature. One of the earliest studies looked at trends in global yearly maximum and minimum temperatures and determined that there was no regular tendency for these temperatures to increase/decrease. Seasonal and monthly air temperature sequences from 1881 to 1997 revealed a significant growing tendency of 0.57 degrees Celsius every 100 years. The magnitude of heat was larger during the post-monsoon and winter seasons. With the exception of a severe negative pattern in northwest India, the monsoon temperature did not show a discernible trend in any significant portion of the world [8].

1.1.3 Wind Speed (in *Kmps*)

It is a fundamental atmospheric quantity created by the movement of air from high to low pressure, mostly as a result of temperature variations. Because of the rotation of the Earth, wind direction is nearly parallel to isobars (rather than perpendicular, as one might anticipate). Wind speed influences weather forecasts, aviation and maritime operations, construction projects, plant growth and metabolic rates, and a variety of other factors. The use of an anemometer to determine wind speed is becoming more widespread [9].

1.1.4 Humidity (in %)

Humidity has a big influence on the weather. It is a natural characteristic of our environment that relates to the amount of water vapour in the air. Humidity levels that are too high or too low can harm people and crops. The combination of high humidity and hot temperatures can be dangerous to one's health, especially for the young and elderly. It indicates whether precipitation, dew, or fog are likely [10].

2 Related work

The following are the most important outcomes of this enormous collection of interconnected works. (1) Between 1901 and 2007, the annual temperatures (mean, maximum, and minimum) all increased at significant rates of 0.51, 0.72, and 0.27 degrees Celsius, respectively. The temperature has gradually and steadily climbed over this time (a hundred years). The warming was mostly caused by higher temperatures throughout the winter and post-monsoon seasons. The annual average temperature climbed by 0.20 degrees Celsius per decade between 1971 and 2007, resulting in substantial swings in both hot and low temperatures. In the same way, the lowest temperature rise was significantly higher than the median. Despite the fact that post-monsoon temperatures climbed drastically in a small number of places, total winter and summer monsoon temperatures rose significantly throughout almost the entire world. (2) Temperature patterns in India were found to be very stable and in line with global and hemispheric trends on a broader geographically aggregated scale. Patterns on smaller regional sizes and for specific sub-periods, on the other hand, have not consistently paralleled Indian aggregate temperatures. Rainfall variability has also altered patterns throughout the monsoon and post-monsoon seasons. Recent temperature increases in some regions of the world might be attributed to the proportional influence of aerosols and greenhouse gases. (3) Rapid warming occurred between 1971 and 2007, with considerable warming occurring between 1998 and 2007. Maximum temperatures in India were somewhat higher than the long-term average (1901–2007) throughout that time period, with a consistent pattern, whereas minimum temperatures exhibited a rising trend, nearly equivalent to that recorded between 1971 and 2007. It's worth remembering that, according to World Meteorological Organization (WMO) data, 2010 was one of the top three warmest years on record since the start of observational climate records in 1850. (4) The average temperature in each season grew dramatically between 1901 and 2007 [11–13].

The research takes use of monthly, seasonal, and annual data. Daily temperature scale increases were also seen at three additional locations during the monsoon and post-monsoon seasons. Temperatures in NE India were fairly steady throughout the winter and pre-monsoon seasons, but they rose dramatically during the monsoon and post-monsoon seasons. Over the annual, seasonal (winter and pre-monsoon), and monthly time periods, there were decreasing trends in sunshine duration. The annual maximum temperature in Central Northeast India rose by 0.008 °C during the monsoon season, 0.014 °C during the post-monsoon season, and 0.008 °C during the post-monsoon season between 1914 and 2003 [14]. During the post-monsoon season, the lowest temperature climbed by 0.012 °C each year, while the maximum temperature declined by 0.002 °C each year. Minimum temperature swings have been demonstrated to be more difficult than maximum temperature swings, both temporally and geographically, and to have less implications [15].

Rainfall patterns during the monsoon season were studied over various divisions, sub-divisions, and the whole nation of India. In India, there has been a declining trend in monsoon rainfall, rainy days, and yearly rainfall since the second half of the 1960s. Growing trends in mean annual and monsoon rainfall were observed over the meteorological subdivisions of Punjab, Haryana, western Rajasthan, eastern Rajasthan, and western Madhya Pradesh from 1901 to 1982. Monsoon rainfall has been decreasing in the northeast peninsula, northeast India, and the northwest peninsula, according to climatic statistics (ranging from -6 to -8 percent of average per 100 years). Rainfall during the monsoon season, on the other hand, rose in the west coast, in the central peninsula, and in northwest India (by around 10 to 12 percent of normal every 100 years) [16].

From 1941 to 2002, the monsoon rainfall in northwest and central India decreased. There was no discernable pattern in yearly, seasonal, or monthly rainfall in India, according to an examination of 135 years of rainfall data (1871 to 2005). Annual and monsoon rainfall have decreased throughout time, however rainfall during the pre-monsoon, post-monsoon, and winter seasons has increased, with the pre-monsoon season highest [17]. During the monsoon months of June, July, and September, precipitation patterns in India decreased, but surged in August. Despite the fact that just three sub-divisions were statistically significant, Haryana, Punjab, and coastal Karnataka, additional investigation on a sub-divisional basis (30 sub-divisions) revealed that half of them had a rising trend in yearly precipitation. Only the Chhattisgarh sub-division had a substantial decline in annual precipitation, showing that annual precipitation is decreasing. For the majority of the months, there was no discernible pattern in annual, seasonal, or monthly precipitation in any of the five zones. Rainfall shows small increases in both the winter and summer seasons [18].

2.1 Background of Marathwada Region *(Maharashtra State)*

Agriculture in Maharashtra's Marathwada region is dependent on rainfall, and the region is currently experiencing the worst drought due to poor rainfall. In this region, agricultural production is also lower than the rate of investment. Agricultural yields are affected by a variety of factors, including erratic weather, low or excessive rainfall, climate change, the lack of soil monitoring, the absence of soil-based crops, or associated fertilizers, the application of too little or too much fertilizer, and planting the same crops every year.

3   Study Area

Maharashtra is India's third biggest state (307,713 km^2) and the second most populous subdivision (118,809 sq mi). Maharashtra is divided into 36 districts, 355 talukas, 535 towns, 63,663 villages, and five regional areas (Konkan, Pune, Marathwada, Vidarbha, and Nashik). Some of the significant rivers are presented in the State (Krishna, Bhima, Godavari, Tapi-Purna, and Wardha-Wainganga). Low rainfall in the state's central region, with several dams on the majority of the rivers in the area.

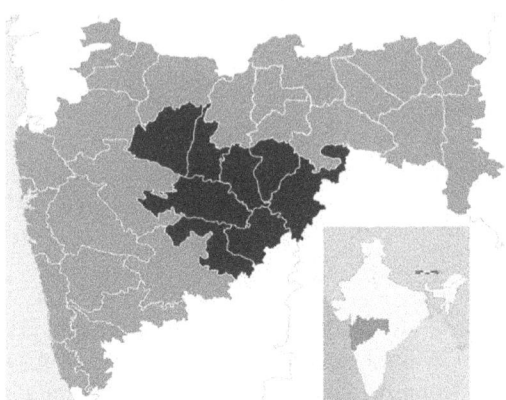

Fig. 1. Study Area (Blue colour shows Marathwada Region)

The Marathwada region occupies 64590 km^2 (24,940 sq mi) and has a population of 18,731,872 people, according to the 2011 census. (See Fig. 1). The region is divided into eight districts (Aurangabad, Beed, Hingoli, Jalna, Parbhani, Latur, Osmanabad, and Nanded). The main city is Aurangabad, which is located in the district of Aurangabad.

3.1 Database

The temperature (in degrees Celsius), rainfall (in millimeters), relative humidity (in percent), pressure (in hpa), and wind speed (in kilometers per hour) are described in the dataset. There are 120 sub-parameters observations of weather parameters (mean and highest maximum temperature, mean and lowest minimum temperature, total rainfall in the month, heavy rainfall in 24 h, number of rainy, mean wind speed, relative humidity, mean station and sea level pressure) in the Marathwada area of Maharashtra State (India) spanning a ten-year period (1976–1985).

IMD is the most widely used climate database. We have taken five districts of Marathwada as Aurangabad, Beed, Parbhani, Nanded, and Osmanabad. The source of the data is credited as the Indian Metrological Department (IMD), Ministry of Earth Science, Pune, India.

4   Methods and Techniques

In order to produce educated estimates that are predictive in identifying the direction of future trends, historical data is used as inputs in the forecasting process. The application of science and technology to anticipate atmospheric conditions for a given area and time is known as weather forecasting. People have been attempting to predict the weather informally and systematically since the nineteenth century. Weather predictions are based on the collection of quantitative data on the present position of the atmosphere, land, and water, as well as the use of meteorology to predict how the atmosphere will change in a particular region. It might be challenging to determine which model will best fit the data from a scatter plot. To identify which model best matches the data, we need first find several models for it, then compare the y-values of each model to the true y-values [19].

4.1   Pre-processing

The raw data is translated into the excel format. We have divided database as district wise and year wise and find the missing of year, month and days.

4.1.1   Missing Values

When no data value is saved for a variable in an observation, it is referred to as missing data or values in statistics. Missing data is a typical occurrence that has a major impact on the conclusions formed from the data. For missing numeric data, the mean and median imputers are utilized (int and float).

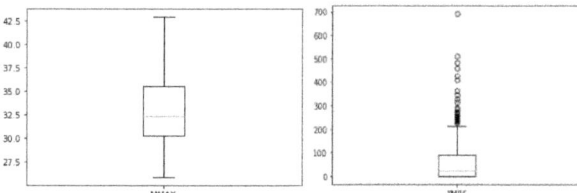

Fig. 2. Data Visualization-Outliers

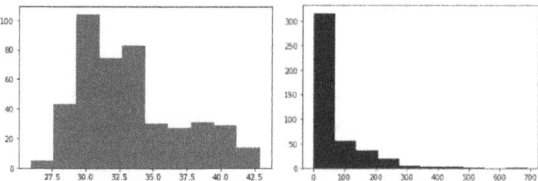

Fig. 3. Data Visualization-Histrogram

4.1.2 Exploratory Data Analysis (EDA)

An outlier is a value in a random sample from a Weather that is abnormally far apart from other values. It is up to the analyst to determine what constitutes aberrant behavior. It is crucial to classify typical observations before identifying anomalous observations. When the distribution is normal, two graphical techniques are employed to discover outliers: Box plots and scatter plots are two types of plots. The box plot is an effective graphical representation for understanding data behavior in the middle and tails of a distribution. The median, as well as the lower and higher quartiles, are used in the box plot (25th and 75th percentiles). The interquartile range, or IQ, is the gap between the lowest and upper quartiles of a population (Q3 - Q1). A moderate outlier is defined as a point on each side of an inner fence, whilst a severe outlier is defined as a point on either side of an outer barrier [20] (Fig. 2).

4.1.3 Histogram

A histogram is a graphical representation of data in the form of groups. It is an accurate method for graphically depicting numerical data distribution. It's a bar plot with the X-axis representing bin ranges and the Y-axis representing frequency [21] (Fig. 3).

4.1.4 Time Series Plot

Visualisation is essential in time series research and forecasting. Raw sample data plots provide important diagnostics for spotting temporal patterns like as trends, cycles, and seasonality, all of which impact model selection. The first and possibly most common time series visualisation is the line plot. The x-axis represents the month, while the y-axis represents the observation data [22] (Fig. 4).

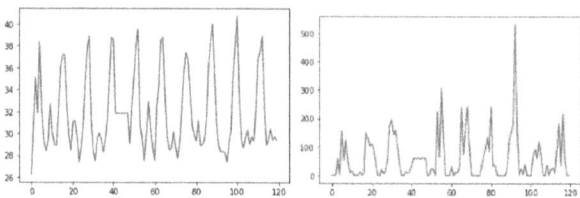

Fig. 4. Data Visualization-Time Series Plot

4.2 Correlation

The mean, standard deviation, variance, and covariance are all statistical numbers that are closely related to correlation. The associations between two or more variables (or features) of a dataset are frequently studied in statistics and data science [23]. The features are the traits or attributes of the observations, and each data point in the dataset is an observation. Variables and observations were used in every dataset we worked with. The features or variables are presented in the dataset (highest and mean maximum temperature, lowest and mean minimum temperature, total monthly rainfall, heavy rainfall in 24 h, number of rainy days, mean wind speed, relative humidity, mean station and mean sea level pressure).

When data is displayed in the form of a table, the observations are usually represented by the rows, while the features are represented by the columns. It is seen in a database table sample (Table 1).

Each entry in this table represents a single observation, or data regarding a single weather characteristic (either month of Jan, Feb, Mar, etc.). For all of the weather data, each column displays one feature (MN). We've looked at any two features in a dataset and discovered some sort of relationship between them. The following pair diagram shows the pairwise correlation between these highly associated qualities (Figs. 5, 6 and Tables 2, 3, 4, 5, 6 and 7).

Each of these plots shows one of three different forms of correlation:

a. **Negative correlation:** The y values tend to drop as the x values increase in the plot on the negative correlation. It was discovered that there is a strong negative association when large values of one trait correspond to small values of the other, and vice versa. The mean and lowest minimum temperatures and as well as the mean wind speed have a substantial negative association with the mean station and the mean sea level pressure.

b. **Weak or no correlation:** The centre plot displays no discernible trend. This is a type of weak correlation that happens when there is no evident or hardly discernible link between two features. The mean and highest maximum temperature, mean and lowest minimum temperature, mean wind speed, mean station and mean sea level pressure have no link with relative humidity.

c. **Positive correlation:** The y values tend to grow when the x values increase in the strong positive correlation. Strong positive correlation arises when large values of one property correspond to large values of the other, and vice versa [24]. Because a greater maximum temperature corresponds to a mean maximum temperature, and mean station level pressure relates to mean sea level pressure and vice versa, the

Table 1. Sample of one year (1985) weather database

MN	MMAX	HMAX	MMIN	LMIN	TMRF	HVYRF	RD	MWS	SLP	MSLP	RH
Jan	30.6	33.9	15	8.4	1	1	0	2	953.3	1009.9	38
Feb	33.1	35.2	13.3	9.6	1	1	0	2.5	949	1004.8	24
Mar	38.3	39.6	20.9	17.8	8.4	8.4	1	2.9	949.8	1004.8	19
Apr	38.1	42.4	22.5	18	8	8	1	4.1	947.2	1002.8	25
May	39.8	43	25.5	18.6	42.4	36.4	2	6	944.2	998.8	23
Jun	34.4	37.5	24.2	22.4	18	10.6	2	7.3	944.2	999.9	50
Jul	29.5	33.6	23	21.4	111.2	35.6	8	5.3	945.4	1001.7	60
Aug	30.1	35.4	22.3	21	11.3	4.4	2	5.7	945.2	1001.4	54
Sep	31.4	35	22.2	20.6	134.4	70.2	8	4.3	947.3	1003.3	51
Oct	30.2	32.8	18.4	13.2	59	28.4	4	4.2	950.1	1006.6	45
Nov	29.5	31.7	13.8	11.4	1	1	0	3.4	953.2	1009.8	31
Dec	29.8	32	13.7	9	1	1	0	3	953.6	1010.5	35

Table 2. Lag sample of temperature (1976 year)

Time (t)	Original data (Y_t)	1 step lagged (Y_{t-1})	2 step lagged (Y_{t-2})
1	29.1		
2	32.4	29.1	
3	36.8	32.4	29.1
4	38.4	36.8	32.4
5	40.1	38.4	36.8
6	34	40.1	38.4
7	31.2	34	40.1
8	30.2	31.2	34
9	31.1	30.2	31.2
10	35	31.1	30.2
11	29.1	35	31.1

connection between mean and highest maximum temperature, mean and lowest minimum temperature, mean wind speed, mean station and sea level pressure are positive correlation.

d. There is a medium (0.71) and negative (-0.55) association between relative humidity and total monthly rainfall.

4.2.1 Heat Map of Weather Dataset

A correlation matrix is a table that shows how two variables in a dataset are related to one another. Each value in this matrix reflects the correlation coefficient between

Table 3. Overall accuracy of weather parameter

Sr. no.	Methods	MMAX	HMAX	MMIN	LMIN	TMRF	HVYRF	RD	MWS	SLP	MSLP	RH
1.	LINEAR	2.59	2.79	2.86	3.26	30.77	13.82	3.36	2.25	1.76	1.84	15.5
2.	Exponential	2.72	2.92	2.85	3.22	37.39	13.8	3.2	2.44	1.74	1.84	13.7
3.	Quadratic	2.85	2.1	2.93	3.32	32.92	13.97	3.21	2.18	1.68	1.84	13.8
4.	Additive seasonality	1.14	1.5	1.14	2.3	28.14	11.46	1.84	1.42	1.21	1.45	5.63
5.	Additive Seasonality Quadratic Trend	1.14	1.42	1.19	1.87	29.3	11.43	1.51	1.06	1.19	1.43	5.07
6.	Multiplicative Seasonality	1.15	1.5	1.12	2.34	24.13	8.74	1.2	1.27	1.21	1.45	5.38
7.	Multiplicative Seasonality Linear Trend	1.2	1.44	1.15	2.32	27.59	10.13	1.35	1.23	1.23	1.48	6.48
	Overall Accuracy	**1.83**	**1.95**	**1.89**	**2.66**	**32.16**	**11.91**	**2.24**	**1.69**	**1.43**	**1.62**	**9.37**

Table 4. Best fit model for weather parameter

Name of Models	MMAX	HMAX	MMIN	LMIN	TMRF	HVYRF	RD	MWS	SLP	MSLP	RH
Additive Seasonality Quadratic Trend	.	✓		✓				✓	✓	✓	✓
Multiplicative Seasonality			✓		✓	✓	✓				
Multiplicative Seasonality Linear Trend	✓										

the variables represented by the relevant row and column, and each row and column represents a variable. The correlation matrix is a vital data analysis metric, it is used to summarize data in order to better understand the link between different variables and make informed decisions. When dimensionality reduction on huge quantities of data is necessary, computing and evaluating the correlation matrix is a crucial pre-processing step in Machine Learning pipelines. Each cell in the correlation matrix represents a correlation coefficient between the two variables denoted by the cell's row and column [25] (Fig. 7).

4.3   Linear Method

Figure 8 depicts a basic technique of imputation that assumes a linear connection between missing and non-missing variables. This method fits a distinct linear polynomial between

Table 5. Original values of Weather parameters

Month	MMAX	HMAX	MMIN	LMIN	TMRF	HVYRF	RD	MWS	SLP	MSLP	RH
Jan	28.7	31.6	12.6	6	0	0	0	9.4	946.6	1010.1	23
Feb	31.2	34	15.6	11.9	3.3	2.5	1	10.8	944.6	1007.4	22
Mar	36	40.2	18.9	13.7	0.1	0.1	0	12.7	942.8	1004.5	14
Apr	39.3	41.2	22.7	12	0	0	0	10.9	940.7	1001.6	15
May	39.9	42	23.6	20.5	0	0	0	18.4	938.9	999.7	18
Jun	33.8	39.4	22.5	18.5	202.3	87.4	9	17.2	936.5	998.7	53
Jul	30.3	34.6	21.8	20.2	102	64	7	22.1	938.5	1001.5	59
Aug	28.7	31.7	20.7	18.7	127.7	45.8	6	17.6	939.1	1002.5	65
Sep	32.4	35	21.1	19	38.3	13.4	4	11.6	941.4	1004	45
Oct	34.5	37.6	18.6	12.7	13.1	13.1	1	6.9	944.3	1006.7	25
Nov	31.1	34	15	9.7	8	7.8	1	5.8	946.1	1009.2	32
Dec	28.2	31.5	11.2	7.1	30.1	18.6	1	6.1	948	1011.9	37

Table 6. Predicted values of Weather parameters

Month	MMAX	HMAX	MMIN	LMIN	TMRF	HVYRF	RD	MWS	SLP	MSLP	RH
Jan	29.33	31.85	11.81	7.01	0	0	0	8.8	946.53	1010.08	27
Feb	32.03	35.17	13.34	8.39	0	0	0	10.09	944.79	1007.48	18
Mar	36.09	39.14	17.58	11.55	0	0	0	11.74	943.5	1005.37	13
Apr	39.07	41.55	21.28	16.46	0	0	0	13.9	940.73	1001.85	12
May	40.29	42.21	23.44	19.05	0	0	0	18.9	938.77	999.53	16
Jun	35.35	40.27	21.92	19.18	165.2	31.25	5	21.29	936.23	998.05	44
Jul	31.12	34.58	21.17	19.5	119.5	37.74	9	20.4	936.67	999.32	61
Aug	29.62	32.56	20.32	18.55	86.89	26.16	8	21.48	937.6	1000.53	63
Sep	31.23	33.79	19.86	17.57	46.58	43.2	6	14.51	940.49	1003.36	55
Oct	32.84	35.09	17.77	13.51	17	14.3	2	9.22	943.92	1006.65	32
Nov	30.59	32.74	14.86	9.74	35.96	23.57	1	9.16	945.61	1008.85	32
Dec	29.13	31.04	11.53	6.11	20.67	14.4	1	7.96	946.92	1010.51	27

each pair of data points for curves, and a different linear polynomial between each set of three points for surfaces.

$$Y_t = \beta_0 + \beta_1 t + \varepsilon \qquad (1)$$

$$y = y_1 + (x - x_1)\frac{(y_2 - y_1)}{(x_2 - x_1)} \qquad (2)$$

The known value is x, while the unknown value is y. The coordinates x1 and y1 are below the known x value, whereas the coordinates x2 and y2 are above the known x value (Fig. 8). If the value at point Z is absent, the value at point Z will be computed using both the last real assessment performed before to point Z, which is point X, and the first actual assessment conducted after point Z, which is point Y [26].

Table 7. Original and Predicted values of Weather parameters

Mean Maximum Temperature Predicted and Original Values

Mean Minimum Temperature Predicted and Original Values

Total Month of Rainfall Predicted and Original Values

Number of Rainy Day Predicted and Original Values

Mean Wind Speed Predicted and Original Values

Relative Humidity Predicted and Original Values

Mean Station Level Pressure Predicted and Original Values

Mean Sea Level Pressure Predicted and Original Values

4.4 Exponential Model

Exponential functions are used to describe many physical phenomena, including populations, interest rates, radioactive decay, and the quantity of drugs in the circulation.

$$\text{Log}(Y_t) = \beta_0 + \beta_1 t + \varepsilon \tag{3}$$

4.5 Quadratic Model

A mathematical model represented by a quadratic equation such as,

$$Y_t = \beta_0 + \beta_1 t + \beta_2 t^2 + \varepsilon \tag{4}$$

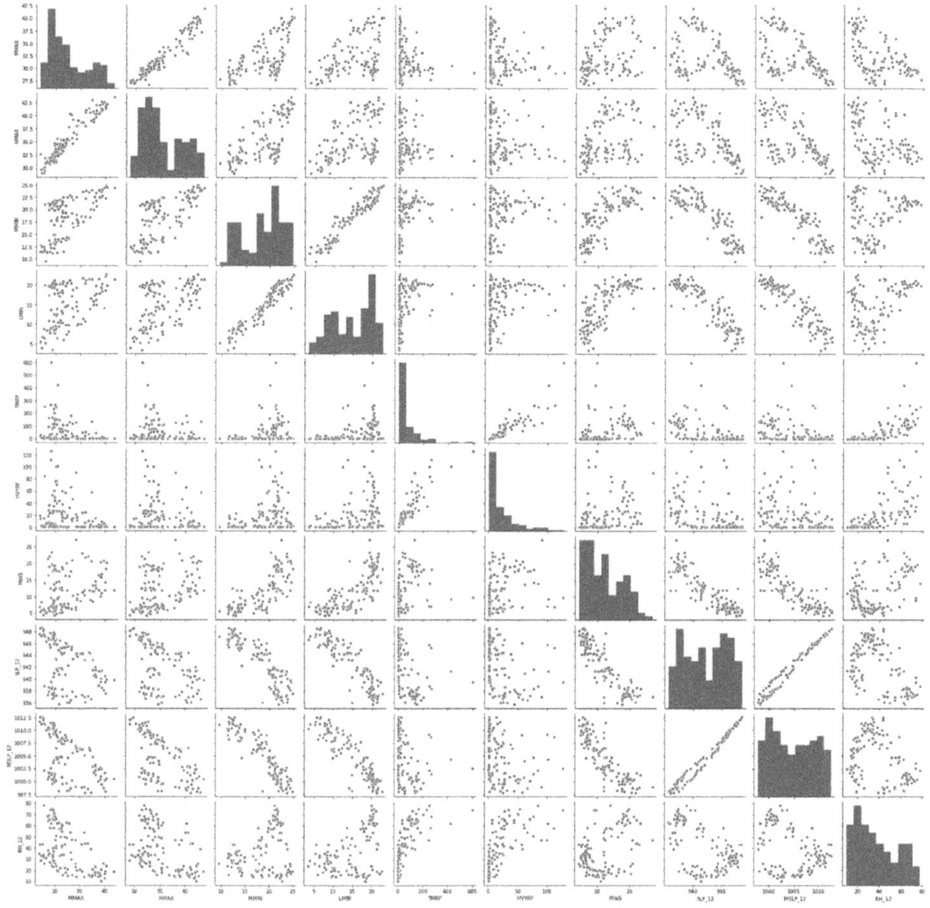

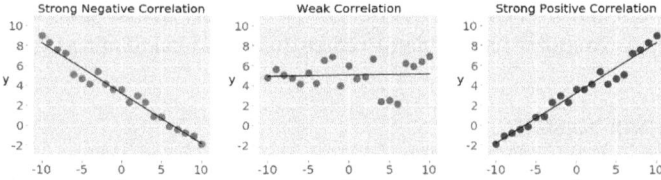

Fig. 5. Correlation of weather parameters

Fig. 6. Three different forms of correlation

A parabola is the graphed link between the variables in a quadratic equation. We plotted the data in scatter plots and used a graphing application to get the least squares regression lines. A similar approach might be used to find a model for nonlinear data. There are several methods to identify the model after utilizing a scatter plot to determine

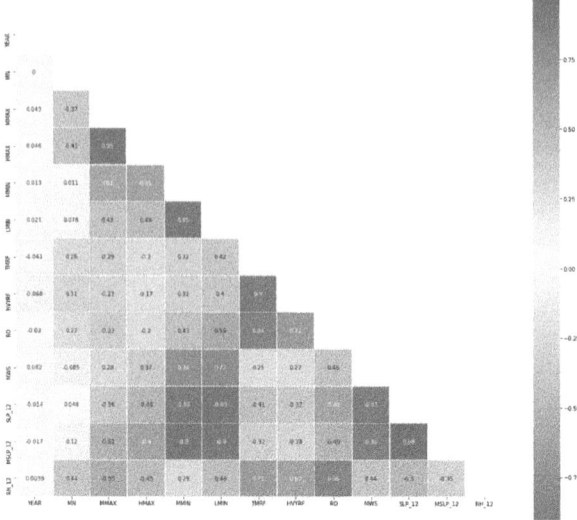

Fig. 7. A correlation matrix of data

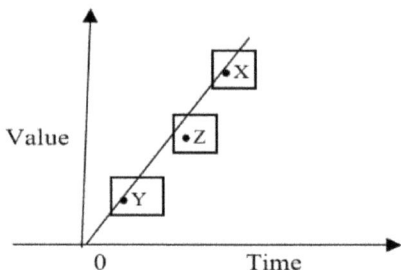

Fig. 8. Linear Relationship between data and missing values.

the type of model that would best suit a collection of data. Each method works effectively when utilizing a computer or calculator rather than hand calculations [27].

4.6 Forecasting Strategy

Seasonality is an important quality to consider when analyzing a Time Series. This property is said to be retained by a Time Series with a default behavior throughout a specified time period. We will have a sample that demonstrates seasonal activity if the pattern repeats itself within the same time range. This study is made easier by the Stats models package, but first, let's define a time series and its analytical properties. The average value of the series is called level. The growing or decreasing value is the series trend. The series' short-term cycle is repeated, which is referred to as seasonality. A noise is a term used to describe the random fluctuation of a series. There are two methods for studying a time series seasonality (additive and multiplicative) [28].

4.6.1 The Additive Model

The additive model is a form of data model that distinguishes and adds the effects of various components to synthetically represent the data. It is a systematic component of the forecasting model. It is represented by:

$$Y_t = L + T + S + N \tag{5}$$

where, L is level, T is the trend, S is seasonality and N is noise. The behavior is linear in the additive model, where adjustments are regularly made by the same amount over time, similar to a linear trend. Following equation is shown the Additive Seasonality (6) and Additive Seasonality with Quadratic Trend Eq. (7).

$$Y_t = \beta_0 + \beta_1 D_{Jan} + \beta_2 D_{Feb} + \beta_3 D_{Mar} + \ldots \ldots + \beta_{11} D_{Nov} + \varepsilon \tag{6}$$

$$Y_t = \beta_0 + \beta_1 t + \beta_2 t^2 + \beta_3 D_{Jan} + \beta_4 D_{Feb} + \beta_5 D_{Mar} + \ldots \ldots + \beta_{13} D_{Nov} + \varepsilon \tag{7}$$

4.6.2 The Multiplicative Model

The error component is compounded and added to the trend and seasonal components. It's a part of a systematic forecasting model [29]. A curving line represents the multiplicative model, which is not linear but might be quadratic or exponential.

$$Y_t = L \times T \times S \times N \tag{8}$$

The multiplicative model, in contrast to the additive model, has an amplitude and frequency that increases or decreases with time. Following equation is shown the Multiplicative Seasonality (9) and Multiplicative Seasonality Linear Trend Eq. (10).

$$Log(Y_t) = \beta_0 + \beta_1 D_{Jan} + \beta_2 D_{Feb} + \beta_3 D_{Mar} + \ldots \ldots \beta_{11} D_{Nov} + \varepsilon \tag{9}$$

$$Log(Y_t) = \beta_0 + \beta_1 t + \beta_2 D_{Jan} + \beta_3 D_{Feb} + \beta_4 D_{Mar} + \ldots \ldots + \beta_{12} D_{Nov} + \varepsilon \tag{10}$$

4.7 Forecasting Error

The discrepancy between the actual and anticipated value of a time series or any other event of interest is known as the forecast error [30]. Because the forecast error is *calculated from the same scale of data, it is only possible* to compare the forecast errors of various series when they are on the same scale. Forecast error (e_t) equation is observed values – predicted values.

$$e_t = Y_t - \hat{Y}_t \tag{11}$$

Where, Y_t is observed values and $\hat{Y}_t$ is forecasted values.

4.7.1 Lag Plot

Plots a variable against its own lagged sample to reveal probable associations between consecutive samples. For example, monthly rainfall/temp/wind/humidity in a year (Y_t = rainfall/temp in time period t, Y_{t+k} = rainfall/temp in time period t-k).

4.7.2 Evaluating Predictive Accuracy Equations

Mean Error

$$ME = \frac{1}{T} \sum_{t-1}^{n} e_t \tag{12}$$

Mean Absolute Deviation

$$MAD = \frac{1}{n} \sum_{t=1}^{n} |e_t| \tag{13}$$

Mean Squared Error.

$$MSE = \frac{1}{n} \sum_{t=1}^{n} e_t^2 \tag{14}$$

Mean Root Squared Error

$$RMSE = \sqrt{\frac{1}{n} \sum_{t=1}^{n} e_t^2} \tag{15}$$

Mean Percentage Error.

$$MPE \frac{1}{n} \sum_{t=1}^{n} \frac{e_t}{y_t} \tag{16}$$

Mean Absolute Percentage Error.

$$MAPE = \frac{1}{n} \sum_{t=1}^{n} \left| \frac{e_t}{y_t} \right| \tag{17}$$

4.7.3 Root Mean Squared Error Values (RMSE)

The square root of the mean of all errors squared is used to calculate the RMSE. Because it is scale-dependent and not across variables, it is only helpful for comparing prediction errors of different models or model configurations for a single variable. RMSE is the residuals' standard deviation (prediction errors). The residuals show how far the data points are from the regression line, and the RMSE shows how widely these residuals are distributed. It represents how tightly the data clusters around the best-fit line. To validate experimental data, RMSE is frequently used in climatology, forecasting, and regression analysis [31].

Additive Seasonality Quadratic Trend is best fit model for the highest maximum temperature (1.42), lowest minimum temperature (1.87), wind speed (1.06), relative humidity (5.07), mean station (1.19), and mean sea level pressure (1.43). Multiplicative Seasonality model is the best model for mean minimum temperature (1.12) total rainfall in the month (24.13), heavy rainfall (8.74), and number of rainy days (1.2). Multiplicative Seasonality Linear Trend is given good accuracy for mean maximum temperature (1.2). The linear, exponential, quadratic and additive seasonality are not given good result for weather parameter.

The temperature (mean and high maximum, mean and lowest minimum), number of rainy day, mean wind speed, mean station and sea level pressure are given good RMSE values such as 1.83, 1.95, 1.89, 2.66, 2.24, 1.69, 1.43, 1.62 respectively. Relative humidity is given 9.37 RMSE values. Total month of rainfall and heavy rainfall is given 32.16 and 11.9 RMSE values. Total month of rainfall accuracy is not good because rainfall is deepened location, time, climate and geographical region. Due to this rainfall is high, medium and low in the rainy season. The mean maximum temperature prediction model gives 98.98% accuracy using Multiplicative Seasonality Linear Trend and rainfall prediction model is given 75.87% accuracy using Multiplicative Seasonality machine learning techniques.

We have used seven machine learning techniques for the prediction of weather model such as linear, exponential, quadratic, additive seasonality, additive seasonality quadratic trend, multiplicative seasonality, and multiplicative seasonality linear trend. The linear, exponential, quadratic and additive seasonality are not given good result for any weather parameter.

The additive seasonality quadratic trend is best fit model for the HMAX, LMIN, MWS, RH, SLP and MSLP. The multiplicative seasonality model is the best model for the MMIN, TMRF, HVYRF and RD. The multiplicative seasonality linear trend is given good accuracy for MMAX.

4.7.4 Time Series Partitioning

We have used one decade historical data for forecasting. We have used 70% data for training. It is fitted the model only to training period and 30% data is used for validation. It assess performance on validation period.

4.8 Autocorrelation

The correlation between a variable and its lagged form is known as autocorrelation (one step, two step or multiple time step).

$$r_k = \frac{\sum_{t=k=1}^{n}\left(Y_t - \overline{Y}\right)\left(Y_{t-k-Y}\right)}{\sum_{i=1}^{n}\left(Y_t - \overline{Y}\right)^2}, \quad K = 0, 1, 2, \dots \tag{18}$$

Where,
  (Y_t) is observation in time period (t).
  (Y_{t-k}) is observation in time period (t-k).
  $(\bar{Y})$ is mean of the values of the series.
  (r_k) is autocorrelation coefficient for k-step lag.

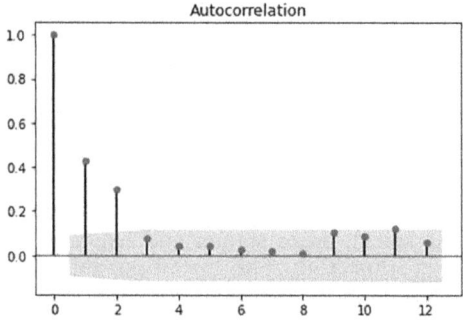

Fig. 9. ACF plot of data

4.8.1 Correlogram or ACF Plot

The ACF is plotted versus the lag. Limits to be exceeded for statistical significance are indicated as plus and minus two standard errors. Identifies lagged variables that is beneficial for predicting [32].

4.8.2 ACF Plot on Residuals

ACF is a (complete) auto-correlation function that returns auto-correlation values for any time series with lagged values (Fig. 9).

4.8.3 Partial Auto-correlation Function (PACF)

It finds correlations of present with lags of the residuals (prediction errors) of the time series (Fig. 10).

We have got the slightly changes in the original and predicted values for mean maximum temperature, mean station and sea level pressure. The rainfall, wind speed and humidity are increased in the monsoon season. Rainfall is highest in the months of July and September, and lowest in the months of June and August. The RMSE value in rainfall is high since rainfall is deepened based on current meteorological knowledge. Sometime rainfall is high and some time it is low or medium. Rainfall is higher in the

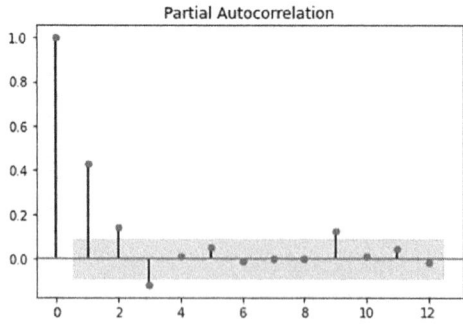

Fig. 10. PACF plot of data

months of June, July, and September, and lower in the month of August. The number of rainy day is depended on how much day rainfall is happened in the month. Number of rainy day is highest in the month of July. The wind speed and relative humidity are increased in the monsoon season. It correlation between rainfall. The station and sea level pressure are decreased in the rainy season. It is increased in the summer and winter season.

5 Conclusions

The weather parameters are playing vital role. The weather parameters are interdependent and current situation. If the extreme events are happened in the year such as flooding, earthquake, cyclone, etc. it will effect on the weather condition. We have taken database form the Indian Metrological Department (IMD), Pune, Maharashtra, India. We have covered the five Marathwada region districts such as Aurangabad, Beed, Parbhani, Osmanabad and Nanded. We have implemented missing imputation, outliers, histogram, scatter plot, barplot and time series plot for preprocessing dataset. It is helped to improve the result accuracy. We have used autocorrelation and seven models for furcating such as linear, exponential, quadratic, additive seasonality, additive seasonality quadratic trend, multiplicative seasonality, and multiplicative seasonality linear trend.

Additive seasonality quadratic trend is the best model for the highest maximum temperature, lowest minimum temperature, wind speed, relative humidity, mean station and sea level pressure. Multiplicative seasonality model is the best model for mean minimum temperature, total rainfall in the month, heavy rainfall, and number of rainy days. Multiplicative Seasonality Linear Trend is given good accuracy for mean maximum temperature. The linear, exponential, quadratic and additive seasonality are not given good result for weather parameter. We have created forecasting system for Marathwada region by using machine learning tools. We have got overall accuracy 1.83, 1.95, 1.89, 2.66, 32.16, 11.91, 2.24, 1.69, 1.43, 1.62, 9.37 for mean and highest maximum temperature, mean and lowest minimum temperature, total month of rainfall, heavy rainfall in the month, number of rainy day, mean wind speed, mean station and sea level pressure and relative humidity respectively.

References

1. Semenov MA, Barrow EM. Use of a stochastic weather generator in the development of climate change scenarios. Climatic Change 1997; 35: 397-414.
2. Wilks DS. Adapting stochastic weather generation algorithms for climate change studies. Climatic Change 1992; 22: 67-84.
3. Pruski FF, Nearing MA. Climate-induced changes in erosion during the 21st century for eight U.S. locations. Water Resour Res 2002; 38: 341–3411.
4. Zhang XC, Nearing MA, Garbrecht JD, Steiner JL. Downscaling monthly forecasts to simulate impacts of climate change on soil erosion and wheat production. Soil Sci Soc Am J 2004; 68: 1376–85.
5. Zhang XC. Spatial downscaling of global climate model output for site-specific assessment of crop production and soil erosion. Agr Forest Meteorol 2005; 135: 215–29.

6. Zhang XC, Liu WZ. Simulating potential response of hydrology, soil erosion, and crop productivity to climate change in Changwu tableland region on the Loess Plateau of China. Agr Forest Meteorol 2005; 131: 127-42.

7. Kilsby CG, Jones PD, Burton A, Ford AC, Fowler HJ, Harpham C, James P, Smith A, Wilby RL. A daily weather generator for use in climate change studies. Environ Modell Softw 2007; 22: 1705-19.

8. Richardson CW. Stochastic simulation of daily precipitation, temperature, and solar radiation. Water Resour Res 1981; 17: 182-90.

9. Richardson CW, Wright DA. WGEN: A model for generating daily weather variables. U.S. Depart. Agr, Agricultural Research Service. Publ. ARS-8; 1984, p. 1–86.

10. Stockle CO, Campbell GS, Nelson R. ClimGen Manual. Biological Systems Engineering Department, Washington State University, Pullman, WA; 1999.

11. Semenov MA, Barrow EM. LARS-WG, A Stochastic Weather Generator for Use in Climate Impact Studies, User Manual; 2002.

12. Dubrovsky M, Buchteke J, Zalud Z. High-frequency and low-frequency variability in stochastic daily weather generator and its effect on agricultural and hydrologic modeling. Climatic Change 2004; 63: 145-79.

13. Hansen JW, Mavromatis T. Correcting low-frequency variability bias in stochastic weather generators. Agr Forest Meteorol 2001; 109: 297-310.

14. Wang QJ, Nathan RJ. A method for coupling daily and monthly time scales in stochastic generation of rainfall series. J Hydrol 2007; 346: 122-30.

15. Chen J, Brissette PF, Leconte R. A daily stochastic weather generator for preserving low-frequency of climate variability. J Hydrol 2010; 388: 480-90.

16. Mehrotra, R., Sensitivity of runoff, soil moisture and reservoir design to climate change in central Indian river basins. Climatic Change, 1999, 42, 725-757.

17. IPCC, Summary for policymakers. In Climate Change 2007: The Physical Science Basis (eds Solomon, S. D. et al.), Cambridge University Press, Cambridge, UK, 2007.

18. Kundzewicz, Z. W., Change detection in hydrological records - a review of the methodology. Hydrol. Sei., J., 2004, 49(1), 7–19.

19. Sen, P. K., Estimates of the regression coefficient based on Kend all's tau. J. Am. Stat. Assoc., 1968, 63, 1379-1389.

20. Lettenmaier, D. P., Wood, E. F. and Wallis, J. R., Hydro climatological trends in the continental United States, 1948-88. J. Climate, 1994, 7, 586-607.

21. Yue, S. and Hashino, M., Temperature trends in Japan: 1900 1990. Theor. Appl. Climatol., 2003, 75, 15-27.

22. Partal, T. and Kahya, E., Trend analysis in Turkish precipitation data. Hydrol. Process, 2006, 20, 2011-2026.

23. Yu, Y. S., Zou, S. and Whittemore, D., Non-parametric trend analysis of water quality data of rivers in Kansas. J. Hydrol., 1993, 150, 61-80.

24. Douglas, E. M., Vogel, R. M. and Knoll, C. N., Trends in flood and low flows in the United States: impact of spatial correlation. J. Hydrol., 2000, 240, 90-105.

25. Yue, S., Pilon, P. and Phinney, B., Canadian streamflow trend detection: impacts of serial and cross-correlation. Hydrol. Sci. J., 2003, 48, 51-63.

26. Burn, D. H., Cunderlik, J. M. and Pietroniro, A., Hydrological trends and variability in the Liard river basin. Hydrol. Sci. J., 2004, 49, 53-67.

27. Singh, P., Kumar, V., Thomas, T. and Arora, M., Changes in rain fall and relative humidity in different river basins in the northwest and central India. Hydrol. Process., 2008, 22, 2982-2992.

28. Singh, P., Kumar, V., Thomas, T. and Arora, M., Basin-wide assessment of temperature trends in the north-west and central India. Hydrol. Sci. J., 2008, 53, 421-433.

29. Salas, J. D., Analysis and modeling of hydrologie time series. In Handbook of Hydrology (ed. Maidment, D. R.), McGraw-Hill, New York, 1993, p. 19.1–19.72.

30. Helsel, D. R. and Hirsch, R. M., Statistical Methods in Water Resources, Elsevier, New York, 1992.

31. Hirsch, R. M., Helsel, D. R., Cohn, T. A. and Gilroy, E. J., Statistical treatment of hydrologie data. In Handbook of Hydrology (ed. Maidment, D. R.), McGraw-Hill, New York, 1993, p. 17.1–17.52.

32. Srivastava, H. N., Sinha Ray, K. C., Dikshit, S. K. and Muk hopadhaya, R. K., Trends in rainfall and radiation over India. Vayu Mandai, 1998, 41–45.

Pest Detection System for Rice Crop Using Pest-Net Model

Sukanya S. Gaikwad[1(✉)] and Mallikarjun Hangarge[2]

[1] Department of Computer Science, Gulbarga University, Kalaburagi, Karnataka, India
gsukanya116@gmail.com
[2] Department of Computer Science, Karnatak Arts Science, and Commerce College, Bidar, Karnataka, India

Abstract. This paper presents a model for automatic pests identification of rice crops using the CNN approach called the Pest-Net model. This model aims to classify six different major pests affecting rice crops. To establish the novelty and credibility of our work, we have also used the transfer learning approach of CNN i.e. AlexNet model for the classification of the same dataset. It is observed from the experimental results and performance measures that the Pest-Net model performed well and gave good recognition accuracy of 88.6% as compared to the AlexNet model.

Keywords: CNN · Pest-Net · AlexNet · Transfer learning · Pest · Rice crop

1 Introduction

The population in India mainly depends on agriculture for their economic income. To cultivate the crop requires adequate irrigation, sufficient sunlight, quality of the soil, and the construction of water dams and water wheels. Among the many crops grown in India, rice is majorly grown and consumed which is around one-fourth of the population of our country. Rice is one of the most significant human food crops, accounting for one-tenth of all arable land on the planet [1]. It is an edible cereal crop whose binomial name is Oryza Sativa (L) commonly known as Asian rice. Asia produces more than 90% of the world's rice, the main production is in China, India, Indonesia, and Bangladesh. Human beings consume 95 percent of the world's rice harvest.

Plant diseases and insect pests cause major yield loss in plants and crops. So, early diagnosis of pests must be very important to the food industry as these might affect the productivity of crops. The general observation method by farmers is time-consuming, costly, and incorrect at times. Due to this reason, we aim to tackle the issue of identification of the pests of rice crops, as rice is the most consumed crop worldwide.

A manual examination can be used to detect pests, but it is a time-consuming and costly procedure. As a result, professionals such as plant pathologists, agriculture experts, and farmers monitor the plants and crops frequently which is a tiresome procedure. Hence the need arises to use the technology in the agriculture sector. This is possible due to

© The Author(s) 2023
R. Manza et al. (Eds.): ACVAIT 2022, AISR 176, pp. 590–601, 2023.
https://doi.org/10.2991/978-94-6463-196-8_45

advancements in technologies such as computer vision, machine learning, and deep learning techniques.

In this work, our goal is to identify and classify pests that cause harm to the rice crop. A pest is an animal, which causes harmful and damaging impacts on the yield of the crops. Here we have collected the pest dataset from Kaggle. The dataset consists of hundred different class labels but we have considered only the pests which affect the rice crop. So a total of six different class labels are considered which include rice gall midge, rice leaf caterpillar, rice leaf roller, rice leafhopper, rice shell pest, and rice water weevil.

The remainder of the article is organized as Sect. 2 narrates the literature survey, Sect. 3 discusses the dataset, Sect. 4 discusses the methods used, Sect. 5 shows the experimental results, and the end conclusions are given in Sect. 6.

2 Literature Survey

T.Y. Kuo et al [2] discuss the recent advances in image processing techniques applied to many aspects of the agriculture industry. They used sparse-representation-based classification algorithms to find a variety of rice grains.

Eusebio L et al [3] identified and classified the rice affecting pests. The transfer learning approach of CNN is utilized, because of fewer data available. Inception v3 model is utilized and after training the model, they got a good recognition accuracy of 90.9% on the collected dataset.

Ebrahimi M. A et al [4] developed an automatic pest detection mechanism for identifying thrips found on strawberry plants. They used the machine learning classifier SVM using color index and choice of region of interest with less than a 2.5% error rate.

Thenmozhi, K et al [5] deployed an automatic crop insect detection system to identify the insect in its early stage. They used the shape detection method for extracting the shapes of the insects like oval, circle, cylindrical, etc. of the sugarcane crop. Using Sobel edge detection the system can identify the insects with good accuracy as compared to the manual methods.

V. Malathi et al [6] worked on the classification of pests present in the paddy crop. They used the transfer learning approach to classify the pest dataset. This pest dataset consists of ten different class labels with 3549 pest images. The ResNet 50 model is fine-tuned over different hyper parameters to obtain a good recognition accuracy of 95.02%.

Pattnaik et al [7] identified and classified 10 different pests present on the tomato plant. The pest dataset consists of 859 images of pests. They used the transfer learning approach to identify the pests. 15 different trained models were exhaustively used to classify the pests. After fine-tuning the models with correct parameters, it is observed that the DenseNet169 model has given an average recognition accuracy of 88.83%, which is the highest compared to the other 14 models.

The watershed approach was employed by Xia et al [8] to segment the insects, and then the Mahalanobis distance was used to extract color information from the YCrCb color space. The closest distance between the retrieved feature vector and the reference vectors associated with each class was used to classify each item as whitefly, aphid, or thrip.

In pictures taken under controlled circumstances, Wen et al. [9] employed the SIFT descriptor to extract features for the characterization of 5 pest species. SVM produced the greatest accuracy results out of the six classifiers examined.

Huang et al [10] worked on classifying the tomato pests. Eight different pests affecting the tomato were taken into consideration. They utilized the hybrid approach of DL to extract the features and classify them using ML methods. For classification, they also utilized the VGG 16 model which gave a good recognition accuracy of 94.95%.

Based on the above analysis of the literature a major gap is noticed that no researcher addressed pests identification that harms the rice crops, though rice is the major crop across the globe. To increase the yield of rice crops, detection of pests and other disease-affecting agents is need to be taken care of at an early stage, so that the spread of the disease is stopped. Hence our main goal of this research is to present a new system for identifying the pests of rice crops in a real-time environment. This may help increase rice yield and help the farmers in the productive production of rice.

3   Dataset Description

The dataset is collected from Kaggle, it contains hundreds of pests that affect different crops and plants. We have collected only the rice affecting pests. These include six different categories which are shown below in Fig. 1.

Table 1 shows the summary of the pest database used.

Fig. 1. Rice Gall Midge, Rice Leaf Caterpillar, Rice Leaf Roller, Rice leaf Hopper, Rice Shell Pest, Rice Water Weevil.

Table 1. Summary of pest database

Category	Training	Testing	Total
Rice Gall Midge	295	74	369
Rice Leaf Caterpillar	209	52	261
Rice Leaf Roller	390	97	487
Rice Leaf Hopper	138	35	173
Rice Shell Pest	688	172	860
Rice Water Weevil	323	81	404
Total	2043	511	2554

4   Proposed Model

Here, we describe the method used for the classification of pests. We introduce a deep learning-based CNN model. Several layers are placed on top of one another, with each layer using the preceding layer as input to the model. CNN requires extremely little pre-processing and excels at picture analysis. To detect pests, we employ the convolution neural network (CNN) architecture, which provides the state of the art results. And to establish the novelty we have created our own deep Convolutional Neural Network, which we call as Pest-Net. Table 2 shows the layer used for creating the Pest-Net model.

Table 2. Pest-Net layers

CNN Layers	Type	Output Size
Conv 1	Convolution	$64 \times 64 \times 32$
Pool 1	Max Pooling	$64 \times 64 \times 32$
Conv 2	Convolution	$63 \times 63 \times 64$
Pool 2	Max Pooling	$63 \times 63 \times 64$
Conv 3	Convolution	$62 \times 62 \times 128$
Pool 3	Max Pooling	$62 \times 62 \times 128$
Conv 4	Convolution	$61 \times 61 \times 256$
Pool 4	Max Pooling	61x61x256
Conv 5	Convolution	$61 \times 61 \times 384$
Pool 5	Max Pooling	$61 \times 61 \times 384$
FC	Fully Connected	4
Probability	Softmax	4

The complete step-by-step process of the Pest-Net model is discussed extensively below.

1. **Pre-processing:** This is the first step in any image processing method, where the given dataset is adjusted according to the need of the problem. Before we train and test the model the dataset needs to be in uniform size and format. Hence we pre-process the dataset to a fixed size of 256 x 256.
2. **Input layer:** This layer accepts the images which are in M x M x N format. Where M x M are dimensions and N is the number of channels. For gray images $N = 2$ and color images it is $N = 3$. Here we are using color images which will be $N = 3$. This layer accepts input as 256 x 256 x 3.
3. **Convolution layer:** This is the layer where actual mathematical operations are performed. In the case of convolution, a bigger convolution filter can extract key information from an input picture, assisting in the more accurate identification of pests. We experimented with different filter sizes for our model like 4×4 and 5×5, which resulted in the time and space complexity of the model as the framework utilized is CPU. Hence, our introduced approach has five convolution layers with a 3×3 filter size. The first convolution layer has a filter size of $32 \times 3 \times 3$, the second has $64 \times 3 \times 3$, the third has $128 \times 3 \times 3$ the fourth has a filter size of $256 \times 3 \times 3$ and the last convolution layer has a filter size of $384 \times 3 \times 3$. These convolution layers help to boost the extraction efficiency. The convolution procedure, which yields Eq. 1, determines the whole feature map. Where P_i is a feature map and * the convolution operators, the nth input channel is designated by X_n, the kernels are defined by Z_{in}, and the bias value is defined by B_i.

$$p_i = B_i + \Sigma Z_{in} * X_n \tag{1}$$

The activation function used is ReLu as it is good at learning nonlinearity. This activation function is used mainly to solve the problem of over-fitting.

4. **Pooling Layer:** Pooling decreases various convolution layer parameters and isolates the important characteristics of these layers. This layer reduces the number of parameters in all areas, boosts computing performance, and calculates significant attributes to reflect all of the qualities of the selected region. We have different types of pooling functions like Max pooling and Average pooling. For our proposed model we have used the Max pooling operation. This function keeps the maximum value from a given sub-window.
5. **Fully Connected Layer (FC):** The proposed model uses FC layers. Before employing the FC layer, the last level, flatten, is where convolution layers and pooling layers' whole output is sent and reshaped into a single linear array of a matrix. The layers use the softmax activation function to learn important characteristics that may be used to recognize and categorize relevant input data. The softmax function is given by Eq. (2)

$$O_x = S(\gamma)_x = \frac{e^{\gamma x}}{\sum_{n=1}^{N} e\gamma n} \tag{2}$$

In Eq. 2, S is the softmax function, which takes an N-dimensional vector and returns a set of real numbers between 0 and 1. Ox is the name of the output vector.

For comparison analysis, we have utilized the transfer learning approach of deep learning, where a pre-trained AlexNet model is used. This model is already trained on thousands of different categories. The Pest-Net and AlexNet model are trained extensively on pest datasets and the observed outputs are discussed in the consequent Section.

5 Experimental Results

In this part, we examine the experimental findings of our research. Pest-Net and the pre-trained deep learning model AlexNet are used for training and testing purposes. We divide the collected dataset into the training and testing part. 80% we utilize for training purposes and the rest 20% we utilize for testing. Hyper-parameter tuning of the models is kept the same so that we can compare both the models with standard parameters, which is shown in Table 3.

We have experimented with different batch sizes, learning rates, and solver types for both models. It is observed from the experiments that the low batch size, learning rate, and solver type as SGDM, both the models have underperformed and have required lot of hours to train the models. Whereas, in the above said table 3 both the models have performed better.

Table 4 and Table 5 show the species-wise recognition accuracy for Pest-Net and AlexNet.

Table 6 and Table 7 shows the Confusion matrix for Pest-Net and AlexNet model respectively.

The below graph Fig. 2 and Fig. 3 shows the accuracy obtained for training and testing datasets by utilizing Pest-Net and AlexNet models respectively.

Below Fig. 4 shows the results obtained using the Pest-Net model and Fig. 5 manifests the relative study of the Pest-Net and AlexNet model.

We have calculated the performance measures for the Pest-Net and AlexNet models which are the required measures to know how well the models perform on the given dataset. Table 8 shows the performance measures of the models.

Table 3. Tuning of Hyperparameters

Sl. No.	Name of the parameter	Parameter
1	Solver type	Adam Optimizer
2	Base learning rate	0.0001
3	Batch size	128
4	Epochs	30
5	Training	80%
6	Validation	20%

Table 4. Species-wise recognition accuracy for Pest-Net

Sl. No.	Species	Accuracy in %
1	Rice Gall Midge	83.1%
2	Rice Leaf Caterpillar	50.3%
3	Rice Leaf Roller	77.6%
4	Rice Leaf Hopper	79.4%
5	Rice Shell Pest	95.8%
6	Rice Water Weevil	82.9%

Table 5. Species-wise recognition accuracy for AlexNet

Sl. No.	Species	Accuracy in %
1	Rice Gall Midge	71.6%
2	Rice Leaf Caterpillar	48.1%
3	Rice Leaf Roller	73.2%
4	Rice Leaf Hopper	74.3%
5	Rice Shell Pest	98.8%
6	Rice Water Weevil	80.2%

Table 6. Confusion Matrix of Pest-Net

	GM	LC	LR	LH	SP	WW
GM	**59**	4	5	0	1	2
LC	10	**30**	6	0	0	5
LR	2	1	**79**	0	5	9
LH	2	4	2	**28**	0	1
SP	1	1	0	1	**171**	0
WW	2	1	7	0	0	**72**
Accuracy in %					**88.6%**	

Experiment findings of this section show that the approach we presented provides effective results that can help with correct pest detection. And the results of the experiments reveal that the presented method's performance is significantly compatible with pest recognition.

Table 7. Confusion Matrix of AlexNet

	GM	LC	LR	LH	SP	WW
GM	53	7	5	1	3	5
LC	12	25	9	0	0	6
LR	5	0	71	0	9	12
LH	2	4	2	26	0	1
SP	0	2	0	0	170	0
WW	3	2	9	1	1	65
Accuracy in %					**80.2%**	

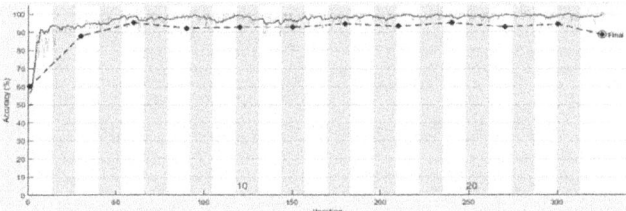

Fig. 2. Graph for accuracy obtained for training (blue) & testing (black) for Pest-Net.

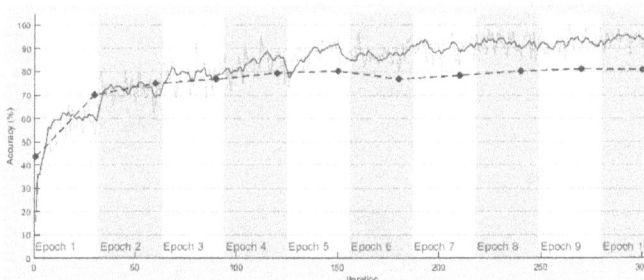

Fig. 3. Graph for accuracy obtained for training (blue) & testing (black) for AlexNet.

5.1 Discussions

The architecture of both the models is different. Many of the parameters like dropout layer, filter size and number of filters used in the model plays an important role in classification task. As the dropout layer is used to focus on the prominent features of the class and drops the not-so significant features. This layer we have avoided in our architecture. The number of filters in our architectures is increasing as we go deep down in the network. This implies we are extracting more number of features as we go down in the network. More number of features implies more accurate results to classify the given class. The Pest-Net model is trained from scratch, and has achieved a final accuracy of

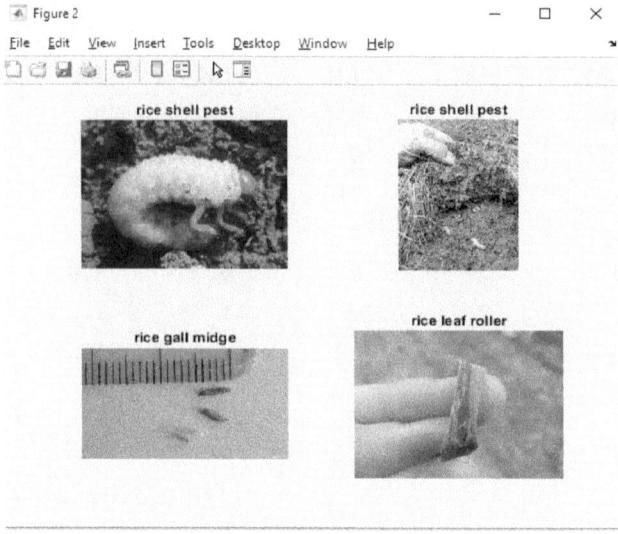

Fig. 4. Obtained result using Pest-Net model

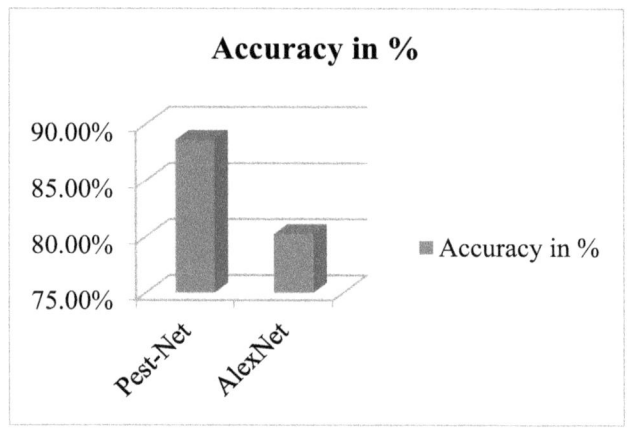

Fig. 5. Comparative analysis of Pest-net and AlexNet model

88.6% with a low error rate to classify the Pest dataset. Hence, the model can be used to predict the rice pests with good accuracy.

The only draw-back of our network is that, it requires more time to train the model, as we are training the model from scratch. The table 9 shows the time elapsed to train both the models.

The main advantages of our work signify as:

1. Our paper aims to work on the most consumed crop in the world i.e., rice. We have worked on the identification of pests present on the rice crop.

Table 8. Performance measures: Precision, Recall, F1 score using Pest-Net and AlexNet

Pest-Net (Own Network)				
	Precision	**Recall**	**F1score**	**Accuracy**
Pest-Net	0.8924	0.7986	0.7889	88.6%
Transfer Learning				
AlexNet	0.7438	0.7765	0.7598	80.2%

Table 9. Comparison based on Time required to train the model.

Sl. No.	Model	Accuracy	Time required to train the model
1	Pest-Net	88.6%	302 min 47 s
2	AlexNet	80.2%	235 min 44 s

2. To the best of our knowledge, we are the first kind to work on six different major pests affecting the rice crop.
3. An exhaustive comparison of transfer learning and own proposed approach is presented. The presented approach is experimented with different hyper parameters to obtain optimized accuracy.
4. Comparison analysis of Pest-Net and AlexNet is made on some standard parameters, to justify the fact that the Pest-Net model has got good accuracy. This is presented in Table 8.

6 Conclusions

In this work, we aim to identify and classify the pests found on rice crops. The dataset is collected from Kaggle. Using the CNN approach, the Pest-Net model is developed from scratch and trained on the pest dataset. For comparison analysis transfer learning approach of CNN is also utilized i.e., a pre-trained AlexNet model is used. It is observed from the experimental results that the developed Pest-Net model performed well and gave promising results compared to the already trained AlexNet model. This is because the Pest-Net model is developed and trained on the pest dataset from scratch. Farmers with smart-phones can use these generated models to help them control rice insect infestations. Once pests have been detected and reported to the Department of Agriculture, these will assist personnel in providing support to farmers.

Acknowledgments. The author would like to thank Dr. Babasaheb Ambedkar Marathwada University, Aurangabad (MS) India for providing the publication support.

References

1. Thorburn, C. 2015. "The rise and demise of integrated pest management in rice in Indonesia," Insects(April 2015), 381–408.
2. T.Y. Kuo , C. L. Chung, S.Y. Chen, H.A. Lin, Y.F. Kuo, "Identifying rice grains using image analysis and sparse-representation-based classification", Computers and Electronics in Agriculture, vol. 127, pp. 716–725, September 2016.
3. Mique Jr, Eusebio L., and Thelma D. Palaoag. "Rice pest and disease detection using convolutional neural network." In Proceedings of the 2018 international conference on information science and system, pp. 147–151. 2018.
4. Ebrahimi, M. A., Mohammad-Hadi Khoshtaghaza, Saeid Minaei, and Bahareh Jamshidi. "Vision-based pest detection based on SVM classification method." *Computers and Electronics in Agriculture* 137 (2017): 52–58.
5. Thenmozhi, K., and U. Srinivasulu Reddy. "Image processing techniques for insect shape detection in field crops." In *2017 International Conference on Inventive Computing and Informatics (ICICI)*, pp. 699–704. IEEE, 2017.
6. Malathi, V., and M. P. Gopinath. "Classification of pest detection in paddy crop based on transfer learning approach." *Acta Agriculturae Scandinavica, Section B—Soil & Plant Science* 71, no. 7 (2021): 552–559.
7. Pattnaik, Gayatri, Vimal K. Shrivastava, and K. Parvathi. "Transfer learning-based framework for classification of pest in tomato plants." *Applied Artificial Intelligence* 34, no. 13 (2020): 981–993.
8. Xia, Chunlei, Tae-Soo Chon, Zongming Ren, and Jang-Myung Lee. "Automatic identification and counting of small size pests in greenhouse conditions with low computational cost." *Ecological informatics* 29 (2015): 139-146.
9. Wen, Chenglu, and Daniel Guyer. "Image-based orchard insect automated identification and classification method." *Computers and electronics in agriculture* 89 (2012): 110-115.
10. Huang, Mei-Ling, Tzu-Chin Chuang, and Yu- Chieh Liao. "Application of transfer learning and image augmentation technology for tomato pest identification." *Sustainable Computing: Informatics and Systems* 33 (2022): 100646.
11. Garcia, J and Barbedo, A.2013. "Digital image processing techniques for detecting, quantifying and classifying plant diseases," Springer Plus, 2 (2013) 660.
12. Alam, M. Z., Crump,A. R., Haque, M. M., Islam, M. S., Hossain, E., Hasan S. B., Hasan ,S. B. and Hossain, M. S. 2016. "Effects of integrated pest management on pest damage and yield components in a rice agro-ecosystem in the Barisal Region of Bangladesh," Environmental Science (March 2016).
13. Patil, J. K. and Kumar,R. 2011. "Advances in image processing for detection of plant diseases," Journal of Advanced Bioinformatics Applications and Research, 2(2)(2011) 135–141.
14. Hong-xing ,X., Ya-jun Y., Yan-hui ,L., Xu-song, Z., Junce ,T. and Feng-xiang, L.2017. "Sustainable management of rice insect pests by non-chemical-insecticide technologies in China," Rice Science, 24(2)(2017) 61–72.
15. Bajwa ,W. I. and Kogan, M. 2017. "Internet-based IPM informatics and decision Support," Integrated Plant Protection Center (IPPC), Retrieved September 2017 from ipmworld: https://ipmworld.umn.edu/bajwa .
16. Azfar,S., Nadeem ,A., and Basit ,A. 2015. "Pest detection and control techniques using wireless sensor network", Journal of Entomology and Zoology Studies, 3(2)(2015) 92- 99.
17. Agnihotri, Vivek. "Machine Learning-based Pest Identification in Paddy Plants." In *2019 3rd International Conference on Electronics, Communication and Aerospace Technology (ICECA)*, pp. 246–250. IEEE, 2019.

Evaluation of the Multispectral Satellites with Object-Based Classifiers for Land Use and Land Cover Classification

Eman A. Alshari[1,2(✉)] and Bharti W. Gawali[2]

[1] Computer Science and Information Technology Department, Thamar University, Dhamar, Yemen
em.alshari3@gmail.com
[2] Dr. Babasaheb Ambedkar, Marathwada University, Aurangabad 431004, India

Abstract. This research aimed to evaluate traditional machine learning to achieve high-resolution LULC classification with multispectral satellites and object-based classifiers. Multispectral satellites have high importance in getting and downloading images of observation land. This article describes the comparative analysis of Sentinel-2A (10 m resolution) and Landsat8 (30 m resolution)Satellites with two classifiers from object-based machine learning methods, Random Forest (RF) and K Nearest Neighbor (KNN), to experiment with the classification of five years (2015, 2016, 2017, 2018, and 2019) with 95 images downloaded, 60 images with sentinal2A, and 35 images with landsat8. Area of Sana'a region. This Study indicated that Random Forest proved efficient for Sentinel 2A and Landsat8. Whereas KNN worked well with Landsat8 and provided higher accuracy than RF. The interpretation of these results may be due to the RF classifier requiring many features for good accuracy. At the same time, KNN works well with a small number of input feature variables and gives good accuracy.

Keywords: Multispectral Satellites · Land Use & Land Cover Classification (LULC C) · Sentinel-2A satellite (10m) · Landsat8 Satellite (30m) · Random Forest (RF) Classifier · K-Nearest Neighbour (KNN) · Sana'a City

1 Introduction

Multispectral sensors are stimulated by incoming energy reflected or released by things on the land's surface, diffused, and collected in sensors sensitive to a wide range of spectral bands [1]. These spectral bands are represented by a small section of the electromagnetic spectrum specified by the sensor's shortest and most effective wavelengths, resulting in a single bitmap for each spectral band. Figure 1 shows the four most often utilized spectral bands in open data multispectral satellite missions worldwide, with black boxes indicating incoming intensity. Optical imaging technologies include near-infrared imaging systems [2].

The energy of the sensor is converted into digital data, which is affected by the weather conditions at the time of measurement. As a result, rather than a quantifiable

R. Manza et al. (Eds.): ACVAIT 2022, AISR 176, pp. 602–625, 2023.
https://doi.org/10.2991/978-94-6463-196-8_46

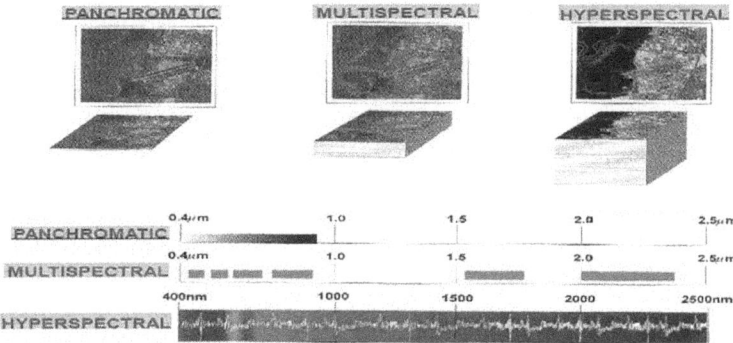

Fig. 1 Types of optical imaging systems and Spectral Resolution Concepts

physical unit, the numerical value indicates the relative relationship of the reversal at the time of observation [3]. It's required to translate numerical figures into an inversion, which is the ratio of the energy reflected for each spectral band to the overall power the sensor receives while analyzing this data. Spectral differences are used to identify and characterize land cover. Every spectral range has its unique personality [4]. When contrasted to the rest of the land, each cover feature has its unique spectral signature, defined by a considerable change in reflectance in one or more spectral bands, as shown in (Fig. 2).

High-resolution satellite images are limited compared to multispectral images in developing countries. This Study compares multispectral satellites using robust accuracy classifiers, Random Forest and KNN. The Pros of multispectral satellites are that it offers a significant number of free imagery: The images' spatial resolution varies (10500 m / pixel). As a result, these satellites may be utilized to get a large area at no cost. The concept is low-cost, easy to implement, and rapid. Significant differences between Landsat8 and Sentinel-2 may have a role in this Study's results. For example: Visiting time Landsat8 16 days and Sentinel-2 ten days per satellite, five days for two satellite constellations. It may be possible to be influenced by this difference from the workbook. Visiting time Sentinel-2 ten days per satellite maybe was not suitable with characters KNN that was my opinion [10].

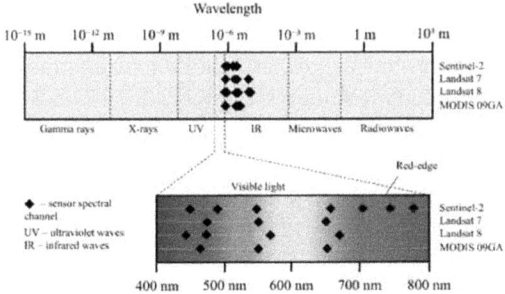

Fig. 2 Comparison of spectral bands for several multispectral satellites.

The machine learning algorithms effectively utilize the sensor images for land cover classification like Random forest and KNN [11]. RF is a collection or group of Classification and Regression Trees created through random resampling on the preparation set on datasets of comparable size to the preparation set, known as bootstraps. It is capable of accurately classifying large amounts of data. It is a learning system built with many decision trees during training, and the individual trees anticipate the modal output [12]. It has become a choice of researchers for classification, prediction, investigating variable importance, and variable selection [13]. The K-Nearest Neighbour method is one of the most fundamental Machine Learning algorithms. It is an approach that saves all available data and categorizes new data points depending on their similarity to the current data. Further data may be swiftly sorted into a well-defined category utilizing the approach [14].

The software used in this study is QGIS and SAGA GIS, a free, open-source software Automated Geoscientific Analysis. SAGA is a GIS application of spatial algorithms which are simple and effective. It includes an easy-to-use user interface with various visualization possibilities and a rich, increasing collection of geoscientific methodologies [15].

This Study attempted to work on the classification of LULC that depends on several factors to obtain a high-resolution characterization and varies according to the classifier used, the image, the time of filming, and the weather conditions in which it was captured., etc. The results showed that selecting only high-resolution satellite images is not enough. The characteristics of the classifier have a significant role in obtaining high-accuracy results in classification. This Study also presented that compatibility of the type of satellite with the typical characteristics of the classifier chosen is critical, which means that the specific features of the classifier selected are essential for this satellite. All of these factors have a role in achieving high-accuracy classification results. The significance of the Study lies in applying multispectral satellites under certain conditions and coming up with significant results. This research will be a helpful way to reveal to new researchers a way to obtain high accuracy in classifying changes in land use and land cover. And it helps specialists in this field decide on the selection type of method and type of satellite and Search in the development of traditional machine learning. This article will effectively plan the future aspects of LULC. This research presented the following: It compared two types of multispectral satellites (Landsat8 and Sentinel-2A) with two object-based classifiers (KNN and RF) of machine learning. It created a database or references for LULC of Sana'a city, the capital of Yemen, consisting of five years (2015, 2016, 2017, 2018, and 2019) with 95 images downloaded, 60 images with sentinal2A, and 35 images with landsat8. The Study presents the experimentation result of two satellite images with machine learning for Sana city –Yemen's capital- which is not yet explored with this approach. The result will assist in monitoring and predicting future land use and cover changes.

2   Literature Review

The summary of the literature survey, this study has concentrated on analyzing the performance of the multispectral satellites presented by research efforts in recent years [16–30]. It focused intensely on factors that influence their performance. This Study dealt with about forty-six studies analyzed systematically. They deal with pixel-based classifiers and other techniques but did not study multispectral satellites with object-based classifiers like this Study in explanation, analysis, and comparisons. Previous studies indicated the gap in studying land change classification with sentinel-2A and landsat8 satellites. In (Fig. 3) has cleared the research line about pixel-based and other techniques with the sentinel-2A versus landsat8 in recent years. The results of these studies show that little research supports that Landsat8 Satellite (30 m) is better than Sentinel2A (10m) [16]. But there are significantly more studies supporting that Sentinel2A (10m) was better than Landsat8 Satellite (30 m) [22–30]. Their findings reveal that the Sentinel2A (10 m) satellite has a superior resolution to the Landsat8 satellite. Their output was that Sentinel2A (10m) is better than Landsat8 Satellite [23] is logical because the pixel classifiers are affected by the location of the images sure gives high accuracy with Sentinel-2A -10-m more than Landsat8 Satellite (30 m). The review of work in this study also revealed that, despite the high resolution of deep learning, machine learning is still widely used and continues to be used today, with classical machine learning outperforming deep learning in terms of features and characteristics. Machine learning is less time-consuming and more accessible to implement than deep learning [29, 30]. The study demonstrated that it is possible without deep learning, we could have achieved a very high resolution for LULC classification using traditional machine learning and multispectral satellites [31–35].

Through Recent Years for pixel-based classifiers.

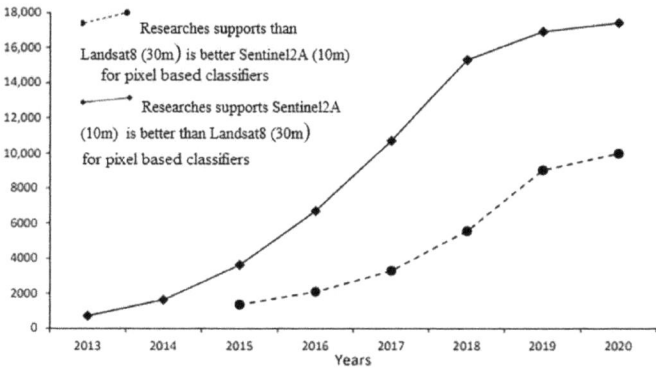

Fig. 3 Research Line Path About The Sentinel2A (10m) Versus Landsat8 Satellite (30m)

2.1 Limitation of This Study

To achieve the high-resolution classification of land changes using multispectral satellites and machine learning in a manner that competes for deep learning and high satellite. It was necessary to study the limitations of methods and satellites used in this Study during the survey literature review. There are essential details for the restriction of Landsat8 and Sentinel-2 described in (Table 1). The limitation of the methods used in this study is mentioned in detail in (Table 2 and Table 3).

Table 1. Differences between Sentinel-2A and Landsat8

Limitation	Landsat 8	Sentinel-2
Bands	Eight color	13 (3 red edge bands have some vegetation and chlorophyll in the ocean, applications)
Thermal bands	2 (band ten is generally better)	None
Swath width	185 km	290 km
Inclination (angle orbit crosses equator)	98.22	98.56
Best spatial Resolution	15 m pan, 30 m MSI	10 m for four bands
Revisit time	16 days	Ten days per satellite, five days for the constellation with two satellites
Coverage limits	81.8 S to 81.8N	systematic coverage: 56S to 84 N
		on request to 84S
Recorded data:	16-bit DN, which can be linearly scaled to TOA radiance or reflectance using constants in metadata	16-bit DN, which can be converted to TOA reflectance by dividing by 10000
Resolution of space (m)	(15),30,100	10,20,60
Temporal reorganization (days)	16	2–3
Resolution of spectral data	11 bands	13 bands
Resolution in radiometric terms	16-bit	12-bit
Width of the swath (km)	185	290
Range of wavelengths (nm)	433–12,500	442–2186
The scale of supported investigations is large.	National,Regional	Local, National

Table 2. Differences between Pixel and Object-based

No	Pixel-based	Object-based
1	The image is classed using spectral information in the pixel-based technique, which is frequently used to extract low-level characteristics. Because the classes are unclear, the pixels in the overlapped region will be incorrectly identified.	The aggregation of picture pixels into spectrally homogenous image objects ensures that the pixels not in an overlapping region will not be misclassified due to the object-based approach, frequently used to extract high-level features from images.
2	Only spectral data (pixel intensity) is used as a training set.	First, using spectral and geographical data (neighborhood pixels) as a training set
3	The techniques directly classify a single pixel.	After first aggregating image pixels into spectrally homogenous things, approaches classify individual objects using an image segmentation algorithm.

3 Materials and Procedures

3.1 Area of Study

Sana'a is Yemen's capital and the administrative seat of the Sana'a Governorate. Sana'a is situated at an altitude of 2150 m above sea level, on the line (15–21) north of the equator and longitude (12–44) east of Greenwich. It is surrounded by two mountains (Jabal Naqum on the east and Jabal Eiban on the west) and the province [36]. The city boasts a unique setting at roughly 2,200 m above sea level [37]. Sana'a is Yemen's largest city and the Governorate's administrative center. The elevation is 2,300 m (7,500 ft). It is the country's highest capital and is near the Sarawat Mountains. It has a population of roughly 3,937,500 (2012)[19]. It covers about 17,707.214 km2 land area in this study (Fig. 4).

3.2 Methodology

A brief explanation of the methodology for processing satellite data is shown in Fig. 5.

3.3 Pre-processing for LULC Classification

It is the primary and essential task in the process LULCC, the coordinate reference system for defining and cutting the map into specific areas. The pre-processing process procedure includes studying the location of the case study exactly, as evident in this study (Fig. 6), and identifying the data after being downloaded from satellites under remote sensing technology precisely (Figs. 7 and 8). The information subject to pre-processing is divided into the images shown in WGS84 or WGS84 / UTM.

Multispectral images from Sentinel-2 and landsat8 are available for the case study (Figs. 7 and 8), showing the pre-processing corrections for band 432. The pre-processing contains valid data with a geometric and radiometric correction, presented in this study

Table 3. Differences between RF and KNN

No	RF	KNN
1	RF classifier is object-based and hyper-parameter.	KNN classifier is object-based. Its algorithm is nonparametric, meaning it doesn't make assumptions about the data.
2	It depends on identifying objects without going into the details of those objects.	It's also known as a lazy learner algorithm since it doesn't immediately learn from the training set; instead, it keeps the dataset and performs a task.
3	It is known as neural networks, which provide estimates for variable relevance.	This method merely saves the information during the training phase. When it receives new data, it classifies it into a category similar to the latest data.
4	It also offers a preferable way of dealing with data that is missing.	Benefits of the KNN Algorithm: It is simple to implement. It can cope with noisy training data. It may be more successful if the training data is vast.
5	Its approach can also handle large datasets with thousands of variables. When a class is rarer than other classes, it can automatically balance data sets.	Disadvantages of the KNN Algorithm: The value of K must constantly be determined, which might sometimes be challenging. The computation cost is high since the distance between the data points for all training samples must be selected [16].
6	The method works quickly with variables suited for more complex jobs [21].	It predicts the output of data points using a labeled input data set. It's one of the most basic Machine Learning algorithms and may be used for a wide range of issues.
7	Missing values are filled in by the variable that appears the most in a given node.	The KNN technique is substantially quicker than earlier training-based algorithms [37].
8	It is implemented using algorithms with built-in feature selection techniques [34].	It's primarily based on visual resemblance.
9	It is effective because they have solid predictive performance, little overfitting, and is simple to comprehend [34].	The training data is saved and only used to produce real-time predictions to learn from it.

[37] with QGIS and SAGA software. These operations improve satellite imagery for classification and rectify the degraded image to generate a more authentic portrayal of the actual scene [37].

3.4 Classification Methods Used in This Study

There are four groups for classification models. Every group contains five categories of the models for five years, 2015, 2016, 2017, 2018, and 2019, as described in

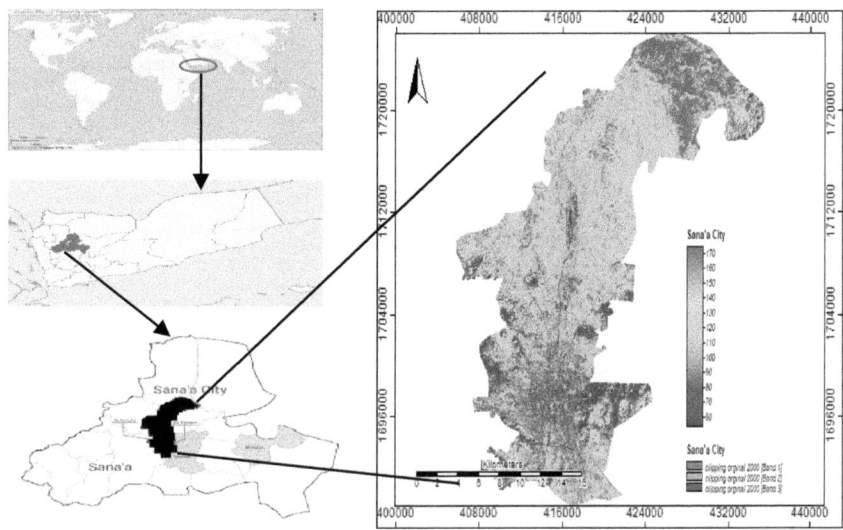

Fig. 4 The location of Sana'a City Study area

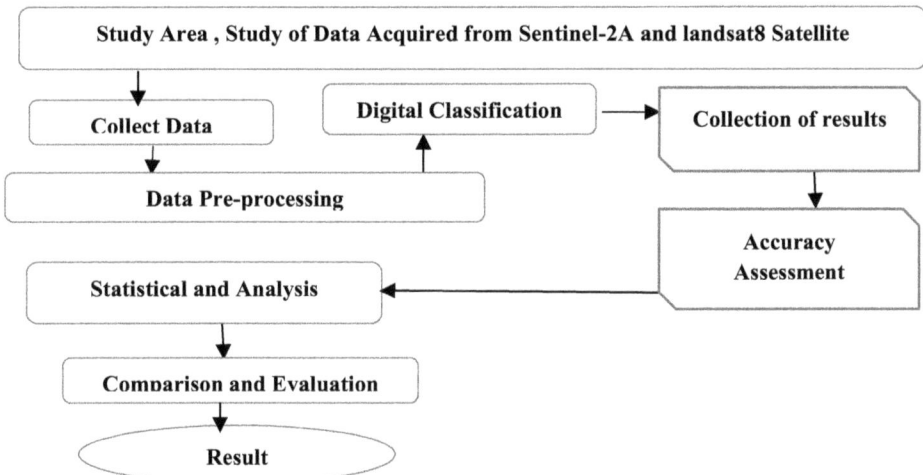

Fig. 5 Workflow Diagram For Proposed Methodology

(Figs. 9, 10, 11, and 12). Twenty images are selected from the found 95 pictures of the database for twenty proposed models to train, validate, and test the methods, five models for landsat8 with RF, five models for landsat8 with KNN, and five models for sentinel-2A with RF, and five models for sentinel-2A with KNN. The band classification used in this study is RGB 432. There are six samples and six parameters for creating model classes: High Land, Mountains, Land Area, Built-up, Vegetation, and Bare Land. Create the samples depending on RGB color composites of Landsat & sentinel-2A satellites, for example, the class Vegetation (red pixels in color composite RGB = 432). This

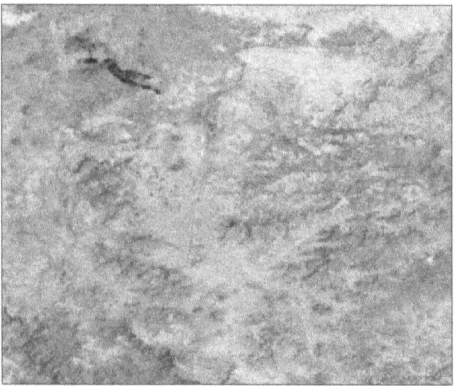

Fig. 6 Sana'a area on google map

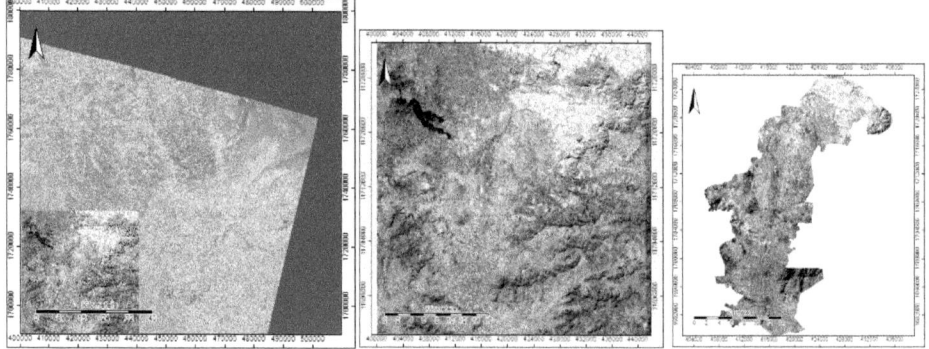

Fig. 7 Data set of Sentinel-2A Satellite Sensor with selection and clipping of area study in Composite

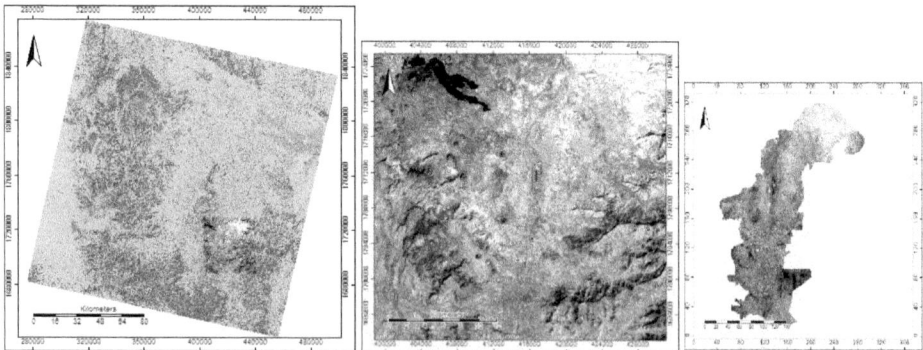

Fig. 8 Data set of Landsat8 Satellite Sensor with selection and clipping of area study in Composite band 432

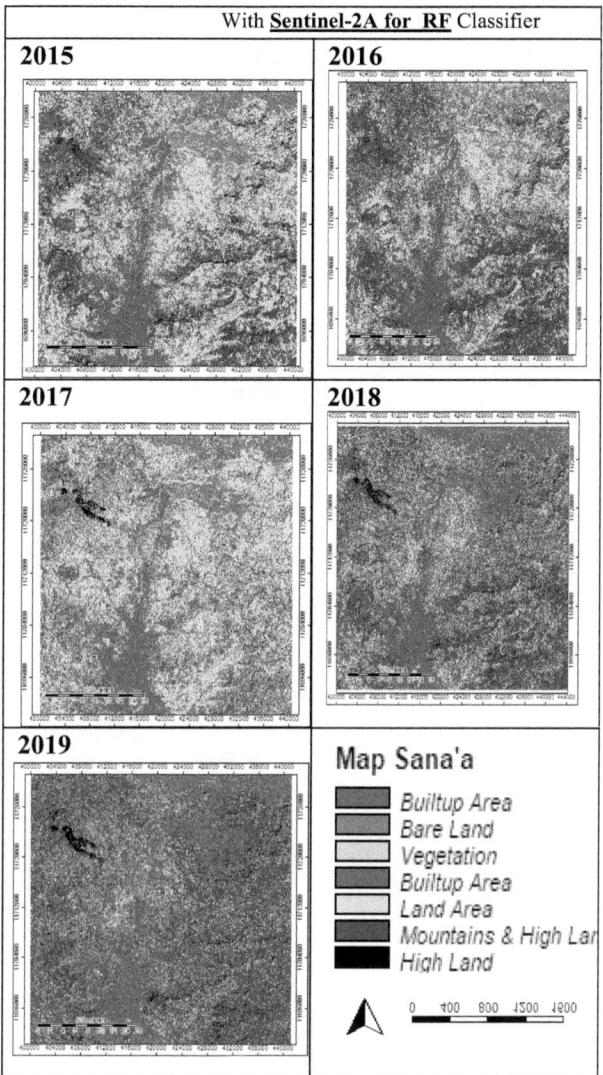

Fig. 9 Group1 of LULC Classification From 2015 To 2019 With **Sentinel-2A for RF** Classifier

article reveals methodology followed by definite outcomes from general level LULCC planning action for Sana'a city utilizing multispectral medium goal satellite information. Our examination shows that the LULC in Sana'a has undergone significant changes from 2015 to 2019.

3.4.1 Random Forest Classifier (RF)

The speed with all test sets is developed to measure the speculation error. Initially intended for AI, the classifier has acquired prominence in the remote detecting local area,

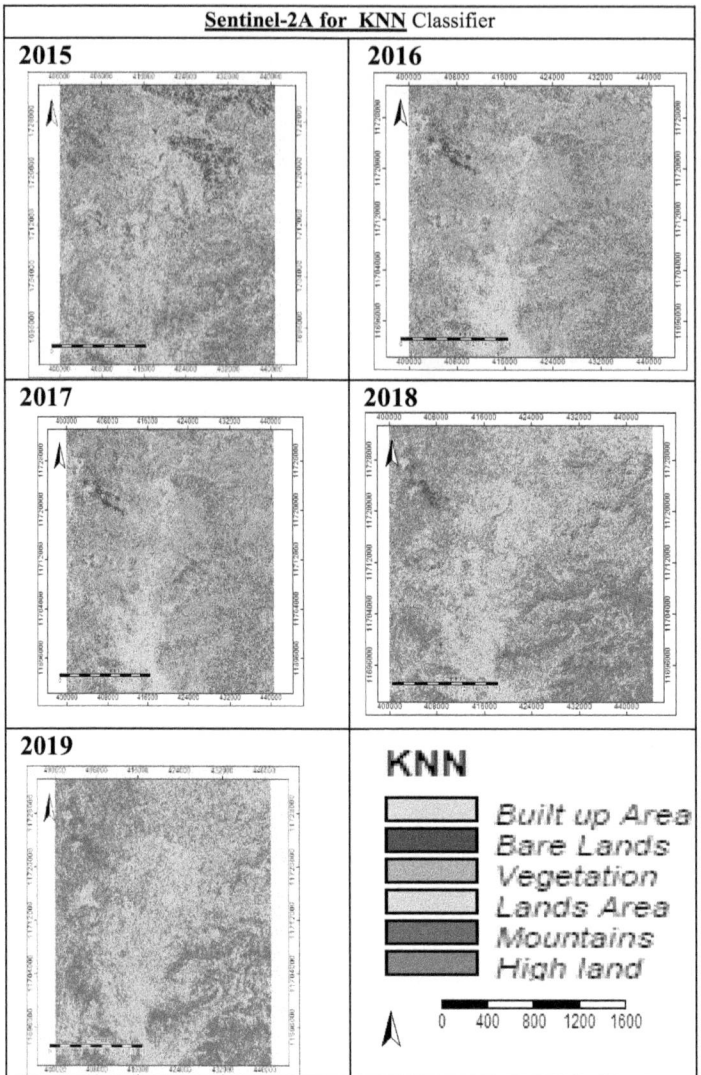

Fig. 10 Group2 of LULC Classification From 2015 To 2019 With **Sentinel-2A for KNN** Classifier

which is applied in distantly detected symbolism characterization because of its high precision. It also accomplishes the appropriate speed required and productive definition. To begin, each tree prepared in the example utilizes arbitrary subsets from the underlying tests. Besides, the ideal split is browsed through the unpruned tree hubs' arbitrarily chosen highlights. Thirdly, every tree develops unbounded [15].

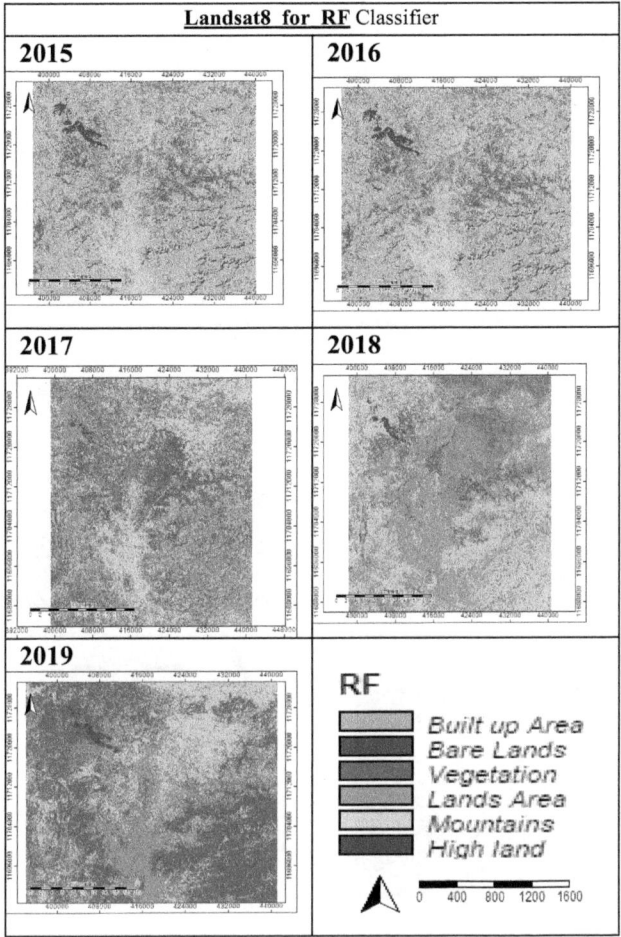

Fig. 11 Group3 of LULC Classification From 2015 To 2019 With **Landsat8 for RF** Classifier

3.4.2 KNN (K-Nearest Neighbor)

It is to discover a collection of k samples from the calibration dataset that are the most similar to unknown models. As a result, the k plays a critical role in its performance for this classifier, and it is the most important tuning parameter. A bootstrap technique was used to calculate the parameter k. This method merely saves the information during the training phase. To explain how it works, use the following algorithm: Step 1: Determine how many neighbors you'll have (K). Step 2: Calculate the Euclidean distance between K neighboring points. Step 3: Determine the K nearest neighbors using the Euclidean distance. Step 4: Among these k neighbors, count the number of data points in each category. Step 5: Assign the newly acquired data points to the class with the most neighbors. Step 6: Our model is now complete. Let's pretend we have a new data point that has to be assigned to the correct category.

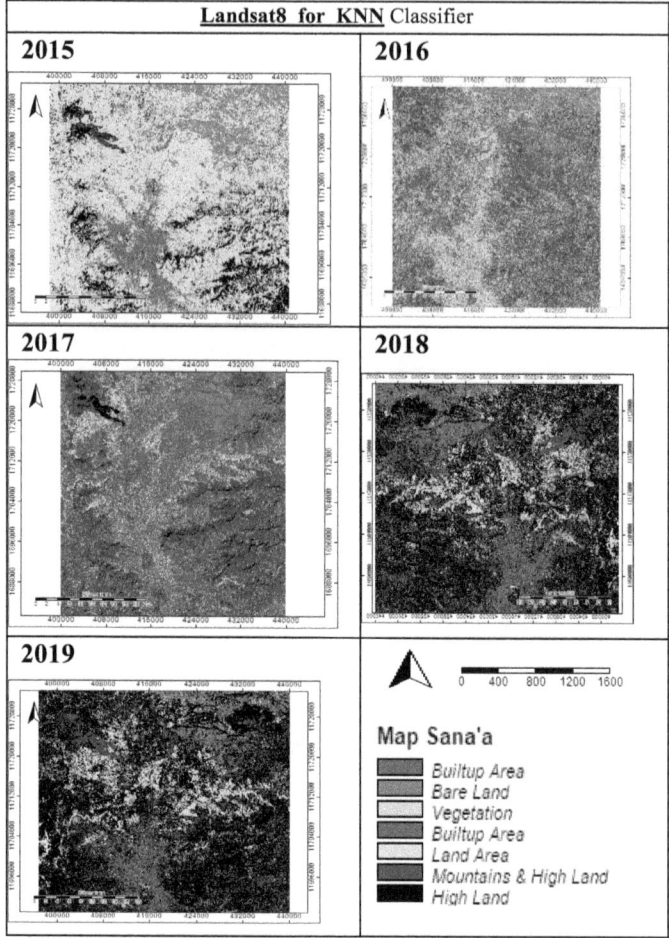

Fig. 12 Group4 of LULC Classification From 2015 To 2019 With **Landsat8 for KNN** Classifier

3.5 Creation of Database and Land Changes Classification

This study used images from Sentinel-2A (10 m) and Landsat 8 multispectral Resolution satellites. The image data was collected from 2015 to 2019, and all photos are from December month. Twelve images are contained each year for Sentinel 2 A. For Landsat8 Satellite, the Spatial Resolution is 30 m. Seven images for respective five years were gathered. The total data size is the number of pictures of multiple years for each satellite 95, as described in (Table 4).

4 Accuracy Assessment

Four measures are available for evaluating classifier performance: Accuracy, confusion matrix, log-loss, and AUC-ROC. This article used the Confusion matrix and A kappa coefficient to estimate classification accuracy. A confusion matrix, also known as an error

Table 4. Creation of Database

SENTINEL-2A Satellite					Landsat 8 Satellite				
The sensor is SENTINEL-2A. Resolution is 10m. The time of the season in December.					The sensor is Operational Land Imager (OLI) & Thermal Infrared Sensor (TIRS). Resolution is 30m. The time of the season in December.				
2015	2016	2017	2018	2019	2015	2016	2017	2018	2019
12	12	12	12	12	7	7	7	7	7

matrix, is a table that describes how well a classification model or classifier performs on a set of test data for which the valid values are known. The kappa measurement joins the off-slanting components of the mistake frameworks and addresses arrangement after eliminating the extent of performance anticipated by change. When the Kappa coefficient equals 1, the transaction is in perfect agreement; when it is close to zero, the bargain is no better than expected by chance. A significant number of pixels are taken from the grouped image and contrasted, and a reference guide of more significant position to assess the accuracy of the grouping process. The kappa coefficient goes from 0 to 1, and values higher than 0.7 are considered adequate. At the same time, those equivalent to or lower than 0.4 recognize an external connection between the characterized image and the ground truth. Generally, Kappa values are apparent in (Table 5).

For each class, the confusion matrix, producer's and user's accuracy, overall accuracy, and the accuracy estimate that removes the effect of unexpected change on the accuracy, known as the Kappa statistic, are calculated.

The confusion matrix is straightforward, but the associated nomenclature might be perplexing. A confusion matrix is calculated in this Study through SAGA GIS software. There are four groups for the results of the confusion matrix. Every group containing five categories of the results for five years, 2015 to 2019, is mentioned in (Figs. 13, 14, 15, and 16). The overall accuracy and kappa coefficient calculated in this study are discussed in (Table 6).

Table 5. Strength of Agreement of A kappa coefficient

No.	Kappa Value	Degree of agreement
1	< 0.00	low
2	0.00–0.20	medium
3	0.21–0.40	Good
4	0.41–0.60	Very Good
5	0.61–0.80	Excellence
6	0.80–1.00	Very Excellence

Table 6. Overall accuracy and Kappa coefficient for Sentinel2A satellite with RF & KNN classifier

		RF Classifier				KNN Classifier			
		Sentinel2A satellite		Landsat8 satellite		Sentinel2A satellite		Landsat8 satellite	
No	Year	Overall Accuracy	Kappa coefficient	Overall Accuracy	Kappa coefficient	Overall Accuracy	Kappa coefficient	Overall Accuracy	Kappa Coefficient
1	2015	99.87%	0.997470	99.66%	0.045511	83.26%	0.919499	92.90%	0.781132
2	2016	99.92%	0.998937	99.83%	0.997137	91.56%	0.977268	96.34%	0.954044
3	2017	99.78%	0.996582	99.59%	-0.056751	91.49%	0.952622	94.88%	0.794250
4	2018	99.82%	0.996878	99.81%	0.997368	84.56%	0.933182	94.88%	0.780590
5	2019	99.79%	0.996686	99.29%	0.653902	83.83%	0.736954	93.86%	0.781132

5   Results and Discussion

The land changes' results are detailed in Tables 7, 8, 9 and 10. Also, the area under major land-use or land-cover classes was calculated for 2015 to 2019. It is observed that the region has changed during the mentioned period. There are differences in the entire geographic space of the Land use and land cover maps. There has been a persistent reduction in Vegetation & Bare Land and increased land cover with expansion in cropland and developed regions. The part was advancing in urban area density, built-up area, and land presence, and the built-up area fell. The land area expanded, and the built-up area was 30.56% in 2015, 25.27% in 2016, 17.78% in 2017, 28.76% in 2018, and 20.24% in 2019, depending on LULC. They were using Sentinel-2A for RF consideration for the highest accuracy. The Land Use & Land cover classification using RF classifier with Sentinel-2A gave accuracy results higher than Landsat8 f with the same period. But, the KNN classifier type with Sentinel-2A gave less accuracy than Landsat8 with the same period. That means Landsat8 results were better than Sentinel-2A with the same period (Table 11). Since the Sentinel-2A satellite has a 10m resolution, which is efficient for object classification, thus proved good with RF and KNN.

2015								
CLASS	High Land	Mountains	Builtup	Land Area	Vegetation	Bare Land	SumUser	AccUser
High Land	0	0	0	0	0	0	250	0
Mountains	1230	0	0	0	0	0	0	
Land Area	0	0	55	0	0	0	120	100
Builtup	0	0	0	0	0	0	44	0
Vegetation	0	0	0	250	0	0	158	0
Bare Land	0	0	0	0	0	0	1235	0
Unclassified	0	0	0	0	0	0	0	0
SumProd	44	55	250	158	1235	120		
AccProd	0	100	0	0	0	100		

2016								
CLASS	High Land	Mountains	Builtup	Land Area	Vegetation	Bare Land	SumUser	AccUser
High Land	222	0	0	0	0	0	82	98.78049
Mountains	0	81	0	1	0	0	165	99.39394
Land Area	0	0	164	1	0	0	107	100
Builtup	0	0	0	107	0	0	2075	99.80723
Vegetation	0	0	0	0	2071	4	824	100
Bare Land	0	0	0	0	0	824	58	100
Unclassified	222	0	0	0	0	0	0	0
SumProd	81	164	109	2071	828	58		
AccProd	100	100	98.16514	100	99.51691	100		

2017								
CLASS	High Land	Mountains	Builtup	Land Area	Vegetation	Bare Land	SumUser	AccUser
High Land	203	0	0	0	0	0	59	0
Mountains	0	0	0	0	438	0	52	0
Land Area	0	59	0	0	0	0	226	0
Builtup	0	0	52	0	0	0	0	
Vegetation	0	0	0	226	0	0	21	0
Bare Land	0	0	0	0	0	0	614	0
Unclassified	203	0	0	0	0	0	0	0
SumProd	203	672	52	226	439	21		
AccProd	100	0	0	0	0	0		

2018								
CLASS	High Land	Mountains	Builtup	Land Area	Vegetation	Bare Land	SumUser	AccUser
High Land	1838	2	0	0	0	1	1841	99.83705
Mountains	3	2178	0	1	0	0	2182	99.81668
Land Area	0	0	205	1	0	0	206	99.51456
Builtup	0	0	0	328	0	0	328	100
Vegetation	0	0	0	1	562	0	563	99.82238
Bare Land	0	0	0	1	0	175	176	99.43182
Unclassified	0	0	0	21	0	0	0	0
SumProd	1841	2180	205	332	562	176		
AccProd	99.83705	99.90826	100	98.79518	100	99.43182		

2019								
CLASS	High Land	Mountains	Builtup	Land Area	Vegetation	Bare Land	SumUser	AccUser
High Land	0	0	0	0	0	0	61	100
Mountains	0	0	56	0	0	0	106	100
Land Area	0	0	0	938	0	0	0	
Builtup	0	0	0	0	376	0	128	99.21875
Vegetation	0	0	0	0	0	0	0	
Bare Land	0	637	0	0	0	0	56	100
Unclassified	0	0	0	0	0	344	0	0
SumProd	127	637	56	938	376	0		
AccProd	100	0	100	100	100			

Fig. 13 Group1 of Confusion Matrix Tables to **Landsat8 with RF** Classifier from 2015 To 2019

2015

CLASS	High Land	Mountains	Builtup	Land Area	Vegetation	Bare Land	SumUser	AccUser
High Land	0	0	0	0	0	0	84	85.71429
Mountains	0	0	0	92	0	1	93	98.92473
Land Area	0	0	0	0	55	0	57	96.49123
Builtup	0	0	0	2	0	370	372	99.46237
Vegetation	0	5	43	1	0	0	356	86.23596
Bare Land	0	0	80	1	0	0	112	0
Unclassified	0	0	0	0	0	0	0	0
SumProd	100	77	124	96	58	371		
AccProd	100	93.50649	0	95.83333	94.82759	99.73046		

2016

CLASS	High Land	Mountains	Builtup	Land Area	Vegetation	Bare Land	SumUser	AccUser
High Land	73	0	7	1	0	0	81	90.12346
Mountains	0	158	7	9	1	0	175	90.28571
Land Area	8	1	94	0	0	0	103	91.26214
Builtup	0	4	1	1978	65	0	2048	96.58203
Vegetation	0	1	0	82	761	0	846	89.95272
Bare Land	0	0	0	0	0	58	58	100
Unclassified	0	0	0	0	0	0	0	0
SumProd	81	164	109	2071	828	58		
AccProd	90.12346	96.34146	86.23853	95.50942	91.90821	100		

2017

CLASS	High Land	Mountains	Builtup	Land Area	Vegetation	Bare Land	SumUser	AccUser
High Land	50	0	0	2	0	0	52	96.15385
Mountains	0	225	1	0	0	0	226	99.55752
Land Area	0	1	399	0	5	0	436	91.51376
Builtup	2	0	0	19	0	0	21	90.47619
Vegetation	0	0	0	0	609	0	609	100
Bare Land	0	0	0	0	0	96	96	100
Unclassified	0	0	6	0	0	0	0	0
SumProd	52	226	433	21	614	96		
AccProd	96.15385	99.55752	92.14781	90.47619	99.18567	100		

2018

CLASS	High Land	Mountains	Builtup	Land Area	Vegetation	Bare Land	SumUser	AccUser
High Land	684	1	1	0	0	0	686	99.70846
Mountains	1	8361	11	8	14	0	8395	99.595
Land Area	0	4	21126	1	5	0	21136	99.95269
Builtup	0	2	0	2924	1	0	2927	99.89751
Vegetation	0	0	0	1	2048	0	2049	99.9512
Bare Land	0	0	0	0	0	28	28	100
Unclassified	0	0	0	0	0	0	0	0
SumProd	685	8368	21138	2934	2068	28		
AccProd	99.85402	99.91635	99.94323	99.65917	99.03288	100		

2019

CLASS	High Land	Mountains	Builtup	Land Area	Vegetation	Bare Land	SumUser	AccUser
High Land	445	0	0	0	0	0	445	100
Mountains	0	2353	0	1	1	2	2357	99.83029
Land Area	0	0	45	0	0	0	45	100
Builtup	0	6	0	13952	1	3	13962	99.92838
Vegetation	0	2	0	0	1511	3	1516	99.67019
Bare Land	0	13	0	3	0	6112	6128	99.7389
Unclassified	0	0	0	0	0	0	0	0
SumProd	445	2374	45	13956	1513	6120		
AccProd	100	99.11542	100	99.97134	99.86781	99.86928		

Fig. 14 Group2 of Confusion Matrix Tables to **Landsat8 with KNN** Classifier from 2015 To 2019

2015

CLASS	High Land	Mountains	Builtup	Land Area	Vegetation	Bare Land	SumUser	AccUser
High Land	770	0	0	0	1	0	771	99.8703
Mountains	0	698	0	0	1	0	699	99.85694
Land Area	0	1	4981	1	1	0	4984	99.93981
Builtup	6	7	1	19285	44	0	19343	99.70015
Vegetation	6	0	0	21	44121	3	44151	99.93205
Bare Land	0	0	0	0	2	816	818	99.7555
Unclassified	837	0	0	0	0	0	0	0
SumProd	782	706	4982	19307	44170	819		
AccProd	98.46547	98.86686	99.97993	99.88605	99.88907	99.6337		

2016

CLASS	High Land	Mountains	Builtup	Land Area	Vegetation	Bare Land	SumUser	AccUser
High Land	497	0	1	1	0	0	499	99.5992
Mountains	0	1123	0	1	0	0	1124	99.91103
Land Area	0	0	482	0	0	0	482	100
Builtup	0	0	1	3015	0	0	3016	99.96684
Vegetation	0	1	0	0	258	0	259	99.6139
Bare Land	0	0	0	0	0	1103	1103	100
Unclassified	0	0	0	0	0	0	0	0
SumProd	497	1124	484	3017	258	1103		
AccProd	100	99.91103	99.58678	99.93371	100	100		

2017

CLASS	High Land	Mountains	Builtup	Land Area	Vegetation	Bare Land	SumUser	AccUser
High Land	11513	11	16	17	5	0	11566	99.54176
Mountains	5	3489	1	0	0	0	3495	99.82833
Land Area	2	0	14202	5	1	0	14210	99.9437
Builtup	0	0	0	935	0	0	935	100
Vegetation	1	0	0	0	485	0	486	99.79424
Bare Land	0	0	0	0	0	290	290	100
Unclassified	0	0	0	0	0	0	0	0
SumProd	11523	3500	14219	957	491	290		
AccProd	99.91322	99.68571	99.88044	97.70115	98.778	100		

2018

CLASS	High Land	Mountains	Builtup	Land Area	Vegetation	Bare Land	SumUser	AccUser
High Land	8355	14	6	14	1	0	8392	99.5591
Mountains	6	21124	3	8	0	0	21141	99.91959
Land Area	3	0	2925	2	0	0	2930	99.82935
Builtup	3	0	0	1883	0	0	1886	99.84093
Vegetation	0	0	0	0	160	0	160	100
Bare Land	0	0	0	0	0	28	28	100
Unclassified	0	0	0	0	0	0	0	0
SumProd	8368	21138	2934	1907	161	28		
AccProd	99.84465	99.93377	99.69325	98.74148	99.37888	100		

2019

CLASS	High Land	Mountains	Builtup	Land Area	Vegetation	Bare Land	SumUser	AccUser
High Land	15187	26	9	22	2	0	15248	99.59995
Mountains	2	22921	1	14	0	0	22938	99.92589
Land Area	5	5	4796	2	0	0	4808	99.75042
Builtup	3	0	1	2124	0	0	2128	99.81203
Vegetation	1	0	0	0	210	0	211	99.52607
Bare Land	0	0	0	0	0	45	45	100
Unclassified	0	0	0	0	0	0	0	0
SumProd	15198	22952	4807	2162	212	45		
AccProd	99.92762	99.86494	99.77117	98.24237	99.0566	100		

Fig. 15 Group3 of Confusion Matrix Tables to **Sentinal-2A with RF** Classifier from 2015 To 2019

2015

CLASS	High Land	Mountains	Builtup	Land Area	Vegetation	Bare Land	SumUser	AccUser
High Land	71	0	0	0	0	0	71	100
Mountains	0	497	0	5	0	0	502	99.00398
Land Area	0	0	1123	4	0	0	1127	99.64508
Builtup	0	0	0	253	0	0	253	100
Vegetation	0	0	1	0	3017	2	3020	99.90066
Bare Land	0	0	0	0	0	1101	1101	100
Unclassified	0	0	0	480	0	0	0	0
SumProd	71	497	1124	262	3017	1103		
AccProd	100	100	99.91103	96.56489	100	99.81868		

2016

CLASS	High Land	Mountains	Builtup	Land Area	Vegetation	Bare Land	SumUser	AccUser
High Land	497	0	1	1	0	0	499	99.5992
Mountains	0	1123	0	1	0	0	1124	99.91103
Land Area	0	0	482	0	0	0	482	100
Builtup	0	0	1	3015	0	0	3016	99.96684
Vegetation	0	1	0	0	258	0	259	99.6139
Bare Land	0	0	0	0	0	1103	1103	100
Unclassified	0	0	0	0	0	0	0	0
SumProd	497	1124	484	3017	258	1103		
AccProd	100	99.91103	99.58678	99.93371	100	100		

2017

CLASS	High Land	Mountains	Builtup	Land Area	Vegetation	Bare Land	SumUser	AccUser
High Land	561	1	0	0	0	0	562	99.82206
Mountains	3	11515	20	11	18	0	11567	99.55045
Land Area	0	4	3479	3	0	0	3486	99.7992
Builtup	0	3	1	14205	4	0	14213	99.94371
Vegetation	0	0	0	0	1426	0	1426	100
Bare Land	0	0	0	0	0	290	290	100
Unclassified	0	0	0	0	0	0	0	0
SumProd	564	11523	3500	14219	1448	290		
AccProd	99.46809	99.93057	99.4	99.90154	98.48066	100		

2018

CLASS	High Land	Mountains	Builtup	Land Area	Vegetation	Bare Land	SumUser	AccUser
High Land	684	1	1	0	0	0	686	99.70846
Mountains	1	8361	11	8	14	0	8395	99.595
Land Area	0	4	21126	1	5	0	21136	99.95269
Builtup	0	2	0	2924	1	0	2927	99.89751
Vegetation	0	0	0	1	2048	0	2049	99.9512
Bare Land	0	0	0	0	0	28	28	100
Unclassified	0	0	0	0	0	0	0	0
SumProd	685	8368	21138	2934	2068	28		
AccProd	99.85402	99.91635	99.94323	99.65917	99.03288	100		

2019

CLASS	High Land	Mountains	Builtup	Land Area	Vegetation	Bare Land	SumUser	AccUser
High Land	445	0	0	0	0	0	445	100
Mountains	0	2353	0	1	1	2	2357	99.83029
Land Area	0	0	45	0	0	0	45	100
Builtup	0	6	0	13952	1	3	13962	99.92838
Vegetation	0	2	0	0	1511	3	1516	99.67019
Bare Land	0	13	0	3	0	6112	6128	99.7389
Unclassified	0	0	0	0	0	0	0	0
SumProd	445	2374	45	13956	1513	6120		
AccProd	100	99.11542	100	99.97134	99.86781	99.86928		

Fig. 16 Group4 of Confusion Matrix Tables to **Sentinal-2A with KNN** Classifier from 2015 To 2019

Table 7. Area and Percentages for LULC Using Sentinel-2A for RF from 2015 to 2019

No.	NAME	2015		2016		2017		2018		2019	
		Area, km^2	%	Area, km^2	%	Area, km^2	%	Area, km^2	%	Area, km^2	%
1	High Land	8712800	0.54%	13669300	0.79%	6743200	0.38%	23567000	1.23%	4077900	0.23%
2	Mountains & High Land	900226900	55.33%	279508700	16.05%	742869700	41.85%	734593900	38.41%	714204300	40.33%
3	Land Area Roads& buildings	61831200	3.80%	704028100	40.44%	605930900	34.14%	472178100	24.69%	585212200	33.05%
4	Builtup Area	497245100	30.56%	440027300	25.27%	315670100	17.78%	550033600	28.76%	361557300	20.42%
5	Vegetation	27778600	9.35%	208762600	11.99%	32317600	1.82%	82921500.00%	4.34%	81325800	4.59%
6	Bare Land	131257500	8.07%	95098700	5.46%	71481500	4.03%	49147800	2.57%	24343900	1.37%
7	Total of area =	1627052100	100.00%	1741094700	100.00%	1775013000	100.00%	1912441900	100.00%	1770721400	100.00%

Table 8. Area and Percentages for LULC Using Sentinel-2A for KNN from 2015 to 2019

No.	NAME	2015		2016		2017		2018		2019	
		Area, km^2	%	Area, km^2	%	Area, km^2	Percentage	Area, km^2	%	Area, km^2	%
1	High Land	15952300	1.02%	13162600	0.76%	6782300	0.38%	23465600	1.23%	30886700	1.74%
2	Mountains & High Land	364087100	23.35%	275873200	15.84%	732874600	41.29%	748233400	39.12%	836821700	47.26%
3	Land Area Roads& buildings	688764900	44.17%	704557400	40.47%	616511800	34.73%	465641400	24.35%	233687900	13.20%
4	Builtup Area	374969400	24.05%	449061900	25.79%	312892200	17.63%	540760200	28.28%	465307600	26.28%
5	Vegetation	11811200	0.76%	210669100	12.10%	33643600	1.90%	85667800	4.48%	161504300	9.12%
6	Bare Land	103773000	6.65%	87770400	5.04%	72308700	4.07%	48673500	2.55%	42513300	2.40%
7	Total of area =	1559357900	100.00%	1741094600	100.00%	1775013200	100.00%	1912441900	100.00%	1770721500	100.00%

Table 9. Area and percentages LULC with Landsat8 for KNN from 2015 to 2019

No.	NAME	2015		2016		2017		2018		2019	
		Area, km^2	%	Area, km^2	%	Area, km^2	%	Area, km^2	%	Area, km^2	%
1	High Land	121965300	2.58%	121965300	4.63%	12273300	0.61%	23465600	1.23%	33465600	2.23%
2	Mountains & High Land	1512416700	31.96%	1512416700	53.08%	205126200	10.23%	748233400	39.12%	848233400	40.12%
3	Land Area	232313400	4.91%	232313400	10.58%	588451500	29.36%	465641400	24.35%	565641400	25.35%
4	Builtup Area	1972601100	41.68%	1116102600	18.75%	228424500	11.40%	540760200	28.28%	640760200	29.28%
5	Vegetation	567041400	11.98%	567041400	8.05%	848327400	42.33%	85667800	4.48%	95667800	5.48%
6	Bare Land	326055600	6.89%	326055600	4.92%	121594500	6.07%	48673500	2.55%	58673500	3.55%
7	Total of area =	4732393500	100.00%	1911456900	100.00%	2004197400	100.00%	1912441900	100.00%	3012441900	100.00%

Table 10. Area and Percentages for LULC Using Landsat8 for RF from 2015 To 2019

| No. | NAME | 2015 | | 2016 | | 2017 | | 2018 | | 2019 | |
		Area, km^2	%	Area, km^2	%	Area, km^2	%	Area, km^2	%	Area, km^2	%
1	High Land	152003700	7.33%	80561700	4.21%	10071900	0.81%	10184400	0.48%	6527700	0.65%
2	Mountains & High Land	791696700	38.18%	890460900	46.59%	501359400	40.28%	861487200	40.94%	219599100	21.87%
3	Land Area	266358600	12.84%	180999900	9.47%	116273700	9.34%	343812600	16.34%	127650600	12.71%
4	Builtup Area	597589200	28.82%	548289900	28.68%	453569400	36.44%	337429800	16.03%	461995200	46.00%
5	Vegetation	141367500	6.82%	155898900	8.16%	15237000	1.22%	344167200	16.35%	67280400	6.70%
6	Bare Land	124767000	6.02%	55244700	2.89%	148232700	11.91%	207279000	9.85%	121186800	12.07%
7	Total of area =	2073782700	100.00%	1911456000	100.00%	1244744100	100.00%	2104360200	100.00%	1004239800	100.00%

Table 11. Overall accuracy for Sentinel-2A & Landsat8 Satellites from 2015 to 2019 with RF & KNN classifiers

| No. | Year | Accuracy LULCC With **RF** | | Accuracy LULCC With **KNN** | |
		Landsat8	**Sentinel-2A**	**Landsat8**	**Sentinel-2A**
1	2015	99.66%	99.87%	92.90%	83.26%
2	2016	99.83%	99.92%	96.34%	91.56%
3	2017	99.59%	99.78%	94.88%	91.49%
4	2018	99.81%	99.82%	94.88%	84.56%
5	2019	99.29%	99.79%	93.86%	83.83%

6 Conclusion

This Study offered criteria for classification using machine learning with multispectral satellites. It is not enough to select high-resolution data. The classifier's type must also be considered. Classifying land-use changes and land cover requires an integrated study of everything related to classification, focusing on three sides: 1) The type of the satellites. 2) The type characteristics of the classifier chosen are suitable for this satellite. 3) Appropriateness of the typical characteristics of the classifier chosen suitable for this satellite is critical. All of these factors have a role in achieving high-accuracy classification results. According to this Study's findings, the effectiveness of any classification system is mainly dependent on precise knowledge of satellite data, classifier features, and the user's skill. Random forest is observed to be efficient for Sentinel 2A satellite images. The RF classifier may have needed numerous features to achieve acceptable accuracy, which could explain how these results were interpreted. At the same time, KNN provides decent accuracy and performs well with few input feature variables. This study also showed that machine learning is still widely utilized and used today, beating deep learning in features and characteristics despite deep learning's high resolution. Deep learning is more challenging to implement and takes more time than machine learning. The study showed that, without deep learning, we could have classified LULC with a very high resolution using multispectral satellites and conventional machine learning.

References

1. Thanh Noi, P., & Kappas, M. Compare random forest, k-nearest neighbor, and support vector machine classifiers for land cover classification using Sentinel-2 imagery. Sensors, 18(1), 18, (2018).
2. Alshari, E. A., & Gawali, B. W. Evaluation of the Potentials and Challenges of Land Observation Satellites. Global Transitions Proceedings. (2021).
3. https://en.wikipedia.org/wiki/Sentinel-2.
4. https://en.wikipedia.org/wiki/Landsat_8
5. Ming, D., Zhou, T., Wang, M., & Tan, T. Land cover classification using random forest with genetic algorithm-based parameter optimization. Journal of Applied Remote Sensing, 10(3), 035021 , (2016).
6. Zhu, L., Suomalainen, J., Liu, J., Hyyppä, J., Kaartinen, H., & Haggren, H. A Review: Remote Sensing Sensors. Multi-Purposeful Application of Geospatial Data. doi:https://doi.org/10.5772/intechopen.71049, (2018).
7. Alshari, E. A., & Gawali, B. W. Development of classification system for LULC using remote sensing and GIS. Global Transitions Proceedings, 2(1), 8-17, (2021).
8. Tewabe, D., & Fentahun, T. Assessment of land use and disclosure of land change using remote sensing in the Tana Lake basin, northwest Ethiopia. Environmental Science Cogent, 6 (1), 1778998, (2020).
9. Fu, W., Ma, J., Chen, P., & Chen, F. Remote Sensing Satellites for Digital Earth. Manual of Digital Earth, 55–123. doi:https://doi.org/10.1007/978-981-32-9915-3_3, (2019).
10. Vali, A., Comai, S., & Matteucci, M. Deep Learning for Land Use and Land Cover Classification Based on Hyperspectral and Multispectral Earth Observation Data: A Review. Remote Sensing, 12(15), 2495. doi:https://doi.org/10.3390/rs12152495, (2020).
11. Radočaj, D., Obhođaš, J., Jurišić, M., & Gašparović, M. Global Open Data Remote Sensing Satellite Missions for Land Monitoring and Conservation: A Review. Land, 9(11), 402. doi:https://doi.org/10.3390/land9110402, (2020).
12. Sarica, A., Cerasa, A., & Quattrone, A. Random forest algorithm for classifying neuroimaging data in Alzheimer's disease: a systematic review. Frontiers in aging neuroscience, 9, 329., (2017).
13. Johnson, D. M., & Mueller, R. Pre-and within-season crop type classification trained with archival land cover information. Remote Sensing of Environment, 264, 112576, (2021).
14. Loi, D. T., Khac, D. V., Hung, D. N., Dong, N. T., Vinh, D. X., & Weber, C. Using Sentinel-2A and Landsat 8 data, a case study of Cam Pha city-Quang Ninh province, monitoring coastline change. Vietnam Journal of Earth Sciences, 43(3), 249-272, (2021).
15. Dhillon, M. S., Dahms, T., Kübert-Flock, C., Steffan-Dewenter, I., Zhang, J., & Ullmann, T. Spatiotemporal Fusion Modelling Using STARFM: Examples of Landsat 8 and Sentinel-2 NDVI in Bavaria. Remote Sensing, 14(3), 677, (2022).
16. Gu, S., Zhang, R., Luo, H., Li, M., Feng, H., & Tang, X. Improved singan integrated with an attentional mechanism for remote sensing image classification. Remote Sensing, 13(9), 1713, (2021).
17. Ahady, A. B., & Kaplan, G. Classification comparison of Landsat-8 and Sentinel-2 data in Google Earth Engine, study case of the city of Kabul. International Journal of Engineering and Geosciences, 7(1), 24-31, (2022).
18. Aksoy, S., Yildirim, A., Gorji, T., Hamzehpour, N., Tanik, A., & Sertel, E. Assessing the performance of machine learning algorithms for soil salinity mapping in Google Earth Engine platform using Sentinel-2A and Landsat-8 OLI data. Advances in Space Research, 69(2), 1072-1086, (2022).

19. Ai, B., Huang, K., Zhao, J., Sun, S., Jian, Z., & Liu, X. Comparison of Classification Algorithms for Detecting Typical Coastal Reclamation in Guangdong Province with Landsat 8 and Sentinel 2 Images. Remote Sensing, 14(2), 385, (2022).
20. Rumora, L., Miller, M., & Medak, D. Contemporary comparative assessment of atmospheric correction influence on radiometric indices between Sentinel-2A and Landsat 8 imagery. Geocarto International, 36(1), 13-27, (2021).
21. Alhedyan, M. A. Change detection of land use and land cover, using landsat-8 and sentinel-2A images (Doctoral dissertation, University of Leicester), (2021).
22. Ghayour, L., Neshat, A., Paryani, S., Shahabi, H., Shirzadi, A., Chen, W., ... & Ahmad, A. Performance evaluation of sentinel-2 and landsat 8 OLI data for land cover/use classification using a comparison between machine learning algorithms. Remote Sensing, 13(7), 1349 (2021).
23. Deliry, S. I., Avdan, Z. Y., & Avdan, U. Extracting urban impervious surfaces from Sentinel-2 and Landsat-8 satellite data for urban planning and environmental management. Environmental Science and Pollution Research, 28(6), 6572-6586, (2021).
24. Nandasena, W. D. K. V., Brabyn, L., & Serrao-Neumann, S. Using Google Earth Engine to classify unique forest and agroforest classes using Sentinel 2a spectral data topographical features: a Sri Lanka case study. Geocarto International, 1–16, (2021).
25. Sheykhmousa, M., Mahdianpari, M., Ghanbari, H., Mohammadimanesh, F., Ghamisi, P., & Homayouni, S. Support vector machine versus random forest for remote sensing image classification: A meta-analysis and systematic review. IEEE Journal of Selected Topics in Applied Earth Observations and Remote Sensing, 13, 6308–6325. Dou, P., Shen, H., Li, Z., Guan, X., & Huang, W. (2021), (2020).
26. Skakun, S., Vermote, E. F., Artigas, A. E. S., Rountree, W. H., & Roger, J. C. An experimental sky-image-derived cloud validation dataset for Sentinel-2 and Landsat 8 satellites over NASA GSFC. International Journal of Applied Earth Observation and Geoinformation, 95, 102253, (2021).
27. Mitri, G., Nader, M., Abou Dagher, M., & Gebrael, K. Investigating the performance of Sentinel-2A and Landsat 8 imagery mapping shoreline changes. Journal of Coastal Conservation, 24(3), 1-9, (2020).
28. Demirkan, D. Ç., Koz, A., & Düzgün, H. S. Hierarchical classification of Sentinel 2-a images for land use and land cover mapping and its use for the CORINE system. Journal of applied remote sensing, 14(2), 026524, (2020).
29. Mansaray, L. R., Wang, F., Huang, J., Yang, L., & Kanu, A. S. Accuracies of support vector machine and random forest in rice mapping with Sentinel-1A, Landsat-8 and Sentinel-2A datasets. Geocarto International, 35(10), 1088-1108, (2020).
30. Xi, Y., Thinh, N. X., & Li, C. Preliminary comparative assessment of various spectral indices for built-up land derived from Landsat-8 OLI and Sentinel-2A MSI imageries. European Journal of Remote Sensing, 52(1), 240-252 , (2019).
31. Najafi, P., Navid, H., Feizizadeh, B., Eskandari, I., & Blaschke, T. Fuzzy object-based image analysis methods using Sentinel-2A and Landsat-8 data to map and characterize soil surface residue. Remote Sensing, 11(21), 2583, (2019).
32. Chastain, R., Housman, I., Goldstein, J., Finco, M., & Tenneson, K. Empirical cross sensor comparison of Sentinel-2A and 2B MSI, Landsat-8 OLI, and Landsat-7 ETM+ top of atmosphere spectral characteristics over the conterminous United States. Remote sensing of environment, 221, 274-285, (2019).
33. Çavur, M., Duzgun, H. S., Kemeç, S., & Demirkan, D. C. Land use and land cover classification of Sentinel 2-A: St Petersburg case study. The International Archives of Photogrammetry, Remote Sensing and Spatial Information Sciences, 42, 13-16, (2019).
34. Varade, D., Sure, A., & Dikshit, O. Potential of Landsat-8 and Sentinel-2A composite for land use land cover analysis. Geocarto International, 34(14), 1552-1567, (2019).

35. Liu, Y., Gong, W., Hu, X., & Gong, J. (2018). Forest type identification with random forest using Sentinel-1A, Sentinel-2A, multi-temporal Landsat-8, and DEM data. Remote Sensing, 10(6), 946.

36. Al-shalabi, M., Pradhan, B., Billa, L., Mansor, S., & Althuwaynee, O. F. Manifestation of remote sensing data in modeling urban sprawl using the SLEUTH model and brute force calibration: a case study of Sana'a city, Yemen. Journal of the Indian Society of Remote Sensing, 41(2), 405-416, (2013).

37. Abdelkareem, O. E. A., Elamin, H. M. A., Eltahir, M. E. S., Adam, H. E., Elhaja, M. E., Rahamtalla, A. M., ... & Elmar, C. Accuracy assessment of land use land cover in umabdalla natural reserved forest, South Kordofan, Sudan. Int J Agric Environ Sci, 3(1), 5–9. (2018).

Real-Time Face Liveness Detection and Face Anti-spoofing Using Deep Learning

Ruchi Zawar$^{(\boxtimes)}$ and Vrishali Chakkarwar

Government Engineering College, Aurangabad, MS, India
ruchi.zawar21@gmail.com, vachakkarwar@geca.ac.in

Abstract. Face recognition biometrics is now widely employed, thanks to the rapid development of computer vision technology. However, since the facial recognition system cannot tell whether a face image is real or not, it is open to impersonation attempts. A face recognition system should be able to recognize not just people's faces but also spoofing attempts using printed images, videos, or 3D masks.

Examining facial liveness, such as landmark detection, eye blinking, and lip movement is a genuine strategy to avoid spoofing. However, when it comes to video-based replay attacks, this strategy is not sufficient. As a result, this study provides a face liveness detection approach that is integrated with a CNN (Convolutional Neural Network) classifier. The landmark detector module identifies the facial landmarks, the eye module analyses eye liveness, and the CNN classifier module makes up the anti-spoofing approach. We created an anti-spoofing model based on MobileNetV2, which was altered and retrained effectively using the LCC FASD dataset, which is freely available for this purpose. In an effort to get rapid inference time with satisfactory precision, a MobileNetV2's transfer learning is used as the classifier. We subsequently merged these landmark detection, eye liveness detection, and anti-spoofing modules and used the combined result to create a simple facial anti-spoofing and liveness detection application. The test results reveal that the built module can distinguish a variety of facial spoof attacks and has a high level of accuracy of 98%.

Keywords: Deep learning · convolution neural network · face liveness detection · face anti-spoofing · Keras and TensorFlow

1 Introduction

With the current growth in computer vision, and because of its simplicity and accuracy Face recognition systems are gaining more impetus. Face recognition biometrics is widely employed in access control systems, payment methods, and various other applications, where a high level of security is necessary. Face recognition functions similarly to how we recognize other people. This facial recognition system works by taking photographs of a person's face using a camera, then processing the image with a specific algorithm to determine whether the face is recognized from a database or not. But on the other hand, these systems cannot tell whether a face image is real or not, making them

R. Manza et al. (Eds.): ACVAIT 2022, AISR 176, pp. 626–636, 2023.
https://doi.org/10.2991/978-94-6463-196-8_47

open to forgery. Expedients to deceive these systems are getting more complicated, and antidote methods are necessary. Photo, video, and three-dimensional face model attacks are all common types of spoofing attacks. Attacks using photos and videos are more common as anyone can get your photos and videos quite easily from various social media sites or the internet. Face-based liveness detection technology arose as the times demanded in order to detect these forgery attacks. Several researchers have been working on developing a robust facial anti-spoofing solution for face recognition systems [1, 2].

Eye blink detection is a highly accurate method of determining whether or not the face in front of the camera is alive. Natural eye movement tracking is a simple method of determining whether or not a face is real. We also used facial landmarks detection along with eye motion detection for our analysis. However, depending on landmark detection and eye liveness detection are not adequate, as the system still remains vulnerable to video replay attacks using smartphones and tablets.

Active Anti-spoofing techniques include challenges and responses. This strategy relates to a one-of-a-kind activity known as a challenge. The system's purpose is to verify that the challenge has occurred during a video sequence. The user must complete these challenges in order to confirm its identity.

However, while successful, this technique necessitates more input and may have a substantial impact on the user experience [2].

Different texture patterns can be found in both real and spoof facial images. This simple truth is that rebuilding faces from camera photos degrades the clarity of facial features and creates gaps in reflectivity. Various prior research has attempted to capture the difference between real and fake facial images using designed color texture characteristics, such as RGB (Red, Green, and Blue) or LBP (Local Binary Pattern) variations. Fu-Mei Chen et al. use CNN to extract deep features and RI-LBP to extract color texture features from facial photos, based on the color information properties of the images [3]. The difference between high-definition color printed paper and high-definition recorded video, on the other hand, is difficult to tell. Color texture analysis was used by Boulkenafet et al. to develop a liveness detection system [4]. To represent the image, the LBP descriptor's combined color texture information (RGB, HSV, and YCbCr) was extracted and submitted to the SVM classifier for evaluating the authenticity.

On the other hand, the dependence on the lighting conditions of the room is a flaw in this texture analysis technology. In conditions where the room is dark, facial textures using illuminations are difficult to distinguish.

Meanwhile, some research uses different input domain names such as histogram or HSL (Hue, Saturation, and Lightness) to precisely extract the visual features that are more biased and counteract the influence of illumination. Because it is sensitive to noise and motion blur, this type of solution is better for pictures or photo attacks but bad for screen attacks.

3D cameras can distinguish between faces and flat objects and specific pixel depth recommendations could provide great precision against demonstration attacks. This would be the most reliable anti-spoofing method. But cameras, on the other hand, remain the most dependable anti-spoofing solution available.

New studies use deep learning and neural networks for face anti-spoofing. It involves training the neural networks to identify the difference between real and fake face images.

However, there are no uniform or defined features that CNN can see or understand and that is the issue.

That is why it is critical to use a combination of liveness detection methods and CNN analysis approaches for classification. We employ landmark detection (which includes brows, eyes, nose, lips, and jawline detection) combined with an eye movement liveness detection model for face liveness detection and a CNN classification model for spoof detection.

As a result, this article recommends using an improved face liveness detection algorithm with CNN to distinguish between legitimate and malicious faces. It is simple and it is more resistant to diverse attack techniques.

The following are some of the work's major contributions:

1. The proposed method is accurate since it reflects the properties of genuine and fake faces employed by CNN and deep transfer learning methods.
2. It can be implemented quickly and easily without the use of any additional hardware.
3. Our face anti-spoofing algorithms are reliable and detectable in real-time and can handle various spoofing techniques (print, replay, and mask).

2 Related Work

There are various approaches in anti-spoofing works that have been historically influential. The first is texture-based approaches, which use the feature descriptors like HOG (Histograms of oriented gradients) and LBP (local binary patterns), along with standard machine learning classifiers like Support vector machines to complete the task. Steps involved in classic machine learning algorithms for solving face spoofing problem includes processing, segmentation, feature extraction, and classifications [5].

On the other hand, to identify the real and fake faces the temporal methods use patterns generated from face motions like eye blinking, mouth movement, or use movements between the face and the image's background. They also use methods like optical flow to trace the facial movements [6].

Some methods use 3D sensors. These 3D sensors collect depth information from 2D images and check 3D face information and compare the 3D model of the input sample to that of a real face.

But this technique even though effective requires the use of 3D sensors which are not widely available and are likely to be costly [7].

Various studies have used deep learning and convolutional neural networks for training the model to distinguish real faces from false face photos. The author of the paper [8] used a deep learning architecture that includes CNN combined with LSTM for achieving face spoof detection in videos and images. The CNN identified local and dense features from the input sequences, whereas the LSTM captured temporal correlations [8]. Similarly, the paper [9] presents a hybrid architecture that combines CNN and LSTM for face anti-spoofing in video sequences by focusing on motion cues across video frames [9].

Active Anti-Spoof Methods entail the user's active participation in the data capture or enrolling process in order to detect spoofs. The user needs to perform a few tasks in front of the camera like smiling, nodding, blinking eyes, etc. to prove that the person is

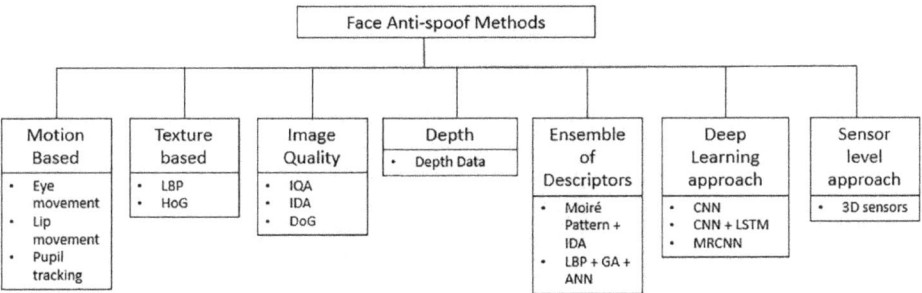

Fig. 1. Face Anti-spoofing methods

real and not fake. On the other hand, Anti-spoofing measures that aren't obtrusive are known as passive anti-spoofing approaches. Here user interaction is not required. The system takes care of everything without the user having to do anything (2). The various types of Face anti-spoof methods are classified as shown in Fig. 1.

3   Methodology

The two key components that we offer for building an anti-spoofing model include the liveness detector and the CNN classifier. The input data will be preprocessed before being sent to the liveness detection module, which will detect face landmarks and eye liveness. The input will then be passed to the CNN classifier module, which will assess if the face is real or fake. If the input passes through both modules, it is declared real. The phases in creating the CNN classifier module include 1) Data preprocessing, 2) model training, 3) model evaluation, and 4) testing (Fig. 2).

3.1   Liveness Detection Module

The Liveness detection module is further divided into two modules: 1) the landmark detection module, and 2) the eye liveness detection module. To find out whether the person in front of the camera is real and alive, more information about the person's face is needed, such as posture, whether the mouth is open or closed, if the eyes are open or closed, whether the person is looking up, and so on.

We use the Dlib library present in python, which provides face detection and landmark detection functions. Dlib employs histogram-oriented methods (HOG) for face

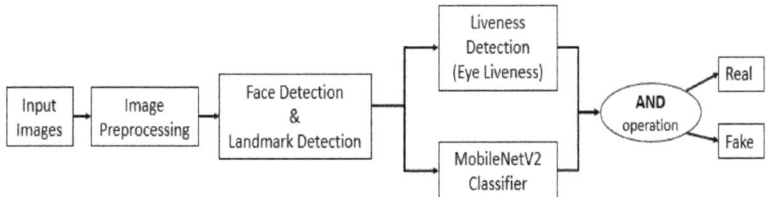

Fig. 2. Proposed Method Overview.

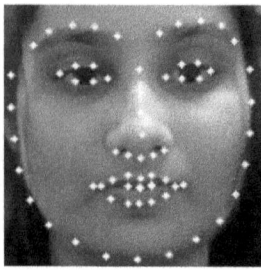

Fig. 3. Example of Landmark Detection on an image.

detection and Kazemi's model for landmark detection [10]. It provides 68 face points (face landmarks) in a swift and objective manner. The dlib's facial landmark detector uses pre-trained models to predict the position of sixty-eight coordinates (x, y) that identify the face features on a person's face as shown in the figure below.

The 68-point iBUG 300-W dataset was used to train the dlib face landmark predictor which detects areas around the eyes, brows, nose, mouth, and jawline. Dlib's landmark detector is fast and reliable and works well in real-time scenarios. It is a crucial element for extracting the movements of the eyes and mouth and detecting liveliness based on the features detected in Realistic scenarios. Also to identify the movement of the eyes of an individual the detected eye features are submitted to the trained KNN model. The model is trained on a labeled dataset of size 200 having different left and right eye ratios to identify whether the eyes are live or not. As input, the Network uses the eyes ratio for the next 20 frames. The eye ratio is defined as the height of the eye divided by the breadth of the eye. We have used the KNN algorithm for training the eye liveness detection model up to 3 epochs and it gives a test accuracy of 93%.

3.2 Classification Module

The second key component of the anti-spoofing model is our classifier model which classifies whether the input image is real or fake.

Dataset
We have used the LCC_FASD dataset which contains three subgroups: training, development, and evaluation. There are 1942 real photos and 16885 spoof faces in the database. The dataset consists of a wide range of high-quality images that are generated using 83 different capturing devices [11]. The table below shows the subject image statistics for each subgroup (Fig. 4 and Table 1).

Pre-processing
Data pre-processing is one of the most important steps that help in removing noisy and unwanted data and keeping only the important data for building our model. We scale, resize the images, perform image augmentation and convert them into array images which pulls the three-channel data from each image's array table. The data is then translated into an average mean value, which aids in extracting the image's best attributes. The

Fig. 4. Examples of real and spoof images.

Table 1. Image statistics in LCC_FASD dataset.

Data	Subject	Real Faces	Spoof Faces
Training	118	1223	7076
Development	25	405	2543
Evaluation	100	314	7266
Total	243	1942	16885

attributes extracted are assigned with the labels which help encode the altered data. After the data is transformed and encoded, it is divided into training, validation, and test data. The train data in the main dataset folder is divided into two groups, with a train and validation ratio of 80–20%. The validation data is used to evaluate the loss during the training.

Model

We have used MobileNetV2 architecture for conducting the binary (real/fake) classification. MobileNet is a network architecture that is better suited for applications where the computational capability is little. In order to give rapid inference time with reasonable precision, a MobileNetV2's transfer learning is used as the classifier. The MobileNetV2 is pre-trained on the imagenet dataset [12]. The pre-trained model is frozen and in the final layers, the model is retrained on the LCC_FASD dataset and customized to give the binary output that is real or fake.

In contrast to traditional residual models, the MobileNetV2 design is based on an inverted residual structure, with the residual block's input and output being narrow bottleneck layers. MobileNetV2 filter features in the intermediate expansion layer with lightweight depth-wise convolutions. Non-linearities in the thin layers were eliminated to maintain representational power [13].

The size of the input has been reduced to 224 x 224 x 3 and the total number of parameters are 3504872. The model network used for training is shown in Fig. 5. The convolution is used to feature out the array of modified values to transmit into subsequent layers and evaluate the best feasible outcome for the categories to predict. The data is processed in MobileNet, with the features being sent to custom layers that aid in understanding the patterns of the picture array and updating its weights and bias using convolution layers. The use of depth-wise convolution, which performs the process in two

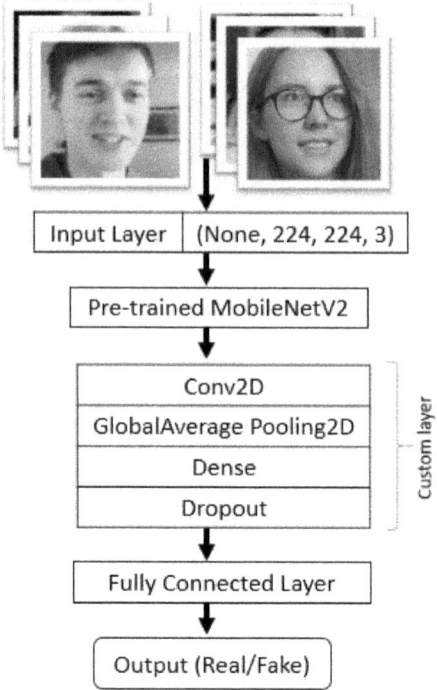

Fig. 5. Training Network Architecture Diagram

parts, first filtering and then combining the features, is one thing that distinguishes our approach. It executes spatial convolution, which is conductedindividually on each channel of a given input, followed by pointwise convolution, which is a 1x1 convolution. The relu as an activation function is used for connecting and processing data with the layers in order to update the bias from one convolution to the next. The Global Average Pooling method generates a median matrix value, which aids in the compression of the array. The dense layer helps to make a decision to evaluate the image's edge and corner array detection and aids in updating the weight parameters for the image pattern prediction process. We have used a dropout to prevent the model from over-fitting. We have used a learning rate of 0.0001, zero-gradient as the optimizer, and binary cross-entropy for calculating the loss. The accuracy is calculated as below.

Accuracy = (TP + TN) / (TP + TN + FP + FN).

The final output is obtained by performing the AND operation on the outputs from both the modules that are the liveness detection module and the classification module. If the output of the liveness module is true, that is the person in front of the web camera is alive, and the output of the CNN classifier is also true, that is the person is classified as real, then the final output (image of the person) is predicted as Real. If anyone of the module gives negative output, then the output (image of the person) is predicted as fake or a spoof.

Testing
We put a variety of face spoofing scenarios to the test, including printed images, digital photos, and digital videos from smartphones. Our model performs quite well in real-time scenarios.

4   Results and Discussion

Deep learning-based techniques integrated with various other cues for life-sign detection give a good outcome for resolving almost all spoof scenarios. The detected landmarks give the points that denote the different facial features which are the eye, brows, nose, lips, and jaw as shown in Fig. 3. The classification module is a neural network-based system that uses images as input to determine if a face is real or not and gives an accuracy of 98% after training on 60 epochs. Photographs, phone photos, video frames, and masks are all examples of fake images. The eye movement liveness module gives accuracy of 97%. The CNN classification module gives a good accuracy of 98%. We have trained our pre-trained neural network model using the LCC_FASD dataset that contains a total of 18827 images, out of which 1942 are real images and 16885 are spoof images. We have used the transfer learning technique for our model to adapt as per the new dataset and customized it to provide binary classification as output. The precision, recall, and f1 score are shown in Table 2 below. The training accuracy, loss and validation accuracy, loss is as depicted in Figs. 6 and 7 respectively. The real-time results of our model are shown in Fig. 8.

The development environment settings used during this research are Windows 11, Intel Core i7-7500U (10th Gen), 6 GB NVIDIA graphics card, and 24 GB RAM. We used Python as the programming language and Keras-OpenCV, Tensorflow framework.

5   Conclusion and Future Work

The aim of this project is to improve the face recognition systems by improving their reliability and protecting it against various types of spoofing attacks. The proposed model performs well on the real and fake discrimination objectives, allowing it to be

Table 2. Precision, Recall, f1-score

	precision	recall	f1-score
spoof	0.94	0.98	0.96
real	0.99	0.98	0.99
accuracy			0.98
Macro avg	0.96	0.98	0.97
weighted avg	0.98	0.98	0.98

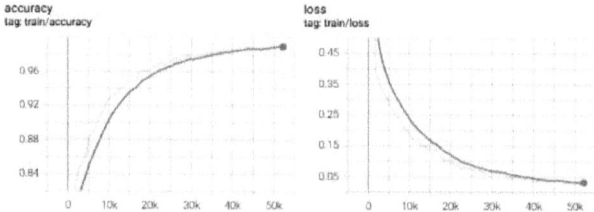

Fig. 6. Training accuracy and loss

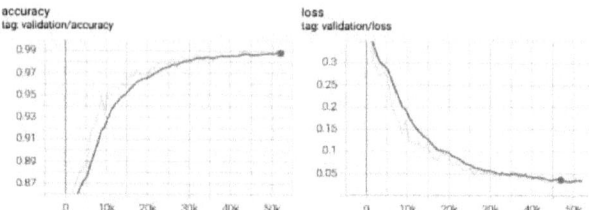

Fig. 7. Validation accuracy and loss

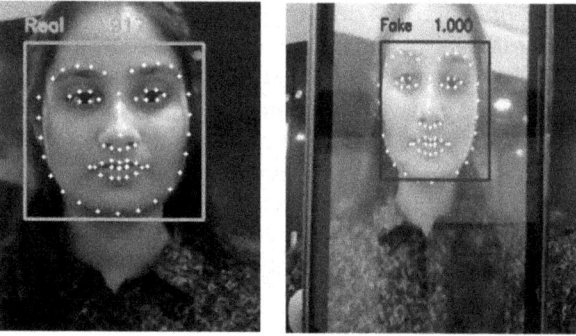

Fig. 8. Examples of real-time results

employed effectively in a variety of applications at low cost and with great accuracy without requiring any new hardware. We suggest in this paper that CNN combined with liveness detection performs remarkably well in real-time scenarios for face anti-spoofing. Various attacks have been tried and tested. The system can efficiently handle printed photos, digital photos, and video replay attacks. We have also discussed various types of spoofing attacks and various facial anti-spoofing approaches that have been proposed in different studies so far. The goal is to give a simple roadmap for the design of more dependable, user-friendly, and effective systems.

When it comes to real-time applications, insufficient light has an impact on classification accuracy. Biases among datasets are inescapable due to varying capture conditions. The future scope for this project could be to develop a mechanism to adapt the learned model to various lighting conditions, and shadowing effects. Another approach is to incorporate deep learning with other cues such as textures, movements, and shapes.

Also, there is a need for an easily available large-size dataset that contains all types of spoofing scenarios and various lighting conditions for further research.

Acknowledgments. I would like to thank Vrishali Chakkarwar ma'am and Dr. Vivek Kshirsagar for their guidance and support. I would like to thank the Department of Computer Science and Information technology, Government college of Engineering, Aurangabad, Maharashtra for providing me with research support. Lastly, I would like to thank Dr. Babasaheb Ambedkar Marathwada University, Aurangabad, Maharashtra, India for providing the publication support.

References

1. R. B. Hadiprakoso, H. Setiawan and Girinoto, "Face Anti-Spoofing Using CNN Classifier & Face liveness Detection," 2020 3rd International Conference on Information and Communications Technology (ICOIACT), 2020, pp. 143–147, https://doi.org/10.1109/ICOIACT50 329.2020.9331977.
2. P. Anthony, B. Ay and G. Aydin, "A Review of Face Anti-spoofing Methods for Face Recognition Systems," 2021 International Conference on INnovations in Intelligent SysTems and Applications (INISTA), 2021, pp. 1-9.
3. Wen C, Chen F M, Xie K, et al. Face liveness detection: fusing color texture feature and deep feature[J]. IET Biometrics, 2019, 8(6):369-377.
4. Boulkenafet Z, Komulainen J, Hadid A. face anti-spoofing based on color texture analysis[C]//Image Processing (ICIP), 2015 IEEE International Conference on. IEEE, 2015: 2636-2640.
5. J. Komulainen and M. Pietikainen, "Face spoofing detection from single images using texture and local shape analysis," International Conference on Computing, Communication and Automation (ICCCA), vol. 1, pp. 3– 10, 2012.
6. Singh, P. Joshi, and G. Nandi, "Face recognition with liveness detection using eye and mouth movement," 07 2014.
7. J. Zhou, C. Ge, J. Yang, H. Yao, X. Qiao, and P. Deng, "Research and application of face anti-spoofing based on depth camera," in 2019 2nd China Symposium on Cognitive Computing and Hybrid Intelligence (CCHI), Sep. 2019, pp. 225–229.
8. Z. Xu, S. Li, and W. Deng, "Learning temporal features using LSTM-CNN architecture for face anti-spoofing," in 2015 3rd IAPR Asian Conference on Pattern Recognition (ACPR), Kuala Lumpur, Malaysia, 3- 6 November 2015, pp. 141–145.
9. X. Tu, H. Zhang, M. Zie, Y. Luo, Y. Zhang, and Z. Ma, "Enhance the motion cues for face anti-spoofing using CNN-LSTM Architecture," retrieved from https://arxiv.org/pdf/1901.05635.pdf (accessed on 07/16/2019).
10. Kazemi, Vahid and Josephine Sullivan. "One millisecond face alignment with an ensemble of regression trees." 2014 IEEE Conference on Computer Vision and Pattern Recognition (2014): 1867–1874.
11. D. Timoshenko, K. Simonchik, V. Shutov, P. Zhelezneva and V. Grishkin, "Large Crowdcollected Facial Anti-Spoofing Dataset," 2019 Computer Science and Information Technologies (CSIT), 2019, pp. 123-126, https://doi.org/10.1109/CSITechnol.2019.8895208.

12. Ghofrani, Ali, Rahil Mahdian Toroghi, and Seyed Mojtaba Tabatabaie. "Attention-Based Face AntiSpoofing of RGB Images, using a Minimal End-2-End Neural Network." arXiv preprint arXiv:1912.08870 (2019).
13. M. Sandler, A. Howard, M. Zhu, A. Zhmoginov and L. -C. Chen, "MobileNetV2: Inverted Residuals and Linear Bottlenecks," 2018 IEEE/CVF Conference on Computer Vision and Pattern Recognition, 2018, pp. 4510-4520, https://doi.org/10.1109/CVPR.2018.00474.

Analysis of Complexities in Patenting AI and Big Data Inventions

Prajakta Kale[✉]

O P Jindal Global University, NCR of Delhi, India
Prajaktak290@gmail.com

Abstract. Legal protection through Intellectual Property Rights has become increasingly vital in the present age of ideas, knowledge, and competition. The paper traces importance of IPR, different forms of IPR and argues why Patent is the most appropriate option when it comes to protection of computer programs or software. It analyses the legal framework in different jurisdictions with regards to software patents. It further focuses on AI and Big Data based inventions and discusses challenges which could come in way of patenting these.

Keywords: Patents · Intellectual Property Rights (IPR) · Artificial Intelligence (AI) · Big Data

1 Introduction

Intellectual Property (IP) is creation of mind or intellect [1]. The word 'property' reflects intangible as opposed to tangible nature of physical property. This intangible nature is peculiar characteristic of IP [2]. Patents, Copyright, Trademark, trade secrets are different forms of IP. These forms create an exclusive set of rights. The protection offered by Intellectual Property Law is important for several reasons. Apart from the economic benefit it provides, it gives recognition to the 'labour' put in by the creator/ inventor and also acts as an incentive to innovate [3].

Legal protection finds particular relevance with computer programs and software as it is susceptible to unauthorized copying, modifying and counterfeiting [4]. Computer programs or software can be protected through Patents, Copyright and trade secrets. The paper intends to analyse protection offered to computer programs or software through patents. The analysis will then be extended to Artificial Intelligence and Big Data based inventions.

1.1 Why Patents?

Copyright is a form of IP which denotes a set of rights given to creators of literary and artistic works [5]. These works include computer programs, technical diagrams, databases amongst others. Copyright however protects the expression of idea and not the idea itself. Therefore, for a computer program a copyright would essentially protect

R. Manza et al. (Eds.): ACVAIT 2022, AISR 176, pp. 637–645, 2023.
https://doi.org/10.2991/978-94-6463-196-8_48

the source code but not the algorithm. It is thus easy for competitors to infringe by using the algorithm with different text [6].

Trade secrets are form of IP for confidential information. Trade secrets appear as viable option as they don't need to be applied for but can be done through internal arrangements of confidentiality or non-disclosure agreements. It does makes difficult for outsiders to misuse the information, but nothing can prevent an independent researcher who works on the same information, benefitting from it. Neither it is possible to stop reverse engineering i.e., deconstructing the innovation and creating similar entity.

Patent on the other hand offers an exclusive set of rights for an invention. Such invention has to be a process or product providing new way of doing something or offers a new 'technical' solution to a problem [7]. An essential requirement to obtain a patent is the disclosure of technical information in the patent application. By its very nature then patents can protect functional aspects of any software [8]. It does not protect the code per se rather it protects a 'software engine' which takes inputs, works upon it and results in some output. Thus 'concept' behind a software is protected. And because this concept is of 'technical nature', patents seem the most appropriate alternative [9]. Apart from this, patent can also protect design of the software. The only pitfall with patents could be the cost and time involved to obtain it compared to other IP forms. Despite this, the advantages outweigh and therefore the paper focuses on patents.

2 Patentability Criteria

Patents are granted based on certain criteria. In Europe, for an invention to be granted a patent, I) the invention must be novel; II) should have an inventive step; III) capable of industrial application and IV) should not contain excluded subject matter. On the same lines, patentability requirement for US is that the invention should be new (novel), non-obvious and useful. In India, an invention is patentable subject matter if it meets the following criteria – i) It should be novel. ii) It should have inventive step or it must be non-obvious iii) It should be capable of Industrial application. iv) It should not attract the provisions of sections 3 and 4 of the Patents Act 1970 [10].

Analysing each criterion with respect to specific jurisdiction is beyond the scope of this paper. Hence, we shall broadly try to understand about these criteria.

2.1 Novelty

Novelty under the European Patents Convention (EPC) depends on whether the invention was part of the 'state of art' on the priority date. Priority date is the date on which application is filed. The scope of the term 'state of art' is hugely wide as it comprises all matter (whether a product, a process, information about either, or anything else) which has at any time before the priority date of that invention been made available to the public (whether in the United Kingdom or elsewhere) by written or oral description, by use or in any other way. The notion of novelty in India and US is broadly same. Prior art or state of the art is the key concept. So, the invention should be novel or new in the sense that nothing from the prior art should be reflected in it. Broadly prior art is all matter prior to filing of the patent but the composition differs slightly from jurisdiction to jurisdiction.

2.2 Inventive Step/Non-obviousness

The EPC provides inventive step as one of the criteria for the invention to be patentable. It further states that this step should be such that it is not 'obvious' to the person skilled in the art. In India an inventive step is that which involves technical advance as compared to the existing knowledge or have economic significance or both and makes the invention not obvious to a person skilled in the art. Thus broadly it can be inferred that inventive step means the invention in question should show some advancement as compared to the existing similar inventions. Further it also calls for non-obviousness and this non-obviousness is judged from the eyes of person skilled in the art. In US, person having ordinary skill in the art (PHOSITA) is a notional person with average technical knowledge of his field. Judges need to look at the case through his eyes not through their own or even a 'reasonable layperson' [11]. In EPC too, he is the key element and his skillset varies on parameter of normalcy in that field. Pertinent to note are the words 'average' and 'ordinary', implying that the said person is not extra-ordinarily brilliant but rather 'uninventive' and 'conservative', hesitant to explore new areas. So, basically this person skilled in the art is someone having knowledge of the concerned field of invention but need not be extra-ordinarily brilliant.

2.3 Subject Matter Eligibility

For an invention to be patented in any jurisdiction, it should fall within the eligible subject matter as specified in the Patent laws of each jurisdiction. The European Patent Convention (EPC), Article 52, paragraph 2, excludes from patentability, in particular 1. discoveries, scientific theories and *mathematical methods*; 2. aesthetic creations; 3. schemes, rules and methods for performing mental acts, playing games or doing business, and *programs for computers*; 4. *presentations of information*." European Patent Office has been following the principle established in the case *T208/84 VICOM/Computer related invention*, wherein a patent may be available for a computer program because it has technical character, a computer programmed to create technical effect and a computer program product which creates technical effects [12]. Thus software as such are not patentable under EPC [13]. EPC instead depends upon the concept of Computer invented inventions (CII) which are inventions using computer, computer network or other programmable apparatus. Broadly, EPC has a two-step approach on subject matter eligibility. First, novelty and second inventive step, both in context of section 56 of EPC.

The US Patent Act 1952 §101 states: 'Whoever invents or discovers any new and useful process, machine, manufacture, or composition of matter, or any new and useful improvement thereof, may obtain a patent therefor, subject to the conditions and requirements of this title'. What is excluded from patentability is laws of nature, natural phenomena and abstract ideas [14]. The approach in US seems to be broad and liberal when it comes to patent eligibility. However, this liberal approach by US has evolved over time. For instance, in cases of *Gottschalk v Benson* [15] and *Parker v Flook* [16], both linked to computer related inventions, an algorithm or mathematical formula was considered like law of nature and thus no patent was granted in each case. US Supreme Court however changed its approach in the case of *Diamond v Diehr* [17] wherein a computer-controlled process for curing synthetic rubber was granted patent. Thus, it made implicitly clear that computer programs and business methods are patentable in principle. However, in case of *Bilski v Kappos*, the Supreme Court emphasised that there is no broad patentability of business methods. The case proposed a 'machine or transformation test' wherein it said that a process can be patented if: 1) It can be performed on an apparatus; and 2) The process can transform an article into a different state [18]. Another notable authority, which was not directly related to software patents but to business methods involving software, is *Alice Corp v CLS Bank International.* In the said case, patent was not granted for a computer invented escrow service for financial transaction as it was an 'abstract idea' and thus did not satisfy subject matter eligibility [19]. The Alice case resulted in two-part test viz.: 1) Whether the claims in issue are directed to a patent ineligibility concept (i.e. law of nature, abstract idea or natural phenomena) and 2) If yes, then whether the claims contain an 'inventive concept' [20]. Uncertainties however still remain on what constitutes 'abstract idea' and what sufficiently more claim is required towards the 'abstract idea'.

3   Challenges in Patentability Due to AI and Big Data

To understand what are the challenges posed by AI, Big data it is important to understand what they mean. The earlier sections have discussed about computer programs, software patents with reference to patentability criteria. This section shall analyse issues with satisfying patentability criteria of inventions related to AI and Big Data.

3.1   About AI and Big Data

Artificial Intelligence (AI) in literal sense can be construed as field of activities in which computer or machines emulate human brain. Despite it being a decade old concept, past few years has witnessed a phenomenal rise in AI Technologies. In purely technical terms, AI are nothing but powerful algorithms which can acquire human like capabilities, for instance speech or vision [21]. Typically then AI systems are learning systems which are better at performing the task otherwise performed by humans, with minimum or no human intervention.

Machine learning is a branch or application of AI which involves analysing of data, learning from data or learning from 'experience' and identify patterns thereby contributing to decision making just as humans do but without any human intervention [22]. Any machine learning model mainly aims to identify and quantify certain 'feature' or characteristic from the data sets. Training data, machine learning algorithm, machine learning model and output are the important elements of machine learning. For instance, in a credit card company which wants to filter applications of customers likely to be filing for bankruptcy, the prior applications will be the training data, the mathematical exercise to extract the information is the machine learning algorithm, the mechanism used for such extraction will be the machine learning model and the result which the company will generate by inputting the personal data of the customers, is the output.

Big Data is intricately linked to Artificial Intelligence and Machine Learning Systems. Although, there cannot be one single definition of what big data is, one thing for sure is its larger scalability in comparison to traditional database systems. Traditional mainstream software cannot grab this huge data. It is characterised by 3 Vs. i.e. Volume, Velocity and Variety. In simple terms thus, big data is larger, has complex data sets and comes from variety of data sources. Broadly therefore, big data means both huge data sets as well as data analytics, data mining and parallel processing capabilities. Complex though it may sound, it helps in tackling seemingly impossible business problems. From the above explanations of AI and Machine learning, their relationship with big data can be deciphered. AI systems are largely data driven. Be it voice assistants like Alexa or Siri, chatbots or other AI applications for fraud detection and prediction, all deal and generate huge data. This convergence of Big Data with AI has triggered rise in AI based solutions [23]. At the same time, AI can analyse huge data sets, recognise patterns which otherwise is not deciphered in small data sets. Thus, big data is used for making evidence-based decision making.

AI being a decades old technology had several scientific publications since its inception. However recent trends show a decrease in the ratio of scientific papers to inventions which essentially implies that commercial application has replaced mere theoretical expositions. AI related patenting has thus grown significantly. Notably, it is the machine learning component of AI which has amounted to maximum patent filings.

3.2   Subject Matter Eligibility

Considering the detailed earlier discussion on Patentable subject matter under US and EPC, and the technicality of AI and related technologies, we now analyse the impact of latter on the former. AI in its very raw form is nothing but a set of complex algorithms. In an advanced form, AI uses trained data sets for output, alternatively there is this machine learning component of AI. This also essentially points out to Big Data- AI, which uses algorithms to find rare relationships from very large 'training data'. Again, AI can be a tool which is giving technical effect. Example being AI in effective decision-making scenario. Thus, broadly there can be three types of AI Patenting: 1) 'Core AI', consisting of pure mathematical algorithms 2) Machine learning/ Trained models and 3) AI as a tool utilised in certain application [24]. Coming to Big Data, it is the extraction feature of big data which has the potential for providing best business solutions. This means best of the big data innovations need to be based on software. These software systems might be used for data collection, analysing unreliable data, aggregation of personal information data without adversely affecting consumer protection laws, etc.

It is evident from earlier explanations that core AI, the first of the three types, consisting of pure algorithms will not satisfy the eligibility criteria under EPC. However, the latter of the two types, which give rise to some 'technical effect', shall make it eligible under EPC. The approach under US, would however differ as Post Alice there remains a grey area with regards to what type of software is patentable. This is particularly relevant for big data innovations as they mostly rely on execution of common and simple algorithms on the computer. There have been instances in US, where patent applications have been rejected as they claimed some concept emulating human activity and the court believed them like 'abstract idea' under section 101 of US Patents Act, 1952 [25]. As the basic idea of AI is itself to emulate human activity, AI Patent applications shall continue to pose such challenge.

3.3 Novelty and Non Obviousness

When AI is used extensively for Research and Development, there are several layers and stages in that system. In such scenario, it is difficult to decide or know who is the actual inventor in the system? These can be conveniently grouped into three stages: 1) Computer as a mere tool to assist human inventor 2) Intermediary stage, for example a text generator being used for filling the gaps in a patent document and 3) Outputs by computers which could be called as patentable inventions [26]. There are projects like 'AllPriorArt' wherein patent claims are generated through autonomous technology [27]. Potential problems arise due to this as these texts can become part of 'state of art', thereby creating problem for novelty and inventive step criteria as discussed earlier. There is a danger of future patents being pre-empted completely [28].

The possibility of computers becoming drivers of innovation in fields like nanotechnology, health and pharmaceuticals is not far from real at all. Artificial Intelligence is used to develop inventive machines like Googles DeepMind or IBM's Watson [29]. Artificial Neural Network, a form of AI, which uses binary switches' collections to stimulate neurons in biological brain, has proved to be an efficient tool to create novel ideas. Dr. Stephen Thalers 'Creativity machines' is the perfect example which has used Artificial Neural Network to create new inventions.

Assessment of obviousness criteria by person having ordinary skills will prove to be challenging due to these developments. As mentioned earlier, for assessment of obviousness, PHOSITA is key element in both the systems. This hypothetical, non – inventive person is supposed to have knowledge only in technical fields of concern. Can the ordinarily skilled person remain central for assessment of inventiveness now? The possibility is that inventive machines are itself used as skilled person. If the skilled person fails to be in pace with real time changes, then this might affect the obviousness bar.

3.4 Inventorship

AI has the ability to learn [30]. Owing to this ability there are instances where AI is able to invent. However, several patent systems in general demand that the inventor is a human being and not machine [31]. It is important to know the inventor because it becomes straightforward to decide liability and other legal consequences. Thus, the issue of Inventorship is a challenge which jurisdictions need to find a way to deal with. A government report in India, for instance admits how the present patent law in India are not adept to tackle the issue of AI Inventorship and how it has created obstacles in patenting 'AI induced innovations' [32].

4   Conclusion

Considering AI based patent applications in US, subject matter ineligibility has been a major problem. Although there has been positive development Post *Alice* case, there is no concrete solution. Therefore, it is important to frame sound strategies while claiming AI as Patent Eligible subject matter. It is vital that the patent claims are made narrowly, the solutions and problem be rooted to specific technology and there is no focus on algorithm [33]. The system under EPO is commendable as interdisciplinary software applications are examined by three examiners with diverse technical backgrounds [34]. Also, there are special EPO Guidelines for Artificial Intelligence and Machine learning which may help simplify AI and Machine Learning claims as it explicitly comments about subject matter eligibility [35].

The main challenge due to AI Inventions Systems will be the role of skilled person and its relevance in the assessment of obviousness. There will certainly be limit on what the skilled person would know. If machines or AI system themselves be the judge, the existence of patent system will itself become questionable. Avoiding this extreme, the change of definition of skilled person as propounded in EPO Conference, seems to be a balanced approach. It has suggested "skilled human using a machine" as the definition of skilled person.

Determination of novelty and inventive step has always been challenging in respect of innovations involving software patents. Sheer volume of state of the art is an issue. Simultaneous innovations take place in the software arena. The pace at which this happens is immense as compared to innovations in another fields. Prior art becomes obsolete quickly as many software have short life spans, so quick that they end even before the patent is issued [36]. Problems are also created when prior art searches are carried on database of existing patents. It is also usually seen that software are granted at higher level of abstraction. Basically, what any software does is to gather and manipulate data as per desired output. And the fact remains that there can be many novel ways to achieve the output. Unfortunately, patents are granted only for such ways thereby ignoring the initial steps. Thus, the patents are broad and overclaim the true novelty. Considering the software innovations which are patented owing to the mentioned emerging technologies, the above problems persist. In fact, they might seem to escalate. For example, AI based tools are used for prior art searches as seen earlier. Most of the software use 'functional claiming' i.e., patenting the problem to be solved rather than method to be solved [37]. When it comes to AI and Big data innovations, functional claims always carry a risk of broad interpretation. Careful drafting of functional claims so that the patent specifications explain functional limitation and providing examples of implementation can be a good strategy.

The relationship between AI and Intellectual Property is sure to see a surge with passing times. While there will be need of patent protection due to these technologies, these technologies shall further contribute for administration of patent technologies. In this dynamic environment, law should adopt a balanced approach, keeping in mind the basic philosophy behind patents.

References

1. WIPO. What is Intellectual Property? wipo.int. [Online] [Cited: May 29, 2022.] https://www.wipo.int/about-ip/en/.
2. Bentley, Lionel. Intellectual Property Law. s.l.: Oxford University Press, 2001.
3. Verkey, Elizabeth. Intellectual Property. s.l.: Eastern Book Company, 2014.
4. Patent, Copyright and Trade Secret Protection in software. Donovan, Stephen. s.l.: IEEE Potentials, 1994, Vol. 13.

5. WIPO. Copyright. wipo.int. [Online] [Cited: May May, 2022.] https://www.wipo.int/copyright/en/.

6. Think Big! The need for patent rights in the era of Big data and Machine Learning. Jin, Hyunjong Ryan. s.l.: New York University Journal of Intellectual Property and Entertainment Law, 2018, Vol. 7 (2).

7. WIPO. Trade Secrets_Everything you need to know. wipo.int. [Online] [Cited: May 29, 2022.] https://www.wipo.int/tradesecrets/en/.

8. Teska, Kirk. Software Patents 101- To protect your Intellectual property, choose the best tool for each stage in its creation. IEEE Spectrum. [Online] [Cited: May 29, 2022.] https://spectrum.ieee.org/software-patents-101.

9. WIPO. Patent Expert Issues: Computer Programs and Business Methods. wipo.int. [Online] [Cited: May 22, 2022.] https://www.wipo.int/patents/en/topics/software.html.

10. Office of CGPDTM, INDIA. Frequently Asked Questions- Patents. ipindia.gov.in. [Online] [Cited: May 30, 2022.] https://ipindia.gov.in/writereaddata/Portal/Images/pdf/Final_FREQUENTLY_ASKED_QUESTIONS_-PATENT.pdf.

11. Rethinking the PHOSITA in Patent Litigation. Reilly, Greg. s.l.: Loyola University Chicago Law Journal, 2016.

12. Bainbridge, David. Information Technology and Intellectual Property Law. s.l.: Bloomsbury Professional, 2014.

13. Piroozi, Christopher J. White and Hamid R. Drafting Patent Applications covering Artificial Intelligence Systems. americanbar.org. [Online] 2019. [Cited: May 30, 2022.] https://www.americanbar.org/groups/intellectual_property_law/publications/landslide/2018-19/january-february/drafting-patent-applications-covering-artificial-intelligence-systems/.

14. WIPO. Patenting Software. wipo.int. [Online] [Cited: May 30, 2022.] https://www.wipo.int/sme/en/documents/software_patents_fulltext.html.

15. Gottschalk v Benson. 409 US 63, 1972.

16. Parker v Flook. 437 US 584, 1978.

17. Diamond v Diehr. 450 US 175, 1981.

18. Bilski v Kappos. 561 US, 2010.

19. Alice Corp v CLS Bank International. 573 US 208, 2014.

20. Pearson, Douglas, Shentoy, Ognion and Kukkanen, Carl. Protecting Artificial Intelligence and Big Data Inventions through Patents: Subject Matter Eligibility. https://www.lexology.com/. [Online] [Cited: May 30, 2022.] https://www.lexology.com/.

21. WIPO Technological Trends 2019: Artificial Intelligence. wipo.int. [Online] [Cited: May 30, 2022.] https://www.wipo.int/edocs/pubdocs/en/wipo_pub_1055.pdf.

22. Li, Hui. Machine Learning: What it is and Why it matters? www.sas.com. [Online] [Cited: May 30, 2022.] https://www.sas.com/en_in/home.html.

23. Katherine Stephens, Toby Bond. Artificial Intelligence: Navigating the IP Challenges. www.twobirds.com. [Online] [Cited: May 30, 2022.] https://www.twobirds.com/en/insights/2018/uk/artifical-intelligence-navigating-the-ip-challenges.

24. Summary Artificial Intelligence Conference. EPO. Munich: EPO, 2018.

25. Intellectual property Protection for Artificial Intelligence. DeCosta, Frank A and Carrano, Alizza. s.l.: Westlaw Journal Intellectual Property, 2017.

26. I Think therefore I Invent: Creative Computers and the Future of Patent Law. Abbott, R. s.l.: Boston College Law Review, 2022, Vol. 57.

27. Fighting Patent trolls with stuff and nonsense. [Online] 2016. [Cited: May 30, 2022.] https://www.cbc.ca/player/play/2686963191.

28. Fraser, Erica. Computers as Inventors: Legal and Policy Implications of Artificial Intelligence on Patent Law. scripted. [Online] 2016. [Cited: May 30, 2022.] https://script-ed.org/wp-content/uploads/2016/12/13-3-fraser-1.pdf.

29. Everything is Obvious. Abbott, Ryan. 2, s.l.: UCLA Law Review, 2019, Vol. 66.
30. Malhotra, Rajiv. Artificial Intelligence and the Future of Power. s.l.: Rupa Publications, 2021.
31. EPO. Artificial Intelligence. epo.org. [Online] [Cited: June 5, 2022.] https://www.epo.org/news-events/in-focus/ict/artificial-intelligence.html.
32. Sabha, Rajya. Review of Intellectual property rights regime in India. s.l.: Rajya Sabha, 2021.
33. Challenges in drafting Patent Applications for AI- related Inventions. Bai, Benjamin. s.l.: EPO- Patenting Artificial Intelligence Conference, 2018.
34. Gin, Aaron and Wilson, Margot. Global Artificial Intelligence Patent Survey. [Online] 2019. [Cited: May 30, 2022.] https://insidebigdata.com/2019/02/22/global-artificial-intelligence-patent-survey/.
35. EPO. Guidelines for Examination. [Online] 2018. https://www.epo.org/law-practice/legal-texts/guidelines.html.
36. Goldman, Eric. The Problem with Software Patent. [Online] 2012. [Cited: May 30, 2022.] https://www.forbes.com/sites/ericgoldman/2012/11/28/the-problems-with-software-patents/?sh=7f95602a4391.
37. —. How to fix Software Patents. [Online] [Cited: May 30, 2022.] https://www.forbes.com/sites/ericgoldman/2012/12/12/how-to-fix-software-patents/?sh=4524726a430f.

Gender Classification from Behavioural Biometric Data using Convolutional Neural Network

Sathish Kumar[1](✉), Shivanand S. Gornale[1], and Rashmi Siddalingappa[2]

[1] Department of Computer Science, Rani Channamma University, Belagavi, India
sathishkumarst25@gmail.com
[2] Department of Computational and Data Sciences, Indian Institute of Science, Bangalore, India

Abstract. Biometric modalities are used to identify the gender of an individual based upon their physiometrics or behaviometric data. Gender plays a crucial role in most applications like banking, security, document authorization, forensics, psychology, human-computer interventions, and many more. Gender classification using handwritten signatures is still considered to be a challenging task due to homogenous variations among male and female handwritten signatures. This paper monologues the gender classification from offline signature images using Convolutional Neural Network features. The results obtained are promising and competitive with state-of-art techniques.

Keywords: Biometrics · Convolutional Neural Network · Offline Handwritten Signature · Gender Classification

1 Introduction

Biometric security systems technologically rely on measurements of an individual's morphological (e.g. Face, Iris, Fingerprint, Hand geometry, etc.) and behavioral (e.g. Voice, Signature, Keystroke, etc.) attributes [1]. Soft biometrics are the demographic information-based biometric modality (e.g. Age, Gender, Ethnicity, Height, etc.) used to differentiate an individual. Recently, identification and authentication from ancillary information of biometric methods are extensively researched issues, whereas soft-biometrics and hard-biometrics work together to ensure best recognition rate for a specific environment [2]. Signatures are behavioural biometrics which is inconsistent and change due to an emotional and physical state like age, mood, and ecological conditions [3]. The word "signature" comes from the Latin word "signure", which means "to mark". It is a special type of person's handwriting, where everyone has their unique style of signature which is due to neuromuscular mechanical variance in the male and female signatures. It is a subconscious habitual act based on his/her habits and mannerism. Gender is one of the physical or social information of a person being male or female, which is used in many applications like forensic science, medical, video surveillance, etc. As a result, handwritten signatures are used to identify a person's various characteristics, such as gender [4], personality analysis [5], emotional state, neurological diseases, age, and also nationality. Handwritten Signatures made on document signifies approval, acceptance, and knowledge of an individual. These are broadly accepted biometric traits, legally and socially everywhere and also help in the court of law as evidence to find the culprit from the suspects [6]. In the past few decades gender classification from offline handwritten signature images is a hot research subject in the areas like health, security, pattern recognition, computer vision, and forensic document examination [7], and an adequate importance in banking agreement, cheque processing methods, official publications, and passport validation.

The biometric data contained in the handwritten signature can also be verified and used to improve the security authentication. In general Handwritten-Signature traits deeply reveal some of the gender-dependent aspects like the writing style, size, and shape of letters, decorativeness, pen pressure, slant/orientation, curvature, speed, irregular spaces, inconsistencies in writing and acceleration. The diversity in shapes of characters is the key challenges in writer identification. In this case, the features extracted from the signature samples may enhance the performance of gender classification. Many current technological studies have focused on the verification and recognition of handwritten signatures; whereas a small number of researchers are working on femininity. Therefore, we aim to propose a deep learning framework for the classification of male and female handwritten signatures using the convolutional neural network. The key contributions of the proposed study is to preprocess the offline scanned handwritten signature images, extract features using deep convolutional neural network and classification employed using state-of-the-art techniques.

The outline of this paper is organized as follows: Sect. 2 presents an overview of previous work done by the researchers. Section 3 is dedicated to the proposed method and feature extraction addresses the state-of-the-art. In Sect. 4 Experimental results are analyzed. Finally, the Comparative study, and the conclusion are presented in Sect. 5.

In the recent past, Biometric modalities like handwritten signatures are extensively accepted for authentication and authorization purpose. Several related studies showcased handwriting-based gender classification. Cavalante Bandeira et al. [8] have investigated the impact of keystrokes and handwritten signatures on gender prediction systems. A total of 100 participants were interviewed, and their handwritten signature images and keystroke information are collected from each participant. The dataset contains each participant's gender, emotion, and hand orientation information. Basic statistical and dynamic features were extracted and classified using the multilayer perceptron technique. An average accuracy of 68.03% is achieved. Pal et al. [9] have proposed work on gender classification using the Euler number as a feature for the offline 500 Hindi handwritten signature images. A backpropagation neural network is used for the classification and a recognition rate of 88.80% is obtained.

2 Related Work

In addition, to the handwritten signature-based gender classification, another aspect worth mentioning is that many works are carried out on handwriting-based independent writer identification and gender classification. In [10], the authors worked on 130 handwriting samples collected between the age group of 18–30 years where 65 males and 65 females. 27 different minute features are extracted and divided into two groups' macro and micro features using a magnifying lens, enlarger scale, and protector for the examination. Hypothesis testing (Z-test) is used to find the statistical significance level of the male and female handwriting and comparative results were obtained. Somaya Al Maadeed et al. [11] have proposed work on age, gender, and nationality prediction using offline handwriting. Several geometric features were extracted from the QUWI dataset and features are combined using random forest classifier and kernel discriminant analysis classification techniques. Recognition rate of 74.05%, 55.76%, and 53.66% for gender, age, and nationality is predicted. Angel Morera et al. [12] proposed a prediction system for Gender and Handedness using offline handwriting. IAM dataset of English texts and KHATT dataset of Arabic texts, two public databases are used for the experimentation. Deep learning and Convolutional Neural Network classification techniques used achieved comparative results. Gender using IAM dataset: accuracy 80.72% and Handedness using IAM dataset accuracy: 90.70%, for KHATT dataset accuracy of Gender, is 68.70% and Handedness is 70.91%. In [13] writer identification based on writer individuality using a combination of features has been proposed. Three types of features were selected namely word, line, and character-based features on English and Bengali handwritten text. Experiments were carried out on writings of both male and female volunteers with different age groups. Extracted features are classified using Multilayer Perceptron and K-Star algorithms. Best recognition results in 93.54% and 95.69% are obtained. Abdeljalil Gattal et al. [14] have proposed work on handwriting-based gender classification. The two new features were introduced in the work, Cloud of Line Distribution and Hinge features on the QUWI dataset. Two types of evaluation techniques were carried out on the database, Script-independent, and Script-dependent evaluations. The extracted features are classified using a Support Vector Machine classifier with an accuracy rate of 73.60% is obtained.

Many previous works have shown that texture features and shape features may enhance the performance of gender classification using offline handwritten signatures and handwriting. However, we observe that there are very little effort is done into gender identification using handwritten signatures that contain multilingual text. Therefore, we proposed a framework of deep convolutional neural network-based features from the offline handwritten signature, which are used to classify the different gender from signature images.

3 Proposed Methodology

In this section, we propose the general architecture of the proposed schema as shown in Fig. 1.

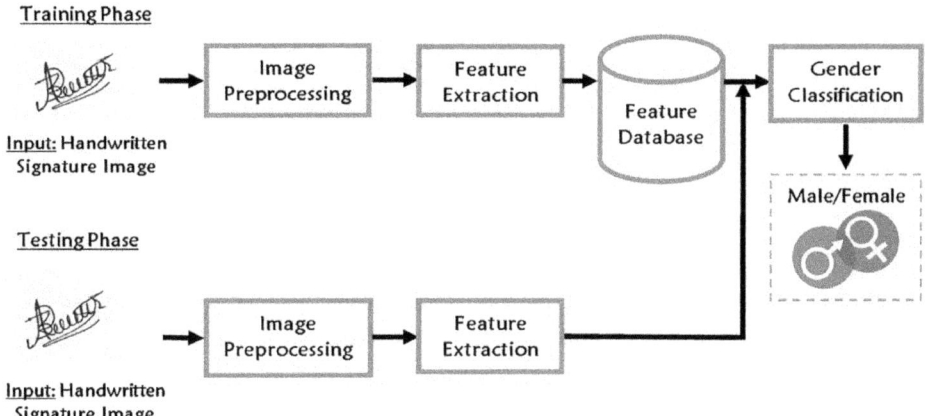

Fig. 1. General architecture for gender classification using handwritten signature

Fig. 2. Samples images from the Handwritten Signature Database

3.1 Dataset

The dataset used in this proposed work is retrieved from the Mendeley database, i.e., Offline Handwritten Signatures based on Gender Annotation [15]. The dataset contains 250 male and 229 female handwritten signatures, an in-house total of 4790 signature samples with different age groups. These samples consist of multilingual handwritten scripts of Kannada, Hindi, Marathi, and English. Signature samples from the dataset are shown in Fig. 2.

3.2 Pre-processing

The sequence of pre-processing steps is carried out to feed the neural network. Pre-processing module consists of enhancing the quality of the collected dataset such as Normalization and Resizing the signature. The neural network assumes that the input is

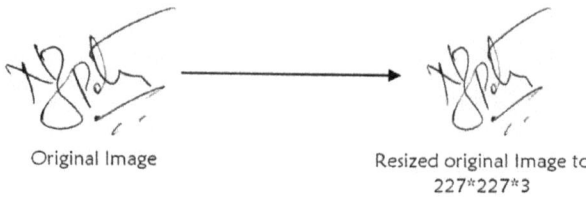

Original Image   Resized original Image to
                           227*227*3

Fig. 3. Pre-processing of the signature image

a fixed size and the shape of the signature significantly varies. Our system consists of the following component: Normalization of the signature into 227*227*3 dimensions (Fig. 3).

Implementation Platform

MATLAB is high-performance language for technical computing and interactive environment for algorithm development. The GUI framework support many different predefined functions/objects in toolbox (https://in.mathworks.com/help/install/).

The proposed work was executed on the MATLAB 2018b with deep learning toolbox (https://in.mathworks.com/products/deep-learning/). A pre trained Convolutional Neural Network (AlexNet) is been trained to extract the features from the input image (Deep Learning Toolbox Model for AlexNet Network - File Exchange - MATLAB Central (mathworks.com)). Classification models trained using Classification Learner application.

3.3 Feature Extraction

Feature extraction is the process of locating or computing influencing and distinguishing qualities that may aid in classifying gender from a given dataset [17]. Feature Extraction converts input data into a set of features. The significant aspects of input data are called features, and they aid in identifying the input patterns. The proposed method exploits the features of a Signature image using a deep Convolutional neural network to differentiate between the two gender classes. A brief description of feature learning techniques is presented in the following.

3.3.1 CNN-Based Feature Extraction

Convolutional Neural Network was firstly introduced in 1980 by Fukushima [18] and developed in 1998 by Y.LeCun et al.[19]. In many computer-vision tasks, CNN is used to achieve better performance in state-of-the-art techniques. CNN architecture is typically composed of a Convolutional layer, a pooling layer, and a fully connected layer. The following Fig. 4 illustrates the general architecture of the CNN model.

The input layer of CNNs directly accepts raw images and convolves them using shared weights across several learning kernels. The number of maps and kernel sizes of the maps are the parameters that define a convolutional layer. Each layer contains M maps (M_x, M_y) of equal size, and (K_x, K_y) is the kernel size which is shifted to the valid region of the input image [16]. In layer l each map is connected to all maps of layer l-1.

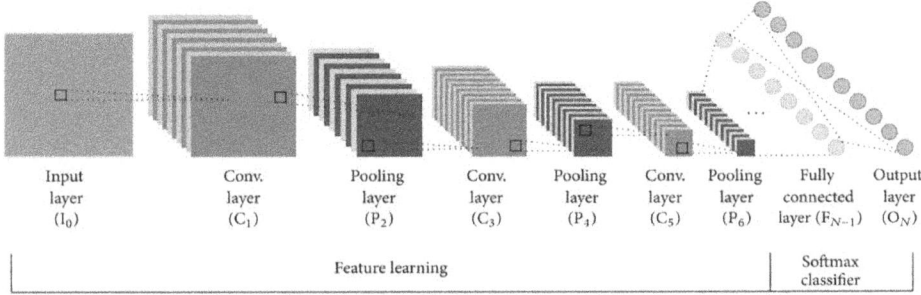

| Input layer (I_0) | Conv. layer (C_1) | Pooling layer (P_2) | Conv. layer (C_3) | Pooling layer (P_4) | Conv. layer (C_5) | Pooling layer (P_6) | Fully connected layer (F_{N-1}) | Output layer (O_N) |

| Feature learning | Softmax classifier |

Fig. 4. A typical general architecture of the CNN model

The weights of neurons in a given map are shared but they have different input fields. Next, the pooling layer reduces the resolutions of the feature maps, the purpose is to achieve spatial invariance or to maintain the information contained in the image. The maximum, mean, or stochastic activation, corresponding to max-pooling, mean-pooling, or stochastic pooling, over non-overlapping rectangular sections of size (K_x, K_y), gives the output of the pooling layer. Feature learning is composed of a convolutional layer and a pooling layer, following which the extracted features are combined and weighted in multiple fully connected layers, and also classification part of the convolutional layer is represented in the fully connected layer. Each neuron in layer l is connected to outputs of all neurons in layer l-1 which corresponds to one character class. Table 1 list of operational modules performed in the above architecture of the CNN model.

Both convolutional layers and fully connected layers have learnable parameters that are optimized during training. After every learnable layer in the network, except for the last layer, the Batch normalization method is applied, followed by a non-linearity ReLU (rectified linear activation function) Layer. Finally, the last full Connected Layer uses the softmax layer of non-linearity, which interprets the assigned probability of each possible use by the network. The result of layer 'fc7' is the input of both output layers [20]. Table 2 describes the list of operations performed in the layers.

Where, $\mathbf{Z}^l$: Pre-activation output of layer l, $\mathbf{h}^l$: activation layer l, $*$: discrete convolution operator, W, γ, , β: learnable parameters, the mean ($E[z_i]$) and variance ($Var[z_i]$).

3.4 Classification

Classification techniques are used to systematically classify given data into one or more sets of classes [21].

3.4.1 Support Vector Machine (SVM)

SVM is one of the supervised and discriminative binary classifiers, which works on decision boundary in feature vector data of closest points using maximal margin hyperplane. It is used to maximize the difference between the two classes and also it gives a hyperplane as a result of classification [22]. SVMs training patterns select feature data

Table 1. Modules of CNN layers

Layer	Size	parameters
ImageInputLayer	$227 \times 227 \times 3$	Name: 'data'
Convolution2DLayer (C1)	$96 \times 11 \times 11$	Stride = 4, pad = 0, Name: 'conv1'
MaxPooling2DLayer	$96 \times 3 \times 3$	Stride = 2, Name: 'pool1'
Convolution2DLayer (C2)	$256 \times 5 \times 5$	Stride = 1, pad = 2, Name: 'conv2'
MaxPooling2DLayer	$256 \times 3 \times 3$	Stride = 2, Name: 'pool2'
Convolution2DLayer (C3)	$384 \times 3 \times 3$	Stride = 1, pad = 1, Name: 'conv3'
Convolution2DLayer (C4)	$384 \times 3 \times 3$	Stride = 1, pad = 1, Name: 'conv4'
Convolution2DLayer (C5)	$256 \times 3 \times 3$	Stride = 1, pad = 1, Name: 'conv5'
MaxPooling2DLayer	$256 \times 3 \times 3$	Stride = 2, Name: 'pool3'
FullyConnected2DLayer (FC6)	4096	Name: 'fc6'
FullyConnected2DLayer (FC7)	4096	Name: 'fc7'
FullyConnected2DLayer (FC8) + Softmax Layer	1000	Name: 'fc8', softmax
Classification Output Layer		Name: 'output', cross entropy

Table 2. Operations performed in the layer

Operation	Formula	
Convolution	$Z^l = h^{l-1} * W^l$	(1)
MaxPooling	$h^l_{xy} = max_{i=0,\ldots S, j=0,\ldots S} h^{l-1}_{(x+i)(y+j)}$	(2)
Fully-connected Layer	$Z^l = W^l h^{l-1}$	(3)
ReLU	$ReLU(Z_i) = \max(0, Z_i)$	(4)
Softmax	$Softmax(Z_i) = \frac{e^{z_i}}{\sum_j e^{z_i}}$	(5)
Batch Normalization	$BN(Z_i) = \gamma_i \widehat{Z}_i + \beta_i, \widehat{Z}_i = \frac{Z_i - E[Z_i]}{\sqrt{Var[Z_i]}}$	(6)

that lies on the hyperplane with maximum margin and the closest point distance in both the classes [23].

3.4.2 K-Nearest Neighbour (K-NN)

K-NN algorithm is firstly developed by Fix and Hodges [24] in the year 1950s. It is a machine learning classifier that is used for classification and also for regression analysis. K-NN classifiers classify data points into predefined classes based on different types of distances. This algorithm selects the feature space to predict the data points into k classes distance measurement as feature similarity. We used city-block distance to find out the shortest neighboring data points. It is calculated as:

$$D_{city-Block}(M, N) = \sum_{J=0}^{n} |M_J - N_J| \qquad (7)$$

where M_J is the new point and N_J is the distribution for distance.

3.4.3 Ensemble Classifier

The ensemble classifier is the combination of multiple classifiers used to classify the number of samples by considering a vote on the predictions of its components to get output. Combining the classifiers generally has two types of methods i.e., classifier selection and classifier fusion [25]. Single classifier applied to get best accuracy for given sample is said to classifier selection, whereas in classifier fusion method different classifiers applied in parallel to get the final decision based on the groups consent [25]. In proposed study, bagging approach is applied for the computed features. The following Fig. 5 demonstrates the bagging the classifier.

The algorithm used for the proposed system is as follows:

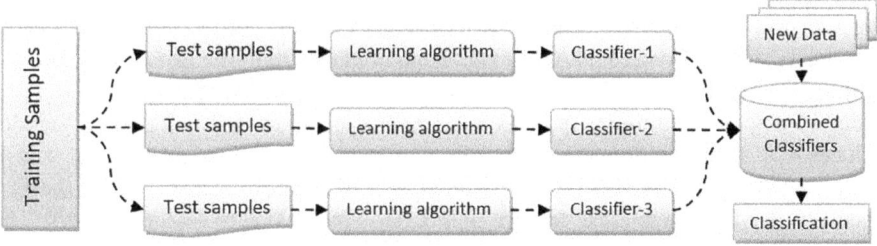

Fig. 5. General representation of bagging approach

<u>Algorithm</u>

> **Input:** Offline Handwritten Signature Image.
>
> **Output:** Gender Classification of the individual.
>
> **Step1:** Input offline handwritten signature image
>
> **Step2:** Pre-processing of the input image into 227x227 fixed sizes.
>
> **Step3:** Compute Features using Convolutional Neural Network.
>
> **Step4:** Classification of feature space using Support Vector Machine, K-Nearest Neighbor, and Ensemble Classifiers and output the gender class of individual.

End

4 Experimental Results

The experimental evaluation of the system carried on the Offline Handwritten Signatures based on Gender Annotation [15], which comprises 4790 offline handwritten signatures of a different gender. An in-house total of 479 writers contributed 10 signatures each, collected from 250 male writers and 229 female writers who belong to different age groups. Firstly, the signatures normalized to a fixed size 227×227. The entire dataset split into 70:30 ratios for training and testing the system shown in Table 3. The proposed work employ Convolutional Neural Network (alexnet) for feature extraction, the input layer accepts raw image followed by the convolution layer 'conv1' with 11×11 filters and 10 maps of size 24×24. Next the sub-sequential max-pooling layer 'pool2' reduces previous layer into 12×12 by 2×2 filters. Similarly 'conv3' also employs 5×5 filters but has 12 maps with dimensions of 8×8 pixels. 'pool4' with 2×2 pooling windows produces 4×4 feature maps that are fully connected to 100 hidden neurons. The 100 dimensional fully connected layer projected into the feature space. Lastly, the series of neurons used to cover these feature points class by class into feature vectors. These features were classified using CNN + KNN, CNN + SVM and CNN + Ensemble classification techniques are tested with 10 cross validation on the signature dataset. It is observed that 95.4% highest accuracy is achieved by the ensemble learning with bagging approach with number of learners = 30. Further, several experiments are carried on K-Nearest Neighbor algorithm with different distance 'k' which ranges from 1 to 20 values, directly impacts the accuracy rate. The proposed work is determines highest accuracy of the KNN model with k = 3 value, the resulted into better overall accuracy of 94.2%. Finally, the SVM algorithm yielded an enhanced accuracy of 84.4% which is less result rate compared to other classifiers. Table 4 represents the experimental results based on classification accuracy, performance analysis and confusion matrix, namely KNN, SVM and Ensemble classifier. In Table 3 Train_x (70% of 4790) indicates the 70% split from the original signature dataset for training, Test_x (30% of 4790) indicates the 30% split reserved for the model validation. The corresponding labels stored at the variable 'y' are again split into 70% for Train_y and the remaining 30% for the Test_y to test the model on the unseen data.

The performance evaluation of the proposed system analysed using performance metrics namely, Accuracy, Precision, Recall (True Positive Rate) and F_score which are defined in following Eqs. 8–11.

$$Accuracy = \frac{TP}{(TP + TN + FP + FN)} \tag{8}$$

$$Precision = \frac{TP}{(TP + FP)} \tag{9}$$

$$Recall = \frac{TP}{(TP + FN)} \tag{10}$$

$$F_{score} = \frac{2 * PRECISION * RECALL}{PRECISION + RECALL} \tag{11}$$

where, TP: True positive value, TN: True Negative value, FP: False Positive Value and FN: False Negative Value. Figure 6 is the graphical representation of classifiers and feature.

Comparative Analysis

Comparative analysis presented in Table 4 the results obtained by the proposed work is compared with similar state-of-the- art techniques used in the related work for gender classification. Pal et al. [9] have worked on gender classification using Euler number as a feature for 500 Hindi handwritten signature database. A Back Propagation Neural Network classification technique is used and obtained an accuracy of 88.80%. Somaya Al Maadeed et al. [11] proposed work on QUWI dataset, several geometric features are extracted and using random forest and kernel discriminant analysis classifiers for gender 74.05%, age 55.76% and for nationality 53.66% is obtained. In [12] authors proposed prediction system of gender and handedness using IAM dataset and KHATT dataset. CNN classification technique is used and achieved an accuracy of 80.72% for gender and 90.70% for handedness using IAM dataset, 68.70% for gender and 70.91% for handedness using KHATT dataset. Abdeljalil Gattal et al. [14] proposed novel feature

Table 3. Training and Test set Split into ratio as 70:20 for the given dataset

No. of Training Samples: 70%	Train_x	No. of Test Samples: 30%	Test_x	Total
	(3353,1000)		(1437,1000)	(4790,66)
	Train_y		Test_y	
	(3353,1)		(1437,1)	(4790,66)

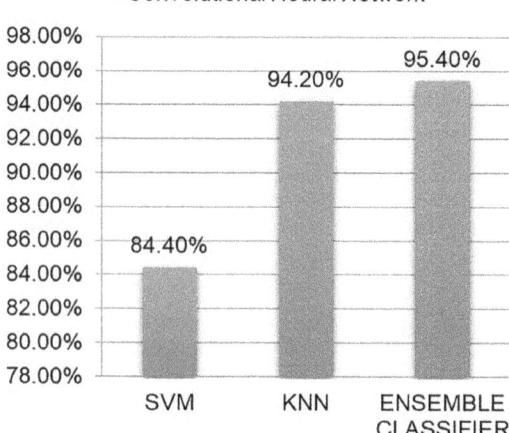

Fig. 6. Graphical illustrations of the obtained results from classifiers and feature

learning techniques such as Cloud of Line Distribution and Hinge features, for handwriting based gender classification using QUWI dataset. An accuracy of 73.60% is achieved using support vector machine classifier. Comparatively, the reported works have drawback of using limited size database for the experiments except the database used in [4]. It observed that the proposed method was able to outperform the other works by using Convolutional Neural Network as feature with Ensemble Classifier which yielded higher accuracy of 95.40%, which is an encouraging result.

Table 4. Summary of related methods in the literature, features, classifiers and datasets.

Authors	Features	Database	Classifiers	Results
Pal et. al [9]	Euler number and statistical features	500 Hindi handwritten signatures	Back Propagation Neural Network	84%
Somaya Al Maadeed et. al[11]	Geometric features	QUWI dataset	Random Forest and Kernel Discriminant analysis	74.05% for gender
Angel Morera et. al [12]	Deep features	IAM dataset and KHATT dataset	Deep CNN	80.72%, 68.70%
Abdeljalil Gattal et al. [14]	COLD features	QUWI dataset	Support Vector Machine	73.60%
Proposed method	**Convolutional Neural Network features**	**Offline Handwritten Signature based on Gender Annotation**	**K-NN classifier, Support Vector Machine, Ensemble Classifier**	**94.20% 84.40% 95.40%**

5   Conclusion

From recent past years the advancement of ML-based algorithms used for gender classification using handwritten signature and handwriting for better recognition. The proposed work presented a competent method to find out gender of the person using handwritten signature sample. The method mainly relies on the feature extraction of Signature samples of male and female writers. A pre-trained deep Convolutional Neural Network (AlexNet) was employed for feature extraction and for classification a number of standard classification techniques are used. Among this ensemble classifier has reported the highest classification result rate. In our further study, we will include study of feature selection and fine tuning of pre-trained models which are used to characterize the writing features, and other demographical biometric analysis such as age and handedness etc. will be studied.

Authors' Contributions.   Sathish Kumar[1]: Conceptualization, Methodology, Software and Field study. Shivanand S. Gornale[2]: Data Curation, Writing-Original draft preparation, Software Validation and Field study. Rashmi Siddalingappa[3]: Visualization, Investigation, Writing-Reviewing and Editing.

Compliance with Ethical Standards.   • Conflict of Interest: The authors state that they do not have any conflicts of interest.

• Research involving Human and Animal Rights: There are no animal trials by any of the authors in this paper.

• Ethical Standards: All procedures used in research involving human volunteers were compatible with the institution's ethical guidelines.

References

1. Thompson, A. F., Alese, B. K., & Olofinlade, F. V. (2013). Nose biometrics verification using linear object technique. In 2013 Pan African International Conference on Information Science, Computing and Telecommunications, PACT 2013 (pp. 182–187). Institute of Electrical and Electronics Engineers Inc. https://doi.org/10.1109/SCAT.2013.7055111
2. Kim, M. G., Moon, H. M., Chung, Y., & Pan, S. B. (2012). A survey and proposed framework on the soft biometrics technique for human identification in intelligent video surveillance system. Journal of Biomedicine and Biotechnology, 2012.https://doi.org/10.1155/2012/614146
3. Wicaksono Putra, A. B., Mulyanto, Suprapty, B., & Onnilita Gaffar, A. F. (2021). A Performance of Combined Methods of VCG and 16BCD for Feature Extraction on HSV. International Journal of Image, Graphics and Signal Processing, 13(3), 13–32. https://doi.org/https://doi.org/10.5815/ijigsp.2021.03.02
4. Gornale, S. S., Kumar, S., Patil, A., & Hiremath, P. S. (2021). Behavioral Biometric Data Analysis for Gender Classification Using Feature Fusion and Machine Learning. Frontiers in Robotics and AI, 8. https://doi.org/https://doi.org/10.3389/frobt.2021.685966
5. Gornale, S. S., Kumar, S., & Hiremath, P. S. (2021). Handwritten Signature Biometric Data Analysis for Personality Prediction System Using Machine Learning Techniques. Transactions on Machine Learning and Artificial Intelligence, 9(5), 1–22. https://doi.org/10.14738/tmlai.95.10808

6. AbdAli, S., & Putz-Leszczynska, J. (2014). Age and gender-invariant features of handwritten signatures for verification systems. In Photonics Applications in Astronomy, Communications, Industry, and High-Energy Physics Experiments 2014 (Vol. 9290, p. 929021). SPIE. https://doi.org/10.1117/12.2075160

7. Sulaiman, A., Omar, K., Nasrudin, M. F., & Arram, A. (2019). Length Independent Writer Identification Based on the Fusion of Deep and Hand-Crafted Descriptors. IEEE Access, 7, 91772–91784. https://doi.org/https://doi.org/10.1109/ACCESS.2019.2927286

8. Cavalcante Bandeira, D. R., De Paula Canuto, A. M., Da Costa-Abreu, M., Fairhurst, M., Li, C., & Nascimento, D. S. C. (2019). Investigating the impact of combining handwritten signature and keyboard keystroke dynamics for gender prediction. In Proceedings - 2019 Brazilian Conference on Intelligent Systems, BRACIS 2019 (pp. 126–131). Institute of Electrical and Electronics Engineers Inc. https://doi.org/10.1109/BRACIS.2019.00031

9. Pal, M., Bhattacharyya, S., & Sarkar, T. (2018). Euler number based feature extraction technique for gender discrimination from offline Hindi signature using SVM & BPNN classifier. In 2018 Emerging Trends in Electronic Devices and Computational Techniques, EDCT 2018 (pp. 1–6). Institute of Electrical and Electronics Engineers Inc. https://doi.org/10.1109/EDCT.2018.8405084

10. Sahu, M., Yadav, A., & Isukapatla, A. R. (2017). Examination of Handwriting for Gender Identifying Features. International Journal of Current Research, 9(1), 45923–45928

11. Al Maadeed, S., & Hassaine, A. (2014). Automatic prediction of age, gender, and nationality in offline handwriting. Eurasip Journal on Image and Video Processing, 2014. https://doi.org/https://doi.org/10.1186/1687-5281-2014-10.

12. Morera, Á., Sánchez, Á., Vélez, J. F., & Moreno, A. B. (2018). Gender and Handedness Prediction from Offline Handwriting Using Convolutional NeuralNetworks. Complexity, 2018. https://doi.org/10.1155/2018/3891624

13. Mukherjee, S., & Ghosh, I. D. (2020). Writer Identification based on Writing Individuality and Combination of Features. In Proceedings of 2020 IEEE Applied Signal Processing Conference, ASPCON 2020 (pp. 324–329). Institute of Electrical and Electronics Engineers Inc. https://doi.org/10.1109/ASPCON49795.2020.9276700

14. Gattal, A., Djeddi, C., Bensefia, A., & Ennaji, A. (2020). Handwriting based gender classification using cold and hinge features. In Lecture Notes in Computer Science (including subseries Lecture Notes in Artificial Intelligence and Lecture Notes in Bioinformatics) (Vol. 12119 LNCS, pp. 233–242). Springer. https://doi.org/10.1007/978-3-030-51935-3_25

15. RCUB, sathish kumar; Gornale, Shivanand (2022), "Offline Handwritten Signature Database based on Gender Annotation", Mendeley Data, V1, doi: https://doi.org/10.17632/22wgmd ppxz.1

16. Zhou, L., Li, Q., Huo, G., & Zhou, Y. (2017). Image classification using biomimetic pattern recognition with convolutional neural networks features. Computational Intelligence and Neuroscience, 2017.https://doi.org/10.1155/2017/3792805

17. Kumar, S., Gornale, S. S., Siddalingappa, R., & Mane, A. (2022). Gender Classification Based on Online Signature Features using Machine Learning Techniques. International Journal of Intelligent Systems and Applications in Engineering, 10(2), 260–268. Retrieved from https://ijisae.org/index.php/IJISAE/article/view/2020

18. Fukushima, K. (1980). Neocognitron: A self-organizing neural network model for a mechanism of pattern recognition unaffected by shift in position. Biological Cybernetics, 36(4), 193–202. https://doi.org/https://doi.org/10.1007/BF00344251

19. LeCun, Y., Bottou, L., Bengio, Y., & Haffner, P. (1998). Gradient-based learning applied to document recognition. Proceedings of the IEEE, 86(11), 2278–2323. https://doi.org/https://doi.org/10.1109/5.726791

20. Hafemann, L. G., Sabourin, R., & Oliveira, L. S. (2017). Learning features for offline handwritten signature verification using deep convolutional neural networks. Pattern Recognition, 70, 163–176. https://doi.org/https://doi.org/10.1016/j.patcog.2017.05.012
21. Gornale, S. S., Kumar, S., Siddalingappa, R., & Hiremath, P. S. (2022). Survey on Handwritten Signature Biometric Data Analysis for Assessment of Neurological Disorder using Machine Learning Techniques. Transactions on Machine Learning and Artificial Intelligence, 10(2). 27-60.
22. Maken, P., & Gupta, A. (2021). A method for automatic classification of gender based on text- independent handwriting. Multimedia Tools and Applications, 80(16), 24573–24602. https://doi.org/https://doi.org/10.1007/s11042-021-10837-9
23. Gornale, S.S., Patil, A., & Prabha (2016). Statistical Features Based Gender Identification Using SVM. International Journal for Scientific Research and Development, 241–244.
24. Anava, O., & Levy, K. Y. (2016). k∗-Nearest neighbors: From global to local. In Advances in Neural Information Processing Systems (pp. 4923–4931). Neural information processing systems foundation.
25. Ahmed, M., Rasool, A. G., Afzal, H., & Siddiqi, I. (2017). Improving handwriting based gender classification using ensemble classifiers. Expert Systems with Applications, 85, 158–168. https://doi.org/https://doi.org/10.1016/j.eswa.2017.05.033

Opinion Mining and Tweet Analysis Using Topic Modeling by LDA with BERT and GLOVE Embedding

Ashwini Pachore[✉] and Vrishali Chakkarwar

Government College of Engineering, Aurangabad, Maharashtra, India
vrush.a143@gmail.com

Abstract. An example of natural language processing is opinion mining. A system is created to gather and process opinions about a product expressed in blog posts, comments, reviews, or tweets in order to assess public sentiment. Data preprocessing is used in this study to clean tweets and remove any punctuation, special symbols, hashtags, and URLs. Topic modelling and LDA are used to extract the themes from the corpus of gathered topics. The Principal Components Analysis (PCA) techniques are described in this article as dimensional reduction strategies with the goal of identifying the fewest possible Principal Components (PCs) that can help achieve the best classification performance. K-means clustering is a technique used to group together comparable words in tweets, along with cluster analysis. Utilizing the glove model, words are represented as vectors. The tweets can be grouped using k-means. Text input is sequentially read using the BERT paradigm. LSTM (long short-term memory) is used to anticipate sequences. In order to maintain the semantic association between words in a low-dimensional embedding space, Word2vec is a potent and effective word embedding technique. It is capable of handling tiny text corpora with a few million unique words (also called as vocabulary). "T-SNE" that places each datapoint on a two- or three-dimensional map to view high-dimensional data. In order to more effectively validate models and outcomes, other performance metrics like accuracy, F1-score, and a confusion matrix were also used.

Keywords: Opinion Mining · Glove Model · BERT Model · LSTM Model · Principal Component Analysis · K-means

1 Introduction

Topic modelling is a probabilistic statistical approach that reveals the hidden theme organization in document collections and makes analyzing massive amounts of unlabeled text simple. By examining distinct patterns present in documents, the fundamental purpose of modelling is to identify patterns of words in text and discover hidden structural terms that run across the corpus [2]. Probabilistic clustering is another term for topic modelling. It's more reliable, and the results are usually more accurate. Grouping that is particularly difficult (e.g. k-mean clustering). Topic modelling differs from traditional

R. Manza et al. (Eds.): ACVAIT 2022, AISR 176, pp. 660–673, 2023.
https://doi.org/10.2991/978-94-6463-196-8_50

clustering algorithms in that it assumes a distance measure between topics and allocates one topic to each text. Allocates a document to a group of subjects with varying degrees of importance Without making any. Assumptions about the distance, weights or probabilities are used of Compared to other subjects.

There are many topic models available, but the latent Dirichlet allocation (LDA) model proposed by David Blei, Andrew Ng and it is the most extensively utilized topic models [1]. Opinion mining is a type of natural language processing that is used to track how people feel about a product. Opinion mining, sometimes referred as sentiment analysis, is the process of developing a system for gathering and analyzing client opinion expressed in blog posts, comments, reviews, or tweets [3] Typically sentiment polarity is classified into three groups. Good, bad, and neutrality. Our text analysis based on the meaning of words in a given context [4]. The model in this work is built on time consuming studies using LSTM and Global Vector's 300-dimensional word embedding features (Glove) [7]. Using the distributional features learned from a large sample of language corpora and creating low dimensional vectors, word embedding allows for identical representation for words with similar meaning. Word2vec and Glove are the most well-known approaches for creating word embeddings in our setting [5]. The first step in the analysis of a tweet is to preprocess the data by removing stop words, special symbols, punctuation, hashtags, and URL, among other things. Next, we create word embeddings and vector forms of textual data from the dataset. Many Natural Language Processing (NLP) tasks benefit from these vector representations of words. So far, Word2Vec and Glove are the two most well-known representation models in this area. Glove is an unlabeled data tool for obtaining word vector representations. The resulting representations highlight intriguing linear substructures of the word vector space, which are trained using aggregated global word to word co-occurrence information from a corpus. Glove word embedding is a global log to bilinear regression model that uses co-occurrence and matrix factorization to produce vectors. The classification of texts using LSTM in this analysis because the structure of LSTM is a sequence in which an integrated whole or cannot be cut, similar to the structure of text documents, which if cut would change the meaning of the phrase.

2   Literature Survey

On the basis of their characteristics, Shrivatava, A., Mayor, S. & Pant, performed a poll of user opinions regarding tweets from Twitter and classified those tweets as positive, negative, or neutral [3]. The glove model, which depicts word representations in glove vector space, was discussed as a current technique for learning matrix factorization representations of words by. Pennington, J., Socher, R., & Manning, C. D. By focusing on the nonzero elements of a verb cooccurrence matrix rather than learning the entire sparse matrix or specific context windows in a huge dataset, the result is seen in global matrix factorization and statistical information [6]. Document clustering is a technique used to group similar documents, and processing and dimensionality reduction techniques (pca and)which aid in document clustering with the use of k-means algorithm were examined in the method provided in [8] Kumar, A. A, & Chandrasekhar, S. The model BERT was developed in by Geetha, M. P., and Renuka, D. K. It is distinctive and different from previous machine learning models in that it is deeply bidirectional, both from left to right and right to left text representation, and pre-trained on a sizable unlabeled text corpus.

3   System Design

Figure 1 depicts the layout of our experiment. To begin, collect tweets from the dataset and pre-process the information so that it may be analysed. Then, using LDA, we execute topic modelling on it, employing glove, PCA, and BERT models, and comparing their accuracy in a graphical approach.

3.1   Dataset

The "omicron tweets" dataset from Kaggle is utilized in this work. The user id, name, user location, user description, user created, tweet, user followers, user friends, user likes, user verified, date, text, hashtags, source, retweets, favorites, and is retweet are the 16 fields that make up each row in the dataset. Omicrons tweet data from 10/2/2022 to 3/3/2022 is the time range of the dataset. The dataset contains 15000 tweets, of which 80% and 20% are used for training and testing, respectively. in order to display the results using graphs and a confusion matrix.

3.2   Data Pre-processing

The reduction of stop - word and punctuations is an important step in the pre-processing of data mining activities involving natural language processing. We utilize the pre-processing module to clean the data after extracting tweets from the dataset. The goal of this module is to remove hashtags, user names, URLs, RT symbols, punctuations, and non-English characters. It also includes data normalization, noise reduction. The tweets returned from Twitter must be pre-processed before we can utilize them to train our

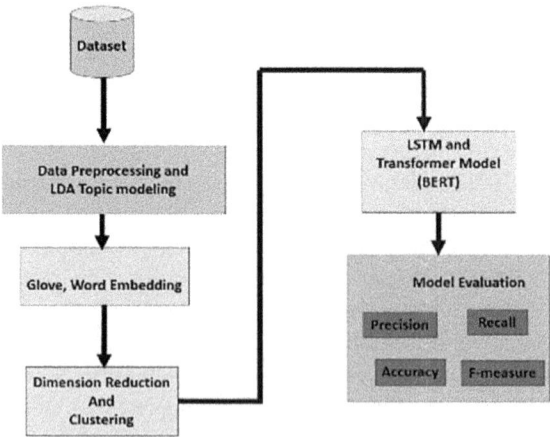

Fig. 1. System design for tweet Analysis

subject modelling algorithms A sample of tweets from each dataset at random URLs, emojis, and other special characters and sequences, such as "RT," are included in the tweets. When you see RT in a tweet, it means it was retweeted by another person [2].

3.2.1 Removing Stop Words

Stop words are words that recur frequently in writings but are irrelevant to the issue at hand. Stop words in the English language include "is," "and," "at," "the," and "it" which do not contribute much to text classification. To remove stop words from our tweets, we are using the NLTK python module's stop word component.

3.2.2 Removing Special Characters and Punctuation

The tweets contain punctuation, standard emoticons, and consumer emoticon built from sequences of special characters. The punctuation field in Python's string class is used to remove punctuation marks. Regular expressions are used to eliminate both user-created and standard emojis.

3.2.3 Tokenization

Tokenization is the process of breaking a text down into words, phrases, or other significant parts, or tokens. Thus, text segmentation includes tokenization. Tweets in the dataset have all been tokenized.

3.2.4 Stemming and Lemmatization

To find the derived words' root forms is the aim of stemming. For instance, "retrieval," "retrieved," and "retrieves" are all stemmed to get "retrieve. "By simply erasing word endings, many stemming systems achieve this outcome in a somewhat rudimentary manner. Stemming can cause a loss of meaning because it ignores the context of the words in a sentence. Using the parts of speech, lemmatization determines whether a word is a noun, verb, pronoun, adverb, or adjective and then converts it accordingly. For instance, the word "better" lemmatizes to corpus to corpora.

3.3 Building LDA Topic Modeling

The Twitter LDA is presented in, and it assumes that each has only one topic. It simulates the tweet generation process by assuming that when a user composes a tweet, he or she first selects a topic from the topic distribution. Then, based on the selected theme or background model, we select a bag of words one at a time. When it came to assigning subjects to a group of tweets, this technique exceeded traditional LDA in terms of quality. With Omicron Tweets processed and clean tweet data, then started topic modelling. Topic modelling is used to locate hidden subjects in enormous volumes of text.

Figure 2 depicts how we construct a model with a number of topics, each of which is made up of a number of keywords, each of which contributes a certain amount of weight to the topic. And we look at the words that appear in that topic, as well as their relative importance.

Topic: 0
Words:0.035*" govern" +0.024*" open" +0.018*" coast" +0.017*" tassanian" +0.017*" gold" + 0.014*" Australia" + 0.015*" beat" +0.010*" win" +0.010*" ahead" +0.009*" shark"
Topic:1
Words:0.023*" world" + 0.014*" final" +0.013*" record" + 0.012*" break" + 0.011*" loss" + 0.011*" Australian" + 0.011*" laugh" + 11*"test" +0.010 *" Australia" + 0.010*" hill"
Topic:2
Words:0.018*" rural" +0.018*" council" + 0.015*" fund" + 0.012*" plan" + 0.011*" health" +0.012*" chang" + 0.011" nation" +0.010*" service" +0.009*" say"
Topic 3:
Words:0.025*" elect" +0.022*" adelaid" + 0.012*" perth" +0.011*" take" + 0.011*" say" + 0.010*" labor" + 0.010*" turnbul" + 0.009*" royal" +0.009*" time"

Fig. 2. Words occurring in that topic and its Relative weight.

3.4 Word Embedding

A method for representing individual words in text as a matrix of numerical values or vectors is called word embedding. For words with comparable meanings, it generates similar vector representations. The word vectorization technique, also known as the word embedding approach, turns each word into a separate vector for use as a neural network input. Although the process of mapping is typically carried out in low- dimensional space, it occasionally depends on the size of the vocabulary. The two main categories of word embedding are probabilistic prediction and count- based methods. Words compiled from a corpus are used in the prediction strategy to train the model. One of the best probabilistic prediction algorithms is Word2Vec [14].

3.4.1 Glove Model

The word context matrix factorization algorithms used in Glove are based on word context matrix factorization algorithms. It begins by constructing a large matrix of co-occurrence data, in which each "word" (row) in a vast corpus is tallied how many times it appears in some "context" (column). The resulting representations highlight relevant linear substructures of the word vectorspace, and training is based on aggregated global word to word co- occurrence statistics from a corpus. The number of "contexts" is enormous because it is essentially combinatorial in scale. Glove embedding, on the other hand, employs a somewhat different working approach than word2vec and is trained using an aggregated co- occurrence matrix of words. The frequency of words occurring together is shown in a corpus [11].

Output of glove model it reads only numeric form of word and show this word id is omicron related or not. And in that Fig. 3. 0 represent means positive tweet of omicron and 1 means negative tweets of omicron.

0	5665	0
1	540	1
2	7845	0
3	4859	1
4	132	0

Fig. 3. Output of glove model

3.5 Dimensionality Reduction and Clustering Technique

3.5.1 PCA (Principal Component Analysis)

A high dimensional dataset frequently contains redundant features because the majority of its features are associated. Dimensionality reduction is the process of locating and removing certain features [9].

The number of variables that are measured for each observation is the data's dimension. The fact that many times not all the measured variables are crucial for comprehending the underlying phenomena of interest is one of the issues with high-dimensional datasets. High dimensionality reduction addresses the issue of inefficient processing and makes it more challenging to find and take advantage of connections between words. Upon receiving the relationship between the keyword relationships, clustering is done quickly and efficiently. The procedure There will be less time. Principal components analysis (PCA) is a dimensionality- reduction approach that is frequently employed to extract a lower-dimensional space from a dataset's existing features, thereby producing new brand components.

3.5.2 K-Means Clustering

A user-specified number of clusters are discovered using the cluster analysis method K-means, which is represented by the centroids of each cluster. One of the frequently employed unsupervised learning techniques for examining the context of text data in natural language form is clustering. It is a mathematical strategy that gathering and grouping documents that are comparable into clusters [10]. The dataset contains four different types of "omicron" tweets, which were separated into four clusters for this study. K-means is helps to grouping the tweets in positive and negative form. The classifications are based on the following: group 1 contains long tweets, group 2 contains tweets with emoji, group 3 contains tweets that have been retweeted, and group 4 contains short tweets.

0	6731
2	3789
1	2989
3	1491

Fig. 4. Groups of tweets

The dataset contains four different types of "omicron" tweets, which were separated into four clusters for this study.

Groups 0, 1, 2, and 3 are divided into 4 groups, and Fig. 1 displays the number of tweets in each group. It contains three groups, with group 0 including 6731 tweets, group 1 containing 2989 tweets, group 2 containing 3789 tweets, and group 3 containing 1491 tweets. And Fig. 4, shows the group 0 contains a greater number of tweets are in there.

3.5.3 Visualization of Tweet with T-SNE

"T-SNE" that places each datapoint on a two- or three- dimensional map to view high-dimensional data. By minimizing the prehensily for points to cluster together in the map's center, the method of a version of stochastic neighbor embedding is generates noticeably superior visualizations. The embedding method known as t-SN is frequently used to display high-dimensional data in scatter plots [13].

Figure 5 shows in this scatter plot, the four colors red, orange, blue, and yellow stand in for the groups of tweets that they represent. Red stands for group 0, orange for group 1, blue for group 2, and yellow for group 3. Using a scatter plot, it is simple to see which group has the most tweets and which types of tweets they belong to.

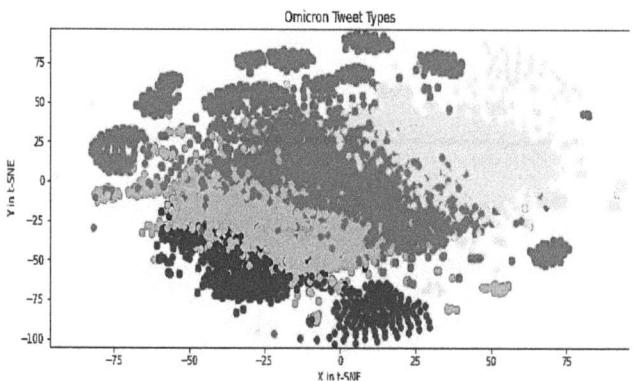

Fig. 5. Visualization of tweet using T-SNE

		id	label
0	hongkong throes worst coronavirus outbreak rec...		0
1	hi feeling slowly back life would would days o...		0
2	spread ba would believed would would times con...		0
3	covid would would covid would would covid omic...		0
4	would would day trends proportion omicronvaria...		0

Fig. 6. Output of BERT model

3.6 Transformer Model BERT and LSTM

3.6.1 BERT

A machine learning framework called Bidirectional Encoder Representations from Transformers (BERT) is intended for processing natural language. BERT is a deep learning model that is intended to pre-train deep learning systems [12]. Every output element is related to every input element. Bidirectional representations by simultaneously using unlabeled text in all layers, there is conditioning on the left and right context. Since BERT features an attention mechanism, also known as Transformer. Which enables analyzing the context of each word in a text separately and determining whether a word has already been used in a text with a similar context, it is characterized as a dynamic technique. As a result, the approach can discover contextual connections among words (or subworlds) in a text. BERT generates a dense vector representation of each word by "looking left and right numerous times." Because BERT learns two representations of each word, one on the right and one on the left, then repeats this learning n times, it is categorized as a fundamentally two- way model. BERT model is also helps to classifying the text if the text is related to omicron or not. The tweets contain word omicron and word related to omicron are in label 1 and this tweet are present in category A and the tweet not containing word related to omicron are in label 0 in label B.it means 0 represent the positive tweets of omicron.

Figure 6 depicts Which contain only positive tweets related to omicron and it contain label 0.

Figure 7 shows 7% of tweets of omicron are positive. And it gains loss is 29%.

3.6.2 LSTM

To identify long-distance dependencies in the sequential data, LSTM is developed. Using specific memory cells, it stores the contextual semantic data for dependencies in a long-range context. The input, forget, and output gates of each LSTM unit are used to coordinate and select the amount of information to hold, toss out, and proceed to the next stage. Additionally, it makes the choice on when to open gates that allow or prevent information from passing through the LSTM unit. Long-term memory in the hidden layer can be used by LSTM as the input for the activation function. Review The LSTM receives text data as input, and it categorizes the input category as output.

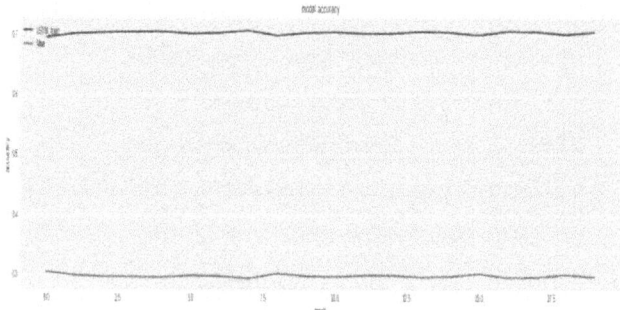

Fig. 7. Graphical representation of BERT models' output.

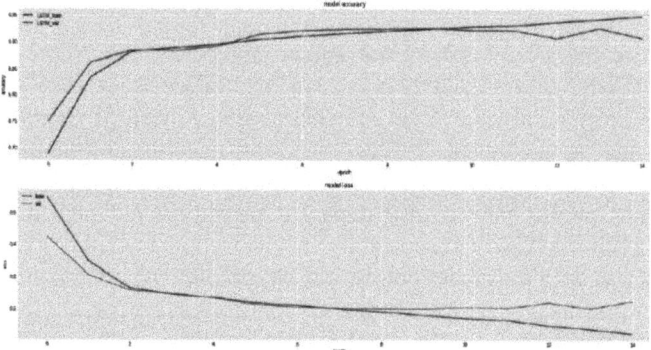

Fig. 8. Graphical representation of LSTM model

The main disadvantages of LSTM are that they take a lot longer to train than neural networks and that they are not really bidirectional because the model learns from left to right and right to left independently before concatenating the context.

Figure 8 illustrates how the LSTM model reveals that Omicron has received the most positive tweets. And it demonstrated 94% accuracy, which is higher than that of other models.

4   Results and Discussion

4.1   Evaluation Measure

The performance indicators that have been developed to gauge the results of the classification algorithms are called evaluation measures. Using the training data sets, the built-in model determines the class of unlabeled text (related to omicron and non-omicron) positive or negative tweets during the assessment phase. The prognostic the created model's performance can be assessed by using the following criteria.

Accuracy: gives the projected instances' percentage of total instances. It counts all instances that were appropriately categorized overall.

$$A = \text{TP} + \text{TNTP} + \text{FP} + \text{TN} + \text{FN}$$

Precision: in the presence of false positive cases, Precision provides model accuracy. As a result, the model's accuracy gives the overall incidence. Incidences of false positives and the rejection of positive instances.

$$p = \text{TP}\text{TP} + \text{FP}$$

Recall: is used to gauge accuracy and displays how well the model performs when a false negative event occurs.

$$r = \text{TP}\text{TP} + \text{FN}$$

F1- score: is a cumulative component that is tested to determine the overall influence of recall and precision in order to determine the overall impact of false negative and false positive instances across the entire accuracy.

$$f1 = 2(\text{TP} + \text{FP}) + (\text{TP} + \text{FN})\text{TP}$$

True Positive (TP): The frequency with which real positive values coincide with predicted positive values.

False positive (FP): The number of times our model incorrectly interpreted negative values as positives.

True Negative (TN): The frequency with which our actual negative values and projected negative values coincide.

False Positive (FP): The number of times the model incorrectly interpreted negative values as positives

$$A = \text{TP} + \text{TN}\text{TP} + \text{FP} + \text{TN} + \text{FN}$$

The actual and anticipated favorable tweets are displayed in Fig. 9 and it illustrates the worth of TP, TN, FP, and FN.

Figure 10 illustrate that 0 represent positive tweets of omicron tweets accuracy and 1 represent negative omicron related tweets accuracy.

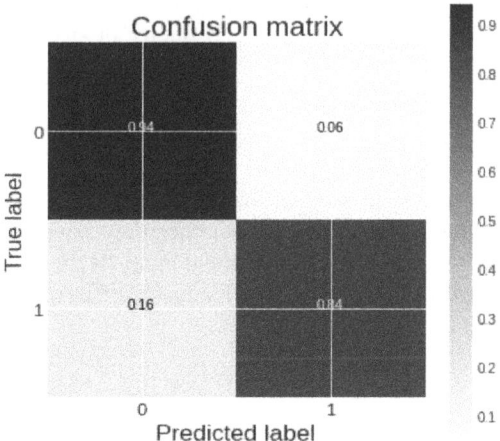

Fig. 9. Confusion matrix of analyzed tweets

	precision	recall	f1-score	support
0	0.96	0.93	0.94	2624
1	0.85	0.91	0.88	1129
accuracy			0.92	3753
macro avg	0.90	0.92	0.91	3753
weighted avg	0.92	0.92	0.92	3753

Fig. 10. Accuracy measure of omicron tweet dataset

Fig. 11. Word cloud of omicron tweets.

4.2 Data Visualization Using Word Cloud

The terms that frequently appear in the document are displayed using word clouds. The output of the word cloud visualization for omicron tweets is shown below. A Word Cloud, sometimes referred as a Label Cloud, is a pictorial display of text data in the form of labels, which are typically single words whose value is indicated by their shape and color. The more commonly a term appears in a text and the more relevant it is, the greater and sharper it is.

The terms connected to the positive tweets of omicron label that appear the most are described in Fig. 11. Examples of words like omicron, coronavirus, and variation that are used frequently. The words are bolder and bigger in size it means the word most related omicron.

4.3 Sentiment Analysis

Opinion mining is another term for sentiment analysis. It's the method of assessing various lines of information to determine whether they have a positive, negative, or neutral emotional tone. Clearly define, sentiment analysis facilitates in determining an author's opinion toward a topic. Sentiment analysis software sorts writing into three categories: positive, neutral, and negative.

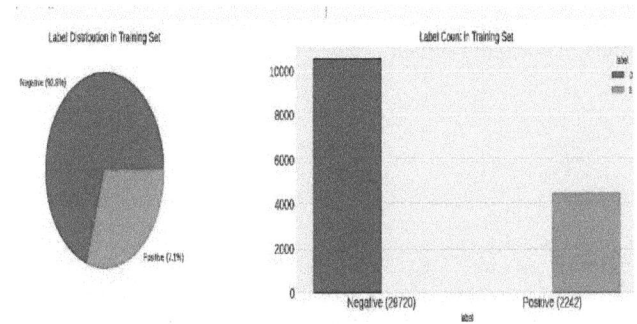

Fig. 12. Twitter Sentiment Analysis of positive and negative tweets

Figure 12 illustrates the sentiment analysis of tweets, which is shown in both positive and negative form. Positive tweets account for 7.1% of total tweets, whereas negative tweets account for 92.9%. The ratio of negative tweets is higher than the ratio of positive tweets, with label 0 indicating negative tweets in blue and label 1 indicating positive tweets in orange. The graph above illustrates that the ratio of negative tweets is the highest.

5 Conclusion

In this experiment, the first step is to clean up all of the tweets and eliminate any hashtags, URLs, special characters, and punctuation from the data. By using topic modelling to identify the abstract topics from our vast corpus after cleaning the data. Then, using the latent Dirichlet allocation (LDA) topic modelling algorithm, it displays Each document has a variety of terms, and each topic also contains a variety of words that correspond to it as well as specify their weight. On the basis of the words it contains, the LDA seeks to identify subjects to which the document belongs.

In our work, by using principal component analysis (PCA) to reduce the dimensionality of data. Based on their co-occurrences and weight, the most frequent words in the omicron language have been compiled in this study. Following the collection of tweets from the dataset, the initial stage is preprocessing, which helps to clean the tweets and make them easier to interpret and analyses. Word embedding is used to display the timing of word occurrences, and the glove represents the word's vector representation. And since the BERT transformer model is bidirectional, it enables readers to read our content from both the left and the right.

Acknowledgments. We would like Thank to Dr. Babasaheb Ambedkar Marathwada University in Aurangabad, India, publication support.

References

1. Lyu, J. C., Le Han, E., & Luli, G. K. (2021). COVID-19 vaccine–related discussion on Twitter: topic modeling and sentiment analysis. Journal of medical Internet research, 23(6), e24435.
2. Culmer, K., & Uhlmann, J. (2021). Examining LDA2Vec and Tweet Pooling for Topic Modeling on Twitter Data. Wseas Trans. Inf. Sci. Appl., 18, 102-115.
3. Shrivatava, A., Mayor, S., & Pant, B. (2014). Opinion mining of real time twitter tweets. International Journal of Computer Applications, 100(19).
4. Das, T. K., Acharjya, D. P., & Patra, M. R. (2014, January). Opinion mining about a product by analyzing public tweets in Twitter. In 2014 International Conference on Computer Communication and Informatics (pp. 1–4). IEEE.
5. Shafi, K. M., & Sheikh, S. A. (2019). Text Embedding Techniques for Sentiment Analysis: A Empirical Review. THE COMMUNICATIONS, 74.
6. Pennington, J., Socher, R., & Manning, C. D. (2014, October). Glove: Global vectors for word representation. In Proceedings of the 2014 conference on empirical methods in natural language processing (EMNLP) (pp. 1532–1543).
7. Sari, W. K., Rini, D. P., & Malik, R. F. (2019). Text Classification Using Long Short-Term Memory with GloVe. Jurnal Ilmiah Teknik Elektro Komputer dan Informatika (JITEKI), 5(1), 85-100.
8. Tam, S., Said, R. B., & Tanriöver, Ö. Ö. (2021). A ConvBiLSTM deep learning model-based approach for Twitter sentiment classification. IEEE Access, 9, 41283- 41293.
9. Noori, M. A. R., & Mehra, R. (2020, November). Fire Emergency Detection from Twitter Using Supervised Principal. In 2020 IEEE 15th International Conference on Industrial and Information Systems (ICIIS) (pp. 403–408). IEEE. Halibas, A. S., Shaffi, A. S., & Mohamed, M. A. K.V. (2018, March). Application of text classification and clustering of Twitter data for business analytics. In 2018 Majan international conference (MIC) (pp. 1–7). IEEE.
10. Es-Sabery, F., Es-Sabery, K., Qadir, J., Sainz-De- Abajo, B., Hair, A., Garcia-Zapirain, B., & De La Torre- Díez, I. (2021). A MapReduce opinion mining for COVID-19-related tweets classification using enhanced ID3 decision tree classifier. IEEE Access, 9, 58706- 58739.
11. Kilimci, Z. H., & Duvar, R. (2020). An efficient word embedding and deep learning based model to forecast the direction of stock exchange market using Twitter and financial news sites: a case of Istanbul stock exchange (BIST 100). IEEE Access, 8, 188186-188198.
12. Van der Maaten, L., & Hinton, G. (2008). Visualizing data using t-SNE. Journal of machine learning research, 9(11).

13. Fávero, E. M. D. B., & Casanova, D. (2021). BERT_SE: A Pre-trained Language Representation Model for Software Engineering. arXiv preprint arXiv:2112.00699.
14. Geetha, M. P., & Renuka, D. K. (2021). Improving the performance of aspect-based sentiment analysis using fine-tuned Bert Base Uncased model. International Journal of Intelligent Networks, 2, 64-69.

Automatic Music Generation Using Deep Learning

Ratika Jadhav[1], Aarati Mohite[2], Debashish Chakravarty[2], and Sanjay Nalbalwar[1(✉)]

[1] Electronics and Telecommunications, Dr. Babasaheb, Ambedkar Technological University, Lonere Raigad, India
nalbalwar_sanjayan@yahoo.com
[2] Electronics and Telecommunications, Indian Institute of Technology Kharagpur, Kharagpur, India

Abstract. This paper aims to build an automatic music generation model for generating musical sequences in ABC notation using a multi-layer Long Short-Term Memory (LSTM) neural network. The model is trained on polyphony such as piano folk and old Scottish flute, merged with various ABC notation tunes by five composers, viz., Nottingham, Jack Campin, Rachael Rae, Quin Abbey, and Rabbie Burns. This approach inputs an arbitrary note from each of the five merged datasets into the neural networks. Depending on the input note, the sequence can process and enlarge until a tune of descent music is generated. With the help of hyperparameter optimization, 95% accuracy is achieved. The model's output efficiency is evaluated using frequency, autocorrelation, PSD, noise filtering, and spectrum analysis. The results show that expressive elements like duration, pitch, and harmony are essential aspects of music composition, and progress has been made to improve these parameters. In addition, the generated note frequency of music is C# (sharp), which evokes sentiments of peace and happiness in mind.

Keywords: Music Generation · Neural Network · RNN · LSTM · Deep Learning · ABC Notation · Duration · Frequency

1 Introduction

Music is the strongest form of magic and universal language, as it relieves stress and produces a kind of pleasure. Music is the time-based harmonization of sounds to create a pleasing pattern, defined as a collection of tones of different frequencies. This paper focuses on generating music automatically using the multi-layer Long Short-Term Memory (LSTM) model. To generate music, one doesn't need to be an expert in music. Even a person who does not have any knowledge of music can generate decent quality music using LSTM. We decided to train the model using ABC music notation. ABC music notation is a type of musical notation in which musical notes are symbolized by the letters from A to G [1]. The model's output data obtained is in the form of ABC music notation.

The model uses a multi-layer Long Short Term Memory Network to generate musical sequences in ABC notation. LSTM is a modified version of Recurrent Neural Networks

© The Author(s) 2023
R. Manza et al. (Eds.): ACVAIT 2022, AISR 176, pp. 674–685, 2023.
https://doi.org/10.2991/978-94-6463-196-8_51

(RNNs) that makes it simpler to recall past information in memory. In machine learning models, the model's previous stages can't be stored. Therefore, previous stages can be stored with Recurrent Neural Networks (RNN). A repeating module in an RNN receives input from previous stages and feeds its output to the next stage. RNNs can only remember information from the most recent stage, therefore a model network that needs to learn long-term dependencies requires additional memory. It is where the LSTM Network comes into the picture [2]. A single LSTM hidden layer is followed by a typical feedforward output layer in the existing LSTM model. The multi-layer LSTM is an extension of this model that contains multiple LSTM hidden layers with numerous memory cells on each layer.

This paper consists of ABC sheet music data merged using two instruments with different ABC notation tunes of five composers and tested on abcjs quick editor. Finally, the merged data is given as input to the model for training. As a result, this model must learn the musical patterns that humans enjoy. The model should be able to generate new music for us once it has learned these patterns. It can't just be copied and pasted from the training data. It should be able to recognize musical patterns to create new music. It is not expected that the model will generate new music of professional quality. Instead, it should generate music of decent quality, melodic, longer duration, and pleasant to hear.

2 Literature Review

Researchers have been working on automatic music generation in artificial intelligence and audio synthesis domains for the past two decades. There are a variety of techniques for making music, and a combination of these approaches can be utilized to construct and design a novel but efficient model. The two primary categories in which these approaches are classified are traditional [3] and autonomous [4]. The traditional method of composing music employs algorithms that operate on predefined functions, but the autonomous model learns from preceding iterations of the notations and then creates new ones. After Artificial Intelligence, many additional models were presented [5], including Anticipation-RNN, probabilistic RNN models, and recursive artificial neural networks (RANN), an updated version of artificial neural networks for generating sequential notes and duration for rhythm composition [6]. "One technique currently being used to make musical sounds is the Generative Adversarial Networks (GANs), which consists of two neural networks: the discriminator network and the generator network. The generator and discriminator network operate together to compare the new data to the original dataset. According to the research, when it comes to fixating on specific sequences, LSTM outperforms GAN; that is, LSTM is better at discovering unique patterns and then reusing them throughout the output sequence" [7]. The LSTM-based models were capable of changing notes and breaking out specific note loops [8]. When it came to GAN-based models, they could only detect basic concepts and had shorter training times [7]. Deep Learning architectures have recently integrated two distinct approaches to automatic music generation. The first uses WaveNet architectures, while the second uses Long Short-Term Memory (LSTM) architectures. WaveNet is Google DeepMind's generative model for raw audio that is based on Deep Learning. WaveNet uses a piece of a raw audio wave as an input. A time-series Recurrent Neural Networks (RNNs)

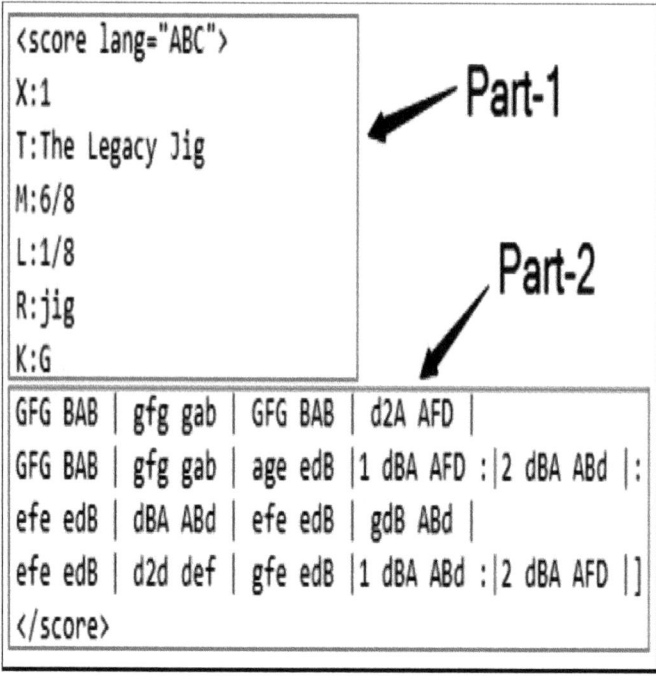

Fig. 1. A Sample of ABC Notation of Music

variation capable of capturing long-term dependencies in the input sequence is referred to as a "raw audio wave" [9].

3 Methodology

3.1 Music Representation Used for the Model

Music can be represented in a variety of ways, including MIDI notation, ABC notation, and sheet music. In this paper, ABC notation is used to train the model for music generation because it is easy to understand and interpret using only a sequence of characters [10]. ABC notation is an ASCII musical notation format that is simple but more effective. It is divided into two parts, as shown in Fig. 1. The first part is the metadata, which includes information about a tune, such as an index, tune type, time signature, and default notes length. The second part represents the real tune, which is expressed as a string of characters. The developed algorithm learns polyphonic musical note sequences using a multi-layered LSTM network.

3.2 Music Dataset and Data Processing

In this paper, the model is trained on polyphony ABC notation, which means that the dataset consists of two instruments, such as piano folks and old Scottish flute, and the dataset is merged with various ABC notation tunes by five composers, namely Nottingham, Jack Campin, Rachael Rae, Quin Abbey, and Rabbie Burns. Tunes selected from this composer's database are Jigs, Reels, Hornpipes, Waltzes, and other dance tunes with bass, Jigs, and Slip Jigs. The model is designed to generate musical notes using integer encoding from a dictionary of 89 unique characters. The dataset is one hot-encoded that is used to categorize the data. The LSTM has been trained using batches of data. The batch specifications used here are as follows: The batch size is 16, and the sequence length is 64. The merged dataset contains a total of 133371 characters.

3.3 Design and Architecture

LSTM is a type of RNN that overcomes the problem or difficulties of training RNNs on sequential data [11]. LSTM learns long-term dependencies as our music has long-term structural patterns. The LSTM unit is composed of a cell and three gates: an input gate, a forget gate and an output gate. The cell retains values for an arbitrary period of time, and these gates control how information in a data sequence enters, is stored in, and exits the network. The forget gate in an LSTM network cell determines whether we should keep or discard information from the previous timestamp. The input gate decides which input value will be used to update the memory, while the output gate sends updated information from the current timestamp to the next timestamp, with the input and memory blocks deciding the output. In this way, LSTM operates sequentially (Fig. 2).

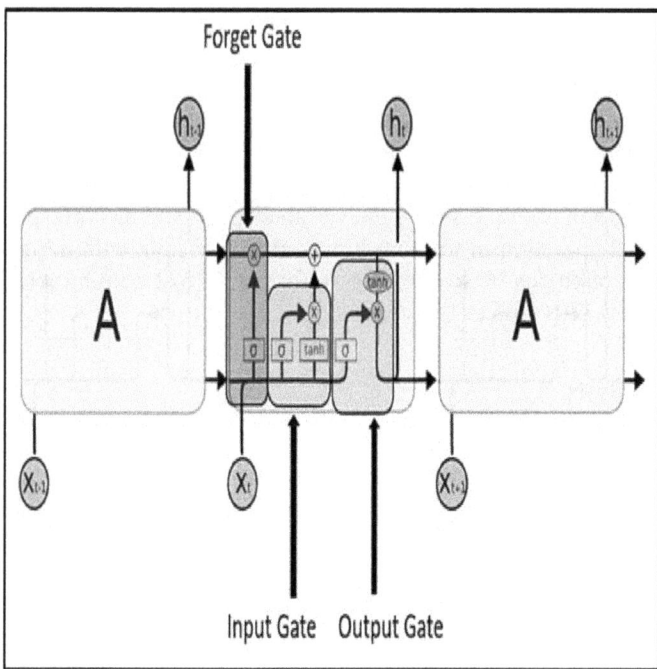

Fig. 2. Architecture of Long Short-Term Memory

The model is built on multi-layer LSTM acting as a core part, along with the dropout layer and time-distributed dense layer. To reduce overfitting, a dropout layer is used. A time-distributed dense layer is used to process the outputs at each timestep. The SoftMax classifier is also used due to the problem statement's multi-class classifying nature. To find predictions for multi-label outputs, the SoftMax classifier is used. SoftMax classifiers use cross-entropy loss to squeeze raw class scores into normalized positive numbers that add up to one to apply cross-entropy loss. To optimize the model, an Adaptive Moment Estimation optimizer is used, also called Adam [12]. It's an excellent choice for LSTM since the model deals with LSTM as input data is fed in sequence (Figs. 3 and 4).

3.4 Music Generation

After training the LSTM network, the model is ready to generate a new pattern of musical notes. The input of the model consists of 89 unique characters, which will generate 89 probability values using the SoftMax classifier. The model then probabilistically selects the next character from the returned 89 probability values and gives back the selected character's input to the model. The model generates music by combining the output characters. In this way, music will be generated.

4 Results and Discussion

The model is implemented over 150 epochs, which results in less training loss per epoch as the number of epochs increases, resulting in a training accuracy of 95%. Figure 5 depicts plotly outputs (visualizations) in the form of graphs representing epochs vs. accuracy. It describes the model's training accuracy values with corresponding epochs. The training accuracy level is observed to be 73% at 20 epochs and then increases linearly from 40 epochs on, that is, from 83% to 95%.

The second graph in Fig. 6 shows the variable epoch and its corresponding training loss. The gradual reduction in training loss is clearly visible with a higher number of epochs. The reduction can be seen in Fig. 6, from a 0.7822 training loss in the first 20 epochs to a final 0.1701 loss at 150 epochs.

4.1 Music Analysis

The model's generated music is analyzed using autocorrelation, PSD, frequency, noise filtering, and spectrum analysis, as illustrated below.

Autocorrelation detects repeated patterns in a signal and describes a signal's similarity to a time-shifted version of itself. The upper waveform in Fig. 7 is a time-domain plot of our model-generated output music file. The duration of the music is 30.348 s, and there are 1338368 samples in total. The music file's downward waveform traces the decreasing and increasing waveforms to the peak point and identifies the first peak position at 78, representing the autocorrelation function. This implies that the pattern will repeat itself after 78 sampled signals.

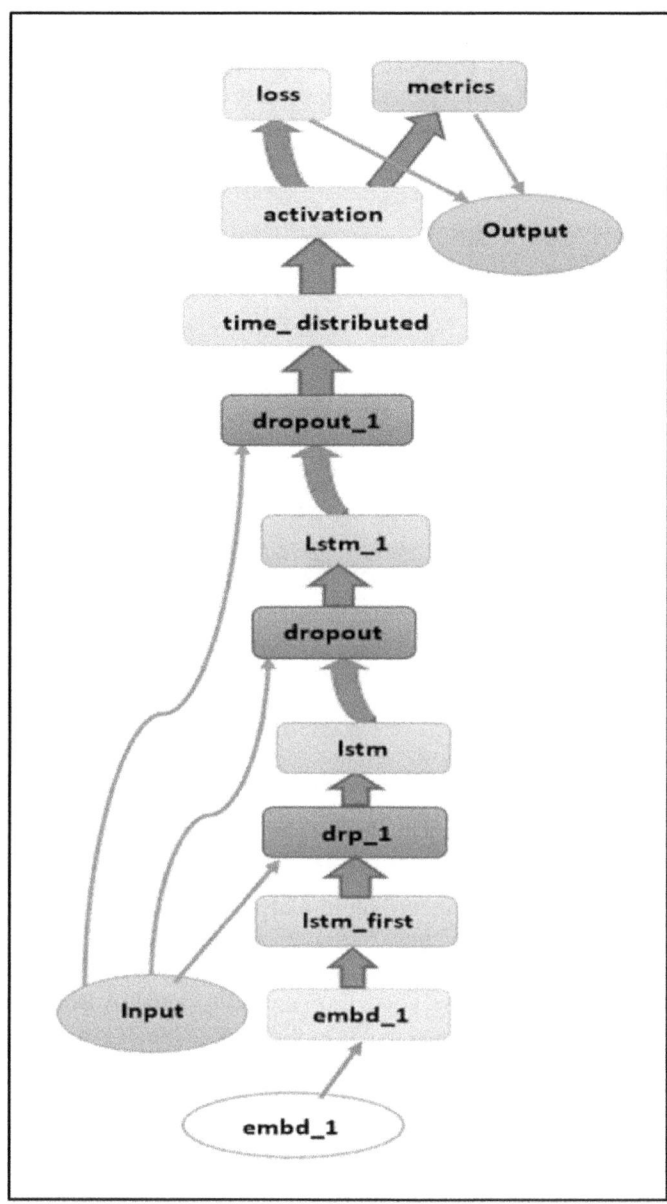

Fig. 3. The figure shows the data flow through the model's layers.

The Power Spectral Density (PSD) plot in Fig. 8 is a frequency-domain plot of power per Hz against frequency. The PSD graph shows that variations between 0 and 5 kHz are strong, while variations between 15 and 20 kHz are weak.

In music, frequency is the speed of vibration, which determines the pitch of the sound. A sound's pitch indicates how high or low a note is. The obtained music signal

```
Number of unique characters: 89
Model: "sequential_1"
```

Layer (type)	Output Shape	Param #
embedding_1 (Embedding)	(16, 64, 512)	45568
lstm_3 (LSTM)	(16, 64, 256)	787456
dropout_3 (Dropout)	(16, 64, 256)	0
lstm_4 (LSTM)	(16, 64, 256)	525312
dropout_4 (Dropout)	(16, 64, 256)	0
lstm_5 (LSTM)	(16, 64, 256)	525312
dropout_5 (Dropout)	(16, 64, 256)	0

Fig. 4. The figure shows the input-output shapes, various layers, and architecture.

has a frequency of 565.38 Hz. According to early research, this frequency is relaxing for the body and mind, as well as more harmonic and pleasant.

As shown in Fig. 9, the most efficient audio noise reduction tool is a Butterworth low pass filter, which is used to remove noise from an audio signal. A Butterworth filter has a frequency response in the passband that is as flat as possible. It is used to remove high-frequency noise with very minimal signal loss. A low-pass filter accepts low-frequency signals while rejecting high-frequency signals. The graph below shows a music signal's filtered and unfiltered time and frequency domain representation. The noise content in the model-generated music is extremely low, resulting in higher-quality music.

Figure 10 shows a graph depicting all of the frequencies present in music at a given time. So, the resulting graph is referred to as a spectrogram. The darker shades in the graph show frequencies with extremely low intensities, whereas the orange and yellow areas, represent frequencies in the music with high intensities.

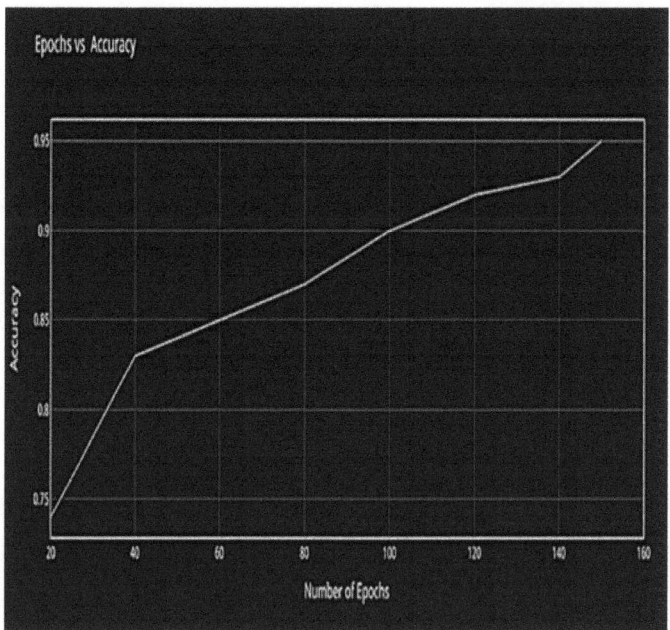

Fig. 5. The graph shows the epochs vs. accuracy of the model for 150 epochs.

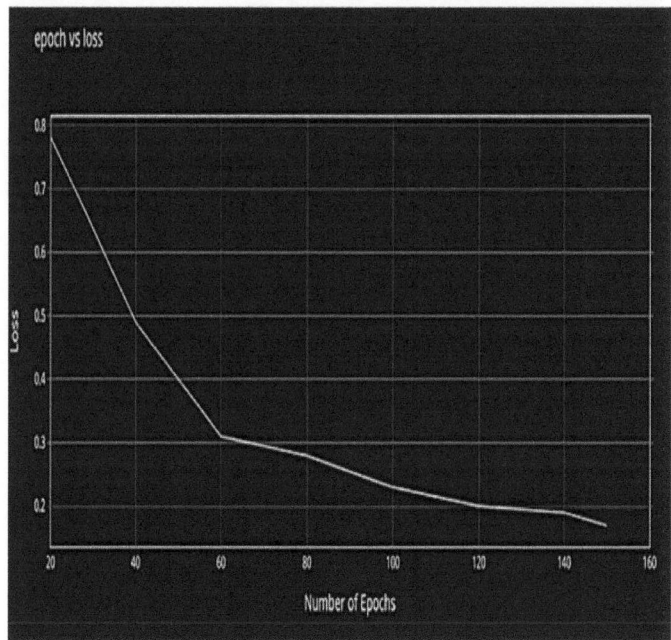

Fig. 6. The graph shows the epochs vs. loss of the model for 150 epochs.

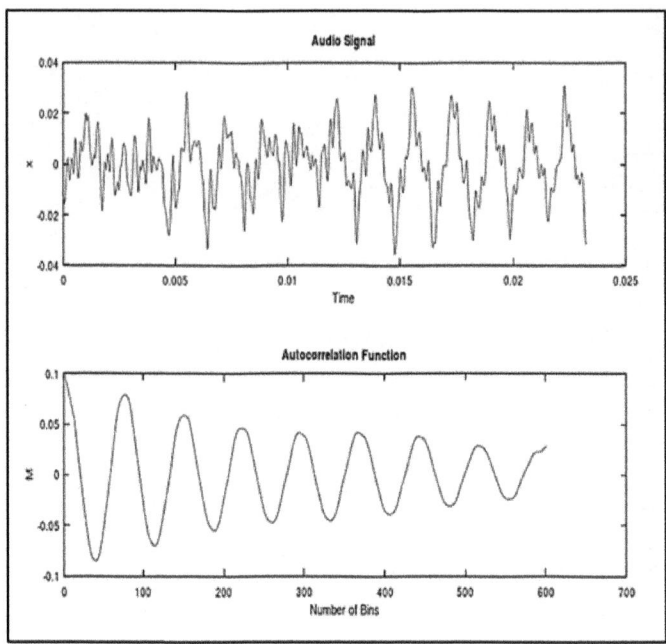

Fig. 7. Autocorrelation function of the model generated audio signal

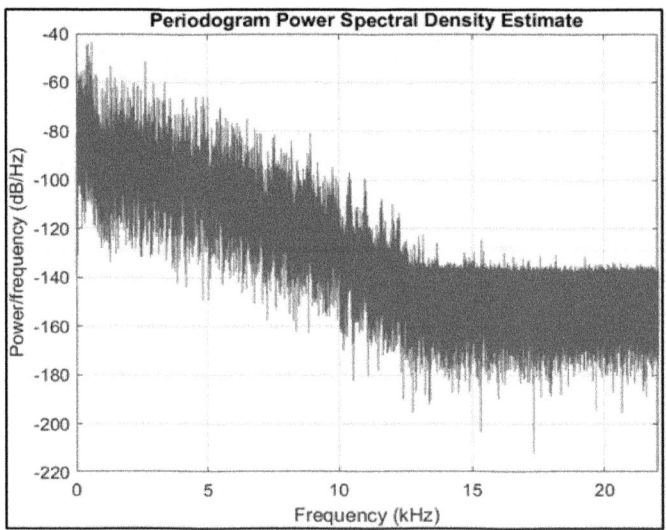

Fig. 8. PSD graph of power vs. frequency

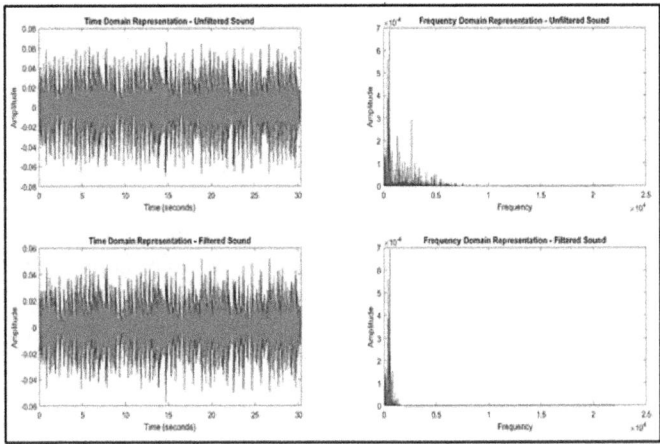

Fig. 9. Noise Filtering using Butterworth low pass filter

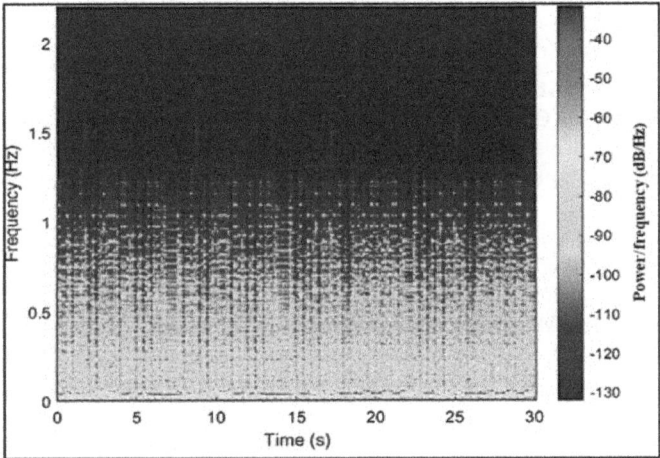

Fig. 10. Spectrogram of Music signal

5 Conclusion

This paper achieves the goal of building a model that is capable of automatically composing melodious music without any human interference. Using a multi-layer LSTM network, the model can recall previous dataset details and generate polyphonic music. It can also learn harmonic and melodic note sequences from the ABC notation dataset. The LSTM is better at analyzing a song structure and creating a more pleasant-sounding composition. After thoroughly analyzing the model, it achieved stellar results in composing new melodies with hyperparameter optimization, yielding an accuracy rate of 95%. The musical note generated from the trained model is C# (sharp), which has a good melody, longer duration, harmony, and decent quality.

In this paper, the overall research agenda is studied and analyzed, which will hopefully help to understand the issues and feasible solutions for music generation using deep learning.

6 Future Scope

As music impacts humans, it is useful to know which genres of music have positive or negative effects on an individual. In the future, we may apply new techniques to enhance learning and produce more enjoyable music, such as predicting emotions in music through audio pattern analysis and generating a model that can conclude the emotional rating of audio patterns on the human brain and act as a buffer for people to decide whether to listen to music or not based on the rating. The purpose of music generation through deep learning is to enhance AI and human interaction, and we can ultimately serve humanity by implementing automatic music-generating technologies in daily life.

References

Sanidhya Mangal, "LSTM Based Music Generation System,"2019.
Ramya Vidiyala, "Music Generation Through Deep Neural Networks," 2020.
A. Joshi," A Comparative Analysis of Algorithmic Music Generation on GPUs and FPGAs" Second International Conference on Inventive Communication and Computational Technologies (ICICCT), 2018.
F. a. H. J. Drewes," An algebra for tree-based music generation," 2007.
Boulanger-Lewandowski," Modeling temporal dependencies in high dimensional sequences Application to polyphonic music generation and transcription," 2012.
N. Hadjeres," Interactive Music Generation with Positional Constraints using Anticipation-RNNs," 2017.
Olof Mogren," C-RNN-GAN: Continuous recurrent neural networks with adversarial training," 2016
Nikhil Kotecha," Generating Music using an LSTM Network", 2018.
Aravind Pai, "Automatic Music Generation." 2020.
Dr.P. SHOBHA RANI, S.V. PRANEETH, "Music Generation Using Deep Learning," 2020.
Nikhil Kotecha," Generating Music using an LSTM Network," 2018.
Vaishali Ingale, "Music Generation Using Three-layered LSTM," 2021.

Customer Churn Analysis and Prediction in Telecommunication Sector Implementing Different Machine Learning Techniques

Samprit Gowd[1], Aarati Mohite[2], Debashish Chakravarty[2], and Sanjay Nalbalwar[1(✉)]

[1] Electronics and Telecommunications, Dr. Babasaheb Ambedkar Technological University,
Lonere, Raigad, India
nalbalwar_sanjayan@yahoo.com
[2] Electronics and Telecommunications, Indian Institute of Technology, Kharagpur, India

Abstract. Nowadays, a large number of telecom industries are dependent on retaining their existing customer base, as retaining customers is found to be more profitable than acquiring new customers. Due to immensely growing competition in this industry, customers get various choices of services and privileges and hence leading them to churn. This problem encourages data scientists to search for solutions to help telecom industries. In this research, 'The orange telecom churn dataset' from Kaggle is analyzed to determine the reasons for customer churning. Different machine learning algorithms viz. Decision Tree, k-nearest neighbor, Random Forest, Naïve Bayes and XGBoost are studied and analyzed for the dataset as mentioned earlier. Results are compared to find the best algorithm to solve the problem for churn prediction. Random Forest and XGBoost algorithms performed best along with the hyperparameter optimization and hence resulted in 95.20% and 95.65% accuracies respectively. Precision-recall curve, accuracy and F-score are the different metrics utilized for the evaluation purpose.

Keywords: Churn · machine learning · XGBoost · precision-recall curve · F-score · Customer churn prediction · Customer Relationship Management

1 Introduction

We live in an era, in which there are fully-fledged businesses and rigorous competitive pressure on the companies. Thus, to survive in the market and increase their income, companies have to maintain their relationship with their customers. This approach is known as "Customer Relationship Management" (CRM), which has the motive of ensuring customers' satisfaction [1]. One of the types of CRM is "Customer churn prediction" (CCP). A company tries to build a model that predicts if a customer is planning to quit the company or minimize its purchases from a company. Companies mostly work with machine learning techniques for customer churn prediction [2]. As there is a need to predict whether customers will stop using services or not, Customer churn is considered to be a classification problem. Customers are always in search of more reassurance and splendor. Therefore, churning has turned into a common trend these days [3]. To

R. Manza et al. (Eds.): ACVAIT 2022, AISR 176, pp. 686–700, 2023.
https://doi.org/10.2991/978-94-6463-196-8_52

provide their customers with more services and offers and increase customer retention, organizations have focused on CRM. Even after focusing on CRM and providing good services, the churning of the customer cannot be stopped. Thus, we can say that churn is an endless process, but it can be predicted to reduce its rate [3].

When it comes to the telecommunications segment, there are a lot of opportunities available for the customers to get better services. The decision of a customer in the telecom industry changes as per needs or experiences. Due to this, there are a lot of chances of customers getting churned to competitors in this telecommunication industry. Collecting new customers is found to be more expensive than retaining the existing customers. Therefore, companies focus on avoiding the churning of customers. As this industry deals with high dimension data, the publication of advanced artificial intelligence and data analytics techniques further help support this rich data to address churn much more effectively.

In this research, analysis of data is carried out to identify the various reasons for churning and a predictive model is built on the telecom-based dataset using different machine learning techniques. Various results are drawn from different algorithms to obtain the best model for our telecom-based dataset. The algorithms used are Decision Tree, Random Forest, k-nearest Neighbor, Naïve Bayes, XGBoost, and Artificial neural network. Grid search is the hyperparameter optimization technique used to improve accuracy. Along with the accuracy of the algorithm time complexity is also considered to find the best algorithm. To compare the results of the build models, different evaluating parameters like Precision-recall curve, loss and accuracy graph, F-score, and accuracy are used.

2 Literature Review

No industry in the market is not affected by customer churning. It is seen that much research is done to find the reasons of customer churning and to predict churning, in the field of data science. "Mr. Saran Kumar A. and Dr. Chandrakala D studied most machine learning algorithms and stated that combining SVM with the boosting algorithms can give higher accuracy for churn prediction" [4]. "Mr. Anurag Bhatnagar Manipal and Dr. Sumit Srivastava implemented Hoeffding Tree and logistic algorithm on the data and comparing the results, concluded that the logistic algorithm works better than the Hoeffding tree algorithm" [3]. "Different machine learning algorithms viz Logistic regression, Decision tree, random forest, K-nearest neighbor are applied to the banking industry dataset in work done by Ms. Ishpreet Kaur and Ms. Jasleen Kaur. Ensembling techniques like voting and averaging are used to improve accuracy. Here Random Forest shows the best results among all the algorithms" [5]. "Xin Hu, Yanfei Yang, Lanhua Chen, and Siru Zhu worked on building the combined customer churn prediction model by using prediction results and confidence of the decision tree prediction model and neural network prediction model. This integrated model compensated for most of the shortcomings of the single prediction model" [6]. "Essam Shaaban, Yehia Helmy, Ayman Khedr, and Mona Nasr are the authors of the research paper, in which data mining techniques like Support Vector Machine, Decision Tree, and Neural Network are used with open-source software called WEKA. The best output is given by the SVM algorithm" [9].

3 Methodology

In the telecommunication industry, it is essential to obtain the causes of customer churning. Data Analysis is the process of methodically implementing statistical or logical techniques to illustrate, describe, and estimate data [7]. In this work, data exploration is carried out to reach the root causes of churning and evaluate the dataset. Several characteristics of the dataset are acquired by exploring the dataset. One of the features is that the dataset is unbalanced. Which is found to be common in the telecommunication industry. This skewness of the dataset declines the performance of algorithms to predict the customers. To solve this problem, we used different algorithms and gain the best-performing predictive model. The steps involved in the proposed work are given in the block Fig. 1.

A. Dataset

The dataset named 'The orange telecom churn dataset' is downloaded from Kaggle. It contains 2666 rows and 20 columns. A single row denotes a customer while a column gives us the customer's attributes. The dataset contains the features such as Area code, State, Account length international plan, Voice mail plan, messages, Total day calls, Total day minutes, Number of vmail, etc. The churn column is the target for prediction.

B. Data Pre-processing

Data pre-processing is the technique of data mining which converts the unprocessed data into convenient and systematic data. It includes data cleaning, data transformation, and data reduction [8]. This technique is used, as the data contain some unrelated features which can be dropped. Exploratory Data Analysis (EDA) is implemented, to carry out

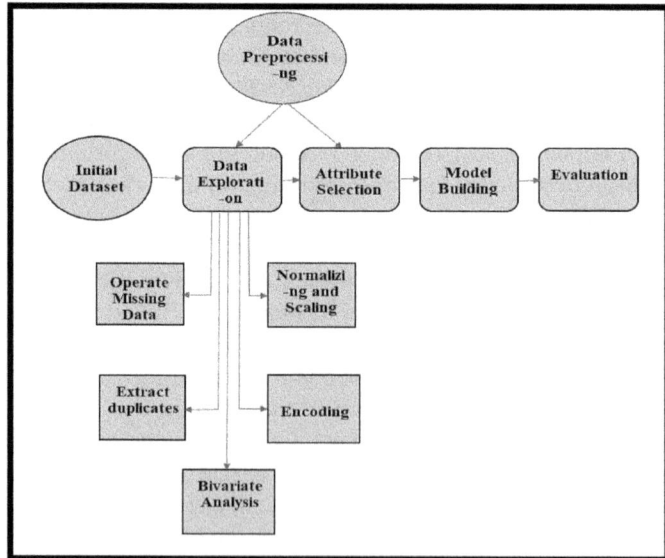

Fig. 1. Block Diagram for the methodology used.

various steps such as finding the missing values, normalizing data and scaling data. To obtain the relationship between two variables Bivariate Analysis is also applied. By finding the correlation between different attributes the unnecessary attributes are removed. Histogram, significant features and heatmap are also plotted.

C. Model Building

Different machine learning algorithms viz. Decision Tree, Random Forest, k-nearest neighbor, Naïve Bayes and XGBoost are implemented to build a churn prediction model. Artificial neural network is also implemented to achieve better churning prediction.

Decision Tree
"The decision tree algorithm falls under the type of supervised learning algorithm which has a predefined target variable. It has two major steps, tree building and tree pruning. The tree-building includes dividing the training sets according to the values of the attributes. The dividing process continues till we get the identical values in the records of the partitions. Some branches can be removed as they may have noisy data. The pruning step includes selecting and removing the branches having a large error rate. Tree pruning is the step that enriches the predictive accuracy of the decision tree and minimizes the difficulty" [9].

Random Forest
Random Forest is the algorithm implemented for the problems of classification and regression. Numerous Decision trees are used to make a final decision. It merges the output of multiple Decision Trees, which are randomly created to generate the final output as it uses the concept of ensemble learning [5]. Each decision tree gives a prediction result during the training phase. The final decision is estimated by the Random Forest based on the majority of the results when a new data point occurs.

k-Nearest Neighbor
k-nearest neighbor algorithm saves all the obtainable data and classifies a new data point according to similarity. KNN algorithm can be applied for both Regression and Classi-fication, but more frequently it is used for Classification problems. KNN is considered a non-parametric algorithm. As KNN does not perceive any knowledge from the training set immediately but reserves the dataset, at the time of classification it acts on the dataset. Therefore, KNN is called a lazy learner algorithm.

Naïve Bayes
A Naive Bayes classifier is considered to be a probabilistic approach. Naïve Bayes' each vector feature is considered to be independent of each other. The assumption of this classifier that the value of each feature has an independent influence on a given class is called as class conditional independence. It is used to make the computations simple, and in this sense, we call it Naïve [10]. The principle of Naïve Bayes is dependent on Bayes' theorem.

XGBoost
XGBoost uses gradient boosting to apply the decision tree algorithm. In gradient boost-ing new models are used to evaluate the inaccuracy of the model which are previ-ously applied. Then both the predictions are combined to make the final prediction [10].

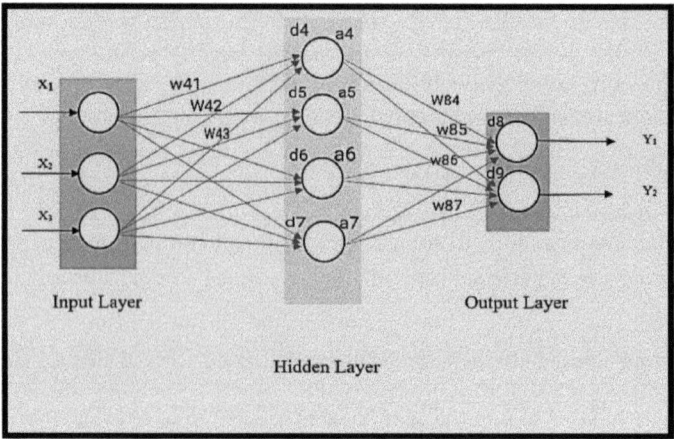

Fig. 2. Layers of ANN

Weights have an essential role in XGBoost. Weights are allocated to all the independent variables which are then fed into the decision tree which predicts results.

Artificial Neural Network

"All the decisions in the brain of a human, are taken by neural networks provided naturally in our body which are created of basic building block called "neuron". All the communications are performed in electrical signals through synapses, a connection point between dendrites and axons from preceding neurons. In the same way, in artificial neuron inputs X1, X2… Xn are taken by each neuron and given as input to the summation and activation function for decision making. The output is carried out on the basis of the joint decision taken by the whole neural network" [11]. The neuron is made up of three layers, which are shown in Fig. 2.

D. Evaluation

Precision-recall curve, F-score, and accuracy are the metrics used for the evaluation of the execution of applied algorithms. Precision and recall are found to be beneficial in cases where there is an imbalanced dataset. "Precision is computed by taking the fraction of the number of true positives divided by the addition of the true positives and false positives. The recall is the ratio of the number of true positives divided by the addition of the true positives and the false negatives" [12]. Integrating the precision and recall of the model gives the F1-score value. "Computational complexity includes the computation of time and space complexity. Time complexity gives us information about how much time is needed to execute the algorithm. It also denotes how complex the problem is to be solved. Space complexity illustrates the space required by the algorithm" [13].

4   Implementation and Results

Initially, the essential step of pre-processing the data is executed. EDA techniques are used here to analyze the data.

After analyzing the data, machine learning algorithms are applied to achieve the best fitting model. The accuracies of the different algorithms are mentioned in Table 1. One of the hyperparameter optimization techniques, Grid Search, is applied to every algorithm to improve accuracy. The improved accuracies can be seen in Table 2. Understanding the time complexity time required for the execution of algorithms is mentioned in Table 3. Best Hyperparameter values are mentioned in Table 4. For evaluation Precision, AUC, Recall, and F-score are the parameters used and precision-recall curves are plotted for the algorithms like Decision Tree, k-nearest neighbor, Random Forest, and all three types of Naïve Bayes. The values of these parameters are shown in Table 5. XGBoost and Artificial Neural Networks are also applied to the dataset.

Results obtained by analyzing the data are as follows (Figs. 3, 4, 5, and 6):

Analyzing data helps us to obtain various relations between the features which are required to gain reasons for customer churning.

Density plots for different features like 'total day charge', 'total eve charge', 'total night charge', and 'total intl charge' are plotted to get the information about distribution. The relation between the customer service calls and churning can be clearly seen in

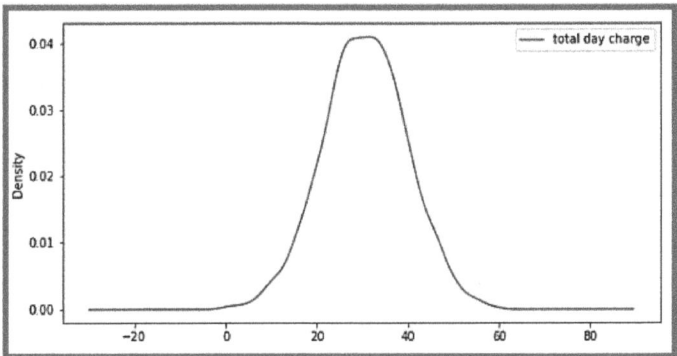

Fig. 3. Density plot for total day charge

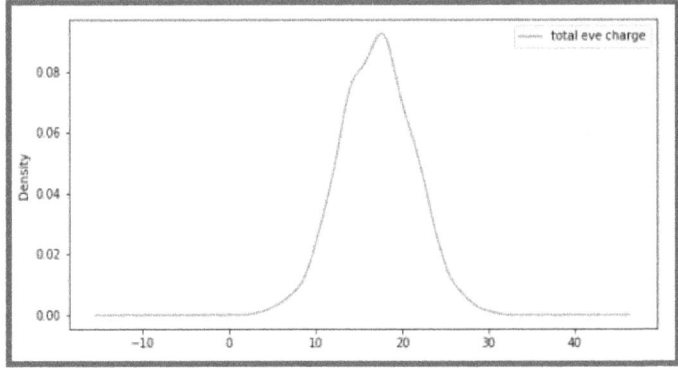

Fig. 4. Density plot for total eve charge

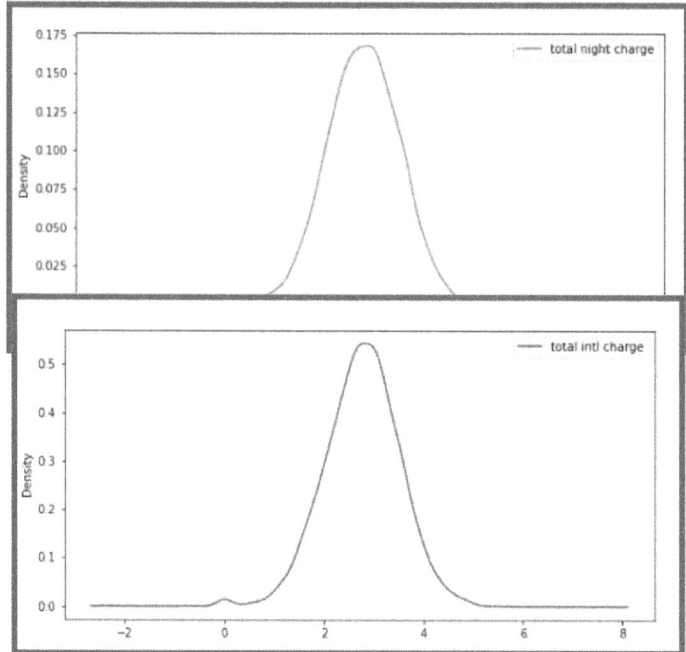

Fig. 6. Density plot for total intl charge

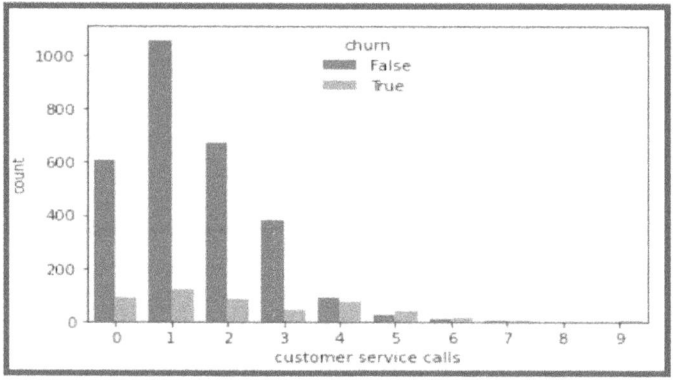

Fig. 7. Relation between Customer Service calls and Customer Churn

Fig. 7. Customer churn can be observed to be increasing after 4 and more Customer service calls. It can be observed from Figs. 8 and 9 that Customers using international plans tend to churn more than Customers with no international plans. This is not the case with the Voice mail plan. In Fig. 10 correlation plot is plotted and it gives us information that four features 'total day charge', 'total eve charge', 'total night charge', 'total intl

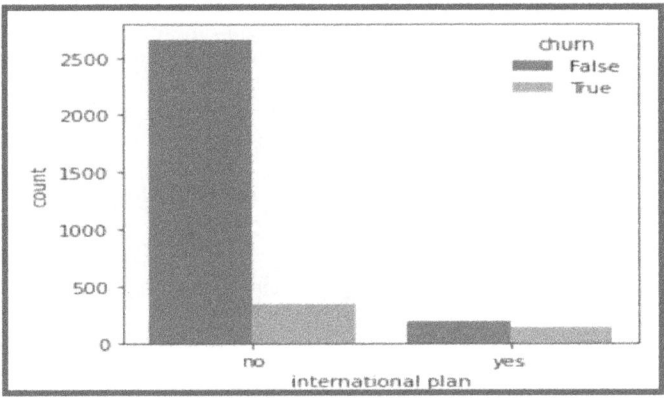

Fig. 8. Relation between International plan and Customer Churn

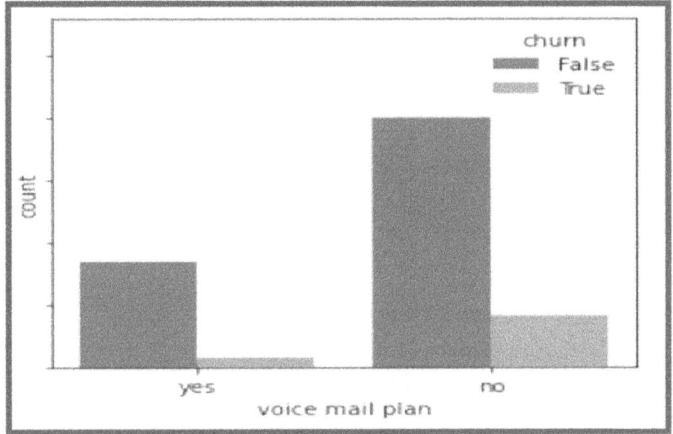

Fig. 9. Relation between Voice mail plan and Customer Churn

charge' are directly dependent on 'total day call', 'total eve calls', 'total night calls', 'total intl calls' respectively.

Precision-recall curves plotted for the applied algorithms are as follows (Figs. 11, 12, 13, 14, 15, and 16):

Artificial Neural Network is implemented on the dataset by using the sigmoid activation function and Adam optimizer. 250 epochs are given for the batch size of 60. Here ANN gives 86.80% of accuracy.

The final accuracies for all the implemented algorithms are mentioned in Table 6.

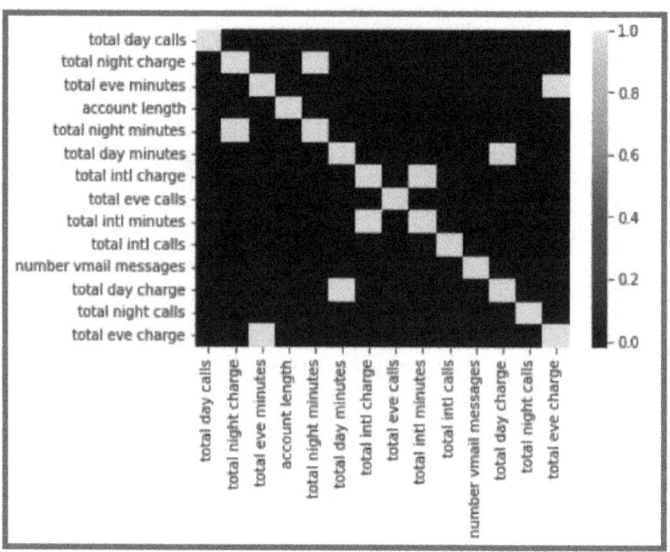

Fig. 10. Heatmap

Table 1. Accuracies of Algorithm without using Grid Search Hyperparameter Optimization

Algorithms	Accuracy (in %)
Decision Tree	93.40
Random Forest	93.85
k-nearest neighbor	88.75
Gaussian Naïve Bayes	85.15
Multinomial Naïve Bayes	63.71
Bernoulli Naïve Bayes	85.60
XGBoost	95.50

Table 2. Accuracies of Algorithm using Grid Search Hyperparameter Optimization

Algorithms	Accuracy (in %)
Decision Tree	93.40
Random Forest	95.20
k-nearest neighbor	88.30
Gaussian Naïve Bayes	88.15
Multinomial Naïve Bayes	63.71
Bernoulli Naïve Bayes	86.20
XGBoost	95.65

Table 3. Time required for execution of Algorithms

Algorithms	Time required for execution (in sec)
Decision Tree	0.010348
Random Forest	1.173684
k-nearest neighbor	0.009588
Gaussian Naïve Bayes	0.007954
Multinomial Naïve Bayes	0.010035
Bernoulli Naïve Bayes	0.010141
XGBoost	0.95737

Table 4. Best Hyperparameter values for Algorithms

Algorithms	Best Hyperparameter values
Decision Tree	random_state = 110 criterion = gini max_depth = 6 min_samples_leaf = 9
Random Forest	n_estimators = 120 random_state = 100 criterion = 'entropy' min_samples_leaf = 7 max_depth = 7
k-nearest neighbor	n_neighbors = 14 p = 2 weights = 'distance' leaf_size = 40 algorithm = 'auto' metric = 'minkowski' metric_params = None n_jobs = None
Gaussian Naïve Bayes	verbose = 1 cv = 10 n_jobs = −1
Multinomial Naïve Bayes	n_jobs = −1 cv = 5 verbose = 5
Bernoulli Naïve Bayes	alpha = 10.0 binarize = 0.0 fit_prior = True class_prior = None
XGBoost	alpha = 1.0

Table 5. Evaluating parameters values.

Algorithms	Precision	Recall	F-score	AUC
Decision Tree	0.74	0.77	0.756	0.80
Random Forest	0.90	0.79	0.80	0.84
k-nearest neighbor	0.67	0.23	0.34	0.37
Gaussian Naïve Bayes	0.62	0.26	0.50	0.47
Multinomial Naïve Bayes	0.38	0.15	0.21	0.29
Bernoulli Naïve Bayes	0.18	0.49	0.26	0.33

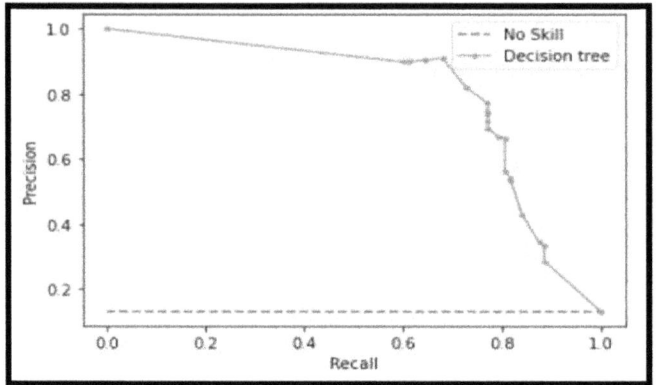

Fig. 11. Precision-recall curve for Decision Tree

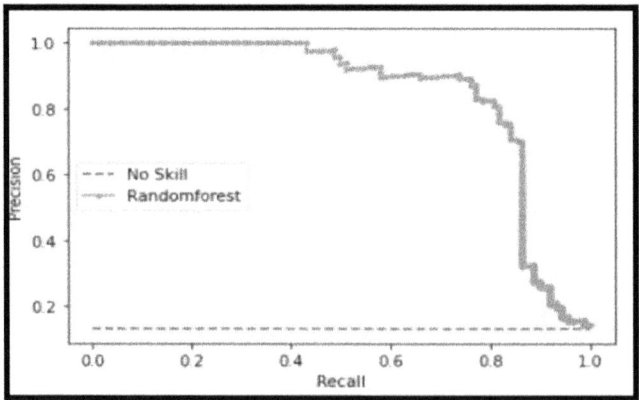

Fig. 12. Precision-recall curve for Random Forest

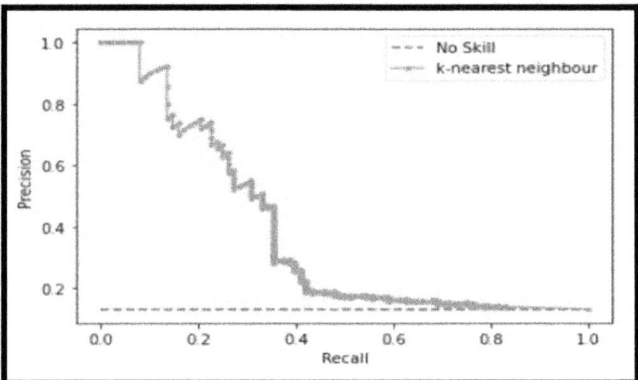

Fig. 13. Precision-recall curve for k-nearest neighbor

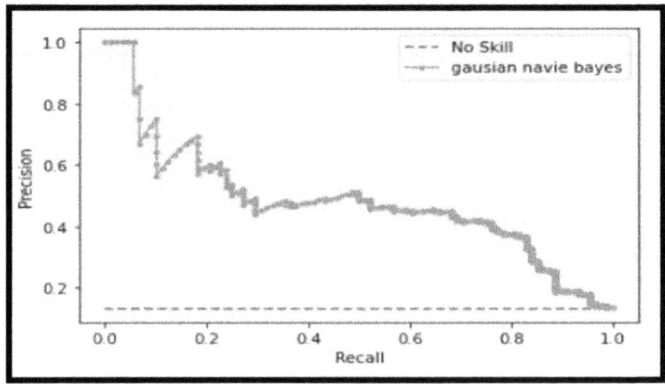

Fig. 14. Precision-recall curve for Gaussian Naïve Bayes

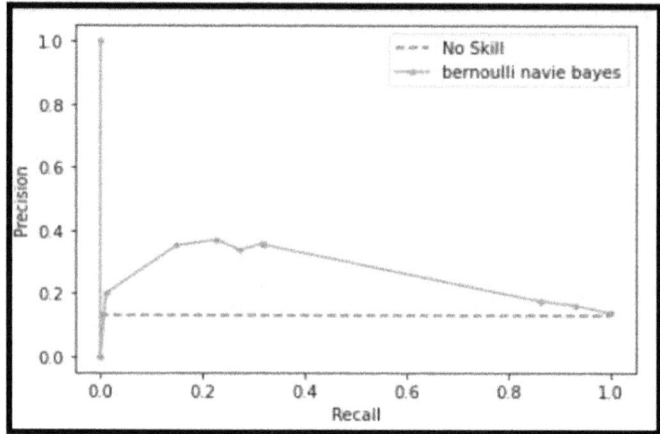

Fig. 15. Precision-recall curve for Bernoulli Naïve Bayes

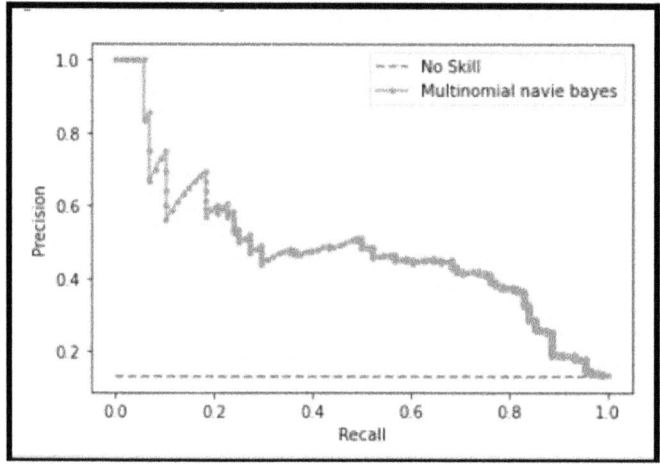

Fig. 16. Precision-recall curve for Multinomial Naïve Bayes

Table 6. Final Accuracy results for the algorithm.

Algorithms	Accuracy (in%)
Decision Tree	93.40
Random Forest	95.20
k-nearest neighbor	88.30
Gaussian Naïve Bayes	88.15
Multinomial Naïve Bayes	63.71
Bernoulli Naïve Bayes	86.20
XGBoost	95.65
Artificial Neural Network	86.80

5 Conclusion

To get the best result for the customer churn prediction in the telecom industry, some commonly known machine learning techniques are imposed on the telecom-based dataset. The use of the Grid Search hyperparameter optimization technique improves the accuracy of the algorithms. The precision-recall curve gives a visual display of the performance of the algorithms. XGBoost and Random Forest are the best performing algorithms with 95.20% and 95.65% accuracies respectively. Comparing these algorithms having the best accuracies with respect to time of execution XGBoost takes less time than Random Forest, which concludes that XGBoost is the best fitting model for this problem.

The future work of the research can involve the implementation of more advanced algorithms and the merging of algorithms to achieve the best outcomes.

References

1. Prof.Andrea Pietracaprina, Prof. Geppino Pucci, "Machine learning techniques for customer churn prediction in banking environments", 2015–16
2. Oskar Sucki, "Predicting the customer churn with machine learning methods - CASE: private insurance customer data", 2019
3. Mr. Anurag Bhatnagar, Dr. Sumit Srivastava "International Conference on Computation, Automation and Knowledge Management (ICCAKM) Performance Analysis of Hoeffding and Logisitic Algorithm for Churn Prediction in Telecom Sector", 2020
4. Saran Kumar A., Chandrakala D., "International Journal of Computer Applications, A Survey on Customer Churn Prediction using Machine Learning Techniques", 2016
5. Ishpreet Kaur, Jasleen Kaur "Customer Churn Analysis and Prediction in Banking Industry using Machine Learning", 2020
6. Xin Hu, Yanfei Yang, Lanhua Chen, Siru Zhu "IEEE 5th International Conference on Cloud Computing and Big Data Analytics Research on a Customer Churn Combination Prediction Model Based on Decision Tree and Neural Network", 2020
7. https://ori.hhs.gov/education/products/n_illinois_u/datamanagement/datopic.html
8. Deepak Jain, "Data Preprocessing in Data mining, Geeks for geeks", 2021

9. Essam Shaaban, Yehia Helmy, Ayman Khedr, Mona Nasr "International Journal of Engineering Research and Applications, A Proposed Churn Prediction Model", 2012
10. Praveen Lalwani, Manas Kumar Mishra, Jasroop Singh Chadha, Pratyush Sethi, "Customer Churn prediction system: a machine learning approach", 2022
11. Yasser Khan, Shahryar Shafiq, Abid Naeem, Sabir Hussain, Sheeraz Ahmed, Nadeem Safwan, "Customers Churn Prediction using Artificial Neural Networks (ANN) in Telecom Industry", 2019
12. Jason Brownlee, "How to use ROC curves and precision Recall curves for classification in python", 2018
13. Qiang Gao, Xinhe Xu "26th Chinese Control and Decision Conference (CCDC), The Analysis and Research on Computational Complexity", 2014

Automated Nutrient Level Determination Using Machine Learning

Shivanand S. Gornale[1]([✉]), A. C. Nuthan[2], and C Sumitha[3]

[1] Department of Computer Science, Rani Chennamma University, Belgavi, Karnataka, India
shivanand1971@gmail.com
[2] Department of Electronics and Communication Engineering, GMIT, Bharathinagara, India
[3] Department of Electrical and Electronics Engineering, GMIT, Bharathinagara, India

Abstract. In present scenario, people look health issues as non-trivial. The primary agenda of life is to have better nutrient food. The calories and nutrition intake as proved harmful worldwide, as it has led to many disease's however dieticians have mistaken that the standard intake of number of calories is essential to maintain the right balance of nutrition and calorie context in the human body. The common people (literate or illiterate) may not able to analyze and decide about nutrient levels in packed food items and even unable to identify the freshness of the food. This system is an aid in such scenarios where if the ingredient list is given, then the system gives a suggestion regarding the nutrition level based on the input. Since the system is to be used by the common (non-technical) people the input to the system is the image of the nutrient list (available at rear end of packaged food items).So our system involves both image processing and machine learning (for automated suggestions based on the input ingredient list).

Keywords: Nutrient Level Determination · Food Freshness · Python · Machine Learning

1 Introduction

Now a day's most of the people look health issues as non-trivial. The primary agenda of life is to have better nutrient food. Our system is an aid in such scenarios where if the ingredient list is given, then the system gives a suggestion regarding the nutrition level based on the input.

Since the systems is to be used by the common (non-technical) people the input to the system is the image of the nutrient list (available at rear end of packaged food items).So our system involves both image processing and machine learning (for automated suggestions based on the input ingredient list).The system has a privilege to detect the freshness of certain food items.

This system helps to dietitians for maintain their weight and also it helps to control the health condition of patients. The system designed here provides users with convenient and intelligent mechanisms that allow them to track their food intake and monitor their calorie count.

R. Manza et al. (Eds.): ACVAIT 2022, AISR 176, pp. 701–710, 2023.
https://doi.org/10.2991/978-94-6463-196-8_53

Calculating food calorie and nutrition level in the intake on a daily basis is mere impossible as it involves dieticians, doctors etc. To treat the patients who suffer from obesity, overweightness, or other food-related health problems there should be correct diagnosis which is challenging issue.

Shervin shirmohammadi et al. [1] gives personal software instrument which can calculate intake calorie and nutrient in any camera equipped device. Image segmentation and preprocessing identifies ROI (region of interest) i.e. food portions from the overall. Amount of each food portion in image is calculated. Level of nutritional facts is calculated using the mass of each portion from its measured volume and matching it against existing nutritional fact tables. As a continuation of the work, in [2] cloud based food calorie measurement system is implemented which is suitable for android devices. Its implementation is analyzed in detail about its functionality on Android system utilizing cloud computing infrastructure. The algorithm is able to withstand huge test and training dataset.

In the paper [3], as against the conventional methods, a novel method is proposed. Vision Based Measurement (VBM) [1] has gained an appreciation as it is simple to use. The algorithm deployed are transferred to the smartphone for real-time implementation.

In the paper [4], the problem caused by the uncertainty of freshness of fruits and vegetables can be overcome by this new and, creative freshness sensor without any chemical treatment which could damage the nutritional value of samples. Additionally, this novel device could be considered as an innovative project which could be a solution for microorganism caused respiratory diseases and allergy like diseases by detecting contamination before microorganism colonies become visible with naked eye by measuring ion concentration changes occurred at samples.

As one more method paper [5] also proposes a method for measuring food nutritional value; this method can be used as a personal assistive application on smart phones. They system analyzes food and fruit images using a set of images processing and analysis procedures, and makes use of a database of images to extract the information needed like color, shape and size properties from the images. It then uses an SVM to the food portion types. Experimental results shows that our image processing technique works better than others in segmenting and extracting the food portions.

In another method [6] uses smart phone to analyse images has many potential applications for people, especially patients. But, the variability of the food objects makes it very difficult to adapt the algorithms with real data. Existing methods can process, analyse and texture features. We have improved the functionality and flexibility of the recognition system by adding shape and size features as well as color and texture. Furthermore, by increasing the number of images in the database the recognition rate can be increased.

2 Objectives

- A person is considered obese when the Body Mass Index is higher than or equal to 30kg. Recent studies have shown that obese people are more likely to have serious health conditions such as hypertension, heart attack, high cholesterol, breast and colon cancer etc.

- High calorie intake as proved harmful worldwide, as it has let too many diseases. However, dieticians have mistaken that a standard intake of number of calories is essential to maintain the right balance of calorie content in the human body
- As per the guidelines of FDA, it has 32 different names of salts,31 different names of sugar,17 different names of fats and 17 different names of allergens based on these, help to decode the ingredient list.
- How it means, with the help of differently mentioned names of sugar, salt, fats and allergens, it measures what type of ingredient is present in the given ingredient list.
- Scenarios which arrive even to common person during the purchase are

  - Even though ingredient list is displayed, the common people may not able to analyze and decide about nutrient levels in packaged food items.
  - May not be able to identify the freshness of the food.

- This system should be able

  - To identify the nutrition level from the input image ingredient list
  - Freshness of the unpacked food item
  - Best suitable suggestions based on identified nutrient level

- **Proposed Methodology & Implementation** (Fig. 1):

  The work handles two of food items.

1. Packed Food.

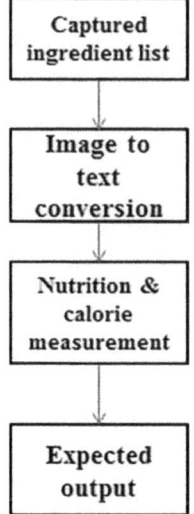

Fig. 1. Proposed Methodology for packed food items

2. Unpacked Fresh vegetable/Fruits.

Capture the food of the image using smart phone. Captured image is preprocessed and is converted into text using character recognition. The text converted image will measures the nutrition and calories by using mathematical calculations which acts like a dataset for machine learning. Using machine learning algorithm a suggestion is given to specific people according to their diet concern. The final outcome of the food measures the nutrition and calories. Same methodology is applied to check the freshness of food.

Let us consider snicker as an example, by capturing ingredient list (like sugar, chocolate, milk fat & so on) by the camera. Such list will convert image to text with the help of image processing (Figs. 2, 3, 4 and 5).

Then the system will measure the nutrition and calorie from the image captured. Then the people will come to know about the nutrition and calorie of the snickers.

Those people who dieting they receive guidance from the dietician. What and how much to be consumes for their health. If the snickers calories and nutrients are matched with dietician guidance, then it is preferable to consume snickers, If it is not matched with dietician guidance, then it is not preferable to consume.

The technical details block will explain how technically it works for both nutrition and calorie measurement as well as for freshness identification of food (vegetables, fruits, meat, etc.).

First we capture the image using smart phone it automatically select ingredient list from the packed food for measurements and capture the food image for freshness identification.

The image to text conversion uses the OCR (optical character recognition) tool to extract the text from image (ingredient list). It helps to analyze the text in the image that what image we upload and converts into text. For freshness identification no need

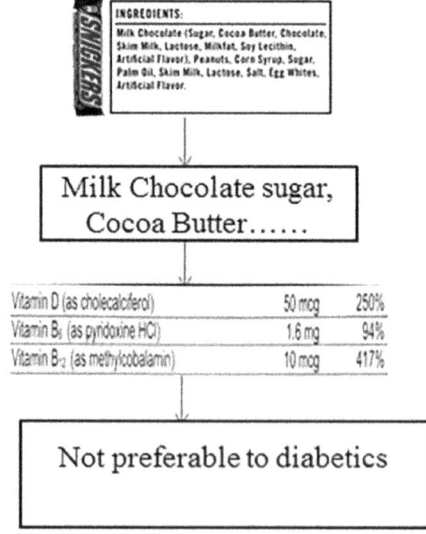

Fig. 2. Example w.r.t packed food

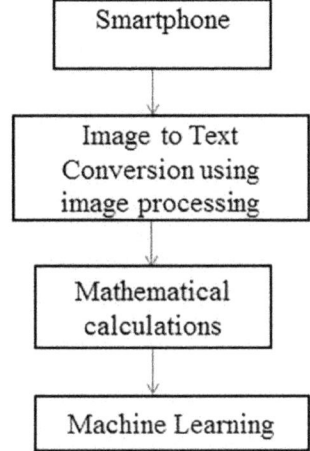

Fig. 3. Technical procedure w.r.t. packed food

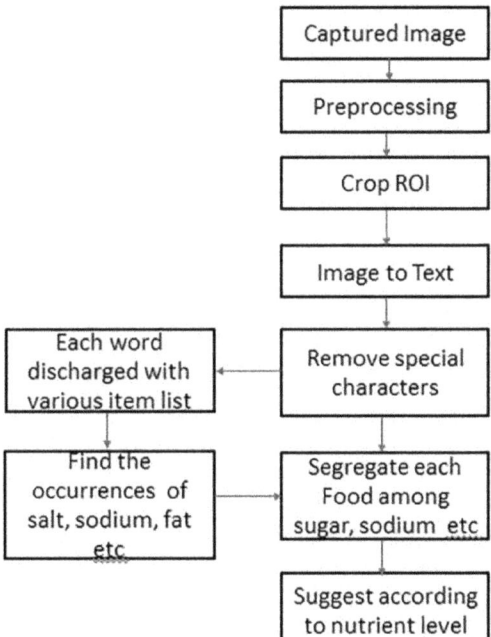

Fig. 4. Flowchart of handling packed food

to convert from image to text but for measuring nutrition and calorie needs to convert from image to text.

The mathematical calculation block will measure the nutrition and calorie in the packed food and freshness identification of the food. Finally it goes to the machine learning block it gives final result to the users.

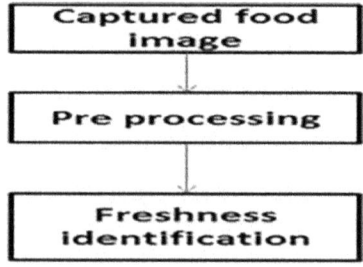

Fig. 5. Block diagram w.r.t. unpacked food

This block will identify the freshness of the food items. The purpose of this,people don't might be know if an food gone bad before buying it and don't know how much foods contaminated by microorganisms this leads to health issue.To overcome this problem freshness identification technology is developed.

The freshness identification technology is done by freshness sensor which identifies the food freshness as helps to know the hidden details present in foods like fruits, vegetables, meat, etc.

Figure 6 shows flowchart of handling the unpacked food.

- First it will choose the colors of the food.
- On the basis of green, red and yellow we are going to implement the freshness identification of the food.
- Based on the green color we decide that the fruit is not ripe, based on the red or yellow color we decide that fruit is ripe.

3 Machine learning

Machine learning deals with the automation of programming where the computer program modifies itself based on the new dataset. At first it should be basically trained using test dataset. It is classified into Supervised learning and unsupervised learning. Data samples are categorized into four types for classification: false negatives (FN), true negatives (TN), true positives (TP), and false positives (FP).

Here lasso regression method is used to check the freshness based on features like color texture, shape etc. The algorithm uses both variable selection and regularization along with soft thresholding. It selects only a subset of the provided covariates for use in the final model. It is mathematical defined by,

$N^{-1} \sum_{i=1}^{N} f(xi, yi, a, b)$.

To check the efficiency of classification, RMSE is evaluated.

- $RMSE = \sqrt{\frac{1}{N} \sum_{i=1}^{n} x_i^2}$
- $RMSE = \sqrt{\frac{\sum_{i=1}^{n} x_i^2}{\sum_{i=1}^{n} n_i^2}} \times 100\%$

Here xi and ni are the error and reference, N is length of the analyzed data which is 125 in this work.

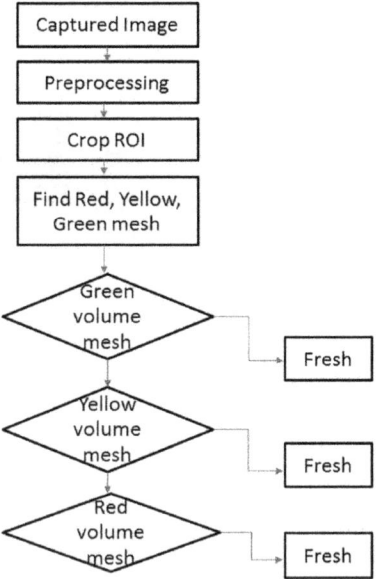

Fig. 6. Flowchart of handling unpacked food

4 Result

To check the freshness the dataset from Kaggle is used. The recognition rate is summarized in the Table.1. About 125 experiments were conducted with the variation types, colours and other parameters. The recognition rate is about 70% which can further be increased.

Since the system is to be used by the common (non-technical) people the input to the system is the image of the nutrient list (available at rear end of packaged food items).The system has a privilege to detect the freshness of certain food items. Figure 7.and Fig. 8 shows the one of the example results of how the system works by handling both packed and unpacked food.

The RMSE for the designed classification is 0.307 which is within the thumb rule of 0.2 to 0.4.

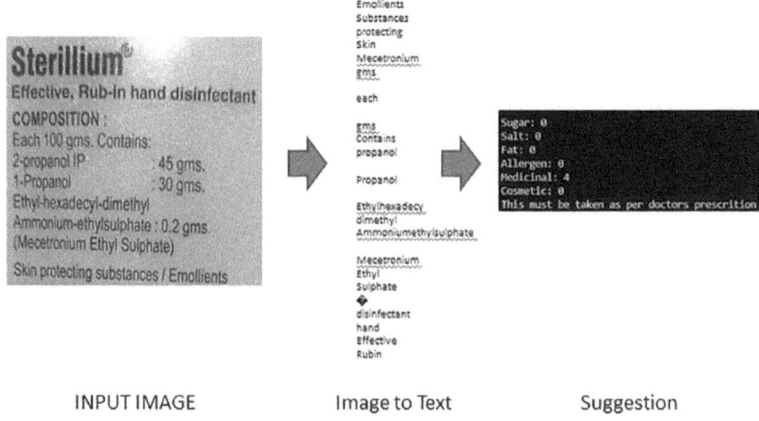

INPUT IMAGE   Image to Text   Suggestion

Fig.7. Results of handling packed food

Table 1. Summary of Food Freshness

FOOD ITEMS		RECOGNITION RATE (%)					
		USING COLOUR FEATURES	USING TEXTURE FEATURES	USING SIZE FEATURES	USING SHAPE FEATURES	USING ALL FEATURES	USING ALL FEATURES (10FOLD CROSS-VALIDATION)
1	apple	60	85	31	23	98	59
2	orange	65	79	41	71	96	70
3	tomato	71	70	48	45	90	65
4	carrot	75	80	69	65	100	78
5	onion	46	80	32	23	90	54
6	bean	77	80	77	65	99	80
Total average		**66**	**79**	**50**	**49**	**96**	**68**

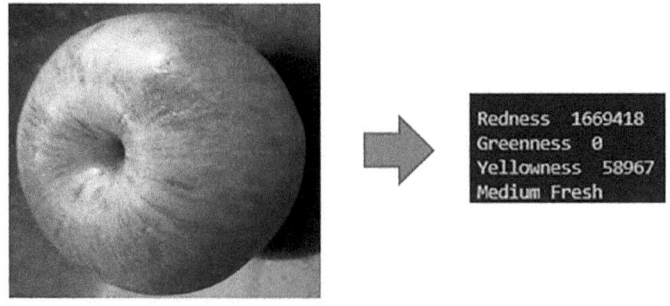

INPUT IMAGE

Fig. 8. Results of handling unpacked food

5 Conclusion

- The proposed system can identify the nutrition level from the input image ingredient list
- Based on nutrient level in the ingredient list the system is able to give appropriate suggestions based on identified nutrient level.
- Freshness of the unpacked food item can also be checked
- Regression models were implemented to classify. Lasso regression showed better results in terms of lesser MSE.
- In future the work can be extended to clustering so that system is more robust even for the non-identified objects which make the system more suitable for real time applications.

References

1. Bharat K.., Broder A., "*A technique for measuring the relative size and overlap of public Web search engines*", Computer Networks, **30**(1–7), pp. 107–117, 1998
2. P. Pouladzadeh, S. Shirmohammadi, and R. Almaghrabi, "*Measuring Calorie and Nutrition from Food Image*", IEEE Transactions on Instrumentation and Measurement, DOI: https://doi.org/10.1109/TIM.2014.2303533, February 25, 2014.
3. P. Pouladzadeh, G. Villalobos, R. Almaghrabi, and S. Shirmohammadi, "*A Novel SVM Based Food Recognition Method for Calorie Measurement Applications*" , Proc. International Workshop on Interactive Ambient Intelligence Multimedia Environments, , p. 495 – 498, in Proc. IEEE International Conference on Multimedia and Expo, Melbourne, Australia, 2012.
4. Wenyan Jia et al., "*A Food Portion Size Measurement System for Image-Based Dietary Assessment*," Bioengineering Conference, IEEE, pp. 3–5, April 2009.
5. R. Almaghrabi, G. Villalobos, P. Pouladzadeh, and S. Shirmohammadi, "*A Novel Method for Measuring Nutrition Intake Based on Food Image*," in Proc. IEEE International Instrumentation and Measurement Technology Conference, Graz, Austria, p. 366 – 370, 2012
6. Food Volume to Weight Conversions: http://www.aqua-calc.com/page/density-table
7. Health Canada Nutrient Values. : http://www.hcsc.gc.ca/fnan/nutrition/fiche-nutridata/nutrient_value-valeurs_nutritives-tc-tmeng.php, November, 2011
8. S. Avancha and A. Baxi, "*Privacy in Mobile Technology for Personal Healthcare*", ACM Computing Surveys, Vol. 45, No. 1, , pp.1–54C., November 2012.
9. Wang and Z. Ma, "*Design of wireless power transfer device for UAV*," in Proc. IEEE Int. Conf. Robot. Automat. (ICRA), , pp. 2449–2454, Aug. 2016
10. H. Hoashi, T. Joutou, and K. Yanai, "*Image recognition of 85 food categories by feature fusion*" in Proc. 2010 IEEE Int. Symp. on Multimedia (ISM), pp. 296–301, 2010
11. F. Takeda et al., "*Dish extraction method with neural network for food intake measuring system on medical use*," Computational Intelligence for Meas. Syst. and Applications, pp. 56–59, Jul. 2003.
12. R. M Haralick, K Shanmugan, and I Dinstein, "*Textural features for image classification*," IEEE Transactions on Systems, Man, and Cybernetics, vol. 3, pp. 610 - 621, 1973.
13. World Health Organization Statistics 2012: http://www.who.int/gho/publications/world_health_statistics/2012/ en/index.html, 2012
14. J. Baxter, "*Food recognition using ingredient-level features*," http://jaybaxter.net/6869_food_project.pdf.

15. Nashat, A. A., & Hassan, N. M. *"Automatic Segmentation and Classification of Olive Fruits Batches Based on Discrete Wavelet Transform and Visual Perceptual Texture Features"* International Journal of Wavelets, Multiresolution and Information Processing, 16(1), 185-193, 2018

16. Pan, C., Yan W., *"Salient Object Detection Based on Perception Saturation. Multimedia Tools and Applications"*, DOI: https://doi.org/10.1007/s11042-020-08866-x), 2020.

17. Davey, M. W., Stals, E., Ngoh-Newilah, G., Tomekpe, K., Lusty, C., Markham, R. *"Sampling Strategies and Variability in Fruit Pulp Micronutrient Contents of West and Central African Bananas and Plantains (Musa Species)"*. Journal of Agricultural and Food Chemistry, 55(7), 2633–2644. 2007.

Development of Multilingual Speech Recognition and Translation Technologies for Communication and Interaction

Ali A. AL-Bakhrani[1,4]([⊠]), Gehad Abdullah Amran[2], Aymen M. Al-Hejri[4,5], S. R. Chavan[3], Ramesh Manza[3], and Sunil Nimbhore[3]

[1] Department of Computer Science, Technique Leaders College, Sana'a, Yemen
albakhrani2017@gmail.com
[2] Department of Management Science and Engineering, Dalian University of Technology, Dalian, Liaoning 116024, China
[3] Department of Computer Science and IT, Dr. Babasaheb Ambedkar Marathwada University, Aurangabad, India
[4] Faculty of Administrative and Computer Sciences, Albaydha University, Albaydha, Yemen
[5] School of Computational Sciences, Swami Ramanand Teerth Marathwada University, Nanded, Maharashtra, India

Abstract. In this study, we find a solution to the problem of recognizing the source language and translating it into the selected target language. This interface is designed to convert the voice or speech into any selected source text, convert it into the targeted text, and save it into wave files. This interface, which in turn solves many problems, including in the field of education and society, can be used in day-to-day life. We have worked on building a software project that solves the problem, as it relies on deep learning techniques in speech recognition. Building the application depends on several main parts: speech recognition, verification of the speaker's language, conversion of speech to text, translation of speech into any language, and conversion into any language. The text of the speaker or translator into voice also allows saving speech in a pdf file and supports translating entire files, as this application has been programmed using the Python programming language.

Keywords: TTS · STT · DNN · Speech Recognition · Translation · Python

1 Introduction

People use speech to communicate with each other, which is the most natural and efficient way to exchange information [1]. From this conclusion, it follows that the next technological advancement will be natural language voice recognition for human-computer interaction. Speech recognition is a branch of computer science and computational linguistics that deals with methodology and technology development for computer speech recognition. Automatic speech recognition (ASR), computer speech recognition, or speech-to-text is sometimes known as ASR, computer speech recognition, or speech

R. Manza et al. (Eds.): ACVAIT 2022, AISR 176, pp. 711–723, 2023.
https://doi.org/10.2991/978-94-6463-196-8_54

recognition (STT) [1]. It integrates technology into the domains of linguistics, computer science, and computer engineering. For voice recognition systems to function correctly, they must be "trained" (sometimes called "enrolled"). By analyzing a person's voice, the system's recognition of that person's speech is more accurate because of the fine-tuning method used. Conversational spoken sentences are quickly translated and spoken aloud in a second language through speech translation [1]. System phrase translation varies from phrase translation because it does not translate phrases that are fixed and finite, but rather anything and everything that can be used in a sentence. Speech translation technology allows people to converse with each other, regardless of their native language [8]. Thus, it is of considerable benefit to humanity in terms of science, intercultural dialogue, and business worldwide. People naturally assume that speaking will be the way communication with computers is conducted. A computer capable of speaking and understanding its native language.

Machine reformation of speech uses a sequence of words and attempts to find the best possible match for the provided speech signal [13]. Virtual reality, multimedia searches, and flight check-in agents are some of the applications for knowledge creation, including informative and on-site accommodations, interpreters, and natural language comprehension. To expand the concept further and make the best use of these technologies, we combined them into one application, which was programmed in the Python language, which supports the user interface with the addition of new features, which serve precisely in the field of education and scientific conferences, and we relied on artificial intelligence techniques [14], which Google translators relied on. It works to solve a problem in education, which in turn provides educational material to the fullest and with high efficiency. For example, the lecturer speaks English, and the students have different languages, such as some of the students speaking Arabic and some of the students speaking Hindi. The student can choose his language, and the application also saves the entire lecture in a pdf file and downloads a file in the speaker's language and another file in the student's language, which helps the student write all observations and focus on the teacher.

2 Related Work

Few surveys have been conducted on voice recognition in this region. Consider, for instance, an evaluation of voice recognition and feedforward networks aided by discriminatively trained networks. The primary purpose of the review was to identify publications that used several processing steps prior to HMM-based word sequence decoding. A number of computational approaches, some of which provide significant improvements in very short vocabulary problems while simultaneously increasing the signal-to-noise ratio (SNR) in very large vocabulary tasks, were discussed in [1]. In addition, the construction techniques outlined offered step-by-step instructions for building structures incorporating many layers, which were built from several layers of MLPs with a high number of hidden layers. This research ultimately concluded that although deep processing structures can develop in this genre, several aspects, such as layer width, have a significant impact on it. Deep neural networks that employ several hidden layers and are trained with new approaches are now being utilized. This is an excellent summation of the results of four separate research groups that cooperate to conclude that feedforward neural networks are best equipped to handle both HMM states and HMM coefficients. In lieu of utilizing standard HMMs and GMMs for acoustic modeling in speech recognition, this alternative was investigated. In a study that has been in progress for several years, deep neural networks that contain many hidden layers and are trained by innovative approaches have demonstrated significant performance gains over GMMs (HMMs) on voice recognition benchmarks [2]. This study states that deep neural networks for acoustic models of speech recognition have an extended history. The overview report concentrates on how deep learning techniques can be further improved. These improved approaches include improved network design and activation functions, improved optimization methods, and new methods for finding neural network parameters. From the overview, we can see that acoustic models that employ deep neural networks (which may or may not use GMMs) are making great progress. Other signal-processing applications, such as voice recognition, may also benefit from using similar acoustic models [3]. To compare Microsoft's recent progress in voice recognition in 2009, a summary was created using deep learning. This study sought to understand recent advancements in voice recognition by investigating the capabilities and limits of deep learning in the field. Microsoft supplied samples from their latest research to facilitate the incorporation of deep learning algorithms for speech-related applications. The incorporation of applications in the field of speech-related technology includes feature extraction, language modeling, acoustic models, speech comprehension, and dialogue estimation. Although traditional GMMs—HMM-based machine learning models—seem better suited to speech spectrogram features, recent experimental results have clearly demonstrated that speech spectrogram features are more deeply learned with neural network-based machine learning models such as GMMs and deep neural networks than with HMMs [4]. This study also highlights that performance enhancements may be obtained by fine-tuning the design of deep neural networks that are state-of-the-art in both computational and phonological terms for automated spoken language recognition. Over the past decade, great progress has been made in the field of spoken language recognition owing to the current advancements in signal processing and cognitive research [7]. Several critical issues in language recognition, such as language classification, modelling methodologies, and software development strategies, have been addressed. The findings show that even though this part of the country has vastly grown in the last several years, it is far from being completely developed, notably in terms of linguistic characterization. Furthermore, this article offers an overview of the current research trends and future objectives, as well as the research techniques and technologies used in the development of the NIST-developed language recognition evaluation (LRE). An exhaustive survey of contemporary noise-robust speech recognition algorithms has been conducted over the past three decades [9]. Greater focus was placed on the established approaches, which are expected to retain and increase their usefulness in the future. The methods under examination were examined and their characteristics were assessed using five different metrics: using prior knowledge about acoustic environment distortion, domain processing method (e.g., model processing versus feature processing) versus process method (e.g., uncertainty processing versus predefined processing), using environment distortion models, and finally using trained acoustic models from the same adaptation process utilized in the testing stage[5]. This research offers information about resilient noise approaches and differentiates among various strategies, making it useful for readers.

3 Methodology

1. Deep Learning Models

One of the deep learning models often used for image categorization is the convolutional neural network (CNN), sometimes known as convent or CNN. Convolution, pooling, and fully linked layers are all key operations in a CNN. Several studies have also included a batch normalization layer. Originally developed for image classification, CNN may be used for sequential data by employing 1-dimensional convolutions instead of traditional 2-dimensional convolutions. Speaker identification systems include 1-dimensional CNN. A similarity function can be trained by employing a Siamese network that consists of two identical networks sharing weights. In [12], a one-shot learning assignment for face verification was performed using a Siamese network. A Siamese network typically employs two identical CNNs to learn the feature representation and compares the similarities between the two inputs. Because the main goal is to determine whether two input voices belong to the same person, this problem can be approached as binary classification. Another frequent way to learn from sequential data is through a long short-term memory network, also known as an LSTM network. Long-term dependencies in the original recurrent neural network were a problem that [10] sought to solve with the LSTM algorithm. The input, forget, candidate, and output gates comprise LSTM, which controls the learning process via four gates. To make things even more complicated, each LSTM cell has two distinct states: visible (cell state) and concealed (hidden). From one moment in time to the next. Both [11], where the authors used LSTM to solve large-vocabulary speech recognition problems, and [8], which uses LSTM for both voice enhancement and automatic speech recognition, have also looked at LSTM in depth.

2. Speech Recognition

Speech recognition is described as the process of voice identification based on spoken words by converting a signal acquired by audio equipment in a book on artificial intelligence (AI) [13]. Speech recognition is also a mechanism for recognizing human speech commands and converting them into data that computers can access. It is important to understand the difference between speech and sound because speech has different signal characteristics. Making a sound recognizable or identifiable so that it can be used necessitates many efforts, including voice or speech recognition. Acoustic-phonetic voice recognition, artificial intelligence voice recognition, and pattern recognition are three approaches to voice recognition. Figure 1 shows a block diagram that explains the pattern recognition approach to speech recognition Fig. 1 [14].

3. Convolutional Neural Networks

Deep learning algorithms such as convolutional neural networks (CNNs) are commonly used in ASR systems. Weight sharing, convolutional filters, and pooling are just a

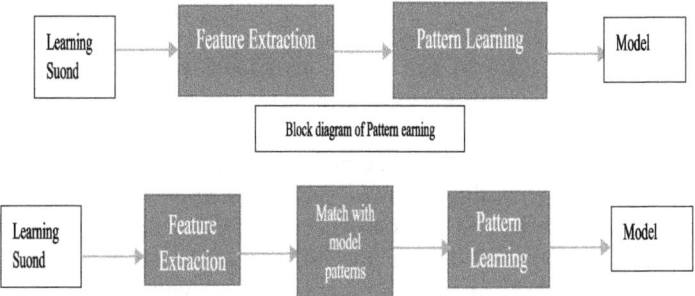

Fig. 1. Speech recognition block diagram

few of the appealing developments in CNNs that have been made. Consequently, CNN's outperformed other ASR technologies in this area. Multiple convolutional layers are used in CNNs to achieve complex functionality. A block diagram of the CNN is shown in Fig. 2.

4. Automatic Speech Recognition

Figure 3 depicts the architecture of an ASR system that uses ASR. This model comprises four parts: signal processing and feature extraction, an acoustic model (AM), a linguistic model (LM), and a hypothetical search. As an audio signal is sent to the system, it is processed to remove noise and channel distortion and then converted to the frequency domain, where it may be extracted as a vector feature that stands out.

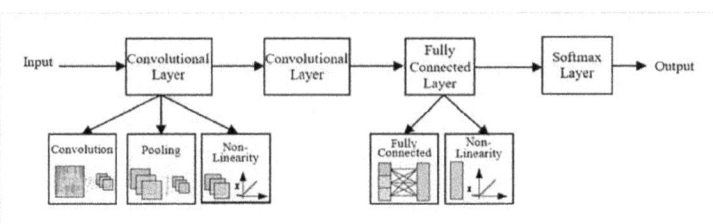

Fig. 2. Block diagram of CNN.

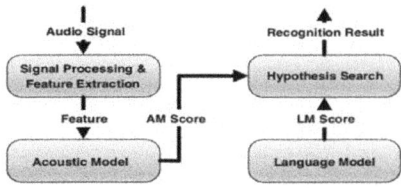

Fig. 3. Architecture of an ASR System

5. Python

Python is an object-oriented and highly structured programming language with dynamic semantics. Scripting or glue language with a higher level of knowledge structure mixed with dynamic and dynamic binding makes it highly marketable for quick creation, as well as the use of existing components. Python's easy-to-read syntax promotes readability while lowering software maintenance costs. Because many offices provide information analysis and data classification, Python supports work on all artificial intelligence algorithms, especially in the field of machine learning and deep learning, which is the core of our [15], as it provides many offices with small code and high and accurate performance in the field of information analysis and data classification.

6. PyCharm

Python programming was made easier with PyCharm, an integrated development environment (IDE). A JetBrains subsidiary in the Czech Republic created it [16]. In addition to code analysis, it has a graphical debugger, an integrated unit tester, and support for version control systems (VCSes). [15] PyCharm is available for Windows, macOS, and Linux and is, therefore, a cross-platform.

7. Python GUI-Tkinter

Python has several graphical user interfaces (GUI) creation options. Tkinters are the most widely used graphical user interface method. The Tk GUI toolbox in Python has a normal Python interface. The fastest and easiest way to create GUI applications is to use Python with a Tkinter. Creating a graphical user interface with a Tkinter is an easy task.

8. Google Cloud Speech

To exploit Google's speech recognition capabilities, a Google Cloud Speech API was created. This API exhibits an excellent speech recognition performance. A neural network was used to recognize 120 languages and dialects. It is possible to use real-time streaming or file input. Because it is a Web API, you will need a way to connect to the internet.

4   Design

The application is designed using the Python language, which supports an interactive user interface that helps users use the application easily:

5   Implementation

In this case, speech recognition systems can be classified by their elegance level.

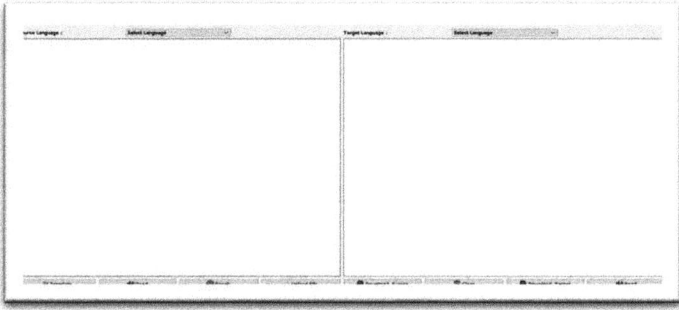

Fig. 4. Snapshot of Main Interface

5.1 Type of Speech

5.1.1 Isolated Word

An isolated word that understands the concept of "attain" usually means that the following two conditions must be met: quietness on both sides of the test window. This method is suitable for single or short utterances. This is a state that has "Listen and Not Listen" written all over it. Another name for this class may be "isolated utterance." [6].

5.1.2 Connected Word

Similar to isolated words, connected word systems are similar to words that are not linked together yet allow independent sentences to be uttered with a minimal pause between them.

5.1.3 Continuous Speech

Artificial intelligence programs that provide continuous voice recognition are said to enable users to talk nearly naturally while the machine decides on the content[1]. Some of the most challenging to develop are continuous speech recognizers because they use unique techniques to identify speech segments.

5.1.4 Spontaneous Speech

This may be defined as natural-sounding speech that has not been rehearsed. If a computer has an ASR system with the capacity to process spontaneous speech, it will be able to handle a wide range of natural speech characteristics, such as running words together.

5.2 Application Work

5.2.1 Run Application

This is the main interface of the application when it starts running (Fig. 5).

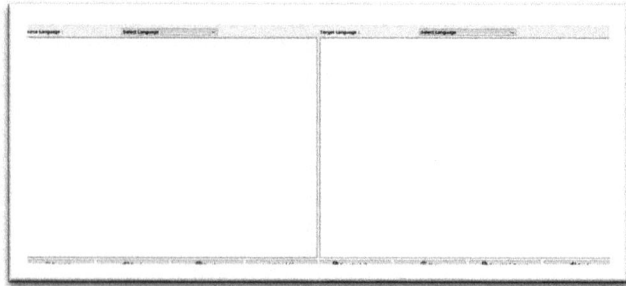

Fig. 5. Snapshot of Main Interface.

5.2.2 Select Source Language

Users can select any source language.

E.g: We will select the English language (Fig. 6).

5.2.3 Select Target Language

Users can select any target language.

E.g: We will select the Arabic language (Fig. 7).

5.2.4 Speak via Microphone

Users can press the speak button to start speaking in lectures.

E.g: We will say "hello how are you" (Fig. 8).

In Fig. 4, the user presses the speaking button to start speaking, and the application listens to and recognizes the sound of the user to convert speech to text and translate it.

5.2.5 Download Source Speech and Target After Translate

Users can download source text as a pdf file or print it using a printer (Fig. 9).

Fig. 6. Snapshot of Select Source language.

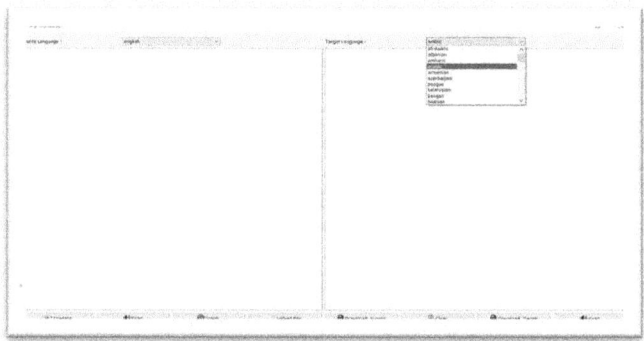

Fig. 7. Snapshot of Select target language

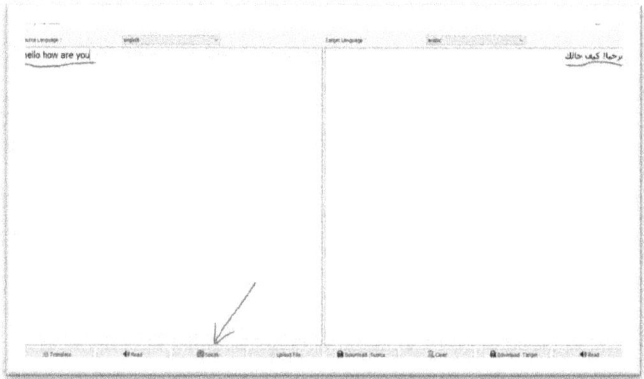

Fig. 8. Snapshot of Speak Process.

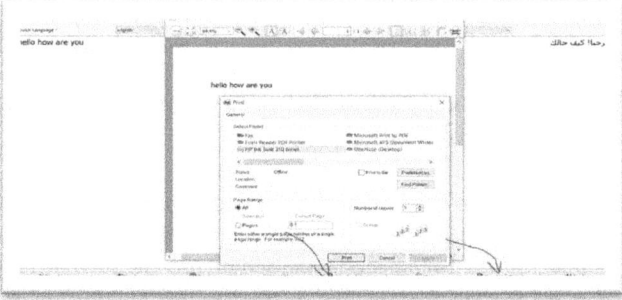

Fig. 9. Snapshot of downloading source text and sending it to printer

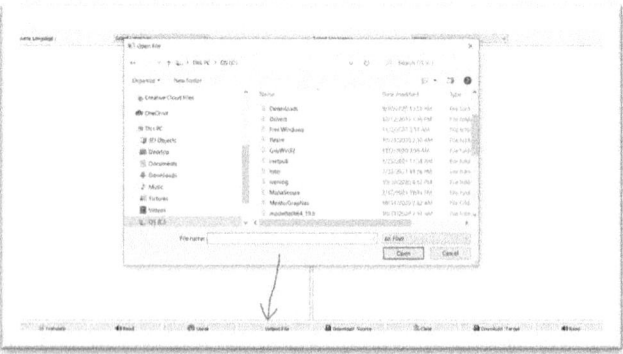

Fig. 10. Snapshot of Upload file

Fig. 11. Snapshot of after Upload file

5.2.6 Upload File

Users can upload the files to translate to any language (Figs. 10 and 11).

6 A Multilingual Voice Translation Processing Architecture That Handles Multilingual Speech

In Fig. 12, an English phrase is transformed into text and subsequenty translated into Arabic, which is then multilingual speech recognition module examines the input speech, comparing it to a large amount of speech data, which are created by representing all the phonemes found in each speech utterance in the English syllabify. Next, the string of phonemes was transformed into a string of words written in the English writing system, resulting in a string of words having the greatest possible probability. An English sentence is created using an engine trained on large quantities of English text by examining the probability of the occurrence of a string of three words. Each English word in the string was replaced with an appropriate Arabic word using a conversational-language translation module. To provide a sequence, the order of Arabic words is altered [7]. A

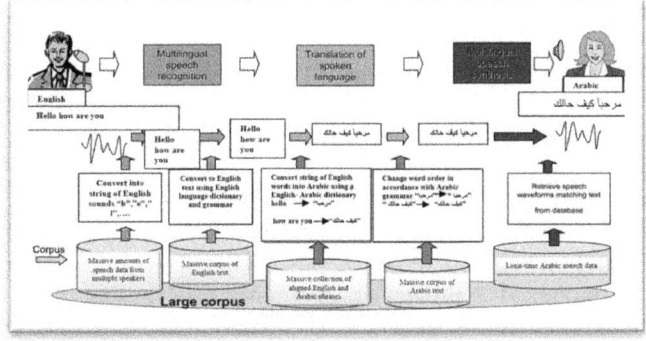

Fig. 12. The Architecture of the speech translation system

translated English-to-Arabic translation model was used to replace the original English words in the strings. An engine trained on large quantities of Arabic text generates an Arabic string of words with the correct probability of occurrence to rearrange them. Once this has been sent to the speech synthesis module, it is sent to the end-user. Speech synthesis connects English words to associated speech sounds, calculates pronunciation and intonation, and selects sounds from a long-term speech data database. Using statistical modeling and machine learning, the method of speech recognition and synthesis known as "corpus-based speech recognition and synthesis" applies massive speech corpora.

7 Discussion

In this study, we focus on how the application fulfills universities' needs for communication improvement between lecturers and students. Artificial intelligence techniques were used to recognize speech, translate speech, convert speech into text, and then save the lecture into text and audio files.

- The lecturers must speak clearly.
- The lecturers should use a wireless microphone that is connected to a computer.
- The application will install on the classroom computer.
- A user interface was designed to facilitate the selection of the present language and target language.
- Creating a display screen for students that displays the process of converting speech to text at present and translating it into the target languages.
- The speech that has been converted into text depends on the translation process; thus, by pressing a translation button, the entire speech is translated.
- At the end of the lecture, the student will be able to save and download the lecture as text, pdf, and audio files by pressing a button.
- In addition, the user can upload a text file to translate it into any language, whether to text or audio files.

8   Conclusion

In this paper, we have included many papers that helped us develop the aforementioned application, as stated above. This application was developed using a high-level programming language called Python. There is a possibility that the application might change educational access for the disabled and for all people. The project has already shown significant gains in the overall understanding and knowledge of how voice recognition, speech-to-text, and translation might be used in educational settings. Project success has a positive effect on business sector support and the consortium of universities that participate in the project. The project's programmer believes that it will attract a large audience due to the emphasis on student accommodation in classrooms. Our view is that a project's objective is to provide everyone with equitable access to knowledge.

References

1. Gaikwad S.K., Gawali B.W., and Yannawar, P., 2010. A review on speech recognition technique. International Journal of Computer Applications, 10(3), pp.16-24.
2. Nimbhore S. , Ramteke G., Ramteke R. ," Pitch Estimation of Marathi Spoken Numbers in Various Speech Signals", International Conference on Communication and Signal Processing, April 3–5, 2013.
3. More S. , P. Borde, S Nimbhore," Isolated Pali Word (IPW) Feature Extraction using MFCC & KNN Based on ASR", IOSR Journal of Computer Engineering (IOSR-JCE) e-ISSN: 2278–0661, p-ISSN: 2278–8727, Volume 20, Issue 6, Ver. II, Nov - Dec 2018.
4. Nimbhore S., Mache S., "Processing of Devnagari Text to Speech Synthesis: A Review, International Journal of Management, Technology And Engineering Volume IX, Issue I, JANUARY/2019 ISSN NO: 2249–745.
5. Morgan N., 2011. Deep and wide: Multiple layers in automatic speech recognition. Ieee transactions on audio, speech, and language processing, 20(1), pp.7-13.
6. Deng, L., Li J., Huang J.T., Yao K., Yu D., Seide F., Seltzer M., Zweig G., He X., Williams J. and Gong Y., 2013, May. Recent advances in deep learning for speech research at Microsoft. In 2013 IEEE International Conference on Acoustics, Speech and Signal Processing (pp. 8604–8608). IEEE.
7. Li H., Ma B. and Lee K.A., 2013. Spoken language recognition: from fundamentals to practice. Proceedings of the IEEE, 101(5), pp.1136-1159.
8. Chen Z., Watanabe S., Erdogan H., and Hershey J. R.2015. Speech enhancement and recognition using multi-task learning of long short-term memory recurrent neural networks. In Proceedings of the 16th Annual Conference of the International Speech Communication Association (Dresden, Germany, September 6–10, 2015). INTERSPEECH '15. 3274–32780.
9. Chowdhury A. and Ross A. 2017. Extracting sub-glottal and supra-glottal features from MFCC using convolutional neural networks for speaker identification in degraded audio signals.In Proceedings of the 2017 IEEE International Joint Conference on Biometrics (Denver, CO, United States, October 1–4, 2017). IJCB '17. IEEE, New York, NY, 608–617.OI=https://doi.org/10.1109/BTAS.2017.8272748.
10. Hochreiter S. and Schmidhuber J. 1997. Long short-term memory. Neural Computation 9, 8 (Nov. 1997), 1735–1780.DOI=https://doi.org/10.1162/neco.1997.9.8.1735.
11. Li X. and Wu X. 2015. Constructing long short-term memory based deep recurrent neural networks for large vocabulary speech recognition. In Proceedings of the 2015 IEEE International Conference on Acoustics, Speech and Signal Processing (Brisbane, Australia, April 19–24,

2015). ICASSP'15.IEEE,NewYork, NY, 4520–4524.DOI=https://doi.org/10.1109/ICASSP.2015.7178826.

12. Taigman Y., Yang M., Ranzato M., and Wolf L. 2014.Deepface: Closing the gap to human-level performance in face verification. In Proceedings of the IEEE Conference on Computer Vision and Pattern Recognition (Columbus, OH, United States, June 23–28, 2014). CVPR '14. IEEE, New York, NY, 1701–1708. https://doi.org/10.1109/FCVPR.2014.220.

13. Amrizal V., Q Aini. Artificial Intellegence (in Indonesia Kecerdasan Buatan). Jakarta Barat. Halaman Moeka Publishing. 2013. E Widiyanto, SN Endah, S Adhy. Speech Application to Text in Bahasa using Mel Frequency Cepstral Coefficients and Hidden Markov Models (in Indonesia Aplikasi Speech To Text Berbahasa Indonesia Menggunakan Mel Frequency Cepstral Coefficients Dan Hidden Markov Model). Prosiding Seminar Nasional Ilmu Komputer Undip. 2014: 39-44.

14. Endah SN., Adhy S., Sutikno S. Comparison of Feature Extraction Mel Frequency Cepstral Coefficients and Linear Predictive Coding in Automatic Speech Recognition for Indonesian.TELKOMNIKA Telecommunication Computer Electronics and Control. 2017; 15(1): 292.

15. AL-Bakhrani Ali A., et al. "Machine Learning and Deep Learning to Do Early Predictions of COVID-19 Infection Using Chest X-Ray Images." Machine Learning 62.07 (2020).

16. Matthew D.Z., Rob F., Visualizing and Understanding Convolutional Networks, Springer International Publishing Switzerland 2014, pp. 818–833.

Milton Keynes UK
Ingram Content Group UK Ltd.
UKHW020938280823
427620UK00007B/554